D

Genetic Programming III

About the Authors

John R. Koza received a B.A. and M.S. in Computer Science and an M.A. in Mathematics from the University of Michigan. He received his Ph.D. in Computer Science from the University of Michigan in 1972. From 1973 to 1987, he was chairman, chief executive officer, and cofounder of Scientific Games, Inc., of Atlanta (a NYSE company). He is currently consulting professor in the Section on Medical Informatics, Department of Medicine, School of Medicine, at Stanford University. Since 1988, he has taught courses in genetic algorithms and genetic programming in the School of Engineering at Stanford University, and since 1995, he has cotaught a course in computational molecular biology in the School of Medicine at Stanford University. From 1987 to the present, he is the president of Third Millennium Venture Capital Limited of Los Altos Hills, California.

Forrest H Bennett III is chief scientist of Genetic Programming, Inc. of Los Altos, California. He received his B.S. degree in Applied Mathematics at the University of Colorado in 1984. He ran a software consulting business for five years, where he designed systems, including industry's leading industrial driveshaft design system. He then became the chief engineer at Manco Systems, where he designed and implemented the company's primary software product, used for data collection in manufacturing environments. He has done research on using functional languages for programming parallel computers. His current research involves using genetic programming to solve problems in areas such as automatic programming of multiagent systems, analog circuit design, and programming field-programmable gate arrays.

David Andre is a Ph.D. candidate in the Computer Science Division of the University of California at Berkeley. He graduated with a B.S. in Symbolic Systems and a B.A. in Psychology from Stanford in 1994. The focus of his research efforts has been to develop techniques that allow evolutionary computation to solve difficult, real-world problems. He is also the author of a public domain genetic programming kernel. In 1996, he was awarded a National Defense Science and Engineering Grant for graduate research. He has also invented a scheduling algorithm for call center workforce management products for Blue Pumpkin Software, Inc.

Martin A. Keane received his Ph.D. from Northwestern University in 1969. He had earlier received a B.S.E.E. from Illinois Institute of technology in 1961 and an M.S. in Mathematics from the University of Hawaii in 1967. Between 1972 and 1976, Dr. Keane supervised the Operations Research group in the Mathematics Department at General Motors Research Laboratory in Warren, Michigan. He joined Bally Manufacturing Corporation of Chicago in 1976 as vice-president of engineering for the amusement game division. He became vice-president for technology for the entire corporation in 1980, supervising over 200 engineers. In this capacity, after the sale of Scientific Games, Inc., to Bally in 1982, Dr. Keane also designed and manufactured various products for Scientific Games, Inc., including video player-activated lottery game machines, interactive laser disk games, and online clerk-activated lottery game terminals with distributed fault-tolerant computer processing. He has also designed specialized equipment for the high-speed computer-controlled imaging operations used in printing instant lottery game tickets. Drs. Keane and Koza have received numerous patents in various areas of computers, electronics, printing, and gaming technology.

GENETIC PROGRAMMING III

Darwinian Invention and Problem Solving

John R. Koza
Forrest H Bennett III
David Andre
Martin A. Keane

MORGAN KAUFMANN PUBLISHERS
San Francisco, California

Senior Editor	Denise E.M. Penrose
Director of Production and Manufacturing	Yonie Overton
Senior Production Editor	Elisabeth Beller
Cover Design	Carron Design
Cover Image	Roberto Brosan/Photonica
Text Design	Mark Ong, Side by Side Studios
Copyeditor	Ken DellaPenta
Proofreader	Jennifer McClain
Compositor	Nancy Logan
Indexer	Steve Rath
Printer	Quebecor Printing

The following illustrations are courtesy of Xilinx, Inc.: Figures 57.1–57.4 and 57.6.

The programs, procedures, and applications presented in this book have been included for their instructional value. The publisher and the authors offer NO WARRANTY OF FITNESS OR MERCHANTABILITY FOR ANY PARTICULAR PURPOSE and do not accept any liability with respect to these programs, procedures, and applications.

Morgan Kaufmann Publishers, Inc.
Editorial and Sales Office
340 Pine Street, Sixth Floor
San Francisco, CA 94104-3205
USA

Telephone	415/392-2665
Facsimile	415/982-2665
Email	mkp@mkp.com
WWW	http://www.mkp.com

Order toll free 800/745-7323

Library of Congress Cataloging-in-Publication Data
Koza, John R.
    Genetic programming III ; darwinian invention and problem solving
    / John R. Koza . . . [et al.].
        p.   cm.
    Includes bibliographical references (p.   and index.
    ISBN 1-55860-543-6
    1. Genetic programming (Computer science)
QA76.623.K69   1999
006.3'1—dc21   99-10099
                                                                          CIP

To our parents—all of whom were best-of-generation individuals

Parts

Abbreviated Contents

Contents

Acknowledgments

We are indebted to Frank Dunlap of Enabling Systems, Inc., of Palo Alto, who, among other things, suggested several of the problems of synthesis of active circuits (and helped us on the implementation of several others) and made numerous helpful comments on the drafts of the part of this book concerning analog electrical circuits.

We collaborated with the following on certain problems in this book:

- Frank Dunlap, Enabling Systems, Palo Alto, California, on frequency discriminator circuits, computational circuits, and various other analog circuits (Koza, Bennett, Andre, Keane, and Dunlap 1997; Koza, Bennett, Lohn, Dunlap, Andre, and Keane 1997a, 1997b, 1997c),
- Jason D. Lohn, NASA Ames Research Laboratory, Mountain View, California, on frequency discriminator circuits and computational circuits (Koza, Bennett, Lohn, Dunlap, Andre, and Keane 1997a, 1997b, 1997c), and
- Jeffrey L. Hutchings and Stephen L. Bade, Convergent Design, L.L.C., Salt Lake City, Utah, on field-programmable gate arrays (Koza, Bennett, Hutchings, Bade, Keane, and Andre 1997a, 1997b, 1997c, 1998).

Computer programming relating to some of the work in this book was done by the following:

- Walter Alden Tackett designed the architecture for the computer processes that are used in the 64-node Transtech parallel computer using INMOS transputers as well as our later implementation of parallel genetic programming.
- Walter Alden Tackett (and David Andre) wrote the computer program to implement the original group of architecture-altering operations.
- Hugh Thomas of SGS-Thompson Microelectronics wrote configuration scripts and assisted in debugging the program and systems for the 64-node Transtech parallel computer using INMOS transputers.
- Jason D. Lohn (and Forrest H Bennett III) wrote the computer programs to implement runs of genetic programming for the source identification circuits and certain computational circuits.
- James Shipman of IBM Corporation, San Jose, on the design and system-level programming of our Beowulf-style parallel computer system (described in Section 62.1.5).
- Oscar Stiffelman of Stanford University on the incorporation of the graph isomorphism algorithm into the problem of synthesizing a lowpass filter (Section 27.6).

- William Mydlowec, Jessen Yu, and Oscar Stiffelman of Stanford University on the programming of the Beowulf-style parallel computer system (described in Section 62.1.5).

Simon Handley of Daimler-Benz Research in Palo Alto, California; David B. Fogel of Natural Selection, Inc., in San Diego, California; and David E. Goldberg of the University of Illinois at Urbana-Champaign made numerous helpful comments and suggestions concerning various versions of the manuscript. We are also indebted to the following people for additional helpful comments and suggestions:

- Wolfgang Banzhaf, University of Dortmund,
- Tobias Blickle, Germany,
- Lashon Booker, the Mitre Corporation,
- Kumar Chellapilla, University of California, San Diego,
- Gary Fogel, Natural Selection, Inc.,
- Edward Feigenbaum, Stanford University,
- John H. Holland, University of Michigan,
- Hitoshi Iba, University of Tokyo,
- Christian Jacob, University of Erlangen,
- Cezary Z. Janikow, University of Missouri, St. Louis,
- William B. Langdon, University of Birmingham,
- Hon-Cheong Leung, Stanford University,
- Thomas Mitchell, Carnegie Mellon University,
- Nancy Mize, Ciphergen, Inc.,
- Peter Nordin, Chalmers University of Technology,
- Zbigniew Michalewicz, University of North Carolina,
- Melanie Mitchell, Santa Fe Institute,
- Bill Mydlowec, Stanford University,
- Una-May O'Reilly, MIT Media Laboratory,
- Justinian Rosca, Siemens Research Laboratory,
- Moshe Sipper, Swiss Federal Institute of Technology,
- Marianne Siroker, Stanford University,
- Oscar Stiffelman, Stanford University,
- Lee Spector, Hampshire College, and
- Jessen Yu, Stanford University.

We gratefully acknowledge useful discussions with various people on portions of this book. One or more of us had useful discussions with

- Arthur O. Bauer, Chairman, Center for German Communication and Related Technology 1920–1945, Germany, concerning history of filters,
- Steve Casselman, Virtual Computer Corporation, concerning field-programmable gate arrays,
- James Crutchfield, Santa Fe Institute, concerning cellular automata,
- Rajarshi Das, IBM T. J. Watson Research Center, concerning cellular automata,
- Lawrence Davis, TICA Associates, concerning cellular automata,
- Phillip Freidin, Silicon Spice, concerning field-programmable gate arrays,
- Thomas Lee, Stanford University, concerning analog circuits,
- Stefan Ludwig, Digital, Inc., concerning field-programmable gate arrays,

- Reading Maley, AMD, concerning analog circuits,
- Melanie Mitchell, Santa Fe Institute, concerning cellular automata,
- John Perry, Cadence, Inc., concerning analog circuits,
- Tom L. Quarles, Meta-Software, Campbell, California, concerning the SPICE simulator,
- Mark J. Roulo, KLA-Tencor Corporation, San Jose, California, concerning multi-agent strategies,
- John Schewel, Virtual Computer Corporation, concerning field-programmable gate arrays,
- Adrian Stroica, JPL, Pasadena, California, concerning the Gaussian computational circuit,
- Andrei Vladimirescu, Cadence, Inc., concerning analog circuits, and
- Bruce Wooley, Stanford University, concerning analog circuits.

Marianne Siroker, Stanford University, and Anat Rubner were helpful in creating some of the figures in this book.

We thank Michael Morgan, Denise Penrose, and Elisabeth Beller of Morgan Kaufmann Publishers and copyeditor Ken DellaPenta for their help with this book.

David Andre is a recipient of a National Defense Science and Engineering Grant.

Note from the Publisher

Support Materials

The authors have prepared a 50-minute videotape that surveys the main points of this book. The videotape briefly presents genetically evolved solutions to many of the problems discussed in the book, with emphasis on the results that are competitive with human-produced results. It describes how genetic programming uses architecture-altering operations to make on-the-fly decisions on whether to use subroutines, loops, recursions, and memory in its evolved program. It also demonstrates that genetic programming possesses the attributes that can reasonably be expected of a system for automatically creating computer programs. Finally, it shows how genetic programming's success arises from the fundamental differences that distinguish it from conventional artificial intelligence and machine learning.

The videotape is available from the publisher in NTSC format (ISBN 1-55860-617-3) and in Pal format (ISBN 1-55860-616-5) and may be ordered from our website, *www.mkp.com/GP3,* or by fax or phone at the numbers listed below.

Contacting the Publisher

We welcome your comments about this book and invite you to contact us with advice, praise, and errors.

Correspondence should be addressed to the Editorial and Sales Office of Morgan Kaufmann Publishers, Inc., 340 Pine Street, Sixth Floor, San Francisco, CA 94104 or sent electronically to *GP3@mkp.com.* If you send your email address to us at *GP3@mkp.com,* we will keep you posted on news about this book and related books from Morgan Kaufmann.

Kindly report any errors you find by email to *GP3bugs@mkp.com.* We suggest you first check the errata page at *www.mkp.com/GP3* to see if the bug has already been reported and fixed.

To order additional copies of this book or to order the video, call 1-800-745-7323, fax 1-800-874-6418, email *orders@mkp.com,* or visit our website at *www.mkp.com.* To obtain an examination copy for a course, please call us at 1-888-864-7547 or fill out the examination request form on our website.

Contacting the Authors

The authors also welcome your comments, and they may be reached by email, surface mail, or through their websites at the following addresses:

John R. Koza
Consulting Professor
Section on Medical Informatics
Department of Medicine
School of Medicine
Medical School Office Building, Stanford
Stanford University
Stanford, CA 94305-5479 USA
koza@genetic-programming.com
www.genetic-programming.com
www.smi.stanford.edu/people/koza

Forrest H Bennett III
Chief Scientist
Genetic Programming, Inc.
Box 1669
Los Altos, CA 94023 USA
forrest@evolute.com
www.genetic-programming.com

David Andre
Ph.D. Candidate
Computer Science Division
University of California
Berkeley, CA 94720 USA
dandre@cs.berkeley.edu
www.cs.berkeley.edu/~dandre

Martin A. Keane
Econometrics, Inc.
111 E. Wacker Dr.
Chicago, IL 60601 USA
makeane@ix.netcom.com

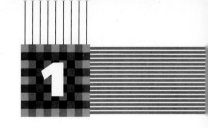

Part 1:
INTRODUCTION

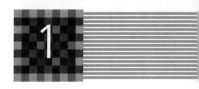

Introduction

One of the central challenges of computer science is to get a computer to solve a problem without explicitly programming it. In particular, the challenge is to create an automatic system whose input is a high-level statement of a problem's requirements and whose output is a working computer program that solves the given problem. Paraphrasing Arthur Samuel (1959), this challenge concerns

> How can computers be made to do what needs to be done, without being told exactly how to do it?

This book is about a biologically inspired, domain-independent method called *genetic programming* that automatically creates a computer program from a high-level statement of a problem's requirements. Genetic programming is an extension of the genetic algorithm described in John Holland's pioneering book *Adaptation in Natural and Artificial Systems* (Holland 1975). Starting with a primordial ooze of thousands of randomly created computer programs, genetic programming progressively breeds a population of computer programs over a series of generations. Genetic programming employs the Darwinian principle of survival of the fittest and analogs of naturally occurring operations such as sexual recombination (crossover), mutation, gene duplication, and gene deletion. It sometimes uses certain mechanisms of developmental biology.

When we talk about a computer program (Figure 1.1), we mean an entity that receives inputs, performs computations, and produces outputs. Computer programs perform basic arithmetic and conditional computations on variables of various types (including integer, floating-point, and Boolean variables), perform iterations and recursions, store intermediate results in memory, contain reusable groups of operations that are organized into subroutines, pass information to subroutines in the form of dummy variables (formal parameters), and receive information from subroutines in the form of return values (or through side effects). The subroutines and main program are typically organized into a hierarchy.

We think that it is reasonable to expect that a system for automatically creating computer programs should be able to create entities that possess most or all of the above capabilities (or reasonable equivalents of them). A capabilities list of attributes for a system for automatically creating computer programs might include the following 16 items:

- **ATTRIBUTE NO. 1** (Starts with "what needs to be done"): It starts from a high-level statement specifying the requirements of the problem.
- **ATTRIBUTE NO. 2** (Tells us "how to do it"): It produces a result in the form of a sequence of steps that satisfactorily solves the problem.

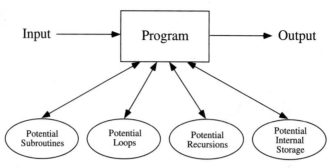

Figure 1.1   A computer program

- **ATTRIBUTE NO. 3** (Produces a computer program): It produces an entity that can run on a computer.
- **ATTRIBUTE NO. 4** (Automatic determination of program size): It has the ability to automatically determine the number of steps that must be performed and thus does not require the user to prespecify the exact size of the solution.
- **ATTRIBUTE NO. 5** (Code reuse): It has the ability to automatically organize useful groups of steps so that they can be reused.
- **ATTRIBUTE NO. 6** (Parameterized reuse): It has the ability to reuse groups of steps with different instantiations of values (formal parameters or dummy variables).
- **ATTRIBUTE NO. 7** (Internal storage): It has the ability to use internal storage in the form of single variables, vectors, matrices, arrays, stacks, queues, lists, relational memory, and other data structures.
- **ATTRIBUTE NO. 8** (Iterations, loops, and recursions): It has the ability to implement iterations, loops, and recursions.
- **ATTRIBUTE NO. 9** (Self-organization of hierarchies): It has the ability to automatically organize groups of steps into a hierarchy.
- **ATTRIBUTE NO. 10** (Automatic determination of program architecture): It has the ability to automatically determine whether to employ subroutines, iterations, loops, recursions, and internal storage, and to automatically determine the number of arguments possessed by each subroutine, iteration, loop, and recursion.
- **ATTRIBUTE NO. 11** (Wide range of programming constructs): It has the ability to implement analogs of the programming constructs that human computer programmers find useful, including macros, libraries, typing, pointers, conditional operations, logical functions, integer functions, floating-point functions, complex-valued functions, multiple inputs, multiple outputs, and machine code instructions.
- **ATTRIBUTE NO. 12** (Well-defined): It operates in a well-defined way. It unmistakably distinguishes between what the user must provide and what the system delivers.
- **ATTRIBUTE NO. 13** (Problem-independent): It is problem-independent in the sense that the user does not have to modify the system's executable steps for each new problem.

- **ATTRIBUTE NO. 14** (Wide applicability): It produces a satisfactory solution to a wide variety of problems from many different fields.
- **ATTRIBUTE NO. 15** (Scalability): It scales well to larger versions of the same problem.
- **ATTRIBUTE NO. 16** (Competitive with human-produced results): It produces results that are competitive with those produced by human programmers, engineers, mathematicians, and designers.

The main point of this book is that genetic programming currently unconditionally possesses 13 of the 16 attributes that can reasonably be expected of a system for automatically creating computer programs and that genetic programming at least partially possesses the remaining three attributes.

The conclusion of this book (Chapter 64) inventories the results demonstrated or cited in this book in relation to the degree to which genetic programming currently possesses the above 16 attributes.

Attribute No. 16 is especially important because it reminds us that the ultimate goal of a system for automatically creating computer programs is to produce useful programs—not merely programs that solve "toy" or "proof of principle" problems. As Samuel (1983) said,

> The aim [is] . . . to get machines to exhibit behavior, which if done by humans, would be assumed to involve the use of intelligence.

In this connection, this book contains 14 specific instances where we claim that genetic programming has automatically created a computer program that is competitive with a human-produced result.

What do we mean when we say that an automatically created solution to a problem is competitive with a result produced by humans? We are not referring to the fact that a computer can rapidly print 10,000 payroll checks or that a computer can compute π to a million decimal places. As Fogel, Owens, and Walsh (1966) said,

> Artificial intelligence is realized only if an inanimate machine can solve problems . . . not because of the machine's sheer speed and accuracy, but because it can discover for itself new techniques for solving the problem at hand.

We think it is fair to say that an automatically created result is competitive with one produced by human engineers, designers, mathematicians, or programmers if it satisfies any of the following eight criteria (or any other similarly stringent criterion):

A. The result was patented as an invention in the past, is an improvement over a patented invention, or would qualify today as a patentable new invention.

B. The result is equal to or better than a result that was accepted as a new scientific result at the time when it was published in a peer-reviewed journal.

C. The result is equal to or better than a result that was placed into a database or archive of results maintained by an internationally recognized panel of scientific experts.

    D.   The result is publishable in its own right as a new scientific result (independent of the fact that the result was mechanically created).

    E.   The result is equal to or better than the most recent human-created solution to a long-standing problem for which there has been a succession of increasingly better human-created solutions.

    F.   The result is equal to or better than a result that was considered an achievement in its field at the time it was first discovered.

    G.   The result solves a problem of indisputable difficulty in its field.

    H.   The result holds its own or wins a regulated competition involving human contestants (in the form of either live human players or human-written computer programs).

Table 1.1 shows 14 instances of results reported in this book where we claim that genetic programming has produced results that are competitive with those produced by human engineers, designers, mathematicians, or programmers. Each claim is accompanied by the particular criterion that establishes the basis for the claim. The instances in Table 1.1 include classification problems from the field of computational molecular biology, a long-standing problem involving cellular automata, a problem of synthesizing the design of a minimal sorting network, and several problems of synthesizing the design of analog electrical circuits. As can be seen, 10 of the 14 instances in Table 1.1 involve previously patented inventions.

Engineering design offers a practical yardstick for evaluating a method for automatically creating computer programs because the design process is usually viewed as requiring human intelligence. Design is a major activity of practicing engineers. The process of design involves the creation of a complex structure to satisfy user-defined requirements. For example, the design process for analog electrical circuits begins with a high-level description of the circuit's desired behavior and characteristics and entails the creation of both the circuit's topology and the values of each of the circuit's components. The design process typically entails trade-offs between competing considerations. The design (synthesis) of analog electrical circuits is especially challenging because there is no previously known general automated technique for creating both the topology and sizing of an analog circuit from a high-level statement of the circuit's desired behavior and characteristics.

In addition, there are numerous instances outside this book where others have used genetic programming to evolve programs that are competitive with human-produced results, including Howley's use of genetic programming to control a spacecraft's attitude maneuvers (Howley 1996) as well as the genetically evolved entries that held their own against the human-written programs in the 1997 and 1998 Robo Cup competitions (Luke and Spector 1998; Andre and Teller 1998).

Of course, we do not claim that genetic programming is the only possible approach to the challenge of getting computers to solve problems without explicitly programming them. However, we are not aware at this time of any other method of artificial intelligence, machine learning, neural networks, adaptive systems, reinforcement learning, or automated logic that can be said to possess more than a few of the above 16 attributes.

Table 1.1   Fourteen instances in this book where genetic programming has produced results that are competitive with human-produced results

	Claimed instance	Basis for the claim	Reference
1	Creation of four different algorithms for the transmembrane segment identification problem for proteins	B, E	Section 16.6
2	Creation of a sorting network for seven items using only 16 steps	A, D	Section 21.4.4
3	Rediscovery of Campbell ladder topology for lowpass and highpass filters	A, F	Section 25.15.1
4	Rediscovery of Zobel's "*M*-derived half section" and "constant *K*" filter topology	A, F	Section 25.15.2
5	Rediscovery of the Cauer (elliptic) topology for filters	A, F	Section 27.3.7
6	Automatic decomposition of the problem of synthesizing a crossover filter	A, F	Section 32.3
7	Rediscovery of a recognizable voltage gain stage and a Darlington emitter-follower section of an amplifier and other circuits	A, F	Section 42.3
8	Synthesis of 60 and 96 decibel amplifiers	A, F	Section 45.3
9	Synthesis of analog computational circuits for squaring, cubing, square root, cube root, logarithm, and Gaussian functions	A, D, G	Section 47.5.3
10	Synthesis of a real-time analog circuit for time-optimal control of a robot	G	Section 48.3
11	Synthesis of an electronic thermometer	A, G	Section 49.3
12	Synthesis of a voltage reference circuit	A, G	Section 50.3
13	Creation of a cellular automata rule for the majority classification problem that is better than the Gacs-Kurdyumov-Levin (GKL) rule and better than all other known rules written by humans over the past 20 years	D, E	Section 58.4
14	Creation of motifs that detect the D–E–A–D box family of proteins and the manganese superoxide dismutase family as well as, or slightly better than, the human-written motifs archived in the PROSITE database of protein motifs	C	Section 59.8

Conspicuously, the above list of 16 attributes does not preordain that formal logic or an explicit knowledge base be the method used to achieve the goal of automatically creating computer programs. Many computer scientists unquestioningly assume that formal logic must play a preeminent role in any system for automatically creating computer programs. Similarly, the vast majority of contemporary researchers in artificial intelligence believe that a system for automatically creating computer programs must employ an explicit knowledge base. Indeed, over the past four decades, the field of artificial intelligence has been dominated by the strongly asserted belief that the goal of getting a computer to solve problems automatically can be achieved *only* by means of formal logic inference methods and knowledge. This approach typically entails the selection of a knowledge representation, the acquisition of the knowledge, the codification of the knowledge into a knowledge base, the depositing of the knowledge base into a computer, and the manipulation of the knowledge in the computer using the inference methods of formal logic. As Lenat (1983) stated,

> All our experiences in AI research have led us to believe that for automatic programming, the answer lies in *knowledge*, in adding a collection of expert rules which guide code synthesis and transformation. [Emphasis in original.]

However, the existence of a strenuously asserted belief for four decades does not, in itself, validate the belief. Moreover, the popularity of a belief does not preclude the possibility that there might be an alternative way of achieving a particular goal.

Genetic programming is different from all other approaches to artificial intelligence, machine learning, neural networks, adaptive systems, reinforcement learning, or automated logic in all (or most) of the following seven ways:

1. **Representation:** Genetic programming overtly conducts its search for a solution to the given problem in program space.
2. **Role of point-to-point transformations in the search:** Genetic programming does not conduct its search by transforming a single point in the search space into another single point, but instead transforms a set (population) of points into another set of points.
3. **Role of hill climbing in the search:** Genetic programming does not rely exclusively on greedy hill climbing to conduct its search, but instead allocates a certain number of trials, in a principled way, to choices that are known to be inferior.
4. **Role of determinism in the search:** Genetic programming conducts its search probabilistically.
5. **Role of an explicit knowledge base:** None.
6. **Role of the inference methods of formal logic in the search:** None.
7. **Underpinnings of the technique:** Biologically inspired.

First, consider the issue of representation. Most techniques of artificial intelligence, machine learning, neural networks, adaptive systems, reinforcement learning, or automated logic employ specialized structures in lieu of ordinary computer programs. These surrogate structures include if-then production rules, Horn clauses, decision trees, Bayesian networks, propositional logic, formal grammars, binary decision diagrams, frames, conceptual clusters, concept sets, numerical weight vectors (for neural nets), vectors of numerical coefficients for polynomials or other fixed expressions (for adaptive systems), genetic classifier system rules, fixed tables of values (as in reinforcement learning), or linear chromosome strings (as in the conventional genetic algorithm).

Tellingly, except in unusual situations, the world's several million computer programmers do not use any of these surrogate structures for writing computer programs. Instead, for five decades, human programmers have persisted in writing computer programs that intermix a multiplicity of types of computations (e.g., arithmetic and logical) operating on a multiplicity of types of variables (e.g., integer, floating-point, and Boolean). Programmers have persisted in using internal memory to store the results of intermediate calculations in order to avoid repeating the calculation on each occasion when the result is needed. They have persisted in using iterations and recursions. They have similarly persisted in organizing useful sequences of operations into reusable groups (subroutines) so that they avoid reinventing the wheel on each occasion when they need a particular sequence of operations. Moreover, they have persisted in passing parameters to subroutines so that they can reuse their subroutines with different instantiations of values. And they have persisted in organizing their subroutines into hierarchies.

All of the above tools of ordinary computer programming have been in use since the beginning of the era of electronic computers in the 1940s. Significantly, none has fallen into disuse by human programmers. Yet, in spite of the manifest utility of these everyday tools of computer programming, these tools are largely absent from existing techniques of automated machine learning, neural networks, artificial intelligence, adaptive systems, reinforcement learning, and automated logic. On one of the relatively rare occasions when one or two of these everyday tools of computer programming is available within the context of one of these automated techniques, they are usually available only in a hobbled and barely recognizable form. In contrast, genetic programming draws on the full arsenal of tools that human programmers have found useful for five decades. It conducts its search for a solution to a problem overtly in the space of computer programs. Our view is that computer programs are the best representation of computer programs. We believe that the search for a solution to the challenge of getting computers to solve problems without explicitly programming them should be conducted in the space of computer programs.

Of course, once you realize that the search should be conducted in program space, you are immediately faced with the task of finding the desired program in the enormous space of possible programs. As will be seen, genetic programming performs this task of program discovery. It provides a problem-independent way to productively search the space of possible computer programs to find a program that satisfactorily solves the given problem.

Second, another difference between genetic programming and almost every automated technique concerns the nature of the search conducted in the technique's chosen search space. Almost all of these nongenetic methods employ a point-to-point strategy that transforms a single point in the search space into another single point. Genetic programming is different in that it operates by explicitly cultivating a diverse population of often-inconsistent and often-contradictory approaches to solving the problem. Genetic programming performs a beam search in program space by iteratively transforming one population of candidate computer programs into a new population of programs.

Third, consider the role of hill climbing. When the trajectory through the search space is from one single point to another single point, there is a nearly irresistible temptation to extend the search only by moving to a point that is known to be superior to the current point. Consequently, almost all automated techniques rely exclusively on greedy hill climbing to make the transformation from the current point in the search space to the next point. The temptation to rely on hill climbing is reinforced because many of the toy problems in the literature of the fields of machine learning and artificial intelligence are so simple that they can, in fact, be solved by hill climbing. However, popularity cannot cure the innate tendency of hill climbing to become trapped on a local optimum that is not a global optimum. Interesting and nontrivial problems generally have high-payoff points that are inaccessible to greedy hill climbing. In fact, the existence of points in the search space that are not accessible to hill climbing is a good working definition of nontriviality. The fact that genetic programming does not rely on a point-to-point search strategy helps to liberate it from the myopia of hill climbing. Genetic programming is free to allocate a certain measured number of trials to points that are known to be inferior. This allocation of trials to known-inferior individuals is not motivated by charity, but in the expectation that it will often unearth an unobvious trajectory through the search space leading to points with an ultimately higher payoff. The fact that genetic programming operates from a population enables it to make a small number of adventurous moves while simultaneously pursuing the more immediately gratifying avenues of advance through the search space. Of course, genetic programming is not the only search technique that avoids mere hill climbing. For example, both simulated annealing (Kirkpatrick, Gelatt, and Vecchi 1983; Aarts and Korst 1989) and genetic algorithms (Holland 1975) allocate a certain number of trials to inferior points in a similar principled way. However, most of the techniques currently used in the fields of artificial intelligence, machine learning, neural networks, adaptive systems, reinforcement learning, or automated logic are trapped on the local optimum of hill climbing.

Fourth, another difference between genetic programming and almost every other technique of artificial intelligence and machine learning is that genetic programming conducts a probabilistic search. Again, genetic programming is not unique in this respect. For example, simulated annealing and genetic algorithms are also probabilistic. However, most existing automated techniques are deterministic.

Fifth, consider the role of a knowledge base in the pursuit of the goal of automatically creating computer programs. In genetic programming, there is no explicit knowledge base. While there are numerous optional ways to incorporate domain knowledge into a run of genetic programming, genetic programming does not require (or usually use) an explicit knowledge base to guide its search.

Sixth, consider the role of the inference methods of formal logic. Many computer scientists unquestioningly assume that every problem-solving technique must be logically sound, deterministic, logically consistent, and parsimonious. Accordingly, most conventional methods of artificial intelligence and machine learning possess these characteristics. However, logic does not govern two of the most important types of complex problem-solving processes, namely, the invention process performed by creative humans and the evolutionary process occurring in nature.

A new idea that can be logically deduced from facts that are known in a field, using transformations that are known in a field, is not considered to be an invention. There must be what the patent law refers to as an "illogical step" (i.e., an unjustified step) to distinguish a putative invention from that which is readily deducible from that which is already known. Humans supply the critical ingredient of "illogic" to the invention process. Interestingly, everyday usage parallels the patent law concerning inventiveness: people who mechanically apply existing facts in well-known ways are summarily dismissed as being uncreative. Logical thinking is unquestionably useful for many purposes. It usually plays an important role in setting the stage for an invention. But, at the end of the day, logical thinking is insufficient for invention and creativity.

Recalling his invention in 1927 of the negative feedback amplifier, Harold S. Black (1977) of Bell Laboratories said

> Then came the morning of Tuesday, August 2, 1927, when the concept of the negative feedback amplifier came to me in a flash while I was crossing the Hudson River on the Lackawanna Ferry, on my way to work. For more than 50 years, I have pondered how and why the idea came, and I can't say any more today than I could that morning. All I know is that after several years of hard work on the problem, I suddenly realized that if I fed the amplifier output back to the input, in reverse phase, and kept the device from oscillating (singing, as we called it then), I would have exactly what I wanted: a means of canceling out the distortion of the output. I opened my morning newspaper and on a page of *The New York Times,* I sketched a simple canonical diagram of a negative feedback amplifier plus the equations for the amplification with feedback.

Of course, inventors are not oblivious to logic and knowledge. They do not thrash around using blind random search. Black did not try to construct the negative feedback amplifier from neon bulbs or doorbells. Instead, "several years of hard work on the problem" set the stage and brought his thinking into the proximity of a solution. Then, at the critical moment, Black made his "illogical" leap. This unjustified leap constituted the invention.

The design of complex entities by the evolutionary process in nature is another important type of problem solving that is not governed by logic. In nature, solutions to design problems are discovered by the probabilistic process of evolution and natural selection. This is not a logical process. Indeed, inconsistent and contradictory alternatives abound. In fact, such genetic diversity is necessary for the evolutionary process to succeed. Significantly, the solutions created by evolution and natural selection almost always differ from those created by conventional methods of artificial intelligence and machine learning in one very important respect. Evolved solutions are not brittle; they are usually able to grapple with the perpetual novelty of real environments.

Similarly, genetic programming is not guided by the inference methods of formal logic in its search for a computer program to solve a given problem. When the goal is the automatic creation of computer programs, all of our experience has led us to conclude that the nonlogical approaches used in the invention process and in natural evolution are far more fruitful than the logic-driven and knowledge-based principles of conventional artificial intelligence. In short, "logic considered harmful."

Seventh, the biological metaphor underlying genetic programming is very different from the underpinnings of all other techniques that have previously been tried in pursuit of the goal of automatically creating computer programs. Many computer scientists and mathematicians are baffled by the suggestion that biology might be relevant to their fields. In contrast, we do not view biology as an unlikely well from which to draw a solution to the challenge of getting a computer to solve a problem without explicitly programming it. Quite the contrary—we view biology as a most likely source. Indeed, genetic programming is based on the only method that has ever produced intelligence—the time-tested method of evolution and natural selection. As Stanislaw Ulam said in his l976 autobiography (1991),

> [Ask] not what mathematics can do for biology, but what biology can do for mathematics.

The notion that artificial intelligence may be realized by using a biological approach is, of course, not new. Turing made the connection between searches and the challenge of getting a computer to solve a problem without explicitly programming it in his 1948 essay "Intelligent Machines" (Ince 1992). (Longer versions of the quotations below appear in Section 2.4.1.)

> Further research into intelligence of machinery will probably be very greatly concerned with "searches" . . .

Turing then identified three broad approaches by which search might be used to automatically create an intelligent computer program.

One approach that Turing identified is a search through the space of integers representing candidate computer programs. Another approach is the "cultural search," which relies on knowledge and expertise acquired over a period of years from others (akin to present-day knowledge-based systems). The third approach that Turing specifically identified is "genetical or evolutionary search." Turing said

> There is the genetical or evolutionary search by which a combination of genes is looked for, the criterion being the survival value. The remarkable success of this search confirms to some extent the idea that intellectual activity consists mainly of various kinds of search.

Turing did not specify in this essay how to conduct a "genetical or evolutionary search" for a computer program. However, his 1950 paper "Computing Machinery and Intelligence" suggested how natural selection and evolution might be incorporated into the search for intelligent machines.

> We cannot expect to find a good child-machine at the first attempt. One must experiment with teaching one such machine and see how well it learns. One can then try another and see if it is better or worse. There is an obvious connection between this process and evolution, by the identifications
>
> Structure of the child machine = Hereditary material
>
> Changes of the child machine = Mutations
>
> Natural selection = Judgment of the experimenter

This book confirms Turing's view that there is indeed a "connection" between machine intelligence and evolution by describing our implementation of Turing's third way to achieve machine intelligence.

1.1 ORGANIZATION OF THIS BOOK

This book has the following 10 parts:

1. Introduction
2. Background
3. Architecture-Altering Operations

4. Genetic Programming Problem Solver
5. Automated Synthesis of Analog Electrical Circuits
6. Evolvable Hardware
7. Discovery of Cellular Automata Rules
8. Discovery of Motifs and Programmatic Motifs for Molecular Biology
9. Parallelization and Implementation Issues
10. Conclusion

Part 1 is the introduction.

Part 2 provides background on genetic algorithms, the LISP programming language, the basic ideas of genetic programming, and sources of additional information about the field of evolutionary computation.

Part 3 describes architecture-altering operations that provide an automatic way, during a run of genetic programming, to

- create, duplicate, and delete subroutines (Chapter 5),
- create, duplicate, and delete arguments to subroutines (Chapter 5),
- create, duplicate, and delete iterations (Chapter 6),
- create, duplicate, and delete loops (Chapter 7),
- create, duplicate, and delete recursions (Chapter 8), and
- create, duplicate, and delete internal storage (Chapter 9).

In addition, Part 3 is intended to demonstrate the breadth of genetic programming with the architecture-altering operations by illustrative applications involving

- Boolean parity problems using the architecture-altering operations for subroutines (Chapter 12),
- time-optimal robot control using the architecture-altering operations for subroutines (Chapter 13),
- multiagent systems using the architecture-altering operations for subroutines (Chapter 14),
- digit recognition using the architecture-altering operations for subroutines (Chapter 15),
- a version of the transmembrane segment identification problem using the architecture-altering operations for subroutines (Chapter 16),
- a problem requiring iteration, namely, a version of the transmembrane segment identification problem using the architecture-altering operations for subroutines and iterations (Chapter 17),
- a problem requiring recursion, namely, creation of a program for the Fibonacci sequence, using the architecture-altering operation of recursion creation (Chapter 18), and
- a problem involving internal storage, namely, the time-optimal cart-centering (isotropic rocket) problem, using the architecture-altering operation of storage creation (Chapter 19).

Chapters 12 and 13 provide especially detailed introductory explanations of how to apply genetic programming to a problem.

Part 4 presents the Genetic Programming Problem Solver (GPPS). Part 4 is intended to demonstrate the generality of genetic programming with the architecture-altering operations. GPPS is intended to provide a general-purpose method for automatically creating computer programs that solve, or approximately solve, problems. GPPS uses a standardized set of functions and terminals and thereby eliminates the need for the user to prespecify a function set and terminal set for the problem. In addition, GPPS uses the architecture-altering operations to create, duplicate, and delete subroutines and loops (and, in GPPS 2.0, recursions and internal storage) during the run of genetic programming. Since the architecture of the evolving program is automatically determined during the run, GPPS eliminates the need for the user to specify in advance whether to employ subroutines, loops, recursions, and internal storage in solving a given problem. It similarly eliminates the need for the user to specify the number of arguments possessed by each subroutine. Chapter 20 describes version 1 of the Genetic Programming Problem Solver. GPPS 1.0 is capable of automatically creating computer programs with

- various numbers of inputs,
- various numbers of outputs,
- an initially unspecified number of subroutines (automatically defined functions), with each automatically defined function possessing an initially unspecified number of arguments,
- an initially unspecified number of automatically defined loops, with each automatically defined loop consisting of a loop initialization branch, a loop condition branch, a loop body branch, and a loop update branch, and
- a fixed number of cells of indexed memory to provide internal storage.

Chapter 21 illustrates GPPS 1.0 by applying it to

- Boolean parity problems (Sections 21.1 and 21.2),
- a time-optimal robot control problem (Section 21.3), and
- a problem of synthesizing the design of a minimal sorting network (Section 21.4).

Chapter 22 describes GPPS 2.0. It has the additional capabilities of handling programs with

- an initially unspecified number of automatically defined recursions, with each automatically defined recursion consisting of a recursion condition branch, a recursion body branch, a recursion update branch, and a recursion ground branch, and
- an initially unspecified amount and type of internal storage as implemented by automatically defined stores.

Chapter 23 illustrates GPPS 2.0 by applying it to

- symbolic regression of a quadratic polynomial (Section 23.1),
- the intertwined spirals problem (Section 23.2),
- the cart-centering (isotropic rocket) problem (Section 23.3),
- the Boolean even-6-parity problem (Section 23.4),
- the time-optimal robot controller problem (Section 23.5), and

- the problem of synthesizing the design of a minimal sorting network (Section 23.6).

Parts 5, 6, 7, and 8 are intended to demonstrate the depth of genetic programming with architecture-altering operations.

Part 5 shows how genetic programming can be used to synthesize analog electrical circuits to satisfy a high-level statement of the circuit's desired behavior and characteristics. There has previously been no general automated technique for automatically synthesizing both the topology and sizing of an analog circuit from high-level design requirements. Automatic synthesis of circuits is accomplished using a developmental process (Chapter 25). The synthesis of circuits by genetic programming is illustrated by designing

- a lowpass filter (with an especially detailed step-by-step explanation) (Chapter 25),
- a highpass filter, bandstop filter, bandpass filter, and frequency-measuring circuit (Chapter 26),
- a lowpass filter using automatically defined functions, architecture-altering operations (Chapter 28), and a quasi-iterative operator (Chapter 27),
- a difficult-to-design asymmetric bandpass filter (Chapter 31),
- a two-band crossover (woofer-tweeter) filter with (and without) the architecture-altering operations (Chapters 32 and 33),
- a three-band crossover (woofer-midrange-tweeter) filter (Chapter 34),
- a double bandpass filter using subcircuits (Chapter 35),
- a double bandpass filter using architecture-altering operations (Chapter 36),
- Butterworth, Chebychev, and elliptic (Cauer) filters (Chapter 37),
- source identification circuits (Chapters 38 and 39),
- amplifiers (Chapters 42, 43, 44, 45, and 46),
- computational circuits (Chapter 47),
- a real-time robot controller circuit (Chapter 48),
- a temperature-sensing circuit (Chapter 49),
- a voltage reference circuit (Chapter 50), and
- a Gaussian computational circuit using MOSFET technology (Chapter 51).

Sections 27.4 through 27.6 focus on the use of genetic programming as a Darwinian invention machine.

Chapter 29 describes the embryos and test fixtures used for circuit synthesis with developmental genetic programming. Chapter 52 describes the handling of special constraints involving subcircuits and topology. Chapter 53 shows how to solve circuit problems using only a minimal embryo.

Chapters 54 and 55 present comparative experiments involving various alternative features of genetic programming. Chapter 56 demonstrates the crucial role of crossover in genetic programming.

Part 6 shows how evolvable hardware and rapidly reconfigurable field-programmable gate arrays can be used to evolve a sorting network (Chapter 57).

Part 7 describes how genetic programming evolved an algorithm for the vexatious majority classification task for one-dimensional two-state cellular automata (Chapter 58).

Part 8 describes two problems of computational molecular biology (in addition to the transmembrane segment identification problem of Chapters 16 and 17) involving

- the automated discovery of motifs in proteins (Chapter 59) and
- the automated discovery of a more powerful type of motif (which we call programmatic motifs) (Chapter 60).

Part 9 discusses the computational requirements of genetic programming (Chapter 61), the implementation of genetic programming on a parallel computing system (Chapter 62), and other practical implementation issues (Chapter 63).

Part 10 reviews the degree to which genetic programming can be currently said to possess the 16 attributes (listed at the beginning of this chapter) that can reasonably be expected of a system for automatically creating computer programs. As will be seen in Chapter 64, genetic programming currently unconditionally possesses the first 13 of the 16 attributes, and genetic programming at least partially possesses the remaining three attributes.

Part 2:
BACKGROUND ON GENETIC PROGRAMMING AND EVOLUTIONARY COMPUTATION

Chapter 2 provides background that makes this book a self-contained explanation of genetic programming.

Background

This chapter describes

- the conventional genetic algorithm (Section 2.1),
- the basic ideas of the LISP programming language that are relevant to understanding genetic programming (Section 2.2),
- the basic ideas of genetic programming (Section 2.3), including automatically defined functions, and
- sources of additional information about genetic algorithms, genetic programming, and other techniques of evolutionary computation, including evolutionary programming, evolution strategies, classifier systems, and evolvable hardware (Section 2.4).

2.1   GENETIC ALGORITHMS

John Holland's pioneering book, *Adaptation in Natural and Artificial Systems* (1975), applied an analog of the naturally occurring evolutionary process to solving problems. This analog, now called the *genetic algorithm*, has proved useful in solving numerous practical problems.

The *genetic algorithm* transforms a *population* of individual objects, each with an associated value of *fitness*, into a new *generation* of the population, using the Darwinian principle of survival and reproduction of the fittest and analogs of naturally occurring genetic operations such as crossover (sexual recombination) and mutation.

The genetic algorithm is a domain-independent algorithm for solving problems by searching a space of candidate solutions. Each possible point in the search space of a given problem is encoded into a representation suitable for applying the genetic algorithm. The genetic algorithm attempts to find the best (or at least a very good) solution to the problem by genetically breeding the population of individual candidates over a number of generations.

There are four major preparatory steps required before applying the genetic algorithm to a problem, namely, determining

1. the representation and encoding scheme,
2. the fitness measure (or other arrangement for explicitly or implicitly measuring fitness),
3. the control parameters for the run, and
4. the termination criterion and method of result designation for the run.

The first preparatory step for applying the genetic algorithm to a problem starts with a determination of the representation. The representation scheme specifies the transformation that maps points in the search space of the problem into a particular fixed-length character string (or other data structure being used by the genetic algorithm) and the inverse transformation that maps each possible string (or structure) into a point in the search space of the problem. The most frequently used representation scheme for the genetic algorithm is a fixed-length character string (resembling a strand of DNA or a chromosome). If the individuals in the population are to be represented in this way, then it is necessary to determine the string length L and the alphabet size K. The most frequently used alphabet size is two (i.e., a binary alphabet). Many other representation schemes and approaches are used with genetic algorithms, including variable-length strings (S. Smith 1980, 1983) and the messy genetic algorithm (Goldberg, Korb, and Deb 1989).

Suppose the problem is to find the values of 12 variables that optimize the performance of some system. The 12-dimensional search space of the problem might be encoded as a fixed-length string of length $L = 120$ over a binary alphabet ($K = 2$). The variables might be scaled so they each range over precisely 1,024 values. Given that decision concerning granularity, the first variable might then be encoded using the first 10 of the 120 bits of the string; the second variable might be encoded using the next 10 bits; and so forth. This transformation maps (codes) points in the 12-dimensional search space of the problem into a particular 120-bit string. An inverse transformation maps (decodes) each possible 120-bit string into a point in the 12-dimensional search space of the problem.

Finding a representation scheme that facilitates solution of a problem by the genetic algorithm often requires considerable insight into the problem as well as good judgment.

A precondition for solving a problem with the genetic algorithm is that the representation scheme satisfy the *sufficiency* requirement in the sense that it is capable of representing a solution to the problem. If, for example, the global optimum for the 12 variables is not among the $1,024^{12}$ combinations of values in the 12-dimensional search space, then the genetic algorithm cannot find the global optimum point.

The genetic algorithm is driven by a problem-specific fitness function. In its most frequently used form, the fitness function assigns a numerical fitness value to each individual in the population. The fitness measure generally satisfies the requirement of being *fully defined* in the sense that it is capable of evaluating any individual that it might encounter.

The purpose of the fitness function in the genetic algorithm is to select individuals for breeding in accordance with the Darwinian principle of survival and reproduction of the fittest. There are several different methods of selection in widespread use by practitioners of genetic algorithms; however, they conform to the following three principles:

- Better individuals are more likely to be selected than inferior individuals.
- Reselection is allowed. That is, better individuals can be selected for breeding more than once.
- Selection is probabilistic.

Because of the probabilistic selection, the best individual in the population is not guaranteed to be selected, and the worst individual in the population is not necessarily overlooked by the selection process. The genetic algorithm favors better individuals; however, it also allocates a certain measured number of trials to individuals that, based on the evidence at hand, are inferior. The selection process in the genetic algorithm does a significant amount of hill climbing, but it is not entirely greedy. This allocation of trials to individuals that do not immediately yield a higher payoff is done in the hope that it will eventually lead to points in the search space with an ultimately higher payoff. Interesting and nontrivial problems always have high-payoff points that are inaccessible to greedy hill climbing. In fact, the existence of points in the search space that are not accessible to hill climbing is a good working definition of nontriviality.

In *fitness-proportionate selection*, individuals are selected with a probability proportional to their fitness. In *tournament selection* (Goldberg and Deb 1991), a specified group of two (or more) individuals is chosen at random from the population. Then the single individual in the chosen group with the best fitness is selected as the winner of the tournament. Tournament selection is especially advantageous when only a partial order exists among the individuals in the population.

It is not necessary to assign an explicit numeric value of fitness to each individual in the population. That is, fitness may be implicit (as it is in natural evolution). Suppose that the goal is to create a strategy for navigating an automobile through traffic. For this problem, a simulation might be performed involving numerous automobiles, each being controlled by a different strategy. The strategies of the automobiles that avoid accidents and survive for a certain length of time might then be selected for breeding. In this situation, no explicit numerical value of fitness is ever assigned to any strategy. Instead, the fitness of competing strategies is implicitly determined by their survival in the simulation.

The primary parameters for controlling the genetic algorithm are the population size, M, and the maximum number of generations to be run, G. Populations can consist of hundreds, thousands, millions, or more individuals. There can be dozens, hundreds, thousands, or more generations in a run of the genetic algorithm. The user typically also specifies the probability of performing the various genetic operations on each generation of the run. In addition, there are a number of secondary control variables for the genetic algorithm (as enumerated in Koza 1992e, Table 27.8).

Each run of the genetic algorithm requires specification of a *termination criterion* for deciding when to terminate a run and a method of result designation. The termination criterion for a run of the genetic algorithm usually consists of either satisfying a problem-specific *success predicate* or completing a specified maximum number of generations, G (or exhausting available computer resources, as measured in some other way).

The success predicate depends on the nature of the problem and the user's goal. For example, the success predicate may consist of achieving a result that exceeds a certain threshold. Sometimes it is possible to recognize a 100%-correct solution to a problem when it is discovered (even though we did not know the answer beforehand). One frequently used method of *result designation* for a run of the genetic algorithm is to designate the best individual obtained in any generation of the population during the run (i.e., the cached *best-so-far* individual) as the result of the run.

Once the user has completed these four preparatory steps for setting up the genetic algorithm, a run of the genetic algorithm can be launched.

The three steps in executing the genetic algorithm in its basic form are

1. Randomly create an initial population (generation 0) of individuals (e.g., fixed-length character strings).
2. Iteratively perform the following substeps (called a *generation*) on the population until the termination criterion has been satisfied:
   a. Assign a fitness value to each individual in the population using the fitness measure for the problem.
   b. Select one or two individual(s) from the population with a probability based on fitness (with reselection allowed) to participate in the genetic operations in (c).
   c. Create individual(s) for the new population by applying the following genetic operations with specified probabilities:
      i. *Reproduction:* Copy the selected individual to the new population.
      ii. *Crossover:* Create new offspring individual(s) for the new population by recombining substrings from two selected individuals at a randomly chosen crossover point.
      iii. *Mutation:* Create one new offspring individual for the new population by randomly mutating randomly chosen position(s) of one selected individual.
3. Designate the individual that is identified by the method of result designation (e.g., the best-so-far individual) as the result of the genetic algorithm for the run. This result may represent a solution (or an approximate solution) to the problem.

The genetic algorithm is a probabilistic algorithm. Probabilistic steps are involved in creating the initial population, selecting individuals from the population on which to perform each genetic operation (e.g., reproduction, crossover, mutation), and choosing a point (i.e., a crossover point or a mutation point) within the selected individual at which to perform the selected genetic operation.

In practice, it is often necessary to make multiple independent runs of a probabilistic algorithm in order to obtain a result that the user considers successful for a given problem. Thus, steps 1, 2, and 3 above are, in practice, embedded in an outer loop representing separate runs.

Figure 2.1 is a flowchart of one popular way of implementing the conventional genetic algorithm. The flowchart handles multiple runs of the genetic algorithm. In the flowchart, RUN is the current run number and N is the maximum number of runs to be made. The variable GEN refers to the current generation number. The population size is M. The index i refers to the current individual in the population.

The flowchart starts in the upper left corner. The overall process consists of several independent runs, so the process starts with the current run number, RUN, being initialized to zero. Each run consists of numerous generations, so the generation number, GEN, is initialized to zero.

The first step of a run is "Create Initial Random Population for Run." This step creates the initial population (generation 0) of M individuals. This step is typically done randomly. The next step is the test for "Termination Criterion Satisfied for Run." This test is typically based on either reaching a certain maximum number of generations, G, or on satisfying some problem-specific criteria. When the "Termination Criterion Satisfied for Run" is satisfied, the next step is "Designate Result for Run." Then the run number, RUN, is incremented. If the run number, RUN, satisfies the test of being equal to the maximum

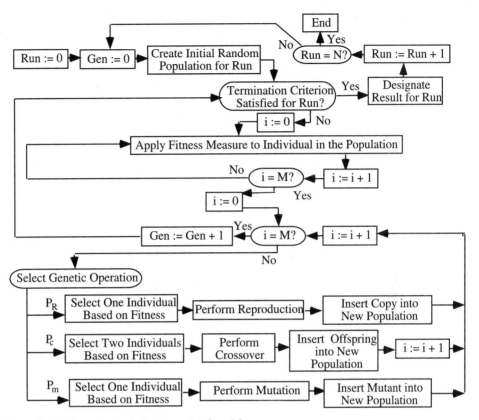

Figure 2.1 Flowchart of the genetic algorithm

number of runs to be run, N, then the entire process ends at "End." Otherwise, the process continues to another run by initializing the generation number, GEN, to zero.

The main generational loop of the genetic algorithm encompasses two loops over the M individuals in the population. In the first of these two main loops (in the middle of the flowchart) the fitness of each individual i in the population is determined. In the second of these two main loops (at the bottom of the flowchart), a total of M genetic operations are performed during the generation.

The first of these two main loops begins by initializing the index, i, for individuals in the population. The index, i, is tested as to whether it equals (or exceeds) the population size, M. If it does not, the fitness of the single individual i in the population is determined. Then the index, i, of the individual in the population is incremented. If the index, i, satisfies the test of being equal to (or greater than) the population size, M, then the first of these main loops over the individuals in the population ends.

The second of these two main loops begins by initializing the index, i. The index, i, is tested as to whether it equals (or exceeds) the population size, M. If it does not, the step of "Select Genetic Operation" is performed. The step of "Select Genetic Operation" is probabilistic. One of the three alternative operations (reproduction, crossover, and mutation) is probabilistically chosen. The sum of the probabilities, p_r, p_c, and p_m, of choosing the operations of reproduction, crossover, and mutation, respectively, being used in the run is 1 (in the so-called generational approach to implementing genetic algorithms).

Each of the three genetic operations begins with a Darwinian selection step. For example, for the genetic operations of reproduction and mutation, the selection step is "Select One Individual Based on Fitness." The selection step for the crossover operation entails the selection of two individuals based on fitness. Individuals in the population may be reselected. If the reproduction operation is chosen, then the operation of reproduction is performed, and one offspring is created. If the crossover operation is chosen, then the crossover operation is performed, and two offspring are created. If the mutation operation is chosen, then the mutation operation is performed, and one offspring is created.

Then the common step of "Insert Copy/Offspring/Mutant into New Population" is performed. The index, i, of the individual in the population is incremented by 1; however, in the case of two-offspring crossover, the index, i, is incremented one additional time. If the index, i, does not satisfy the test of being equal to (or greater than) the population size, M, this second main loop continues. If the index, i, satisfies the test, then the second of these main loops over the individuals in the population ends. The generation number, GEN, is then incremented. If exactly $M - 1$ operations have been previously chosen for the current generation, the two-offspring crossover is not permitted to be chosen as the last operation of the generation.

The best individual produced by looping over i is the *best-of-generation* individual; the best individual produced by looping over GEN is the *best-of-run* individual; and the best individual produced by looping over RUN is the *best-of-all* individual. If there is a tie for any of these classes of best individual, the single individual that first produced the best result is arbitrarily designated as the best.

The genetic operation of *reproduction* is based on the Darwinian principle of survival and reproduction of the fittest. In the reproduction operation, an individual is probabilistically selected from the population on the basis of its fitness (with reselection allowed), and the individual is then copied, without change, into the next generation of the population. The selection is done in such a way that the better an individual's fitness, the more likely it is to be selected.

The genetic operation of *crossover* allows new individuals to be created and new points in the search space to be tested. The operation of crossover starts with two parents that are independently selected probabilistically from the population on the basis of their fitness (with reselection allowed). As before, the selection is done in such a way that the better an individual's fitness, the more likely it is to be selected. The crossover operation produces two offspring. Each offspring contains some genetic material from each of its parents.

Individuals from the population can be selected—and, in general, are selected—more than once during a generation to participate in the operations of reproduction and crossover. Indeed, the differential rate of reproduction and participation in genetic operations by more fit individuals is an essential part of the genetic algorithm.

Now we will illustrate the commonly used single-point crossover operation being applied to the two parental strings 011 and 110 of length $L = 3$ over an alphabet of size $K = 2$. We start with the two *parents*:

Parent 1	Parent 2
011	110

The crossover operation begins by randomly choosing a number between 1 and $L - 1$ using a uniform probability distribution. There are $L - 1 = 2$ interstitial locations lying between the positions of a character string of length $L = 3$. One of these interstitial locations (say, the second) becomes the *crossover point*. Each parent is then split at this crossover point into a crossover fragment and a remainder. The *crossover fragments* of parents 1 and 2 are

Crossover fragment 1	Crossover fragment 2
01–	11–

The part of each parent that remains after the crossover fragment is identified is called the *remainder*:

Remainder 1	Remainder 2
– – 1	– – 0

The crossover operation recombines crossover fragment 1 with remainder 2 to create offspring 1. Similarly, the crossover operation recombines crossover fragment 2 with remainder 1 to create offspring 2:

Offspring 1	Offspring 2
111	010

The two offspring are usually different from their two parents and different from each other. Crossover is a creative operation that produces new individuals that are composed entirely of genetic material from their two parents. If a character string represents a somewhat effective approach to solving a given problem, then certain values at certain positions of the string may have some merit. More importantly, some combinations of values situated at two (or k) positions of the string may have some merit when they occur together in the string. These combinations of values at multiple positions of the chromosome string are what Holland (1975) calls "co-adapted sets of alleles." By recombining randomly chosen parts of fit strings, a new string that represents an even better approach to solving the problem may be produced.

In the special case where the two parents selected to participate in crossover are identical, the two offspring are, regardless of the crossover point, identical to each other and identical to their parents. This incestuous case occurs frequently because of the Darwinian selection of individuals to participate in the reproduction and crossover operations on the basis of their fitness. Consequently, identical copies of a highly fit individual may come to dominate a population. If the domination is total, the population is said to have *converged. Premature convergence* occurs when an individual becomes dominant in a population, but that individual does not represent the global optimum of the search space.

The operation of *mutation* begins by probabilistically selecting an individual from the population on the basis of its fitness. A *mutation point* along the string is randomly chosen using a uniform probability distribution, and the single character at that point is changed. More than one mutation may be applied to a particular individual. The mutated individuals are then copied into the next generation of the population. Mutation is potentially useful in restoring genetic diversity that may be lost in a population because of premature convergence. Mutation is generally used sparingly in genetic algorithm work.

Now we will illustrate the mutation operation being applied to the parental string 011:

Parent 1

011

The mutation operation begins by randomly choosing a number between 1 and $L = 3$ using a uniform probability distribution. In the mutation operation, the chosen point (say, the third) becomes the *mutation point*. The character at that position is then randomly mutated (e.g., the 1 in the third position of the string becomes a 0):

Offspring 1

010

In implementing the genetic algorithm on a computer, the reproduction, crossover, and mutation operations are performed nondestructively on copies of the selected individuals. The selected individuals remain unchanged in the population until the end of the current generation (thereby making it possible for them to be reselected to participate in additional genetic operations during the current generation).

The Darwinian selection of individuals to participate in the operations of reproduction, crossover, and mutation on the basis of their fitness is an essential aspect of the genetic algorithm. When an individual is selected on the basis of its fitness to be copied (with or without mutation) into the next generation of the population, the effect is that the new generation contains the characteristics of the selected individual. These characteristics include particular gene values (alleles) at certain positions (loci) of the character string. More importantly, these characteristics include certain combinations of values situated at two or more positions of the string. When two individuals are selected on the basis of their fitness to be recombined, each of the offspring in the new generation contains some of the characteristics (and some of the combinations of characteristics) of both parents.

The probabilistic nongreedy selection used in the genetic algorithm is an essential aspect of the algorithm. That is, the genetic algorithm is not merely a greedy hill-climbing algorithm that always selects the best individual. The genetic algorithm gives every individual, however poor its fitness, some chance of being selected to participate in the operations of reproduction, crossover, and mutation. In this regard, the genetic algorithm resembles simulated annealing (Kirkpatrick, Gelatt, and Vecchi 1983; Arts and Korst 1989) in that individuals that are known to be inferior are selected in a principled way.

The fact that the genetic algorithm operates on a population of individuals, rather than a single point in the search space of the problem, is an essential aspect of the algorithm. The population serves as the reservoir of the potentially valuable genetic material that the crossover operation uses to create new individuals with new combinations of characteristics.

The success of the genetic algorithm in solving problems also arises from the creative role of the crossover operation. Indeed, a once-controversial point in *Adaptation in Natural and Artificial Systems* (Holland 1975) concerns the preeminence of the crossover operation and the relative unimportance of mutation in the evolutionary process in nature and in solving artificial problems of adaptation using the genetic algorithm. Mutation is an important part of the genetic algorithm, but crossover is the predominant operation.

The genetic algorithm works in a domain-independent way on the fixed-length character strings in the population. The genetic algorithm searches the space of possible character strings in an attempt to find high-fitness strings. The space may be highly non-linear, and its fitness landscape may be very rugged. To guide this search, the genetic algorithm uses only the fitness associated with the explicitly tested strings. Regardless of the particular problem domain, the genetic algorithm carries out its search by performing the same disarmingly simple operations of copying, recombining, and occasionally randomly mutating the strings.

In practice, the genetic algorithm is often surprisingly rapid in effectively searching complex, highly nonlinear, multidimensional search spaces. This is all the more surprising because the genetic algorithm does not have any knowledge about the problem domain except for the information indirectly provided by the fitness measure and the representation scheme.

Genetic algorithms superficially seem to process only the particular individual character strings actually present in the current generation of the population. However, *Adaptation in Natural and Artificial Systems* (Holland 1975) focused attention on the remarkable fact that the genetic algorithm implicitly processes, in parallel, a large amount of information about unseen Boolean hyperplanes (schemata) in the search space. A *schema* (plural: *schemata*) is a set of points from the search space of a problem with certain specified similarities. For the genetic algorithm operating on fixed-length character strings, a schema is described by a string over an extended alphabet consisting of the alphabet of the representation scheme (e.g., 0 and 1 if the alphabet is binary) and a *don't care symbol* (denoted by an asterisk).

The genetic algorithm creates individual strings in the new generation of the population in such a way that each schema can be expected to be represented in proportion to the ratio of its *schema fitness* (i.e., the average of the fitness of all the points from the search space contained in the population and contained in the schema) to the *average population fitness* (i.e., the average of the fitness of all the points from the search space that are contained in the population).

As previously mentioned, there are numerous variations in implementations of the genetic algorithm. The flowchart (Figure 2.1) depicts only one of many possible alternative implementations. For example, mutation is performed hand in hand with the crossover operation in many implementations of the genetic algorithm (Goldberg 1989a). Also, crossover is sometimes performed at two or more crossover points (Goldberg 1989a). The flowchart depicts the so-called *generational* genetic algorithm, in which the genetic operations are organized into major temporal stages called *generations*. In this approach, the number of reproduction, crossover, and mutation operations in each generation is chosen so that the total number of offspring equals the population size (thereby creating a new population that replaces the entire old population). The algorithm then evaluates the fitness of all the individuals of the new generation of the population. The generational version of the genetic algorithm differs from the *steady-state* version of the algorithm (Syswerda 1989, 1991; Reynolds 1993, 1994a, 1994d). In the steady-state genetic algorithm, a single genetic operation is performed; the offspring is immediately inserted into the population; and the fitness of the new offspring is immediately computed. A considerable number of published papers have been devoted to the mathematical analysis and experimental study of the numerous alternative implementations of the genetic algorithm. Section 2.4 provides references and sources of additional information on genetic algorithms and evolutionary computation.

2.2 BACKGROUND ON LISP

Virtually any programming language is capable of implementing genetic programming. Today, C is the most widely used. Genetic programming is also implemented in C++, Java, Mathematica (Nachbar 1995), assembly code (Nordin 1994, 1997; Nordin and Banzhaf 1995; Banzhaf, Nordin, Keller, and Francone 1998), and LISP.

All the work presented in this book was done using the C programming language (for reasons stated in Section 63.1). In contrast, the work presented in *Genetic Programming* (Koza 1992e) and *Genetic Programming II* (Koza 1994g) was done in the LISP programming language using a LISP machine.

Genetic programming is most easily understood by thinking of a computer program as a sequence of applications of functions (operations) to arguments (values). Although any computer program—whether it is written in C, C++, FORTRAN, PASCAL, Java, assembly code, or any other programming language—can be viewed in this way, the multiplicity of different types of statements and syntactic constraints of most programming languages tends to obscure this view. The LISP programming language overtly treats programs as sequences of applications of functions to arguments.

In addition, LISP treats programs and data in a like manner. Consequently, LISP permits a computer program to be manipulated first as data and then enables the just-modified program to be effortlessly executed as a program. In particular, the EVAL function provided by LISP permits a LISP expression to be evaluated on the fly within a genetic programming system. Moreover, the COMPILE function in LISP permits a LISP expression to be dynamically compiled. Since genetic programming manipulates computer programs using various genetically motivated operations, it was convenient (especially during the formative period of genetic programming) to implement genetic programming in LISP. The LISP programming language is useful in explaining genetic programming. The results of runs of genetic programming are presented in LISP in this book (and many published papers) even though LISP may not have been used to produce the results. New operators are explained in this book in terms of LISP.

For the purpose of this book, LISP can be viewed as having only two types of entities: atoms and lists. The constant 7 and the variable TIME are examples of *atoms* in LISP. A *list* in LISP is written as an ordered collection of items inside a pair of parentheses. (A B C D) and (+ 1 2) are examples of lists in LISP. Both lists and atoms in LISP are called *symbolic expressions (S-expressions)*. There is no syntactic distinction between programs and data in LISP. The S-expression is the only syntactic form in pure LISP. In particular, all data in LISP are S-expressions, and all programs in LISP are S-expressions.

A LISP system (software or hardware) works so as to evaluate its input. When seen by LISP, a constant atom (such as 7) evaluates to itself, and a variable atom (such as TIME) evaluates to the current value of the variable. When a list is the input to LISP, the list is evaluated by treating the first element of the list (i.e., whatever is just inside the opening parenthesis) as a function and by then applying that function to the results of evaluating the remaining elements of the list. That is, all the remaining elements of the list are treated as arguments to the function. If an argument is a constant atom or a variable atom, the evaluation is immediate; however, if an argument is itself a list, the evaluation of such an argument entails a recursive application of the above steps for evaluation.

For example, in the LISP S-expression (+ 1 2), LISP treats the item just inside the outermost left parenthesis as a function and then applies that function to the remaining items of the list. The addition function + appears just inside the opening parenthesis. The S-expression (+ 1 2) calls for the application of the addition function + to two arguments, namely, the constant atoms 1 and 2. Since both arguments are atoms, they can be immediately evaluated. The value returned as a result of the evaluation of the entire S-expression (+ 1 2) is 3. Because the function + appears to the left of the arguments, LISP S-expressions are examples of *prefix notation.*

If any of the arguments in an S-expression are themselves lists (rather than constant or variable atoms that can be immediately evaluated), LISP first evaluates these arguments. In Common LISP (Steele 1990), evaluation is done in a recursive, depth-first way, starting from the left. This convention of Common LISP is used throughout this book (except for the construction-continuing subtrees used in analog circuit synthesis in Part 5). The S-expression

```
(+ (* 2 3) 4)
```

illustrates the way that computer programs in LISP can be viewed as a sequence of applications of functions to arguments. This S-expression calls for the application of the addition function + to two arguments, namely, the sub-S-expression (* 2 3) and the constant atom 4. In order to evaluate the entire S-expression, LISP must first evaluate the sub-S-expression (* 2 3). This argument (* 2 3) calls for the application of the multiplication function * to the two constant atoms 2 and 3, so it evaluates to 6 and the entire S-expression evaluates to 10.

In contrast, ordinary mathematical expressions and programming languages such as C, FORTRAN, and PASCAL employ *infix notation* for two-argument functions. The above LISP program would be written using infix notation as

```
2 * 3 + 4.
```

One of the advantages of the prefix notation used in LISP is that a k-argument function is handled in a more uniform fashion than is the case with ordinary infix notation (which requires establishment of rules of precedence among the operators).

The term "computer program," of course, carries the connotation of the ability to do more than merely perform compositions of ordinary arithmetic functions. Computer programs are expected to perform alternative computations conditioned on the outcome of intermediate calculations, to perform computations on variables of many different types, to perform iterations and recursions, to store and retrieve information from the computer's internal memory, to reuse code by means of subprograms (subroutines), to communicate information between the main program and the program's subroutines, and to perform operations in a hierarchical way. Unlike most other programming languages, LISP implements all these different tasks with S-expressions.

For example, the LISP S-expression

```
(+ 1 2 (IF (> TIME 10) 3 4))
```

illustrates how LISP views conditional and relational elements of computer programs as applications of functions to arguments. The three-argument addition function + at the top level calls for the application of the addition function to its three arguments: the constant atom 1, the constant atom 2, and the sub-S-expression (IF (> TIME 10) 3 4). In the sub-sub-S-expression (> TIME 10), the relation > is viewed as a function and is applied to the variable atom TIME and the constant atom 10. The sub-subexpression (> TIME 10) then evaluates to either T (true) or NIL (false), depending on the current value of the variable atom TIME. The conditional operator IF is viewed as a function and is then applied to the logical value (T or NIL) returned by the sub-subexpression (> TIME 10). If the first argument of an IF function evaluates to T (more precisely, anything other than NIL), the function returns the result of evaluating its second argument (the constant atom 3 here), but if the first argument evaluates to NIL, the function returns the result of evaluating its third argument (the constant atom 4 here). The S-expression as a whole evaluates to either 6 or 7, depending on whether the current value of the variable atom TIME is or is not greater than 10.

Most other programming languages employ a variety of syntactic forms and statement types. For example, both prefix and infix notation are used in many programming languages. In that event, rules of precedence are required to ensure the correct and unambiguous application of functions to arguments. In contrast, pure LISP employs a common syntax.

Any LISP S-expression can be graphically depicted as a rooted point-labeled tree with ordered branches. Figure 2.2 shows the tree corresponding to the S-expression

```
(+ 1 2 (IF (> TIME 10) 3 4)).
```

This tree has a total of nine *points* (i.e., functions and terminals). In this graphical depiction, the three internal points of the tree are labeled with functions, namely, +, IF, and >. The root of the tree is labeled with the function appearing just inside the leftmost opening parenthesis of the S-expression (i.e., the +). The six external points (leaves) of the tree are labeled with terminals (the variable atom TIME and the five constant atoms 1, 2, 3, 4, and 10). The branches are ordered because the order of the arguments matters for many functions (e.g., IF and >). Of course, the order does not matter for commutative functions (such as +).

This tree form of a LISP S-expression is equivalent to the parse tree (unseen by the programmer) that is internally constructed by most compilers of high-level programming languages to represent programs.

An important feature of LISP is that all LISP computer programs have just one syntactic form (the S-expression). The programs of the LISP programming language are S-expressions, and an S-expression is, in effect, the parse tree of the program. Moreover, data is also represented in LISP by S-expressions. For these reasons, LISP is used throughout this book for explaining the genetic operations and presenting evolved computer programs. Nonetheless, as previously mentioned, genetic programming is most commonly implemented today in programming languages other than LISP.

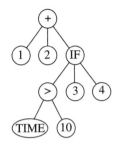

Figure 2.2 LISP symbolic expression depicted as a rooted point-labeled tree with ordered branches

At a high level, genetic programming can be viewed as a combination of some of the features of John Holland's genetic algorithm (and other techniques of evolutionary computation) and some of the features of John McCarthy's LISP programming language (and other techniques of symbolic artificial intelligence that have been closely associated with LISP).

2.3   BACKGROUND ON GENETIC PROGRAMMING

Genetic programming is a domain-independent method that genetically breeds populations of computer programs to solve problems. Genetic programming is an extension of the genetic algorithm in which the genetic population contains computer programs.

Genetic programming starts with a primordial ooze of randomly generated computer programs composed of the available programmatic ingredients and then applies the principles of Darwinian evolution to breed a new (and often improved) population of programs. The breeding is done in a domain-independent way using the Darwinian principle of survival and reproduction of the fittest, an analog of the naturally occurring genetic operation of crossover (sexual recombination), and occasional mutation. The crossover operation is designed to create structurally valid offspring programs. Genetic programming combines the expressive high-level symbolic representations of computer programs with the near-optimal search efficiency of the genetic algorithm. A computer program that solves (or approximately solves) a given problem often emerges from this process.

The basic elements of genetic programming were introduced in the paper "Hierarchical Genetic Algorithms Operating on Populations of Computer Programs," presented at the 11th International Joint Conference on Artificial Intelligence in Detroit (Koza 1989); a Stanford University Computer Science Department technical report (Koza 1990b); the book *Genetic Programming: On the Programming of Computers by Means of Natural Selection* (Koza 1992e); and its accompanying videotape, *Genetic Programming: The Movie* (Koza and Rice 1992e). The first runs of genetic programming were made in 1987, and genetic programming was first described in detail in Koza 1988.

The book *Genetic Programming II: Automatic Discovery of Reusable Programs* (Koza 1994g) and its accompanying videotape, *Genetic Programming II Videotape: The Next Generation* (Koza 1994h), focused on subroutines (automatically defined functions) and scalability of genetic programming.

Genetic programming is further described in *Genetic Programming—An Introduction* (Banzhaf, Nordin, Keller, and Francone 1998).

The first book, *Genetic Programming,* introduced the basic principles of genetic programming and established the following two main points:

- A wide variety of seemingly different problems from many different fields can be recast as requiring the discovery of a computer program that produces some desired output when presented with particular inputs. That is, they can be reformulated as problems of program induction.
- Genetic programming provides a way to do program induction.

Genetic programming automatically determines the program's size (i.e., the total number of steps) and automatically determines the exact sequence of primitive functions and terminals that are executed by the program. Specifically, *Genetic Programming* demonstrated that it is possible to

- automatically create computer programs consisting of a single main branch (a result-producing branch),
- automatically create multibranch programs (programs with two or more result-producing branches) (Chapter 19 of *Genetic Programming*),
- automatically create programs whose branches are constructed in accordance with a constrained syntactic structure (Chapter 19 of *Genetic Programming*), and
- automatically create multibranch programs consisting of a main program (result-producing branch) and one or more subroutines (referred to as function-defining branches or automatically defined functions) that can hierarchically refer to one another (Chapters 20 and 21 of *Genetic Programming*).

The problems solved in *Genetic Programming* involved symbolic regression (system identification, empirical discovery, modeling, forecasting, data mining), classification, control, optimization, equation solving, game playing, induction, problems exhibiting emergent behavior, problems involving coevolution, cellular automata programming, randomizer construction, image compression, symbolic integration and differentiation, inverse problems, decision tree induction, and many others. The problems in *Genetic Programming* include many then-current benchmark problems from the fields of machine learning, artificial intelligence, and neural networks.

Additional problems were solved in *Genetic Programming II,* including problems involving symbolic regression, control, pattern recognition, classification, computational molecular biology, and discovery of the impulse response function for an electrical circuit.

The present book contains solutions to problems from the fields of system identification, time-optimal control, classification, synthesis of cellular automata rules, synthesis of minimal sorting networks, multiagent programming, and synthesizing both the topology and sizing for analog electrical circuits.

Between 1987 and September 1998, over 300 authors published 1,382 papers that have described numerous creative and innovative extensions to the basic idea of genetic programming. Genetic programming has been demonstrated to be capable of solving several hundred different problems. Admittedly, genetic programming has not been demonstrated to be capable of solving all problems of all types from all fields. It has not solved the protein-folding problem nor has it evolved a competitor to the Microsoft Windows operating system. Nonetheless, it is fair to say that there is "considerable evidence in favor" of the assertion that genetic programming possesses the following attribute of a system for automatically creating computer programs (Chapter 1):

- **ATTRIBUTE NO. 14** (Wide applicability): It produces a satisfactory solution to a wide variety of problems from many different fields.

Some people express the above attribute by saying that a problem-solving technique "scales well" to many types of problems. However, we reserve the phrase "scales well" (Attribute No. 15) to refer to the ability of a problem-solving technique to solve larger versions of the same problem by expending a reasonable amount of computational effort (e.g., linear or polynomial, as opposed to, say, exponential computational effort).

2.3.1 Preparatory Steps

Arthur Samuel (1959) characterized machine learning by asking

> How can computers be made to do what needs to be done, without being told exactly how to do it?

In other words, a system for automatically creating computing programs should start from a high-level statement of the requirements for a solution to a problem. Of course, no system for automatically creating computer programs is clairvoyant. As Friedberg (1958), another pioneer in machine learning, observed,

> If a machine is not told *how* to do something, at least some indication must be given of *what* it is to do; otherwise we could not direct its effort toward a particular problem. [Emphasis in original.]

That is, there must be some method for communicating "what it is to do" to the system before it can start. The preparatory steps of genetic programming are the user's way of communicating the high-level statement of the problem to the genetic programming system. The preparatory steps identify what the user must provide to the genetic programming system before launching a run of genetic programming. The preparatory steps serve to unmistakably distinguish between what the user must supply to the genetic programming system and what the system delivers.

The five major preparatory steps for genetic programming entail determining

1. the set of terminals (e.g., the actual variables of the problem, zero-argument functions, and random constants, if any) for each branch of the to-be-evolved computer program,
2. the set of primitive functions for each to-be-evolved branch,
3. the fitness measure (or other arrangement for explicitly or implicitly measuring fitness),
4. the parameters for controlling the run, and
5. the termination criterion and the method of result designation for the run.

Figure 2.3 shows the five major preparatory steps for the basic version of genetic programming. The preparatory steps (shown in the left part of the figure) are the input to the genetic programming system. The result (shown in the right part of the figure) is a computer program produced by a run of genetic programming. The program evolved by genetic programming may solve, or approximately solve, the user's problem.

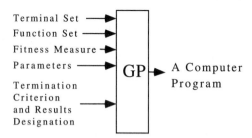

Figure 2.3   Five major preparatory steps for basic genetic programming

The first two preparatory steps concern the ingredients that are to be used to create the computer programs. The universe of possible compositions of the available functions and terminals defines the search space of possible computer programs for the run. Often these ingredients consist only of the four arithmetic operations of addition, subtraction, multiplication, and division, a conditional branching operator, the inputs, and constants. A run of genetic programming is a competition (beam search) among a diverse population of programs composed of the available functions and terminals. The search is directed to the goal of discovering a satisfactory program for solving the given problem.

The third preparatory step concerns the fitness measure for the problem. The fitness measure provided by the user is the primary mechanism for communicating a high-level statement of the requirements for a problem's solution to the genetic programming system. The first two preparatory steps define the search space, and the fitness measure determines the outcome of the search.

For example, if the problem entails navigating a robot with a nonzero turning radius to a destination in minimum time (as it does in Chapter 13), the fitness measure for the problem is based on elapsed time. This fitness measure indicates "what needs to be done"—namely, get the robot to the destination in a time-optimal way. This fitness measure assigns a numerical value (total elapsed time) to each control strategy that may be encountered during the run of genetic programming. This fitness measure provides a method of comparing any two candidate control strategies to determine which is quicker (i.e., it establishes a partial order between any two candidate points in the search space of the problem). However, the fitness measure does not specify "how to do it." In particular, the fitness measure conveys no hint about the critical (and counterintuitive) tactic needed to minimize elapsed time in time-optimal control problems—namely, that it is sometimes necessary to veer away from the destination in order to reach it in minimal time. It is the job of genetic programming to discover "how to do it."

Similarly, correlation is the fitness measure for the various classification problems of molecular biology in this book (Chapters 16, 17, 59, and 60). In particular, fitness is the correlation between the classification produced by a candidate program and the correct answer. The fitness measure is concerned with "what needs to be done"—namely, get the correct answer (by maximizing correlation). The fitness measure does not reveal "how to do it." This fitness measure provides no information about the biochemistry of living cells that may aid in making the correct classification. It is the job of genetic programming to discover "how to do it."

The fitness measure for the problem of learning Boolean parity functions (Chapter 12 and Sections 21.1, 21.2, and 23.4) scores a candidate program according to the number of errors that it makes. This fitness measure indicates "what needs to be done" (i.e., make no errors), not "how to do it." In particular, the fitness measure does not instruct genetic programming to use, say,

- an iteration (counting the number of ones among the inputs),
- a decision tree (containing a chain of conditional tests),
- a subroutine (in a hierarchy of lower-order parity functions),
- a recursion (taking successive two-parities until some base case is reached),
- disjunctive or conjunctive normal form,
- some different approach, or
- some combination of the above approaches.

Instead, the fitness measure merely indicates "what needs to be done" without conveying any information about the way of doing it.

The fitness measure for each problem of analog circuit synthesis (Part 5) is couched in terms of the high-level behavior (and other measurable characteristics) of the desired circuit. For example, if a lowpass filter is desired, the fitness measure calls for delivery of a near-maximum output voltage for low frequencies and a near-zero output voltage for high frequencies. The fitness measure is concerned with "what needs to be done"—namely, produce the desired output voltage at the specified frequencies. The fitness measure does not disclose "how to do it." The fitness measure provides no information about the number of components that may be needed in order to achieve the desired behavior, the topological arrangement of the components, or the numerical values of the components. Similarly, the fitness measure does not encapsulate or represent the considerable expertise that human engineers bring to bear in designing filters.

Likewise, the fitness measure for the problem of devising a rule for a cellular automaton (Chapter 58) is couched in terms of the accuracy of the automaton at performing the majority classification task. The fitness measure indicates "what needs to be done" (i.e., get the right answer), not "how to do it." This fitness measure conveys no hint that it is advisable to construct, transmit, receive, and decode space-time signals in order to solve this problem. Achieving high accuracy is the problem's high-level requirement. Creating space-time signals is an advisable approach to solving the problem; however, it is the job of genetic programming to discover this approach.

The fourth and fifth preparatory steps are administrative. The fourth preparatory step entails specifying the control parameters for the run. The fifth preparatory step consists of specifying the termination criterion and the method of result designation for the run.

The number of major preparatory steps for a run of genetic programming may be more or less than five. If the Genetic Programming Problem Solver (GPPS) in Part 4 of this book is being used, the user is relieved of performing the first and second preparatory steps (concerning the choice of the terminal set and the function set). Figure 20.2 shows the abbreviated set of three preparatory steps required by GPPS.

When developmental genetic programming is used for problems of analog circuit synthesis (Part 5), the user must perform an additional preparatory step (consisting of specifying a test fixture and embryo). Figure 25.42 shows the enlarged set of required preparatory steps.

If automatically defined functions (Section 2.3.6), automatically defined iterations (Chapter 6), automatically defined loops (Chapter 7), automatically defined recursions (Chapter 8), or automatically defined stores (Chapter 9) are being used on a particular problem, genetic programming automatically determines, during the run of genetic programming, the particular sequence of steps in each of the branches (which, in turn, establishes the size and shape of each of the branches). However, the automatic determination of the steps within each branch does not involve determining the number and type of branches in the program in the first place. Thus, when a multibranch program is involved, the question arises as to how to determine the architecture of the overall program.

The *architecture* of a multipart program consists of

- the total number of branches,
- the type of each branch (e.g., result-producing branch, automatically defined function, automatically defined iteration, automatically defined loop, automatically defined recursion, and automatically defined store),
- the number of arguments (if any) possessed by each branch,
- if there is more than one branch, the nature of the hierarchical references (if any) allowed among the branches.

There are two ways of determining the architecture for a computer program that is to be evolved using genetic programming. The user may either

- prespecify the architecture of the overall program (i.e., perform an additional architecture-defining preparatory step in addition to the five steps shown in Figure 2.3) or
- use the architecture-altering operations (Part 3) to enable genetic programming to automatically create the architecture of the overall program during the run.

The preparatory steps define what we mean when we say that genetic programming starts from a high-level statement of the requirements for solving a problem. When we say this, we do not mean that genetic programming starts with a statement of the problem spoken into a microphone in real time in colloquial English and then creates a computer program that solves the problem. We do mean that genetic programming starts with a high-level statement of the problem couched in terms of the user-supplied preparatory steps described above.

Thus, genetic programming possesses the following attribute of a system for automatically creating computer programs (Chapter 1):

- **ATTRIBUTE NO. 1** (Starts with "what needs to be done"): It starts from a high-level statement specifying the requirements of the problem.

2.3.2 Executional Steps

After the user has performed the preparatory steps for a problem, the run of genetic programming is launched on a computer. Once the run is launched, a series of well-defined, problem-independent steps is executed. These steps (described below) consist of first creating the initial population and then iteratively executing the main generational loop. The fitness of each individual in the population is determined and the genetic operations are performed in this main generational loop. The steps for executing genetic programming in its basic form are

1. Randomly create an initial population (generation 0) of individual computer programs.
2. Iteratively perform the following substeps (called a *generation*) on the population until the termination criterion has been satisfied:
    a. Execute each program in the population and assign it (explicitly or implicitly) a fitness value using the fitness measure for the problem.
    b. Select one or two individual program(s) from the population with a probability based on fitness (with reselection allowed) to participate in the genetic operations in (c).
    c. Create new individual program(s) for the population by applying the following genetic operations with specified probability:
        i.   *Reproduction:* Copy the selected individual program to the new population.
        ii. *Crossover:* Create new offspring program(s) for the new population by recombining randomly chosen parts from two selected programs.
        iii. *Mutation:* Create one new offspring program for the new population by randomly mutating a randomly chosen part of one selected program.
        iv. *Architecture-altering operations:* Choose an architecture-altering operation from the available repertoire of such operations and create one new offspring program for the new population by applying the chosen architecture-altering operation to the one selected program (as described in Chapters 5 through 9 in Part 3 of this book).
3. After satisfaction of the termination criterion (which usually entails a maximum number of generations to be run as well as a problem-specific success predicate), the single best computer program in the population produced during the run (the best-so-far individual) is harvested and designated as the result of the run. This result may (or may not) be a solution (or approximate solution) to the problem.

Figure 2.4 shows a flowchart of genetic programming showing the basic genetic operations of crossover, reproduction, and mutation along with the architecture-altering operations (Part 3). The flowchart is identical to that of Figure 2.1 except for the inclusion of a new step involving the architecture-altering operations. In this new step, one of the architecture-altering operations is first chosen (in accordance with its preestablished probability). Then one individual is selected probabilistically based on fitness (in the same manner as for reproduction and mutation). One offspring is then created and inserted into the new population. This flowchart shows a two-offspring version of the crossover operation (although, in practice, a one-offspring crossover is used throughout this book).

The preparatory steps specify what the user must provide in advance to the genetic programming system. Once the run is launched, the sequence of steps in the flowchart for genetic programming (Figure 2.4) is executed. There are no hidden preparatory steps and no hidden executional steps in genetic programming. In particular, there is no discretionary human intervention or interaction during a run of genetic programming (although the user may optionally decide when to terminate the run). Thus, genetic

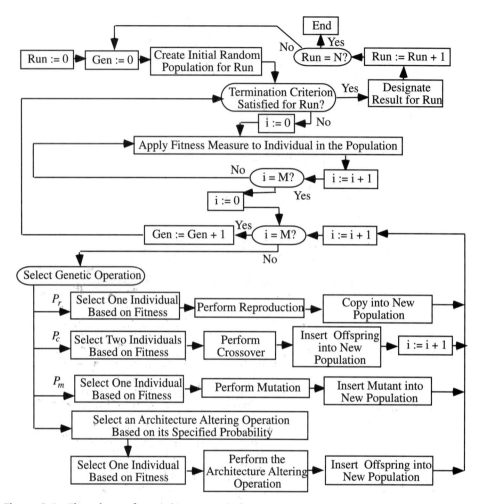

Figure 2.4   Flowchart of genetic programming

programming possesses the following attribute of a system for automatically creating computer programs (Chapter 1):

- **ATTRIBUTE NO. 12** (Well-defined): It operates in a well-defined way. It unmistakably distinguishes between what the user must provide and what the system delivers.

Genetic programming is problem-independent in the sense that the flowchart (Figure 2.4) specifying the basic sequence of executional steps does not have to be modified for each new problem. Thus, genetic programming possesses the following attribute of a system for automatically creating computer programs (Chapter 1):

- **ATTRIBUTE NO. 13** (Problem-independent): It is problem-independent in the sense that the user does not have to modify the system's executable steps for each new problem.

Genetic programming starts with an initial population of computer programs composed of functions and terminals appropriate to the problem. The functions are frequently merely standard arithmetic functions and standard logical functions. The terminals typically include the external inputs to the program (and may also include constants and zero-argument functions). The individual programs in the initial population are typically generated by recursively generating a rooted point-labeled program tree composed of random choices of functions and terminals (usually subject to a preestablished maximum size). In general, the individual programs in the initial population are of different size (i.e., number of primitive functions and terminals) and different shape (i.e., the particular arrangement of primitive functions and terminals). The simplest programs have a single result-producing branch; however, many programs have multiple branches.

The work produced by computer programs is typically the creation of output values (e.g., the value returned by a result-producing branch), the side effects of the functions on the state of the world (e.g., a robotic control program), or a combination of return values and side effects.

For example, consider the following one-branch computer program (presented as a LISP S-expression):

```
(+ (* 0.234 Z) (- X 0.789)).
```

This expression is ordinarily written in mathematical notation as

$$0.234 Z + X - 0.789.$$

This program takes two externally supplied floating-point variables (X and Z) as input. It produces a single floating-point output by applying the two-argument addition (+) function to the results produced by two subexpressions,

```
(* 0.234 Z)
```

and

```
(- X 0.789).
```

The first subexpression applies the two-argument multiplication (*) function to the constant 0.234 and the input Z; the second subexpression applies the subtraction (-) function to the input X and the constant 0.789.

Now consider a second program:

```
(* (* Z Y) (+ Y (* 0.314 Z))).
```

These two programs are depicted in Figure 2.5 as rooted point-labeled trees with ordered branches. Internal points (i.e., internal nodes) of the tree correspond to functions (e.g., addition, subtraction, multiplication) and external points (i.e., leaves, endpoints, external nodes) correspond to terminals (i.e., the external inputs X, Y, and Z). Both programs consist of a single result-producing branch. The work of each program here consists of performing an arithmetic calculation on its inputs and producing a single numerical value as its output (i.e., the numerical value returned by the program's single branch). These two illustrative computer programs are typical of the computer programs created for the initial generation of the population in genetic programming in that they have

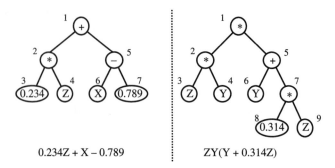

$$0.234Z + X - 0.789 \qquad ZY(Y + 0.314Z)$$

Figure 2.5   Two computer programs

different size (i.e., the total number of primitive functions and terminals) and have a different shape (i.e., the particular arrangement of primitive functions and terminals). The numbers beside the functions and terminals in the program tree are for reference only.

The initial population may, if desired, be seeded with particular promising individuals. Such seeding provides an opportunity to introduce available problem-specific knowledge into the operation of genetic programming (although we do not do this anywhere in this book). In any event, the initial population consists of structurally valid computer programs.

Not all computer programs are composed only of standard arithmetic functions and logical functions. Some problems involve problem-specific functions or functions that have a side effect on the state of some system (e.g., special functions that move and turn a robot).

Not all computer programs produce only single floating-point values. Depending on the particular problem, the computer program may produce a result that is Boolean-valued, integer-valued, complex-valued, vector-valued, or symbolic-valued, or it may produce a result in the form of a more complex data structure.

In any event, each individual computer program in the population is executed and then measured in terms of how well it performs the task at hand. For many problems, this measurement yields a specific numerical value, called *fitness*. Depending on the problem, the fitness of a computer program may be measured in terms of the amount of error between its output and the desired output, the amount of time (fuel, money, etc.) required to bring a system to a desired target state, the accuracy of the program in recognizing patterns or classifying objects into classes, the payoff that a game-playing computer program produces for the player of a game, and so forth.

Typically, each computer program in the population is executed over a number of different *fitness cases* so that its fitness is measured over a representative sample of different values of the program's input(s) or a representative sample of different initial conditions of the state of a system. Sometimes the fitness cases are chosen probabilistically (e.g., randomly chosen values of the independent variable[s] or randomly chosen values for the system's initial condition[s]).

The creation of the initial random population is, in effect, a blind random search of the search space of the problem. Unless the problem is so trivial that it can be easily solved by blind random search, the individual computer programs in generation 0 will all have exceedingly poor fitness. Nonetheless, some individuals in the population will be more fit than others. These differences in fitness are then exploited as genetic programming applies Darwinian selection and the genetic operations to create a new population of offspring programs from the current population of parental programs.

After the genetic operations are performed on the current population, the population of offspring (i.e., the new generation) replaces the old population (i.e., the old generation). This iterative process of measuring fitness and performing the genetic operations is repeated over many generations.

Reproduction Operation

The Darwinian reproduction operation operates on one individual computer program selected with a probability based on fitness and makes a copy of the program for inclusion in the next generation of the population.

Crossover Operation

The crossover operation operates on two parental computer programs selected with a probability based on fitness and creates one (or two) new offspring programs consisting of parts of each parent (depending on whether one-offspring or two-offspring crossover is being used). The offspring are inserted into the new population at the next generation.

Suppose the two illustrative computer programs in Figure 2.5 have been selected to participate in the crossover operation. These two programs are typical of the computer programs that participate in the crossover operation in that they have different size (i.e., the total number of primitive functions and terminals) and have a different shape (i.e., the particular arrangement of primitive functions and terminals).

The crossover operation begins by randomly choosing a number between 1 and the size of the first parent (i.e., seven) and by randomly and independently choosing a second random number between 1 and the size of the second parent (i.e., nine). These two independent random choices identify a crossover point in each parent. A crossover point may be an internal point of the program tree or an external point. Suppose, for sake of example, that point 2 (out of the seven points of the first parent in Figure 2.5) is randomly chosen as the crossover point for the first parent and that point 5 (out of the nine points of the second parent in Figure 2.5) is randomly chosen as the crossover point for the second parent. The chosen crossover points are therefore the * for the first parent and the + for the second parent. Both of these crossover points are internal points. The *crossover fragment* of an individual program is the subtree rooted at the crossover point. The two crossover fragments for this example are shown in Figure 2.6.

The crossover fragment of the first parent corresponds to the underlined subexpression (i.e., sublist, subprogram, sub-S-expression) in the expression below:

```
(+ (* 0.234 Z) (- X 0.789)).
```

The crossover fragment of the second parent corresponds to the underlined subexpression in the expression below:

```
(* (* Z Y) (+ Y (* 0.314 Z))).
```

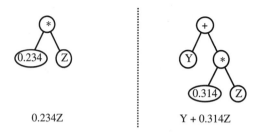

0.234Z   Y + 0.314Z

Figure 2.6　Two crossover fragments

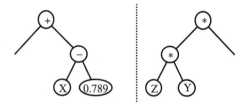

Figure 2.7　Two remainders

Figure 2.7 shows the remainders produced by removing the crossover fragments from the two parents.

The crossover operation creates offspring by exchanging subtrees. Specifically, the first offspring is produced by deleting the crossover fragment of the first parent and implanting the crossover fragment of the second parent at the crossover point of the first parent (i.e., by implanting the crossover fragment of the second parent in the remainder of the first parent). Thus, the first offspring resulting from the crossover operation is

```
(+ (+ Y (* 0.314 Z)) (- X 0.789)).
```

In producing this offspring, the second parent is the contributing (male) parent and the first parent is the receiving (female) parent.

Similarly, the second offspring is produced by deleting the crossover fragment of the second parent and implanting the crossover fragment of the first parent at the crossover point of the second parent. Thus, the second offspring is

```
(* (* Z Y) (* 0.234 Z)).
```

In producing this offspring, the first parent is the contributing (male) parent and the second parent is the receiving (female) parent.

The two offspring are shown in Figure 2.8. Note that there are 63 possible pairs of choices of crossover points for a crossover involving a seven-point parent and a nine-point parent; hence there were 63 possible outcomes of the crossover operation for these particular two parents. These two illustrative offspring are typical of the vast majority of the offspring produced by the crossover operation in that they are different than their parents (and each other).

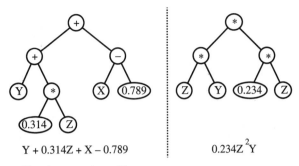

$$Y + 0.314Z + X - 0.789 \qquad 0.234Z^2Y$$

Figure 2.8   Two offspring produced by crossover

Because entire subtrees are swapped, the crossover operation always produces structurally valid programs as offspring regardless of the choice of the two crossover points (assuming closure among the functions and terminals involved). When we say that the set of functions and terminals is closed, we mean that every function in the function set is able to accept, as its arguments, any value that may possibly be returned by any function in the function set that may appear as its arguments and any value that may possibly be assumed by any terminal in the terminal set that may appear.

Because programs are selected to participate in the crossover operation with a probability based on fitness, crossover allocates future trials to regions of the search space whose programs contain parts from promising programs.

In the one-offspring version of crossover, only the first of the above two offspring is produced. The one-offspring version of crossover is used throughout this book.

The crossover operation is regulated so that it does not produce excessively large offspring (typically measured in terms of a preestablished maximum number of points in the offspring tree, but sometimes in terms of a preestablished maximum depth for the offspring tree).

It is common for practitioners of genetic programming to bias the choices of the two crossover points so as to favor the internal points of the parental program trees. The bias in the distribution of crossover points that is used throughout this book results in approximately 90% of the crossover points being internal points. Without this bias, the crossover fragment would be a mere terminal (instead of a subtree) in a significant fraction of the cases (approximately half when the functions predominantly take two arguments). The result would be that many instances of the crossover operation would degenerate to a point mutation. After this bias in favor of internal points is applied, the choice of crossover points is made with a uniform probability distribution. This bias is controlled by one of the default control parameters described in Appendix D.

Mutation Operation

The mutation operation operates on one parental computer program selected with a probability based on fitness and creates one new offspring program to be inserted into the new population at the next generation.

In the mutation operation, a point is randomly chosen in the parental program. The subtree rooted at the chosen mutation point is deleted from the program, and a new subtree is randomly grown using the available functions and terminals in the same manner as trees are grown in creating the initial random population of generation 0. Then the random subtree is implanted at the chosen mutation point.

For example, consider the following parental program (presented as a LISP S-expression) composed of Boolean functions and terminals:

```
(OR (AND D2 D1 (NOR D0 D1))).
```

This program has three Boolean variables (D0, D1, and D2) as its inputs. It produces a single Boolean output by applying the two-argument Boolean OR (disjunction) function to the result produced by evaluating two subexpressions, namely, (AND D2 D1) and (NOR D0 D1).

Figure 2.9 shows this one-branch parental computer program as a rooted point-labeled tree with ordered branches. The three internal points of the tree correspond to functions (i.e., OR, AND, and NOR) and four external points correspond to terminals (i.e., the three external inputs D0, D1, and D2, of which D1 appears twice).

Suppose that the AND (labeled 2) is randomly chosen as the mutation point (out of the seven points in the program tree). The subtree rooted at this chosen mutation point corresponds to the underlined portion of the LISP S-expression above. This subtree is deleted. In this example, the subtree consists of the three points (AND D2 D1). A new subtree, such as

```
(NOR (NOT D0) (NOT D1)),
```

is randomly grown using the available functions and terminals and inserted in lieu of the three-point subtree (AND D2 D1) rooted at AND (labeled 2). Figure 2.10 shows the offspring produced by this mutation operation. This illustrative nine-point offspring is typical of the offspring produced by the mutation operation in that it is different than its parent in size and shape. The result of the mutation operation is

```
(OR (NOR (NOT D0) (NOT D1)) (NOR D0 D1)).
```

Since the initial population consists of structurally valid computer programs and the subtree grown at the mutation point is grown in the same manner that is used for creating the initial random population of generation 0, the mutation operation always produces a structurally valid program as its offspring regardless of the choice of the mutation point (assuming closure among the functions and terminals involved).

The mutation operation is regulated so that it does not produce excessively large offspring (measured typically by a preestablished maximum number of points or a preestablished maximum depth for offspring trees). The mutation operation is generally used sparingly in genetic programming.

2.3.3   Automatic Creation of an Executable Program

The initial population consists of structurally valid, executable computer programs composed of ingredients from a user-supplied repertoire of functions and terminals. The operations of reproduction, crossover, and mutation (and all the architecture-altering operations defined later in Part 3) always produce offspring that are structurally valid, executable computer programs. Therefore, all individuals in all generations of the popu-

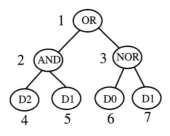

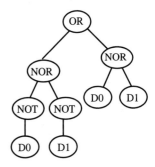

Figure 2.9 One parental program

Figure 2.10 Offspring produced by mutation

lation in a run of genetic programming are always structurally valid, executable computer programs.

A run of genetic programming ends when the termination criterion is satisfied. The result of the run is a certain designated individual (usually the best-so-far individual encountered in any generation) so that the result of the run is a structurally valid, executable computer program. Thus, genetic programming possesses the following attribute of a system for automatically creating computer programs (Chapter 1):

- **ATTRIBUTE NO. 3** (Produces a computer program): It produces an entity that can run on a computer.

2.3.4 Automatic Creation of a Program's Sequence of Steps

The individual computer programs in the initial population are a random composition of the user-supplied repertoire of programmatic ingredients (i.e., the terminals in the terminal set and the functions in the function set as provided by the user in the first and second major preparatory steps of genetic programming). That is, a run of genetic programming starts with a population of programs, each with a different random sequence of programmatic steps. Crossover, mutation, and all architecture-altering operations (Part 3) manipulate sequences of steps taken from the one or two individual programs in the population. These operations almost always produce offspring containing a different sequence of steps than their parent(s).

The run of genetic programming is a competition (beam search) among a diverse population of computer programs to discover a satisfactory program for solving the given problem. The competitive pressures of the environment (as expressed by the problem's fitness measure provided by the user in the third major preparatory step of genetic programming) determines the outcome of the competition. A run of genetic programming ends when the termination criterion is satisfied and the result of the run is determined by the method of result designation (as provided by the user in the fifth major preparatory step for genetic programming). The exact sequence of functions and terminals in the designated final result of a run is not predetermined by the user, but instead emerges from the evolutionary process during the run.

In this system, the fitness measure specifies "what needs to be done" in terms of a high-level statement of the requirements for a solution to a problem. The particular sequence of steps that emerges in the designated final result of a run of genetic programming tells the user "how to do it." Thus, genetic programming possesses the following attribute of a system for automatically creating computer programs (Chapter 1):

- **ATTRIBUTE NO. 2** (Tells us "how to do it"): It produces a result in the form of a sequence of steps that satisfactorily solves the problem.

2.3.5   Automatic Creation of Program Size

Genetic programming is an open-ended process in the sense that the size of the solution is part of the *answer* produced by the process, not part of the *question* posed by the user.

The individual programs in the initial population are of different size. Crossover, mutation, and all architecture-altering operations defined later (Part 3) usually yield offspring of different size than their parent(s). Thus, the individuals in each generation of the population during the run are diverse in terms of size. A run of genetic programming is a competition among a population of computer programs of different sizes that is governed by the competitive pressures of the environment (as expressed by the fitness measure). The size of the designated final result of a run of genetic programming is not predetermined by the user, but instead emerges from the evolutionary process during the run. Thus, genetic programming possesses the following attribute of a system for automatically creating computer programs (Chapter 1):

- **ATTRIBUTE NO. 4** (Automatic determination of program size): It has the ability to automatically determine the number of steps that must be performed and thus does not require the user to prespecify the exact size of the solution.

Of course, genetic programming is not unique in automatically determining the exact size of the solution during the run. For example, algorithms for creating decision trees from empirical data (Quinlan 1986) do not require the user to prespecify the exact number of attribute-testing functions (the internal points of a decision tree) that must be executed or the exact sequence in which the attribute tests must be performed.

Nonetheless, many techniques of machine learning, reinforcement learning, adaptive systems, neural networks, artificial intelligence, and automated logic require the user to analyze the problem in advance and to make the important decision concerning the exact size of the solution in advance. For example, in most neural network learning algorithms (e.g., Rumelhart, McClelland, and the PDP Research Group 1986), the user (not the connectionist learning algorithm) prespecifies the exact number of neurons in the neural network. In addition, the user (not the learning algorithm) usually prespecifies how the output of each neuron is connected to the input of other neurons. By prespecifying the number of neurons and their connectivity, the user preordains the exact number of primitive operations (weighted sums) that will be performed by the solution.

Note that the foregoing characterization of neural network techniques applies to most, but not all, connectionist algorithms. Some techniques (e.g., Lee 1991) adaptively determine the architecture of the neural network during the run. Frederic Gruau's technique of cellular encoding (1992a, 1992b, 1993, 1994a, 1994b) uses genetic programming to dynamically evolve the architecture of the neural network at the same time as the weights, thresholds, and biases of the neural network are being evolved.

A clarification is necessary when we say that the program size in genetic programming is "open-ended." We mean this in the same vein as statements such as "A Turing machine has an infinite amount of storage in the form of a linear tape" or "A Pentium computer can be programmed to perform any computation." In practice, if a Turing machine were to be implemented on a real-world computer, its nominally infinite tape would be constrained by the computer's virtual memory. Similarly, the computations that can be performed by a Pentium computer are manifestly constrained by the size of the computer's virtual memory. No particular finite implementation of a Turing machine has the computational power of a theoretical Turing machine, and no particular actual computer can realize the power of an abstract computing machine. The preestablished maximum limits in this book on the size of the various branches of programs are simply the amount of memory that is allocated for storing the program in the computer that is running the genetic programming system. They should not be confused with the (generally smaller) actual size of the evolved program that actually emerges from a run of genetic programming. These preestablished limits exist because they are convenient in programming our system that implements genetic programming—not because we are trying to preordain the exact size of the result that finally emerges from the run. These preestablished limits are always generously chosen so as to permit the individual programs in the population to freely expand and contract from generation to generation. It is, of course, possible, in principle, to program genetic programming with a dynamic allocation of memory. However, even when we have implemented genetic programming on a LISP machine (where such dynamic memory allocation is especially convenient), we imposed preestablished limits on the size of each individual program in the population because practical experience indicates that extraordinarily large individuals are rarely useful in evolving solutions to problems.

2.3.6 Automatically Defined Functions

Computer programmers commonly organize sequences of primitive steps into useful groups (subroutines). Typically, programmers repeatedly invoke a particular subroutine. This reuse is usually done with different instantiations of the subroutine's dummy variables (formal parameters). Reuse exploits the modularities, symmetries, and regularities of problems and eliminates the need to "reinvent the wheel" on each occasion when a particular sequence of steps is required. Programmers also commonly organize subroutines into hierarchies.

Genetic programming provides a mechanism for the parameterized reuse and hierarchical invocation of evolved code in the form of automatically defined functions (ADFs). Automatically defined functions are the mechanism by which genetic programming implements subroutines (subprograms, procedures, DEFUNs). An ADF consists of a function-defining branch that possesses zero, one, or more dummy variables (formal parameters) and whose body is subject to evolutionary modification during the run of genetic programming.

Each automatically defined function resides in a separate function-defining branch within a multipart computer program. That is, it belongs to a particular individual program in the population. The body of the function-defining branch (automatically defined function) is coevolved with the body of its calling subprogram during the run of genetic programming.

An automatically defined function may, in general, be called by a main result-producing branch of the overall program, another automatically defined function, an automatically defined iteration, an automatically defined loop, or an automatically defined recursion.

When automatically defined functions are being used, a program in the population consists of a hierarchy of one (or more) *reusable* function-defining branch(es) (i.e., automatically defined functions) along with one (or sometimes more) main result-producing branch(es). Typically, the automatically defined functions are reused with different instantiations of their dummy variables. During a run, genetic programming coevolves subprograms in the function-defining branches of the overall program, main programs in the result-producing branch, different instantiations of the dummy variables in the function-defining branches, and different hierarchical references between the branches.

Automatically defined functions are the main focus of *Genetic Programming II: Automatic Discovery of Reusable Programs* (Koza 1994g) and *Genetic Programming II Videotape: The Next Generation* (Koza 1994h). Automatically defined functions were conceived and developed by James P. Rice and John R. Koza.

Automatically defined functions can be implemented within the context of genetic programming by establishing a constrained syntactic structure for the programs in the population (Koza 1992f; Koza 1992e, Chapters 20 and 21; Koza and Rice 1992a).

Constrained syntactic structures are defined by means of syntactic rules of construction for each overall program. When constrained syntactic structures are used,

- the initial population must be created so that every individual program in the population conforms to the requirements of the syntactic structure, and
- when crossover, mutation, or any other operation is performed, the requirements of the syntactic structure must be preserved.

Figure 2.11 shows a two-branch program consisting of one result-producing branch in the right part of the figure and one function-defining branch (automatically defined function ADF0) in the left part of the figure. The topmost point of the overall program in Figure 2.11 is the PROGN (labeled 400). In LISP, a PROGN sequentially executes its arguments and returns only the value of its final argument. The automatically defined function is defined by DEFUN 410. This definitional process enables the automatically defined function to be called by other branches of the overall program. Execution of the DEFUN does not itself return anything of interest. More specifically, the DEFUN in LISP returns the name of the just-defined function, ADF0. Because PROGN 400 returns only the value returned by its final (second) argument, the function name returned by the DEFUN is simply lost.

The function definition for ADF0 has three parts. First, the function definition specifies the name of the function (i.e., ADF0 411). Second, the function definition includes the argument list of the function (appearing beneath the function LIST 412). Here the function list includes two dummy variables (formal parameters), ARG0 413 and ARG1 414. Third, the function definition consists of the body of ADF0. In the figure, the body of ADF0 is a value-returning subtree that begins with VALUES 419. In LISP, VALUES is a function that is used to return the value(s) produced by execution of a subtree. The body of ADF0 contains the five points labeled 420, 421, 422, 423, and 424. Specifically, the body of ADF0 performs the following Boolean calculation on the two dummy variables ARG0 and ARG1:

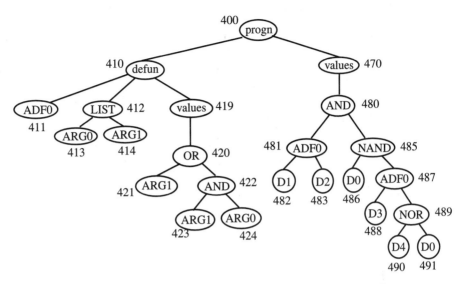

Figure 2.11 Program consisting of one two-argument automatically defined function (ADF0) and one result-producing branch

```
(OR ARG1 (AND ARG0 ARG1)).
```

Now consider the result-producing branch in the right part of the figure. The PROGN executes the VALUES 470 that returns the value produced by the 11-point subtree rooted at the AND 480. This subtree performs a Boolean calculation on the actual variables of the problem (i.e., the externally provided inputs to the overall program), namely, D0, D1, D2, D3, and D4. In the course of performing this calculation, the result-producing branch invokes the automatically defined function ADF0 twice (once at 481 and once at 487). In the first invocation of ADF0 at 481, ADF0 is called by instantiating the first dummy variable (formal parameter) of the automatically defined function with D1 482 and by instantiating the second dummy variable with D2 483. In the second invocation of ADF0 at 481, ADF0 is called by instantiating the first dummy variable with D3 488 and by instantiating the second dummy variable with the subexpression

```
(NOR D4 D0)
```

at 489, 490, and 491.

The value returned by the overall program consists of the value returned by the result-producing branch. In this figure, this is the single value returned at VALUES 470.

If the program in Figure 2.11 were to have more than one automatically defined function, there would be an additional DEFUN for each such additional automatically defined function. There would be a new name, an argument list, and a body beneath each such additional DEFUN.

The result-producing branch does not contain dummy variables. It typically contains the external input to the overall computer program (i.e., the actual variables of the problem, such as D0, D1, D2, D3, and D4). The result-producing branch also contains various primitive functions of the problem (i.e., AND, OR, NAND, and NOR in the case of the

Boolean calculation here). The result-producing branch may invoke all, some, or none of the automatically defined function(s) that may be present within the overall program.

The automatically defined functions of a particular overall program are usually named sequentially (from left to right) as ADF0, ADF1, and so forth.

Automatically defined functions typically each possess a certain number of dummy variables. Here, ADF0 possesses two dummy variables, ARG0 413 and ARG1 414.

If the overall program has more than one automatically defined function, there may (or may not) be hierarchical references between automatically defined functions. It is common for an automatically defined function to be allowed to refer nonrecursively to any previously defined automatically defined function. Thus, if the automatically defined functions are numbered sequentially (from left to right), a higher-numbered automatically defined function is permitted to refer to a lower-numbered one (but not vice versa). (Recursion is discussed in Chapter 8.)

References within a particular program to automatically defined functions are to the automatically defined functions belonging to that particular program (not to the automatically defined functions of other individual programs in the population).

Actions (with side effects) may be performed within the function-defining branches, the result-producing branches, or both.

The argument map describes the architecture of a multipart program in terms of the number of its function-defining branches and the number of arguments that they each possess. The *argument map* of the ordered set of automatically defined functions belonging to an overall program is a list containing the number of arguments possessed by each of the program's automatically defined functions. The argument map for the overall program in Figure 2.11 is {2} because there is one automatically defined function and it possesses two arguments.

When automatically defined functions are being used, generation 0 of the population must be created so that each individual program in the population has the intended architecture. In Figure 2.11, the architecture of the overall program consists of one result-producing branch and one two-argument function-defining branch.

The function-defining branch for the automatically defined function ADF0 is a random composition of functions from the function set, F_{adf}, and terminals from the terminal set, T_{adf}. The function set for the automatically defined function, F_{adf}, consists of four two-argument Boolean functions:

F_{adf} = {AND, OR, NAND, NOR}.

The terminal set for the automatically defined function, T_{adf}, consists of two dummy variables (formal parameters):

T_{adf} = {ARG0, ARG1}.

The result-producing branch is a random composition of functions from the function set, F_{rpb}, and terminals from the terminal set, T_{rpb}. The function set for the result-producing branch, F_{rpb}, consists of the above four two-argument Boolean functions and the now-defined automatically defined function, ADF0:

F_{rpb} = {AND, OR, NAND, NOR, ADF0}.

The terminal set for the result-producing branch, T_{rpb}, consists of the problem's five actual variables (external inputs):

$$T_{rpb} = \{D0, D1, D2, D3, D4\}.$$

Genetic Programming II (Koza 1994g) focused on subroutines (automatically defined functions) and scalability of genetic programming to larger versions of the same problem and established eight main points:

1. Automatically defined functions enable genetic programming to solve a variety of problems in a way that can be interpreted as a decomposition of a problem into subproblems, a solving of the subproblems, and an assembly of the solutions to the subproblems into a solution to the overall problem (or that can alternatively be interpreted as a search for regularities in the problem environment, a change in representation, and a solving of a higher-level problem).

2. Automatically defined functions discover and exploit the regularities, symmetries, homogeneities, similarities, patterns, and modularities of the problem environment in ways that are very different from the style employed by human programmers.

3. For a variety of problems, genetic programming requires less computational effort (fewer fitness evaluations to yield a solution with a satisfactorily high probability) with automatically defined functions than without them, provided the difficulty of the problem is above a certain relatively low break-even point.

4. For a variety of problems, genetic programming usually yields solutions with smaller overall size (lower average structural complexity) with automatically defined functions than without them, provided the difficulty of the problem is above a certain break-even point.

5. For the three problems in *Genetic Programming II* for which a progression of several scaled-up versions is studied, the average size of the solutions produced by genetic programming increases as a function of problem size at a lower rate with automatically defined functions than without them.

6. For the three problems in *Genetic Programming II* for which a progression of several scaled-up versions is studied, the number of fitness evaluations required by genetic programming to yield a solution (with a specified high probability) increases as a function of problem size at a lower rate with automatically defined functions than without them.

7. For the three problems in *Genetic Programming II* for which a progression of several scaled-up versions is studied, the improvement in computational effort and average structural complexity conferred by automatically defined functions increases as the problem size is scaled up.

8. Genetic programming is capable of simultaneously solving a problem and selecting the architecture of the overall program (consisting of the number of automatically defined functions and the number of their arguments).

In addition, *Genetic Programming II* demonstrated that it is possible to

- automatically create multibranch programs containing an iteration-performing branch along with a main program and subroutines (e.g., the transmembrane identification problem of Chapter 18 and the omega loop problem of Chapter 19),

- automatically create multibranch programs containing multiple iteration-performing branches and iteration-terminating branches (e.g., the lookahead version of the transmembrane problem in Chapter 20), and
- automatically determine the architecture for a multibranch program in an architecturally diverse population by means of evolutionary selection (e.g., Chapters 21 and 25).

The above mechanisms for automatically identifying useful groups of steps in computer programs and then automatically reusing the groups can be illustrated by the "two boxes" problem (Koza 1994g, Chapter 4). The "two boxes" problem is a problem of symbolic regression (system identification, empirical discovery, modeling, forecasting, data mining) entailing the discovery of a computer program (i.e., mathematical expression, formula, composition of primitive functions and terminals) that produces the observed values of the dependent variable(s) as its output when given the values of the independent variable(s) as input.

Table 2.1 shows examples of the values of the dependent variable, D, associated with 10 combinations of values of the six independent variables (L_0, W_0, H_0, L_1, W_1, and H_1). The underlying relationship among the variables in the six-dimensional symbolic regression problem of Table 2.1 is that the dependent variable, D, is the difference in volume between a first box (whose length, width, and height are L_0, W_0, and H_0, respectively) and a second box (whose length, width, and height are L_1, W_1, and H_1, respectively). Figure 2.12 shows the two boxes.

If the user happens to know (or suspect) that the data in a problem of symbolic regression comes from a physical system that is composed of two three-dimensional subspaces as shown in Table 2.1 and Figure 2.12, the user could advantageously choose a program architecture consisting of one three-argument automatically defined function and one result-producing branch.

The following LISP program implements the above decomposition involving one three-argument automatically defined function:

```
1  (PROGN
2   (DEFUN ADF0 (ARG0 ARG1 ARG2)
3    (VALUES
4     (* ARG0 (* ARG1 ARG2)))))
5   (VALUES
6    (- (ADF0 L0 W0 H0)
7     (ADF0 L1 W1 H1)))))
```

In the program, the DEFUN on line 2 defines a subroutine called ADF0. The subroutine possesses three dummy variables (formal parameters): ARG0, ARG1, and ARG2. The body of the subroutine (on line 4) computes the product of the three arguments. The VALUES function (on line 3) specifies that the value returned by the subroutine is the product of the three arguments. The main program appears on lines 5, 6, and 7. The main program has six external outputs: the length, width, and height of the first box (i.e., L0, W0, and H0) and the length, width, and height of the second box (i.e., L1, W1, and H1). The main program on line 6 calls the subroutine ADF0 with the length, width, and height of the first box. Line 7 calls the subroutine ADF0 with the length, width, and

Table 2.1   Data for a six-dimensional symbolic regression problem

Fitness case	L_0	W_0	H_0	L_1	W_1	H_1	D
1	3	4	7	2	5	3	54
2	7	10	9	10	3	1	600
3	10	9	4	8	1	6	312
4	3	9	5	1	6	4	111
5	4	3	2	7	6	1	−18
6	3	3	1	9	5	4	−171
7	5	9	9	1	7	6	363
8	1	2	9	3	9	2	−36
9	2	6	8	2	6	10	−24
10	8	1	10	7	5	1	45

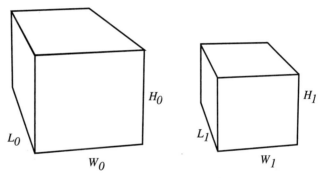

Figure 2.12   Boxes representing the two subspaces of this problem

height of the second box. Line 6 subtracts the value returned by the call to ADF0 for the first box from the value returned by the call to ADF0 for the second box. The resulting difference is the value returned by the main program by the VALUES function on line 5.

Table 2.2 is similar to Table 2.1; however, two new columns (labeled V_0 and V_1) have been inserted. These two columns represent the volume of the first and second boxes, respectively. By recognizing the importance of the two three-dimensional subspaces (representing the volumes of the two boxes), the given six-dimensional symbolic regression problem can be recast into a new two-dimensional problem involving the new variables, V_0 and V_1, and the original dependent variable, D. This recasting is highly advantageous for this problem because it converts a six-dimensional *nonlinear* regression problem into a much simpler two-dimensional *linear* regression problem. After this recasting, it can be easily seen that the dependent variable, D, is merely the difference between V_0 and V_1.

This recasting may be viewed as a top-down or bottom-up way of solving a problem. When a human implements the top-down approach (often called "divide and conquer"), the first step of the process involves finding a way to decompose the given problem into subproblems. Second, the user solves each of the now-identified subproblems. Third, the

Table 2.2 Eight-dimensional version

Fitness case	L_0	W_0	H_0	L_1	W_1	H_1	V_0	V_1	D
1	3	4	7	2	5	3	84	30	54
2	7	10	9	10	3	1	630	30	600
3	10	9	4	8	1	6	360	48	312
4	3	9	5	1	6	4	135	24	111
5	4	3	2	7	6	1	24	42	−18
6	3	3	1	9	5	4	9	180	−171
7	5	9	9	1	7	6	405	42	363
8	1	2	9	3	9	2	18	54	−36
9	2	6	8	2	6	10	96	120	−24
10	8	1	10	7	5	1	80	35	45

user solves the given problem by assembling the now-available solutions to the subproblems into a solution to the given problem. The result is a hierarchical solution to the problem.

Figure 2.13 depicts the three-step top-down hierarchical problem-solving process. In the figure, the given problem is shown at the left. In the step labeled "decompose" near the left of the figure, the original problem is decomposed into two subproblems. In the step labeled "solve subproblems" in the middle of the figure, the two subproblems are solved. Finally, in the step labeled "solve original problem" near the right, the solutions of the two subproblems are assembled into a solution to the original problem. In the case of the problem of two boxes, there are two subproblems, namely, finding the volume of the two boxes. Once these two subproblems are solved, the solution to the original given problem can be assembled (by mere subtraction) from the solutions to the two subproblems.

When a human implements the bottom-up approach (often called a "change of representation"), the first step of the process is to find useful low-level patterns in the given data. Second, the user changes the representation of the problem and restates the problem in terms of the now-discovered low-level patterns. In effect, a new problem is created. Third, the user solves the presumably simpler new problem.

Figure 2.14 depicts the three-step bottom-up hierarchical problem-solving process. In the figure, the given problem is shown at the left. The step labeled "identify regularities" near the left of the figure identifies two recoding rules that can be applied to the original representation of the problem. The step labeled "change representation" in the middle of the figure recodes the original given data using the two recoding rules and creates a new representation of the problem. Finally, the step labeled "solve" near the right solves the problem in terms of the new representation. After the change in representation of the problem of two boxes, it is easy to solve the problem.

The bottom-up approach is especially pertinent to problems of pattern recognition and grammar induction. In such problems, low-level features (e.g., a group of pixels representing an edge or corner of an image, frequently used substrings) are identified and the original image is recoded as a composition of features. An image is often easier to identify after this change in representation.

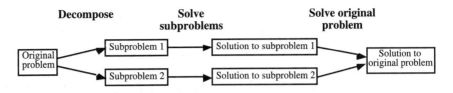

Figure 2.13 **Top-down ("divide and conquer") approach to problem solving**

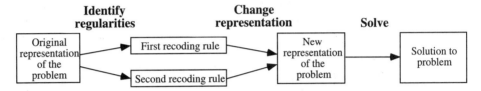

Figure 2.14 **Bottom-up ("change of representation") approach to problem solving**

Both the top-down and bottom-up approach to problem solving exploit the modularities, symmetries, and regularities that are inherent in most practical problems. Both the top-down and bottom-up approach create the opportunity to reuse code. Code reuse is important because it obviates the necessity of repeatedly rewriting code to solve an already-solved subproblem (in the top-down approach) or to rediscover an already-identified change of representation (in the bottom-up approach). Reuse facilitates problem solving because ever-more complex problems can be solved by leveraging already-obtained solutions to subproblems and already-obtained changes of representation.

Code reuse goes hand in hand with generality. Because a subroutine's steps are repeatedly executed (often with different instantiations of the subroutine's dummy variables), there is usually a high degree of generality to the steps executed by a subroutine.

Code reuse is especially advantageous in an adaptive process. If the code within a subroutine is incrementally improved, the benefit of the improvement is leveraged because it will be automatically conferred on all parts of the overall program that refer to the improved subroutine. It is not necessary to separately rediscover the improvement for each separate part of the overall program.

The sequence of primitive operations in automatically defined functions is evolved during the run of genetic programming. Once such a sequence of steps in an automatically defined function is defined, it can (and typically is) reused repeatedly within the overall program. In addition, automatically defined functions can be parameterized. That is, it is possible to communicate information between a calling program and an automatically defined function so that the behavior of the automatically defined function varies in response to the passed parameters.

The architecture-altering operations for subroutines (Chapter 5) provide a mechanism for reuse. Iterations, loops, and recursion provide additional mechanisms for reuse (as described in Chapters 6, 7, and 8, respectively). Thus, genetic programming possesses the following attribute of a system for automatically creating computer programs (Chapter 1):

- **ATTRIBUTE NO. 5** (Code reuse): It has the ability to automatically organize useful groups of steps so that they can be reused.

As far as we know, genetic programming is unique among existing techniques for artificial intelligence, machine learning, neural networks, adaptive systems, reinforcement learning, or automated logic in providing a general mechanism for automatically identifying useful groups of steps and automatically reusing them. We know of no analogous general mechanism for automatic reuse in decision trees, Bayesian networks, inductive logic programming, adaptive systems, production systems, reinforcement learning, genetic classifier systems, genetic algorithms, or most neural network learning algorithms.

Nonetheless, some attention has been devoted in several of these fields to exploring the possibilities of implementing a capability for reuse. The weight-sharing approach in neural network research (Le Cun et al. 1990) and the neocognitron (Fukushima and Miyake 1982; Fukushima, Miyake, and Takatuki 1983; Fukushima 1989) contemplate reuse, but do not provide an automatic mechanism for identifying the opportunities for such reuse. As discussed in *Genetic Programming II* (Koza 1994g, Section 3.5), SOAR (Laird, Rosenbloom, and Newell 1986a, 1986b; Rosenbloom, Laird, and Newell 1993) has some capability for reuse, but does not have a general mechanism for automatically identifying and implementing reuse. Parameters are sometimes reused in reinforcement learning. Notwithstanding these and other isolated efforts, it is fair to say that reuse is not a major component of most techniques of artificial intelligence, machine learning, neural networks, adaptive systems, reinforcement learning, or automated logic.

We now consider scalability. Once a sequence of steps is evolved for a subroutine, iteration, loop, or recursion during a run of genetic programming, the sequence of steps can be (and typically is) reused repeatedly in the overall program. This reuse means that it is not necessary to evolve a sequence of steps anew on each separate occasion in which it is needed. We believe that reuse is a precondition for a scalable system for automatically creating computer programs.

Main points 5, 6, and 7 of *Genetic Programming II* (listed above) provide some evidence that automatically defined functions provide a basis for a scalable system for automatically creating computer programs. In addition, this book provides some additional evidence on this point in the form of comparisons (Chapter 55) of the computational effort (Section 12.6.1) associated with evolving the design of a succession of increasingly stringent filters and the computational effort associated with the automatically defined copy (a variation of the automatically defined function). There are, of course, many practical difficulties associated with attempting to study scaling experimentally. Experimental evidence concerning the scaling of genetic programming is admittedly limited. Clearly, more experimental evidence as well as theoretical work is needed on the important question of scalability.

We merely say, at this time, that there is "some evidence in favor" of the assertion that genetic programming possesses the following attribute of a system for automatically creating computer programs (Chapter 1):

- **ATTRIBUTE NO. 15** (Scalability): It scales well to larger versions of the same problem.

2.3.7 Internal Storage

The usefulness of genetic programming today is the result of the innovative advances made by various researchers who have implemented a broad range of useful programming constructs and technique extensions in the context of genetic programming. In particular, there are a number of advances in genetic programming concerning the implementation of internal storage, including the following:

- named memory (Koza 1992e, 1994g),
- indexed memory (Teller 1994a, 1994b),
- matrix memory (Andre 1994b),
- data structures, such as stacks, queues, lists (Langdon 1995, 1996a, 1996b, 1996c, 1998),
- stack-based program structures (Perkis 1994; Spector and Stoffel 1996a, 1996b),
- state (Raik and Browne 1997), and
- relational memory (Brave 1995a, 1996c).

This book describes additional approaches to internal storage in Chapter 9.

2.3.8 Iteration and Recursion

Various researchers have increased the usefulness of genetic programming by implementing iterations and recursion, including the following:

- iterations and statistic computing zones (Handley 1996a, 1998),
- recursion (Brave 1995b, 1996b; Wong and Leung 1996, 1998; Yu and Clack 1997b; Teller 1998),
- iterations (Andre 1994c; Koza 1992e, Chapter 18), and
- iterations and recursions in genetic programming with graphlike structures and neural programming and PADO (Teller 1998; Poli 1997a, 1997b).

This book describes additional approaches to iteration and recursion in Chapters 6, 7, and 8.

2.3.9 Technique Extensions

Various researchers have increased the usefulness of genetic programming with technique extensions, such as

- control structures involving multiple result-producing branches (Luke and Spector 1996b; Bennett 1996a; Svingen 1997),
- adaptive, self-modifying, ontogenetic genetic programming (Spector and Stoffel 1996a, 1996b),
- cultural storage and transmission (Spector and Luke 1996a, 1996b),
- hierarchical problem solving (Rosca and Ballard 1994a, 1994b; Rosca 1995, 1997),
- modules (Angeline and Pollack 1993, 1994; Angeline 1993, 1994; Kinnear 1994a),
- logic grammars (Wong and Leung 1995a, 1995b, 1995c, 1995d, 1995e, 1997),
- cellular encoding (developmental genetic programming) for evolving neural networks (Gruau 1992a, 1992b, 1993, 1994a, 1994b; Gruau and Whitley 1993; Esparcia-Alcazar and Sharman 1997),

- developmental methods for evolving finite automata using genetic programming (Brave 1996a),
- automatic parallelization of computer programs that are provably equivalent to the original serial program (Ryan 1996a, 1997)
- evolutionary art and interactive graphics (Sims 1991a, 1991b, 1992, 1993)
- application of genetic programming to Lindenmayer systems (Jacob 1995, 1996, 1997)
- developmental methods for shape optimization (Kennelly 1997),
- evolving graphs and networks (Luke and Spector 1996a),
- using a grammar to represent bias and background knowledge (Whigham 1995a, 1995b, 1996a, 1996b),
- developmental methods for fuzzy logic systems (Tunstel and Jamshidi 1996),
- Turing completeness of genetic programming (Teller 1994c; Nordin and Banzhaf 1995),
- evolution of chemical topological structures (Nachbar 1998),
- diploidy and dominance (Greene 1997a, 1997b),
- interactive fitness measures (Poli and Cagnoni 1997)
- variations in crossover operations (Poli and Langdon 1997),
- distributed processes and multiagent systems (Haynes and Sen 1997; Ryan 1995; Luke and Spector 1996b; Iba 1996b; Iba, Nozoe, and Ueda 1997; Qureshi 1996; Crosbie and Spafford 1995),
- complexity-based fitness measures using minimum description length (Iba, Kurita, de Garis, and Sato 1993; Iba, deGaris, and Sato 1994),
- coevolution (Reynolds 1994b),
- steady-state genetic programming (Reynolds 1993, 1994a, 1994d),
- use of noise in fitness cases (Reynolds 1994c),
- balancing parsimony and accuracy (Zhang and Mühlenbein 1993, 1994, 1995; Blickle 1997),
- a multistrategy approach combining genetic programming with rules produced by concept induction or other machine-learning algorithms (Aler, Barrajo, and Isasi 1998),
- automatically defined features using genetic algorithms in conjunction with genetic programming (Andre 1994a), and
- graphical program structures and neural programming (Teller and Veloso 1996, 1997; Teller 1998; Poli 1997a, 1997b).

2.3.10 Other Programming Constructs

Various researchers have implemented a broad range of useful and familiar programming constructs in the context of genetic programming, including the following:

- automatically defined macros (ADMs) for simultaneous evolution of programs and their control structures (Spector 1996),
- libraries (Koza 1990b; Koza and Rice 1991b; Koza 1992e, Section 6.5.4; Angeline and Pollack 1993, 1994; Angeline 1993, 1994; Kinnear 1994a),
- strong typing (Montana 1995; Montana and Czerwinski 1996; Janikow 1996; Yu and Clack 1997a) and constrained syntactic structures (Koza 1992e),

- explicit pointers (Andre 1994c), and
- evolution of machine code (Nordin 1994, 1997) and linear genomes (Banzhaf, Nordin, Keller, and Francone 1998).

Moreover, basic genetic programming implements conditional operations, logical functions, integer functions, floating-point functions, complex-valued functions, multiple inputs, and multiple outputs.

Based on the above, genetic programming possesses the following attribute of a system for automatically creating computer programs (Chapter 1):

- **ATTRIBUTE NO. 11** (Wide range of programming constructs): It has the ability to implement analogs of the programming constructs that human computer programmers find useful, including macros, libraries, typing, pointers, conditional operations, logical functions, integer functions, floating-point functions, complex-valued functions, multiple inputs, multiple outputs, and machine code instructions.

As stated in Chapter 1, the 16 attributes of a system for automatically creating computer programs are not intended to be definitional, but instead to provide a list of attributes that such a system might reasonably be expected to possess. We do not contend that every programming construct that human programmers find useful must be present in order to have a useful system for automatically creating computer programs. Nonetheless, it would be a cause for concern if a putative system for automatically creating computer programs lacked a way to implement a large fraction of the constructs that human computer programmers regularly use.

2.4   THE FIELD OF EVOLUTIONARY COMPUTATION

The field of evolutionary computation includes

- evolutionary programming,
- evolution strategies,
- classifier systems,
- evolvable hardware,
- genetic algorithms (Section 2.1), and
- genetic programming (Section 2.3).

Section 2.4.1 briefly mentions the early history of the field of evolutionary computation. Section 2.4.2 describes sources of additional information for all six parts of the field of evolutionary computation.

2.4.1   History of Evolutionary Computation

The ideas underlying the field of evolutionary computation can be traced back to the earliest years of the field of electronic computers. In his 1948 essay "Intelligent Machines" (edited by D. C. Ince in *Mechanical Intelligence: Collected Works of A. M. Turing*, 1992), Turing speculated on the possibility of automatically creating a computer program composed of perhaps 1,000 to 1,000,000 bits. Turing (1948) said

> If the untrained infant's mind is to become an intelligent one, it must acquire both discipline and initiative. . . . [D]iscipline is certainly not enough in itself to produce intelligence. That

which is required in addition we call initiative. . . . Our task is to discover the nature of this residue as it occurs in man, and to try and copy it in machines. . . .

A very typical sort of problem requiring some sort of initiative consists of those of the form "Find a number n such that . . .". This form covers a very great variety of problems. For instance problems of the form "See if you can find a way of calculating the function which will enable us to obtain the values for arguments . . . to accuracy . . . within a time . . . using the [Universal Practical Computing Machine]. . ." are reducible to this form, for the problem is clearly equivalent to that of finding a program to put into the machine in question, and it is easy to put the programs into correspondence with the positive integers in such a way that given either the number or the program the other can easily be found. We should not go far wrong for the time being if we assumed that all problems were reducible to this form. It will be time to think again when something turns up which is obviously not of this form. [All ellipses in this paragraph are in original.]

The crudest way of dealing with such a problem is to take the integers in order and to test each one to see whether it has the required property, and to go on until one is found which has it. Such a method will only be successful in the simplest cases. For instance in the case of problems of the kind mentioned above, where one is really searching for a program, the number required will normally be somewhere between $2^{1,000}$ and $2^{1,000,000}$. For practical work therefore some more expeditious method is necessary.

Continuing, Turing made the connection between searches and artificial intelligence by saying,

Further research into intelligence of machinery will probably be very greatly concerned with "searches" . . .

Turing then identified three broad approaches by which search might be used to automatically create an intelligent computer program. One approach that Turing identified is a search through the space of integers representing candidate computer programs. Another approach is the "cultural search," which relies on knowledge and expertise acquired over a period of years from others (akin to present-day knowledge-based systems and expert systems). The third approach that Turing specifically identified is the "genetical or evolutionary search." Turing said

There is the genetical or evolutionary search by which a combination of genes is looked for, the criterion being the survival value.

Turing did not specify how to conduct the "genetical or evolutionary search" for a computer program composed of 1,000 to 1,000,000 bits. However, his 1950 paper "Computing Machinery and Intelligence" suggested how natural selection and evolution might be incorporated into such a search:

We cannot expect to find a good child-machine at the first attempt. One must experiment with teaching one such machine and see how well it learns. One can then try another and see if it is better or worse. There is an obvious connection between this process and evolution, by the identifications

Structure of the child machine = Hereditary material

Changes of the child machine = Mutations

Natural selection = Judgment of the experimenter

Then, in 1953, the mathematician Nils Aall Barricelli prevailed on John von Neumann to give him computer time on the new computer of the Institute for Advanced Studies in Princeton so that he could conduct experiments in simulated evolution (Dyson 1997).

In 1962, Barricelli described how he created a population of 500 eight-bit strings representing simple program instructions and reported (Barricelli 1962),

> We have created a class of numbers which are able to reproduce and to undergo hereditary changes.
>
> The conditions for an evolution process according to the principle of Darwin's theory would appear to be present. The numbers which have the greatest survival in their environment . . . will survive. The other numbers will be eliminated little by little. A process of adaptation to the environmental conditions, that is, a process of Darwinian evolution, will take place.

David Fogel has compiled reprints of 30 papers of historical interest from the field of evolutionary computation (including two from Barricelli) in *Evolutionary Computation: The Fossil Record* (1998). Fogel's compilation includes a historical discussion of each paper.

2.4.2   Sources of Information on Evolutionary Computation

The field of evolutionary computation includes genetic algorithms, genetic programming, evolutionary programming, evolution strategies, classifier systems, and evolvable hardware. We do not undertake a detailed explanation of the latter four areas here; however, this section describes sources of additional information on all six of these areas of evolutionary computation.

Evolution Strategies

Evolution strategies (*Evolutionsstrategie* in German or *evolution artificiel* in French) originated at the Technical University in Berlin with the work in the 1960s of Ingo Rechenberg (1965, 1973), Hans-Paul Schwefel, and Peter Bienert on airfoil design and other problems. Evolution strategies (ES) rely primarily on selection and mutation (as opposed to crossover) for evolving solutions to problems.

Books on evolution strategies and evolutionary computation and evolutionary algorithms include the following:

- *Die Theorie der Evolutionsstrategien* (Beyer 1998),
- *Evolutionsstrategie* (Rechenberg 1994), and
- *Evolution and Optimum Seeking* (Schwefel 1995).

The edited collection of Quagliarella, Periaux, Poloni, and Winter (1998) includes many papers on evolution strategies. Recent work on evolution strategies is primarily published by conferences such as Parallel Problem Solving from Nature (Voigt, Ebeling, Rechenberg, and Schwefel 1996) and Artificial Evolution (Alliot et al. 1995). In addition, most of the conferences mentioned at the end of this chapter include some papers on evolution strategies.

Evolutionary Programming

The idea of evolutionary programming was first published in 1962 (Lawrence Fogel 1962) and extended in the 1966 book by Lawrence Fogel, Alvin Owens, and Michael J. Walsh, who originally worked together at Convair and later formed Decision Science, Inc.

Evolutionary programming (EP), like evolution strategies, relies on Darwinian selection and mutation (as opposed to crossover) for evolving solutions to problems. Evolutionary programming differs from evolution strategies in that evolutionary programming does not always select the known best individual, but instead uses probabilistic selection based on fitness.

Books on evolutionary programming include the following:

- *Artificial Intelligence through Simulated Evolution* (Lawrence Fogel, Owens, and Walsh 1966),
- *System Identification through Simulated Evolution* (David Fogel 1991), and
- *Intelligent System Applications in Power Engineering: Evolutionary Programming and Neural Networks* (Lai 1998).

Recent work on evolutionary programming is primarily published by the Evolutionary Programming conferences (Angeline, Reynolds, McDonnell, and Eberhart 1997). In addition, most of the other conferences mentioned at the end of this chapter include papers on evolutionary programming.

Genetic Algorithms

Books that survey the field of genetic algorithms (and are often used as textbooks) include the following:

- *Genetic Algorithms and Engineering Design* (Gen and Cheng 1997),
- *Genetic Algorithms in Search, Optimization, and Machine Learning* (Goldberg 1989a),
- *Adaptation in Natural and Artificial Systems: An Introductory Analysis with Applications to Biology, Control, and Artificial Intelligence* (Holland 1975),
- *Genetic Algorithms + Data Structures = Evolution Programs* (Michalewicz 1996), and
- *An Introduction to Genetic Algorithms* (Mitchell 1996).

More specialized books on genetic algorithms include the following:

- *Genetic Algorithms and Investment Strategies* (Bauer 1994),
- *Genetic Learning for Adaptive Image Segmentation* (Bhanu and Lee 1994),
- *Genetic Algorithms* (Buckles and Petry 1992),
- *Genetic Algorithms and Robotics* (Davidor 1990),
- *Adaptive Learning by Genetic Algorithms* (Dawid 1996),
- *Evolutionary Learning Algorithms for Neural Adaptive Control* (Dracopoulos 1997),
- *Genetic Algorithms and Grouping Problems* (Falkenauer 1997),
- *Fuzzy Rule-Based Expert Systems and Genetic Machine Learning* (Geyer-Schulz 1995),
- *Practical Genetic Algorithms* (Haupt and Haupt 1998),
- *Genetic Algorithms for Control and Signal Processing* (Man, Tang, Kwong, and Halang 1997),
- *Evolutionary Search and the Job Shop* (Mattfield 1996),
- *Genetic Algorithms and Pattern Recognition* (Pal and Wang 1996),
- *Genetic Algorithms in Optimization, Simulation, and Modeling* (Stender, Hillebrand, and Kingdon 1994),

- *Evolution and Optimization: An Introduction to Solving Complex Problems by Replicator Networks* (Voigt 1989), and
- *The Simple Genetic Algorithm: Foundations and Theory* (Vose 1999).

Edited collections of papers on genetic algorithms include Biethahn and Nissen (1995); Chambers (1995); Dasgupta and Michalewicz (1997); Davis (1987, 1991); Dawid (1996); Kitano (1993, 1995, 1997); Stender (1993); Winter, Periaux, Galan, and Cuesta (1996); Quagliarella, Periaux, Poloni, and Winter (1998); and Zalzala and Fleming (1997).

Genetic Programming

Additional information about genetic programming can be found in the following books:

- *Genetic Programming—An Introduction* (Banzhaf, Nordin, Keller, and Francone 1998),
- *Emergence, Evolution, Intelligence: Hydroinformatics* (Babovic 1996b),
- *Theory of Evolutionary Algorithms and Application to System Synthesis* (Blickle 1997),
- *Principia Evolvica: Simulierte Evolution mit Mathematica* (Jacob 1997, in German; English translation forthcoming),
- *Genetic Programming* (Iba 1996b, in Japanese),
- *Genetic Programming: On the Programming of Computers by Means of Natural Selection* (Koza 1992e),
- *Genetic Programming II: Automatic Discovery of Reusable Programs* (Koza 1994g),
- *Genetic Programming and Data Structures: Genetic Programming + Data Structures = Automatic Programming!* (Langdon 1998),
- *Evolutionary Program Induction of Binary Machine Code and Its Application* (Nordin 1997).

Edited collections of papers on genetic programming include *Advances in Genetic Programming* (Kinnear 1994b), *Advances in Genetic Programming 2* (Angeline and Kinnear 1996). A third book in this series from the MIT Press, *Advances in Genetic Programming 3*, is forthcoming (Spector, Langdon, O'Reilly, and Angeline 1999).

A series of books on genetic programming has been started by Kluwer Academic Publishers. The first book in this series is *Genetic Programming and Data Structures: Genetic Programming + Data Structures = Automatic Programming!* (Langdon 1998).

Recent research in genetic programming is often published in the proceedings of the annual Genetic Programming Conferences (Koza, Goldberg, Fogel, and Riolo 1996; Koza, Deb, Dorigo, Fogel, Garzon, Iba, and Riolo 1997; Koza, Banzhaf, Chellapilla, Deb, Dorigo, Fogel, Garzon, Goldberg, Iba, and Riolo 1998), and the annual European Workshops on Genetic Programming (Banzhaf, Poli, Schoenauer, and Fogarty 1998). In addition, most of the other conferences mentioned at the end of this chapter include some papers on genetic programming. Information about the annual Genetic Programming Conferences can be obtained from the World Wide Web at *www.genetic-programming.org*. Additional information about genetic programming and links to many other sources of information about genetic programming can also be obtained from this Web site.

Between 1989 and September 1998, 1,382 papers are known to have been published on genetic programming. William Langdon of the University of Birmingham has an extensive bibliography on genetic programming at *www.cs.bham.ac.uk/~wbl/*.

Thirty-two Ph.D. degrees have been awarded involving research in genetic programming—Peter Angeline (1993), Vladan Babovic (1996a), Tobias Blickle (1997), Wilker Shane Bruce (1995), K. Govinda Char (1998), Gary Diplock (1996), Anna I. Esparcia-Alcazar (1998), Chris Gathercole (1998), Francis Greene (1997a), Frederic Gruau (1994a), Simon Handley (1998), Christopher Harris (1997), Thomas Haynes (1998), Christian Jacob (1995), M. Jiang (1992), William B. Langdon (1996b), Wei-Po Lee (1997), Frank Moore (1997), Peter Nordin (1997), Una-May O'Reilly (1995), Mouloud Oussaidene (1996), Justinian P. Rosca (1997), Carolyn P. Rose (1997), Gerry P. Roston (1994), Conor Ryan (1996b), Eric Siegel (1998), Terence Soule (1998), Walter Alden Tackett (1994), Astro Teller (1998), Edward Tunstel (1996), Peter Whigham (1996a), and Man Leung Wong (1995).

As of September 1998, 51 additional students are known to be working on Ph.D. theses involving genetic programming. These students (listed on a Web page accessible from *www.genetic-programming.org*) include those whose topic has been approved by their university and who have passed their university's necessary examinations to proceed toward a Ph.D. A workshop at which current Ph.D. and other graduate students present their work to a faculty panel is held as part of the annual Genetic Programming Conference.

Two other techniques, PIPE (Probabilistic Incremental Program Evolution) (Salustowicz and Schmidhuber 1997) and ADATE (Olsson 1994a, 1994b), deal with issues closely related to genetic programming.

Classifier Systems

Genetic classifier systems are a cognitive architecture that applies the genetic algorithm to a set of if-then rules (Holland and Reitman 1978; Holland 1986; Holland, Holyoak, Nisbett, and Thagard 1986; Holland 1987; Holland and Burks 1987, 1989; Goldberg 1983; Forrest 1991; Booker, Goldberg, and Holland 1989; Smith and Valenzuela-Rendon 1994). Books on classifier systems include the following:

- *Robot Shaping: An Experiment in Behavior Engineering* (Dorigo and Colombetti 1997) and
- *Parallelism and Programming in Classifier Systems* (Forrest 1991).

Recent work on classifier systems is most frequently published at conferences such as the International Conference on Genetic Algorithms (ICGA) (Bäck 1997) and the annual Genetic Programming Conferences (Koza, Goldberg, Fogel, and Riolo 1996; Koza, Deb, Dorigo, Fogel, Garzon, Iba, and Riolo 1997; Koza, Banzhaf, Chellapilla, Deb, Dorigo, Fogel, Garzon, Goldberg, Iba, and Riolo 1998). In addition, most of the other conferences mentioned at the end of this chapter include papers on classifier systems.

Evolvable Hardware

Field-programmable gate arrays (FPGAs) are massively parallel computational devices containing thousands of logical function units whose functionality and connectivity can be configured by the user in the field (as opposed to the factory). Once a field-programmable gate array is configured, its thousands of logical function units operate in parallel at the chip's clock rate (see Chapter 57).

The advent of FPGAs that are rapidly reconfigurable and infinitely reprogrammable has led to the idea of evolvable hardware (Higuchi et al. 1993a, 1993b). In this technique, each individual of the evolving population is first embodied into hardware and then executed for a (typically very short) period of time (Hemmi, Hikage, and Shimohara 1994; Hemmi, Mizoguchi, and Shimohara 1994; Higuchi et al. 1996; de Garis 1993, 1996: Korkin, de Garis, Gers, and Hemmi 1997; Thompson 1995, 1996a, 1996b, 1996c, 1997, 1998; Harvey and Thompson 1996; Thompson, Harvey, and Husbands 1996). The conventional genetic algorithm is the technique of evolutionary computation that is currently most frequently used in conjunction with evolvable hardware.

Books on evolvable hardware include *Evolution of Parallel Cellular Machines* (Sipper l997a). Recent work on evolvable hardware is primarily published at the International Conference on Evolvable Systems (Higuchi, Iwata, and Liu 1997). This conference also meets in 1998. An earlier workshop entitled "Toward Evolvable Hardware" was held in Lausanne in 1995 (Sanchez and Tomassini 1996). The edited collection *Bio-Inspired Computing Machines* (Mange and Tomassini 1998) contains a number of papers covering current research on evolvable hardware. The annual Genetic Programming Conferences (Koza, Goldberg, Fogel, and Riolo 1996; Koza, Deb, Dorigo, Fogel, Garzon, Iba, and Riolo 1997; Koza, Banzhaf, Chellapilla, Deb, Dorigo, Fogel, Garzon, Goldberg, Iba, and Riolo 1998) include some papers on evolvable hardware.

Evolutionary Computation in General

There are a number of books that encompass the field of evolutionary computation (evolutionary algorithms) as a whole, including the following:

- *Adaptability* (Conrad 1983),
- *Evolutionary Algorithms in Theory and Practice* (Bäck 1996),
- *Evolutionary Algorithms for VLSI CAD* (Drechsler 1998),
- *Evolutionary Computation: Toward a New Philosophy of Machine Intelligence* (David Fogel 1995),
- *Evolutionary Computation: The Fossil Record* (David Fogel 1998),
- *Evolutionaere Algorithmen. Darstellung, Beispiele* (Nissen 1994),
- *Einfuehrung in Evolutionaere Algorithmen. Optimierung nach dem Vorbild der Evolution* (Nissen 1997), and
- *Convergence Properties of Evolutionary Algorithms* (Rudolph 1997).

Edited volumes on evolutionary computation include Pedrycz (1997), Bentley (1998) and the periodically updated *Handbook of Evolutionary Computation* (Bäck, Fogel, and Michalewicz 1997), containing contributions from over a hundred authors.

Conferences and Journals

Twenty regularly scheduled conferences on evolutionary computation are listed below along with a reference to a recent edition of the proceedings of the conference:

- ACDM—Adaptive Computing in Design and Manufacture (Parmee 1998),
- AE—Artificial Evolution (Alliot et al. 1995),

- EC—Evolutionary Computing (Fogarty 1995; Corne and Shaprio 1997),
- EP—Evolutionary Programming Conference (Angeline, Reynolds, McDonnell, and Eberhart 1997),
- ER—Evolutionary Robotics Symposium (Gomi 1998),
- EUROGEN (Winter, Periaux, Galan, and Cuesta 1996),
- EuroGP—European Workshop on Genetic Programming (Banzhaf, Poli, Schoenauer, and Fogarty 1998),
- EvCA—Evolutionary Computation and Its Applications (Goodman 1996),
- EvoRobot—Evolutionary Robotics (Husbands and Meyer 1998),
- FEA—Frontiers of Evolutionary Algorithms (Wang 1997),
- FOGA—Foundations of Genetic Algorithms (Belew and Vose 1997),
- GALESIA—Genetic Algorithms in Engineering Systems: Innovations and Applications (IEE 1995),
- GP—Genetic Programming Conference (Koza, Goldberg, Fogel, and Riolo 1996; Koza, Deb, Dorigo, Fogel, Garzon, Iba, and Riolo 1997; Koza, Banzhaf, Chellapilla, Deb, Dorigo, Fogel, Garzon, Goldberg, Iba, and Riolo 1998),
- ICANNGA—International Conference on Artificial Neural Networks and Genetic Algorithms (Smith, Steele, and Albrecht 1997),
- ICEC—International Conference on Evolutionary Computation (IEEE 1997),
- ICES—International Conference on Evolvable Systems (Higuchi, Iwata, and Liu 1997; Sipper, Mange, and Perez-Uribe 1998),
- ICGA—International Conference on Genetic Algorithms (Bäck 1997),
- NWGA—Nordic Workshop on Genetic Algorithms and Their Applications (Alander 1997),
- PPSN—Parallel Problem Solving from Nature (Voigt, Ebeling, Rechenberg, and Schwefel 1996), and
- SEAL— Simulated Evolution and Learning (Yao, Kim, and Furuhashi 1997).

In addition, the following conferences in artificial life usually contain numerous papers that employ the techniques of evolutionary computation:

- ALIFE—Artificial Life conferences (Langton and Shimohara 1997),
- BCEC—Bio-Computing and Emergent Computation (Lundh, Olsson, and Narayanan 1997),
- ECAL—European Artificial Life conference (Husbands and Harvey 1997), and
- SAB—Simulation of Adaptive Behavior conference (Maes et al. 1996).

Recent research in evolutionary computation is often published in journals such as the *Evolutionary Computation,* published by MIT Press, and the *IEEE Transactions on Evolutionary Computation* as well as in numerous other journals including, but not limited to, *Artificial Life, BioSystems,* and *Complex Systems.* In addition, the series of books, *Advances in Genetic Programming* (Kinnear 1994b), *Advances in Genetic Programming 2* (Angeline and Kinnear 1996), and *Advances in Genetic Programming 3* (Spector, Langdon, O'Reilly, and Angeline 1999) contain longer papers that are edited in the manner of journal papers. Kluwer Academic Publishers is starting a journal on genetic programming.

Part 3: ARCHITECTURE- ALTERING OPERATIONS

A system for automatically creating computer programs should require that the human user make as few decisions as possible prior to presenting the problem to the system. One of the shortcomings of existing techniques has been the requirement that the human user predetermine the size, shape, and character of the ultimate solution to the problem. The size, shape, and character of the solution should be part of the *answer* produced by the automated system, not part of the *question* posed by the human user.

Earlier work on genetic programming has addressed various aspects of this problem. Genetic programming in its most basic form (such as in Koza 1989, 1992e) automatically determines the size and the sequence of primitive operations (steps) in the to-be-created computer programs. Genetic programming is also capable of automatically creating the size and the sequence of primitive operations in reusable and parameterizable subroutines (automatically defined functions) in the to-be-created computer programs (Koza 1992e, Chapters 20 and 21; Koza 1992f; Koza and Rice 1992a; Koza 1994g). Moreover, genetic programming is also capable of automatically selecting the architecture of the to-be-created program in a competitive and evolutionary process during the run of genetic programming (Koza 1994g, Chapters 21 and 25).

This part of this book describes another way to eliminate the advance specification by the user of the architecture of the to-be-created computer program.

Chapter 3 describes previous methods for determining the architecture of automatically created computer programs.

Chapter 4 discusses the origin of new functionality in nature and relates it to the problem of automatically determining the architecture of computer programs that are evolved by means of genetic programming. The chapter also describes the naturally occurring processes of gene duplication and gene deletion. The chapter also reviews the artificial analogs of gene duplication and gene deletion appearing in previous work in the field of evolutionary computation.

Chapter 5 describes the architecture-altering operations for subroutines. These operations provide an automated way to evolve the architecture of a multipart program during the run. In particular, the architecture-altering operations for subroutines provide an automated way to dynamically create, duplicate, and delete a program's automatically defined functions. These architecture-altering operations determine, during the run, whether or not to employ ADFs, how many ADFs to employ, the number of arguments possessed by each ADF, and the hierarchical references among the ADFs. Viewed from a higher level, the architecture-altering operations provide an automated way to decompose a problem into a nonprespecified number of subproblems of nonprespecified dimensionality, to solve the subproblems, and to assemble the solutions of the subproblems into a solution of the overall problem. Alternatively, they can be viewed as providing an automated way to change the representation of a problem. They can also be interpreted as providing an automated way to specialize and generalize during the problem-solving process.

Chapter 6 describes a restricted form of iteration, called an automatically defined iteration (ADI), that makes a single pass over a preestablished, problem-specific finite sequence, vector, or array. The chapter also describes several architecture-altering operations for ADIs that enable genetic programming to dynamically create, duplicate, and delete automatically defined iterations during the run of genetic programming.

Chapter 7 describes a more general form of iteration, called an automatically defined loop (ADL), and various architecture-altering operations for ADLs that enable genetic programming to dynamically create, duplicate, and delete automatically defined loops during a run.

Chapter 8 describes automatically defined recursions (ADRs) and various architecture-altering operations for ADRs that enable genetic programming to dynamically create, duplicate, and delete automatically defined recursions.

Chapter 9 describes automatically defined stores (ADSs) and various architecture-altering operations for ADSs that enable genetic programming to dynamically create, duplicate, and delete internal storage during the run of genetic programming.

Chapter 10 summarizes how the architecture-altering operations for ADFs, ADIs, ADLs, ADRs, and ADSs enable genetic programming to automatically determine a program's overall architecture and enable the self-organization of hierarchies in the programs evolved by genetic programming. Chapter 11 contains a gedankenexperiment that illustrates the roles of ADFs, ADIs, ADLs, ADRs, and ADSs in solving problems.

Chapter 12 demonstrates the principle that it is possible to evolve a solution to the Boolean parity problem while concurrently evolving the architecture of the solution using the architecture-altering operations for subroutines. The existence of parameterizable subroutines, the number of such subroutines, the size of such subroutines, and the steps contained in such subroutines are all evolved dynamically during the run of genetic programming using the architecture-altering operations. In addition, hierarchical references among the subroutines are dynamically created during the run. This chapter contains a comparative experiment showing that the benefit of the architecture-altering operations can be achieved at a computational cost that is intermediate between that of solving the problem without automatically defined functions and that required using a user-supplied architecture that is known in advance to be a good choice for the problem.

Chapter 13 applies the architecture-altering operations for subroutines to a problem of discovering a time-optimal controller. Chapter 14 applies them to a problem involving multiagent strategies. Chapter 15 applies them to a problem of digit recognition.

Chapter 16 applies the architecture-altering operations for subroutines to evolve a computer program to classify a given protein segment as being a transmembrane domain or nontransmembrane area of the protein. This problem requires the global integration of information. In this chapter, the role of subroutines is open-ended, but the existence of one iteration is preordained.

Chapter 17 revisits the transmembrane segment identification problem of Chapter 16. This chapter demonstrates how automatically defined iteration(s) can be added during the run by the architecture-altering operation of iteration creation. In other words, neither the role of iteration nor the role of subroutines is preordained in this chapter. Instead, their roles are discovered by the evolutionary process. The evolved solutions for the transmembrane segment identification problem in both Chapters 16 and 17 perform slightly better than the algorithms written by knowledgeable human investigators.

Chapter 18 presents a problem involving recursion—creation of a program for the Fibonacci sequence. The automatically defined recursions are created during the run by the architecture-altering operation of recursion creation.

Chapter 19 describes a problem requiring internal storage—the time-optimal cart-centering (isotropic rocket) problem. This problem is solved by adding internal storage during the run using the architecture-altering operations for automatically defined stores.

3

Previous Methods of Determining the Architecture of a Multipart Program

Before applying genetic programming to a problem, the user usually must perform five major preparatory steps (Section 2.3.1).

In addition, when automatically defined functions (Section 2.3.6) are used, the architecture of the to-be-evolved programs must be determined in some way. One approach is for the user to specify the architecture prior to the run of genetic programming. In this approach, the user performs an architecture-defining preparatory step prior to the run of genetic programming. Figure 3.1 shows the addition of this architecture-defining preparatory step to the five major preparatory steps of Figure 2.3.

Sometimes the architectural choices for automatically defined functions are obvious to the user because they flow directly from the nature of the problem. However, in general, there is no way of knowing a priori the optimal (or minimum) number of automatically defined functions that will prove to be useful for solving a given problem. Similarly, there is no way of knowing in advance the optimal (or minimum) number of arguments for each automatically defined function or the optimal (or sufficient) arrangement of hierarchical references among the automatically defined functions.

Five methods have been used previously for making the necessary architectural choices (Koza 1994g). The first four of these methods are manual; the fifth is an automated technique:

1. prospective analysis of the nature of the problem (Section 3.1),
2. retrospective analysis of the results of actual runs of similar problems (Section 3.2),
3. seemingly sufficient capacity (overspecification) (Section 3.3),
4. affordable capacity (Section 3.4), and
5. evolutionary selection of the architecture (Section 3.5).

Chapters 5 through 9 will describe a set of architecture-altering operations that provide a new additional automated method for determining the architectures of evolving programs.

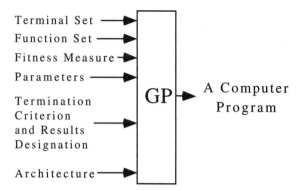

Figure 3.1 Six major preparatory steps for genetic programming with automatically defined functions

3.1 PROSPECTIVE ANALYSIS

One method of making architectural choices for the yet-to-be-evolved programs is for the user to analyze the problem in advance and use human insight to determine that a certain subspace, subsystem, or decomposition is likely to be helpful in solving the problem. This insight may then be used to establish an advantageous (or at least nondeleterious) architecture for the yet-to-be-evolved programs.

When applying genetic programming with automatically defined functions to a problem where the user knows (or suspects) the existence of a relevant subspace, subsystem, or subproblem of a certain dimensionality, the user can specify that number (or a somewhat larger number) of arguments for the function-defining branches. Similarly, if it is known that there are a certain number of subspaces or subsystems, the user can specify that number of function-defining branches.

When the user specifies a maximum number of function-defining branches and a maximum number of arguments for each branch, the user is, of course, not actually solving the problem. The choice of a maximum number of branches and arguments still leaves genetic programming with the substantial task of discovering a sequence of primitive steps that will solve the problem, and with the task of deciding on the number of branches and arguments that it will actually use in solving the problem. Moreover, if hierarchical references are permitted among the branches of the overall problem, genetic programming is still left with the nontrivial additional task of deciding on whether to actually make any hierarchical references.

3.2 RETROSPECTIVE ANALYSIS

If the user is dealing with a series of related problems, a thorough retrospective analysis of one problem may provide guidance for making an advantageous architectural choice for a similar problem.

In this approach, the user makes a statistically significant number of independent runs of genetic programming of the problem with different architectures and retrospectively calculates the computational effort (Section 12.6.1) required to solve the problem with each such architecture. A retrospective analysis of the results of a series of such runs of one problem may suggest an advantageous or optimal architectural choice for a related problem.

3.3 OVERSPECIFICATION

For many problems, the choice of the common architecture for the programs in the population can be made on the basis of providing seemingly sufficient capacity. In this approach, the user overspecifies the number of function-defining branches and the number of arguments possessed by each function-defining branch. Overspecification often works well because genetic programming exhibits considerable ability to ignore extraneous automatically defined functions, to ignore extraneous dummy variables of an automatically defined function, and to ignore unproductive hierarchical references among already-defined automatically defined functions.

3.4 AFFORDABLE CAPACITY

The amount of computer resources that you can afford to devote to a particular problem often influences or dictates the choice of the architecture for the programs in the population. Often the architectural choice is made on the basis of hoping that the resources that you can afford to devote to the problem will prove to be sufficient to solve the problem.

The computer resources consumed by a run of genetic programming include both memory and computer time. Resources are consumed by each automatically defined function and each argument possessed by an automatically defined function. Additional resources are consumed if the automatically defined functions are permitted to invoke each other hierarchically.

Automatically defined iterations, automatically defined loops, and automatically defined recursions typically consume large amounts of computer time. For many problems, the least-fit individuals in the population consume the most resources. Since runs of genetic programming start at generation 0 with a blind random search, large amounts of computer time are often consumed in the early generations of a run.

The total amount of memory available to store the population often influences or dictates the choice of the number of ADFs, ADIs, ADLs, ADRs, and ADSs in an individual program.

3.5 EVOLUTIONARY SELECTION OF ARCHITECTURE

The fifth technique for establishing the architecture of the to-be-evolved program is to evolutionarily select the architecture during the run of genetic programming (Koza 1994g, Chapters 21–25).

The technique of evolutionary selection starts with an architecturally diverse initial random population. After generation 0, there is a competition among the existing architectures during the course of the run. As the evolutionary process proceeds, individuals with certain architectures may prove to be more fit than others in solving the problem.

Individuals with better architectures will tend to prosper, while the individuals with less-fit architectures will tend to wither away. Eventually a program with a particular architecture may emerge that solves the problem at hand. In this technique, no architectures are ever created after the beginning of the run, and no architectures are altered during the run.

Each of the five foregoing methods for determining the architecture of a to-be-evolved program have significant shortcomings. As will be seen shortly, the problem of automating the determination of program architecture can be approached using a process that is similar to the evolutionary process by which new proteins are created in nature.

4

On the Origin of New Functions

Deoxyribonucleic acid (DNA) is a long threadlike biological molecule that has the ability to carry hereditary information. The DNA molecule consists of a backbone that encases a long sequence of four nucleotide bases: adenine (A), guanine (G), cytosine (C), and thymine (T). DNA has the ability to serve as a model for the production of replicas of itself. All known life-forms on this planet (including bacteria, fungi, plants, animals, and humans) are based on the DNA molecule (Stryer 1995; Lewin 1994; Watson et al. 1987).

Proteins determine the structure, function, and behavior of living organisms. Protein molecules are polypeptides that are composed of sequences of between about 50 and several thousand amino acid residues. The sequence of amino acid residues appearing in a protein is specified by the sequence of nucleotide bases appearing in the DNA. Subsequences consisting of three nucleotide bases of DNA (called a *codon*) are translated, using the genetic code, into one of 20 amino acid residues (Creighton 1993).

Proteins are responsible for such a wide variety of biological structures and functions that it can be said that the structure and functions of living organisms are primarily determined by proteins (Stryer 1995). For example, some proteins transport particles such as electrons, atoms, or large macromolecules within living organisms (e.g., hemoglobin transports oxygen in blood). Some proteins store particular particles for later use (e.g., myoglobin stores oxygen in muscles). Some proteins generate nerve impulses (e.g., rhodopsin is the photoreceptor protein in retinal rod cells), while other proteins enable signals to be communicated in the nervous system. Some proteins provide physical structure (e.g., collagen gives skin and bone their high tensile strength). Other proteins create physical contractile motion (e.g., actin and myosin). Proteins are the basis of the immune system (e.g., antibodies recognize and combine in highly specific ways with foreign entities such as bacteria). Hormonal proteins transmit chemical instructions throughout the living organism. Other proteins control the expression of the genetic information contained in the nucleic acids that are responsible for the reproduction of the organism. Growth factor proteins control growth and differentiation.

The human genome consists of about three billion nucleotide bases of DNA. About 100,000 different proteins are expressed (manufactured) from the hereditary information in human DNA.

Since less complex living organisms generally perform fewer different functions, they generally manufacture a smaller number of different proteins. The number of proteins manufactured by humans is about 50 times greater than the number manufactured by various simpler organisms. The entire genomes of 15 freestanding living organisms have already been determined (Rost 1998). These organisms include representatives of the three major kingdoms of life (bacteria, archaea, and eukarya). For example, the genome of the *Haemophilus influenzae* bacterium translates into 1,680 different protein sequences, *Methanococcus jannaschii* has 1,735 sequences, and the yeast *Saccharomyces cerevisiae* has 6,218 sequences (Gerstein 1997).

Since organisms with a greater number of functions and structures apparently evolved (in most cases) from organisms with fewer functions and structures, the question arises as to how these new functions and structures were created.

In nature, sexual recombination (crossover) exchanges genes at particular locations (loci) along the chromosome (a molecule of DNA). The DNA then controls the manufacture of various proteins that determine the structure, function, and behavior of the living organism. The resulting organism then spends its life grappling with its environment. Some organisms in a given population do better than others in the sense that they survive to the age of reproduction, successfully produce offspring, and thereby pass on all or part of their genetic makeup to the next generation of the population. Over a period of many generations, the population as a whole evolves so as to contain an increasing representation of traits (and, more importantly, coadapted combinations of traits) that contribute to survival of the organism to the age of reproduction (and that facilitate large numbers of offspring). Charles Darwin (1859) called this process *natural selection*:

> I think it would be a most extraordinary fact if no variation ever had occurred useful to each being's own welfare . . . . But if variations useful to any organic being do occur, assuredly individuals thus characterised will have the best chance of being preserved in the struggle for life; and from the strong principle of inheritance they will tend to produce offspring similarly characterised. This principle of preservation, I have called, for the sake of brevity, Natural Selection.

Analogous to the process of natural selection is the genetic algorithm (Holland 1975). Before applying the genetic algorithm (Section 2.1) to a problem, the user designs an artificial chromosome of a certain size and then defines a mapping (encoding) between the points in the search space of the problem and the artificial chromosome. For example, in applying the genetic algorithm to a multidimensional optimization problem (such as the one described in Section 2.1, where the goal is to find the global optimum of an unknown multidimensional function), the artificial chromosome is often a linear fixed-length character string (modeled directly after the linear string of information found in DNA). A specific location (a gene) along this artificial chromosome is associated with each of the variables of the problem. A specific gene value that is located at a particular position along the chromosome denotes the value of a particular variable. Each individual in the population has a fitness value (which, for a multidimensional optimization problem, is the value of the unknown function). The genetic algorithm then manipulates a population of such artificial chromosomes using the operations of reproduction, crossover, and mutation.

In both the natural and artificial evolutionary processes, the reproduction operation makes accurate copies of an already established fixed-size chromosome. The genetic operation of mutation randomly alters one or more genes at particular locations along a preestablished fixed-size chromosome in various ways. The genetic operation of crossover inserts genes from a particular group of contiguous locations of one already-existing fixed-size chromosome into corresponding locations of another already-existing fixed-size chromosome. However, none of these operations alters the already-existing architecture of the chromosome.

So how do totally new structures, new functions, new behaviors, and new species arise? In nature, there is not only short-term optimization of genes in their preestablished locations within a preestablished fixed-size chromosome, but long-term emergence of new proteins (which, in turn, create new structures, functions, and behaviors and thereby create new and more complex organisms).

The emergence of new proteins requires a change in the architecture of the chromosome—that is, a change in the structure of the genome. Genome lengths have generally increased with the emergence of new and more complex organisms and the emergence of new proteins (Dyson and Sherratt 1985; Brooks Low 1988).

Returning to genetic algorithms, the analog of a genome change is an alteration, during a run of the genetic algorithm, of the user-created mapping (the encoding and decoding) between points from the search space of the problem and instances of the artificial chromosome. Focusing on genetic programming, the analog of a genome change is an alteration, during a run of genetic programming, of the architecture (Section 2.3.1) of an overall multibranch computer program.

The computer programs involved in genetic programming may be single-branch programs (consisting of merely one main result-producing branch) or multibranch programs (containing one or more result-producing branches, automatically defined functions, automatically defined iterations, automatically defined loops, automatically defined recursions, or automatically defined stores).

When single-branch programs are involved, genetic programming automatically determines, during the run of genetic programming, the sequence of steps in the evolved solution. The sequence of steps, in turn, establishes the size and shape of the program tree.

When multibranch programs are involved, genetic programming automatically determines, during the run of genetic programming, the particular sequence of steps in each of the branches (which, in turn, establishes the size and shape of each of the branches). However, the automatic determination of the steps within each branch does not involve determining the number and type of branches in the program in the first place.

For multibranch programs, the question arises as to how to determine the architecture of the overall program. Is it possible to determine the architecture of a multipart program dynamically during a run of genetic programming (rather than require that the user predetermine that architecture before the run starts)? That is, is it possible to make the architecture of the solution part of the answer provided by genetic programming, rather than part of the question presented to the genetic programming system?

In genetic programming (with a fixed arrangement of automatically defined functions and other types of branches), crossover is analogous to the exchanging of gene values (alleles) in a preexisting chromosome. Subtrees (containing a composition of the primitive functions and terminals of the problem) are exchanged by the crossover operation within a preexisting architectural arrangement.

Since the analog of a genome change in nature is a dynamic alteration, during a run of genetic programming, of the architecture of an overall multibranch computer program, we might ask, So how does the genome change in nature?

In nature, part of the chromosome of one parent is recombined with a corresponding (homologous) part of a corresponding chromosome from the second parent. However, in certain very rare and unpredictable instances, this recombination does not occur in the usual way. A *gene duplication* is an illegitimate recombination event that results in the duplication of a lengthy subsequence of a chromosome. A gene duplication lengthens the chromosome and constitutes a genome change.

Susumu Ohno's seminal book *Evolution by Gene Duplication* (1970) proposed the provocative thesis that the creation of new proteins (and hence new structures and behaviors in living things) begins with a gene duplication and that gene duplication is "the major force of evolution."

Chapters 5 through 9 describe architecture-altering genetic operations for genetic programming that are suggested by the naturally occurring mechanism of gene duplication (and the complementary mechanism of gene deletion). These architecture-altering operations enable genetic programming to evolve the architecture of a multipart program during a run of genetic programming.

4.1 GENE DUPLICATION AND DELETION IN NATURE

Biological populations display the ability to adapt, survive, and reproduce in their natural environments and to rapidly and robustly adapt in response to changes in the environment. Nature's methods for adapting biological populations to their environments and nature's methods of adapting these populations to successive changes in their environments provide a potentially useful model for creating automated problem-solving techniques for problems that are generally thought to require "intelligence" to solve (Lawrence Fogel, Owens, and Walsh 1966).

The naturally occurring genetic operations of mutation and crossover (sexual recombination) provide one way to alter the linear string of nucleotide bases. Mutation, for example, alters the chromosomal string by changing one nucleotide base of the string. When the changed DNA is then translated into proteins in the living cell, the mutation may lead either to the manufacture of a variant of the original protein or, as is often the case, to no viable protein being manufactured from the altered portion of the DNA. The variant of the protein (or absence of the original protein) may then affect the structure and behavior of the living thing in some advantageous or disadvantageous way. If the change is advantageous, natural selection will tend to perpetuate the change. In the more common situation where the random mutant is disadvantageous, natural selection will tend to eliminate the mutant.

When crossover is performed, the linear string of nucleotide bases of an offspring is created by recombining portions of the DNA from two individuals.

In addition to frequent changes introduced by mutation and crossover, chromosomes are occasionally also modified by other naturally occurring genetic operations, such as gene duplication and gene deletion. Gene duplications are rare and unpredictable events in the evolution of genomic sequences. In gene duplication, there is a duplication of a portion of the linear string of nucleotide bases of the DNA in the living cell. When a gene duplication occurs, there is no immediate change in the proteins that are manufactured by the living cell. The immediate effect of a gene duplication is merely to create two identical ways of manufacturing the same protein.

Then, over a period of time, other genetic operations (e.g., mutation or crossover) may change one of the two identical genes. Assuming the new gene is not actively deleterious, the changed gene is simply carried along from generation to generation. Thus, over short periods of time, the changes accumulating in a gene usually have no discernible effect. As long as one of the genes remains unchanged, the original protein manufactured from the unchanged gene continues to be manufactured, and the structure and behavior of the organism involved will probably continue as before.

Natural selection exerts considerable force in favor of maintaining a gene that encodes for the manufacture of a protein that is important for the successful performance and survival of the organism in its environment. But, after a gene duplication occurs, there is usually no disadvantage associated with the loss of the *second* way of manufacturing the original protein. Consequently, natural selection usually exerts little or no pressure to maintain a second way of manufacturing the same protein. Over a period of time, the second gene may accumulate additional changes and diverge more and more from the original gene. Eventually the changed gene may lead to the manufacture of a distinctly new and different protein that actually does affect the structure and behavior of the living thing in some advantageous or disadvantageous way. When a changed gene leads to the manufacture of a viable and advantageous new protein, natural selection again starts to work to preserve that new gene.

Ohno (1970) corrects the mistaken notion that natural selection is a mechanism for promoting change. Ohno emphasizes the essentially conservative role of natural selection in the evolutionary process:

> . . . the true character of natural selection . . . is not so much an advocator or mediator of heritable changes, but rather it is an extremely efficient policeman which conserves the vital base sequence of each gene contained in the genome. As long as one vital function is assigned to a single gene locus within the genome, natural selection effectively forbids the perpetuation of mutation affecting the *active* sites of a molecule. [Emphasis in original.]

Ohno further points out that simple point mutation and crossover are insufficient to explain major evolutionary changes:

> . . . while allelic changes at already existing gene loci suffice for racial differentiation within species as well as for adaptive radiation from an immediate ancestor, they cannot account for large changes in evolution, because large changes are made possible by the acquisition of new gene loci with previously non-existent functions.

Ohno continues:

> Only by the accumulation of *forbidden* mutations at the *active* sites can the gene locus change its basic character and become a new gene locus. An escape from the ruthless pressure of natural selection is provided by the mechanism of gene duplication. By duplication, a redundant copy of a locus is created. Natural selection often ignores such a redundant copy, and, while being ignored, it accumulates formerly forbidden mutations and is reborn as a new gene locus with a hitherto non-existent function. [Emphasis in original.]

Ohno concludes:

> Thus, gene duplication emerges as the major force of evolution.

Ohno's provocative thesis is supported by the discovery of pairs of proteins with similar sequences of DNA and similar sequences of amino acids, but different functions (Nei 1987; Maeda and Smithies 1986; Dyson and Sherratt 1985; Brooks Low 1988; Patthy 1991; Go 1991; Hood and Hunkapiller 1991). Examples include

- myoglobin and the single subunits of monomeric hemoglobin of lamprey and hagfish,

- myoglobin (used for storing oxygen in muscle cells of vertebrates) and the four subunits of hemoglobin (used for transporting oxygen in red blood cells),
- trypsin and chymotrypsin,
- the protein of microtubules and actin of the skeletal muscle, and
- the light and heavy immunoglobin chains.

For the *Escherichia coli* bacterium, a relatively simple organism, it is known that more than 30% of its proteins are the result of gene duplications (Lazcano and Miller 1994; Riley 1993). These proteins include its DNA polymerases, dehydrogenases, ferredoxins, glutamine synthetases, carbamoyl-phosphate synthetases, F-type ATPases, and DNA topoisomerases.

The midge, *Chironomus tentans,* provides an additional example of gene duplication (Galli and Wislander 1993, 1994). In particular, consider the contiguous sequence of 3,959 nucleotide bases from this midge that is archived under accession number X70063 in the European Molecular Biology Laboratory (EMBL) database and the Gen Bank database. The 732 nucleotide bases located at positions 918–1,649 of the 3,959 bases of the DNA sequence involved become expressed as a protein containing 244 (i.e., one-third of 732) amino acid residues. The 759 nucleotide bases at positions 2,513–3,271 become expressed as a protein containing 253 residues. The 732-base subsequence is called the *C. tentans* Sp38–40.A gene and the 759-base subsequence is called the *C. tentans* Sp38–40.B gene. The bases of DNA before position 918, the bases between positions 1,650 and 2,512, and the bases after position 3,271 of this sequence of length 3,959 do not become expressed as any protein.

Both the "A" and the "B" proteins are secreted from the midge's salivary gland to form two similar, but different, kinds of water-insoluble fibers. The two kinds of fibers are, in turn, spun into one of two similar, but different, kinds of tubes. One tube is for larval protection and feeding, while the other tube is for pupation (the stage in the development of an insect in which it lies in repose and from which it eventually emerges in the winged form).

Figure 4.1 shows the bases of DNA in positions 900 through 3,399 of the 3,959 nucleotide bases of X70063. In the DNA sequence, A represents the nucleotide base adenine, C represents cytosine, G represents guanine, and T represents thymine. Each group of three consecutive bases (a codon) of DNA becomes expressed as one of the 20 amino acid residues of the protein. For example, the letters A, T, and G appearing at positions 918, 919, and 920, respectively, in this reading frame, of the DNA sequence are translated into the amino acid residue methionine (denoted by the single letter M using the 20-letter coding for amino acid residues in proteins). Thus, methionine is the first amino acid residue (i.e., N-terminal) of the "A" protein. Positions 921, 922, and 923 contain the bases A, G, and A, respectively, and these three bases, in this reading frame, are translated into arginine (an amino acid residue denoted by the letter R). Thus, arginine is the second amino acid residue of the "A" protein, and the protein sequence begins with the residues M and R. The DNA up to position 1,649 encodes the first protein. Positions 1,647, 1648, and 1,649 code for the amino acid residue lysine (denoted by the letter K). Thus, lysine is the last (244th) residue (i.e., C-terminal) of the "A" protein.

Figure 4.2 shows the 244 amino acid residues of the *C. tentans* Sp38–40.A protein. Figure 4.3 shows the 253 amino acid residues of the *C. tentans* Sp38–40.B protein. The two proteins are similar, but not identical. For example, the first 14 amino acid residues of Figures 4.2 and 4.3 are identical. Residue 15 of the "A" protein is phenylalanine (F), while the residue 15 of the "B" protein is leucine (L), a chemically similar amino acid. Residues 16–50 are identical. Residue 51 of the "A" protein is glutamic acid (E), while residue 51 of the "B" protein is aspartic acid (D). D and E are similar in that both are electrically negative at normal pH values. However, for some positions, such as 76, the amino acid residues (threonine T and alanine A) are not chemically similar.

Notice that the last few residues of each protein are identical. Since the proteins are of different lengths, identification of the similarity between the two protein sequences requires aligning the two proteins in some way. Protein alignment algorithms, such as the Smith-Waterman algorithm (Smith and Waterman 1981), provide a way to align two proteins and to measure the degree of similarity or dissimilarity between them. The Smith-Waterman algorithm is a progressive alignment method employing dynamic programming. Since the proteins being aligned are typically of different lengths, gaps may be introduced (and then progressively lengthened) in an attempt to best align the residues making up the proteins. A penalty is assessed to open a gap (5 here) and another penalty is assessed to lengthen a gap (25 here). An additional penalty is assessed when one residue disagrees with another. This penalty is smaller for substitutions involving evolutionarily close amino acid residues. The PAM-250 ("percentage of accepted point mutations") matrix is used to reflect the likelihood of one amino acid residue being mutated into another. The overall algorithm performs a trade-off employing dynamic programming between the penalties assessed by the PAM-250 matrix, the gap-opening penalty, and the gap-lengthening penalty. The Smith-Waterman algorithm has been implemented in GeneWorks, a software package available from Intelligenetics Inc. of Mountain View, California. A total cost of zero is associated with a perfect alignment.

Figure 4.4 shows the alignment of the *C. tentans* Sp38–40.A protein and the *C. tentans* Sp38–40.B protein. Identical residues are boxed. The alignment shows that there is 81% identity between the two protein sequences. As can be seen, the first disagreement between the two aligned sequences occurs at position 15 and the second occurs at residue 51. The first gap is introduced at residue 112, where the "A" protein has an alanine (A) residue. A gap of length 3 is introduced at positions 147, 148, and 149, where the "A" protein has three proline (P) residues. Note that this alignment recognizes the identity between the last five residues of the two proteins. This alignment has a total cost of 265.

Galli and Wislander (1993) point out that these two similar proteins arise as a consequence of a gene duplication. Immediately after the gene duplication occurred at some time in the distant past, there were two identical copies of the duplicated sequence of DNA. Over a period of millions of years since the initial gene duplication, additional mutations accumulated so that the two proteins are now only 81% identical (after alignment). More importantly, the two proteins now perform different (but similar) functions in the midge.

More complex organisms have a general tendency to perform more distinct functions and have more expressed proteins and longer genomes (Dyson and Sherratt 1985). The rise of new functions as a consequence of gene duplication is consistent with the longer genomes generally associated with more complex organisms.

Gene deletion also occurs in nature. In gene deletion, there is a deletion of a portion of the linear string of nucleotide bases that would otherwise be translated and manu-

TGAAGTAATA	TTAAGCTATG	AGAATTAAGT	TCCTAGTAGT	ATTAGCAGTT	950
	M	R I K F	L V V	L A V	
ATCTGCTTGT	TTGCACATTA	TGCCTCAGCT	AGTGGTATGG	GGGGTGATAA	1000
I C L F	A H Y	A S A	S G M G	G D K	
AAAACCCAAA	GATGCCCCAA	AACCCAAAGA	TGCCCCAAAA	CCCAAGAAG	1050
K P K	D A P K	P K D	A P K	P K E V	
TGAAGCCTGT	CAAAGCTGAG	TCATCAGAGT	ATGAGATAGA	AGTCATTAAA	1100
K P V	K A E	S S E Y	E I E	V I K	
CACCAGAAAG	AAAAGACCGA	GAAGAAGGAG	AAGGAGAAGA	AGACTCACGT	1150
H Q K E	K T E	K K E	K E K K	T H V	
TGAAACCAAG	AAAGAAGTTA	AAAAGAAGGA	GAAGAAGCAA	ATCCCTTGTT	1200
E T K	K E V K	K K E	K K Q	I P C S	
CTGAAAAACT	CAAGGATGAA	AAACTTGATT	GTGAGACCAA	GGGCGTCCCT	1250
E K L	K D E	K L D C	E T K	G V P	
GCAGGCTACA	AAGCAATCTT	CAAATTCACA	GAAAACGAGG	AGTGCGATTG	1300
A G Y K	A I F	K F T	E N E E	C D W	
GACGTGCGAT	TATGAAGCAC	TTCCACCACC	TCCAGGAGCA	AAGAAAGACG	1350
T C D	Y E A L	P P P	P G A	K K D D	
ACAAGAAAGA	AAAGAAGACA	GTTAAAGTCG	TTAAGCCACC	AAAGGAGAAA	1400
K K E	K K T	V K V V	K P P	K E K	
CCACCAAAGA	AGCTTAGAAA	GGAATGCTCT	GGCGAAAAAG	TGATCAAATT	1450
P P K K	L R K	E C S	G E K V	I K F	
CCAAAACTGT	CTCGTTAAGA	TTAGAGGACT	TATTGCCTTT	GGTGATAAGA	1500
Q N C	L V K I	R G L	I A F	G D K T	
CAAAGAACTT	TGATAAGAAG	TTCGCAAAGC	TTGTCCAAGG	AAAGCAGAAG	1550
K N F	D K K	F A K L	V Q G	K Q K	
AAGGGCGCAA	AAAAAGCTAA	AGGCGGTAAG	AAGGCAGCAC	CAAAACCAGG	1600
K G A K	K A K	G G K	K A A P	K P G	
ACCAAAACCA	GGGCCAAAAC	AAGCTGATAA	ACCAAAAGAT	GCAAAAAAAT	1650
P K P	G P K Q	A D K	P K D	A K K	
AAACTGACAT	AGTAAGAATA	ATAAAATAAA	CATTATTTGA	GCAACATCAC	1700
AACACAAGAA	AAAAATCATA	TCAACATAAT	TAAGACCTAA	AAATTCTCGC	1750
TATTCACTTT	TTTTCAAATG	AATATCCAAA	ACAACATCAT	TAAGGGATCT	1800
TACACAATTT	TATCCCAAAT	TAGTTTTAAG	TCTATTTTTT	AGTTTTAAGT	1850
AAAACATTAG	TTAGAGAAAT	TTCAAATGCG	AAAAAAAGAC	AAAATCAAAA	1900
TTAACTCCAA	CTAATTGTCT	AGATCTAATC	ACCACTGAAA	AACAATATTT	1950
TTTTCAATAA	TATCTGAGAT	GAAAATTTTG	TAAGATACGA	TTCAAAAAAA	2000
AAAAAACAAA	AACTTAAATA	TTTTCTTTAT	AAGAAAGTAA	AAAACTTACA	2050
TGAACAACAA	GTAGACTAAG	GGCTTAAAAA	TACTAAGGAA	TTTAAAGAAA	2100
CTGAACCAAT	AACATCCAAT	AAATATAAGC	GTGTATTTAA	CATCCATTCA	2150
TGCAAAATTT	GACTTGTTTT	ATTCTAAACT	TTTGAATTGT	GAATATTTTT	2200
GATGATTATT	GAATATTTTA	CAGCATTTTT	CGACAAAATC	CAAGGAAACT	2250
GTTTTGTTTA	ATATATACTA	CAGCTCAGTA	TCTATGCACA	CGAAAAACTG	2300

Figure 4.1 Portion of a DNA sequence containing the two expressed proteins

TAACAGACCA	GACCATAAAA	CCTACACATC	ACCAAGATAC	GTATTTTAAA	2350
TTCATGTGAC	TGACAAAAGC	TGGAAACACT	TGTGTCACGT	CATGAAAACC	2400
TCGTTGAAAT	AAAACTTCTA	GAAAGGTTAT	CATGAAAGAG	TATAAAAGAG	2450
ATCTCAAACG	AGGCTCAGTC	AGTTCAGTTT	AGCTTGGACT	TCATATGAAG	2500
TAATATTTAG	CTATGAGAAT	TAAGTTCCTA	GTAGTATTAG	CAGTTATCTG	2550

	M R I	K F L	V V L A	V I C	
CTTGCTTGCA	CATTATGCCT	CAGCTAGTGG	TATGGGGGGT	GATAAAAAC	2600
L L A	H Y A S	A S G	M G G	D K K P	
CCAAAGATGC	CCCAAAACCC	AAAGATGCCC	CAAAACCCAA	AGAAGTGAAG	2650
K D A	P K P	K D A P	K P K	E V K	
CCTGTCAAAG	CTGACTCATC	AGAGTATGAG	ATAGAAGTCA	TTAAACACCA	2700
P V K A	D S S	E Y E	I E V I	K H Q	
GAAAGAAAAG	ACCGAGAAGA	AGGAGAAGGA	GAAGAAGCT	CACGTCGAAA	2750
K E K	T E K K	E K E	K K A	H V E I	
TCAAGAAAAA	GATTAAAAAT	AAGGAGAAGA	AGTTTGTCCC	ATGTTCTGAA	2800
K K K	I K N	K E K K	F V P	C S E	
ATTCTCAAGG	ATGAAAAACT	TGAATGTGAG	AAAAATGCTA	CTCCAGGCTA	2850
I L K D	E K L	E C E	K N A T	P G Y	
TAAAGCACTC	TTCGAATTCA	AAGAAAGCGA	AAGTTTTTGC	GAATGGGAGT	2900
K A L	F E F K	E S E	S F C	E W E C	
GCGATTATGA	AGCAATTCCA	GGAGCAAAGA	AAGACGAAAA	AAAGGAGAAG	2950
D Y E	A I P	G A K K	D E K	K E K	
AAGGTAGTTA	AAGTCATTAA	GCCACCAAAG	GAAAAACCAC	CAAAGAAGCC	3000
K V V K	V I K	P P K	E K P P	K K P	
TAGAAAGGAA	TGCTCTGGCG	AAAAAGTGAT	CAAATTCCAA	AACTGTCTCG	3050
R K E	C S G E	K V I	K F Q	N C L V	
TTAAGATTAG	AGGACTTATT	GCCTTTGGTG	ATAAGACAAA	GAACTTTGAT	3100
K I R	G L I	A F G D	K T K	N F D	
AAGAAGTTTG	CAAAGCTTGT	CCAAGGAAAG	CAAAAGAAGG	GCGCAAAAAA	3150
K K F A	K L V	Q G K	Q K K G	A K K	
AGCTAAAGGC	GGTAAGAAGG	CAGAACCAAA	ACCAGGACCA	AAACCAGCAC	3200
A K G	G K K A	E P K	P G P	K P A P	
CAAAACCAGG	ACCAAAACCA	GCACCAAAAC	CAGTACCAAA	ACCAGCTGAT	3250
K P G	P K P	A P K P	V P K	P A D	
AAACCAAAAG	ATGCAAAAAA	ATAAACTGAC	ATAGTGAGAA	TAATAAAATA	3300
K P K D	A K K				

Figure 4.1   (continued)

factured into proteins in the living cell. After a gene deletion occurs, some particular protein that may formerly have been manufactured will no longer be manufactured. Consequently, there may be a change in the structure or behavior of the living thing in some advantageous or disadvantageous way. If the deletion is advantageous, natural selection will tend to perpetuate the change, but if the deletion is disadvantageous, natural selection will tend to lead to the extinction of the change.

```
MRIKFLVVLA   VICLFAHYAS   ASGMGGDKKP   KDAPKPKDAP   KPKEVKPVKA    50
ESSEYEIEVI   KHQKEKTEKK   EKEKKTHVET   KKEVKKKEKK   QIPCSEKLKD   100
EKLDCETKGV   PAGYKAIFKF   TENEECDWTC   DYEALPPPPG   AKKDDKKEKK   150
TVKVVKPPKE   KPPKKLRKEC   SGEKVIKFQN   CLVKIRGLIA   FGDKTKNFDK   200
KFAKLVQGKQ   KKGAKKAKGG   KKAAPKPGPK   PGPKQADKPK   DAKK         244
```

Figure 4.2 Protein sequence of "A" protein

```
MRIKFLVVLA   VICLLAHYAS   ASGMGGDKKP   KDAPKPKDAP   KPKEVKPVKA    50
DSSEYEIEVI   KHQKEKTEKK   EKEKKAHVEI   KKKIKNKEKK   FVPCSEILKD   100
EKLECEKNAT   PGYKALFEFK   ESESFCEWEC   DYEAIPGAKK   DEKKEKKVVK   150
VIKPPKEKPP   KKPRKECSGE   KVIKFQNCLV   KIRGLIAFGD   KTKNFDKKFA   200
KLVQGKQKKG   AKKAKGGKKA   EPKPGPKPAP   KPGPKPAPKP   VPKPADKPKD   250
AKK                                                            253
```

Figure 4.3 Protein sequence of "B" protein

```
First.protein    MRIKFLVVLA VICLFAHYAS ASGMGGDKKP KDAPKPKDAP KPKEVKPVKA
Second.protein   MRIKFLVVLA VICLLAHYAS ASGMGGDKKP KDAPKPKDAP KPKEVKPVKA

First.protein    ESSEYEIEVI KHQKEKTEKK EKEKKTHVET KKEVKKKEKK QIPCSEKLKD
Second.protein   DSSEYEIEVI KHQKEKTEKK EKEKKAHVEI KKKIKNKEKK FVPCSEILKD

First.protein    EKLDCETKGV PAGYKAIFKF TENEE-CDWT CDYEALPPPP GAKKDDKKEK
Second.protein   EKLECEKNAT P-GYKALFEF KESESFCEWE CDYEAI---P GAKKDEKKEK

First.protein    KTVKVVKPPK EKPPKKLRKE CSGEKVIKFQ NCLVKIRGLI AFGDKTKNFD
Second.protein   KVVKVIKPPK EKPPKKPRKE CSGEKVIKFQ NCLVKIRGLI AFGDKTKNFD

First.protein    KKFAKLVQGK QKKGAKKAKG GKKAAPKPGP KPGPK----Q ADKP------
Second.protein   KKFAKLVQGK QKKGAKKAKG GKKAEPKPGP KPAPKPGPKP APKPVPKPAD

First.protein    --KDAKK
Second.protein   KPKDAKK
```

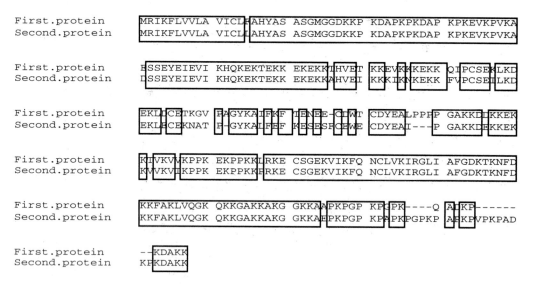

Figure 4.4 Protein alignment of the "A" and "B" proteins

4.2 PREVIOUS WORK

Analogs of the naturally occurring operation of gene duplication have been previously used in connection with genetic algorithms and other forms of evolutionary computation.

A form of gene duplication and gene deletion was used as early as the late 1960s for the design of a convergent-divergent two-phase nozzle (Schwefel 1968; Klockgether and

Schwefel 1970). This work used a variable-length chromosome consisting of a string of integers representing the diameter of the nozzle at equidistant points along the length of the to-be-designed nozzle. The nozzle's entry and throat diameters were fixed. The nozzle's overall length was variable and was determined by the total number of integers in the chromosome. If a chromosome had k integers, the nozzle consisted of $k - 1$ conical sections such that the diameter of the bottom of the jth conical section was specified by the integer j of the chromosome and the diameter of the top of the jth conical section was specified by integer $j + 1$ of the chromosome. The first part of the chromosome contained integers representing the convergent part of the nozzle, and the second part of the chromosome contained integers representing the nozzle's divergent part. A zero-mean small-variance mutation operator was used to randomly perturb the values of integers in the chromosome. As explained by Hans-Paul Schwefel (1998) to the authors, gene duplication and gene deletion were part of this early work on evolution strategies. Gene duplication and gene deletion operated on randomly chosen subsequences of consecutive integers along the chromosome. In gene duplication, a randomly chosen subsequence of one or more integers was duplicated (thereby lengthening the nozzle). In the case of gene deletion, a randomly chosen subsequence of one or more integers was deleted (thereby shortening the nozzle). Thus, the nozzle's overall length as well as its diameter at each point was determined during the evolutionary process. Mutation was the only genetic operator used.

Cavicchio (1970) used intrachromosomal gene duplication in early work on pattern recognition with the genetic algorithm (Goldberg 1989a).

Holland (1975, page 116) suggested that intrachromosomal gene duplication might provide a means of adaptively modifying the effective mutation rate by making two or more copies of a substring of adjacent gene values (alleles). If there are k copies of an allele, the probability of a mutation of any one particular allele would be k times greater than if there were only one occurrence of the allele.

Gene duplication is implicitly used in the messy genetic algorithm (Goldberg, Korb, and Deb 1989).

Lindgren (1991) analyzed the prisoner's dilemma game using an evolutionary algorithm that employed an operation that is analogous to naturally occurring gene duplication. The prisoner's dilemma is a problem in game theory with numerous psychological, sociological, and geopolitical interpretations. In this nonzero-sum game, two players can either cooperate or not cooperate. The players make their moves simultaneously and without communication. Each player then receives a payoff that depends on his move and the simultaneous move of the other player. The payoffs in the prisoner's dilemma game are arranged so that a noncooperative choice by one player always yields a greater payoff to that player than a cooperative choice (regardless of what the other player does). But, if both players are selfishly noncooperative, they are both worse off than if both cooperated.

For a single encounter, the best strategy for each player is to be noncooperative even though both are worse off than if they cooperated. However, the situation becomes considerably more interesting and complex if the two players engage in this game over a series of plays. In this so-called iterated version of the prisoner's dilemma, it becomes advantageous for cooperation to evolve (Axelrod 1984, 1987).

In Lindgren's work, strategies for playing the game over a series of plays are expressed as fixed-length binary character strings of length 2, 4, 8, 16, or 32. Strings of length 2 represent game-playing strategies that take account of only the one previous action by the opponent. For example, the string 01 instructs the player to make a noncooperative move (indicated by the 0 in the first position of the string) if the opponent made a non-cooperative move on his previous move and to make a cooperative move (indicated by 1) if the opponent just made a cooperative move. This particular strategy is called "tit-for-tat" since the player mimics his opponent's previous move. The string 10 is called "anti-tit-for-tat" because it instructs the player to do the opposite of what the opponent did on the previous move. String 11 is "Mr. Nice Guy," and 00 is "Darth Vader."

The 16 strategies represented by strings of length 4 take account of the player's own previous action as well as the opponent's previous action. Strings of length 8 look back even farther and take account of the opponent's action two moves ago in addition to both players' actions one move ago. Similarly, strings of length 16 and 32 take account of additional previous moves of the opponent and/or the player.

Lindgren used an evolutionary algorithm to evolve a population of game-playing strategies with varying degrees of look-back. Lindgren started with a population of 1,000 consisting of 250 copies of each of the four possible strings of length 2. The fitness of a string is measured according to the average score achieved by the strategy when that strategy is played interactively against all other strategies in the population. At each generational step of the process, a string is copied (reproduced) in proportion to its fitness.

The strings in the population are occasionally modified by Lindgren's evolutionary algorithm using three operations:

1. A mutation operation randomly alters a single bit in a single string.
2. A gene duplication operation doubles a given character string. For example, the gene duplication operation transforms the string 01 into 0101. This operation has no immediate effect on the play. The lengthened string takes the previous move of the player himself into account; however, because the 01 is repeated, it causes the very same action to be taken—regardless of the previous move. That is, the semantics of the strategy is preserved even though the structure of the genome is changed by lengthening.
3. A gene deletion operation (which Lindgren calls "split mutation") cuts the length of a string in half by randomly deleting either the first or second half of the string. For example, when this operation is applied to the string 1100, the result is (with equal probability) either the string 11 or 00. Unlike the operation of gene duplication, this operation does not preserve the semantics of the strategy.

Lindgren's evolutionary algorithm did not contain the crossover (recombination) operation.

Over a period of many generations, Lindgren (1991) found that the dynamics of this population of game-playing strategies exhibited many interesting evolutionary phenomena. Strategies with varying degrees of look-back spontaneously emerged in the population, became prominent in the population, and, in some cases, became extinct. As the evolutionary process progressed, phenomena such as mass extinctions and punctuated equilibria were observed.

Architecture-Altering Operations for Subroutines

This chapter describes six architecture-altering operations that create, duplicate, or delete a subroutine (automatically defined function, function-defining branch) or that create, duplicate, or delete dummy variables (formal parameters) possessed by a subroutine.

The architecture-altering operations are performed during the main generational loop of a run of genetic programming in tandem with the ordinary genetic operations of reproduction, crossover, and mutation (as shown in the flowchart of Figure 2.4). During each generation of the run of genetic programming, a certain (usually small) percentage of the individuals in the population are selected to participate in an architecture-altering operation. The participating individuals are selected by the usual Darwinian process that probabilistically selects individuals based on fitness. The architecture-altering operations each operate on one individual. The architecture-altering operations differ from the ordinary genetic operations of reproduction, crossover, and mutation in that they modify the architectural structure of the participating individual. The architecture-altering operations create architectural diversity in the population. As the run proceeds from generation to generation, a competition ensues among individuals with various architectures. The evolutionary process will tend to select against an individual in the population with an architecture that is not well suited for solving the problem at hand. Individuals with unsuitable architectures will tend to be driven to extinction. Meanwhile, individuals with architectures that facilitate solving the given problem will tend to be fruitful and multiply.

The six architecture-altering operations that operate on automatically defined functions are the following:

1. *Subroutine duplication* creates one new offspring program for the new population by duplicating a preexisting function-defining branch of one program.
2. *Argument duplication* creates one new offspring program for the new population by duplicating a preexisting argument of one function-defining branch of one program.
3. *Subroutine creation* creates one new offspring program for the new population by adding one new function-defining branch containing a portion of a preexisting branch and by creating a reference to the new branch.

4. *Argument creation* creates one new offspring program for the population by adding one new argument to the argument list of a preexisting function-defining branch and by appropriately modifying references to the branch.

5. *Subroutine deletion* creates one new offspring program for the new population by deleting a preexisting function-defining branch of one program.

6. *Argument deletion* creates one new offspring program for the new population by deleting a preexisting argument of one function-defining branch of one program.

5.1   SUBROUTINE DUPLICATION

The architecture-altering operation of subroutine duplication duplicates one of a program's function-defining branches (automatically defined functions). Subroutine duplication operates on one individual selected from the population probabilistically on the basis of fitness. The offspring program contains a new branch that consists of a duplicate of one of its parent's preexisting branches. Thus, a program with k branches begets an offspring program with $k + 1$ branches. The operation creates an appropriate name for the new function-defining branch and an argument list for the new branch. The operation also provides a way to create an invoking reference to the new branch.

The architecture-altering operation of subroutine duplication operates in the following way:

1. Select an individual program from the population to participate in this architecture-altering operation.

2. Pick one of the function-defining branches of the selected program as the branch-to-be-duplicated. If the selected program has only one function-defining branch, that branch is automatically picked. If the selected program has no function-defining branches (or already has the maximum number of function-defining branches established for the problem), this operation is aborted.

3. Add a uniquely named new function-defining branch to the selected program, thus increasing, by one, the number of function-defining branches in the selected program. The new function-defining branch has the same argument list and the same body as the branch-to-be-duplicated.

4. For each occurrence of an invocation of the branch-to-be-duplicated anywhere in the selected program, randomly choose (with equal probability) either to leave that invocation unchanged or to replace that invocation with an invocation of the newly created branch. If the choice is to make the replacement, the arguments in the invocation of the newly created branch are identical to the arguments of the preexisting invocation.

5. The terminal set of the newly created branch is identical to that of the branch-to-be-duplicated. Likewise, the function set of the newly created branch is identical to that of the branch-to-be-duplicated. The name of the newly created branch is added to the function set of any branch whose function set includes the branch-to-be-duplicated (i.e., any branch that actually calls the branch-to-be-duplicated or that is permitted to call the branch-to-be-duplicated). The arity of the newly created branch (equal to that of the branch-to-be-duplicated) is inserted into the list containing the number of arguments possessed by each function for any

branch whose function set includes the branch-to-be-duplicated. If hierarchical references are permitted between the newly created branch and the branch-to-be-duplicated, the function set of the newly created branch is enlarged to include the name of the branch-to-be-duplicated. Note that the function set of the branch-to-be-duplicated is not so enlarged in order to avoid unintended recursions. The terminal set of any branch whose function set includes the branch-to-be-duplicated (i.e., any branch that actually calls the branch-to-be-duplicated or that is permitted to call the branch-to-be-duplicated) is not affected by this operation.

The step of selecting a program is performed probabilistically on the basis of fitness for subroutine duplication (and all the other architecture-altering operations subsequently described in this book), so that a program that is more fit has a greater probability of being selected to participate in the operation than a less-fit program. A copy is first made of the selected program, and the operation is then performed on the copy. Thus, the unchanged original program remains in the population and is therefore available to be reselected if its fitness so warrants.

Suppose that the program in Figure 2.11 has been selected, in step 1, as the program to participate in the operation of subroutine duplication. Since this program happens to have only one function-defining branch (defining two-argument automatically defined function ADF0), its sole function-defining branch is necessarily picked, in step 2, as the branch-to-be-duplicated.

In step 3, a new function-defining branch is added to the selected program, thus increasing the number of function-defining branches in the selected program. The new branch is given the new name of ADF1. This new name is unique within this program.

Figure 5.1 shows the program resulting after applying the operation of subroutine duplication to the program in Figure 2.11. The program in Figure 2.11 possesses one two-argument automatically defined function (ADF0) and has an argument map of {2}. The program in Figure 5.1 has two automatically defined functions—ADF0 and the newly created one (ADF1). It has an argument map of {2, 2} because the operation of subroutine duplication duplicated the original two-argument function-defining branch.

The function-defining branch starting at the DEFUN labeled 410 of Figure 2.11 defining ADF0 (also shown as 510 of Figure 5.1) is duplicated. The duplicated branch is added at DEFUN 540 of Figure 5.1, thereby giving the new overall program three branches: a first function-defining branch starting at DEFUN 510, a new second function-defining branch starting at DEFUN 540, and a result-producing branch starting at VAL-UES 570. The new function-defining branch is given the unique new name, ADF1, at 541. The argument list of the new function-defining branch is the same as the argument list of the branch-to-be-duplicated and consists of ARG0 543 and ARG1 544. The body of the new function-defining branch starting with VALUES 549 is the same as the body of the first function-defining branch starting at VALUES 419 of Figure 2.11 (also shown as 519 in Figure 5.1).

There are two occurrences of invocations of the branch-to-be-duplicated, ADF0, in the result-producing branch of the selected program, namely, ADF0 481 and ADF0 487 of Figure 2.11. For each of these two occurrences, a random choice is made to either leave the occurrence of ADF0 unchanged or to replace it with the newly created ADF1. For the first invocation of ADF0 at 481 of Figure 2.11, the choice is made to replace ADF0 with ADF1. Thus, ADF1 appears at 581 in Figure 5.1. The arguments for the invocation of

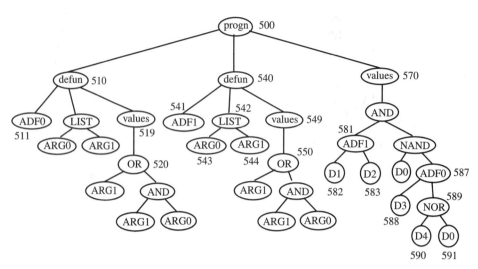

Figure 5.1 Program with argument map of {2, 2} created using subroutine duplication

ADF1 581 are D1 582 and D2 583 in Figure 5.1 (i.e., they are identical to the arguments D1 482 and D2 483 for the invocation of ADF0 at 481 in Figure 2.11). For the second invocation of ADF0 at 487 of Figure 2.11, the choice is randomly made to leave ADF0 unchanged. Thus, ADF0 appears at 587 of Figure 5.1.

There are two parameters for controlling the operation of subroutine duplication:

1. The subroutine duplication operation is controlled by a parameter specifying the probability of executing the operation on each generation, $p_{\text{subroutine-duplication}}$.
2. There is a preestablished maximum number of automatically defined functions, $N_{\text{max-adf}}$, for each program in the population.

The general rule, throughout this book, is that when execution of an operation would cause the creation of an individual that would violate a preestablished maximum (or pre-established minimum), the operation is aborted, and a reproduction operation is performed instead.

Subroutine duplication broadens the hierarchy of references in the computer program on which it operates. The operation of subroutine duplication and the other architecture-altering operations described subsequently in this book are designed so that they always produce a structurally valid program (when applied to a structurally valid program). Since the initial population in generation 0 of a run of genetic programming starts with structurally valid programs and since the genetic operations of crossover, mutation, and reproduction always produce structurally valid programs (when applied to structurally valid programs), every individual in the population at each generation of a run of genetic programming with subroutine duplication (and all of the other architecture-altering operations) is always a structurally valid program.

Because the duplicated new function-defining branch is identical to the previously existing function-defining branch (except for the name ADF1 at 541) and because the new function-defining branch ADF1 is invoked with the very same arguments as ADF0, the value(s) returned and the action(s) performed by the overall program are unchanged by the architecture-altering operation of subroutine duplication. That is, the offspring program produced by subroutine duplication is semantically equivalent to its parent (while, of course, being structurally different).

The semantic equivalence of the offspring program produced by the operation of subroutine duplication and the selected parental program permits a time-saving optimization in implementing this operation on a computer. As long as the problem's fitness measure is oblivious to the program's structure (e.g., the fitness measure for the problem does not incorporate program size) and the fitness measure does not vary from generation to generation (e.g., no randomly changing fitness cases), there is no need to compute anew the fitness of the offspring program. This same optimization is frequently used in connection with the reproduction operation. This optimization is applicable to all the other architecture-altering operations that preserve program semantics (e.g., argument duplication and subroutine creation).

When the six architecture-altering operations in this chapter were first described in *Architecture-Altering Operations for Evolving the Architecture of a Multi-Part Program in Genetic Programming* (Koza 1994a) and various early papers (Koza 1995a, 1995b, 1995e), they were called branch duplication, branch creation, and branch deletion. Since there are now additional architecture-altering operations that duplicate, create, and delete other types of branches, these three operations have been renamed in this book as subroutine duplication, subroutine creation, and subroutine deletion, respectively.

5.1.1 **The Relation of Duplication to Specialization, Refinement, and Case Splitting**

As just mentioned, subroutine duplication preserves program semantics when it first occurs. Subsequent genetic operations (such as crossover and mutation) may (and, in general, do) alter the sequence of steps in one or both of the two initially identical automatically defined functions that are present immediately after a subroutine duplication. This subsequent change constitutes a divergence (to use the biological term) in structure. A divergence in structure usually results in a divergence in behavior.

The parent that spawned the new individual program is, more often than not, a reasonably fit member of its generation (as suggested by its selection in the first place to participate in the operation of subroutine duplication). Its reasonably good fitness in the current generation may enable it to survive in the population for some time into the future. The offspring produced by the subroutine duplication operation is equally fit (assuming that the problem's fitness measure is oblivious to the program's structure and that the fitness cases do not vary from generation to generation). Thus, the parent, the offspring produced by the subroutine duplication, or both have a good chance of surviving in the population. Thus, the parent and offspring and the descendents of both will compete with one another (and, of course, other individuals in the population) for survival during subsequent generations of the evolutionary process. As the descendents of the parent and offspring diverge over a period of generations, the fitness of some descendent of one will generally turn out to be better than the fitness of some descendent of the other. In other words, the operation of subroutine duplication creates an experimental trial, undertaken over a period of generations within the run of genetic programming, as to whether two slightly different subroutines are better than one subroutine at solving the given problem. The competitive pressures of the environment (as expressed by the problem's fitness measure) ultimately determine the outcome of this trial.

In the terminology of artificial intelligence and machine learning, the operation of subroutine duplication is a *case splitting*. After the subroutine duplication, the result-producing branch invokes both automatically defined functions ADF0 587 and ADF1 581—instead of just ADF0 (Figure 2.11). The two automatically defined functions can be viewed as separate and specialized procedures for handling the two separate cases (subproblems). Prior to the subroutine duplication, the two cases (subproblems) are handled in precisely the same way. Immediately after the subroutine duplication, the two cases (subproblems) are also handled in the same way. However, subsequent operations (such as crossover and mutation) cause the two initially identical procedures to diverge in structure (and, almost always, behavior). In artificial intelligence and machine learning, this divergence is sometimes called a *specialization* or *refinement*. ADF0 can be viewed as a specialization for handling the now-split-off cases associated with the particular parts of the overall program that call ADF0. Similarly, ADF1 is a specialization for handling a second set of now-split-off cases. Time will tell whether it is beneficial to have specialized procedures for handling the two separate cases.

Since the individuals participating in subroutine duplication (and all other architecture-altering operations subsequently described in this book) are selected probabilistically on the basis of fitness, more-fit individuals are more likely to be selected than less-fit ones. That is, more experimental trials concerning the utility of specialization are conducted on the more-fit individuals in the population. The experimentation is concentrated in the best currently known regions of the search space. Meanwhile, genetic programming (as always) allocates a certain measured number of trials to individuals that are known to be inferior (based on the fitness measure). This allocation of experimental trials to known inferior individuals is done in the hope that it will unearth a trajectory through the search space leading to individuals with an ultimately higher payoff.

Most such experimental trials are unproductive. Sometimes a particular architectural change cannot be beneficial until the search moves into a better region of the search space. Sometimes an architectural change cannot be fruitful until some stage-setting change occurs in individuals in the population. Nonetheless, a certain number of trials are untiringly conducted on each generation (typically involving 1% or less of the population of each generation).

The fact that genetic programming operates from a population enables it to make a small number of adventurous moves while primarily pursuing the more immediately gratifying avenues of advance through the search space. This experimentation is done in the hope that it will unearth a trajectory through the search space leading to points with an ultimately higher payoff.

The architecture-altering operation of subroutine duplication implements a mechanism for considering the potential usefulness of specialization (case splitting, refinement). Selective pressures internal to the run of genetic programming—not the user's intelligent decision prior to the run—ultimately determine whether a specialization will become part of the solution to the problem.

5.1.2 Self-Organization of Hierarchies by Subroutine Duplication

We believe that the automatic creation of hierarchies is indispensable for solving ever-larger problems and achieving scalability in a system for automatically creating computer programs.

Subroutine duplication broadens the hierarchy of references between the automatically defined functions in a program; however, it does not itself immediately deepen the hierarchy. In the foregoing example, the result-producing branch invoked the function-defining branch ADF0 twice prior to the subroutine duplication (Figure 2.11). The depth of the hierarchy of calls between the branches of the overall program was one. After the subroutine duplication, the result-producing branch calls ADF0 once and calls ADF1 once (Figure 5.1). That is, the operation of subroutine duplication increased the number of different function-defining branches that are called by the result-producing branch but did not change the depth of the hierarchy.

Although subroutine duplication does not immediately deepen the hierarchy, it often sets the stage for a deepening of the hierarchy of references in the program on a subsequent generation of the run.

Continuing with the foregoing example, the function set for the result-producing branch includes ADF0 prior to the subroutine duplication. The function set for ADF1 includes ADF0 as a consequence of step 5 of the branch duplication operation. Then, when a crossover operation is subsequently performed on the result-producing branch, a portion of the result-producing branch containing an invocation of ADF0 may be inserted into ADF1, thereby creating a hierarchical reference from ADF1 to ADF0. Since the result-producing branch almost always contains reference(s) to ADF1 (as a result of step 4 of the original subroutine duplication operation), a hierarchy is formed in which the result-producing branch refers to ADF1 and in which ADF1, in turn, refers to ADF0. Thus, a subroutine duplication operation in conjunction with a subsequent crossover operation may deepen the hierarchy of references in the overall program.

Similarly, the subroutine duplication operation may set the stage for a deepening of the hierarchy of references by a subsequent mutation operation. When a mutation operation is performed on ADF1, the randomly created subtree created and inserted by the mutation operation into ADF1 will often include a reference to ADF0 (since ADF0 is the function set of ADF1). Thus, the mutation operation can create a hierarchical reference from ADF1 to ADF0. Since the result-producing branch almost always contains reference(s) to ADF1 (as a result of step 4 of the original subroutine duplication operation), a hierarchy is thus formed in which the result-producing branch refers to ADF1 and in which ADF1, in turn, refers to ADF0.

As a run continues, function-defining branches that were created earlier in the run by an early subroutine duplication operation may themselves be duplicated by a later subroutine duplication operation. Thus, the potential exists for further deepening of the hierarchy of references among the various branches of the overall program.

In other words, the operation of subroutine duplication permits the self-organization of hierarchies in computer programs during a run of genetic programming. As will be seen shortly (Section 5.3), the operation of subroutine creation is an even more prolific engine for automatically creating a deepened hierarchy of references among automatically defined functions.

5.2 ARGUMENT DUPLICATION

The architecture-altering operation of argument duplication duplicates one of the arguments (dummy variables, formal parameters) of one of a program's function-defining branches (automatically defined functions). Argument duplication operates on one individual selected from the population probabilistically on the basis of fitness. A program with k branches begets an offspring program with k branches; however, one of the offspring's function-defining branches has one more argument than the corresponding branch of its parent. The operation creates an appropriate name for the new argument and appropriately modifies the argument list for the branch involved.

The architecture-altering operation of argument duplication operates in the following way:

1. Select an individual program from the population to participate in this operation.
2. Pick one of the function-defining branches of the selected program. If the selected program has only one function-defining branch, that branch is automatically chosen. If the selected program has no function-defining branches, this operation is aborted.
3. Choose one of the arguments of the picked function-defining branch of the selected program as the argument-to-be-duplicated. If the picked function-defining branch has no arguments (or already has the maximum number of arguments established for the problem), this operation is aborted.
4. Add a uniquely named new argument to the argument list of the picked function-defining branch of the selected program, thus increasing the number of arguments in its argument list by one.
5. For each occurrence of the argument-to-be-duplicated anywhere in the body of the picked function-defining branch of the selected program, randomly choose (with equal probability) either to leave that occurrence unchanged or to replace that occurrence with the new argument.
6. For each occurrence of an invocation of the picked function-defining branch anywhere in the selected program, identify the argument subtree in that invocation corresponding to the argument-to-be-duplicated and duplicate that argument subtree in that invocation, thereby increasing the number of arguments in the invocation by one.
7. The terminal set of the picked branch is enlarged to include the name of the newly created argument. The function set of the picked branch is not changed. The function set of any branch whose function set includes the picked branch (i.e., any branch that actually calls the picked branch or that is permitted to call the picked branch) is unchanged. The arity of the picked branch is incremented by one in the list containing the number of arguments possessed by each function for any branch whose function set includes the picked branch. The terminal set of any branch whose function set includes the picked branch (i.e., any branch that actually calls the picked branch or that is permitted to call the picked branch) is unchanged.

Figure 5.2 shows the result of applying the operation of argument duplication to the program in Figure 2.11. The argument list of the automatically defined function ADF0 in

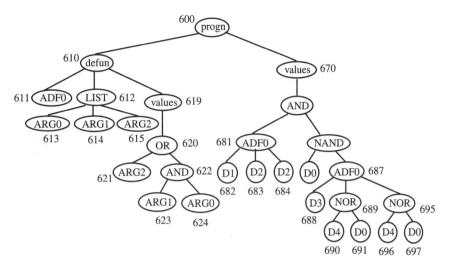

Figure 5.2 **Program with argument map of {3} created using argument duplication**

the program in Figure 2.11 contains two dummy variables (formal parameters), ARG0 and ARG1. After the operation of argument duplication, the argument list of the automatically defined function ADF0 in Figure 5.2 contains three dummy variables, ARG0, ARG1, and ARG2. The original program in Figure 2.11 has an argument map of {2}. The new program in Figure 5.2 has an argument map of {3} because the operation of argument duplication added the new argument ARG2 to the function-defining branch.

ADF0 in Figure 2.11 takes two dummy variables, ARG0 413 and ARG1 414. Suppose that the second argument, ARG1 414, is chosen as the argument-to-be-duplicated. The argument list of ADF0 in Figure 5.2 is changed by adding a uniquely named new argument, ARG2 at 615, thereby increasing the size of this argument list from two to three. There are two occurrences of the argument-to-be-duplicated in the body of the picked function-defining branch of the selected program, namely, at 421 and 423 in Figure 2.11. For each of these two occurrences, a random choice is made to either leave the occurrence of ARG1 unchanged or to replace it with the newly created argument, ARG2. Figure 5.2 shows that the choice is in favor of a replacement for the first occurrence of ARG1 at 421. Consequently, the new name, ARG2, appears at 621 of Figure 5.2. The choice is against replacement for the second occurrence of ARG1 at 423 of Figure 2.11, so ARG1 appears at 623 of Figure 5.2.

There are two occurrences of an invocation of ADF0 in the result-producing branch at 481 and 487 of Figure 2.11. The second argument, ARG1, is the argument-to-be-duplicated in this example. In the first invocation of ADF0 at 481, the variable D2 483 corresponds to the argument-to-be-duplicated because it is the second argument of ADF0 481. In the second invocation of ADF0 at 487, the entire argument subtree consisting of (NOR D4 D0) at 489, 490, and 491 corresponds to the argument-to-be-duplicated.

Because of the argument duplication, ADF0 681 and ADF0 687 in Figure 5.2 now each possess three arguments, instead of only two. For the first invocation of ADF0 at 681, D2 683 has been duplicated so that D2 now appears at both 683 and 684. For the second invocation of ADF0 at 687, the entire argument subtree (NOR D4 D0) has been duplicated so that it appears at 689, 690, and 691 as well as 695, 696, and 697.

Because the function-defining branch containing the duplicated argument is invoked with an identical copy of the previously existing argument, the value(s) returned and the action(s) performed by the overall program are unchanged by the operation of argument duplication. That is, the architecture-altering operation of argument duplication preserves program semantics.

There are several parameters for controlling the operation of argument duplication:

1. The argument duplication operation is controlled by a parameter specifying the probability of executing the operation on each generation, $p_{argument-duplication}$.
2. There is a maximum number of arguments for each automatically defined function, $N_{max-argument-adf}$, for each program.
3. The maximum size, S_{rpb}, for the result-producing branch (usually established for reasons unrelated to the operation of argument duplication) indirectly impacts this operation.

Subsequent crossovers and mutations will usually alter the sequence of steps in one or both of the initially identical instantiations of the two arguments that are present immediately after an argument duplication. This subsequent divergence in structure usually causes a divergence in behavior.

The parent that spawned the new individual program is usually a reasonably fit member of its generation. The offspring produced by the argument duplication operation is equally fit (assuming that the problem's fitness measure is oblivious to the program's structure and the fitness cases do not vary from generation to generation). Thus, both parent and offspring have a good chance of surviving in the population for some time into the future. As the two diverge over a period of generations, the fitness of some descendent of one will generally turn out to be better than the fitness of some descendent of the other. That is, the parent and offspring and their descendents will compete with one another (and, of course, other individuals in the population) for survival during subsequent generations of the evolutionary process.

Thus, the argument duplication operation sets up an experimental trial during the run of genetic programming as to whether increasing the number of arguments in an automatically defined function and differentiating them is, in fact, beneficial. The competitive pressures of the environment (as expressed by the problem's fitness measure) ultimately determine the outcome of this trial. Time will tell whether a particular argument duplication is beneficial to the overall goal of solving the problem at hand.

The operation of argument duplication can be interpreted as a specialization or refinement in the same sense that the operation of subroutine duplication is so interpreted. Although the two cases (subproblems) are handled in precisely the same way immediately after the argument duplication operation, subsequent evolution may introduce changes in the instantiations of the second and third arguments (from the example above) in each invocation of ADF0 and thereby create different ways of handling the two separate cases. Subsequent genetic operations may alter one or both of these two initially identical arguments, and these subsequent changes can lead to a divergence in structure and behavior. Once the second and third arguments diverge, this divergence may be interpreted as a specialization or refinement.

5.3   SUBROUTINE CREATION

The architecture-altering operation of subroutine creation creates a new automatically defined function (function-defining branch) within a given program. Subroutine creation operates on one individual selected from the population probabilistically on the basis of fitness. The offspring program contains a new branch that consists of a portion of one of its parent's preexisting branches. Thus, a program with k branches begets an offspring program with $k + 1$ branches. The operation creates an appropriate name for the new function-defining branch and an appropriate argument list for the new branch. The operation also creates an invoking reference to the new branch.

The operation of subroutine creation differs from the previously described operation of subroutine duplication (Section 5.1). Subroutine duplication creates a new branch that is identical to the preexisting branch (except for its name). Subroutine creation dismantles a preexisting branch and divides its steps among the preexisting branch and the newly created branch.

The architecture-altering operation of subroutine creation operates in the following way:

1. Select an individual program from the population to participate in this operation (provided that the selected program must not, after the addition of a function-defining branch, have more than the maximum number of function-defining branches established for the problem).

2. Pick a point in the body of one of the function-defining branches, result-producing branches, or other branches of the selected program. This picked point will become the topmost point of the body of the branch-to-be-created.

3. Starting at the picked point, begin traversing the subtree below the picked point (e.g., in a depth-first manner).

4. As each point below the picked point in the picked branch is encountered during the traversal, make a random determination as to whether to designate that point as being the topmost point of an argument subtree for the branch-to-be-created (provided that the number of such designated points cannot exceed the preestablished maximum number of arguments for the problem). If such a designation is made, no traversal is made of the subtree below that designated point. The traversal continues, and this step (4) is repeatedly applied to each point encountered during the traversal so that when the traversal of the subtree below the picked point is completed, zero, one, or more points are so designated during the traversal.

5. Add a uniquely named new function-defining branch to the selected program. The argument list of the new branch consists of the same number of consecutively numbered dummy variables (formal parameters) as the number of points (zero, one, or more) that were randomly designated during the traversal. The body of the new branch consists of a modified copy of the subtree starting at the picked point. The modifications to the copy are made in the following way: For each point in the copy corresponding to a point designated during the traversal of the original subtree, replace the designated point in the copy (and the subtree in the copy below that designated point in the copy) by a unique dummy variable.

The result is a body for the new function-defining branch that contains as many uniquely named dummy variables as there are dummy variables in the argument list of the new function-defining branch.

6. Replace the picked point in the picked branch by the name of the new function-defining branch. If no points below the picked point were designated during the traversal, the operation of subroutine creation is now complete.

7. If one or more points below the picked point were designated during the traversal, the subtree below the just-inserted name of the new function-defining branch will be given as many argument subtrees as there are dummy variables in the new function-defining branch in the following way: For each point in the subtree below the point designated during the traversal, attach the designated point and the subtree below it as an argument to the function defined by the new function-defining branch.

8. The terminal set of the newly created branch is identical to that of the picked branch, minus the dummy variables of the picked branch, plus the dummy variables of the newly created branch. The function set of the newly created branch is identical to the original function set of the picked branch. The function set of the picked branch is enlarged to include the name of the newly created function-defining branch. The terminal set of the picked branch is unchanged. The arity of the newly created branch is inserted into the list containing the number of arguments possessed by each function for the picked branch and any branch whose function set includes the picked branch (i.e., any branch that actually calls the picked branch or that is permitted to call the picked branch). The function set of any branch whose function set includes the picked branch is enlarged to include the name of the newly created function-defining branch. The terminal set of any branch whose function set includes the picked branch is not affected by this operation.

Several different methods may be used in step 4 to choose the zero, one, or more points below the picked point that are designated during the traversal described above. In the subroutine creation operation, internal points below the picked point are designated independently at random. We disallow picking a point in the subtree of other picked points (i.e., the subtrees below all the picked points are disjoint). Other methods of designation may be used. For example, in *depth compression*, the points at a certain distance (depth) below the picked point would be designated; in *leaf compression*, all of the external points (leaves) below the picked point would be designated (Angeline and Pollack 1993, 1994; Angeline 1993, 1994).

The operation of subroutine creation does not have any immediate effect on the value(s) returned and the action(s) performed by the selected program. That is, subroutine creation preserves program semantics. However, subsequent genetic operations may alter the branch that is created by this architecture-altering operation, thereby eventually producing a divergence in structure and behavior between the parent program and offspring.

The operation of subroutine creation described here differs from the compression (module acquisition) operation described by Angeline and Pollack (Angeline and Pollack 1993, 1994; Angeline 1993, 1994) in at least three ways. First, the compression operation places each new function (called a module) into a public "genetic library."

When the new function is deposited into a public library, the new function is not exclusively associated with the program that gave rise to it. Instead, a function in the library may be invoked by any program in the population. In this regard, the compression operation is similar to the "define building block" operation (Koza 1990b; Koza and Rice 1991b; Koza 1992e, Section 6.5.4) that created a library of subtrees that was available to the entire population. (The "define building block" operation was renamed "encapsulation" in Koza 1992e, Section 6.5.4). In contrast, in the subroutine creation operation, each newly created function is a branch of a specific selected program. The newly created function coevolves with the particular program that spawned it.

Second, after the compression operation (or the encapsulation operation) places a new function into the genetic library, the function is insulated from subsequent change (e.g., from crossover or mutation). Functions that may be useful and relevant early in a run may become irrelevant as the run progresses. In contrast, when the subroutine creation operation is used, the body of the new branch continues to be susceptible to evolutionary change in later generations.

A third difference between the compression operation and the operation of subroutine creation is that the subroutine creation operation may be applied to any branch. It is particularly salient that branch creation can operate on a function-defining branch. When the subroutine creation operation is applied to a function-defining branch, a hierarchical reference is created between two function-defining branches, and there is a deepening of hierarchical references in the program. The compression operation does not change the architecture of the preexisting program in the sense of creating additional branches in the preexisting program. Subsequent applications of the compression operation to the same program are necessarily limited to a preexisting branch (e.g., the result-producing branch) and therefore cannot deepen the hierarchy of references in a program.

The compression operation is similar to the earlier "define building block" ("encapsulation") operation (Koza 1990b; Koza and Rice 1991b; Koza 1992e, Section 6.5.4) in that its ability to actually aid the evolutionary process is doubtful (Kinnear 1994a). Our own unpublished efforts with encapsulation confirm Kinnear's conclusion. Accordingly, we have not used the "define building block" ("encapsulation") operation since our early work with it.

There are several parameters for controlling the operation of subroutine creation:

1. The subroutine creation operation is controlled by a parameter specifying the probability of executing the operation on each generation, $p_{subroutine-creation}$.
2. There is a maximum size, S_{adf}, for each automatically defined function in a program.
3. There is a maximum number of automatically defined functions, $N_{max-adf}$, for each program in the population.
4. There is a maximum number of arguments for each automatically defined function, $N_{max-argument-adf}$, for each program.
5. There is a minimum number of arguments for each automatically defined function, $N_{min-argument-adf}$, for each program.

5.3.1   Self-Organization of Hierarchies by Subroutine Creation

As explained in Section 5.1, a subroutine duplication operation, in conjunction with a subsequent crossover or mutation, may sometimes deepen the hierarchy of references among automatically defined functions of a program. However, this phenomenon depends on the sequential occurrence of more than one event. As will be seen momentarily, the subroutine creation operation is a far more prolific engine for creating ever-deeper hierarchical references among function-defining branches of a program.

The operation of subroutine creation is more general than the operation of subroutine duplication in that the picked point need not be the topmost point of the body of a pre-existing function-defining branch. There are several possibilities for the location of the picked point. First, the picked point may be somewhere in the result-producing branch. Second, the picked point may be a nontop point of the body of a preexisting function-defining branch. Third, the picked point may potentially be somewhere in an automatically defined iteration (Chapter 6), an automatically defined loop (Chapter 7), or an automatically defined recursion (Chapter 8).

The first possibility enables a function-defining branch to be created from the result-producing branch dynamically during the run of genetic programming (thereby creating a hierarchical reference from the result-producing branch to the newly created function-defining branch). This possibility is of special importance when all the programs in the population consist of only a single result-producing branch (as may be the case in generation 0 of a run). In this case, the operation of subroutine creation provides the means to introduce a hierarchical reference into a program with no preexisting hierarchical reference.

The second possibility arises whenever a subroutine creation operation is applied to a nontop point of the body of a preexisting function-defining branch. In this case, a hierarchical reference is created between the preexisting function-defining branch and the newly created function-defining branch. Since the preexisting function-defining branch is (almost always) invoked by some calling branch, a chain of hierarchical references is created from the preexisting calling branch to the preexisting function-defining branch to the newly created function-defining branch. This chain is deeper than the chain from the preexisting calling branch to the preexisting function-defining branch.

The third possibility is similar to the second. As before, a hierarchical reference is created between the preexisting branch and the newly created branch (an automatically defined iteration, an automatically defined loop, or an automatically defined recursion). The hierarchy of references is deepened.

The operation of subroutine creation is explained below with the aid of three examples.

Example 1

Figure 5.3 shows the result of applying the operation of subroutine creation to a point in the result-producing branch of the program in Figure 2.11 (which has an argument map of {2}). Since a three-argument function-defining branch ADF1 is created, the resulting program in Figure 5.3 has an argument map of {2, 3}.

Suppose the point NAND 485 is picked from the result-producing branch starting at VALUES 470 in Figure 2.11. Starting at the picked point, NAND 485, a depth-first traversal of the subtree below this point will visit 486, 487, 488, 489, 490, and 491, in that

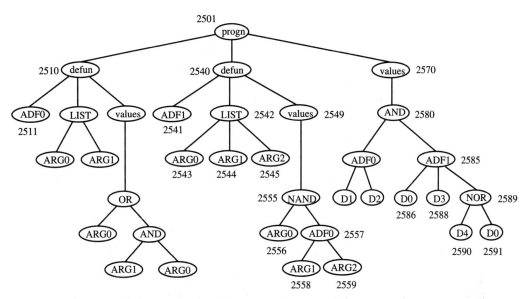

Figure 5.3   Program with a three-argument function-defining branch (ADF1) created from a result-producing branch using subroutine creation

order. Suppose, while making this depth-first traversal, three points are designated during the traversal of points. The fact that three points were designated means that the branch-to-be-created will be a three-argument function-defining branch. The three-argument subtrees rooted at these three designated points will become arguments for the branch-to-be-created. For purposes of illustration, suppose that points 486, 488, and 489 of Figure 2.11 were the three points that were designated during the traversal. Note that once point 489 was designated, points D4 490 and D0 491 were excluded from the traversal.

The subroutine creation operation causes a new branch to be added to the overall selected program. The new branch starts at DEFUN 2540 in Figure 5.3. The new branch is given a new name, ADF1 2541, that is unique within the new overall program. The argument list of this new branch in Figure 5.3 contains three consecutively numbered dummy variables, namely, ARG0 2543, ARG1 2544, and ARG2 2545, appearing below LIST 2542.

The body of this new branch starts at VALUES 2549. The body of the new branch in Figure 5.3 consists of a modified copy of the seven-point subtree starting at the picked point, NAND 485 of Figure 2.11. In modifying the copy, each of the three designated points from Figure 2.11 (486, 488, and 489) is replaced by a different consecutively numbered dummy variable, ARG0, ARG1, and ARG2 in Figure 5.3. Specifically, the first designated point, D0 486, from Figure 2.11 is replaced by ARG0 and appears as ARG0 2556 in Figure 5.3. The second designated point, D3 488, from Figure 2.11 is replaced by ARG1 and appears as ARG1 2558 in Figure 5.3. The third designated point, NOR 489, and the entire subtree below this designated point (i.e., D4 490 and D0 491) from Figure 2.11 are replaced by ARG2 and appear as ARG2 2559 in Figure 5.3.

The picked point, NAND 485, from Figure 2.11 is now replaced by the name, ADF1, of the new function-defining branch. Thus, ADF1 appears at 2585 in Figure 5.3. Since three points below NAND 485 from Figure 2.11 were designated during the traversal, ADF1 2585 will be given three argument subtrees. The first designated point, D0 486, from Figure 2.11 appears below ADF1 2585 as D0 2586 in Figure 5.3 as the first argument to ADF1 2585. Because D0 is a terminal, D0 2586 appears alone in Figure 5.3. The second designated point, D3 488, from Figure 2.11 appears below ADF1 2585 as D3 2588 in Figure 5.3 (where it is the second argument to ADF1 2585). The third designated point, NOR 489, from Figure 2.11 appears below ADF1 2585 as NOR 2589 in Figure 5.3 as the third argument to ADF1 2585. Unlike the previous two designated points, NOR 489 has a subtree below it in Figure 2.11. The entire subtree is (NOR D4 D0) at 489, 490, and 491 in Figure 2.11. Thus, the entire subtree (NOR D4 D0) appears at 2589, 2590, and 2591 of Figure 5.3.

The argument map of the original overall program in Figure 2.11 is {2}, and the argument map of the new overall program in Figure 5.3 is {2, 3} because the new branch takes three arguments.

Example 2

As a second example of the operation of the subroutine creation operation, consider Figure 5.4. This figure shows the special case of applying the operation of subroutine creation to a point in the result-producing branch of the program in Figure 2.11 in which a zero-argument new function-defining branch ADF1 is created.

Suppose the point NAND 485 is again picked from the result-producing branch starting at VALUES 470 in Figure 2.11 within the overall program starting at PROGN 400. However, now suppose that, while making the depth-first traversal, no points at all were designated. As before, the subroutine creation operation causes a new branch to be added to the overall selected program. The new branch starts at DEFUN 2640 of Figure 5.4. The new branch is given a unique new name, ADF1 (at 2641), in Figure 5.4. Since no points were designated during the traversal, the argument list of this new branch contains no dummy variables, and no dummy variables appear below LIST 2642 in Figure 5.4. The body of this new branch starts at VALUES 2649. However, since no points were designated during the traversal, the body of the new branch consists of an exact copy of the seven-point subtree starting at the picked point, NAND 485, of Figure 2.11. In particular, several of the actual variables of the problem (D0 2656, D3 2658, D4 2650, and D0 2651) are imported into the body of the function definition for ADF1 in Figure 5.4. As before, the picked point, NAND 485, of Figure 2.11 is replaced in Figure 5.4 by the name, ADF1 2685, of the new function-defining branch. Since no points below NAND 485 were designated during the traversal of Figure 2.11, ADF1 2685 in Figure 5.4 has no argument subtrees. Thus, in this special case, the entire subtree containing the picked point, NAND 485, and the subtree below it is encapsulated in the zero-argument automatically defined function ADF1 in Figure 5.4. In this example, the argument map of the original overall program in Figure 2.11 is {2}, and the argument map of the new overall program in Figure 5.4 is {2, 0}.

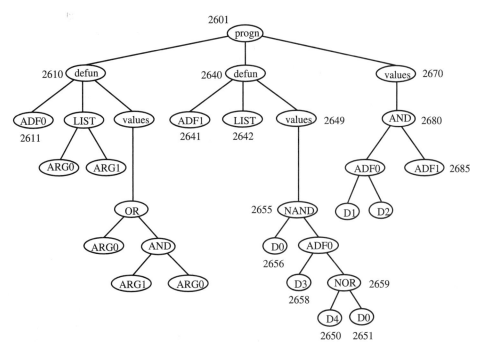

Figure 5.4 **Program with a zero-argument function-defining branch (ADF1) created from a result-producing branch using subroutine creation**

Example 3

As a third example of the subroutine creation operation, consider Figures 5.5 and 5.6. These two figures illustrate the important fact that whenever a subroutine creation operation is applied to a point of the body of a preexisting function-defining branch, a hierarchical reference is created between the preexisting function-defining branch and the newly created branch. Since the preexisting function-defining branch is, in general, invoked by some calling branch, a deepened network of hierarchical references is created from the preexisting calling branch, to the preexisting function-defining branch, and to the newly created function-defining branch.

Figure 5.5 shows a program with one function-defining branch (ADF0) and an argument map of {2}. The hierarchy has a depth of one in the sense that the result-producing branch refers to ADF0.

Suppose the point NOR 425 is picked from the body of the function-defining branch for ADF0 starting at DEFUN 410 in Figure 5.5. Starting at this picked point, NOR 425, a depth-first traversal of the subtree below this point will visit 425, 426, 427, 428, and 429. Suppose, while making this depth-first traversal, a total of two points (ARG1 426 and NAND 427 of Figure 5.5) are designated. The fact that two points were designated means that the branch-to-be-created will be a two-argument function-defining branch. The argument subtrees starting at these two designated points will become arguments for the branch-to-be-created. The first of these argument subtrees will consist only of the single

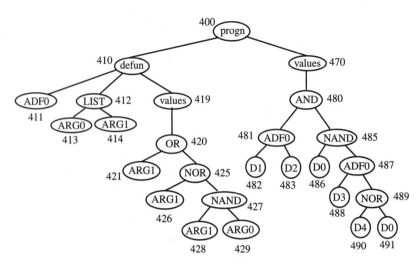

Figure 5.5 **Program with one function-defining branch and an argument map of {2}**

point ARG1 426, while the second will consist of the three-point subtree (NAND ARG1 ARG0).

When hierarchical references are possible, it is often convenient to give the newly created branch a lower number. Since the branch from which the point NOR 425 was picked was originally called ADF0, it may be convenient (in order to maintain a consistent left-to-right order for calls) to rename ADF0 of Figure 5.5 as ADF1 in Figure 5.6. Specifically, ADF1 in Figure 5.6 is the renamed branch and has steps starting with OR 550 (derived from OR 420 of ADF0 of Figure 5.5). ADF1 also possesses two dummy variables, ARG0 543 and ARG1 544 (derived from ARG0 413 and ARG1 414 of ADF0 of Figure 5.5). Having now renamed the preexisting branch as ADF1, the newly created branch will be called ADF0 in Figure 5.6. Note that other preexisting branches in the program must be modified to reflect this renaming. Specifically, the call ADF0 at 481 of the result-producing branch of Figure 5.5 is renamed as ADF1 581 in Figure 5.6. Similarly, ADF0 487 of the result-producing branch of Figure 5.5 is renamed as ADF1 587 in Figure 5.6. Thus, after the renaming, the result-producing branch invokes ADF1, and the newly created branch is called ADF0.

Figure 5.6 shows the result of applying the operation of subroutine creation to the program in Figure 5.5. The newly created program in Figure 5.6 has two function-defining branches (ADF0 and ADF1) and an argument map of {2, 2}. After the subroutine creation, there is a hierarchy of depth two in the sense that the result-producing branch refers to ADF1 (at both 581 and 587), and ADF1, in turn, refers to ADF0 (at 557). Prior to the subroutine creation (Figure 5.6), the depth of the hierarchy was one.

The subroutine creation operation causes a new branch to be added to the overall selected program. The new branch starts at DEFUN 510 and is now called ADF0 511 in Figure 5.6. The argument list of the new branch contains two consecutively numbered dummy variables, ARG0 513 and ARG1 514, appearing below LIST 512. The body of the new branch starts at VALUES 519. The body of the new branch consists of a modified

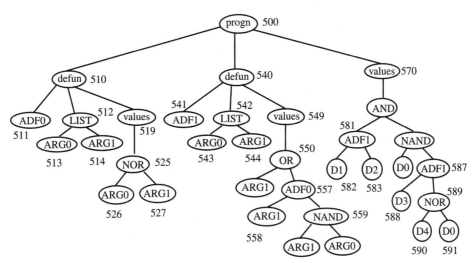

Figure 5.6 Hierarchical reference from the result-producing branch to ADF1 to ADF0

copy of the five-point subtree starting at the picked point (NOR 425 of Figure 5.5). In modifying the copy, both of the two designated points (ARG1 426 and NAND 427 of Figure 5.5) are replaced by different consecutively numbered dummy variables (ARG0 and ARG1, respectively, in Figure 5.6). Specifically, the first designated point, ARG1 426, of Figure 5.5 is replaced by ARG0 526 of ADF0 in Figure 5.6. The second designated point, NAND 427, of Figure 5.5 and the remainder of the subtree below this NAND (i.e., ARG1 428 and ARG0 429 of Figure 5.5) are replaced by ARG1 527 of ADF0 in Figure 5.6. In other words, the newly created ADF0 of Figure 5.6 is a two-argument automatically defined function whose work consists of taking the NOR of its two arguments.

The preexisting branch (renamed as ADF1 in Figure 5.6) is now modified so that it calls the newly created branch (now called ADF0 in Figure 5.6). The picked point (NOR 425 of ADF0 from Figure 5.5) is now replaced by the name (ADF0) of the newly created function-defining branch. Thus, ADF0 appears at 557 of ADF1 in Figure 5.6 in lieu of the picked point NOR 425 of Figure 5.5. This substitution is what creates the reference from the preexisting branch to the newly created branch. Since two points below NOR 425 from Figure 5.5 were designated during the traversal, ADF0 557 will have two argument subtrees below it. The first designated point (ARG1 426 from Figure 5.5) happens to be a terminal. It appears below ADF0 557 as ARG1 558 in Figure 5.6 and becomes the first argument to ADF0 557. The second designated point (NAND 427 from Figure 5.5) happens to be the top of a three-point subtree. This entire three-point subtree, (NAND ARG1 ARG0), appears below ADF0 557 in Figure 5.6 and becomes the second argument to ADF0 557. In other words, the preexisting branch (now renamed as ADF1) calls ADF0 with two arguments.

Whenever a subroutine creation operation is applied to a point of the body of a preexisting function-defining branch, a hierarchical reference is created between the preexisting function-defining branch and the newly created function-defining branch. Since the preexisting function-defining branch (now renamed as ADF1) is (usually) invoked by some calling branch (namely, the result-producing branch at ADF1 581 and ADF1 587 in Figure 5.6), a chain of hierarchical references is created from the preexisting calling branch (the result-producing branch) to the preexisting function-defining branch (now renamed as ADF1) to the newly created function-defining branch (the new ADF0). This chain of hierarchical references is one layer deeper than the preexisting chain.

5.4   ARGUMENT CREATION

The architecture-altering operation of argument creation creates a new argument within one of a program's function-defining branches (automatically defined functions). Argument creation operates on one individual selected from the population probabilistically on the basis of fitness. A program with k branches begets an offspring program with k branches; however, one of the offspring's function-defining branches has one more argument than the corresponding branch of its parent. The operation creates an appropriate name for the new argument, appropriately modifies the argument list for the branch involved, and appropriately modifies the calls to the branch involved.

The architecture-altering operation of argument creation operates in the following way:

1. Select an individual program from the population to participate in this operation.
2. Pick a point in the body of one of the function-defining branches of the selected program (provided that the picked point must not, after the addition of an argument at that point, have more than the maximum number of arguments established for the problem).
3. Add a uniquely named new argument to the argument list of the picked function-defining branch for the purpose of defining the argument-to-be-created.
4. Replace the picked point (and the entire subtree below it) in the picked function-defining branch by the name of the newly created argument.
5. For each occurrence of an invocation of the picked function-defining branch anywhere in the selected program, add an additional argument subtree to that invocation. In each instance, the added argument subtree consists of a modified copy of the picked point (and the entire subtree below it) in the picked function-defining branch. The modification is made in the following way: For each dummy variable in a particular added argument subtree, replace the dummy variable with the entire argument subtree of that invocation corresponding to that dummy variable.
6. The terminal set of the picked function-defining branch is enlarged to include the name of the newly created argument. The function set of the picked function-defining branch is unchanged. The now-incremented arity of the picked branch is inserted into the list containing the number of arguments possessed by each function for any branch whose function set includes the picked branch (i.e., any branch that actually calls the picked branch or that is permitted to call the picked branch). The function set of any branch whose function set includes the picked branch is unchanged. The terminal set of any branch whose function set includes the picked branch is unchanged.

Figure 5.7 shows the result of applying the operation of argument creation to the program in Figure 2.11 (which has an argument map of {2}). The newly created program in Figure 5.7 has an argument map of {3}.

Suppose the point AND 422 of Figure 2.11 is the picked point, from step 2, in the body of the function-defining branch starting at DEFUN 410. This picked point, AND 422, is the topmost point of the three-point subtree (AND ARG1 ARG0) at 422, 423, and 424 of Figure 2.11. ARG2 is the name given to the newly created argument that will appear in Figure 5.7. Thus, ARG2 3015 is added to the argument list starting at LIST 3012 of Figure 5.7. In Figure 5.7, ARG2 3022 has replaced the picked point (AND 422 of Figure 2.11) and the entire subtree in Figure 2.11 below the picked point.

In Figure 2.11, there are two occurrences of invocations of the picked function-defining branch (ADF0), namely, at 481 and 487.

The first invocation of ADF0 in the selected program is the two-argument invocation (ADF0 D1 D2) at 481, 482, and 483 in Figure 2.11. A new third argument is added for the invocation of ADF0 at 481. The new argument subtree is manufactured by starting with a copy of the picked point and the entire subtree below that picked point, namely, (AND ARG1 ARG0) at 422, 423, and 424 in Figure 2.11. This copy is first modified by replacing the dummy variable ARG1 423 by the argument subtree of the invocation of ADF0 at 481 corresponding to the dummy variable ARG1 423 (i.e., the single point D2 483). Note that it is D2 483 that corresponds because D2 483 is the second argument subtree of ADF0 481 and because ARG1 is the second dummy variable of DEFUN 410. The copy is further modified by replacing the dummy variable ARG0 424 by the argument subtree of the invocation of ADF0 at 481 corresponding to that dummy variable (i.e., the single point D1 482). The result is that ADF0 is now invoked at 3081 in Figure 5.7 with three arguments (instead of two), namely,

    (ADF0 D1 D2 (AND D2 D1)).

The added (third) argument is (AND D2 D1) rooted at 3084 of Figure 5.7.

The second invocation of ADF0 in the selected program is the two-argument invocation

    (ADF0 D3 (NOR D4 D0))

rooted at 487 in Figure 2.11. A new third argument is added for the invocation ADF0 487. The new argument subtree is manufactured by starting with a copy of the picked point and the entire subtree below that picked point from Figure 2.11, namely, (AND ARG1 ARG0) at 422, 423, and 424. This copy is first modified by replacing the dummy variable ARG1 423 by the argument subtree of the invocation of ADF0 at 487 corresponding to the dummy variable ARG1 423, namely, the entire argument subtree (NOR D4 D0) at 489, 490, and 491. Note that a three-point subtree, (NOR D4 D0), corresponds because it is the second argument subtree of ADF0 487 in Figure 2.11 and because ARG1 is the second dummy variable of DEFUN 410. The copy is further modified by replacing the dummy variable ARG0 424 by the argument subtree of the invocation of ADF0 at 487 corresponding to that dummy variable (i.e., the single point D3 488). The result is that ADF0 is now invoked at 3087 in Figure 5.7 with three arguments (instead of two),

    (ADF0 D3 (NOR D4 D0) (AND (NOR D4 D0) D3)).

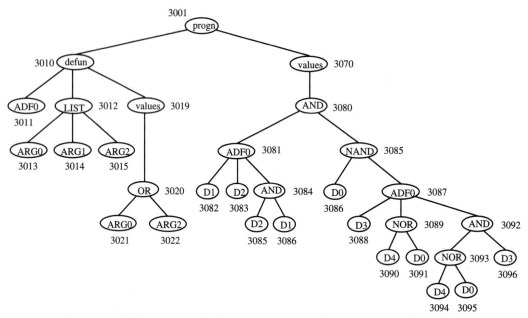

Figure 5.7   Program with argument map of {3} created using argument creation

The added (third) argument is

```
(AND (NOR D4 D0) D3)
```

rooted at 3092 of Figure 5.7.

The operation of argument creation changes the argument map of the selected program from {2} to {3} because ADF0 now takes three arguments, instead of two.

The operation of argument creation does not have any immediate effect on the value(s) returned and the action(s) performed by the selected program. However, subsequent genetic operations may cause a divergence in the structure and behavior of the parent and offspring of this architecture-altering operation.

There are several parameters for controlling the operation of argument creation:

1. The argument creation operation is controlled by a parameter specifying the probability of executing the operation on each generation, $p_{argument\text{-}creation}$.
2. There is a maximum number of arguments for each automatically defined function, $N_{max\text{-}argument\text{-}adf}$, for each program.
3. The maximum size, S_{rpb}, for the result-producing branch (usually established for reasons unrelated to the operation of argument creation) indirectly impacts this operation.

5.5   SUBROUTINE DELETION

The architecture-altering operation of subroutine deletion deletes one of a program's function-defining branches (automatically defined functions). Subroutine deletion operates on one individual selected from the population probabilistically on the basis of fitness. The offspring program lacks one of its parent's preexisting branches. That is, a program with k branches begets one with $k - 1$ branches.

The architecture-altering operation of subroutine deletion operates in the following way:

1. Select an individual program from the population to participate in this operation. If the selected program has no function-defining branches (or already has the minimum number of function-defining branches established for the problem), this operation is aborted.
2. Pick one of the function-defining branches of the selected program as the branch-to-be-deleted.
3. Delete the branch-to-be-deleted from the selected program, thus decreasing the number of branches in the selected program by one.
4. For each occurrence of an invocation of the branch-to-be-deleted anywhere in the selected program, replace the invocation of the branch-to-be-deleted with an invocation of a surviving branch (described below).
5. The function set of any branch whose function set includes the picked branch (i.e., any branch that actually calls the picked branch or that is permitted to call the picked branch) is changed by deleting the name of the picked branch. The terminal set of any branch whose function set includes the picked branch is unchanged.

Subroutine deletion provides a mechanism for narrowing the hierarchy of a program. There are several parameters for controlling the operation of subroutine deletion.

1. The subroutine deletion operation is controlled by a parameter specifying the probability of executing the operation on each generation, $p_{\text{subroutine-deletion}}$.
2. There is a minimum number of automatically defined functions, $N_{\text{min-adf}}$, for each program in the population.
3. When a function-defining branch is deleted, the question arises as to how to modify invocations of the branch-to-be-deleted by the other branches of the overall program. The following three alternatives will be considered: subroutine deletion by consolidation, subroutine deletion with random regeneration, and subroutine deletion by macro expansion.

   The first alternative, *subroutine deletion by consolidation*, involves choosing a suitable second function-defining branch of the overall program and replacing (consolidating) each invocation of the branch-to-be-deleted with an invocation to this second branch. Subroutine deletion by consolidation almost never preserves the semantics of the overall program. Subroutine deletion by consolidation can be interpreted as a way to achieve generalization in a problem-solving procedure.

   The second alternative, *subroutine deletion with random regeneration*, involves randomly generating new subtrees composed of the available functions and terminals in lieu of an invocation of the branch-to-be-deleted. Subroutine deletion with random regeneration almost never preserves the semantics of the overall program.

   The third alternative, *subroutine deletion by macro expansion*, involves inserting the entire body of the (nonrecursive) branch-to-be-deleted for each instance of an invocation of that branch. Subroutine deletion by macro expansion preserves the semantics of the overall program (usually at the expense of a substantial increase in the size of the overall program).

5.5.1   Subroutine Deletion by Consolidation

The first alternative (subroutine deletion by consolidation) begins by finding a suitable choice for the surviving branch. Since subroutine deletion by consolidation involves two branches (i.e., the branch-to-be-deleted and the surviving branch), it is necessary that the selected program have at least two function-defining branches. Thus, when subroutine deletion by consolidation is being used and the selected program has less than two function-defining branches, this operation is aborted.

When subroutine deletion by consolidation is performed, the number of arguments possessed by the proposed surviving branch may be

1. equal to,
2. less than, or
3. greater than

the number of arguments possessed by the branch-to-be-deleted.

Figure 5.1 illustrates the first of these three possibilities for subroutine deletion by consolidation (where the number of arguments possessed by the proposed surviving branch is equal to the number of arguments possessed by the branch-to-be-deleted). Suppose that the first function-defining branch (defining ADF0) of the program in Figure 5.1 is picked as the branch-to-be-deleted and that the second function-defining branch (defining ADF1) is to be the surviving branch. In that event, the first function-defining branch is deleted; the invocation of ADF0 at 587 in Figure 5.1 is replaced by an invocation of ADF1; and the two argument subtrees below the invocation of ADF0 at 587 are retained as the argument subtrees for the invocation at 587 of ADF1. That is, the branch-to-be-deleted is merged into ADF1. The original program in Figure 5.1 has an argument map of {2, 2}, and the resulting program has an argument map of {2}.

In the second possibility, the number of arguments required by the proposed surviving branch is less than the number of arguments possessed by the branch-to-be-deleted. Any superfluous argument subtrees below the invocation of the branch-to-be-deleted are simply deleted. The subroutine deletion may also be viewed as a generalization of a procedure with an accompanying generalization of its arguments.

In the third possibility, the number of arguments required by the proposed surviving branch is greater than the number of arguments possessed by the branch-to-be-deleted. The required additional argument subtrees may be randomly created (or duplicated). This random creation is accomplished using the same method of generation originally used to create the invoking branch at the time of creation of the initial random population in generation 0 (with the branch-to-be-deleted, of course, being unavailable during this random regeneration).

5.5.2   Subroutine Deletion with Random Regeneration

When the second alternative (subroutine deletion with random regeneration) is being used, all of the argument subtrees required by the invocation of the branch-to-be-deleted are randomly generated.

Except when random regeneration is used, the operations of subroutine deletion and argument deletion (described in Section 5.6) are recombinative in the sense that the offspring produced by each operation consists entirely of genetic material that comes from an existing member of the population. When random regeneration is used, subroutine deletion and argument deletion are partially recombinative and partially mutational.

5.5.3   Subroutine Deletion by Macro Expansion

In the third alternative (subroutine deletion by macro expansion), each of the argument subtrees in each invocation of the branch-to-be-deleted is substituted into a copy of the body of the branch-to-be-deleted, and the now-expanded body then replaces the invocation of the branch-to-be-deleted. This alternative has the advantage of preserving the semantics of the overall program (usually at the expense of a substantial increase in the size of the overall program). Preservation of program semantics may be viewed as either desirable or undesirable. To the extent that the objective of a deletion is to change the semantics of the overall program (i.e., to achieve generalization), this alternative defeats that objective.

5.5.4   Self-Organization of Hierarchies by Subroutine Deletion

As previously noted, the operations of subroutine duplication, subroutine creation, argument duplication, and argument creation generally create larger and more complex programs.

Assuming the alternative of subroutine deletion by macro expansion (described above) is not used, the operations of subroutine deletion and argument deletion (subsequently described in Section 5.6) create generally smaller and less complex programs. Thus, these two deletion operations provide a mechanism for counterbalancing the growth that would otherwise occur because of subroutine duplication, subroutine creation, argument duplication, and argument creation.

The significance of the two deletion operations goes beyond parsimony. The operation of subroutine deletion sets up an experimental trial during the run of genetic programming as to whether a particular automatically defined function in a program is useful. After the deletion, the downsized program competes with other individuals in the population (frequently including the reasonably fit parent that spawned it) for survival during subsequent generations of the evolutionary process. If an offspring that is shorn of one of its automatically defined functions still performs reasonably well, it will tend to survive in the population in future generations. If the downsized program is ineffective in grappling with its environment, it will tend to be driven to extinction. Time will tell whether a particular subroutine deletion is beneficial to the overall goal of solving a given problem.

5.5.5   The Relation of Deletion to Generalization

It was previously mentioned (Section 5.1.1) that a subroutine duplication can be viewed as a mechanism for implementing specialization, refinement, and case splitting in the context of genetic programming. Again assuming the alternative of subroutine deletion by macro expansion (described in Section 5.5.3) is not used, subroutine deletion may be viewed as providing a mechanism for generalization. Before a subroutine deletion, the two preexisting automatically defined functions constitute different procedures for handling different cases (subproblems) of the given problem. The two automatically defined functions do different things and are invoked from different parts of the overall program. That is, prior to a subroutine deletion, there is specialization. After the subroutine deletion, both cases (subproblems) are handled in the same way by the one surviving automatically defined function. Generalization has occurred.

Since the individuals that participate in subroutine deletion are selected probabilistically on the basis of fitness, more-fit individuals are more likely to be selected than less-fit ones. That is, more experimental trials of the utility of generalization are (likely) made on more-fit individuals in the population.

Argument deletion is, similarly, a form of generalization (just as argument duplication is a form of specialization).

Thus, the architecture-altering operations of genetic programming, as a group, implement two mechanisms—generalization and specialization—that are generally considered to be useful problem-solving mechanisms. Of course, a particular generalization can be beneficial, neutral, or detrimental in the efforts to solve a particular problem. Selective pressures internal to the run of genetic programming—not the user's intelligent decision prior to the run—ultimately determine whether the generalization or specialization will become part of the ultimate solution to the problem.

5.6 ARGUMENT DELETION

The architecture-altering operation of argument deletion deletes an argument of one of a program's function-defining branches (automatically defined functions). One of the function-defining branches of the offspring lacks one of its arguments possessed by the corresponding branch of its parent. A program with k branches begets an offspring program with k branches; however, one of the offspring's branches has one less argument than the corresponding branch of its parent.

The architecture-altering operation of argument deletion operates in the following way:

1. Select an individual program from the population to participate in this operation.
2. Pick one of the function-defining branches of the selected program. If the selected program has only one function-defining branch, that branch is automatically picked. If the selected program has no function-defining branches, this operation is aborted.
3. Choose one of the arguments of the picked function-defining branch of the selected program as the argument-to-be-deleted. If the picked function-defining branch has no arguments (or already has the minimum number of arguments established for the problem), this operation is aborted.
4. Delete the argument-to-be-deleted from the argument list of the picked function-defining branch of the selected program, thus decreasing the number of arguments in each of their argument lists by one.
5. For each occurrence of an invocation of the picked function-defining branch anywhere in the selected program, delete the argument subtree in that invocation

corresponding to the argument-to-be-deleted, thereby decreasing the number of arguments in the invocation by one.

6. For each occurrence of the argument-to-be-deleted anywhere in the body of the picked function-defining branch of the selected program, replace the argument-to-be-deleted with a surviving argument (using one of the options detailed below).

7. The terminal set of the picked branch is changed by deleting the name of the argument-to-be-deleted. The function set of the picked branch is not changed. The function set of any branch whose function set includes the picked branch (i.e., any branch that actually calls the picked branch or that is permitted to call the picked branch) is unchanged; however, the arity of the picked branch is decremented by one in the list containing the number of arguments possessed by each function for any branch whose function set includes the picked branch. The terminal set of any branch whose function set includes the picked branch is unchanged.

There are several parameters for controlling the operation of argument deletion:

1. The operation is controlled by a parameter specifying the probability of executing the operation on each generation, $p_{\text{argument-deletion}}$.

2. There is a minimum number of arguments, $N_{\text{min-adf-arg}}$, for each automatically defined function.

3. When an argument is deleted, the question arises as to how to modify references to the argument-to-be-deleted within the picked branch. The following three alternatives will be considered: argument deletion by consolidation, argument deletion with random regeneration, and argument deletion by macro expansion.

The first alternative, *argument deletion by consolidation*, involves identifying another argument of the picked branch as the surviving argument and replacing (consolidating) the argument-to-be-deleted with the surviving argument in the picked branch. Argument deletion by consolidation almost never preserves the semantics of the overall program. When this alternative is employed, the operation of argument deletion may be viewed as a generalization in the sense that some information that was formerly considered in executing a procedure is now no longer considered.

The second alternative, *argument deletion with random regeneration*, involves generating a new subtree in lieu of an invocation of the argument-to-be-deleted using the same method of generation originally used to create the picked branch at the time of creation of the initial random population (with the argument-to-be-deleted being unavailable during this random regeneration). Argument deletion with random regeneration almost never preserves program semantics.

The third alternative, *argument deletion by macro expansion*, may also be used. This alternative has the advantage of preserving the semantics of the overall program (usually at the expense of a substantial increase in the size of the overall program). The characteristic of preserving program semantics may be viewed as either desirable or undesirable. To the extent that the objective of a deletion is to change the semantics of the overall program (i.e., to achieve generalization), this alternative defeats that objective.

5.6.1 Argument Deletion by Consolidation

Suppose, in employing the first alternative (argument deletion by consolidation), that ARG2 615 in Figure 5.2 is chosen as the argument-to-be-deleted and that ARG1 at 614 is chosen (from among the remaining two arguments) as the surviving argument. The one occurrence of ARG2 at 621 in Figure 5.2 is replaced by ARG1. The two invocations of ADF0 by the result-producing branch (at 681 and 687) are modified by deleting the third argument subtree in each invocation. Specifically, the argument subtree D0 684 is deleted from the invocation of ADF0 at 681, and the argument subtree (NOR D4 D0) at 695, 696, and 697 is deleted from the invocation of ADF0 at 687. The result is the program shown in Figure 2.11. The original program in Figure 5.2 has an argument map of {3}, and the resulting program in Figure 2.11 has an argument map of {2}.

Since argument deletion by consolidation involves two arguments (i.e., the argument-to-be-deleted and the surviving argument), it is necessary that the picked branch have at least two arguments. Thus, when argument deletion by consolidation is being used and the picked function-defining branch has less than two arguments, this operation is aborted.

It is often advisable to set a minimum permissible number of arguments for any function. For example, in a problem involving Boolean functions and no side effects, there are only four possible Boolean functions of one argument, so it may be more efficient to exclude such one-argument functions for a Boolean problem. If this approach is adopted, whenever the picked function-defining branch has less than three arguments, the operation of argument deletion is aborted.

5.6.2 Argument Deletion with Random Regeneration

When the second alternative (argument deletion with random regeneration) is being used, a new subtree is randomly generated in lieu of an invocation of the argument-to-be-deleted using the same method of generation originally used to create the picked branch at the time of creation of the initial random population (with the argument-to-be-deleted being unavailable during this random regeneration). The subtree may consist of either a single available terminal or an entire generated argument subtree composed of the available functions and terminals.

5.6.3 Argument Deletion by Macro Expansion

When the third alternative (argument deletion by macro expansion) is used, the first step is to delete the argument-to-be-deleted from the argument list of the picked branch. The second step is then to create as many copies of the now-modified picked branch as there are invocations of the picked branch in the overall program (e.g., in the result-producing branch or other branches) and to give each such copy of the picked branch a unique name. The third step is to replace each invocation of the picked branch in the overall program with an invocation to a particular one of the uniquely named copies of the now-modified picked branch. The fourth step is, for each uniquely named copy of the now-modified picked branch, to insert the argument subtree corresponding to the argument-to-be-deleted for every occurrence of the argument-to-be-deleted in that particular copy.

Argument deletion by macro expansion has the characteristic of preserving the semantics of the overall program. It has the disadvantage of usually creating a vast number of additional branches and large overall programs. Of course, to the extent that the objective of a deletion is to change the semantics of the overall program (i.e., to achieve generalization), this alternative defeats that objective.

5.7   IMPLEMENTATION ISSUES FOR AN ARCHITECTURALLY DIVERSE POPULATION

When the architecture-altering operations are used in a run of genetic programming, there is a proliferation of different architectures in the population. This section describes two implementation issues associated with architecturally diverse populations:

- the method of creating the initial random population (Section 5.7.1) and
- the modifications required to the crossover operation (Section 5.7.2).

5.7.1   Creation of an Architecturally Diverse Initial Population

The initial random population of programs may be created in any one of several possible ways when the architecture-altering operations are being used. One possibility is that each program in the initial population has a uniform architecture with no automatically defined functions at all (i.e., each program consists of only a result-producing branch). In this approach, the argument map of every individual in generation 0 is the bare minimum, namely, {}. When this approach is used, the operation of subroutine creation must be used to create function-defining branches. In order to accelerate the appearance of automatically defined functions in the population, the operation of subroutine creation is often used with an abnormally high frequency on generation 0 or the first few generations of the run (where it is called the "big bang"). In later generations, the operation of subroutine creation is used sparingly.

A second possibility is that each multipart program in the initial random population at generation 0 has a uniform architecture with exactly one automatically defined function possessing a minimal number of arguments. For example, for a problem involving floating-point variables, the argument map of every individual in generation 0 might uniformly be {}. A zero-argument automatically defined function is effectively a vehicle for storing a constant. It resembles (but differs from) a "let" or a "set" in LISP. A zero-argument automatically defined function is minimally useful for problems involving floating-point variables. For a problem involving Boolean functions, the argument map of every individual in generation 0 might be {1} since there are only four one-argument Boolean functions (two of which are constant) and they all are minimally useful in solving problems.

A third possibility is that the population at generation 0 is architecturally diverse. This approach is mandatory with the technique of evolutionary selection of the architecture (Koza 1994g, Chapter 21) and is optional with the architecture-altering operations. In this approach, the creation of an individual program in the initial random population begins with a random choice of the number of automatically defined functions, if any, that will belong to the program. Then a series of independent random choices is made for the number of arguments possessed by *each* automatically defined function, if any, in the program. All of these random choices are made within a wide range that includes every number that might reasonably be thought to be useful for the problem at hand.

Zero is included in the range of choices for the number of automatically defined functions, so the initial random population also includes some programs without any automatically defined functions. Once the number of automatically defined functions is chosen for a particular overall program, the automatically defined functions, if any, are systematically named in the usual sequential manner from left to right.

The range of possibly useful numbers of arguments for the automatically defined functions cannot, in general, be predicted with certainty for an arbitrary problem. There are occasional problems involving only a few actual variables where it is useful to have an automatically defined function that takes a large number of arguments. However, most problem-solving efforts focus primarily on solving problems by decomposing them into problems of lower dimensionality. Accordingly, it is often reasonable to cap the range of the number of arguments for each automatically defined function by the number of actual variables of the problem. There is no guarantee that this cap (motivated by an expectation of decomposing the problem) or any other cap is necessarily optimal, desirable, or sufficient to solve a given problem. In any event, practical considerations concerning computer resources frequently play a controlling role in setting the upper bound on the number of arguments to be permitted.

Similarly, the range of potentially useful numbers of automatically defined functions cannot, in general, be predicted in advance for an arbitrary problem. The number of potentially useful automatically defined functions is not necessarily less than the dimensionality of the problem. However, once again, considerations of computer resources play a controlling role in setting the upper bound on the allowed number of automatically defined functions. In practice, the allowed number of automatically defined functions is typically capped by the number of actual variables of the problem.

In practice, a zero-argument automatically defined function may or may not be a meaningful option for a given problem. In problems involving floating-point or integral numbers, it may be useful to include zero-argument automatically defined function(s) to house an evolvable constant that can then be repeatedly called from elsewhere in the overall program. However, in the special case of the Boolean domain, the two possible Boolean constants (T or NIL) have negligible usefulness because all compositions of these two constants merely evaluate to one of these two values. If an automatically defined function has no access to the actual variables of the problem, has no dummy variables, does not contain any side-effecting primitive functions, and does not contain any random constants, nothing is available to serve as terminals (leaves) of the program tree in the body of such a zero-argument automatically defined function.

Random choices occurring during the creation of the initial random population determine whether the body of any particular function-defining branch of any particular program in the population actually hierarchically calls all, none, or some of the automatically defined functions that it is theoretically permitted to call. Subsequent crossovers during the run may, of course, change the body of a particular function-defining branch and thereby change the automatically defined functions that a branch actually calls hierarchically. Thus, the function-defining branches have the ability to organize themselves into arbitrary disjoint hierarchies of dependencies among the available automatically defined functions. For example, within an overall program with five automatically defined functions at generation 0, ADF4 might actually refer only to ADF2 and

ADF3, with ADF2 and ADF3 not referring at all to either ADF0 or ADF1. Meanwhile, ADF1 might refer only to ADF0. In this situation, there would be two disjoint hierarchies of dependencies. A subsequent crossover might change this organization. For example, after such a crossover, ADF3 might refer to ADF0, but still not to ADF1, thereby establishing a different hierarchy of dependencies. A wide variety of hierarchical dependencies may thus be created during the evolutionary process.

5.7.2   Structure-Preserving Crossover with Point Typing

In the crossover operation in genetic programming, a crossover point is randomly and independently chosen in each of two parents, and genetic material from one parent is then inserted into a part of the other parent to create an offspring.

A population may be architecturally diverse either because it is initially created with architectural diversity or because the architecture-altering operations create a diversity of new architectures during the run. If the population is architecturally diverse, the parents selected to participate in the crossover operation will usually possess different numbers of automatically defined functions. Moreover, an automatically defined function with a certain name (e.g., ADF2) belonging to one parent will often possess a different number of arguments than the same-named automatically defined function belonging to the other parent (if indeed ADF2 is present at all). After a crossover is performed, each call to an automatically defined function actually appearing in the crossover fragment from the contributing parent will no longer refer to the automatically defined function of the contributing parent, but instead will refer to the same-named automatically defined function of the receiving parent. Thus, the crossover operation must be modified when it is employed in an architecturally diverse population.

In the implementation of genetic programming exemplified throughout most of Koza 1992e, no syntactic constraints are involved in constructing individual programs in the population (except, arguably, the constraint as to the overall size of the program measured in terms of the depth of the program tree or in terms of the total number of points in the program tree). Subject only to the size limit established for generation 0, any function from the function set of the problem and any terminal from the terminal set may appear at any point in a program during the initial random creation of programs in generation 0. Because of the closure property for the function and terminal sets, the crossover operation produces a structurally valid offspring regardless of what points are chosen as crossover points from the two parents (subject only to the size limit established for offspring).

When automatically defined functions are involved, each program in the population conforms to a constrained syntactic structure (such as shown in Figure 2.11) that distinguishes between the result-producing branch, the function-defining branches (automatically defined functions), the topmost connective PROGN, the DEFUN associated with each automatically defined function, the name of each automatically defined function, the argument list of each automatically defined function, and the VALUES function of each automatically defined function. The initial random population is created in accordance with this constrained syntactic structure. Crossover must be performed so as to preserve the structural validity of all offspring. For example, an overall program consisting of a result-producing branch and automatically defined function(s) has the following points that constitute the fixed structure of the program:

- the topmost connective PROGN,
- the DEFUN associated with each automatically defined function (under the PROGN),
- the name of each automatically defined function (under the DEFUN),
- the argument list of each automatically defined function (under the DEFUN),
- the VALUES function of each automatically defined function (under the DEFUN), and
- the VALUES function of the result-producing branch (under the PROGN).

The points constituting the fixed structure of the overall program are never eligible to be chosen as crossover points and are never altered by crossover. Instead, structure-preserving crossover is restricted to the points in the bodies of the various branches of the overall program.

In structure-preserving crossover, each point in the body of each branch is assigned a type. Types may be assigned in several different ways (as described below). The type of a point is based on either the functions and terminals that are allowed to occur in the branch in which the particular point resides or on the functions and terminals that actually appear in the subtree rooted at the particular point.

In structure-preserving crossover, any point in the body of any branch of the overall program may be chosen, without restriction, as the crossover point of the first parent. The type of the chosen point is then ascertained. Once the type of the crossover point of the first parent is ascertained, the choice of the crossover point in the second parent is restricted (as described below).

The typing of the points in the bodies of the branches of the overall program constrains the set of subtrees that can potentially replace the chosen crossover point and the subtree below it. This typing is done so that the structure-preserving crossover operation will always produce structurally valid offspring.

There are several ways of assigning types to the points in the bodies of the branches of the overall program, including

- branch typing,
- like-branch typing, and
- point typing.

Branch typing assigns a separate type to each separate branch of the overall program. When branch typing is used, the number of types of points equals the number of branches in the program. All the points in each branch are assigned the same type. For example, if a program has two automatically defined functions (ADF0 and ADF1) and one result-producing branch (RPB), separate types are assigned to ADF0, ADF1, and RPB. Branch typing is the approach used almost exclusively in *Genetic Programming* and *Genetic Programming II*.

Like-branch typing assigns the same type to all points in branches that share the same function and terminal sets. When like-branch typing is used, the number of types of points is typically less than (but, in any event, does not exceed) the number of branches in the program. All the points in each branch are assigned the same type. Like-branch typing is the same as branch typing, except if the function sets and terminal sets of two or more branches are identical in every respect (including the arity of the functions), all the points of such branches are assigned the same type. Note that the assignment is based on the function and terminal sets of the branches (i.e., the allowable functions and terminals in the branches), not the functions and terminals that actually appear in the branches. Like-branch typing is used when a problem has a multiplicity of similar automatically defined functions. For example, branch typing could reasonably have been used for the five feature detectors of the letter recognition problem of Chapter 15 of *Genetic Programming II* because all five branches shared a common function and terminal set, although it was not actually used on that problem.

Point typing assigns a type to each point in the body of each branch. The type reflects the actual contents of the subtree rooted at the point (i.e., not the allowable contents). Because the contents of the actual subtree starting at the point are relevant in determining if the subtree may be inserted at a particular point of another program in an architecturally diverse population, point typing facilitates genetic recombination in an architecturally diverse population. The type of a point in a branch of an overall program is obtained by flattening the subtree starting at the point (i.e., creating a list of the names of all functions and terminals in the subtree using LISP's FLATTEN function or its equivalent). Each function name in the list is then converted to an ordered pair consisting of the function name and the arity of that particular occurrence of the function (thereby making, for example, a two-argument addition function distinct from a three-argument addition function). Duplicates are then removed from this list of ordered pairs. As can be seen, when point typing is used, the number of distinct types of points is typically large. Point typing is described in detail in Section 21.2 of *Genetic Programming II* and used in Chapters 21–25 of *Genetic Programming II*. Point typing is used throughout this book for all problems involving the architecture-altering operations.

When all the programs in the population have a common architecture, any of the three methods of typing may be used in conjunction with the crossover operation. In practice, branch typing is most commonly used. However, when the population is architecturally diverse, point typing is usually used. If a program is subject to any additional problem-specific constrained syntactic structure, that additional structure must also be respected and preserved in performing structure-preserving crossover.

When point typing is used, the crossover operation acquires a directionality that did not exist with branch typing or like-branch typing. A distinction must be made between the contributing (male) parent and the receiving (female) parent. Consequently, single-offspring crossover is used with point typing. That is, the crossover operation for point typing starts with two parents, but produces only one offspring.

In single-offspring structure-preserving crossover with point typing, a point anywhere in the body of some branch of the contributing (male) parent is randomly chosen, without restriction. The crossover point of the receiving (female) parent (sometimes called the *point of insertion*) must be chosen from the set of points for which the crossover fragment from the contributing parent may be inserted without violating the constrained syntactic structure of the receiving parent. When genetic material is inserted into the receiving parent during structure-preserving crossover with point typing, the offspring inherits its architecture from the receiving parent (the maternal line).

Point typing is governed by three general principles:

1. Every terminal and function actually appearing in the crossover fragment from the contributing parent must be in the terminal set or function set of the branch of the receiving parent containing the point of insertion.
2. The number of arguments of every function actually appearing in the crossover fragment from the contributing parent must equal the number of arguments specified for the same-named function in the argument map of the branch of the receiving parent containing the insertion point. This requirement applies to all functions. This name-based requirement is especially pertinent to automatically defined functions, automatically defined iterations, automatically defined loops, automatically defined recursions, and automatically defined stores because the same function name (e.g., ADF0) is used to represent entirely different entities (with different numbers of arguments) in different individuals in the population.
3. All additional problem-specific syntactic rules of construction, if any, must be satisfied.

Additional details on structure-preserving crossover with point typing can be found in *Genetic Programming II* (Koza 1994g).

Each of the comments made above concerning the implementation of structure-preserving crossover for a function-defining branch defined by a DEFUN apply to automatically defined iterations defined by a DEFITERATE (Section 6.1.3), automatically defined loops defined by a DEFLOOP (Section 7.1), and automatically defined recursions defined by a DEFRECURSION (Chapter 8). For example, the following points in a program tree that are associated with a DEFITERATE associated with an automatically defined iteration are ineligible to be chosen as a crossover point:

- the DEFITERATE itself,
- the name of the automatically defined iteration (e.g., ADI0),
- the argument list of the automatically defined iteration, and
- the VALUES associated with the iteration-performing branch of the automatically defined iteration.

Structure-preserving crossover with point typing permits reasonably unrestrained recombination while simultaneously guaranteeing that any pair of architecturally different parents will produce structurally valid offspring. In addition, when the architecture-altering operations are being used, structure-preserving crossover with point typing enables the architecture appropriate for solving the problem to be evolved during a run while the problem is being solved, in the sense of actually changing the architecture of programs in the population dynamically during the run.

Automatically Defined Iterations

Subroutines are extremely useful in computer programming because

- subroutines reuse code,
- there is usually a high degree of generality in the code found in the body of a subroutine, and
- the benefit of an improvement made to the body of a subroutine is automatically conferred on every part of the overall program that calls the subroutine.

Code reuse is important because it obviates the necessity of repeatedly rewriting code to solve an already-solved subproblem. Reuse facilitates problem solving because evermore complex problems can be solved by leveraging already-obtained solutions to subproblems. We believe that code reuse is the essential precondition for achieving scalability in a system for automatically creating computer programs.

Code reuse goes hand in hand with generality. Because a subroutine's steps are repeatedly executed (often with different instantiations of the subroutine's dummy variables), there is usually a high degree of generality to the steps of a subroutine.

Code reuse is especially advantageous in an adaptive process. If the code within a subroutine is incrementally improved, the benefit of the improvement is leveraged because it is automatically conferred on all parts of the overall program that invoke the improved subroutine. It is not necessary to independently reinvent the improvement for each part of the overall program where it may be useful.

One of the main points of *Genetic Programming II: Automatic Discovery of Reusable Programs* (Koza 1994g) is that the automatic creation of computer programs by genetic programming can be accelerated by exploiting the reuse inherent in subroutines (i.e., automatically defined functions).

Iterations are similar to subroutines in that

- iterations reuse code,
- there is usually a high degree of generality in the code in the body of an iteration, and
- the benefit of an improvement made to the body of an iteration is realized on every occasion that the body of the iteration is executed.

6.1   ITERATIONS

In its most general form, an iteration consists of four elements:

- an initialization step,
- a continuation (or termination) condition,
- a body, and
- an update step.

An iteration starts with the execution of an initialization step. In one frequently used implementation of an iteration, the continuation condition is then tested. If the continuation condition is satisfied, the body of the iteration is executed. Then, an update step of the iteration is executed. After that, the last three elements (i.e., the continuation condition, the body of the iteration, and the update step) are repeatedly executed while the continuation condition is satisfied.

For example, the code for computing the average of the numbers stored in a vector V of length LEN might be written in the C programming language using a `for` loop as follows:

```
M0 = 0;
for (i = 0; i < LEN; i++)
{
   M0 = M0 + V[i];
}
AVERAGE = M0 / LEN;
```

In this program, the variable M0 is first set to 0. The iteration is implemented in C by the `for` statement. The initialization step of the `for` loop consists of setting the index i to 0. The continuation condition of the `for` loop consists of testing whether i < LEN. In C, the body of the `for` loop (located between the opening and closing brackets) is executed if the continuation condition is satisfied (i.e., i < LEN). The body here consists of computing a running sum that increments the variable M0 by the ith element of the vector V. The index i is used to access the ith element of the vector V. The update step of the `for` loop is then executed. The update step sets the index i to i + 1. This incrementation is written in C by writing i++ in the `for` statement. After completion of the `for` loop, the AVERAGE is computed by dividing the accumulated running sum M0 by LEN.

There are numerous alternative ways of structuring an iteration. For example, some iterations employ a termination condition instead of a continuation condition. Also, the update step and the continuation test might be consolidated into the body, or the update step might be placed in a different location relative to the body of the iteration.

6.1.1   Rationing Resources for Iterations

As every computer programmer knows, the inclusion of even one iteration in a computer program creates the possibility of an infinite loop. In genetic programming, the programs in the initial population are typically created at random. In addition, the programs in later generations of a run are the offspring of operations containing one or more random steps. When iteration is permitted in evolving populations of computer programs, the vicissitudes of these random operations virtually guarantee the creation of some infinite loops (as well as the creation of some exceedingly time-consuming noninfinite loops). Therefore, when iterations are permitted, it is a practical necessity to impose some mechanism for rationing the computer resources that may be consumed by iterations.

This rationing may be implemented in numerous ways. For example, the rationing may be in the form of a straightforward time-out limit based on a maximum number of executions (or a maximum amount of computer time) consumed by a single iteration in a program. This rationing can be extended to deal with the effects of multiple iterations or nested iterations by imposing an additional independent limit based on a maximum cumulative number of executions (or a maximum cumulative amount of computer time) consumed by all iterations in a given program.

Rationing may also be implemented by allocating computer time in a round-robin fashion to various individuals in the evolving population (Maxwell 1994). This approach eliminates the arbitrariness of time-out limits (which genetic programming sometimes shamelessly exploits in fashioning a solution). However, to properly implement the round-robin approach, the amount of time allocated to each program must be judiciously decreased as the run of genetic programming proceeds so that the population does not become progressively overrun with programs with infinite (or very time-consuming) loops.

6.1.2   Memory and Iterations

Unless an iteration operates solely through side-effecting functions (e.g., robotic actions), it is necessary to have an avenue for communicating information between the iteration and other parts of a program. This communication can be accomplished in several different ways.

The value returned by the last execution of the body of the iteration is one avenue for communicating information between the iteration and the other branches of the overall program. However, since only a single value is returned, this approach is of limited usefulness.

Memory provides a far more flexible avenue for communicating information between the iteration and other parts of a program. Memory is implemented in genetic programming by various functions and terminals for reading and writing memory. During the iteration, one or more values may be written to memory. The communication may be to or from the iteration. For example, after an iteration is executed, another branch of the program may read the values that were produced and stored by the iteration. Or, prior to execution of an iteration, another branch of the program (possibly another iterative branch) may write values into the memory. The iteration may read the values that were produced and stored by the other branch.

Memory can be implemented in genetic programming in numerous ways. Named memory (Koza 1992e, 1994g) is the simplest kind of memory used in genetic programming. In this approach, information is stored in a named (settable) variable. The variables are given names such as M0, M1, M2, . . . in this approach. The value of the variable is set using a setting function that is specifically associated with the particular named variable.

The one-argument memory-setting function, SETM0, writes the value of its argument into the named memory cell M0. For example,

```
(SETM0 (+ X Y))
```

side-effects memory cell M0 by setting it to the sum of X and Y. The return value of the SETM0 function is the value it just wrote to M0.

An additional uniquely named memory-setting function is required for each additional cell of named memory (e.g., SETM1 for M1, SETM2 for M2). Named memory is read by simply referring to the appropriate named (settable) variable (e.g., the terminals M0, M1, M2, . . .). Named memory has the disadvantage of requiring a separate uniquely named function and a separate uniquely named terminal for each cell of named memory. Since the distinguishing parts of the names (e.g., 0, 1, 2, . . .) are not themselves variables, the different cells of named memory cannot be referenced with a parameter.

Indexed memory (Teller 1994a, 1994b) alleviates this limitation of named memory. Indexed memory consists of a linear vector of memory cells that are addressed by a single indexing variable.

Indexed memory is implemented by a reading function and a writing function. Specifically, the WIM ("write indexed memory") function is a two-argument function that writes the value returned by the first argument into the location of indexed memory specified by the second argument. The return value of a WIM function is the value it writes. For example, if there are 20 cells of indexed memory,

```
(WIM (+ X Y) 17)
```

side-effects location 17 of indexed memory by setting it to the sum of X and Y. The second argument is adjusted by flooring it (i.e., reducing it to the largest integer less than or equal to it) and then taking it modulo the size (NINDEXED) of the indexed memory. Thus, if there are 20 cells of indexed memory,

```
(WIM (+ X Y) 37)
```

also side-effects location 17 of indexed memory.

The RIM ("read indexed memory") function is a one-argument function that returns the value of the element of the vector of indexed memory specified by the argument (adjusted in the same manner as above based on the size of the indexed memory). For example, (RIM 57) returns the value currently stored in location 17 of indexed memory.

Matrix memory (Andre 1994b) involves a two-dimensional array of memory cells that are addressed by a pair of indexing variables. Higher-dimensional memory arrays can be similarly defined.

Other more powerful forms of memory include data structures such as stacks, queues, and lists (Langdon 1995, 1996a, 1996c, 1998). Brave (1995a, 1996c) has implemented relational memory in genetic programming.

6.1.3 Iterations over a Finite Sequence, Vector, or Array

For certain problems, it may be reasonable to consider a restricted form of iteration that makes a single pass over a preestablished, problem-specific finite sequence, vector, or array. Rationing can be implemented in a very unobtrusive way for such problems. For example, in economic time series problems, it is common to perform an iterative calculation over a certain known finite number of discrete time steps (representing perhaps days, months, quarters, or years). In protein or genomic sequence problems, it is often natural to perform an iteration over a given sequence of amino acid residues or nucleotide bases. In many discrete-time signal-processing problems (and many continuous-time problems employing discrete-time sampling), a one-dimensional iteration over a finite sequence of time steps may be useful. In two-dimensional pattern recognition or computer vision problems, it is often useful to perform an iterative calculation over a given two-dimensional array of pixels, or perhaps a particular subarray of pixels.

The remainder of this chapter is devoted to iteration-performing branches that make a single pass over a preestablished, problem-specific finite sequence, vector, or array. When such restricted iterations are appropriate, three of the four elements of a general iteration (namely, the initialization step, the continuation condition, and the update step) become fixed so that they are not subject to evolutionary modification during the run of genetic programming. This approach immediately eliminates the possibility of infinite loops (as well as excessively time-consuming loops). Moreover, since the size of the sequence, vector, or array is known, it is usually possible to compute a reasonably accurate estimate or bound on the amount of computer time that will be consumed by the iteration.

Automatically defined iterations provide a mechanism by which genetic programming can iteratively execute certain steps for each element in a preestablished sequence, vector, or array. An automatically defined iteration (ADI) consists of an iteration-performing branch, the body of which is subject to evolutionary modification during the run of genetic programming. A fixed structure (not subject to evolutionary modification) causes the iteration-performing branch of an automatically defined iteration to be executed one time for each element in a preestablished sequence, vector, or array.

An automatically defined iteration resembles an automatically defined function in that it has a name (allowing it to be invoked in the same manner as any other function), an argument list (which may or may not be empty), and a body. An automatically defined iteration differs from an automatically defined function in that the body of the automatically defined iteration is, in general, executed multiple times for a single invocation of the automatically defined iteration.

An automatically defined iteration may be called from a result-producing branch, an automatically defined function, an automatically defined loop (Chapter 7), an automatically defined recursion (Chapter 8), or another automatically defined iteration. For example, when an expression such as

```
(ADI2 ARG0 ARG1)
```

is encountered during the execution of a program, the iteration-performing branch of the automatically defined iteration ADI2 is repeatedly executed for each member of the preestablished finite sequence, vector, or array. During the execution of the iteration-performing branch of ADI2, the values of the two dummy variables (formal parameters), ARG0 and ARG1, of ADI2 are available to the iteration-performing branch. The value returned by the above expression is the value returned by the last execution of the iteration-performing branch.

The overall program may contain arbitrarily many automatically defined iterations (up to some preestablished limit), each possessing arbitrarily many arguments (again, up to a preestablished limit). A computer program may potentially contain nested automatically defined iterations (subject to a preestablished limit on the depth of nesting).

In genetic programming, external input(s) are often supplied to a computer program by means of terminals that are instantiated with different values of the input variables. In some programs employing automatically defined iterations, it may be appropriate for the preestablished sequence, vector, or array to be the program's input. Examples include the sequence of amino acid residues in a protein sequence, the sequence of nucleotide bases of a genomic sequence, the sequence of values of an economic variable, and the sequence of values of a signal at various times, t. For these problems, it is often useful or convenient to define a special terminal that returns the ith value of the sequence, vector, or array (or some other value directly derived from the ith value) during the ith execution of the iteration-performing branch.

Figure 6.1 shows an example of a multipart program consisting of one result-producing branch in the right part of the figure and one automatically defined iteration, ADI0, in the left part of the figure. The subtree rooted at VALUES 214 constitutes the iteration-performing branch, IPB, of this automatically defined iteration. This illustrative overall program computes the numerical average of a set of numbers stored in a vector of length LEN. The topmost function of the overall program is PROGN (labeled 200). A PROGN sequentially executes its arguments and returns only the value of its final argument. An automatically defined iteration is defined by a DEFITERATE. The DEFITERATE of an automatically defined iteration resembles the DEFUN that defines an automatically defined function (Section 2.3.6). This definitional process enables the automatically defined iteration to be invoked by other branches of the overall program. Execution of the DEFITERATE 211 returns nothing of interest to PROGN 200. The automatically defined iteration has a name, ADI0. If ADI0 212 possesses arguments, the arguments appear under the LIST 213; however, the automatically defined iteration in this figure possesses no arguments and hence no dummy variables appear. The topmost PROGN 200 then proceeds to execute VALUES 221 in the right part of the figure. This VALUES executes PROGN 234. PROGN 234 begins by invoking zero-argument ADI0 235. The call to ADI0 causes the iteration-performing branch (i.e., the steps under the VALUES 214 of ADI0) to be iteratively executed once for each member of the preestablished vector of LEN numbers. On each of the executions of the iteration-performing branch, the terminal V returns the ith value of the vector of length LEN. Each execution of the iteration-performing branch takes the current value of the named memory (settable variable) M0 (which is initially zero), adds M0 to the value of the terminal V, and uses the setting function SETM0 237 to set M0 to the just-incremented running sum. After the LEN executions of the iteration-performing branch, the iteration is complete. The return value at ADI0 235 in the result-producing branch is ignored because PROGN 234 returns only the value of its final argument. The result-producing branch divides the accumulated running sum contained in memory cell M0 by LEN to obtain the numerical average. PROGN 234 then returns the result of protected division % 236 (Section 13.3.2) to the VALUES 221 of the result-producing branch. This value becomes the value returned by the overall program (i.e., the topmost PROGN 200). The cell of named memory, M0, is the avenue of communication from the iteration-performing branch of the automatically defined iteration to the result-producing branch.

There are numerous alternative ways in which an automatically defined iteration can be used to perform this same calculation. For example, since the return value of ADI0 happens to be equal to M0, ADI0 (instead of M0) can be referenced in the result-

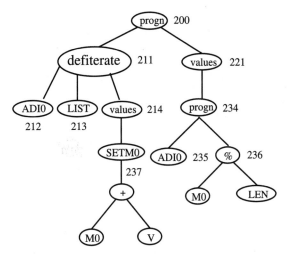

Figure 6.1 Illustrative program with an automatically defined iteration (ADI0) and a result-producing branch

producing branch in this particular example. That is, the entire result-producing branch can be reduced to merely

```
(% (ADI0) LEN)
```

instead of

```
(PROGN (ADI0) (% M0 LEN)).
```

As another (somewhat inefficient) example, the division can be repeatedly performed as the topmost step of the iteration-performing branch. That is, the iteration-performing branch can be

```
(% (SETM0 (+ M0 V)) LEN)
```

and the result-producing branch can be simply

```
(ADI0).
```

Upon completion of the iteration, the return value of the result-producing branch is the desired average.

If an iteration-performing branch (say, ADI2) happens to contain a reference to another automatically defined iteration (say, ADI1), then ADI1 is executed when the reference to ADI1 is encountered in ADI2, thereby creating a nested iteration.

When using iterations, it is often convenient to introduce an explicit indexing terminal (called INDEX) that counts the number of executions of the iteration.

The user can make automatically defined iterations available for solving a problem either by

- prespecifying the architecture of the overall program (i.e., by performing an additional architecture-defining preparatory step), or

- using architecture-altering operations (Section 6.2) to enable genetic programming to automatically create the automatically defined iterations for the overall program dynamically during the run.

6.1.4 Simplified Version of the Automatically Defined Iteration

Because of limited computer resources, only a constrained form of automatically defined iteration is used in this book. In this simplified model, each automatically defined iteration is executed exactly once prior to execution of the result-producing branch. Then the result-producing branch is executed once. Thus, in this simplified model, the appearance of the name of an automatically defined iteration (e.g., ADI2) in a program does not cause the execution of the iteration. Instead, ADI2 merely returns the appropriate value from the already-executed iteration (i.e., the value of the last execution of the iteration-performing branch).

Specifically, in the simplified model for automatically defined iterations:

- There may be multiple automatically defined iterations in a program (up to some preestablished limit).
- The automatically defined iterations are each invoked once prior to the invocation of the single result-producing branch.
- The return value of an automatically defined iteration is available to the result-producing branch as a terminal.
- The automatically defined iterations do not possess arguments.
- The automatically defined iterations may contain references to automatically defined functions, and the automatically defined functions may refer to one another hierarchically.
- The automatically defined iterations may contain functions and terminals that read and write memory.
- The result-producing branch has access to memory (which may have been written during the execution of the automatically defined iterations).
- There are no nested automatically defined iterations; however, an automatically defined iteration may access the value returned by already-executed automatically defined iterations as well as whatever may have been written into memory by already-executed automatically defined iterations.

The execution of an overall program in this simplified model consists of the following steps:

1. For each fitness case, all locations of all types of memory are initialized to zero.
2. If the overall program contains an automatically defined iteration, ADI0, its iteration-performing branch is executed once for each member of the problem-specific preestablished finite sequence, vector, or array. The return value of the automatically defined iteration consists of the value returned by the last execution of its iteration-performing branch and is available to the result-producing branch as a terminal (called IPB0 or ADI0).
3. If the overall program contains additional automatically defined iterations (e.g., ADI1, ADI2, . . .), they are each executed once in the same manner as step 2.
4. The result-producing branch, RPB, is executed once.

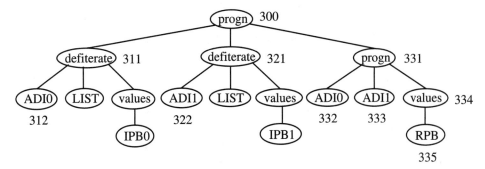

Figure 6.2 Simplified model of program with two automatically defined iterations, `ADI0` and `ADI1`

5. If an automatically defined function appears in an iteration-performing branch, the result-producing branch, or an automatically defined function, it is executed at the time when it is encountered in the usual way.

6. If an iteration index (INDEX) is being used, it is externally initialized to zero at the beginning of execution of a program and prior to the first execution of the iteration-performing branch. It is externally incremented by one after each execution of the iteration-performing branch.

Figure 6.2 illustrates this simplified model with two automatically defined iterations, ADI0 and ADI1. The execution of the first two arguments (i.e., DEFITERATE 311 and DEFITERATE 321) of PROGN 300 does not return anything interesting. The execution of the third argument of PROGN 300 (that is, PROGN 331 at the second level of the hierarchy) first causes the first automatically defined iteration (ADI0 332) to be executed once. The continuation of the execution of PROGN 331 then causes the second automatically defined iteration (ADI1 333) to be executed once. The values returned by ADI0 332 and ADI1 333 are ignored by PROGN 331. The continuation of the execution of PROGN 331 then causes the execution of VALUES 334, which, in turn, causes the execution of the entire result-producing branch RPB 335. The value returned by PROGN 331 (and hence the value returned by topmost PROGN 300) is the value returned via VALUES 334 from the execution of the result-producing branch, RPB 335.

6.2   ARCHITECTURE-ALTERING OPERATIONS FOR AUTOMATICALLY DEFINED ITERATIONS

When first looking at a problem, it is usually not obvious whether an automatically defined iteration will prove to be necessary, helpful, or useless in solving the problem. If iterations are useful, it is usually not obvious whether a particular problem requires one, two, or more automatically defined iterations. Even when the needed number of iterations is known, the precise sequence of steps within the body of each iteration-performing branch must be discovered. Therefore, it would be desirable to automate the decision as to how many times, if ever, to employ automatically defined iterations in solving a problem (along with the related decision of exactly what iterative computation to perform).

This automation can be realized by using architecture-altering operations for automatically defined iterations. In particular, automatically defined iterations and their arguments may be created, duplicated, or deleted using architecture-altering operations that are analogous to the operations applicable to automatically defined functions (Chapter 5). We first describe an architecture-altering operation analogous to subroutine creation (Section 5.3) for introducing an automatically defined iteration into a program. Chapter 17 illustrates the use of this new operation of iteration creation.

6.2.1   Iteration Creation

The architecture-altering operation of iteration creation operates on one individual in the population selected probabilistically on the basis of fitness. It creates one new offspring program for the new population by adding one new automatically defined iteration containing an iteration-performing branch consisting of a portion of an existing branch. A program with k branches begets a program with $k + 1$ branches. The operation also creates a DEFITERATE for the newly created iteration-performing branch, a unique name for the new automatically defined iteration, an argument list for the automatically defined iteration, and an invoking reference to the new automatically defined iteration. The automatically defined iteration may or may not possess arguments. The steps of the operation of iteration creation resemble those of subroutine creation:

1. Select, based on fitness, an individual program from the population to participate in this operation. A copy is first made of the selected program and the operation is then performed on the copy. Thus, the original selected program remains unchanged in the population and is therefore available to be reselected for another operation.
2. Randomly pick one of the branches of the selected program. If the selected program has only one branch, that branch is automatically picked. The picking of the branch may, as an option, be restricted to a result-producing branch or other specified category of branches.
3. Randomly choose a point in the picked branch of the selected program. This chosen point will become the topmost point of the body of the to-be-created iteration-performing branch of the automatically defined iteration.
4. Add a uniquely named new iteration-performing branch to the selected program consisting of the subtree rooted at the chosen point, thus increasing the number of iteration-performing branches in the selected program by one.
5. Replace the chosen point in the picked branch by the name of the newly created automatically defined iteration.
6. The terminal set of the newly created iteration-performing branch is identical to that of the picked branch. The function set of the newly created iteration-performing branch is identical to the function set of the picked branch. The function set of the picked branch is unchanged. The terminal set of the picked branch is enlarged to include the name of the newly created iteration-performing branch. The function set of any branch in the program whose function set includes the picked branch (i.e., any branch that actually calls the picked branch or that is permitted to call the picked branch) is enlarged to include the name of the newly created iteration-performing branch. The terminal set of any branch in the program whose function set includes the picked branch is not affected by this operation.

The operation of iteration creation is, in general, not semantics-preserving.

There are several parameters for controlling the operation of iteration creation.

1. The iteration creation operation is controlled by a parameter specifying the probability of executing the operation on each generation, $p_{\text{iteration-creation}}$.
2. There is a maximum size, S_{adi}, for each iteration-performing branch.
3. There is a maximum number of automatically defined iterations, $N_{\text{max-adi}}$, for each program.
4. The iteration creation operation is controlled by a parameter specifying the maximum number of arguments for the newly created iteration-performing branch of the automatically defined iteration, $N_{\text{max-argument-adi}}$. If this maximum is greater than zero, the branch acquires arguments in the same manner as for the subroutine creation operation.
5. The terminal INDEX may be included in the terminal set of the iteration-performing branch of the automatically defined iteration (and other branches of the overall program) so that it is available as an ingredient for the evolving programs.

Iteration creation deepens the hierarchy of references in a computer program. The new iteration-performing branch consists of a subtree that was formerly executed (usually once) in its original location in the picked branch of a program selected on the basis of fitness. Moving such a subtree into an iteration-performing branch sets up an experimental trial, during the run of genetic programming, as to whether iteratively executing that particular subtree (over the preestablished problem-specific sequence, vector, or array) is beneficial to the overall effort to solve the given problem. Repeated execution of a particular subtree may be detrimental, neutral, or beneficial.

The new operation of iteration creation is demonstrated later in this book by applying it to the transmembrane segment identification problem (Chapter 17).

6.2.2 Iteration Duplication

Automatically defined iterations may be duplicated using an architecture-altering operation analogous to subroutine duplication. A program with k branches begets an offspring program with $k + 1$ branches.

The operation of iteration duplication operates on one individual in the population selected probabilistically on the basis of fitness. It creates one new offspring program for the new population by duplicating the automatically defined iteration of the selected program and creating invocations of the newly created automatically defined iteration. The duplicated automatically defined iteration is executed over the same problem-specific sequence, vector, or array as the original automatically defined iteration. The steps of this operation resemble those of subroutine duplication of automatically defined functions:

1. Select, based on fitness, an individual program from the population to participate in this operation.
2. Pick one of the iteration-performing branches of the selected program as the branch-to-be-duplicated. If the selected program has only one iteration-performing branch, that branch is automatically picked. If the selected program has no iteration-performing branches (or already has the maximum number of iteration-performing branches established for the problem), this operation is aborted.

3. Add a uniquely named new automatically defined iteration to the selected program, thus increasing the number of automatically defined iterations in the selected program by one. The newly created automatically defined iteration has the same argument list and the same body as the branch-to-be-duplicated.

4. For each occurrence of an invocation of the branch-to-be-duplicated anywhere in the selected program, randomly choose either to leave that invocation unchanged or to replace that invocation with an invocation of the newly created branch. If the choice is to make the replacement, the arguments in the invocation of the newly created branch are identical to the arguments of the preexisting invocation.

5. The terminal set of the newly created iteration-performing branch is identical to that of the picked branch. The function set of the newly created iteration-performing branch is identical to the function set of the picked branch. The function set of the picked branch is enlarged to include the name of the newly created iteration-performing branch. The terminal set of the picked branch is unchanged. The function set of any branch whose function set includes the picked branch (i.e., any branch that actually calls the picked branch or that is permitted to call the picked branch) is enlarged to include the name of the newly created iteration-performing branch. The terminal set of any branch whose function set includes the picked branch is not affected by this operation.

Iteration duplication broadens the hierarchy of references in the computer program on which it operates. The offspring produced by an iteration duplication is semantically equivalent to its parent.

6.2.3   Iteration Deletion

Automatically defined iterations may be deleted from a computer program during the run of genetic programming using an architecture-altering operation analogous to subroutine deletion. A program with k branches begets a program with $k - 1$ branches.

The operation of iteration deletion operates on one individual in the population selected probabilistically on the basis of fitness and creates one new offspring program for the new population by deleting one automatically defined iteration of an existing program.

The deletion of an iteration-performing branch raises the question of how to modify invocations of the branch-to-be-deleted in the surviving branches of the selected program. The options include random regeneration, consolidation, and potentially (at the expense of exceedingly large size) macro expansion (all originally discussed in Section 5.5 in connection with subroutine deletion).

Appropriate changes in the function and terminal sets of the affected branches of the program must be made to reflect the deletion.

Iteration deletion narrows the hierarchy of references in a computer program. The operation of iteration deletion sets up an experimental trial, during the run of genetic programming, as to whether a particular iteration-performing branch is, in fact, useful. After being shorn of its former iteration-performing branch, the resulting program competes with other individuals in the population (frequently including the reasonably fit parent that gave rise to it) for survival during subsequent generations of the evolutionary process.

6.2.4   Iteration Argument Creation, Iteration Argument Duplication, and Iteration Argument Deletion

The automatically defined iterations appearing in this book do not possess arguments; however, such arguments would be useful for certain problems. If automatically defined iterations were to possess arguments, then it would be appropriate to employ additional architecture-altering operations for creating, duplicating, and deleting their arguments. These architecture-altering operations for automatically defined iterations are defined in a manner analogous to the operations of argument creation, argument duplication, and argument deletion that are applicable to automatically defined functions.

Automatically Defined Loops

The previous chapter dealt with a restricted form of iteration (namely, the automatically defined iteration) in which the iteration consists of an iteration-performing branch that makes a single pass over a preestablished problem-specific finite sequence, vector, or array. This chapter deals with a more general form of iteration—the automatically defined loop.

7.1   LOOPS

Automatically defined loops provide a mechanism by which genetic programming implements a general form of iteration involving an initialization step, a termination condition, a loop body, and an update step.

An automatically defined loop (ADL) consists of four distinct branches:

- a loop initialization branch, LIB,
- a loop condition branch, LCB,
- a loop body branch, LBB, and
- a loop update branch, LUB.

The bodies of all four branches of an ADL are subject to evolutionary modification during the run of genetic programming. When the loop is invoked, a fixed structure (not subject to evolutionary modification) causes the loop initialization branch, LIB, of the automatically defined loop to be executed. The loop condition branch, LCB, is then executed, and the loop is either continued or terminated based on whether the condition specified by the loop condition branch is satisfied. If the loop is not terminated, the loop body branch, LBB, is executed. Then, the loop update branch, LUB, is executed. Thereafter, the loop condition branch, the loop body branch, and the loop update branch are repeatedly executed. The convention for the automatically defined loops in this book is that the loop is continued while the return value of the loop condition branch, LCB, returns a positive numerical value. That is, the loop is terminated as soon as the loop condition branch becomes zero or negative.

Using the above terminology for LIB, LCB, LBB, and LUB, an automatically defined loop might be written as the following for loop in the C programming language:

```
float ADL(void)
{
float result = 0;

for (LIB(); LCB() > 0; LUB())
 {
 result = LBB();
 }
return(result);
}
```

An automatically defined loop resembles an automatically defined function and an automatically defined iteration in that it has a name (allowing it to be invoked) and an argument list (which may or may not be empty). An automatically defined loop differs from an automatically defined function and an automatically defined iteration in that the automatically defined loop has four distinct branches.

An automatically defined loop may be invoked by a result-producing branch, an ADF, an ADI, an automatically defined recursion (Chapter 8), or another ADL. When an expression such as

(ADL3 ARG0 ARG1)

is encountered during the execution of a program, the loop initialization branch, LIB3, of automatically defined loop ADL3 is executed first. Then the loop condition branch, LCB3, is executed. The loop is either continued or terminated based on the value produced by LCB3. If the loop is not terminated, the loop body branch, LBB3, is then executed. Finally, the loop update branch, LUB3, is executed. After that, a loop consisting of three branches (LCB3, LBB3, and LUB3) is repeatedly executed while the loop condition branch, LCB3, is positive. During the execution of the loop, the values of the arguments, if any, of the loop (i.e., ARG0 and ARG1 above) are available to any of the four branches. The value returned by the above expression is the value returned by the last execution of the loop body branch, LBB3.

The overall program may contain arbitrarily many automatically defined loops (up to some preestablished limit), each possessing arbitrarily many arguments (again, up to a preestablished limit).

If any of the four branches of the automatically defined loop contains a reference to another automatically defined loop or to an automatically defined iteration, then the ADL or ADI is executed when it is encountered, thereby creating a nested iterative structure. A computer program may contain nested automatically defined loops (subject to a preestablished limit on the depth of nesting).

It is a practical necessity to ration the computer resources that may be consumed by the automatically defined loop. This rationing may be implemented as a time-out limit based on a maximum number of executions (or a maximum amount of computer time) consumed by a single automatically defined loop in a program and an additional separate limit based on the maximum cumulative number of executions (or the maximum cumulative amount of computer time) consumed by all automatically defined loops in a program.

The idea of an automatically defined loop can be illustrated by applying it to the problem of computing the numerical average of LEN numbers in a vector V. Such a computa-

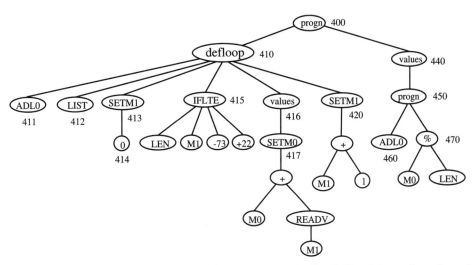

Figure 7.1 Illustrative program with an automatically defined loop (ADL0) and a result-producing branch

tion might be performed with a `for` loop in the C programming language in the following way:

```
M0 = 0;
for (i = 0; i < LEN; i++)
{
  M0 = M0 + V[i];
}
AVERAGE = MO/LEN;
```

Figure 7.1 shows an example of a multipart program consisting of one result-producing branch in the right part of the figure and one automatically defined loop, ADL0, consisting of four branches in the left part of the figure. The subtree rooted at SETM1 413 constitutes the loop initialization branch, LIB0, of this automatically defined loop. The subtree rooted at IFLTE 415 constitutes the loop condition branch, LCB0. The subtree rooted at VALUES 416 constitutes the loop body branch, LBB0. The subtree rooted at SETM1 420 constitutes the loop update branch, LUB0. The overall program computes the average of a set of numbers stored in a vector of length LEN. The topmost point in the overall program is PROGN (labeled 400).

The topmost PROGN 400 begins by executing the DEFLOOP 410. An automatically defined loop is defined by a DEFLOOP. The DEFLOOP resembles the DEFUN that defines an automatically defined function (Section 2.3.6) and the DEFITERATE that defines an automatically defined iteration (Section 6.1.3). This definitional process enables the automatically defined loop to be invoked by other branches of the overall program. Execution of the DEFLOOP 410 returns nothing of interest to PROGN 400.

The automatically defined loop has a name, ADL0, within the overall program. If ADL0 possesses arguments, the arguments appear under LIST 412; however, the particular automatically defined loop here possesses no arguments.

After the automatically defined loop is defined, the topmost PROGN 400 then proceeds to execute VALUES 440 in the right part of the figure. This VALUES begins with its own PROGN (labeled 450). PROGN 450 begins by invoking ADL0 460. When ADL0 460 is invoked, the loop initialization branch, LIB0, is executed first. The topmost point of the LIB0 is the setting function SETM1 413. The LIB0 sets named memory cell M1 to the constant 0. As it happens, this action is redundant since all cells of memory are always initialized to zero prior to execution of every fitness case for every overall program.

The topmost point of the loop condition branch, LCB0, is IFLTE 415. The IFLTE ("if less than or equal") conditional branching operator (Section 13.3.2) tests whether LEN is less than or equal to M1. If so, the IFLTE operator 415 returns –73, and, since this value is nonpositive, the loop terminates. If not, the IFLTE operator returns +22, and, since the value is positive, the loop continues. As can be seen, this particular loop executes exactly LEN times (for positive LEN).

The topmost point of the loop body branch, LBB0, is VALUES 416. The LBB0 computes a running sum by setting M0 to the sum of the current value of M0 and the value of the M1th element of the vector. The one-argument function READV returns the element of the vector designated by its argument (modulo the length of the vector). Note that this loop is relying on M0 having been initialized to zero prior to execution of the overall program.

The topmost point of the loop update branch, LUB0, is SETM1 420. The LUB0 sets M1 to the sum of the current value of M1 and the constant 1. Control then returns to the loop condition branch, LCB0, which again tests whether LEN is less than or equal to M1. The loop continues while the loop condition branch, LCB0, is positive. This occurs when the loop is executed exactly LEN times. The return value of this particular ADL0 is ignored because PROGN 450 returns only the value of its final argument. The result-producing branch then computes the quotient (at 470) of the running sum stored in M0 and the length LEN of the vector. PROGN 450 then returns this quotient to VALUES 440. This value becomes the value produced by the overall program (i.e., the value returned by PROGN 400). The cell of named memory, M0, is the conduit for communication from the automatically defined loop to the result-producing branch.

When using automatically defined loops, it is often convenient to introduce an explicit indexing terminal (called INDEX) that counts the number of executions of the loop. When INDEX is used, an automatically defined loop might be written as the following for loop in the C programming language:

```
float ADL(void)
{
float result = 0;
int index = 0;

for (LIB(); LCB() > 0; LUB(), index++)
  {
  result = LBB();
  }
return(result);
}
```

There are, of course, numerous ways of structuring an automatically defined loop to perform a particular calculation. For example, the steps performed in the loop condition branch, the loop body branch, and the loop update branch in the above example need not be partitioned into the three branches in the manner described. Instead, these steps can be consolidated or distributed among any one, two, or three of these branches in any computationally equivalent way. As another example, if the index variable, INDEX, were available, it could be used in lieu of M1 in the program shown in Figure 7.1. As yet another example, the value of ADL0 could be referenced (in lieu of M0) in the result-producing branch because the return value of ADL0 happens to be equal to M0 after completion of the loop in the above illustrative example. That is, the entire result-producing branch could be reduced to merely

    (% ADL0 LEN)

instead of

    (PROGN ADL0 (% M0 LEN)).

The user can make automatically defined loops available for solving a problem either by

- prespecifying the architecture of the overall program (i.e., by performing an additional architecture-defining preparatory step), or
- using architecture-altering operations (Section 7.2) to enable genetic programming to automatically create the automatically defined loops for the overall program dynamically during the run.

The automatically defined loop is illustrated by the solution of the Boolean parity problem using version 1.0 of the Genetic Programming Problem Solver (GPPS 1.0) (Sections 21.1 and 21.2) and the minimal sorting network problem (Section 21.4).

Chapters 30 and 55 describe another quasi-iterative structure, called an automatically defined copy (ADC), that is applicable to developmental genetic programming (and, in particular, the synthesis of electrical circuits).

7.1.1 Simplified Version of the Automatically Defined Loop

Only a constrained form of the automatically defined loop is used in this book. In this simplified model, each automatically defined loop is executed exactly once prior to execution of the result-producing branch; the result-producing branch is executed once; and nested loops are not allowed. Thus, in this simplified model, the appearance of the name of an automatically defined loop (e.g., ADL3) in a program does not cause the execution of the loop. Instead, ADL3 merely returns the appropriate value from the already-executed loop (i.e., the value returned by the last execution of the loop body branch, LBB3, of ADL3).

Specifically, in the simplified model for automatically defined loops:

- There may be multiple automatically defined loops in a program (up to some pre-established limit).
- The automatically defined loops are each invoked once prior to the invocation of the single result-producing branch.

- The return value of each automatically defined loop is available to the result-producing branch as a terminal.
- There are no nested automatically defined loops.
- The automatically defined loops do not possess arguments.
- The automatically defined loops may contain references to automatically defined functions, and the automatically defined functions may refer to one another hierarchically.
- The automatically defined loops may contain functions and terminals that write and read memory.
- The result-producing branch has access to memory (which may have been written during the execution of the automatically defined loop).

The execution of an overall program in this simplified model consists of the following steps:

1. For each fitness case, all locations of all types of memory are initialized to zero.
2. If there are no automatically defined loops, step 4 is executed next. If there are one or more automatically defined loops, the first automatically defined loop (ADL0) is now executed once. The execution of automatically defined loop ADL0 consists of the following substeps:
   a. An index, called INDEX, is externally initialized to zero as if the initialization step were located at the beginning of the loop initialization branch, LIB, of each automatically defined loop.
   b. The loop initialization branch, LIB0, is executed exactly one time for the automatically defined loop.
   c. This substep is the beginning of the loop. The loop condition branch, LCB0, is executed. The loop continues provided LCB0 is positive and provided INDEX is less than a preestablished maximum number of executions of the loop, $N_{max\text{-}adl\text{-}executions}$. When LCB0 causes the termination of ADL0, step 3 is executed.
   d. The loop body branch, LBB0, is executed. The final return value of this branch is available to the invoking branch as ADL0.
   e. The loop update branch, LUB0, is executed.
   f. INDEX is externally incremented by one for each execution of the automatically defined loop as if the incrementing step were located at the end of the loop update branch, LUB0.
   g. The loop then returns to substep c.
3. If there are additional automatically defined loops (e.g., ADL1, ADL2, . . .), they are each executed once in the same manner as step 2.
4. The result-producing branch, RPB, is executed once.
5. If an automatically defined function appears in any branch of the automatically defined loop, the result-producing branch, or another automatically defined function, it is executed in the usual way at the time that it is referenced.

Figure 7.2 illustrates this simplified model with two automatically defined loops, ADL0 and ADL1. The execution of the first two arguments (i.e., DEFLOOP 811 and DEFLOOP 821) of PROGN 800 does not return anything interesting. The execution of the third argument of PROGN 800 (that is, PROGN 831 at the second level of the hierarchy)

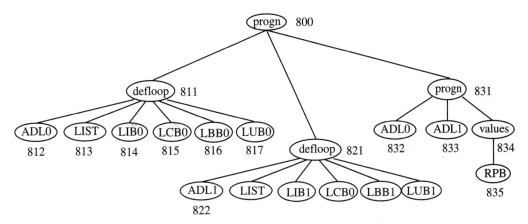

Figure 7.2   Simplified model of program with two automatically defined loops (ADL0 and ADL1)

first causes the first automatically defined loop (ADL0 832) to be executed once. As explained above, the execution of ADL0 832 begins with the execution of its loop initialization branch (LIB0 814) followed by the repeated execution of a loop consisting of the loop condition branch (LCB0 815), the loop body branch (LBB0 816), and the loop update branch (LUB0 817) while the loop condition branch (LCB0 815) is positive. The continuation of the execution of PROGN 831 then causes the branches of the second automatically defined loop (ADL1 822) to be executed once in a similar manner. The values returned by ADL0 832 and ADL1 833 are ignored by PROGN 831. The continuation of the execution of PROGN 831 then causes the execution of VALUES 834, which, in turn, causes the execution of the result-producing branch, RPB 835. The result-producing branch may refer to the values returned by the automatically defined loop. The value returned by PROGN 831 (and hence the value returned by topmost PROGN 800) is the value returned via VALUES 834 from the execution of the result-producing branch, RPB 835.

7.2   ARCHITECTURE-ALTERING OPERATIONS FOR AUTOMATICALLY DEFINED LOOPS

Architecture-altering operations for automatically defined loops can be used to automate the decision as to how many times, if ever, to employ automatically defined loops in solving a problem (along with the related decision of exactly what computation to perform within each loop). In particular, automatically defined loops and their arguments may be created, duplicated, or deleted using architecture-altering operations that are analogous to the operations applicable to automatically defined functions (Chapter 5) and automatically defined iterations (Chapter 6).

7.2.1   Loop Creation

The architecture-altering operation of loop creation operates on one individual in the population selected probabilistically on the basis of fitness. It creates one new offspring program for the new population by adding a loop initialization branch, a loop condition branch, a loop body branch, and a loop update branch. A program with k branches begets a program with $k + 4$ branches. Each of these four new branches is composed of a portion of a preexisting branch of the given program. The operation also creates a DEFLOOP to define the four newly created branches, unique names for the automatically defined loop and its four branches, an argument list for the automatically defined loop, and an invoking reference to the new automatically defined loop. The automatically defined loop may or may not possess arguments.

The steps in the architecture-altering operation of loop creation are as follows:

1. Select, based on fitness, an individual program from the population to participate in this operation. A copy is first made of the selected program, and the operation is then performed on the copy. Thus, the original unchanged program remains available to be reselected for another operation.

2. Randomly pick one of the branches of the selected program. If the selected program has only one branch, that branch is automatically picked. The picking of the branch may, as an option, be restricted to a result-producing branch or other specified category of branches. Randomly choose a point in this first picked branch of the selected program. Add a uniquely named new loop initialization branch, LIB, to the selected program. The newly created loop initialization branch consists of a copy of the subtree rooted at the first chosen point. No change is made in the picked branch of the selected program.

3. Randomly pick, independently from step 2, one of the branches of the selected program in the same manner as step 2. Randomly choose a point in this second picked branch of the selected program. Add a uniquely named new loop condition branch, LCB, to the selected program. The newly created loop condition branch consists of a copy of the subtree rooted at the second chosen point. No change is made in the picked branch of the selected program.

4. Randomly pick, independently from steps 2 and 3, one of the branches of the selected program in the same manner as steps 2 and 3. Randomly choose a point in this third picked branch of the selected program. Add a uniquely named new loop update branch, LUB, to the selected program. The newly created loop update branch consists of a copy of the subtree rooted at the third chosen point. No change is made in the picked branch of the selected program.

5. Randomly pick, independently from steps 2, 3, and 4, one of the branches of the selected program in the same manner as steps 2, 3, and 4. Randomly choose a point in this fourth picked branch of the selected program. Add a uniquely named new loop body branch, LBB, to the selected program. The newly created loop body branch consists of a copy of the subtree rooted at this fourth chosen point. However, unlike steps 2, 3, and 4, the picked branch of the selected program is changed by removing the subtree starting at this fourth chosen point and replacing the subtree with the name of the newly created automatically defined loop. The reason for the removal of this subtree from the fourth picked branch is that the newly created automatically defined loop is intended to repeatedly execute the steps of the removed subtree.

6. The terminal set of each branch of the new automatically defined loop is identical to that of the branch of the selected program that was picked to create the particular branch of the automatically defined loop. The function set of each branch of the new automatically defined loop is identical to that of the branch of the selected program that was picked to create the particular branch of the automatically defined loop. The function set of the branch of the selected program that was picked to create the loop body branch is enlarged to include the name of the newly created automatically defined loop. The terminal set of each of the four branches of the picked automatically defined loop is unchanged. The function set of any branch in the program whose function set includes the picked branch (i.e., any branch that actually calls the picked automatically defined loop or that is permitted to call the picked automatically defined loop) is enlarged to include the name of the newly created automatically defined loop. The terminal set of any branch in the program whose function set includes the picked automatically defined loop is not affected by this operation.

The operation of loop creation is, in general, not semantics-preserving.

There are several parameters for controlling the operation of loop creation for automatically defined loops.

1. The loop creation operation is controlled by a parameter specifying the probability of executing the operation on each generation, $p_{loop\text{-}creation}$.
2. There is a maximum number of automatically defined loops, N_{adl}, for each program in the population.
3. There is a maximum size, S_{adl}, for all four branches of each newly created automatically defined loop.
4. The loop creation operation is controlled by a parameter specifying the minimum number, $N_{min\text{-}argument\text{-}adl}$, and the maximum number, $N_{max\text{-}argument\text{-}adl}$, of arguments for each newly created automatically defined loop. If automatically defined loops possess arguments, each branch is given arguments in the same manner as for the subroutine creation operation (with appropriate changes being made in the picked branch of the selected program).
5. Since the loop condition branch and loop update branch are executed once for each loop, the loop creation operation can, if desired, be simplified so that it creates only two new branches, instead of four. In this event, the two new branches would be the loop initialization branch, LIB, and the loop body branch, LBB. Updating (if any) would occur within the loop body branch. The value returned by the loop body branch would determine whether the loop is terminated (in the same manner as the value returned by the loop condition branch determines whether the loop is terminated in the four-branch arrangement).
6. The terminal INDEX may be included in the terminal set of the four branches of the automatically defined loop (and other branches of the overall program) so that it is available as an ingredient for the evolving programs.

Loop creation deepens the hierarchy of references in a computer program.

The new operation of loop creation is included in the Genetic Programming Problem Solver in Part 4 of this book and is illustrated by various problems in Chapters 21 and 23.

7.2.2   Loop Duplication

The group of four branches that constitute an automatically defined loop may be duplicated using an architecture-altering operation analogous to subroutine duplication and iteration duplication.

The operation of loop duplication operates on one individual in the population selected probabilistically on the basis of fitness and creates one new offspring program for the new population by duplicating all four branches of an existing automatically defined loop of one existing program and making additional appropriate changes to reflect this change. The steps of the architecture-altering operation of loop duplication are very similar to that of subroutine duplication and iteration duplication, as shown below:

1. Select, based on fitness, an individual program from the population to participate in this operation.

2. Pick one of the automatically defined loops of the selected program as the loop-to-be-duplicated. If the selected program has only one automatically defined loop, that loop is automatically picked. If the selected program has no automatically defined loops (or already has the maximum number of automatically defined loops established for the problem), this operation is aborted.

3. Add a uniquely named new automatically defined loop to the selected program, thus increasing the number of automatically defined loops in the selected program by one. The newly created automatically defined loop has the same argument list and the same body as the to-be-duplicated automatically defined loop.

4. For each occurrence of an invocation of the to-be-duplicated automatically defined loop anywhere in the selected program, randomly choose either to leave that invocation unchanged or to replace that invocation with an invocation of the to-be-duplicated automatically defined loop. If the choice is to make the replacement, the arguments in the invocation of the newly created automatically defined loop are identical to the arguments of the preexisting invocation.

5. The terminal sets of each of the four branches of the new automatically defined loop are identical to that of the corresponding branch of the picked automatically defined loop. The function sets of each of the four branches of the new automatically defined loop are identical to that of the corresponding branch of the picked automatically defined loop. The function set of the loop body branch of the picked automatically defined loop is enlarged to include the name of the newly created automatically defined loop. The terminal set of each of the four branches of the picked automatically defined loop is unchanged. The function set of any branch in the program whose function set includes the picked automatically defined loop (i.e., any branch that actually calls the picked automatically defined loop or that is permitted to call the picked automatically defined loop) is enlarged to include the name of the newly created automatically defined loop. The termi-

nal set of any branch in the program whose function set includes the picked automatically defined loop is not affected by this operation.

Loop duplication broadens the hierarchy of references in a computer program. A program with k branches begets a program with $k + 4$ branches. The offspring produced by a loop duplication is semantically equivalent to its parent.

7.2.3   Loop Deletion

The group of four branches that constitute an automatically defined loop may be deleted from a computer program during the run of genetic programming using an architecture-altering operation analogous to subroutine deletion and iteration deletion.

The operation of *loop deletion* operates on one individual in the population selected probabilistically on the basis of fitness and creates one new offspring program for the new population by deleting all four branches of one automatically defined loop of the existing program.

The deletion of an automatically defined loop raises the question of how to modify invocations of the to-be-deleted branches in the remaining branches of the overall program. The options include random regeneration, consolidation, and macro expansion (originally discussed in Section 5.5 in connection with subroutine deletion).

Appropriate changes in the function and terminal sets of the affected branches of the program must be made to reflect the deletion.

Loop deletion provides a mechanism for narrowing the hierarchy of the overall program. A program with k branches begets one with $k - 4$ branches.

The operation of loop deletion sets up an experimental trial, during the run of genetic programming, as to whether a particular looping structure is, in fact, useful. After being shorn of its former four branches, the downsized program competes with other individuals in the population (frequently including the reasonably fit parent that spawned it) for survival during subsequent generations of the evolutionary process.

7.2.4   Loop Argument Creation, Loop Argument Duplication, and Loop Argument Deletion

The automatically defined loops in this book do not possess arguments. However, such arguments would be useful for certain problems. If automatically defined loops were to possess arguments, then it would be appropriate to employ additional architecture-altering operations to create, duplicate, and delete their arguments. These architecture-altering operations for automatically defined loops are defined in a manner analogous to the operations of argument creation, argument duplication, and argument deletion that are applicable to automatically defined functions.

8

Automatically Defined Recursion

Human-computer programmers often find recursions useful in writing programs. Recursions are similar to subroutines and iterations in that they provide a mechanism for reusing computer code. In addition, there is usually a high degree of generality in the code in the body of a recursion.

Automatically defined recursions provide a mechanism by which genetic programming implements a general form of recursion involving a termination condition, a recursion body, an update step, and a base (ground) case. Specifically, an automatically defined recursion (ADR) consists of

- a recursion condition branch, RCB,
- a recursion body branch, RBB,
- a recursion update branch, RUB, and
- a recursion ground branch, RGB.

The bodies of the four branches of an ADR are subject to evolutionary modification during the run of genetic programming. When the recursion is invoked, a fixed structure (not subject to evolutionary modification) first causes the recursion condition branch, RCB, to be executed. The recursion is continued while the recursion condition branch returns certain specified values. The convention for the automatically defined recursions in this book is that the recursion is continued as long as the recursion condition branch, RCB, returns a positive numerical value. If the recursion is continued, the recursion body branch, RBB, is executed. The distinguishing feature of an automatically defined recursion is that the recursion can invoke itself. In particular, the recursion body branch, RBB, is unique in that it may recursively reference the automatically defined recursion of which it is a part. After the RBB completes, the recursion update branch, RUB, is executed. When the recursion is terminated (because the recursion condition branch returns a nonpositive value), the recursion ground branch, RGB, is executed exactly once.

When the recursion condition branch, RCB, returns a positive numerical value, the return value of the automatically defined recursion is the value returned by the recursion body branch, RBB. When the recursion condition branch, RCB, returns a nonpositive numerical value, the return value of the automatically defined recursion is the value returned by the recursion ground branch, RGB.

Using the above terminology for RCB, RBB, RUB, and RGB, a recursion in C might be written as follows:

```
float ADR0 (float ARG0)
{
 float result;

 if (RCB (ARG0)>0)
 {
  result = RBB (ARG0); /* This may call ADR0 */
  RUB (ARG0);
 }
 else
  result = RGB (ARG0);
return (result);
}
```

The following handwritten program for the Boolean even-6-parity problem illustrates an automatically defined recursion in genetic programming. In this illustrative problem, the six Boolean input values (0 and 1) reside in a vector. The RLI ("read linear input") function is a one-argument function that returns the value of the element of the input vector specified by the RLI's one argument (modulo 6). The program consists of one result-producing branch and one automatically defined recursion consisting of four branches.

The result-producing branch, RPB, of the program is

```
(ADR0 5).
```

That is, the RPB invokes the ADR0 with an argument of 5.

The recursion condition branch, RCB0, of the automatically defined recursion possesses one argument (ARG0):

```
(IFGTZ ARG0 1 -1).
```

IFGTZ ("if greater than zero") is a conditional branching operator (Section 13.3.2).

The recursion body branch, RBB0, possesses one argument (ARG0):

```
(IFGTZ
   (ADR0 (- ARG0 1))
   (IFGTZ (RLI ARG0) -1 1)
   (IFGTZ (RLI ARG0) 1 -1)
).
```

The recursion update branch, RUB0, possesses one argument (ARG0) and is irrelevant to this example. It might contain

```
(* 2 3).
```

The recursion ground branch, RGB0, possesses one argument (ARG0):

```
(IFGTZ (RLI ARG0) -1 1).
```

An automatically defined recursion resembles an automatically defined function, an automatically defined iteration, and an automatically defined loop in that it has a name (allowing it to be invoked in the same manner as any other function) and an argument list. An ADR differs from an ADF and an ADI in that the ADR has four distinct branches. An ADR differs from an ADF in that the branches of an ADR are, in general, executed multiple times for a single invocation. Moreover, an ADR differs from an ADF, an ADI, and an ADL in that its recursive body branch (RBB) is allowed to contain a recursive reference to the ADR itself.

A multipart computer program may contain arbitrarily many automatically defined recursions (up to some preestablished limit).

An automatically defined recursion may be called from a result-producing branch, an ADF, an ADI, an ADL, or another ADR. In addition, an ADR may call itself.

Since the recursion condition branch of an automatically defined recursion is subject to evolutionary modification during the run, it is a practical necessity to ration the computer resources that may be consumed by the automatically defined recursion. This rationing may be implemented in numerous ways. For example, the rationing may be in the form of a preestablished limit based on the maximum depth for any one recursion and on the total number of recursive calls allowed in any one program. The fitness of any individual exceeding a preestablished limit is a high penalty value (e.g., 10^{10}).

Figure 8.1 depicts the above program for the Boolean even-6-parity problem. It shows a multipart program consisting of one result-producing branch in the right part of the figure and one automatically defined recursion, ADR0 (consisting of four branches) in the left part of the figure. The topmost point in the overall program is PROGN (labeled 600). The subtree rooted at VALUES 620 constitutes the recursion condition branch, RCB0, of automatically defined recursion ADR0. The subtree rooted at IFGTZ 630 constitutes the recursion body branch, RBB0, of ADR0. The subtree rooted at the multiplication (*) at 650 constitutes the recursion update branch, RUB0. The subtree rooted at IFGTZ 660 constitutes the recursion ground branch, RGB0.

The overall program computes the Boolean even-6-parity function of six Boolean variables residing in an input vector of length 6. The topmost PROGN 600 begins by executing the DEFRECURSION 610. An automatically defined recursion is defined by a DEFRECURSION. The DEFRECURSION resembles the DEFUN that defines an automatically defined function (Section 2.3.6), the DEFITERATE that defines an automatically defined iteration (Section 6.1.3), and the DEFLOOP that defines an automatically defined loop (Section 7.1). This definitional process enables the automatically defined recursion to be invoked by other branches of the overall program. Execution of the DEFRECURSION 610 returns nothing of interest to PROGN 600.

The automatically defined recursion has a unique name, ADR0, within the overall program. An automatically defined recursion always possesses at least one argument. The argument list of ADR0 611 appears under LIST 612. In this example, there is one dummy variable (formal parameter) ARG0 613 in the argument list.

After the automatically defined recursion is defined, the topmost PROGN 600 then proceeds to execute VALUES 670 in the right part of the figure. This VALUES 670 begins by invoking automatically defined recursion ADR0 680 with an argument consisting of the constant 5 (labeled 681). When ADR0 is invoked the first time, the recursion condition branch, RCB, is executed first. The recursion condition branch, RCB0, returns 1 in this example because the current value of ARG0 is 5. Since RCB0 returns a positive value, the recursion body branch, RBB0, is executed. The topmost point of the RBB0 is IFGTZ 630. The first argument of IFGTZ 630 recursively invokes ADR0 with an argument of

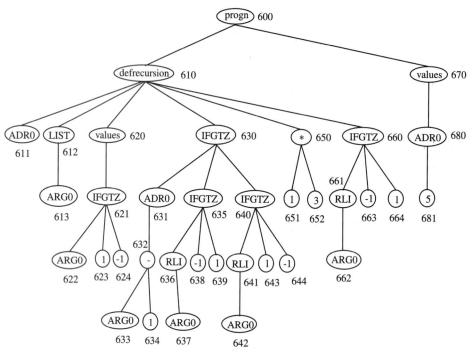

Figure 8.1 Illustrative program with an automatically defined recursion (ADR0) and a result-producing branch

ARG0 minus 1. The recursion body branch, RBB0, computes the even-2-parity of the ARG0th location of the input and the value returned from the recursive call (ADR0 (− ARG0 1)). In particular:

- If the value returned for (ADR0 (− ARG0 1)) is positive (i.e., the parity of the ARG0 − 1 inputs is even), the Boolean value (0 or 1) in location ARG0 of the input vector is examined. If this value in the input vector is positive, a −1 is returned by IFGTZ 635. Otherwise, a 1 is returned by IFGTZ 635 and, in turn, by IFGTZ 630 and, in turn, by the call to ADR0.
- If the value returned for (ADR0 (− ARG0 1)) is negative (i.e., the parity of the ARG0 − 1 inputs is odd), the Boolean value in location ARG0 of the input vector is examined. If this value in the input vector is positive, a 1 is returned by IFGTZ 640. Otherwise, a −1 is returned by IFGTZ 640 and, in turn, by IFGTZ 630 and, in turn, by the call to ADR0.

The recursion update branch (whose topmost point is the multiplication function labeled 650) is irrelevant in this example.

The topmost point of the recursion ground branch, RGB0, is IFGTZ 660. The recursion ground branch, RGB0, computes the even-1-parity of the ARG0th location of the input vector. This is the base case of the recursion. In particular:

- If the value (0 or 1) in location ARG0 of the input vector is positive (i.e., odd parity), IFGTZ 660 returns −1.
- If the value (0 or 1) in location ARG0 of the input vector is nonpositive (i.e., even parity), IFGTZ 660 returns 1.

Although the distinguishing feature of an automatically defined recursion is that the recursion is permitted to invoke itself, the recursion body branch of a particular automatically defined recursion may or may not actually do so.

There are various alternative ways of implementing automatically defined recursions in the context of genetic programming. For example, the recursion body branch and recursion update branch might be consolidated so that an automatically defined recursion has only three branches. In this three-branch approach, the updating would occur within the recursion body branch.

The user can make automatically defined recursions available for solving a problem either by

- prespecifying the architecture of the overall program (i.e., by performing an additional architecture-defining preparatory step) or
- using architecture-altering operations (Section 8.1) to enable genetic programming to automatically create the architecturally defined recursions for the overall program dynamically during the run.

The automatically defined recursion is illustrated with the Fibonacci sequence problem (Chapter 18).

8.1 ARCHITECTURE-ALTERING OPERATIONS FOR AUTOMATICALLY DEFINED RECURSIONS

The decision as to how many times, if ever, to employ automatically defined recursions in solving a problem can be made during the run of genetic programming by means of architecture-altering operations. Specifically, automatically defined recursions may be created using an architecture-altering operation that is analogous to the operation of subroutine creation for ADFs (Section 5.3), the operation of iteration creation for ADIs (Section 6.2.1), and the operation of loop creation for ADLs (Section 7.2.1).

8.1.1 Recursion Creation

The architecture-altering operation of recursion creation operates on one individual in the population selected probabilistically on the basis of fitness. It creates one new offspring program by adding a recursion condition branch, a recursion body branch, a recursion update branch, and a recursion ground branch. A program with k branches begets an offspring program with $k + 4$ branches. Each of these four new branches is composed of a portion of a preexisting branch of the given program. The operation also creates a DEFRECURSION to define the four newly created branches, creates unique names for the automatically defined recursion and its four branches, creates an argument list for the automatically defined recursion, and creates an invoking reference to the new automatically defined recursion. An automatically defined recursion always has at least one argument.

The steps in the architecture-altering operation of recursion creation are as follows:

1. Select, based on fitness, an individual program from the population to participate in this operation. A copy is first made of the selected program, and the operation is then performed on the copy. Thus, the original unchanged program remains available to be reselected for another operation.

2. Randomly pick one of the branches of the selected program. If the selected program has only one branch, that branch is automatically picked. The picking of the branch may, as an option, be restricted to a result-producing branch or other specified category of branches. Randomly choose a point in this first picked branch of the selected program. Add a uniquely named new recursion ground branch, RGB, to the selected program. The newly created recursion ground branch consists of a copy of the subtree rooted at the first chosen point. Randomly pick one terminal of this subtree and change it to ARG0.

3. Randomly pick, independently from step 2, one of the branches of the selected program in the same manner as step 2. Randomly choose a point in this second picked branch of the selected program. Add a uniquely named new recursion condition branch, RCB, to the selected program. The newly created recursion condition branch consists of a copy of the subtree rooted at the second chosen point. Randomly pick one terminal of this subtree and change it to ARG0.

4. Randomly pick, independently from steps 2 and 3, one of the branches of the selected program in the same manner as steps 2 and 3. Randomly choose a point in this third picked branch of the selected program. Add a uniquely named new recursion update branch, RUB, to the selected program. The newly created recursion update branch consists of a copy of the subtree rooted at the third chosen point. Randomly pick one terminal of this subtree and change it to ARG0.

5. Randomly pick, independently from steps 2, 3, and 4, one of the branches of the selected program in the same manner as steps 2, 3, and 4. Randomly choose a point in this fourth picked branch of the selected program. Add a uniquely named new recursion body branch, RBB, to the selected program. The newly created recursion body branch consists of a copy of the subtree rooted at this fourth chosen point. However, unlike steps 2, 3, and 4, the picked branch of the selected program is changed by removing the subtree starting at this fourth chosen point and replacing the subtree with the name of the newly created automatically defined recursion. The reason for the removal of this subtree from the selected program is that the body of the recursion is intended to repeatedly perform the steps of the subtree. Randomly pick one terminal of this subtree and change it to ARG0.

6. The terminal set of each branch of the new automatically defined recursion contains the dummy variables (formal parameters) of the automatically defined recursion along with the terminals in the terminal set of the branch of the selected program that was picked to create that particular branch of the automatically defined recursion. The function set of each branch of the new automatically defined recursion is identical to that of the branch of the selected program that was picked to create the particular branch of the automatically defined recursion with the following important exception: The function set of the recursion body branch additionally includes the name of the newly created automatically defined

recursion. The function set of the branch of the selected program that was picked to create the recursion body branch is enlarged to include the name of the newly created automatically defined recursion. The terminal set of each of the four branches of the new automatically defined recursion is enlarged by ARG0. The function set of any branch in the program whose function set includes the picked branch (i.e., any branch that actually calls the picked automatically defined recursion or that is permitted to call the picked automatically defined recursion) is enlarged to include the name of the newly created automatically defined recursion. The terminal set of any branch in the program whose function set includes the picked branch is not affected by this operation.

The operation of recursion creation is, in general, not semantics-preserving.

There are several parameters for controlling the operation of recursion creation for automatically defined recursions:

1. The recursion creation operation is controlled by a parameter specifying the probability of executing the operation on each generation, $p_{recursion-creation}$.
2. There is a maximum number, N_{adr}, of automatically defined recursions for each program in the population.
3. There is a maximum size, S_{adr}, for all four branches of each newly created automatically defined recursion.
4. The recursion creation operation is controlled by a parameter specifying the minimum number, $N_{min-argument-adr}$, of arguments for each newly created automatically defined recursion. This minimum must be at least one.
5. The recursion creation operation is controlled by a parameter specifying the maximum number, $N_{max-argument-adr}$, of arguments for each newly created automatically defined recursion.

The new operation of recursion creation is included in the Genetic Programming Problem Solver in Part 4 of this book and is illustrated by various problems in Chapters 21 and 23.

8.1.2   Recursion Deletion

The group of four branches that constitute an automatically defined recursion may be deleted from a computer program during the run of genetic programming using an architecture-altering operation analogous to subroutine deletion, iteration deletion, and loop deletion. A program with k branches begets an offspring program with $k - 4$ branches.

The operation of recursion deletion operates on one individual in the population selected probabilistically on the basis of fitness and creates one new offspring program for the new population by deleting all four branches of one automatically defined recursion of the existing program.

The deletion of an automatically defined recursion raises the question of how to modify invocations of the to-be-deleted branches in the remaining branches of the selected program. The realistic options include random regeneration and consolidation (both originally discussed in Section 5.5 in connection with subroutine deletion), but not macro expansion.

Appropriate changes in the function and terminal sets of the affected branches of the program must be made to reflect the deletion.

The operation of recursion deletion creates the opportunity to conduct a trial, during the run of genetic programming, as to whether a particular recursive structure is, in fact, useful. After being shorn of its former four branches, the downsized program competes with other individuals in the population (frequently including the reasonably fit parent that spawned it) for survival during subsequent generations of the evolutionary process.

8.1.3   Recursion Duplication

The group of four branches that constitute an automatically defined recursion may be duplicated during the run of genetic programming using an architecture-altering operation analogous to the operations of subroutine duplication, iteration duplication, and loop duplication. A program with k branches begets an offspring program with $k + 4$ branches.

The operation of recursion duplication operates on one individual in the population selected probabilistically on the basis of fitness and creates one new offspring program for the new population by duplicating the entire group of four branches of one automatically defined recursion of the existing program and making additional appropriate changes in the function and terminal sets of the affected branches of the program to reflect the duplication.

8.1.4   Recursion Argument Creation, Recursion Argument Duplication, and Recursion Argument Deletion

Architecture-altering operations may be used to create, duplicate, and delete arguments of automatically defined recursions. These architecture-altering operations are defined in a manner analogous to the operations of argument creation, argument duplication, and argument deletion that are applicable to automatically defined functions.

8.2   SUMMARY

Recursion has been successfully implemented in the context of genetic programming in various ways (Brave 1995b, 1996b; Wong and Leung 1996, 1998; Yu and Clack 1997b; Teller 1998; Poli 1997a, 1997b). (See also the related work in Olsson 1994a and 1994b involving the ADATE system.) Iteration has also been successfully implemented previously in genetic programming in various ways (Koza 1992e, Chapter 18; Andre 1994c; Handley 1996a, 1998; Teller 1998).

In addition, this book describes a general approach to creating, using, and deleting automatically defined iterations (Chapter 6), automatically defined loops (Chapter 7), and automatically defined recursions (this chapter) in evolving computer programs.

Iterations, loops, and recursions are mechanisms for code reuse. Reused code provides leverage that can accelerate an automated learning system. Because the code appearing in iterations, loops, and recursions is reused, it tends to be general.

Thus, genetic programming possesses the following attribute of a system for automatically creating computer programs (Chapter 1):

- **ATTRIBUTE NO. 8** (Iterations, loops, and recursions): It has the ability to implement iterations, loops, and recursions.

Automatically Defined Storage

Internal storage (memory) is convenient, and often necessary, in writing computer programs. Memory can be implemented in genetic programming in numerous ways, including named memory, indexed (vector) memory, matrix and array memory, stacks, queues, lists, other data structures, and relational memory (Sections 2.3.7 and 6.1.2).

When first looking at a problem, it is usually not obvious whether internal storage would be necessary, helpful, or useless in solving the problem. Moreover, even if internal storage is known to be necessary or helpful, it is often not obvious as to what amount of internal storage is sufficient for a particular problem. In addition, it may not be obvious as to what type and dimensionality of internal storage may be advantageous for a given problem. Even if the amount, type, and dimensionality of internal memory are known, it is not trivial to decide exactly what to store in memory and exactly when to retrieve the stored information during the course of a program's execution. Therefore, it would be desirable to automate the decision as to whether to use internal storage on a particular problem, how much internal storage to use, what type of internal storage to use, what dimensionality of internal storage to use, and, of course, the specific way in which it is used.

There are several possible ways to implement the automatic creation and deletion of internal storage during a run of genetic programming. We use an approach that closely parallels our implementation of automatically defined functions, automatically defined iterations, automatically defined loops, and automatically defined recursions. Automatically defined stores provide a mechanism by which genetic programming implements a general form of internal storage.

In this approach, an automatically defined store (ADS) is implemented by adding two new branches to the given computer program:

- a storage writing branch, SWB, and
- a storage reading branch, SRB.

The storage writing branch, SWB, may be thought of as simply a WRITE function, and the storage reading branch, SRB, may be viewed as simply a READ function. In this approach, the pair of branches of an automatically defined store are not used for housing any executable code. Instead, when internal storage is added to (or deleted from) an existing computer program, the branches provide an administratively convenient (albeit somewhat artificial) way to expand (or contract) the program's function sets so as to include (or delete) the functions necessary to write and access the newly created memory.

Table 9.1 Types of internal storage

Dimension	Possible types
0	Named memory, pushdown stack, queue
1	Indexed (vector) memory, list
2	Two-dimensional matrix, relational memory
3	Three-dimensional array
4	Four-dimensional array

A program may contain arbitrarily many automatically defined stores (subject to a preestablished maximum number of automatically defined stores, $N_{\text{max-ads}}$). Each automatically defined store has a name, dimensionality, type, and size. Each automatically defined store in a given program has a unique name. The automatically defined stores in a given program are named sequentially, ADS0, ADS1, etc.; the storage writing branches are named sequentially, SWB0, SWB1, etc.; and the storage reading branches are similarly named sequentially.

The dimensionality of an automatically defined store is the number of arguments necessary to address it. The dimensionality of each automatically defined store is established at the time it is created. The choice of dimensionality for each automatically defined store is made independently for each newly created automatically defined store. The choice is typically made randomly (subject to a preestablished maximum dimensionality for the automatically defined stores). Thus, if a program contains more than one automatically defined store, the automatically defined stores may (and are likely) to have different dimensionality.

The type of an automatically defined store is established at the time it is created. The choice of type is made independently for each newly created automatically defined store. The choice of type for an automatically defined store is typically made randomly; however, this random choice is constrained by its already-chosen dimensionality (and by preestablished limits on the types of internal storage permitted for this already-chosen dimensionality). Thus, if a program contains more than one automatically defined store, the automatically defined stores may (and are likely) to be of different types. Table 9.1 shows some of the possible types of internal storage of dimensionality 0, 1, 2, 3, and 4.

The types of internal storage of dimensionality 0 include named memory, a pushdown stack, and a queue. Named memory is an example of internal storage with dimensionality 0 because no argument is required for specifying the address of named memory. For example, when the zero-argument SRB2 function for named memory is invoked, it returns the contents of named memory cell 2. The SRB2 function operates in the same manner as the terminal M2 associated with named memory cell 2 described in Section 6.1.2. When the one-argument SWB2 function is invoked, it writes the contents of named memory cell 2 with the value returned by evaluating its one argument. This same value becomes the return value of the SWB2 function. That is, the SWB2 function operates in the manner identical to the setting function, SETM2, associated with named memory cell 2 (Section 6.1.2).

A pushdown stack and a FIFO (first in, first out) queue are also of dimensionality 0 because an address is not required to access either of these data structures. For example, suppose the automatically defined store, ADS1, of a given program is a pushdown stack. In that event, the execution of the storage writing function, SWB1, pushes the value provided by its argument onto the stack associated with ADS1. The execution of the storage reading function, SRB1, pops the topmost value from the pushdown stack associated with ADS1.

And, as another example, suppose the first automatically defined store, ADS0, of a given program is a queue. In that event, the execution of the storage writing function, SWB0, appends the value provided by its one argument to the end of the queue associated with ADS0. The execution of the storage reading function, SRB0, returns the front element of the queue.

The types of internal storage of dimensionality 1 include indexed (vector) memory and lists. Indexed (vector) memory is internal storage of dimensionality 1. When indexed (vector) memory is being implemented, the SRB and the SWB each possess an argument for specifying the address of indexed memory that is being read or written. The SRB function for indexed memory possesses one argument (i.e., the address), and the SWB function possesses two arguments (i.e., the address and the value to be written into the designated memory cell). In the case of indexed memory, execution of the two-argument SWB function writes the result of evaluating its second argument into the cell of indexed memory designated by its second argument. The SWB function returns the value of its second argument. Execution of the one-argument storage reading branch, SRB, returns the current value of the cell of indexed memory designated by its argument. List memory is an additional example of internal storage of dimensionality 1.

The types of internal storage of dimensionality 2 include two-dimensional matrix memory and relational memory. In the case of two-dimensional matrix memory, the execution of the three-argument SWB function writes the result of evaluating its third argument into the cell of two-dimensional matrix memory designated by its first two arguments. Execution of the two-argument SRB function returns the current value of the cell of the matrix designated by its two arguments.

In relational memory, there is a fixed palette of points. Initially, there are no connections between any of the points in the palette. The writing function for relational memory provides a way to record the existence of a relation between two points of the palette. The reading function provides a way to determine whether a relation exists between two points. Execution of the two-argument SWB function draws a directed line from the point in the palette specified by its first argument to the point specified by its second argument. Execution of the two-argument SRB function returns +1 if there is a directed line connecting the point in the palette specified by its first argument to the point specified by its second argument.

The size of the indexed (vector) memory is determined at the time the memory is created. The choice is typically made randomly (subject to a preestablished maximum size). All references to an address in indexed memory are modulo the size of the indexed memory. The choice of memory size is made separately and independently for each newly created automatically defined store. Thus, vector memories of sizes that are appropriate for solving a given problem will tend to grow and prosper within the evolving population, while vector memories of inappropriate sizes will tend to disappear.

Two-dimensional matrix memory is an example of array memory of dimensionality two. Higher-dimensional array memory may also be created. When array memory of dimensionality k is being used, the SRB function possesses k arguments (to specify the k addresses in the k-dimensional array that is being read). The SWB function possesses $k + 1$ arguments (to specify the k addresses as well as the value that is to be written into the designated cell of the array). The dimensions of an array are determined at the time the memory is created. The choices are typically made randomly and independently for each separate dimension of the array at the time it is created, subject to a preestablished maximum size associated with each separate dimension of the array. For example, for two-dimensional array (matrix) memory, $N_{\text{max-ads-size-index-1}}$ is the maximum size for the array's first dimension and $N_{\text{max-ads-size-index-2}}$ is the maximum size for the array's second dimension. If an individual program in the population possesses more than one array, the choices of dimensions are made anew at the time each separate array is created. Each index of an address of the array is taken modulo the actual chosen size for that particular dimension. For example, suppose that the maximum size for a two-dimensional array's first dimension, $N_{\text{max-ads-size-index-1}}$, is 5 and the maximum size for an array's second dimension, $N_{\text{max-ads-size-index-2}}$, is 6. Suppose further that the actual size of the matrix is chosen to be 3×4. Then, when the matrix is addressed, the first index of the address in the matrix is taken modulo 3, and the second index is taken modulo 4.

Chapter 19 applies automatically defined stores in the form of named memory to the cart-centering (isotropic rocket) problem.

9.1 ARCHITECTURE-ALTERING OPERATIONS FOR AUTOMATICALLY DEFINED STORES

The architecture-altering operations described in this section provide a way to automate the decision as to whether to use internal storage on a particular problem, how much internal storage to use, what type of internal storage to use, and, of course, the specific way in which it is used.

9.1.1 Storage Creation Operation

The architecture-altering operation of storage creation operates on one individual in the population selected probabilistically on the basis of fitness. It creates one new offspring program for the new population by adding a storage writing branch, SWB, and a storage reading branch, SRB. The operation also creates appropriate names for referencing the two new branches, an invoking reference to the storage writing branch, SWB, and an invoking reference to the storage reading branch, SRB.

The steps in the architecture-altering operation of storage creation are as follows:

1. Select, based on fitness, an individual program from the population to participate in this operation. A copy is first made of the selected program, and the operation is then performed on the copy. Thus, the original unchanged program remains available to be reselected for another operation.
2. Randomly choose a dimension for the new memory (subject to a preestablished maximum dimensionality for the automatically defined stores, $N_{\text{max-ads-dimension}}$).
3. If it is appropriate for the chosen dimension of memory, randomly choose a type for the new memory from the preestablished repertoire of allowable types for the problem.

4. If it is appropriate for the chosen dimension and the chosen type of memory, randomly choose a size for the new memory subject to a preestablished maximum size associated with each separate dimension of the type of memory (e.g., $N_{\text{max-ads-size-index-1}}$ for the size of indexed memory for an array's first dimension, $N_{\text{max-ads-size-index-2}}$ for an array's second dimension, etc.).

5. Add a uniquely named new storage writing branch, SWB, to the selected program. The storage writing branch contains only fixed code necessary to implement writing the chosen type of memory.

6. Add a uniquely named new storage reading branch, SRB, to the selected program. The storage reading branch contains only fixed code necessary to implement reading the chosen type of memory.

7. Randomly pick one of the branches of the selected program. If the selected program has only one branch, that branch is automatically picked. The picking of the branch may, as an option, be restricted to a result-producing branch or other specified category of branches.

8. Randomly choose a point in this first picked branch of the selected program. Temporarily delete the entire subtree rooted at this chosen point. Insert a two-argument PROG2 connective function at this chosen point. Insert an invocation of the storage writing branch, SWB, as the first argument of the PROG2 and insert an invocation of the storage reading branch, SRB, as the second argument of the PROG2. Now restore the temporarily deleted subtree as the first argument of the invocation of the storage writing branch, SWB.

9. In the event that the dimensionality of the newly created memory is equal to or greater than 1, create an appropriate number of additional address arguments to both the invocation of the storage writing branch, SWB, and the invocation of the storage reading branch, SRB. The kth address argument of the storage writing branch, SWB, will be identical to the kth address argument of the storage reading branch, SRB. To create each such twice-needed address argument, randomly pick (independently from step 7 and all other address arguments) one of the branches of the selected program in the same manner as step 7. Then randomly choose (independently from step 8 and all other address arguments) a point in this newly picked branch of the selected program. Insert one copy of the entire subtree rooted at this newly chosen point in this newly picked branch of the selected program as the kth address argument of the storage writing branch, SWB, and insert a second copy of this entire subtree as the kth address argument of the storage reading branch, SRB.

10. The function set and terminal set of both branches of the new automatically defined store are empty. The function set of the picked branch of the selected program is enlarged to include the names of the storage writing branch, SWB, and the storage reading branch, SRB, of the newly created automatically defined store. The terminal set of the picked branch of the selected program is unchanged. (Note that, in discussing automatically defined stores, we treat the SRB for named memory as a zero-argument function, rather than as a terminal.) The function set of any branch in the program whose function set includes the picked branch (i.e., any branch that actually calls the picked branches or that is permitted to call the picked branches) is enlarged to include the names of the storage writing branch,

SWB, and the storage reading branch, SRB, of the newly created automatically defined store. The terminal set of any branch in the program whose function set includes the picked branches is not affected by this operation.

Suppose that the illustrative result-producing branch of a computer program shown in Figure 9.1 is the branch that is picked in step 7 during the operation of storage creation. Suppose that point 5 is the point chosen in step 8 from the branch picked in Figure 9.1 during the operation of storage creation. If so, the three-point subtree

```
(- X 0.789)
```

rooted at point 5 is temporarily deleted from the branch (and held aside for later use). As shown in Figure 9.2, a two-argument PROG2 connective function (labeled 8) is inserted at this chosen point. An invocation of SWB 9 is inserted as the first argument of this PROG2 and an invocation of SRB 10 is inserted as the second argument of this PROG2. The temporarily deleted three-point subtree is now inserted as the argument of the invocation of SWB 9. If the newly created internal storage is of dimensionality 0 (e.g., named memory, a pushdown stack, or a queue), the figure shows the result of the operation of storage creation. If the newly created internal storage is of dimensionality 1 or higher, both the SWB and SRB would possess additional argument(s) specifying address(es) in the newly created memory.

When the program is executed, the PROG2 8 first executes the SWB 9. The SWB writes the value returned by the three-point subtree into the newly created memory. The SWB 9 returns this just-written value, but the PROG2 ignores the value returned by the execution of its first argument. The PROG2 then executes SRB 10. The SRB reads the value in the newly created memory and returns this just-read value. The PROG2 then returns the value returned by the SRB. Consequently, the value returned by PROG2 8 is identical to the value returned by the original three-point subtree rooted at point 5 (Figure 9.1). Moreover, if the original subtree contains side-effecting functions, these functions are executed in precisely the same sequential order as before the storage creation operation. Once the architecture becomes open to evolution by means of the architecture-altering operations, functions and terminals often migrate from one part of the evolving overall program to another. This subsequent migration occurs because of crossover, because of mutation (since newly created functions and terminals enter the set of ingredients from which new subtrees are randomly created), and because of subsequent architecture-altering operations.

The value(s) returned and the action(s) performed by the overall program are unchanged by the operation of storage creation. That is, the offspring program produced by the architecture-altering operation of storage creation is semantically equivalent to the original selected program (its parent).

The parent that spawned the new individual program is usually a reasonably fit member of its generation. The offspring produced by the storage creation operation is equally fit (assuming that the problem's fitness measure is oblivious to the program's structure and the fitness cases do not vary from generation to generation). Thus, both parent and offspring have a good chance of surviving in the population for some time into the future. As the two diverge over a period of generations, the fitness of some descendent of one will generally become better than the fitness of some descendent of the other. That is, the parent and offspring and their descendents will compete with one another (and, of

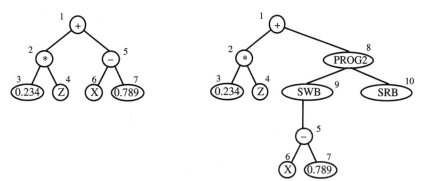

Figure 9.1   Illustrative program before storage creation

Figure 9.2   Illustrative program after storage creation

course, other individuals in the population) for survival during subsequent generations of the evolutionary process. Thus, the storage creation operation sets up an experimental trial, during the run of genetic programming, as to whether a program with internal storage is, in fact, beneficial. The competitive pressures of the environment (as expressed by the problem's fitness measure) ultimately determine the outcome of the trial. Time will tell whether internal storage is beneficial to the overall goal of solving the problem at hand. If internal storage is necessary to solve a given problem, individuals with internal storage should be fruitful and should multiply in the population.

The operation of storage creation can be implemented without explicitly introducing the PROG2 connective into the function set of the problem. In this alternative implementation, the functionality of the PROG2 is incorporated into the storage writing branch, SWB. The modified version of the SWB possesses one additional final argument, namely, the SRB. The modified version of the SWB is inserted in lieu of the chosen subtree (i.e., the three-point subtree in the example). The modified version of the SWB first writes the desired value into the newly created memory (as before) and then executes this final argument, the SRB.

There are several parameters for controlling the operation of storage creation:

1. The storage creation operation is controlled by a parameter specifying the probability of executing the operation on each generation, $p_{storage\text{-}creation}$.
2. There is a maximum number of automatically defined stores, $N_{max\text{-}ads}$, for each program in the population.
3. The storage creation operation is controlled by a parameter specifying the maximum dimensionality, $N_{max\text{-}ads\text{-}dimension}$, of the memory being created.
4. The storage creation operation is controlled by a data structure specifying the allowable types of internal storage for each allowable dimensionality.
5. The storage creation operation is controlled by a set of parameters specifying the maximum size associated with each separate dimension of the vector, matrix, or array (e.g., $N_{max\text{-}ads\text{-}size\text{-}index\text{-}1}$ for the first dimension, $N_{max\text{-}ads\text{-}size\text{-}index\text{-}2}$ for the second dimension, if any, and so forth).

9.1.2 Storage Deletion

The storage writing branch, SWB, and the storage reading branch, SRB, that constitute an automatically defined store may be deleted from a computer program during the run of genetic programming using an architecture-altering operation analogous to subroutine deletion, iteration deletion, loop deletion, and recursion deletion.

The operation of storage deletion operates on one individual in the population selected probabilistically on the basis of fitness and creates one new offspring program for the new population by deleting both branches of one automatically defined store of the existing program.

The deletion of an iteration-performing branch raises the question of how to modify invocations of the to-be-deleted branches in the remaining branches of the overall program. The options include random regeneration, consolidation, and even potentially (at the expense of size) macro expansion (all originally discussed in Section 5.5 in connection with subroutine deletion).

Appropriate changes in the function and terminal sets of the affected branches of the program must be made to reflect the deletion.

The operation of storage deletion creates the opportunity to conduct an experimental trial, during the run of genetic programming, as to whether a particular automatically defined store is, in fact, useful. After the deletion, the program with the reduced amount of storage competes with other individuals in the population (often including the reasonably fit parent that gave rise to it) for survival in subsequent generations of the evolutionary process.

9.1.3 Storage Duplication

Storage may be duplicated using an architecture-altering operation analogous to subroutine duplication, iteration duplication, loop duplication, and recursion duplication. The architecture-altering operation of storage duplication preserves the semantics of the program.

The operation of storage duplication operates on one individual in the population selected probabilistically on the basis of fitness and creates one new offspring program for the new population by duplicating both branches of one automatically defined store of the existing program and creating invocations of the newly created automatically defined store.

Appropriate changes in the function and terminal sets of the affected branches of the program must be made to reflect the duplication.

9.2 DYNAMIC CHANGES IN THE DIMENSIONALITY OF MEMORY

Named memory can be viewed as array memory of dimensionality 0, and indexed (vector) memory can be viewed as array memory of dimensionality 1. The architecture-altering operations of storage argument duplication and storage argument deletion provide a mechanism for dynamically altering the dimensionality of an already-created memory array during the run of genetic programming. These operations act on the pair of branches that constitute an automatically defined store. Since there is no body to the storage reading and writing branches, there is no analog, in the realm of internal storage, to the operation of argument creation.

9.2.1   Storage Argument Duplication

The architecture-altering operation of storage argument duplication changes the storage reading branch function (SRB) and the storage writing branch function (SWB) by increasing the number of arguments that they each possess. Storage argument duplication operates on one individual selected from the population probabilistically on the basis of fitness. A program with k storage reading and writing branches begets an offspring program with k storage reading and writing branches. However, there is one more argument in one pair of storage reading and writing branches of the offspring (compared to the corresponding pair of branches in the parent). The operation appropriately modifies the argument list for the pair of branches involved.

The architecture-altering operation of storage argument duplication operates in the following way:

1. Select an individual program from the population to participate in this operation.
2. Pick one pair of storage reading and writing branches for named memory, indexed (vector) memory, or array memory from the selected program. If the selected program has only one such pair of branches, that pair is automatically chosen. If the selected program has no such pair of branches, this operation is aborted.
3. Choose one of the arguments of the picked pair of storage reading and writing branches of the selected program as the argument-to-be-duplicated. If the picked function-defining branch already has the maximum number of arguments established for the problem, this operation is aborted.
4. Add a uniquely named new argument to the argument list of the picked pair of storage reading and writing branches, thus increasing the number of arguments in their argument lists by one.
5. For each occurrence of an invocation of the picked storage reading branch anywhere in the selected program, identify the argument subtree in that invocation corresponding to the argument-to-be-duplicated and duplicate that argument subtree in that invocation, thereby increasing the number of arguments in the invocation by one.
6. Similarly perform step 5 for each occurrence of an invocation of the picked storage writing branch anywhere in the selected program. Note that the storage writing branch always has one more argument than its associated storage reading branch.
7. Replicate the preexisting internal storage for the selected program so it becomes an array with one additional dimension. If argument j is chosen in step 3 and $N_{\text{max-ads-size-index-j}}$ is the maximum size for the array's jth dimension, then the amount of internal storage will increase by a factor of $N_{\text{max-ads-size-index-j}}$ after this replication.
8. The function set of any branch whose function set includes the picked storage reading branch or the picked storage writing branch (i.e., any branch that actually calls or that is permitted to call them) is unchanged; however, the arity of both the picked storage reading branch and the picked storage writing branch is

incremented by one in the list containing the number of arguments possessed by each function for any branch whose function set includes the picked branches. The terminal set of any branch whose function set includes the picked storage reading branch or the picked storage writing branch is unchanged.

The difference between array memory of dimensionality k versus array memory of dimensionality $k + 1$ is that higher-dimensional internal storage permits information to be accessed with a greater degree of refinement. The operation of storage argument duplication sets up an experimental trial, during the run of genetic programming, as to whether higher-dimensional internal storage is necessary or superfluous.

9.2.2   Storage Argument Deletion

The architecture-altering operation of storage argument deletion changes the storage reading branch function (SRB) and the storage writing branch function (SWB) by decreasing the number of arguments that they each possess. Storage argument deletion operates on one individual selected from the population probabilistically on the basis of fitness. A program with k storage reading and writing branches begets an offspring program with k storage reading and writing branches. However, there is one less argument in one pair of storage reading and writing branches of the offspring (compared to the corresponding pair of branches in the parent). The operation appropriately modifies the argument list for the pair of branches involved.

The architecture-altering operation of storage argument deletion operates in the following way:

1. Select an individual program from the population to participate in this operation.
2. Pick one pair of storage reading and writing branches for named memory, indexed (vector) memory, or array memory from the selected program. If the selected program has only one such pair of branches, that pair is automatically chosen. If the selected program has no such pair of branches, this operation is aborted.
3. Choose one of the arguments of the picked pair of storage reading and writing branches of the selected program as the argument-to-be-deleted. If the picked function-defining branch already has the minimum number of arguments established for the problem, this operation is aborted.
4. Delete the argument-to-be-deleted from the argument list of both branches of the picked pair of storage reading and writing branches of the selected program, thus decreasing the number of arguments in each of their argument lists by one.
5. For each occurrence of an invocation of the picked storage reading branch anywhere in the selected program, delete the argument subtree in that invocation corresponding to the argument-to-be-deleted, thereby decreasing the number of arguments in the invocation by one.
6. Similarly perform step 5 for each occurrence of an invocation of the picked storage writing branch anywhere in the selected program.
7. Compress the preexisting internal storage for the selected program so it becomes an array with fewer dimensions. If argument j is chosen in step 3 and $N_{\text{max-ads-size-index-}j}$ is the maximum size for the array's jth dimension, then the amount of internal storage will decrease by a factor of $N_{\text{max-ads-size-index-}j}$ after this compression.

8. The function set of any branch whose function set includes the picked storage reading branch or the picked storage writing branch (i.e., any branch that actually calls or that is permitted to call them) is unchanged; however, the arity of both the picked storage reading branch and the picked storage writing branch is decremented by one in the list containing the number of arguments possessed by each function for any branch whose function set includes the picked branches. The terminal set of any branch whose function set includes the picked storage reading branch or the picked storage writing branch is unchanged.

Higher-dimensional array memory is superfluous for many problems. The operation of storage argument deletion creates the opportunity to conduct an experimental trial, during the run of genetic programming, as to whether all of the information in a particular array and the prevailing method of accessing it are useful for solving the problem at hand. After the deletion, the program with less information (and with a less specific way to access it) competes with other individuals in the population for survival in subsequent generations of the run.

9.3   SUMMARY

Genetic programming can implement internal storage in numerous forms, including named memory (Koza 1992e, 1994g), indexed (vector) memory (Teller 1994a, 1994b), matrix memory (Andre 1994b), state (Raik and Browne 1997), and relational memory (Brave 1995a, 1996c).

Langdon (1995, 1996a, 1996b, 1996c) and *Genetic Programming and Data Structures: Genetic Programming + Data Structures = Automatic Programming!* (Langdon 1998) describes the implementation of a wide variety of data structures in genetic programming, including stacks, queues, and lists. This chapter provides a general approach to creating, using, and deleting internal storage in evolving computer programs in the form of the automatically defined stores. Based on this work, genetic programming possesses the following attribute of a system for automatically creating computer programs (Chapter 1):

*   **ATTRIBUTE NO. 7** (Internal storage): It has the ability to use internal storage in the form of single variables, vectors, matrices, arrays, stacks, queues, lists, relational memory, and other data structures.

Self-Organization of Hierarchies and Program Architecture

Hierarchies are central to efficient and effective computer programming. As D. C. Ince (1992) said, in reviewing Turing's 1945 "Proposals for Development in the Mathematics Division of an Automatic Computer Engine (ACE)":

> The third feature of [Turing's 1945] proposal—and almost certainly the most important—was the idea of a hierarchy of programs. This was the first instance of a developer drawing attention to the fact that *certain operations for a computer would be required time and time again, and that some facilities would be required for storing the programs . . . that implement these operations, and for controlling the hierarchical execution of these programs.* Turing's solution . . . is still the preferred method for controlling the execution of software.

> It has been claimed that Turing's ideas represent the invention of the art of programming (Hodges 1983). This claim can be seen as something of a slight exaggeration as Conrad Zuse had, during World War II, worked out some similar ideas; indeed, a good case could be made that Babbage was the real father of programming. Nevertheless, *the description of a software system as a hierarchic series of programs which communicate with each other* is a unique insight which represents a major leap forward from the rather primitive programming ideas that were current in 1945 and 1946. [Emphasis added.]

Chapter 5 presented architecture-altering operations for creating, duplicating, and deleting subroutines and for creating, duplicating, and deleting the arguments possessed by them during the run of genetic programming. The dummy arguments (formal parameters) that are passed to a subroutine and the value(s) returned by a subroutine are the means for communicating between subroutines and between subroutines and the main program.

In addition, architecture-altering operations were described for dynamically creating, duplicating, and deleting automatically defined iterations (Chapter 6), automatically defined loops (Chapter 7), and automatically defined recursions (Chapter 8) and for dynamically creating, duplicating, and deleting the arguments possessed by them. The dummy arguments (formal parameters) that are passed to an ADI, ADL, or ADR and the value(s) returned by them constitute their means of communication with other parts of the overall program.

The hierarchy of references among the branches of the program can be broadened by the operations of

- subroutine duplication (Section 5.1.2),
- iteration duplication (Section 6.2.2),
- loop duplication (Section 7.2.2), and
- recursion duplication (Section 8.1.3).

The hierarchy of references among the branches of the program can be deepened by the operations of

- subroutine creation (Section 5.3.1),
- iteration creation (Section 6.2.1),
- loop creation (Section 7.2.1), and
- recursion creation (Section 8.1.1).

Broadening may set the stage for subsequent deepening of the hierarchy by crossover.

The hierarchy of references among the branches of the program can be pruned by the operations of

- subroutine deletion (Section 5.5.4),
- iteration deletion (Section 6.2.3),
- loop deletion (Section 7.2.3), and
- recursion deletion (Section 8.1.2).

The amount of information that is communicated within the hierarchy of a program can be dynamically changed by the operations of argument duplication (Section 5.2), argument creation (Section 5.4), and argument deletion (Section 5.6) and their counterparts for automatically defined iterations (Chapter 6), automatically defined loops (Chapter 7), and automatically defined recursions (Chapter 8).

In summary, the architecture-altering operations for ADFs, ADF arguments, ADIs, ADLs, and ADRs enable genetic programming to automatically create a hierarchical organization of the groups of useful steps and to create what Ince (1992) calls "a hierarchic series of programs which communicate with each other." Thus, genetic programming possesses the following attribute of a system for automatically creating computer programs (Chapter 1):

- **ATTRIBUTE NO. 9** (Self-organization of hierarchies): It has the ability to automatically organize groups of steps into a hierarchy.

Chapter 9 described the automatically defined store and architecture-altering operations for dynamically creating, duplicating, and deleting internal storage. The operations of storage argument duplication and storage argument deletion permit the dynamic changing of internal storage.

Each offspring created by an architecture-altering operation (for ADFs, ADF arguments, ADIs, ADLs, ADRs, and ADSs) constitutes an experimental trial, undertaken during the run of genetic programming, as to whether a particular subroutine, argument, iteration, loop, recursion, or element of internal storage structure is, in fact, beneficial to the overall effort of solving the problem at hand. The competitive pressures of the environment (as expressed by the problem's fitness measure) ultimately determine the outcome of the trial. These trials are conducted automatically as a part of the ongoing competition for survival among the evolving individuals in the population during the run of genetic programming. Thus, genetic programming possesses the following attribute of a system for automatically creating computer programs (Chapter 1):

- **ATTRIBUTE NO. 10** (Automatic determination of program architecture): It has the ability to automatically determine whether to employ subroutines, iterations, loops, recursions, and internal storage, and to automatically determine the number of arguments possessed by each subroutine, iteration, loop, and recursion.

Later sections of this book will demonstrate that the ability of genetic programming to automatically construct a hierarchy of intercommunicating programs enables genetic programming to address a wide variety of problems and produce results that are competitive with human-produced results.

Rotating the Tires on an Automobile

This chapter describes a gedankenexperiment in which we visualize several different ways of using genetic programming to evolve a problem-solving procedure to perform the hypothetical task of rotating the tires on an automobile. In this task, the goal is to remove the four tires from their axles and remount them on specified different axles.

The experiment will visualize the use of genetic programming on this task in the following ways:

1. without automatically defined functions (i.e., in the fashion of most of Koza 1992e),
2. with automatically defined functions (Section 2.3.6) (i.e., in the fashion of most of Koza 1994g),
3. with automatically defined functions and with the technique of evolutionary selection of the architecture (as described in Koza 1994g, Chapters 21–25),
4. with the architecture-altering operations for automatically defined functions (Chapter 5 of this book), including the operations of
   • subroutine duplication,
   • argument duplication,
   • subroutine creation,
   • argument creation,
   • subroutine deletion, and
   • argument deletion,
5. with the architecture-altering operations for automatically defined iterations (Chapter 6), including the operation of iteration creation,
6. with the architecture-altering operations for automatically defined loops (Chapter 7), including the operation of loop creation,
7. with the architecture-altering operations for automatically defined recursions (Chapter 8), including the operation of recursion creation, and
8. with the architecture-altering operations for automatically defined stores (Chapter 9), including the operation of storage creation.

The to-be-evolved procedure has access to independent variables (terminals) providing all necessary information about the problem environment (including, among other things, the size of the bolts for fastening a tire to an axle, the number of bolts on a tire, and the presence or absence of a hubcap). In addition, the to-be-evolved procedure has access to a repertoire of primitive functions that is sufficient to perform the task at hand (including, among other things, functions for removing a hubcap, unfastening a bolt, and sliding the tire off the axle). In addition, the to-be-evolved problem-solving procedure has access to certain extraneous information (such as the color of the car) and certain extraneous functions (such as opening and closing the windows of the car).

There is considerable underlying modularity, symmetry, and regularity in this hypothetical task. In fact, this task offers numerous opportunities for reuse of sequences of procedural steps because all four tires can be removed and remounted in essentially the same way for any particular car. The task also presents opportunities for specialization and generalization because the only difference in the procedure for different models of cars lies in what a human planner would consider to be details of the problem (e.g., whether there is a hubcap to remove and remount). In addition, the task presents opportunities for parameterization of the procedures (e.g., based on the size and number of the bolts on each tire).

Before proceeding to the gedankenexperiment, we first list the architecture-altering operations (Chapters 5 through 9) that we will be discussing in this chapter as items 2.c.iv–xiii of the executional steps for a run of genetic programming.

The steps for executing genetic programming are as follows:

1. Generate an initial random population (generation 0) of computer programs.
2. Iteratively perform the following substeps until the termination criterion of the run has been satisfied:
   a. Execute each program in the population and assign it (explicitly or implicitly) a fitness value according to how well it solves the problem.
   b. Select program(s) from the population to participate in the genetic operations in c below.
   c. Create new program(s) for the population by applying the following genetic operations:
      i. *Reproduction*: Copy an existing program to the new population.
      ii. *Crossover*: Create new offspring program(s) for the new population by recombining randomly chosen parts of two existing programs.
      iii. *Mutation*: Create one new offspring program for the new population by randomly mutating a randomly chosen part of one existing program.
      iv. *Subroutine duplication*: Create one new offspring program for the new population by duplicating one function-defining branch of one existing program and making additional appropriate changes to reflect this change.
      v. *Argument duplication*: Create one new offspring program for the new population by duplicating one argument of one function-defining branch of one existing program and making additional appropriate changes to reflect this change.
      vi. *Subroutine deletion*: Create one new offspring program for the new population by deleting one function-defining branch of one existing program and making additional appropriate changes to reflect this change.
      vii. *Argument deletion*: Create one new offspring program for the new population by deleting one argument of one function-defining branch of one

existing program and making additional appropriate changes to reflect this change.

viii. *Subroutine creation*: Create one new offspring program for the new population by adding one new function-defining branch containing a portion of an existing branch and creating a reference to that new branch.

ix. *Argument creation*: Create one new offspring program for the population by adding one new argument to the argument list of an existing function-defining branch and appropriately modifying the contents of the branch and references to the branch.

x. *Iteration creation*: Create one new offspring program for the new population by adding an automatically defined iteration consisting of one new iteration-performing branch (composed of a portion of an existing branch) and by creating an invoking reference to the newly created automatically defined iteration.

xi. *Loop creation*: Create one new offspring program for the new population by adding an automatically defined loop consisting of a loop initialization branch, a loop condition branch, a loop body branch, and a loop update branch (each composed of a portion of an existing branch) and by creating an invoking reference to the newly created automatically defined loop.

xii. *Recursion creation*: Create one new offspring program for the new population by adding an automatically defined recursion consisting of a recursion condition branch, a recursion body branch, a recursion update branch, and a recursion ground branch (each composed of a portion of an existing branch) and by creating an invoking reference to the newly created automatically defined iteration.

xiii. *Storage creation*: Create one new offspring program for the new population by adding an automatically defined store consisting of a storage writing branch and a storage reading branch.

3. After satisfaction of the termination criterion (which usually entails a maximum number of generations to be run as well as a problem-specific success predicate), the single best computer program in the population produced during the run (the best-so-far individual) is designated as the result of the run. This result may (or may not) be a solution (or approximate solution) to the problem.

11.1   APPROACH WITHOUT ADFs

First consider the task of rotating tires from the perspective of the predominant approach used in *Genetic Programming: On the Programming of Computers by Means of Natural Selection* (Koza 1992e). When genetic programming without automatically defined functions is applied to a particular problem, the user must perform five preparatory steps prior to the run.

The user must first decide upon the ingredients from which the to-be-evolved programs will be composed. The terminal set for this hypothetical problem consists of the information-carrying independent variables (i.e., terminals) such as the number of bolts, the size of the bolts, the presence or absence of hubcaps, and the color of the car. The function set consists of the various primitive operations (e.g., unfastening a bolt, sliding the tire off the axle, opening the windows, and closing the windows).

Fitness is the total number of tires that end up on their specified axles after the complete execution of the program or after some reasonable amount of time. The fitness of a program is computed over a suite of fitness cases consisting of various models of cars. The fitness cases include cars of different colors, with and without hubcaps, and with the tires being fastened by different numbers and sizes of bolts.

When automatically defined functions are not being used, the evolved programs typically consist only of a result-producing branch. In principle, genetic programming should be able to evolve a solution to this problem without employing automatically defined functions, provided the population size is sufficiently large and provided that the run is allowed to continue for a sufficiently large number of generations.

Although each run of genetic programming is different, we can nevertheless make certain statements about the likely characteristics of the evolved solution. Since automatically defined functions are not being used, each identical or marginally different situation must necessarily be handled by a uniquely crafted and separately learned sequence of steps. Although all four tires can be removed and remounted in essentially the same way for any particular car, it is most unlikely that one common procedure would be evolved and used four times (once for each of the tires). Instead, the overall evolved solution will almost certainly contain four uniquely crafted (and therefore different) sequences of steps for handling each of the four tires. Similarly, it is most unlikely that one common procedure would be evolved and reused for each of the bolts belonging to each tire. Instead, the solution will contain a uniquely crafted sequence of steps for unfastening each bolt on each of the four tires.

Moreover, since automatically defined functions are not being used, there would be no parameterization of the sequence of steps for unfastening the bolts. Thus, models of cars whose tires are fastened by one size of bolts cannot be handled with a common sequence of reusable code in the same way as models with another size of bolts. Instead, there will be one sequence of code that causes the $\frac{1}{2}$-inch wrench to be used when the bolt size is determined to be $\frac{1}{2}$ inch, and an additional, separate sequence of code that causes the $\frac{5}{8}$-inch wrench to be used on $\frac{5}{8}$-inch bolts. Moreover, there will be one sequence of code for handling models of cars whose tires have six bolts, and separate sequences of code for handling tires that have five or four bolts.

A run of genetic programming without automatically defined functions will not be able to exploit the considerable underlying modularity, symmetry, and regularity of the tire-changing task. Because the evolved solution will not have parameterized and reused sequences of code, it is safe to say that the program necessary to perform this task will be large. The evolution of large amounts of code typically requires the expenditure of a considerable amount of computational effort (Section 12.6.1).

11.2 APPROACH WITH ADFs

Now consider the task of rotating tires from the perspective of the predominant approach used in *Genetic Programming II: Automatic Discovery of Reusable Programs* (Koza 1994g) (and in Chapters 20 and 21 of Koza 1992e).

The fact that all four tires can be removed and remounted in essentially the same way for any particular car suggests that the task of rotating the tires of a car can be performed with the aid of automatically defined functions.

When automatically defined functions are being used, a solution to a problem can be interpreted such that each automatically defined function represents a subproblem; the body of each automatically defined function represents the way to solve the subproblem; and the result-producing branch represents the assembly of the solutions to the subproblems into a solution of the overall problem. If there are four tires, the result-producing branch will likely invoke the automatically defined function four times in order to perform the overall task of rotating the tires.

Each automatically defined function also can be interpreted as a change of representation. If, for example, we compare a solution to an overall problem by a result-producing branch that does not invoke any automatically defined functions to one that does, the difference can be viewed as a change of representation. The version of the solution with automatically defined functions solves the problem in terms of the new representation created by the application of the automatically defined functions. The result-producing branch of the solution with automatically defined functions operates in the new world of the changed representation. Details are usually invisible at the new and higher level of the changed representation.

If automatically defined functions are added to genetic programming, genetic programming will probably produce a solution to the overall problem that will *reuse* and *parameterize* certain sequences of steps, rather than handling each identical or marginally different situation with a uniquely crafted and separately learned sequence of steps.

For example, it is reasonably safe to anticipate that genetic programming will produce a solution in which a tire-dismounting function evolves within the overall multipart program so that the result-producing branch of the overall program is able to invoke this function with the bolt size as a parameter. When the bolt-unfastening function is parameterized by the bolt size, separate code will not be necessary for handling each different size of bolt.

The ability to generalize is an important aspect of artificial intelligence and automated programming. A parameterized automatically defined function can be interpreted as a generalization in the sense that a parameterized function-defining branch is a generalized procedure for performing some subtask. A particular instantiation of the parameter has the effect of specializing the general procedure to a particular situation.

It is reasonably safe to anticipate that genetic programming with automatically defined functions will evolve a solution such that the size of the overall program will be considerably smaller than the size of the program evolved without them. That is, parsimony is an emergent consequence of the availability of automatically defined functions. This parsimony arises because of the generalization that is inherent in reuse.

In addition, it is reasonable to anticipate (based on Koza 1994g and voluminous subsequent work by numerous researchers) that the evolution of a solution to this inherently repetitive problem will require the expenditure of less computational effort with automatically defined functions than without them.

When automatically defined functions are being used, the evolved program would, of course, consist of a result-producing branch and one or more function-defining branches. The question arises, how many automatically defined functions will there be? And how many arguments will each automatically defined function possess?

Before the user can apply genetic programming with automatically defined functions to a problem, the user must employ some technique for determining the architecture of the overall solution. These techniques include evolutionary selection of the architecture (Section 11.3) or the architecture-altering operations (Section 11.8). Of course, determining the architecture is not the same as determining the particular sequence of steps in each automatically defined function. However, once chosen, the architecture of the overall program constrains the decomposition of the original problem into subproblems. Each particular architecture permits and prohibits certain ways of decomposing the overall problem into subproblems. Each particular architecture favors the emergence of certain decompositions while making others less likely.

The number of available automatically defined functions affects, in general, the character of the solution. If, for example, two or more automatically defined functions are available, it is reasonable to anticipate that genetic programming will evolve a solution in which separate automatically defined functions are devoted to the tire-dismounting and bolt-unfastening subtasks. However, if only one automatically defined function is available, then either both the tire-dismounting and the bolt-unfastening subtasks would have to be performed inside one automatically defined function, or one of these subtasks would have to be performed in the result-producing branch (where there would be no opportunity for parameterized reuse of code).

The number of arguments possessed by each automatically defined function also generally affects the character of the solution. If, for example, each automatically defined function possesses only one argument, then it would not be possible to take an action inside any of the automatically defined functions based on two or more variables.

11.3 APPROACH WITH EVOLUTIONARY SELECTION OF THE ARCHITECTURE

As previously mentioned (Section 3.5), evolutionary selection of the architecture during the run of genetic programming (Koza 1994g, Chapters 21–25) is one of the techniques by which the user can determine the architecture of the overall program. In this technique, the population is architecturally diverse starting with the initial random population of generation 0. Then there is a competition among the preexisting architectures in the population. However, no new architectures are ever created (or altered) during the run with this approach.

11.4 APPROACH WITH ADIs

The task of rotating tires is now considered from the perspective of an automatically defined iteration (Chapter 6). When the automatically defined iteration is invoked, it applies a common sequence of steps to the problem-specific finite sequence of four tires. An automatically defined iteration is similar to an automatically defined function in that both mechanisms exploit the fact that all four tires can be removed and remounted in essentially the same way for any particular car. The two approaches differ in that the automatically defined iteration need be invoked only once, while the automatically defined function must be invoked on four separate occasions.

When an automatically defined iteration is being used, the body of the automatically defined iteration can be interpreted as the way to solve the subproblem of changing tire i. When the automatically defined iteration is executed for all four values of i from 1 to 4, the automatically defined iteration is, in effect, assembling the solution to the subproblem into a solution of the overall problem. The result-producing branch invokes the automatically defined iteration once in order to perform the task of rotating the four tires.

It is reasonable to anticipate that the evolution of a solution to this inherently iterative problem will require the expenditure of less computational effort with automatically defined iterations than without them.

In addition, it is safe to anticipate that parsimony is an emergent consequence of the availability of automatically defined iterations. Automatically defined iterations are a mechanism for code reuse. The reuse inherent in automatically defined iterations enables genetic programming to produce solutions whose size is smaller than the size of programs evolved without a mechanism for code reuse.

11.5   APPROACH WITH ADLs

Now consider the task of rotating tires from the perspective of an automatically defined loop (Chapter 7). An automatically defined loop has a loop initialization branch, loop condition branch, loop body branch, and loop update branch.

An automatically defined loop is similar to an automatically defined iteration in that both approaches iteratively execute a common sequence of steps. The two approaches have similarities and differences. The automatically defined iteration is provided with external information that the car has four tires. The ADI then executes its body a predetermined number of times (four). It executes its body once for each of the four preidentified tires. In contrast, the automatically defined loop is not provided with the information that the car has four tires. Its loop condition branch must terminate the loop after a satisfactory number of executions of the loop's body.

Automatically defined loops are a mechanism for code reuse. Thus, it is safe to anticipate that genetic programming will produce a solution using ADLs whose size is smaller than the size of programs evolved without such a mechanism for code reuse.

Again, because of the inherently iterative nature of the tire-changing problem, it is reasonable to anticipate that the evolution of a solution will require the expenditure of considerably less computational effort with automatically defined loops than without any iterative mechanism. It is also reasonable to anticipate that solving this problem with automatically defined loops may take more computational effort than solving this problem with automatically defined iterations. Ideally, the automatically defined loop would be invoked once by the result-producing branch and would execute its body four times. However, since the four branches of the automatically defined loop are all subject to modification during the evolutionary process, it is likely that a far less efficient sequence of steps will evolve. For example, the automatically defined loop might conceivably execute its body six times (thereby doing two additional and unnecessary dismounts and remounts). Or, all four tires might be handled by invoking the automatically defined loop on two different occasions, with each invocation causing two of the four tires to be dismounted and mounted.

11.6 APPROACH WITH ADRs

The task of rotating tires can also be considered from the perspective of automatically defined recursions (Chapter 8). An automatically defined recursion has a recursion condition branch, a recursion body branch, a recursion update branch, and a recursion ground branch.

An automatically defined recursion resembles an automatically defined loop in that both have four branches and both repeatedly execute a common sequence of steps while some condition is satisfied. Presumably an ADR for the tire-rotating task would proceed from axle to axle and execute the steps required for dismounting one tire and mounting the tire that was dismounted from the axle handled previously (until such time as no such previous axle remains).

Because ADRs (like ADLs) are a mechanism for code reuse, it is safe to anticipate that genetic programming will produce a solution using ADRs whose size is smaller than the size of programs evolved without such a mechanism for code reuse.

Because of the inherently repetitive nature of the tire-changing problem, it is reasonable to anticipate that the evolution of a solution will require the expenditure of considerably less computational effort with automatically defined recursions than without any recursive or iterative mechanism.

11.7 APPROACH WITH ADSs

The task of rotating tires can also be considered from the perspective of automatically defined stores (Chapter 9).

Although the task of rotating the tires can certainly be performed without the use of memory, it is possible to perform the task by first doing some of the steps for each tire, storing certain information in memory, and then doing some additional steps for each tire based on the contents of the memory. For example, the tires could be inspected one by one to see if they have hubcaps. The result of each of the four inspections is a single bit of information that could be stored in memory. After examining all four tires in this manner, each tire could be dismounted. At the time each tire is dismounted, no inspection concerning hubcaps is made. Instead, the memory is referenced, and the appropriate action is taken based on the contents of the memory.

Internal storage can be viewed as yet another mechanism for reuse in computer programs. Code is reused in programs by means of subroutines, iterations, loops, and recursions. An intermediate result (which is produced by the execution of code) can be reused by means of internal memory.

11.8   RELATION OF ARCHITECTURE-ALTERING OPERATIONS TO GENERALIZATION AND SPECIALIZATION

The architecture-altering operations described here provide a way to determine the architecture. The architecture-altering operations enable the architecture to be evolved dynamically and automatically during the run of genetic programming in the sense of actually creating new architectures and altering existing architectures during the run.

The architecture-altering operations can be viewed from five perspectives:

1.   The architecture-altering operations provide a new way to solve the problem of determining the architecture of the overall program in the context of genetic programming.

2.   They provide an automatic implementation of the ability to specialize and generalize in the context of automated problem solving.

3.   The architecture-altering operations, in conjunction with automatically defined functions, provide a way to automatically and dynamically decompose problems into subproblems and then automatically solve the overall problem by assembling the solutions of the subproblems into a solution of the overall problem.

4.   These operations, in conjunction with automatically defined functions, provide a way to automatically and dynamically change the representation of the problem while simultaneously solving the problem.

5.   These operations, in conjunction with automatically defined functions, provide a way to automatically and dynamically discover useful subspaces (usually of lower dimensionality than that of the overall problem) and then automatically assemble a solution to the overall problem from solutions applicable to the individual subspaces.

Now consider the second perspective above involving specialization and generalization. As previously mentioned, the initial random population may be uniform and ADF-less, it may be uniform and consist of programs with the minimal ADF structure (the minimalist approach), or it may be architecturally diverse. The minimalist approach is used in the discussion below.

11.8.1   Generalization by Subroutine Deletion and Argument Deletion

The architecture-altering operations enable arguments and branches of programs to be deleted during a run of genetic programming. These deletions may be interpreted as generalizations in the sense that a generalization ignores some previously available information or deletes some previously performed step in carrying out a task. The deletion of an argument or branch may be interpreted as a generalization of the procedure represented by the branch.

Of course, some generalizations are useful and some are not. The process of generalizing a procedure is often useful because it permits the development of a procedure that is applicable to a wider variety of situations. Generalization may also be desirable because it shortens the description of the procedure (i.e., improves parsimony).

First, consider the deletion of an argument. The deletion of the color of the car from the argument list of a branch would be a helpful simplification of the procedure performed by the branch since there is no possible benefit from this extraneous variable in solving the problem of rotating the tires. If the color of the car is actually used by the branch, deleting this argument will make the branch applicable to a wider variety of situations (with no degradation in performance as measured by the problem's fitness measure). If the color is ignored, deleting this argument will make the branch more parsimonious.

On the other hand, deletion may make vital information unavailable. Assuming that argument deletion by consolidation or argument deletion by random regeneration is being used, deleting an argument communicating vital information would (almost always) be an unhelpful generalization. The size of the tire's bolts is a necessary argument because the task cannot be performed with a wrench of unsuitable size. The tire-dismounting function cannot properly be performed without knowing how many bolts to remove.

Now consider deletion of a branch. The operation of subroutine deletion may be viewed as a generalization at the procedural level. After subroutine deletion by consolidation or random regeneration is performed, the overall program will (usually) be less specialized than before. For example, the deletion of a branch that lifts the car's hood would be a helpful simplification of the procedure performed by the overall program since lifting the hood is not helpful in solving the problem of rotating the tires. On the other hand, it would not be helpful to delete a branch that checks whether a hubcap is present because the wrench is useless for removing bolts if the bolts are inaccessible because of an unremoved hubcap. In either event, the operation of subroutine deletion usually produces a procedure with improved parsimony.

There is no way of knowing in advance whether a particular generalization will be helpful. However, natural selection will ultimately judge whether the offspring produced by a particular deletion prove to be more fit or less fit in grappling with the problem environment.

11.8.2   Specialization by Subroutine Duplication and Argument Duplication

In many instances of automated problem solving, it is desirable to have the ability to split the problem environment into different cases and treat the cases slightly differently. The operations of subroutine duplication and argument duplication set the stage for enabling a procedure to be specialized and refined at a later time. Such a specialization or refinement permits such slightly differing treatments of two similar but different situations. This specialization can occur at the argument level or procedure level.

For example, even though the procedure for changing the tire may be similar for all cars, the procedure must be specialized to each particular type of car by including a certain argument, such as the size of the bolts. Argument duplication provides a way to set the stage so that subsequent evolution can incorporate this additional information.

Subroutine duplication can provide a way to set the stage so that subsequent evolution can create a slightly different procedure for two models of cars. The procedure for changing the tire on a Cadillac may differ from the procedure for a Honda because the Cadillac may have a hubcap that must be removed to expose the bolts so that the wrench can then unfasten the bolts.

During the run, branches and arguments will be duplicated. For example, consider a program with a branch that hastily tries to unfasten the bolts without checking for the presence of a hubcap. Such a branch works satisfactorily for a car without hubcaps. A program with this branch will accrue a certain amount of fitness for correctly handling the subset of fitness cases involving cars with no hubcaps. However, this program will not receive the maximum possible value of fitness because it will not correctly handle the fitness cases involving cars with hubcaps. After a subroutine duplication, there are two branches, and both start by hastily trying to unfasten the bolts without checking for the presence of a hubcap. Each of these identical branches is invoked under different (randomly chosen) circumstances by their calling branches. Although subroutine duplication has no immediate effect, subsequent genetic operations may alter one or the other branch. Some of these alterations will make the overall program more fit at grappling with the problem environment by specializing one branch to some particular situation. For example, one of these branches may be modified by a subsequent genetic operation (e.g., a crossover or mutation) so that it checks for the presence of a hubcap, removes the hubcap, and then continues as before. This specialization is a potential benefit of a subroutine duplication.

Arguments may also be duplicated during the run. Although argument duplication has no immediate effect, the presence of an additional argument may, after subsequent operations, make the altered program more fit at grappling with certain fitness cases from the problem environment by enabling it to specialize its behavior in response to the additional information provided by the additional argument. Of course, a specialization may be productive, counterproductive, useless, or harmless when applied to a particular problem. For example, an argument duplication may make the color of the car available to a branch. This useless information will, at best, be harmless. This argument duplication may be harmful if it overspecializes the branch or reduces the efficiency of the operation of the branch.

11.8.3   Specialization by Subroutine Creation and Argument Creation

When the initial random population is uniformly ADF-less, the operation of subroutine creation is necessary to create function-defining branches so that part of the initial result-producing branch can become parameterized and generalized. The existence of some parameterized branches is necessary if there are to be multiple invocations of portions of the overall program (and the associated benefit in terms of the overall computational effort necessary to solve the problem). In any event, regardless of how the initial random population is created, the operation of subroutine creation provides the potential benefit of achieving specialization in the future. Similarly, the operation of argument creation provides the potential benefit of achieving specialization in the future.

The architecture-altering operations are useful in enabling the evolution of the architecture of the overall program while solving the problem. That is, the architecture of the eventual solution to the problem need not be preordained by the user during the preparatory steps. Instead, the architecture can emerge from the competitive fitness-driven process that occurs during the run at the same time as the problem is being solved.

Boolean Parity Problem Using Architecture-Altering Operations for Subroutines

This chapter demonstrates the architecture-altering operations for subroutines (Chapter 5) on the problem of evolving a computer program with the behavior of Boolean even-parity functions.

The Boolean even-parity function takes k Boolean arguments, D0, D1, D2, and so forth (up to a total of k arguments). Each argument can take on the value T (true or 1) or NIL (false or 0). The even-k-parity function returns T if an even number of its Boolean arguments are T, but otherwise returns NIL. There are 2^k combinations of the k Boolean inputs for a Boolean even-k-parity function. Parity functions are used in computers to check the accuracy of stored or transmitted binary data because a change in the value of any single bit always toggles the value of the function.

Run A (of the four runs in the first portion of this chapter) will demonstrate the principle that genetic programming can evolve, by means of the architecture-altering operations, the architecture of a computer program at the same time that it is solving a problem. A complete genealogical audit trail will be shown for 11 generations of one run of the problem of symbolic regression of the Boolean even-3-parity function.

Run B will demonstrate the automatic creation of hierarchical references among automatically defined functions by means of the architecture-altering operations. A maternal lineage will be shown for 16 generations for one solution of the problem.

Run C demonstrates the evolution, by means of the architecture-altering operations, of two automatically defined functions (one a nonparity function and one a lower-order parity function) that are then used together to solve the Boolean even-5-parity problem. The solution is assembled from the two lower-order Boolean functions represented by the two automatically defined functions.

Run D illustrates a different decomposition of the even-5-parity problem.

Each of these runs shows how genetic programming conducts a broad search in program space for a solution to a problem. The search involves, in part, a search for useful subtrees for each program's main result-producing branch and for each program's automatically defined functions (subroutines). However, when architecture-altering operations are used, the search also involves a search among possible architectures for the overall program. This aspect of the search involves settling on the number of automatically defined functions, the number of arguments that they each possess, and the hierarchical references among them. All three of these aspects are resolved automatically during the run of genetic programming using the architecture-altering operations. Each of these illustrative runs starts with a population having a uniform basic architecture that is sufficient, but not helpful, in solving the problem. However, each run will quickly create a variety of program architectures. In the resulting architecturally diverse population of computer programs, multibranch programs with different numbers of automatically defined functions (each possessing different numbers of arguments) compete with one another in attempting to find a solution to the problem. In each run, the evolutionary process creates numerous architectures that were not present in the initial random population at generation 0 and uses them to solve the problem. In each of the illustrative runs, one or more automatically defined functions that implement lower-order Boolean functions (each of higher arity than that of any automatically defined function in generation 0) are brought to bear to solve the problem.

12.1 PREPARATORY STEPS

There are six major preparatory steps when applying genetic programming with automatically defined functions to a problem. Throughout this book, we frequently find it convenient to focus first on the question of the architecture of the to-be-evolved problem (i.e., the sixth major step).

12.1.1 Program Architecture

When applying genetic programming with automatically defined functions to a problem, the sixth major preparatory step entails specifying the program architecture.

Each run of this problem will start with each program in the initial random population (i.e., generation 0) having a uniform architecture. Starting in generation 1, the architecture-altering operations will create an architecturally diverse population. The architectural variation will involve the number of automatically defined functions, the number of dummy variables possessed by each of the automatically defined functions, and the nature of the hierarchical references among the automatically defined functions.

Each program in generation 0 has a uniform and minimalist architecture. The minimalist initial architecture is intended to provide nothing that is useful in solving the problem at hand. For a Boolean problem, an automatically defined function with only one dummy variable (formal parameter) can be considered minimalist. Indeed, there are only four possible Boolean functions of one Boolean variable, namely, two constant functions ("always true" and "always false"), the NOT function, and the identity function. Thus, each program in generation 0 of this problem has a uniform architecture consisting of one result-producing branch, one automatically defined function, and one dummy variable. The argument map of each program in generation 0 of the population is {1}.

Since there is only one automatically defined function in the programs in generation 0, there is no question of hierarchical references among the automatically defined functions in generation 0. Hierarchical references among the automatically defined functions will be permitted as soon as the architecture-altering operations increase the number of automatically defined functions in individual programs.

Figure 12.1 Uniform architecture for generation 0 consisting of a result-producing branch (RPB) and a single one-argument automatically defined function (ADF0)

This minimalist architecture in generation 0 provides a starting point for the subsequent emergence of a diversity of architectures that are created by the architecture-altering operations. Since lower-order Boolean functions (at least those with two or more arguments) can greatly simplify the writing of programs for higher-order Boolean functions, some of the automatically defined functions created by the architecture-altering operations may be helpful in solving the 3- and 5-parity problems. Over the generations, an architectural arrangement that is beneficial in solving a problem will tend to propagate in the population, while unhelpful architectures will tend to become extinct.

Figure 12.1 shows the common architecture of all the programs in generation 0. The architecture consists of a result-producing branch, RPB, and a single automatically defined function, ADF0, possessing one dummy variable (formal parameter), ARG0. The bodies of the result-producing branch and the function-defining branch are not shown in the figure.

For reasons of both practicality and convenience in programming, a maximum number of automatically defined functions, a maximum number of arguments for each automatically defined function, a maximum size for the result-producing branch, and a maximum size for each automatically defined function are established for each problem. These maxima are usually chosen liberally so as not to constrain the diversity of architectures that may be created by the architecture-altering operations and so as not to constrain the evolution of the branches of the overall program.

For this problem, the maximum number of automatically defined functions, $N_{\text{max-adf}}$, is established to be five. The maximum number of arguments for each automatically defined function, $N_{\text{max-argument-adf}}$, is established to be three. The maximum size for the result-producing branch, S_{rpb}, is 200 points. The maximum size for each automatically defined function, S_{adf}, is 150 points. Thus, an individual program with five automatically defined functions could have as many as 950 points.

These maximum sizes are almost certainly more than sufficient for creating computer programs for the Boolean 3- and 5-parity problems. For more complex problems (where the population size may be hundreds of thousands of individuals), considerations of available computer memory may influence the choice of these maxima.

12.1.2 Functions and Terminals

The first major step in preparing to use genetic programming is to identify the terminal set for the problem, and the second major step is to identify the function set.

The function and terminal sets specify the ingredients of the to-be-discovered computer program. The function and terminal sets define the particular space of computer programs that genetic programming will consider in solving the problem. Each program considered during the run of genetic programming will be a composition of the available functions and terminals. For this problem, the ingredients consist of

- the three Boolean arguments, D0, D1, and D2, constituting the inputs to the to-be-discovered program and
- the Boolean functions AND, OR, NAND, and NOR.

A precondition for solving a problem with genetic programming is that the function and terminal sets satisfy the *sufficiency* requirement in the sense that they are capable of representing a solution to the problem. Thus, for example, if the terminal set includes D0 and D2, but not D1, it would be impossible for genetic programming to evolve a computer program for the even-3-parity function of D0, D1, and D2. If the function set includes only the AND and OR functions, it would be impossible for genetic programming to evolve a solution to this problem because it is known that no composition of the AND and the OR functions is sufficient to represent the even-3-parity function. On the other hand, if the function set is sufficient (say, it contains NAND), the inclusion of extraneous functions (e.g., AND, OR, NOR, or NOT) would not prevent genetic programming from finding a solution. Similarly, if the terminal set is sufficient (i.e., D0, D1, and D2), genetic programming would not be prevented from finding a solution by the inclusion of an extraneous Boolean noise terminal (say, the terminal BTIME, which returns a Boolean value depending on whether the exact time, in nanoseconds, when the terminal is actually referenced during the program's execution is odd or even).

Notice how little domain knowledge is used in determining these function and terminal sets for this problem. Indeed, the above ingredients could be suitable for virtually any three-input problem involving Boolean function learning.

When the architecture-altering operations are used, the notion of function and terminal sets must be refined. There are typically at least eight separate function and terminal sets for a program in the population. These eight sets arise because there are

- both initial and potential members of
- both function and terminal sets for
- both the result-producing branches and the function-defining branches.

Specifically, the eight sets are as follows:

- the initial terminal set, $T_{\text{rpb-initial}}$, that consists of the terminals of the result-producing branch that are available to individuals of the initial population (generation 0),
- the initial function set, $F_{\text{rpb-initial}}$, that consists of the functions of the result-producing branch that are available to individuals of generation 0,
- the potential terminal set, $T_{\text{rpb-potential}}$, that consists of the terminals of the result-producing branch that may potentially be made available during the run by the architecture-altering operations,
- the potential function set, $F_{\text{rpb-potential}}$, that consists of the functions of the result-producing branch that may potentially be made available during the run by the architecture-altering operations,
- four similar sets for the function-defining branches (automatically defined functions): $F_{\text{adf-initial}}$, $T_{\text{adf-initial}}$, $F_{\text{adf-potential}}$, and $T_{\text{adf-potential}}$.

The initial terminal set for the result-producing branch, $T_{rpb\text{-}initial}$, consists of the three externally supplied Boolean inputs of the as-yet-undiscovered computer program for the even-3-parity function:

$T_{rpb\text{-}initial} = \{D0, D1, D2\}.$

Dummy variables (formal parameters) do not appear in the result-producing branch.

The initial function set for the result-producing branch, $F_{rpb\text{-}initial}$, consists of four two-argument Boolean functions (AND, OR, NAND, and NOR) and the single one-argument automatically defined function, ADF0, that is present in generation 0:

$F_{rpb\text{-}initial} = \{AND, OR, NAND, NOR, ADF0\}.$

This initial function set has an argument map of $\{2, 2, 2, 2, 1\}$. Thus, the result-producing branch can call the automatically defined function, ADF0.

The initial function set, $F_{adf0\text{-}initial}$, for automatically defined function ADF0 is

$F_{adf0\text{-}initial} = \{AND, OR, NAND, NOR\},$

each taking two arguments. Note that the automatically defined function is not allowed to recursively call itself (in this chapter).

The initial terminal set, $T_{adf0\text{-}initial}$, for automatically defined function ADF0 consists of one dummy variable (formal parameter), ARG0:

$T_{adf0\text{-}initial} = \{ARG0\}.$

The function-defining branch of programs in generation 0 is composed of functions from $F_{adf0\text{-}initial}$ and terminals from $T_{adf0\text{-}initial}$; the result-producing branch of programs in generation 0 is composed of functions from $F_{rpb\text{-}initial}$ and terminals from $T_{rpb\text{-}initial}$.

After generation 0, the architecture-altering operations can add additional automatically defined functions to individual programs in the population and can also add additional dummy variables to each automatically defined function (including ADF0).

After generation 0, the architecture-altering operations add automatically defined functions to certain individuals in the population. They also add arguments to certain automatically defined functions. Consequently, the population becomes architecturally diverse after generation 0.

The set of potential terminals, $T_{adf\text{-}potential}$, for each automatically defined function includes two new dummy variables that may be created by the architecture-altering operations in addition to the preexisting ARG0. That is,

$T_{adf\text{-}potential} = \{ARG1, ARG2\}.$

Since dummy variables do not appear in the result-producing branch, the set of potential terminals, $T_{rpb\text{-}potential}$, for the result-producing branch is empty. That is,

$T_{rpb\text{-}potential} = \phi.$

The set of potential functions, $F_{rpb\text{-}potential}$, for the result-producing branch is

$F_{rpb\text{-}potential} = \{ADF1, ADF2, ADF3, ADF4\}.$

each taking a yet-to-be-determined number of arguments (up to three).

Unless recursions are being used (as in Chapter 18), automatically defined functions are not allowed to call themselves (either directly or indirectly). Thus, the set of potential functions, $F_{adf4\text{-}potential}$, for automatically defined function ADF4 does not include ADF4. In particular,

$F_{adf4\text{-}potential}$ = {AND, OR, NAND, NOR, ADF3, ADF2, ADF1, ADF0}.

Similarly,

$F_{adf3\text{-}potential}$ = {AND, OR, NAND, NOR, ADF2, ADF1, ADF0}.
$F_{adf2\text{-}potential}$ = {AND, OR, NAND, NOR, ADF1, ADF0}, and
$F_{adf1\text{-}potential}$ = {AND, OR, NAND, NOR, ADF0}.

In the remainder of this book, we will not write out multiple separate function sets when it is understood that only nonrecursive references are permitted among the automatically defined functions.

All three terminals as well as all the functions in the function set are Boolean-valued. Thus, the set of functions and terminals is closed. This remains the case even as new automatically defined functions (with varying numbers of arguments) are created.

Note that it is convenient, for purposes of presentation, to distinguish between terminals and functions. However, when it comes time to write a program to implement genetic programming on a computer, terminals are usually treated as if they were zero-argument functions.

12.1.3 Fitness

The third major step in preparing to use genetic programming is identifying the fitness measure. An individual program in the population is evaluated by executing its result-producing branch. The result-producing branch for the even-3-parity problem (runs A and B below) has access to the program's three external inputs (D0, D1, and D2). In general, the result-producing branch contains calls to one or more function-defining branches (automatically defined functions). The result-producing branch eventually returns a single Boolean value as the result of executing the overall program. Since the result-producing branch yields a Boolean value, there is no need for a wrapper (output interface) to transform the value produced by the result-producing branch. That value may agree or disagree with the correct value of the Boolean even-3-parity function for a particular combination of the three inputs.

The fitness cases for this problem consist of the universe of $2^3 = 8$ possible combinations of the three Boolean inputs (D0, D1, and D2).

The raw fitness (and number of hits) of an individual program in the population is the number of fitness cases for which the value returned by the result-producing branch of the program equals the correct value of the Boolean even-3-parity function. Raw fitness ranges from 0 to 8, with 8 being the best.

The standardized fitness of an individual program in the population is the sum, over the 8 fitness cases, of the absolute value of the difference (Hamming distance) between the value returned by the result-producing branch of the program and the correct value of the Boolean even-3-parity function. That is, standardized fitness is 8 minus the raw fitness. A smaller value of standardized fitness is better. A standardized fitness of zero is best and indicates a program that correctly computes the Boolean even-3-parity function.

Notice how little domain knowledge is used in determining the fitness measure for this problem. This fitness measure is concerned with "what needs to be done"—namely, make no errors. The fitness measure does not reveal "how to do it." In fact, the same fitness measure could be used for matching any three-input Boolean function.

For the even-5-parity problem (runs C and D below), there are five Boolean inputs (D0, D1, D2, D3, and D4). Hence there are $2^5 = 32$ fitness cases, and fitness ranges from 0 to 32.

12.1.4 Parameters

The fourth major step in preparing to use genetic programming involves determining the values of certain parameters that control the runs.

For the even-3-parity problem (runs A and B below), the population size, M, is 1,000. The maximum number of generations to be run, G, is 51. The problem was run on a 486-type PC (serial) computer.

For the even-5-parity problem (runs C and D below), a population size, M, of 96,000 is used. Runs C and D were run on a Transtech parallel computer system (described in Chapter 62). The subpopulation size, Q, is 1,500 at each of the $D = 64$ processing nodes (demes), and the migration rate is $B = 2\%$ between processing nodes on each generation of the run.

The control parameters for the frequency of performing the genetic operations for runs A, B, C, and D are atypical. Normally, the architecture-altering operations are performed sparingly (e.g., with percentages such as 0.5% and 1% on each generation). However, the goal here is to present a complete genealogical audit trail of a successful run employing the architecture-altering operations. Since an individual at generation i can have as many as 2^i ancestors in an audit trail, it is a practical necessity to encourage the discovery of a solution in a small number of generations. Consequently, the architecture-altering operations are performed with an atypically high frequency in this chapter. The percentage of operations is 45% one-offspring crossover, 8% reproduction, 15% subroutine duplication, 15% subroutine creation, 15% argument duplication, 1% subroutine deletion, and 1% argument deletion.

The other control parameters for runs in this chapter are either in the tableau (Table 12.1) or are the default values specified in Appendix D of Koza 1994g.

12.1.5 Termination

The fifth major step in preparing to use genetic programming involves specifying the method for designating the result and the criterion for terminating a run. In a run of genetic programming on a parallel computer system with asynchronous generations, a *pace-setting program* is a program from a processing node whose fitness is better than any previously reported value of fitness. The method of result designation used throughout this book is to designate the best-so-far pace-setting individual as the result of the run.

The termination criterion varies from problem to problem in this book; however, termination is commonly triggered in this book by one (or a combination) of the following events:

- completion of the maximum number of generations to be run (G),
- satisfaction of the success predicate of the problem (which is, for this problem, the achievement of 100% of the maximum possible number of hits), or
- manual observation that the values of fitness for the best-of-generation individual and other individuals in the population appear to have reached a plateau.

12.1.6   Tableau

Table 12.1, called a *tableau*, summarizes the main choices made while applying the major preparatory steps of genetic programming to the problem of symbolic regression of the even-3-parity function. This tableau is the first of 39 similar tables in this book.

The second row of each tableau in this book describes how the architecture of each program in the population is determined. This row corresponds to the sixth major preparatory step for genetic programming. The architecture may be determined either by

- specific choices made by the user prior to the run or
- the architecture-altering operations that create and modify the architecture during the run.

The next eight rows of each tableau present the choices for the terminal and function sets for the problem. These rows correspond to the first and second major preparatory steps for genetic programming. These eight rows apply to both the initial and potential members of both the function and terminal sets for both the result-producing branches and the automatically defined functions. Additional rows are necessary in the tableau for a problem in which some automatically defined functions have different function or terminal sets than others, for problems with constrained syntactic structures, and for problems with automatically defined iterations, automatically defined loops, and automatically defined recursions.

Four rows of the tableau present the choices made concerning the fitness measure for the problem (for fitness cases, raw fitness, standardized fitness, and hits). These rows correspond to the third major preparatory step for genetic programming.

The fourth-to-last row of each tableau indicates whether a wrapper (output interface) is needed for the particular problem.

The third-to-last row of each tableau presents the choices of control parameters for the problem. This row always includes the population size, M, and the maximum number of generations to be run, G. These parameters correspond to the fourth major preparatory step for genetic programming. The default control parameters are not specifically mentioned unless they differ from the default values in Appendix D of this book. If a parallel computer is being used, this row also shows the subpopulation size, Q, for each of the D demes (processing nodes) and the migration rate, B.

This third-to-last row of the tableau also presents the maximum size of each branch in the to-be-evolved program. It presents the maximum size of the result-producing branch(es), S_{rpb}, and, if more than one result-producing branch is being used, the number, N_{rpb}, of result-producing branches in each program. If automatically defined functions, automatically defined iterations, automatically defined loops, automatically defined recursions, or automatically defined stores are being used, the tableau includes additional parameters. For example, if automatically defined functions are being used, the tableau also presents the size of each function-defining branch of each automatically defined function, S_{adf}, the maximum number of ADFs, $N_{max-adf}$, the maximum number of arguments of each ADF, $N_{max-argument-adf}$, and the minimum number of arguments of each ADF, $N_{min-argument-adf}$. Appendix D of this book describes the additional parameters associated with the use of ADIs, ADLs, ADRs, and ADSs.

Table 12.1 Tableau for even-3-parity problem

Objective	Find a computer program that produces the value of the Boolean even-3-parity function as its output when given the value of the three independent Boolean variables as its input.
Program architecture	One result-producing branch, RPB, and a single initial one-argument function-defining branch, ADF0, in generation 0. Additional automatically defined functions (ADF1, ADF2, . . .) and additional arguments (ARG0, ARG1, . . .) will be created during the run by the architecture-altering operations.
Initial function set for the RPBs	$F_{\text{rpb-initial}}$ = {AND, OR, NAND, NOR, ADF0}
Initial terminal set for the RPBs	$T_{\text{rpb-initial}}$ = {D0, D1, D2}
Initial function set for the ADFs	$F_{\text{adf0-initial}}$ = {AND, OR, NAND, NOR}
Initial terminal set for the ADFs	$T_{\text{adf0-initial}}$ = {ARG0}.
Potential function set for the RPBs	$F_{\text{rpb-potential}}$ = {ADF1, ADF2, ADF3, ADF4}
Potential terminal set for the RPBs	$T_{\text{rpb-potential}}$ = ϕ.
Potential function set for the ADFs	$F_{\text{adf-potential}}$ = {ADF0, ADF1, ADF2, ADF3}
Potential terminal set for the ADFs	$T_{\text{adf-potential}}$ = {ARG1, ARG2}
Fitness cases	All 2^3 = 8 combinations of the three Boolean arguments D0, D1, and D2
Raw fitness	Raw fitness of an individual program in the population is the number of fitness cases for which the value returned by the result-producing branch of the individual program equals the correct value of the even-3-parity function.
Standardized fitness	Standardized fitness of an individual program in the population is the sum, over the 8 fitness cases, of the absolute value of the difference (i.e., the Hamming distance) between the value returned by the individual program and the correct value of the even-3-parity function.
Hits	Same as raw fitness
Wrapper	None
Parameters	M = 1,000. G = 51. N_{rpb} = 1. S_{rpb} = 200. S_{adf} = 150. $N_{\text{max-adf}}$ = 5. $N_{\text{max-argument-adf}}$ = 3. $N_{\text{min-argument-adf}}$ = 1.
Result designation	Best-so-far pace-setting individual
Success predicate	A program scores the maximum number (8) of hits.

The second-to-last row of the tableau shows the method of result designation (typically, the best-so-far pace-setting individual).

The last row of the tableau shows the success predicate for the problem.

12.2 RUN A—A COMPLETE GENEALOGICAL AUDIT TRAIL

The first run (run A) of the Boolean even-3-parity problem starts with the random creation of a population of $M = 1,000$ individual programs. Each program in the population is evaluated as to how well it solves the problem. In particular, the fitness of each program in the population of 1,000 programs is measured according to how well that program mimics the target function for all eight possible combinations of the three Boolean inputs, D0, D1, and D2.

The initial random population of a run of genetic programming is a blind random search of the search space of the problem. As such, it provides a baseline for comparing the results of subsequent generations.

The best program from among the 1,000 randomly created programs in generation 0 of this run has the following one-argument function-defining branch (automatically defined function ADF0):

(OR (AND (NAND ARG0 ARG0) (OR ARG0 ARG0)) (NOR (NOR ARG0 ARG0)
(AND ARG0 ARG0))).

The result-producing branch, RPB, of the best-of-generation program from generation 0 is

(NOR (AND D0 (NOR D2 D1)) (AND (AND D2 D1))).

The behavior of ADF0 is that of the Boolean constant zero ("always false") function; however, the uselessness of ADF0 does not matter since the result-producing branch fails to call it. The minimalist approach is not intended to provide a useful automatically defined function in generation 0, but merely a starting point for the subsequent emergence of useful automatically defined functions.

Table 12.2 shows the behavior of this best-of-generation program from generation 0. The first three columns show the values of the three Boolean variables, D0, D1, and D2. The fourth column shows the value produced by the best-of-generation program. The fifth column shows the correct value of the target function, the even-3-parity function. The last column shows how well the program performed at matching the behavior of the target function. As is shown, the program is correct for six of the eight possible combinations (fitness cases). Thus, the program achieves a raw fitness of 6 (out of a possible 8) and a standardized fitness of 2. It scores 6 hits.

A new population of 1,000 programs is then created from the current population of 1,000 programs. Each successive generation of the population is created from the existing population by applying the genetic operations of crossover, mutation, the reproduction operation, and the architecture-altering operations.

The raw fitness of the best-of-generation program for generation 5 improves to 7. That is, this program correctly computes the target even-3-parity function for seven of the eight fitness cases. The program achieving this new and higher level of fitness has a total of four branches – one result-producing branch and three function-defining

Table 12.2 Operation of the best-of-generation program from generation 0

D0	D1	D2	Output of best-of- generation program for generation 0	Correct value of the even-3-parity function	Score
0	0	0	1	1	correct
0	0	1	1	0	wrong
0	1	0	1	0	wrong
0	1	1	1	1	correct
1	0	0	0	0	correct
1	0	1	1	1	correct
1	1	0	1	1	correct
1	1	1	0	0	correct

Figure 12.2   The {2, 2, 3} architecture of the best-of-generation program from generation 5

branches (Figure 12.2). The change in the number of branches from two at generation 0 to four at generation 5 is the consequence of the architecture-altering operations. This program has function-defining branches defining a two-argument ADF0, a two-argument ADF1, and a three-argument ADF2, so that its argument map is {2, 2, 3}.

The result-producing branch of this best-of-generation program from generation 5 is

```
(NOR (ADF2 D0 D2 D1) (AND (ADF1 D2 D1) D0)).
```

The first function-defining branch,

```
(OR (AND (NAND ARG0 ARG0) (OR ARG1 ARG0)) (NOR (NOR ARG1 ARG0)
(AND ARG0 ARG1))),
```

of this program takes two dummy variables (ARG0 and ARG1). Recall that ADF0 started with one dummy variable at generation 0. The existence of two dummy variables in this function-defining branch is a consequence of an argument duplication operation that increased the number of its arguments from one to two. As it happens, the behavior of this function-defining branch is not important because ADF0 is not referenced by the result-producing branch.

The second function-defining branch (defining ADF1) of this program also takes two dummy variables:

```
(OR (AND ARG0 ARG1) (NOR ARG0 ARG1)).
```

The existence of this second function-defining branch is a consequence of a subroutine duplication operation.

Table 12.3 shows the behavior of ADF1 of the best-of-generation program for generation 5. As can be seen, ADF1 is equivalent to the even-2-parity function. In evolving a computer program for the Boolean even-3-parity function, it is often useful to evolve a lower-order parity function and then use a lower-order parity function in solving the higher-order parity problem.

The function-defining branch for ADF2 of the best-of-generation program for generation 5 takes three dummy variables (ARG0, ARG1, and ARG2):

```
(AND ARG1 (NOR ARG0 ARG2)).
```

This third function-defining branch exists as a consequence of yet another subroutine duplication operation. Its three arguments exist as a consequence of the argument duplication operation.

Table 12.4 shows that ADF2 returns 1 only when ARG0 and ARG2 are 0 and ARG1 is 1. ADF2 operates as a detector for this particular combination of three inputs.

Note that the run of genetic programming did not begin at generation 0 with any three-argument Boolean functions. Three-argument functions emerged from the evolutionary process as a consequence of the architecture-altering operations. The ultimate usefulness of an emergent higher-order function is determined by the competitive Darwinian process for survival that occurs at each generation of the run.

The raw fitness of the best individual program in the population remains steady at a value of 7 for generations 6, 7, 8, and 9; however, the average fitness of the population as a whole improves during these generations.

On generation 10, the best individual program in the population of 1,000 perfectly computes the behavior of the even-3-parity function. This 100%-correct solution to the problem has a total of six branches: a result-producing branch (RPB), a two-argument ADF0, a two-argument ADF1, a three-argument ADF2, a two-argument ADF3, and a two-argument ADF4 (Figure 12.3). The argument map of this best-of-run program from generation 10 is {2, 2, 3, 2, 2}. This multiplicity of branches is a consequence of the repeated application of the subroutine duplication operation and the subroutine creation operation. Notice that all five function-defining branches of this program have more than one dummy variable. All of these additional arguments exist as a consequence of the repeated application of the argument duplication operation.

The result-producing branch of the best-of-run program for generation 10 is

```
(NOR (ADF4 D0(ADF1 D2 D1)) (AND (ADF1 D2 D1) D0)).
```

The function-defining branch for ADF0 of this program takes two dummy variables (ARG0 and ARG1):

```
(OR (AND (NAND ARG0 ARG0) (OR ARG1 ARG0)) (NOR (NOR ARG1 ARG0)
(AND ARG0 ARG1))).
```

The behavior of ADF0 is equivalent to the odd-2-parity function. However, ADF0 is ignored by the result-producing branch.

The function-defining branch for ADF1 takes two dummy variables:

```
(OR (AND ARG0 ARG1) (NOR ARG0 ARG1)).
```

Table 12.3 ADF1 **of the best-of-generation program of generation 5**

ARG0	ARG1	ADF0
0	0	1
0	1	0
1	0	0
1	1	1

Table 12.4 ADF2 **of the best-of-generation program of generation 5**

ARG0	ARG1	ARG2	ADF2
0	0	0	0
0	0	1	0
0	1	0	1
0	1	1	0
1	0	0	0
1	0	1	0
1	1	0	0
1	1	1	0

Figure 12.3 The {2, 2, 3, 2, 2} architecture of the best-of-run program from generation 10

ADF1 is equivalent to the even-2-parity function. ADF1 is called twice by the result-producing branch.

The function-defining branch for ADF2 takes three dummy variables (ARG0, ARG1, and ARG2):

```
(AND ARG1 (NOR ARG0 ARG2)).
```

ADF2 returns 1 only when ARG0 and ARG2 are 0 and ARG1 is 1. However, ADF2 is ignored by the result-producing branch.

The function-defining branch for two-argument ADF3 is the one-argument identity function for one of its two variables. This useless branch is ignored by the result-producing branch.

The function-defining branch for ADF4 takes two dummy variables (ARG0 and ARG1):

```
(OR (AND ARG0 ARG1) (NOR ARG0 ARG1)).
```

ADF4 is equivalent to the even-2-parity function. ADF4 is called once by the result-producing branch.

The result-producing branch calls ADF1 twice and ADF4 once. Since both ADF1 and ADF4 are even-2-parity functions, the result-producing branch can be simplified to

```
(NOR (EVEN-2-PARITY D0 (EVEN-2-PARITY D2 D1)) (AND (EVEN-2-
PARITY D2 D1) D0)).
```

This expression is equivalent to the even-3-parity function.

Note that this evolved solution advantageously used (and, in fact, reused) a two-argument function (the even-2-parity) that did not exist in generation 0 of the run. The even-2-parity function arose as a consequence of the architecture-altering operations.

An examination of the genealogical audit trail shows the interplay between the Darwinian reproduction operation, the crossover operation, and the architecture-altering operations. Figure 12.4 shows all of the ancestors of the just-described 100%-correct best-of-run program from generation 10 of run A. The generation numbers (from 0 to 10) are shown on the left edge of the figure. The figure also shows the sequence of reproduction operations, crossover operations, and architecture-altering operations that gave rise to every program that is an ancestor of the 100%-correct program in generation 10. The 100%-correct best-of-run solution from generation 10 is represented by the box labeled M10 at the bottom of the figure. The argument map of each program in this figure is shown in a box. For example, {2, 2, 3, 2, 2} is the argument map for the best-of-run program at the bottom of the figure.

The two lines flowing into the box M10 indicate that the solution in generation 10 is produced by a crossover operation acting on two programs from the previous generation (generation 9). Figure 12.4 uses the convention of placing the mother (the receiving parent) (e.g., M9) on the right and father (the contributing parent) (e.g., P9) on the left. Recall that, in a one-offspring crossover operation using point typing, the bulk of the structure of a multipart program comes from the mother since the father contributes only one subtree into only one of the many branches of the mother. Thus, the 11 boxes on the right side of this figure (consecutively numbered from M0 to M10) represent the maternal genetic lineage (from generation 0 through generation 10) of the 100%-correct best-of-run individual (M10) that emerged in generation 10. The best-of-run individual M10 in generation 10 has the same argument map, {2, 2, 3, 2, 2}, as its mother M9 because the crossover operation is not an architecture-altering operation. That is, crossover does not change the architecture (or argument map) of the offspring (relative to the mother). As can be seen, there are ultimately a total of only seven ancestors from generation 0 for the best-of-run individual for this particular run. In the extreme, if every offspring were created by crossover, an individual in generation 10 would have $2^{10} = 1,024$ ancestors from generation 0. Of course, Darwinian selection drastically reduces the number of different ancestors because highly fit individuals tend to be reselected many times to participate in the genetic operations.

We will now examine the maternal lineage in detail in order to illustrate the overall process of evolving the architecture of a solution to a problem.

The mother M9 from generation 9 (shown on the right side of Figure 12.4) has an argument map of {2, 2, 3, 2, 2}, has a raw fitness of 7, and is the result of a crossover of

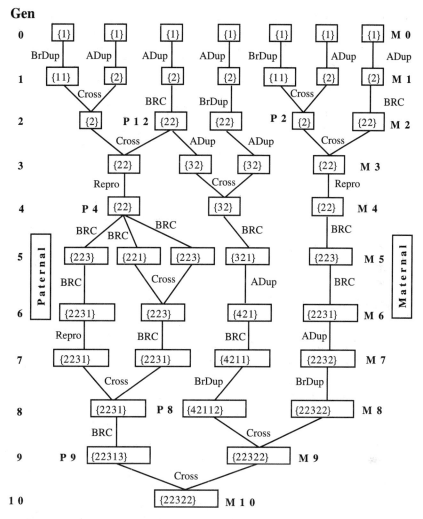

Figure 12.4   Complete genealogical audit trail showing all ancestors since generation 0 of the best-of-run program (M10) from generation 10 for run A

two parents from generation 8. The grandfather of the 100%-correct solution M10 in generation 10 (and the father of M9) is P8. The grandmother of the 100%-correct solution M10 in generation 10 (and the mother of M9) is M8.

The grandmother M8 from generation 8 of the 100%-correct solution M10 in generation 10 has an argument map of {2, 2, 3, 2, 2}, has a raw fitness of 7, and is the offspring produced by a subroutine duplication applied to M7 from generation 7.

Because of the subroutine duplication operation (sometimes also called branch duplication or "BrDup"), the program M7 from generation 7 of the maternal lineage at the far right of Figure 12.4 has one fewer branch than its offspring M8. Program M7 has an argument map of {2, 2, 3, 2}. Program M7 is the result of an argument duplication from a single ancestor from generation 6.

Because of the argument duplication operation, the fourth function-defining branch of the program M6 from generation 6 of the maternal lineage at the far right of Figure 12.4 has one less argument than its offspring M7. Program M6 from generation 6 has an argument map of {2, 2, 3, 1}; program M7 from generation 7 has an argument map of {2, 2, 3, 2}. Program M6 is the result produced by a subroutine creation (sometimes also called branch creation or "BRC") operating on the single ancestor M5 from generation 5.

Because of the subroutine creation operation, the program M5 from generation 5 (shown on the right side of Figure 12.4) has one fewer function-defining branch than program M6. Program M5 has an argument map of {2, 2, 3}. In turn, program M5 is the result of a subroutine creation from a single ancestor M4 from generation 4.

Program M4 from generation 4 has one less function-defining branch than its offspring program M5. Program M4 has an argument map of {2, 2}. Program M4 is the result of a reproduction operation from a single ancestor M3 from generation 3.

Program M3 from generation 3 has an argument map of {2, 2} and is the result of a crossover involving father P2 and mother M2 from generation 2.

Program M2 from generation 2 has an argument map of {2, 2} and is the result of a subroutine creation from a single ancestor M1 from generation 1.

Program M1 from generation 1 has an argument map of {2} and is the result of an argument duplication of a single ancestor M0 from generation 0.

Program M0 from generation 0 at the upper right corner of Figure 12.4 has an argument map of {1} and has a raw fitness of 6. It necessarily has an argument map of {1} because all programs at generation 0 have a uniform architecture consisting of one result-producing branch and a single one-argument function-defining branch, ADF0.

This run demonstrates the creation, by means of the architecture-altering operations, of the architecture of a computer program. This automatic evolution of architecture occurs during a run of genetic programming while genetic programming is creating a program to solve the problem. The evolved solution advantageously used a two-argument automatically defined function (the even-2-parity) even though no two-argument automatically defined function existed in generation 0 of the run. The architecture-altering operations created automatically defined functions possessing two arguments, and the evolutionary process exploited their availability to solve the problem.

12.3 RUN B—EVOLUTION OF HIERARCHICAL REFERENCES BETWEEN SUBROUTINES

This second run (run B) of the even-3-parity problem illustrates the evolution of a hierarchical reference of one function-defining branch by another. It also illustrates the operation of subroutine deletion. In this run, a 100%-correct best-of-run solution emerges in generation 15 to the problem of symbolic regression of the even-3-parity problem.

The best-of-generation program from generation 0 of this run has a raw fitness of only 5. There are many programs in the population with this mediocre level of fitness. As will be seen, this program (called M0 in Figure 12.5) is an early ancestor of the 100%-correct solution that eventually emerges in generation 15. The result-producing branch of this best-of-generation program from generation 0 is

```
(OR (NOR D2 (ADF0 (AND D1 D0))) (AND D2 (ADF0 (NAND D0 D0)))).
```

ADF0 of this program is

```
(AND (NAND (OR ARG0 (OR ARG0 ARG0))) (AND (AND ARG0 ARG0) (OR
ARG0 ARG0))) (AND (NAND (OR ARG0 ARG0) (NOR ARG0 ARG0)) (OR
(AND ARG0 ARG0) (OR ARG0 ARG0)))).
```

ADF0 illustrates the use of an automatically defined function to augment the original set of primitive functions. ADF0 is equivalent to the one-argument negation (NOT) function (which was not one of the original four primitive functions for this problem).

Figure 12.5 shows all of the maternal ancestors of the 100%-correct individual from generation 15 (labeled M15 at the bottom of the figure) for run B. Because 16 generations are involved, this figure does not show all of the ancestors of the 100%-correct solution, M15; however, it shows a few selected ancestors. Each box in this figure shows the raw fitness (hits) of each program to the left of its argument map. The program labeled M0 at the upper right of this figure is the best-of-generation program from generation 0 (discussed above), with an argument map of {1} and a raw fitness of 5. Program M0 is the 15th-generation ancestor, entirely along the maternal line, of the ultimate best-of-run individual, M15.

A subroutine duplication operates on program M0 to produce program M1 in generation 1 with an argument map of {1, 1}.

Two crossovers occurring in generations 2 and 3 raise the raw fitness of the maternal ancestor M3 in generation 3 from 5 to 6. Program M3 has two one-argument function-defining branches. Its ADF0 is "always false":

```
(AND (NAND (OR ARG0 (OR ARG0 ARG0))) (AND (AND ARG0 ARG0) (OR
ARG0 ARG0))) (AND (NAND (OR ARG0 ARG0) (NOR ARG0 ARG0)) (OR
(AND ARG0 ARG0) (OR ARG0 ARG0)))).
```

ADF1 of this program M3 is exactly the same as ADF0 of ancestor M0 at generation 0 (i.e., the NOT function). The subroutine duplication that created program M1 in generation 1 duplicated ADF0 of ancestor M0 of generation 0. Then the intervening crossovers modified ADF0 so as to convert it into the useless "always false" function.

Then a subroutine deletion removed the now-always-false ADF0 of program M3 to produce program M4 in generation 4. This is an example of the removal of an extraneous function-defining branch by the subroutine deletion operation. The surviving function-defining branch of program M4 is exactly the same as ADF0 of ancestor M0 at generation 0 (i.e., it is the NOT function). Program M4 retains a fitness level of 6. The result-producing branch of program M4 from generation 4 is

```
(OR (NOR D2 (ADF0 (AND D1 D0))) (AND D2 (OR D1 D0))).
```

Next, a subroutine creation operation creates a new branch, ADF1, of program M5 of generation 5 from the underlined portion of the result-producing branch of program M4 above. The new branch, ADF1, is

```
(ADF0 (AND ARG1 ARG0)).
```

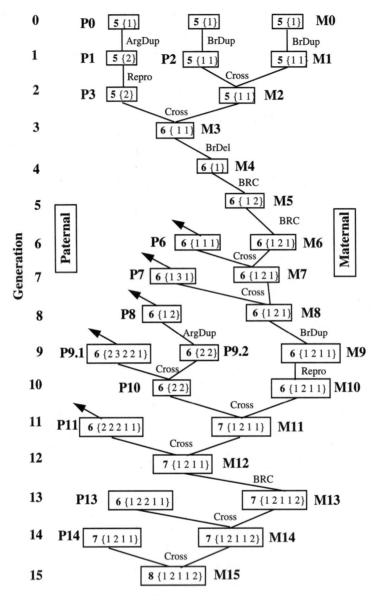

Figure 12.5 Partial genealogical audit trail showing all the maternal ancestors from generations 0 through 14 (and selected other ancestors) for the best-of-run individual (M15) from generation 15 for run B

The result-producing branch of program M4 of generation 4 is also modified, and the modified version is part of program M5 of generation 5:

```
(OR (NOR D2 (ADF1 D1 D0)) (AND D2 (OR D1 D0))).
```

Two crossovers, one reproduction, one subroutine creation, and one subroutine duplication then occur on the maternal lineage between generations 6 and 10.

The ADF0 of program M10 of generation 10 is the NOT function. ADF1 of program M10 from generation 10 uses the just-created hierarchical reference to emulate the behavior of the NAND function:

```
(ADF0 (AND ARG1 ARG0)).
```

Mother M10 mates with father P10 to produce offspring M11 in generation 11. ADF0 of father P10 performs the even-2-parity function:

```
(AND (NAND (OR ARG1 ARG0) (AND (NAND ARG1 ARG0) (OR ARG1
ARG1))) (AND (NAND ARG0 (NOR ARG1 ARG0)) (OR (AND ARG1 ARG1)
(NOR ARG0 ARG0)))).
```

In the crossover, this entire branch from father P10 is inserted into ADF1 of mother M10, replacing (AND ARG1 ARG0) and producing a new ADF1 that performs the odd-2-parity function (since ADF0 performs the NOT function).

Three crossovers and one subroutine creation then occur on the maternal lineage. However, ADF1 (created in generation 11) remains intact. ADF1 performs the odd-2-parity function.

The 100%-correct solution that emerged in generation 15 has an argument map of {1, 2, 1, 1, 2}. Only ADF0 and ADF1 of this best-of-run program are referenced by the result-producing branch. ADF0 performs the NOT function:

```
(AND (NAND (OR ARG0 ARG0) (AND (AND ARG0 ARG0) (OR ARG0 ARG0)))
(AND (NAND (OR ARG0 ARG0) (NOR ARG0 ARG0)) (OR (AND ARG0 ARG0)
(NOR ARG0 ARG0)))).
```

ADF1 defines the odd-2-parity function by hierarchically referring to ADF0:

```
(**ADF0** (AND (NAND (OR ARG1 ARG0) (AND (NAND ARG1 ARG0) (OR ARG1
ARG1))) (AND (NAND ARG0 (NOR ARG1 ARG0)) (OR (AND ARG1 ARG1)
(NOR ARG0 ARG0))))).
```

It is often useful to use a call tree to show the hierarchy of references among branches of a multipart program. The call tree of Figure 12.6 shows that a particular program consists of one result-producing branch, RPB; that RPB contains a reference to one automatically defined function, ADF0; and that ADF0 possesses one argument (as indicated inside the parentheses in the box for ADF0). Of course, the existence of a reference in the body of the result-producing branch, RPB, does not guarantee that RPB actually invokes ADF0 when RPB is executed for a particular combination of inputs. For example, a reference to ADF0 may never be executed because of a conditional operation in RPB. The call tree in this figure applies to every program from generation 0 of this problem that contains a reference to ADF0 (i.e., almost all programs in generation 0). The figure does not apply to the minority of programs in generation 0 whose result-producing branches do not actually contain a reference to ADF0.

Figure 12.7 is the call tree for the 100%-correct best-of-run program from generation 15. The figure shows that the result-producing branch, RPB, calls a one-argument

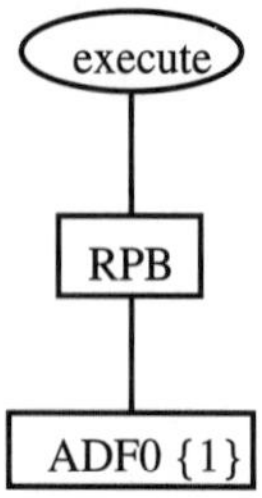

Figure 12.6 Call tree for almost all programs in generation 0

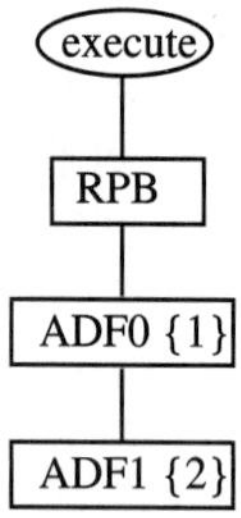

Figure 12.7 Call tree for the best-of-run program from generation 15 for even-3-parity problem

automatically defined function, ADF0, and that the RPB indirectly calls two-argument ADF1 by first calling ADF0.

This run demonstrates the creation, by means of the architecture-altering operations, of a hierarchical reference by one automatically defined function to another automatically defined function in the process of solving the problem of symbolic regression of the Boolean even-3-parity problem.

Runs A and B together demonstrate the automatic determination, during the run of genetic programming, of

- the number of subroutines,
- the number of arguments possessed by each subroutine,
- the sequence of steps of (and hence the task performed by) each subroutine,
- the hierarchical references among the subroutines, and
- the sequence of steps of (and hence the task performed by) the main result-producing branches.

The subroutines and the main result-producing branch communicate with each other by

- the arguments supplied to the subroutines by their calling subprogram and
- the values returned by the subroutines.

Thus, there is an automatic determination, during the run of genetic programming, of both the hierarchy of subroutines and the flow of information between the subroutines and the main result-producing branch of the overall program.

12.4 RUN C—PROBLEM DECOMPOSITION

We now consider the even-5-parity problem.

On generation 0 of run C, the best program in the population scores 19 hits (out of 32). Fitness improves to 24 hits on generation 1, and 25 hits on generation 2 with programs having an argument map of {2}. This new level of fitness is attained in conjunction with the availability of two-argument automatically defined functions (none of which existed on generation 0).

On generation 8, a best-of-generation program with 26 hits emerges with two automatically defined functions and an argument map of {2, 1}. In this program, ADF1 takes only one argument and is equivalent to the NOT function.

A program with 28 hits with an argument map of {2, 2} emerges on generation 10. Another program with an argument map of {2, 2} emerges on generation 11 with 29 hits.

On generation 13, a 100%-correct solution to the even-5-parity problem appears. This best-of-run program has two automatically defined functions and an argument map of {3, 2}. The architecture-altering operations are responsible for the increase in the number of automatically defined functions and their increased arity.

The result-producing branch of the best-of-run program from generation 13 refers to both ADF0 and ADF1:

```
(AND (OR (ADF0 (NAND D1 D2) (ADF0 D2 D0 D0) (ADF0 D2 D0 D0))
(NAND (OR D3 D1) (ADF1 D3 D3))) (ADF0 (ADF1 (NAND D1 D2) (NOR D4
D4)) (ADF1 (ADF1 D3 D0) (NOR D1 D2)) (ADF1 (ADF1 D3 D0) (NOR D1
D2))))).
```

Three-argument ADF0 is

```
(NOR (OR (AND (OR (OR ARG0 ARG2) (NAND ARG0 ARG2)) (AND (NAND
ARG0 ARG1) (NOR ARG2 ARG0))) (AND (AND (NOR ARG1 ARG0) (OR ARG2
ARG0)) (OR (NAND ARG0 ARG1) (NOR ARG2 ARG0)))) (NAND (NAND (AND
(NOR ARG0 ARG2) (NAND ARG0 ARG0)) (NOR (NAND ARG0 ARG0) (NOR
ARG2 ARG1))) (OR (NAND (AND ARG1 ARG0) (OR ARG1 ARG0)) (OR
(NAND ARG2 ARG2) (NOR ARG0 ARG0))))).
```

Table 12.5 is the truth table for ADF0.

ADF0 performs Boolean rule 106, a nonparity rule. When presented in disjunctive normal form, ADF0 is

```
(OR (AND ARG0 (NOT ARG1))
(AND ARG0 (NOT ARG2))
(AND (NOT ARG0) ARG1 ARG2)).
```

Two-argument ADF1 is equivalent to the odd-2-parity function:

```
(NOR (OR (AND (OR (OR ARG0 ARG1) (NAND ARG0 ARG1)) (AND (NAND
ARG0 ARG1) (NOR ARG1 ARG0))) (AND (AND (NOR ARG1 ARG0) (OR ARG1
ARG0)) (OR (NAND ARG0 ARG1) (NOR ARG1 ARG0)))) (NAND (NAND (AND
(NOR ARG0 ARG1) (NAND ARG0 ARG0)) (NOR (NAND ARG0 ARG0) (NOR
ARG1 ARG1))) (OR (NAND (AND ARG1 ARG0) (OR ARG1 ARG0)) (OR
(NAND ARG1 ARG1) (NOR ARG0 ARG0))))).
```

Figure 12.8 shows the call tree for the above best-of-run program from generation 13. As can be seen, the result-producing branch directly calls three-argument ADF0 and two-argument ADF1. The hierarchy for this solution is not as deep as that shown in Figure 12.7.

In this run, the architecture-altering operations evolved two automatically defined functions (one a nonparity three-argument function and one a two-argument parity function) and solved a fifth-order Boolean problem by assembling a solution from them.

Table 12.5 Truth table for ADF0

Fitness case	ARG2	ARG1	ARG0	ADF0
0	0	0	0	0
1	0	0	1	1
2	0	1	0	0
3	0	1	1	1
4	1	0	0	0
5	1	0	1	1
6	1	1	0	1
7	1	1	1	0

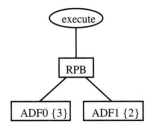

Figure 12.8 Call tree for the best-of-run program from generation 13 for even-5-parity problem

No three-argument automatically defined functions existed at the beginning of this run. The existence of three-argument Boolean functions is a consequence of the architecture-altering operations. Moreover, no two-argument automatically defined functions existed at the beginning of this run, and the existence and availability of the odd-2-parity function as a building block for constructing the fifth-order parity function is also a consequence of the architecture-altering operations. The {3, 2} argument map is known to be a good choice of architectures for solving the Boolean even-5-parity problem (Koza 1994g).

12.5   RUN D—ANOTHER DECOMPOSITION

On generation 13 of a run of the even-5-parity problem (run D), a 100%-correct solution to the even-5-parity problem was created. This program has three automatically defined functions and an argument map of {2, 3, 2}. The result-producing branch refers to ADF0 and ADF2:

```
(ADF0 (NAND (NAND (AND D0 D4) (NAND (OR D1(NAND D2 D0))D4))
(NAND D0 D0)) (ADF2 (ADF2 (NAND D2 D2) (NOR D3 D3)) (NAND (NAND
D4 D1) (ADF2 D1 D4)))).
```

ADF0 and ADF2 are identical. They realize the even-2-parity function:

(AND (NAND ARG0 ARG1) (OR ARG0 ARG1)).

ADF1 takes three arguments, ignores one of them, and consists merely of the primitive AND function. In turn, ADF1 is ignored by all the other branches.

It would never occur to a human programmer to write two identical subroutines (ADF0 and ADF2) or to write a three-argument subroutine (ADF1) for a two-argument function that is already in the repertoire of primitive functions for the problem (and then never bother to call it). In spite of the many foibles of this program, a solution was evolved in a relatively early generation (13). Discovery of a computer program that matches the output of the even-5-parity is, on average, considerably accelerated by the use of subroutines (Koza 1994g, Chapter 6). In this instance, the discovery of a lower-order parity function (ADF0 and ADF2) is a particularly useful subroutine for constructing the desired higher-order parity function.

12.6   COMPARISON OF COMPUTER TIME AND PROGRAM SIZE

A price must be paid for the benefit of having genetic programming dynamically determine the architecture of an evolving computer program. Thus, the question arises as to the price associated with the benefits of architecture-altering operations.

This chapter describes an experiment that compares the computational effort, E; the wallclock time, $W(M,t,z)$ (Koza 1994g); and the average structural complexity, $\bar{s}$, for solving the Boolean even-5-parity problem using the following five approaches:

A. without automatically defined functions (corresponding to the style of runs discussed throughout most of Koza 1992e),

B. with automatically defined functions, evolutionary selection of the architecture (corresponding to the style of runs discussed in Chapters 21–25 of Koza 1994g), an architecturally diverse initial population, and structure-preserving crossover with point typing,

C. with automatically defined functions, the architecture-altering operations, a potentially architecturally diverse population, and structure-preserving crossover with point typing (representing the architecture-altering operations described here),

D. with automatically defined functions, a fixed architecture known from Koza 1994g to be a good choice of architecture for the problem (i.e., an argument map of {3, 2}), and structure-preserving crossover with point typing, and

E. with automatically defined functions, a fixed architecture known to be a good choice of architecture for the problem (i.e., an argument map of {3, 2}), and structure-preserving crossover with branch typing (corresponding to the style of runs discussed throughout most of Koza 1994g).

It should be emphasized that all five approaches involve the automatic creation of the particular sequence of steps of the to-be-evolved computer program (and all its branches, if any) for the Boolean even-5-parity problem. This comparative experiment relates only to the price to be paid for various levels of automation in the process of determining the architecture of the solution.

12.6.1 Computational Effort

We start by considering the approach involving the architecture-altering operations (approach C) and then consider the four alternatives.

Approach C

Consider first a series of runs employing the architecture-altering operations (the approach used earlier in this chapter). A probabilistic algorithm may or may not yield a successful result on a particular run. Once there is a failed run in a series of runs of a given problem, a straightforward arithmetic average of the duration of each run is not a satisfactory way to compute the expected computational effort required to solve a given problem. One way to measure the performance of a probabilistic algorithm is to use performance curves (described in detail in Koza 1994g, Section 4.11) that provide a measure of the computational effort required to solve the problem with a certain probability (say, $z = 99\%$).

Figure 12.9 presents the performance curves based on 25 runs using approach C. The $N = 25$ runs were made by running the problem 25 separate times on a 64-node parallel computer with $D = 64$ subpopulations of size $Q = 1,500$ (for a total population of size 96,000) and a migration rate of $B = 8\%$ (in each of four directions on each generation of each subpopulation). The values of M, D, Q, B, z, $R(z)$ (explained below), and N are shown in the larger box inside each performance curve in this book.

The main horizontal axis of Figure 12.9 represents x, the number of fitness evaluations. The second horizontal axis (shown below the main axis) represents the *equivalent number* of generations, i, if all the processing nodes happened to be synchronized (where $x = 96,000i$).

Almost all of the work in this book was done on a parallel computer (Chapter 62). There is a slight difference between creating performance curves for runs on a single serial computer with a single population and *panmictic* selection (i.e., where the individual selected to participate in a genetic operation can come from anywhere in the population) versus runs made on a parallel computer in which the processing nodes contain semi-isolated subpopulations (demes) that operate asynchronously (i.e., where different nodes are working on different generations). For the panmictic selection from a population of size M on a single serial processor, the number of fitness evaluations, x, that are performed on a particular single run is simply $x = M(i + 1)$, where i is the generation number on which the solution emerged. However, in a parallel computing system in which the processing nodes operate asynchronously, the number of fitness evaluations is

$$x = Q \sum_d (i(d) + 1),$$

where the summation index d is over the D processing nodes, where Q is the subpopulation (deme) size, and where $i(d)$ is the number of the last reporting generation from processor d at the time when a program satisfied the success criterion.

The rising curve in Figure 12.9 shows the experimentally observed cumulative probability of success, $P(M, x)$, of solving the problem after making x fitness evaluations. The left vertical axis ranges from 0.0 to 1.0 and applies to $P(M, x)$. $P(M, x)$ is obtained experimentally. First, a table is made in which each row represents an independent run of the problem. The entry in the table associated with each independent run represents the

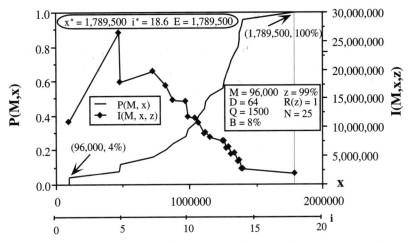

Figure 12.9 Performance curves for the problem of symbolic regression of the even-5-parity function using the architecture-altering operations (approach C)

time of the first appearance during that run of an individual that satisfies the success criterion of the problem (e.g., 32 hits out of a possible 32 for the even-5-parity problem). The time is measured in terms of the generation number, i, for a serial computer or in terms of the number of fitness evaluations, x, for a parallel computer. Second, another table is derived from this first table in which each row represents an increasing generation number (for a serial computer) or an increasing number of fitness evaluations (for a parallel computer). Each entry in this second table is the cumulative probability of success, $P(M, x)$, of solving the problem after i generations (for a serial computer) or after x fitness evaluations (for a parallel computer).

The first value of x for which $P(M, x)$ is nonzero occurs when $x = 96,000$ fitness evaluations ($i = 1.0$ equivalent synchronous generations). The experimentally observed cumulative probability of success, $P(M, x)$, is 4% (1 in 25) for $x = 96,000$. The experimentally observed value of $P(M, x)$ over the runs reaches 100% after making $x = 1,789,500$ fitness evaluations ($i = 18.6$ equivalent synchronous generations).

The second curve in Figure 12.9 shows the number of individuals that must be processed, $I(M, x, z)$, to yield, with probability z, a solution to the problem. The right vertical axis applies to $I(M, x, z)$. $I(M, x, z)$ is derived from the experimentally observed values of $P(M, x)$. It is the product of the number of fitness evaluations, x, and the number of independent runs, $R(z)$, necessary to yield a solution to the problem with a required probability, z, after making x fitness evaluations. In turn, $R(z)$ is given by

$$R(z) = \left\lceil \frac{\log(1-z)}{\log(1 - P(M, x))} \right\rceil,$$

where the brackets indicate the ceiling function for rounding up to the next highest integer. The required probability, z, will be 99% for all performance curves in this book. The rounding up is not required for computing $R(z)$ and, in fact, is not used in Section 21.2 and Chapters 54 and 55.

The $I(M, x, z)$ curve reaches a minimum value of 1,789,500 at the best value $x^* = $ 1,789,500 ($i^* = 18.6$ equivalent synchronous generations) as shown by the shaded vertical line. For the observed value of $P(M, x^*)$ (i.e., 100%) associated with this best x^*, the number of independent runs necessary to yield a solution to the problem with a 99% probability is $R(z) = 1$. This minimum is called E. E is a measure of the computational effort necessary to yield a solution to a problem with 99% probability. The three summary numbers in the oval ($x^* = 1,789,500$, $i^* = 18.6$, and $E = 1,789,500$) indicate that making runs involving processing a total of $x^* = 1,789,500$ individuals (i.e., 96,000 population size $\times$ 18.6 equivalent synchronous generations $\times$ 1 run) is sufficient to yield a solution (with 99% probability) to this problem after making a total computational effort of $E = 1,789,500$ fitness evaluations. Note that the number 1,789,500 appears twice in this particular oval since $R(z) = 1$.

The frequencies of usage for the genetic operations for this comparative study are found using the tables of percentages of genetic operations in Appendix D of this book. The other control parameters are the default values specified in Koza (1994g, Appendix D).

Approach A

Figure 12.10 presents the performance curves based on 14 runs of the problem of symbolic regression of the Boolean even-5-parity function without automatically defined functions (approach A). For the runs in approach A, the maximum size, S_{rpb}, for the result-producing branch is 500 points.

As will be seen, the ADF-less approach makes the slowest progress toward solution of the problem among the five approaches. The first value of x for which the experimentally observed cumulative probability of success, $P(M, x)$, is nonzero occurs at $x = 3,275,000$ individuals ($i = 34.1$ equivalent synchronous generations); $P(M, x)$ is 7% for that x. The cumulative probability of success, $P(M, x)$, reaches 100% when $x = 5,025,000$ ($i = 52.3$ equivalent synchronous generations). The three summary numbers in the oval ($x^* = $ 5,025,000, $i^* = 52.3$, and $E = 5,025,000$) indicate that making runs involving processing a total of $x^* = 5,025,000$ individuals (i.e., 96,000 population size $\times$ 52.3 equivalent synchronous generations $\times$ 1 run) is sufficient to yield a solution to this problem after making a total computational effort of $E = 5,025,000$ fitness evaluations with 99% probability.

By way of comparison, when the Boolean even-5-parity problem was solved in *Genetic Programming II* (Koza 1994g, Figure 6.4) without automatically defined functions, a roughly similar value of computational effort, E, was obtained (albeit with a significantly different population size, significantly different choices of minor parameters, and with a single population with panmictic selection on a serial computer). Specifically, the first occasion when the experimentally observed cumulative probability of success is nonzero occurs in generation 34 in *Genetic Programming II* (compared to 34.1 equivalent synchronous generations here). The cumulative probability of success is 44% by generation 50 in *Genetic Programming II* (compared to over 90% here). The numbers in the oval in Figure 6.4 in *Genetic Programming II* indicate that running this problem eight times through to generation 50 and thereby processing a total computational effort of $E = $ 6,528,000 individuals (i.e., $16,000 \times 51$ generations $\times$ 8 runs) is sufficient to yield a solution to this problem with 99% probability. This computational effort, E, of 6,528,000

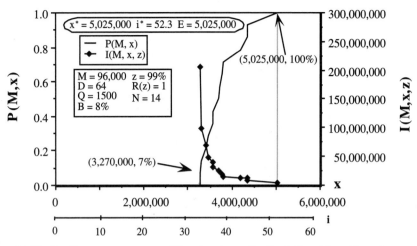

Figure 12.10   Performance curves without automatically defined functions (approach A)

compares to a total computational effort of E = 5,025,000 fitness evaluations here (Figure 12.10). Although differences in control parameters, of course, affect runs of genetic programming, it is interesting to note the closeness of these two values of computational effort.

Approach B

Figure 12.11 presents the performance curves based on 14 runs of this problem with evolutionary selection of the architecture (approach B). For the runs in approach B, the maximum number of function-defining branches is 4; the minimum number of automatically defined functions is 0; the minimum number of arguments for any automatically defined function is 2; and the maximum number of arguments for any automatically defined function is 4.

The first value of x for which the experimentally observed cumulative probability of success, $P(M, x)$, is nonzero occurs at x = 97,500 individuals (i = 1.02 equivalent synchronous generations); $P(M, x)$ is 7% for that x. The cumulative probability of success, $P(M, x)$, reaches 100% when x = 4,263,000 (i = 44.4 equivalent synchronous generations). As can be seen, these milestones are reached considerably earlier for approach B than approach A (the ADF-less approach). The three summary numbers in the oval (x^* = 4,263,000, i^* = 44.4, and E = 4,263,000) indicate that making runs involving processing a total of x^* = 4,263,000 individuals (i.e., 96,000 population size $\times$ 44.4 equivalent synchronous generations $\times$ 1 run) is sufficient to yield a solution to this problem after making a total computational effort of E = 4,263,000 fitness evaluations with 99% probability.

Approach D

Since approaches B and C use point typing, approach D is included so that the additional computational effort required by point typing can be separately identified by direct

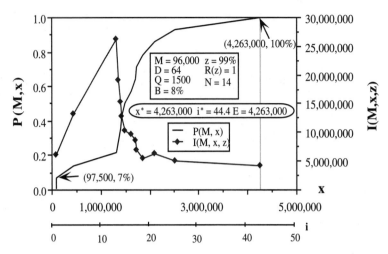

Figure 12.11 Performance curves with evolutionary selection of the architecture (approach B)

comparison with approach E. For the runs in approaches D and E, the size of the result-producing branch is limited to 166 points; the size of both function-defining branches is limited to 167 points.

Figure 12.12 presents the performance curves based on 25 runs of this problem with the fixed {3, 2} architecture with point typing (approach D). The first value of x for which the experimentally observed cumulative probability of success, $P(M, x)$, is nonzero occurs at $x = 100,500$ fitness evaluations ($i = 1.05$ equivalent synchronous generations); $P(M, x)$ is 4% for that x. The cumulative probability of success, $P(M, x)$, reaches 100% when $x = 1,705,500$ ($i = 17.8$ equivalent synchronous generations). The three summary numbers in the oval ($x^* = 1,705,500$, $i^* = 17.8$, and $E = 1,705,500$) indicate that making runs involving processing a total computational effort of $x^* = 1,705,500$ individuals (i.e., 96,000 population size × 17.8 equivalent synchronous generations × 1 run) is sufficient to yield a solution to this problem after making a total computational effort of $E = 1,705,500$ fitness evaluations with 99% probability.

Approach E

Figure 12.13 presents the performance curves based on 25 runs of this problem with the fixed {3, 2} architecture with branch typing (approach E). As can be seen, these runs make the fastest progress toward a solution to the problem among the five approaches. The first value of x for which the experimentally observed cumulative probability of success, $P(M, x)$, is nonzero occurs at $x = 100,500$ fitness evaluations ($i = 1.05$ equivalent synchronous generations); $P(M, x)$ is 4% for that x. The cumulative probability of success, $P(M, x)$, reaches 100% when $x = 1,261,500$ ($i = 13.1$ equivalent synchronous generations). The three summary numbers in the oval ($x^* = 1,261,500$, $i^* = 13.1$, and $E = 1,261,500$) indicate that making runs involving processing a total of $x^* = 1,261,500$ individuals (i.e., 96,000 population size × 13.1 equivalent synchronous generations × 1 run)

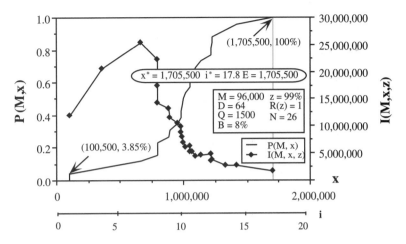

Figure 12.12   Performance curves for the fixed {3, 2} architecture and point typing (approach D)

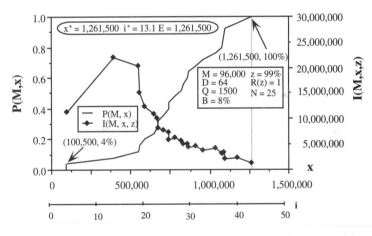

Figure 12.13   Performance curves for the fixed {3, 2} architecture and branch typing (approach E)

is sufficient to yield a solution to this problem after making a total computational effort of $E = 1,261,500$ fitness evaluations with 99% probability.

By way of comparison, when automatically defined functions were used in solving this same even-5-parity problem in *Genetic Programming II* (Koza 1994g, Figure 6.17), the first occasion when the experimentally observed cumulative probability of success is nonzero occurs in generation 9 (compared to 3.05 equivalent synchronous generations here). The cumulative probability of success is 100% by generation 28 in *Genetic Programming II* (compared to 100% by 42.05 equivalent synchronous generations here).

The numbers in the oval in Figure 6.17 in *Genetic Programming II* indicate that running this problem one time through to generation 50 and thereby processing a total computational effort of E = 464,000 individuals (i.e., 16,000 × 29 generations × 1 run) is sufficient to yield a solution to this problem with 99% probability (compared to a total computational effort of E = 1,261,500 fitness evaluations here).

12.6.2   Discussion

Table 12.6 compares the computational effort, E; wallclock time (in seconds), $W(M,t,z)$; and average structural complexity, $\bar{s}$, for the Boolean even-5-parity problem using the five approaches. As can be seen from the table, all runs with all five approaches yield solutions to the problem well before the targeted maximum number (i.e., 76) of generations (a value of x = 7,296,000). Note also that size of the search space for five-argument Boolean functions consists of $2^{2^5} = 2^{32} \sim 4 \times 10^9$ different functions.

The observed values of computational effort, E, for the five approaches are related as follows:

$$E(A) > E(B) > E(C) > E(D) > E(E).$$

That is, all four approaches (B, C, D, or E) employing automatically defined functions require less computational effort than the approach not using them (approach A).

Approach E requires the least computational effort. It enjoys both the advantages of automatically defined functions and of the known-good, user-supplied architecture.

At the other extreme, approach A (with no automatically defined functions at all) has no such advantages and requires the most computational effort.

Approach C (discovering the architecture using the architecture-altering operations) requires less computational effort than solving the problem without automatically defined functions (approach A), but more computational effort than with a good user-supplied choice of architecture for the automatically defined functions (approach E).

Approach B (discovering the architecture using evolutionary selection of the architecture) requires greater computational effort than using the architecture-altering operations (approach C), but less than that for runs without automatically defined functions (approach A). Even though both approaches B and C involve architecturally diverse populations and use point typing, the reason for the larger computational effort for approach B may be that approach B involves such an extensive range of different architectures that many of these architectures are inappropriate for the problem. Moreover, since there are so many different architectures in approach B, the effective working size of the subpopulation for each architecture is very small.

Point typing (used by approaches B and C) apparently increases the computational effort. To isolate the effect of point typing, approach D uses point typing on the same good fixed architecture used in approach E. The table shows that greater computational effort is required by approach D than approach E. Since the computational effort for approach C is almost tied with approach D, the cost of employing the architecture-altering operations for this problem is not much greater than the cost of employing point typing.

In summary, a price must be paid for dynamically determining the architecture of a computer program that can solve a given problem. For the specific problem studied in this chapter (and the specific choices of parameters), discovering the architecture using the architecture-altering operations (approach C) requires less computational effort than

Table 12.6 Comparison of five approaches to solving the even-5-parity problem

Approach	Computational effort	Wallclock time	Average structural complexity
A no ADFs	5,025,000	36,950	469.1
B evolutionary selection	4,263,000	66,667	180.9
C architecture-altering operations	1,789,500	13,594	88.8
D fixed architecture and point typing	1,705,500	14,088	130.0
E fixed architecture and branch typing	1,261,500	6,481	112.2

solving the problem without automatically defined functions (approach A), but more computational effort than with a good user-supplied choice of architecture for the automatically defined functions (approach E). That is, the price for dynamically determining the architecture appears to be intermediate between the extreme of not using automatically defined functions at all and using automatically defined functions with a fixed, known-good, user-supplied architecture. Of course, this conclusion is necessarily limited by the specific problem (and choices of parameters and limited statistical significance) of this experimental comparison.

12.6.3   Wallclock Time

The observed values of wallclock time, $W(M,t,z)$, are related as follows:

$$W(A) > W(C) > W(E).$$

That is, approach E (with both automatically defined functions and a good user-supplied choice of architecture) consumes less wallclock time than approach C (using the architecture-altering operations), which, in turn, consumes less wallclock time than approach A (without automatically defined functions).

The reason why the most wallclock time is consumed by approach B (discovering the architecture using evolutionary selection of the architecture) is perhaps that the population (starting at generation 0) contains many deep hierarchies of calls to automatically defined functions (even though the problem does not actually require such depth).

The amount of wallclock time consumed by approach D is very close (but greater than) the wallclock time for approach C.

Note that the wallclock times reported here are not comparable to the wallclock times reported in *Genetic Programming II* because they were run on different machines and because of certain optimizations that were unique to the earlier runs on the LISP machine (Section 6.9 of Koza 1994g).

12.6.4   Average Structural Complexity

The average structural complexity, š, is the average number of points (i.e., number of work-performing functions and terminals in all branches of a program) in the first reported solution (if any) of each run. As it happened, all runs of this problem with the population size, M, of 96,000 produced solutions.

The average structural complexity, $\bar{s}$, for all four approaches employing automatically defined functions (B, C, D, or E) is less than the average structural complexity for approach A (without automatically defined functions):

$$\bar{s}(A) > \bar{s}(B, C, D, E)$$

Approach C (using the architecture-altering operations) has the lowest value of average structural complexity:

$$\bar{s}(A, B, D, E) > \bar{s}(C).$$

The reason may be that this approach starts with a "minimalist" architecture and judiciously expands programs by adding function-defining branches and arguments.

12.6.5 Summary

The even-parity problem was solved in runs A, B, C, and D of this chapter. For each of these four runs, we did not prespecify any of the following characteristics of the solution:

- that subroutines should be used,
    - if subroutines were to be used at all, the number of subroutines,
    - if subroutines were to be used at all, the number of arguments that they would each possess,
- the precise number of steps in
    - the result-producing branch,
    - the subroutines,
- the exact sequence of steps that would be performed in
    - the result-producing branch,
    - the subroutines,
- the hierarchical organization for the program's different branches.

All of the above characteristics of the evolved solution emerged during the run of genetic programming as a result of the architecture-altering operations for subroutines.

Time-Optimal Robot Control Problem Using Architecture-Altering Operations for Subroutines

This chapter illustrates the use of the architecture-altering operations on a time-optimal control problem. The goal is to find a strategy for continuously specifying the direction for moving a constant-speed object with a nonzero turning radius to an arbitrary destination point.

If the moving object (e.g., an aircraft or a robot) has a nonzero turning radius, this problem cannot be solved by greedily reducing the distance between the robot and the destination at every intermediate point along the robot's trajectory. Instead, momentarily disadvantageous actions must be taken in the short term in order to achieve the long-term objective (Clements 1990).

This same problem is solved using version 1.0 of the Genetic Programming Problem Solver (GPPS 1.0) in Section 21.3 and by GPPS 2.0 in Section 23.5. In Chapter 48, genetic programming is used to create an analog electrical circuit to implement the time-optimal solution to this same problem as a real-time robot controller.

13.1 BACKGROUND

In Figure 13.1, the robot is initially positioned at the origin (0, 0) of the coordinate system and is headed east (i.e., along the positive x-axis). The robot moves at a constant speed, A. The robot's maximum turn angle, Θ_{max}, defines a turning radius, R. The radius of each of the two circles centered at $(0, +R)$ and $(0, -R)$ along the vertical axis in the figure are equal to this turning radius. The robot's trajectory is controlled by the turn angle, Θ, which controls the robot's change in heading. Angles are measured in radians counterclockwise from the positive x-axis.

Suppose the destination point lies on the positive x-axis, such as point (x_1, y_1) in Figure 13.1. In this first case, the robot's time-optimal control strategy is to move straight ahead (east) along the positive x-axis (i.e., with $\Theta = 0$ radians). The time-optimal trajectory is the straight line between the origin and the target (x_1, y_1) along the positive x-axis.

Now suppose that the target point, such as (x_3, y_3), lies on the circumference of the upper circle of radius R. In this second case, the time-optimal control strategy is to turn with a heading equal to the maximum turn angle $\Theta = +\Theta_{max}$. The robot's time-optimal trajectory will be the portion of the circumference of the circle between the origin and the target point (x_3, y_3). By symmetry, the minimum-time control strategy for any point on the circumference of the lower circle, such as (x_6, y_6), consists of proceeding at the maximum turn angle of $\Theta = -\Theta_{max}$.

The remaining points can be classified into two additional cases based on whether they are outside or inside the circles. The strategies for these next two cases employ portions of the robot trajectories used by one or both of the above strategies.

In the third case (Figure 13.2), the target point is in the first or second quadrants (i.e., positive values of y) but *outside* the upper circle. For a point such as (x_2, y_2), there is a unique first point **P** on the circumference of the upper circle such that the tangent line to the upper circle at point **P** passes through (x_2, y_2). For this third case, the minimum-time control strategy for the robot is to turn at the maximum angle $\Theta = +\Theta_{max}$ until the robot reaches point **P** on the circumference of the upper circle and then to move straight ahead (i.e., with an angle of $\Theta = 0$) to the target. The robot's time-optimal trajectory will be the portion of the circumference of the upper circle between the origin and **P** combined with the tangent line between **P** and the target (x_2, y_2). Note that this strategy works regardless of the location of (x_2, y_2) in the first or second quadrants and outside the upper circle including, specifically, points in the second quadrant (i.e., negative values of x, but positive values of y) behind the robot's initial position. By symmetry, a similar strategy (of first turning southeast at the maximum angle of $\Theta = -\Theta_{max}$ and then moving straight) works for target points *outside* the lower circle, such as (x_5, y_5). Points on the negative x-axis (i.e., directly behind the robot's initial position) can be reached equally well in this manner (initially going around the circle in either direction).

In the fourth case (Figure 13.3), the target point is in the first or second quadrants but *inside* the upper circle. None of the points inside the upper circle can be reached by pursuing a strategy that tries to greedily reduce the distance between the robot and the target at every intermediate point along the robot's trajectory. Such destinations can only be reached by veering away from the destination and incurring a temporary increase in the distance between the robot and the target. As can be seen in Figure 13.3, for a point such as (x_4, y_4), there is a unique point **Q** to the east of the origin on the circumference of a unique third circle of radius R such that the circumference of the third circle is tangent to the lower circle at point **Q** and passes through (x_4, y_4) of the upper circle. For this fourth case, the minimum-time control strategy for the robot is to turn at the maximum angle $\Theta = -\Theta_{max}$ (i.e., initially turning southeast, thereby increasing the distance between the robot and the target) until the robot reaches point **Q** and then to reverse directions and turn at the maximum angle $+\Theta_{max}$ until the robot reaches the target. The robot's time-optimal trajectory will be the portion of the circumference of the lower circle between the origin and **Q** and the portion of the circumference of the new tangent circle between **Q** and the target. Note that this strategy works regardless of the location of (x_4, y_4), in the first or second quadrants and inside the upper circle (including, specifically, points behind the robot's initial position in the second quadrant). By symmetry, a similar strat-

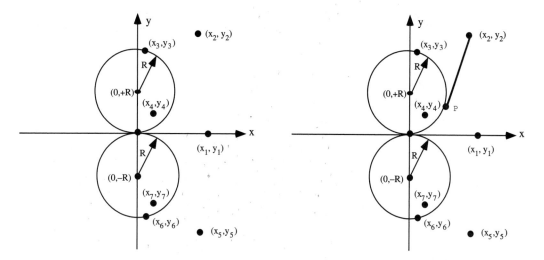

Figure 13.1 The first two cases of the robot controller problem

Figure 13.2 The third case of the robot controller problem

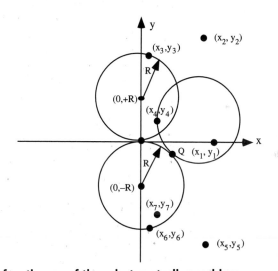

Figure 13.3 The fourth case of the robot controller problem

egy (of first turning northeast at the maximum angle of $\Theta = +\Theta_{max}$ and then turning at the maximum angle of $\Theta = -\Theta_{max}$) works for target points *inside* the lower circle, such as (x_7, y_7).

The above optimal control strategies and trajectories were described as if the state of the system were expressed in terms of the robot's changing position relative to the ground, namely, $(x_{ground}(t), y_{ground}(t))$. If the control variable for the robot is the turn angle Θ, then the state transition equations for the system are

$$x_{robot}(t + 1) = x_{robot}(t) + A \, \Delta t \, \text{Cos} \, \Theta$$

and

$$y_{robot}(t + 1) = y_{robot}(t) + A\,\Delta t\,\text{Sin}\,\Theta.$$

In practice, the more natural viewpoint for a robot controller is the view from the robot. In this view, whenever the robot travels in a particular direction, the coordinate system is immediately adjusted so that the robot is repositioned to the origin $(0, 0)$ of the coordinate system with the robot heading due east. In this view, the state of the system is the changing location of the destination point relative to the robot, namely, $(x_{dest\text{-}robot}(t), y_{dest\text{-}robot}(t))$. The equations for transforming the coordinates are

$$x_{dest\text{-}robot}(t + 1) = (y_{dest\text{-}ground} - y_{robot})\,\text{Sin}\,\Theta + (x_{dest\text{-}ground} - x_{robot})\,\text{Cos}\,\Theta$$

$$y_{dest\text{-}robot}(t + 1) = (y_{dest\text{-}ground} - y_{robot})\,\text{Cos}\,\Theta - (x_{dest\text{-}ground} - x_{robot})\,\text{Sin}\,\Theta$$

Each of the above four optimal control strategies can be restated in accordance with this new view from the robot:

- For the first case, the strategy of moving straight ahead toward a target on the positive x-axis has the effect of moving the target point west along the positive x-axis until it reaches the robot.
- For the second case, the strategy of turning with an angle Θ_{max} for a target point on the circumference of the upper circle has the effect of moving the target point around the circumference of the circle until it reaches the robot.
- For the third case, the strategy for a target point in the first or second quadrants and outside the upper circle has the effect of first rotating the target to the positive x-axis and then moving the target west along the positive x-axis until it reaches the robot.
- For the fourth case, the strategy for a target point inside the upper circle has the effect of first rotating the target away from the robot to the circumference of the third circle and then moving the target point around the circumference of the third circle until it reaches the robot.

13.2 THE PROBLEM

The goal in this navigation problem is to find a time-optimal strategy for continuously controlling the movement of a constant-speed moving object with a nonzero turning radius (such as a robot) to an arbitrary destination point in the plane. Specifically, the robot has a constant speed, A, of 200 meters per hour and a maximum performance rate of turn that corresponds to a turn angle of 0.197 radians per time step of 0.001 hour (Clements 1990).

13.3 PREPARATORY STEPS

13.3.1 Program Architecture

Our intent is that each program in generation 0 have a minimalist architecture. For a problem involving real-valued variables, even one automatically defined function might

Figure 13.4   Common architecture for generation 0

be considered useful. Accordingly, each program in generation 0 has a uniform architecture consisting of one result-producing branch and no automatically defined functions, as shown in Figure 13.4.

After generation 0, the architecture-altering operations can create automatically defined functions and determine the number of arguments that they each possess. As multiple automatically defined functions begin to appear in the population, hierarchical references will be allowed between them. Thus, if a program contains two automatically defined functions (ADF0 and ADF1), ADF1 may refer to ADF0.

Since this problem involves only two independent variables, the maximum number of arguments, $N_{\text{max-argument-adf}}$, for each automatically defined function is established to be two. The maximum number of automatically defined functions, $N_{\text{max-adf}}$, is two. The maximum size, S_{rpb}, for the result-producing branch is 400 points. The maximum size, S_{adf}, for each automatically defined function is 200 points. Thus, an individual program in the population can have as many as 800 points.

13.3.2   Functions and Terminals

The first major step in preparing to use genetic programming is to identify the terminal set for the problem. The second major step is to identify the function set.

The function and terminal sets specify the ingredients of the to-be-discovered computer program. The function and terminal sets define the particular space of computer programs that genetic programming will consider in solving the problem. Each program considered during the run of genetic programming will be a composition of the available functions and terminals. For this problem, the ingredients consist of

- the two floating-point variables, X and Y, constituting the inputs to the to-be-discovered program,
- the arithmetic operations of addition, subtraction, multiplication, and division,
- an "if less than or equal" conditional branching operator, and
- floating-point numerical constants.

Notice that no significant domain knowledge concerning time-optimal control is used in determining the function and terminal sets for this problem. Notice, specifically, that we did not employ any of the mathematical analysis or any problem-specific background information concerning time-optimal control (such as found in Section 13.1) in selecting this generic function set and terminal set for this problem. In fact, the above generic terminals are suitable for any control problem involving two floating-point inputs (and, indeed, for a wide variety of other types of two-input problems outside of the field of control, including problems of system identification, optimization, and classification). The above generic functions are completely unremarkable—they constitute the core of the repertoire of primitive machine code instructions for virtually every general-purpose computer that has ever been built. They are the basic functions used by control engineers (and mathematicians and others) in their everyday work on a wide variety of problems. Some critics of genetic programming have asserted that the user's choice of the function and terminal set prior to the run of genetic programming is tantamount to solving the problem. If so, the entire universe of two-input control problems has just been solved!

When the architecture-altering operations are used, separate function and terminal sets are needed to identify both the initial and potential members of both the function and terminal sets for both the result-producing and the function-defining branch(es).

The initial terminal set for the result-producing branch, $T_{\text{rpb-initial}}$, consists of the two externally supplied floating-point inputs (X and Y) and floating-point random constants:

$$T_{\text{rpb-initial}} = \{X, Y, \Re_{\text{smaller-reals}}\}.$$

Here X and Y are the coordinates of the target point, and $\Re_{\text{smaller-reals}}$ are floating-point random constants between −1.0 and +1.0.

During the creation of the individual programs in generation 0, whenever $\Re_{\text{smaller-reals}}$ is the terminal at a particular point of a program tree, a constant between −1.0 and +1.0 is inserted into the program tree at that point. The particular random constant that is inserted at a particular point is drawn from a fixed repertoire of floating-point random constants between −1.0 and +1.0 that were generated at the start of the run. In the "one-byte" representation used in our implementation of genetic programming, each point (terminal or function) of each program tree in the population is encoded into one byte of computer memory. The number of different floating-point random constants is the difference between 256 and the sum of the number of functions (initial and potential) in the problem's function set and the number of terminals (initial and potential) in the problem's terminal set. For most problems in this book, there are over 200 different random constants in this fixed repertoire. These initial random constants are typically recombined in many different ways using various arithmetic functions in the program trees. For purposes of constructing individuals for generation 0, the family of floating-point random constants is weighted as if it were a single terminal (as explained in Appendix D of this book).

The initial function set for the result-producing branch, $F_{\text{rpb-initial}}$, consists of the four two-argument arithmetic functions and the one four-argument conditional branching operator (IFLTE):

$$F_{\text{rpb-initial}} = \{+, -, *, \%, \text{IFLTE}\},$$

taking 2, 2, 2, 2, and 4 arguments, respectively.

The two-argument *protected division function*, %, returns the number 1 when division by 0 is attempted (including 0 divided by 0) and, otherwise, returns the normal quotient.

When thousands of different randomly created computer programs are each exposed to dozens of combinations of inputs over hundreds of generations, it is only a matter of time before every conceivable error condition will arise. Thus, all four arithmetic functions (+, −, *, %) require additional protection against floating-point overflows and underflows. This protection can be implemented most easily by writing magnitude-protected subroutines for all four of these functions. This protection can also be implemented by trapping the overflow or underflow errors in the manner appropriate to the user's computer and appropriately returning control to the executing program or by globally disabling the effect of such errors (as is done with machine code genetic programming; see Nordin 1994, 1997; Nordin and Banzhaf 1995; Banzhaf, Nordin, Keller, and Francone 1998). In any event, whenever the magnitude of the result obtained by performing any of the four arithmetic operations is larger than a certain limit (e.g., 10^9) or is smaller than a certain limit (e.g., 10^{-9}), then some nominal value is instead returned (e.g., 10^9 or 10^{-9}, respectively, with the appropriate sign).

The four-argument conditional branching operator IFLTE evaluates and returns its third argument if its first argument is less than or equal to its second argument, but otherwise evaluates and returns its fourth argument. The IFLTE operator is implemented as a macro (in the sense that the term is used in the LISP programming language). That is, exactly one (never both) of the two alternative argument subtrees (the third and fourth arguments) is executed. Specifically, the third argument subtree of the IFLTE operator is executed if and only if the condition is satisfied (i.e., the first argument of the IFLTE operator is less than or equal to its second argument), and the fourth argument subtree is executed otherwise.

This same approach is used for similar conditional operators in this book, such as

- the three-argument IFGTZ ("if greater than zero") conditional branching operator used in the transmembrane segment identification problem (Chapters 16 and 17), the Genetic Programming Problem Solver (Chapters 20 through 23 of Part 4), the digit recognition problem (Chapter 15), and the cellular location problem (Chapter 60),
- the three-argument IFEQZ ("if equal zero") conditional branching operator, used in version 1.0 of the Genetic Programming Problem Solver (Chapter 20),
- the short-circuiting versions of the two-argument logical functions—the ORN function used in the transmembrane segment identification problem (Chapters 16 and 17) and the TAND and TOR functions used in the Genetic Programming Problem Solver (Chapters 20 through 23 of Part 4), and
- the problem-specific conditional branching operators of the multiagent problem involving ants (Chapter 14).

Additional details of the implementation of such conditional operators are provided in Section 6.1.1 of *Genetic Programming* and Section 12.2 of *Genetic Programming II*.

Since there are no automatically defined functions in generation 0 of this problem, $T_{\text{adf-initial}}$ and $F_{\text{adf-initial}}$ are empty:

$$T_{\text{adf-initial}} = \phi$$

and

$$F_{\text{adf-initial}} = \phi.$$

There are no automatically defined functions (ADF0, ADF1, . . .) or dummy variables (ARG0, ARG1, . . .) in any individual in generation 0 of the run. After generation 0, the architecture-altering operations can add automatically defined functions and dummy variables. For this problem involving two independent variables, the maximum number of dummy variables for any one automatically defined function is preestablished to be two.

The set of potential terminals, $T_{\text{adf-potential}}$, for each automatically defined function includes two new dummy variables that may be created by the architecture-altering operations:

$$T_{\text{adf-potential}} = \{\texttt{ARG0, ARG1}\}.$$

Since dummy variables do not appear in the result-producing branch, the set of potential terminals, $T_{\text{rpb-potential}}$, for the result-producing branch is empty:

$$T_{\text{rpb-potential}} = \phi.$$

The set of potential functions, $F_{\text{rpb-potential}}$, for the result-producing branch is

$$F_{\text{rpb-potential}} = \{\texttt{ADF0, ADF1}\},$$

each taking a yet-to-be-determined number of arguments (up to two).

The set of potential functions, $F_{\text{adf1-potential}}$, for automatically defined function ADF1 is

$$F_{\text{adf1-potential}} = \{\texttt{ADF0}\}.$$

Because of our usual limitation that a function-defining branch can refer hierarchically only to a previously defined function-defining branch, the set of potential functions, $F_{\text{adf0-potential}}$, for automatically defined function ADF0 is empty:

$$F_{\text{adf0-potential}} = \phi.$$

Since the two independent variables, the random constants, the four arithmetic functions, and the IFLTE operator all evaluate to a floating-point value, the set of functions and terminals is closed. This remains the case even as new automatically defined functions (with varying numbers of arguments) are created.

13.3.3 Fitness

Fitness is measured over 72 fitness cases, each representing a different destination (x_i, y_i) for the robot. The x_i and y_i coordinate of each destination lies between −4.0 and +4.0 meters. Fitness is the sum, over the 72 destinations, of the time for the robot to reach the destination. A smaller sum is better.

For each fitness case, the robot is assumed to start at the origin of a coordinate system representing a world that extends 4 meters in each of the four directions. A total of 80 time steps, each representing 0.001 hour, are used to simulate the trajectory of the robot. The total simulation time of 0.080 hours generously permits a trajectory equivalent to the robot moving twice across its world of 64 square meters.

The robot is controlled by a turn angle Θ that must lie between $-\Theta_{\max}$ and $+\Theta_{\max}$. An individual program in the population is evaluated by executing its result-producing branch. The result-producing branch typically contains numerous invocations of various function-defining branches (automatically defined functions) that are created during the run by the architecture-altering operations. When an individual program in the population is executed, it produces an arbitrary floating-point value, x. Thus, a wrapper (output interface) is needed for this problem to map this numerical value into the permissible range for a turn angle Θ. Figure 13.5 shows how the wrapper interprets the numeric value, x, returned by execution of an individual program. The wrapper takes the value, x,

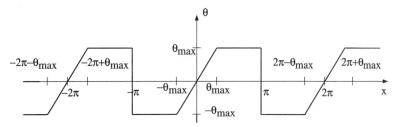

Figure 13.5 Wrapper (output interface) for the robot controller

modulo 2π and clamps the result so that its absolute value is always less than or equal to Θ_{max} (i.e., so that the final output Θ lies between $-\Theta_{max}$ and $+\Theta_{max}$).

If the robot comes within a capture radius of 0.28 meters of its target point before the end of the 80 time steps allowed for a particular fitness case, the robot is regarded as having reached its destination, and the detrimental contribution (penalty) to the fitness measure for that fitness case is the actual travel time.

If the robot fails to come within the capture radius during the 80 time steps, the detrimental contribution to fitness for that fitness case is a penalty value of 0.160 hours (twice the worst possible amount of time). Because Darwinian selection is used at each step of genetic programming, the practical effect of a penalty on one or more fitness case(s) is that the penalized individuals are less likely to be selected to be reproduced (copied) into the next generation or to participate in genetic operations (e.g., crossover and mutation). That is, the evolutionary search tends to work around penalized individuals.

The number of hits is defined as the number of fitness cases (from 0 to 72) for which the robot arrives at its destination within the available 80 time steps (i.e., does not time out).

Notice how little domain knowledge is used in determining the fitness measure for this problem. In essence, the fitness measure for this problem is (when divided by 72) the average amount of time it takes the robot to reach its destination. Except for certain details that are artifacts of the discretization that enables the problem to be simulated on a computer within a reasonable amount of time, this same fitness measure could be used for almost any other two-dimensional control problem involving the minimization of time. These details include the exact number of fitness cases (which ideally would be infinite), the size of the time step (which ideally would be infinitesimal), the maximum amount of time (which ideally would not be artificially capped at all), the penalty value for exceeding the maximum amount of time (which would be irrelevant if the time were not capped), and the capture radius (which ideally would be zero). Notice that these details concerning measurement do not, under any reasonable interpretation, constitute domain knowledge about how to maneuver a robot to a destination in a time-optimal way. In particular, the one item of domain knowledge that is crucial for solving this problem (namely, the necessity of veering away from a destination that is inaccessible because of the robot's turning radius) is not used at all in constructing the fitness measure. Moreover, none of the above details arise because of any demands peculiar to genetic programming. It is necessary to address these same issues in order to solve this problem with a neural network learning algorithm, a reinforcement learning algorithm, an adaptive system algorithm, a machine learning algorithm, an artificial intelligence search, or virtually any other automated technique.

In problems involving complex multistep simulations, it is often possible to save a considerable amount of computer time by using approximate values of fitness that are prestored in lookup tables. In this problem, the calculation of fitness requires up to 5,760 executions (72×80) of each individual program in the population. For this particular problem, the world of 64 square meters is discretized into a 40×40 grid of 1,600 discrete squares (with each square being 0.2×0.2 meters). For each individual program in the population, a table is computed giving the value of the control variable, Θ, as if the target point were in the exact center of each of the 1,600 squares and as if the robot were located at (0,0). When an individual program is executed for a particular time step of a particular fitness case, the new state of the system is computed from the state transition equations (Section 13.1) using floating-point arithmetic. However, the value of the control variable, Θ, is obtained from the table as if the target were located in the exact center of its square (and not its precise actual location within its square). Note that the precise actual new state of the system is passed along to the next time step of the state transition equations; only the value of the control variable, Θ, is based on the discretization and approximation. If the robot happens to move outside of its world of 64 square meters or if the target point ever moves out of the world relative to the robot's frame of reference, the simulation is terminated for that fitness case and a penalty value of fitness of 0.160 hours is assigned for that fitness case. The worst value of fitness is 11.52 hours, and it occurs when all 72 fitness cases are assigned a time of 0.160 hours. This same discretization is used in Chapter 48 (where this same problem is solved by means of an analog electrical circuit and where capping computer time is even more important than it is in this chapter).

13.3.4   Parameters

The population size, M, is 40,000. The problem was run on a Parsytec parallel computer system (described in detail in Chapter 62). The subpopulation size, Q, is 10,000 at each of the $D = 4$ processing nodes (demes) of a four-node Parsytec parallel computer system. The migration rate is $B = 2\%$.

If we were not using the architecture-altering operations, the percentage of reproduction for a typical run of genetic programming would typically be 10%, the percentage of mutation would typically be 1%, and the percentage of crossover would typically be 89%. The architecture-altering operations are generally used sparingly on each generation (e.g., in the neighborhood of 0.5% and 1%). In order to accommodate the architecture-altering operations, we slightly reduce the percentage for the crossover operation. When we use operations that add branches (e.g., subroutine creation and subroutine duplication) or when we use operations that add arguments, we usually compensate for the increase in the number of branches and arguments by using subroutine deletion or argument deletion. Since each program at the start of the run in generation 0 usually consists of only one result-producing branch and no automatically defined functions (or one automatically defined function with a minimal number of arguments), the percentage of operations that delete branches and arguments is smaller than the percentage of operations that add them. This policy promotes a net growth in the number of automatically defined functions over the generations and compensates for the fact that the run starts with a population having a minimalist architecture. Thus, the percentage of the subroutine deletion operation is typically 0.5%. We use the above percentages for the vast majority of the run (specifically, for all generations after generation 5). Thus, the percentages of the genetic operations on each generation after generation 5 are

- 10% reproduction,
- 1% mutation,
- 1% subroutine duplication,
- 1% subroutine creation,
- 0.5% subroutine deletion, and
- 86.5% one-offspring crossover.

Since all the programs in generation 0 typically have a minimalist architecture, we accelerate the appearance of automatically defined functions in the population by increasing the percentage of the architecture-altering operations on each generation up to and including generation 5. Thus, the percentages for the genetic operations on each generation up to and including generation 5 are

- 10% reproduction,
- 1% mutation,
- 5% subroutine duplication,
- 5% subroutine creation,
- 1% subroutine deletion, and
- 78% one-offspring crossover.

The percentages of genetic operations are presented in Appendix D for most of the remaining problems in this book. Unless otherwise specified, all control parameters that are not included in the description or tableau for a particular problem are the default values listed in Appendix D of this book.

13.3.5 Termination

The optimal attainable value is sometimes known in advance even though the strategy necessary to achieve that value is not known. However, in most optimal control problems, the best possible value of the to-be-optimized quantity is unknown in advance. In this event, one approach to deciding when to terminate a run is to manually monitor the run and to terminate the run when the to-be-optimized quantity appears to have reached a plateau. Thus, the termination criterion for this problem involves manually monitoring the run to see if the value of fitness for the best-of-generation individual in several consecutive generations (after there are 72 hits) appears to have reached a plateau.

For reference, if the optimal control strategy in Clements 1990 is applied to this problem's 72 fitness cases, the optimum time is 1.518 hours (an average of about 21 time steps of 0.001 hours each).

13.3.6 Tableau

Table 13.1 summarizes the key features of the robot controller problem.

Table 13.1 Tableau for the robot controller problem

Objective	Find a control strategy for controlling the trajectory of a constant-speed robot with nonzero turning radius such that the robot moves to an arbitrary destination point in minimal time.
Program architecture	One result-producing branch, RPB, in generation 0. Automatically defined functions (with various number of arguments) will be created during the run by the architecture-altering operations.
Initial function set for the RPBs	$F_{rpb-initial} = \{+, -, *, \%, \text{IFLTE}\}$.
Initial terminal set for the RPBs	$T_{rpb-initial} = \{x, y, \Re_{smaller-reals}\}$
Initial function set for the ADFs	No automatically defined functions in generation 0. $F_{adf-initial} = \phi$.
Initial terminal set for the ADFs	No automatically defined functions in generation 0. $T_{adf-initial} = \phi$.
Potential function set for the RPBs	$F_{rpb-potential} = \{\text{ADF0}, \text{ADF1}\}$
Potential terminal set for the RPBs	$T_{rpb-potential} = \phi$
Potential function set for the ADFs	$F_{adf1-potential} = \{\text{ADF0}\}$ $F_{adf0-potential} = \phi$
Potential terminal set for the ADFs	$T_{adf-potential} = \{\text{ARG0}, \text{ARG1}\}$
Fitness cases	72 random destinations (x_i, y_i) for the robot
Raw fitness	Fitness is the sum, over the 72 destinations, of the time for the robot to reach the destination.
Standardized fitness	Same as raw fitness
Hits	Number of fitness cases (from 0 to 72) for which the robot arrives at its destination within the available 80 time steps (i.e., does not time out)
Wrapper	The wrapper modularizes and clamps the value returned by the result-producing branch so that the final turn angle Θ lies between $-\Theta_{max}$ and $+\Theta_{max}$)
Parameters	$M = 40{,}000. G = 51. Q = 10{,}000. D = 4. B = 2\%. N_{rpb} = 1. S_{rpb} = 400. S_{adf} = 200. N_{max-adf} = 2. N_{max-argument-adf} = 2.$
Result designation	Best-so-far pace-setting individual
Success predicate	Fitness appears to have reached a plateau (after there are 72 hits).

13.4 RESULTS

On generation 0 of one run, the best program in the population achieves a fitness of 3.01 hours and scores 61 hits (out of 72). This program is

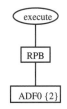

Figure 13.6   Call tree for all programs of generation 0

Figure 13.7   Call tree for best-of-generation program from generation 6

```
(% (IFLTE X X Y X) (IFLTE X Y X Y)).
```

Like all programs of generation 0, it has one result-producing branch and no automatically defined functions.

Figure 13.6 shows the call tree for all programs of generation 0, including the best-of-generation program.

13.4.1   Emergence of Subroutines

In subsequent generations, the programs in the population acquire additional structure in terms of automatically defined functions and dummy variables, and they exhibit improved fitness.

The first pace-setting program containing an automatically defined function appears in generation 6. This program achieves a fitness of 2.03 and scores 69 hits. Its 31-point result-producing branch is

```
(IFLTE (ADF0 7.155755E-01 Y) (% X(IFLTE 6.117399E-01 (-
2.209775E-01 Y) (- -2.874621E-01 -1.965841E-01 ) (IFLTE
(IFLTE Y X Y 4.392818E-01 ) (+ Y X) (IFLTE 4.143711E-01
5.257213E-01 Y -8.257957E-01 ) -1.100833E-01 ))) 7.907724E-01
-2.957690E-01 ).
```

The 13-point ADF0 has two arguments (ARG0 and ARG1):

```
(* (IFLTE ARG0 ARG1 1.647886E-01 1.008279E-01 ) (* (- ARG0 Y)
(% ARG0 ARG1))).
```

Figure 13.7 shows the call tree for the best-of-generation program from generation 6. Although this program has an automatically defined function, it is called only once by the result-producing branch.

13.4.2   Emergence of Reuse

Numerous pace-setting programs with one or two automatically defined functions (each possessing either one or two arguments) appear in subsequent generations. However, the first pace-setting program containing a reused automatically defined function appears in generation 15. This program achieves a fitness of 1.520 and scores 72 hits. It calls two-argument ADF0 twice.

Figure 13.8 Call tree for best-of-generation program from generation 25

Figure 13.9 Call tree for best-of-generation program from generation 70

13.4.3 Emergence of Multiple Invocations of Multiple Subroutines

The first pace-setting program containing multiple uses of multiple automatically defined functions appears in generation 25. This program scores 72 hits and achieves a fitness of 1.454. The program calls its two-argument ADF0 twice and its one-argument ADF1 twice. Figure 13.8 shows the call tree for the best-of-generation program from generation 25.

13.4.4 Best-of-Run Individual with Thrice-Used Subroutine

The best-of-run program appears in generation 70. This program achieves a fitness of 1.366 and scores 72 hits.

Note that a successful run of this problem may achieve a value of fitness that is slightly better than the mathematically known optimum value because of the 0.28-meter capture radius, the granularity of the 40×40 grid, the random choices of the 72 destinations, and the policy of treating the destination as if it were in the center of a square on the grid.

This best-of-run program calls its lone one-argument automatically defined function three times. Its result-producing branch has 340 points; its ADF0 has 121 points; and its ADF1 has 51 points. Figure 13.9 shows the call tree for the best-of-generation program from generation 70.

Figure 13.10 shows the trajectory for the fitness case where the destination is (–2.58, –2.28) in the third quadrant (i.e., negative values of x and y). The circle in this figure represents the capture radius of 0.28 meters. The destination in this figure lies outside the lower circle of Figure 13.3. As can be seen, the robot begins its time-optimal trajectory by circling until it faces the destination. It then proceeds straight to the destination.

Figure 13.11 shows the trajectory for the fitness case where the destination is (0.409, –0.892) in the fourth quadrant (i.e., positive values of x and negative values of y). The circle in this figure represents the capture radius of 0.28 meters. This destination, like point (x_7, y_7), is inside the lower circle of Figure 13.3. As can be seen, the trajectory begins by veering away from the destination (thereby increasing the distance to the destination). The robot then continues by following a circular trajectory to the destination.

We attempted to solve this time-optimal control problem several years ago with a single 40 MHz Texas Instruments Explorer II+ LISP machine. Because this problem entails a time-consuming multi step simulation, it was feasible to expose each individual in the population to only a paltry 10 destination points (compared to the 72 fitness cases used above), and it was feasible to use only a population of 2,000 (compared to 40,000 here).

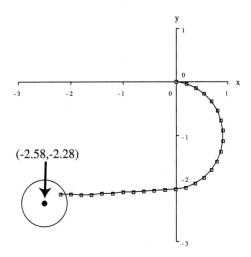

Figure 13.10 Evolved time-optimal trajectory for a fitness case in the third quadrant that is outside the lower circle

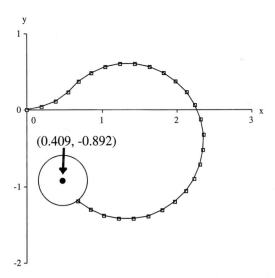

Figure 13.11 Evolved time-optimal trajectory for a fitness case in the fourth quadrant that is inside the lower circle

In spite of the limited computer resources, genetic programming evolved control strategies on the LISP machine that reliably moved the robot to 100% of the given destination points (and 100% of an additional larger set of out-of-sample destination points that were tested only on the best evolved solutions). The evolved trajectories from the LISP machine were time-optimal only for the subset of fitness cases for which the destination was in front of the robot. For the more challenging fitness cases (such as shown in Figure 13.11), the trajectories usually exhibited some resemblance to the time-optimal trajectory in that they did indeed veer away from the destination; however, they were nonoptimal because they veered too far. In other words, the LISP machine was capable of solving the robotic path-planning problem (but not the *time-optimal* path-planning problem) in a reasonable amount of time. It was our opinion, at the time, that there was no reason that this problem could not be solved with genetic programming if additional computer resources were available. The results above vindicate that opinion. We maintain this same opinion regarding the problems in this book for which genetic programming finds a good but not quite perfect solution. We believe that imperfect results can usually be improved by applying additional computer resources. Thus, we view all the problems in this book as illustrative of the potential of genetic programming for automatically creating computer programs—not its outer limits.

13.4.5 Summary

The solution evolved in this chapter for the time-optimal robot controller problem employed a thrice-used one-argument automatically defined function.

When we set up this problem, we specified the problem's fitness measure (the third major preparatory step for a run of genetic programming). The fitness measure indicates "what needs to be done"—namely, get the robot to the destination in minimal time. The fitness measure provides a method of comparing any two candidate control strategies as to which is quicker (i.e., it establishes a partial order between any two candidates). However, the fitness measure does not specify "how to do it." In particular, the fitness measure conveys no hint about the critical (and counterintuitive) tactic needed to minimize elapsed time in this time-optimal control problem—namely, that it is sometimes necessary to veer away from the destination in order to reach it in minimal time.

Similarly, when we performed the first and second preparatory step, we specified the ingredients of the to-be-discovered computer program. The ingredients consisted of the two externally supplied floating-point inputs (X and Y), floating-point random constants, the four arithmetic functions, and one conditional branching operator. The specification of these functions and terminals defines the search space of the problem. However, in providing these generic ingredients, we did not, in any way, prespecify "how to do it." In fact, the four arithmetic and one conditional operator used in this problem are generic functions found in the repertoire of virtually every general-purpose computer that has ever been built.

Likewise, when we performed the sixth preparatory step relating to program architecture, we did not prespecify that the solution should employ subroutines. That is, we did not specify "how to do it" in terms of the program architecture of the solution.

Using generic programmatic ingredients and a fitness measure that merely expressed the high-level requirements of the problem, genetic programming discovered the critical tactic needed to solve the problem. Genetic programming also decided, during the run, to create a hierarchy containing a one-argument subroutine and to invoke the subroutine three times.

Multiagent Problem Using Architecture-Altering Operations for Subroutines

Systems composed of concurrently executed independent processes are of special interest in the field of artificial intelligence. Minsky (1985) argued that minds are organized into such processes:

> I'll call "Society of Mind" this scheme in which each mind is made of many smaller processes. These we'll call agents. Each mental agent by itself can only do some simple thing that needs no mind or thought at all. Yet when we join these agents in societies—in certain very special ways—this leads to true intelligence.

> To explain the mind, we have to show how minds are built from mindless stuff, from parts that are much smaller and simpler than anything we'd consider smart. Unless we can explain the mind in terms of things that have no thoughts or feelings of their own, we'll only have gone around in circles.

Similar arguments have been made by Baars (1988), who argued that minds are implemented as a "distributed society of specialists." Dennett (1991) argued that "there is no central Headquarters" in the mind but instead that "specialist circuits" operate in "parallel pandemoniums."

The alluring potential of systems composed of multiple concurrently executed independent processes is tempered by the reality that such systems are often exceedingly difficult to construct. The difficulty arises, in large part, from the fact that the human designer of a multiagent system cannot begin writing the detailed sequence of steps in each process until certain high-level decisions are made. In particular, the human designer of a multiagent system is typically required to predetermine the number of distinct processes, the specific tasks to be performed by each process, and the relationships between the processes. In practice, it is usually very difficult to make these high-level architectural decisions about the size and shape of the solution.

In this chapter, the term "agents" is used in Minsky's sense—that is, the narrow specialist processes that operate in parallel to create an effective overall problem-solving organism. Thus, in this chapter, an agent corresponds to a single branch of an overall program tree for an individual in the population. As will be seen, the architecture-altering operations offer a mechanism for automatically determining the architecture of a multiagent system.

Social insects such as ants, wasps, bees, and termites dominate the insect fauna and together constitute more than 75% of the insect biomass (Fittkau and Klinge 1973). The success of such insects is due in large part to the survival advantages accruing from the efficiencies of specialization (e.g., queens and workers) made possible by their cooperation in a complex social organization. Of the social insects, ants have the most complex social organizations (Hölldobler and Wilson 1990).

Complex behavior may arise in nature as the consequence of multiagent systems. For example, an individual ant in a typical species of ants may have as many as 50 different categories of behaviors (Oster and Wilson 1978). It is possible that each of these behaviors corresponds to one or more agents.

This chapter deals with the cooperative behavior of simulated ants in a colony and, in particular, the central-place foraging problem. The goal is to discover a common program that, when simultaneously executed by the ants in a colony, causes all of the available food to be transported to the nest of an ant colony.

A single worker ant can perform food foraging competently. However, in nature and in the version of the problem presented here, cooperation yields more efficient foraging.

In the *Solenopsis invicta* species, individual ants initially use random search to locate food sources. Once a food source is located, individual ants collect the food and disperse an α-farnesene recruitment pheromone on the ground as they return to the nest, thereby creating a pheromone trail connecting the food source and the nest. Other worker ants are attracted and recruited by the odor of this pheromone and respond by following the pheromone trail to the food. Recruited ants are able to go much more directly to a food source that has already been found since they do not have to search randomly for the food. The combination of the pheromone-dropping behavior and the trail-following behavior enables the ants of the colony to cooperate in the task of food foraging. This cooperative behavior is accomplished with each ant responding only to locally available information.

The repetitive application of seemingly simple rules can lead to complex overall behavior (Steels 1990, 1991; Forrest 1990). Such emergent behavior arises in cellular automata (Chapter 58), dynamical systems (Devaney 1989), fractals (Barnsley 1988), Lindenmayer systems (Lindenmayer 1968; Lindenmayer and Rozenberg 1976; Prusinkiewicz and Hanan 1980; Prusinkiewicz and Lindenmayer 1990), artificial life (Langton 1989; Langton, Taylor, Farmer, and Rasmussen 1991; Langton 1991; Langton 1994; Langton and Shimohara 1997), and distributed artificial intelligence (Huhns 1987; Gasser and Huhns 1989).

Andre (1994b, 1995a) used genetic programming to evolve the sequence of steps for two agents—a map maker and map user. However, the number of agents (two) and the task of each agent was prespecified by him. Ryan (1995) used genetic programming to evolve teams of robots; however, Ryan prespecified both the number of robots and the conditions under which each robot would be activated. In their work on evolving a team using genetic programming, Haynes and Sen (1997) and Luke and Spector (1996b) prespecified the number (four) of members of a cooperating team. Similarly, the work of Hitoshi Iba and his colleagues (Iba 1996a; Iba, Nozoe, and Ueda 1997) prespecified the number of cooperating entities (two). Qureshi (1996) similarly prespecified the number of entities. Crosbie and Spafford (1995) used genetic programming to evolve entities to protect a computer against intrusion. In this particular work, each entity came from a separate run. Likewise, Trenaman (1998) prespecified the number of concurrent agents (two) in his work involving the *Tartarus* world (Teller 1994b).

Resnick (1991) conceived and wrote a computer program for the central-place food foraging problem in which each ant executes a common sequential program. Genetic programming has been used to evolve a common sequential program for this problem (Koza 1992e, Section 12.1; Koza and Rice 1992a); however, the number of cooperating ants (20) was predetermined and the function and terminal set was powerful in the sense that several more elementary steps were incorporated into some of the functions and terminals.

Deneubourg, Aron et al. (1986) and Deneubourg, Goss et al. (1991) conceived and wrote a set of rules that, when simultaneously executed by a group of independent ants, can cause them to consolidate widely dispersed pellets of food into one pile. Beckers, Holland, and Deneubourg (1994) implemented this problem using physical robots. Genetic programming has been used to evolve a common sequential program for this problem (Koza 1992e, Section 12.2; Koza and Rice 1992e); however, the number of cooperating ants was predetermined.

14.1   THE CENTRAL-PLACE FOOD FORAGING PROBLEM

The goal in the central-place food foraging problem is to discover a common program that, when simultaneously executed by all the ants of a colony, causes all of the available food to be transported to the nest of the colony.

The behavior of each individual ant is controlled by a multiagent strategy (multibranch computer program) in which each agent (branch) is executed in parallel. Each of the 20 ants in the colony is controlled by the same multiagent program (i.e., an individual multibranch program tree in the population).

The colony's world is a 32×32 toroidal grid as shown in Figure 14.1. Location $(0, 0)$ is in the lower-left corner of the figure. A 3×3 nest is centered at location $(21, 11)$. There are a total of 144 food pellets located in two separate grid locations, each with 72 food pellets. One food area is at $(5, 17)$ and the other at $(15, 29)$. Each of the colony's ants begins each fitness evaluation at a random location within 5 squares of the center of the nest. Each ant initially faces in a random direction.

The multiple agents (branches) are useful for this problem because the task of food collection requires many different kinds of activities.

14.2   PREPARATORY STEPS

14.2.1   Program Architecture

Each program in generation 0 has a uniform architecture consisting of one result-producing branch (the first agent).

After generation 0, the architecture-altering operations will add and subtract agents (branches). The maximum number of branches is established to be seven (the original

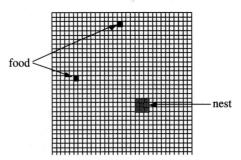

food

nest

Figure 14.1   Central-place food foraging problem

one plus up to six additional branches added by the architecture-altering operations). The parallel execution model used on this problem (explained below) makes the branches coequal and makes their order immaterial. There is no operational distinction between the original result-producing branch and the function-defining branches that are created by the architecture-altering operations during the run. However, for consistency with the terminology used throughout this book, we will consider the added branches as automatically defined functions. None of the automatically defined functions possess arguments. Since the automatically defined functions do not refer to one another in this problem, there are no hierarchical references between the automatically defined functions.

Two operations (subroutine duplication and subroutine deletion) are used to create the multiagent architecture. Duplicated branches initially have no effect, since the new branch does the same thing as the branch of which it is a copy. The subroutine deletion operation generally affects the behavior of the individual program unless the deleted branch is a duplicate of another branch, the deleted branch did nothing, or the effects of the deleted branch are the same as the effects of some combination of one or more of the remaining branches.

14.2.2   Functions and Terminals

All the terminals in this problem are zero-argument functions that operate by their side effects on the simulated world. None of them return any value.

The initial terminal set for the result-producing branch, $T_{rpb\text{-}initial}$, is

$T_{rpb\text{-}initial}$ = {MOVE-FORWARD, TURN-RIGHT, TURN-LEFT, MOVE-RANDOM, GRAB-FOOD, UNCONDITIONAL-DROP-PHEROMONE, NO-ACTION}.

MOVE-FORWARD changes the ant's location to the adjacent grid location in the direction that the ant is currently facing.

TURN-RIGHT changes the direction the ant is facing by 90° clockwise.

TURN-LEFT changes the direction the ant is facing by 90° counterclockwise.

MOVE-RANDOM changes the direction the ant is facing to one of the four possible directions (north, east, south, and west) with equal probability and then moves the ant two squares forward in that direction.

GRAB-FOOD takes one food pellet from the grid location where the ant is currently located provided there is a food pellet at that location and the ant is not already carrying a food pellet.

UNCONDITIONAL-DROP-PHEROMONE drops a pheromone cloud into a 3 × 3 square centered at the current location of the ant. The pheromones decay linearly such that they are no longer present on the grid locations 20 time steps after they are dropped.

NO-ACTION does nothing. It enables an agent to take no action on a given time step.

Note that many of these terminals are considerably weaker than the terminals used in Koza 1992e (Chapter 12) for the central-place foraging problem for an ant colony. For example, the DROP-PHEROMONE terminal in Koza 1992e is a powerful operator that contains a built-in internal test as to whether the ant is already carrying food; it only drops pheromone when the ant is carrying food. In contrast, the UNCONDITIONAL-DROP-PHEROMONE terminal here drops pheromone unconditionally. In order to be effective, it must be combined with a test (described below) to determine if the ant is already carrying food. As another example, the MOVE-TO-NEST terminal in Koza 1992e combines the perception of the direction of the nest with the action of movement toward the nest. In contrast, the MOVE-FORWARD terminal here must be combined with a test (described below) to determine if the ant is facing the nest.

All the functions in this problem are two-argument conditional (IF) operators (percepts).

The initial function set for the result-producing branch, $F_{rpb\text{-}initial}$, is

$F_{rpb\text{-}initial}$ = {IF-FOOD-HERE, IF-FOOD-FORWARD, IF-CARRYING-FOOD, IF-SMELL-FOOD, IF-NEST-HERE, IF-FACING-NEST, IF-SMELL-PHEROMONE, IF-PHEROMONE-FORWARD}.

IF-FOOD-HERE is a two-argument conditional branching operator that executes its first branch if there is a food pellet at the same location on the grid as the ant, but otherwise executes its second branch. The IF-FOOD-HERE operator (and all the other conditional branching operators in this problem) is implemented as a macro in the same manner as the IFLTE operator (Section 13.3.2). That is, exactly one (never both) of the two alternative argument subtrees is executed.

IF-FOOD-FORWARD is a two-argument conditional branching operator that executes its first branch if there is a food pellet in the grid location adjacent to the ant's location in the direction the ant is facing, but otherwise executes its second branch.

IF-CARRYING-FOOD is a two-argument conditional branching operator that executes its first branch if the ant is carrying a food pellet, but otherwise executes its second branch. This conditional will be satisfied if the ant has grabbed a food pellet but has not yet returned to the nest.

IF-SMELL-FOOD is a two-argument conditional branching operator that executes its first branch if there is at least one food pellet on one (or more) of the five grid locations at or adjacent to (north, east, south, and west) the ant's current location; otherwise, its second branch is executed.

IF-NEST-HERE is a two-argument conditional branching operator that executes its first branch if the ant is currently in a grid location that is one of the grid locations of the nest, but otherwise executes its second branch. When an ant carrying food enters the nest, that food pellet is implicitly taken from the ant and deposited into the nest.

IF-FACING-NEST is a two-argument conditional branching operator that executes its first branch if the ant is currently facing in the direction of the nest, but otherwise executes its second branch. The ant is considered to be facing in the direction of the nest if and only if the execution of a MOVE-FORWARD terminal would not increase the ant's Manhattan distance (i.e., measured along edges of a uniform square grid) from the center of the nest. In nature, some species of ants are able to navigate to their nest using polarized light in the sky (Hölldobler and Wilson 1990).

IF-SMELL-PHEROMONE is a two-argument conditional branching operator that executes its first branch if there is at least one pheromone on one or more of the five grid locations at or adjacent to the ant's current location, but otherwise executes its second branch.

IF-PHEROMONE-FORWARD is a two-argument conditional branching operator that executes its first branch if there is a pheromone in the grid location adjacent to the ant's location in the direction the ant is facing, but otherwise executes its second branch.

Note, again, that these functions are considerably weaker than the functions used in Koza 1992e (Chapter 12) for the central-place foraging problem for an ant colony. For example, the MOVE-TO-ADJACENT-FOOD-ELSE function in Koza 1992e combines a test of all the adjacent positions in the ant's environment with a move into the location with the food pellet in it. Thus, the evolutionary process did not have to learn to find the location containing the food pellet, and did not have to learn to link this information with the action of moving into that location. In the version of the problem presented here, genetic programming has to discover an equivalent to the MOVE-TO-ADJACENT-FOOD-ELSE function by using some combination of the above more-primitive functions. The same point applies to the MOVE-TO-ADJACENT-PHEROMONE-ELSE function in Koza 1992e.

Since all programs in generation 0 consist of only a result-producing branch, $F_{\text{adf-initial}}$ and $T_{\text{adf-initial}}$ are empty. The same terminal set and function set are available to every branch (agent) that is subsequently created by the architecture-altering operations.

Accordingly, the set of potential terminals, $T_{\text{rpb-potential}}$, for the result-producing branch is the same as the set of potential terminals, $T_{\text{adf-potential}}$, for the automatically defined functions. In turn, they both are the same as that of the initial set of terminals for the result-producing branch:

$$T_{\text{rpb-potential}} = T_{\text{rpb-initial}}.$$

$$T_{\text{adf-potential}} = T_{\text{rpb-initial}}.$$

$$F_{\text{rpb-potential}} = F_{\text{rpb-initial}}.$$

$$F_{\text{adf-potential}} = F_{\text{rpb-initial}}.$$

The set of functions and terminals is closed in the sense that every combination of functions and terminals in any branch yields a permissible and unambiguous sequence of steps.

14.2.3 Fitness

The ant colony is simulated until either all the food pellets have been transported to the nest or the maximum number of allotted time steps (4,000) is reached.

On each time step of the simulation, the individual from the population is evaluated once for each of the 20 ants in the colony. Evaluating an individual program for a single ant involves evaluating each branch (agent) of the program.

Each branch (agent) of a program is executed independently in parallel. The execution of the agent (branch) ends when the first terminal (action) is encountered. This single terminal (action) is the only result of executing the branch. The action of each agent is not actually performed in the world until all of the branches (agents) have been evaluated. This delay in the actual performance of the actions ensures that all the functions (conditional tests) are evaluated with the world and the ants in the same state. Thus, the order of the branches (agents) in the overall program tree is irrelevant. If more that one agent evaluates to the same action, then that action will be executed only once.

The actions (terminals) are executed in the following order of precedence (regardless of the branch in which they are located):

- GRAB-FOOD,
- UNCONDITIONAL-DROP-PHEROMONE,
- TURN-LEFT,
- TURN-RIGHT,
- MOVE-RANDOM, and
- MOVE-FORWARD.

Figure 14.2 shows an illustrative three-branch (three-agent) program tree that illustrates the parallel execution of each branch (agent) of an individual program tree for this problem. Suppose the program tree in the figure is evaluated for an ant that is not currently carrying food and that is situated on a grid location containing food. Since IF-FOOD-HERE is true, the result of the first (leftmost) agent (branch) is the GRAB-FOOD terminal. The result of the second (middle) agent is the MOVE-FORWARD terminal. Since the ant is not currently carrying food, the result of the third (rightmost) agent is the MOVE-RANDOM terminal. The set of three actions (terminals) obtained by evaluating the three agents (branches) is

```
S = {GRAB-FOOD, MOVE-FORWARD, MOVE-RANDOM}.
```

These three actions (terminals) identified from the parallel execution of the three branches (agents) are now executed. First, GRAB-FOOD (located in the leftmost branch) removes one food pellet from the current grid location and sets the state of the ant to indicate that it is carrying food. Second, the MOVE-RANDOM (from the rightmost branch) is executed. Third, the MOVE-FORWARD (from the middle branch) changes the ant's grid location by one square in the direction the ant is currently facing. Note that the MOVE-RANDOM (from the rightmost branch) is executed before the MOVE-FORWARD (from the middle branch) because the former appears higher on the above order of precedence.

The above parallel execution model is motivated, in part, because it is a reasonable way to implement a "distributed society of specialists" (Baars 1988), a "society of mind" (Minsky 1985), and "parallel pandemoniums" (Dennett 1991). This parallel execution model is, in addition, a reasonable approach to representing the simultaneous interaction of chemical molecules (say, proteins) in three-dimensional space.

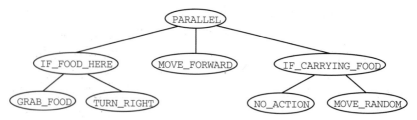

Figure 14.2   A program consisting of three agents (branches)

The fitness measure for this problem considers several factors:

1. It imposes a heavy penalty for each food pellet that is not transported to the nest before the time runs out. An ant colony can become more competitive by transporting more of the food to the nest.
2. The fitness measure imposes a penalty for the time it takes to find and transport each food pellet to the nest. A colony in which each ant separately searches for each food pellet in a random manner will take a long time to gather the food and thus will be less fit. An ant colony can become more competitive by accelerating the transportation of food to the nest by learning to cooperate.
3. The fitness measure penalizes execution time inefficiency by incorporating a count of the greatest number of functions executed in any one of the agents. For example, a program that executes 100 functions in four agents (with 25 functions per agent) will be twice as execution time efficient as a program that executes 100 functions in two agents (with 50 functions per agent). An ant colony can become more competitive by distributing the functions and terminals of the program tree into as many agents as is consistent with still solving the problem. The architecture-altering operations directly address the trade-off between the greatest number of functions executed in any one of the agents (which tends to decrease as the number of agents is increased) while still solving the problem.

Fitness is

$$\frac{\sum_{1}^{n} t_{food}\, f_{food} + \sum_{1}^{m} t_{max}\, f_{max}\, d_{food}}{1{,}000{,}000}$$

where

- n is the number of food pellets transported to the nest,
- t_{food} is the number of time steps elapsed when the food pellet arrived at the nest,
- f_{food} is the number of sequential IF functions (as defined below) executed by the ant that transported the particular food pellet,
- m is the number of food pellets not transported to nest,
- t_{max} is the maximum allotted time steps (4,000),
- S_{agent} is the maximum number of points (i.e., functions and terminals) per agent (100),

- f_{max} is the maximum possible value of f_{food} (t_{max} * S_{agent} or 400,000), and
- d_{food} is the Manhattan distance between a food pellet and the nest at the end of the simulation.

The number of sequential IF functions executed by an ant to transport a food pellet to the nest is determined as follows. When the agents in the program tree are evaluated for a single time step for a single ant, the maximum number of functions evaluated by any agent is measured in terms of the maximum number of sequential IF functions executed by any of that ant's agents for that time step. A running total of this count is stored for each ant, and the count for an ant is incorporated into the fitness as noted above and then cleared each time the ant arrives at the nest with a food pellet.

A penalty is imposed on any program that ends by leaving some food pellets not transported to the nest when the time runs out. The penalty is computed as if the food pellet were transported the remaining distance to the nest by a hypothetical agent of maximum size that takes the maximum number of time steps to transport the food to the nest.

Fitness is calculated for a single fitness case (i.e., for a single configuration of nest location, food pellet locations, and total number of food pellets).

Note that a program cannot rely on a particular sequence of MOVE-RANDOM executions to solve the problem because successive executions of the MOVE-RANDOM terminal, in general, move the ant in different directions and because the starting position and orientation of each ant is, in general, different in each generation.

Even though the food is located in the same places in each fitness evaluation, the colony has no way to encode the location of the food with the given function and terminal set. Therefore, the colony must actually search for the food in each fitness evaluation.

The number of hits is defined as the number (0 to 144) of food pellets that the colony transports to the nest before the time runs out.

The four distinct levels of parallelism employed in this problem are

- the simulated parallelism of the multiple agents controlling a single ant,
- the simulated parallelism of the 20 ants within one ant colony,
- the conceptual parallelism of the individuals in the population of programs in the genetic programming system, and
- the physical parallelism of the 64 processors of the actual hardware used.

14.2.4 Parameters

A population size, M, of 64,000 is used. The subpopulation size, Q, is 1,000 at each of the D = 64 processing nodes (demes). The migration rate is B = 2%.

The architecture-altering operations are used sparingly on each generation. The percentage of operations on each generation is 3% subroutine duplication, 1% subroutine deletion, 10% reproduction, 1% mutation, and 85% one-offspring crossover.

The other control parameters for runs in this chapter are either in the tableau below or are the default values specified in Koza (1994g, Appendix D).

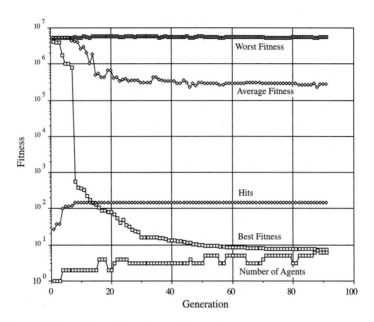

Figure 14.3 Fitness, hits, and number of agents

14.2.5 Termination

Since a fitness of zero is not possible for this problem and there is no way of predicting in advance the value of fitness that might be achieved, there is no explicit success predicate for this problem. The run was terminated manually after the fitness value of the best-of-run individual appeared to plateau.

14.2.6 Tableau

Table 14.1 summarizes the key features of the multiagent problem.

14.3 RESULTS

The best individual of generation 0 has a fitness value of 4,258,013 and scores 26 hits. Like all the individuals of generation 0, it consists of a single agent (branch). The behavior of this single agent is to wander randomly until it finds food, to grab any food that it finds, and to wander randomly back to the nest. It does not use smell, it does not attempt to orient itself in the direction of the nest, and it does not cooperate in any way with the other ants in the colony. The program tree for this individual is, after simplification,

```
(IF-FOOD-HERE (IF-CARRYING-FOOD (MOVE-FORWARD) (GRAB-FOOD))
(MOVE-RANDOM)).
```

Figure 14.3 shows, by generation, the fitness of the worst-of-generation individual, the average fitness of the population as a whole, the number of hits of the best-of-generation individual, the fitness of the best-of-generation individual, and the number of

Table 14.1 Tableau for the multiagent problem

Objective	Discover a common program that, when simultaneously executed by the 20 ants of a colony, causes all of the available food to be transported to the colony's nest.
Program architecture	One result-producing branch in generation 0. Additional branches (agents) will be created during the run by the architecture-altering operations.
Initial function set for the RPBs	$F_{rpb\text{-}initial}$ = {IF-FOOD-HERE, IF-FOOD-FORWARD, IF-CARRYING-FOOD, IF-SMELL-FOOD, IF-NEST-HERE, IF-FACING-NEST, IF-SMELL-PHEROMONE, IF-PHEROMONE-FORWARD}
Initial terminal set for the RPBs	$T_{rpb\text{-}initial}$ = {MOVE-FORWARD, TURN-RIGHT, TURN-LEFT, MOVE-RANDOM, GRAB-FOOD, UNCONDITIONAL-DROP-PHEROMONE, NO-ACTION}
Initial function set for the ADFs	No automatically defined functions in generation 0. $F_{adf\text{-}initial} = \phi$.
Initial terminal set for the ADFs	No automatically defined functions in generation 0. $T_{adf\text{-}initial} = \phi$.
Potential function set for the RPBs	$F_{rpb\text{-}potential} = F_{rpb\text{-}initial}$
Potential terminal set for the RPBs	$T_{rpb\text{-}potential} = T_{rpb\text{-}initial}$
Potential function set for the ADFs	$F_{adf\text{-}potential} = F_{rpb\text{-}initial}$
Potential terminal set for the ADFs	$T_{adf\text{-}potential} = T_{rpb\text{-}initial}$
Fitness cases	One fitness case
Raw fitness	The fitness measure imposes penalties according to a formula (see text) for food that is not transported to the nest before the time runs out, for the amount of time it takes to transport the food to the nest, and for the number of functions executed by the least-efficient agent (branch).
Standardized fitness	Same as raw fitness
Hits	The number of food pellets (0 to 144) that have been transported to the nest within the allotted time steps
Wrapper	None
Parameters	M = 64,000. G = 901. Q =1,000. D = 64. B = 2%. N_{rpb} = 1. S_{rpb} = 100. $N_{max\text{-}rpb}$ = 7.
Result designation	Best-so-far pace-setting individual
Success predicate	Fitness appears to have reached a plateau.

agents of the best-of-generation individual. The vertical axis for fitness and hits is a logarithmic scale.

The best individual of generation 4 has distinctly better fitness (998,714), more hits (115), and more agents (3) than its predecessors. This individual does better than its predecessors because it can both MOVE_FORWARD and MOVE_RANDOM in its search for food. Moreover, it does not move on the turn when it grabs food. The improved performance of this best-of-generation individual is the consequence of the additional agents created by the architecture-altering operations for this individual.

There is an even more significant change in hits and fitness in generation 7. The first best-of-generation individual in the run to score the maximum number of hits (144) appears in generation 7. This individual has a fitness value of 568 and consists of two agents, with 79 points in the first agent and 93 points in the second agent. The existence of the second agent is a consequence of the architecture-altering operation of subroutine duplication. Note that the fitness of the best-of-generation individual (Figure 14.3) drops by three orders of magnitude between generations 6 and 7. This large drop in fitness occurs because the best-of-generation colony in generation 7 transports all the food to the nest and thus does not incur the large fitness penalty for nontransported food.

After generation 7, all the best-of-generation individuals score 144 hits. However, the best-of-generation fitness continues to decrease (or remain the same) in every generation because the best-of-generation individuals become more efficient between generations 7 and 90. Also, between generations 7 and 90, the number of agents in the best-of-generation individual tends to increase as the best-of-generation fitness tends to improve (decrease).

This run produced numerous individuals that scored the maximum possible 144 hits, including some with two, three, four, five, six, and seven agents.

In generation 87, the best-of-generation individual consists of seven agents. This is the only generation in which the best individual has the maximum number of agents. All the other best-of-generation individuals consist of six (or fewer) agents. The fact that most of the high-scoring agents in later generations of the run consist of six agents suggests that seven (the maximum) is not the most appropriate number of agents for solving this problem.

The best-of-run individual appears in generation 90. It has a fitness value of 7.4 and scores 144 hits. This individual consists of six agents. These six branches have a total of 380 points. The evolved code for agents 0, 1, 2, and 4 in the best-of-run individual from generation 90 is shown below (with agents 3 and 5 being omitted since they are almost the same as agent 1).

Agent 0 is

```
(IF-FACING-NEST (IF-FACING-NEST (MOVE-FORWARD) (TURN-LEFT))
(IF-SMELL-FOOD (IF-FOOD-FORWARD (IF-NEST-HERE (IF-FACING-NEST
(MOVE-FORWARD) (TURN-LEFT)) (IF-FOOD-HERE (DROP-PHER)
(MOVE-FORWARD))) (IF-NEST-HERE (MOVE-FORWARD) (TURN-LEFT))
(MOVE-FORWARD))).
```

Agent 1 is

```
(IF-CARRYING-FOOD (IF-FACING-NEST (IF-CARRYING-FOOD (IF-SMELL-
PHER (DROP-PHER) (IF-FACING-NEST (IF-FACING-NEST (IF-FOOD-HERE
(MOVE-FORWARD) (MOVE-FORWARD)) (TURN-RANDOM)) (TURN-RIGHT)))
(IF-FACING-NEST (MOVE-FORWARD) (TURN-LEFT))) (IF-FACING-NEST
(IF-FOOD-FORWARD (MOVE-FORWARD) (TURN-RIGHT)) (TURN-LEFT)))
(IF-SMELL-FOOD (IF-FOOD-FORWARD (IF-NEST-HERE (IF-CARRYING-
```

```
FOOD (IF-FACING-NEST (IF-FACING-NEST (MOVE-FORWARD) (TURN-
LEFT)) (IF-PHER-FORWARD (GRAB-FOOD) (MOVE-FORWARD))) (IF-FOOD-
HERE (TURN-RIGHT) (IF-FACING-NEST (MOVE-FORWARD) (TURN-
RIGHT)))) (IF-CARRYING-FOOD (IF-FACING-NEST (IF-SMELL-PHER
(GRAB-FOOD) (GRAB-FOOD)) (IF-PHER-FORWARD (GRAB-FOOD) (MOVE-
FORWARD))) (IF-FOOD-HERE (IF-FOOD-HERE (GRAB-FOOD) (DROP-
PHER)) (IF-FOOD-FORWARD (MOVE-FORWARD) (IF-FOOD-HERE (TURN-
RIGHT) (TURN-RANDOM)))))) (IF-NEST-HERE (MOVE-FORWARD) (TURN-
LEFT))) (IF-PHER-FORWARD (GRAB-FOOD) (IF-FACING-NEST (IF-CAR-
RYING-FOOD (TURN-RIGHT) (TURN-RANDOM)) (IF-SMELL-PHER (TURN-
LEFT) (TURN-RANDOM)))))).
```

Agent 2 is

```
(IF-CARRYING-FOOD (IF-FACING-NEST (IF-NEST-HERE (IF-NEST-HERE
(IF-FACING-NEST (TURN-RIGHT) (IF-SMELL-PHER (TURN-LEFT) (NO-
ACTION))) (MOVE-FORWARD)) (IF-SMELL-PHER (MOVE-FORWARD) (IF-
SMELL-PHER (TURN-LEFT) (DROP-PHER)))) (IF-NEST-HERE (GRAB-
FOOD) (IF-SMELL-PHER (IF-FACING-NEST (TURN-RIGHT) (IF-SMELL-
PHER (TURN-LEFT) (NO-ACTION))) (IF-SMELL-FOOD (NO-ACTION) (IF-
FOOD-FORWARD (MOVE-FORWARD) (MOVE-FORWARD)))))) (IF-NEST-HERE
(IF-CARRYING-FOOD (IF-FOOD-HERE (IF-FACING-NEST (NO-ACTION)
(IF-NEST-HERE (TURN-RANDOM) (MOVE-FORWARD))) (IF-PHER-FORWARD
(GRAB-FOOD) (NO-ACTION))) (IF-NEST-HERE (IF-SMELL-FOOD (IF-
FOOD-HERE (IF-FACING-NEST (NO-ACTION) (IF-NEST-HERE (TURN-
RANDOM) (MOVE-FORWARD))) (IF-PHER-FORWARD (GRAB-FOOD) (NO-
ACTION))) (IF-FOOD-HERE (IF-FACING-NEST (IF-CARRYING-FOOD
(GRAB-FOOD) (GRAB-FOOD)) (IF-FACING-NEST (IF-FOOD-HERE (MOVE-
FORWARD) (MOVE-FORWARD)) (TURN-RANDOM))) (IF-CARRYING-FOOD
(GRAB-FOOD) (GRAB-FOOD)))) (IF-SMELL-FOOD (GRAB-FOOD) (MOVE-
FORWARD)))) (IF-SMELL-FOOD (GRAB-FOOD) (MOVE-FORWARD)))).
```

Agent 4 is

```
(IF-FACING-NEST (IF-CARRYING-FOOD (IF-FACING-NEST (IF-FACING-
NEST (MOVE-FORWARD) (TURN-LEFT)) (IF-PHER-FORWARD (GRAB-FOOD)
(MOVE-FORWARD))) (IF-FOOD-FORWARD (IF-NEST-HERE (IF-CARRYING-
FOOD (IF-FACING-NEST (IF-FACING-NEST (MOVE-FORWARD) (TURN-
LEFT)) (IF-PHER-FORWARD (GRAB-FOOD) (MOVE-FORWARD))) (IF-FOOD-
HERE (IF-FOOD-HERE (GRAB-FOOD) (DROP-PHER)) (IF-FOOD-FORWARD
(IF-NEST-HERE (IF-PHER-FORWARD (GRAB-FOOD) (MOVE-FORWARD))
(TURN-LEFT)) (TURN-RIGHT)))) (IF-FOOD-HERE (DROP-PHER) (MOVE-
FORWARD))) (IF-NEST-HERE (IF-CARRYING-FOOD (IF-FACING-NEST
(IF-FACING-NEST (MOVE-FORWARD) (TURN-LEFT)) (IF-PHER-FORWARD
(IF-FOOD-FORWARD (IF-NEST-HERE (IF-FOOD-HERE (IF-FACING-NEST
(TURN-LEFT) (GRAB-FOOD)) (IF-SMELL-PHER (TURN-RANDOM) (IF-
NEST-HERE (DROP-PHER) (TURN-LEFT)))) (IF-FOOD-FORWARD (IF-
FOOD-HERE (TURN-RIGHT) (NO-ACTION)) (GRAB-FOOD))) (IF-NEST-
```

```
HERE (TURN-LEFT) (MOVE-FORWARD))) (MOVE-FORWARD))) (IF-FOOD-
HERE (IF-FOOD-HERE (GRAB-FOOD) (DROP-PHER)) (IF-FOOD-FORWARD
(IF-NEST-HERE (MOVE-FORWARD) (TURN-LEFT)) (TURN-RIGHT))))
(TURN-LEFT)))) (IF-SMELL-FOOD (IF-FOOD-FORWARD (IF-FOOD-HERE
(IF-FOOD-HERE (GRAB-FOOD) (DROP-PHER)) (IF-FOOD-FORWARD (MOVE-
FORWARD) (IF-FOOD-HERE (TURN-RIGHT) (IF-FOOD-FORWARD (IF-NEST-
HERE (IF-FACING-NEST (IF-FACING-NEST (MOVE-FORWARD) (TURN-
LEFT)) (IF-FOOD-FORWARD (MOVE-FORWARD) (IF-FOOD-HERE (TURN-
RIGHT) (TURN-RANDOM)))) (MOVE-FORWARD)) (IF-NEST-HERE (MOVE-
FORWARD) (TURN-LEFT)))))) (IF-NEST-HERE (MOVE-FORWARD) (TURN-
LEFT))) (MOVE-FORWARD))).
```

An animated display was used in order to analyze the strategy by which the 20 six-agent ants of the best-of-run individual from generation 90 collectively solve the problem. Each ant begins by wandering randomly until it finds food, whereupon it grabs a food pellet and proceeds directly back to the nest while dropping pheromones along the way. Other randomly wandering ants that chance upon the pheromone trail follow it to the food and are thereby recruited into carrying food and dropping pheromone. The recruitment, carrying, and pheromone dropping continue until the food source is exhausted. Then the ants resume random wandering, and the pheromone trail dries up. Sometimes the second food source is discovered while the first food source is still being exploited. In this case, the colony works on both food sources at the same time. Then, when one of the food sources is exhausted, all of the recruited ants focus their attention on the remaining food source.

In order to understand the qualitative behavior of each of the six agents, six separate animations were run. In each animation, a single agent was allowed to control one half of the ants of the colony, while the ants in the other half of the colony were controlled by all six agents.

The qualitative behavior of the six agents, as determined from the animation of the ants controlled only by a single agent, is as follows:

- Agent 0: The ant only moves in a straight line in the direction that it is initially facing and doesn't pick up any food or drop pheromones.
- Agent 1: The ant wanders randomly until it finds either a pheromone or food, then it stops next to that pheromone or food and does nothing else. When the pheromone adjacent to the ant decays or the food pellet adjacent to the ant is carried away, the ant resumes random wandering.
- Agent 2: When the ant arrives at the nest, it stops there and does nothing else. Otherwise, it only moves in a straight line in the direction that it is initially facing and doesn't pick up any food or drop pheromones.
- Agent 3: The ant behaves as it does when under the control of agent 1, except that the ant stops at the same location as the food instead of next to the food.
- Agent 4: The ant moves to the point in the world farthest away from the nest, stops there, and does nothing else. However, if it encounters a food pellet on the way to the corner, it stops on top of that food pellet and stays there until the food pellet is carried away, whereupon the ant travels to the point in the world farthest away from the nest and stops.

- Agent 5: The ant behaves the same as agent 3.

In a post-run experiment in which both agent 0 and agent 1 are used together to control the colony, the ants perform random foraging, grab available food, and transport it to the nest. However, the ants do not drop pheromones or cooperate in any way.

In another post-run experiment in which the three agents 0, 1, and 2 are run together to control the colony, the ants perform the full cooperative pheromone-dropping and pheromone-trail-following behavior, but still do not perform as efficiently as all six agents run together.

An interesting new tactic appears when agents 2 and 3 control half of the ants in the colony and all six agents control the other half. The ants controlled only by agents 2 and 3 move randomly either until they find a pheromone trail and follow it to the food or until they stumble upon food. Once they discover food, they carry it to the nest if there are no pheromones around the food; otherwise the ants just stop at the food. This behavior has two consequences for food foraging. If an ant controlled only by agents 2 and 3 is the first to find food (so there would be no pheromone trail around the food), it carries the food to the nest and lays the pheromone trail as expected. However, if one of these ants finds food that already has pheromones around it (and is thus already being exploited), the ant just stops there and waits. Then, if the pheromones around the food decay completely, any ant sitting at food will then pick the food up and proceed back to the nest and rebuild the pheromone trail. Thus, ants controlled only by agents 2 and 3 build a new pheromone trail to a food pile when a pheromone trail dries up because of a lack of recruitment. The benefit of this waiting tactic is that the food does not have to be discovered again by random searching. The cost of this tactic is that these waiting ants are not doing anything else. This waiting tactic does not appear when all six agents are controlling an ant. If the food pile where the ant is waiting becomes exhausted, the ant resumes random searching.

The best individual was tested 10,000 times to determine how well it would generalize over many different random sequences of MOVE-RANDOM. For 100% of these 10,000 trials this individual scored the maximum possible of 144 hits. The average fitness in these 10,000 trials was 14.6 (compared to 7.4 for the same individual measured during the run). The standard deviation was 6.3.

In summary, genetic programming evolved both the overall architecture and the particular sequence of steps in each of the agents (branches) of an overall program for the central-place foraging problem for an ant colony. Specifically, the satisfactory evolved architecture distributes the functions and terminals across multiple agents (branches) in such a way as to reduce the maximum number of functions executed per agent, while still solving the problem.

Digit Recognition Problem Using Architecture-Altering Operations for Subroutines

One of the persistent issues surrounding automated pattern recognition is the degree to which the human user must predetermine the feature detectors, and the size and shape of the ultimate solution employing the feature detectors (Samuel 1959; Uhr and Vossler 1966).

This chapter shows how the architecture-altering operations can be used to automatically determine the number of feature detectors, the sequence of steps to be performed by the feature detectors, and the sequence of steps to be performed by the main program that invokes the feature detectors.

15.1 PROBLEM OF RECOGNIZING DIGITS

The goal in this digit recognition problem is to create a computer program that can map an input consisting of any of the 2^{24} possible 6×4 pixel patterns of bits into a correct identification for the pattern—0, 1, 2, 3, 4, or NIL (i.e., not any of the digits).

Figure 15.1 shows the digits 0, 1, 2, 3, and 4, each presented in a 6×4 pixel binary grid. The 6×4 pixel pattern of the given pattern may be examined by moving a *turtle* around the 24 pixels. The turtle starts at a designated location on the grid and can move one step at a time to the north (up), south (down), east (right), west (left), northeast, southeast, southwest, and northwest. The turtle's vision is limited to its immediate 3×3 neighborhood of the nine pixels centered at its current location. The pixel where the turtle is currently located is called X (center), and the eight neighboring pixels are called N, NE, E, SE, S, SW, W, and NW.

The problem of recognizing stick digits discussed here is similar to the letter recognition problem in *Genetic Programming II* (Koza 1994g, Chapter 15). Note that the correct identification of a pattern of pixels requires not only establishing that all the specific pixels that should be ON are indeed ON, but also inspecting other pixels on the grid to exclude the possibility that the pattern is a nondigit or another digit.

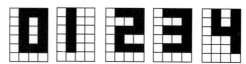

Figure 15.1   The digits 0, 1, 2, 3, and 4

Let us make clear what we are doing in this section and what we are *not* trying to do. We are *not* trying to evolve a practical pattern recognizer. The domain of 6×4 stick digits is admittedly simple. We are not trying to identify a pattern embedded in a noisy background, and we are not trying to demonstrate translation invariance, rotation invariance, or size invariance. We are also not interested in demonstrating that the evolved solution can generalize to any unseen versions of the "same" pattern (an ability that has been previously established for genetically evolved pattern-recognizing programs). By excluding all of these other interesting and important aspects of pattern recognition, we can focus our attention and concentrate our computing resources on a demonstration of two novel capabilities: the automatic creation of reusable feature detectors and the automatic determination of the number of automatically created feature detectors.

15.2   PREPARATORY STEPS

15.2.1   Program Architecture

Each program in generation 0 has a uniform architecture consisting of one result-producing branch and no automatically defined functions.

After generation 0, the architecture-altering operations will create zero-argument automatically defined functions. The maximum number of automatically defined functions, $N_{\text{max-adf}}$, is 10. The maximum number of arguments, $N_{\text{max-argument-adf}}$, for each automatically defined function is zero. The maximum size, S_{rpb}, for the result-producing branch is 500 points. The maximum size, S_{adf}, for each automatically defined function is 200 points. Thus, an individual program in the population can have as many as 2,500 points. Hierarchical references are allowed among the automatically defined functions.

15.2.2   Functions and Terminals

There will be a total of 30 functions and terminals in this problem:

- 14 initial terminals,
- 6 initial functions,
- 10 potential functions, and
- no potential terminals.

The initial terminal set for the result-producing branch, $T_{\text{rpb-initial}}$, is

$T_{\text{rpb-initial}} =$
{0, 1, 2, 3, 4, NIL, (GO-N), (GO-NE), (GO-E), (GO-SE), (GO-S), (GO-SW), (GO-W), (GO-NW)}.

The six terminals 0, 1, 2, 3, 4, or NIL are the categories into which a given 6×4 pixel pattern is to be classified. The eight zero-argument side-effecting operators, (GO-N), (GO-NE), (GO-E), (GO-SE), (GO-S), (GO-SW), (GO-W), and (GO-NW), move the turtle one step in any one of the eight possible directions from its current location in the grid.

The initial function set for the result-producing branch, $F_{rpb\text{-initial}}$, is

$$F_{rpb\text{-initial}} = \{\text{AND, OR, NOT, IFGTZ, HOMING, PROGN}\},$$

taking 2, 2, 1, 3, 1, and 2 arguments, respectively.

AND is the two-argument numerical-valued conjunctive function returning +1 if both of its arguments are positive, but returning −1 otherwise. AND is a short-circuiting (optimized) function in the sense that its second argument subtree will not be evaluated (leaving any side-effecting operator therein unexecuted) if its first argument is negative. This short-circuiting is relevant for programs that include side-effecting functions (as is the case here).

OR is the two-argument numerical-valued disjunctive function with similar short-circuiting.

NOT is the one-argument numerical-valued negation function.

The three-argument conditional branching operator IFGTZ ("if greater than zero") evaluates and returns its second argument if its first argument (the condition) is greater than zero, but otherwise evaluates and returns its third argument. The IFGTZ operator is implemented as a macro in the same manner as the IFLTE operator (Section 13.3.2).

The one-argument HOMING operator works in conjunction with a turtle. When the HOMING operator is executed, the current location of the turtle is remembered; the argument of HOMING is then executed, and the turtle is then rubber-banded back to its remembered location. HOMING is equivalent to the brackets in a Lindenmayer system (Prusinkiewicz and Lindenmayer 1990).

Each function above returns the value (T or NIL) of the pixel to which the turtle moves (i.e., it returns the new X).

The two-argument connective PROGN evaluates each of its two arguments sequentially and returns the result of evaluating its last argument.

Since there are no automatically defined functions in generation 0 of this problem, $F_{adf\text{-initial}}$ and $T_{adf\text{-initial}}$ are empty. After generation 0, the architecture-altering operations can add zero-argument automatically defined functions to programs in the population.

The set of potential functions for the result-producing branch, $F_{rpb\text{-potential}}$, is

$$F_{rpb\text{-potential}} = \{\text{ADF0, ADF1, . . . , ADF9}\}.$$

The set of potential functions for the automatically defined functions, $F_{adf\text{-potential}}$, is

$$F_{adf\text{-potential}} = \{\text{ADF0, ADF1, . . . , ADF9}\}.$$

subject to our usual limitation that a function-defining branch can refer hierarchically only to a previously defined function-defining branch.

Since the automatically defined functions for this problem all possess zero arguments, the set of potential terminals, $T_{adf\text{-potential}}$, for each automatically defined function is empty:

$$T_{adf\text{-potential}} = \phi.$$

Since dummy variables do not appear in the result-producing branch, the set of potential terminals, $T_{rpb\text{-}potential}$, for the result-producing branch is empty:

$$T_{rpb\text{-}potential} = \phi.$$

Each program operates as a decision tree. When a program is executed for a particular fitness case, the result-producing branch of the program returns a classification (0, 1, 2, 3, 4, or NIL) or a Boolean value (TRUE or FALSE). A wrapper (output interface) interprets the value returned by the result-producing branch at face value if it is a classification (0, 1, 2, 3, 4, or NIL) and interprets both of the Boolean values (TRUE and FALSE) as a classification of NIL (i.e., not any of the five digits).

The comprehensibility of evolved programs for this problem can be greatly enhanced by imposing a constrained syntactic structure that segregates the two distinct kinds of activity in a decision tree. The partition involves placing the decision-making calculations into the first (antecedent) argument of each IFGTZ operator and placing the category-specifying terminals into second (then) and third (else) arguments of each IFGTZ operator. Specifically, the first (antecedent) argument of each IFGTZ operator is constrained to be a composition of the three Boolean functions (AND, OR, NOT), the HOMING function, the PROGN connective function, and the eight turtle-moving operators, namely, (GO-N), (GO-NE), (GO-E), (GO-SE), (GO-S), (GO-SW), (GO-W), and (GO-NW). The second (then) and third (else) arguments of each IFGTZ operator are constrained to be compositions of the IFGTZ operator and the category-specifying terminals (0, 1, 2, 3, 4, or NIL). The initial random population is randomly generated to conform to these constraints; structure-preserving crossover is used to preserve this constrained syntactic structure during the run.

The set of functions and terminals is closed for this problem. This remains the case even as new automatically defined functions are created by the architecture-altering operations.

15.2.3   Fitness Measure

The fitness measure assigns a value indicating how well a particular pattern-recognizing program classifies a given 6×4 pixel pattern into the correct category (out of the available six categories).

The fitness cases for this problem consist of various 6×4 arrangements of binary pixels. Because there are 2^{24} possible arrangements of pixels, it is not practical to include all arrangements in the set of fitness cases. Each individual in the population is tested against an environment consisting of 199 fitness cases, each consisting of a 6×4 pixel pattern and its correct identification (0, 1, 2, 3, 4, or NIL). The set of fitness cases is constructed to include the five positive fitness cases (0, 1, 2, 3, and 4) and 194 different negative fitness cases. The negative cases include (among other things) every version of the digits 0, 1, 2, 3, and 4 with one of its ON pixels deleted; every version of the digits 0, 1, 2, 3, and 4 with one extraneous ON pixel added adjacent to one of its correct pixels; and various random combinations of pixels.

When an individual program in the population is executed for a particular fitness case, the result-producing branch of the program may return a symbol, such as 0, 1, 2, 3, or 4, or a Boolean value (TRUE or FALSE). For purposes of interpreting the program's output, both TRUE and FALSE are considered to be a classification of NIL (i.e., not any of the five digits). When the program's classification (0, 1, 2, 3, 4, or NIL) for a particular fitness case is compared to the correct classification for that fitness case, the outcome can be one of the following:

- a *true positive* (i.e., the program correctly identifies a digit such as 2 as a 2, etc.),
- a *true negative* (i.e., the program correctly identifies a pattern that is a nondigit as NIL),
- a *false positive* (i.e., the program incorrectly identifies a nondigit as 0, 1, 2, 3, or 4),
- a *false negative* (i.e., the program incorrectly identifies a digit, such as a 2, as a NIL, etc.), or
- a *wrong positive* (i.e., the program incorrectly identifies a digit, such as a 2, as a different digit, say, 3).

For this problem, the standardized fitness of an individual program is the sum, over the fitness cases, of the weighted errors produced by the program plus a penalty for an extreme lack of diversity among its responses (described below). True positives and true negatives contribute 0 to this sum of the weighted errors; false positives and wrong positives contribute 1; and false negatives contribute 30. The smaller the sum of the weighted errors and the penalty, the better. A 100%-correct pattern recognizer would have a fitness of 0 (i.e., zero weighted errors and no penalties).

This problem highlights a difficulty that can potentially occur with any run of the genetic algorithm or genetic programming. In general, evolution occurs when there is a population of replicating entities, there is some variation in the structure of the entities in the population, and there is some variation in fitness associated with the structural variations. Generation 0 of a run of the genetic algorithm or genetic programming is a blind random search of the space of alternative possibilities. Genetic algorithms and genetic programming exploit (usually small) variations in the fitness of various individuals in the population to direct the search.

In the extreme, if there is no variation in fitness among any of the individuals in generation 0, then Darwinian fitness-based selection degenerates to mere random selection among the individuals in the population. That is, there is no selective pressure in favor of one individual over another. In this extreme case, the crossover operation in generation 0 degenerates to blind random search in the sense that crossover merely inserts a random subtree from a random individual in the population into a random location in a second random individual. Similarly, if there is no variation in fitness in the population, the mutation operation degenerates to blind random search in the sense that mutation implants a freshly grown random subtree into a random location in a random individual. These insertions of random material at random locations in random individuals are, in a practical sense, indistinguishable from the random growth process by which individuals were constructed in generation 0. In other words, if there is no variation in fitness among any of the individuals in generation 0, the genetic algorithm degenerates to blind random search: it constructs the population for generation 1 in a manner that is indistinguishable, in a practical sense, from the method it used in generation 0.

If the absence of exploitable variation in fitness persists in generation 1 and subsequent generations, the genetic algorithm continues to be nothing more than blind random search in the later generations. Enormous amounts of computer time will then be expended and wasted in what amounts to a blind random search. To put it another way, variation in fitness in the randomly created population is a precondition for successful operation of the genetic algorithm or genetic programming. Obtaining some variation in fitness among randomly created individuals in generation 0 is, ultimately, a matter of population size. If the population size at generation 0 could approach the (usually enormous) size of the search space as a whole, some variation in fitness will necessarily appear (assuming there is some variation in fitness in the search space in the first place). However, if the population is very small in relation to the size of the search space (as it necessarily is in practice for runs of the genetic algorithm or genetic programming on a computer), it is sometimes difficult to get any variation in any particular random population for a nontrivial problem.

A run in which there is no variation (or little variation) in fitness for many generations can be viewed as equivalent to a run involving the decimation operation (Koza 1992e, Section 6.5.5). As an example, if decimation with a 10% survival rate is invoked on generation 0, the run starts out in generation 0 with 10 times the population that is used for subsequent generations of the run. Immediately after fitness is calculated for generation 0, all but 10% of the population is deleted using Darwinian fitness-based selection.

This digit recognition problem suffers from this difficulty. The randomly created individuals in generation 0 are not merely poor, but are almost always uniformly worthless at performing the task at hand.

If computational resources are not available to increase the population size, a problem-specific approach can be devised to jump-start the run of genetic programming. In this problem, the fitness of the individual is adjusted by penalizing programs that do not produce a minimal amount of diversity in their responses to the 199 fitness cases. Specifically, if a program fails to classify at least one of the 199 fitness cases into each of the six categories (0, 1, 2, 3, 4, and NIL), a penalty of 500 is added for each category to which no fitness case is assigned. Thus, a penalty of between 0 and 2,500 is added to the fitness of individuals in this problem. Note that if a program classifies at least one of the 199 fitness cases into each of the six categories, no penalty is assessed. This penalty proved to be sufficient to jump-start genetic programming for this problem.

15.2.4 Parameters

The control parameters for this chapter are in the tableau (Table 15.1), the tables of percentages of genetic operations in Appendix D of this book, and the default values specified in Koza (1994g, Appendix D).

15.2.5 Tableau

Table 15.1 summarizes the key features of the digit recognition problem.

15.3 RESULTS

The first run of this problem (taking about 46 hours of computer time) evolved a program with a standardized fitness of zero.

Table 15.1 Tableau for the digit recognition problem

Objective	Find a computer program that classifies a given 6×4 pixel pattern as 0, 1, 2, 3, 4, or other.
Program architecture	One result-producing branch, RPB, in generation 0. Zero-argument automatically defined functions will be created during the run by the architecture-altering operations. Hierarchical references are allowed among the yet-to-be-created automatically defined functions.
Initial function set for the RPBs	$F_{rpb\text{-}initial}$ = {OR, AND, NOT, IFGTZ, HOMING, PROGN}
Initial terminal set for the RPBs	$T_{rpb\text{-}initial}$ = {0, 1, 2, 3, 4, NIL, (GO-N), (GO-NE), (GO-E), (GO-SE), (GO-S), (GO-SW), (GO-W), (GO-NW)}
Initial function set for the ADFs	No automatically defined functions in generation 0. $F_{adf\text{-}initial} = \phi$.
Initial terminal set for the ADFs	No automatically defined functions in generation 0. $T_{adf\text{-}initial} = \phi$.
Potential function set for the RPBs	$F_{rpb\text{-}potential}$ = {ADF0, ADF1, . . . , ADF9}
Potential terminal set for the RPBs	$T_{rpb\text{-}potential} = \phi$
Potential function set for the ADFs	$F_{adf\text{-}potential}$ = {ADF0, ADF1, . . . , ADF9}
Potential terminal set for the ADFs	$T_{adf\text{-}potential} = \phi$
Fitness cases	199 fitness cases, each consisting of a 6×4 pixel pattern
Raw fitness	Fitness is the sum, over the 199 fitness cases, of the weighted errors produced by the program plus a penalty for an extreme lack of diversity among the classifications.
Standardized fitness	Same as raw fitness
Hits	Not used
Wrapper	A wrapper (output interface) interprets the value returned by the result-producing branch at face value if it is a classification (0, 1, 2, 3, 4, or NIL) and interprets both of the Boolean values (TRUE and FALSE) as a classification of NIL (i.e., not any of the five digits).
Parameters	M = 512,000. G = 201. Q = 8,000. D = 64. B = 5%. N_{rpb} = 1. S_{rpb} = 500. S_{adf} = 200. $N_{max\text{-}adf}$ = 10. $N_{max\text{-}argument\text{-}adf}$ = 0.
Result designation	Best-so-far pace-setting individual
Success predicate	A program achieves a standardized fitness of zero.

All of the randomly generated programs in generation 0 lacked diversity in their classifications of the 199 fitness cases. Accordingly, penalties of between 1,500 and 2,500 are assessed on all individuals in generation 0.

The best-of-generation program for generation 0 has a standardized fitness of 1,681. This program scores no true positives, 119 true negatives, 31 false positives, 5 false negatives, and no wrong positives. This program receives a penalty of 1,500 because there are three categories (out of the six) into which this program failed to classify at least one of the 199 fitness cases.

The best-of-generation program for generation 1 has a standardized fitness of 1,181.

The penalty for lack of diversity among responses proved to be very effective on this problem. By generation 3, the best-of-generation program has a standardized fitness of 296 (i.e., it incurred no penalty for lack of diversity).

On generation 5, a program emerged with a fitness of 177. This program scores no true positives, 123 true negatives, 27 false positives, 5 false negatives, and no wrong positives. This program has acquired three automatically defined functions. Since automatically defined functions did not exist in generation 0, these automatically defined functions are present in this program because of the architecture-altering operations.

Fitness of the best-of-generation individual improves to 163, 150, 131, 119, 58, 23, 12, and 1 in generations 6, 11, 15, 20, 53, 101, 126, and 158, respectively. The number of automatically defined functions in the best-of-generation individual is 2, 1, 3, 3, 3, 6, 7, and 10, respectively, for these generations.

On generation 165, one program with 10 automatically defined functions scored a perfect value of 0 for standardized fitness. This program scores 5 true positives, 194 true negatives, no false positives, no false negatives, and no wrong positives.

Six of the 10 automatically defined functions (ADF1, ADF2, ADF3, ADF4, ADF5, and ADF7) each consist of only one point and merely invoke another automatically defined function. After references to these six automatically defined functions have been removed, the result-producing branch refers to ADF0 21 times; ADF6 refers to ADF8 and ADF9 once each; and ADF0, ADF8, and ADF9 do not refer to any other automatically defined function.

After editing, the 381-point result-producing branch of this program is

```
(IFGTZ (IFGTZ (IFGTZ (AND (GO_N) 3) (IFGTZ (GO_SW) 4 (IFGTZ
(GO_SW) (IFGTZ (IFGTZ (GO_N) (IFGTZ (GO_SW) 5 (GO_S)) (IFGTZ
(GO_SW) (IFGTZ (GO_N) 3 (IFGTZ (GO_SW) 4 (GO_S))) (IFGTZ (IFGTZ
3 4 4) 3 2))) 5 (IFGTZ (GO_SW) 5 (ADF0))) (IFGTZ (IFGTZ (GO_SW)
5 (ADF0)) (IFGTZ (AND (GO_N) 3) 3 4) (PROGN 4 (IFGTZ (GO_SW) 5
(ADF0)))))) (IFGTZ (IFGTZ (IFGTZ (GO_N) (IFGTZ (GO_SW) 4
(IFGTZ (GO_SW) (IFGTZ (IFGTZ (GO_SW) 5 (GO_S)) 5 (GO_S)) (IFGTZ
(IFGTZ (GO_N) 3 (GO_S)) 5 (GO_S)))) (GO_S)) (HOMING (IFGTZ
(GO_N) 3 (IFGTZ (GO_SW) (IFGTZ (NOT (IFGTZ (GO_SW) 5 (AND
(GO_N) 3))) (IFGTZ (GO_SW) (IFGTZ (HOMING (GO_SE)) (IFGTZ
(GO_SW) (IFGTZ (GO_SW) 5 (GO_S)) (IFGTZ (GO_SW) (IFGTZ (GO_N) 3
(IFGTZ (GO_SW) 5 (GO_S))) 2)) (HOMING (IFGTZ (IFGTZ (GO_SW) 5
(ADF0)) (IFGTZ (IFGTZ (GO_SW) 5 (ADF0)) 3 (PROGN 4 (IFGTZ
(GO_SW) 5 (IFGTZ (GO_SW) 4 (GO_S))))) (PROGN 4 (IFGTZ (GO_SW) 5
(ADF0)))))) (IFGTZ (IFGTZ (IFGTZ (GO_NW) (IFGTZ (IFGTZ (IFGTZ
(IFGTZ (GO_N) (IFGTZ (AND (IFGTZ (GO_NW) 3 (IFGTZ (IFGTZ
(GO_SW) 5 (GO_S)) 5 (GO_S))) 3) (IFGTZ (GO_SW) (IFGTZ (IFGTZ
```

(GO_SW) (ADF0) (GO_S)) 3 (IFGTZ (GO_N) 3 (IFGTZ (GO_SW) 5
(GO_S)))) (GO_S)) 4) (PROGN 4 (IFGTZ (GO_SW) 5 4))) (ADF0)
(GO_S)) 3 (IFGTZ (IFGTZ (GO_SW) (IFGTZ (IFGTZ (GO_SW) 5 (ADF0))
(GO_SW) (GO_S)) (ADF0)) (GO_SW) (GO_S))) 3 (AND 4 (GO_NE))) 4)
(IFGTZ (GO_SW) 4 (IFGTZ (GO_SW) 5 (GO_S))) (IFGTZ (IFGTZ
(GO_SW) 5 (GO_S)) 5 (GO_S))) (IFGTZ (PROGN 4 (IFGTZ (GO_SW) 5
(ADF0))) 5 (HOMING (GO_NW))) (IFGTZ (GO_N) 3 (GO_S)))) (GO_N))
(GO_S)))) (IFGTZ (GO_SW) 5 (IFGTZ (GO_SW) (AND (GO_N) 3) (PROGN
2 (GO_S))))) (IFGTZ (GO_SW) (IFGTZ (IFGTZ (GO_SW) (IFGTZ
(GO_SW) 5 (GO_S)) (ADF0)) 5 (GO_S)) (ADF0)) (ADF0))) 4 (IFGTZ
(GO_SW) 5 (IFGTZ (GO_SW) (IFGTZ (IFGTZ (GO_SW) 5 (GO_S)) 5
(GO_S)) (IFGTZ (GO_N) 3 (PROGN (PROGN 3 (IFGTZ (IFGTZ 2 (IFGTZ
4 (GO_SE) 4) 5) (IFGTZ (IFGTZ (GO_SW) (IFGTZ (NOT (OR (GO_NW)
(GO_W))) 4 (GO_N)) (IFGTZ (GO_SW) (PROGN 4 (IFGTZ (GO_SW) 5
(ADF0))) (GO_S))) (IFGTZ (AND 4 (GO_N)) 4 3) (HOMING (GO_N)))
2)) (IFGTZ (GO_SW) (NOT (OR (GO_NW) (GO_W))) (ADF0)))))))
(IFGTZ (IFGTZ (GO_SW) 4 (HOMING (IFGTZ (IFGTZ (GO_SW) (GO_SW)
(IFGTZ (GO_SW) 5 (IFGTZ (GO_SW) (AND (GO_N) 3) (PROGN 2
(GO_S))))) (PROGN 4 (IFGTZ (GO_SW) 5 (ADF0))) (IFGTZ (GO_SW)
(IFGTZ (IFGTZ (GO_SW) 4 (IFGTZ (HOMING (GO_SE)) (IFGTZ (IFGTZ
(GO_SW) (ADF0) (GO_S)) 5 (GO_S)) (GO_S))) 5 (GO_S)) (IFGTZ
(GO_SW) 4 (ADF0)))))) (NOT (IFGTZ 3 4 5)) (ADF0)) (ADF0)).

Automatically defined function ADF0 has 192 points:

(IFGTZ (GO_SW) (IFGTZ (GO_N) (IFGTZ (GO_N) (IFGTZ (AND (GO_N)
3) (IFGTZ (GO_SW) (IFGTZ (IFGTZ (GO_SW) (IFGTZ (GO_SW) 5
(GO_S)) (GO_S)) (IFGTZ (OR 5 (GO_W)) 3 5) (GO_S)) (GO_S)) 4)
(IFGTZ (GO_SW) 5 (GO_S))) 2) (IFGTZ (GO_SW) (IFGTZ (IFGTZ
(IFGTZ (IFGTZ (GO_N) (IFGTZ (GO_SW) 5 (IFGTZ (IFGTZ (GO_NW) 3
(IFGTZ (IFGTZ (GO_SW) 5 (GO_S)) 5 (GO_S))) 3 (IFGTZ (GO_SW)
(IFGTZ (GO_SW) 5 (IFGTZ (IFGTZ (IFGTZ (GO_N) 3 (IFGTZ (GO_SW) 4
(GO_S))) 5 (GO_S)) 5 (HOMING (IFGTZ (GO_SW) (IFGTZ (IFGTZ 2
(IFGTZ (GO_N) 3 (IFGTZ (GO_SW) 5 (GO_S))) 5) (IFGTZ (GO_SW)
(IFGTZ (GO_SW) 5 (GO_S)) (GO_S)) 2) (GO_S))))) (GO_S))))
(GO_S)) 5 (GO_S)) (IFGTZ (IFGTZ (GO_SW) 5 (GO_S)) 5 (GO_S))
(PROGN (IFGTZ (IFGTZ (GO_NW) 3 4) (IFGTZ (GO_SW) 5 (IFGTZ
(GO_SW) (AND (GO_N) 3) (PROGN 2 (GO_S)))) (IFGTZ (GO_SW) 5
(GO_S))) (GO_W))) (IFGTZ (IFGTZ (GO_SW) (IFGTZ (GO_SW) (IFGTZ
(GO_SW) 5 (GO_S)) (GO_S)) (GO_S)) (IFGTZ (OR (GO_NW) (GO_W)) 3
5) (GO_S)) (GO_S)) (HOMING (IFGTZ (GO_SW) (IFGTZ (IFGTZ
(GO_SW) (IFGTZ (GO_SW) 5 (GO_S)) (GO_S)) (IFGTZ (GO_SW) (GO_S)
(HOMING (IFGTZ (IFGTZ (GO_SW) 5 (GO_SW)) (IFGTZ (GO_N) (IFGTZ
(IFGTZ (GO_SW) (OR (GO_NW) (GO_W)) (GO_S)) 5 (GO_S)) (IFGTZ
(GO_SW) 5 (GO_S))) (IFGTZ (GO_SW) (IFGTZ (GO_SW) 5 (GO_S))
(GO_S))))) (GO_S)) (GO_S))))).

Automatically defined function ADF6 has 111 points:

```
(IFGTZ (GO_SW) (IFGTZ (GO_N) (ADF9) 2) (IFGTZ (GO_SW) (IFGTZ
(IFGTZ (IFGTZ (IFGTZ (GO_N) (IFGTZ (GO_SW) 5 (IFGTZ (IFGTZ
(GO_NW) 3 (IFGTZ (IFGTZ (GO_SW) 5 (GO_S)) 5 (GO_S))) 3 (IFGTZ
(GO_SW) (IFGTZ (GO_SW) 5 (IFGTZ (GO_SW) 5 (GO_S))) (GO_S))))
(GO_S)) 5 (GO_S)) (IFGTZ (IFGTZ (GO_SW) 5 (GO_S)) 5 (GO_S))
(PROGN (IFGTZ (IFGTZ (GO_NW) 3 4) (IFGTZ (GO_SW) 5 (IFGTZ
(GO_SW) (AND (GO_N) 3) (PROGN 2 (GO_S)))) (IFGTZ (GO_SW) 5
(GO_S))) (GO_W))) (ADF8) (GO_S)) (HOMING (IFGTZ (GO_SW) (IFGTZ
(IFGTZ (GO_SW) (IFGTZ (GO_SW) 5 (GO_S)) (GO_S)) (IFGTZ (GO_SW)
(GO_S) (HOMING (IFGTZ (IFGTZ (GO_SW) 5 4) (IFGTZ (GO_N) 3
(IFGTZ (IFGTZ (IFGTZ (GO_SW) 5 (GO_S)) 4 (GO_S)) 5 (GO_S)))
(IFGTZ 4 (GO_SE) 4)))) (GO_S)) (GO_S))))).
```

Automatically defined function ADF8 has 18 points:

```
(IFGTZ (IFGTZ (GO_SW) (IFGTZ (GO_SW) (IFGTZ (GO_SW) 5 (GO_S))
(GO_S)) (GO_S)) (IFGTZ (OR (GO_NW) (GO_W)) 3 5) (GO_S)).
```

Automatically defined function ADF9 has 35 points:

```
(IFGTZ (GO_N) (IFGTZ (AND (GO_N) 3) (IFGTZ (GO_SW) (IFGTZ
(IFGTZ (GO_SW) (IFGTZ (GO_SW) 5 (GO_S)) (GO_S)) (IFGTZ (OR
(GO_NW) (GO_W)) 3 5) (GO_S)) (NOT (IFGTZ (GO_SW) 5 (AND (GO_N)
3)))) 4) (IFGTZ (GO_SW) 5 (GO_S))).
```

Thus, we have demonstrated that the architecture-altering operations can be used to automatically determine the number of feature detectors, the sequence of steps to be performed by the feature detectors, and the sequence of steps to be performed by the main program that invokes the feature detectors.

Transmembrane Segment Identification Problem Using Architecture-Altering Operations for Subroutines

Automated methods of machine learning may prove to be useful in discovering biologically meaningful information hidden in DNA sequences and protein sequences. The computational analysis of genomic sequences and protein sequences can be viewed, in part, as one-dimensional pattern recognition problems.

In one approach to solving pattern recognition problems, a human examines sample data and handcrafts a certain number of feature detectors that recognize certain low-level patterns in the data. Then, automation is used to create a higher-level procedure that makes the final classification decision by integrating information about the presence or absence of the low-level features. The low-level feature detectors are typically reused many times in making the final classification decision.

In a more general approach to automating the problem of pattern recognition, both the creation of the low-level feature detectors and the creation of the procedure for making the final classification decision are simultaneously created in an automated way. In this more general approach, the user is not required to prespecify the number of low-level feature detectors, the specific pattern recognized by each low-level feature detector, or the higher-level procedure for making the final classification decision. That is, the low-level feature detectors and the higher-level procedure are part of the *answer* provided by an automated technique—not part of the *question* supplied by the human user.

This chapter considers the problem of deciding whether a given protein segment is a transmembrane domain or nontransmembrane area of the protein.

Algorithms written by biologists for the problem of identifying transmembrane domains in protein sequences are based on biochemical knowledge about amino acid residues, properties of membrane-spanning proteins, and hydrophobicity (Kyte and Doolittle 1982; von Heijne 1992; Engelman, Steitz, and Goldman 1986).

This problem provides an opportunity to illustrate the automatic discovery of reusable feature detectors, the evolution of the architecture of multipart computer programs, the use of restricted iteration, the use of state (in the form of named memory) in evolved computer programs, and the handling of input sequences of different lengths. Genetic programming will be used to create a computer program for predicting whether a given subsequence of amino acids in a protein is a transmembrane domain or a nontransmembrane area of the protein.

Weiss, Cohen, and Indurkhya (1993) reported an algorithm for the transmembrane segment identification problem that was created with the aid of machine learning. Using domain knowledge of hydrophobicity in the form of the numerical Kyte-Doolittle hydrophobicity scale (Kyte and Doolittle 1982), Weiss, Cohen, and Indurkhya handcrafted a three-way division of the 20 amino acid residues. They then counted the number of occurrences of residues in the given protein segment from each of their three groups. Next they computed the difference between the counts for two of their three groups. After all of this preliminary work, they then employed machine learning (the SWAP-1 induction technique) to discover a numerical threshold for making the final two-way classification decision based on the two counts. If the difference between the two group counts exceeded the threshold discovered by the machine learning technique, the protein segment was identified as being a transmembrane domain. In their first experiment, the error rate of their approach equaled the error rate of the best of three known human-written algorithms for this classification task. As can be seen, machine learning played a relatively small role in solving the problem.

Genetic programming previously demonstrated its ability to evolve a classifying program for the transmembrane segment identification problem without using any biochemical knowledge about amino acid residues, properties of membrane-spanning proteins, and hydrophobicity (Koza 1994b, 1994c, 1994g, 1994j). In this previous work, the architecture of the evolved program consisted of three initially unspecified detectors (i.e., automatically defined functions), an initially unspecified iterative calculation incorporating the as-yet-undiscovered detectors, and an initially unspecified final calculation incorporating the results of the as-yet-undiscovered iteration.

The transmembrane segment identification problem was solved in *Genetic Programming II* (Koza 1994g) using two different approaches. First, in the set-creating approach, the problem was solved using three automatically defined functions (detectors) whose function set consisted of set-creating operators (Koza 1994g, Sections 18.5–18.9). This choice of the function set predisposed the solutions to contain counts reminiscent of the approach of Weiss, Cohen, and Indurkhya. Second, in the arithmetic-performing approach, the problem was solved using three detectors whose function set consisted of ordinary arithmetic functions and an ordinary conditional operator (Koza 1994g, Sections 18.10 and 18.11). This approach removed the predisposition toward the set-creating operators reminiscent of Weiss, Cohen, and Indurkhya. The evolved solutions for both the set-creating version and the arithmetic-performing version of this problem achieved a better error rate than that of the three known human-written algorithms cited in Weiss, Cohen, and Indurkhya (1993) and that of the algorithm developed by Weiss, Cohen, and Indurkhya. These evolved solutions are instances where an evolutionary computation technique has produced results that are superior to those written by knowledgeable human investigators.

The question arises as to whether it is possible to solve the same problem using the architecture-altering operations that dynamically determine, during the run, the existence and number of detectors (automatically defined functions).

16.1   PROTEINS

Proteins are composed of a chain of amino acid residues in a linear arrangement (Stryer 1995). The same 20 amino acid residues (denoted by the letters A, C, D, E, F, G, H, I, K, L, M, N, P, Q, R, S, T, V, W, and Y) are used for virtually all proteins of all species on earth. Thus, a protein can be viewed as a linear sequence over a 20-letter alphabet (called the *primary structure* of the protein). The length of protein sequences varies widely, with the average being about 300.

Subject to only minor qualifications and exceptions, the three-dimensional location (called its *conformation* or *tertiary structure*) of every atom of a protein molecule in a living organism is determined (within a small variation) by this linear sequence over the 20-letter alphabet (Anfinsen 1973). The three-dimensional spatial location of the atoms, in turn, determines the protein's biological function within a living organism. Thus, broadly speaking, all the information about the protein's biological function is contained (albeit hidden) in the linear sequence over the 20-letter alphabet.

Ever-growing numbers of primary sequences are being archived in computerized databases (e.g., the SWISS-PROT database of Bairoch and Boeckmann 1991) as a consequence of the various ongoing genome projects around the world. As newly sequenced proteins are archived, they are typically immediately tested by various computerized algorithms for clues as to their biological structure and function. A major goal of the field of computational molecular biology is to determine a protein's biological function within a living organism by analyzing the protein's primary sequence.

16.2   TRANSMEMBRANE DOMAINS

Membranes play many important roles in living things. The cellular membrane, for example, plays the crucial role of creating the distinctive environment in which life exists. The nuclear membrane defines the cell nucleus within a living cell (in eukaryotes).

A *transmembrane protein* (Yeagle 1993) is a protein that is embedded in a membrane in such a way that part of the protein is located outside the membrane, part is embedded within the membrane, and part is inside the membrane. Transmembrane proteins perform functions such as sensing the presence of certain particles or certain stimuli on one side of the membrane and transporting particles or transmitting signals to the other side of the membrane. Transmembrane proteins often thread in and out of the membrane several times. They thus have portions that are immersed in the different milieu on each side of the membrane. Understanding the behavior of transmembrane proteins requires identification of the portion(s) of the protein that are actually embedded within the membrane, such portion(s) being called the *transmembrane domain(s)* of the protein.

The lengths of the transmembrane domains of a protein are usually different from one another, and the lengths of the nontransmembrane areas are also usually different from one another.

The goal in this chapter is to evolve a computer program for predicting whether or not a particular protein segment (i.e., a subsequence of amino acid residues extracted from an entire protein sequence) is a transmembrane domain of the protein.

Biological membranes have an oily *hydrophobic* (water-hating) composition. Certain amino acid residues are likewise hydrophobic and tend to associate with chemical structures that are hydrophobic. The hydrophobicity of the amino acid residues in a protein segment plays an important role in determining whether a segment is a transmembrane domain.

Many transmembrane domains are α-helices. In this case, all the amino acid residues of the transmembrane domain of a protein are exposed to the oily membrane. The residues have a pronounced, but not overwhelming, tendency to be hydrophobic. About 25% of the proteins in *Haemophilus influenzae* bacterium and *Saccharomyces cerevisiae* yeast (two of the first dozen organisms for which the entire genome has been published) have at least one helical transmembrane domain (Rost 1998). The percentage of helical transmembrane proteins and other transmembrane proteins is thought to be around 10% for higher-level organisms.

Other transmembrane domains are β-sheets (Schirmer and Cowan 1993). Protein segments of this type can be identified as being transmembrane domains by the pronounced, but not overwhelming, hydrophobic nature of the particular half of the residues of the β-sheet that are actually exposed to the oily membrane. Because they are extremely difficult to handle in the laboratory, very few transmembrane segments of this type currently appear in the computerized databases. This bias in the computerized databases has the practical effect of excluding transmembrane proteins of the β-sheet type from the discussion here.

The amino acid residues vary considerably in their degree of hydrophobicity. Table 16.1 shows the names of the 20 residues in the fourth column, the standard one-letter code for the residue in the third column, and the standard three-letter code in the fifth column. The hydrophobicity scale of Kyte and Doolittle (1982) assigns a numerical value (second column) to each of the 20 residues. The table presents the 20 residues in decreasing order according to their Kyte-Doolittle hydrophobicity. The 20 hydrophobicity values can reasonably be clustered into the three broad categories, as shown in the first column. Seven of the 20 residues can be categorized as hydrophobic, six as neutral, and seven as *hydrophilic* (water-loving). As can be seen, isoleucine (I) has the largest positive value in the table and is therefore the most hydrophobic residue according to this scale. On the other hand, the four electrically charged residues (D, E, K, and R) are the most hydrophilic.

Hydrophobicity is not a precisely defined characteristic. For example, 43 different hydrophobicity scales are listed in Trinquier and Sanejouand (1998). These alternative scales differ considerably from one another as to the relative numerical value assigned to the 20 amino acids as well as the rank order of the amino acids and the categories into which the amino acids are most naturally clustered. There is no consensus on which hydrophobicity scale, if any, is best suited for this particular problem. Nonetheless, the Kyte-Doolittle scale and the three broad categories above are suitable for the limited pur-

Table 16.1 Kyte-Doolittle hydrophobicity values for the 20 amino acid residues

Category	Kyte-Doolittle value	One-letter code	Amino acid	Three-letter code
Hydrophobic	+4.5	I	Isoleucine	Ile
	+4.2	V	Valine	Val
	+3.8	L	Leucine	Leu
	+2.8	F	Phenylalanine	Phe
	+2.5	C	Cysteine	Cys
	+1.9	M	Methionine	Met
	+1.8	A	Alanine	Ala
Neutral	−0.4	G	Glycine	Gly
	−0.7	T	Threonine	Thr
	−0.8	S	Serine	Ser
	−0.9	W	Tryptophan	Trp
	−1.3	Y	Tyrosine	Tyr
	−1.6	P	Proline	Pro
Hydrophilic	−3.2	H	Histidine	His
	−3.5	Q	Glutamine	Gln
	−3.5	N	Asparagine	Asn
	−3.5	E	Glutamic acid	Glu
	−3.5	D	Aspartic acid	Asp
	−3.9	K	Lysine	Lys
	−4.0	R	Arginine	Arg

pose of discussing how hydrophobicity relates to whether a protein segment is a transmembrane domain.

Figure 16.1 shows the 161 amino acid residues of mouse peripheral myelin protein 22. This protein is one of the 33,329 proteins appearing in release 27 in late 1993 of the SWISS-PROT computerized database of proteins (Bairoch and Boeckmann 1991) and is identified in that database by the locus name "PM22_MOUSE." The first residue (at the N-terminal end of the protein) is methionine (M); the 161st residue (at the C-terminal end) is leucine (L). This protein has transmembrane domains located at residues 2–31, 65–91, 96–119, and 134–156. These four transmembrane domains are underlined in the figure.

For example, the third transmembrane domain of mouse peripheral myelin protein 22 consists of the 24 residues (the third underlined subsequence in Figure 16.1) between positions 96 and 119, namely,

FYITGFFQILAGLCVMSAAAIYTV.

The 27 residues between positions 35 and 61 are

TTDLWQNCTTSALGAVQHCYSSSVSEW

and are an example of a randomly chosen nontransmembrane area of this protein.

MLLLLLGILF LHIAVLVLLF VSTIVSQWLV GNGHTTDLWQ NCTTSALGAV   50

QHCYSSSVSE WLQSVQATMI LSVIFSVLAL FLFFCQLFTL TKGGRFYITG   100

FFQILAGLCV MSAAAIYTVR HSEWHVNTDY SYGFAYILAW VAFPLALLSG   150

IIYVILRKRE L   161

Figure 16.1   Primary sequence of mouse peripheral myelin protein 22 with four trans-membrane domains (underlined)

16.3   TRANSMEMBRANE SEGMENT IDENTIFICATION PROBLEM

The goal in the transmembrane segment identification problem is to classify a given protein segment (i.e., a subsequence of amino acid residues from a protein sequence) as being a transmembrane domain or nontransmembrane area of the protein (without using biochemical knowledge concerning hydrophobicity used by human-written algorithms for this task).

A correct classification cannot be made by merely examining a particular position in the given protein segment, testing for the presence or absence of any one particular amino acid residue in the segment, or analyzing any small combination of positions within the segment. Success in this problem involves integrating information over the entire protein segment.

16.4   PREPARATORY STEPS

16.4.1   Program Architecture

In the set-creating version (Koza 1994g, Sections 18.5–18.9) and the arithmetic-performing version (Koza 1994g, Sections 18.10 and 18.11) of this problem, we began by envisioning the roles that might be played by each branch of the yet-to-be-evolved classifying program. We prespecified that there would be three automatically defined functions (ADF0, ADF1, and ADF2).

In the set-creating version of this problem, we envisioned that the automatically defined functions would create sets that would categorize the amino acid residues into useful categories (i.e., perform what is sometimes called an *alphabet reduction* on the 20-letter alphabet of amino acids).

In the arithmetic-performing version of this problem, we envisioned that the automatically defined functions would perform various arithmetic and conditional operations.

For both versions, we further envisioned that the iteration-performing branch, IPB, would refer to the automatically defined functions, perform arithmetic and conditional operations, and access and modify various memory variables. In addition, we envisioned that the result-producing branch, RPB, would access (but not modify) the memory vari-

$$\mathbf{F}_{\text{rpb-initial}} = \{+, \ -, \ *, \ \%, \ \text{SETM0}, \ \text{IFGTZ}, \ \text{ORN}\},$$

taking 2, 2, 2, 2, 1, 3, and 2 arguments, respectively.

The one-argument setting function SETM0 is used to set the named memory variable, M0, to the value of its one argument.

The three-argument conditional branching operator IFGTZ evaluates and returns its second argument if its first argument is greater than or equal to zero, but otherwise evaluates and returns its third argument. The IFGTZ operator is implemented as a macro in the same manner as the IFLTE operator (Section 13.3.2) in the sense that either its second or third argument, but not both, will be executed (so that any side-effecting function, such as SETM0, contained in the unexecuted branch will not be executed).

ORN is the two-argument numerical-valued disjunctive function returning +1 if either or both of its arguments are positive, but returning –1 otherwise. ORN is a short-circuiting (optimized) disjunction function in the sense that its second argument will not be evaluated (and any side-effecting function, such as SETM0, contained therein will remain unexecuted) if its first argument is positive.

The initial function set for the iteration-performing branch, $\mathbf{F}_{\text{adi-initial}}$, is identical to that of the result-producing branch:

$$\mathbf{F}_{\text{adi-initial}} = \mathbf{F}_{\text{rpb-initial}} = \{+, \ -, \ *, \ \%, \ \text{SETM0}, \ \text{IFGTZ}, \ \text{ORN}\}.$$

Since there are no automatically defined functions in generation 0 of this problem, the initial function set for automatically defined functions, $\mathbf{F}_{\text{adf-initial}}$, is empty:

$$\mathbf{F}_{\text{adf-initial}} = \phi.$$

Automatically defined functions (ADF0, ADF1, . . .) and their dummy variables (ARG0, ARG1, . . .) are not present in generation 0. After generation 0, the architecture-altering operations can add them to some individuals in the population.

The set of potential functions for the result-producing branch, $\mathbf{F}_{\text{rpb-potential}}$, is

$$\mathbf{F}_{\text{rpb-potential}} = \{\text{ADF0}, \ \text{ADF1}, \ \text{ADF2}, \ \text{ADF3}\},$$

each taking an as-yet-unknown number of arguments (between zero and four).

The set of potential functions for the iteration-performing branch, $\mathbf{F}_{\text{adi-potential}}$, is identical to that of the result-producing branch:

$$\mathbf{F}_{\text{adi-potential}} = \mathbf{F}_{\text{rpb-potential}} = \{\text{ADF0}, \ \text{ADF1}, \ \text{ADF2}, \ \text{ADF3}\},$$

each taking an as-yet-unknown number of arguments (between 0 and 4).

Since there are no hierarchical references between the potential function set for the automatically defined functions, $\mathbf{F}_{\text{adf-potential}}$, is

$$\mathbf{F}_{\text{adf-potential}} = \mathbf{F}_{\text{adi-initial}} = \{+, \ -, \ *, \ \%, \ \text{SETM0}, \ \text{IFGTZ}, \ \text{ORN}\}.$$

The initial terminal set for the result-producing branch, $\mathbf{T}_{\text{rpb-initial}}$, is

$$\mathbf{T}_{\text{rpb-initial}} = \{\Re_{\text{bigger-reals}}, \ \text{M0}, \ \text{LEN}\}.$$

Here $\Re_{\text{bigger-reals}}$ represents floating-point random constants between –10.0 and +10.0. M0 is a settable variable of named memory. M0 is zero when execution of a given fitness case begins. LEN is the length of the protein segment (fitness case) currently under consideration. As will be seen, LEN varies between 15 and 42 for the protein segments used in this problem.

The terminal set for the iteration-performing branch, $T_{\text{adi-initial}}$, is

$$T_{\text{adi-initial}} = \{\Re_{\text{bigger-reals}}, \text{ MO, LEN, (A?), (C?), } . . . , \text{ (Y?)}\}.$$

The alanine-detecting function (A?) is the zero-argument residue-detecting function returning a numerical +1 if the current residue is alanine (**A**) but otherwise returning a numerical –1. A similar residue-detecting function—from the cysteine-detecting function (C?) to the tyrosine-detecting function (Y?)—is defined for each of the 19 other amino acid residues. Each time the body of the iteration-performing branch is executed, the current residue of the protein is advanced to the next residue of the protein segment until the end of the entire protein segment is encountered. If a residue-detecting function is directly called from the iteration-performing branch (or indirectly called by virtue of being within a yet-to-be-created automatically defined function that is called by the iteration-performing branch), the residue-detecting function is evaluated for the current residue of the iteration.

Since there are no automatically defined functions in generation 0 of this problem, $T_{\text{adf-initial}}$ is empty.

The set of potential terminals for the automatically defined functions, $T_{\text{adf-potential}}$, is

$$T_{\text{adf-potential}} = \{\text{ARG0, ARG1, ARG2, ARG3}\}.$$

Since dummy variables do not appear in the result-producing branch, the set of potential terminals, $T_{\text{rpb-potential}}$, for the result-producing branch consists of the residue-detecting functions that may migrate into the result-producing branch as a consequence of the architecture-altering operations. That is,

$$T_{\text{rpb-potential}} = \{\text{(A?), (C?), } . . . , \text{ (Y?)}\}.$$

If a residue-detecting function migrates into the result-producing branch, it is evaluated for the leftover value of the iterative index (i.e., the last residue of the protein segment). This treatment mirrors what happens when a programmer carelessly references an array using a leftover index from a consummated loop.

The set of potential terminals, $T_{\text{adf-potential}}$, for the automatically defined functions consists of the residue-detecting functions that may migrate into the automatically defined functions as a consequence of the architecture-altering operations:

$$T_{\text{adf-potential}} = T_{\text{adi-initial}} = \{\Re_{\text{bigger-reals}}, \text{ MO, LEN, (A?), (C?), } . . . , \text{ (Y?)}\}.$$

Once the architecture becomes open to evolution by means of the architecture-altering operations, functions and terminals often migrate from one part of the evolving overall program to another. This subsequent migration occurs because of crossover, because of mutation (since newly created functions and terminals enter the set of ingredients from which new subtrees are randomly created), and because of subsequent architecture-altering operations.

Thus, a residue-detecting function may migrate into the body of a yet-to-be-created automatically defined function, which may, in turn, become referenced by some yet-to-be-created call from the result-producing branch. This possibility is handled by specifying that when a residue-detecting function is called directly by the result-producing branch (or called indirectly by virtue of being inside a yet-to-be-created automatically defined function that is referenced by a yet-to-be-created call from the result-producing branch), the residue-detecting function is evaluated for the leftover value of the iterative index (i.e., the last residue of the protein segment). This treatment mirrors what happens when a programmer carelessly references a vector using a leftover index from a consummated loop.

It would have been reasonable to include the 20 residue-detecting functions in the initial function set for the result-producing branch; however, their absence has several potential advantages:

1   The absence of the 20 residue-detecting functions from the result-producing branch simplifies the function set. The result-producing branch is executed once per protein segment. If the residue-detecting functions are to play a nontrivial role in the result-producing branch, they would (most reasonably) have to possess an argument so that they could access different positions of the protein segments. Since the protein segments are of different lengths, the argument would necessarily have to be subject to rectification (for example, modulo LEN) whenever it would otherwise point to a residue beyond the length of a particular protein segment.

2.   The absence of these 20 functions from the result-producing branch (and their presence in the iteration-performing branch) creates pressure toward generality in the program that eventually evolves. The result-producing branch is executed once per protein segment, while the sequence of steps in the iteration-performing branch is executed once for each position along the protein segment. This pressure toward generalization is important because the ultimate goal here is to discover an algorithm for correctly performing the desired classification on previously unseen out-of-sample protein segments (i.e., not merely to discover an algorithm that learns to faithfully replicate the correct classifications associated with the in-sample training cases).

3.   The absence of these 20 functions from the result-producing branch makes the result-producing branch potentially understandable. Without the residue-detecting functions, the result-producing branch is a function of only two variables, namely, M0 and LEN. The applicable range for LEN is constrained because it is a consequence of the relatively narrow range of possible thicknesses for biological membranes and because of the known bond lengths of the atoms in a polypeptide chain. Moreover, the range for LEN is known in advance since it is the range (15 through 42 here) of the actual lengths of the transmembrane domains in the set of fitness cases. The applicable range for M0 is not known in advance; however, experience indicates that there is a good possibility of establishing post hoc a range of values for M0 after the run is completed.

The closure property for the function and terminal set of this problem is satisfied because of the use of numerically valued logic (i.e., the ORN function), numerically valued residue-detecting functions (e.g., (A?)), the numerically valued arithmetic functions, the floating-point random constants, and the initialization of the named memory variable, M0, to zero. This remains the case even after automatically defined functions (with varying numbers of arguments) begin to be created.

A wrapper is used to convert the floating-point value produced by the result-producing branch into a binary outcome. If the result-producing branch returns a positive value, the segment will be classified as a transmembrane domain, but otherwise it will be classified as a nontransmembrane area of the protein. The wrapper is, in effect, an IFGTZ ("if greater than zero") operator.

16.4.3 Fitness

Fitness measures how well a particular classifying program predicts whether the segment is or is not a transmembrane domain. Fitness is measured over a number of fitness cases. The fitness cases consist of protein segments. The classification made by the evolved program for each protein segment in the *in-sample* set of fitness cases (the *training set*) is compared to the known correct classification for the protein segment. Fitness is based on the correlation between these two classifications.

The fitness cases for this problem come from the same proteins used in *Genetic Programming II* (Koza 1994g, Chapter 18). One of the transmembrane domains of each of these proteins was selected at random as a positive fitness case for this in-sample set. One segment that was of the same length as the chosen transmembrane segment but not contained in any of that protein's transmembrane domains was selected from each protein as a negative fitness case. There are a total of 246 fitness cases (123 positive and 123 negative) in the in-sample set of fitness cases.

When an individual program in the population is tested against a particular fitness case, the outcome is one of the following four possibilities:

- a true positive (i.e., the program correctly predicts that the given segment is a transmembrane domain when the segment is, in fact, transmembrane),
- a true negative (i.e., the program correctly predicts that the given segment is not a transmembrane domain when the segment is, in fact, not transmembrane),
- a false positive (i.e., the program *overpredicts* that the given segment is a transmembrane domain when the segment is, in fact, not transmembrane), or
- a false negative (i.e., the program *underpredicts* that the given segment is not a transmembrane domain when the segment is, in fact, transmembrane).

The sum of the number of true positives (N_{tp}), the number of true negatives (N_{tn}), the number of false positives (N_{fp}), and the number of false negatives (N_{fn}) equals the total number of fitness cases, N_{fc}:

$$N_{fc} = N_{tp} + N_{tn} + N_{fp} + N_{fn}.$$

In a two-way classification problem, correlation is an especially appropriate measure of raw fitness for a classifying program. For a two-way classification problem, the *correlation*, C, of an individual program in the population can be computed (Matthews 1975) as

$$C = \frac{N_{tp}N_{tn} - N_{fn}N_{fp}}{\sqrt{(N_{tn} + N_{fn})(N_{tn} + N_{fp})(N_{tp} + N_{fn})(N_{tp} + N_{fp})}}$$

The correlation, C, ranges between -1.0 and $+1.0$ (with higher values being better). The correlation coefficient indicates how much better a particular classifying program is than a random classifying program. The correlation, C, may be viewed as the cosine of the angle in a space of dimensionality N_{fc} between the zero-mean vector (obtained by subtracting the mean value of all components of the vector from each of its components) of correct answers and the zero-mean vector of predictions made by the classifying program. A correlation, C, of -1.0 indicates that the pair of vectors point in opposite directions in N_{fc}-space (i.e., greatest negative correlation). A correlation of $+1.0$ indicates coincident vectors (i.e., greatest positive correlation). A correlation, C, of 0.0 indicates orthogonality (i.e., no correlation).

The raw fitness of a classifying program is correlation, C. Standardized fitness ("zero is best") can then be defined as $1 - C/2$. Standardized fitness ranges between 0.0 and $+1.0$, with lower values being better and a value of 0 being the best. Thus, a standardized fitness of 0 indicates perfect agreement between the classifying program and the observed reality. A standardized fitness of $+1.0$ indicates perfect disagreement. A standardized fitness of 0.50 indicates that the classifying program is no better than random.

The *in-sample correlation*, C, is the correlation computed from the set of in-sample fitness cases. Note that this fitness measure is concerned with "what needs to be done"—namely, get the correct answer (by maximizing correlation). The fitness measure does not reveal "how to do it." The fitness measure provides no information about proteins or amino acids, hydrophobicity, or the biochemistry of living cells.

The *error rate* is the number of fitness cases for which the classifying program is incorrect divided by the total number of fitness cases. Since Weiss, Cohen, and Indurkhya (1993) use the error rate as their yardstick for comparing three methods in the biological literature with their algorithm created with the aid of the SWAP-1 induction technique, our results are presented in terms of both correlation and error rate. Error rate is used for the purpose of comparing results.

The evolutionary process is driven by fitness as measured by the set of in-sample fitness cases. However, the true measure of performance for a classifying program is how well it generalizes to previously unseen fitness cases from the same problem environment. Thus, 250 out-of-sample fitness cases (125 positive and 125 negative) were created from the 125 different proteins in a manner similar to that used to create the in-sample fitness cases. These out-of-sample fitness cases (i.e., the *out-of-sample* data or *testing set*) were then used to validate the performance of the evolved classifying programs.

16.4.4   Parameters

The control parameters for this chapter are in the tableau (Table 16.2), the tables of percentages of genetic operations in Appendix D of this book, and the default values specified in Koza 1994g, Appendix D.

16.4.5   Termination

Since perfect classification performance is unlikely to be achieved and there is no way of predicting the highest correlation that might be achieved, no explicit success predicate is used for this problem. The run is manually monitored and terminated manually after the fitness value of the best-of-run individual appears to plateau. As it happens, the best-of-run program appears in generation 28, and the run was manually terminated in generation 179.

16.4.6 Tableau

Table 16.2 summarizes the key features of the transmembrane segment identification problem with architecture-altering operations.

16.5 RESULTS

A program was evolved on the first run of this problem that is superior to the human-written algorithm. Accordingly, only one run (taking about 23 hours of computer time) was made of this problem.

The vast majority of the randomly generated programs in generation 0 perform no better than random chance in identifying whether a protein segment is a transmembrane domain. Thus, they have a zero or near-zero correlation, C. However, even in the initial random population, some individuals are better than others.

The first pace-setting individual from generation 0 scores an in-sample correlation of 0.0690 and an in-sample error rate of 48%. The next pace-setting individual from generation 0 scores an in-sample correlation of 0.2265 and an in-sample error rate of 46%. On each iteration along the protein segment, the iteration-performing branch of this program sets the settable variable M0 to +1 if the current residue is glutamic acid (**E**) and −1 otherwise. Glutamic acid is electrically charged and highly hydrophobic. Since the iteration-performing branch resets M0 for each position along the protein segment, the only setting of M0 that matters, upon completion of all the iterations, is the setting for the last position of the segment. The 93-point result-producing branch of this program then uses M0 (after reversing its sign) to classify the entire protein segment.

This myopic program from generation 0 is fundamentally flawed. First, it makes a decision for the entire protein segment based on an examination of only one residue. Since the average length of the transmembrane domains here is about 23, M0 is overwritten repeatedly, and this myopic program is oblivious to 96% of the protein segment. It is known that a correct decision requires integration of information over the entire protein segment. Second, this myopic program makes its decision based on a manifestly inadequate test (checking only on glutamic acid while ignoring the other 19 amino acid residues). The fact that this highly myopic program is the best of the 2,000 initial random programs from its processing node illustrates the principle that in the valley of the blind, the one-eyed man is king.

The best-of-generation program for generation 0 becomes known only after all 64 processing nodes of the parallel computer system finish generation 0 and report their results to the host computer. In practice, this occurs well after some of the 64 processing nodes are finished with their generation 1. The best-of-generation program for generation 0 has an in-sample correlation of 0.3604 and an in-sample error rate of 34%. This program has 30 points in its iteration-performing branch and 17 points in its result-producing branch. Its out-of-sample correlation is 0.3632, and its out-of-sample error rate is 35%. Figure 16.3 shows the call tree for this best-of-generation program from generation 0.

The best-of-generation program for generation 1 is a pace-setting program with an in-sample correlation of 0.7107 and an in-sample error rate of 15%. This program has no

Table 16.2 Tableau for the transmembrane segment identification problem with architecture-altering operations for subroutines

Objective	Discover, using the architecture-altering operations for automatically defined functions, a computer program to classify whether or not a segment of a protein sequence is a transmembrane domain.
Program architecture	One result-producing branch, RPB, and one iteration-performing branch, IPB, in generation 0. Automatically defined function(s) and their argument(s) will be created during the run by the architecture-altering operations.
Initial function set for the RPBs	$F_{rpb-initial} = \{+, -, *, \%, SETM0, IFGTZ, ORN\}$
Initial terminal set for the RPBs	$T_{rpb-initial} = \{\Re_{bigger-reals}, M0, LEN\}$
Initial function set for the ADFs	No automatically defined functions in generation 0. $F_{adf-initial} = \phi$.
Initial terminal set for the ADFs	No automatically defined functions in generation 0. $T_{adf-initial} = \phi$.
Initial function set for the IPBs	$F_{adi-initial} = \{+, -, *, \%, SETM0, IFGTZ, ORN\}$
Initial terminal set for the IPBs	$T_{adi-initial} = \{\Re_{bigger-reals}, M0, LEN, (A?), (C?), \ldots, (Y?)\}$
Potential function set for the RPBs	$F_{rpb-potential} = \{ADF0, ADF1, ADF2, ADF3\}$
Potential terminal set for the RPBs	$T_{rpb-potential} = \{(A?), (C?), \ldots, (Y?)\}$
Potential function set for the ADFs	$F_{adf-potential} = \phi$
Potential terminal set for the ADFs	$T_{adf-potential} = \{ARG0, ARG1, ARG2, ARG3\}$
Potential function set for the IPBs	$F_{adi-potential} = \{ADF0, ADF1, ADF2, ADF3\}$
Potential terminal set for the IPBs	$T_{adi-potential} = \phi$
Fitness cases	The in-sample set of fitness cases consists of 246 protein segments (half transmembrane domains and half not). The out-of-sample set of fitness cases consists of 250 protein segments (half transmembrane domains and half not).
Raw fitness	Correlation C (ranging from –1.0 to +1.0)
Standardized fitness	$1 - C/2$ (ranging from 0.0 to 1.0)
Hits	Not used for this problem
Wrapper	If the result-producing branch returns a number greater than 0, the segment is classified as a transmembrane domain; otherwise, the segment is classified as nontransmembrane.

(continued)

Table 16.2 (continued)

Parameters	$M = 128{,}000$. $G = 1{,}001$. $Q = 2{,}000$. $D = 64$. $B = 5\%$. $N_{rpb} = 1$. $S_{rpb} = 200$. $S_{adf} = 200$. $N_{max\text{-}adf} = 4$. $N_{max\text{-}argument\text{-}adf} = 4$.
Result designation	Best-so-far pace-setting individual
Success predicate	Fitness appears to have reached a plateau.

automatically defined functions. Like the best-of-generation program from generation 0, this program bases its decision only on the last residue of the protein segment. The only operative part of its 37-point iteration-performing branch sets M0 to the difference between the value returned by the arginine-detecting function, (R?), and the length, LEN, of the segment. Apparently it is better to be myopic with arginine (**R**) than with glutamic acid (**E**). The part of the 32-point result-producing branch that meaningfully uses M0 begins by adding LEN to M0. That is, the iteration-performing branch and the result-producing branch coevolved so as to pass the value of (R?) between the two branches (by first coding it by subtracting the irrelevant value of LEN and then decoding and restoring it by adding LEN). This program is typical of many programs that appear as best-of-generation programs in runs of genetic programming: it is an incremental improvement over its immediate ancestors.

16.5.1 Emergence of Hierarchy

The best-of-generation program for generation 4 has an in-sample correlation of 0.7150 and is another pace-setting program. This program has a 19-point iteration-performing branch and a 28-point result-producing branch (which refers to ADF0 and M0). This program has two automatically defined functions, each possessing two arguments. Since automatically defined functions did not exist in generation 0, these automatically defined functions are present in this program because of the architecture-altering operations. Although many programs with automatically defined functions were created as early as generation 1, this program is the first program with automatically defined functions in this run that is also a pace-setting program.

This program illustrates the emergence of hierarchy that often occurs as a result of the architecture-altering operations. The program contains a hierarchy in which ADF0 refers to ADF1. ADF1 performs a three-way arithmetic product as follows:

```
(* (* ARG0 -3.529439) ARG1).
```

ADF0 then refers to ADF1 as follows:

```
(ADF1 ARG0 (ORN M0 ARG1)).
```

As usual, only a nonrecursive hierarchy of function-defining branches is allowed to form. Figure 16.4 shows the call tree for this best-of-generation program from generation 4.

In generation 5, the best-of-generation program does not have any automatically defined functions. It has an in-sample correlation of 0.7170.

The next pace-setting program is the second-best program of generation 6 (with in-sample correlation of 0.7212). It is interesting because it has four automatically defined functions (possessing 0, 3, 2, and 1 arguments, respectively) and a somewhat more com-

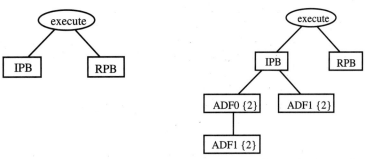

Figure 16.3   Call tree for best-of-generation program from generation 0

Figure 16.4   Call tree for best-of-generation program from generation 4

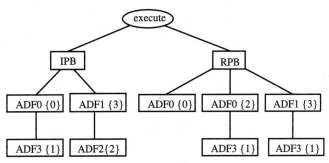

Figure 16.5   Call tree for best-of-generation program from generation 6

plicated hierarchy. ADF0 hierarchically refers to ADF3, and ADF1 refers to ADF2. One-argument ADF3 is degenerate and merely returns its one dummy variable, ARG0. Two-argument ADF2 merely multiplies its dummy variables, ARG0 and ARG1, together. However, ADF0 and ADF1 are larger and perform significant calculations. The result-producing branch refers to ADF1 (which, in turn, refers to ADF2), and it also refers to ADF0 (which, in turn, refers to ADF3); the iteration-performing branch refers to ADF2. Figure 16.5 shows the call tree for this best-of-generation program from generation 6.

The second-best program of generation 7 is another pace-setting program (with in-sample correlation of 0.7315). It does not have any automatically defined functions, and not surprisingly, it is a rather large program (with a total of 115 points). This program is the last program without automatically defined functions that qualifies as a pace-setting program in this run. That is, after generation 7, no program lacking automatically defined functions ever again sets the pace for the run. In the competitive race to accrue fitness, programs without automatically defined functions are less fit. This observation from this particular problem is a small additional piece of evidence in favor of the general proposition (which we believe, after the test of time, will prove to be usually true) that genetic programming tends to produce solutions to problems with less computational effort with automatically defined functions than without them.

Table 16.3 Pace-setting values for in-sample correlation

Generation	Number of ADFs	Argument map of the ADFs	In-sample correlation	In-sample error rate	Out-of-sample correlation	Out-of-sample error rate
0	None	{}	0.0690	48%	0.0772	48%
0	None	{}	0.2265	46%	0.2245	46%
0	None	{}	0.2546	41%	0.2245	43%
0	None	{}	0.3604	34%	0.3632	35%
1	None	{}	0.4849	31%	0.4736	32%
1	None	{}	0.7107	15%	0.7389	14%
4	2	{2 2}	0.7150	15%	0.7142	15%
5	None	{}	0.7107	15%	0.7213	15%
6	4	{0 3 2 1}	0.7212	15%	0.6929	13%
7	1	{1}	0.7315	14%	0.6340	19%
7	None	{}	0.7479	14%	0.7842	12%
6	1	{2}	0.7510	13%	0.7871	11%
8	4	{0 0 2 2}	0.7645	12%	0.7760	12%
9	1	{3}	0.7663	13%	0.7861	12%
8	1	{0}	0.7700	12%	0.7897	11%
9	4	{2 1 2 2}	0.7849	11%	0.7871	11%
11	1	{3}	0.8101	10%	0.8165	10%
11	1	{3}	0.8378	9%	0.8738	7%
13	2	{1 3}	0.8700	7%	0.8320	9%
16	1	{0}	0.9108	5%	0.9440	3%
19	1	{0}	0.9206	5%	0.9448	3%
20	2	{3 2}	0.9271	4%	0.9365	4%
22	1	{3}	0.9361	4%	0.9295	4%
28	**1**	**{0}**	**0.9596**	**3%**	**0.9681**	**1.6%**
34	1	{0}	0.9675	2%	0.9521	3%
37	2	{0 1}	0.9676	2%	0.9520	3%
39	2	{0 0}	0.9756	2%	0.9520	3%
47	3	{0 0 0}	0.9837	1%	0.9440	3%
56	4	{0 0 0 0}	0.9839	1%	0.9361	4%
71	4	{0 0 0 1}	0.9919	1%	0.9361	4%

There were 30 occasions in this run when a processing node reported a pace-setting new best level of in-sample correlation. Twenty-three of these occasions were prior to generation 28 (the generation that produces the best-of-run individual).

Table 16.3 shows the generation on which each pace-setting program was created, the number of automatically defined functions in each pace-setting program, the number of arguments possessed by these automatically defined functions (if any), the in-sample correlation, the in-sample error rate, the out-of-sample correlation, and the out-of-sample error rate. Note that since the generations are run asynchronously on the 64 nodes of a parallel computing system, the reports are occasionally out of generational order (e.g., pace-setting values from generations 6 and 8 report in after other processors have reported pace-setting values from later generations). Note also for generations (such as 0, 1, 6, 7, and 8) where more than one pace-setting value is reported, it is the last entry in the table for the generation that contains the best-of-generation value of in-sample correlation. No additional improvement occurs in in-sample correlation between generations 71 and 179.

As can be seen from the table, the architectures of the successive pace-setting programs in the table vary considerably. The table also shows that the out-of-sample correlation generally increases in tandem with the in-sample correlation until generation 28 (highlighted in bold). The best program of generation 28 scores an in-sample correlation of 0.9596, an out-of-sample correlation of 0.9681, an in-sample error rate of 3%, and an out-of-sample error rate of 1.6%. These scores arise from 122 true positives, 119 true negatives, 4 false positives, and 1 false negative for the in-sample set of fitness cases and 124 true positives, 122 true negatives, 3 false positives, and 1 false negative for the out-of-sample fitness cases. In other words, this program only makes five mistakes on the in-sample fitness cases and four mistakes on the out-of-sample fitness cases.

After generation 28, the in-sample correlation continues to rise while its out-of-sample counterpart begins to drop off. Similarly, after generation 28, the in-sample error rate continues to drop while its out-of-sample counterpart begins to rise. Based on this, the best-of-generation program from generation 28 was designated as the best-of-run program.

Figure 16.6 shows the architecture of the best-of-run program from generation 28. This program has one automatically defined function, ADF0; one iteration-performing branch, IPB; and one result-producing branch, RPB.

Figure 16.7 shows the call tree for this best-of-generation program from generation 28. As can be seen from the call tree, ADF0 is called by both the iteration-performing branch, IPB, and the result-producing branch, RPB.

ADF0 of the best-of-run program from generation 28 contains an arithmetic multiplication of two numerically valued residue-detecting functions:

```
(* (F?) (L?)).
```

Note that phenylalanine (F) and leucine (L) are the third and fourth most hydrophobic residues on the Kyte-Doolittle scale. Since there can be only one amino acid residue at any one position in a protein sequence, the phenylalanine-detecting function (F?) and the leucine-detecting function (L?) cannot both return +1. However, ADF0 will return +1 when the current residue is neither F nor L. On the other hand, if the current residue is either F or L, ADF0 will return −1. That is, ADF0 is a negative disjunctive detector (NOR) for these particular two hydrophobic amino acid residues.

The 36-point iteration-performing branch, IPB, is

```
(IFGTZ (IFGTZ (IFGTZ (SETM0 (+ (SETM0 (+ (+ (E?) (+ M0 (* (A?)
(M?)))) (* (V?) (SETM0 (I?))))) (ADF0))) -4.636735 (V?)) -
4.636735 (+ (C?) (V?))) (- (IFGTZ LEN M0 2.720462) (* LEN M0))
(+ (C?) (V?)))).
```

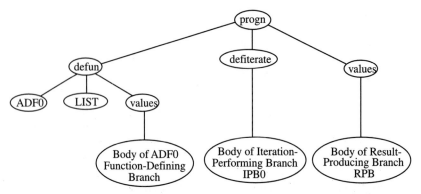

Figure 16.6 Architecture of best-of-run program from generation 28 with one zero-argument automatically defined function, ADF0; one iteration-performing branch, IPB0; and one result-producing branch, RPB

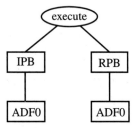

Figure 16.7 Call tree for best-of-generation program from generation 28

When simplified, this iteration-performing branch uses addition and multiplication to set M0 to the following sum (presented using infix notation):

```
M0 + (E?) + (A?)*(M?) + (V?)*(I?) + ADF0.
```

Substituting for ADF0 yields

```
M0 + (E?) + (A?)*(M?) + (V?)*(I?) + (F?)*(L?).
```

This running sum in the iteration-performing branch involves A, F, I, L , M, and V. These amino acids are six of the seven most hydrophobic residues on the Kyte-Doolittle scale. Glutamic acid (E) is, in turn, electrically charged and one of the most highly hydrophilic amino acid residues on the Kyte-Doolittle scale.

The net effect of this expression is that if the residue is E, the increment to the running sum, M0, is +4; if the residue is A, F, I, L, M, or V, the increment to M0 is 0; or if the residue is any of the other 13 residues, the increment to M0 is +2.

The 169-point result-producing branch, RPB, is

```
(IFGTZ (+ (* (IFGTZ (IFGTZ -3.982617 M0 M0) (% LEN M0) (ORN M0
LEN)) (ORN (% -4.636735 (IFGTZ (IFGTZ (ORN -2.670227 M0) (IFGTZ
-2.817162 M0 LEN) (% 2.043147 1.479118)) (ORN (% -1.234550 M0)
```

```
(- M0 M0)) (+ (+ LEN -2.222740) (* LEN LEN)))) (IFGTZ LEN -
3.982617 2.533069))) (+ (ORN M0 0.399343) (- (IFGTZ LEN M0 (+
M0 LEN)) (* LEN 3.929935)))) (- (+ (- (+ -1.017916 -4.526229)
(% LEN -1.111554)) (IFGTZ (- M0 -4.862647) (% LEN LEN) (*
4.953630 M0))) (% (* (% M0 (+ (- -4.478793 LEN) (IFGTZ LEN M0
M0))) (* M0 M0)) (% (% (+ (- (* (* LEN LEN) (- LEN M0)) (+
(- -3.574382 4.751522) (IFGTZ LEN LEN M0))) (ORN (* (% LEN LEN)
(* 0.719815 M0)) (% LEN LEN))) 2.750320) (ORN 2.043147 LEN))))
(+ (- (* (% LEN 4.173654) (- LEN M0)) (+ (- -3.574382 4.751522)
(IFGTZ (ORN (+ (- M0 -4.303949) (ADF0)) (* (IFGTZ -4.303949 LEN
-2.738661) (* -0.809109 (+ LEN LEN)))) LEN (IFGTZ (ORN LEN
(* LEN 3.929935)) M0 LEN)))) LEN)).
```

After genetic programming evolves a satisfactory solution to a problem, the user may want to understand the operation of the evolved program (Wheeler 1998). Such an understanding may increase confidence in the result (beyond that provided by cross-validation on out-of-sample data) or may be important because it may suggest future scientific experiments. This same issue of comprehensibility arises in understanding weight matrices in neural networks and in understanding the often baffling sequence of attribute tests in decision trees for nontrivial problems.

Of course, a program performs a well-defined sequence of steps using well-defined operations. However, the programs created by an evolutionary process often appear, at first glance, to be incomprehensible. It is common for evolved programs to contain large segments of unused material (sometimes called an "appendix" or an "intron") as well as large segments that have very little impact on the final result produced by the overall program. Nonetheless, our experience has been that it is usually possible, after some effort, to come to understand the seemingly incomprehensible programs created by evolution.

This particular evolved program can be deciphered. First, although a reference to ADF0 migrated into the result-producing branch, ADF0 plays no role in the result produced by the result-producing branch. Second, no residue-detecting function appears in the result-producing branch. The interpretation of this particular evolved program is greatly simplified by these two fortuitous events. The value returned by the result-producing branch is dependent only on the value of the settable variable M0 (communicated from the iteration-performing branch) and the length, LEN, of the current protein segment. That is, the result-producing branch, RPB, is simply a function of two variables, namely, M0 and LEN.

The behavior of this 169-point result-producing branch can then be analyzed by embedding it (along with the problem's wrapper) into a simple test program that loops over a range of reasonable values for M0 and LEN. The applicable range for LEN is the known range of actual values for the lengths of the transmembrane domains among the fitness cases (i.e., between 15 and 42). The range for M0 is constrained to a narrow band because the 36-point iteration-performing branch of the evolved program is fortuitously equivalent to a running sum of the integers 0, 2, and 4. Thus, only attainable values of M0 are integral and lie between 0 and 168 (4×42).

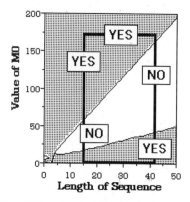

Figure 16.8   Behavior of the 169-point result-producing branch from the best-of-run program from generation 28

Figure 16.8 shows a graph of the behavior of the 169-point result-producing branch from the best-of-run program from generation 28 for various values of MO and LEN. This figure plots the output of the test problem described above. The wrapperized output of the result-producing branch classifies a protein segment as a transmembrane domain for the shaded region (labeled "yes") and classifies the segment as a nontransmembrane area of the protein for the nonshaded region (labeled "no"). The heavy black frame highlights the area where LEN lies between 15 and 42 and where MO lies between 0 and 168. Although there is a small triangular unshaded region adjacent to the vertical axis where the result-producing branch returns both positive and nonpositive values for marginally different values of LEN and MO, this small anomalous region can be ignored since no actual protein sequences have such small values of LEN and MO.

Although MO can conceivably attain a value as high as 168, a value of 168 can only be attained if the segment consists of 42 consecutive electrically charged residues of glutamic acid (E). There is no actual protein segment that even remotely approaches this degree of electrical activity among the fitness cases. In fact, all actual values of MO are less than 50.

Figure 16.9 is a cutaway portion of Figure 16.8 that shows the behavior of the result-producing branch only for the biologically plausible values of LEN between 15 and 42 and for realistic values of MO (i.e., less than 50). Remarkably, the region inside the heavy black frame of this cutaway figure is neatly divided by a straight line. In other words, the region of biologically plausible combinations of values of LEN and MO for this problem is linearly separable. A linear regression on the boundary that so neatly partitions Figure 16.9 reveals that

MO = 3.1544 + 0.9357 LEN.

The Kyte-Doolittle rule (and other similar human-written rules) are linear. Note, however, that the linear functional form that emerged from the run of genetic programming is linear because that is what the evolutionary process produced. It was not preordained by any of the user-supplied preparatory steps for this problem.

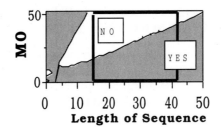

Figure 16.9 Cutaway portion of graph showing behavior of the 169-point result-producing branch from the best-of-run program from generation 28

The evolved solution for classifying a protein segment as a transmembrane domain or a nontransmembrane area of the protein can then be restated as the following relatively simple rule (which we call the "0-2-4 rule"):

- Increment the running sum, SUM, by adding 4 for each **E** in the protein segment.
- Increment the running sum, SUM, by adding 0 for each **A, F, I, L, M,** or **V** in the protein segment.
- Increment the running sum, SUM, by adding 2 for each of the 13 other residues (i.e., **C, D, G, H, K, N, P, Q, R, S, T, W,** or **Y**) in the protein segment.
- If

$$\left\lceil \frac{\text{SUM} - 3.1544}{0.9357} \right\rceil < \text{LEN},$$

then classify the protein segment as a transmembrane domain; otherwise, classify the segment as a nontransmembrane area of the protein.

Table 16.4 shows the increments for the evolved "0-2-4 rule" above. The evolved "0-2-4" rule resembles the Kyte-Doolittle rule in that it involves a linear expression based on accumulated values. However, the three increments (0, 2, and 4) are far simpler than the 20 (mostly different) floating-point values of the Kyte-Doolittle hydrophobicity scale (Table 16.1). The fact that the six residues **A, F, I, L, M,** and **V** are all known to be highly hydrophobic and **E** is known to be highly hydrophilic (electrically charged) makes the "0-2-4" rule biologically plausible. Of course, this "0-2-4" rule was evolved without using any knowledge of biochemistry, hydrophobicity, or amino acid residues.

Table 16.4 Increments for the evolved "0-2-4 rule"

Residue	Increment
A, F, I, L, M, or V	0
C, D, G, H, K, N, P, Q, R, S, T, W, or Y	+2
E	+4

16.6 COMPARISON OF EIGHT METHODS OF SOLVING THE TRANSMEMBRANE SEGMENT IDENTIFICATION PROBLEM

Table 16.5 shows the out-of-sample error rate for eight different approaches to the transmembrane segment identification problem. The first three rows of the table refer to human-written algorithms described in Weiss, Cohen, and Indurkhya 1993. The seventh row of the table relates to the approach described above in this chapter. The eighth row relates to the approach described in Chapter 17. The eight methods are as follows:

- the human-written algorithm of von Heijne (1992),
- the human-written algorithm of Engelman, Steitz, and Goldman (1986),
- the human-written algorithm of Kyte and Doolittle (1982),
- the machine learning approach (incorporating a machine learning technique that relied upon a considerable amount of human ingenuity) of Weiss, Cohen, and Indurkhya (1993),
- the set-creating version using genetic programming with prespecification by the user of the architecture consisting of exactly three zero-argument automatically defined functions and exactly one iteration-performing branch (Koza 1994g, Sections 18.5–18.9),
- the arithmetic-performing version using genetic programming with prespecification by the user of the architecture consisting of exactly three zero-argument automatically defined functions and exactly one iteration-performing branch (Koza 1994g, Sections 18.10 and 18.11),
- the "0-2-4" rule evolved in this chapter using the architecture-altering operations for subroutines, but with prespecification by the user of exactly one iteration-performing branch (Koza and Andre 1996a), and
- the result described in Chapter 17 using the architecture-altering operations for automatically defined functions and for automatically defined iterations such that there is no prespecification by the user of the architecture for either subroutines or iterations (Koza and Andre 1996b).

As can be seen from the last four rows of the table, the out-of-sample error rates for all four algorithms created by genetic programming (two in this book and two in *Genetic Programming II*) are better than the error rates for the three human-written algorithms (the first three rows of the table).

Referring to the eight criteria in Chapter 1 for establishing that an automatically created result is competitive with a human-produced result, these four results satisfy the following two of the eight criteria:

B. The result is equal to or better than a result that was accepted as a new scientific result at the time when it was published in a peer-reviewed journal.

E. The result is equal to or better than the most recent human-created solution to a long-standing problem for which there has been a succession of increasingly better human-created solutions.

Table 16.5 Comparison of eight methods

Method	Error
von Heijne 1992	2.8%
Engelman, Steitz, and Goldman 1986	2.7%
Kyte and Doolittle 1982	2.5%
Weiss, Cohen, and Indurkhya 1993	2.5%
Genetic programming—set-creating version (Koza 1994g)	1.6%
Genetic programming—arithmetic-performing version (Koza 1994g)	1.6%
Genetic programming with architecture-altering operations for subroutines ("0-2-4" rule of this chapter)	1.6%
Genetic programming with architecture-altering operations for subroutines and iterations (Chapter 17 of this book)	1.6%

Therefore, we make the following claim:

- **CLAIM NO. 1** We claim that the four different algorithms for the transmembrane segment identification problem discovered by genetic programming are instances where genetic programming has produced a result that is competitive with an algorithm produced by creative and inventive humans.

These four instances of automatically created algorithms satisfy Arthur Samuel's criterion (1983) for artificial intelligence and machine learning:

> The aim [is] . . . to get machines to exhibit behavior, which if done by humans, would be assumed to involve the use of intelligence.

Transmembrane Segment Identification Problem Using Architecture-Altering Operations for Iterations

The previous chapter showed that the transmembrane segment identification problem can be solved using the architecture-altering operations for automatically defined functions (i.e., subroutine duplication, subroutine creation, and subroutine deletion). That is, the decision on whether or not to employ automatically defined functions was dynamically made by the genetic programming system during the run—not by the human user prior to the start of the run.

The evolved program also included a single hard-wired automatically defined iteration consisting of an iteration-performing branch. Genetic programming successfully performed the nontrivial task of creating the particular sequence of steps contained in the iteration-performing branch. However, the human user made the decision, prior to the start of the run of genetic programming, that every individual in the evolving population would contain exactly one iteration-performing branch.

For many problems, it is not obvious in advance whether the solution of a particular problem requires an iteration-performing branch. If the problem requires iteration, it is usually not obvious in advance whether the problem requires exactly one such iteration-performing branch or multiple iteration-performing branches. It is therefore desirable to automate the decision as to whether to employ iteration and, if iteration is to be employed, how many times to employ iteration in solving the problem. This automation can be realized using the architecture-altering operation of iteration creation. This operation adds an automatically defined iteration to an individual program during a run of genetic programming. The operation of iteration creation is illustrated by applying it to the transmembrane segment identification problem (described in Chapter 16).

17.1 PREPARATORY STEPS

17.1.1 Program Architecture

Each program in generation 0 has a uniform architecture consisting of one result-producing branch. There are no iteration-performing branches or automatically defined functions.

Any automatically defined functions or iteration-performing branches that will be used to solve the problem will be created dynamically during the run of genetic programming. After generation 0, the architecture-altering operations will create iteration-performing branches and automatically defined functions and determine the number of arguments that each automatically defined function possesses. For practical reasons, a maximum number of three iteration-performing branches is established. Similarly, a maximum of four automatically defined functions, each possessing between zero and four arguments, is established. Hierarchical references are allowed among the automatically defined functions.

The transmembrane segment identification problem deals with protein segments, each of which is of a known, finite length. Therefore, each iteration (after it is created) is restricted in the sense that it will consist of one pass over the current protein segment. This decision to use restricted iteration effectively caps the amount of computer time that can be expended in executing any one program. Specifically, the iteration will start by pointing to the first position of the protein segment; the transition rule for the iteration entails advancing the pointer to the next position of the protein segment; and the iteration terminates when it points to the last position of the protein segment. The iteration-performing branch(es) do not have access to the iterative index. The residue-detecting functions sense the presence or absence of a particular amino acid residue at the current position of the protein segment.

17.1.2 Functions and Terminals

There are a total of 51 functions and terminals in this problem:

- 12 initial functions,
- 28 initial terminals,
- 4 potential functions, and
- 7 potential terminals.

These 51 functions and terminals will appear in 12 different sets defining

- both the initial and potential members of
- both the function and terminal sets for
- the three types of branches (the result-producing branch, the function-defining branches, and the iteration-performing branch).

The initial function set for the result-producing branch, $F_{\text{rpb-initial}}$, is

$F_{\text{rpb-initial}} = \{+, -, *, \%, \text{SETM0}, \text{SETM1}, \text{SETM2}, \text{SETM3}, \text{SETM4}, \text{SETM5}, \text{IFGTZ}, \text{ORN}, (A?), (C?), \ldots, (Y?)\}.$

The one-argument setting functions, SETM0, SETM1, SETM2, SETM3, SETM4, and SETM5, are used to set named memory variables, (M0, M1, M2, M3, M4, and M5, respectively) to the value of their one argument. The residue-detecting functions return +1 or –1 based on the "current residue" of the protein segment. When a residue-detecting function appears within a newly created iteration-performing branch, it is, of course, evaluated for the current residue of the protein segment as the iteration proceeds along the protein segment. When such a function appears within a newly created automatically defined function that is called from within a newly created iteration-performing branch, it is similarly evaluated for the current residue of the protein segment as the iteration proceeds along the protein segment. The other functions were defined in the previous chapter.

When a residue-detecting function appears in a program with no iteration-performing branch, the "current residue" to which it is pointing is formally undefined. This situation arises for 100% of the individuals in generation 0 (where the programs consist of only a result-producing branch). It arises for numerous additional programs in virtually every later generation. In situations where the "current residue" is formally undefined, a residue-detecting function is evaluated for the first position of the protein segment (i.e., as if the iterative index were pointing to the first residue of the protein sequence). This convention reflects the idea that, if no iteration has been performed, it is reasonable to say that the value of the iterative index should be its starting value.

When a residue-detecting function appears within the result-producing branch of a program with one or more iteration-performing branches, the residue to which it is pointing is also formally undefined. In this situation, the function is evaluated for the leftover value of the iterative index (i.e., as if the iterative index were pointing to the last residue of the protein sequence). This convention reflects the idea that if one or more iterations have already been performed, it is reasonable to say that the value of the iterative index should be its terminating value.

Similarly, for a program with one or more iteration-performing branches, when a residue-detecting function appears within an automatically defined function that is not called by an iteration-performing branch (i.e., is called by the result-producing branch), the residue to which it is pointing is also formally undefined. In this situation, the function is evaluated for the leftover value of the iterative index (i.e., as if the iterative index is pointing to the last residue of the protein sequence).

Since there are no automatically defined functions in generation 0 of this problem, the initial function set for automatically defined functions, $F_{\text{adf-initial}}$, is empty:

$$F_{\text{adf-initial}} = \phi.$$

Since there are no iteration-performing branches in generation 0 of this problem, the initial function set for the iteration-performing branch, $F_{\text{adi-initial}}$, is empty:

$$F_{\text{adi-initial}} = \phi.$$

Neither iteration-performing branches nor automatically defined functions are present in generation 0. After generation 0, the architecture-altering operations can add them to some individuals in the population.

The set of potential functions for the result-producing branch, $F_{\text{rpb-potential}}$, is

$$F_{\text{rpb-potential}} = \{\text{ADF0, ADF1, ADF2}\},$$

each taking an as-yet-unknown number of arguments (between zero and four).

The set of potential functions for the iteration-performing branch, $F_{\text{adi-potential}}$, is identical to that of the result-producing branch:

$$F_{\text{adi-potential}} = F_{\text{rpb-potential}} = \{\text{ADF0, ADF1, ADF2}\}.$$

Since there are no hierarchical references between the potential function set for the automatically defined functions, $F_{\text{adf-potential}}$ is

$$F_{\text{adf-potential}} = F_{\text{adi-initial}} = \{\text{+, -, *, \%, SETM0, SETM1, SETM2, SETM3,}$$
$$\text{SETM4, SETM5, IFGTZ, ORN}\}.$$

The initial terminal set, $T_{\text{rpb-initial}}$, for the result-producing branch is

$$T_{\text{rpb-initial}} = \{\Re_{\text{bigger-reals}}, \text{M0, M1, M2, M3, M4, M5, LEN, (A?), (C?),}$$
$$\text{. . . , (Y?)}\}.$$

M0, M1, M2, M3, M4, and M5 are settable memory variables. Each is zero when execution of a given fitness case begins.

Since there are no automatically defined functions in generation 0 of this problem, $T_{\text{adf-initial}}$ is empty. Since there are no iteration-performing branches in generation 0 of this problem, $T_{\text{adi-initial}}$ is empty.

After generation 0, iteration-performing branches (and the terminals representing their return values, IPB0, IPB1, and IPB2) and automatically defined functions (ADF0, ADF1, ADF2, and ADF3) and their dummy variables (ARG0, ARG1, ARG2, and ARG3) begin to appear in the population.

The set of potential terminals for the result-producing branch, $T_{\text{rpb-potential}}$, is

$$T_{\text{rpb-potential}} = \{\text{IPB0, IPB1, IPB2}\}.$$

The set of potential terminals for the automatically defined functions, $T_{\text{adf-potential}}$, is

$$T_{\text{adf-potential}} = \{\text{ARG0, ARG1, ARG2, ARG3, } \Re_{\text{bigger-reals}}, \text{ M0, M1, M2, M3,}$$
$$\text{M4, M5, LEN, (A?), (C?), . . . , (Y?)}\}.$$

The set of potential terminals for the iteration-performing branches, $T_{\text{adi-potential}}$, is

$$T_{\text{adi-potential}} = T_{\text{rpb-initial}} = \{\Re_{\text{bigger-reals}}, \text{ M0, M1, M2, M3, M4, M5, LEN, (A?),}$$
$$\text{(C?), . . . , (Y?)}\}.$$

The closure property for the function and terminal set of this problem is satisfied because of the use of numerically valued logic, numerically valued residue-detecting functions, the numerically valued arithmetic functions, the floating-point random constants, and the initialization of the named memory variables to zero. This remains the case even after automatically defined functions (with varying numbers of arguments) and iteration-performing branches are created.

A wrapper (output interface) is used to convert the floating-point value produced by the result-producing branch into a binary outcome. If the result-producing branch returns a positive numerical value, the segment will be classified as a transmembrane domain, but otherwise the segment will be classified as a nontransmembrane area of the protein.

17.1.3 Fitness

The fitness cases and fitness measure (correlation) are the same as in Chapter 16.

17.1.4 Parameters

This problem has several control parameters that have not appeared previously in this book:

- The maximum number, $N_{\text{max-adi}}$, of automatically defined iterations is 3.
- The maximum size, S_{adi}, for the iteration-performing branch of each automatically defined iteration is 200 points.
- The range of number of arguments for each automatically defined function is 0 to 4, so that $N_{\text{min-argument-adf}} = 0$ and $N_{\text{max-argument-adf}} = 4$.

The control parameters for this chapter are in the tableau (Table 17.1), the tables of percentages of genetic operations in Appendix D of this book, and the default values specified in Koza (1994g, Appendix D).

17.1.5 Termination

The run is monitored and manually terminated when the correlation appears to have reached a plateau.

17.1.6 Tableau

Table 17.1 summarizes the key features of the problem of symbolic regression of the transmembrane segment identification problem with iteration creation.

17.2 RESULTS

It is usually difficult to understand the workings of genetically evolved computer programs. One practical way to obtain understandable evolved programs is to harvest more than a single best-of-run program from a run. When this approach is used, the run is not terminated as soon as the first satisfactory high-fitness program is created, but is instead continued until a number of high-fitness programs have been created. For simplicity, only pace-setting best-of-generation programs are harvested. Specifically, five different evolved programs were harvested from generations 34, 37, 40, 42, and 43 of our first run of this version of the problem. The programs harvested from generations 40 and 42 have an out-of-sample error rate of 1.6%, and the other three harvested programs have an out-of-sample error rate of 2%. All five of these programs are superior to the three human-written algorithms shown in Table 16.5 (with error rates of between 2.5% and 2.8%) based on the Kyte-Doolittle hydrophobicity values (Table 16.1). Other runs of this problem also produced programs with error rates that are superior to the error rates of human-produced algorithms for this problem.

Table 17.1 Tableau for the transmembrane segment identification problem with iteration creation

Objective	Discover, using architecture-altering operations including the operation of restricted iteration creation, a computer program to classify whether or not a segment of a protein sequence is a transmembrane domain.
Program architecture	One result-producing branch. Iteration-performing branch(es) and automatically defined function(s) and their arguments will be created during the run by the architecture-altering operations including the operation of restricted iteration creation.
Initial function set for the RPBs	$F_{rpb\text{-}initial}$ = {+, -, *, %, SETM0, SETM1, SETM2, SETM3, SETM4, SETM5, IFGTZ, ORN, (A?), (C?), . . . , (Y?)}
Initial terminal set for the RPBs	$T_{rpb\text{-}initial}$ = {$\Re_{bigger\text{-}reals}$, M0, LEN}
Initial function set for the ADFs	No automatically defined functions in generation 0. $F_{adf\text{-}initial}$ = ϕ.
Initial terminal set for the ADFs	No automatically defined functions in generation 0. $T_{adf\text{-}initial}$ = ϕ.
Initial function set for the IPBs	No iteration-performing branches in generation 0. $F_{adi\text{-}initial}$ = ϕ.
Initial terminal set for the IPBs	No iteration-performing branches in generation 0. $T_{adi\text{-}initial}$ = ϕ.
Potential function set for the RPBs	$F_{rpb\text{-}potential}$ = {ADF0, ADF1, ADF2}
Potential terminal set for the RPBs	$T_{rpb\text{-}potential}$ = {IPB0, IPB1, IPB2}
Potential function set for the ADFs	$F_{adf\text{-}potential}$ = {+, -, *, %, SETM0, SETM1, SETM2, SETM3, SETM4, SETM5, IFGTZ, ORN}
Potential terminal set for the ADFs	$T_{adf\text{-}potential}$ = {ARG0, ARG1, ARG2, ARG3, $\Re_{bigger\text{-}reals}$, M0, M1, M2, M3, M4, M5, LEN, (A?), (C?), . . . , (Y?)}.
Potential function set for the IPBs	$F_{adi\text{-}potential}$ = $F_{rpb\text{-}potential}$ = {ADF0, ADF1, ADF2}
Potential terminal set for the IPBs	$T_{adi\text{-}potential}$ = {$\Re_{bigger\text{-}reals}$, M0, M1, M2, M3, M4, M5, LEN, (A?), (C?), . . . , (Y?)}
Fitness cases	The in-sample set of fitness cases consists of 246 protein segments (half transmembrane domains and half not). The out-of-sample set of fitness cases consists of 250 protein segments (half transmembrane domains and half not).
Raw fitness	Correlation C (ranging from −1.0 to +1.0).
Standardized fitness	$1 - C/2$ (ranging from 0.0 to 1.0)
Hits	Not used for this problem

Wrapper	If the result-producing branch returns a number greater than 0, the segment is classified as a transmembrane domain; otherwise, the segment is classified as nontransmembrane.
Parameters	$M = 64{,}000$. $G = 1{,}001$. $Q = 1{,}000$. $D = 64$. $B = 5\%$. $N_{rpb} = 1$. $S_{rpb} = 200$. $S_{adf} = 200$. $S_{adi} = 200$. $N_{max\text{-}adf} = 4$. $N_{max\text{-}argument\text{-}adf} = 4$. $N_{min\text{-}argument\text{-}adf} = 0$. $N_{max\text{-}adi} = 3$.
Result designation	Best-so-far pace-setting individual
Success predicate	Fitness appears to have reached a plateau.

17.2.1 The Myopic Performance of the Best of Generation 0

The best-of-generation program for generation 0 has an in-sample correlation of 0.3108. Like all programs in generation 0, this program consists only of the result-producing branch. This 18-point program is

```
(SETM2 (* (SETM5 (SETM0 (ORN LEN M0))) (* (* (SETM4 LEN) (SETM4
(M?))) (% (SETM1 (W?)) (SETM4 (V?)))))).
```

Since this program has no iteration-performing branch, the residue-detecting functions (i.e., (M?), (W?), and (V?)) refer to the first residue of the protein segment. When simplified, this program returns +1 if the first residue of the protein segment is M (methionine), V (valine), or W (tryptophan), but returns –1 otherwise. M and V are hydrophobic on the Kyte-Doolittle hydrophobicity scale (Kyte and Doolittle 1982), and W is neutral.

This myopic best-of-generation program from generation 0 is fundamentally flawed in several respects. First, the character of the computation is Boolean, thereby ignoring the fact that different amino acid residues have different degrees of hydrophobicity and hydrophilicity. Second, this myopic program makes its decision for the entire protein segment based on an examination of only one residue, even though it is known that a correct decision requires integration of information over the entire segment. Third, this myopic program makes its decision based on checking only M or V and remains oblivious to the role of the other 18 amino acid residues. Thus, this program returns –1 for the approximately 90% of the protein segments that do not begin with M or V.

17.2.2 A Myopic Automatically Defined Iteration

Iteration-performing branches, automatically defined functions, and arguments for them are created by the architecture-altering operation during generation 1 (and all later generations of the run).

One early pace-setting program from generation 1 has a 26-point result-producing branch and a 14-point iteration-performing branch. The iteration-performing branch was created by the iteration creation operation. This individual achieves an in-sample correlation of 0.4702. However, even though the structure of this program includes an iteration-performing branch and even though this branch is iteratively executed, no avenue of communication is established between successive iterations of the iteration-

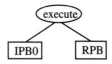

Figure 17.1 Architecture of early pace-setting program from generation 1

performing branch. Thus, there is no global integration of information across the protein segment. The classification of the entire protein segment is myopically made on the basis of just the last residue from the protein segment. Figure 17.1 shows the architecture of this program.

17.2.3 An Automatically Defined Iteration That Globally Integrates Information

A later pace-setting program from generation 1 uses its newly created iteration-performing branch to achieve a distinctly better value of in-sample correlation (0.5760). This program globally integrates information over the entire protein segment (although, as will be seen momentarily, the way that it globally integrates information is of limited utility).

The three-point result-producing branch of this program is

```
(ORN (IPB0) (L?)).
```

The value returned by the iteration-performing branch, IPB0, is used to communicate information between the iteration-performing branch and the result-producing branch.

The six-point iteration-performing branch, IPB0, of this program is

```
(% (SETM3 (ORN (K?) M3)) (E?)).
```

The amino acid residue K (lysine) is electrically charged and hydrophilic and therefore is comparatively rare in a transmembrane domain. The settable variable M3 is iteratively set to the ORN of the previous value of M3 and the value (−1 or +1) returned by the lysine-detecting function (K?). Since the value returned by the SETM3 on the final iteration equals −1 if there are no Ks in the segment, the effect is to scan the protein segment (averaging 23 residues) for the absence of Ks.

Note that the outcome of the test for E (glutamic acid) in the iteration-performing branch does not affect the value stored in M3 on each of the LEN executions of the iteration-performing branch. The (E?) function only becomes relevant for the very last residue of the segment (when the value returned by the entire iteration-performing branch is about to be passed to the result-producing branch). If there is no E at the end of the segment (and an E is comparatively rare in a transmembrane domain), (E?) returns −1, and the value (i.e., the quotient) returned by the iteration-performing branch, IPB0, is +1 if there are no Ks anywhere in the segment.

The result-producing branch then classifies the entire segment as a transmembrane domain if either the last residue is the hydrophobic residue L (leucine) or if there is an absence of hydrophilic Ks in the entire segment (and the segment does not end in E).

This program is superior to its predecessors in the run because it globally integrates information from the entire protein segment in order to make its classification decision. Tellingly, all succeeding pace-setting programs in this run have at least one iteration-performing branch that globally integrates information about the entire protein segment. This reflects the fact that iteration and global integration of information is so important for this problem that no program without it can be very fit. Notice that we did not tell genetic programming that this problem requires global integration of information and we did not instruct genetic programming to use iteration to accomplish the necessary integration. The decision to use iteration emerged during the run as a result of the competitive pressures of the problem's fitness measure.

This individual is flawed in many ways. First, it gives the last residue of the protein segment considerably more influence than the rest (both with respect to L and with respect to E). The first and last few residues of a protein segment are, in fact, least likely to accurately reflect the overall characteristics of the segment. Second, all 20 amino acid residues appear in both transmembrane domains and nontransmembrane areas of a protein (albeit with different frequencies). While a total absence of Ks is somewhat correlated with a protein segment being a transmembrane domain, there are many transmembrane domains with one (and sometimes more) Ks. Checking for the total absence of one particular amino acid residue is a very inadequate test.

17.2.4 An Automatically Defined Iteration That Computes a Running Sum

The first pace-setting program from generation 2 globally integrates information about the protein segment and achieves an in-sample correlation of 0.7224. Unlike its predecessor above, this program treats all residues in the protein segment in a uniform way. In particular, it does not do anything different for the last residue of the segment.

The one-point result-producing branch of this program returns the value of its eight-point iteration-performing branch, IPB0.

The iteration-performing branch, IPB0, of this program is

```
(SETM3 (+ (* (H?) (E?)) (+ (V?) M3))).
```

This iteration-performing branch computes a running sum and stores it in settable variable M3. Each hydrophobic V residue (+4.2 on the Kyte-Doolittle scale) contributes +1 to the running sum. Each residue that is neither E (–3.5 on the scale) nor H (–3.2 on the scale) contributes +1. An E or an H contributes –1.

A running sum is a much more sophisticated computation than the previously seen test for a total absence of Ks in the protein segment.

17.2.5 Emergence of a Subroutine

The pace-setting program from generation 6 consists of a one-argument automatically defined function, one iteration-performing branch, and a result-producing branch. Figure 17.2 shows the architecture of this program from generation 6, and Figure 17.3 shows its call tree. Although automatically defined functions were, of course, created by the architecture-altering operations as early as generation 1, this program is the first pace-setting program using an automatically defined function.

17.2.6 Emergence of Multiple Automatically Defined Iterations

The first pace-setting program from generation 8 has multiple iteration-performing branches. One of these iteration-performing branches globally integrates information over the entire protein segment.

Figure 17.2 Architecture of the best-of-generation program from generation 6

Figure 17.3 Call tree for the best-of-generation program from generation 6

17.2.7 Emergence of Cooperativity among Two Automatically Defined Iterations

The second pace-setting program from generation 11 has two iteration-performing branches that cooperatively integrate global information about the protein segment. The outcome of the overall program is significantly affected by both iteration-performing branches.

Its 12-point first iteration-performing branch, IPB0, is

```
(SETM3 (+ (* (H?) (E?)) (+ (ORN (SETM2 M0) (SET2 (W?))) M3))).
```

This first branch, IPB0, computes a running sum in settable variable M3. An increment of +2 is contributed by W (tryptophan), and −2 is contributed by either an E or an H (histidine). Other residues contribute nothing. The settable variable, M3, is used for communication between the first and second iteration-performing branches.

The eight-point second iteration-performing branch, IPB1 (which, interestingly, is identical to IPB0 of the program from generation 2 cited above), makes an additional contribution to memory cell M3 based on H, E, and V (valine) as follows:

```
(SETM3 (+ (* (H?) (E?)) (+ (V?) M3))).
```

This second branch, IPB1, makes an additional contribution to settable variable M3. An increment of +2 is contributed by V, and −2 is contributed by either an E or an H.

The one-point result-producing branch of this program is simply IPB1. That is, the terminal IPB1 is used for communication between the second iteration-performing branch and the final result-producing branch. The value of the result-producing branch can be expressed as a running sum in which an increment of +2 is contributed by each W and V, and −4 is contributed by each E and H.

Neither iteration-performing branch uses any automatically defined functions.

Figure 17.4 shows the call tree for the best-of-generation program from generation 11.

It would never occur to a human programmer to use two cooperating iteration-performing branches to compute a single running sum (such as M3 above). However, such cooperativity (to use the term used in the field of molecular biology) is commonplace among branches created by the architecture-altering operations. In this run, the first iteration-performing branch was part of the best-of-generation individual from generation 2. It made a positive contribution toward solving the problem as early as generation 2. An architecture-altering operation subsequently added the second iteration-performing branch. The second branch appearing in generation 11, in cooperation with

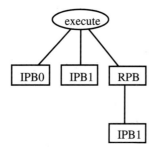

Figure 17.4 Call tree for the best-of-generation program from generation 11

the first branch, incrementally enhances the performance of the program over all its predecessors.

Cooperativity is commonplace among subunits of protein molecules in nature (Stryer 1995). For example, oxygen is transported in lamprey and hagfish by a molecule of hemoglobin possessing a single oxygen-binding site. This form of hemoglobin is monomeric—the molecule consists of a single subunit (with one oxygen-binding site). However, in most vertebrates, the hemoglobin molecule is tetrameric—it has four (nearly identical) subunits (each with its own oxygen-binding site). When a protein alignment (Section 4.1) is done, each of the four subunits of tetrameric hemoglobin is, in turn, similar to the monomeric form of hemoglobin found in lamprey and hagfish. The four subunits of tetrameric hemoglobin are known to be the consequence of a gene duplication arising from the earlier monomeric forms of hemoglobin found in lamprey and hagfish (Ohno 1970).

The four oxygen-binding sites of the four subunits of tetrameric hemoglobin are physically distant from one another. In spite of the physical distance, the four subunits of tetrameric hemoglobin cooperate: once oxygen manages to bind to one of the four binding sites, it becomes progressively easier for additional oxygen to bind to the molecule's remaining binding sites. This cooperative activity maximizes the amount of oxygen that binds to the molecule as it rushes through the lungs in blood. The cooperativity between the molecule's four distant binding sites occurs because information concerning the number of sites to which oxygen has already bound is mechanically communicated throughout the molecule (Perutz 1990, 1997; Dickerson and Geis 1983; Stryer 1995). Specifically, each successive insertion of an additional oxygen into the hemoglobin molecule progressively changes the conformation of the molecule. The conformation changes because of the breaking of certain chemical bonds (salt bridges) connecting the molecule's subunits and because of the physical expulsion of a companion molecule from the central cavity of the hemoglobin molecule. These physical changes relax the conformation of the molecule and make it more receptive to receiving additional oxygen.

The cooperativity of the two iteration-performing branches (which exist as a consequence of an architecture-altering operation in genetic programming) in computing M3 in the best-of-generation program from generation 11 resembles the cooperativity of the subunits of tetrameric hemoglobin (which exist as a consequence of a gene duplication in nature).

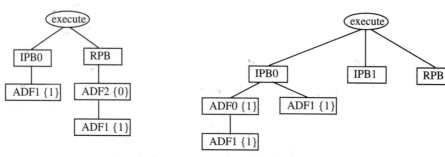

Figure 17.5 Call tree showing emergence of hierarchy in a pace-setting individual from processing node 48 of generation 26

Figure 17.6 Call tree for the best-of-generation program from generation 26

17.2.8 Emergence of Hierarchy among Subroutines

Computer programmers commonly organize sequences of primitive steps into useful groups (subroutines) and organize subroutines into hierarchies.

A pace-setting program from processing node 48 of generation 26 has a one-argument ADF1 and a zero-argument ADF2 such that ADF2 refers to ADF1. Figure 17.5 shows the call tree for the best-of-generation program from processing node 48 of generation 26.

17.2.9 Emergence of Multiple Subroutines and Multiple Automatically Defined Iterations

The next pace-setting program of generation 26 has two one-argument automatically defined functions as well as two iteration-performing branches. Figure 17.6 shows the call tree for the best-of-generation program from processing node 55 of generation 26.

17.2.10 Best-of-Run Program

The best-of-generation program of generation 42 scores 122 true positives, 122 true negatives, 1 false positive, and 1 false negative and has an in-sample correlation of 0.9938. For the out-of-sample fitness cases, this program scores 123 true positives, 123 true negatives, 2 false positives, and 2 false negatives and has an out-of-sample error rate of 1.6%. This error rate is superior to the error rate of the three human-written algorithms shown in Table 16.5 (with error rates of between 2.5% and 2.8%) based on the Kyte-Doolittle hydrophobicity values (Table 16.1). This best-of-run program (whose architecture is shown in Figure 17.7) has one result-producing branch, two one-argument automatically defined functions (ADF0 and ADF1), and two iteration-performing branches (IPB0 and IPB1) that cooperatively integrate global information about the protein segment. Figure 17.8 shows the call tree for the best-of-generation program from generation 42.

The one-point result-producing branch returns the value returned by the second iteration-performing branch, IPB1. The first automatically defined function, ADF0, has six points:

```
(ADF1 (+ (SETM0 (E?)) (SETM4 (Q?)))).
```

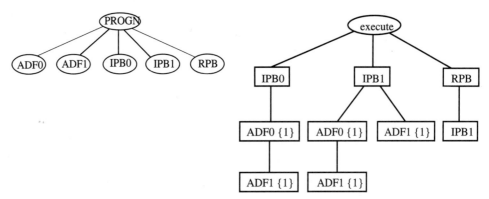

Figure 17.7 Architecture of the best-of-run program from generation 42

Figure 17.8 Call tree for the best-of-run program from generation 42

Notice that ADF0 hierarchically refers to ADF1. Since ADF1 merely returns its one argument, ADF0 returns 0 if the current residue is **E** or **Q** (glutamine) and otherwise returns −2. ADF0 also side-effects the settable variables M0 and M4.

The first iteration-performing branch, IPB0, has 112 points:

```
(SETM1 (- (- (SETM1 (SETM1 (- (SETM1 M1) (SETM3 (SETM3 (% (-
(I?) (R?)) (ADF0 (H?)))))))) (SETM3 (SETM3 (% (- (+ (V?) M3)
(SETM2 (+ (- (D?) (+ (V?) (SETM3 (+ (ORN (Y?) (* (E?) (SETM5
(ORN (P?) (D?))))) (+ (SETM5 (ORN M0 (L?))) M3))))) (SETM3
(R?))))) (ADF0 (% (SETM1 (- (- (SETM1 (SETM1 (- (SETM1 M1)
(SETM3 (SETM3 (% (- (I?) (R?)) (ADF0 (H?)))))))) (SETM3 (SETM3
(% (- (+ (V?) M3) (SETM2 (+ (- (* (SETM5 (ORN (P?) (R?)))
(SETM5 (ORN (P?) (D?)))) (L?)) (SETM3 (ORN (Q?) (% M5
(V?))))))) (SETM5 (ORN M0 (L?))))))) (SETM3 (SETM3 (% (- (F?)
(R?)) (ADF0 (H?)))))) (E?)))))) (SETM3 (SETM3 (% (- (F?)
(R?)) (ADF0 (H?)))))).
```

The second iteration-performing branch, IPB1, has 45 points:

```
(SETM1 (- (SETM1 M1) (SETM3 (SETM3 (% (- (I?) (ADF1 (* (SETM0
(SETM1 (ORN (ORN (P?) (R?)) (- (SETM1 M1) (SETM3 (SETM3 (IFGTZ
(SETM4 (- (Y?) (R?))) (SETM1 (Y?)) IPB0)))))) (SETM0 (* (SETM0
(ORN (K?) M0)) (SETM1 (ORN (SETM4 (SETM1 (SETM4 (P?))))
(Q?))))))))) (ADF0 (H?)))))).
```

Both possible avenues of communication between iterative branches are employed by this program. First, two of the six settable variables (M0 and M1) are set in IPB0 and referenced by IPB1 (as highlighted and underlined in boldface type in IPB1). Second, IPB1 contains a reference to the value returned by IPB0 (also highlighted and underlined in boldface type in IPB1).

In summary, genetic programming evolved a successful classifying program for the transmembrane segment identification problem using the architecture-altering operation of iteration creation for automatically defined iterations (along with the previously described architecture-altering operations for subroutines). The evolved program has two subroutines and two iterations. The subroutines are organized hierarchically, and the iterations work cooperatively. The evolved program has an error rate of 1.6%. This error rate is equal to that achieved with three other approaches using genetic programming (as shown in Table 16.5). This error rate of 1.6% for all four approaches using genetic programming is better than the error rate for the four algorithms described in Weiss, Cohen, and Indurkhya 1993. All four versions using genetic programming (none of which employs any foreknowledge of the biochemical concept of hydrophobicity) are instances of an automatically created algorithm whose performance is slightly superior to that of the algorithms written by knowledgeable human investigators.

We did not prespecify any of the following characteristics of the solution evolved in this chapter:

- that iterations should be used,
  - if iterations were to be used at all, the number of iterations,
- that subroutines should be used,
  - if subroutines were to be used at all, the number of subroutines,
  - if subroutines were to be used at all, the number of arguments that they would each possess,
- the precise number of steps in
  - the result-producing branch,
  - the subroutines,
  - the iteration-performing branches,
- the exact sequence of steps that would be performed in
  - the result-producing branch,
  - the subroutines,
  - the iteration-performing branches,
- the hierarchical organization of the program's branches.

All of the above characteristics of the evolved solution emerged during the run of genetic programming as a result of the architecture-altering operations for subroutines and iterations.

Fibonacci Sequence

Recursions are sometimes convenient in writing computer programs. Personal preference would largely determine whether a programmer writes a program for, say, the Boolean parity function using an iteration (counting the number of 1s among the inputs), one or more subroutines (as a hierarchy of lower-order parity functions), a decision tree containing a chain of conditional tests, or a recursion (taking successive two-parities until some base case is reached).

When first looking at a problem, it is usually not obvious whether recursion is necessary, helpful, or superfluous in solving a given problem. Even if recursion is known to be necessary, the number of recursions is usually not obvious. Even if the needed number of recursions is known, the construction of a useful recursion is nontrivial and requires the expenditure of a certain amount of programming effort. Therefore, it would be desirable to automate the decision of how many times, if any, to employ automatically defined recursions in solving a problem along with the related (and even more important) decision of exactly what recursive computation to perform. The architecture-altering operation for recursion creation provides a way to automate these decisions.

In attempting to illustrate the use of recursion in solving problems with genetic programming, we started with the even-parity problem. The problem invariably solved; however, the evolved solution was always based on one of the simpler programming constructs (e.g., iterations, subroutines, decision trees, or some combination of them). The reason was that solving a problem with recursion is often more intricate than solving the same problem by other means. Accordingly, we focus our attention on a problem whose solution is most conveniently expressed with a recursion.

18.1 STATEMENT OF THE PROBLEM

The goal is to find a one-input, one-output computer program that produces the values of the Fibonacci sequence. The well-known Fibonacci sequence

```
1, 1, 2, 3, 5, 8, 13, 21, 34, 55, 89, 144, 233, 377, 610, 987,
1,597, 2,584, 4,181, 6,765, . . .
```

can be computed for $j \geq 2$ using the recursive expression

$$s_j = s_{j-1} + s_{j-2}$$

(where s_0 and s_1 are both 1).

18.2 PREPARATORY STEPS

18.2.1 Program Architecture

Each program in generation 0 has a uniform architecture consisting of one result-producing branch and no automatically defined recursions.

After generation 0, the architecture-altering operation of recursion creation can create one-argument automatically defined recursions. The maximum size, S_{rpb}, for the result-producing branch is 100 points. The maximum size, S_{adr}, for each branch of an automatically defined recursion is 100 points. The maximum number of automatically defined recursions, $N_{max\text{-}adr}$, is one. Thus, an individual program in the population can have as many as 500 points.

18.2.2 Functions and Terminals

The initial function set for the result-producing branch, $F_{rpb\text{-}initial}$, is

$$F_{rpb\text{-}initial} = \{+, -, \text{IFLTZ}, \text{READ\_INPUT}, \text{WRITE\_OUTPUT}\},$$

taking 2, 2, 3, 1, and 2 arguments, respectively. The READ_INPUT function reads the problem's one input from the input vector. The WRITE_OUTPUT function deposits the program's answer into the output vector.

Since there are no automatically defined recursions in generation 0, the initial function set for the recursion condition branch, the recursion body branch, the recursion update branch, and the recursion ground branch are all empty:

$$F_{rcb\text{-}initial} = \phi,$$
$$F_{rbb\text{-}initial} = \phi,$$
$$F_{rub\text{-}initial} = \phi, \text{ and}$$
$$F_{rgb\text{-}initial} = \phi.$$

After generation 0, the architecture-altering operation of recursion creation can add an automatically defined recursion (consisting of four branches) and its dummy variable (ARG0) to individuals in the population.

The result-producing branch can invoke an automatically defined recursion that is created by the architecture-altering operation of recursion creation. Thus, the set of potential functions for the result-producing branch, $F_{rpb\text{-}potential}$, is

$$F_{rpb\text{-}potential} = \{\text{ADR0}\}.$$

The set of potential functions for the recursion condition branch (RCB), the recursion update branch (RUB), and the recursion ground branch (RGB) are

$$F_{rcb\text{-}potential} = \{+, -, \text{IFLTZ}, \text{READ\_INPUT}, \text{WRITE\_OUTPUT}\},$$
$$F_{rub\text{-}potential} = \{+, -, \text{IFLTZ}, \text{READ\_INPUT}, \text{WRITE\_OUTPUT}\}, \text{ and}$$
$$F_{rgb\text{-}potential} = \{+, -, \text{IFLTZ}, \text{READ\_INPUT}, \text{WRITE\_OUTPUT}\}.$$

Since the recursion body branch may refer to itself, the set of potential functions for the recursion body branch (RBB) is

$$F_{rbb\text{-}potential} = \{\text{ADR0}, +, -, \text{IFLTZ}, \text{READ\_INPUT}, \text{WRITE\_OUTPUT}\}.$$

The initial terminal set for the result-producing branch, $T_{rpb\text{-}initial}$, is

$$T_{rpb\text{-}initial} = \{\Re_{integers}\},$$

where $\Re_{integers}$ are integer random constants between −10 and +10.

Since there are no automatically defined recursions in generation 0, the initial terminal set for the recursion condition branch, the recursion body branch, the recursion update branch, and the recursion ground branch are all empty:

$$T_{rcb\text{-}initial} = \phi,$$
$$T_{rbb\text{-}initial} = \phi,$$
$$T_{rub\text{-}initial} = \phi, \text{ and}$$
$$T_{rgb\text{-}initial} = \phi.$$

The set of potential terminals for the result-producing branch, $T_{rpb\text{-}potential}$, is

$$T_{rpb\text{-}potential} = \phi.$$

The set of potential terminals for the recursion condition branch (RCB), the recursion body branch (RBB), the recursion update branch (RUB), and the recursion ground branch (RGB) are identical:

$$T_{rcb\text{-}potential} = \{\text{ARG0}, \Re_{integers}\},$$
$$T_{rbb\text{-}potential} = \{\text{ARG0}, \Re_{integers}\},$$
$$T_{rub\text{-}potential} = \{\text{ARG0}, \Re_{integers}\}, \text{ and}$$
$$T_{rgb\text{-}potential} = \{\text{ARG0}, \Re_{integers}\}.$$

18.2.3 Fitness

There are 12 fitness cases representing the first 12 elements of the Fibonacci sequence. Fitness is the sum, over the 12 fitness cases, of the absolute value of the difference between the value returned by the result-producing branch of the program and the correct value of the Fibonacci sequence.

The number of hits is defined as the number of fitness cases (from 0 to 12) for which the correct value of the Fibonacci sequence is returned by the result-producing branch of the program.

18.2.4 Parameters

This problem has several control parameters that have not appeared previously in this book.

The maximum number, $N_{max\text{-}adr\text{-}executions}$, of executions of an automatically defined recursion is 300. Note that this number must be chosen generously in order to accommodate the pyramid of recursive calls necessary to solve this problem. Also, this limit was chosen so that it could not be exploited by genetic programming in solving the problem.

Normally, the architecture-altering operations are performed sparingly (e.g., with percentages such as 0.5% and 1% on each generation). However, the goal here is to illustrate the dynamic creation during the run of genetic programming of an automatically defined recursion. Consequently, the architecture-altering operations are performed with an atypically high frequency on this particular problem. Up to generation 5, the percentage of operations is 25% recursion creation, 64% one-offspring crossover, 10% reproduction, and 1% mutation. Thereafter, the percentage of operations is 1% recursion creation, 89% one-offspring crossover, 9% reproduction, and 1% mutation.

The other control parameters for this problem are found in the tableau (Table 18.1), the tables of percentages of genetic operations in Appendix D, and the default values specified in Appendix D.

18.2.5 Tableau

Table 18.1 summarizes the key features of the Fibonacci sequence problem.

Table 18.1 Tableau for the Fibonacci sequence problem

Objective	Find a computer program that produces the values of the Fibonacci sequence.
Program architecture	One result-producing branch, RPB, in each program in generation 0. A one-argument automatically defined recursion (ADR0) and its dummy argument (ARG0) can be created during the run by the architecture-altering operation of recursion creation.
Initial function set for the RPBs	$F_{\text{rpb-initial}} = \{+, -, \text{IFLTZ}, \text{READ\_INPUT}, \text{WRITE\_OUTPUT}\}$
Initial terminal set for the RPBs	$T_{\text{rpb-initial}} = \{\Re_{\text{integers}}\}$
Initial function set for RCB, RUB, and RGB	$F_{\text{rcb-initial}} = \phi.$ $F_{\text{rub-initial}} = \phi.$ $F_{\text{rgb-initial}} = \phi.$
Initial terminal set for RCB, RUB, and RGB	$T_{\text{rcb-initial}} = \phi.$ $T_{\text{rub-initial}} = \phi.$ $T_{\text{rgb-initial}} = \phi.$
Initial function set for RBB	$F_{\text{rbb-initial}} = \phi$
Initial terminal set for RBB	$T_{\text{rbb-initial}} = \phi$
Potential function set for the RPBs	$F_{\text{rpb-potential}} = \{\text{ADR0}\}$
Potential terminal set for the RPBs	$T_{\text{rpb-potential}} = \phi$
Potential function set for RCB, RUB, and RGB	$F_{\text{rcb-potential}} = \{+, -, \text{IFLTZ}, \text{READ\_INPUT}, \text{WRITE\_OUTPUT}\}.$ $F_{\text{rub-potential}} = \{+, -, \text{IFLTZ}, \text{READ\_INPUT}, \text{WRITE\_OUTPUT}\}.$ $F_{\text{rgb-potential}} = \{+, -, \text{IFLTZ}, \text{READ\_INPUT}, \text{WRITE\_OUTPUT}\}.$
Potential terminal set for RCB, RUB, and RGB	$T_{\text{rcb-potential}} = \{\text{ARG0}, \Re_{\text{integers}}\}.$ $T_{\text{rub-potential}} = \{\text{ARG0}, \Re_{\text{integers}}\}.$ $T_{\text{rgb-potential}} = \{\text{ARG0}, \Re_{\text{integers}}\}.$
Potential function set for RBB	$F_{\text{rbb-potential}} = \{\text{ADR0}, +, -, \text{IFLTZ}, \text{READ\_INPUT}, \text{WRITE\_OUTPUT}\}$

Potential terminal set for RBB	$T_{\text{rbb-potential}} = \{\text{ARGO}, \Re_{\text{integers}}\}$.
Fitness cases	12 fitness cases representing the first 12 elements of the Fibonacci sequence
Raw fitness	The sum, over the 12 fitness cases, of the absolute value of the difference between the value returned by the result-producing branch of the program and the correct value of the Fibonacci sequence
Standardized fitness	Same as raw fitness
Hits	The number of fitness cases (0 to 12) for which the result-producing branch returns the correct value of the Fibonacci sequence
Wrapper	None
Parameters	$M = 600{,}000$. $G = 501$. $Q = 10{,}000$. $D = 60$. $B = 2\%$. $N_{\text{rpb}} = 1$. $S_{\text{rpb}} = 100$. $S_{\text{adr}} = 100$. $N_{\text{max-adr}} = 1$. $N_{\text{max-argument-adf}} = 1$.
Result designation	Best-so-far pace-setting individual
Success predicate	A program scores the maximum number (12) of hits.

18.3   RESULTS

The best-of-generation program from generation 0 of one run has a fitness of 195 and scores two hits. Like all programs in generation 0, the program consists of a single result-producing branch. The program has 70 points:

```
(+ (READ_INPUT -7) (+ (WRITE_OUTPUT (- (- (WRITE_OUTPUT
(READ_INPUT 1) (READ_INPUT 9)) (WRITE_OUTPUT (IFGTZ
(READ_INPUT -2) (- 1 -9) (+ 9 -1E+01)) (READ_INPUT 5))) (-
(READ_INPUT -7) (+ (+ (READ_INPUT 5) (READ_INPUT -9)) (+
(READ_INPUT 5) (READ_INPUT 3))))) (READ_INPUT 6)) (IFGTZ
(READ_INPUT (IFGTZ (READ_INPUT -2) (READ_INPUT -7) (READ_INPUT
0))) (READ_INPUT 8) (IFGTZ (READ_INPUT 9) (+ (- (READ_INPUT -3)
(IFGTZ (READ_INPUT 8) (READ_INPUT 5) (+ 5 7))) (READ_INPUT 6))
(READ_INPUT -1))))).
```

Starting in generation 1, some of the programs in the population have an automatically defined recursion. However, the best-of-generation program from generation 1 (which has fitness of 179 and scores one hit) does not employ recursion.

The first pace-setting individual to employ recursion appears in generation 2. This program has the following three-point result-producing branch:

```
(ADR0 (READ_INPUT -7))
```

and the following 17-point recursion body branch that invokes itself:

```
(+ (- (READ_INPUT 7) (- (IFGTZ (READ_INPUT 5) -4 1) (READ_INPUT
0))) (+ (ADR0 -3) (READ_INPUT 1))).
```

However, the fitness of this recursive program is poor (156), and it scores no hits.

By generation 24, all of the pace-setting individuals from the various processing nodes of the parallel computer system have a recursion. This reflects the discovery by genetic programming that recursion is helpful in solving this problem.

In generation 103, a pace-setting program appears that has a fitness of 0 and that scores 12 hits. The 34-point result-producing branch refers to automatically defined recursion ADR0:

```
(ADR0 (+ (READ_INPUT 1) (READ_INPUT (+ (READ_INPUT (READ_INPUT
(+ (+ (READ_INPUT (READ_INPUT (READ_INPUT (READ_INPUT -7))))
(READ_INPUT (+ (READ_INPUT (+ (+ 0 8) (READ_INPUT 5)))
(READ_INPUT (READ_INPUT -2))))) (+ (ADF3 2) -10))))
(READ_INPUT (READ_INPUT -2))))))).
```

The three-point recursion condition branch, RCB, is

```
(+ ARG0 -9).
```

The two-point recursion update branch, RUB, is

```
(READ_INPUT -9).
```

The 100-point recursion ground branch, RGB, is

```
(IFGTZ (WRITE_OUTPUT (READ_INPUT (+ (READ_INPUT (+ -2 (IFGTZ 5
-7 -7))) (READ_INPUT 8))) (READ_INPUT (READ_INPUT 1))) (IFGTZ
(- (WRITE_OUTPUT (WRITE_OUTPUT (READ_INPUT (READ_INPUT
(READ_INPUT -2))) (READ_INPUT (+ (WRITE_OUTPUT (READ_INPUT 1)
7) (READ_INPUT (READ_INPUT 0))))) (- (+ ARG0 -9) (WRITE_OUTPUT
(READ_INPUT -4) (READ_INPUT -4)))) (+ ARG0 -4)) (WRITE_OUTPUT
(WRITE_OUTPUT (READ_INPUT (+ (+ ARG0 -7) -1E+01)) (READ_INPUT
-3)) (READ_INPUT -4)) (WRITE_OUTPUT (- (+ ARG0 -9)
(WRITE_OUTPUT (WRITE_OUTPUT (READ_INPUT (READ_INPUT
(READ_INPUT -2))) (READ_INPUT -3)) (READ_INPUT -4)))
(READ_INPUT -1))) (IFGTZ (WRITE_OUTPUT -4 (READ_INPUT ARG0)) 3
(+ (IFGTZ (READ_INPUT (READ_INPUT -7)) (READ_INPUT (READ_INPUT
1)) (+ ARG0(- 5 0))) (+ (READ_INPUT 8) (+ -4 (READ_INPUT
5))))))).
```

The 97-point recursion body branch, RBB, has five invocations of ADR0:

```
(+ (+ (ADR0 (+ ARG0 -7)) (ADR0 (+ ARG0 -5))) (IFGTZ (- (ADF3 (+
ARG0 -4)) (IFGTZ ARG0(+ 8 1) (READ_INPUT 0))) (IFGTZ (IFGTZ (-
(IFGTZ (READ_INPUT 5) (READ_INPUT (ADR0 -7)) (READ_INPUT -9))
(+ ARG0 -5)) (READ_INPUT (+ (+ (READ_INPUT -4) (READ_INPUT (+
(- 9 -7) (- (ADR0 2) (- 9 -8))))) 5)) (WRITE_OUTPUT (- (+ ARG0
-9) (+ (READ_INPUT (+ -4 (READ_INPUT (READ_INPUT 0))))) (IFGTZ
(+ (READ_INPUT -9) -7) 0 -5))) (READ_INPUT (+ ARG0 -9))))
```

```
(READ_INPUT (+ ARG0 -9)) (+ ARG0(- (ADR0 2) (- 9 -7)))) (+
ARG0(- (READ_INPUT -3) (- 9 -8)))))).
```

The above evolved program accurately generates the first 12 elements of the Fibonacci sequence. Moreover, automatically defined recursions are used in a nondegenerate way. The recursion is actively controlled and terminated at the correct moment by the recursion condition branch. In particular, the program never reaches the preestablished maximum number, $N_{\text{max-adr-executions}}$, of executions of an automatically defined recursion (300 for this problem).

The evolved program did not generalize beyond the first 12 elements of the Fibonacci sequence.

Cart Centering

Memory (internal storage) is convenient, and sometimes necessary, when writing computer programs. But it is usually not obvious, when first looking at a problem, whether memory is necessary, helpful, or superfluous in solving a given problem. Even if memory is known to be necessary, the amount and type of memory may not be obvious. The architecture-altering operations for creating or deleting automatically defined stores (ADSs) provide a way to automate the decision as to the amount and type of internal storage, if any, to use in solving a problem.

This chapter considers a special version of the well-known cart-centering (isotropic rocket) problem in which internal storage is necessary in order to solve the problem.

19.1 STATEMENT OF THE PROBLEM

The goal is to find a time-optimal strategy for continuously controlling the movement of a cart along a frictionless one-dimensional track that brings the cart to rest at the origin, using only information about the cart's current position.

In this problem, the position of the cart can be changed by applying a fixed-magnitude (bang-bang) force to the cart so as to accelerate the cart toward the left (the negative direction) or the right (the positive direction) along the horizontal track. The goal is to bring the cart to rest (i.e., velocity 0.0) at the origin (i.e., position 0.0) in minimal time.

Figure 19.1 shows a cart at position $x(t)$ at time t. The position of the cart in the figure is negative, its velocity $v(t)$ is positive, and the bang-bang force is being applied so as to accelerate the cart in the positive direction (i.e., toward the right).

The well-known time-optimal solution to this problem (Macki and Strauss 1982; Bryson and Ho 1975; Koza 1992e, Section 7.1) is to apply the bang-bang force F to accelerate the cart in the positive direction if

$$
-x(t) > \frac{v(t)^2 \operatorname{Sign} v(t)}{\dfrac{2|F|}{m}}
$$

and, otherwise, to apply the bang-bang force F to accelerate the cart in the negative direction. The Sign function returns +1 for a positive argument and −1 otherwise. If the mass of the cart m happens to be 2.0 kilograms and the force F is 1.0 newtons, the denominator $\dfrac{2|F|}{m}$ equals 1.0 and can be hereafter ignored.

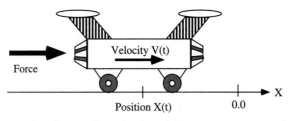

Figure 19.1 Cart-centering (isotropic rocket) problem

In the special and more difficult version of this problem being considered in this chapter, the goal is to bring the cart to rest at the origin in minimal time *while using only information about the cart's horizontal position*. The time-optimal solution to this problem is known to require consideration of both the cart's current velocity $v(t)$ and position $x(t)$. The problem simply cannot be solved without $v(t)$. In fact, for every positive (and negative) value of position, there exists a range of values of velocity for which the optimal strategy calls for a negative bang-bang force, and another range of values of velocity for which the optimal strategy calls for a positive bang-bang force. Nonetheless, if the control strategy has access to an earlier position of the cart, the velocity $v(t)$ can be closely estimated by subtracting the remembered position and the cart's current horizontal position $x(t)$. That is, if the control strategy has internal storage, it becomes possible to solve the problem using only $x(t)$ as input.

The user can make internal storage available for solving a problem either by

- explicitly including one or more memory reading and memory writing functions in the function set of the problem (as part of the second preparatory step for a run of genetic programming) or
- using the architecture-altering operation of storage creation (Section 9.1.1) to enable genetic programming to add automatically defined stores during the run.

We illustrate the latter approach below.

19.2 PREPARATORY STEPS

19.2.1 Program Architecture

Each program in generation 0 has a minimalist architecture consisting of one result-producing branch. In particular, the programs in generation 0 do not contain any automatically defined stores.

After generation 0, the architecture-altering operation of storage creation will add internal storage to some programs in the population. The maximum number of automatically defined stores for any program, $N_{\text{max-ads}}$, is 3. The maximum dimensionality of the created memory, $N_{\text{max-ads-dimension}}$, is 0, and named memory is the only type of memory permitted. Thus, after generation 0, programs in the population will have 0, 1, 2, or 3 cells of named memory.

19.2.2   Functions and Terminals

The initial terminal set for the result-producing branch, $T_{rpb\text{-}initial}$, consists of the one externally supplied floating-point input (i.e., the cart's current position) and floating-point random constants:

$$T_{rpb\text{-}initial} = \{X, \Re_{smaller\text{-}reals}\}.$$

Note that the velocity of the cart is not included in the terminal set.

The initial function set for the result-producing branch, $F_{rpb\text{-}initial}$, consists of four two-argument arithmetic functions and the one three-argument IFGTZ ("if greater than zero") conditional branching operator:

$$F_{rpb\text{-}initial} = \{+, -, *, \%, IFGTZ\}.$$

Since there are no automatically defined functions in this problem, $T_{adf\text{-}initial}$, $F_{adf\text{-}initial}$, $T_{adf\text{-}potential}$, and $T_{rpb\text{-}potential}$ are empty.

The set of potential terminals, $T_{rpb\text{-}potential}$, for the result-producing branch is

$$T_{rpb\text{-}potential} = \{SRB0, SRB1, SRB2\}.$$

The set of potential functions, $F_{rpb\text{-}potential}$, for the result-producing branch is

$$F_{rpb\text{-}potential} = \{SWB0, SWB1, SWB2\}.$$

19.2.3   Fitness

Fitness is measured over 20 randomly chosen initial conditions for the cart, each consisting of the cart's initial position $x(0)$ and initial velocity $v(0)$. The initial positions range between –0.75 and +0.75 meters. The initial velocities range between –0.75 and +0.75 meters per second. Note that although the cart has an initial velocity, this value is not available to the control strategy.

For each fitness case, the behavior of the cart is simulated over a total of 500 time steps, each representing 0.02 seconds. The individual program is executed for each of these time steps. A wrapper interprets the numeric value returned by the execution of an individual program. Any positive value is interpreted as calling for a positive bang-bang force and any nonpositive value is interpreted as calling for a negative bang-bang force. As usual, the memory is initialized to zero at the beginning of each fitness case (but not at each time step of the simulation for a particular fitness case).

If the square root of the sum of the square of the cart's velocity and the square of the cart's position is less than 0.01 (the capture radius), the cart is considered to have come to rest at the origin. If the cart fails to come to rest for a particular fitness case within the allotted time (10 seconds), the contribution to fitness for that fitness case is 10 seconds (the maximum).

Fitness is the sum, over the 20 fitness cases, of the times for the cart to come to rest at the origin. A smaller value of fitness is better.

The number of hits is defined as the number of fitness cases (from 0 to 20) for which the cart comes to rest at the origin within the allotted time (i.e., does not time out).

19.2.4 Parameters

The control parameters for this chapter are in the tableau (Table 19.1), the tables of percentages of genetic operations in Appendix D of this book, and the default values specified in Appendix D of this book.

19.2.5 Termination

The optimal value of fitness for the 20 randomly chosen fitness cases actually used in this problem is known to be 46.54 seconds.

19.2.6 Tableau

Table 19.1 summarizes the key features of the cart-centering problem.

19.3 RESULTS

The best-of-generation program for generation 0 scores 3 hits (out of 20) and has a fitness of 176.1.

The first pace-setting program with internal storage appears at generation 3. The program has two cells of named memory, but only one of the two is actually referenced. The individual scores 4 hits and has a fitness of 170.1.

The first pace-setting program to score 20 hits (out of 20) appears in generation 11 and has a fitness of 81.83.

The best-of-run program emerges on generation 104, scores 20 hits (out of 20), and has a fitness of 46.54 (i.e., the known optimal value). The result-producing branch of the best-of-run program has 486 points. The best-of-run program has two automatically defined stores. The best-of-run program does indeed use internal storage. Specifically, it contains one reference to the first storage writing branch, SWB0, and two references to the first storage reading branch, SRB0. It also contains one reference to the second storage writing branch, SWB1, and one reference to the second storage reading branch, SRB1. An examination of the step-by-step operation of the best-of-run program over the 500 time steps for each of the 20 fitness cases indicates that the automatically created internal storage is actively used.

This problem establishes the principle that internal storage can be automatically created and successfully used in solving a problem.

Table 19.1 Tableau for the cart-centering problem

Objective	Find, using only information about the cart's current position, a time-optimal strategy for continuously controlling the movement of a cart along a frictionless one-dimensional track that brings the cart to rest at the origin.
Program architecture	One result-producing branch, RPB, in generation 0. Automatically defined stores will be created during the run by the architecture-altering operation of storage creation.
Initial function set for the RPBs	$F_{rpb\text{-}initial}$ = {+, -, *, %, IFGTZ}
Initial terminal set for the RPBs	$T_{rpb\text{-}initial}$ = {x, $\Re_{smaller\text{-}reals}$}
Initial function set for the ADFs	No automatically defined functions
Initial terminal set for the ADFs	No automatically defined functions
Potential function set for the RPBs	$F_{rpb\text{-}potential}$ = {SWB0, SWB1, SWB2}
Potential terminal set for the RPBs	$T_{rpb\text{-}potential}$ = {SRB0, SRB1, SRB2}
Potential function set for the ADFs	No automatically defined functions
Potential terminal set for the ADFs	No automatically defined functions
Fitness cases	20 randomly chosen initial conditions for the cart's velocity and position
Raw fitness	The sum, over the 20 fitness cases, of the times for the cart to come to rest at the origin
Standardized fitness	Same as raw fitness
Hits	Number of fitness cases (from 0 to 20) for which the cart comes to rest at the origin within the allotted time (i.e., does not time out)
Wrapper	The wrapper interprets any positive value as a positive bang-bang force and any nonpositive value as a negative bang-bang force.
Parameters	M = 128,000. G = 201. Q = 2,000. D = 64. B = 2%. N_{rpb} = 1. S_{rpb} = 500. $N_{max\text{-}ads}$ = 3. $N_{max\text{-}ads\text{-}dimension}$ = 0.
Result designation	Best-so-far pace-setting individual
Success predicate	Fitness attains a value of 46.54 seconds.

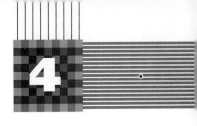

Part 4: THE GENETIC PROGRAMMING PROBLEM SOLVER

The Genetic Programming Problem Solver (GPPS) is a general-purpose method for automatically creating a computer program to solve a problem. GPPS addresses the central aim of machine learning and artificial intelligence—to get a computer to solve a problem without explicitly telling it how to do it. In particular, GPPS is a form of genetic programming that eliminates the need for the user to specify the function set and terminal set prior to applying genetic programming to a problem. GPPS eliminates the first and second major preparatory steps of genetic programming by employing a standardized set of functions and terminals.

In addition, GPPS eliminates the need for the user to prespecify whether to employ subroutines and loops in solving a given problem by using the architecture-altering operations during the run of genetic programming to create, duplicate, and delete subroutines and loops (and, in version 2 of GPPS, recursions and internal storage). Moreover, if a program contains subroutines (automatically defined functions), GPPS also eliminates the need for the user to prespecify the number of arguments possessed by each subroutine and whether and how the subroutines refer to one another.

Specifically, Chapter 20 describes version 1 of the Genetic Programming Problem Solver. GPPS 1.0 is capable of automatically creating computer programs with

- various numbers of inputs,
- various numbers of outputs,
- a main result-producing branch consisting of a to-be-evolved sequence of steps,
- to-be-evolved numbers of automatically defined functions, each possessing
  - a to-be-evolved number of arguments and to-be-evolved hierarchical references to one another
  - a to-be-evolved sequence of steps,
- to-be-evolved numbers of automatically defined loops, each consisting of
  - a loop initialization branch consisting of a to-be-evolved sequence of steps,
  - a loop condition branch consisting of a to-be-evolved sequence of steps,

- a loop body branch consisting of a to-be-evolved sequence of steps, and
- a loop update branch consisting of a to-be-evolved sequence of steps, and
- a fixed number of cells of indexed memory.

Chapter 21 illustrates GPPS 1.0 by applying it to the following problems:

- symbolic regression of Boolean parity functions (originally solved in Chapter 12 using architecture-altering operations and solved yet again in Section 23.4 using GPPS 2.0),
- the time-optimal robot controller (originally solved in Chapter 13, solved again in Section 23.5 using GPPS 2.0, and solved yet again in Chapter 48 using an electrical circuit), and
- synthesis of the design of a minimal sorting network (solved in Section 23.6 using GPPS 2.0 and solved yet again in Chapter 57 using evolvable hardware and field-programmable gate arrays).

Chapter 22 describes GPPS 2.0. It has the additional capability of handling programs with

- an initially unspecified number of automatically defined recursions, each consisting of
  - a recursion condition branch consisting of a to-be-evolved sequence of steps,
  - a recursion body branch consisting of a to-be-evolved sequence of steps,
  - a recursion update branch consisting of a to-be-evolved sequence of steps,
  - a recursion ground branch consisting of a to-be-evolved sequence of steps, and
- internal storage of an initially unspecified number and type as implemented by automatically defined stores (which are in lieu of the indexed memory of GPPS 1.0).

Chapter 23 illustrates GPPS 2.0 by applying it to

- symbolic regression of a quadratic polynomial (Section 23.1),
- the intertwined spirals problem (Section 23.2),
- the cart-centering problem (Section 23.3),
- the Boolean even-6-parity problem (Section 23.4),
- the time-optimal robot controller problem (Section 23.5), and
- the problem of synthesizing the design of a minimal sorting network (Section 23.6).

Subroutines, iterations, recursions, and internal storage are all included in the problem-solving arsenal of one or both versions of the Genetic Programming Problem Solver. The decision to use (or not use) subroutines, iterations, recursions, and internal storage is an automatic and integral part of the evolutionary process during the run of genetic programming. Both versions of GPPS rely on Darwinian selection to cause programs with architectures that are suitable for solving a given problem to grow and prosper in the evolving population. Thus, the human user is relieved of the task of deciding whether to use subroutines, iterations, recursions, and internal storage.

Elements of GPPS 1.0

When we talk about a computer program, we mean an entity (as depicted in Figure 1.1) that receives certain inputs, performs various operations on them, and produces certain outputs. The vast majority of problems in *Genetic Programming* (Koza 1992e), *Genetic Programming II* (Koza 1994g), and this book involve the four arithmetic functions of addition, subtraction, multiplication, and division and a conditional branching operator (e.g., the three-argument "if greater than zero" IFGTZ). It should be no surprise that arithmetic and conditional functions have proven to be well suited for a broad range of problems. These primitive functions constitute the core of the repertoire of primitive machine code instructions for virtually every general-purpose computer that has ever been built. Human programmers have found them very useful in solving a broad range of problems.

Computer programs typically process variables of many different types (e.g., Boolean-valued variables, integer-valued variables, and floating-point variables). Floating-point variables subsume both Boolean and integer variables since a floating-point variable can be readily interpreted as a Boolean or integer variable. Specifically, an integer variable can be represented by a floating-point number by adopting the convention that each variable that is required to be integral will be floored (i.e., reduced to the largest integer less than or equal to it). Similarly, a Boolean variable can be represented by a floating-point number by adopting the convention that a positive floating-point number represents the Boolean value of TRUE and a zero or negative floating-point number represents FALSE.

The inputs to the to-be-evolved computer programs can, without loss of generality and without a significant sacrifice in convenience, be received in an input vector. The outputs can be similarly handled by means of an output vector. Problem-specific side-effecting functions (e.g., robotic control functions) can be handled, without loss of generality, by means of an output vector (and interpreter).

Figure 20.1 shows the flow of information in a computer program using version 1.0 of the Genetic Programming Problem Solver. The program in the figure has an input vector (of size N1), an output vector (of size N2), and indexed memory (of size N3). GPPS 1.0 programs potentially may have zero, one, or more automatically defined functions and zero, one, or more automatically defined loops. The automatically defined function(s) can each possess zero, one, or more arguments.

Specifically, GPPS 1.0 employs the following functions and terminals:

- arithmetic functions:
  - addition (+),
  - subtraction (−),

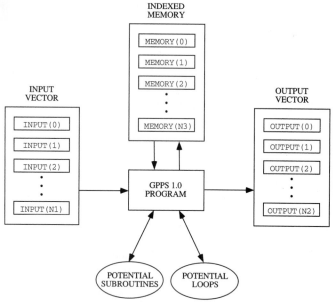

Figure 20.1 Flow of information in a computer program using GPPS 1.0

- multiplication (*), and
- protected division %.
- conditional branching operators:
  - "if greater than zero" IFGTZ and
  - "if equal zero" IFEQZ.
- numerically valued logical functions:
  - conjunction TAND,
  - disjunction TOR, and
  - negation TNOT.
- input reading function:
  - "read linear input" RLI.
- writing and reading functions for indexed memory:
  - "write indexed memory" WIM and
  - "read indexed memory" RIM.
- output writing and reading functions:
  - "write linear output" WLO and
  - "read linear output" RLO.
- conversion function:
  - FLOOR.
- terminals:
  - floating-point random constants, $\Re_{\text{bigger-reals}}$,
  - a constant specifying the number of inputs, NINPUTS,
  - a constant specifying the number of outputs, NOUTPUTS, and
  - the loop index, INDEX.

- potential automatically defined functions (Chapter 5), such as
  - ADF0,
  - ADF1,
  - ADF2, and
  - ADF3.
- potential terminals representing the dummy variables (formal parameters) of the potential automatically defined functions (Chapter 5), such as
  - ARG0,
  - ARG1,
  - ARG2, and
  - ARG3.
- potential terminals representing the return value of the loop body branch of each potential automatically defined loop (Chapter 7), such as
  - LBB0 and
  - LBB1.

Let's look at some of these in more detail. In addition to the floating-point random constants (Section 13.3.2), the terminal set of GPPS 1.0 includes the following terminals:

- NINPUTS is an externally established, invariant terminal that specifies the number of input(s) for the problem in the input vector.
- NOUTPUTS is an externally established, invariant terminal that specifies the number of output(s) for the problem in the output vector.
- INDEX is the loop index for automatically defined loops. It is externally initialized to zero prior to execution of a program for each fitness case. It remains zero if there are no automatically defined loops in the program. It is externally initialized to zero at the beginning of execution of each automatically defined loop. It is externally incremented by one after the end of each execution of a loop update branch. If it is referenced outside of an automatically defined loop, it returns its leftover value.

In addition to the IFGTZ conditional branching operator (Section 13.3.2) and the arithmetic functions (Section 13.3.2), the function set of GPPS 1.0 includes IFEQZ. IFEQZ ("if equal zero") is the three-argument conditional branching operator that evaluates and returns its second argument if its first argument (the condition) is equal to zero, but otherwise evaluates and returns its third argument (Section 13.3.2).

There are three numerically valued logical functions:

- TAND is the two-argument numerical-valued conjunctive function returning a floating-point +1.0 if both of its arguments are positive, but returning –1.0 otherwise. TAND is a short-circuiting (optimized) function. In particular, its second argument will not be evaluated (and any side-effecting function contained therein will remain unexecuted) if its first argument is negative.
- TOR is the two-argument numerical-valued disjunctive function returning a floating-point +1.0 if one or both of its arguments are positive, but returning –1.0 otherwise. TOR is also a short-circuiting (optimized) function.
- TNOT is the one-argument numerical-valued negation function returning a floating-point +1.0 if its argument is negative, but returning –1.0 otherwise.

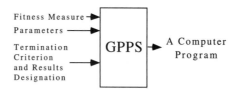

Figure 20.2   Three preparatory steps with the Genetic Programming Problem Solver

Additional functions include the following:

- RLI ("read linear input") is a one-argument function that returns the value of the element of the input vector specified by the argument. The argument is adjusted by flooring it and then taking it modulo the size (NINPUTS) of the input vector.
- WIM ("write indexed memory") is a two-argument function that writes the value returned by the first argument into the location of indexed memory specified by the second argument (adjusted in the same manner as above based on the size of indexed memory).
- RIM ("read indexed memory") is a one-argument function that returns the value of the element of the vector of indexed memory specified by the argument (adjusted in the same manner as above based on the size of the indexed memory).
- WLO ("write linear output") is a two-argument function that writes the value returned by the first argument into the location in the output vector specified by the second argument (adjusted in the same manner as above based on the size, NOUTPUTS, of the output vector).
- RLO ("read linear output") is a one-argument function that reads the location in the output vector specified by the argument (adjusted in the same manner as for WLO). This function enables the output vector to be used as an additional area of indexed memory.
- FLOOR is the one-argument conversion function that floors its argument by reducing it to the next lower integer.

All cells of indexed memory and all cells of the output vector are initialized to zero for each set of inputs (i.e., each fitness case). Note that if the fitness evaluation of a program requires that it be run through a series of time steps, neither the indexed memory nor the output vector are initialized between time steps.

For practical reasons, since the initialization, updating, and terminating of the iteration is controlled by branches that will be subject to vicissitudes of the evolutionary process, the total number of iterations that can be performed by any one iteration-performing branch is rationed.

When GPPS is used to solve a problem, the program architecture, the function set, and the terminal set do not change from problem to problem. That is, the first and second preparatory steps of genetic programming are eliminated. Thus, as shown in Figure 20.2, there are only three problem-specific preparatory steps with GPPS: determining the fitness measure, determining the run's control parameters, and determining the termination criterion and the method of result designation. GPPS makes it especially clear that the determination of the fitness measure (the third major preparatory step of genetic programming) is, as a general rule, the most important preparatory step in applying genetic programming to a problem.

Three Problems Illustrating GPPS 1.0

This chapter illustrates GPPS 1.0 by applying it to the following problems:

- symbolic regression of Boolean parity functions of order 6, 5, 4, and 3 (Sections 21.1 and 21.2),
- the time-optimal robot controller problem (Section 21.3), and
- synthesis of the design of a minimal sorting network (Section 21.4).

21.1 EVEN-6-PARITY PROBLEM WITH GPPS 1.0

This section applies GPPS 1.0 to the six-input, one-output problem of symbolic regression of the Boolean even-6-parity function. This problem was originally solved in Chapter 12 using architecture-altering operations and is solved yet again in Section 23.4 using GPPS 2.0.

A Boolean parity problem is especially suitable for purposes of illustration of GPPS because this problem can be solved in several distinct ways:

1. The problem can be solved with a single result-producing branch without subroutines or loops. A one-branch solution to this problem might contain a composition of the primitive Boolean functions of disjunction, conjunction, and negation and conditional branching operations (such as IFEQZ and IFGTZ).
2. The even-6-parity problem can be solved using one or more automatically defined functions. Such subroutines might perform some useful lower-order Boolean function (such as a lower-order parity function). The subroutines may or may not call each other.
3. The problem can be solved using an automatically defined loop that sums the six Boolean inputs and tests the sum to see whether it is even or odd.
4. The problem can be solved in the style of a decision tree with a chain of conditional branching operations.
5. The foregoing approaches can be combined in numerous different ways.

We specifically chose the six-argument version of the Boolean parity problem (as opposed to a lower-order version of this problem) in the hope of discouraging pedestrian solutions that employ only a single result-producing branch.

21.1.1 Preparatory Steps

Program Architecture

When GPPS 1.0 is being used, each program in generation 0 has a uniform architecture consisting of one result-producing branch. There are no automatically defined functions or automatically defined loops in generation 0.

After generation 0, GPPS 1.0 uses the architecture-altering operations to create, duplicate, and delete automatically defined functions and to determine the number of arguments possessed by each automatically defined function. Hierarchical references are allowed among the automatically defined functions created by the architecture-altering operations. Similarly, GPPS 1.0 uses the architecture-altering operations to create, duplicate, and delete automatically defined loops.

For practical reasons, a maximum of four automatically defined functions, each possessing between zero and four arguments, is established for this problem. Similarly, a maximum of two automatically defined loops (each consisting of a loop initialization branch, a loop condition branch, a loop body branch, and a loop update branch) is established for this problem.

Functions and Terminals

When GPPS 1.0 is being used, the function and terminal sets do not change from problem to problem.

The initial function set for the result-producing branch, $F_{rpb\text{-}initial}$, is

$F_{rpb\text{-}initial}$ = {+, -, *, %, IFLTE, IFEQZ, TOR, TAND, TNOT, RLI, WIM, RIM, WLO, RLO, FLOOR},

taking 2, 2, 2, 2, 4, 3, 2, 2, 1, 1, 2, 1, 2, 1, and 1 arguments, respectively.

Since there are no automatically defined functions in generation 0, the initial function set for automatically defined functions, $F_{adf\text{-}initial}$, is empty:

$F_{adf\text{-}initial} = \phi$.

Since there are no automatically defined loops in generation 0, the initial function set for the four branches of the automatically defined loops, $F_{adl\text{-}initial}$, is empty:

$F_{adl\text{-}initial} = \phi$.

After generation 0, the architecture-altering operations introduce automatically defined loops (each consisting of four branches), automatically defined functions, and the dummy variables possessed by the automatically defined functions. As a result, individuals in the population begin to contain invocations of the newly created automatically defined functions (ADF0, ADF1, ADF2, and ADF3), and references to terminals representing the dummy variables of the newly created automatically defined functions (ARG0, ARG1, ARG2, and ARG3). In addition, individuals in the population begin to contain terminals representing the return values of the loop body branches (LBB0 and LBB1) of automatically defined loops ADL0 and ADL1.

The set of potential functions for the result-producing branch, $F_{rpb\text{-}potential}$, is

$$F_{\text{rpb-potential}} = \{\text{ADF0, ADF1, ADF2, ADF3}\}.$$

The potential automatically defined functions take an as-yet-unknown number of arguments (between zero and four).

The set of potential functions for the four branches of each automatically defined loop, $F_{\text{adl-potential}}$, is

$$F_{\text{adl-potential}} = \{\text{ADF0, ADF1, ADF2, ADF3, +, -, *, \%,IFLTE, IFEQZ,}$$
$$\text{TOR, TAND, TNOT, RLI, WIM, RIM, WLO, RLO, FLOOR}\}.$$

Similarly, the potential function set for the automatically defined functions, $F_{\text{adf-potential}}$, is

$$F_{\text{adf-potential}} = \{\text{ADF0, ADF1, ADF2, ADF, +, -, *, \%,IFLTE, IFEQZ,}$$
$$\text{TOR, TAND, TNOT, RLI, WIM, RIM, WLO, RLO, FLOOR}\},$$

subject to our usual limitation that a function-defining branch can refer hierarchically only to a previously defined function-defining branch.

The initial terminal set for the result-producing branch, $T_{\text{rpb-initial}}$, is

$$T_{\text{rpb-initial}} = \{\text{NINPUTS, NOUTPUTS, INDEX, } \Re_{\text{bigger-reals}}\}.$$

For the even-6-parity problem, the size, NINPUTS, of the input vector is 6 and the size, NOUTPUTS, of the output vector is 1.

Since there are no automatically defined functions in generation 0, the initial terminal set for automatically defined functions, $T_{\text{adf-initial}}$, is empty:

$$T_{\text{adf-initial}} = \phi.$$

Since there are no automatically defined loops in generation 0, the initial terminal set for the four branches of the automatically defined loops, $T_{\text{adl-initial}}$, is empty:

$$T_{\text{adl-initial}} = \phi.$$

The set of potential terminals for the result-producing branch, $T_{\text{rpb-potential}}$, is

$$T_{\text{rpb-potential}} = \{\text{LBB0, LBB1}\}.$$

The set of potential terminals for the automatically defined functions, $T_{\text{adf-potential}}$, is

$$T_{\text{adf-potential}} = \{\text{ARG0, ARG1, ARG2, ARG3, NINPUTS, NOUTPUTS, INDEX,}$$
$$\Re_{\text{bigger-reals}}\}.$$

The set of potential terminals for the four branches of the automatically defined loops, $T_{\text{adl-potential}}$, is

$$T_{\text{adl-potential}} = \{\text{NINPUTS, NOUTPUTS, INDEX, } \Re_{\text{bigger-reals}}\}.$$

Note that a program tree in GPPS contains floating-point random constants and floating-point arithmetic functions. Thus, the programs typically deposit a floating-point value in the output vector. For the even-6-parity problem, a wrapper (output interface) consisting of the IFGTZ ("if greater than zero") operator is used to convert the value deposited into the output vector (a floating-point number) into a binary outcome (+1.0 and −1.0).

Fitness

The fitness cases for this problem consist of the set of $2^6 = 64$ possible combinations of the six Boolean inputs (0.000 and +1.000) in the input vector. The standardized fitness of an individual program in the population is the sum, over the 64 fitness cases, of the absolute value of the difference (Hamming distance) between the value returned by the result-producing branch (after interpretation by the wrapper) and the correct value of the Boolean even-6-parity function.

Parameters

This problem has several control parameters that have not appeared previously in this book:

- The size, NINDEXED, of indexed memory is 20.
- The maximum number, $N_{max\text{-}adl}$, of automatically defined loops is 2.
- The maximum size, S_{adl}, for each of the four branches of each automatically defined loop is 100 points.
- None of the four branches of the automatically defined loops possess arguments, so that $N_{min\text{-}argument\text{-}adl} = 0$ and $N_{max\text{-}argument\text{-}adl} = 0$.
- The maximum number, $N_{max\text{-}adl\text{-}executions}$, of executions of an automatically defined loop is 7.

The other control parameters for this problem are found in the tableau (Table 21.1), the tables of percentages of genetic operations in Appendix D, and the default values specified in Appendix D.

Tableau

Table 21.1 summarizes the key features of the problem of symbolic regression of the Boolean even-6-parity function with GPPS 1.0. When GPPS 1.0 is used to solve a problem, the program architecture, the function set, and the terminal set do not change from problem to problem (and are the same as shown in this tableau).

21.1.2   Results

Six runs were made of this problem. Correct solutions were produced on all six runs (on generations 10, 15, 16, 17, 18, and 58).

Run A demonstrates the wide variety of architectural arrangements of automatically defined loops and automatically defined functions that can be created as part of the competitive evolutionary process of a single run of GPPS 1.0. The best-of-run solution employs subroutines but not loops.

Run B illustrates the use of two automatically defined loops in a particularly interesting iterative solution to the problem.

Architectural Diversity of a Run

The best-of-generation program for generation 0 of Run A scores 33 hits (out of 64).

A pace-setting individual (scoring 34 hits) from generation 2 has one automatically defined loop.

Table 21.1 Tableau for the even-6-parity problem with GPPS 1.0

Objective	Discover, using the Genetic Programming Problem Solver, a computer program that takes the values of the six independent Boolean variables in the input vector and deposits the value of the Boolean even-6-parity function into the output vector.
Program architecture	One result-producing branch, RPB. Automatically defined loops and automatically defined function(s) and their arguments will be created during the run by the architecture-altering operations.
Initial function set for the RPBs	$F_{rpb\text{-}initial}$ = {+, −, *, %, IFLTE, IFEQZ, TOR, TAND, TNOT, RLI, WIM, RIM, WLO, RLO, FLOOR}
Initial terminal set for the RPBs	$T_{rpb\text{-}initial}$ = {$\mathfrak{R}_{bigger\text{-}reals}$, NINPUTS, NOUTPUTS, INDEX}
Initial function set for the ADFs	No automatically defined functions in generation 0. $F_{adf\text{-}initial}$ = ϕ.
Initial terminal set for the ADFs	No automatically defined functions in generation 0. $T_{adf\text{-}initial}$ = ϕ.
Initial function set for ADLs	No automatically defined loops in generation 0. $F_{adl\text{-}initial}$ = ϕ.
Initial terminal set for ADLs	No automatically defined loops in generation 0. $T_{adl\text{-}initial}$ = ϕ.
Potential function set for the RPBs	$F_{rpb\text{-}potential}$ = {ADF0, ADF1, ADF2, ADF3}
Potential terminal set for the RPBs	$T_{rpb\text{-}potential}$ = {LBB0, LBB1}
Potential function set for the ADFs	$F_{adf\text{-}potential}$ = {ADF0, ADF1, ADF2, ADF3, +, −, *, %, IFLTE, IFEQZ, TOR, TAND, TNOT, RLI, WIM, RIM, WLO, RLO, FLOOR}
Potential terminal set for the ADFs	$T_{adf\text{-}potential}$ = {ARG0, ARG1, ARG2, ARG3, NINPUTS, NOUTPUTS, INDEX, $\mathfrak{R}_{bigger\text{-}reals}$}
Potential function set for ADLs	$F_{adl\text{-}potential}$ = {ADF0, ADF1, ADF2, ADF3, +, −, *, %, IFLTE, IFEQZ, TOR, TAND, TNOT, RLI, WIM, RIM, WLO, RLO, FLOOR}
Potential terminal set for ADLs	$T_{adl\text{-}potential}$ = {NINPUTS, NOUTPUTS, INDEX, $\mathfrak{R}_{bigger\text{-}reals}$}
Fitness cases	All 2^6 = 64 combinations of the six Boolean arguments in the input vector
Raw fitness	The number of fitness cases for which the value deposited in the output vector equals, after interpretation by the wrapper, the correct Boolean value of the even-6-parity function
Standardized fitness	The sum, over the 64 fitness cases, of the absolute value of the difference (i.e., the Hamming distance) between the value deposited in the output vector and the correct value of the even-6-parity function. Standardized fitness is 64 minus the raw fitness.

(continued)

Table 21.1 *(continued)*

Hits	Same as raw fitness
Wrapper	A wrapper (output interface) consisting of the IFGTZ ("if greater than zero") operator is used to convert the floating-point value deposited into the output vector to a binary outcome.
Parameters	$M = 640{,}000$. $G = 1{,}001$. $Q = 10{,}000$. $D = 64$. $B = 2\%$. $N_{rpb} = 1$. $S_{rpb} = 500$. $S_{adf} = 100$. $N_{max\text{-}adf} = 4$. $N_{max\text{-}argument\text{-}adf} = 4$. $N_{min\text{-}argument\text{-}adf} = 0$. $N_{max\text{-}adl} = 2$. $S_{adl} = 100$. $N_{max\text{-}adl\text{-}executions} = 7$. $N_{max\text{-}argument\text{-}adl} = 0$. $N_{min\text{-}argument\text{-}adl} = 0$. NINDEXED $= 20$.
Result designation	Best-so-far pace-setting individual
Success predicate	A program scores the maximum number of hits (64).

In generation 6, the first pace-setting individual with two automatically defined loops appears.

The first pace-setting individual (scoring 38 hits) with both an automatically defined loop and an automatically defined function appears later in generation 6. This individual has one automatically defined loop, one zero-argument automatically defined function, and a single one-argument automatically defined function. One automatically defined function hierarchically referred to the other one. The result-producing branch referred to the automatically defined function at the top of the hierarchy and to the automatically defined loop. Thus, as early as generation 6, a rather complex architecture has emerged that is competitively superior to all other programs so far in the run.

In generation 15, the first pace-setting individual with a two-argument automatically defined function appeared. This individual (scoring 42 hits) also has one automatically defined loop.

In generation 17, the first pace-setting individual with two two-argument automatically defined functions appeared. This individual (scoring 44 hits) also has one automatically defined loop.

In generation 29, the first pace-setting individual with four two-argument automatically defined functions appeared. This individual (scoring 55 hits) also has one automatically defined loop.

In generation 38, the first pace-setting individual with a three-argument automatically defined function appeared. This individual (scoring 56 hits) also has one automatically defined loop and one two-argument automatically defined function.

The 100%-correct individual scoring 64 hits (out of 64) emerged in generation 58. This best-of-run program consists of the following seven branches:

- one result-producing branch, RPB,
- one automatically defined loop, ADL0, consisting of the following four branches:
  - a loop initialization branch, LIB0,
  - a loop condition branch, LCB0,
  - a loop body branch, LBB0, and
  - a loop update branch, LUB0
- two two-argument automatically defined functions created by the architecture-altering operations.

The result-producing branch of the best-of-run individual from generation 58 has 444 points:

```
(WLO (WLO (IFEQZ (WLO (RLI -7.274451) (TNOT NINPUTS)) (+ (-
(TAND (+ (FLOOR LBB0) (RLI -0.405153)) (WLO (TOR (RIM INDEX)
(IFEQZ NINPUTS NINPUTS 3.323932)) (RLI NINPUTS))) (IFGTZ (WIM
(RLI (RLI 3.058891)) (RLI 1.327383)) (IFEQZ (RLI 2.908941)
(WLO (RIM INDEX) (TNOT -3.737233)) (WIM (FLOOR INDEX) (RLI
NINPUTS))) (+ (WIM (IFEQZ (IFGTZ (RLI (RLI 2.606788)) (IFEQZ
(% (TOR (WLO NINPUTS 3.628510) (% 7.265455 (WLO (RLI (FLOOR
INDEX)) (TNOT (TNOT (TNOT (TNOT -3.737233))))))))) (TOR (RLI
-9.592547) (% -4.329314 3.872723))) (RLI INDEX) (IFEQZ (WIM
(WLO -8.701645 6.955063) (RIM INDEX)) (IFGTZ (RLO -1.110111)
(* -6.981014 9.976995) (RLI 1.327383)) (RLI NINPUTS))) (IFGTZ
(RLI 3.239255) (* (WIM (RLI 3.058891) LIB0) (- -8.536102 (RLI
-7.274451))) (IFEQZ (TAND (WLO (FLOOR (RLI 7.648451)) (FLOOR
LBB0)) (% 0.705781 INDEX)) (IFEQZ (* 8.318048 NINPUTS) (TNOT
(RLI -1.110111)) (* -5.550876 -2.956903)) (TAND (+ (+ (FLOOR
LBB0) (RLI -0.405153)) NINPUTS) (FLOOR 1.436937))))) (RLO (WIM
(* (IFGTZ -8.995371 INDEX 9.470537) LCB0) 2.151551)) (RIM (RLI
(IFEQZ (RLI 2.908941) (WLO (RIM INDEX) (TNOT -3.737233)) (WIM
(FLOOR (+ (IFEQZ NINPUTS (RIM INDEX) 3.323932) (TOR -2.793060
-6.639519))) (RLI NINPUTS)))))) INDEX) (RIM (RLO 6.757090)))))
(TAND (TNOT (TAND (RIM -5.206735) (RLO -0.405153))) (% (FLOOR
(RLI (RIM (IFGTZ (WIM (RLI (RLI -8.004584)) (RLI 1.327383))
(IFEQZ (RLI 2.908941) (WLO (RIM INDEX) (TNOT (TNOT INDEX)))
(WIM -1.633354 (RLI NINPUTS))) (+ (TNOT (RLI (RLI 2.908941)))
(RIM (RLO 6.757090))))))) (RLI NINPUTS)))) (- (+ (FLOOR LBB0)
(RLI -0.405153)) (+ (- (TAND (+ (FLOOR LBB0) (RLI -0.405153))
(WLO (TOR (RIM INDEX) (IFEQZ NINPUTS NINPUTS 3.323932)) (IFGTZ
(RIM (RLO 6.757090)) (TOR (* (IFGTZ -8.995371 INDEX 9.470537)
LCB0) (+ (IFEQZ INDEX -2.302380 9.834745) (RIM LCB0))) (WLO
(RIM INDEX) (TNOT -3.737233))))) (IFGTZ (WIM (RLI (RLI
3.058891)) (RLI 1.327383)) (IFEQZ (RLI 2.908941) (WLO (RIM
INDEX) (TNOT -3.737233)) (WIM (FLOOR INDEX) (RLI NINPUTS)))
(+ (WIM (IFEQZ (IFGTZ (RLI (RLI 2.606788)) (IFEQZ (% (TOR (WLO
NINPUTS 3.628510) (% 7.265455 (WLO (RLI (FLOOR INDEX)) (TNOT
(TNOT (TNOT INDEX))))))) (TOR (RLI -9.592547) (% -4.329314
3.872723))) (RLI INDEX) (IFEQZ (WIM (WLO -8.701645 6.955063)
(RIM INDEX)) (IFGTZ (RLO -1.110111) (* -6.981014 9.976995)
(RLI 1.327383)) (RLI NINPUTS))) (IFGTZ (RLI 3.239255) (* (WIM
(RLI 3.058891) LIB0) (- -8.536102 (RLI -7.274451))) (IFEQZ
(TAND (WLO NINPUTS NINPUTS) (% 0.705781 INDEX)) (IFEQZ
(* 8.318048 NINPUTS) (TNOT (RLI -1.110111)) (* -5.550876
-2.956903)) (TAND (+ (+ (FLOOR LBB0) (RLI -0.405153)) NINPUTS)
(FLOOR 1.436937))))) (RLO (WIM (* (IFGTZ -8.995371 INDEX
```

```
(IFEQZ (RLI 2.908941) (WLO (RIM INDEX) (TNOT -3.737233)) (WIM
(FLOOR (+ (FLOOR LBB0) (RLI -0.405153))) (RLI NINPUTS))))
LCB0) 2.151551)) (RIM (RLI (IFEQZ (RLI 2.908941) (WLO (RIM
INDEX) (TNOT -3.737233)) (WIM (FLOOR (+ (IFEQZ NINPUTS (RIM
INDEX) 3.323932) (RLI -0.405153))) (RLI NINPUTS)))))) INDEX)
(RIM (RLO 6.757090))))) (TAND (TNOT (% (IFEQZ (RLI 4.258403)
(WIM -0.405153 2.151551) (TNOT INDEX)) (% (RLI NINPUTS)
INDEX))) (% (FLOOR (RIM INDEX)) (RLI NINPUTS)))))) (RLI
6.757090)) (RLI 6.757090)).
```

The loop initialization branch, `LIB0`, of automatically defined loop `ADL0` consists of the following 10 points:

```
(IFGTZ (RLI 0.617464) (WIM (RLI 3.058891) (RLO 1.971325))
(FLOOR -5.550876)).
```

The loop condition branch, `LCB0`, of automatically defined loop `ADL0` consists of the following eight points:

```
(IFGTZ (RIM INDEX) (* -6.981014 9.976995) (RLI 1.327383)).
```

The loop body branch, `LBB0`, of automatically defined loop `ADL0` consists of the following 31 points:

```
(* (RIM (FLOOR (RLO (- (WLO (RLI 1.225266) (TNOT (IFGTZ
-8.403739 NINPUTS (RIM -5.206735)))) (RIM (% (TNOT (TAND (RIM
-5.206735) (RLO (+ (IFEQZ INDEX -2.302380 9.834745) (RIM
LCB0))))) (RLI 7.648451))))))) 2.256185).
```

The loop update branch, `LUB0`, of automatically defined loop `ADL0` consists of the following eight points:

```
(TOR (RIM INDEX) (IFEQZ NINPUTS (RIM INDEX) 3.323932)).
```

Neither `ADF4` nor `ADF5` are referenced by the result-producing branch. (Note that the numbering of the two automatically defined functions starts at 4 because the automatically defined loop has four branches.) `ADF4` is a two-argument automatically defined function created by the architecture-altering operations. `ADF4` consists of one point and returns the numerical constant –6.981014. `ADF5` is a two-argument automatically defined function created by the architecture-altering operations. It is equivalent to the two-argument disjunction function:

```
(TOR (TOR ARG0 ARG1) ARG1).
```

Subroutines, iterations, and indexed memory were all available to the Genetic Programming Problem Solver. As it turned out, only iteration was used in solving this problem on this particular run. The decision to use (or not use) subroutines, iterations, and indexed memory was made by the evolutionary process—not by the human user prior to presenting the problem to the Genetic Programming Problem Solver.

Evolution of an Iterative Solution

Now consider the 100%-correct best-of-run individual produced in generation 10 of run B of GPPS on this problem. The evolved solution consists of one result-producing branch and two automatically defined loops.

The six-point result-producing branch of the best-of-run individual from generation 10 is shown below:

```
(TOR LBB1 (TNOT (FLOOR (RLI NINPUTS)))).
```

This branch is irrelevant in this program because it does not write anything to the output vector.

First consider the four branches of automatically defined loop 0 of the best-of-run individual from generation 10. The loop initialization branch, LIB0, of automatically defined loop ADL0 consists of the following five points:

```
(WLO (RLI NINPUTS) (RLI 8.521336)).
```

The loop condition branch, LCB0, of automatically defined loop ADL0 consists of the following two points:

```
(RLI INDEX).
```

The loop body branch, LBB0, of automatically defined loop ADL0 consists of the following three points:

```
(RLO (RLI 2.832704)).
```

The loop update branch, LUB0, of automatically defined loop ADL0 consists of the following two points:

```
(RLI -7.182307).
```

The last three of these four branches (i.e., LCB0, LBB0, and LUB0) merely read information from the input and output vectors and therefore contribute nothing to the final output of the overall program.

The first of these four branches (i.e., the loop initialization branch, LIB0) executes one WLO ("write linear output") function. Since NOUTPUTS is 1, this WLO writes to the sole location of the output vector, regardless of the value of (RLI 8.521336). Since (RLI NINPUTS) is equivalent to (RLI 0), this RLI ("read linear input") function reads the contents of location 0 of the input vector. That is, the RLI reads external input D0 (of the six external inputs to the even-6-parity problem). The WLO of LIB0 then writes external input D0 into the single location of the output vector. As will be seen momentarily, the loop body branch, LBB1, of automatically defined loop ADL1 begins by executing an RLO ("read linear output") and thereby gains access to this deposited value of external input D0. The passing of this single external input D0 to LBB1 is the sole consequence of automatically defined loop ADL0.

Now consider the four branches of automatically defined loop ADL1 of the best-of-run individual from generation 10. The loop initialization branch, LIB1, of automatically defined loop ADL1 consists of the following two points:

```
(RLO NINPUTS).
```

The loop condition branch, LCB1, of automatically defined loop ADL1 consists of the following four points:

    (IFEQZ -6.530157 4.493470 NINPUTS).

The loop body branch, LBB1, of automatically defined loop ADL1 consists of the following 46 points:

    (**WLO** (IFGTZ (**RLO** (- (RLI -0.045897) (IFEQZ (RLI 0.157271)
    (RLI -7.182307) (RLI -1.983282)))) (RLI INDEX) (**WIM** (TNOT (RLI
    INDEX)) (**RIM** (TNOT (**WIM** (RLI -5.498105) (% (- (**WIM** 9.525654
    8.521336) (FLOOR INDEX)) (FLOOR (FLOOR -9.943804)))))))))
    (% (RLI (TNOT (IFGTZ (- INDEX 9.230116) (FLOOR -6.570716)
    -8.528593))) (RLI 6.669161))).

The loop update branch, LUB1, of automatically defined loop ADL1 consists of the following two points:

    (RLI NINPUTS).

Since −6.530157 is not equal to zero, the loop condition branch, LCB1, always returns NINPUTS (the positive constant 6). Thus, the loop is not terminated until INDEX reaches 7 (and is therefore no longer less than $N_{\text{max-adl-executions}}$, which is 7).

The topmost point of the loop body branch, LBB1, is a WLO ("write linear output") function (underlined and emboldened). LBB1 also executes three WIM ("write indexed memory") functions and one RIM ("read indexed memory") function (all also underlined and emboldened). LBB1 also contains one RLO ("read linear output") function.

    (**WLO** (IFGTZ (**RLO** (- (RLI -0.045897) (IFEQZ (RLI 0.157271)
    (RLI -7.182307) (RLI -1.983282)))) (RLI INDEX) (**WIM** (TNOT (RLI
    INDEX)) (**RIM** (TNOT (**WIM** (RLI -5.498105) (% (- (**WIM** 9.525654
    8.521336) (FLOOR INDEX)) (FLOOR (FLOOR -9.943804)))))))))
    (% (RLI (TNOT (IFGTZ (- INDEX 9.230116) (FLOOR -6.570716)
    -8.528593))) (RLI 6.669161))).

The loop body branch, LBB1, of automatically defined loop ADL1 can be simplified by making the following 10 substitutions:

- (FLOOR -6.570716) = −7.
- (FLOOR (FLOOR -9.943804)) = −10.
- Since NINPUTS is 6, (RLI 6.669161) = (RLI 0).
- (RLI -0.045897) = (RLI 5).
- (RLI -5.498105) = (RLI 0).
- (RLI 0.157271) = (RLI 0).
- (RLI -7.182307) = (RLI 4).
- (RLI -1.983282) = (RLI 4).
- Since INDEX is a nonnegative integer, (FLOOR INDEX) = INDEX.
- Since the size of indexed memory is 20, (WIM 9.525654 8.521336) = (WIM 9.525654 8).

The effects of these 10 changes (each underlined and emboldened) on the loop body branch, LBB1, are shown below:

```
(WLO (IFGTZ (RLO (- (RLI 5) (IFEQZ (RLI 0) (RLI 4) (RLI 4))))
(RLI INDEX) (WIM (TNOT (RLI INDEX)) (RIM (TNOT (WIM (RLI 0) (%
(- (WIM 9.525654 8) INDEX) -10)))))) (% (RLI (TNOT (IFGTZ
(- INDEX 9.230116) -7 -8.528593))) (RLI 0))).
```

Since both the second and third arguments to the IFEQZ (the seventh point in the expression above) are identical, the entire seven-point subexpression

```
(IFEQZ (RLI 0) (RLI 4) (RLI 4))
```

can be replaced with (RLI 4). The effect of this additional change on LBB1 (underlined and emboldened) is shown below:

```
(WLO (IFGTZ (RLO (- (RLI 5) (RLI 4))) (RLI INDEX) (WIM (TNOT
(RLI INDEX)) (RIM (TNOT (WIM (RLI 0) (% (- (WIM 9.525654 8)
INDEX) -10)))))) (% (RLI (TNOT (IFGTZ (- INDEX 9.230116) -7
-8.528593))) (RLI 0))).
```

Since NOUTPUTS is 1, the entire second argument of the topmost WLO function is irrelevant. That is, the 11-point subexpression

```
(% (RLI (TNOT (IFGTZ (- INDEX 9.230116) -7 -8.528593))) (RLI
0))
```

can be replaced by a placeholder (say, 1). The effect of this additional change on LBB1 (underlined and emboldened) is shown below:

```
(WLO (IFGTZ (RLO (- (RLI 5) (RLI 4))) (RLI INDEX) (WIM (TNOT
(RLI INDEX)) (RIM (TNOT (WIM (RLI 0) (% (- (WIM 9.525654 8)
INDEX) -10)))))) 1).
```

Since there is only one output, the argument to the RLO ("read linear output") function can be replaced with 0 (underlined and emboldened) and LBB1 can then be further simplified to

```
(WLO
  (IFGTZ
    (RLO 0)
    (RLI INDEX)
    (WIM (TNOT (RLI INDEX))
      (RIM (TNOT (WIM (RLI 0) (% (- (WIM 9.525654 8) INDEX)
      10))))))
  1).
```

Because WIM returns the value of its first argument, the loop body branch, LBB1, of automatically defined loop ADL1 can then be further simplified to

```
(WLO (IFGTZ
       (RLO 0)
```

```
(RLI INDEX)
(TNOT (RLI INDEX)))
1).
```

As mentioned earlier, the sole role of ADL0 is to deposit the single external input D0 into the output vector. This action of ADL0 has the effect of offsetting the extra iteration of the loop.

On the first occasion when the loop body branch, LBB1, is executed, INDEX is 0. If the content of the output vector is positive (as determined by ADL0), the IFGTZ returns (RLI 0), namely, external input D0, thereby rewriting a positive value into the output vector. If the content of the output vector is nonpositive, the IFGTZ returns the negation of (RLI 0), namely, (NOT D0), thereby writing a positive value into the output vector.

On the second occasion when LBB1 is executed, INDEX is 1 and the content of the output vector is unconditionally positive. The IFGTZ returns (RLI 1), namely, external input D1, thereby writing D1 into the output vector. Thus, this second execution of LBB1 cancels the effect of the first execution of LBB1 and deposits D1 into the output vector.

The third execution of LBB1 is typical of all later executions. On the third occasion when LBB1 is executed, INDEX is 2 and the output vector contains D1. If D1 is positive, the IFGTZ returns (RLI 2), namely, external input D2, and writes D2 into the output vector. If D1 is nonpositive, the IFGTZ returns the negation (TNOT (RLI INDEX)) of external input D2, and writes the nonpositive of D2 into the output vector. Thus, the output vector contains the even-2-parity function (E2P) of D1 and D2.

(E2P D2 D1).

After the fourth execution of LBB1, the output vector contains

(E2P D3 (EOP D2 D1)).

After the fifth execution of LBB1, the output vector contains

(E2P D4 (E2P D3 (EOP D2 D1))).

After the sixth execution of LBB1, the output vector contains

(E2P D5 (E2P D4 (E2P D3 (EOP D2 D1)))).

On the seventh execution of LBB1, INDEX is 6 and (RLI INDEX) returns the external input D0. After the seventh execution of LBB1, the output vector contains

(E2P D0 (E2P D5 (E2P D4 (E2P D3 (EOP D2 D1))))

into the output vector.

This is the final execution of LBB1 because an INDEX of 7 will cause the loop condition branch, LCB1, to terminate automatically defined loop ADL1. This iterative computer program is a perfect solution to the even-6-parity problem.

In other words, the second execution of LBB1 places D1 into the output vector. Then, the third, fourth, fifth, sixth, and seventh executions of LBB1 place the even-2-parity of the previously written output and another input into the output vector. Thus, this iterative computer program is a perfect solution to the even-6-parity problem. This iterative solution can also be viewed as an unrolled recursive solution to this problem.

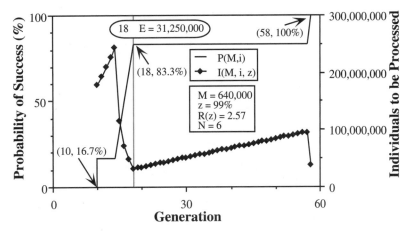

Figure 21.1   Performance curves for the even-6-parity problem using GPPS 1.0

Subroutines, iterations, and indexed memory were all available to the Genetic Programming Problem Solver. The solution evolved for this problem on this particular run does not use subroutines at all. The evolved solution makes nominal, but unimportant, use of indexed memory. The evolved solution actively employed iteration. The decision to use (or not use) subroutines, iterations, and memory was made as part of the evolutionary process—not by the human user prior to presenting the problem to the Genetic Programming Problem Solver.

Only six runs were made of the even-6-parity problem using GPPS 1.0. Although all six runs were successful, this number of successful runs is insufficient to compute an accurate performance curve. Nonetheless, we can get a rough idea of the computational effort involved by constructing a performance curve in the usual fashion. Figure 21.1 presents the performance curve based on six independent runs for the even-6-parity problem using GPPS 1.0. The first generation for which the experimentally observed cumulative probability of success, $P(M, x)$, is nonzero is generation 10; $P(M, x)$ is 16.7% for that generation. The cumulative probability of success, $P(M, x)$, reaches 100% at generation 58. The $I(M, x, z)$ curve reaches a minimum value at the best generation $i^* = 18$. The cumulative probability of success, $P(M, x)$, is 83.3% at generation 18, so $R(z)$ is 2.57. The two numbers in the oval indicate that running this problem 2.57 times through to generation 18 and thereby processing a total computational effort of $E = 31,250,000$ individuals (i.e., $640,000 \times 19$ generations $\times 2.57$ runs) is sufficient to yield a solution to this problem with 99% probability.

21.2   RESULTS FOR 3-, 4-, AND 5-PARITY PROBLEMS

This section shows the computational effort, E, for solving the problems of symbolic regression of the 3-, 4-, and 5-parity functions using the GPPS 1.0.

The computational effort is computed from 60 independent runs, each with a population size of 12,000. The runs are implemented by making one run on each of 60 nodes of a parallel computer with migration squelched. The performance curves in this chapter

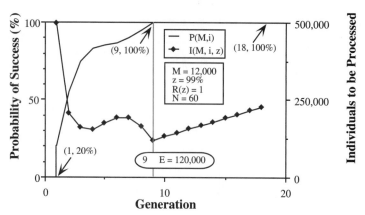

Figure 21.2 **Performance curves for the even-3-parity problem using GPPS 1.0**

are constructed in the manner described in Section 12.6.1 (except that the ceiling function for rounding up to the next highest integer is not used).

Figure 21.2 presents the performance curve based on 60 independent runs of the problem of symbolic regression of the even-3-parity function using GPPS 1.0. The first generation for which the experimentally observed cumulative probability of success, $P(M, x)$, is nonzero is generation 1; $P(M, x)$ is 20% for that generation. The cumulative probability of success, $P(M, x)$, reaches 100% at generation 9. The $I(M, x, z)$ curve reaches a minimum value at the best generation $i^* = 9$. The cumulative probability of success, $P(M, x)$, is 100% at generation 9, so $R(z)$ is 1. The two numbers in the oval indicate that running this problem one time through to generation 9 and thereby processing a total computational effort of $E = 120,000$ individuals (i.e., $12,000 \times 10$ generations $\times 1$ run) is sufficient to yield a solution to this problem with 99% probability.

Figure 21.3 presents the performance curve based on 60 independent runs for the even-4-parity problem using GPPS 1.0. The first generation for which the experimentally observed cumulative probability of success, $P(M, x)$, is nonzero is generation 11; $P(M, x)$ is 1.67% for that generation. The cumulative probability of success, $P(M, x)$, reaches 93.3% at generation 54. The $I(M, x, z)$ curve reaches a minimum value at the best generation $i^* = 32$. The cumulative probability of success, $P(M, x)$, is 88.3% at generation 32, so $R(z)$ is 2.14. The two numbers in the oval indicate that running this problem one time through to generation 32 and thereby processing a total computational effort of $E = 848,826$ individuals (i.e., $12,000 \times 33$ generations $\times 2.14$ runs) is sufficient to yield a solution to this problem with 99% probability.

Figure 21.4 presents the performance curve based on 60 independent runs for the even-5-parity problem using GPPS 1.0. The first generation for which the experimentally observed cumulative probability of success, $P(M, x)$, is nonzero is generation 24; $P(M, x)$ is 1.67% for that generation. The cumulative probability of success, $P(M, x)$, reaches 45% at generation 148. The $I(M, x, z)$ curve reaches a minimum value at the best generation $i^* = 50$. The cumulative probability of success, $P(M, x)$, is 26.7% at generation 50, so $R(z)$ is 14.8. The two numbers in the oval indicate that running this problem one time through to generation 50 and thereby processing a total computational effort of

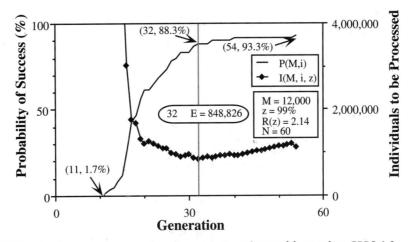

Figure 21.3 Performance curves for the even-4-parity problem using GPPS 1.0

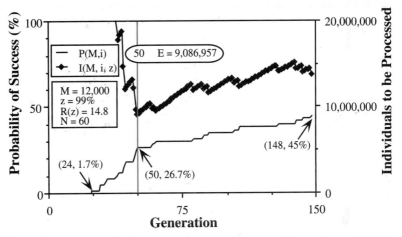

Figure 21.4 Performance curves for the even-5-parity problem using GPPS 1.0

Table 21.2 Computational effort for 3-, 4-, 5-, and 6-parity problems using GPPS 1.0

Order	Computational effort, E
3	120,000
4	848,826
5	9,086,957
6	31,250,000

$E = 9,086,957$ individuals (i.e., $12,000 \times 51$ generations $\times 14.8$ runs) is sufficient to yield a solution to this problem with 99% probability.

Table 21.2 summarizes the computational effort, E, for the 3-, 4-, 5-, and 6-parity problems using GPPS 1.0. The value of computational effort for the even-6-parity problem is the rough estimate made in the previous section (and is based on a different population size).

21.3 ROBOT CONTROLLER PROBLEM WITH GPPS 1.0

This section demonstrates the application of GPPS 1.0 to the time-optimal robot controller problem. This problem was originally solved in Chapter 13, is solved yet again in Section 23.5 using GPPS 2.0, and solved yet again in Chapter 48 using an electrical circuit.

21.3.1 Preparatory Steps

When GPPS 1.0 is used to solve a problem, the program architecture, the function set, and the terminal set do not change from problem to problem (and are the same as Table 21.1 for the even-6-parity problem). Thus, there are only three problem-specific preparatory steps: determining the fitness measure, determining the parameters, and determining the termination criterion and the method of result designation.

Fitness

For each fitness case and each time step, the evolved program receives the current values of x and y in the input vector (whose size, NINPUTS, is 2). The single value deposited in the output vector (whose size, NOUTPUTS, is 1) steers the robot. The details are the same as those found in Section 13.3.3.

Parameters

The control parameters for this problem are found in the tableau (Table 21.3), the tables of percentages of genetic operations in Appendix D, and the default values specified in Appendix D. Except for NINPUTS and NOUTPUTS, these parameters are the same as the parameters for the even-6-parity problem with GPPS 1.0 (Table 21.1).

Termination

The termination criterion and the method of result designation are the same as in Section 13.3.5 for the robot controller.

Tableau

Table 21.3 is an abbreviated tableau for the robot controller problem using GPPS 1.0. This tableau is abbreviated since the program architecture, the function set, and the terminal set do not change in GPPS 1.0 from problem to problem (and are the same as Table 21.1 for the even-6-parity problem).

21.3.2 Results

The best-of-generation individual from generation 0 of one illustrative run has a fitness of 2.55 hours, scores 64 hits, and consists of a 65-point result-producing branch.

The first best-of-generation program with an automatically defined function appears in generation 5. It scores 71 hits.

Table 21.3 Abbreviated tableau for robot controller problem using GPPS 1.0

Objective	Find a control strategy for controlling the trajectory of a constant-speed robot with nonzero turning radius such that the robot moves to an arbitrary destination point in minimal time.
Fitness cases	72 random destinations (x_i, y_i) for the robot
Raw fitness	The sum, over the 72 destinations, of the time for the robot to reach the destination
Standardized fitness	Same as raw fitness
Hits	Number of fitness cases (from 0 to 72) for which the robot arrives at its destination within the available 80 time steps (i.e., does not time out)
Wrapper	The wrapper modularizes and clamps the value returned by the result-producing branch so that the final turn angle Θ lies between $-\Theta_{max}$ and $+\Theta_{max}$).
Parameters	$M = 640{,}000$. $G = 1{,}001$. NINPUTS $= 2$. NOUTPUTS $= 1$. $Q = 10{,}000$. $D = 64$. $B = 2\%$. $N_{rpb} = 1$. $S_{rpb} = 500$. $S_{adf} = 100$. $N_{max\text{-}adf} = 4$. $N_{max\text{-}argument\text{-}adf} = 4$. $N_{min\text{-}argument\text{-}adf} = 0$. $N_{max\text{-}adl} = 2$. $S_{adl} = 100$. $N_{max\text{-}adl\text{-}executions} = 7$. $N_{max\text{-}argument\text{-}adl} = 0$. $N_{min\text{-}argument\text{-}adl} = 0$. NINDEXED $= 20$.
Result designation	Best-so-far pace-setting individual
Success predicate	Fitness appears to have reached a plateau (and, as a minimum, there are 72 hits).

The first program to achieve 72 hits appears in generation 5 and has a fitness of 1.87 hours. It has two one-argument three-point automatically defined functions (one unreferenced) that create an indirect addressing scheme.

The first best-of-generation program with an automatically defined loop (in fact, two) appears in generation 6. This program has a fitness of 1.69 hours and scores 71 hits.

The best-of-run individual appears in generation 24, scores 72 hits, and has a fitness of 1.44 hours. It consists of six branches: a 260-point result-producing branch, an eight-point automatically defined function, and one automatically defined loop (consisting of a two-point loop initialization branch, a two-point loop condition branch, a six-point loop body branch, and a two-point loop update branch).

The automatically defined function of the best-of-run individual is not referenced by any other branch and is therefore irrelevant.

Neither the loop initialization branch nor the loop condition branch of the best-of-run individual writes anything to indexed memory or the output vector. The loop condition branch causes the immediate unconditional termination of the loop. The loop body branch is referenced once by the result-producing branch. It produces a constant (15.10) that is used by the result-producing branch and that is written, at the time of reference, into location 0 of indexed memory.

The 260-point result-producing branch of the best-of-run individual from generation 24 is

(WLO (- (WLO (- (* (IFGTZ (IFGTZ -3.068030 INDEX 2.608109)
(IFEQZ 1.293460 6.271305 7.182295) (RLI 3.167868)) INDEX)
NINPUTS) (RLI (WLM (- (IFGTZ (TNOT (TNOT -8.563198)) (WLM (FLOOR
-6.586866) (+ 7.761524 7.346823)) (RLI 6.271305)) (IFGTZ
(IFEQZ (RLI -9.910165) (TAND INDEX INDEX) (RLI 2.206976)) (TOR
(- NOUTPUTS INDEX) (RLO -6.005774)) (RLO (TNOT -1.394406))))
(IFGTZ (RLI INDEX) (TOR (IFGTZ (RLM 2.458234) (RLI NINPUTS) (%
NOUTPUTS -5.504727)) (TNOT (TNOT -3.240778))) (RLI NIN-
PUTS))))) (% (IFGTZ (RLI -7.387192) (FLOOR (RLI 6.176998))
(FLOOR (% (RLO (+ (TOR (IFEQZ (RLI (TNOT 4.128504E-01)) (RLM
(RLO (IFEQZ (RLI (TNOT 4.128504E-01)) (RLM (% (RLM (% (TAND
-7.466449 -5.814634) (TOR INDEX 9.171734))) -2.230111)) (WLM
(RLM NOUTPUTS) 3.023518)))) (WLM (RLM NOUTPUTS) (RLO NIN-
PUTS))) INDEX) INDEX)) (TNOT (IFEQZ 8.630079 4.385998 (RLI
(TNOT 4.128504E-01))))))) (* (+ (IFEQZ (RLM (RLI INDEX)) (+ (+
(FLOOR 1.609247) 5.095557) (RLO NINPUTS)) (* (RLI 5.580121)
(TOR 3.424158E-01 INDEX))) (IFEQZ (TNOT (+ 7.745760
-3.604181)) (TAND (IFGTZ INDEX -3.671995 NINPUTS) (TNOT INDEX))
(RLI -4.805269E-01))) (RLI (RLI -7.147597))))) (TAND (WLM
(IFGTZ (WLO (WLO (+ (RLI (RLI INDEX)) (IFEQZ INDEX NOUTPUTS
-6.524444) (RLI 4.953274)) (WLM (ADF3) (RLI INDEX))) (WLM
(IFEQZ (RLO (TNOT -7.898183)) (RLI NOUTPUTS) (WLM (RLO
NINPUTS) (IFEQZ INDEX -2.312283 (TOR -5.710949 -7.314668))))
(RLI -6.162939)) (RLM (RLI 6.176998))) (IFGTZ (WLM (TAND (WLO
(TOR 8.569630 -6.524444) (RLI -6.005774)) (* (WLO (- (RLI
INDEX) (RLI NOUTPUTS)) (RLO (RLI -1.230717E-01))) (TNOT
(IFGTZ -5.014982 -7.097149E-01 9.171734)))) (RLI 2.458234))
(TAND (RLI NINPUTS) (RLO (TOR (RLI 8.746576E-01) (+ NOUTPUTS
-4.805269E-01)))) (TOR (RLM (IFEQZ (RLI -2.163548) (FLOOR
7.761524) (TOR -9.910165 5.417677))) (RLI 1.582668)))) (RLO
(RLM (WLM (TOR (RLI 1.582668) (TOR (RLM 4.814925) (+ 6.760324
-5.014982))) (* (RLI INDEX) (RLI 3.858910)))))))).

The two-point loop initialization branch, LIB0, of the first automatically defined
loop, ADL0, is

(RLI -6.162939).

The two-point loop condition branch, LCB0, of ADL0 is

(RLI -6.162939).

The six-point loop body branch, LBB0, of ADL0 is

(WLO (+ 7.761524 7.346823) (FLOOR -3.793905)).

The two-point loop update branch, LUB0, of ADL0 is:

(RLI 3.858910).

The unreferenced eight-point automatically defined function, `ADF0`, is

`(IFEQZ (WLM (RLM NOUTPUTS) (RLO NINPUTS)) 4.496870 NINPUTS)`.

Subroutines, iterations, and indexed memory were all available to the Genetic Programming Problem Solver. Indexed memory did not appear at all in the evolved solution to this problem on this particular run. Two programming constructs (automatically defined functions and automatically defined loops) appeared nominally in the above evolved solution; however, both were effectively ignored in the evolved solution. Of course, there is no reason why subroutines, iterations, or indexed memory should be used at all in solving this particular problem. Indeed, it is difficult to imagine a human programmer using any of them. The important point is that the decision to use (or not use) subroutines, iterations, and indexed memory was made by the evolutionary process—not by the human user prior to presenting the problem to the Genetic Programming Problem Solver.

21.4   MINIMAL SORTING NETWORK PROBLEM WITH GPPS 1.0

This section applies GPPS 1.0 to a problem involving symbolic manipulation—the problem of synthesizing the design of minimal sorting networks.

Chronologically, we first solved this problem using evolvable hardware (field-programmable gate arrays) as described in Chapter 57 of this book. We subsequently decided to try to apply GPPS to this problem on the belief (mistaken, as it turns out) that GPPS would have difficulty with a nonnumerical problem involving symbolic manipulation. As will be seen momentarily, GPPS not only solved the problem, but it exploited the features of GPPS (specifically, its ability to use loops in solving a problem) in an unexpected and highly effective way. This problem will be solved again in Section 23.6 using GPPS 2.0.

21.4.1   Minimal Sorting Networks

A sorting network is an algorithm for sorting items consisting of a sequence of comparison-exchange operations that are executed in a fixed order. Sorting networks are oblivious to their inputs in the sense that they always perform the same fixed sequence of comparison-exchange operations, regardless of the inputs. Figure 21.5 shows a five-step sorting network for four items.

The to-be-sorted items (`D0`, `D1`, `D2`, and `D3` in the figure) start at the left on the dotted horizontal lines. A vertical line connecting horizontal line i and j indicates that a `(COMPARE-EXCHANGE i j)` function is to be performed on items i and j. Specifically, items i and j are to be compared and, if necessary, exchanged so that the larger of the two is on the bottom. The five steps in this sorting network are

- `(COMPARE-EXCHANGE 2 3)`,
- `(COMPARE-EXCHANGE 0 1)`,
- `(COMPARE-EXCHANGE 1 3)`,
- `(COMPARE-EXCHANGE 0 2)`, and
- `(COMPARE-EXCHANGE 1 2)`.

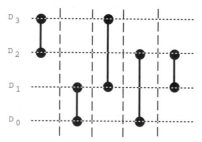

Figure 21.5   Minimal sorting network for four items

The first step of this sorting network causes items D2 and D3 to be exchanged if and only if D2 < D3. Collectively, the first four steps of this sorting network cause the largest of the four items to be routed down and the smallest of the four items up. The fifth step ensures that the remaining two items end up in the correct order. The correctly sorted output appears at the right. A five-step network is known to be minimal for four items. There are, of course, many different four-step five-sorters.

Sorting networks are of considerable practical importance. For one thing, sorting networks are part of the internal machinery of many computers. Sorting networks can be easily implemented in hardware because they perform a fixed sequence of comparison-exchange operations. This hardware is used to sort internal variables for scheduling or channeling data. In addition, sorting networks are often implemented in software. Sorting networks are more efficient than the better-known nonoblivious algorithms (such as Quicksort) for sorting small numbers of items. In fact, in speed-sensitive commercial sorting applications, sorting network software complements the capabilities of the nonoblivious software. Thus, there is considerable interest in sorting networks (hardware or software) with a minimum number of comparison-exchange operations.

There has been a lively search over the years for smaller sorting networks (Knuth 1973) for various numbers of items. In U.S. patent 3,029,413, O'Connor and Nelson (1962) described sorting networks for 4, 5, 6, 7, and 8 items employing 5, 9, 12, 18, and 19 comparison-exchange operations, respectively.

During the 1960s, Floyd and Knuth devised a 16-step seven-sorter. Their sorter had two fewer steps than the sorter of O'Connor and Nelson. Floyd and Knuth proved their sorter to be a minimal seven-sorter. They also proved that the four other sorting networks in the 1962 O'Connor and Nelson patent are minimal.

The 16-sorter has received considerable attention. In 1962, Bose and Nelson devised a 65-step sorting network for 16 items. In 1964, Batcher and Knuth presented a 63-step 16-sorter. In 1969, Shapiro discovered a 62-step 16-sorter, and in the same year, Green discovered one with 60 steps. Hillis (1990, 1992) used the genetic algorithm to evolve 16-sorters with 65 and 61 steps. In this work, Hillis incorporated the first 32 steps of Green's 60-step 16-sorter as a fixed beginning for all sorters (Juille 1995). Hillis's work is particularly noteworthy because of his novel coevolutionary technique involving competing populations of sorting networks and fitness cases. In the coevolutionary approach, the fitness of each sorting network is the number of input vectors (fitness cases) that the sorting network properly sorts; the fitness of each fitness case is the number of sorting networks that cannot properly handle the fitness case.

Juille (1995) used an evolutionary algorithm to evolve a 13-sorter with 45 steps, thereby improving on the 13-sorter with 46 steps presented in Knuth (1973). Juille (1997) has also evolved networks for sorting 14, 15, and 16 items having the same number of steps (i.e., 51, 56, and 60, respectively) as reported in Knuth (1973).

As the number of items to be sorted increases, construction of a minimal sorting network becomes increasingly difficult. Verification that a network is a correct sorting network does not require consideration of all $n!$ permutations of n different quantities to be sorted. Thanks to the "zero-one principle" (Knuth 1973, page 224; Ahlswede and Wegener 1979), if a sorting network for n items correctly sorts n bits into nondecreasing order (i.e., all the 0s ahead of all the 1s) for all 2^n possible sequences of n bits, it necessarily will correctly sort any set of n distinct numbers into nondecreasing order. Thus, it is sufficient to test a putative 16-sorter against only $2^{16} = 65,536$ combinations of binary inputs (instead of all $16! \sim 2 \times 10^{13}$ permutations of 16 inputs). Nonetheless, in spite of this very helpful "zero-one principle," testing a putative 16-sorter consisting of around 60 steps on 65,536 different 16-bit input vectors is a formidable amount of computation when it appears in the inner loop of a genetic algorithm on a contemporary single workstation.

For a discussion of an application of genetic programming to a different type of sorting problem, see Kinnear 1993a, 1993b.

21.4.2 Statement of the Problem

The goal is to synthesize the design of a sorting network composed of COMPARE-EXCHANGE operations for sorting seven items.

21.4.3 Preparatory Steps

When the GPPS 1.0 is used to solve a problem, the program architecture, the function set, and the terminal set do not change from problem to problem (and are the same as shown in Table 21.1 for the even-6-parity problem). Thus, there are only three problem-specific preparatory steps: determining the fitness measure, determining the parameters, and determining the termination criterion and the method of result designation.

Fitness

The fitness of an individual sorting network is based on the correctness of its sorting of 2^k vectors consisting of all possible arrangements of k bits. For sorting $k = 7$ items, there are $2^k = 128$ vectors. If, after an individual program is executed on a particular vector, all the 1s appear below all the 0s, the program is deemed to have correctly sorted all seven bits in that particular vector.

The Genetic Programming Problem Solver evolves a computer program that deposits its results into an output vector. One straightforward way of using a vector to represent a sorting network is for the to-be-evolved program to deposit the first argument of the first COMPARE-EXCHANGE into the vector's first position, to deposit the second argument of the first COMPARE-EXCHANGE into the vector's second position, and so forth, until the output vector contains the entire desired sequence of COMPARE-EXCHANGE operations.

Thus, for example, a vector of length 32 would be required to represent 16 COMPARE-EXCHANGE functions (the now-known minimal number for a seven-sorter). However, an important part of the problem of creating a sorting network entails determining the number of COMPARE-EXCHANGE operations in the network. Thus, we do not want to specify the exact number of COMPARE-EXCHANGE operations in advance. One straightforward way of achieving this flexibility is for the user to choose an overly large output vector and let the to-be-evolved program insert as many COMPARE-EXCHANGE operations into the output vector as it will. Thus, for this problem, the size, NOUTPUTS, of the output vector is 42. An output vector of this size is sufficient to accommodate 21 COMPARE-EXCHANGE operations. Twenty-one is larger than the number of steps (18) used for the seven-sorter in the 1962 O'Connor and Nelson patent, so we know that 21 is a generous overspecification. In fact, 21 is five more than the now-known minimal number (16) of COMPARE-EXCHANGE operations for a seven-sorter.

Exchanges where $i = j$ and exchanges that are identical to the previous exchange are ignored. That is, a (COMPARE-EXCHANGE X X) operation (where there is an X in positions $2j$ and $2j + 1$ of the output vector) is ignored. (This is the same convention used in solving this problem using field-programmable gate arrays in Chapter 57). Since all elements of the output vector are initialized to zero for each of the 128 vectors, the output vector begins, in effect, with 21 degenerate (COMPARE-EXCHANGE 0 0) operations. Adoption of this convention provides a convenient means for permitting variation in the number of COMPARE-EXCHANGE operations in the output vector. A 16-step seven-sorter in an output vector of length 42 would then have five (COMPARE-EXCHANGE X X) operations.

Since the to-be-evolved computer program is intended to write a sorting network into the output vector, the input vector is not relevant. The size, NINPUTS, of the input vector is 1. The input is nominal and consists of the constant number 7 (the number of items to be sorted).

The fitness of an individual program in the population is then determined in several steps:

1. The individual program in the population is executed.
2. The output vector of length 42 is interpreted as a sorting network (with between 0 and 21 steps).
3. The sorting network is exposed to all $2^k = 128$ vectors. The fitness measure for this problem is multiobjective in that it involves both the correctness of the sorting network and its size (i.e., number of COMPARE-EXCHANGE operations that are actually executed). Standardized fitness is defined in a lexical fashion to be 1 plus the number of bits (0 to 7×128) that are incorrectly positioned upon completion of the sort plus 0.01 times the number of COMPARE-EXCHANGE operations that are actually executed (i.e., excluding those COMPARE-EXCHANGE operations for which $i = j$ or that are identical to the previous exchange). Since there are 128 vectors, the number of incorrect bits ranges from 0 to 7×128 (896). For example, the fitness of an imperfect sorting network for seven items with 18 COMPARE-EXCHANGE functions that correctly handles all but 12 bits is 13.18, while the fitness of a perfect zero-error 16-step seven-sorter is 1.16. Since we use tournament selection throughout this book, this multiobjective fitness

measure operates in a lexical way in the sense that considerations concerning the correctness of the sort dominate all considerations of parsimony.

The number of hits is defined as the number of COMPARE-EXCHANGE functions that are actually executed.

Parameters

The control parameters for this problem are found in the tableau (Table 21.4), the tables of percentages of genetic operations in Appendix D, and the default values specified in Appendix D. Except for NINPUTS and NOUTPUTS, they are the same as the parameters for the even-6-parity problem with GPPS 1.0 (Table 21.1).

Termination

The termination criterion involves monitoring the run (after a fitness of less than 2.0 is attained) to see if the number of COMPARE-EXCHANGE functions appears to have reached a plateau.

Tableau

Table 21.4 is an abbreviated tableau for the problem of synthesizing the design of a sorting network for seven items using GPPS 1.0. When GPPS 1.0 is used to solve a problem, the program architecture, the function set, and the terminal set do not change from problem to problem (and are the same as shown in Table 21.1 for the even-6-parity problem).

21.4.4 Results

The best individual for generation 0 has a fitness of 239.03. The program consists of one result-producing branch with 107 points.

As the run proceeds from generation to generation, automatically defined functions and automatically defined loops are added to some programs in the population. In addition, arguments are added to some automatically defined functions.

The best-of-generation individual from generation 1 has a fitness of 219.04. Its architecture consists of one result-producing branch (with 90 points) and one automatically defined loop (consisting of a 39-point loop initialization branch, an 18-point loop condition branch, a 3-point loop body branch, and a 5-point loop update branch).

The best-of-generation individual from generation 3 has a fitness of 167.08 and an architecture consisting of one result-producing branch and two automatically defined loops.

The best-of-generation individual from generation 6 has a fitness of 159.07 and an architecture consisting of one result-producing branch and one three-argument automatically defined function.

The best-of-generation individual from generation 7 has a fitness of 131.08 and an architecture consisting of one result-producing branch and two automatically defined loops.

The best-of-generation individual from generation 14 (with a fitness of 87.11) has a total of 11 branches. It consists of one result-producing branch, two one-argument automatically defined functions, and two automatically defined loops.

Table 21.4 Abbreviated tableau for the sorting network problem using GPPS 1.0

Objective	Synthesize the design of a minimal sorting network for seven items.
Fitness cases	The $7 \times 128 = 896$ bits appearing in all possible vectors of seven bits
Raw fitness	1 plus the number of bits (0 to $7 \times 2^7 = 128$) for which the bits are incorrectly positioned upon completion of the sort, plus 0.01 times the number of COMPARE–EXCHANGE functions that are actually executed
Standardized fitness	128 minus raw fitness
Hits	The number of COMPARE–EXCHANGE functions that are actually executed
Wrapper	Exchanges where $i = j$ and consecutive identical exchanges are ignored
Parameters	$M = 640,000$. $G = 1,001$. NINPUTS = 1 and NOUTPUTS = 42. $Q = 10,000$. $D = 64$. $B = 2\%$. $N_{rpb} = 1$. $S_{rpb} = 500$. $S_{adf} = 100$. $N_{max-adf} = 4$. $N_{max-argument-adf} = 4$. $N_{min-argument-adf} = 0$. $N_{max-adl} = 2$. $S_{adl} = 100$. $N_{max-adl-executions} = 7$. $N_{max-argument-adl} = 0$. $N_{min-argument-adl} = 0$. NINDEXED = 20.
Result designation	Best-so-far pace-setting individual
Success predicate	Fitness reaches 1.16.

A 100%-correct 16-step seven-sorter emerged in generation 31. This best-of-run program consists of 11 branches, including one result-producing branch, two one-argument automatically defined functions, and two automatically defined loops (each consisting of a loop initialization branch, a loop condition branch, a loop body branch, and a loop update branch).

Before analyzing this evolved 11-branch best-of-run program in detail, we note the remarkable fact that it has only 24 WLO ("write linear output") functions. Without some form of reuse, this number of WLO functions is insufficient to yield a 16-step sorting network (which requires 32 usable entries in the 42-item output vector). Thus, the best-of-run program must be reusing code in some way. As will be seen shortly, this reuse comes from the automatically defined loops. To demonstrate this behavior, we first show this 11-branch program. Second, we will show the 16 COMPARE–EXCHANGE operations that it produces as both a table and a sorting network. Third, we will show the progressive temporal formation of the 42-item output vector by the two automatically defined loops and the result-producing branch of the program.

The 96-point result-producing branch of this best-of-run individual from generation 31 contains seven WLO functions:

```
(- (TOR (TNOT (RLI 1.423951)) (RLI -0.663916)) (* (RLO (% (WLM
(ADF8 (% (+ (RLI (WLO (RLI -1.450035) (RLI (TAND (TOR 2.718654
-0.983453) (RLI 8.494635))))))) (RLI (% (WLM (% (+ (RLI INDEX)
(RLI NOUTPUTS)) (LBB1)) (WLO (+ (IFGTZ 2.609941 -5.032810
```

```
9.230534) (RLO -1.435415)) (RLI -9.329263))) (- -3.620759
NOUTPUTS)))) (LBB1))) (WLO 2.203066 -9.737621)) (% (WLM (% (+
(RLI INDEX) (RLI NOUTPUTS)) (LBB1)) (WLO (+ (IFGTZ 2.609941
-5.032810 9.230534) (LBB0) (RLI (- (WLO (- (+ INDEX INDEX)
(IFGTZ -9.737621 INDEX -4.461124)) (- (WLO INDEX 5.510109)
(TNOT 2.414358))) (RLI 2.414358))))) (+ (WLO -3.620759
-1.339846) (+ 4.916246 NINPUTS))))) (RLI 7.964794))).
```

The 96-point loop initialization branch, LIB0, of the first automatically defined loop, ADL0, contains four WLO functions:

```
(% (WLM (% (+ (RLI INDEX) (RLI NOUTPUTS)) (RLI (IFGTZ -9.737621
(WLO (% (+ (+ (FLOOR 3.635883) (IFEQZ (- (+ INDEX -7.642968)
(TNOT 2.414358)) 0.000000 -8.097490)) (- (WLO INDEX INDEX)
(RLI 2.414358))) (% (TOR (- (WLO INDEX 5.510109) (TNOT
2.414358)) (TNOT 6.013577)) (RLI NINPUTS))) (IFGTZ (RLO (*
(IFEQZ 0.513199 5.854084 INDEX) (IFGTZ INDEX -3.575161
0.960634))) (+ (* (- 7.153162 7.628452) (IFEQZ 6.123299
-3.620759 -5.346760)) (RLI -4.709143)) (IFEQZ (TOR (RLM
-5.152097) (% 6.013577 NINPUTS)) (RLI -0.663916) (TNOT (TAND
9.951460 NOUTPUTS))))) -4.461124))) (WLO (+ (IFGTZ 2.609941
-5.032810 9.230534) (+ INDEX -2.569815)) (RLI -9.329263)))
(- INDEX (- -3.620759 NOUTPUTS))).
```

The 41-point loop condition branch, LCB0, of the first automatically defined loop, ADL0, contains six WLO functions:

```
(- (WLO (- (+ INDEX INDEX) (IFGTZ -9.737621 INDEX -4.461124))
(- (WLO INDEX (- (WLO INDEX 5.510109) (IFGTZ -9.737621 INDEX (*
(WLO -2.406623 -0.640701) NOUTPUTS)))) (TNOT 2.414358))) (RLI
(WLO INDEX (WLO (+ (IFGTZ 2.609941 -5.032810 9.230534) (+ INDEX
-2.569815)) (RLI -9.329263)))))).
```

The first branches of the first automatically defined loop do not read or write to indexed memory at all. The last two branches of the first automatically defined loop do not read or write to indexed memory and, more pertinently, do not contain any WLO functions. They are thus irrelevant to the operation of the overall program with one minor exception, namely, that LBB0 is referenced once by the result-producing branch and once in the second automatically defined loop, ADL1.

The five-point loop update branch, LUB0, of the first automatically defined loop, ADL0, contains no WLO functions:

```
(+ (RLI INDEX) (RLI NOUTPUTS)).
```

The three-point loop body branch, LBB0, of the first automatically defined loop, ADL0, contains no WLO functions and evaluates to a constant value of –4.461124:

```
(+ -5.461124 1.000000).
```

The two-point loop initialization branch, LIB1, of the second automatically defined loop, ADL1, of the best-of-run individual from generation 31 contains no WLO functions:

```
(RLI NOUTPUTS).
```

The 64-point loop condition branch, LCB1, of the second automatically defined loop, ADL1, contains seven WLO functions:

```
(- (WLO (- (+ (- (WLO INDEX (WLO (+ (IFGTZ 2.609941 -5.032810
9.230534) (+ INDEX -2.569815)) (RLI -9.329263))) (TNOT
2.414358)) (- INDEX (- -3.620759 NOUTPUTS))) (IFGTZ -9.737621
INDEX -4.461124)) (- (WLO INDEX 5.510109) -9.737621)) (RLI
(- (WLO (WLO (- (+ INDEX INDEX) (IFGTZ -9.737621 INDEX
-4.461124)) (- (WLO INDEX (RLI 7.818230)) (- (+ INDEX INDEX)
(IFGTZ (+ INDEX -4.461124) INDEX -4.461124)))) 5.510109) (RLI
2.414358)))).
```

The seven-point loop update branch, LUB1, of the second automatically defined loop, ADL1, contains no WLO functions:

```
(+ (IFGTZ 2.609941 (RLI NOUTPUTS) 9.230534) (LBB0)).
```

The two-point loop body branch, LBB1, of the second automatically defined loop, ADL1, contains no WLO functions and evaluates to a constant value of –1:

```
(TNOT 2.414358).
```

The one-point automatically defined function, ADF8, of the best-of-run individual from generation 31 is referenced once by the result-producing branch:

```
ARG0.
```

The six-point automatically defined function, ADF9, of the best-of-run individual from generation 31 is not referenced at all:

```
(- (RLI 7.818230) (TAND 3.285362 -2.823500)).
```

The best-of-run individual from generation 31 causes the execution of 16 COMPARE–EXCHANGE operations. Table 21.5 shows the 16 nondegenerate COMPARE–EXCHANGE operations in the best-of-run individual from generation 31. For convenience, the lower-numbered item is shown first for each COMPARE–EXCHANGE operation in this table.

Figure 21.6 shows the 100%-correct 16-step sorting network for seven items produced by the best-of-run individual from generation 31. In the figure, the horizontal rows are numbered 0 to 6 from bottom to top. Thus, the first step is a (COMPARE–EXCHANGE 4 6) operation. The dotted vertical lines show that certain COMPARE–EXCHANGE operations operate on disjoint items (and could, if desired, be performed in parallel). The three COMPARE–EXCHANGE operations appearing in the fourth group formed by the vertical lines are

- (COMPARE–EXCHANGE 1 2),
- (COMPARE–EXCHANGE 3 4), and
- (COMPARE–EXCHANGE 5 6).

Table 21.5 The 16 COMPARE–EXCHANGE operations of the 100%-correct 16-step seven-sorter evolved with GPPS

Step	First argument	Second argument
0	4	6
1	1	3
2	0	5
3	2	4
4	0	1
5	3	5
6	0	2
7	4	6
8	1	2
9	3	4
10	5	6
11	2	5
12	1	3
13	2	3
14	4	5
15	3	4

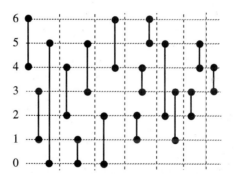

Figure 21.6   The 100%-correct 16-step minimal sorting network evolved with GPPS 1.0 on generation 31

These three operations act on consecutively numbered pairs of items (1, 2, 3, 4, 5, and 6) and will be mentioned prominently in the discussion below. Similarly, the two COMPARE–EXCHANGE operations appearing in the sixth group formed by the vertical lines are

- (COMPARE–EXCHANGE 2 3) and
- (COMPARE–EXCHANGE 4 5).

These two operations act on consecutively numbered items (2, 3, 4, and 5) and will also be mentioned below.

Table 21.6 shows the progressive formation of the 42-item output vector by the two loops (ADL0 and ADL1) and the result-producing branch (RPB). The vertical axis represents increasing time (downwards in the table). The first column identifies the branch of the overall program (one of the four branches of the two automatically defined loops or, on the last row of the table, the result-producing branch) that is executed at a particular time. Since the output vector is initialized at the beginning of each fitness case that is presented to the overall program, the first row of the table (labeled "**begin**") contains an output vector consisting of 42 zeros (shown as 42 dashes). The second column of the table shows INDEX (which runs from 0 to 6 for ADL0 and then runs from 0 to 6 for ADL1). The third column of the table shows the state of the 42-item output vector after execution of the branch involved.

The second row of the table (labeled "**After LIB0**") shows that the loop initialization branch, LIB0, of the first automatically defined loop, ADL0, writes a 6 in position 0 (the leftmost position) of the output vector. The next row shows that the loop condition branch, LCB0, writes a 4 in position 41 (i.e., the rightmost position of the 42-item output vector). The next two rows show that LBB0 and LUB0 do not affect the output vector.

The last row of the table shows the effect of the result-producing branch (RPB). The result-producing branch affects five of the positions of the output vector (positions 0, 5, 7, 32, and 40). These five changes can be interpreted as a "wrap-up" phase that occurs after execution of the two automatically defined loops. The 42-item output vector in this row represents a 16-step sorter (rather than a 21-step sorter) because the five pairs of consecutive zeros (shown as dashes) in positions 16–17 and 24–25, 26–27, 28–29, and 30–31 represent degenerate (COMPARE–EXCHANGE 0 0) operations that are deleted by the wrapper (output interface).

Return now to the fifth row of the table (where INDEX first becomes 1) and notice positions 18–23 of the output vector. The next 18 rows (as INDEX increases from 1 to 6) show that six consecutive positions (18–23) of the output vector are progressively filled in by a growing consecutive sequence of numbers (1, 2, 3, 4, 5, and 6). The sequence is lengthened by each execution of the loop condition branch, LCB0, of ADL0. Once this sequence of six consecutive numbers is formed, neither the second automatically defined loop, ADL1, nor the result-producing branch affects positions 18–23. These six entries in positions 18–23 of the output vector correspond to the three COMPARE–EXCHANGE operations appearing in the fourth group formed by the vertical lines in Figure 21.6. This iterative reuse of code (six times) is part of what enables an overall program containing only 24 WLO functions to produce the 32 entries in the output vector necessary to specify a 16-step sorting network.

A similar structure is simultaneously produced by ADL0 in positions 35–40 of the output vector in the same 18 lines of Table 21.6. The six consecutive numbers (1, 2, 3, 4, 5, and 6) remain intact until the result-producing branch alters the 6 in position 40 to a 3. The 2, 3, 4, and 5 in positions 36–39 ultimately yield the two COMPARE–EXCHANGE operations appearing in the sixth group formed by the vertical lines in Figure 21.6.

A sequence of three even numbers (2, 4, and 6) is inserted into positions 13–15 of the output vector by the action of LCB1 when INDEX is 4, 5, and 6. This sequence of three

Table 21.6 Progressive formation of the 42-item output vector of the 100%-correct 16-step seven-sorter evolved with GPPS

Time	INDEX	State of the 42-item output vector
Begin		`------------------------------------------`
After LIB0	—	`6-----------------------------------------`
After LCB0	0	`6---------------------------------------4`
After LBB0	0	`6---------------------------------------4`
After LUB0	0	`6---------------------------------------4`
After LCB0	1	`-6---1------------1----------------1-----4`
After LBB0	1	`-6---1------------1----------------1-----4`
After LUB0	1	`-6---1------------1----------------1-----4`
After LCB0	2	`161--2-----------12---------------12----4`
After LBB0	2	`161--2-----------12---------------12----4`
After LUB0	2	`161--2-----------12---------------12----4`
After LCB0	3	`2613-3-----------123-------------123---4`
After LBB0	3	`2613-3-----------123-------------123---4`
After LUB0	3	`2613-3-----------123-------------123---4`
After LCB0	4	`361354-----------1234------------1234--4`
After LBB0	4	`361354-----------1234------------1234--4`
After LUB0	4	`361354-----------1234------------1234--4`
After LCB0	5	`46135------------12345-----------12345-4`
After LBB0	5	`46135------------12345-----------12345-4`
After LUB0	5	`46135------------12345-----------12345-4`
After LCB0	6	`5613562----------123456----------1234564`
After LBB0	6	`5613562----------123456----------1234564`
After LUB0	6	`5613562----------123456----------1234564`
After LIB1	0	`5613562----------123456----------1234564`
After LCB1	0	`-613542--1-------123456----------1244564`
After LBB1	0	`-613542--1-------123456----------1244564`
After LUB1	0	`-613542--1-------123456----------1244564`
After LCB1	1	`1613562--13------123456----------1644564`
After LBB1	1	`1613562--13------123456----------1644564`
After LUB1	1	`1613562--13------123456----------1644564`
After LCB1	2	`2613512--135-----123456----------1244564`
After LBB1	2	`2613512--135-----123456----------1244564`
After LUB1	2	`2613512--135-----123456----------1244564`
After LCB1	3	`3613532--135-----123456----------31234564`
After LBB1	3	`3613532--135-----123456----------31234564`
After LUB1	3	`3613532--135-----123456----------31234564`
After LCB1	4	`4613552--135-2----123456---------531234564`
After LBB1	4	`4613552--135-2----123456---------531234564`
After LUB1	4	`4613552--135-2----123456---------531234564`
After LCB1	5	`-6135-2--135-24---123456---------531234564`
After LBB1	5	`-6135-2--135-24---123456---------531234564`
After LUB1	5	`-6135-2--135-24---123456---------531234564`
After LCB1	6	`2613522--135-246--123456---------531234564`
After LBB1	6	`2613522--135-246--123456---------531234564`
After LUB1	6	`2613522--135-246--123456---------531234564`
After RPB		`46135-24-135-246--123456--------2531234534`

even numbers is created by the iterative action of LCB1. When INDEX is ≥ 4, LCB1 performs the equivalent of the following:

```
(WLO (- (* 2 INDEX) 6) (+ INDEX 9)).
```

Similarly, a sequence of three odd numbers (1, 3, and 5) is inserted into positions 2–4 of the output vector by the action of LCB0 when INDEX is 2, 3, and 4. This sequence of three odd numbers is created by the iterative action of LCB0. When 2 ≤ INDEX ≤ 4, LCB0 performs the equivalent of the following:

```
(WLO (- (* 2 INDEX) 3) INDEX).
```

Also, a sequence of three odd numbers (1, 3, and 5) is inserted into positions 9–11 of the output vector by the iterative action of LCB0 when INDEX is 0, 1, and 2. When INDEX ≤ 2, LCB0 performs the equivalent of the following:

```
(WLO (+ (* 2 INDEX) 1) (+ INDEX 9)).
```

Subroutines, iterations, and indexed memory were all available to the Genetic Programming Problem Solver. Indexed memory played no role in the solution evolved for this problem on this particular run. One automatically defined function appeared nominally in the above evolved solution; however, it played no practical role in the solution. Loops played a critical role in fashioning the solution to the problem. The important point is that the decision to use (or not use) subroutines, iterations, and indexed memory was made by the evolutionary process—not by the human user prior to presenting the problem to the Genetic Programming Problem Solver.

The sorting network evolved in this chapter using GPPS 1.0, the solution evolved in Chapter 23 using GPPS 2.0, and the solution evolved in Chapter 57 using field-programmable gate arrays are all superior to that presented by the inventors of sorting networks in their 1962 patent (O'Connor and Nelson 1962). Specifically, the 16-step seven-sorter evolved using GPPS has two fewer steps than the sorting network described in the 1962 patent. In fact, GPPS rediscovered what Floyd and Knuth (Knuth 1973) discovered several years after the 1962 patent, namely, that 16 steps are sufficient for a sorting network for seven items. That is, genetic programming evolved a solution here that is better than that devised by the inventors of sorting networks (O'Connor and Nelson) and equal to that devised by two well-known subsequent human researchers of computer algorithms (Floyd and Knuth).

Referring to the eight criteria in Chapter 1 for establishing that an automatically created result is competitive with a human-produced result, this result satisfies the following two of the eight criteria:

A. The result was patented as an invention in the past, is an improvement over a patented invention, or would qualify today as a patentable new invention.

D. The result is publishable in its own right as a new scientific result (independent of the fact that the result was mechanically created).

Therefore, we make the following claim:

- **CLAIM NO. 2** We claim that the rediscovery by genetic programming of a sorting network for seven items with only 16 steps is an instance where genetic programming has produced a result that is competitive with a result produced by creative and inventive humans.

This instance of an automatically synthesized solution to a problem satisfies Arthur Samuel's criterion (1983) for artificial intelligence and machine learning:

> The aim [is] . . . to get machines to exhibit behavior, which if done by humans, would be assumed to involve the use of intelligence.

Elements of GPPS 2.0

Automatically defined stores (Chapter 9) were developed after the original design of version 1.0 of the Genetic Programming Problem Solver (Chapter 20). Automatically defined stores provide a way to automate the decision as to whether to use internal storage on a particular problem, how much internal storage to use, and what type of internal storage to use. Similarly, automatically defined recursions (Chapter 8) were developed after the original design of GPPS 1.0. GPPS 2.0 incorporates both ADSs and ADRs.

Subroutines, loops, recursions, and internal storage are all available to GPPS 2.0 in solving problems. The decision to use (or not use) automatically defined functions, automatically defined loops, automatically defined recursions, and automatically defined stores on a particular problem is dynamically made by GPPS 2.0 during the run—not by the human user prior to the run.

Version 2.0 of the Genetic Programming Problem Solver differs from GPPS 1.0 in the following ways:

1. Automatically defined stores (Chapter 9) and automatically defined recursions (Chapter 8) are added to the repertoire of programming constructs available to GPPS 2.0. The architecture-altering operations of storage creation (Section 9.1.1) and recursion creation (Section 8.1.1) are added to GPPS 2.0.

2. Because we are using automatically defined stores, the built-in indexed (vector) memory of GPPS 1.0 is removed. For the same reason, the WIM ("write indexed memory") and the RIM ("read indexed memory") functions are also removed.

3. Experience indicated that GPPS 1.0 sometimes commandeered the output vector as indexed memory (i.e., the RLO and WLO functions were used to read and write the output vector). Since our intent is to automate the decision as to whether to employ internal storage, we also removed the RLO function.

4. The three-argument IFEQZ ("if equal zero") conditional branching operator was removed.

Figure 22.1 shows the flow of information in a computer program using version 2.0 of the Genetic Programming Problem Solver. The program in the figure has an input vector (of length size N1) and an output vector (of length size N2). The GPPS 2.0 program potentially has zero, one, or more automatically defined functions, automatically defined loops, automatically defined recursions, and automatically defined stores.

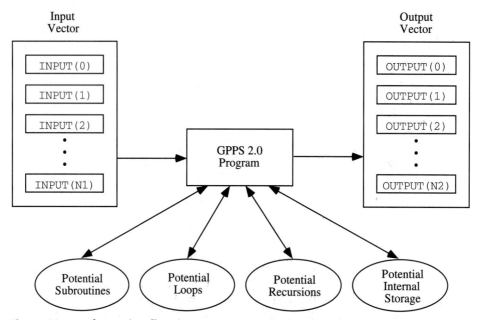

Figure 22.1 Information flow in a computer program using GPPS 2.0

Version 2.0 of the Genetic Programming Problem Solver contains the following functions and terminals:

- arithmetic functions:
  - addition (+),
  - subtraction (−),
  - multiplication (*), and
  - protected division %.
- conditional branching operators:
  - "if greater than zero" IFGTZ.
- numerically valued logical functions:
  - conjunction TAND,
  - disjunction TOR, and
  - negation TNOT.
- input reading function:
  - read linear input RLI.
- output writing function:
  - write linear output WLO.
- conversion function:
  - FLOOR.
- terminals:
  - floating-point random constants, $\Re_{\text{bigger-reals}}$,
  - constant for number of inputs, NINPUTS,

- constant for number of outputs, NOUTPUTS, and
- iteration index, INDEX.
- potential automatically defined functions (Chapter 5), such as
  - ADF0,
  - ADF1,
  - ADF2, and
  - ADF3.
- potential terminals representing the dummy variables (formal parameters) of the potential automatically defined functions (Chapter 5), such as
  - ARG0,
  - ARG1,
  - ARG2, and
  - ARG3.
- potential terminals representing the return value of the loop body branch of each potential automatically defined loop (Chapter 7), such as
  - LBB0 and
  - LBB1.
- potential writing and reading functions for implementing automatically defined stores (Chapter 9), such as
  - storage writing branch, SWB0, and storage reading branch, SRB0, and
  - storage writing branch, SWB1, and storage reading branch, SRB1.

Unless otherwise stated in the text or tableau, all the details of GPPS 1.0 apply to GPPS 2.0.

Six Problems Illustrating GPPS 2.0

This chapter applies version 2.0 of the Genetic Programming Problem Solver to the following problems from the fields of system identification (symbolic regression), classification, control, Boolean function leaning, and design:

- symbolic regression of a quadratic polynomial,
- the intertwined spirals problem,
- the cart-centering problem (originally solved in Chapter 19 using automatically defined stores),
- the Boolean even-6-parity problem (originally solved in Chapter 12 using architecture-altering operations for subroutines and solved again in Chapter 21 using GPPS 1.0),
- the time-optimal robot controller problem (originally solved in Chapter 13, solved again in Chapter 21 using GPPS 1.0, and solved yet again in Chapter 48 using electrical circuits), and
- the problem of synthesizing the design of a minimal sorting network (solved in Chapter 21 using GPPS 1.0 and solved later in Chapter 57 using evolvable hardware and field-programmable gate arrays).

23.1 QUADRATIC POLYNOMIAL PROBLEM WITH GPPS 2.0

This problem calls for the automatic creation, using the Genetic Programming Problem Solver 2.0, of a one-input, one-output computer program that takes the value of one independent floating-point variable x in the input vector and deposits a value into the output vector that closely matches certain given data. The input is related to the output by the quadratic polynomial $2.718x^2 + 3.1416x$. This problem first appeared in Section 10.2 of *Genetic Programming* (Koza 1992e).

23.1.1 Preparatory Steps

Program Architecture

When GPPS 2.0 is being used, each program in generation 0 has a uniform architecture consisting of one result-producing branch. There are no automatically defined functions, no automatically defined loops, no automatically defined recursions, and no automatically defined stores.

After generation 0, GPPS 2.0 uses the architecture-altering operations to create, duplicate, and delete automatically defined functions and to determine the number of arguments possessed by each automatically defined function. Hierarchical references are allowed among the automatically defined functions created by the architecture-altering operations. Similarly, GPPS 2.0 uses the architecture-altering operations to create, duplicate, and delete ADLs, ADRs, and ADSs from individual programs.

For practical reasons, a maximum of four automatically defined functions, each possessing between zero and two arguments, is established for this problem. Similarly, there is a maximum of one automatically defined loop, one automatically defined recursion, and two automatically defined stores. The type of internal storage that may be created by an automatically defined store is limited to named memory.

Functions and Terminals

When GPPS 2.0 is being used, the function and terminal sets do not change from problem to problem.

The initial function set for the result-producing branch, $F_{rpb\text{-}initial}$, is

$$F_{rpb\text{-}initial} = \{+, -, *, \%, \text{IFGTZ}, \text{TOR}, \text{TAND}, \text{TNOT}, \text{RLI}, \text{WLO}, \text{FLOOR}\},$$

taking 2, 2, 2, 2, 3, 2, 2, 1, 1, 2, and 1 arguments, respectively. Notice that four functions appearing in GPPS 1.0 (WIM, RIM, RLO, and IFEQZ) are not used in GPPS 2.0.

Since there are no automatically defined functions in generation 0, the initial function set for automatically defined functions, $F_{adf\text{-}initial}$, is empty:

$$F_{adf\text{-}initial} = \phi.$$

Since there are no automatically defined loops or automatically defined recursions in generation 0, the initial function sets for the four branches of the automatically defined loops and automatically defined recursions are empty:

$$F_{adl\text{-}initial} = \phi$$

and

$$F_{adr\text{-}initial} = \phi.$$

After generation 0, the architecture-altering operations introduce automatically defined functions, the dummy variables possessed by the automatically defined functions, automatically defined loops (each consisting of four branches), automatically defined recursions (each consisting of four branches), and automatically defined stores (each consisting of two branches). As a result, individuals in the population begin to contain functions and terminals associated with the newly created branches.

The set of potential functions for the result-producing branch, $F_{rpb\text{-}potential}$, is

$$F_{rpb\text{-}potential} = \{\text{ADL0}, \text{ADR0}, \text{SWB0}, \text{SWB1}, \text{ADF0}, \text{ADF1}, \text{ADF2}, \text{ADF3}\}.$$

Here SWB0 and SWB1 are the storage writing branches of automatically defined stores ADS0 and ADS1, respectively. The automatically defined functions take an as-yet-unknown number of arguments (between zero and four).

The potential function set for the automatically defined functions, $F_{adf\text{-}potential}$, is

$$F_{adf\text{-}potential} = \{\text{ADF0}, \text{ADF1}, \text{ADF2}, \text{ADF3}, +, -, *, \%, \text{IFLTE}, \text{TOR}, \text{TAND}, \text{TNOT}, \text{RLI}, \text{WLO}, \text{FLOOR}\},$$

subject to our usual limitation that a function-defining branch can refer hierarchically only to a previously defined function-defining branch.

The set of potential functions for the four branches of each automatically defined loop, $F_{\text{adl-potential}}$, is

$F_{\text{adl-potential}} = \{$ADF0, ADF1, ADF2, ADF3, +, -, *, %, IFLTE, TOR, TAND, TNOT, RLI, WLO, FLOOR$\}$.

The set of potential functions for the four branches of each automatically defined recursion, $F_{\text{adr-potential}}$, includes the recursion body branch, RBB0, along with the automatically defined functions:

$F_{\text{adr-potential}} = \{$ADR0, ADF0, ADF1, ADF2, ADF3, +, -, *, %, IFLTE, TOR, TAND, TNOT, RLI, WLO, FLOOR$\}$.

The initial terminal set for the result-producing branch, $T_{\text{rpb-initial}}$, is

$T_{\text{rpb-initial}} = \{\Re_{\text{bigger-reals}},$ NINPUTS, NOUTPUTS, INDEX$\}$.

For this problem, the size, NINPUTS, of the input vector is 1, and the size, NOUTPUTS, of the output vector is 1. INDEX is the index of the automatically defined loops.

Since there are no automatically defined functions in generation 0, the initial terminal set for automatically defined functions, $T_{\text{adf-initial}}$, is empty:

$T_{\text{adf-initial}} = \phi$.

Since there are no automatically defined loops or automatically defined recursions in generation 0, the initial terminal sets for the four branches of the automatically defined loops and automatically defined recursions are empty:

$T_{\text{adl-initial}} = \phi$

and

$T_{\text{adr-initial}} = \phi$.

The set of potential terminals for the result-producing branch, $T_{\text{rpb-potential}}$, is

$T_{\text{rpb-potential}} = \{$LBB0, SRB0, SRB1$\}$.

Here LBB0 is the return value from the loop body branch of automatically defined loop ADL0. SRB0 and SRB1 are the return values of the storage reading branches of automatically defined stores ADS0 and ADS1, respectively.

The set of potential terminals for the automatically defined functions, $T_{\text{adf-potential}}$, is

$T_{\text{adf-potential}} = \{$ARG0, ARG1, NINPUTS, NOUTPUTS, INDEX, $\Re_{\text{bigger-reals}}\}$.

The set of potential terminals for the four branches of the automatically defined loops, $T_{\text{adl-potential}}$, is

$T_{\text{adl-potential}} = \{$NINPUTS, NOUTPUTS, INDEX, $\Re_{\text{bigger-reals}}\}$.

The set of potential terminals for the four branches of the automatically defined recursions, $T_{\text{adr-potential}}$, is

$T_{\text{adr-potential}} = \{$NINPUTS, NOUTPUTS, INDEX, $\Re_{\text{bigger-reals}}\}$.

Fitness

The fitness cases for this problem consist of 20 randomly chosen values of the independent variable x between -1.0 and $+1.0$. Standardized fitness is the sum, over the 20 fitness cases, of the absolute value of the difference between the value deposited in the output vector and the value of the quadratic polynomial $2.718x^2 + 3.1416x$.

The number of hits is defined as the number of fitness cases (0 to 20) for which the value deposited in the output vector is within 0.01 of the value of the quadratic polynomial $2.718x^2 + 3.1416x$.

Parameters

This problem has several control parameters that have not appeared previously in this book:

- The maximum number, $N_{max-ads}$, of automatically defined stores is 2.
- The maximum number, $N_{max-adr}$, of automatically defined recursions is 1.
- The maximum size, S_{adr}, for each of the four branches of each automatically defined recursion is 100 points.
- None of the four branches of the automatically defined recursions possess arguments, so that $N_{min-argument-adr} = 0$ and $N_{max-argument-adr} = 0$.
- The maximum number, $N_{max-adr-executions}$, of recursive calls for automatically defined recursions is 9.

The other control parameters for this problem are found in the tableau (Table 23.1), the tables of percentages of genetic operations in Appendix D, and the default values specified in Appendix D.

Tableau

Table 23.1 summarizes the key features of the problem of symbolic regression of the quadratic polynomial $2.718x^2 + 3.1416x$ using GPPS 2.0. When GPPS 2.0 is used to solve a problem, the program architecture, the function set, and the terminal set do not change from problem to problem (and are the same as shown in this tableau).

23.1.2 Results

During our only run of the problem of symbolic regression of the quadratic polynomial $2.718x^2 + 3.1416x$ using GPPS 2.0, the best-of-generation program from generation 0 has a fitness of 16.457 and scores no hits (out of 20). Like all programs in generation 0 of any run of GPPS 2.0, this program has no automatically defined functions, no automatically defined loops, no automatically defined recursions, and no automatically defined stores.

After generation 0, GPPS 2.0 uses the architecture-altering operations to create, duplicate, and delete ADFs, ADLs, ADRs, and ADSs from individual programs in the population.

Table 23.2 shows the generation on which each of 34 pace-setting programs was created during the run; the number of ADFs, ADLs, ADRs, and ADSs in each pace-setting program; and the fitness and the number of hits for each pace-setting program. Note that the entries in the table reflect the order of reporting by the 64 nodes of the parallel

Table 23.1 Tableau for symbolic regression of a quadratic polynomial

Objective	Create, using the Genetic Programming Problem Solver 2.0, a computer program that takes the values of one independent floating-point variable x in the input vector and deposits a value into the output vector that closely matches the quadratic polynomial $2.718x^2 + 3.1416x$.
Program architecture	One result-producing branch, RPB. Automatically defined loops, automatically defined recursions, automatically defined stores, and automatically defined function(s) and their arguments will be created during the run by the architecture-altering operations.
Initial function set for the RPBs	$F_{rpb\text{-}initial}$ = {+, −, *, %, IFGTZ, TOR, TAND, TNOT, RLI, WLO, FLOOR}
Initial terminal set for the RPBs	$T_{rpb\text{-}initial}$ = {$\Re_{bigger\text{-}reals}$, NINPUTS, NOUTPUTS, INDEX}
Initial function set for the ADFs	No automatically defined functions in generation 0. $F_{adf\text{-}initial} = \phi$.
Initial terminal set for the ADFs	No automatically defined functions in generation 0. $T_{adf\text{-}initial} = \phi$.
Initial function set for ADLs	No automatically defined loops in generation 0. $F_{adl\text{-}initial} = \phi$.
Initial terminal set for ADLs	No automatically defined loops in generation 0. $T_{adl\text{-}initial} = \phi$.
Initial function set for ADRs	No automatically defined recursions in generation 0. $F_{adr\text{-}initial} = \phi$.
Initial terminal set for ADRs	No automatically defined recursions in generation 0. $T_{adr\text{-}initial} = \phi$.
Potential function set for the RPBs	$F_{rpb\text{-}potential}$ = {ADL0, ADR0, SWB0, SWB1, ADF0, ADF1, ADF2, ADF3}
Potential terminal set for the RPBs	$T_{rpb\text{-}potential}$ = {LBB0, SRB0, SRB1}
Potential function set for the ADFs	$F_{adf\text{-}potential}$ = {ADF0, ADF1, ADF2, ADF3, +, −, *, %, IFLTE, TOR, TAND, TNOT, RLI, WLO, FLOOR}
Potential terminal set for the ADFs	$T_{adf\text{-}potential}$ = {ARG0, ARG1, NINPUTS, NOUTPUTS, INDEX, $\Re_{bigger\text{-}reals}$}
Potential function set for ADLs	$F_{adl\text{-}potential}$ = {ADF0, ADF1, ADF2, ADF3, +, −, *, %, IFLTE, TOR, TAND, TNOT, RLI, WLO, FLOOR}
Potential terminal set for ADLs	$T_{adl\text{-}potential}$ = {NINPUTS, NOUTPUTS, INDEX, $\Re_{bigger\text{-}reals}$}
Potential function set for ADRs	$F_{adr\text{-}potential}$ = {ADR0, ADF0, ADF1, ADF2, ADF3, +, −, *, %, IFLTE, TOR, TAND, TNOT, RLI, WLO, FLOOR}
Potential terminal set for ADRs	$T_{adr\text{-}potential}$ = {NINPUTS, NOUTPUTS, INDEX, $\Re_{bigger\text{-}reals}$}.

(continued)

Table 23.1 *(continued)*

Fitness cases	20 randomly chosen values of the independent variable x between −1.0 and +1.0
Raw fitness	The sum, over the 20 fitness cases, of the absolute value of the difference between the value deposited in the output vector and the value of the quadratic polynomial $2.718x^2 + 3.1416x$
Standardized fitness	Same as raw fitness
Hits	The number of fitness cases (0 to 20) for which the value deposited in the output vector is within 0.01 of the value of the quadratic polynomial $2.718x^2 + 3.1416x$.
Wrapper	None
Parameters	$M = 120,000$. $G = 1,001$. NINPUTS = 1. NOUTPUTS = 1. $Q = 2,000$. $D = 60$. $B = 2\%$. $N_{rpb} = 1$. $S_{rpb} = 500$. $S_{adf} = 100$. $N_{max-adf} = 4$. $N_{max-argument-adf} = 2$. $N_{min-adf-arg} = 0$. $N_{max-adl} = 1$. $S_{adl} = 100$. $N_{max-argument-adl} = 0$. $N_{min-argument-adl} = 0$. $N_{max-adl-executions} = 3$. $N_{max-adr} = 1$. $S_{adr} = 100$. $N_{max-argument-adr} = 0$. $N_{min-argument-adr} = 0$. $N_{max-adr-executions} = 9$. $N_{max-ads} = 2$.
Result designation	Best-so-far pace-setting individual
Success predicate	A program scores 20 hits.

computer system. Hence, pace-setting programs (such as the ones from generations 15 and 22) are sometimes listed out of order in the table.

There is no compelling need to use ADFs, ADLs, ADRs, or ADSs in solving this problem. As can be seen from Table 23.2, ADFs, ADLs, and ADRs appear only sporadically among the pace-setting individuals during the run. ADSs never appear in any pace-setting individual.

The best-of-run program emerges on generation 29. This program scores 20 hits (out of 20) and has a fitness of 0.063 (an average error of only about 0.003 per fitness case). It has three two-argument ADFs, no ADLs, no ADRs, and no ADSs. The three automatically defined functions are present in this best-of-run program as a consequence of the architecture-altering operations. The result-producing branch has two references to ADF0 and two references to ADF2. The 34-point result-producing branch of the best-of-run program is

```
(ADF2 (* (RLI INDEX) (+ (TOR (ADF2 -6.903925 (IFGTZ INDEX (RLI
INDEX) -1.767983)) NOUTPUTS) (% (+ (TOR (ADF0 -6.903925 (RLI
8.720865)) NOUTPUTS) (% (TOR (ADF0 -6.903925 (RLI INDEX))
NOUTPUTS) (+ 8.936079 NOUTPUTS))) 8.288404))) 8.902800).
```

Automatically defined function ADF0 possesses two arguments and has 45 points:

```
(WLO (* ARG0 (- (+ (* (* ARG0 (- (+ (* (WLO 2.447521 -9.375271)
(RLI 3.350736)) NOUTPUTS) (IFGTZ INDEX (RLI INDEX)
-1.767983))) (RLI (IFGTZ INDEX (* (RLI (TOR NOUTPUTS
NOUTPUTS)) ARG1) -1.767983))) NOUTPUTS) (IFGTZ INDEX (* (RLI
```

```
(TOR NOUTPUTS NOUTPUTS)) ARG1) -1.767983))) (+ 2.163702
NOUTPUTS)).
```

Table 23.2 Pace-setting values of fitness for symbolic regression of the quadratic polynomial with GPPS 2.0

Generation	Number of ADFs	Number of ADLs	Number of ADRs	Number of ADSs	Fitness	Hits
0	0	0	0	0	16.457	0
0	0	0	0	0	13.824	0
0	0	0	0	0	12.064	0
0	0	0	0	0	11.718	0
0	0	0	0	0	11.217	0
1	0	0	0	0	10.674	0
1	0	0	0	0	9.265	0
2	0	0	0	0	6.470	0
3	0	0	0	0	5.554	0
4	0	0	1	0	5.551	1
4	0	0	0	0	5.100	0
4	0	1	0	0	4.054	0
4	0	0	0	0	3.930	2
5	0	0	0	0	3.030	0
5	1	0	1	0	3.030	0
6	1	0	1	0	3.004	0
6	0	1	1	0	2.761	0
7	1	1	0	0	2.379	1
7	0	0	1	0	2.052	1
9	1	0	1	0	1.854	0
10	0	0	0	0	1.646	4
10	1	0	1	0	1.537	1
11	1	1	0	0	1.456	3
12	2	0	0	0	1.210	4
14	2	0	1	0	1.191	0
16	1	0	1	0	1.144	3
15	1	0	0	0	0.611	5
17	2	0	0	0	0.394	4
21	2	0	0	0	0.285	11
24	2	0	0	0	0.186	12
22	3	0	0	0	0.127	19
24	2	0	0	0	0.123	19
24	3	0	0	0	0.112	19
29	3	0	0	0	0.063	20

Automatically defined function `ADF2` possesses two arguments and has 21 points:

```
(WLO (WLO (* ARG0 (- (+ (* (WLO 2.397371 2.506599) (RLI
NOUTPUTS)) NOUTPUTS) (IFGTZ INDEX ARG1 -1.767983)))
(+ 2.163702 NOUTPUTS)) NOUTPUTS).
```

The above program demonstrates that GPPS 2.0 can evolve a solution to the problem of symbolic regression of the quadratic polynomial $2.718x^2 + 3.1416x$. Subroutines, loops, recursions, and internal storage were all available to GPPS 2.0. The decision to use (or not use) ADFs, ADLs, ADRs, and ADSs was made by GPPS 2.0 during the run—not by the human user prior to the run.

23.2   INTERTWINED SPIRALS PROBLEM WITH GPPS 2.0

This problem calls for the automatic creation, using the Genetic Programming Problem Solver 2.0, of a two-input, one-output classification program that distinguishes between two intertwined spirals. The inputs to the classification program are the Cartesian coordinates of a point in the plane. The goal in the problem is to tell whether the point belongs to the first or second of two spirals. This problem was solved by Lang and Witbrock (1989) using neural networks and appeared in Section 17.3 of *Genetic Programming* (Koza 1992e).

Each spiral in Figure 23.1 coils around the origin of a Cartesian coordinate system three times. There are 97 points in the first spiral (indicated by squares) and 97 points in the second spiral (indicated by circles). The first spiral belongs to class +1 and the second spiral belongs to class –1. The task as defined by Lang and Witbrock (1989) is limited to the 194 points in the three turns of these two spirals and does not involve dealing with points that would lie on a fourth or later turn of the extensions of the same spirals.

23.2.1   Parameters

The tableau for the quadratic polynomial problem (Table 23.1) provides the details applicable to this run of the intertwined spirals problem using GPPS 2.0 with the following exceptions: `NINPUTS` is 2; `NOUTPUTS` is 1; and the population size, *M*, is 700,000 (with *Q* = 12,500; *D* = 56). This run was made on 56 nodes of our 70-node Beowulf-style parallel computer (described in Section 62.1.5). Notice how few changes there are between this problem and the previous problems using GPPS 2.0.

23.2.2   Tableau

Table 23.3 is an abbreviated tableau for the intertwined spirals problem using GPPS 2.0. When GPPS 2.0 is used to solve a problem, the program architecture, the function set, and the terminal set do not change from problem to problem (and are the same as Table 23.1 for the quadratic equation problem).

23.2.3   Results

In our second run of the intertwined spirals problem using GPPS 2.0, the best-of-generation program from generation 0 has a fitness of 76.0 and scores 118 hits (out of 194). Like all programs in generation 0 of any run of GPPS 2.0, this program has no

Table 23.3 Abbreviated tableau for the intertwined spirals problem using GPPS 2.0

Objective	Create, using the Genetic Programming Problem Solver 2.0, a computer program that takes the Cartesian coordinates of a point in the plane and tells whether the point belongs to the first or second of two intertwined spirals.
Fitness cases	194 points (x_i, y_i) on one or the other spiral
Raw fitness	The number of points that are correctly classified
Standardized fitness	The maximum raw fitness (i.e., 194) minus the raw fitness
Hits	Same as raw fitness for this problem
Wrapper	The wrapper maps a positive value in the output vector to +1 and maps nonpositive values to class –1.
Parameters	M = 700,000. G = 501. NINPUTS = 1. NOUTPUTS = 1. Q = 12,500. D = 56. B = 2%. N_{rpb} = 1. S_{rpb} = 500. S_{adf} = 100. $N_{max\text{-}adf}$ = 4. $N_{max\text{-}argument\text{-}adf}$ = 2. $N_{min\text{-}adf\text{-}arg}$ = 0. $N_{max\text{-}adl}$ = 1. S_{adl} = 100. $N_{max\text{-}argument\text{-}adl}$ = 0. $N_{min\text{-}argument\text{-}adl}$ = 0. $N_{max\text{-}adl\text{-}executions}$ = 3. $N_{max\text{-}adr}$ = 1. S_{adr} = 100. $N_{max\text{-}argument\text{-}adr}$ = 0. $N_{min\text{-}argument\text{-}adr}$ = 0. $N_{max\text{-}adr\text{-}executions}$ = 9. $N_{max\text{-}ads}$ = 2.
Result designation	Best-so-far pace-setting individual
Success predicate	A program scores 194 hits.

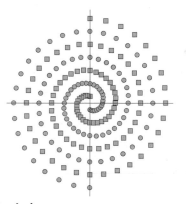

Figure 23.1 The intertwined spirals

automatically defined functions, no automatically defined loops, no automatically defined recursions, and no automatically defined stores.

After generation 0, GPPS 2.0 uses the architecture-altering operations to create, duplicate, and delete ADFs, ADLs, ADRs, and ADSs from individual programs.

Table 23.4 shows the generation on which each pace-setting program of the run was created; the number of ADFs, ADLs, ADRs, and ADSs in each pace-setting program; and the fitness and the number of hits for each pace-setting program. As can be seen, ADLs appear sporadically in pace-setting individuals during the run.

Table 23.4 Pace-setting values of fitness for intertwined spirals problem with GPPS 2.0

Generation	Number of ADFs	Number of ADLs	Number of ADRs	Number of ADSs	Fitness	Hits
0	0	0	0	0	80	114
0	0	0	0	0	77	117
0	0	0	0	0	76	118
1	0	0	0	0	72	122
1	0	0	0	0	70	124
2	0	0	0	0	69	125
3	0	0	0	0	66	128
3	0	0	0	0	64	130
4	0	0	0	0	61	133
7	0	0	0	0	56	138
8	1	4	0	0	55	139
9	1	0	1	1	54	140
9	0	4	0	1	53	141
10	1	0	0	0	52	142
10	0	4	1	0	51	143
13	0	4	0	1	50	144
13	0	4	0	1	48	146
14	0	0	0	2	47	147
15	0	4	1	0	46	148
15	0	0	0	2	45	149
17	0	0	0	2	44	150
19	0	0	0	2	42	152
19	1	0	1	1	41	153
21	1	0	1	1	40	154
20	1	0	1	1	39	155
21	1	4	1	1	38	156
23	1	0	1	1	37	157
24	1	0	1	2	36	158
29	1	0	1	1	35	159
27	1	0	1	1	34	160
30	1	0	1	1	33	161
31	1	0	1	1	32	162
32	1	0	1	1	31	163
33	1	0	1	1	30	164
33	1	0	1	1	29	165
38	2	0	1	1	28	166
37	1	0	1	1	27	167
42	1	0	1	1	26	168
42	1	0	1	2	25	169

44	1	0	1	2	24	170
48	1	0	1	2	23	171
49	1	0	1	2	22	172
45	1	0	1	2	21	173
55	1	0	1	2	20	174
58	1	0	1	2	19	175
58	1	0	1	2	18	176
58	2	0	1	2	17	177
61	1	0	1	2	16	178
53	1	0	1	2	15	179
60	1	0	1	2	14	180
52	1	0	1	2	13	181
70	2	0	1	2	12	182
76	1	0	1	2	11	183
81	1	0	1	2	10	184
83	1	0	1	2	9	185
83	1	0	1	2	8	186
84	1	0	1	2	7	187
96	1	0	1	2	6	188
103	1	0	1	2	5	189
111	1	0	1	2	4	190
130	2	0	1	2	3	191
142	3	0	1	2	2	192
195	4	0	1	2	1	193

The best-of-run program emerges on generation 195. This program scores 193 hits (out of 194) and has a fitness of 1. It has four ADFs, no ADLs, one ADR, and two ADSs. The ADFs, ADRs, and ADSs are present in this best-of-run program as a consequence of the architecture-altering operations.

The 476-point result-producing branch reads internal storage in four places; however, since no branch ever writes anything to either element of internal storage, these references to SRB0 and SRB1 merely return zero. The result-producing branch invokes ADF3 in three places. None of the other automatically defined functions are invoked by any branch. This result-producing branch is

```
(- (TAND (FLOOR (+ (FLOOR (WLO (FLOOR (RLI (+ (- -9.294943
1.259354) (RLI (- (RLI (RLI 9.474991)) NINPUTS))))) (% (TAND
(TNOT (- 3.043689 -3.236099)) (% -3.027544E-01 9.049971))
(FLOOR (- (RLI NOUTPUTS) (RLI (FLOOR (RLI (RLI
-7.449758)))))))))) INDEX)) (IFGTZ (- (* (WLO (% (RLI
-3.613539) (RLI (FLOOR (RLI -8.270741)))) (RLI (ADF3))) (RLI (+
(IFGTZ (- (* (WLO (% (RLI (RLI -7.186990)) (RLI (FLOOR (RLI
```

```
-8.270741)))) (RLI -3.199815)) (+ (% -4.810277 (- (RLI (FLOOR
(RLI (RLI NOUTPUTS)))) NINPUTS)) (RLI (- (RLI NOUTPUTS) (+
9.243441E-01 1.403765))))) -1.931131) (RLI (- (IFGTZ (- (*
(TOR (RLI NINPUTS) (% (RLI -8.270741) (RLI (FLOOR (RLI
(RLI NOUTPUTS)))))) (RLI 6.217785E-01)) (* (WLO (- (RLI (RLI
-7.186990)) (RLI 6.245180)) (IFGTZ (TAND NOUTPUTS 1.566558)
2.956152E-01 (TAND -7.760544E-01 -7.703409))) (RLI NOUTPUTS)))
(WLO (* (RLI NINPUTS) (RLI (RLI NOUTPUTS))) (- (RLI 4.344521E-
01) (RLI (TOR (RLI -2.245080) (WLO (RLI 6.661274) (**SRB0**))))))
(RLI NINPUTS)) (RLI 3.191200))) (IFGTZ (IFGTZ (TNOT (WLO (%
(- (RLI (% INDEX (RLI NOUTPUTS))) -8.957327) (FLOOR (- (RLI
NOUTPUTS) (RLI (FLOOR (RLI -7.618966)))))) (RLI 3.702745E-
01))) (TOR -2.293921E-01 -2.111530E-01) (**SRB1**)) (RLI (* (TNOT
(RLI -3.072415)) NINPUTS)) (TOR (* (TOR (RLI -2.245080) (WLO
(RLI 6.661274) (**SRB0**))) (- (RLI (RLI NINPUTS)) (RLI
-3.888663))) 4.344521E-01))) 1.403765))) (RLI NOUTPUTS)) (RLI
(- (IFGTZ (+ (% -4.810277 (- (RLI (RLI 9.474991)) NINPUTS))
(RLI 6.842735)) (RLI NOUTPUTS) (WLO -9.196673 (IFGTZ (FLOOR
-9.196673) NINPUTS (WLO (RLI (FLOOR (RLI (RLI -7.449758))))
5.964897)))) (RLI -3.027544E-01))) (IFGTZ (IFGTZ (TNOT (WLO (%
(TAND (% -3.027544E-01 -7.186990) (% -3.027544E-01 9.049971))
(RLI (RLI 3.191200))) (IFGTZ (RLI NINPUTS) -4.807597
5.762297))) (FLOOR -7.618966) (RLI 6.842735)) (RLI NOUTPUTS)
(TOR (RLI 4.344521E-01) (% (RLI 1.259354) -1.617459))))) (*
(IFGTZ (+ (RLI (RLI (WLO (- (RLI -7.618966) (% (RLI (RLI
NOUTPUTS)) (RLI NOUTPUTS))) (% INDEX (TOR (RLI -2.245080)
(WLO (RLI 6.661274) (**SRB0**))))))) (RLI NINPUTS)) (RLI 8.551830)
(RLI (IFGTZ (+ (RLI (RLI (WLO (- (RLI -7.618966) (% (RLI
(RLI NOUTPUTS)) (RLI NOUTPUTS))) (% INDEX (TOR (RLI -2.245080)
(RLI -8.270741)))))) (RLI NINPUTS)) (RLI 8.551830) (IFGTZ (-
(* (WLO (% (RLI (RLI 3.191200)) (RLI (FLOOR (RLI (RLI
NOUTPUTS))))) (RLI -3.199815)) (RLI 6.427534)) -1.931131)
(RLI (IFGTZ (+ (% -4.810277 (- (RLI (RLI 9.474991)) NINPUTS))
(RLI (- (RLI NOUTPUTS) (+ 9.243441E-01 1.403765)))) (WLO
(* (RLI NINPUTS) (RLI (RLI NOUTPUTS))) (- (RLI 4.344521E-01)
(% NINPUTS -1.617459))) (WLO -9.196673 (IFGTZ (FLOOR
-9.196673) NINPUTS (WLO NOUTPUTS 5.964897))))) (IFGTZ (WLO
(WLO (% (TAND (TNOT (- 3.043689 -3.236099)) (RLI NOUTPUTS))
(FLOOR (- (RLI NOUTPUTS) (RLI (+ (TAND (+ (% (RLI INDEX)
(- -5.538187 (RLI 3.191200))) (% (RLI (RLI (* (RLI INDEX)
NINPUTS))) 1.318227)) (* (% -4.810277 (- (RLI (RLI 9.474991))
(* (+ (TNOT NOUTPUTS) (TOR -2.336568 (TNOT -7.703409))) (- (RLI
(TOR (RLI -2.245080) (WLO (FLOOR (RLI (**ADF3**))) (**SRB0**))))
(RLI -3.888663))))) (WLO -7.223339E-01 6.217785E-01))) (RLI
8.081902)))))) (RLI -3.027544E-01)) (RLI (RLI -7.186990)))
(RLI (* (TNOT (RLI -3.072415)) NINPUTS)) (% (RLI 1.403765)
```

```
-1.617459)))))) (- (TAND (FLOOR (RLI (ADF3))) (TAND (WLO (RLI
(% (- 3.043689 -5.470221) (- (RLI NOUTPUTS) (+ (+ -9.114832
6.172256E-01) 1.403765)))) (RLI (RLI -8.270741))) (RLI
9.422867))) (FLOOR (RLI -8.270741)))))).
```

The 42-point automatically defined function ADF3 is

```
(WLO (* (RLI NINPUTS) (RLI (RLI NOUTPUTS))) (- (RLI NOUTPUTS)
(IFGTZ (RLI NINPUTS) -4.807597 (% (- (% NINPUTS (+ (%
(RLI INDEX) (- -5.538187 (RLI (FLOOR (RLI -7.618966)))))
(% (RLI (RLI 1.403765)) 1.318227))) -8.957327) (FLOOR
(- (RLI NOUTPUTS) (RLI (FLOOR (RLI -7.618966))))))))))).
```

The above program demonstrates that GPPS 2.0 can evolve an almost perfect solution to the intertwined spirals problem. Although subroutines, loops, recursions, and internal storage were all available to GPPS 2.0, the decision to use (or not use) them was dynamically made by GPPS 2.0 during the run.

23.3   CART-CENTERING PROBLEM WITH GPPS 2.0

The time-optimal cart-centering (isotropic rocket) problem was originally described in Chapter 19 using automatically defined stores (and in the tableau of Table 19.1).

23.3.1   Parameters

The tableau for the quadratic polynomial problem (Table 23.1) provides the details applicable to GPPS 2.0, except that NINPUTS is 1; NOUTPUTS is 1; and the population size, M, is 120,000 (with $Q = 2,000$; $D = 60$). Notice how few changes there are between this problem and the previous problems using GPPS 2.0.

23.3.2   Results

During our only run of the cart-centering problem using GPPS 2.0, the best-of-generation program from generation 0 has a fitness of 195.0 and scores only 1 hit (out of 20).

Table 23.5 shows the generation on which each pace-setting program of the run was created; the number of ADFs, ADLs, ADRs, and ADSs in each pace-setting program; and the fitness and the number of hits for each pace-setting program.

It is known that it is not possible to make significant progress on this problem without internal storage. The architecture-altering operations in GPPS 2.0 introduced the necessary storage in the evolving program dynamically during the run. As can be seen from Table 23.5, all the pace-setting programs after generation 8 have at least one cell of named memory.

On the other hand, loops or recursions are not necessary for solving this problem. Accordingly, ADLs and ADRs appear sporadically (19 times in the 42 rows of the table).

Although subroutines are also not necessary for solving this problem, one, two, or three automatically defined functions appear in 36 of the 42 pace-setting individuals of this run.

The best-of-run program emerges on generation 56. This program scores 20 hits (out of 20) and has a fitness of 46.68 (100.3% of the known optimum). It has two ADFs, one

Table 23.5 Pace-setting values of fitness for cart-centering problem with GPPS 2.0

Generation	Number of ADFs	Number of ADLs	Number of ADRs	Number of ADSs	Fitness	Hits
0	0	0	0	0	195.0	1
0	0	0	0	0	192.1	1
0	0	0	0	0	185.1	2
5	3	0	0	1	184.8	2
5	0	1	0	0	183.0	3
6	1	1	0	0	180.4	5
7	0	0	1	1	178.5	3
8	1	1	0	1	178.3	3
8	1	1	0	0	177.5	3
9	0	1	0	1	176.8	3
10	1	0	0	1	162.2	7
10	3	0	0	1	129.3	15
14	2	0	0	1	87.2	19
14	2	0	0	1	74.1	20
17	3	0	0	1	66.7	20
24	2	0	0	1	66.2	20
19	2	0	0	1	61.1	20
25	2	0	0	1	59.3	20
28	2	0	0	1	57.8	20
31	2	0	0	1	56.9	20
31	2	0	0	1	56.8	20
27	2	0	0	2	56.0	20
33	3	1	0	1	55.2	20
35	3	0	0	1	53.7	20
28	3	0	0	2	53.6	20
29	2	0	0	2	51.9	20
41	2	0	0	1	51.7	20
36	2	1	0	1	51.7	20
42	3	0	1	2	51.2	20
42	2	0	0	1	50.3	20
43	2	0	0	1	49.9	20
44	2	1	0	1	49.8	20
43	2	1	0	1	49.6	20
44	2	1	0	1	49.6	20
54	2	0	0	1	49.3	20
46	2	1	0	1	49.1	20
51	2	1	0	1	49.0	20
51	2	1	0	1	48.8	20

52	2	1	0	1	48.7	20
52	2	1	0	1	47.4	20
59	2	1	0	1	47.1	20
56	2	1	0	1	46.7	20

ADL, no ADRs, and one ADS. The ADFs, ADL, and ADS are present in this best-of-run program as a consequence of the architecture-altering operations.

The result-producing branch of the best-of-run program has 451 points. It has 10 invocations (in bold below) of the storage writing branch, SWB, and 11 invocations (in bold below) of the storage reading branch, SRB. It also has three invocations of automatically defined function ADF0 and five invocations of automatically defined function ADF3. In turn, ADF3 has one invocation of the storage writing branch, SWB. The result-producing branch of this program is

```
(WLO (+ (SRB) (* (RLI INDEX) -4.011031)) (IFGTZ (FLOOR (WLO
(IFGTZ (FLOOR (+ (SWB (* (RLI -2.236637) (+ 3.599064 (- (FLOOR
(TAND 6.936476 6.918259E-01 )) (FLOOR (RLI 8.133572)))))) (-
(- (FLOOR (TAND 6.936476 6.918259E-01 )) (TOR NOUTPUTS (% (%
-9.464722 NOUTPUTS) INDEX))) (ADF3 (TOR (* -6.567883 NINPUTS)
-4.372463))))) (FLOOR (RLI (RLI 3.632965))) (WLO (- (* -
6.567883 NINPUTS) (RLI -4.160260)) (FLOOR (WLO (IFGTZ (FLOOR
(+ (SWB (* (RLI -2.236637) (+ 3.443432 (IFGTZ (- (RLI (TNOT
(RLI INDEX))) (- (WLO NINPUTS 6.172361E-01 ) (* (* (RLI
-6.611924) (RLI (TNOT (* -3.409420 (TNOT (RLI INDEX))))))) (*
INDEX 7.344950)))) (IFGTZ (- (RLI INDEX) NINPUTS) NINPUTS
(IFGTZ (FLOOR (RLI 8.133572)) (RLI (% (IFGTZ NINPUTS -7.529213
-3.908672E-01 ) 2.935582)) (% (- -8.818617E-01 NOUTPUTS)
(- -1.580816 (FLOOR (+ 3.443432 (RLI (RLI NINPUTS)))))))))))
(IFGTZ (FLOOR (RLI 8.133572)) (RLI (% -2.982692 2.935582)) (%
(- -8.818617E-01 NOUTPUTS) (- -1.580816 (- (* -6.567883 (SWB (*
(RLI -2.236637) (+ 3.443432 (RLI 1.827848))))) (* -6.567883
NINPUTS))))))))) INDEX)) (FLOOR (RLI NOUTPUTS)) (RLI (WLO (+
(SRB) (WLO (IFGTZ (FLOOR (+ (SWB (* (RLI -2.236637) (+ 3.443432
(IFGTZ (- (RLI (TNOT (RLI INDEX))) (- (FLOOR (SRB)) (* (* (RLI
-6.611924) (RLI (TNOT (* -3.409420 (TNOT (RLI (TNOT
(* -3.409420 (TNOT (RLI INDEX))))))))))))) (* (FLOOR (SRB))
7.344950)))) (WLO (- (* -6.567883 (SWB (* (RLI -2.236637)
(+ 3.443432 (RLI 1.827848))))) (* -6.567883 NINPUTS)) (TOR
(RLI (RLI NOUTPUTS)) (IFGTZ NINPUTS -7.529213 -3.908672E-01
))) (IFGTZ (FLOOR (RLI 8.133572)) (RLI (% -2.982692 2.935582))
(% (- -8.818617E-01 (SWB (* (RLI -2.236637) (+ 3.599064
(- (FLOOR (TAND 6.936476 6.918259E-01 )) (RLI INDEX))))))
(- -1.580816 3.582714)))))))) INDEX)) (FLOOR (* -4.370489
NOUTPUTS)) (RLI (WLO (+ (SRB) (* (RLI INDEX) -4.011031)) (IFGTZ
```

```
(+ (SWB (* (RLI -2.236637) (+ 3.599064 (- (FLOOR (TAND 6.936476
6.918259E-01 )) (RLI INDEX))))) (- (- (FLOOR (TAND 6.936476
6.918259E-01 )) (TOR NOUTPUTS (% (% -9.464722 NOUTPUTS)
INDEX))) (ADF3 (TOR (TAND (* (RLI (RLI -4.160260)) -4.011031)
1.642557) -4.372463)))) (ADF0) (WLO -5.533132 NOUTPUTS)))))
(FLOOR (SRB)))) (IFGTZ (* (IFGTZ (FLOOR (WLO (IFGTZ (FLOOR
(+ (SWB (* (RLI (FLOOR (WLO (IFGTZ (RLI INDEX) (FLOOR (RLI
NOUTPUTS)) (RLI 8.904701)) (FLOOR (SRB))))) (+ 3.443432
(- (- (FLOOR (TAND 6.936476 6.918259E-01 )) (RLI NOUTPUTS))
(RLI -3.193890))))) (RLI -1.580816))) (FLOOR (RLI NOUTPUTS))
(* (RLI (RLI -9.080980)) (ADF3 3.599064))) (FLOOR (SRB))))
-9.387218 (FLOOR (WLO (IFGTZ (FLOOR (+ (SWB (* (RLI -2.236637)
(+ 3.443432 (IFGTZ (- (RLI INDEX) NINPUTS) 3.443432 (% (-
-8.818617E-01 (+ (* (RLI (+ 3.443432 (RLI (+ (SRB) (* (% (ADF3
-6.654253E-01 ) (RLI 2.350081)) -4.011031))))) (ADF3
3.599064)) (ADF0))) (- -1.580816 3.582714)))))) (RLI
-1.580816))) (FLOOR (RLI NOUTPUTS)) (RLI -9.241910)) (FLOOR
(- (WLO NINPUTS 6.172361E-01 ) (* (* (RLI -6.611924) (RLI (TNOT
(* -3.409420 (TNOT (RLI (TNOT (* -3.409420 (TNOT (RLI
INDEX)))))))))) (* INDEX 7.344950)))))))  1.642557) (ADF0) (WLO
-5.533132 NOUTPUTS))))) (FLOOR (SRB)))))) (FLOOR (SRB))))
-9.387218 (WLO -5.533132 (SWB (% (RLI (TOR 3.962722 NINPUTS))
(- (- (FLOOR NINPUTS) (RLI NOUTPUTS)) (TAND 6.936476
6.918259E-01 ))))))).
```

Automatically defined function ADF0 has seven points:

```
(TOR NOUTPUTS (% (% -9.464722 NOUTPUTS) INDEX)).
```

Automatically defined function ADF3 has 10 points:

```
(SWB (* (RLI (RLI (RLI (FLOOR (* -4.370489 NOUTPUTS)))))))
3.882782)).
```

The automatically defined loop of this best-of-run program is not referenced.

The above program demonstrates that GPPS 2.0 can evolve a solution to the time-optimal cart-centering problem. This problem is known to require the use of internal storage. Subroutines, loops, recursions, and internal storage were all available to GPPS 2.0. The crucial decision to use an automatically defined store, as well as the decisions to use (or not use) ADFs, ADLs, and ADRs, was made dynamically by GPPS 2.0 during the run—not by the human user prior to the run.

23.4 EVEN-6-PARITY PROBLEM WITH GPPS 2.0

The Boolean even-6-parity problem was originally solved in Chapter 12 using architecture-altering operations for subroutines and solved again in Chapter 21 using GPPS 1.0. See the tableau (Table 12.1) for details.

23.4.1   Parameters

The tableau for the quadratic polynomial problem (Table 23.1) provides the details applicable to GPPS 2.0, except that NINPUTS is 6; NOUTPUTS is 1; and the population size, M, is 120,000 (with Q = 2,000; D = 60). The maximum number of iterations for any one execution of any one automatically defined loop, $N_{\text{max-adl-executions}}$, is 9.

23.4.2   Results

During our only run of the even-6-parity problem using GPPS 2.0, the best-of-generation program from generation 0 has a fitness of 32 and scores 32 hits (out of 64).

Table 23.6 shows the generation on which each pace-setting program of the run was created; the number of ADFs, ADLs, ADRs, and ADSs in each pace-setting program; and the fitness and the number of hits for each pace-setting program. As can be seen, ADFs, ADLs, ADRs, and ADSs each appear sporadically during the run.

The best-of-run program for the even-6-parity problem emerges on generation 77. This program scores 64 hits (out of 64) and has a fitness (error) of 0. It has one ADF, one ADL, no ADRs, and one ADS.

The result-producing branch of the best-of-run program has 498 points. Automatically defined function ADF0 is referenced twice by the result-producing branch. The storage write branch, SWB, and the storage read branch, SRB, are each referenced once by the result-producing branch. The result-producing branch refers four times to the value returned by the loop body branch, LBB, of the program's automatically defined loop. The program is

```
(IFGTZ (WLO (* (* (IFGTZ (TNOT (RLI (- (TNOT (% -8.075199E-01
(FLOOR (% INDEX NINPUTS)))) (RLI (TNOT 6.000711))))) (% (IFGTZ
NOUTPUTS (% (TOR (% 9.738825 INDEX) (FLOOR (+ (WLO (LBB) (RLI
INDEX)) (FLOOR (RLI -8.212069))))) (TAND (RLI 8.977148) (-
(TNOT (% -8.075199E-01 (FLOOR (% INDEX NINPUTS)))) (RLI (TNOT
6.000711))))) (- (WLO (RLI -2.156086) (* 4.381680 INDEX)) (RLI
-1.447678))) (TAND (RLI 8.977148) (IFGTZ -3.081552 3.976555
-7.128815))) (- (WLO (RLI -2.156086) (* 4.381680 INDEX)) (RLI
-1.447678))) (RLI -9.882646)) (RLI -9.882646)) (RLI (+ (WLO
(FLOOR (% -2.435598E-01 (RLI -8.065310E-01 ))) (RLI NINPUTS))
(TOR (TOR (* -9.024844 NOUTPUTS) (RLI INDEX)) (* (% INDEX
7.173054) (% (RLI NINPUTS) -3.955457))))))) (IFGTZ (+ (+ (RLI
1.111267) (% INDEX (RLI (RLI NOUTPUTS)))) (% (TAND (RLI
3.256218) (FLOOR (% NINPUTS INDEX))) (+ (WLO (LBB) (RLI INDEX))
(FLOOR (RLI -8.212069))))) (SWB (RLI -5.770931E-01 )) (RLI
4.759479)) (- (RLI NINPUTS) (IFGTZ (WLO (* (IFGTZ (TNOT (RLI
(RLI (RLI 2.087852)))) (% (TOR (% 9.738825 INDEX) (FLOOR
NOUTPUTS)) (- (RLI -4.211002) (- (WLO (RLI -2.156086) (*
4.381680 INDEX)) (RLI -1.447678)))) (- (WLO (RLI -2.156086)
(* 4.381680 INDEX)) (RLI -1.447678))) (RLI (- (RLI -4.211002)
(- (WLO (RLI -2.156086) (* 4.381680 INDEX)) (RLI
-1.447678))))) (RLI NOUTPUTS)) (IFGTZ (+ (FLOOR (RLI (+ (- (RLI
-4.211002) (RLI INDEX)) (RLI (- (WLO (RLI -2.156086) (FLOOR (%
```

```
-2.435598E-01 -8.010729))) (RLI -1.447678)))))) (% (TAND (RLI
-4.834002) (FLOOR (% NINPUTS INDEX))) (+ (WLO (RLI -8.065310E-
01 ) (RLI (RLI NINPUTS))) (LBB)))) (RLI -5.770931E-01 ) (RLI
4.759479)) (- (RLI NINPUTS) (IFGTZ (WLO (* (IFGTZ (TNOT (RLI
(RLI -4.108169))) (% (TOR (% 9.738825 INDEX) (FLOOR NOUTPUTS))
(TAND (RLI 8.977148) (IFGTZ -3.081552 3.976555 -7.128815)))
(- (WLO (RLI -2.156086) (* 4.381680 INDEX)) (% INDEX (RLI
1.111267)))) (RLI -9.882646)) (RLI NOUTPUTS)) (IFGTZ (+ (+
(RLI 1.111267) (% INDEX 5.010924)) (% (TAND (* 4.381680 (RLI
-4.108169)) -4.108169) (+ (WLO (TOR (RLI -4.834002) (RLI
INDEX)) (RLI INDEX)) (FLOOR (RLI -8.212069))))) (RLI INDEX)
-4.355075) (- (RLI (RLI -2.156086)) (IFGTZ (IFGTZ (WLO (*
(IFGTZ (TNOT (RLI (RLI (RLI -2.156086)))) (+ (RLI (WLO (+
4.950438 NINPUTS) (FLOOR (* INDEX (TOR (TOR (* -9.024844
NOUTPUTS) (RLI INDEX)) (* (TAND (RLI 3.256218) (FLOOR (RLI
-8.065310E-01 ))) (% NOUTPUTS -3.955457))))))) INDEX) (- (WLO
(RLI INDEX) (RLI -4.048536)) (RLI -1.447678))) (RLI
-9.882646)) (RLI (FLOOR (* (RLI -4.355075) (RLI (WLO (FLOOR
(% -2.435598E-01 -8.010729)) (TAND (ADF0 -1.014584 4.222528)
(- -5.528134 8.375563)))))))) (IFGTZ (+ (FLOOR (RLI (+ (FLOOR
6.581360) (RLI 4.936962E-01 )))) (% (TAND (RLI 3.256218)
(FLOOR (% NINPUTS (TNOT 6.000711)))) (+ (WLO (RLI -8.065310E-
01 ) (RLI INDEX)) (FLOOR (RLI (RLI -4.108169)))))) (RLI (RLI
NINPUTS)) (RLI 4.759479)) (- (RLI NINPUTS) (IFGTZ (* (RLI (RLI
NOUTPUTS)) (% NINPUTS INDEX)) (TNOT (FLOOR (* (+ (RLI NOUTPUTS)
-7.780355) (RLI NINPUTS)))) (+ (WLO (FLOOR (% -2.435598E-01
-8.010729)) (TAND (ADF0 -1.014584 4.222528) (- -5.528134
8.375563))) (TOR (TOR (* INDEX (TOR (TOR (* -9.024844 NOUTPUTS)
(RLI INDEX)) (* (TAND (RLI 4.759479) (FLOOR (% NINPUTS (+ (WLO
(LBB) (RLI INDEX)) (FLOOR (RLI -8.212069)))))) (% NOUTPUTS
-3.955457)))) (RLI INDEX)) (* (% INDEX 7.173054) (% NOUTPUTS
-6.547245))))))) (TNOT (SRB)) (+ (WLO (FLOOR (% -2.435598E-01
(RLI -8.065310E-01 ))) (RLI NINPUTS)) (TOR (TOR (* -9.024844
NOUTPUTS) (RLI INDEX)) (* (% INDEX 7.173054) (% NOUTPUTS
-3.955457)))))))))))).
```

Automatically defined function ADF0 has 52 points:

```
(* (IFGTZ (TNOT (TOR (% 9.738825 INDEX) (FLOOR NOUTPUTS))) (%
(+ (RLI 1.111267) (% INDEX 5.010924)) (TAND (RLI 8.977148)
(IFGTZ -3.081552 3.976555 -7.128815))) (- (WLO (RLI -2.156086)
(* 4.381680 INDEX)) (RLI -1.447678))) (IFGTZ (TNOT (RLI (RLI
(RLI -2.156086)))) (+ (RLI (RLI 4.759479)) INDEX) (- (* (RLI
(RLI NOUTPUTS)) (RLI -9.927546)) (RLI -1.447678)))).
```

The loop iteration branch, LIB, has two points:

```
(RLI 4.759479).
```

Table 23.6 Pace-setting values of fitness for even-6-parity problem with GPPS 2.0.

Generation	Number of ADFs	Number of ADLs	Number of ADRs	Number of ADSs	Fitness	Hits
0	0	0	0	0	32	32
0	0	0	0	0	31	33
0	0	0	0	0	30	34
4	1	1	0	0	29	35
5	0	1	0	0	28	36
6	2	0	1	0	27	37
9	1	1	0	0	26	38
11	1	1	0	0	25	39
14	1	1	1	0	24	40
15	1	1	0	0	22	42
21	1	1	1	0	21	43
20	1	1	0	0	20	44
21	0	1	0	0	19	45
22	1	1	0	0	18	46
24	1	1	0	0	17	47
25	1	1	0	0	16	48
27	1	1	0	0	15	49
31	1	1	0	0	14	50
34	1	1	0	0	13	51
31	1	1	0	0	12	52
35	1	1	0	0	11	53
40	1	1	0	0	10	54
42	1	1	1	0	9	55
47	2	1	1	0	8	56
43	1	1	0	0	7	57
52	1	1	0	0	6	58
57	1	1	1	0	5	59
57	1	1	0	0	4	60
64	1	1	0	0	3	61
67	1	1	0	1	2	62
72	1	1	0	1	1	63
77	1	1	0	1	0	64

The loop condition branch, LCB, has seven points:

```
(TNOT (FLOOR (* (RLI -4.355075) (RLI NINPUTS)))).
```

The loop update branch, LUB, has 21 points:

```
(% (TAND (RLI (WLO (RLI -8.065310E-01 ) (RLI INDEX))) (FLOOR (%
NINPUTS INDEX))) (+ (WLO (RLI -8.065310E-01 ) (RLI INDEX))
(FLOOR (RLI -8.212069))))).
```

The loop body branch, LBB, has two points:

```
(RLI -8.065310E-01 ).
```

The above program demonstrates that GPPS 2.0 can evolve a solution to the Boolean even-6-parity problem. Although subroutines, loops, recursions, and internal storage were all available to GPPS 2.0, the decision to use (or not use) them was dynamically made by GPPS 2.0 during the run.

23.5 ROBOT CONTROLLER PROBLEM WITH GPPS 2.0

The time-optimal robot controller problem was originally solved in Chapter 13, solved again in Chapter 21 using GPPS 1.0, and is solved yet again in Chapter 48 using electrical circuits. The problem is described in the tableau (Table 13.1).

23.5.1 Parameters

The tableau for the quadratic polynomial problem (Table 23.1) provides the details applicable to GPPS 2.0 for this problem, except that NINPUTS is 2; NOUTPUTS is 1; and the population size, M, is 120,000 (with $Q = 5,000$; $D = 60$).

23.5.2 Results

During our only run of the robot controller problem using GPPS 2.0, the best-of-generation program from generation 0 has a fitness of 3.204 and scores 60 hits (out of 72).

Table 23.7 shows the generation on which each pace-setting program of the run was created; the number of ADFs, ADLs, ADRs, and ADSs in each pace-setting program; and the fitness and the number of hits for each pace-setting program. The ADFs, ADLs, ADRs, and ADSs in the pace-setting programs are present as a consequence of the architecture-altering operations.

Table 23.7 Pace-setting values of fitness for robot controller problem with GPPS 2.0

Generation	Number of ADFs	Number of ADLs	Number of ADRs	Number of ADSs	Fitness	Hits
0	0	0	0	0	3.204	60
0	0	0	0	0	2.548	64
3	0	0	1	0	2.009	69
3	0	0	1	0	1.687	72
4	0	1	1	0	1.671	72
5	0	0	1	0	1.670	72
8	0	0	1	0	1.579	72
8	0	0	1	0	1.573	72

9	0	0	1	0	1.560	72
15	0	1	1	0	1.556	72
14	0	0	1	0	1.553	72
15	1	0	0	0	1.502	72
18	1	0	0	0	1.482	72
21	2	0	0	0	1.476	72
20	0	1	1	0	1.474	72
21	0	1	1	0	1.462	72
21	0	1	0	0	1.450	72
24	0	0	1	0	1.442	72
27	0	1	1	0	1.441	72
28	0	0	1	0	1.433	72
31	0	0	1	0	1.430	72
32	0	0	1	0	1.429	72
32	0	0	1	0	1.424	72
33	1	0	1	0	1.420	72
34	0	0	1	0	1.415	72
35	0	0	1	0	1.408	72
37	0	0	1	0	1.404	72
40	0	0	1	0	1.403	72
40	1	0	1	0	1.400	72
40	0	0	1	0	1.394	72
43	0	0	1	0	1.390	72
41	0	1	1	0	1.389	72
44	0	0	1	0	1.387	72
44	0	0	1	0	1.386	72
49	0	0	1	0	1.384	72
47	0	1	1	0	1.382	72
53	0	0	1	0	1.381	72
50	1	0	1	0	1.378	72
57	0	0	1	0	1.376	72
54	0	0	1	0	1.374	72
54	1	0	1	0	1.370	72
57	0	0	1	0	1.368	72
62	0	0	1	0	1.368	72
66	0	0	1	0	1.367	72
69	1	0	1	0	1.366	72
69	0	0	1	0	1.366	72
74	0	0	1	0	1.365	72
73	0	0	1	0	1.365	72
76	0	0	1	0	1.364	72
76	0	0	1	0	1.363	72

Subroutines, loops, and recursions are not necessary for solving this problem; however, they are not deleterious. Accordingly, ADFs, ADLs, and ADRs each appear sporadically during the run.

At every time step, the optimal action for the robot is a function of the program's two inputs. Any information that might be stored in one time step and actually used in a later time step would not be helpful in solving this problem. As can be seen from Table 23.7, there are no automatically defined stores in any of the pace-setting programs.

The best-of-run program for the robot controller problem emerges on generation 76. This program scores 72 hits (out of 72) and has a fitness of 1.363. It has no ADFs, no ADLs, one ADR, and no ADSs. The result-producing branch has 10 invocations (in bold below) of the recursion body branch, RBB, of the program's one automatically defined recursion. However, the 3-point recursion body branch, RBB, does not contain a reference to itself, and hence there is no actual recursion in this program. The 345-point result-producing branch is

```
(IFGTZ (+ (IFGTZ (IFGTZ (RLI 4.009863) (RLI -4.441402) (* (-
(TNOT (+ NOUTPUTS -5.122842)) (+ (+ 4.904263 -2.153238) (RLI
7.318499))) (RLI -5.842543))) (FLOOR (TOR INDEX 1.609404))
(RLI 5.410130)) (TNOT (IFGTZ (- (- (- (TNOT INDEX) 1.434870)
(RLI (+ NOUTPUTS -5.122842))) (RLI -3.296044)) (* (TAND (RLI
NOUTPUTS) (WLO (TAND 9.328573 (% 9.291887 INDEX)) (RLI (RBB))))
-1.555272) (RLI (- (RLI 7.318499) (WLO (TNOT (RLI (TOR (RLI
7.964893) (RLI (RLI NINPUTS))))) (* -4.160453 NOUTPUTS))))))))
(RLI (RLI (TOR (RBB) (RLI (TOR (TOR (RBB) (RLI (RLI (TOR (WLO
(IFGTZ (WLO (- (RLI 1.822424E-01 ) (* 2.168889 (+ (TOR (RLI
9.291887) 3.654995) (WLO -7.397127E-01 (TOR (RLI NINPUTS) (RLI
-1.230136))))))) (RLI 9.328573)) 7.953329 (- 7.301870 (RLI (RLI
(TOR INDEX (TOR (RBB) (WLO 7.964893 (IFGTZ -9.261286 INDEX
9.896755E-01 )))))))) (RBB)) (WLO (- (FLOOR (TOR INDEX (TOR (+
(% (RLI -2.903260) (TOR (* (RLI 4.009863) (TAND 5.410130 (RLI
INDEX))) (IFGTZ (RLI NOUTPUTS) (* 4.597404 (WLO (IFGTZ (WLO
(RLI NINPUTS) (RLI 9.328573)) 7.953329 (- 7.301870 (RLI (RLI
6.348879)))) (RBB))) (IFGTZ (FLOOR INDEX) (* NINPUTS
-1.555272) (RLI 8.034996))))) (RLI (IFGTZ (+ NINPUTS 9.927290)
(TOR (RLI NINPUTS) (RLI -1.433177)) (RLI -4.417305)))) (WLO
7.964893 (IFGTZ -9.261286 INDEX (RLI -6.810165)))))) (RLI
INDEX)) (IFGTZ (+ -6.082267 NOUTPUTS) (TNOT (RLI (RLI (TOR (WLO
(IFGTZ (WLO (RLI NINPUTS) (% (FLOOR (RLI -6.860714E-01 ))
7.526743)) (TNOT (IFGTZ (- (- (- (TNOT INDEX) 1.434870) (RLI (+
NOUTPUTS -5.122842))) (RLI -3.296044)) (* NINPUTS -1.555272)
(RLI 8.034996))) (- 7.301870 (RLI (RLI 6.348879))))) (RBB)) (WLO
(- (FLOOR (TOR INDEX (TOR (RBB) (WLO 7.964893 (IFGTZ -9.261286
(+ (* NINPUTS -5.696434) (WLO -7.397127E-01 INDEX)) 9.896755E-
01 ))))) (RLI INDEX)) (% -5.007554 7.526743)))))) (* INDEX
```

```
-6.746701))))))) (RLI (RLI (TOR (WLO (IFGTZ (WLO (RLI NINPUTS)
(RLI 9.328573)) 7.953329 (- (* (FLOOR NINPUTS) (+ (TOR (RLI
9.291887) 3.654995) (IFGTZ (- (- (- (TNOT INDEX) 1.434870)
(RLI (+ NOUTPUTS -5.122842))) (RLI -3.296044)) (* NINPUTS
-1.555272) (RLI 8.034996)))) (RLI (RLI 6.348879)))) (**RBB**))
(WLO (- (FLOOR (TOR -6.810165 (TOR (**RBB**) (WLO 7.964893
(IFGTZ -9.261286 -2.153238 9.896755E-01 ))))) (RLI INDEX))
(IFGTZ -9.261286 INDEX (+ -3.451916 (RLI (IFGTZ (+ NINPUTS
9.927290) (TOR (RLI NINPUTS) (RLI -1.433177)) (RLI
-4.417305))))))))))))) (- (RLI (TOR INDEX 1.609404))
(* (RLI -6.810165) (+ (* NINPUTS -5.696434) (WLO -7.397127E-01
INDEX))))).
```

The recursion condition branch, RCB, has 75 points:

```
(RLI (WLO (% (IFGTZ (RLI (FLOOR NINPUTS)) (RLI NOUTPUTS))
(- (RLI 6.522041) (+ (TAND (RLI 5.456662) (* (TOR NINPUTS
NINPUTS) (RLI -8.401497)))) (TOR (- (RLI (WLO (TNOT -7.807952)
-4.383421)) (WLO (FLOOR (RLI 4.631721)) NINPUTS)) (TOR (*
-4.160453 NOUTPUTS) (RLI INDEX)))))) (* (RLI NINPUTS) (- (RLI
1.822424E-01 ) (* (RLI -6.810165) (+ (TOR (TOR (RLI (* 8.956333
NOUTPUTS)) 3.654995) 3.654995) (RLI 6.348879)))))) (- (RLI
7.318499) (WLO (TNOT (RLI (TOR (RLI 7.964893) (RLI (RLI
NINPUTS))))) (* -4.160453 NOUTPUTS))))).
```

The three-point recursion update branch, RUB, is

```
(+ -6.082267 NOUTPUTS).
```

The three-point recursion body branch, RBB, is

```
(* 1.729506 INDEX).
```

The three-point recursion ground branch, RGB, is

```
(- 7.953329 -9.058321).
```

The above program demonstrates that GPPS 2.0 can evolve a solution to the time-optimal robot controller problem. Subroutines, loops, recursions, and internal storage were all available to GPPS 2.0. The decision to use (or not use) ADFs, ADLs, ADRs, and ADSs was made by GPPS 2.0 during the run—not by the human user prior to the run.

23.6 MINIMAL SORTING NETWORK WITH GPPS 2.0

The sorting network problem was solved in Chapter 21 using GPPS 1.0 and is solved later in Chapter 57 using evolvable hardware and a field-programmable gate array. See Table 21.4 for details.

23.6.1 Parameters

The tableau for the quadratic polynomial problem (Table 23.1) provides the details applicable to GPPS 2.0, except that NINPUTS is 1; NOUTPUTS is 42; and the population size, M, is 300,000 (with $Q = 5,000$; $D = 60$).

23.6.2 Results

During our only run of this problem using GPPS 2.0, the best-of-generation program from generation 0 has a fitness of 289.02. Like all programs in generation 0 of any run of GPPS 2.0, there are no automatically defined functions, no automatically defined loops, no automatically defined recursions, and no automatically defined stores.

After generation 0, GPPS 2.0 uses the architecture-altering operations to create, duplicate, and delete ADFs, ADLs, ADRs, and ADSs from individual programs.

Table 23.8 shows the generation on which each pace-setting program of the run was created; the number of ADFs, ADLs, ADRs, and ADSs in each pace-setting program; the fitness of each pace-setting program; and the number of COMPARE–EXCHANGE operations (steps) for each pace-setting program.

The best-of-run program for the sorting network problem emerges on generation 33. This sorting network has the known minimum number of steps (16) for sorting seven items. Figure 23.2 shows the best-of-run sorting network from generation 33.

The best-of-run program from generation 33 has no ADFs, one ADL, one ADR, and one ADS. The result-producing branch has four references to the value returned by the loop body branch, LBB, of the program's automatically defined loop. It has three references to the recursion body branch, RBB, of the program's automatically defined recursion. The storage reading branch, SRB, is referenced twice; however, since there is no reference to the storage writing branch, SWB, anywhere in the program, these references simply return zero (the value to which the cell of named memory was initialized). The 250-point result-producing branch of the best-of-run program is

```
(TOR RBB(TOR (TOR (TOR (TOR RBB(TOR (TOR RBB SRB) (TAND (RLI
8.674055) (WLO -8.756800 (WLO 6.187817 -3.372040)))))))SRB) (WLO
(IFGTZ (WLO (* NINPUTS (- (TAND (TAND (RLI -2.223262) (- LBB (%
(- (WLO -1.852163 -8.041438) 4.018015) (% INDEX 8.574966))))
(% (+ (TAND (RLI (- 9.360512 -4.402980)) (RLI INDEX)) (RLI (TOR
(TOR (WLO (- -5.397911E-01 INDEX) (WLO (* INDEX 9.175266)
INDEX)) (TAND (WLO NINPUTS (TAND (RLI 8.674055) (WLO -9.735246
(FLOOR (FLOOR (TNOT (* (TOR (RLI 2.800743) (WLO (WLO INDEX
INDEX) (- (WLO -6.001205E-01 NINPUTS) 4.018015))) (RLI NIN-
PUTS))))))))) (+ NOUTPUTS -2.443494))) (RLI (% (IFGTZ NINPUTS
NOUTPUTS -9.397069) (RLI NINPUTS))))))) (- (RLI NINPUTS) (WLO
INDEX INDEX)))) 7.383869)) (- (TAND (TAND (RLI -2.223262) (-
LBB (% (IFGTZ NINPUTS (- 9.360512 NOUTPUTS) 2.450953) (% INDEX
8.574966)))) (% (+ (TAND (RLI (- 9.360512 NOUTPUTS)) (RLI (-
(WLO (- (FLOOR (- (WLO -6.001205E-01 NINPUTS) (TOR (RLI
9.750521) (WLO (RLI NINPUTS) -1.112901))))) (IFGTZ (TNOT (WLO
(WLO INDEX -5.397911E-01 ) (TOR (RLI 9.750521) (% (RLI
```

```
8.496822) INDEX)))) (WLO -2.782498 (WLO -1.852163 -7.439513))
(WLO (RLI 3.023534) (TNOT 1.539941)))) 4.018015) (WLO (WLO
(IFGTZ NOUTPUTS -9.602212 -6.973456) (FLOOR -5.921524))
INDEX)))) (RLI (TOR (TOR (WLO (- -5.397911E-01 INDEX) (WLO (*
INDEX 9.175266) (RLI NINPUTS))) (TAND (WLO NINPUTS (TAND (RLI
8.674055) (WLO -9.735246 (FLOOR (WLO -9.735246 (FLOOR (* (TAND
NINPUTS -2.598114) LBB))))))) (+ NOUTPUTS -2.443494))) (RLI (%
(IFGTZ NINPUTS NOUTPUTS -9.397069) (RLI NINPUTS)))))) (- (RLI
NINPUTS) (WLO INDEX INDEX)))) 7.383869)) LBB (RLI 8.292118)) (+
(WLO (* 2.595102 4.018015) (WLO (* 2.595102 (- -5.397911E-01
INDEX)) -6.842794E-01 )) (+ (FLOOR NINPUTS) INDEX)))) (TAND
(RLI 8.674055) -2.431063))).
```

The three-point loop initialization branch, LIB0, of the automatically defined loop is

```
(- 9.168068 4.020708).
```

The 27-point loop condition branch, LCB0, of the automatically defined loop is

```
(IFGTZ 4.872396 (IFGTZ (WLO INDEX INDEX) (IFGTZ 4.872396
(IFGTZ (WLO INDEX (WLO (- -5.397911E-01 INDEX) (* 8.348608
5.749842))) (- 9.168068 4.020708) (FLOOR 8.746222)) NINPUTS)
(FLOOR 8.746222)) NINPUTS).
```

The 44-point loop update branch, LUB0, of the automatically defined loop is

```
(TOR (WLO (IFGTZ 4.872396 (IFGTZ (WLO INDEX (WLO (- -9.775822
INDEX) (WLO (* INDEX 9.175266) INDEX))) (- 9.168068 4.020708)
(FLOOR 8.746222)) NINPUTS) (- (% (FLOOR (RLI (WLO (- 9.168068
4.020708) (- -4.413715 7.383869)))) (TNOT (WLO (* 8.348608
5.749842) (- 9.360512 NOUTPUTS)))) NINPUTS)) (RLI -4.402980)).
```

The eight-point loop body branch, LBB0, of the automatically defined loop is

```
(- (RLI (- (TAND 5.632193 -7.691397) NOUTPUTS)) 8.039476).
```

The three-point recursion condition branch, RCB, is

```
(- NOUTPUTS 7.383869).
```

The 21-point recursion update branch, RUB, is

```
(- (% (+ (TAND (RLI 3.267426) (RLI INDEX)) (RLI (* 8.348608
5.749842))) (- (RLI (WLO 6.187817 -3.372040)) (RLI -5.980978E-
01 ))) (RLI 9.168068)).
```

The 17-point recursion body branch, RBB, contains a reference to the value returned by the loop body branch, LBB:

```
(WLO (IFGTZ (WLO (* NINPUTS (WLO INDEX INDEX)) (- -4.413715
7.383869)) LBB NINPUTS) (- 9.360512 (RLI 9.168068))).
```

The above program demonstrates that GPPS 2.0 can evolve a solution to the problem of synthesizing the design of a minimal sorting network for seven items. Although subroutines, loops, recursions, and internal storage were all available to GPPS 2.0, the decision to use (or not use) them was dynamically made by GPPS 2.0 during the run.

Table 23.8 Pace-setting values of fitness for sorting network problem with GPPS 2.0

Generation	Number of ADFs	Number of ADLs	Number of ADRs	Number of ADSs	Fitness	Number of COMPARE–EXCHANGE operations
0	0	0	0	0	289.02	2
0	0	0	0	0	273.02	2
0	0	0	0	0	261.02	2
0	0	0	0	0	245.03	3
1	0	0	0	0	241.03	3
1	0	0	0	0	239.03	3
2	0	1	0	0	229.08	8
2	0	0	0	0	227.04	4
2	0	1	0	0	217.05	5
3	0	0	0	0	217.04	4
3	0	0	0	0	207.05	5
3	0	1	0	0	201.06	6
4	0	1	0	0	201.05	5
4	0	1	0	0	199.05	5
4	0	1	0	0	195.06	6
4	0	2	0	0	177.06	6
5	0	1	0	0	169.07	7
5	0	1	0	0	165.06	6
5	0	1	1	0	147.07	7
6	0	1	1	0	133.07	7
7	0	1	1	0	127.09	9
8	2	1	0	0	125.08	8
8	0	1	1	0	123.09	9
8	0	1	1	0	123.08	8
9	0	1	0	0	117.09	9
9	0	1	0	0	111.12	12
9	0	1	1	0	109.08	8
10	0	1	1	0	103.09	9
10	0	1	1	0	99.12	12
11	0	1	1	0	61.15	15
13	0	1	1	0	55.15	15
14	1	1	1	0	47.14	14
14	0	1	1	0	27.18	18
16	0	1	1	0	27.16	16
18	0	1	1	0	15.19	19

18	0	1	1	0	11.18	18
20	0	1	1	0	9.20	20
21	0	1	1	0	9.19	19
22	1	1	1	0	7.20	20
16	0	1	1	0	7.19	19
17	0	1	1	0	5.19	19
23	0	1	1	0	3.19	19
21	0	1	1	0	3.18	18
25	0	1	1	0	1.19	19
25	0	1	1	0	1.18	18
25	0	1	1	1	1.17	17
33	0	1	1	1	1.16	16

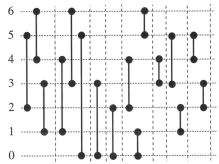

Figure 23.2   Best-of-run sorting network from generation 33 with GPPS 2.0

23.7   COMPUTER RESOURCES FOR GPPS

GPPS may occasionally solve certain problems more rapidly than other forms of genetic programming. However, in general, we have observed that GPPS consumes between two and three orders of magnitude more computer time than an ordinary run of genetic programming.

As an example, the evolved solution for the sorting network problem using GPPS 2.0 (created on generation 33 with a population of 120,000 in Section 23.6) and the evolved solution in Chapter 21 using GPPS 1.0 (created on generation 31 with a population of 640,000 in Section 21.4) are typical of solutions produced by GPPS in that they consumed considerably more computational resources than an ordinary run of genetic programming on the same problem. To put these two runs with GPPS in perspective, a similar minimal sorting network for seven items is successfully evolved in Chapter 57 using ordinary genetic programming with a population of only 1,000 by generation 31 (using a field-programmable gate array for the task of fitness evaluation). Since solutions were obtained between generations 31 and 33 with all three approaches, the number of fitness evaluations performed is about 640 times greater with GPPS 1.0 than with ordinary genetic programming and is about 120 times greater with GPPS 2.0 than with ordinary genetic programming. It is likely that GPPS 2.0 is more efficient than GPPS 1.0

on this particular problem because indexed memory is built into GPPS 1.0 and internal storage is superfluous for this problem.

Similarly, the evolved solution for the problem of symbolic regression of the quadratic polynomial $2.718x^2 + 3.1416x$ (created on generation 29 with a population of 120,000 using GPPS 2.0 in Section 23.1) consumed considerably more computational resources than an ordinary run of genetic programming on this problem. Specifically, the computational effort, E, for this problem was reported to be 305,500 in *Genetic Programming* (Koza 1992e, Figure 10.3) with a population size of 500.

The reason for the difference of between two and three orders of magnitude in computer time between GPPS and ordinary genetic programming is that a price must be paid for the high degree of generality and convenience provided by GPPS. The main motivation for GPPS is that it provides a very general and convenient approach to automatic problem solving—not that it is computationally efficient.

Of course, humans frequently prefer convenience over efficiency. Even though 10 numbers can be added together in a few dozen nanoseconds using the basic machine code instructions of any desktop computer, humans frequently find it to be a better use of their time to obtain the sum from spreadsheet software composed of tens of millions of instructions. The spreadsheet employs a multiplicity of complex technologies and programming techniques to display the 10 numbers and the sum in the user's favorite font on a large video screen.

Similarly, if a human wants a problem to be solved in an automated way without specifying in advance whether the solution should employ subroutines, loops, recursions, or internal storage, it may be preferable to pay a price of two or three orders of magnitude for generality and convenience.

In practice, it is possible to ameliorate the greater amount of computer time associated with GPPS in two ways. First, GPPS has an *extremely* reduced instruction set. Moreover, the handful of primitive functions in a GPPS program correspond one-for-one to the basic machine code operations of most general-purpose computers. It does not require an enormous amount of effort to write a compiler to dynamically compile a program with such a tiny repertoire of instructions and constructions into machine code. Compilation of evolved programs into machine code eliminates the time-consuming interpretative procedure commonly used in genetic programming to execute evolved programs. In fact, James Gochee wrote such a dynamic compiler (with only slightly different functions than those of GPPS) for use on our parallel computer. This on-the-fly compiler is invoked during the run of genetic programming every time a new individual is created by a genetic operation. Dynamic compilation of evolved programs is most beneficial when each evolved program is executed a large number of times (e.g., for problems involving a large number of fitness cases, a large number of time steps, or both).

Second, it has previously been demonstrated that genetic programming can be implemented directly in machine code instructions (Nordin 1994, 1997; Nordin and Banzhaf 1995; Banzhaf, Nordin, Keller, and Francone 1998). Since the primitive functions of GPPS are included among the basic machine code operations of virtually every general-purpose computer, the greater expenditure of computer time required to solve a problem using GPPS may be ameliorated by implementing GPPS directly in machine code. Nordin (1994) reported acceleration by factors of between 200 and 500 with his technique.

23.8 FUTURE WORK ON GPPS

We intend to modify GPPS to reflect our experience in using it and to implement certain additional features (including operations concerned with the automatic creation of arguments for the various types of branches).

23.9 SUMMARY

The central goal of machine learning and artificial intelligence concerns the question of getting a computer to solve a problem without telling it how to do it. The Genetic Programming Problem Solver directly addresses this goal by

- eliminating the need for the user to prespecify the function set and terminal set by standardizing the set of functions and terminals,
- eliminating the need for the user to prespecify whether to employ subroutines, loops, recursions, or internal storage in solving a given problem,
- eliminating the need for the user to prespecify the number of arguments possessed by each subroutine, and
- eliminating the need for the user to prespecify whether and how subroutines hierarchically refer to one another.

Part 5: AUTOMATED SYNTHESIS OF ANALOG ELECTRICAL CIRCUITS

The process of design involves the creation of a complex structure to satisfy user-defined requirements. Design is a major activity of practicing electrical, mechanical, civil, and aeronautical engineers. The design process typically entails trade-offs between competing considerations. The end product of the design process is usually a satisfactory and compliant design as opposed to a perfect design. Design is usually viewed as requiring human intelligence. Consequently, the field of design is a source of challenging problems for automated techniques of machine learning and artificial intelligence. In particular, design problems are useful for determining whether an automated technique can perform tasks that are competitive with human-created designs.

The design (synthesis) of analog electrical circuits is especially challenging. Although considerable progress has been made in automating the synthesis of certain categories of purely digital circuits, the synthesis of analog circuits and mixed analog-digital circuits has not proved to be as amenable to automation (Rutenbar 1993). There is no previously known general technique for automatically creating an entire analog circuit (i.e., both the topological arrangement of the components and the values of all of its components) from a high-level statement of the design goals of the circuit (e.g., the circuit's measurable behaviors and characteristics).

In discussing "the analog dilemma," O. Aaserud and I. Ring Nielsen (1995) observe:

Analog designers are few and far between. In contrast to digital design, most of the analog circuits are still handcrafted by the experts or so-called "zahs" of analog design. The design process is characterized by a combination of experience and intuition and requires a thorough knowledge of the process characteristics and the detailed specifications of the actual product.

Analog circuit design is known to be a knowledge-intensive, multiphase, iterative task, which usually stretches over a significant period of time and is performed by designers with a large portfolio of skills. It is therefore considered by many to be a form of art rather than a science.

The design for an electrical circuit includes both its topology and sizing. The *topology* of a circuit consists of the total number of components in the circuit, the type of each component (e.g., resistor) at each location in the circuit, and a list of all the connections between the components. The *sizing* of a circuit consists of the component value(s) associated with each component. The sizing of a component is typically a numerical value (e.g., the capacitance of a capacitor).

The problem of analog circuit synthesis is of considerable practical importance. Ultimately, all electrical circuits are analog circuits. Most digital circuitry is surrounded by a layer (eggshell) of analog circuitry that provides the interface between the digital circuit and the outside world. In particular, about 60% of *CMOS*-based application-specific integrated circuit (ASIC) designs incorporate analog circuitry (Lohn and Colombano 1998). Because analog design is part art and part science, analog design is exceedingly time-consuming. There is an ongoing shortage of analog design engineers. Moreover, each advance in semiconductor process technology necessitates the redesign of the commonly used analog circuits. Time-to-market considerations often dominate the design process for analog circuits.

Thus, it would be ideal if there were an automatic technique for creating both the topology and sizing of an analog electrical circuit from a high-level statement of the circuit's behavior and characteristics. This part of this book shows how the problem of analog circuit synthesis can be recast as a problem of automatically creating a computer program. Recasting this problem in this way enables genetic programming to search for a solution to the problem of analog circuit synthesis. The goal is to use genetic programming as an automated general technique for synthesizing an analog circuit from a high-level statement of the circuit's desired behavior and characteristics.

First, Chapter 24 reviews previous work. Next, Chapter 25 serves as a detailed introduction and a tutorial that shows, step by step, how genetic programming can be applied to the problem of automatically synthesizing the design for a lowpass filter. This chapter introduces a small subset of component-creating functions, topology-modifying functions, and development-controlling functions that are sufficient to carry you through Chapter 40. (Chapter 41 presents the full repertoire of circuit-constructing functions.)

Chapters 26 through 40 present additional examples of the automatic synthesis of passive circuits composed of resistors, capacitors, and inductors. These examples include various types of filters and frequency discrimination (source identification) circuits. Automatically defined functions, architecture-altering operations, and the quasi-iterative automatically defined copy are employed. Chapter 29 describes the embryos and test fixtures used for circuit synthesis with developmental genetic programming.

Chapters 42 through 51 contain numerous examples of the genetically synthesized circuits composed of transistors, including amplifiers, computational circuits, a time-optimal real-time robot controller circuit, a voltage reference circuit, and a temperature-sensing circuit.

Chapter 52 describes the special handling of constraints involving subcircuits and topology. Chapter 53 shows a minimal embryo. Chapters 54 and 55 present comparative experiments involving various alternative features of genetic programming. Chapter 56 demonstrates the crucial role of crossover in genetic programming.

Previous Work on Automated Analog Circuit Synthesis

Numerous techniques have been applied to various parts of the problem of automating the design process for analog and mixed analog-digital circuits. Many existing techniques require the user to supply both the topology and sizing of a reasonably good prototype circuit as a starting point; the automated technique then adjusts the sizing of the components. Many existing techniques are limited to certain highly specialized types of circuits. Also, existing techniques typically require repeated interactive intervention by the user. The decisions that are automated are frequently only a small subset of the decisions that must be made; the outcomes that the automated system can produce are frequently only a small subset of the universe of possibilities.

Because of the importance of computer-aided design (CAD) for circuits, there has been extensive research in the fields of optimization, artificial intelligence, mathematics, and, of course, electrical engineering on the problem of automating the design of electrical circuits. We mention a few of these efforts here.

In early papers on artificial intelligence, Sussman and Stallman (1975, 1977, 1979) discuss how constraint propagation might be applied to analog circuits. However, this effort focused on the problem of *analyzing* circuits, not *synthesizing* (designing, creating) them.

In an interactive design tool for synthesizing analog integrated circuits, called IDAC (Degrauwe 1987), the user selects various possible topologies for the circuit. IDAC then determines the values of the components in each circuit (in relation to the desired behavioral characteristics), and the user chooses the best circuit.

In the OASYS system (Harjani 1989), a knowledge-based approach to analog circuit synthesis has been applied to the problem of synthesis of the design of operational amplifiers and comparators. The OASYS system starts with analog circuit topologies and associated design knowledge and hierarchically breaks the design task into smaller tasks. (See also Harjani, Rutenbar, and Carley 1987, 1989.)

In OPASYN (Koh, Sequin, and Gray 1987), a topology is chosen beforehand based on heuristic rules, and the synthesis tool attempts to size the circuit. If the synthesis tool cannot size the chosen topology correctly, the tool creates a new topology using other heuristic rules, and the process continues. The success of these systems depends on the effectiveness of the knowledge base of heuristic rules.

Maulik, Carley, and Rutenbar (1992) attempt to handle topology selection and circuit sizing simultaneously using expert design knowledge.

In SEAS (Ning, Kole, Mouthaan, and Wallings 1992), evolution is used to modify the topology, and simulated annealing (Kirkpatrick, Gelatt, and Vecchi 1983; Aarts and Korst 1989) is used to size the circuit.

Ochotta (1994) describes the ASTRX/OBLX system, which starts with the circuit topology and performance specifications of the desired circuit. The system first produces an executable performance prediction module that is customized for the particular circuit synthesis problem at hand. The prediction module is then used to guide simulated annealing to the sizing and biasing of a satisfactory circuit. (See also Ochotta, Rutenbar, and Carley 1996.)

Jones (1996) enhanced the ASTRX/OBLX system by giving it the ability to modify a user-supplied topology while retaining its ability to do sizing and biasing. In this enhancement, binary variables indicate the presence or absence of certain connections and components contained in a user-supplied topology. Simulated annealing is used to perturb the topology by subtracting certain elements from this user-supplied superset.

24.1   AUTOMATED DESIGN USING EVOLUTIONARY COMPUTATION

The earliest work in the field of evolutionary computation recognized the possibility of applying it to the problem of designing complex structures. This pioneering work on automated design included the application of evolution strategies to airfoil design (Rechenberg 1965, 1973), the application of evolutionary programming to the design of finite automata (Fogel, Owens, and Walsh 1966), and the application of evolution strategies to nozzle design (Schwefel 1968; Klockgether and Schwefel 1970).

There have been numerous instances where evolutionary computation has been applied to the design of electrical circuits. Evolution strategies have been used to evolve the length and structure of a recursive digital filter with infinite impulse response (IIR) as well as numerical coefficients (Gorne and Schneider 1993).

Genetic algorithms have been applied to the problem of circuit synthesis. Powers-of-two coefficients for finite impulse response (FIR) filters have been evolved using the genetic algorithm (Gentilli, Piazza, and Uncini 1994).

In the first known fielded application of genetic programming, Oakley (1994) designed a filter for a medical application using genetic programming.

Numerical filter coefficients and numerical time delays for analog IIR filters have been evolved using the genetic algorithm (Neubauer 1994).

Miller, Thomson, and Fogarty have used genetic algorithms to discover novel designs for digital arithmetic circuits such as adders and multipliers that are more efficient, in many cases, than human-designed equivalents (Fogarty, Miller, and Thomson 1998; Miller, Thomson, and Fogarty 1998).

In the DARWIN system (Kruiskamp 1996; Kruiskamp and Leenaerts 1995), operational amplifier (op amp) circuits are evolved using a genetic algorithm. Each circuit in the population is represented by a chromosome string consisting of zeros and ones. The initial population of circuits in the DARWIN system is created to ensure that each circuit behaves as an op amp by choosing one of a preestablished hand-designed set of 24 suitable op amp topologies. The behavior of each op amp is evaluated using a small-signal equivalent circuit and analytical calculations specialized to op amp circuits. The fitness of each op amp is computed using a combination of factors, including the power dissipation of the circuit and the deviation between the actual behavior of the circuit and the desired behavior. Offspring chromosome strings are created by a crossover operation that is specialized to op amps (and incorporates knowledge about the mandatory and optional stages of a typical op amp). At each step, a set of constraints are employed to ensure that all transistors operate in their proper range and that all transistor sizes lie between certain maximum and minimum values. The DARWIN system has successfully designed op amps that deliver gains of 40, 60, and 100 decibels.

In an innovative paper, Grimbleby (1995) used the genetic algorithm to evolve the topology of passive linear circuits composed of two-leaded components such as capacitors, resistors, and inductors. Component values were then determined by a subsequent numerical optimization process.

Evolvable hardware is one approach to automated synthesis of digital circuits. Early pioneering work in this field includes that of Higuchi, Niwa et al. (1993a, 1993b); Hemmi, Hikage, and Shimohara (1994); Higuchi, Hitoshi, and Manderick 1994; Hemmi, Mizoguchi, and Shimohara (1994); and Mizoguchi, Hemmi, and Shimohara (1994). Hemmi, Hikage, and Shimohara (1994) employed genetic methods to the design of digital circuits using a hardware description language (HDL). Additional work in the field of evolvable hardware was presented at the 1995 workshop on evolvable hardware in Lausanne, Switzerland (Sanchez and Tomassini 1996), and the first international conference on evolvable systems held in Tsukuba, Japan, in 1996 (Higuchi, Iwata, and Liu 1997).

Thompson (1995) used a digital field-programmable gate array operating in analog mode to evolve an oscillator, robot controller, and frequency discriminator (see also Thompson 1996a, 1996b, 1996c, 1997, 1998; Harvey and Thompson 1996; Thompson, Harvey, and Husbands 1996).

Keane, Koza, and Rice (1993) used genetic programming to find the impulse response function for circuits.

24.2 AUTOMATED DESIGN OF NEURAL NETWORKS

Recent work on automating the design of artificial neural networks contains elements that are relevant to the design of electrical circuits.

A neural network is a structure consisting of one or more neural processing units (neurons). A neural network can be represented by a line-labeled, point-labeled, directed graph. The points of the graph are either neural processing units, input points, or output points. Each line in the graph represents a connection between two points. Each line is labeled with a numerical weight to represent the amplification or attenuation of the signal along the connection. The neural processing units are labeled with two numbers indicating the neuron's threshold and the neuron's bias. The only type of component in a neural network is a neural processing unit.

Neural networks are dynamical systems in the sense that the state of the network at a future time depends on the state of the network at the current time and the inputs to the network at the current time. There is a directional flow of information in time. In a feedforward neural network, information flows from the inputs to the network, through the neurons, to the outputs of the network without any cycles within the directed graph representing the network. In a recurrent neural network, the output of one neuron at a particular instant in time may be sent back to become the input of another neuron at a future instant so as to create a cycle within the directed graph representing the network.

Neural network training paradigms (e.g., back propagation) usually presuppose that the user has predetermined the architecture of the neural network. That is, they presuppose that selections have been made for the number of layers of neurons, the number of neurons in each layer, and the connectivity between the neurons. (An exception to this general statement is found in Lee 1991, where both the architecture of the network and the weights of its neurons are adaptively determined.)

The conventional genetic algorithm operating on fixed-length character strings provides a way to search the highly nonlinear multidimensional search space of weight vectors to discover the numerical weights for the connections as well as the thresholds and biases of a neural network (Miller, Todd, and Hegde 1989). However, the architecture of the neural network must usually be specified in advance (Schaffer and Whitley 1992).

The major difficulty in automating the discovery of the architecture of a neural network using genetic methods has centered on finding a malleable representation for the line-labeled, point-labeled graph representing the neural network that is receptive to the kinds of operations performed by genetic methods (notably the crossover operation).

Early work applied genetic programming to the problem of discovering both the architecture and weights of a neural network (Koza 1990b; Koza and Rice 1991b; Koza 1992e). In this work, the neural network was represented as a point-labeled tree. Some subtrees were used to establish the weights on input lines of the neural network. Some internal points of the trees were used to represent neurons. Since a tree representation does not provide a direct way to broadcast a signal (either an outside input or an output of a neuron) to more than one neuron, the "define building block" ("encapsulation") operation of genetic programming was introduced to provide such connectivity.

In almost all of the early work using genetic algorithms to design neural networks (Miller, Todd, and Hegde 1989; Schaffer and Whitley 1992), each element of the neural network (i.e., each weight, threshold, and bias) was directly encoded into the chromosome string of the genetic algorithm. Kitano (1990, 1994, 1996) described an innovative technique using a graph generation system to create the design of a neural network using the genetic algorithm. Kitano's graph generation grammar is an extension of Lindenmayer's L-system (Lindenmayer 1968; Lindenmayer and Rozenberg 1976; Prusinkiewicz and Hanan, 1980; Prusinkiewicz and Lindenmayer 1990). In Kitano's approach, the graph generation grammar is encoded into a chromosome string. The neural network is then created by a developmental process in which the grammar is used to create the neural network.

In his *Cellular Encoding of Genetic Neural Networks*, Frederic Gruau (1992a) described a clever technique, called *cellular encoding*, in which genetic programming is used to concurrently evolve the architecture of a neural network, along with the weights, thresholds, and biases of the individual neurons in the neural network. In this technique, each individual program tree in the population of the run of genetic programming is a specification for developing a complete neural network from a starting point consisting of a single neuron. Genetic programming is applied to populations of these network-constructing program trees in order to evolve neural networks capable of solving various problems. (See also Gruau 1992b, 1993, 1994a, 1994b.)

In cellular encoding, each program tree is a composition of functions and terminals that are used to construct the neural network. The program tree is the genotype, and the neural network constructed in accordance with the trees instructions is the phenotype. The fitness of an individual program tree in the population is measured by how well the neural network that is constructed in accordance with the instructions contained in the program tree performs the desired task. Fitness is measured by exposing the neural network to all (or a sample) of possible combinations of inputs (e.g., binary signals) and testing whether the output(s) of the neural network match the correct output(s) for the particular combination of inputs. For many problems, fitness is computed from the number of incorrect and correct output(s) produced by the neural network. Genetic programming then breeds the population of program trees using the usual genetic operations of Darwinian reproduction, crossover, and mutation.

The construction process for a neural network starts from an embryonic neural network consisting of a single neuron. This single neuron has a threshold of 0, and its bias is 0. Its input is connected to all of the networks input nodes with connections with weights of +1; its output is connected to all of the networks output nodes. The functions in the program tree specify how to develop the embryonic neural network into a full neural network. Certain context-free functions permit a particular neuron to be subdivided in a parallel or sequential manner. Other functions can change the threshold of a neuron, the weight of a connection, or the bias on a neuron.

Gruau (1992a, 1992b, 1993, 1994a, 1994b), Gruau and Whitley (1993), and Esparcia-Alcazar and Sharman (1997) have used genetic programming to create the topology for recurrent neural networks.

Luke and Spector (1996a) showed that graphs and networks can be evolved using a clever domain-independent edge encoding scheme.

De Garis (1996) is working on a large cellular automata representing a neural network using field-programmable gate arrays. (See also de Garis 1993; Korkin, de Garis, Gers, and Hemmi 1997.)

Synthesis of a Lowpass Filter

This chapter is an introductory and tutorial chapter that shows, step by step, how genetic programming can be applied to the problem of automatically synthesizing the design for a lowpass filter:

- Section 25.1 provides basic information about electrical circuits and netlists.
- Section 25.2 describes circuit simulators, notably the SPICE simulator.
- Section 25.3 discusses the mapping between circuits and program trees, Section 25.4 describes the idea of an embryo and a test fixture, and Section 25.5 introduces the developmental process.
- A small repertoire of component-creating functions (Section 25.6), value-setting sub-trees (Section 25.7), topology-modifying functions (Section 25.8), and development-controlling functions (Section 25.9) are introduced. This small repertoire will prove to be sufficient for until Chapter 41, where the complete repertoire of circuit-constructing functions is described.
- Section 25.10 contains a detailed step-by-step example of the developmental process by which a circuit-constructing program tree creates a fully developed electrical circuit from an initial circuit consisting of a test fixture and an embryo. Section 25.11 presents a grammar for the constrained syntactic structure used in creating the circuit-constructing program trees.
- Section 25.12 describes filters, and Section 25.13 contains a high-level statement of the design goals for a lowpass filter.
- Section 25.14 states the preparatory steps for applying genetic programming to the problem of synthesizing a lowpass filter.
- Section 25.15 presents the results of various runs of genetic programming.
- Section 25.16 discusses harvesting multiple solutions from a single run of genetic programming.
- Section 25.17 describes the multiple roles of the crossover operation in evolving a circuit.
- Section 25.18 describes implementation details for the fitness measure, including required modifications to the simulator (Section 25.18.4).

25.1 CIRCUITS AND NETLISTS

Electrical circuits are complex structures composed of a multiplicity of components whose leads (ends, interface points) are connected together in a particular topological arrangement. (Since the word "terminal" has a distinct meaning in the field of genetic programming, the term "lead" is used in this book to describe a point at which an electrical component becomes connected to another component.)

Circuits receive input signals from zero, one, or more input sources and produce output signals at one or more output ports (probe points).

Some analog circuits contain only passive linear components (such as resistors, capacitors, and inductors). Others contain active components (e.g., transistors) whose behavior is nonlinear. Large circuits are typically created by reusing identical (or slightly modified) copies of various smaller substructures. (Note that the word "substructure" is used in this book because the more commonly used word, "subcircuit," has a specialized meaning in SPICE.) Anyone who has ever glanced at the schematic diagram of an electrical circuit can testify that modularity and the reuse of substructures is very important in the design of circuits.

All electrical circuits have at least one energy source (e.g., an incoming signal, a power supply).

One or more component values are necessary to completely specify most components. The sizing of a component is usually a numerical value such as

- the resistance of a resistor,
- the capacitance of a capacitor,
- the inductance of an inductor, and
- the length and width occupied on a silicon chip by the channel of a variable-sized MOSFET transistor.

Sometimes the sizing of a component is a symbolic value. For example, a voltage source may be "DC" (direct current) or "AC" (alternating current). Some components (e.g., a diode, a nonsized transistor) may not carry any explicit component values.

Digital circuits are often composed of analog modules that perform logical operations (e.g., NAND gates, flip-flops, and multiplexers).

Mixed analog-digital circuits contain combinations of analog and digital components. Such mixed analog-digital circuits are becoming increasingly important because of the current trend toward placing an entire system onto a single chip.

Figure 25.1 shows a simple one-input, one-output analog electrical circuit. The input to this circuit is located between node 1 and node 0 (the ground) and is labeled **VSOURCE**. The input **VSOURCE** is a sinusoidal voltage source as indicated by the circular icon containing a tiny sine wave. The output of this circuit (the probe point labeled **VOUT**) is the voltage at node 5. This circuit also contains a 1 microhenry (μH) inductor **L1** between nodes 2 and 3, and a 1 nanofarad (nF) capacitor **C2** between nodes 3 and 4. Practical electrical circuits often contain source and load resistors. This circuit contains a 1,000 ohm (Ω) source resistor **RSOURCE** between nodes 1 and 2 and a 1,000 Ω load resistor **RLOAD** between node 5 and ground (node 0). The wire **ZOUT** connects node 3 with node 5. The wire **ZGND** connects node 4 with node 0 (ground). Electrical engineers do not ordinarily assign names to wires in circuit diagrams; however, wires are often labeled in this book for reasons that will become apparent shortly.

Note that every component (including wires) of a circuit is part of a cycle (closed loop); that is, there are no dangling components (or wires). Although the load resistor

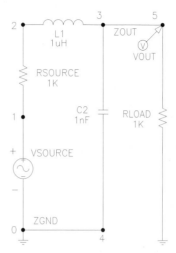

Figure 25.1   Simple electrical circuit

RLOAD in Figure 25.1 may appear, at first glance, to be a dangling component, it is, in fact, part of a closed loop, namely, between node 5 and node 0 (ground).

An electrical circuit is a nontree graphical structure in which every component and every wire is part of a cycle and in which the components are labeled with a component type and component value(s).

A *component* is an object that has a type, some number of component values, and some number of leads. For example, a resistor is a component of the type "resistor" that carries a single numerical component value (e.g., 1,000 Ω) and that possesses two leads.

The *netlist* for an electrical circuit is a data structure consisting of an unordered list that defines both the topology and sizing of a circuit. Each line of the netlist contains the name of a component, the nodes to which each lead of that component is connected, and the value(s), if any, of that component. The netlist for the circuit in Figure 25.1 consists of the following five lines:

```
RSOURCE 1 2 1000OHM
L1 2 3 1UH
C2 3 0 1NF
RLOAD 3 0 1000OHM
VSOURCE 1 0 SIN (0VOLTS 5VOLTS 60HERTZ 0SECONDS 0PERSECOND)
```

The first line of the above netlist indicates that there is a resistor named RSOURCE between nodes 1 and 2. By convention, the first letter of the name of a component in a netlist indicates its type. For example, "R" denotes a resistor, "L" denotes an inductor, "C" denotes a capacitor, "D" denotes a diode, "Q" denotes a bipolar transistor, "V" denotes a voltage source, and "I" denotes a current source. The value (sizing) of RSOURCE is 1,000 Ω.

The second line of the netlist indicates that there is an inductor L1 between nodes 2 and 3 whose component value is 1 μH.

The third line indicates that there is a 1 nF capacitor **C2** between nodes 3 and 0. By convention, node 0 is always considered to be ground. Since wires (such as **ZGND** between nodes 4 and 0 in Figure 25.1) do not usually appear in a netlist, **C2** is shown in the netlist as being directly connected to nodes 3 and 0.

The fourth line indicates that there is a 1,000 Ω resistor **RLOAD** between nodes 3 and 0 (ground). Again, the wire **ZOUT** between nodes 3 and 5 does not appear in the netlist.

The fifth line indicates there is an independent alternating-current sinusoidal voltage source **VSOURCE** connected between nodes 1 and 0 (ground). Although resistors and inductors each carry one component value, a voltage source carries six component values. The additional information on the fifth line of the netlist specifies that **VSOURCE**

- is sinusoidal (`SIN`),
- has an offset (bias) of 0 volts (i.e., the sine wave oscillates up and down around 0 volts),
- has an amplitude of 5 volts,
- has a frequency of 60 hertz (Hz) (cycles per second),
- has a time delay of 0 seconds (before the sine wave starts oscillating), and
- has a damping factor of 0 (so that the voltages are multiplied by $e^0 = 1$). If $k < 0$, the voltages would be progressively suppressed by multiplication by e^{kt}).

Note that "`SIN`" is an example of a symbolic component value.

A netlist is an unordered set of lines, so all 120 permutations of the above five-line netlist are equivalent.

In writing a netlist, it is conventional to give all components with two leads a positive (+) and negative (–) end. The first-listed node in each line of the netlist is interpreted as the component's positive end, and the second-listed node represents the negative end. Although there is no electrical significance to the polarity of a component such as a resistor, polarity is critical for components such as diodes. There is a conventional order for components with more than two leads (e.g., transistors, transformers).

Netlists are most commonly created today using an interactive schematic editor (schematic capture tool). A schematic editor enables an electrical engineer to sit at a computer and draw a schematic diagram of the circuit on the computer screen. The tool then automatically converts the schematic diagram on the computer screen into a textual netlist. As will be seen shortly, when circuits are created using genetic programming, the netlist is created in an automated way. In fact, the problem of automated circuit synthesis (design) may be restated as a problem of creating a netlist representing a circuit that satisfies the user's specified high-level design goals (e.g., the circuit's measurable behaviors and characteristics).

The nontree structure of an electrical circuit is different from the point-labeled program trees with ordered branches commonly employed in genetic programming. The nontree structure of an electrical circuit also differs from the alternative nontree graphical programmatic structures used in PADO and neural programming (Teller and Veloso 1996, 1997; Teller 1998; Poli 1997a, 1997b) and the linear sequences of assembly code used in Nordin's approach to program evolution (Nordin 1994, l997; Nordin and Banzhaf 1995; Banzhaf, Nordin, Keller, and Francone 1998).

25.2 CIRCUIT SIMULATORS

In designing a circuit, the goal is to create the topology and sizing of a circuit that satisfies high-level requirements that are stated in terms of the circuit's measurable behaviors and characteristics. The salient behavioral quantities typically include the circuit's output voltages or currents (often in response to certain input voltages or currents). These output voltages or currents are often viewed in either the time or frequency domain. Numerous other behavioral quantities (e.g., power consumption) may be relevant for particular circuits. The behavioral quantities are typically measured under specified environmental conditions (e.g., room temperature). Other salient characteristics of a circuit include structural characteristics such as the number of components in the circuit, the dollar cost of the components, or the total surface area of silicon occupied by the circuit.

In practice, the behavior of a circuit may be determined in several ways:

1. The circuit may be built. This can sometimes be done on a breadboard on a workbench; however, it sometimes must be done in silicon. In any event, the circuit's behavior can then be directly measured while the circuit is operating. In some cases, it may be possible to embody the circuit using rapidly reconfigurable hardware (e.g., field-programmable gate arrays or field-programmable analog arrays as discussed in Part 6 on evolvable hardware).

2. It is sometimes possible to mathematically solve the equations that describe the behavior of a given circuit. The behavior of linear, time-invariant analog circuits is specified by a system of integro-differential equations (one equation for each node in the circuit in accordance with Kirchhoff's laws). The time behavior of voltage across and current passing through inductors and capacitors can be represented by derivatives and integrals. The voltage across and current passing through a resistor are represented by Ohm's law. It is sometimes practical to solve the resulting system of linear integro-differential equations (e.g., by using Laplace transforms). However, when the circuit contains active and nonlinear components (e.g., transistors and diodes), solution of the equations becomes vexatious.

3. The circuit may be simulated. A circuit simulator analyzes a given circuit and calculates its behavior in response to specified inputs under specified conditions.

SPICE (Simulation Program with Integrated Circuit Emphasis) is an industrial-strength electrical circuit simulator. SPICE is a large family of programs written over several decades at the University of California at Berkeley for the simulation of analog, digital, and mixed analog-digital electrical circuits. The SPICE simulator (and its many variants) dominates the field of simulation for general-purpose electrical circuits. There are over 100,000 copies of SPICE in use (Perry 1998) by practicing electrical engineers throughout the world. Don Pederson of the University of California at Berkeley was awarded the 1998 IEEE Medal of Honor "for the creation of the SPICE program, universally used for computer aided design of circuits."

SPICE3 (Quarles, Newton, Pederson, and Sangiovanni-Vincentelli 1994) is currently the most recent version of Berkeley SPICE. It consists of about 217,000 lines of C source code residing in 878 separate files. When compiled, it occupies about 6.1 megabytes of storage.

SPICE3 performs various types of analysis on circuits containing various types of electrical devices. The devices include

- resistors,
- capacitors,
- inductors,
- diodes,
- transistors,
- voltage and current sources (both dependent and independent),
- transmission lines, and
- switches.

The types of analysis that SPICE3 can perform include

- DC analysis,
- transient analysis,
- AC small-signal analysis,
- temperature analysis,
- pole-zero analysis,
- small-signal distortion analysis,
- sensitivity analysis, and
- noise analysis.

There are over 20 commercial derivatives (Perry 1998) of Berkeley SPICE including PSpice from MicroSim Corporation of Irvine, California; HSPICE from Meta-Software (now part of Avanti) of Campbell, California; IS-SPICE from Intusoft of San Pedro, California; T-Spice from Tanner Research Inc. of Pasadena, California; ZSPICE from ZTEC of College Place, Washington; Smart SPICE from Silvaco Inc. of Santa Clara, California; and Circuit Maker from Micro Code Engineering of Orem, Utah. PSpice was introduced in 1984 and was the first commercial version of SPICE available for personal computers (Tuinenga 1995; Monsseen 1993; Fenical 1992). (Additional information about SPICE can be found in sources such as Vladimirescu 1994, Kielkowski 1994, and Lamey 1995.)

Some commercial versions of SPICE are advantageous for certain types of circuits in terms of convergence, accuracy, or computer time. In addition, commercial versions of SPICE usually come with libraries providing detailed performance characteristics for thousands of different commercially available electrical components. Most conspicuously, commercial versions of SPICE all have attractive multifeatured interactive graphical user interfaces that enable the design engineer to conveniently enter a circuit into the simulator and graphically display the circuit's behavior in many useful and appealing ways. In contrast, the basic SPICE simulator available from the University of California at Berkeley takes input only in the form of a netlist in text form (mirroring its original version whose input was by means of punched cards). The basic Berkeley SPICE simulator produces output in the form of text (in the form of tables or plots produced with asterisks and spaces).

Over the years, the SPICE simulator (and its many derivatives) has proved to be a robust industrial-strength simulator that is capable of accurately simulating a vast range of practical electrical circuits. SPICE and other simulators in the field of electrical engineering have earned a reputation considerably different from that of, say, most robotics simulators used in artificial intelligence research (where there frequently is a significant divergence between the robot's real-world behavior and the simulator's prediction).

In addition to SPICE, there are numerous other robust and reliable simulators available to electrical engineers, including, for example, specialized simulators for radio frequency (RF) circuits.

It is important to note the difference between circuit synthesis and circuit simulation (circuit analysis). Circuit simulators, such as SPICE, do analysis. Although commercial circuit simulators are often marketed using phrases such as "design tool," circuit simulators do not create (synthesize) the design of anything. A circuit simulator takes, as its input, a circuit that has already been designed (typically by a human). A circuit simulator then analyzes the given circuit and produces output (in the form of tables and graphs) that shows the circuit's behavior in response to certain specified inputs under certain specified conditions. That is, circuit simulators do *analysis* of already designed circuits; they do not do *synthesis* (creation) of circuits. Circuit simulators are useful in the design process because they are used by human engineers as part of an interactive design process in which the engineer initially creates a circuit design, studies the circuit's behavior using the simulator, and then employs human intelligence to adjust the current version of the circuit to better comply with the design goals. These interactive steps are typically iterated by the engineer in order to produce better and better circuits. In contrast, genetic programming synthesizes (creates) the design for a circuit without this kind of iterative and interactive involvement by a human engineer.

25.2.1 Sample Run of the SPICE Simulator

In order to simulate a circuit with SPICE, the user must provide SPICE with

- a netlist describing the circuit to be analyzed, and
- SPICE commands that instruct SPICE as to the type of analysis to be performed and the nature of the output to be produced.

For example, the complete input to an illustrative run of SPICE follows:

```
* SIMPLE CIRCUIT
RSOURCE 1 2 1000OHM
L1 2 3 1HENRY
C2 3 0 1FARAD
RLOAD 3 0 1000OHM
VSOURCE 1 0 SIN (0VOLTS 5VOLTS 60HERTZ 0SECONDS 0PERSECOND)
.PLOT V(3)
.TRAN 0.002 0.02 0.0
.END
```

The input to SPICE always begins with a command line that provides a name for the circuit ("SIMPLE CIRCUIT" here).

The netlist (the same five lines as explained in detail in Section 25.1) follows the name for the circuit.

The commands that instruct SPICE to perform certain types of analysis or to perform certain other tasks follow the netlist. Some of these commands may identify the probe (output) points of the circuit and may specify the desired types of analyses to be performed on the signals. A circuit may be probed for voltage or current. SPICE may be instructed to perform a PLOT on more than one node of a circuit.

For example, the command

```
.PLOT V(3)
```

instructs SPICE to capture the behavior of the circuit in terms of its output voltage V(3) at node 3. As another example, the command

```
.TRAN 0.002 0.020 0.000
```

instructs SPICE to perform a transient analysis in the time domain in step sizes of 0.002 seconds ranging from a starting time of 0.000 to an ending time of 0.020 seconds.

SPICE may be instructed to perform more than one type of analysis for a particular circuit. For example, the command

```
.AC DEC 25 1 10000
```

instructs SPICE to perform AC small-signal analysis. Specifically, the AC command causes the analysis to be performed in the frequency domain ranging from a starting frequency of 1 Hz to an ending frequency of 10,000 Hz and with 25 equal steps per decade (on a logarithmic scale). There will be numerous examples of other types of analysis by SPICE throughout this book.

The input to SPICE is always delimited by an END command.

25.3 THE MAPPING BETWEEN CIRCUITS AND PROGRAM TREES

There are numerous differences between the labeled cyclic graphs germane to electrical circuits and the rooted point-labeled trees with ordered branches that have been discussed throughout this book in connection with genetic programming.

Figure 25.2 shows a rooted point-labeled tree (acyclic graph) with ordered branches representing the even-2-parity function. The internal points are labeled with Boolean functions (such as AND, OR, and NOT) and the external points are labeled with the terminals or inputs (such as D0 and D1).

One difference between the trees used in genetic programming and the graphs germane to electrical circuits is that circuits are cyclic graphs. They are not only cyclic graphs (in the usual sense of having at least one cycle), but *every* component and wire in an electrical circuit is included in a cycle. There are no dangling components or wires anywhere in a circuit.

Another difference between the trees used in genetic programming and the graphs germane to electrical circuits is their labeling. The points of the trees used in genetic programming each carry a single label, namely, that of a function or terminal. In contrast, the components of an electrical circuit carry a variable number of labels. For electrical components, one label identifies the type of electrical component (e.g., a capacitor such as C2). Additional label(s), if any, specify the value(s) of the component (i.e., 12 nF). A single explicit numerical value is sufficient to specify some components (e.g., resistors, capacitors, and inductors); however, multiple explicit values are required to specify

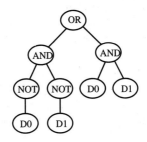

Figure 25.2   A rooted point-labeled tree (acyclic graph) with ordered branches representing a computer program

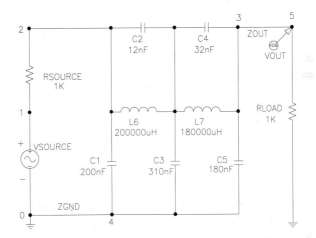

Figure 25.3   A labeled cyclic graph representing an electrical circuit

other components (e.g., the length and width of the channel in a MOSFET transistor on a chip). The values of some components are nonnumerical and symbolic (e.g., whether a voltage source is "AC" or "DC"). Some components (e.g., diodes and nonsized transistors) do not carry any explicit component value at all. Figure 25.3 shows an electrical circuit.

Yet another difference between the trees used in genetic programming and the graphs germane to electrical circuits is that there is a distinct orientation to the leads of many electrical components (e.g., the positive and negative leads of a diode; the base, collector, and emitter leads of a transistor; and the four leads of a transformer).

In addition, the method of evaluation of an electrical circuit differs in a fundamental way from the evaluation of a program tree. The functions in a program tree (such as Figure 25.2) are evaluated separately in sequential order. For example, the NOT function is applied to D0 (and to D1) before the AND function is applied to the two results (NOT D0) and (NOT D1). The OR function at the root of the program tree is evaluated only after the two AND functions are evaluated. In contrast, an electrical circuit operates in continuous time. There is no separate and sequential order to the evaluation of a circuit's components. Instead, all of a circuit's components interact continuously with all the other components in the circuit. In particular, each loop (and node) in an electrical circuit obeys Kirchhoff's loop (or node) law. The time behavior of voltage across and current passing through each inductor and capacitor is expressed by a derivative or integral. The voltage across and current passing through each resistor is expressed by Ohm's law. There is one integro-differential equation for each separate loop (and node) in the circuit. The overall behavior of an electrical circuit (say, the voltage across and the current passing through each component) is expressed by the solution to the resulting system of integro-differential equations. These voltages and currents change continuously over time.

25.4   EMBRYO AND TEST FIXTURE

Genetic programming can be applied to the automated synthesis of complex structures such as electrical circuits if a bridge can be established between the particular kind of structures bred by genetic programming and the particular kind of labeled cyclic graphs that represent electrical circuits.

In nature, the life of a complex multicellular organism begins with a single embryonic cell. In the first stage of the developmental process, the embryo divides. In subsequent stages, the original cell and the successor cells divide. In complex multicellular organisms, there is typically differentiation of cell types during the developmental process so that the fully developed organism consists of many different types of cells (Gilbert 1991).

The innovative work of Kitano (1990) and Gruau (1992a, 1992b, 1993, 1994a, 1994b) applied the principles of developmental biology to design neural networks with evolutionary algorithms. Our approach to the automatic synthesis of electrical circuits applies similar principles from nature.

The starting point of the developmental process for transforming an individual program tree in the population into a potentially useful electrical circuit is an initial circuit. The initial circuit consists of two parts: an embryo and a test fixture. Both parts are very simple. Neither the embryo alone nor the test fixture alone is a valid electrical circuit. After an embryo is embedded into its test fixture, the combination of the two (called the *initial circuit*) constitutes a valid electrical circuit (albeit a degenerate one). The typical initial circuit in this book yields only a trivial output (usually a constant-valued output). The two parts of an initial circuit are as follows:

- **The embryo:** The embryo is an electrical substructure that contains at least one modifiable wire or modifiable component. A modifiable wire is a wire that is capable of being converted into an electrical component, another modifiable wire, or a nonmodifiable wire during the developmental process. The developmental process transforms the initial circuit into a fully developed electrical circuit. An embryo has one or more ports that enable it to be embedded into its test fixture. Occasionally, an embryo will also contain nonmodifiable wires, nonmodifiable electrical components, or modifiable electrical components.
- **The test fixture:** A test fixture incorporates certain fixed elements that are required to test the type of circuit being designed. The test fixture is a fixed (hard-wired) substructure composed of nonmodifiable wires and nonmodifiable electrical compo-

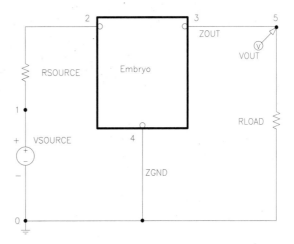

Figure 25.4   One-input, one-output test fixture with three ports to the embryo

nents. Its purpose is to provide a means for testing another electrical substructure. The test fixture provides access to the circuit's external input(s) and permits probing of the circuit's output. A test fixture has one or more ports that enable an embryo to be embedded into it. In the initial circuit, the test fixture encases the embryo. After the embryo is fully developed, the test fixture encases the nontrivial substructure that is developed from the embryo. For example, the test fixture often contains a source resistor, reflecting the reality that all sources have resistance, and a load resistor, representing the load that must be driven by the output.

The distinctive feature of the test fixture is that it contains no modifiable wires and no modifiable components. The distinctive feature of the embryo is that it contains at least one modifiable wire.

Figure 25.4 shows a one-input, one-output test fixture with three ports that is used frequently in this book. Nodes 2, 3, and 4 are the three ports of this test fixture that are intended to be attached to an embryo. This test fixture consists of the following six elements:

- an incoming signal (input to the overall circuit) in the form of voltage source **VSOURCE**, whose negative end is connected to node 0 (ground) and whose positive end is connected to node 1,
- a source resistor **RSOURCE** between nodes 1 and 2,
- a nonmodifiable wire **ZOUT** between nodes 3 and 5,
- a voltage probe point **VOUT** (the output of the overall circuit) at node 5,
- a load resistor **RLOAD** between nodes 5 and 0, and
- a nonmodifiable wire **ZGND** between nodes 4 and 0.

The test fixture usually contains certain components that are appropriate to the circuit being synthesized. For example, the incoming signal **VSOURCE** might be a 2 volt (peak) alternating-current (AC) source, the load resistor **RLOAD** of this test fixture might be 1,000 Ω, and the source resistor **RSOURCE** might also be 1,000 Ω.

Figure 25.5 shows an embryo with two modifiable wires and three ports that is used frequently in this book. The two modifiable wires of this embryo are **Z0** and **Z1**. The three ports of this embryo are **Embryo_Input**, **Embryo_Output**, and **Embryo_Ground**. This embryo consists of the following two elements:

- a modifiable wire **Z0** between the **Embryo_Output** and the **Embryo_Ground**, and
- a modifiable wire **Z1** between the **Embryo_Input** and the **Embryo_Output**.

The initial circuit is the result of embedding an embryo into a test fixture. The initial circuit is a valid electrical circuit. In contrast, neither the embryo nor the test fixture is a valid electrical circuit. An embryo can be embedded in a test fixture by attaching the ports of the embryo to the ports of the test fixture. Figure 25.6 shows the initial circuit that is created when the embryo of Figure 25.5 is embedded in the test fixture of Figure 25.4. This embedding occurs by attaching

- node 2 of the test fixture to the **Embryo_Input**,
- node 3 of the test fixture to the **Embryo_Output**, and
- node 4 of the test fixture to the **Embryo_Ground**.

Note that the output of this initial circuit (Figure 25.6) at its probe point **VOUT** at node 5 is entirely uninteresting. It is a constant-zero signal; it is entirely independent of the incoming signal **VSOURCE**. More pointedly, this output does not satisfy the design requirements of any problem of circuit synthesis in this book.

Note that this initial circuit (and all the other initial circuits appearing in this book) contain only resistors and wires in addition to the circuit's input, the circuit's output, and a connection to ground. (Section 52.2 describes a special embryo in which two transistors are purposefully hard-wired into the embryo; however, even this exceptional embryo contains only a tiny fraction of the circuitry required to perform the desired task.)

It is known that the design requirements of no problem in this book can be satisfied merely by wires and resistors. The initial circuit is merely the starting point of a multistep developmental process that transforms the initial circuit into a potentially useful, fully developed circuit. This transformation is accomplished by side-effecting functions contained in an individual circuit-constructing program tree in the population being evolved by genetic programming.

Note, specifically, that the initial circuits used in this book are entirely different in character from the kind of "pretty good" human-designed "prototype circuits" that are used as the starting points for various circuit-perfecting techniques (Chapter 24). The starting points in such circuit-perfecting techniques are complete working circuits whose topology has been created by the human engineer. These techniques then make small adjustments (typically affecting only the sizing of the prototype's preexisting components, but occasionally involving the deletion of a preexisting connection).

The above test fixture (Figure 25.4) is one of eight different test fixtures shown in Section 29.1. The above embryo (Figure 25.5) is one of eight different embryos shown in Section 29.2. (Other special embryos and test fixtures are shown in Chapter 52.)

The choice of a particular embryo for a particular problem of circuit synthesis primarily reflects the number of external inputs and outputs of the circuit and the desired ini-

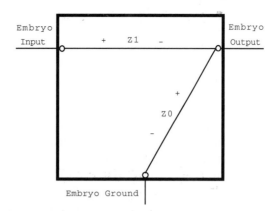

Figure 25.5   Embryo with two modifiable wires, Z0 and Z1, and three ports (Embryo_Input, Embryo_Output, and Embryo_Ground)

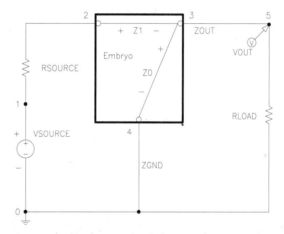

Figure 25.6   Initial circuit consisting of an embryo with two modifiable wires, Z0 and Z1, embedded in a one-input, one-output test fixture with three ports to the embryo

tial number of modifiable wires (which, as will be seen momentarily, equals the number of result-producing branches in the overall circuit-constructing program tree).

Since the purpose of the test fixture is to test the substructure that it surrounds, the choice of test fixture for a particular problem reflects, in practice, the number of external inputs and outputs for the overall circuit. Thus, a different test fixture is required for, say, a circuit with two external inputs and one external output than a circuit with one input and three outputs. As will be seen later (Chapter 52), the test fixture may also contain (or omit) certain hard-wired components and connections for various problem-specific reasons.

25.5 THE DEVELOPMENTAL PROCESS

The developmental process for transforming an individual program tree in the population into an electrical circuit begins with the initial circuit. Each circuit-constructing program tree in the population of a run of genetic programming yields one fully developed electrical circuit.

The embryo's modifiable wire(s) are transformed as the embryo develops. These transformations occur as side effects of the execution of the functions in a circuit-constructing program tree. The population of individuals being bred by genetic programming is a population of such circuit-constructing program trees. When the first function in a particular circuit-constructing program tree is executed, it is applied to a particular designated modifiable wire of the embryo to produce the first successor to the initial circuit in the developmental process. Thereafter, the remaining functions in the circuit-constructing program tree are executed, one by one, in breadth-first order. Each function is applied, one by one, to the current state of the developing circuit in order to produce a successor circuit. That is, the functions in the circuit-constructing program tree operate by means of their side effects on the initial circuit and its successors during the developmental process. After all the circuit-constructing functions of the program tree have been executed, the developmental process is completed. The final successor circuit is the circuit produced by the circuit-constructing program tree.

The circuit-constructing functions are, in almost all cases, defined so that they manipulate the initial circuit (and its successors in the developmental process) in such a way that every successor constitutes a valid electrical circuit at each step of the developmental process. That is, validity is preserved throughout the developmental process. Since each circuit-constructing program tree is composed of such validity-preserving circuit-constructing functions, every individual circuit-constructing program tree in the population necessarily creates a valid electrical circuit. Furthermore, because all the elements of the test fixture are permanently fixed (hard-wired), all fully developed circuits are guaranteed to possess all elements of the test fixture. As will be seen shortly, the circuit-constructing functions that we use here are designed to also preserve certain additional desirable properties (such as the allowable number of lines impinging on each node of the circuit) at each step of the developmental process.

Certain functions (e.g., the CUT function [Section 25.8.8] and the PAIR_CONNECT function [Section 25.8.10]) do not necessarily preserve structural validity during the developmental process. However, when these functions are used, we restore structural validity by automated postdevelopmental editing, when possible.

When a component-creating function in a circuit-constructing program tree creates a component requiring one or more component values, the sizing of the component is simultaneously established by the component-creating function. The component value(s) are established by executing value-setting subtree(s) that appear as arguments of the component-creating function. If the component value is numerical, the value is established by an arithmetic-performing subtree consisting of a composition of arithmetic functions and numerical constants that together yield the numerical value for the component.

The result of the entire developmental process is the topology of the circuit, the choice of the types of components that are situated at each location within the topology, and the sizing of all the components of the circuit. In other words, the developmental process starts with a trivial and useless initial circuit consisting of a test fixture and embryo and ends with a fully developed electrical circuit. The circuit-constructing program tree is the genotype, and the fully developed circuit constructed in accordance with the tree's instructions is the phenotype.

The circuit-constructing program trees can contain the following five categories of functions:

- topology-modifying functions for modifying the topology of the developing circuit structure,
- component-creating functions for inserting a particular component into a location within the topology of the developing circuit structure in lieu of a modifiable wire (or a modifiable component) and for specifying the sizing of each such inserted component by means of value-setting subtree(s),
- development-controlling functions for controlling the process of developing the initial circuit and its successors into a fully developed circuit,
- automatically defined functions (subroutines) whose existence, number, arity, and hierarchical references are either specified in advance by the user or come into existence (or are deleted) dynamically during the run as a consequence of the architecture-altering operations (Part 3), and
- arithmetic-performing functions in the value-setting subtrees of the component-creating functions for specifying the numerical value (sizing) of components.

Program trees conform to a constrained syntactic structure. Each component-creating function, topology-modifying function, and development-controlling function has zero, one, or more value-setting subtrees and zero, one, or more construction-continuing subtrees. Construction-continuing subtrees specify how the construction of the circuit is to be continued. Many component-creating functions have one or more value-setting subtree(s) (i.e., arithmetic-performing subtree(s)). An arithmetic-performing subtree consists of a composition of arithmetic functions and numerical constant terminals that together yield the numerical value for the component. By convention, the value-setting subtree(s) of a component-creating function are the first argument(s) of the component-creating function. That is, the value-setting subtree(s) appear on the left under each component-creating function in figures in this book, and the construction-continuing subtree(s) appear on the right.

Figure 25.7 is an illustrative circuit-constructing program tree shown as a rooted point-labeled tree with ordered branches. This program tree is not a contrived example; it is a best-of-generation individual from the initial random generation of one of our first runs of the problem of synthesizing a lowpass filter. The details of each function in this program tree will be presented in Sections 25.6 through 25.9. The developmental process by which this particular tree creates a fully developed circuit will be presented in Section 25.10. In the meantime, let us make a few high-level preliminary observations about the structure and content of this circuit-constructing program tree. The overall program consists of two result-producing branches joined by the connective LIST function (labeled 1). The first (left) result-producing branch is rooted at the capacitor-creating C function (labeled 2). The second result-producing branch is rooted at the polarity-reversing FLIP function (labeled 3). This figure also contains four occurrences of the inductor-creating

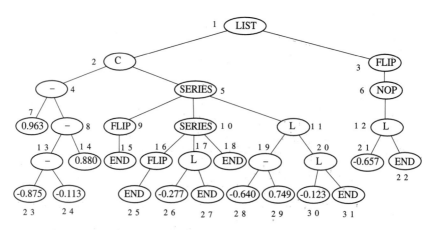

Figure 25.7   Illustrative circuit-constructing program tree

L function (at 17, 11, 20, and 12). This figure contains two occurrences of the topology-modifying SERIES function (at 5 and 10). The figure also contains five occurrences of the development-controlling END function (at 15, 25, 27, 31, and 22) and one occurrence of the development-controlling "no operation" NOP function (at 6). There is a seven-point arithmetic-performing subtree rooted at 4 and located under the capacitor-creating C function at 2, a three-point arithmetic-performing subtree at 19 under the inductor-creating L function at 11, and one-point arithmetic-performing subtrees (i.e., constants) at 26, 30, and 21. Each of these five arithmetic-performing subtrees is the first (leftmost) argument of its respective component-creating function.

The program tree in Figure 25.7 (and all other individual circuit-constructing program trees in the population) is constructed in accordance with a constrained syntactic structure (described in Section 25.11). The random program trees in the initial population (generation 0) and all random subtrees generated by the mutation operation in later generations are created so as to conform to this constrained syntactic structure (as described in Section 5.7.1). A *type* is assigned to each potential crossover point in a program tree on the basis of the actual contents of the subtree below the potential crossover point (called *point typing*). When crossover is to be performed, this constrained syntactic structure is preserved using structure-preserving crossover with point typing (as described in Section 5.7.2).

At the beginning of the execution of a program tree, the topmost point of each result-producing branch in the circuit-constructing program tree is associated with a particular modifiable wire of the embryo of the initial circuit. For example, the capacitor-creating C function (labeled 2 in Figure 25.7) of the program tree is associated with modifiable wire Z0 of the embryo. Similarly, the polarity-reversing FLIP function (labeled 3) of the program tree is associated with modifiable wire Z1 of the embryo. This association can be thought of as an arc linking a particular function in the program tree with a particular modifiable wire (or, as development proceeds, a modifiable component). We sometimes refer to this association by saying that a particular internal point (function) in a program tree (or a particular modifiable wire or modifiable component in a developing circuit) possesses a *writing head*.

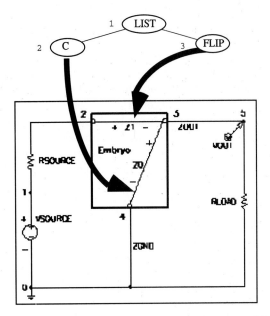

Figure 25.8 One-input, one-output initial circuit with two writing heads associated with the two modifiable wires (Z0 and Z1) of the embryo

Figure 25.8 shows the topmost three points of the program tree of Figure 25.7 along with the initial circuit of Figure 25.6. Figure 25.8 shows the initial two writing heads (one for each of the two result-producing branches under the connective LIST function). The first writing head is initially associated with the C function (labeled 2) of the circuit-constructing program tree and links the C function to modifiable wire Z0 of the embryo of the initial circuit. The second writing head is initially associated with the FLIP function (labeled 3) and links the FLIP function to modifiable wire Z1 of the embryo.

Each component-creating, topology-modifying, and development-controlling function in a circuit-constructing program tree modifies the developing circuit structure in a particular way. Most of the functions have one or more construction-continuing subtrees that specify the successor function(s) in the program tree. For example, the capacitor-creating C function (labeled 2 in Figure 25.7) has one construction-continuing subtree. The topology-modifying SERIES function (labeled 5 in Figure 25.7) is the topmost function of the construction-continuing subtree of the capacitor-creating C function. The execution of the C function of the program causes the writing head linked to the C function to move from the C function to the SERIES function (labeled 5) of the program tree.

Similarly, the polarity-reversing FLIP function (labeled 3) has one construction-continuing subtree. The topmost function of the construction-continuing subtree of the FLIP function is the development-controlling NOP ("no operation") function (labeled 6). The execution of the FLIP function causes the writing head linked to the FLIP function to move and become linked to the NOP function.

The three-argument SERIES topology-modifying function (at 5) has three construction-continuing subtrees (rooted at 9, 10, and 11). The topmost functions of the three construction-continuing subtrees of the SERIES function are the FLIP function (labeled 9), another SERIES function (at 10), and an inductor-creating L function (at 11). The execution of the SERIES function (at 5) causes a trifurcation of the writing head at SERIES 5 and creates three writing heads linked to 9, 10, and 11. A circuit is progressively developed by modifying each modifiable wire (or modifiable component) to which a writing head is currently pointing. The development-controlling END function occurs only at external points of the tree. The END function has no construction-continuing subtree. In other words, execution of the END function causes its writing head to be discarded. The development of a circuit is complete when all the writing heads have been discarded.

Because the elements of the test fixture are permanently fixed, all fully developed circuits that arise from an initial circuit are guaranteed to possess all hard-wired elements of the test fixture. Thus, all fully developed circuits arising from the initial circuit of Figure 25.6 (containing the embryo of Figure 25.5) will possess an incoming signal source **VSOURCE**, the source resistor **RSOURCE**, the probe point **VOUT**, and the fixed load resistor **RLOAD**.

Modifiable wires (such as **Z0** and **Z1** in the initial circuit of Figure 25.6) are the starting point of the developmental process that ends with an eventual fully developed circuit. Modifiable wires appear only in the embryo (not the test fixture) of the initial circuit. Each modifiable wire is associated with a particular function in the circuit-constructing program tree (i.e., there is a writing head linking the function in the program tree with the modifiable wire in the initial circuit or its successors). All development of the circuit begins with the modifiable wires. All subsequent development continues from the modifiable wires (or modifiable components) to which the writing head(s) currently point. A circuit is developed by modifying the modifiable wire (or modifiable component) to which a writing head is pointing (sometimes in conjunction with a node or nearby component) in the way specified by the particular circuit-constructing function.

Note that the embryo of Figure 25.5 (and all of the other embryos in this book) and the test fixture of Figure 25.4 (and all other test fixtures in this book) are designed such that the number of lines impinging at any node in the developing circuit structure is always either two or three. Each of the topology-modifying and component-creating functions (described below) in the circuit-constructing program tree are designed to preserve, during the developmental process, this constraint concerning the number of impinging lines. This constraint significantly streamlines the definition of the topology-modifying and component-creating functions used in this book. However, this approach is, by no means, the only possible approach for evolving circuits or other complex structures using genetic programming. Note that this constraint does not preclude the connection of more than three components at a single point in a circuit because both wires and vias (Sections 25.8.4, 25.8.6, and 25.8.10) provide ways to create virtual nodes of degree greater than three.

Nonmodifiable wires (such as **ZGND** and **ZOUT** in Figure 25.6) do not have writing heads. They are most commonly used for purposes of isolation (e.g., in the test fixture). Nonmodifiable wires prevent alteration of fixed elements of the test fixture by putting them beyond the reach of the topology-modifying and component-creating functions. For example, isolating wire **ZOUT** protects the probe point **VOUT** and the load resistor **RLOAD** from getting separated from one another during the developmental process.

Similarly, isolating wire **ZGND** protects the negative terminal of **VSOURCE** and the ground from getting separated from one another during the developmental process.

No wires appear in the netlist that is actually submitted to SPICE. Nonmodifiable wires are edited out before the netlist is submitted to SPICE. Moreover, modifiable wires have either become nonmodifiable or disappeared by the time that the circuit structure is fully developed. In fact, the completion of the developmental process is defined by the disappearance of the last modifiable wire.

Note that, except for minor details of the test fixture (such as the value of the load and source resistors and the voltage level of the incoming signal), the initial circuit of Figure 25.6 is *potentially applicable to any one-input, one-output circuit*. As will be seen, this particular initial circuit will be used for numerous one-input, one-output circuits throughout this book (e.g., filters, source identification circuits, computational circuits). Of course, various alternative initial circuits can also be used for one-input, one-output circuits.

25.6 SMALL REPERTOIRE OF CIRCUIT-CONSTRUCTING FUNCTIONS

In the interests of quickly presenting one complete and detailed example of the application of genetic programming to a problem of circuit synthesis, the following sections describe a small subset of three basic component-creating functions (Section 25.6), ten basic topology-modifying functions (Section 25.8), and two development-controlling functions (Section 25.9). Value-setting subtrees are described right after the component-creating functions (Section 25.7).

This small subset of 15 functions will be sufficient for discussing the design of numerous circuits composed of only resistors, capacitors, and inductors (Chapters 25 to 40). Then, prior to discussing active circuits involving transistors, Chapter 41 will present the full repertoire of circuit-constructing functions.

Circuit-constructing program trees can contain component-creating functions, topology-modifying functions, development-controlling functions, (optionally) automatically defined functions (subroutines), and arithmetic-performing functions (in value-setting subtrees).

The small repertoire of component-creating functions (Section 25.6) includes the following three functions:

- resistor-creating R function,
- capacitor-creating C function, and
- inductor-creating L function.

The small repertoire of topology-modifying functions (Section 25.8) includes the following 10 function families:

- SERIES division function,
- two parallel division functions, PARALLEL0 and PARALLEL1,
- polarity-reversing FLIP function,
- eight two-argument TWO_VIA functions,
- the two-argument grounding function TWO_GROUND,

- eight three-argument THREE_VIA functions,
- two three-argument THREE_GROUND functions,
- the CUT function,
- the SAFE_CUT function, and
- the PAIR_CONNECT functions.

The entire repertoire of development-controlling functions (Section 25.9) consists of the following two functions:

- the "no operation" NOP function and
- the development-terminating END function.

Each component-creating function inserts a component into the developing circuit structure and assigns component value(s) to the component. A component-creating function usually has one construction-continuing subtree (so that its writing head moves to one successor function). The polarity of each two-leaded component that is introduced into a circuit by a component-creating function matches that of the modifiable wire or modifiable (two-leaded) component it replaces.

Each topology-modifying function in a program tree is associated with a particular component in the developing circuit structure and modifies the topology of the developing circuit structure in some way. A topology-modifying function may have one (and often more than one) construction-continuing subtree. When a circuit-constructing function has k construction-continuing subtrees, it spawns k writing heads.

Development-controlling functions control the progressive development of the circuit.

In general, each component-creating, topology-modifying, and development-controlling function starts with a valid electrical circuit and transforms it into another valid circuit. In general, each component-creating function and topology-modifying function leaves either two or three lines impinging at each of the circuit's nodes. That is, all the circuit-constructing functions are designed to preserve both circuit validity and the property that either two or three lines impinge at each node.

25.6.1 The R Function

The two-argument resistor-creating R function causes the modifiable wire or modifiable component in the developing circuit structure that is linked to this function in the circuit-constructing program tree to be changed into a resistor. The arity of the R function is two because one of the arguments of the R function is its value-setting (arithmetic-performing) subtree and the other is its construction-continuing subtree.

The value of the newly created resistor is established by the arithmetic-performing subtree (the first argument of the R function). The value of the resistor is the antilogarithm (base 10) of the intermediate value U (described in Section 25.7) in kilo-ohms. This mapping gives the resistor a value within a range of plus or minus 5 orders of magnitude centered around 1 kΩ.

Figure 25.9 shows a modifiable wire Z0 located between nodes 1 and 2 of a partial circuit that also contains four capacitors (C2, C3, C4, and C5). Figure 25.10 shows that the result of applying the R function to the modifiable wire Z0 of Figure 25.9 is the creation of a resistor R1 connecting nodes 1 and 2 in lieu of the modifiable wire Z0 of Figure 25.9. Note that the polarity of the newly created resistor R1 matches that of the

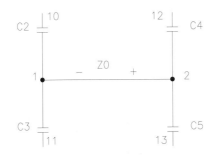

Figure 25.9 Modifiable wire Z0 connecting nodes 1 and 2

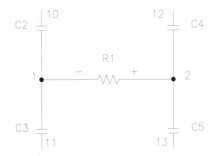

Figure 25.10 Modifiable resistor R1 connecting nodes 1 and 2

modifiable wire Z0 that it replaces. The newly created resistor R1 remains modifiable. That is, R1 is linked to the topmost function of the construction-continuing subtree of the R function (the second argument of the R function). In other words, R1 retains the writing head that originally linked the R function of the program tree to the modifiable wire Z0 of the developing partial circuit of Figure 25.9.

In practice, the netlist for a circuit is not created until the circuit is fully developed and is ready to be submitted to the SPICE simulator. Moreover, netlists are not typically made for partial circuits. Also, since the modifiable wires are purely artifacts of the developmental process, the netlist that is eventually passed to the SPICE simulator does not contain any wires (modifiable or nonmodifiable). However, for the sake of argument, if a netlist were created for the partial circuit of Figure 25.9, it would consist of the following five lines:

```
C2 1 10
C3 1 11
Z0 2 1
C4 2 12
C5 2 13
```

The interpretation of the third line of the above netlist is that there is a component named Z0 of type "wire" whose positive end is connected to node 2 and whose negative end is connected to node 1. By convention, the first-listed node in a netlist is the node connected to the positive end of a two-leaded component, so Z0 is shown as being connected from node 2 to node 1.

The effect of the R function (creating, say, a 5 Ω resistor) is to change the third line of this five-line netlist:

```
C2 1 10
C3 1 11
R1 2 1 5OHMS
C4 2 12
C5 2 13
```

The interpretation of the third line of the above modified netlist is that there is a resistor named **R1** that is connected between nodes 2 and 1 of the circuit and that this component has a value of 5 Ω.

The R function is defined so that it overwrites the modifiable component or modifiable wire to which its writing head is currently linked. Thus, if the R function of a circuit-constructing program tree happens to be linked to a modifiable wire of a developing circuit, the R function inserts a modifiable resistor in lieu of the modifiable wire. If the R function is linked to a preexisting nonwire component, it inserts a modifiable resistor in lieu of the preexisting component. The component-creating functions for two-leaded components might, alternatively, have been defined so that a component always remains in the circuit once a modifiable wire is converted into a component. In this alternative implementation, there would be no construction-continuing subtree for the component-creating function (so that a component-creating function such as the R function would have only one argument, instead of two). A comparative experiment involving this alternative approach for two-leaded components appears in Section 54.9.

25.6.2 The C Function

The two-argument capacitor-creating C function causes the modifiable wire or modifiable component to which it is linked to be changed into a capacitor. The value of the newly created capacitor is established by the arithmetic-performing subtree (the first argument of the C function). The value of the capacitor is the antilogarithm (base 10) of the intermediate value U (described in Section 25.7) in nanofarads. This mapping gives the capacitor a value within a range of plus or minus 5 orders of magnitude centered around 1 nF.

Figure 25.11 shows that the result of applying the C function to the modifiable wire **Z0** of Figure 25.9 is the creation of a capacitor **C1** connecting nodes 1 and 2 in lieu of the modifiable wire **Z0** of Figure 25.9. The newly created capacitor **C1** remains modifiable. That is, **C1** is linked to the topmost function in the construction-continuing subtree (the second argument of the C function).

25.6.3 The L Function

The two-argument inductor-creating L function causes the modifiable wire or modifiable component to which it is linked to be changed into an inductor. The value of the inductor is the antilogarithm (base 10) of the intermediate value U (described in Section 25.7) in microhenrys. This mapping gives the inductor a value within a range of plus or minus 5 orders of magnitude centered around 1 μH.

Figure 25.12 shows that the result of applying the L function to the modifiable wire **Z0** of Figure 25.9 is the creation of an inductor **L1** connecting nodes 1 and 2 in lieu of the modifiable wire **Z0** of Figure 25.9. The newly created inductor **L1** remains modifiable. That is, **L1** is linked to the topmost function in the construction-continuing subtree (the second argument of the L function).

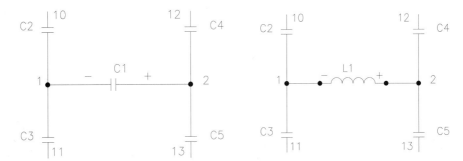

Figure 25.11   Result of applying the C function to the modifiable wire Z0 that previously connected nodes 1 and 2

Figure 25.12   Result of applying the L function to the modifiable wire Z0 that previously connected nodes 1 and 2

25.7   VALUE-SETTING SUBTREES FOR THE COMPONENT-CREATING FUNCTIONS

Most electrical components carry one or more component values. For example, a resistor has a resistance, a capacitor has a capacitance, and an inductor has an inductance. Component values are established by value-setting subtrees. A component-creating function has as many value-setting subtrees as it has component values. For example, the R, L, and C functions each carry one numerical component value. The most common type of component value is numerical. Thus, the R function has one value-setting subtree to establish the value of its resistance (and similarly for the L and C functions). The R, L, and C functions each take a total of two arguments—the first being the single value-setting subtree and the second being the construction-continuing subtree. Some components (e.g., a diode) carry no explicit component values and hence have no value-setting subtree.

Value-setting subtrees for components are implemented in this book as arithmetic-performing subtrees. An arithmetic-performing subtree of a component-creating function is a composition of arithmetic functions and random constants. When evaluated, an arithmetic-performing subtree returns a floating-point value. This approach for implementing value-setting subtrees has a number of very convenient features; however, it is, by no means, the only possible approach.

Arithmetic-performing subtrees are implemented in this book using a particular range of numerical values that we arrived at after examining a large number of practical circuits in contemporary electrical engineering books (Van Valkenburg 1982, page 13; Tuinenga 1995; Monsseen 1993; Fenical 1992; Vladimirescu 1994; Kielkowski 1994; Lamey 1995).

The breadth of the range of values appearing in practical circuits suggested a logarithmic scale for the numerical values of components. The use of a logarithmic scale suggested, in turn, the use of addition and subtraction (but not multiplication and division) as the arithmetic functions in the arithmetic-performing subtrees.

Specifically, the function set, F_{aps}, for each arithmetic-performing subtree is

$$F_{aps} = \{+, -\},$$

each taking two arguments.

The terminal set, T_{aps}, for each arithmetic-performing subtree is

$$T_{aps} = \{\Re_{smaller\text{-}reals}\},$$

where $\Re_{smaller\text{-}reals}$ represents random floating-point constants between -1.0 and $+1.0$ (as described in detail in Section 13.3.2).

The functions in arithmetic-performing subtrees are executed in depth-first order (as for functions in LISP), not breadth-first order.

We examined various practical circuits in several contemporary electrical engineering books. This examination showed that the values for the commonly used components seemed to span a range of 10 orders of magnitude or less. Moreover, the centers of these observed ranges of 10 orders of magnitude did not correspond to one full electrical unit for the commonly used components. For example, the values of resistance that we observed appeared to vary within a range of plus or minus 5 orders of magnitude centered around 1,000 Ω (rather than 1 Ω). The value of capacitance appeared to vary within a range of plus or minus 5 orders of magnitude centered around 1 nF. The value of inductance appeared to vary within a range of plus or minus 5 orders of magnitude centered around 1 μH.

The logarithmic scale, the limited range of values, and the center of the ranges of value together suggested that the floating-point value returned by an arithmetic-performing subtree must be interpreted in some manner before being attached to a component. A three-step process is used to interpret the arithmetic-performing subtree:

1. The arithmetic-performing subtree is evaluated. We call the floating-point number that it returns X.
2. X is used to produce an intermediate value U in the range of -5 to $+5$ in the following way:

    -   If the return value X is between -5.0 and $+5.0$, an intermediate value U is set to the value X returned by the subtree.
    -   If the return value X is less than -100 or greater than $+100$, U is set to a saturating value of zero.
    -   If the return value X is between -100 and -5.0, U is found from the straight line connecting the points $(-100, 0)$ and $(-5, -5)$.
    -   If the return value X is between $+5.0$ and $+100$, U is found from the straight line connecting $(5, 5)$ and $(100, 0)$.

    Figure 25.13 shows the mapping between the value of X returned by the subtree and U.

3. The actual value of the component is the antilogarithm (base 10) of the intermediate value U in a unit that is appropriate for the type of component. That is, the component's value is 10^U. The units are kilo-ohms for resistors, nanofarads for capacitors, and microhenrys for inductors.

The program tree of Figure 25.7, when written in the style of the LISP programming language, is

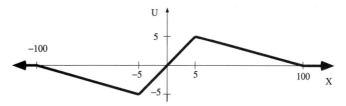

Figure 25.13 Mapping between X and U

(LIST (C **(- 0.963 (- (- -0.875 -0.113) 0.880))**) (SERIES (FLIP
END) (SERIES (FLIP END) (L **-0.277** END) END) (L **(- -0.640 0.749)**
(L **-0.123** END))))
      (FLIP (NOP (L **-0.657** END))))).

The underlined seven-point subtree

(- 0.963 (- (- -0.875 -0.113) 0.880))

associated with the capacitor-creating C function at the beginning of the above expression (which corresponds to the subtree rooted at the point labeled 4 in Figure 25.7) is an example of an arithmetic-performing subtree. The return value of this particular seven-point arithmetic-performing subtree is 2.605. When 2.605 is interpreted and scaled (in the manner described by Figure 25.13), it establishes 403 nF as the component value for the capacitor created by the C function.

Similarly, the underlined three-point subtree

(- -0.640 0.749)

associated with the L function corresponding to the three-point subtree rooted at the point labeled 19 in Figure 25.7 is another example of an arithmetic-performing subtree. Also, the three one-point subtrees (-0.277, -0.123, and -0.657) associated with the L functions (at the points labeled 17, 20, and 12, respectively, in Figure 25.7) are additional examples of arithmetic-performing subtrees.

During the run of genetic programming, the evolutionary process (particularly, the operation of structure-preserving crossover with point typing and the operation of mutation) will modify the arithmetic-performing subtrees so as to change the individual program of which it is a part (as described in Koza 1992e, Sections 10.1 and 10.2).

Of course, there are many acceptable alternatives to using 10 orders of magnitude as the range of values for the electrical components. Also, there are numerous alternative ways of converting the floating-point value returned by an arithmetic-performing subtree into a component value within a specified range. For example, if a circuit must be manufactured using certain commercially available parts, you might choose the commercially available part whose value is nearest to the value returned by the arithmetic-performing subtree.

In addition, there are numerous alternatives to arithmetic-performing subtrees for establishing the values of components. One approach is to establish the numerical component values by means of the conventional genetic algorithm operating on fixed-length

Table 25.1 Potential functions and terminals for arithmetic-performing subtrees

Name	Short description	Arity
$\Re_{\text{smaller-reals}}$	Floating-point random constants ranging between –1.0 and +1.0 (from a set of around 200 or so different values as explained in Section 13.3.2)	0
+	Addition	2
–	Subtraction	2
ADF0, ...	Automatically defined functions (Section 2.3.6)	Various
ARG0, ...	Dummy variables (formal parameters)	0

character strings. This could be implemented within genetic programming using a constrained syntactic structure in which the value-setting subtree is a binary character string (implemented, say, by a LIST function for a fixed-length list and the terminals 0 and 1). A second approach is to establish the numerical component value by means of a genetic algorithm using real-valued genes and, possibly, a Gaussian creep operator (Montana and Davis 1989; Davis 1991) or the Gaussian mutation operation often used in evolutionary programming (Chellapilla 1997b). Alternatively, if the number of possible component values is small, a separate component-creating function can be defined for each differently valued component (so that the component's value is implicit in the component-creating function and there is no value-setting subtree at all).

It is also possible for automatically defined functions and dummy variables to appear in arithmetic-performing subtrees. Automatically defined functions permit a useful value to be computed once and then reused to control the setting of the value of many different components. Dummy variables permit the value returned by the automatically defined function to vary in a consistent way based on a value provided by the calling arithmetic-performing subtree. In this event, the function set, F_{aps}, for each arithmetic-performing subtree becomes

$$F_{\text{aps}} = \{+, \ -, \ \text{ADF0, ADF1, } . \ . \ .\}.$$

The terminal set, T_{aps}, for each arithmetic-performing subtree becomes

$$T_{\text{aps}} = \{\Re_{\text{smaller-reals}}, \ \text{ARG0, ARG1, } . \ . \ .\},$$

where $\Re_{\text{smaller-reals}}$ are floating-point random constants ranging between –1.0 and +1.0.

Table 25.1 lists the functions and terminals that might potentially appear in an arithmetic-performing subtree.

25.8   SMALL REPERTOIRE OF TOPOLOGY-MODIFYING FUNCTIONS

This section describes a small repertoire of 10 topology-modifying function families that are used in Chapters 25 through 40:

- the SERIES division function,
- two parallel division functions, PARALLEL0 and PARALLEL1,
- the polarity-reversing FLIP function,

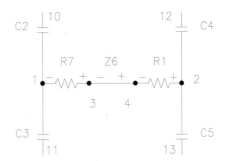

Figure 25.14   Result after applying the SERIES division function to resistor R1

- eight two-argument TWO_VIA functions,
- the two-argument grounding function TWO_GROUND,
- the three-argument THREE_VIA functions,
- two three-argument THREE_GROUND grounding functions,
- the CUT function,
- the SAFE_CUT function, and
- the PAIR_CONNECT functions.

25.8.1   SERIES Division Function

The three-argument SERIES division function operates on one modifiable wire or modifiable component and creates two new nodes and a series composition consisting of the original modifiable wire or modifiable component, one new modifiable wire, and a copy of the original modifiable wire or modifiable component. Since there are three modifiable items (the original modifiable component, its copy, and the new modifiable wire) after execution of the SERIES function, the arity of the SERIES function is three, and there are three construction-continuing subtrees.

Figure 25.14 illustrates the result of applying the SERIES division function to resistor R1 from Figure 25.10. Modifiable resistors R1 and R7 and modifiable wire Z6 are each linked to the topmost function of one of the three construction-continuing subtrees of the SERIES function.

First, the SERIES function creates two new nodes, 3 and 4.

Second, SERIES disconnects the negative end of the original modifiable component (R1) from node 1 and connects this negative end to the first new node, 4 (while leaving its positive end connected to the original node 2).

Third, SERIES creates a new wire (named Z6 in Figure 25.14) between new nodes 3 and 4. The negative end of the new wire is connected to the first new node 3 and the positive end is connected to the second new node 4.

Fourth, SERIES inserts a duplicate (named R7 in Figure 25.14) of the original component (including all its component values) between new node 3 and original node 1. The positive end of the duplicate is connected to the new node 3 and its negative end is connected to original node 1.

The netlist for the partial circuit of Figure 25.10 containing the four capacitors and the single 5 Ω resistor R1 is as follows:

```
C2 1 10
C3 1 11
R1 2 1 5OHMS
C4 2 12
C5 2 13
```

The SERIES function changes the above five-line netlist into the following seven-line netlist (representing Figure 25.14):

```
C2 1 10
C3 1 11
R1 2 4 5OHMS
Z6 4 3
R7 3 1 5OHMS
C4 2 12
C5 2 13
```

Note that modifiable wires (such as Z6) are used only during the developmental process; all such wires are edited out prior to the submission of the netlist to SPICE.

When the SERIES function is applied to a modifiable wire, the result is a series composition of three modifiable wires.

Note our convention of globally numbering components consecutively as the developmental process proceeds. This convention contrasts with the convention of maintaining a separate series of consecutive numbers (with each series starting at 1) for each type of component (e.g., resistors are named R1, R2, R3, . . . , while capacitors are named C1, C2, C3, . . .). Our global numbering convention serves as a timestamp for events in the developmental process and plays a symmetry-breaking role in the outcome of certain functions (e.g., the PARALLEL0 and PARALLEL1 parallel division functions described in the next section).

25.8.2 PARALLEL Division Functions

Parallel division is somewhat more complicated than series division because there sometimes are two topologically distinct outcomes for a parallel division. Since we want the outcome of all circuit-constructing functions to be deterministic, there are two members (called PARALLEL0 and PARALLEL1) in the PARALLEL family of topology-modifying functions. The two functions in the family operate differently depending on degree and numbering of the preexisting components in the developing circuit. One of the two functions is associated with each of the two topologically distinct outcomes.

When the initial random population of individuals is created in generation 0, the functions belonging to a two-member family (e.g., the PARALLEL0 and PARALLEL1) are each chosen with a probability equal to 50% of that used for a circuit-constructing function that does not belong to a multiple-member family (as explained in Appendix D).

The four-argument PARALLEL function causes the modifiable wire or modifiable component to which it is linked to be replaced by two new nodes and a parallel composition consisting of the original modifiable wire or modifiable component, two modifiable new wires, and a duplicate of the original modifiable wire or modifiable component. Since there are four modifiable items (the original modifiable component, its copy, and the two new modifiable wires) after execution of the PARALLEL function, the arity of the PARALLEL function is four and there are four construction-continuing subtrees.

First Case

First consider the case where both nodes of the preexisting modifiable component are of degree 3. This case is illustrated in Figure 25.10 (which shows resistor R1 connecting nodes 1 and 2 of a partial circuit containing four capacitors). In Figure 25.10, node 1 is of degree 3 (because R1, capacitor C2, and capacitor C3 are connected to it), and node 2 is also of degree 3 (because R1, capacitor C4, and capacitor C5 are connected to it).

The next two figures show the different outcomes resulting from the application of the PARALLEL0 function versus the PARALLEL1 function to resistor R1 of Figure 25.10. Figure 25.15 shows the result of applying the PARALLEL0 function to resistor R1 of Figure 25.10. Modifiable resistors R1 and R7 and modifiable wires Z6 and Z8 are each linked to the topmost function in one of the four construction-continuing subtrees of the PARALLEL0 function.

First, the PARALLEL0 parallel division function creates two new nodes, 3 and 4, and also creates two new wires, Z6 (between original node 2 and new node 3 of Figure 25.15) and Z8 (between original node 1 and new node 4). The negative leads of both new wires are connected to the nodes (i.e., 1 and 2) of the original component, thereby establishing the polarity of the new wires.

Second, the PARALLEL0 parallel division function inserts a duplicate of the original modifiable component (including all of its component values) between the new nodes 3 and 4 of Figure 25.15. The negative end of the duplicate is connected to node 4 (the new node connected by the new wire that is connected to the negative end of the original component, namely, Z8). The positive end of the duplicate is connected to node 3 (the new node connected by the new wire that is connected to the positive end of the original component, namely, Z6). This establishes the polarity of the new component.

Third, the topology of the new component in relation to the original components must be established. The two parallel division functions operate in slightly different ways in this regard. The PARALLEL0 function connects the negative end of the new component to the smaller-numbered component (of the two components that were originally connected to the negative end of the original modifiable component), while the PARALLEL1 connects the negative end of the new component to the larger-numbered component.

The netlist for the partial circuit of Figure 25.10 containing the four capacitors and the single 5 Ω resistor R1 is as follows:

```
C2  1  10
C3  1  11
R1  2  1  5OHMS
C4  2  12
C5  2  13
```

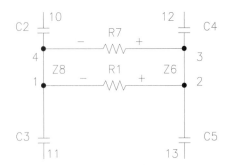
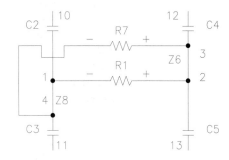

Figure 25.15 Result after applying the PARALLEL0 parallel division function to resistor R1

Figure 25.16 Result after applying the PARALLEL1 parallel division function to resistor R1

The parallel division function PARALLEL0 changes the above five-line netlist to the following eight-line netlist (representing Figure 25.15):

```
C2 4 10
C3 1 11
Z6 3 2
Z8 4 1
R1 2 1 5OHMS
R7 3 4 5OHMS
C4 3 12
C5 2 13
```

C2 and C3 are the two original components that were originally connected to the negative end of original component R1 (at original node 1). When the resistor is duplicated, the question arises as to whether C2 or C3 should be connected to the new resistor (as opposed to the original resistor, R1). Since C2 bears a smaller number than C3, the PARALLEL0 function causes C2 (the component with the smaller number) to become connected to new node 4 (emboldened above) while leaving C3 connected to original node 1 (emboldened above). The polarity of the four capacitors in Figure 25.10 is not shown because it is simply assumed, in presenting the above netlist, that the positive leads of C2 and C3 are connected to original node 1 (so that node 4 precedes node 10 on the line of the netlist relating to C2, and node 1 precedes node 11 for C3). The important aspect of the PARALLEL0 function is not the polarity of C2 and C3, but the fact that node 4 appears on C2's line of the netlist (and node 1 appears on C3's line).

The PARALLEL1 function operates slightly differently than the PARALLEL0 function. Figure 25.16 shows the results of applying the PARALLEL1 function to resistor R1 of Figure 25.10. Modifiable resistors R1 and R7 and modifiable wires Z6 and Z8 are each linked to the topmost function in one of the four construction-continuing subtrees of the PARALLEL1 function.

The PARALLEL1 function changes the original netlist above to the following new netlist (representing Figure 25.16):

```
C2 1 10
C3 4 11
R1 2 1 5OHMS
Z6 3 2
Z8 4 1
R7 3 4 5OHMS
C4 3 12
C5 2 13
```

Since **C3** bears a larger number than **C2**, the PARALLEL1 function causes **C3** (the component with the larger number) to become connected to new node 4 (emboldened above), while leaving **C2** connected to original node 1 (emboldened above).

Second Case

PARALLEL0 and PARALLEL1 produce identical results in the case where both nodes of the original modifiable component are of degree 2.

Figure 25.17 shows a modifiable resistor **R1** connecting nodes 1 and 2 of a partial circuit containing two capacitors. Node 1 is of degree 2 (because **R1** and capacitor **C2** are connected to it), and node 2 is of degree 2 (because **R1** and capacitor **C4** are connected to it).

Figure 25.18 shows the result of applying either the PARALLEL0 division function or the PARALLEL1 function to resistor **R1** of Figure 25.17 in which nodes 1 and 2 are of degree 2. Modifiable resistors **R1** and **R7** and modifiable wires **Z6** and **Z8** are each linked to the topmost function in one of the four construction-continuing subtrees of the PARALLEL function.

First, the PARALLEL0 (or PARALLEL1) function creates two new nodes (3 and 4 in Figure 25.18) and also creates two new wires **Z6** (between original node 2 and new node 3) and **Z8** (between original node 1 and new node 4). The negative leads of both new wires are connected to the nodes (i.e., 1 and 2) of the original component, thereby establishing the polarity of the new wires.

Second, the PARALLEL0 (or PARALLEL1) function inserts a duplicate of the original modifiable component (including all of its component values) between the new nodes 3 and 4 (as shown in Figure 25.18). The negative end of the duplicate is connected to node 4 (the new node connected by the new wire that is connected to the negative end of the original component, namely, new wire **Z8**). The positive end of the duplicate is connected to node 3 (the new node connected by the new wire that is connected to the positive end of the original component, namely, new wire **Z6**). This establishes the polarity of the new component.

Third Case

Finally, consider the case where one node of the original modifiable component is of degree 3 while the other node is of degree 2. Figure 25.19 shows a resistor **R1** connecting nodes 1 and 2 of a partial circuit containing three capacitors in which node 1 is of degree 3 and node 2 is of degree 2.

Figure 25.17 A circuit containing a modifiable resistor R1 in which nodes 1 and 2 are of degree 2

Figure 25.18 Result after applying the PARALLEL0 or PARALLEL1 function to resistor R1 in which both nodes 1 and 2 are of degree 2

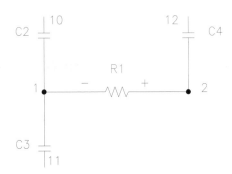

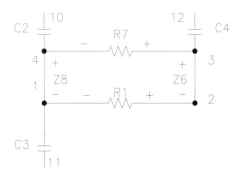

Figure 25.19 A circuit containing a modifiable resistor R1 in which node 1 is of degree 3 and node 2 is of degree 2

Figure 25.20 Result after applying PARALLEL0 to a circuit in which node 1 is of degree 3 and node 2 is of degree 2

Figure 25.20 shows the result of applying the PARALLEL0 division function to resistor R1 of Figure 25.19. Modifiable resistors R1 and R7 and modifiable wires Z6 and Z8 each have writing heads upon completion of this four-argument function.

The PARALLEL1 division function operates in a similar manner. PARALLEL1 connects the negative end of the new component to the larger-numbered component (of the two components that were originally connected to the negative end of the original modifiable component).

First, the PARALLEL1 function creates two new nodes (3 and 4) and also creates two new wires, Z6 (between original node 2 and new node 3) and Z8 (between original node 1 and new node 4). The negative leads of both new wires are connected to the nodes (i.e., 1 and 2) of the original component, thereby establishing the polarity of the new wires.

Second, the PARALLEL1 function inserts a duplicate of the original modifiable component (including all of its component values) between new nodes 3 and 4. The negative end of the duplicate is connected to node 4 (the new node connected by the new wire that is connected to the negative end of the original component, namely, new wire Z8). The positive end of the duplicate is connected to node 3 (the new node connected by the new wire that is connected to the positive end of the original component, namely, new wire **Z6**). This establishes the polarity of the new component.

Since **C3** bears a larger number than **C2**, the PARALLEL1 function causes **C3** (the component with the larger number) to become connected to the negative end of the new component at new node 4 while leaving **C2** connected to original node 1. Since the node at the positive end of the original modifiable component **R1** is of degree 2, the PARALLEL1 function leaves **C4** connected to original node 2.

25.8.3   **FLIP Function**

All two-leaded electrical components have a polarity in SPICE in the sense that they each have a designated positive end and a designated negative end. The polarity of two-leaded components is reflected by the fact that the first-listed node in each line of the netlist is the node connected to the positive end of a component, and the second-listed node is the node connected to the component's negative end. Polarity clearly matters for components such as diodes. Polarity also matters for components whose electrical behavior is independent of its polarity (e.g., resistors) because it sometimes affects the sequential course of the developmental process that transforms an initial circuit into a fully developed circuit.

The one-argument polarity-reversing FLIP function provides a method for reversing the polarity of any two-leaded component. Figure 25.21 shows a modifiable diode **D1** located between nodes 1 and 2 of a partial circuit containing four capacitors (**C2**, **C3**, **C4**, and **C5**). The one-argument FLIP function attaches the positive end of the original modifiable component to the node to which its negative end is currently attached and vice versa. After execution of the FLIP function, the writing head points to the now-flipped original component.

Figure 25.22 shows the result of applying the FLIP function to the diode **D1** of Figure 25.21, thereby creating a diode **D2** with its polarity reversed. The now-flipped diode **D2** remains modifiable. That is, **D2** is linked to the topmost function in the construction-continuing subtree (the only argument of the FLIP function).

The portion of the netlist for Figure 25.21 describing the diode **D1** consists of the following line:

```
D1 2 1
```

Since diodes do not carry component values, the above netlist does not contain a component value.

The FLIP function changes the above one-line partial netlist into the following partial netlist (representing Figure 25.22):

```
D2 1 2
```

25.8.4   **Two-Argument TWO_VIA Functions**

The two-argument TWO_VIA functions enable distant parts of a circuit to be connected together. The eight two-argument functions in the TWO_VIA family of functions (called TWO_VIA0, . . . , TWO_VIA7) each create a new node and a composition of two modifiable wires and one nonmodifiable wire such that the nonmodifiable wire makes a connection, called a *via*, to a designated one of eight imaginary numbered layers (0 to 7) of

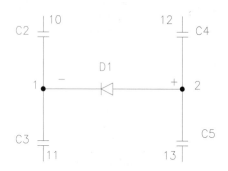

Figure 25.21 Modifiable diode D1 connecting nodes 1 and 2

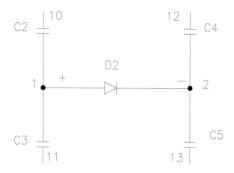

Figure 25.22 Result of applying the FLIP function to diode D1

an imaginary silicon wafer on which the circuit resides. For example, the TWO_VIA0 function uses a via called M0 to make a connection to imaginary layer 0, the TWO_VIA1 function uses a via called M1 to make a connection to imaginary layer 1, and so forth.

If more than one via makes a connection to a particular numbered layer, they all become connected electrically. The TWO_VIA function provides a way to escape the planarity of the other circuit-constructing operations. The TWO_VIA function also provides a way to connect more than three nodes together (thereby overcoming the limitation imposed by our requirement that each node of the embryo and the developing circuit have degree 2 or 3).

If only one via makes a connection to a particular numbered layer in the fully developed circuit, then the nonmodifiable wire of the via connecting to the layer is deleted just before the netlist is submitted to SPICE (so that there are no dangling wires in the final netlist).

Figure 25.23 shows the results of applying the TWO_VIA0 function to modifiable wire **Z0** of Figure 25.9. Modifiable wire **Z0** is replaced by modifiable wire **Z6** between node 1 and new node 3 and modifiable wire **Z7** between node 2 and new node 3. Thus, the TWO_VIA0 function provides a way to connect new node 3 to distant parts of the overall circuit using layer 0. Via M0 is connected to the layer numbered 0. Note that if, prior to execution of the TWO_VIA function, a modifiable component (instead of a modifiable wire) in the developing circuit structure were linked to the TWO_VIA function in the program tree, then that modifiable component would be replaced by the two new modifiable wires **Z6** and **Z7**. The two new modifiable wires, **Z6** and **Z7**, are linked to the topmost functions in the construction-continuing subtree of the TWO_VIA function.

25.8.5 Two-Argument TWO_GROUND Function

The two-argument TWO_GROUND ("ground") function enables any part of a circuit to be connected to ground. The TWO_GROUND function operates in a manner similar to a TWO_VIA function; however, the direct connection to ground is unconditionally made (even if only one TWO_GROUND function is ever executed).

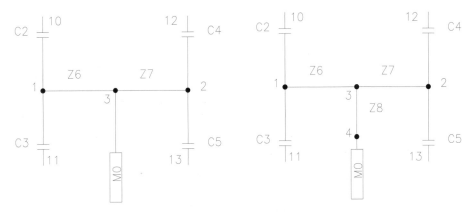

Figure 25.23   Result after applying the TWO_VIA0 function to modifiable wire Z0

Figure 25.24   Result after applying the THREE_VIA0 function to modifiable wire Z0

25.8.6   Three-Argument THREE_VIA Functions

The THREE_VIA functions are similar to the TWO-VIA functions. The eight three-argument functions in the THREE_VIA family of functions (called THREE_VIA0, . . . , THREE_VIA7) each create two new nodes, a T-shaped composition of three modifiable wires, and a numbered via.

Figure 25.24 shows the results of applying the THREE_VIA0 function to modifiable wire **R1** of Figure 25.10. The THREE_VIA0 function creates via M0. Via M0 is connected to an imaginary layer numbered 0 of the imaginary silicon wafer on which the circuit resides. The THREE_VIA0 function replaces **R1** by a new modifiable wire **Z6** between node 1 and new node 3, a new modifiable wire **Z7** between node 2 and new node 3, and a new modifiable wire **Z8** between new node 3 and new node 4. The via M0 is connected to new node 4 by a nonmodifiable wire. Thus, the THREE_VIA0 function provides a way to potentially connect node 4 to distant parts of the overall circuit. The three new modifiable wires, **Z6**, **Z7**, and **Z8**, are linked to the topmost functions in the construction-continuing subtree of the THREE_VIA function.

The two-argument TWO_VIA functions (and the two-argument TWO_GROUND functions) were used on the first group of analog circuit synthesis problems that we solved using genetic programming. After a few months, we switched to the three-argument THREE_VIA functions and the three-argument THREE_GROUND functions on the belief that they would introduce greater variety into the evolved topologies. We later abandoned the THREE_VIA functions in favor of the PAIR_CONNECT functions (Section 25.8.10). Note that the presentation order of problems in this book is a topical order that seemed logical at the time that we wrote the book—not the chronological order in which the problems were actually solved. Therefore, do not attach any significance to unexplained variations in the choice of particular circuit-constructing functions from chapter to chapter. Unless otherwise stated, our use of a particular function usually merely reflects the time when the reported work was done—not the result of any insightful analysis on our part that a particular circuit-constructing function was especially suited for a particular problem. If any lesson is to be inferred from our experience with different circuit-constructing functions in different problems, it is that there are many different ways to successfully apply genetic programming to the problem of circuit synthesis. Chapter 54 reinforces this point by presenting several comparative experiments on various alternative ways of applying genetic programming to problems of circuit synthesis. In most of these experiments, each of the alternative approaches studied was about equally successful.

25.8.7 Three-Argument THREE_GROUND Function

The three-argument THREE_GROUND function enables a part of a circuit to be connected directly to ground. The THREE_GROUND function creates a via to ground in a manner similar to a THREE_VIA function; however, the connection to ground is unconditionally made (i.e., even if there is only one THREE_GROUND function). After execution of a THREE_GROUND function, there are three writing heads. They point to the three new modifiable wires.

25.8.8 The CUT Function

The zero-argument CUT function (i.e., the CUT terminal) causes the modifiable wire or modifiable component to which it is linked to be deleted from the developing circuit structure. Since the modifiable wire or modifiable component is removed from the developing circuit structure, the CUT function has no construction-continuing subtree. CUT, SAFE_CUT, and END are among the terminals that appear as the external points (leaves) of circuit-constructing program trees.

Figure 25.25 shows the result of applying the CUT function to the modifiable resistor **R1** of Figure 25.10. The CUT function creates a dangling component when the degree of either node at the leads of the original modifiable component is two. Before a netlist is submitted to the SPICE simulator, it is checked for dangling components. Depending on the problem, if a dangling component is found, it is either pruned from the circuit, or the entire circuit is assigned a high penalty value of fitness.

We used the CUT function for a period of time during the early phase of our research on applying genetic programming to the problem of circuit synthesis. We subsequently switched to the SAFE_CUT function.

25.8.9 The SAFE_CUT Function

The zero-argument SAFE_CUT function (i.e., the SAFE_CUT terminal) is similar to the CUT function, except that it only removes the modifiable wire or modifiable component to which it is linked if the degree of the nodes at both leads of the modifiable wire or modifiable component is three. This proviso reduces the creation of dangling components or wires. SAFE_CUT, CUT, and END are among the terminals that appear as the external points (leaves) of circuit-constructing program trees.

After using the original CUT function for a period of time on several problems, we concluded that the SAFE_CUT function would produce superior results to the CUT function because it would reduce the number of unsimulatable circuits.

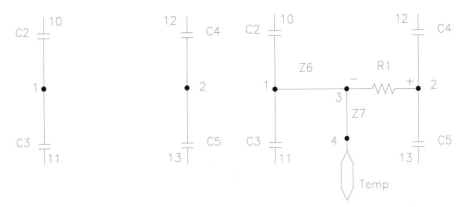

Figure 25.25 Result after applying the CUT function to modifiable resistor R1

Figure 25.26 Result after applying the PAIR_CONNECT_0 function to resistor R1

25.8.10 The PAIR_CONNECT Functions

The two three-argument PAIR_CONNECT functions (called PAIR_CONNECT_0 and PAIR_CONNECT_1) enable distant parts of a circuit to be connected together in a somewhat less disruptive manner than the THREE_VIA functions.

One arguable shortcoming of the THREE_VIA functions (and the TWO_VIA functions) is that when a THREE_VIA-X function is called, if no other similarly numbered THREE_VIA-X function is called, some portion of the developing circuit structure will be left dangling (and will be pruned out of the final circuit when it is edited just prior to its submission to SPICE). The PAIR_CONNECT functions minimize this likelihood because each newly created potentially dangling piece created by a PAIR_CONNECT function is connected to the next dangling piece created by the next call to PAIR_CONNECT. The difficulty of getting different parts of the tree to agree on a particular numbered via is thus eliminated.

The first PAIR_CONNECT to occur in the developmental process creates two new wires, two new nodes, and one temporary port (named **Temp**). The next PAIR_CONNECT (whether PAIR_CONNECT_0 or PAIR_CONNECT_1) to be executed creates two new wires and one new node, connects the temporary port to the end of one of these new wires, and then removes the temporary port. Subsequent pairs of PAIR_CONNECT functions enable other parts of the developing circuit structure to become connected.

Figure 25.26 shows the results of applying the first PAIR_CONNECT function to resistor **R1** of Figure 25.10. This first PAIR_CONNECT creates two new modifiable wires (**Z6** and **Z7**), two new nodes (3 and 4), and one temporary port (**Temp**).

PAIR_CONNECT_0 leaves the positive end of the original component connected and attaches its negative end to the new node (3 in Figure 25.26). PAIR_CONNECT_1 leaves the negative end of the original component connected and attaches its positive end to the new node (3 in Figure 25.26). A PAIR_CONNECT_0 function can connect to a PAIR_CONNECT_1.

Figure 25.27 shows a partial circuit with resistors R1 and R9 that will be used to illustrate the operation of a sequence consisting of a PAIR_CONNECT_0 function and a PAIR_CONNECT_1 function.

Figure 25.28 shows the result of applying the PAIR_CONNECT_0 function to preexisting R1. PAIR_CONNECT_0 causes the creation of new nodes 5 and 6 and new modifiable wires Z12 and Z13. The negative end of R1 is attached to new node 5, new modifiable wire Z12 is inserted between node 1 and node 5, and new modifiable wire Z13 is inserted between new node 5 and the temporary port (Temp).

Figure 25.29 shows the result of applying the PAIR_CONNECT_1 to preexisting R9. This function causes the creation of new node 7 and new modifiable wires Z15 and Z14. The negative end of R9 remains attached to node 3, while the positive end becomes attached to new node 7. New modifiable wire Z15 is inserted between new node 7 and node 4. New modifiable wire Z14 is inserted between new node 7 and the node (6) at the end of the temporary port Temp (created by the earlier PAIR_CONNECT_0), thereby connecting the leads of Z13 and Z14. The net effect of the PAIR_CONNECT_0 and PAIR_CONNECT_1 is to make a connection between two distant parts of the original circuit (R1 and R9 of Figure 25.27).

25.9 REPERTOIRE OF DEVELOPMENT-CONTROLLING FUNCTIONS

This section describes the entire repertoire of development-controlling functions:

- the no-operation NOP function and
- the development-terminating END function.

The zero-argument CUT function (Section 25.8.8) and the SAFE_CUT function (Section 25.8.9) have characteristics of both development-controlling functions and topology-modifying functions. We have listed them among the topology-modifying functions.

25.9.1 The NOP Function

The one-argument NOP ("no operation") function has no effect on the modifiable wire or modifiable component to which it is linked. However, the NOP function delays the developmental activity on the path from the topmost point of the program tree on which it appears in relation to other paths in the overall program tree. Thus, the NOP function frequently affects the fully developed circuit that is eventually produced by the developmental process. The modifiable wire or modifiable component linked to the NOP function remains modifiable. It is linked to the topmost function in the construction-continuing subtree (the one argument) of the NOP function.

25.9.2 The END Function

The zero-argument development-terminating END function (i.e., the END terminal) causes the modifiable wire or modifiable component to which it is linked to become nonmodifiable. In other words, the modifiable wire or modifiable component to which the END function is linked loses its writing head. Since the modifiable wire or modifiable

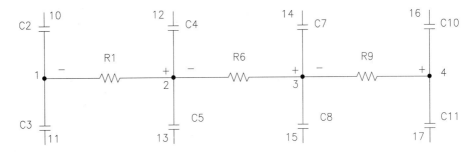

Figure 25.27   Circuit with R1 and R9

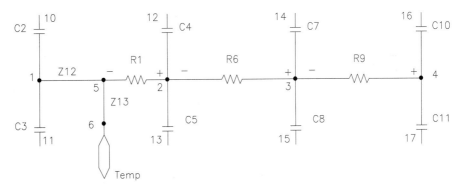

Figure 25.28   Result of applying PAIR_CONNECT_0 to R1

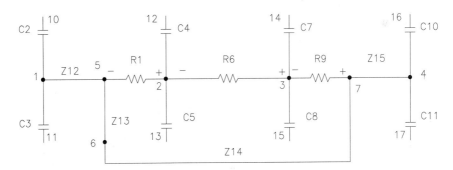

Figure 25.29   Result of applying PAIR_CONNECT_1 to R9

component is no longer modifiable, the END function has no construction-continuing subtree. Thus, the END function appears at the external points (leaves) of a circuit-constructing program tree.

25.10 DETAILED EXAMPLE OF THE DEVELOPMENT OF AN INITIAL CIRCUIT INTO A FULLY DEVELOPED CIRCUIT

This section presents, in detail, an example of the process of developing an initial circuit into a fully developed circuit.

Figure 25.7 presents an illustrative circuit-constructing program as a rooted point-labeled tree with ordered branches. The connective LIST function (labeled 1) at the top of the program tree joins the two result-producing branches. The first result-producing branch of this program tree has 25 points (i.e., functions and terminals), and the second result-producing branch has 5 points. The two result-producing branches correspond to the two modifiable wires of the embryo. The first result-producing branch is rooted at the capacitor-creating C function (labeled 2), and the second is rooted at the polarity-reversing FLIP function (labeled 3). When written in the style of the LISP programming language, the entire individual program tree of Figure 25.7 is

```
(LIST (C (- 0.963 (-(- -0.875 -0.113) 0.880)) (SERIES (FLIP
END) (SERIES (FLIP END) (L -0.277 END) END) (L (- -0.640 0.749)
(L -0.123 END))))
     (FLIP (NOP (L -0.657 END))))).
```

In executing a program tree, the functions in the result-producing branches below the connective LIST function at the root of the program tree are executed in a breadth-first order with one exception: Whenever a component-creating function is encountered, any arithmetic-performing subtree (such as the seven-point subtree rooted at the point labeled 4; the three-point subtree rooted at 19; and the one-point subtrees rooted at 17, 29, and 12) is immediately executed, in its entirety, in a depth-first order (as for functions in LISP). Thus, the capacitor-creating C function (labeled 2) in Figure 25.7 is executed first in the normal breadth-first order. Next, the seven-point arithmetic-performing subtree (labeled 4) is immediately executed in its entirety in a depth-first way. It yields a single numerical value that is used by the capacitor-creating function C to establish the value of the new capacitor. Then, the breadth-first order of evaluation is resumed and the topology-modifying FLIP function (labeled 3) is executed. The policy of using breadth-first order follows Gruau (1992a, 1992b, 1993, 1994a, 1994b). (See Section 54.10 for an experiment involving the alternative of depth-first order.)

Figure 25.30 shows the result of executing the capacitor-creating C function (labeled 2 in Figure 25.7 and underlined below) acting on the modifiable wire Z0 of the embryo in the initial circuit of Figure 25.8. The execution of this C function creates a new capacitor C3 as shown in Figure 25.30. This C function is at the top of the first result-producing branch of the program tree (Figure 25.7)

```
(LIST (C (- 0.963 (- (- -0.875 -0.113) 0.880)) (SERIES (FLIP
END) (SERIES (FLIP END) (L -0.277 END) END) (L (- -0.640 0.749)
(L -0.123 END))))
     (FLIP (NOP (L -0.657 END))))).
```

The seven-point subtree (rooted at the point labeled 4 in Figure 25.7),

```
(- 0.963 (- (- -0.875 -0.113) 0.880)),
```

is an arithmetic-performing subtree associated with the C function. It is executed in its entirety in conjunction with its C function (labeled 2 in Figure 25.7). The return value of the seven-point subtree is 2.605. When 2.605 is interpreted and scaled (in the manner described in Section 25.7), it establishes 403 nF as the component value for the new capacitor **C3**. After applying the C function to modifiable wire **Z0**, its writing head points to 403 nF **C3**. Thus, **C3** remains subject to subsequent modification during the development process.

The FLIP function (labeled 3 in Figure 25.7 and underlined below) at the top of the second result-producing branch of the program tree is now executed.

```
(LIST (C (- 0.963 (- (- -0.875 -0.113) 0.880)) (SERIES (FLIP
END) (SERIES (FLIP END) (L -0.277 END) END) (L (- -0.640 0.749)
(L -0.123 END))))
       (FLIP (NOP (L -0.657 END))))).
```

Figure 25.31 shows the result of executing the FLIP function (labeled 3) on the modifiable wire **Z1** (whose positive end was originally at node 2) so as to change its polarity (so that its negative end is now at node 2). The FLIP function has no immediate electrical effect on a wire (or, for that matter, on a capacitor, resistor, or inductor); however, a change of polarity usually affects the later development of the circuit's topology. After execution of the FLIP function, one writing head points to the now-flipped (and still modifiable) wire **Z1**.

Execution of the breadth-first search of the program tree now proceeds to the third level of the tree. Since the seven-point arithmetic-performing subtree (rooted at 4) has already been entirely executed, the SERIES function (labeled 5) is executed next.

Figure 25.32 shows the result of executing the SERIES function (labeled 5 in Figure 25.7 and underlined below) acting on 403 nF capacitor **C3** to create a series composition consisting of the preexisting capacitor **C3**, new node 6, new modifiable wire **Z4**, new node 7, and new capacitor **C5** (with the same component value, 403 nF, as the preexisting capacitor **C3**).

```
(LIST (C (- 0.963 (- (- -0.875 -0.113) 0.880)) (SERIES (FLIP
END) (SERIES (FLIP END) (L -0.277 END) END) (L (- -0.640 0.749)
(L -0.123 END))))
       (FLIP (NOP (L -0.657 END))))).
```

The execution of the three-argument SERIES function creates three writing heads (pointing to **C3**, **Z4**, and **C5**). Of course, a writing head still points to **Z1**.

The NOP ("no operation") function (labeled 6 in Figure 25.7 and underlined below) in the second result-producing branch of the overall program tree is now executed.

```
(LIST (C (- 0.963 (- (- -0.875 -0.113) 0.880)) (SERIES (FLIP
END) (SERIES (FLIP END) (L -0.277 END) END) (L (- -0.640 0.749)
(L -0.123 END))))
       (FLIP (NOP (L -0.657 END))))).
```

This NOP function affects the timing of execution of subsequent functions. In effect, it delays the execution of the remaining unexecuted functions in the second result-producing branch relative to the unexecuted functions in the first result-producing branch.

Execution now proceeds to the fourth level of the program tree of Figure 25.7. Figure 25.33 shows the result of executing the FLIP function (labeled 9 in Figure 25.7 and underlined below) acting on capacitor **C3** (whose positive end was originally at node 3) to change its polarity (so that its negative end is now at node 3).

```
(LIST (C (- 0.963 (- (- -0.875 -0.113) 0.880)) (SERIES (FLIP
END) (SERIES (FLIP END) (L -0.277 END) END) (L (- -0.640 0.749)
(L -0.123 END))))
        (FLIP (NOP (L -0.657 END)))))).
```

After execution of this FLIP function, one writing head points to the now-flipped capacitor **C3**. Writing heads still point to **Z4**, **C5**, and **Z1**.

Figure 25.34 shows the result of executing the SERIES function (labeled 10 in Figure 25.7 and underlined below) acting on modifiable wire **Z4** to create a series arrangement consisting of modifiable wire **Z4**, new node 8, modifiable wire **Z6**, new node 9, and modifiable wire **Z5**.

```
(LIST (C (- 0.963 (- (- -0.875 -0.113) 0.880)) (SERIES (FLIP
END) (SERIES (FLIP END) (L -0.277 END) END) (L (- -0.640 0.749)
(L -0.123 END))))
        (FLIP (NOP (L -0.657 END)))))).
```

After execution of this SERIES function, there are a total of six writing heads (pointing to **C3**, **Z4**, **Z6**, **Z5**, **C5**, and **Z1**).

Figure 25.35 shows the result of executing the L function (labeled 11 in Figure 25.7 and underlined below) acting on the capacitor **C5**.

```
(LIST (C (- 0.963 (- (- -0.875 -0.113) 0.880)) (SERIES (FLIP
END) (SERIES (FLIP END) (L -0.277 END) END) (L (- -0.640 0.749)
(L -0.123 END))))
        (FLIP (NOP (L -0.657 END)))))).
```

This L function converts capacitor **C5** into an inductor (**L7**). The three-point arithmetic-performing subtree (rooted at 19) associated with this L function is

```
(- -0.640 0.749).
```

Its return value is –1.389. After being interpreted, this return value establishes 0.041 μH as the component value for the newly created inductor **L7**. After execution of this L function, there are still six writing heads (pointing to **C3**, **Z4**, **Z6**, **Z5**, **L7**, and **Z1**).

After the FLIP, SERIES, and L functions (9, 10, and 11, respectively) on the fourth level of the first result-producing branch are executed, execution moves to the L function (labeled 12 in Figure 25.7 and underlined below) on the fourth level of the second result-producing branch.

```
(LIST (C (- 0.963 (- (- -0.875 -0.113) 0.880)) (SERIES (FLIP
END) (SERIES (FLIP END) (L -0.277 END) END) (L (- -0.640 0.749)
(L -0.123 END))))
        (FLIP (NOP (L -0.657 END)))))).
```

Figure 25.36 shows the result of executing the L function (labeled 12 in Figure 25.7) acting on the modifiable wire Z1 to create inductor L8. The one-point arithmetic-performing subtree consisting of the constant −0.657 (labeled 21 in Figure 25.7) establishes 0.220 µH as the component value for L8. After execution of this L function, there are still six writing heads (pointing to C3, Z4, Z6, Z5, L7, and L8).

Execution now passes to the fifth level of the program tree of Figure 25.7. The developmental-terminating END function (labeled 15) is now executed, thereby ending the developmental process for the path running through 1, 2, 5, 9, and 15 of the first result-producing branch of Figure 25.7. The END function eliminates the writing head associated with C3, so there are now only five writing heads (pointing to Z4, Z6, Z5, L7, and L8). The FLIP function (labeled 16) operates on wire Z4.

Figure 25.37 shows the result of executing the L function (labeled 17 in Figure 25.7 and underlined below) acting on the modifiable wire Z6 to create a new inductor L9.

```
(LIST (C (- 0.963 (- (- -0.875 -0.113) 0.880)) (SERIES (FLIP
END) (SERIES (FLIP END) (L -0.277 END) END) (L (- -0.640 0.749)
(L -0.123 END))))
        (FLIP (NOP (L -0.657 END))))).
```

When interpreted, the one-point arithmetic-performing subtree consisting of the constant −0.277 (labeled 26) establishes 0.528 µH as the component value for the newly created inductor L9. There are still five writing heads (pointing to Z4, L9, Z5, L7, and L8).

The END function (labeled 18) is now executed, thereby ending the developmental process for Z5 and causing the writing head associated with Z5 to be eliminated. Thus, there are now only four writing heads (pointing to Z4, L9, L7, and L8).

The L function (labeled 20 in Figure 25.7 and underlined below) from the first result-producing branch is now executed. It overwrites existing 0.47 µH inductor L7 to create a new inductor L10.

```
(LIST (C (- 0.963 (- (- -0.875 -0.113) 0.880)) (SERIES (FLIP
END) (SERIES (FLIP END) (L -0.277 END) END) (L (- -0.640 0.749)
(L -0.123 END))))
        (FLIP (NOP (L -0.657 END))))).
```

When interpreted, the one-point arithmetic-performing subtree consisting of the constant −0.123 (labeled 30) establishes 0.753 µH as the component value for the newly created inductor L10. Writing heads now point to Z4, L9, L10, and L8.

This overwriting provides a way to change the value of an already inserted component during the developmental process. Thus, there are two ways, operating on different time scales, that the value of a component can be changed. First, the value of a component may be changed during the developmental process when one component-creating function overwrites another. Second, the value of a component may be changed during the evolutionary process when the genetic operations (such as crossover and mutation) operate on the arithmetic-performing subtree of a component-creating function.

The END function at 22 is now executed, thereby completing the execution of the second result-producing branch of the program tree. This END function releases the writing

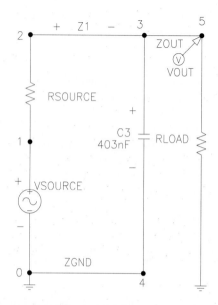

Figure 25.30 Result of executing the C function (labeled 2) acting on modifiable wire Z0 of the embryo to create 403 nF capacitor C3

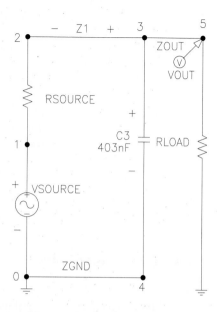

Figure 25.31 Result of executing the FLIP function (labeled 3) acting on modifiable wire Z1 of the embryo

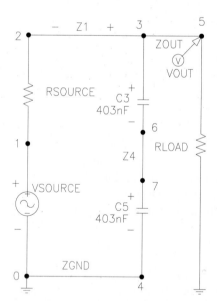

Figure 25.32 Result of executing the SERIES function (labeled 5) acting on 403 nF capacitor C3 to create a series composition of C3, new modifiable wire Z4, and new 403 nF capacitor C5

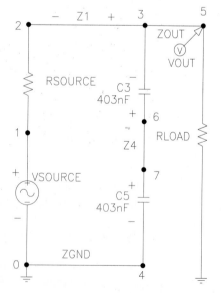

Figure 25.33 Result of executing the FLIP function (labeled 9) acting on capacitor C3

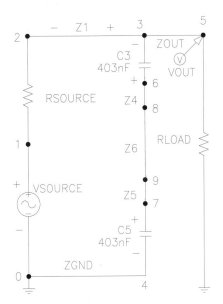

Figure 25.34   Result of executing the SERIES function (labeled 10) acting on modifiable wire Z4 to create modifiable wires Z4, Z6, and Z5

Figure 25.35   Result of executing the L function (labeled 11) acting on capacitor C5 to convert it into new 0.041 μH inductor L7

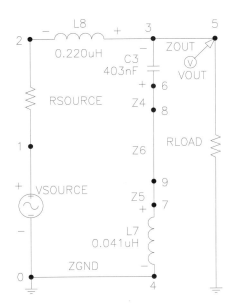

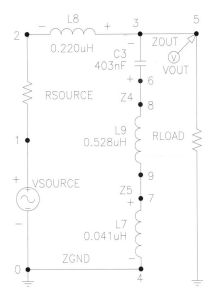

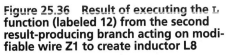

Figure 25.36   Result of executing the L function (labeled 12) from the second result-producing branch acting on modifiable wire Z1 to create inductor L8

Figure 25.37   Result of executing the L function (labeled 17) acting on modifiable wire Z6 to create inductor L9

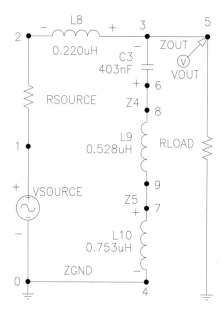

Figure 25.38 Fully developed circuit resulting from the circuit-constructing program tree of Figure 25.7

head associated with **L8** so that there are now only three writing heads (pointing to **Z4**, **L9**, and **L10**).

Execution now proceeds to the sixth (bottom) level of the program tree of Figure 25.7. The END functions at 25, 27, and 31 are now executed, thereby eliminating the writing heads on **Z4**, **L9**, and **L10**. Since all writing heads have been eliminated, the developmental process is now finished. Figure 25.38 shows the fully developed circuit resulting from the execution of the circuit-constructing program tree of Figure 25.7.

25.11 GRAMMAR FOR CIRCUIT-CONSTRUCTING PROGRAM TREES

The program tree in Figure 25.7 and all other individual circuit-constructing program trees in the population are constructed in accordance with a constrained syntactic structure specified by the following rules of construction.

First, the overall program can consist of at least one result-producing branch and zero or more function-defining branches (automatically defined functions):

    <PROGRAM> := <RPB> <RPB>* <ADF>*

Second, a result-producing branch can consist of a construction-continuing subtree appropriate for result-producing branches:

    <RPB> := <CCS-RPB>

Third, each automatically defined function can consist of a construction-continuing subtree appropriate for automatically defined functions:

```
<ADF> := <CCS-ADF>
```

Each construction-continuing subtree of a result-producing branch can consist of a component-creating function, a topology-modifying function, a development-controlling function, or zero or more automatically defined functions (each of which may have zero or more arithmetic-performing subtrees as its arguments). ADFs are named using consecutive numbers (e.g., ADF0, ADF1, . . .). Our usual convention is that when there are hierarchical references between automatically defined functions, a higher numbered ADF refers to a lower numbered one.

```
<CCS-RPB> := <CCF-RPB>
             |<TMF-RPB>
             |<DCF>
             |(<ADF-NUM> <APS-RPB>*)*
```

Each construction-continuing subtree of an automatically defined function can consist of a component-creating function, a topology-modifying function, a development-controlling function, or zero or more automatically defined functions (each of which may have zero or more arithmetic-performing subtrees as its arguments). ADFs are named using consecutive numbers (e.g., ADF0, ADF1, . . .). Our preferred convention is that when there are hierarchical references between automatically defined functions, a higher numbered ADF is only allowed to refer to a lower numbered one.

```
<CCS-ADF> := <CCF-ADF>
           | <TMF-ADF>
           | <DCF>|
           |(<ADF-NAME> <APS-RPB>*)*
```

Each component-creating function of a result-producing branch can consist of a resistor, capacitor, or inductor (each with an arithmetic-performing subtree and a construction-continuing subtree):

```
<CCF-RPB> := (RESISTOR <APS-RPB> <CCS-RPB>)
           | (CAPACITOR <APS-RPB> <CCS-RPB>)
           | (INDUCTOR <APS-RPB> <CCS-RPB>)
```

Each component-creating function of an automatically defined function can consist of a resistor, capacitor, or inductor (each with an arithmetic-performing subtree and a construction-continuing subtree):

```
<CCF-ADF> := (RESISTOR <APS-ADF> <CCS-ADF>)
           | (CAPACITOR <APS-ADF> <CCS-ADF>)
           | (INDUCTOR <APS-ADF> <CCS-ADF>)
```

Each topology-modifying function of a result-producing branch can consist of one of 10 functions (each with a certain number of construction-continuing subtrees):

```
<TMF-RPB> := (SERIES <CCS-RPB> <CCS-RPB> <CCS-RPB>)
             | (PARALLEL0 <CCS-RPB> <CCS-RPB> <CCS-RPB> <CCS-RPB>)
             | (PARALLEL1 <CCS-RPB> <CCS-RPB> <CCS-RPB> <CCS-RPB>)
             | (FLIP <CCS-RPB>)
             | (TWO_VIA <CCS-RPB> <CCS-RPB>)
             | (TWO_GROUND <CCS-RPB> <CCS-RPB>)
             | (THREE_VIA <CCS-RPB> <CCS-RPB> <CCS-RPB>)
             | (THREE_GROUND <CCS-RPB> <CCS-RPB> <CCS-RPB>)
             | (PAIR_CONNECT0 <CCS-RPB> <CCS-RPB> <CCS-RPB>)
             | (PAIR_CONNECT1 <CCS-RPB> <CCS-RPB> <CCS-RPB>)
```

Each topology-modifying function of an automatically defined function can consist of one of 10 functions (each with a certain number of construction-continuing subtrees):

```
<TMF-ADF> := (SERIES <CCS-ADF> <CCS-ADF> <CCS-ADF>)
             | (PARALLEL0 <CCS-ADF> <CCS-ADF> <CCS-ADF> <CCS-ADF>)
             | (PARALLEL1 <CCS-ADF> <CCS-ADF> <CCS-ADF> <CCS-ADF>)
             | (FLIP <CCS-ADF>)
             | (TWO_VIA <CCS-ADF> <CCS-ADF>)
             | (TWO_GROUND <CCS-ADF> <CCS-ADF>)
             | (THREE_VIA <CCS-ADF> <CCS-ADF> <CCS-ADF>)
             | (THREE_GROUND <CCS-ADF> <CCS-ADF> <CCS-ADF>)
             | (PAIR_CONNECT0 <CCS-ADF> <CCS-ADF> <CCS-ADF>)
             | (PAIR_CONNECT1 <CCS-ADF> <CCS-ADF> <CCS-ADF>)
```

Each development-controlling function in a result-producing branch can consist of one of four functions:

```
<DCF-RPB> := CUT
             | SAFE_CUT
             | NOP <CCS-RPB>
             | END
```

Each development-controlling function in an automatically defined function can consist of one of four functions:

```
<DCF-ADF> := CUT
             | SAFE_CUT
             | NOP <CCS-ADF>
             | END
```

Each arithmetic-performing subtree of a result-producing branch can consist of a sum of two terms or a difference between two terms:

```
<APS-RPB> := <APS-TERM-RPB> + <APS-TERM-RPB>
             | <APS-TERM-RPB> - <APS-TERM-RPB>
```

Each arithmetic-performing subtree of an automatically defined function can consist of a sum of two terms or a difference between two terms:

```
<APS-ADF>  :=  <APS-TERM-ADF> + <APS-TERM-ADF>
             | <APS-TERM-ADF> - <APS-TERM-ADF>
```

Also, for result-producing branches, each terminal <APS-TERM-RPB> can consist of an arithmetic-performing subtree or a constant:

```
<APS-TERM-RPB>  :=  <APS-RPB>
                  | <CONSTANT>
```

Also, for automatically defined functions, each terminal **<APS-TERM-ADF>** can consist of an arithmetic-performing subtree, a constant, or an argument name (e.g., **ARG0**, **ARG1**, ...):

```
<APS-TERM-ADF>  :=  <APS-ADF>
                  | <CONSTANT>
                  | <ARG-NAME>
```

25.12   DEFINITION OF A FILTER

A simple *filter* is a one-input, one-output electronic circuit that receives a signal as its input and passes the frequency components of the incoming signal that lie in a specified range (called the *passband*) while suppressing the frequency components that lie in all other frequency ranges (the *stopband*).

A *lowpass filter* passes all frequencies below a certain specified frequency, but stops all higher frequencies.

Suppose 1,000 Hz is the boundary of the passband, and 2,000 Hz is the boundary of the stopband of an illustrative lowpass filter. Figure 25.39 shows the output, in the time domain, of an illustrative lowpass filter that is receiving an input consisting of a 1,000 Hz 1-volt perfect sinusoidal signal. The horizontal axis of this figure represents time on a linear scale from 0 to 20 milliseconds. The vertical axis represents output voltage on a linear scale from −2.00 to +1.00 volts. As can be seen, after a brief transient period of about 5 milliseconds (i.e., five cycles of a 1,000 Hz signal), the circuit's output (transient response) is an almost perfect 1,000 Hz sinusoidal signal with a full 1-volt amplitude. In other words, the circuit passes the incoming 1,000 Hz signal. References to alternating current voltages in this book always refer to the peak voltage (e.g., a 1-volt sinusoidal signal oscillates between a low of −1 and a high of +1 volts) and not to the root mean square (RMS) voltage or the peak-to-peak voltage.

Figure 25.40 shows the output of the illustrative lowpass filter in response to a 2,000 Hz 1-volt sinusoidal input signal. Note that the vertical axis of this figure is in millivolts. As can be seen, after a brief transient period of about 3 or 4 milliseconds, the lowpass filter attenuates (suppresses) the incoming 1-volt signal to a tiny fraction of a volt.

If we exposed this same illustrative lowpass filter circuit to any frequency below 1,000 Hz, we would get a transient response similar to that of Figure 25.39—that is, after a brief transient period, the circuit's output would be a near-perfect sinusoid of like frequency with a full 1-volt amplitude. If we exposed this circuit to any frequency above 2,000 Hz, we would get a nearly complete attenuation of the incoming signal, similar to that of Figure 25.40. That is, after a brief transient period, the output would be essentially 0 volts in the time domain. Since it would be highly inconvenient to make a large

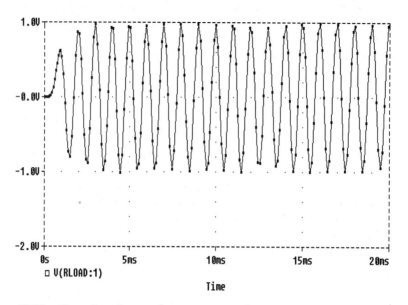

Figure 25.39 Time domain transient response of a lowpass filter to a 1,000 Hz sinusoidal input signal

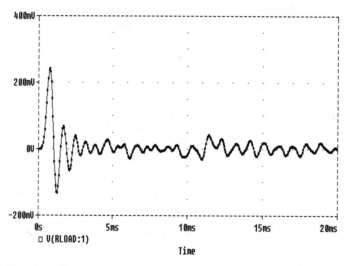

Figure 25.40 Time domain transient response of a lowpass filter to a 2,000 Hz sinusoidal input signal

collection of graphs of a circuit's response in the time domain to a multiplicity of frequencies, the behavior of a filter circuit is usually viewed in the frequency domain.

Figure 25.41 shows the frequency domain behavior of this same illustrative lowpass filter. The horizontal axis represents the frequency of the incoming signal and ranges

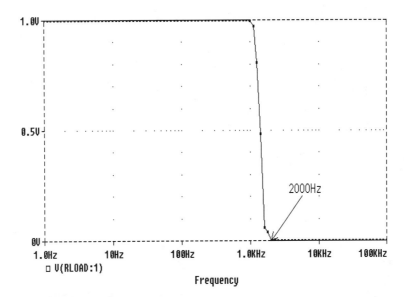

Figure 25.41   Frequency domain behavior of a lowpass filter

over five decades of frequencies between 1 Hz and 100,000 Hz on a logarithmic scale. The vertical axis represents the peak voltage of the output and ranges between 0 to 1 volts on a linear scale. When the input to the circuit consists of a sinusoidal signal with any frequency from 1 Hz to 1,000 Hz (1 KHz), the output is a sinusoidal signal with an amplitude of a full 1 volt. On the other hand, when the input to the circuit consists of a sinusoidal signal with any frequency from 2,000 Hz to 100,000 Hz, the amplitude of the output is essentially 0 volts. The region between 1 KHz and 2 KHz is the transition region for the filter. The voltage drops off from 1 to 0 volts in this transition region.

A *highpass filter* passes all frequencies above a certain specified frequency, but stops all lower frequencies. A *bandpass filter* passes all frequencies in a specified range while stopping all other frequencies. A *bandstop filter* (also called a band-reject, band-elimination, or notch filter) stops all frequencies in a specified range while passing all other frequencies. A two-band *crossover filter* is a one-input, two-output circuit that passes all frequencies below a certain specified frequency to its first output port and that passes all higher frequencies to a second output port. Some filters have multiple passbands and stopbands. Filters with a succession of equal passbands and equal stopbands are called *comb filters*.

Filters of various types are ubiquitous in analog electrical circuitry. For example, in a high-fidelity sound system, a crossover filter may channel the low frequencies to the woofer speaker, while channeling the high frequencies to the tweeter speaker. In a modem, a bandpass filter may be used to sense the presence or absence of a signal at (or near) a prescribed frequency. Filters are often used to suppress unwanted noise.

Filters may be constructed from passive components (such as inductors and capacitors) or active components (such as transistors).

The starting point for the design of a filter is the specification by the user of the frequency ranges for the filter's passband(s) and stopband(s). The *attenuation* of the filter is defined in terms of the output signal relative to a reference signal. The incoming signal is never fully passed in the passband nor fully suppressed in the stopband. Since ideal behavior cannot usually be realized in practice, the acceptable deviation from the ideal is part of the specification of a filter.

The design of filters becomes increasingly difficult as the user imposes more stringent constraints (Zverev 1967; Van Valkenburg 1982; Williams and Taylor 1995). In general, it is more difficult to design filters with high stopband attenuation and low passband attenuation. It is generally also more difficult to design a lowpass or highpass filter when the passband and stopband are close together (i.e., the transitional region between the two bands is small). In the example above, there is a 2-to-1 ratio between 2,000 Hz (the stopband cutoff frequency) and 1,000 Hz (the passband cutoff frequency).

25.13   DESIGN GOALS FOR A LOWPASS FILTER

Design problems begin with a high-level statement of the specifications. The goal in this chapter is to evolve the design of a lowpass filter composed of inductors and capacitors with a passband below 1,000 Hz and a stopband above 2,000 Hz.

Design problems are often couched in terms of a three-way distinction concerning that which is ideal (and often unattainable in practice), that which is acceptable (tolerable), and that which is unacceptable (intolerable):

- Ideal: It is ideal if the output voltage is exactly 1 volt for frequencies in the desired passband (below 1,000 Hz) and is exactly 0 volts for frequencies in the desired stopband (above 2,000 Hz).
- Acceptable: It is acceptable if the output voltage in the desired passband is between 970 millivolts and 1 volt. Also, it is acceptable if the output voltage in the desired stopband is between 0 volts and 1 millivolt.
- Unacceptable: It is unacceptable if the output voltage in the desired passband is lower than 970 millivolts. Also, it is unacceptable if the output voltage in the desired stopband is higher than 1 millivolt.

Figure 25.41 shows the behavior, in the frequency domain, of a circuit that complies with the above design requirements. The output voltage is between 970 millivolts and 1 volt up to 1,000 Hz, and the voltage is between 0 volts and 1 millivolt above 2,000 Hz. The transitional region between 1,000 and 2,000 Hz is a "don't care" region.

The above constitutes what we regard to be the high-level statement of the requirements of this design problem. The remainder of this section provides some information about electrical engineering that may help explain the meaning of these requirements. However, none of this information about electrical engineering is used by genetic programming in solving the problem.

The circuit will be driven by an incoming AC voltage source with a 2-volt amplitude. There is a source (internal) resistance of 1,000 Ω and a load resistance of 1,000 Ω. Note that a 2-volt input is connected through two equal resistors to the output.

The ratio of the ideal signal in the passband (1 volt) to the maximum acceptable signal in the stopband (1 millivolt) is 1,000-to-1. A *decibel* is a unitless measure of relative voltage that is defined as 20 times the common logarithm of the ratio between the two voltages. Thus, the above goal of at least 1,000-to-1 attenuation can be expressed as a requirement for an attenuation (suppression) of at least 60 decibels (i.e., 20 times the common logarithm of 1,000).

A practicing electrical engineer would recognize that the above design goals can be satisfied by a fifth-order *elliptic (Cauer) filter* with a modular angle Θ of 30° and a reflection coefficient ρ of 24.3% (Van Valkenburg 1982; Williams and Taylor 1995; Zverev 1967). The modular angle Θ is the arcsin of the ratio of the frequencies at the boundaries of the passband and stopband of a lowpass filter:

$$\theta = \sin^{-1}\left(\frac{w_p}{w_s}\right)$$

Thus, for example, a modular angle Θ of 30° corresponds to a 1-to-2 ratio (i.e., 1,000 Hz to 2,000 Hz) between the two boundary frequencies. The modular angle is important in filter design because it is more difficult to design a lowpass or highpass filter when the passband and stopband are close together. The reflection coefficient ρ is

$$\rho = \sqrt{1 - 10^{\frac{-\alpha_{max}}{10}}}$$

where α_{max} is the maximum allowable passband attenuation. Thus, for example, a reflection coefficient ρ of 24.3% corresponds to a value of α_{max} of 20 times the common logarithm of the quotient of 970 millivolts to 1,000 millivolts.

25.14   PREPARATORY STEPS FOR A LOWPASS FILTER

This section details the step-by-step process by which the user converts the above high-level design goals for a lowpass filter into the specific preparatory steps necessary to apply genetic programming to the problem of automatically synthesizing the filter's design.

Before applying genetic programming to a circuit synthesis problem, the user must perform the following seven major preparatory steps:

1. identifying the terminals of the to-be-evolved circuit-constructing program trees,
2. identifying the primitive functions contained in the to-be-evolved program trees,
3. creating the fitness measure for evaluating how well a given circuit (developed from the program tree) satisfies the design goals of the problem at hand,
4. choosing certain control parameters for the run,
5. determining the termination criterion and method of result designation for the run,
6. determining the architecture of the circuit-constructing program trees, and
7. specifying an embryo and test fixture that is suitable for the problem.

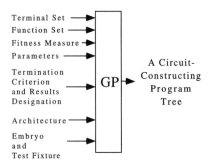

Figure 25.42   Seven preparatory steps

Figure 25.42 shows the above seven major user-supplied preparatory steps in the left part of the figure. Genetic programming then evolves a population of circuit-constructing program trees under the guidance of the fitness measure. After a number of generations, the evolving population may contain a circuit-constructing program tree that, when fully developed, produces an electrical circuit that satisfies the design goals for the problem at hand.

Steps 7 and 6 are considered first.

25.14.1   Embryo and Test Fixture

When applying genetic programming to a problem of circuit synthesis, the seventh major preparatory step entails specifying an embryo and test fixture.

The one-input, one-output initial circuit (Figure 25.6) for this problem is created by embedding the embryo with two modifiable wires and three ports (Figure 25.5) into the one-input, one-output test fixture with three ports to the embryo (Figure 25.4).

Role of Knowledge

In studying automated learning techniques, it is important to precisely identify what information is provided to the automated process by the human user and what information is actually produced by the automated process. Accordingly, we will identify (in this section and the six succeeding similar subsections) the domain-specific knowledge that we employ in performing each of the seven preparatory steps for this problem.

The domain-specific knowledge that goes into creating the initial circuit for this problem consists (at most) of the following six items:

- The initial circuit has one input.
- The initial circuit has one output.
- The elements of the to-be-evolved circuit are to be located between the Embryo_Input, Embryo_Output, and Embryo_Ground in lieu of the two modifiable wires of the embryo.
- The initial circuit is a structurally valid circuit.
- The source resistor of the test fixture (reflecting the reality that all real sources in electrical circuits have resistance) has a value of 1,000 Ω.
- The load resistor of the test fixture (reflecting the requirement that a circuit's output must drive a load) has a value of 1,000 Ω.

As can be seen, the first three items of information concern the nature of the inputs and outputs of the problem. They are not what we would ordinarily call domain knowledge about the field of electrical engineering. Some would regard these three items as part of the statement of the problem. We used the first and second items above when we decided to use the one-input, one-output test fixture (Figure 25.4). We used the third item when we decided that an embryo (Figure 25.5) with two modifiable wires and three ports (Embryo_Input, Embryo_Output, and Embryo_Ground) was an acceptable choice as the embryo.

The fourth item concerns electrical engineering. We used the fourth item when we constructed the initial circuit consisting of the chosen embryo and test fixture to be a complete, structurally valid electrical circuit (e.g., an entity with no dangling wires or components).

The knowledge involved in the last two items concerns testing the to-be-evolved circuit. The remaining two items entail a small amount of domain knowledge about electrical engineering. Again, some would regard these two items as part of the statement of the problem. Specifically, we used the fifth item when we decided that 1,000 Ω is a reasonable size for a source resistor in a test fixture with an incoming 2-volt AC incoming signal. We used the sixth item when we decided that 1,000 Ω is a reasonable size for a load resistor in the test fixture.

The test fixture is not part of the to-be-evolved circuit, but merely a device for testing its compliance with the design requirements of the problem. The embryo, of course, disappears entirely as the circuit is developed. The embryo, the test fixture, and the way they are interconnected do not incorporate any knowledge about the particular circuit that is sought. In fact, the embryo, the test fixture, and these interconnections are equally applicable to a wide variety of one-input, one-output circuits, including filters of all types, source identification circuits, and so on. In any event, the small amount of knowledge incorporated into the initial circuit is not similar in character to the kind of knowledge that we might collect into a knowledge base if we were contemplating building a knowledge-based system to synthesize filters. It certainly does not represent or codify the considerable knowledge, mathematical abstractions, and expertise that human engineers bring to bear in designing filters (e.g., knowledge about inductors, capacitors, circuit topology, Kirchhoff's node law, integro-differential equations, Laplace transforms, poles, zeros, etc.).

25.14.2   Program Architecture

When applying genetic programming to a problem of circuit synthesis, the sixth major preparatory step entails specifying the program architecture.

Since the embryo of the initial circuit has two modifiable wires (one associated with each of the result-producing branches), there are necessarily two result-producing branches in each program tree in the population. That is, the choice of the embryo made in the previous section dictates the number of main result-producing branches in each program tree.

In this introductory chapter, we decided not to use automatically defined functions on this problem. Therefore, the architecture of each program tree consists only of the two just-mentioned result-producing branches joined by a connective LIST function. The program tree of Figure 25.7 is an example of this two-branch architecture.

This introductory problem will be solved again shortly using automatically defined functions (Chapter 27), architecture-altering operations (Chapter 28), and the quasi-iterative automatically defined copy (Chapter 30).

Role of Knowledge

The above choice of program architecture reflects our preference (at the time of this run) on how to make runs of genetic programming—not any domain knowledge from the field of electrical engineering.

25.14.3   Functions and Terminals

The first major step in preparing to use genetic programming is to identify the terminal set for the problem. The second major step is to identify the function set.

Since there are no automatically defined functions for this problem, the functions and terminals are divided into the following four categories:

- component-creating functions,
- topology-modifying functions,
- development-controlling functions, and
- arithmetic-performing functions that appear in the value-setting subtrees of the component-creating functions.

The component-creating functions specify the particular electrical components that can be inserted into locations within the topology of the developing circuit structure in lieu of modifiable wires (and other components). For this problem, the set of component-creating functions is determined by the fact that the desired circuit is to be composed of inductors and capacitors. Thus, the set of component-creating functions consists of the previously described

- inductor-creating L function (Section 25.6.3) and
- capacitor-creating C function (Section 25.6.2).

The topology-modifying functions specify the ways the topology of the developing circuit structure (starting with the initial circuit) can be modified. For this problem, the set of topology-modifying functions consists of the

- series division function SERIES (Section 25.8.1),
- parallel division function PARALLEL0 (Section 25.8.2),
- polarity-reversing FLIP function (Section 25.8.3),
- ground function TWO_GROUND (Section 25.8.5), and
- the eight TWO_VIA functions (Section 25.8.4).

The construction-continuing subtree(s) of each topology-modifying function continue the developmental process. Different topology-modifying functions have different numbers of construction-continuing subtrees. For example, the SERIES function has three construction-continuing subtrees, the PARALLEL0 function has four construction-continuing subtrees, the FLIP function has one construction-continuing subtree, and the TWO_GROUND function and the eight TWO_VIA functions each have two construction-continuing subtrees. The topology-modifying functions require no arithmetic-performing subtrees. Thus, the number of arguments taken by these functions equals their respective number of construction-continuing subtrees. The set of development-controlling functions consists of

- the no-operation NOP function (Section 25.9.1) and
- the development-terminating END function (Section 25.9.2).

The construction-continuing subtree of the NOP function continues the developmental process and takes one construction-continuing subtree; however, the END function has no construction-continuing subtree. The development-controlling functions require no arithmetic-performing subtrees. Thus, the number of arguments taken by these functions equals their respective number of construction-continuing subtrees, namely, one and zero, respectively.

The value-setting (arithmetic-performing) subtrees of these component-creating functions specify the numerical value (sizing) for each inductor or capacitor that they insert. The value returned by the arithmetic-performing subtree(s) specifies the numerical value of the inserted components. Since the inductors and capacitors involved in this problem each take one numerical component value, there is one arithmetic-performing subtree associated with both of these component-creating functions. The construction-continuing subtree(s) of each function continue the developmental process after the component is inserted. Since the L and C functions each have one construction-continuing subtree and one arithmetic-performing subtree, they each take two arguments. The arithmetic-performing subtree(s) contain

- addition,
- subtraction, and
- random constants (Section 13.3.2).

Each result-producing branch (beneath the connective LIST function at the top of each program tree) is created in accordance with the constrained syntactic structure.

The terminal sets are identical for both result-producing branches of the program trees for this problem. The function sets are identical for both result-producing branches of the program trees.

The initial function set, $F_{\text{ccs-rpb-initial}}$, for the construction-continuing subtrees of the result-producing branches is

$F_{\text{ccs-rpb-initial}}$ = {C, L, SERIES, PARALLEL0, FLIP, NOP, TWO_GROUND, TWO_VIA0, TWO_VIA1, TWO_VIA2, TWO_VIA3, TWO_VIA4, TWO_VIA5, TWO_VIA6, TWO_VIA7}.

The first seven of these functions take 2, 2, 3, 4, 1, 1, and 2 arguments, respectively. The eight TWO_VIA functions each take 2 arguments.

The initial terminal set, $T_{\text{ccs-rpb-initial}}$, for the construction-continuing subtrees of the result-producing branches is

$T_{\text{ccs-rpb-initial}}$ = {END}.

The function set, F_{aps}, for each arithmetic-performing subtree is,

F_{aps} = {+, -},

each taking two arguments.

The terminal set, T_{aps}, for each arithmetic-performing subtree is

$$T_{aps} = \{\Re_{smaller-reals}\},$$

where $\Re_{smaller-reals}$ represents random floating-point constants between -1.0 and $+1.0$.

Since F_{aps} and T_{aps} are the same for all result-producing branches and automatically defined functions for all problems of circuit synthesis in this book, no distinction is made as to whether they appear in result-producing branches or automatically defined functions or whether they appear initially or potentially (i.e., are added by the architecture-altering operations during the run).

Since there are no automatically defined functions and no architecture-altering operations in this problem, $T_{adf-initial}$, $F_{adf-initial}$, $T_{rpb-potential}$, $F_{rpb-potential}$, $T_{adf-potential}$, and $F_{adf-potential}$ are all empty.

In each arithmetic-performing subtree for all problems of circuit synthesis in this book, the functions and terminals satisfy the closure property because such subtrees contain only numerically valued arithmetic functions and floating-point random constants. Closure is similarly satisfied for all other subtrees and branches of the overall circuit-constructing program tree for all problems of circuit synthesis in this book because they operate solely through their side effects on the initial circuit (and its successors) in the developmental process. No value is returned by any construction-continuing subtree, any result-producing branch, or the overall circuit-constructing program tree.

Since no value is returned by the overall program, no wrapper (output interface) is used for this problem of circuit synthesis in this book.

Role of Knowledge

Domain knowledge about electrical engineering is used in choosing the function and terminal set for this problem. However, note the small amount of knowledge that goes into the choice of function set and terminal set for this problem. The problem-specific knowledge that we use in making these choices consists *only* of the fact that a lowpass filter can be constructed from capacitors and inductors.

Genetic programming cannot design a circuit unless it is supplied with a sufficient set of components from which to construct the desired circuit. Genetic programming does not know that a lowpass filter can be constructed from capacitors and inductors. The above piece of knowledge concerning the sufficiency of capacitors and inductors is explicitly contained in the high-level statement of the problem and is communicated to genetic programming by including the capacitor-creating C function and the inductor-creating L function in the function set for this problem. These two component-creating functions establish the *parts bin* for the problem (i.e., the electrical components that are available to be used to construct the circuit).

Of course, there are alternative choices for a sufficient parts bin for this problem. For example, filters can be constructed from transistors, resistors, and capacitors (i.e., without inductors). Operational amplifiers can also be used as a primitive component in constructing filters (Sections 41.1.27–41.1.29 and 48.5). Filters are often also constructed from resistors (along with inductors and capacitors) since resistors often broaden a filter's bandwidth.

If the user did not know that a lowpass filter satisfying the requirements of this design problem can be constructed from capacitors and inductors (or preferred not to use this knowledge), the user could have supplied genetic programming with a parts bin containing both necessary and extraneous components. For example, a user knowing nothing about electrical engineering might include neon bulbs, transformers, and diodes in addition to inductors and capacitors. It is well known that genetic programming is generally able to operate (albeit usually less efficiently) when extraneous functions are included in its function set (Koza 1992e). Section 54.4 verifies that this general observation applies to this particular problem and reports on two comparative experiments in which extraneous components are added to the parts bin of this problem. In one experiment, diodes (which are completely extraneous) are included along with inductors and capacitors in the parts bin; in a second experiment, resistors (which are possibly helpful) are included.

25.14.4   Fitness

The third major step in preparing to use genetic programming is identifying the fitness measure.

Before proceeding to define the fitness measure for the problem of synthesizing the lowpass filter, it is worth reemphasizing that *everything we have said so far can be applied to any one-input, one-output circuit composed of inductors and capacitors.* We have not yet done anything to specify that our goal is a lowpass filter, as opposed to, say, a highpass filter, a bandpass filter, a bandstop filter, a double bandpass filter, a frequency discrimination circuit, or any of numerous other types of one-input, one-output circuits composed of inductors and capacitors. It is the user-provided fitness measure that directs the evolutionary process (within the search space of circuit-constructing program trees) to a satisfactory design for a lowpass filter.

In general, the fitness measure may incorporate any calculable or measurable behavior or characteristics of the circuit (or combination of such behaviors or characteristics). These may include, but are not limited to, the circuit's behavior in the time domain, its behavior in the frequency domain, its power consumption, the total number of components (parts count), the dollar cost of the components (a cost-weighted parts count), the surface area that is occupied by the components (after layout), the circuit's sensitivity to ambient conditions such as temperature, the circuit's sensitivity to variations in the externally supplied source of electrical power, the circuit's sensitivity to variations of manufactured components from their nominal value, the circuit's emissions, and so forth. Multiobjective fitness measures are common in design problems because most practical design problems involve trade-offs among several competing considerations.

Since the design of a filter is being evolved, the focus is on the behavior of the circuit in the frequency domain. For this problem, the voltage **VOUT** is probed at node 5 (Figure 25.6). The SPICE simulator is instructed to perform an AC small-signal analysis and to report the circuit's behavior for values chosen over five decades of frequency between 1 Hz and 100,000 Hz. We chose this particular range of frequencies because the boundaries of the passband and the stopband (i.e., 1,000 and 2,000 Hz) are roughly in the middle of this range. Each of the five decades of frequency is divided into 20 parts (using a logarithmic scale). Thus, there are 101 fitness cases (sampled frequencies) for this problem.

The fitness measure for this problem is based on a weighted sum of the discrepancies between the circuit's actual behavior in the frequency domain and the desired behavior. Specifically, standardized fitness is measured in terms of the sum, over the 101 fitness cases, of the absolute weighted deviation between the actual value of the voltage that is produced by the circuit at the probe point **VOUT** at node 5 and the target value for voltage. The smaller the value of fitness, the better. A fitness of zero represents an ideal lowpass filter.

Specifically, the standardized fitness is

$$F = \sum_{i=0}^{100} [W(d(f_i), f_i) d(f_i)]$$

where f_i is the frequency (in Hertz) of fitness case i; $d(x)$ is the absolute value of the difference between the target and observed values at frequency x; and $W(y, x)$ is the weighting for difference y at frequency x.

The high-level design specifications for this particular design problem are couched in terms of what is ideal, acceptable, and unacceptable. Indeed, many design problems from many fields of engineering are couched in this way because ideal values are usually unattainable, and a practicing design engineer is usually seeking a design that is tolerable versus one that is intolerable. This three-way division suggests a simple and straightforward way to construct a fitness measure. Specifically, the fitness measure is designed to

- not penalize ideal values,
- slightly penalize acceptable deviations, and
- heavily penalize unacceptable deviations.

We will use this three-way division repeatedly in this book.

The procedure for each of the 61 points in the three-decade interval between 1 Hz and 1,000 Hz (the desired passband) is as follows:

- If the voltage equals the ideal value of 1.0 volt in this interval, the deviation is 0.0.
- If the voltage is between 970 millivolts and 1,000 millivolts, the absolute value of the deviation from 1,000 millivolts is weighted by a factor of 1.0.
- If the voltage is less than 970 millivolts, the absolute value of the deviation from 1,000 millivolts is weighted by a factor of 10.0.

This arrangement for the desired passband reflects the fact that the ideal output voltage is 1.0 volt, that a shortfall of up to 30 millivolts is acceptable in the passband, and that a voltage below 970 millivolts is unacceptable. This arrangement also recognizes that an acceptable 990 millivolts in the desired passband is better than an acceptable 980 millivolts, and that an unacceptable 960 millivolts is better than an unacceptable 950 millivolts. Note that the "ideal" category above is rhetorical and is, in fact, merely a special case of the acceptable category.

The procedure for each of the 35 points in the interval from 2,000 Hz to 100,000 Hz (the desired stopband) is as follows:

- If the voltage equals the ideal value of 0.0 volts in this interval, the deviation is 0.0.
- If the voltage is between 0 millivolts and 1 millivolt, the absolute value of the deviation from 0 millivolts is weighted by a factor of 1.0.

- If the voltage is more than 1 millivolt, the absolute value of the deviation from 0 millivolts is weighted by a factor of 10.0.

This arrangement for the desired stopband reflects the fact that the ideal output voltage is 0.0 volts, that a voltage of up to 1 millivolt is acceptable in the stopband, and that a voltage above 1 millivolt is not acceptable.

The above calculation of fitness employing a discrete number of sampled frequencies may be viewed as a numerical approximation to the integral of a weighted error function over the continuous domain from 1 Hz to 100,000 Hz. The above trifurcation between ideal, acceptable, and unacceptable points is, of course, merely an artifact of the way that many design problems are couched. There are numerous alternative ways of constructing fitness measures reflecting design constraints.

For each of the five points in the transitional region (i.e., the "don't care" band) from 1,000 Hz to 2,000 Hz, the deviation is deemed to be zero. That is, these five points contribute nothing to the accumulated value of fitness.

The fitness values produced by this fitness measure range from 0 to a maximum of 960 using SPICE's AC small-signal analysis. The worst (largest) value of fitness of 960 is attained when the voltages for all 96 sampled frequencies (outside the "don't care" band) are a full 1.0 volt away from their target voltages (as they would, in fact, be for an ideal *highpass* filter with the roles of the desired passband and stopband reversed).

The number of hits is defined as the number of fitness cases for which the voltage is acceptable or ideal or that lie in the "don't care" band. Since there are five points in the "don't care" band, the number of hits ranges from a low of 5 to a high of 101 for this problem. The goal is that 100% of the sampled frequencies (fitness cases) be in compliance with the design specifications. That is, the goal is to achieve 101 hits.

The SPICE simulator is remarkably robust; however, it cannot simulate every conceivable circuit. In particular, many circuits that are randomly created for the initial population of a run of genetic programming and many circuits that are created by the crossover and mutation operations in later generations of a run are so pathological that SPICE cannot simulate them. Circuits that cannot be simulated by SPICE are assigned, throughout this book, a penalty value of fitness (10^8). This penalty value is far larger than the worst value of fitness that can be attained by any simulatable circuit for the problem involved. The assignment of a harsh penalty value of fitness to unsimulatable individuals directs the evolutionary process away from such individuals. The unsimulatable circuits automatically become the worst-of-generation circuits for each generation. Because Darwinian selection is used at each step of genetic programming, the practical effect of this penalty is that unsimulatable individuals are almost never selected to be reproduced (copied) into the next generation or to participate in genetic operations (e.g., crossover and mutation). That is, the evolutionary search is forced to work around certain portions of the search space. As will be seen, since genetic programming operates on a large population of individuals, the fact that some individuals in a particular generation are effectively eliminated does not prevent genetic programming from solving problems.

Note that there are a different number of fitness cases in the passband and stopband (61 and 35, respectively). This discrepancy is an artifact of our somewhat arbitrary decision to use five decades of frequency between 1 Hz and 100,000 Hz and the fact that the "don't care" band is not centered exactly in the middle of the chosen five decades. An argument can be made in favor of choosing the range of frequencies so as to perfectly center the "don't care" band in the entire range. However, we regard 61 and 35 to be sufficiently close that there is no compelling need to bother with such equalization for this particular problem. In addition, an argument can also be made in favor of equalizing the influence of the deviations that are considered acceptable in the passband versus the stopband. A deviation as small as 1.001 millivolts triggers the invocation of the onerous penalty factor of 10 in the stopband, whereas it takes a deviation of 30.001 millivolts to trigger this same penalty factor in the passband. Again, we felt that there is no compelling need for such equalization for this particular problem. Indeed, the relatively simple and straightforward fitness measure described above turns out to be sufficient for solving this particular problem.

The evaluation of fitness for each individual circuit-constructing program tree in the population begins by executing the program. This execution applies the functions in the program tree to a starting point consisting of the initial circuit, thereby developing the initial circuit and its successors, step by step, into a fully developed circuit. A netlist describing the fully developed circuit is then created. The netlist identifies each component of the circuit, the nodes to which the leads of that component are connected, and the value of that component. Each circuit is then simulated to determine its behavior. The 217,000-line SPICE simulator was modified to run as a submodule within the genetic programming system (as explained in detail in Section 25.18.4). The input to a SPICE simulation consists of a netlist describing the circuit to be analyzed and certain commands that instruct SPICE as to the type of analysis to be performed and the type of output to be produced. SPICE can produce tabular information (text) describing the circuit's electrical behavior. This tabular information is then used to calculate fitness. The SPICE simulation for this problem (and, unless otherwise stated, all other problems in this book) is run at room temperature (27° Celsius). This is the default value in the SPICE simulator.

Figure 25.43 summarizes the steps involved in the calculation of fitness for a circuit. The calculation starts by initializing the current CIRCUIT to the initial circuit. The individual circuit-constructing program tree from the population is then executed. This execution causes the component-creating, topology-modifying, and development-controlling functions in the program tree to be applied to the current developing circuit structure (i.e., the functions in the program tree side-effect the current developing circuit structure). When this execution is completed, the fully developed CIRCUIT is translated into a NETLIST. The NETLIST is then simplified to create a SIMPLIFIED NETLIST. Finally, the SPICE simulator is run on the SIMPLIFIED NETLIST to create tabular values of the electrical behavior of the circuit. An example of the coding of the fitness measure using the C programming language and details on the creation of the SIMPLIFIED NETLIST are found in Sections 25.18.1 and 25.18.2.

Role of Knowledge

Carefully note the small amount of domain knowledge about electrical engineering that goes into the construction of the fitness measure supplied by the user prior to the run of genetic programming. This knowledge consists of the following:

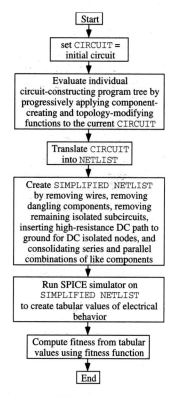

Figure 25.43 Steps in the calculation of fitness for a circuit

1. The circuit should be probed in the frequency domain (as opposed to, say, the time domain or by means of a DC sweep) because the purpose of a filter is to differentially pass incoming signals of various frequencies.

2. The behavior of the circuit should be examined over a generous range of frequencies on both sides of the desired boundaries of the passband and stopband (thus making the choice of 1 Hz to 100,000 Hz a good choice for a filter with a transition region between 1,000 and 2,000 Hz).

3. The behavior of the circuit should be sampled over a sufficiently large number of different frequencies to establish the nature of its behavior (such as the 101 points chosen above).

4. The design goals of this problem (Section 25.13) state:

    a. It is ideal if the output voltage is exactly 1 volt for frequencies in the desired passband (below 1,000 Hz) and is exactly 0 volts for frequencies in the desired stopband (above 2,000 Hz).

    b. It is acceptable if the output voltage in the desired passband is between 970 millivolts and 1 volt. Similarly, it is acceptable if the output voltage in the desired stopband is between 0 volts and 1 millivolt.

    c. It is unacceptable if the output voltage in the desired passband is lower than 970 millivolts. Similarly, it is unacceptable if the output voltage in the desired stopband is higher than 1 millivolt.

All four items above concern the *testing* of a candidate circuit—not the *design* of the circuit. Although a certain amount of knowledge is embedded in these four items, these items are most accurately characterized as a high-level statement of the requirements of the problem. These items deal with "what needs to be done"—not "how to do it." This knowledge is not at all similar in character to the kind of knowledge that we might collect and codify into a knowledge base if we were contemplating building some kind of knowledge-based system to synthesize filters. In any event, this knowledge does not resemble the mathematical abstractions, knowledge, or expertise that human engineers bring to bear in designing filters.

Notice, in particular, what we did not use. We did not employ knowledge about

- Kirchhoff's node law,
- the fact that the time behavior of the voltage and current passing through inductors and capacitors can be represented by derivatives and integrals,
- methods for solving the integro-differential equations resulting from substituting the appropriate derivatives and integrals into Kirchhoff's node law,
- knowledge about Laplace transforms, poles, zeros, or any other mathematical techniques or insights that are used by electrical engineers for analyzing filters or circuits,
- anything about the nature of Campbell, Zobel, Johnson, Butterworth, Chebychev, or Cauer (elliptic) filters,
- anything about good circuit topologies for filters, or
- anything about good sizing of components for filters.

Of course, an enormous amount of knowledge about electrical engineering is incorporated into the Berkeley SPICE simulator to enable it to compute the behavior of a circuit. However, the input to the SPICE simulator is an already designed circuit whose topology and sizing has already been created by genetic programming. Genetic programming does not have direct access to any of the knowledge that may have been used to create the SPICE simulator. Instead, a complete circuit that was created by genetic programming is supplied to the SPICE simulator, and the simulator then provides information about the circuit's behavior in the frequency domain.

25.14.5 Parameters

The fourth major step in preparing to use genetic programming involves determining the values of certain parameters that control the runs.

The population size, M, is 320,000 for runs A and B, 40,000 for runs C, D, E, and F, and 30,000 for run G. As will be seen later (Section 54.3), the problem of synthesizing a lowpass filter can be run with a population size as small as 1,000 with only a moderate reduction in efficiency.

The other control parameters for this chapter are in the tableau (Table 25.2), the tables of percentages of genetic operations in Appendix D, and the default values specified in Appendix D.

Role of Knowledge

The above choice of population size (and the default choices of control parameters from Appendix D) reflects our preferences concerning how to manage a run of genetic programming—not any domain knowledge that is specific to the field of electrical engineering.

25.14.6 Termination

The fifth major step in preparing to use genetic programming involves specifying the method for designating a result and the criterion for terminating a run.

When we first ran this problem, we did not know whether it would be possible to evolve a 100%-compliant individual (i.e., a circuit scoring 101 hits for the 101 sampled frequencies). Similar uncertainty surrounded each new circuit synthesis problem in this book. Thus, our uniform practice for problems of circuit synthesis in this book is to set the maximum number of generations, G, to some arbitrary large number (e.g., 501) and to manually monitor and manually terminate the run. As it turns out, 100%-compliant individuals are routinely evolved for this particular problem (usually within a few dozen generations).

The best-so-far pace-setting individual is always harvested from each run. Since a parallel computer system is used for all circuit synthesis problems in this book, additional high-fitness individuals are also harvested (to varying degrees) from other processing nodes in the expectation that evolved designs from other evolutionary threads may be interesting.

Role of Knowledge

The above choices concerning the termination criterion and the method of result designation reflect our preferences concerning how to manage a run of genetic programming—not any domain knowledge from the field of electrical engineering.

25.14.7 Tableau

Table 25.2 summarizes the key features of the problem of synthesizing a lowpass filter.

25.15 RESULTS FOR A LOWPASS FILTER

This section contains the results of several different runs of genetic programming on the problem of evolving the design for a lowpass filter.

25.15.1 Classical Campbell Ladder Circuit from Run A

A run of genetic programming starts with the random creation of an initial population of circuit-constructing program trees (each consisting of two result-producing branches) composed of the functions and terminals identified in Section 25.14.3 and in accordance with the constrained syntactic structure described in Section 25.11.

The initial random population (generation 0) of a run of genetic programming is a blind random search of the search space of the problem. As such, it provides a baseline for comparing the results of subsequent generations.

Table 25.2 Tableau for lowpass filter

Objective	Design a lowpass filter composed of inductors and capacitors with a passband below 1,000 Hz, a stopband above 2,000 Hz, a maximum allowable passband deviation of 30 millivolts, and a maximum allowable stopband deviation of 1 millivolt.
Test fixture and embryo	One-input, one-output initial circuit with a source resistor, load resistor, and two modifiable wires
Program architecture	Two result-producing branches, RPB0 and RPB1
Initial function set for the RPBs	For construction-continuing subtrees: $F_{ccs\text{-}rpb\text{-}initial}$ = {C, L, SERIES, PARALLEL0, FLIP, NOP, TWO_GROUND, TWO_VIA0, TWO_VIA1, TWO_VIA2, TWO_VIA3, TWO_VIA4, TWO_VIA5, TWO_VIA6, TWO_VIA7}. For arithmetic-performing subtrees: F_{aps} = {+, -}.
Initial terminal set for the RPBs	For construction-continuing subtrees: $T_{ccs\text{-}rpb\text{-}initial}$ = {END}. For arithmetic-performing subtrees: $T_{aps} = \{\Re_{smaller\text{-}reals}\}$.
Initial function set for the ADFs	Automatically defined functions are not used.
Initial terminal set for the ADFs	Automatically defined functions are not used.
Potential function set for the RPBs	Architecture-altering operations are not used.
Potential terminal set for the RPBs	Architecture-altering operations are not used.
Potential function set for the ADFs	Architecture-altering operations are not used.
Potential terminal set for the ADFs	Architecture-altering operations are not used.
Fitness cases	101 frequency values in an interval of five decades of frequency values between 1 Hz and 100,000 Hz
Raw fitness	Fitness is the sum, over the 101 sampled frequencies (fitness cases), of the absolute weighted deviation between the actual value of the output voltage that is produced by the circuit at the probe point and the target value for voltage. The weighting penalizes unacceptable output voltages much more heavily than deviating, but acceptable, voltages.
Standardized fitness	Same as raw fitness
Hits	The number of hits is defined as the number of fitness cases (out of 101) for which the voltage is acceptable or ideal or that lie in the "don't care" band.
Wrapper	None
Parameters	M = 320,000 (for runs A and B). G = 501. Q = 1,000. D = 64. B = 2%. N_{rpb} = 2. S_{rpb} = 200.

Table 25.2 *(continued)*

Result designation	Best-so-far pace-setting individual
Success predicate	A program scores the maximum number (101) of hits.

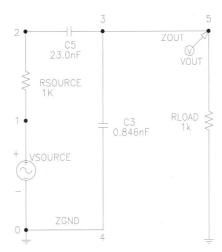

Figure 25.44   Worst simulatable circuit of generation 0

The circuits in generation 0 have a wide variety of sizes and shapes. The branches of the program trees in generation 0 vary in size up to the preestablished maximum size. The circuits in generation 0 have between 0 and 151 components (not counting the source and load resistors in the test fixture of the initial circuit).

The worst circuits in generation 0 are so pathological that the SPICE simulator cannot simulate them. In fact, 72% of the 320,000 program trees of generation 0 for this problem produce circuits that cannot be simulated by SPICE. These circuits are assigned a high penalty value of fitness (i.e., 10^8).

The worst simulatable individual circuit (Figure 25.44) from generation 0 has a fitness of 892.0 (with the worst possible value of fitness being 960 for this problem). This circuit has two capacitors and no inductors. This circuit is developed from a program tree that has 11 points in its first result-producing branch and 14 points in its second result-producing branch. The behavior of this circuit is not in compliance for any of the 96 points in the desired passband or the desired stopband. Accordingly, this circuit scores the minimum possible number of hits (representing the five "don't care" points in the transitional region between 1,000 Hz and 2,000 Hz).

Figure 25.45a shows the behavior, in the frequency domain, of the worst simulatable circuit of generation 0. Like most figures in this book depicting the behavior of electrical circuits in the frequency domain, the horizontal axis is logarithmic. The horizontal axis represents the frequency of the incoming signal and ranges logarithmically over the five decades of frequency between 1 Hz and 100,000 Hz. The 101 equally spaced filled circles along the curve represent the 101 fitness cases (sampled frequencies). There are 20

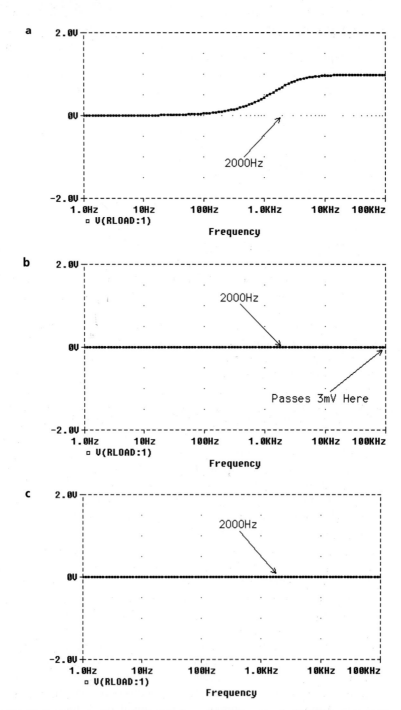

Figure 25.45 Frequency domain behavior of (*a*) the worst, (*b*) 25th percentile, (*c*) 50th percentile (median)

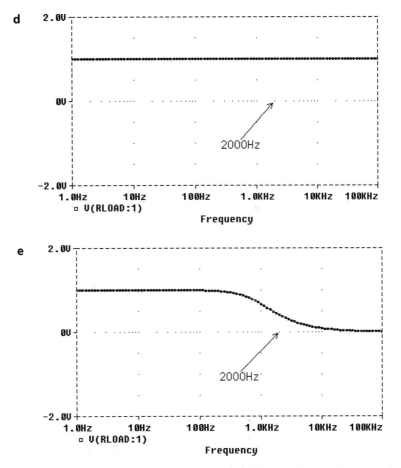

Figure 25.45 *(continued)*   (*d*) 75th percentile, and (*e*) best circuits of generation 0

fitness cases per decade. The vertical axis represents the peak voltage of the circuit's output signal. The vertical axis ranges linearly between –2 and +2 volts in this figure (and the other four figures of this series). As can be seen, the amplitude of the voltages produced by the best circuit of generation 0 for frequencies below 1,000 Hz are all zero or near-zero. They are nowhere near the desired values near 1 volt (between 970 millivolts and 1 volt) required by the design specifications of the desired lowpass filter. Equally bad, the amplitudes of many of the voltages produced for frequencies above 2,000 Hz approach 1 volt. They are nowhere near the desired near-zero values (between 0 millivolts and 1 millivolt). In other words, the behavior of this circuit is nothing like that of the desired lowpass filter. To the extent that the behavior of this circuit resembles any filter at all, it resembles the behavior of a poor highpass filter.

However, even in a population of random individuals, some individuals are better than others. Figure 25.46 shows the circuit from the 25th percentile of fitness of simulatable circuits from generation 0. (Since 72% of the circuits in generation 0 are unsimulat-

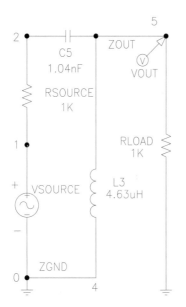

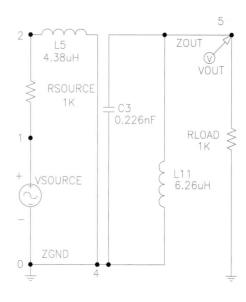

Figure 25.46   25th percentile simulatable circuit of generation 0

Figure 25.47   Median simulatable circuit of generation 0

able, the 25th percentile of simulatable circuits corresponds to the 79th percentile of the entire population.) Unlike the previous circuit that entirely lacked inductors, this circuit has one inductor (**L3**) and one capacitor (**C5**). This circuit has a fitness of 610.1 and scores 29 hits (out of 101). The topological arrangement of the inductor and capacitor in this circuit is one of the worst possible ways of realizing a lowpass filter. The topology consisting of a capacitor positioned horizontally "in series" (as filter designers say) with the incoming signal and an inductor positioned vertically as a "shunt" (as filter designers say) from the output of the capacitor to ground is a reasonable topology for a rudimentary highpass filter, but not for a lowpass filter.

Figure 25.45b shows the behavior, in the frequency domain, of the 25th percentile simulatable circuit from generation 0. The graph here is not exactly a straight line; this feeble highpass filter actually passes 3 millivolts at frequencies near 100,000 Hz. This circuit scores 29 hits (24 because of the near-zero values of voltage above 2,000 Hz and 5 because of the "don't care" band between 1,000 Hz and 2,000 Hz).

Figure 25.47 shows the median (50th percentile) simulatable circuit from generation 0. This circuit has a fitness of 610.0 and scores 40 hits. Since inductor **L5** is connected directly to ground at node 4, the output probe point **VOUT** at node 5 is completely disconnected from the incoming signal **VSOURCE**. The probe point **VOUT** at node 5 receives no energy from the incoming signal **VSOURCE**. The result is that this circuit produces a constant output of 0 volts that is independent of the incoming signal.

Figure 25.45c shows the behavior in the frequency domain of this median simulatable circuit of generation 0. The graph is a straight flat line at 0 volts. This circuit scores 40

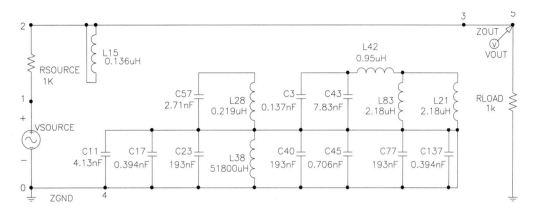

Figure 25.48 75th percentile simulatable circuit of generation 0

hits because of the zero value for voltage in the two decades of frequency above 1,000 Hz (5 hits for the five "don't care" points and 35 hits for the points above 2,000 Hz). The discrepancy between the actual voltage (0 volts) for each of the 61 points of the desired passband and the target voltage is 1 volt per point. Since these 61 discrepancies are each weighted by 10, the fitness of the circuit is exactly 610. This circuit is not a filter because it exhibits no differential treatment of the incoming frequencies.

Figure 25.48 shows the circuit from the 75th percentile of fitness of simulatable circuits from generation 0. This circuit has a fitness of 350.0 and scores 66 hits. The two result-producing branches of the circuit-constructing program tree for this circuit have 272 and 14 points, respectively. Excluding the two resistors of the test fixture of the initial circuit, this circuit has 16 components (six inductors and 10 capacitors). However, inductor L15 is useless because both of its leads are tied together. Moreover, the remaining 15 components are useless because they are entirely disconnected from the incoming signal VSOURCE. In fact, the output probe point VOUT at node 5 is directly connected to the incoming signal VSOURCE (through source resistor RSOURCE). That is, the circuit passes the incoming signal directly to the output probe point.

Figure 25.45d shows the behavior, in the frequency domain, of this 75th percentile simulatable circuit from generation 0. The graph is a straight flat line at 1 volt. This circuit scores 66 hits (5 because of the "don't care" band between 1,000 Hz and 2,000 Hz and 61 because of the 1-volt output for the 61 points from 1 Hz to 1,000 Hz). This circuit has a fitness of exactly 350 because the discrepancy between the actual voltage for the 35 points of the desired stopband and the target voltage is 1 volt and because these 35 discrepancies are then each weighted by 10. This allpass filter exhibits no differential treatment of the incoming frequencies. The fact that this circuit is accorded a better value of fitness than the median circuit above is an artifact of the asymmetric influence of the passband and stopband in the fitness measure used for this problem.

The best circuit from generation 0 (Figure 25.49) has a fitness of 61.7. Note that the values of fitness for the simulatable circuits of generation 0 span approximately one order of magnitude (with the worst having a fitness of 892.0). The circuit scores 52 hits. The circuit-constructing program tree has 23 points in its first result-producing branch

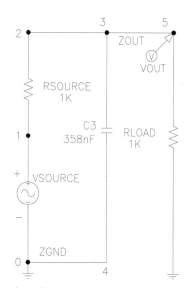

Figure 25.49   Best circuit of generation 0

and 3 points in its second result-producing branch. Excluding the source and load resistors of the test fixture of the initial circuit, the circuit has only one component (358 nF capacitor **C3**).

Figure 25.45e (and Figure 25.55a) shows the behavior in the frequency domain of this best-of-generation circuit from generation 0. As can be seen, the voltages produced by this circuit in the two-decade interval between 1 Hz and 100 Hz are very close to the required 1 volt (thereby accounting for most of the hits scored by this individual). However, the voltages produced between 100 Hz and 1,000 Hz deviate considerably from the minimum acceptable value of 970 millivolts required by the design specifications for the passband. In fact, the deviations amount to hundreds of millivolts near 1,000 Hz. Similarly, most of the voltages produced above 2,000 Hz deviate considerably (again by hundreds of millivolts) from the maximum acceptable value of 1 millivolt required by the design specifications for the stopband. Nonetheless, the behavior of this highly noncompliant best-of-generation circuit from generation 0 bears some resemblance to that of a poor lowpass filter in two ways. First, the voltage is near 1 volt for the first two decades of frequency in the left portion of the figure. Second, the voltage is near 0 for a handful of sample points in the far right part of the figure.

Thus, after creating and simulating 320,000 circuits (some with as many as 151 components) in the blind random search phase of genetic programming (i.e., generation 0), the best circuit consists of a single capacitor connected to ground. A circuit satisfying the design requirements of this problem cannot be created from a single capacitor. However, in the valley of the blind, the one-eyed man is king.

Generation 1 (and each subsequent generation of the run) is created in the usual way from the population of the preceding generation by performing reproduction, crossover, and mutation on individuals selected probabilistically on the basis of fitness.

The best individual program in generation 1 has a slightly better fitness than generation 0. As the run proceeds from generation to generation, the fitness of the best-of-generation

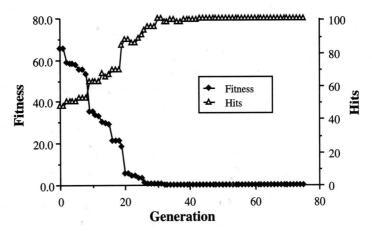

Figure 25.50 Fitness and hits

individual tends to improve. Figure 25.50 shows, by generation, the standardized fitness and number of hits for the best-of-generation program of each generation of a typical run of this problem.

As previously mentioned, 72% of the programs of generation 0 for this problem produce circuits that cannot be simulated by SPICE. However, the percentage of unsimulatable circuits drops precipitously on subsequent generations. It drops to 31% by generation 1, 16% by generation 2, 15% by generation 3, and 7% by generation 10. The vast majority of the circuits in the population are simulatable after just a few generations.

Figure 25.51 shows, by generation, the percentage of unsimulatable circuits for a typical run of this problem. This figure shows that the evolutionary process works around unsimulatable circuits and quickly directs future search into regions of the search space that are rich in simulatable circuits.

When we first embarked on our research as to whether it is possible to evolve the design of analog circuits using genetic programming, we had two major threshold concerns. Our first concern was whether any significant percentage of the randomly created circuits of generation 0 from the highly epistatic space of analog electrical circuits would be simulatable at all. A second concern was whether the probabilistic operations of crossover and mutation would beget any significant number of simulatable offspring.

Figure 25.51 shows that neither of these threshold concerns materialized on this particular problem (which was, in fact, the first problem of analog circuit synthesis that we attempted). Moreover, we have subsequently observed the same kind of precipitous drop-off in the percentage of unsimulatable circuits for *every* other problem of analog circuit synthesis that we have attempted using genetic programming. Darwinian selection, crossover, and mutation are apparently very effective in quickly steering the search on successive generations into a portion of the search space where simulatable parents beget simulatable offspring.

This observation is consistent with the general principle that the characteristics of individuals in the population in intermediate generations of a run of genetic programming (and random subtrees picked from them) differ markedly from that of the individuals (and their randomly picked subtrees) in the randomly created population of

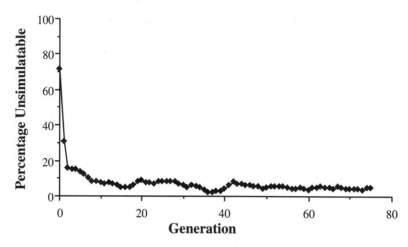

Figure 25.51   Percentage of unsimulatable circuits

generation 0 of the same run. That is, the statistical characteristics of crossover fragments drawn from intermediate generations of a run of genetic programming are very different from the statistical characteristics of randomly grown subtrees of generation 0 (and hence very different from the randomly grown subtrees provided by the mutation operation). This observation is experimental evidence that, for a nontrivial problem, the population serves a vital role in the genetic algorithm—the role of providing a reservoir of useful fragments by which crossover can rapidly advance the search. (The role of the crossover operation in genetic programming is discussed in detail in Section 25.7 and in Chapter 56.)

In genetic programming, the improvement from generation to generation is not limited to just the best single individual in the population. In fact, the entire population generally improves from generation to generation. The hits histogram is a useful monitoring tool for visualizing the progressive learning of the population as a whole during a run of genetic programming.

Figure 25.52 shows hits histograms for generations 0, 10, 20, 30, 40, and 50 of a run of this problem of synthesizing a lowpass filter. Since we do not ordinarily collect data for hits histograms on runs of genetic programming, the data for this figure comes from a separate (identically structured) run of this problem. The horizontal axis represents the number of hits (0 to 101 here); the vertical axis represents the percentage of individuals in the population scoring that number of hits. The horizontal axis has 21 buckets (20 representing five consecutive numbers of hits and the final one representing exactly 101 hits). Note the left-to-right undulating movement of both the high point and the center of mass of the population over the generations. This movement reflects the improvement of the population as a whole. Note also the left-to-right advance of the rightmost edge of the histogram (denoting the general improvement in the number of hits for the best-of-generation individual).

The improvement, from generation to generation, in the fitness of the population as a whole can also be seen by examining the average fitness of the population by generation.

The average fitness of the population of generation 1 is 3,240,415 (as compared to 7,232,192 for generation 0). That is, the entire population improves from generation 0 to generation 1. Part of this improvement reflects the smaller number of unsimulatable individuals in the population at generation 1 (i.e., those assigned the penalty value of fitness of 10^8). The average fitness of the population as a whole reaches 1,328,221 for generation 5 and 924,046 for generation 13 (again reflecting the many fewer individuals in the population receiving the penalty value of fitness).

Figure 25.53 shows, by generation, the average fitness of the simulatable circuits in the population (i.e., after all individuals receiving the penalty value of fitness are excluded from consideration). As can be seen, the average fitness of the population as a whole is 443 for generation 2, 213 for generation 5, 58.2 for generation 10, 38.0 for generation 20, and 16.5 by generation 30.

The best circuit from generation 10 (Figure 25.54) has a fitness of 21.4. The circuit scores 76 hits. The circuit-constructing program tree has 72 points in its first result-producing branch and 61 points in its second result-producing branch. Excluding the source and load resistors of the test fixture of the initial circuit, the circuit has three components (inductors **L5** and **L10** and capacitor **C12**). Notice that the capacitor **C12** is connected to ground (as was the capacitor in the best circuit of generation 0 shown in Figure 25.49). That is, this circuit from generation 10 built on what was learned in the blind random search phase of the run (i.e., generation 0) using Darwinian selection, crossover, and mutation over 10 generations. The best circuit from generation 10 represents a considerable evolutionary advance over its ancestors from the earlier generations. In fact, it is a recognizable "T" section of a classical ladder topology for lowpass filters in that there are two inductors in series (horizontally across the top of the figure) with the incoming signal and one shunt capacitor to ground. Although this circuit from generation 10 has only the beginnings of a ladder, a full ladder will emerge later in the run.

Figure 25.55a shows the behavior in the frequency domain of the best-of-generation circuit from generation 0 with a vertical axis ranging linearly from 0 to 1 volt.

Figure 25.55b shows the behavior in the frequency domain of the best-of-generation circuit from generation 10. The vertical axis ranges linearly from 0 to 1 volt. As can be seen, the voltages produced by this circuit are very close to the desired 1 volt for about $2\frac{1}{2}$ decades in the left part of the figure and very close to the desired 0 volts for about $1\frac{1}{4}$ decades in the right part of the figure. A comparison with the adjoining graph for the best circuit from generation 0 (Figure 25.55a) shows that the behavior of the best circuit from generation 10 is much closer to the desired behavior than the best circuit from generation 0.

The best circuit from generation 15 (Figure 25.56) has a fitness of 19.6. The circuit scores 90 hits. The circuit-constructing program tree has 73 points in its first result-producing branch and 186 points in its second result-producing branch. Excluding the source and load resistors of the test fixture of the initial circuit, the circuit has six components (three inductors and three capacitors). This circuit has a recognizable ladder topology consisting of two inductors in series with the incoming signal and three shunts (two consisting of just one capacitor each and one consisting of an inductor and a capacitor).

Figure 25.55c shows the behavior in the frequency domain of this best-of-generation circuit from generation 15. As can be seen, the voltages produced by this circuit are very close to the desired 1 volt for about $2\frac{1}{2}$ decades in the left part of the figure and very close to the desired 0 volts for about $1\frac{1}{4}$ decades in the right part of the figure.

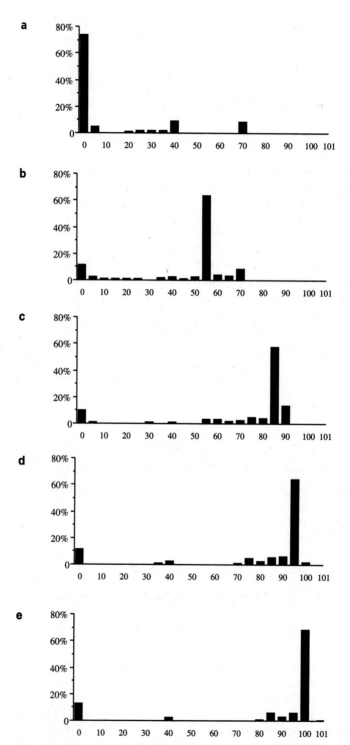

Figure 25.52 Hits histograms for generations (*a*) 0, (*b*) 10, (*c*) 20, (*d*) 30, (*e*) 40

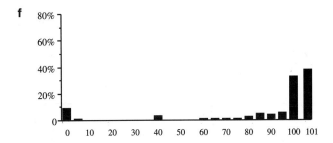

Figure 25.52 *(continued)*   *(f)* **50**

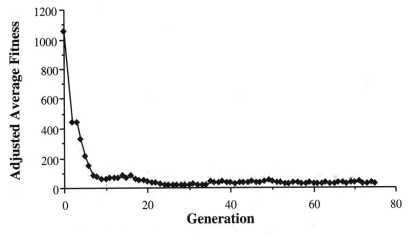

Figure 25.53   Average fitness of the simulatable circuits

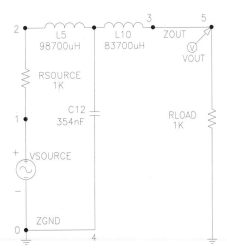

Figure 25.54   Best circuit of generation 10

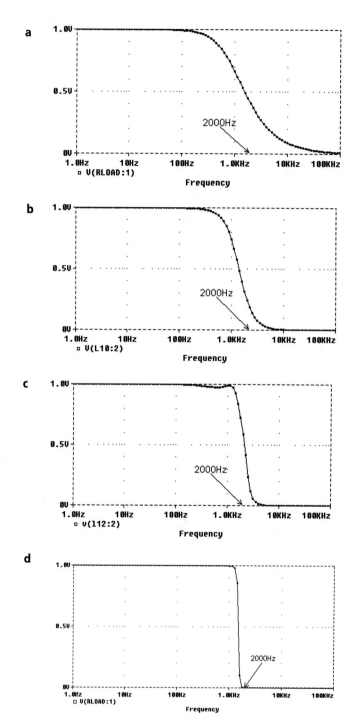

Figure 25.55 Frequency domain behavior of best circuits of generations (*a*) 0, (*b*) 10, (*c*) 15, and (*d*) 49

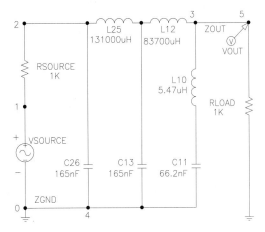

Figure 25.56   Best circuit of generation 15

The best individual program tree of generation 49 has a fitness of 0.00781 and scores 101 hits. That is, by generation 49, all 101 sample points are in compliance with the design goals for this problem. The fitness of this best-of-generation circuit from generation 49 is approximately five orders of magnitude less than that of the worst simulatable circuit from generation 0. The deviation averages only about 0.8 millivolts over the 101 sampled frequencies for this best-of-generation circuit. The voltages produced by this circuit (Figure 25.55d) are very close to the desired 1 volt from 1 Hz to 1,000 Hz, there is a much sharper drop-off after 1,000 Hz, and more points in the right part of the figure are near the desired 0-volt level.

The first result-producing branch, RPB0, of this best-of-generation circuit from generation 49 has 179 points:

```
(C (− (+ (+ (+ −8.841827E−01 −1.351154E−01 ) (+ (− −1.547141E−
01 3.394866E−01 ) 2.785355E−01 )) 6.216426E−01 ) −7.385337E−01
) (− (C (− (− 7.200445E−01 (− −7.729423E−01 7.037411E−01 )) (−
−6.136844E−01 −8.752375E−01 )) (PARALLEL0 (C (− (+ 9.450361E−
01 6.216426E−01 ) −7.385337E−01 ) (− (C (− (+ 9.450361E−01
6.216426E−01 ) −7.385337E−01 ) (− (PARALLEL0 (END) (END) (L (+
(− (+ 8.564349E−01 (+ −5.572846E−01 −3.846784E−01 )) (+ (−
8.245459E−01 (− −5.314455E−01 9.118310E−01 )) (− −6.136844E−01
−8.752375E−01 ))) (− (+ −9.233361E−01 (+ −8.310153E−01
−7.556455E−01 )) (+ (− 0.06303740 (+ −1.030779E−01 −5.122700E−
01 )) 6.002918E−01 ))) (+ (− 8.245459E−01 (− −5.314455E−01 (−
8.245459E−01 (− −5.314455E−01 9.118310E−01 )))) (− −6.136844E−
01 −8.752375E−01 ))) (END)) (− (+ 9.030429E−01 (− (PARALLEL0
(END) (END) (END) (END)) (− 0.02472150 4.826100E−01 )))
6.216426E−01 ))) (− (− (+ −9.233361E−01 (+ −8.310153E−01
−7.556455E−01 )) (L (+ (+ −1.943367E−01 (− (+ 9.450361E−01
6.216426E−01 ) −7.556455E−01 )) (+ −8.310153E−01 −7.556455E−01
```

```
)) (END))) -8.999599E-01 ))) (FLIP (END)) (NOP (L (+ (- (+ (-
(+ -5.306351E-01 3.485614E-01 ) 8.691459E-01 ) (+ -5.572846E-
01 (+ -8.310153E-01 -7.556455E-01 ))) (+ (+ 0.06190884
-8.310153E-01 ) (- -6.136844E-01 -8.752375E-01 ))) (- (+
-9.233361E-01 (+ -8.310153E-01 -7.556455E-01 )) (END))) (+
8.564349E-01 (+ -5.572846E-01 -3.846784E-01 )))) (PARALLEL0
(END) (END) (END) (END)))) (- (+ 9.030429E-01 (- (PARALLEL0
(END) (END) (+ 1.069093E-01 (- 9.030429E-01 -1.547141E-01 ))
(END)) (- 0.02472150 4.826100E-01 ))) -8.999599E-01 ))).
```

The second result-producing branch, RPB1, of this best-of-generation circuit from generation 49 has 179 points:

```
(- 7.200445E-01 (- (+ -9.233361E-01 (+ (NOP (L 9.856515E-01 (+
(+ -8.841827E-01 -1.351154E-01 ) (- (+ (+ -9.338167E-01 -
8.841827E-01 ) 3.485614E-01 ) (- (+ (END) 3.485614E-01 ) (-
-4.092255E-01 -7.092842E-01 )))))) 6.216426E-01 )) (+ (- (FLIP
(SERIES (SERIES (END) (END) (END)) (TWO_VIA5 (END) (END))
(TWO_VIA5 (END) (END)))) (TWO_VIA7 (+ -8.310153E-01 -
7.556455E-01 ) (END))) (C (+ (+ (- (- (PARALLEL0 (END) (END) (L
(+ (- (+ (- -3.839042E-01 8.691459E-01 ) (+ -5.572846E-01 (+
-8.310153E-01 (FLIP (END))))) -2.832756E-01 ) (- (+ -
9.233361E-01 (+ -8.310153E-01 -7.556455E-01 )) (END))) (FLIP
(NOP (NOP (- -5.122700E-01 -4.977509E-01 ))))) (END)) (+ (-
-8.310153E-01 -4.588416E-01 ) (- -5.177572E-01 (+ (+
0.04709685 5.398288E-01 ) (- (+ (- 7.460642E-01 (- (- (+
-1.943367E-01 (- (- -3.444579E-01 (+ -9.233361E-01 (+
-8.310153E-01 -7.556455E-01 ))) -8.310153E-01 )) (+ -
2.161386E-01 -4.546671E-01 )) -4.079809E-01 )) (L (-
5.449004E-01 -2.349250E-01 ) (END))) -5.177572E-01 ))))) (-
-3.821788E-01 -1.156657E-01 )) (+ -5.572846E-01 -3.846784E-01
)) -3.846784E-01 ) (END))))).
```

As usual, the two branches of this circuit-constructing program tree are applied to the embryo. The fully developed circuit is then translated into a netlist, which is then simplified and edited. The netlist is then surrounded with the SPICE commands necessary to perform a SPICE simulation. The result is as follows:

```
* BEST-OF-GENERATION OF GENERATION 49
V0 2 0 SIN(0 2 166 0 0) AC 2
C3 3 0 2.02E+02NF
L5 4 5 9.68UH
R6 2 4 1.00K
R8 1 0 1.00K
L10 5 6 1.82E-05UH
C12 0 5 8.61E+01NF
L13 1 7 1.82E-05UH
C15 0 1 8.61E+01NF
```

```
L22 6 8 2.09E-05UH
C24 6 0 2.02E+02NF
L25 7 9 2.09E-05UH
C27 7 0 2.02E+02NF
L28 8 3 2.09E-05UH
C30 8 0 2.02E+02NF
L31 9 3 2.09E-05UH
C33 9 0 2.02E+02NF
* COMPONENT_COUNT = 17
.AC DEC 20 1 100000
.PLOT AC VM(1)
.OPTIONS NOPAGE NOMOD
.END
```

Figure 25.57 shows the best circuit from generation 49 for run A of this problem. This circuit has the recognizable ladder topology (Williams and Taylor 1995). This particular ladder has seven rungs. The ladder topology consists of repeated instances of inductors (L5, L10, L22, L28, L31, L25, and L13) arranged in series with the incoming signal horizontally across the top of the figure along with repeated instances of capacitors (C12, C24, C30, C3, C33, C27, and C15) located on seven vertical shunts to ground. Note that the numbers on nodes in the evolved circuits in this book usually correspond to the netlist actually produced by the run of genetic programming (and therefore are not necessarily consistent with the more orderly numbering of nodes of nonevolved illustrative circuits).

Figure 25.55d shows the behavior in the frequency domain of the best-of-run circuit from generation 49. As can be seen, the 100%-compliant lowpass filter delivers a voltage of essentially 1 volt in the entire passband from 1 Hz to 1,000 Hz and suppresses the voltage of essentially 0 volts in the entire stopband starting at 2,000 Hz. There is a sharp drop-off from 1 volt to 0 volts in the transitional ("don't care") region between 1,000 Hz and 2,000 Hz.

Almost all of the components in the seven-rung ladder of Figure 25.57 are necessary to achieve 100% compliance (101 hits). Table 25.3 shows the number of hits achieved by a circuit created by deleting each particular inductor or capacitor from this seven-rung ladder. For purposes of this analysis, a deletion is implemented by setting the component's value to zero (so that a capacitor becomes an open circuit and an inductor

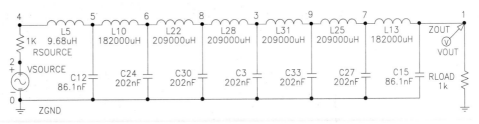

Figure 25.57   Seven-rung ladder lowpass filter from generation 49 of run A

Table 25.3 Effect of deleting particular components from seven-rung ladder filter

Component	Value	Number of hits
C3	202 nF	91
C12	86.1 nF	99
C15	86.1 nF	99
C24	202 nF	92
C27	202 nF	92
C30	202 nF	91
C33	202 nF	91
L5	9.68 μH	101
L10	182,000 μH	92
L13	182,000 μH	92
L22	209,000 μH	93
L25	209,000 μH	93
L28	209,000 μH	92
L31	209,000 μH	92

becomes a wire). As can be seen, all but one of these single-component deletions significantly degrade the circuit's behavior and reduce the number of hits below 101 (the exception being the deletion of the minuscule 9.68 μH inductor L5).

Notice that four of the seven rungs of the ladder of the best-of-run circuit from generation 49 are identical. That is, four of the rungs consist of a 209,000 μH inductor and a 202 nF capacitor. This duplication is the consequence of crossovers operating on the circuit-constructing program trees in the population during the run. This duplication will be discussed again in Section 25.17 and Chapter 56.

The circuit of Figure 25.57 has the recognizable features of the circuit for which George Campbell of American Telephone and Telegraph received U.S. patent 1,227,113 (Campbell 1917a). As Campbell said, in describing his patent entitled *Electric Wave Filter,*

My invention in one or more of its embodiments has important applications in connection with wireless telegraphy, wireless telephony, multiplex high frequency wire telephony, composite telegraph and telephone lines, and in particular with telephone repeater circuits, wherein it is highly important that means be provided for selecting a range or band of frequencies, such as, for instance, the range or band of frequencies necessary for intelligible telephonic transmission of speech, while at the same time excluding from the receiving or translating device currents of all other frequencies.

Claim 2 of patent 1,227,113 covered

An electric wave filter consisting of a connecting line of negligible attenuation composed of a plurality of sections, each section including a capacity element and an inductance element, one of said elements of each section being in series with the line and the other in shunt across the line, said capacity and inductance elements having precomputed values dependent upon the upper limiting frequency and the lower limiting frequency of a range of frequencies it is desired to transmit without attenuation, the values of said capacity and inductance elements being so proportioned that the structure transmits with practically negligible attenuation sinusoidal currents of all frequencies lying between said two limiting frequencies, while attenuating and approximately extinguishing currents of neighboring frequencies lying outside of said limiting frequencies.

An examination of the evolved circuit of Figure 25.57 shows that it indeed consists of "a plurality of sections" (specifically, seven). In the figure, "each section includ[es] a capacity element and an inductance element." Specifically, the first of the seven sections consists of inductor L5 and capacitor C12, the second section consists of inductor L10 and capacitor C24, and so forth. Moreover, "one of said elements of each section [is] in series with the line and the other in shunt across the line." As can be seen in the figure, inductor L5 of the first section is indeed "in series with the line" and capacitor C12 is "in shunt across the line." This is also the case for the remaining six sections of the evolved circuit. Furthermore, Figure 25.57 exactly matches Figure 7 of Campbell's 1917 patent. In addition, this circuit's frequency domain behavior (shown in Figure 25.55d) confirms the fact that the values of the inductors and capacitors are such as to transmit "with practically negligible attenuation sinusoidal currents" of the passband frequencies "while attenuating and approximately extinguishing currents" of the stopband frequencies. In short, the evolved circuit has all the features contained in claim 2 of Campbell's 1917 patent. But for the fact that this patent has long since expired, this evolved circuit would infringe that patent.

In addition to possessing the topology of the Campbell filter, the evolved circuit of Figure 25.57 also approximately possesses the numerical values described in Campbell's 1917 patent (Campbell 1917a). In fact, this evolved circuit is almost equivalent to what is now known as a cascade of six identical symmetric π-sections (Johnson 1950). To see this, we modify the evolved circuit of Figure 25.57 in four minor ways.

First, we replace the 9.68 µH inductor L5 near the upper left corner of the figure with a wire. The value of this inductor is more than five orders of magnitude less than the value of the other six inductors (L10, L22, L28, L31, L25, and L13) in series across the top of the figure. This replacement does not noticeably affect the behavior of the evolved circuit for the frequencies of interest in this problem.

Second, we replace each of the five identical 202 nF capacitors (C24, C30, C3, C33, C27) by a composition of two parallel 101 nF capacitors. The capacitance of a composition of two parallel capacitors equals the sum of the two individual capacitances. Thus, these five changes do not change the behavior of the evolved circuit at all.

Third, we note that the two 86.1 nF capacitors (C12 and C15) at the two ends of the ladder are each approximately equal to the (now) ten 101 nF capacitors. Suppose, for sake of argument, that these 12 approximately equal capacitors are replaced by 12 equal capacitors with capacitance equal to their average value (98.5 nF). The behavior of the evolved circuit is only slightly changed by these replacements.

Fourth, we note also that the six nontrivial inductors (L10, L22, L28, L31, L25, and L13) are approximately equal. Suppose, for sake of argument, that these six approximately equal inductors are replaced by six equal inductors with inductance equal to their average value (200,000 µH). Again, the behavior of the evolved circuit is only slightly changed by these replacements.

The behavior in the frequency domain of the circuit resulting from the above four changes is substantially the same as that of the evolved circuit of Figure 25.57. In particular, the modified circuit is still 100%-compliant with the problem's design requirements (i.e., it still scores 101 hits).

The modified circuit is what is now known as a cascade of six identical symmetric π-sections. Each π-section consists of an inductor of inductance L (where L equals 200,000 µH) and two equal capacitors of capacitance C/2 (where C equals 197 nF). In each π-section, the two 98.5 nF capacitors constitute the vertical legs of the π and the one 200,000 µH inductor constitutes the horizontal bar across the top of the π.

Such π-sections are characterized by two key parameters. The first parameter is the section's characteristic impedance (resistance). This characteristic resistance should match the circuit's fixed load resistance (1,000 Ω) established by **RLOAD** in the circuit's test fixture. The second parameter is the nominal cutoff frequency that separates the filter's passband from its stopband. This second parameter should lie somewhere in the transition region between the end of the passband (1,000 Hz) and the beginning of the stopband (2,000 Hz).

The characteristic resistance, R, of each π-section is given by the formula (Johnson 1950)

$$R = \sqrt{(L/C)}.$$

When the inductance, L, is 200,000 µH and the capacitance, C, is 98.5 nF, this formula yields a characteristic resistance, R, of 1,008 Ω. This value is very close to the value of the 1,000 Ω load resistance of this problem.

The nominal cutoff frequency, f_c, of each of the π-sections of a lowpass filter is given by the formula (Johnson 1950)

$$f_c = 1/(\pi\sqrt{(LC)}).$$

When the inductance, L, is 200,000 µH and the capacitance, C, is 98.5 nF, this formula yields a nominal cutoff frequency, f_c, for a lowpass filter of 1,604 Hz (i.e., roughly in the middle of the transition region between the passband and stopband of the desired lowpass filter).

In other words, both of these key parameters of the evolved π-sections of Figure 25.57 are very close to the textbook values (Johnson 1950) of π-sections that are consistent with this problem's design requirements. After compensating for the historical differences in notation, the formulae found in Johnson (1950) are equivalent to the formulae that George Campbell presented in U.S. patent 1,227,113 as his preferred numerical values for the filter's capacitors and inductors (Campbell 1917a, page 5). That is, the differences in component sizing between the evolved circuit of Figure 25.57 and the circuit taught by Campbell in his 1917 patent are minor and unsubstantial. Under the "doctrine of equivalences" of the patent law, the evolved circuit of Figure 25.57 infringes on the claims of the now-expired Campbell patent.

The legal criteria for obtaining a U.S. patent are that the proposed invention be "new" and "useful" and the differences between the subject matter sought to be patented and the prior art are such that the subject matter as a whole would [not] have been obvious at the time the invention was made to a person having ordinary skill in the art to which said subject matter pertains. (35 United States Code 103a).

George Campbell was part of the renowned research team of the American Telephone and Telegraph Corporation that played a major role in the development of the electronics industry for most of the 20th century. He received a patent for his filter design in 1917 because his idea was new in 1917, because it was useful, and because it satisfied the statutory test for unobviousness. The fact that genetic programming rediscovered an electrical circuit that was unobvious "to a person having ordinary skill in the art" establishes that this evolved result satisfies Arthur Samuel's criterion (1983) for artificial intelligence and machine learning, namely

The aim [is] . . . to get machines to exhibit behavior, which if done by humans, would be assumed to involve the use of intelligence.

This run (made on October 31, 1995) established the principle that it is possible to synthesize both the topology and sizing of an analog electrical circuit using genetic programming.

It is important to note that when we performed the preparatory steps for applying genetic programming to this problem of synthesizing a lowpass filter, we did not employ any significant domain knowledge from the field of filter design or electrical engineering. In fact, we explicitly inventoried our use of information and knowledge about electrical engineering as we performed each of the preparatory steps for this problem (Section 25.14).

The ladder topology emerged during this run of genetic programming as a natural consequence of the problem's fitness measure and natural selection—not because we primed the run with domain knowledge about electrical engineering in general or information from Campbell's 1917 patent in particular. That is, the evolutionary process opportunistically *reinvented* the Campbell filter in this run because it was helpful in solving the problem at hand. Thus, in spite of the absence of explicit domain knowledge about electrical engineering and filters, genetic programming evolved a 100%-compliant circuit that is well known in the field of electrical engineering.

Referring to the eight criteria in Chapter 1 for establishing that an automatically created result is competitive with a human-produced result, this result satisfies the following criteria:

A. The result was patented as an invention in the past, is an improvement over a patented invention, or would qualify today as a patentable new invention.
F. The result is equal to or better than a result that was considered an achievement in its field at the time it was first discovered.

Therefore, we make the following claim:

- **CLAIM NO. 3** We claim that the reinvention by genetic programming of the Campbell filter is an instance where genetic programming has produced a result that is competitive with a result produced by creative and inventive humans.

25.15.2   Cascade of T-Sections

Genetic programming involves probabilistic steps in at least four places: creating the initial population of generation 0, selecting individuals from the population based on fitness on which to perform the genetic operations, selecting the particular operation to perform, and selecting a point (e.g., the crossover point, mutation point) within the selected individual at which to perform the operation. Moreover, in the parallel implementation of genetic programming, individuals are probabilistically selected from the population based on fitness to migrate from one processing node to another in the parallel computer system. Thus, different runs of genetic programming on the same problem almost always produce different results.

As shown in the previous section, the evolved 100%-compliant lowpass filter (Figure 25.57) from generation 49 of run A of this problem is approximately equivalent to what is now known as a cascade of six identical symmetric π-sections. The 100%-compliant circuit (Figure 25.58) from generation 38 of another run of this problem (run B) is an example of another well-known type of lowpass filter. This evolved circuit from generation 38 consists of five inductors (L36, L19, L30, L45, and L37) arranged horizontally "in series" with the incoming signal and the source resistor. It also contains four shunt capacitors (C62, C12, C82, and C73).

In addition to possessing the topology of the Campbell filter, the evolved circuit of Figure 25.58 also approximately possesses the numerical values described in Campbell's 1917 patent (Campbell 1917a) for what is now known as a cascade of four identical symmetric T-sections (Johnson 1950). To see this, we modify the evolved circuit of Figure 25.58 in three ways.

First, we note that the value of three of the four capacitors is 221 nF, and the value of the fourth capacitor is similar (namely 246 nF). Suppose, for sake of argument, that each of these four capacitors is replaced by a capacitor with capacitance equal to their average value (227 nF). This change does not appreciably affect the behavior of the circuit for the frequencies of interest.

Second, we replace each of the three largest inductors (L19, L30, and L45) by a series composition of two equal inductors whose inductances are half of the value of the given inductor. That is, L19 is replaced by a series composition of two 138,500 μH inductors; L30 is replaced by a series composition of two 129,000 μH inductors; and L45 is replaced by a series composition of two 118,500 μH inductors. This change does not affect the behavior of the circuit at all.

Third, we note also that the values of the (now) eight inductors in series horizontally across the top of the figure are approximately equal. Suppose, for sake of argument, that each of these approximately equal inductors are replaced by an inductor with inductance equal to their average value (133,000 μH). Again, these changes do not appreciably affect the behavior of the circuit for the frequencies of interest.

The modified circuit is what is now known as a cascade of four identical symmetric T-sections. Each T-section consists of two equal inductors of inductance $L/2$ (where L equals 266,000 μH) and one capacitor of capacitance C (where C equals 227 nF). In each T-section, the two 133,000 μH inductors constitute the horizontal arms of the "T," and the one capacitor constitutes the vertical stem of the "T." Such T-sections are characterized by two key parameters. The first parameter is the characteristic resistance (imped-

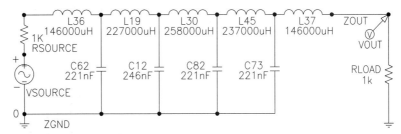

Figure 25.58   Four-rung lowpass filter consisting of four T-sections from generation 38 of run B

ance) of the T-sections. This characteristic resistance should match the circuit's fixed load resistance (1,000 Ω). The second parameter is the nominal cutoff frequency that separates the filter's passband from its stopband. This second parameter should lie somewhere in the transition region between the end of the passband (1,000 Hz) and the beginning of the stopband (2,000 Hz).

The characteristic resistance, R, of each of the T-sections is given by the formula

$$\sqrt{(L/C)}.$$

This formula yields a characteristic resistance, R, of 1,083 Ω (i.e., close to the value of the 1,000 Ω load resistance of this problem). The nominal cutoff frequency, f_c, of each of the T-sections of a lowpass filter is given by the formula

$$1/(\pi\sqrt{(LC)}).$$

This formula yields a nominal cutoff frequency, f_c, of 1,295 Hz (i.e., within the transition region between the passband and stopband of the desired lowpass filter). In other words, both of these key parameters for the T-sections of Figure 25.58 are very close to the textbook values (Johnson 1950) of T-sections that are consistent with this problem's design requirements.

25.15.3   Zobel's M-Derived Half Section

In another run of this same problem, a 100%-compliant circuit was evolved in generation 34 of run C. This evolved circuit is approximately equivalent to what is known as a combination of a cascade of three symmetric T-sections and an M-derived half section (Johnson 1950). To see this, we modify the evolved circuit from generation 34 in three ways.

First, we replace the two 0.138 μH inductors of the evolved circuit by wires. The value of these two inductors is about six orders of magnitude smaller than the value of the other inductors in the circuit, so these two replacements do not noticeably affect the behavior of the evolved circuit for frequencies of interest in this problem. The resulting circuit is shown in Figure 25.59.

Second, we replace each of the three 198,000 μH inductors in the figure (**L16**, **L13**, and **L10**) with a series composition of two 99,000 μH inductors. Since the inductance of two inductors in series is equal to the sum of their inductances, this change does not affect the behavior of the circuit at all. The circuit can now be viewed as having one

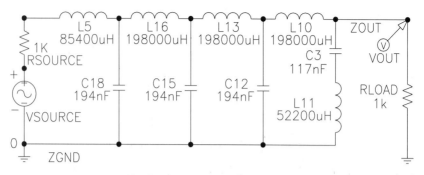

Figure 25.59 **Slightly modified version of the evolved lowpass filter circuit from run C consisting of three symmetric T-sections and an *M*-derived half section**

incoming 85,400 µH inductor (**L5**) and six 99,000 µH inductors in series horizontally at the top of the figure.

Third, we note also that the values of the (now) seven inductors in series horizontally across the top of Figure 25.59 are approximately equal. Suppose, for sake of argument, that each of these seven approximately equal inductors are replaced by an inductor with inductance equal to their average value (97,000 µH). This change does not appreciably affect the behavior of the circuit for the frequencies of interest.

After the above changes, the circuit is approximately equivalent to what is called a cascade of three identical symmetric T-sections and an "M-derived half section." Consider first the T-sections. Each T-section consists of an incoming inductor of inductance $L/2$ (where L equals 194,000 µH), a junction point from which a capacitor of capacitance C (where C equals 194 nF) is shunted off to ground, and an outgoing inductor of inductance $L/2$. The two inductors are the horizontal arms of the "T." The final "half section" (so named because it has only one arm of the two arms of a "T") has one incoming inductor of inductance $L/2$ and a junction point from which a capacitive-inductive shunt (**C3** and **L11**) is connected to ground.

The first three symmetric T-sections are referred to as "constant K" filter sections (Johnson 1950, page 331). Such filter sections are characterized by two key parameters. The first parameter is the section's characteristic resistance (impedance). This characteristic resistance should match the circuit's fixed load resistance (1,000 Ω). The second parameter is the nominal cutoff frequency that separates the filter's passband from its stopband. This second parameter should lie somewhere in the transition region between the end of the passband (1,000 Hz) and the beginning of the stopband (2,000 Hz).

The characteristic resistance, R, of each of each of the three T-sections is given by the formula

$$R = \sqrt{(L/C)}.$$

When the inductance, L, is 194,000 µH and the capacitance, C, is 194 nF, then the characteristic resistance, R, is 1,000 Ω according to this formula (i.e., exactly equal, in this instance, to the value of the actual load resistor). The nominal cutoff frequency, f_c, of each of the three T-sections of a lowpass filter is given by the formula

$$f_c = 1/(\pi \sqrt{(LC)}).$$

This formula yields a nominal cutoff frequency, f_c, of 1,641 Hz (i.e., near the middle of the transition band for the desired pass filter). In other words, both of the key parameters of the three T-sections are very close to the canonical values of "constant K" sections designed with the aim of satisfying this problem's design requirements.

The remaining half section of the evolved circuit closely approximates what is called an "M-derived half section." This final section is said to be "derived" because it is derived from the foregoing three identical "constant K" prototype sections. In the derivation, m is a real constant between 0 and 1. Let m be 0.6 here. In a canonical "M-derived half section" that is derived from the above "constant K" prototype sections, the value of the capacitor in the vertical shunt of the "M-derived half section" is given by the formula mC. This formula yields a value of 116.4 nF, while the actual value of **C3** in the evolved circuit is 117 nF.

The value of the inductor in the vertical shunt of an "M-derived half section" is given by the formula

$$L(1 - m^2)/(4m).$$

This formula yields a value of 51,733 while the actual value of **L5** in the evolved circuit is 52,200 μH.

The frequency, f_∞, where the attenuation first approaches infinity, is given by the formula

$$f_\infty = f_c / \sqrt{(1 - m^2)}.$$

This formula yields a value of f_∞ of 2,051 Hz. This value is near the beginning of the desired stopband.

Taken as a whole, the topology and component values of the evolved circuit of Figure 25.59 are reasonably close to the canonical values for the three identical symmetric T-sections and a final "M-derived half section" that is designed with the aim of satisfying this problem's design requirements.

Otto Zobel was another member of the American Telephone and Telegraph Company research team in the 1920s. He invented the idea of adding an "M-derived half section" to one or more "constant K" sections. As he explains in U.S. patent 1,538,964 (Zobel 1925),

> The principal object of my invention is to provide a new and improved network for the purpose of transmitting electric currents having their frequency within a certain range and attenuating currents of frequency within a different range. . . . Another object of my invention is to provide a wave-filter with recurrent sections not all of which are alike, and having certain advantages over a wave-filter with all its sections alike.

The advantage of Zobel's approach is a "sharper transition" in the frequency domain behavior of the filter. Claim 1 of Zobel's 1925 patent covers

> A wave-filter having one or more half-sections of a certain kind and one or more other half-sections that are M-types thereof, M being different from unity.

Claim 2 covers

> A wave-filter having its sections and half-sections so related that they comprise different M-types of a common prototype, M having several values for respectively different sections and half-sections.

Claim 3 goes on to cover

A wave-filter having one or more half-sections of a certain kind and one or more half-sections introduced from a different wave-filter having the same characteristic and the same critical frequencies and a different attenuation characteristic outside the free transmitting range.

Viewed as a whole, the differences between the teachings of Zobel's 1925 patent and the evolved circuit of Figure 25.59 are minor and unsubstantial. Thus, under the "doctrine of equivalences," the evolved circuit infringes on the claims of the now-expired Zobel patent.

We have encountered numerous other instances of an "M-derived half section" appended to various numbers of "constant K" prototype sections on other runs on other problems of circuit synthesis in this book. For example, both the topology and numerical values of the components in the evolved highpass filter of Figure 26.5 are those of an "M-derived half section" appended to two "constant K" prototype sections. In addition, both the topology and numerical values of the components in the highpass portion of the evolved crossover filter of Figure 32.10 are those of an "M-derived half section" appended to two "constant K" prototype sections. In other words, both of these evolved circuits also infringe on the claims of Zobel's 1925 patent.

Referring to the eight criteria in Chapter 1 for establishing that an automatically created result is competitive with a human-produced result, this result satisfies the following criteria:

A. The result was patented as an invention in the past, is an improvement over a patented invention, or would qualify today as a patentable new invention.
F. The result is equal to or better than a result that was considered an achievement in its field at the time it was first discovered.

Therefore, we make the following claim:

• **CLAIM NO. 4** We claim that the reinvention by genetic programming of Zobel's "M-derived half section" in conjunction with a number of "constant K" filter sections is an instance where genetic programming has produced a result that is competitive with a result created by a creative and inventive human.

The automatic discovery of this result satisfies Arthur Samuel's criterion (1983) for artificial intelligence and machine learning, namely

The aim [is] . . . to get machines to exhibit behavior, which if done by humans, would be assumed to involve the use of intelligence.

25.15.4 "Bridged T" Topology

Figure 25.60 shows a 100%-compliant best-of-run circuit from another run of genetic programming on this problem. This circuit from generation 64 of run D scores 101 hits and has a fitness of 0.04224 (somewhat better than the 0.00781 for the best-of-run circuit from run A). The right part of this figure contains a recognizable "bridged T" substructure. Specifically, the 0.796 µH inductor **L11** constitutes the vertical part of the "T," the two 118 nF capacitors **C3** and **C15** constitute the two horizontal parts of the "T," and the 214,000 µH inductor **L14** is the bridge over the "T." That is, this run of genetic

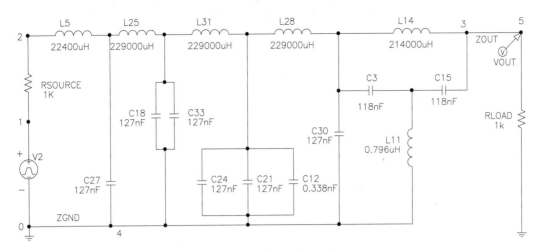

Figure 25.60 **"Bridged T" circuit from generation 6 of run D**

programming produced a 100%-compliant lowpass filter containing a topological sub-structure that is distinct from the ladder topology of runs A, B, and C and that is well known in the field of electrical engineering. After consolidating the parallel capacitors (i.e., the pair **C18** and **C33** and the triplet **C24**, **C21**, and the insignificant 0.338 nF capacitor **C12**), it can be seen that this circuit contains three rungs of a ladder to the left of the "bridged T."

Figure 25.61 shows another 100%-compliant best-of-generation circuit from generation 53 of the same run (D). This circuit has a fitness of 0.06507 and also scores 101 hits. A recognizable "bridged T" arrangement involving **L16**, **C17**, **C3**, **L28**, and **L13** appears on the left portion of this circuit (as opposed to the right portion of Figure 25.60). The circuit also contains three rungs of a ladder in the right portion of this figure (after the parallel capacitors are consolidated). This circuit can be simplified by consolidating series inductors **L5** and **L11** and series inductors **L28** and **L13**. It can be further simplified by consolidating **C26**, **C23**, and **C14**.

The "bridged T" was invented by Kenneth S. Johnson of Western Electric Company and patented in 1926. As U.S. patent 1,611,916 (Johnson 1926) states,

In accordance with the invention, a section of an artificial line, such as a wave filter, comprises in general four impedance paths, three of which are arranged in the form of a T network with the fourth path bridged across the transverse arms of the T. The impedances of this network, which for convenience, will be referred to as a bridged T network, bear a definite relationship to a network of the series shunt type, the characteristics of which are well known.

In the forms of the invention described herein, the arms of the bridged T network consist of substantially pure reactances. Its most useful forms are found to be wave filter networks in which there is a substantially infinite attenuation at a frequency within the band to be suppressed and the network may be designed so that this frequency is very near the cut-off frequency of the filter, thus producing a very sharp separation between the transmitted and suppressed bands.

Claim 1 of patent 1,611,916 covers

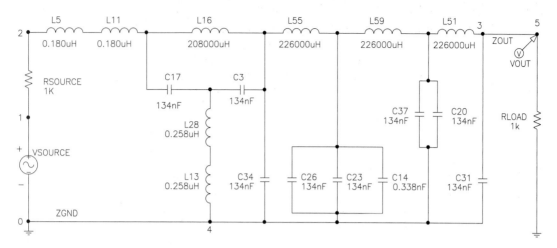

Figure 25.61 "Bridged T" circuit from generation 53 of run D

An electrical network comprising a pair of input terminals and a pair of output terminals, an impedance path connected directly between an input terminal and an output terminal, a pair of impedance paths having a common terminal and having their other terminals connected respectively to the terminals of said first path, and a fourth impedance path having one terminal connected to said common terminal and having connections from its other terminal to the remaining input terminal and output terminal, each of said paths containing a substantial amount of reactance, the impedances of said network having such values that said network is the equivalent of a series-shunt network having desired transmission characteristics.

Figures 25.60 and 25.61 of run D establish that the general topological form of Johnson's "bridged T" filter can be evolved by genetic programming. However, neither of these 100%-compliant filters have the substance of a bona fide "bridged T" filter. In fact, these two evolved circuits are approximately equivalent to ordinary ladder filters once the minuscule shunt inductors (**L11** of Figure 25.60 and the series composition of **L28** and **L13** of Figure 25.61) are replaced by wires. We made several additional runs with a specific detector (similar to that employed in Section 27.6) for the "bridged T" construction; however, we did not encounter a bona fide example of a "bridged T" filter in any run.

The "bridged T" topology is extremely useful in designing filters and other circuits. Numerous patents were issued for the "bridged T" topology in the 1920s and 1930s. Bode received U.S. patent 2,002,216 for one version of the "bridged T" topology in 1935 (Bode 1935). Bode's 1935 patent employs a resistor in the bridge above the "T" instead of an inductor (e.g., at the position occupied by **L14** in Figure 25.60 and **L16** in Figure 25.61). Bode also received U.S. patent 1,828,454 for the "bridged T" topology in which the two inductors at the top of the "T" of the filter are mutually connected (Bode 1931). Stevenson (1926) received U.S. patent 1,606,817 for a "bridged T" employing both an inductor and capacitor in the bridge above the "T." Zobel (1934) received U.S. patent 1,977,751 for three additional variations of the "bridged T" topology.

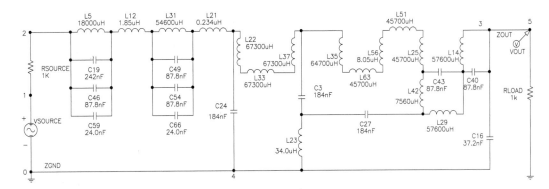

Figure 25.62   Best circuit from generation 212 of run E

25.15.5   Novel Topologies

Additional runs of this problem yield various 100%-compliant circuits with various novel topologies. Figure 25.62 shows another 100%-compliant circuit from another run (run E) of genetic programming on this problem. This circuit from generation 212 has a fitness of 0.00114 and scores 101 hits. This circuit has three capacitors in parallel with inductors L5 and L31 at the top left end of the circuit. It also has a highly unusual arrangement of components at its right end.

Figure 25.63 shows another 100%-compliant circuit from another run (run F) of genetic programming on this problem. This circuit (from generation 58 of its run) has a fitness of 0.03201. The right part of this circuit has numerous instances of parallel capacitors and series inductors that, when combined, constitute a classical ladder structure. However, the left half of this circuit has a novel topology. The bypassing of capacitor C29 is an example of the kind of anomaly that often appears in genetically evolved structures. Of course, anomalies can sometimes be removed by standard manual or automated editing and simplification methods. Figure 25.64 shows the behavior in the frequency domain of the best circuit from generation 58.

Note that the figures for the frequency domain behavior of the circuits in this book were not created online from the numerical data produced internally by our genetic programming system. Instead, they were all separately created offline using a different SPICE simulator. Specifically, after each circuit is created using our genetic programming system (containing our modified version of the public-domain SPICE3 simulator from the University of California at Berkeley), the circuit is simulated anew offline using the commercially available PSPICE simulator from MicroSim. The PSPICE simulator is based on the original SPICE simulator from the University of California at Berkeley; however, many of PSPICE's algorithms and internal parameter settings are different from those of Berkeley SPICE. In the offline simulation, the netlist produced by the run of genetic programming is submitted to PSPICE, the circuit is simulated by PSPICE, and the results of the PSPICE simulation are examined to verify compliance with the original design goals of the problem.

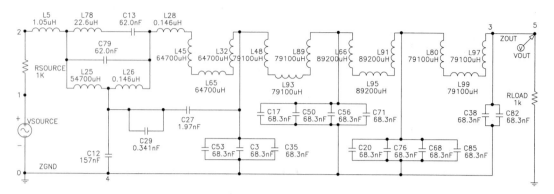

Figure 25.63 Best circuit from generation 58 of run F

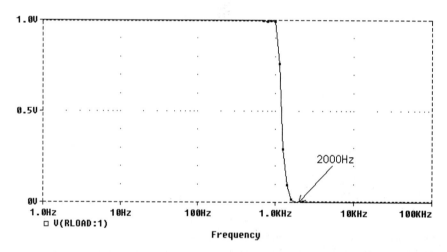

Figure 25.64 Frequency domain behavior of the best circuit from generation 58 of run F

25.16 HARVESTING MULTIPLE SOLUTIONS FROM A RUN

More than one 100%-compliant circuit can be harvested from a single run of genetic programming. This harvesting can be accomplished in two ways.

First, if a run of genetic programming is continued after the emergence of the first 100%-compliant individual, it is common for even more fit 100%-compliant individuals to be created in later generations. These additional solutions sometimes have entirely different topologies and sometimes have different values for the homologous components. For example, when run A (the run that produced the seven-rung ladder of Figure 25.57 in generation 49) was continued beyond generation 49, the best-of-generation circuit from generation 76 achieves a fitness of 0.000995. This new and improved value of fitness is about an order of magnitude better than that of the 100%-compliant individual harvested from generation 49. The new 100%-compliant circuit from generation 76 (Figure 25.65) is a 19-rung ladder.

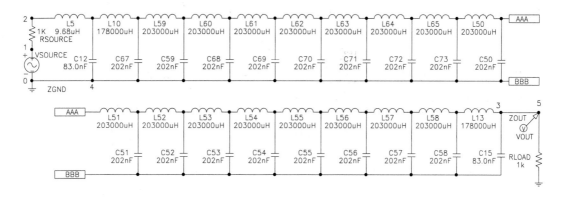

Figure 25.65   Best-of-run 100%-compliant 19-rung ladder circuit from generation 76 of run A

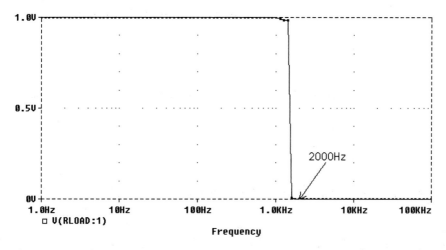

Figure 25.66   Frequency domain behavior of best-of-run 19-rung ladder circuit from generation 76 of run A

Figure 25.66 shows the behavior in the frequency domain of the best-of-run circuit from generation 76. Notice that the drop-off in the transition region is far sharper here than in Figure 25.55d from generation 49.

Second, when a parallel computing system with semi-isolated subpopulations is used for a run of genetic programming, there are often differences between the solutions created on different processing nodes. Thus, several other circuits scoring 101 hits were harvested from this particular run that employed the ladder topology (but with different numbers of rungs and different component values).

By harvesting multiple 100%-compliant circuits from a single run, genetic programming can provide a design engineer with a set of good solutions for a given problem. The various solutions will typically solve the given problem in different ways. Occasionally, a solution may employ a novel construction that would never occur to a human engineer. In any event, the design engineer has the option of selecting from among a multiplicity of solutions (perhaps choosing one that satisfies secondary criteria that were not incorporated into the fitness measure used in the actual run).

25.17 THE MULTIPLE ROLES OF CROSSOVER IN IMPROVING A CIRCUIT

The crossover operation improves the population of circuit-constructing program trees in the following three distinct ways:

- changing component sizing,
- changing circuit topology, and
- operating as a mechanism for reuse.

25.17.1 Crossover as a Mechanism for Changing Component Sizing

The crossover that created the best-of-generation individual of generation 10 of run G of the lowpass filter problem illustrates how the crossover operation can improve the sizing of a component in a circuit.

The two parents that produced the best-of-generation individual of generation 10 were typical of the parents selected to participate in the crossover operation from a population of 30,000 in that they were far from being the best individuals of their generation. In fact, the best-of-generation individual of generation 9 had a fitness of 25.83 and scored 69 hits. On the other hand, the two parents were reasonably good individuals from their generation, and in any event they were considerably better than any individual (including the best) from generation 0 of the run.

The receiving (female) parent came from generation 9 and had a fitness of 33.13 and scored 64 hits. Figure 25.67 shows that this receiving parent consisted of a series of two inductors (L205 and L214) appearing horizontally across the top of the figure and one capacitive shunt C212. Note that the value of inductor L214 is a minuscule and insignificant 0.0997 μH.

The contributing (male) parent came from generation 17 and had a fitness of 35.05 and scored 63 hits (out of 101). Figure 25.68 shows that this contributing parent was a one-rung ladder consisting of one 83,700 μH inductor L105 and one vertical capacitive shunt C112.

The contributing (male) parent has the topology of a second-order Butterworth filter (Section 37.1.1). The topology of the receiving (female) parent has the topology of a third-order Butterworth filter since the receiving parent has a series of two inductors (L205 and L214) horizontally across the top of the figure (along with a capacitive shunt C212 to ground). Although the minuscule inductor L214 of the receiving parent (Figure 25.67) has very little impact on this circuit's actual behavior, its presence gives this circuit a superior topology to that of the contributing parent (Figure 25.68). In other words, the receiving (female) parent has good topology, but bad sizing (the component value of L214).

The offspring produced in generation 10 by the crossover of the above two parents is a significant improvement over both of its parents. The offspring has a fitness of 21.36 and scores 76 hits. The offspring's fitness is a substantial improvement (reduction) over the fitness of its male and female parents (35.05 and 33.13, respectively). The offspring's number of hits is also a substantial improvement over the number of hits of the two parents (63 and 64 hits, respectively). Moreover, 21.36 is considerably better than the fitness (25.83) of the best-of-generation individual from the parents' generation (9).

Figure 25.69 shows that this offspring consists of a series of two inductors (L205 and L105) and one vertical capacitive shunt C212). The one component numbered in the 100s (the 83,700 µH inductor L105) is created by circuit-constructing functions from the crossover fragment of the contributing parent. The two components numbered in the 200s (L205 and C212) are created by circuit-constructing functions from the remainder of the receiving parent. The 83,700 µH inductor L105 from the contributing parent replaced the minuscule 0.0997 µH inductor L214 of the receiving parent. The topology of the offspring is identical to that of its receiving (female) parent; however, the sizing of the inductor has been drastically changed (and improved) as a result of the crossover with the contributing (male) parent.

Figures 25.70a, 25.70b, and 25.70c show the frequency domain behavior of the contributing parent, the receiving parent, and the offspring, respectively. The vertical axis represents output voltage on a linear scale. As can be seen, the offspring in generation 10 has a somewhat more rapid roll-off than either of its parents from generation 9. The improved behavior of the offspring in generation 10 is a consequence of the change in sizing of inductor L105.

The improvement of the offspring in generation 10 over its two parents from generation 9 is more clearly depicted by Figure 25.71. In this figure, the vertical axis represents attenuation in decibels (i.e., on a logarithmic scale). As can be seen, the offspring produces much greater (i.e., more negative) attenuation above 1,000 Hz than either of its two parents (i.e., the offspring produces a larger negative number on the decibel scale at all frequencies above 1,000 Hz). The offspring is a big improvement over its parents.

We now examine the circuit-constructing program trees of the two parents and the offspring to see how the crossover operation brings the one component numbered in the 100s (inductor L105) together with the two components numbered in the 200s in the offspring (L205 and C212).

In the crossover operation of interest, the crossover point of the receiving parent is in its first result-producing branch; the crossover point of the contributing parent is in its second result-producing branch.

The first result-producing branch of the receiving parent from generation 9 has 24 points. This branch is the source of the remainder for the crossover of interest. The remainder is underlined below and consists of all except one point (an END function):

```
(L 0.478299 (C (- (- 0.444189 -0.774646) (+ -0.7498
-0.580390)) (PARALLEL0 CUT END (SERIES END END (L (- (-
-0.569258 -0.179734) 0.611633) END)) END))).
```

The second result-producing branch of the receiving parent from generation 9 has 61 points. This branch of the receiving parent is not changed by the crossover of interest and becomes the second result-producing branch of the offspring. It is shown here for completeness:

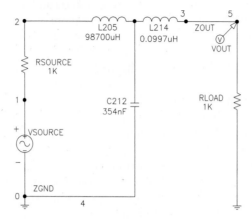

Figure 25.67   Receiving (female) parent from generation 9 of run G

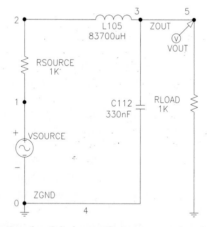

Figure 25.68   Contributing (male) parent from generation 9 of run G

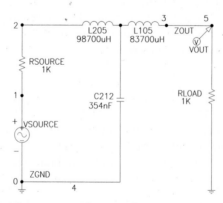

Figure 25.69   Offspring from generation 10 of run G

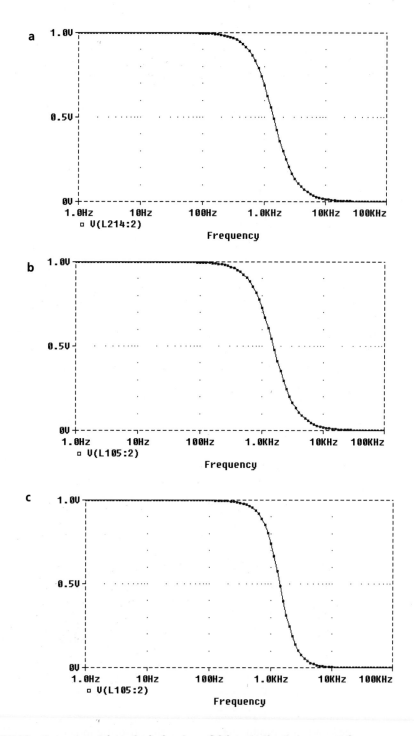

Figure 25.70   Frequency domain behavior of (*a*) contributing parent from generation 9, (*b*) receiving parent from generation 9, and (*c*) offspring from generation 10 of run G

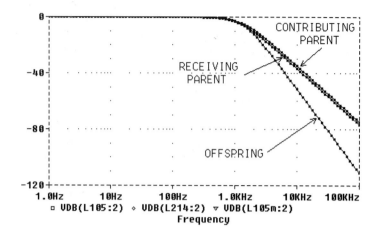

Figure 25.71 Frequency domain behavior of the two parents from generation 9 and the offspring from generation 10 of run G

```
(L (+ (+ (- (+ (+ (+ (- 0.827789 -0.754247) 0.000000)
-0.640660) (- (+ (+ (+ (- 0.827789 -0.754247) 0.000000)
-0.774646) (- 0.539290 -0.715978)) -0.569258)) (- 0.449309
-0.715978)) -0.179734) (+ 0.168843 (- (+ (- (+ (+ (+
(- 0.827789 -0.754247) 0.000000) -0.640660) (- (+ (+ (+
(- 0.827789 -0.754247) 0.000000) -0.774646) (- 0.539290
-0.715978)) -0.569258)) (- 0.449309 -0.715978)) -0.179734)
-0.369041))) END).
```

The first result-producing branch of the contributing parent from generation 9 has 19 points. This branch of the contributing parent is not used by the crossover operation of interest, but is shown here for completeness:

```
(NOP (PARALLEL0 CUT (C 0.900357 (C (- (- 0.994883 -0.553163) -
0.668930) (FLIP (PARALLEL0 END END END END)))) END END)).
```

The second result-producing branch of the contributing parent from generation 9 has 50 points. All except one point of this branch (the NOP function at the root) is the crossover fragment for the crossover of interest. The 49-point crossover fragment is shown in bold:

```
(NOP (C 0.994883 (L (+ (+ (+ 0.892785 (- (- 0.666146 -0.627331)
(- 0.541529 -0.281568))) (- (+ (+ 0.298456 0.828372) (+
-0.666898 -0.702825)) (- (- -0.225407 0.828372) (- -0.375366
-0.427176)))) (- (- (+ (+ 0.994883 0.900357) -0.986587)
(+ 0.611633 -0.754247)) (- 0.059892 (- (+ -0.224230 0.805176)
(+ -0.369041 -0.755410))))) END))).
```

The first result-producing branch of the offspring in generation 10 has 72 points. This branch is created by a crossover in which 49 of the 50 points of the second result-

producing branch of the contributing parent from generation 9 (i.e., the crossover fragment shown above in bold) is inserted into the underlined portion of the first result-
producing branch of the receiving parent from generation 9 (i.e., the remainder shown
with underlining). The inserted crossover fragment is inserted at the point of insertion
(i.e., the root of the one-point subtree consisting of the END function) of the receiving
parent. The inserted crossover fragment replaces the subtree rooted at the point of insertion (i.e., the one-point subtree consisting of the END function).

```
(L 0.478299 (C (- (- 0.444189 -0.774646) (+ -0.749839
-0.580390)) (PARALLEL0 CUT END (SERIES (C 0.994883 (L (+ (+ (+
0.892785 (- (- 0.666146 -0.627331) (- 0.541529 -0.281568)))
(- (+ (+ 0.298456 0.828372) (+ -0.666898 -0.702825)) (- (-
-0.225407 0.828372) (- -0.375366 -0.427176)))) (- (- (+ (+
0.994883 0.900357) -0.986587) (+ 0.611633 -0.754247)) (-
0.059892 (- (+ -0.224230 0.805176) (+ -0.369041 -0.755410)))))))
END)) END (L (- (- -0.569258 -0.179734) 0.611633) END)) END))).
```

As previously mentioned, the second result-producing branch of the receiving parent
is unaffected by the crossover and becomes the second result-producing branch of the
offspring.

Thus, we have seen how crossover can improve the sizing of a circuit.

25.17.2   Crossover as a Mechanism for Changing Circuit Topology

The crossover that created the best-of-generation individual of generation 18 of run G of
the lowpass filter problem illustrates how the crossover operation can improve the topology of a circuit.

The two parents that produced the best-of-generation individual of generation 18
were not the best individuals of generation 17 (where the best-of-generation individual
had a fitness of 5.99).

The contributing (male) parent came from generation 17 and had a fitness of 12.20
and scored 85 hits (out of 101). To put these values in perspective, the best value of fitness in the blind random search of 1,920,000 individuals (64 runs of 30,000) for this
problem (Section 54.2) is 90.5, and the best number of hits in this blind random search
is 72. Thus, this parent from generation 17 is considerably better than any individual
found in generation 0 of the 64 runs involving the 1,920,000 individuals (and, of course,
better than any individual found in generation 0 of its own run). Figure 25.72 shows that
this contributing parent was a two-rung ladder circuit consisting of a series of two inductors (L105 and L111) and two vertical shunts (C112 and C103). That is, the contributing parent has the topology of a fourth-order Butterworth filter (Section 37.1.1).

The receiving (female) parent came from generation 17 and had a fitness of 12.22 and
scored 77 hits. Figure 25.73 shows that this receiving parent consisted of a series of two
inductors (L225 and L212) appearing horizontally across the top of the figure, two
capacitive shunts (C226 and C213), and one inductive-capacitive shunt consisting of
inductor L210 and capacitor C211.

The offspring produced in generation 18 by the crossover of the above two parents is
a significant improvement over both of its parents. The offspring has a fitness of 3.143
and scores 95 hits. The offspring's fitness is a substantial improvement (reduction) over

the fitness of its male and female parents (12.20 and 12.22, respectively). The offspring's number of hits is also a substantial improvement over the number of hits for the two parents (85 and 77 hits, respectively). Moreover, 3.143 is considerably better than the fitness (5.99) of the best-of-generation individual from the parents' generation (17).

Figure 25.74 shows that this offspring consists of a series of three inductors (**L225**, **L212**, and **L111**) and four vertical shunts (**C226**, **C213**, **C112**, and **C103**). The three components numbered in the 100s (**C112**, **L111**, and **C103** in the right portion of the figure) are created by the circuit-constructing functions from the crossover fragment of the contributing parent. The four components numbered in the 200s (**L225**, **L212**, **C226**, and **C213** in the left portion of the figure) are created by the circuit-constructing functions from the remainder of the receiving parent.

Figures 25.75a, 25.75b, and 25.75c show the frequency domain behavior of the contributing parent, the receiving parent, and the offspring, respectively. The vertical axis represents voltage on a linear scale. As can be seen, the offspring in generation 18 is an improvement over both of its parents.

The improvement of the offspring in generation 18 over its two parents from generation 17 is more clearly depicted by Figure 25.76. The vertical axis represents attenuation in decibels (i.e., on a logarithmic scale). As can be seen, the offspring produces much greater attenuation above 1,000 Hz than either of its two parents (i.e., the offspring produces a larger negative number on the decibel scale for all frequencies above 1,000 Hz).

We now examine the circuit-constructing program trees of the two parents and the offspring to see how the crossover operation brings the three components numbered in the 100s in the offspring (**C112**, **L111**, and **C103** of Figure 25.74) together with the four components numbered in the 200s in the offspring (**L225**, **L212**, **C226**, and **C213** of Figure 25.74).

In the crossover operation of interest, the crossover point of both parents happens to be in their first result-producing branches.

The first result-producing branch of the receiving parent from generation 17 has 60 points. This branch is the source of the remainder for the crossover of interest. The remainder is underlined below:

```
(C (+ (- (+ 0.721217 (+ (- 0.549634 0.946380) 0.629899)) (+ (-
(+ -0.668930 0.168843) (+ -0.754247 -0.569258)) (+ (+ 0.016991
0.478232) (- -0.702825 0.298456)))) (- 0.737948 (- (- (+
0.611633 0.994883) (+ 0.507170 0.752239)) (+ 0.507170
0.312889)))) (SERIES (TWO_VIA5 END (PARALLEL0 END END END END)
END) (L 0.098189 (L 0.737948 (NOP END))) (PARALLEL0 END END END
(NOP (NOP END))))).
```

The second result-producing branch of the receiving parent from generation 17 has 186 points. This branch of the receiving parent is not changed by the crossover of interest and becomes the second result-producing branch of the offspring. It is shown here for completeness:

```
(NOP (TWO_GROUND END (C 0.994883 (L (+ (+ (+ 0.892785 (-
(- 0.666146 -0.627331) (- (+ (- 0.549634 0.468420) 0.629899)
-0.281568))) (- (+ (+ 0.298456 0.828372) (+ -0.666898
-0.702825)) (- (- -0.225407 0.828372) (- -0.375366
```

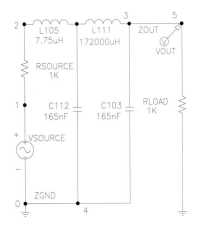

Figure 25.72   Contributing (male) parent from generation 17 of run G

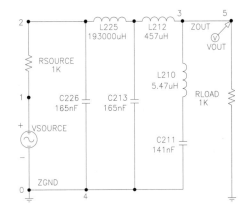

Figure 25.73   Receiving (female) parent from generation 17 of run G

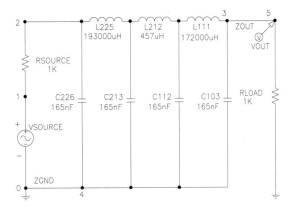

Figure 25.74   Offspring from generation 18 of run G

```
-0.427176)))) (- (- (+ -0.197980 -0.986587) (+ 0.611633
-0.754247)) (- 0.059892 (- (+ -0.224230 0.805176) (+ -0.369041
-0.755410))))) END)) (C 0.411444 (C (- (- 0.994883 -0.553163)
-0.668930) (FLIP (PARALLEL0 END END END (SERIES (NOP (C
0.539290 (L (- (+ (- (+ (- -0.160969 0.666146) (+ -0.702825
0.721217)) (+ (+ -0.986159 -0.837154) (- 0.886660 0.498312)))
(- (+ (+ -0.174744 0.500782) (- 0.835152 -0.627331)) (+ (-
-0.197206 0.994883) (+ -0.427176 -0.959580)))) 0.059892)
END))) END (L (+ (- (- (- (- (- (+ -0.754247 0.835152)
(- 0.257694 -0.427176)) (+ (+ 0.449309 -0.369041) (+ 0.611633
0.185220))) (- (- (- -0.976637 0.947680) (+ (- (- 0.444189
-0.774646) (+ -0.749839 -0.580390)) 0.512571)) (+ (+ 0.507170
0.855712) (+ -0.224230 0.444189)))) (- (+ (+ (- -0.179734
-0.640660) (- -0.788463 -0.627331)) (- (+ 0.500782 0.500782)
```

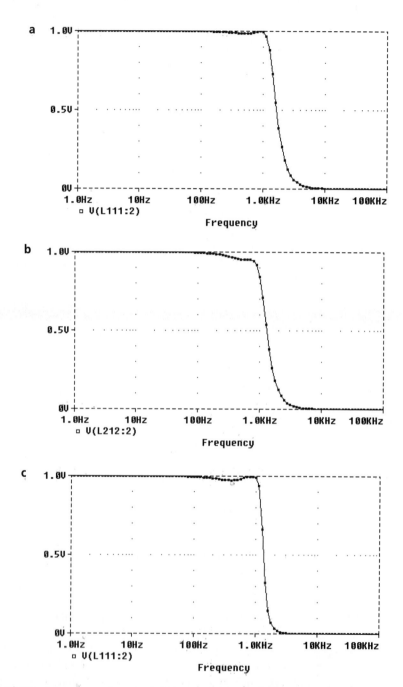

Figure 25.75 Frequency domain behavior of (a) contributing parent from generation 17, (b) receiving parent from generation 17, and (c) offspring from generation 18 of run G

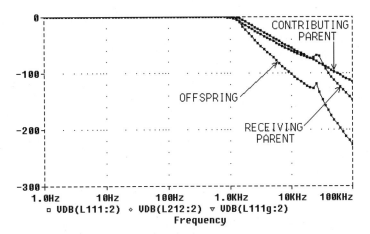

Figure 25.76   Frequency domain behavior of the two parents from generation 17 and the offspring from generation 18 of run G

```
(- 0.449309 -0.263866))) (- (- (+ -0.627331 0.312889) (-
-0.347332 0.044719)) (- (- -0.837154 0.946380) 0.666146)))) (+
0.500782 0.478232)) -0.627331) (NOP (SERIES END END
END)))))))))).
```

The first result-producing branch of the contributing parent from generation 17 has 69 points. The crossover fragment for the crossover of interest (shown later in this book as Figure 56.7) consists of the entirety of this branch. This crossover fragment is shown in bold:

**(FLIP (FLIP (C 0.411444 (C (- (- 0.994883 -0.553163) -0.668930)
(FLIP (PARALLEL0 END END END (L (- (- (- (- (+ 0.947680
0.500782) (- -0.224230 -0.427176)) (+ (+ (- -0.179734 -0.640660)
(- -0.788463 -0.627331)) (- (+ 0.500782 0.500782) (- 0.449309
-0.263866)))) (+ (+ (+ -0.217665 -0.553163) (+ 0.669445 -
0.746141)) (- (+ 0.312889 0.189004) (+ 0.428589 0.629899)))) (-
-0.986159 (- (+ 0.507170 0.752239) -0.627331))) (FLIP (SERIES
END END (NOP END))))))))))).**

The second result-producing branch of the contributing parent from generation 17 has 152 points. This branch of the contributing parent is not used by the crossover operation of interest, but is shown here for completeness:

```
(L (- (- (- (+ (- (+ (- (+ 0.629899 -0.746141) (- 0.428589
0.189004)) (- (+ -0.837154 0.428589) (+ -0.986159 0.721217)))
(- (- (+ 0.666146 -0.788463) (- -0.969031 -0.567546)) (+
0.947680 (- -0.774646 (- 0.208993 0.298456))))) (- (- (- (+
0.947680 0.500782) (- -0.224230 -0.427176)) (+ -0.754247
-0.569258)) (+ (+ (+ -0.217665 -0.553163) (+ 0.669445
-0.746141)) (- (+ 0.312889 0.189004) (+ 0.428589 0.629899)))))
```

```
(- (+ (- (- (- -0.197980 0.298456) (- -0.553163 0.213009)) (+
(+ -0.781101 -0.755410) (+ 0.946380 0.649394))) (- (- (+
(- 0.827789 -0.754247) (+ (- (- 0.444189 -0.774646) (+ -
0.749839
-0.580390)) (+ 0.666146 0.855712))) (+ 0.835152 0.189004)) (-
(- 0.737948 (- 0.994883 (+ (+ -0.788463 0.498312) (+ -0.349945
0.855712)))) (+ 0.189004 -0.640660)))) (- (+ (- (+ 0.578057
-0.886602) (- -0.442093 -0.347332)) (- (+ -0.281568 0.500782)
(+ -0.754247 -0.369041))) (+ (+ (- -0.263866 -0.347332) (-
-0.749839 0.549634)) (+ (+ -0.715978 (+ 0.611633 -0.754247))
(+ 0.892785 -0.451277)))))) 0.044719) 0.855712) (NOP END)).
```

The first result-producing branch of the offspring in generation 18 has 107 points. This branch is created by a crossover in which the entirety of the 69-point first result-producing branch of the contributing parent from generation 17 (i.e., the crossover fragment shown above in bold) is inserted into the underlined portion of the first result-producing branch of the receiving parent from generation 17 (i.e., the remainder shown with underlining). Notice that the final parenthesis of this offspring comes from the remainder.

```
(C (+ (- (+ 0.721217 (+ (- 0.549634 0.946380) 0.629899)) (+ (-
(+ -0.668930 0.168843) (+ -0.754247 -0.569258)) (+ (+ 0.016991
0.478232) (- -0.702825 0.298456)))) (- 0.737948 (- (- (+
0.611633 0.994883) (+ 0.507170 0.752239)) (+ 0.507170
0.312889)))) (FLIP (FLIP (CAP 0.411444 (CAP (- (- 0.994883
-0.553163) -0.668930) (FLIP (PARALLEL0 END END END (L (- (- (-
(- (+ 0.947680 0.500782) (- -0.224230 -0.427176)) (+ (+ (-
-0.179734 -0.640660) (- -0.788463 -0.627331)) (- (+ 0.500782
0.500782) (- 0.449309 -0.263866)))) (+ (+ (+ -0.217665
-0.553163) (+ 0.669445 -0.746141)) (- (+ 0.312889 0.189004) (+
0.428589 0.629899)))) (- -0.986159 (- (+ 0.507170 0.752239)
-0.627331))) (FLIP (SERIES END END (NOP END)))))))))))).
```

As previously mentioned, the second result-producing branch of the receiving parent is unaffected by the crossover and becomes the second result-producing branch of the offspring.

Thus, we have seen how the crossover operation can improve the topology of a circuit.

25.17.3 Crossover as a Mechanism for Reuse

Practitioners of genetic algorithms and genetic programming usually (and correctly) view the crossover operation as a mechanism for creating new individuals. The automatically defined functions of general programming are usually (and correctly) viewed as a mechanism for reuse.

The basic crossover operation can also serve as an important mechanism for reuse in genetic programming. This distinct and important additional role of the crossover operation is usually not evident in "toy" problems that lack modularity, symmetry, and regularity.

Recall that 17 of the 19 rungs in Figure 25.65 are identical (each consisting of a 203,000 µH inductor and a 201 nF capacitor). Recall also that four of the seven rungs of the best-of-generation circuit from generation 49 (Figure 25.57) were identical (each consisting of a 209,000 µH inductor and a 202 nF capacitor). It is well known that, if you start with a reasonably good ladder filter, it is sometimes possible to improve the circuit by replicating one of the existing rungs (thereby extending the ladder). Adding rungs to a ladder often makes a filter's frequency response steeper in the transition band. The observed repetition of rungs in the two ladders here reflects the application of this principle.

This observed repetition of rungs is a consequence of the crossover operation operating on the population of circuit-constructing program trees. In the crossover operation, individuals with relatively good fitness are more likely to be selected to participate in the crossover than their less fit cohorts in the population. The crossover operation takes a subtree from one good circuit-constructing program tree and implants it into other good circuit-constructing program tree. Some of the implanted subtrees from already good parents develop into a rung of a ladder. Thus, the crossover operation can lengthen an existing ladder by adding a rung. The addition of a rung (from an already good circuit) often makes the offspring produced by the crossover operation more fit than either of its parents. Thus, in a problem with inherent modularity, the crossover operation can be a mechanism for reusing fitness-enhancing subtrees. In particular, the crossover operation can increase the number of occurrences of a fitness-enhancing substructure (the rung) and thereby modularly construct a progression of ever-more fit individuals. It should be noted that operations such as the mutation operation do not have this ability to promote the reuse of good substructures. The mutation operation implants a randomly created subtree in a single good individual in the population. It is very unlikely that a freshly created random subtree will create (much less replicate) a fitness-enhancing rung of a ladder. The role of the basic crossover operation in promoting the reuse of good substructures is further discussed in Chapter 56.

25.18 IMPLEMENTATION DETAILS FOR THE FITNESS MEASURE

This section contains implementation details concerning the calculation of fitness for problems of circuit synthesis, including

- an example of how the fitness measure is coded in the C programming language for the lowpass filter problem,
- implementation details on the simplification of netlists,
- implementation details on how to optimize the netlist and how to identify in advance certain circuits that cannot be simulated by SPICE, and
- a brief description of the changes that were made in Berkeley SPICE3 to embed it in our genetic programming system.

25.18.1 C Code for the Fitness Measure

The following code illustrates how the above fitness measure might be coded in the C programming language.

```
fitness = 0.0;
hits = 0;
for (i = 0;i<number_of_fitness_cases;i++)
{
  deviation = fabs(observed_value[i] - desired_value[i]);
  switch (type_of_fitness_case[i])
  {
  case CONCERNED_ONLY_ABOUT_LOWER_BOUND:
    if (observed_value[i] < desired_value[i])
    if (deviation < allowable_deviation[i])
    {
      fitness += compliant_weight[i] * deviation;
      hits++;
    } else fitness += non_compliant_weight[i] * deviation;
    else hits++;
    break;
  case CONCERNED_ONLY_ABOUT_UPPER_BOUND:
    if (observed_value[i] > desired_value[i])
      if (deviation < allowable_deviation[i])
      {
        fitness += compliant_weight[i] * deviation;
        hits++;
      } else fitness += non_compliant_weight[i]*deviation;
    else hits++;
    break;
  case CONCERNED_ABOUT_DEVIATIONS_IN_BOTH_DIRECTIONS:
    if (deviation < allowable_deviation[i])
    {
      fitness += compliant_weight[i] * deviation;
      hits++;
    }
    else fitness += non_compliant_weight[i]*deviation;
    break;
  case DONT_CARE:
    hits++;
    break;
  }
}
```

The code begins by initializing the standardized fitness, called fitness, and the number of hits, called hits, to zero. The code iterates over the fitness cases in a loop indexed by i. The deviation, called deviation, is the absolute value of the difference between the observed value of a certain quantity (voltage here) at the designated probe point in the circuit and the desired value. The fitness cases are organized into the following four types:

1. "CONCERNED_ONLY_ABOUT_LOWER_BOUND" is the case where you want the observed_value to be above a certain lower bound (e.g., the passband between 1 Hz and 1,000 Hz of this problem).

2. "CONCERNED_ONLY_ABOUT_UPPER_BOUND" is the case where you want the observed_value to be below a certain upper bound (e.g., the stopband above 2,000 Hz in this problem).

3. "CONCERNED_ABOUT_DEVIATIONS_IN_BOTH_DIRECTIONS" is the case where you want the observed_value to be in a range around some ideal central value (as is the case for the passband in the problem described in Chapter 31).

4. "DONT_CARE" is the case where the observed_value does not matter (as is the case for the five points above 1,000 Hz and below 2,000 Hz).

For this problem, we are "CONCERNED_ONLY_ABOUT_LOWER_BOUND" for the 61 points in the three-decade passband from 1 Hz to 1,000 Hz. For these 61 fitness cases, if the observed_value is less than the desired_value (1,000 millivolts) and the deviation is less than the allowable_deviation (30 millivolts here), then fitness is incremented by the deviation times the compliant_weight (1.0) and hits is incremented. If the deviation is not less than the allowable_deviation, then fitness is incremented by the deviation times non_compliant_weight (10.0) and hits is not incremented. If the observed_value is not less than the desired_value, then hits is incremented, but there is no increment to fitness.

We are "CONCERNED_ONLY_ABOUT_UPPER_BOUND" for this problem for the 35 points in the stopband from 2,000 Hz to 100,000 Hz. The desired_value is 0.0 for this problem, the compliant_weight is 1.0, and the non_compliant_weight is 10.0.

There are five fitness cases above 1,000 Hz and below 2,000 Hz for which we "DONT_CARE" and for which hits is unconditionally incremented.

There are no fitness cases for this particular problem for which we are "CONCERNED_ABOUT_DEVIATIONS_IN_BOTH_DIRECTIONS." This feature is illustrated in Section 31.2.4.

25.18.2   Simplification of Netlists

The NETLIST is simplified in five ways in order to create a SIMPLIFIED NETLIST. The typical procedure is as follows:

1. All wires are removed, and the two nodes at each end of each wire are merged into a single node.

2. A very large resistance (a 1-gigaohm resistor named **RHUGE**) is inserted between ground and any node for which there is no DC path to ground (e.g., a path to ground that does not go through a capacitor). The introduction of a very large resistance between such a node and ground has no significant electrical effect; however, it is essential for enabling SPICE to simulate the circuit.

3. The netlist is simplified to accelerate the SPICE simulation. The time required for a SPICE simulation generally increases nonlinearly as a function of the number of nodes in the netlist (in an approximately subquadratic to quartic way, depending on the type of circuit). Thus, it is highly advantageous to shorten the netlist provided to SPICE. All series and parallel compositions of like passive components are consolidated and replaced, for purposes of the simulation only, by a single component of appropriate value. For example, two resistors R1 and R2 in series are consolidated and replaced by a single resistor whose value is the sum of the two resistances; two resistors in parallel are replaced by a single resistor whose value is the reciprocal of the sum of the reciprocal of the two resistances. Similarly, two capacitors in parallel are consolidated in the same manner as two resistors in series; two capacitors in series are consolidated in the same manner as two resistors in parallel. Inductors are consolidated in the same manner as resistors. Note that this consolidation and replacement is for the purpose of simulation only. No change is made in the actual circuit-constructing program tree residing in the population.

4. All dangling components (i.e., components that are connected to a node of degree one) are removed. This step is repeated until no dangling components remain.

5. Any isolated substructures (i.e., substructures that are not connected to the test fixture) are removed.

25.18.3   Netlist Optimizations

A considerable amount of computer time can be saved by advance identification of certain circuits that cannot be simulated by SPICE.

Note that some of the characteristics below cannot occur for certain types of problems and some apply only when certain functions are present in the function set. Moreover, some of the simplifications described in the previous subsection may obviate the need for some of the optimization below.

If the netlist of a circuit has any of the following pathological characteristics, it is not passed along to SPICE for simulation, but instead is immediately assigned the high penalty value of fitness:

- The circuit contains a voltage source with both leads connected to the same node.
- The circuit contains an inductor with both leads connected to the same node.

If any of the following types of errors occur during the SPICE simulation, the simulation is stopped, and the circuit is assigned the high penalty value of fitness:

- The number of memory allocation requests exceeds a preestablished upper limit (e.g., 2,000 requests).
- The amount of memory allocated exceeds a preestablished upper limit (e.g., 300 kilobytes). This limit indirectly acts as a time limit on the simulation.
- A floating-point error (e.g., division by zero, underflow, overflow) occurs. For example, during the simulation of the behavior of transistors, a floating-point overflow will sometimes occur. During the probe output setup, divisions by zero sometimes occur.

- A null (invalid) pointer appears in one of the matrix routines.
- An attempt is made to free a block of memory that has not previously been allocated.

25.18.4 Modifications Required to Import the SPICE Simulator into the Genetic Programming System

The Berkeley SPICE3 simulator consists of about 217,000 lines of C source code residing in 878 separate files occupying about 6.1 megabytes of storage.

A number of modifications are required in order to embed a complex simulator into a genetic programming system. These modifications relate to the following issues:

- changing from batch-oriented to serially reusable code,
- changing the source of the input to the simulation (the netlist),
- changing the destination of the output of the simulation,
- handling nonconvergent cases,
- removing unnecessary system overhead, and
- changing the handling of errors that the simulator was already capable of recognizing in advance and trapping and, most importantly, that the simulator was not previously capable of recognizing in advance and trapping.

The Berkeley SPICE3 simulator was originally a batch-oriented system. In order to embed this simulator in our genetic programming system, it was necessary to make it an invokable submodule of our system. This entailed making the simulator serially reusable by adding code to initialize variables that were noninitialized global variables in the Berkeley SPICE version.

The Berkeley SPICE3 simulator originally accepted input in the form of text files. We changed this so that the circuit netlist was passed to the simulator as a parameter. Similarly, the Berkeley SPICE3 simulator originally deposited its output into an output file or displayed it on a video screen. We changed this so that all output was passed directly to the genetic programming system.

Nonconvergence can be a problem in complex simulators such as SPICE (Kielkowski 1994). We changed the simulator so that the simulation is terminated when an inordinate amount of computational resources (as measured by both time and memory usage) is being consumed on the simulation of any one circuit. A special error code is then returned to the genetic programming system (which then assigns a penalty value of fitness to the nonconverging circuit). This change entailed implementing our own memory manager (on top of the standard C memory manager) so that we could control the amount of memory requested and used by SPICE.

The Berkeley SPICE3 simulator contains numerous time-consuming system calls that are not necessary when the simulator is operating as a submodule of a genetic programming system.

A run of genetic programming presents issues that are very different from those encountered when a human engineer uses a complex simulator. For one thing, a human engineer generally does not present a simulator with the kind of pathological circuits that are routinely created by a run of genetic programming. Also, an engineer will typically present only a handful of circuits to a simulator during a day or week. A 1-in-1,000 chance of a simulator crash would be almost unnoticeable to a practicing engineer. In contrast, a single run of genetic programming may entail the simulation of tens of millions of circuits (as shown in Table 61.1), so even a small probability of a crash is unacceptable inside the genetic programming system.

The most important changes required in embedding any complex simulator into a run of genetic programming are to ensure that every possible error is captured so that the overall process never halts. The changes concerning error handling fall into two categories.

First, the SPICE simulator was written to halt upon detection of certain error conditions during a simulation. We modified the simulator so that it never halts, but instead returns a special error code to the genetic programming system. This approach enables the genetic programming system to assign a penalty value of fitness to the unsimulatable circuit and then to proceed with the run.

Second, the SPICE simulator crashes when it encounters certain error conditions. As we discovered each such unrecoverable error condition, we progressively modified the SPICE code so as to detect each impending crash in advance of its occurrence. We modified the simulator so that it never halts, but instead returns a special error code to the genetic programming system. This approach enables the genetic programming system to assign a penalty value of fitness to the unsimulatable circuit. Over a period of time, we progressively lengthened the time between crashes of SPICE. At the time of writing of this book, the last known crash of SPICE occurred about a year ago. Our modified SPICE simulator has simulated about two billion circuits during that one-year period.

Lohn and Colombano (1998) invoked SPICE as an independent process using Unix pipes. This approach greatly simplifies the incorporation of a complex simulator into a genetic programming system (at the expense of increased computer time).

All (or almost all) of the above issues are generic to the task of embedding any complex simulator into a run of genetic programming.

Emergence of Structure from Fitness

The previous chapter demonstrated that a satisfactory design for a lowpass filter can be successfully synthesized using genetic programming. How can genetic programming be used to design other circuits?

This chapter (and succeeding chapters) will demonstrate that very few changes are necessary in order to apply genetic programming to the design of different types of circuits. The requisite information required to initiate a run of genetic programming is specified by the seven major preparatory steps (Figure 25.42). In practice, a surprising variety of circuits can be synthesized merely by changing the fitness measure. Numerous additional circuits can be evolved by changing the parts bin (i.e., adding or subtracting certain component-creating functions from the function set) or changing the test fixture and embryo.

26.1 HIGHPASS FILTER

26.1.1 Design Goals

A highpass filter passes all frequencies above a certain specified frequency, but stops all lower frequencies. Suppose that the design goal is to evolve a highpass filter with a stopband below **1,000 Hz** and a passband above **2,000 Hz**. In particular, the goal is to design a filter where the roles of the passband and stopband are reversed from those of a lowpass filter of the previous chapter. That is, it is acceptable for the output voltage in the passband above 2,000 Hz for the highpass filter to be between 970 millivolts and 1 volt and for the output voltage in the stopband of the highpass filter below 1,000 Hz to be between 0 volts and 1 millivolt.

26.1.2 Preparatory Steps

Six of the seven preparatory steps are the same for this highpass filter as they were for the lowpass filter (Section 25.14). Only the fitness measure is different.

The fitness cases for the highpass filter are the same 101 points in the six decades of frequency between 1 Hz and 1,000,000 Hz as for the lowpass filter (Section 25.14.4).

The procedure for each of the 61 points in the three-decade interval between 1 Hz and 1,000 Hz (the desired stopband of the highpass filter) is as follows:

- If the voltage equals the ideal value of 0.0 volts in this interval, the deviation is 0.0.
- If the voltage is between 0 millivolts and 1 millivolt, the absolute value of the deviation from 0 millivolts is weighted by a factor of 1.0.
- If the voltage is more than 1 millivolt, the absolute value of the deviation from 0 millivolts is weighted by a factor of 10.0.

This arrangement for the desired stopband reflects the fact that the ideal output voltage is 0.0 volts, that a voltage of up to 1 millivolt is acceptable in the stopband, and that a voltage above 1 millivolt is not acceptable.

The procedure for each of the 35 points in the interval from 2,000 Hz to 1,000,000 Hz (the desired passband of the highpass filter) is as follows:

- If the voltage equals the ideal value of 1.0 volt in this interval, the deviation is 0.0.
- If the voltage is between 970 millivolts and 1,000 millivolts, the absolute value of the deviation from 1,000 millivolts is weighted by a factor of 1.0.
- If the voltage is less than 970 millivolts, the absolute value of the deviation from 1,000 millivolts is weighted by a factor of 10.0.

This arrangement for the desired passband reflects the fact that the ideal output voltage is 1.0 volt, that a shortfall of up to 30 millivolts is acceptable in the passband, and that a voltage below 970 millivolts is unacceptable.

26.1.3 Results

We made two runs using the modified fitness measure for a highpass filter. Both runs yielded 100%-compliant highpass filter circuits. Run A yielded a recognizable circuit topology that is well known to electrical engineers. Run B yielded a novel topology.

Run A

In one run (run A), the best-of-run circuit from generation 27 (Figure 26.1) has a fitness of 0.213 and scores 101 hits. This circuit has four capacitors and five inductors (in addition to the fixed components of the initial circuit). The two result-producing branches of the program tree have 260 and 246 points.

Figure 26.2 shows the behavior in the frequency domain of the best-of-run circuit from generation 27 of run A. The horizontal axis ranges from 1 Hz to 1 MHz on a logarithmic scale. The vertical axis presents peak voltage and ranges from 0 to 1 volt on a linear scale. As can be seen, the 100%-compliant highpass filter delivers a voltage of essentially 0 volts in the entire stopband from 1 Hz to 1,000 Hz and essentially 1 volt in the entire passband above 1,000 Hz. There is a sharp rise from 0 volts to 1 volt in the transitional ("don't care") region between 1,000 Hz and 2,000 Hz.

The best-of-run circuit from generation 27 (Figure 26.1) has a ladder topology (Williams and Taylor 1995) consisting of repeated instances of capacitors in series horizontally across the top of the figure (C33, C5, C10, and C19) and repeated instances of inductors (L23, L12, L3, and L21) appearing on the vertical shunts to ground. In contrast, in the previously seen ladders for lowpass filters (e.g., the seven-rung ladder low-

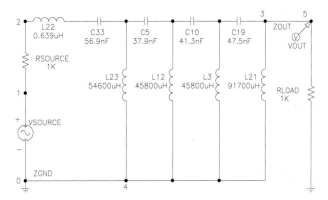

Figure 26.1   Four-rung ladder highpass filter from generation 27 of run A

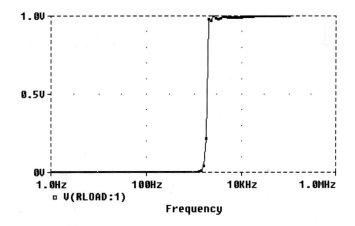

Figure 26.2   Frequency domain behavior of best-of-run 4-rung ladder filter from generation 27 of run A

pass filter of Figure 25.57), the inductors ran horizontally across the top of the figure, while the capacitors appeared on the vertical shunts. Why have the inductors and capacitors exchanged locations within the ladder of these evolved highpass and lowpass filters?

This reversal of roles for the capacitors and inductors in lowpass and highpass ladder filters is well known to electrical engineers and is the consequence of the duality of the single terms (derivatives versus integrals) in the integro-differential equations that represent the voltages and currents of the inductors and capacitors in the loops and nodes of a circuit. Note that genetic programming was not given any domain knowledge concerning this duality. In the problem of synthesizing a highpass filter, genetic programming searched the very same space as it did for the lowpass filter problem (i.e., the space of circuit-constructing program trees composed from the same function set and terminal set). The fitness measure was the only difference between the preparatory steps for the highpass filter (immediately above) and for the lowpass filter (Chapter 25). Using the fitness measure appropriate for highpass filters, genetic programming evolved a 100%-compliant highpass filter embodying the appropriate highpass ladder topology (with the roles of the capacitors and inductors exchanged).

The evolved highpass filter circuit of Figure 26.1 has all the elements of claim 2 of U.S. patent 1,227,113 (Campbell 1917a), as discussed in detail in Section 25.15.1. In particular, this evolved circuit matches Figure 6 of Campbell's 1917 patent. But for the fact that this patent has long since expired, this evolved circuit would infringe Campbell's patent.

A Novel Topology from Run B

As previously mentioned, genetic programming often produces unconventional solutions to problems. In another run (run B) of this same problem, the best-of-generation circuit from generation 28 (Figure 26.3) has a fitness of 0.156 and scores 101 hits. The two result-producing branches of the program tree have 222 and 289 points. This circuit has six capacitors and four inductors (in addition to the fixed components of the initial circuit).

The parts count (10) of this circuit from generation 28 of run B compares favorably to the parts count of 9 (four capacitors and five inductors) for the best-of-run circuit from run A. The fitness (0.156) of this circuit from generation 28 of run B also compares favorably to the fitness (0.213) for the best-of-run circuit from run A. Figure 26.4 shows the frequency domain behavior of the evolved highpass filter from generation 28 from run B.

An *M*-Derived Half Section from Run B

Later in run B, the best-of-generation circuit from generation 30 (Figure 26.5) has a fitness of 0.0475 and scores 101 hits. This fitness is about an order of magnitude better than that of the best-of-run circuit from run A and the best-of-generation circuit from generation 28 from run B. The two result-producing branches of the program tree have 290 and 198 points. This circuit has five capacitors and five inductors (in addition to the fixed components of the initial circuit). Figure 26.6 shows the frequency domain behavior of the best-of-generation circuit from generation 30 of run B.

Figure 26.5 can be simplified without noticeably affecting its behavior by replacing the tiny 0.31 µH inductor L36 with a wire. Since the capacitance of a composition of two parallel capacitors equals the sum of the two individual capacitances, the figure can be further simplified (without changing its behavior at all) by combining the two parallel capacitors C20 and C18 into an equivalent 105.7 nF capacitor. Since the capacitance of two equal capacitors in series is half the capacitance of either of them, Figure 26.5 can be further rearranged (without changing its behavior at all) by replacing the 47.4 nF capacitor C15 with a series composition of two 94.8 nF capacitors and by replacing the 54.4 nF capacitor C10 with a series composition of two 108.8 nF capacitors. If, for sake of argument, we are willing to regard 105.7, 94.8, and 108.8 as being approximately equal and are willing to replace these values by their average (103 nF), the top of the figure can be viewed as five identical 103 nF capacitors in series (one to the left of the first vertical shunt containing L16, two lying between the first and second vertical shunts containing L12, and two lying between the second and third vertical shunts containing L3, C13, and

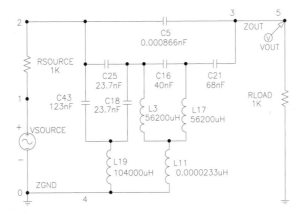

Figure 26.3   Highpass filter from generation 28 of run B

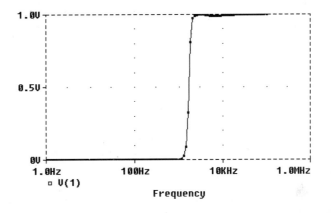

Figure 26.4   Frequency domain behavior of evolved highpass filter from generation 28 from run B

C14). If we were also willing to regard the 53,300 µH inductance of L16 in the first vertical shunt as being approximately equal to the 44,800 µH (the common value for the inductance of L12 in the second vertical shunt and inductors L3 and L14 in the third vertical shunt), we can say that the inductance of the first two vertical inductive shunts are equal and that the inductance of the third shunt (L3 and L14 in series) is equal to twice the inductance of either of the first two vertical inductive shunts.

After the above approximations and simplifications, the evolved highpass filter circuit of Figure 26.5 can be viewed as consisting of a cascade of two identical symmetric T-sections. Each T-section consists of an incoming capacitor of capacitance 2C (where C equals 51.5 nF), a junction point from which an inductor of inductance L (where L equals 44,800 µH) is shunted off to ground, and an outgoing capacitor of identical capacitance 2C. The third and final section of the filter has one incoming capacitor of

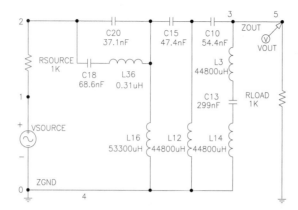

Figure 26.5   Evolved highpass filter from generation 30 of run B

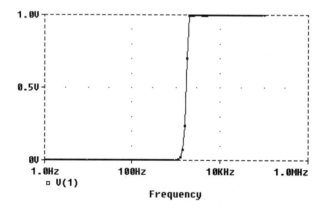

Figure 26.6   Frequency domain behavior of evolved highpass filter from generation 30 of run B

capacitance $2C$ and a junction point from which an inductor of inductance $2L$ is shunted off to ground.

The first two symmetric T-sections are referred to as "constant K" filter sections (Johnson 1950, page 331). Such filter sections are characterized by two key parameters. The first parameter is the section's characteristic resistance (impedance). This characteristic resistance should match the circuit's fixed load resistance (1,000 Ω). The second parameter is the nominal cutoff frequency that separates the filter's passband from its stopband. This second parameter should lie somewhere in the transition region between the end of the stopband (1,000 Hz) and the beginning of the passband (2,000 Hz).

The characteristic resistance, R, of each of each of the two T-sections is given by the formula

$$R = \sqrt{L/C}.$$

When the inductance, L, is 44,800 µH and the capacitance, C, is 51.5 nF, then the characteristic resistance, R, is 933 Ω according to this formula. This value is very close to the value of the fixed load resistance of 1,000 Ω.

The nominal cutoff frequency, f_c, of each of the T-sections of a highpass filter is given by the formula

$$f_c = 1/(4\pi\sqrt{(LC)}).$$

When the inductance, L, is 44,800 µH and the capacitance, C, is 51.5 nF, then the nominal cutoff frequency, f_c, for a highpass filter is 1,657 Hz. This value is roughly in the middle of the transition band for the desired highpass filter. In other words, both of the key parameters of the evolved T-sections of Figure 26.5 are very close to the canonical values of "constant K" sections designed with the aim of satisfying this problem's design requirements. Note that the formula for the characteristic resistance of a highpass filter is the same as that of the corresponding formula for a lowpass filter but that the formula for the nominal cutoff frequency of a highpass filter has a factor of 4 that is not present in the corresponding formula for a lowpass filter.

The third and final section of the evolved circuit closely approximates a section now called an "M-derived half section" (Section 25.15.3). This final section is said to be "derived" because it is derived from the foregoing two identical "constant K" prototype sections. In the derivation, m is a real constant between 0 and 1. Let m be the ratio of the assumed common inductive value in the first two "constant K" sections (44,800 µH) to the inductive value in the final section, so that m is 0.5 here. In a canonical "M-derived half section" that is derived from the above "constant K" prototype section, the series capacitance in the horizontal part of the half section is C/m (which is $2C$ in this instance because $m = 0.5$ here) and the inductance in the vertical shunt of the half section is L/m (which is $2L$ in this instance because $m = 0.5$ here). This is, in fact, the case in Figure 26.5. The value of **C13** in an "M-derived half section" is given by the formula

$$4\,m\,C\,/\,(1-m^2).$$

The actual value of **C13** in Figure 26.5 is about twice what we calculate to be the canonical value (136 nF). The purpose of the "M-derived half section" appended to the two symmetric T-sections is to sharpen the edge of the filter's stopband. In fact, this particular "M-derived half section" introduces almost an order of magnitude of additional attenuation at about 980 Hz (i.e., right at the edge of the stopband). In other words, this "M-derived half section" nails down the edge of the filter's stopband.

Thus, taken as a whole, the topology and component values of Figure 26.5 are reasonably close to the canonical values for the two T-sections and the final "M-derived half section" that is designed with the aim of satisfying this problem's design requirements. Otto Zobel invented filters composed of one or more "constant K" sections appended to an "M-derived half section" and received U.S. patent 1,538,964 for this invention. Viewed as a whole, the differences between the teachings of Zobel's 1925 patent and the evolved circuit here are minor and unsubstantial. Thus, this evolved circuit infringes on the claims of the now-expired Zobel patent.

Minimal information was required in order to apply genetic programming to the problem of synthesizing the above highpass filter (as opposed to the lowpass filter of the previous chapter). The highpass filter synthesized above is an example of what we call "what you want is what you get" ("WYWIWYG"—pronounced "wow-eee-wig") design. It demonstrates that structure does indeed arise from fitness in the evolutionary process.

26.2 BANDSTOP FILTER

The design of numerous other one-input, one-output circuits composed of inductors and capacitors can be automatically synthesized merely by changing the fitness measure.

A *bandstop filter* (also called a *band-reject, band-elimination,* or *notch filter*) stops all frequencies in a specified range while passing all other frequencies. We can evolve the design for a bandstop filter whose stopband lies between 500 Hz and 1,000 Hz merely by changing the fitness measure. Specifically, the fitness of a circuit for the bandstop filter problem is the weighted sum (over the same 101 fitness cases that were used in Chapter 25 on the lowpass filter) of the absolute value of the difference between the output voltage of a candidate circuit and a target value appropriate for a bandstop filter. In a bandstop filter, there are two passbands, one stopband, and two transition bands. Suppose that the first passband of the desired bandstop filter runs from 1 Hz to 250 Hz and the second one runs from 2,000 Hz to 100,000 Hz. Suppose further that the first transition ("don't care") band lies between 250 Hz and 500 Hz and the second one runs from 1,000 Hz to 2,000 Hz. The desired stopband lies between 500 Hz and 1,000 Hz. The acceptable deviation in the two passbands is 30 millivolts (i.e., the same as for the single passband of the previously discussed lowpass and highpass filters). The acceptable deviation in the stopband between 500 Hz and 1,000 Hz is 1 millivolt (again, the same as for the stopband of the lowpass and highpass filters).

A 100%-compliant evolved bandstop filter (Figure 26.7) with 9 capacitors and 13 inductors was evolved on generation 101 in our only run of this problem.

Figure 26.8 shows the frequency domain behavior of this 100%-compliant bandstop filter (scoring 101 hits). Note that the output is nearly a full volt in the two desired passbands and that it is essentially zero in the desired stopband (between 500 Hz and 1,000 Hz).

26.3 FREQUENCY-MEASURING CIRCUIT

Similarly, a frequency-measuring circuit can be evolved merely by changing the fitness measure and adding the resistor-creating function (Section 25.6.1) to the function set.

Specifically, the goal here is to synthesize the design for a frequency-measuring circuit whose output in millivolts (from 1 millivolt to 1,000 millivolts) is linearly proportional to the logarithm of the frequency of the incoming signal (between 1 Hz and 100,000 Hz). The fitness of an individual circuit for this problem is the sum (over the same 101 fitness cases used for the bandstop filter in this chapter and the lowpass filter in Chapter 25) of the absolute value of the difference between the circuit's actual output and the desired output voltage.

An evolved frequency-measuring circuit (Figure 26.9) with 17 resistors, 18 capacitors, and one inductor appeared on generation 56 in our only run of this problem. Figure 26.10 shows the frequency domain behavior of this evolved frequency-measuring circuit.

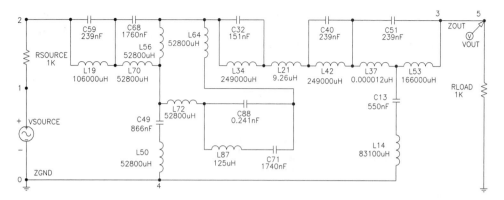

Figure 26.7   Evolved bandstop filter

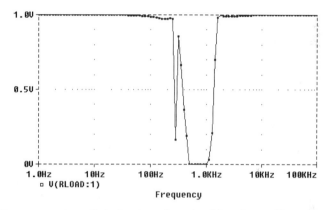

Figure 26.8   Frequency domain behavior of evolved bandstop filter

26.4   BANDPASS FILTER

A bandpass filter passes all frequencies in a specified range while stopping all other frequencies. In a bandpass filter, there are two stopbands, one passband, and two transition bands.

Suppose the goal is to evolve the design for a bandpass filter whose passband lies between 500 Hz and 1,000 Hz. This can be accomplished merely by changing the fitness measure used for the previously discussed circuits in this chapter. Specifically, the fitness of a circuit for this new problem of circuit synthesis is the weighted sum (over the same 101 fitness cases that were used earlier in this chapter for the bandstop filter and frequency-measuring circuit and for the lowpass filter in Chapter 25) of the absolute value of the difference between the output voltage of a candidate circuit and a target value appropriate for the desired bandpass filter. Suppose that the first stopband runs from 1 Hz to 250 Hz and the second one runs from 2,000 Hz to 100,000 Hz. Suppose further that the first transition ("don't care") band lies between 250 Hz and 500 Hz and the

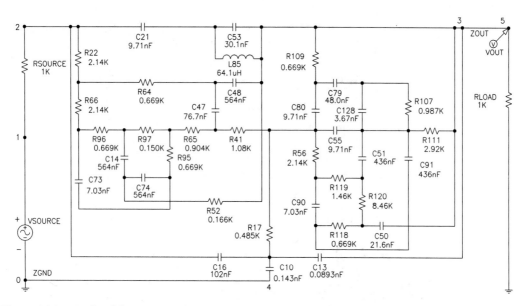

Figure 26.9   **Evolved frequency-measuring circuit**

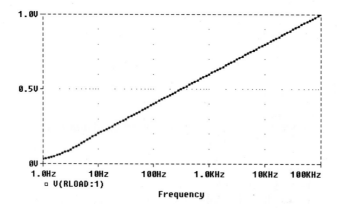

Figure 26.10   **Frequency domain behavior of evolved frequency-measuring circuit**

second one runs from 1,000 Hz to 2,000 Hz. The acceptable deviation in the two stopbands is 1 millivolt (i.e., the same as for the stopbands of the previously discussed lowpass, highpass, and bandstop filters). The acceptable deviation in the passband is 30 millivolts (again, the same as for the passbands of the previously discussed filters).

This problem was run on a medium-grained parallel Beowulf-style computer (described in Section 62.1.5) arranged in a 7 × 10 toroidal mesh with a population size of 1,400,000 (with Q = 20,000 at each of the D = 70 processing nodes).

Figure 26.11 shows the 100%-compliant bandpass filter that emerged on generation 718.

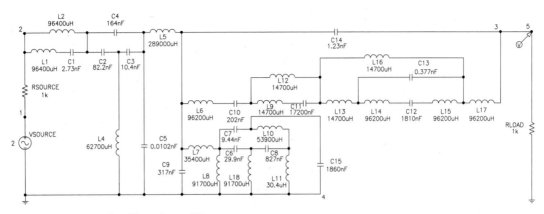

Figure 26.11   Evolved bandpass filter

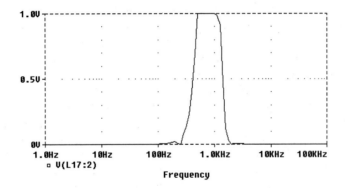

Figure 26.12   Frequency domain behavior of evolved bandpass filter

Figure 26.12 shows the frequency domain behavior of this 100%-compliant bandpass filter (scoring 101 hits). Note that the output is nearly a full volt in the desired passband between 500 Hz and 1,000 Hz and that it is essentially zero in the desired stopbands (i.e., between 1 Hz and 250 Hz and between 2,000 Hz and 100,000 Hz).

Chapter 31 demonstrates the synthesis of a 100%-compliant difficult-to-design asymmetric bandpass (merely by altering the fitness measure from that of Sections 26.1 and 26.2).

Synthesis of a Lowpass Filter Using Automatically Defined Functions

Anyone who has ever looked at an architectural floor plan of a building, a corporate or military organization chart, a map of a city, the layout of a railroad switchyard, a three-dimensional rendering of a protein molecule, a musical score, a large electrical circuit diagram, or almost any other complex human-created structure has noticed the massive reuse of certain basic substructures within the overall structure. Indeed, designs of complex structures are almost always replete with modularities, symmetries, and regularities.

Substructures are sometimes reused exactly. However, substructures are more commonly reused with some minor variation. In the case of subroutines in computer programs, variations can be introduced into a reused group of steps by invoking the subroutine with a different instantiation of the subroutine's dummy variables (formal parameters). Moreover, the reused substructures (whether reused exactly or with variation) are typically organized into hierarchies.

These observations suggest that an approach to automated design should incorporate some hierarchical mechanism to exploit, *by reuse* and *parameterization*, the modularities, symmetries, and regularities inherent in complex structures.

In ordinary computer programs, subroutines provide the basic mechanism by which segments of computer code can be reused exactly, by which segments of code can be used with different instantiations of the formal parameters, and by which segments of code can be conveniently organized into hierarchies. In genetic programming, automatically defined functions provide the mechanism for reuse, parameterized reuse, and hierarchical organization.

Given the pervasiveness of modularities, symmetries, and regularities in complex structures, it seems appropriate to include automatically defined functions in runs of genetic programming for evolving the design for complex structures, such as analog electrical circuits.

Automatically defined functions may be used in two distinct ways in problems of circuit synthesis. First, they may be composed of topology-modifying, component-creating, and development-controlling functions and invoked as part of the process of creating the topology and inserting sized components into the topology. Second, they may be composed of arithmetic functions and invoked from an arithmetic-performing subtree as part of the process of sizing components.

This chapter applies the first of these two ways to the problem of synthesizing a low-pass filter with the same design specification as Section 25.13. You will see a direct link between the repeated invocations of automatically defined functions and the progressive improvement in performance of the evolving circuits from generation to generation.

27.1 DESIGN GOALS

The goal is to evolve, using automatically defined functions, the design for a lowpass filter that satisfies the same design characteristics as in Section 25.13.

27.2 PREPARATORY STEPS

27.2.1 Embryo and Test Fixture

The initial circuit (Figure 25.6) for this problem is the same as that of Chapters 25 and 26. It is created by embedding the embryo with two modifiable wires and three ports (Figure 25.5) into the one-input, one-output test fixture with three ports to the embryo (Figure 25.4).

27.2.2 Program Architecture

Since the embryo of the initial circuit has two modifiable wires, there are two result-producing branches in each program tree in the population.

No architecture-altering operations are used for this problem in this chapter; however, they will be used on this same problem in the next chapter (Chapter 28).

We decided that there would be four zero-argument automatically defined functions (named ADF0, ADF1, ADF2, and ADF3) in each program and no hierarchical references among the automatically defined functions.

How are these architectural choices made? One (or a combination) of the four manual methods described in Chapter 3 can be used:

1. prospective analysis of the nature of the problem (Section 3.1),
2. retrospective analysis of the results of actual runs of similar problems (Section 3.2),
3. seemingly sufficient capacity (overspecification) (Section 3.3), and
4. affordable capacity (Section 3.4).

For example, if we prospectively analyze the problem (method 1), we would conclude that repetitive structures are useful in solving the problem. We would then conclude that four repetitive structures would be more than enough for this problem (method 3).

Alternatively, since this problem was just solved in Chapter 25, we could retrospectively analyze the architectural needs of the problem (method 2). We would then conclude that repetitive structure(s) are useful and that four repetitive structures are more than sufficient for this problem (method 3).

If we were concerned with computer resources, we might use method 4 and simply hope that four automatically defined functions would prove to be sufficient to solve the problem.

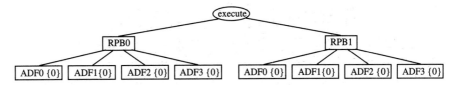

Figure 27.1 Call tree for program consisting of two result-producing branches and four function-defining branches

Regardless of which method is used, the above choice of four automatically defined functions is certainly nonconstraining and generous for this problem.

A practicing engineer whose goal is to solve the problem at hand would probably proceed as we did and simply choose a generous and nonconstraining number of automatically defined functions. On the other hand, if the goal is to study the minimal amount of user-supplied information required by genetic programming, we might make no architectural choices and instead employ the architecture-altering operations (as we, in fact, do in the next chapter).

In any event, the architecture of each program in the population consists of a total of six branches (i.e., two result-producing branches and four function-defining branches). These six branches are joined by a connective LIST function to create the overall program tree.

Figure 27.1 shows the call tree (explained in detail in connection with Figure 12.6) for a program consisting of two result-producing branches and four function-defining branches.

27.2.3 Functions and Terminals

The function set, $F_{ccs-rpb-initial}$, for each construction-continuing subtree of the result-producing branches is

$F_{ccs-rpb-initial}$ = {ADF0, ADF1, ADF2, ADF3, C, L, SERIES, PARALLEL0, FLIP, NOP, THREE_GROUND, THREE_VIA0, THREE_VIA1, THREE_VIA2, THREE_VIA3, THREE_VIA4, THREE_VIA5, THREE_VIA6, THREE_VIA7}.

The four automatically defined functions each take zero arguments. The next seven functions take 2, 2, 3, 4, 1, 1, and 3 arguments, respectively. The eight THREE_VIA functions each take 3 arguments.

The terminal set, $T_{ccs-rpb-initial}$, for each construction-continuing subtree of the result-producing branches is

$T_{ccs-rpb-initial}$ = {END, CUT}.

The initial function set, $F_{ccs-adf-initial}$, for each construction-continuing subtree of the function-defining branches (automatically defined functions) is

$F_{ccs-adf-initial}$ = {C, L, SERIES, PARALLEL0, FLIP, NOP, THREE_GROUND, THREE_VIA0, THREE_VIA1, THREE_VIA2, THREE_VIA3, THREE_VIA4, THREE_VIA5, THREE_VIA6, THREE_VIA7}.

The terminal set for the function-defining branches of each program tree is the same as that of the result-producing branches. The initial terminal set, $T_{ccs-adf-initial}$, for each construction-continuing subtree of the function-defining branches is

$$T_{ccs-adf-initial} = T_{ccs-rpb-initial} = \{END, CUT\}.$$

Since there are no architecture-altering operations in this problem, $T_{rpb-potential}$, $F_{rpb-potential}$, $T_{adf-potential}$, and $F_{adf-potential}$ are empty.

The function set, F_{aps}, for each arithmetic-performing subtree in any branch and the terminal set, T_{aps}, for each arithmetic-performing subtree in any branch are the same as for the lowpass filter problem in Section 25.14.3.

27.2.4 Fitness

The fitness measure is the same as in Section 25.14.4.

27.2.5 Parameters

The control parameters are the same as in Section 25.14.5.

27.2.6 Termination

The termination criterion and the method of result designation are the same as in Section 25.14.6.

27.2.7 Tableau

Table 27.1 summarizes the key features of the problem of designing a lowpass filter using automatically defined functions.

27.3 RESULTS

The best circuit from generation 0 (Figure 27.2) has a fitness of 58.6 and scores 52 hits (out of 101). The program tree for the best circuit from generation 0 has 283 points in its first result-producing branch, 3 points in its second result-producing branch, and 52, 284, 20, and 33 points in its automatically defined functions (ADF0, ADF1, ADF2, and ADF3), respectively. However, neither of the two result-producing branches actually references any of the four automatically defined functions. The best-of-generation circuit consists of a single inductor and a single capacitor. The topological arrangement of these two components is that of the first rung of a classical ladder topology for a filter.

Figure 27.3a shows the behavior of the best-of-generation circuit from generation 0 in the frequency domain. The horizontal axis represents the frequency of the incoming signal and ranges from 1 Hz to 100,000 Hz on a logarithmic scale. The vertical axis represents peak output voltage and ranges from 0 to 1 volt on a linear scale. As can be seen, the behavior of this largely noncompliant best-of-generation circuit from generation 0 is similar to the best circuit of generation 0 from run A without automatically defined functions (Section 25.15.1).

Figure 27.4 shows, by generation, the standardized fitness and number of hits for the best-of-generation program of each generation of this run. Note that there are two

Table 27.1 Tableau for lowpass filter using automatically defined functions

Objective	Design, using automatically defined functions, a lowpass filter composed of inductors and capacitors with a passband below 1,000 Hz, a stopband above 2,000 Hz, a maximum allowable passband deviation of 30 millivolts, and a maximum allowable stopband deviation of 1 millivolt.
Test fixture and embryo	One-input, one-output initial circuit with a source resistor, load resistor, and two modifiable wires
Program architecture	Two result-producing branches, RPB0 and RPB1, and four zero-argument automatically defined functions, ADF0, ADF1, ADF2, and ADF3
Initial function set for the RPBs	For construction-continuing subtrees: $F_{ccs-rpb-initial}$ = {ADF0, ADF1, ADF2, ADF3, C, L, SERIES, PARALLEL0, FLIP, NOP, THREE_GROUND, THREE_VIA0, THREE_VIA1, THREE_VIA2, THREE_VIA3, THREE_VIA4, THREE_VIA5, THREE_VIA6, THREE_VIA7}. For arithmetic-performing subtrees: F_{aps} = {+, -}.
Initial terminal set for the RPBs	For construction-continuing subtrees: $T_{ccs-rpb-initial}$ = {END, CUT}. For arithmetic-performing subtrees: T_{aps} = {$\Re_{smaller-reals}$}.
Initial function set for the ADFs	For construction-continuing subtrees: $F_{ccs-adf-initial}$ = {C, L, SERIES, PARALLEL0, FLIP, NOP, THREE_GROUND, THREE_VIA0, THREE_VIA1, THREE_VIA2, THREE_VIA3, THREE_VIA4, THREE_VIA5, THREE_VIA6, THREE_VIA7}. For arithmetic-performing subtrees: F_{aps} = {+, -}.
Initial terminal set for the ADFs	For construction-continuing subtrees: $T_{ccs-adf-initial}$ = {END, CUT}. For arithmetic-performing subtrees: T_{aps} = {$\Re_{smaller-reals}$}.
Potential function set for the RPBs	Architecture-altering operations are not used.
Potential terminal set for the RPBs	Architecture-altering operations are not used.
Potential function set for the ADFs	Architecture-altering operations are not used.
Potential terminal set for the ADFs	Architecture-altering operations are not used.
Fitness cases	101 frequency values in an interval of five decades of frequency values between 1 Hz and 100,000 Hz
Raw fitness	The sum, over these 101 fitness cases, of the absolute weighted deviation between the actual value of the voltage that is produced by the circuit at the probe point and the target value for voltage

(continued)

Table 27.1 *(continued)*

Standardized fitness	Same as raw fitness
Hits	The number of hits is defined as the number of fitness cases (out of 101) for which the voltage is acceptable or ideal or that lie in the "don't care" band.
Wrapper	None
Parameters	$M = 640,000$. $G = 501$. $Q = 10,000$. $D = 64$. $B = 2\%$. $S_{rpb} = 300$. $N_{rpb} = 2$. $S_{adf} = 300$. $N_{max\text{-}adf} = 4$. $N_{max\text{-}argument\text{-}adf} = 0$.
Result designation	Best-so-far pace-setting individual
Success predicate	A program scores the maximum number (101) of hits.

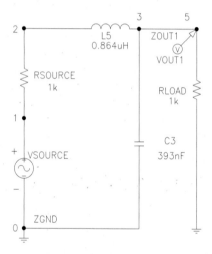

Figure 27.2   Best circuit from generation 0 is a one-rung ladder

instances of a decrease in the number of hits for the best-of-generation individual in conjunction with an improvement (decrease) in the fitness.

Fully 98% of the programs of generation 0 for this problem produce circuits that cannot be simulated by SPICE; however, the percentage of unsimulatable circuits drops to 84% by generation 1, 77% by generation 2, 41% by generation 3, and 15% by generation 4. Thereafter, the percentage ranges between 6% and 12% for the rest of the run. That is, the vast majority of the circuits are simulatable after just a few generations.

27.3.1   Performance Improves by Optimizing Component Values

The best-of-generation individual from processing node 18 of generation 9 (Figure 27.5) has a fitness of 29.5 and scores 65 hits. The program tree has 14 points in its RPB0 and 29 points in its RPB1 and has 22, 27, 225, and 68 points in ADF0, ADF1, ADF2, and ADF3, respectively.

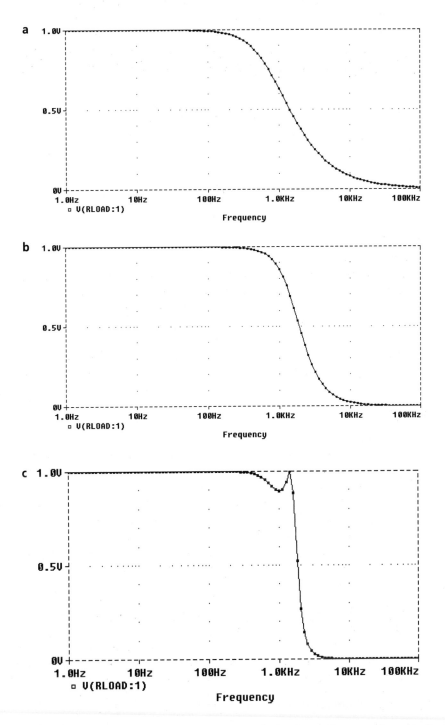

Figure 27.3 Frequency domain behavior of the best-of-generation circuits from generation (a) 0, (b) 9 (processing node 18), (c) 9 (processing node 21) *(continued)*

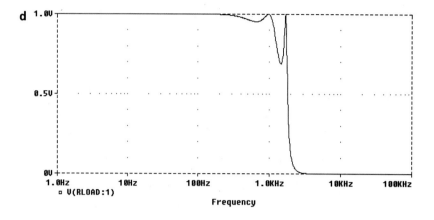

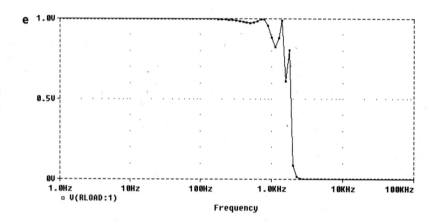

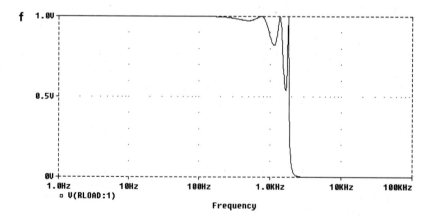

Figure 27.3 *(continued)* *(d)* 16, *(e)* 19, *(f)* 20

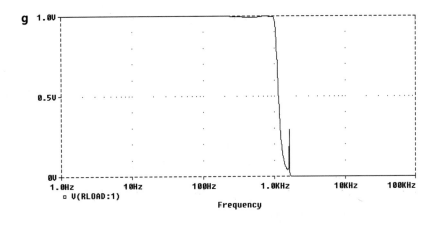

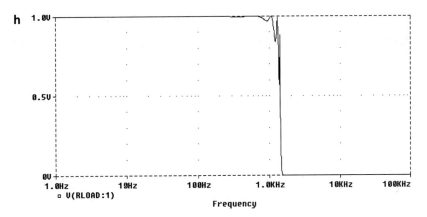

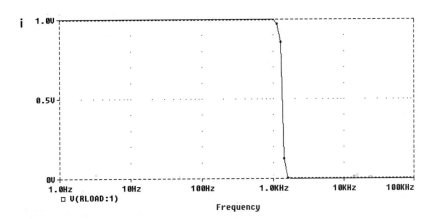

Figure 27.3 *(continued)* *(g)* 24, *(h)* 31, and *(i)* 35

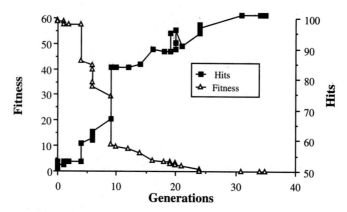

Figure 27.4 Fitness and hits

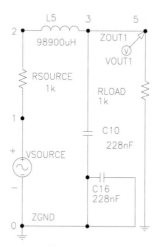

Figure 27.5 Best circuit from processing node 18 and generation 9 is an improved one-rung ladder

Ignoring the electrically useless capacitor **C16**, the topology of this circuit is effectively the same as the simple topology of the best-of-generation circuit of generation 0. This circuit achieves considerably better fitness (29.5 versus 58.6) and scores more hits (65 versus 52) primarily as a consequence of the better choice of the numerical value for series inductor **L5** (98,000 μH instead of only 0.864 μH).

Curiously, this circuit is the first pace-setting individual where an automatically defined function is called more than once. The twice-used automatically defined function ADF3 creates a 228 nF capacitor. However, as can be seen in the figure, the second occurrence of this 228 nF capacitor at **C16** is electrically useless since both of its leads are tied together.

Figure 27.3b shows the behavior in the frequency domain of the best circuit from processing node 18 and generation 9. The behavior of this improved one-rung ladder is considerably better than that of the best circuit of generation 0; however, it still does not satisfy the design requirements.

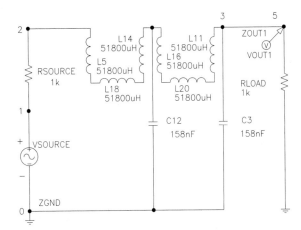

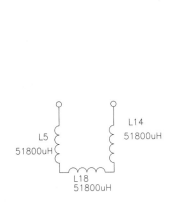

Figure 27.6 Twice-used automatically defined function ADF0 from processing node 21 and generation 9

Figure 27.7 Best circuit from processing node 21 and generation 9 is a two-rung ladder

27.3.2 Emergence of Reuse—A Two-Rung Ladder Is Created by a Twice-Used Automatically Defined Function

Code reuse is advantageous in a system for automatically solving problems because it obviates the necessity of repeatedly rewriting code (reinventing the wheel) to solve an already-solved subproblem. Reuse leverages the benefit of an already-obtained solution to a subproblem.

The best individual circuit from processing node 21 of generation 9 has a fitness of 10.3 and scores 84 hits. The program tree has 19 points in its RPB0, 8 points in its RPB1, and 48, 283, 6, and 2 points in ADF0, ADF1, ADF2, and ADF3, respectively. Figure 27.6 shows the twice-used automatically defined function ADF0 from processing node 21 and generation 9.

This new pace-setting circuit from processing node 21 in generation 9 (Figure 27.7) differs from all previous pace-setting best-of-generation circuits in this run in that it has the topology of a two-rung ladder. The induction elements that appear horizontally across the top of the figure each arise from a series composition of three inductors (L5, L18, and L14 for the first rung and L16, L20, and L11 for the second rung). Both of these identical groups of inductors are spawned by the automatically defined function ADF0. ADF0 creates a useful substructure that is reused in order to create this two-rung ladder circuit.

The fitness of this two-rung ladder circuit is superior to all previously seen one-rung ladder circuits from this run. Designers of Campbell, Zobel, Johnson, Butterworth, Chebychev, or Cauer (elliptic) filters know that it is often possible to make a filter's frequency response steeper in the transition band by increasing the order of the filter (which can be accomplished by adding an additional rung to the ladder). The automatically defined function here causes a rung to be duplicated and is directly responsible for the improved fitness of this circuit.

Figure 27.3c shows the behavior in the frequency domain of the best circuit from processing node 21 and generation 9. As can be seen, the two-rung ladder is a marked improvement over the behavior of the previously seen one-rung ladders. This figure (but not the fitness calculation) was made with 200 sample points per decade (i.e., a total of 1,000 points) in order to show the finer details of the circuit's behavior in the frequency domain. Notice that the curve starts dropping off and then rebounds to the 1-volt level just before its sharp drop in voltage.

27.3.3   A Thrice-Used Substructure Further Enhances Performance

The best-of-generation circuit from generation 16 has a fitness of 4.1 and scores 90 hits. It came from processing node 20 (which is neat to nodes 18 and 21 of the parallel computing system). The program tree has 24 points in its RPB0 and 8 points in its RPB1. It has 78, 210, 6, and 3 points in ADF0, ADF1, ADF2, and ADF3, respectively. This new pace-setting circuit from generation 16 differs from all previous pace-setting circuits in this run in that it has a thrice-used automatically defined function ADF0 (Figure 27.8).

Figure 27.9 shows the best circuit of generation 16. It has a different topology from all earlier pace-setting individuals, namely, that of a three-rung ladder. Note that the first group of three 55,000 μH inductors (e.g., L5, L21, and L17) can be consolidated into a single inductor so that the first segment of the ladder can be viewed as consisting of one 158 nF capacitor (C15) and one inductor. Similarly, the second and third groups of three inductors can be consolidated into a single inductor so that the second and third segments of the ladder can also each be viewed as consisting of one 158 nF capacitor and one inductor. Thus, this circuit can be viewed as consisting of three identical segments, each consisting of an inductor positioned horizontally across the top of the figure and a capacitor that is shunted vertically to ground.

Figure 27.3d (made with 200 sample points per decade) shows the behavior in the frequency domain of the best circuit from generation 16. The drop-off in the transition band is much steeper for this circuit than for that of any previous circuit from this run. Filter designers know that it is often possible to improve a filter by adding rungs.

The evolved circuit consists of three repetitions of a two-element inductor-capacitor pair. This circuit has the topology of what is now called a Butterworth filter. Such filters were described by S. Butterworth of the British Admiralty Research Laboratory in 1930 in *Experimental Wireless and the Wireless Engineer* (Butterworth 1930). In this paper, Butterworth showed

> how to obtain the best results from a two-element filter and then how to combine any number of elementary pairs . . . so as to approach closer and closer to the ideal filter as the number of stages are increased.

The three-rung ladder of Figure 27.9 emerged as a natural consequence of the fitness-driven evolutionary process—not because the user primed genetic programming with the domain knowledge contained in Butterworth's 1930 article concerning the advantage of increasing the number of rungs of a ladder. The three rungs that are responsible for this circuit's improved fitness are the consequence of the three invocations of the automatically defined function.

Figure 27.8 Thrice-used automatically defined function ADF0 from generation 16

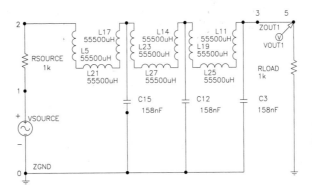

Figure 27.9 Best circuit of generation 16 is a three-rung ladder

27.3.4 A Quadruply Used Substructure Further Enhances Performance

The best individual program in generation 19 has a fitness of 4.1 and scores 95 hits. It came from processing node 20. The program has 29 points in its RPB0 and 12 points in its RPB1 and has 78, 215, 6, and 3 points in ADF0, ADF1, ADF2, and ADF3, respectively. Figure 27.10 shows the best circuit of generation 19. Note that it has a different topology from its predecessors, namely, a four-rung ladder.

ADF0 is used four times in this new pace-setting individual. The enhanced performance of this circuit as shown in Figure 27.3e (as compared with the best circuit from generation 16) is the consequence of an additional reuse of ADF0 (which happens to be the same as ADF0 for the best-of-generation circuit from generation 16). This structural difference corresponds to the improvement in performance.

We noticed that the best-of-generation individual of generation 19 came from the same processing node as the best-of-generation individual from generation 16; that three of its six branches have exactly the same number of points as their counterparts from generation 16; that the other three branches have approximately the same number of points as their counterparts from generation 16; that ADF0 is identical (in topology, components, component values, and component numbering); and that the actual contents of the result-producing branches and the automatically defined functions are very similar. These observations together suggest that this individual is a descendent of the best-of-generation individual from generation 16. The difference between these two pace-setting individuals is the fourth use of ADF0.

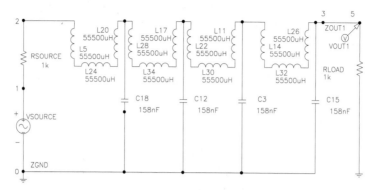

Figure 27.10   Best circuit of generation 19 is a four-rung ladder

27.3.5   A Different Quadruply Used Substructure Further Enhances Performance

Code reuse is advantageous in an automatic problem-solving system because it obviates the necessity of repeatedly rediscovering the solution to an already-solved subproblem. This important aspect of genetic programming has already been demonstrated by the use of an automatically defined function two, three, and four times (in generations 9, 16, and 19).

There is an additional reason why code reuse is advantageous in an adaptive problem-solving process. If the code within an automatically defined function is incrementally improved, the benefit of the improvement is leveraged in the sense that the benefits will be automatically conferred on all parts of the overall program that refer to the improved automatically defined function. It is not necessary to separately rediscover the improvement for each separate part of the overall program.

The best program in generation 20 has a fitness of 2.8 and scores 96 hits. It also came from processing node 20. The program tree has 29 points in its RPB0 and 14 points in its RPB1 and has 50, 285, 6, and 3 points in ADF0, ADF1, ADF2, and ADF3, respectively.

ADF0 (Figure 27.11) is used four times. As can be seen, the value of the three inductors in this ADF0 are each 56,300 µH (as compared to 55,500 µH for their counterparts in ADF0 from the best-of-generation individual from generation 19).

Figure 27.12 shows the best circuit of generation 20. Figure 27.3f (made with 200 sample points per decade) shows the behavior in the frequency domain of the best circuit from generation 20.

27.3.6   Emergence of Two Inductive-Capacitive Shunts

The best individual program in generation 24 has a fitness of 0.139 and scores 76 hits. The program tree has 29 points in its RPB0 and 12 points in its RPB1 and has 62, 287, 10, and 3 points in ADF0, ADF1, ADF2, and ADF3, respectively. ADF0 is invoked four times.

Quadruply called ADF0 from the best-of-generation individual of generation 24 develops in two distinct ways. (Section 27.3.9 provides a detailed description of the way that a given automatically defined function can develop into different ways on different invocations.)

Figure 27.13 shows the two-ported substructure that develops from ADF0 on two of its four invocations. Figure 27.14 shows the three-ported substructure that develops from ADF0 on two of its four invocations.

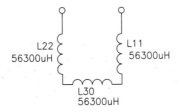

Figure 27.11 Quadruply called automatically defined function ADF0 from generation 20

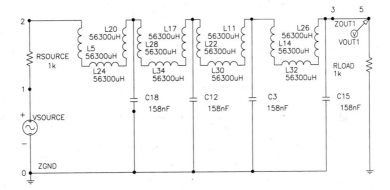

Figure 27.12 Best circuit of generation 20 is a four-rung ladder

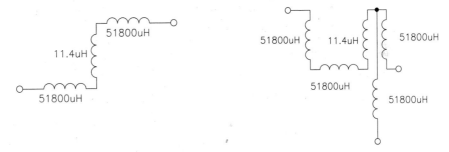

Figure 27.13 Two-ported substructure that sometimes develops from ADF0 of generation 24

Figure 27.14 Three-ported substructure that sometimes develops from ADF0 of generation 24

Figure 27.15 shows the best circuit of generation 24. Note that all the previous pace-setting individuals in this run had vertical shunts containing only a capacitor (i.e., they were shunts such as you find in Campbell, Butterworth, and Chebychev filters). Two of the four vertical shunts of this best-of-generation circuit contain an inductor as well as a capacitor. In one (of the two) standard topologies for an elliptic lowpass filter, all the vertical shunts consist of one inductor and one capacitor. Thus, the elliptic topology is

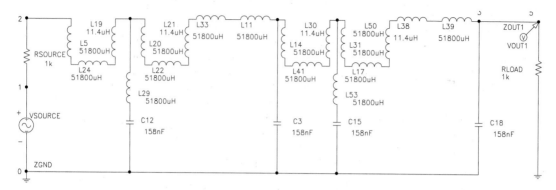

Figure 27.15   Best circuit of generation 24 is a four-rung ladder

making its first appearance (among pace-setting individuals of this run) in two of this circuit's four vertical shunts.

Figure 27.3g shows the behavior in the frequency domain of the best circuit from generation 24. This figure was made with 200 sample points per decade (i.e., 1,000 points).

27.3.7   Emergence of an Elliptic (Cauer) Topology

As already demonstrated in generation 20 of this run, code reuse is especially advantageous in an adaptive process because the benefit of an improvement can be leveraged by repeatedly applying it. This important principle is illustrated again in generation 31 of this run. As will be seen momentarily, the helpful twice-used inductive-capacitive shunt that appeared in the best-of-generation individual of generation 24 will be used four times in generation 31.

The best individual program in generation 31 is especially interesting because it has the exact topology (after consolidation of all multiple inductors in series into one inductor) of a tenth-order elliptic filter. This individual scores 101 hits (out of 101) and has a fitness of 0.0850. The program tree has 41 points in its RPB0 and 7 points in its RPB1; it has 52, 297, 22, and 2 points in ADF0, ADF1, ADF2, and ADF3, respectively. ADF0 (Figure 27.16) is used five times.

Figure 27.17 shows the best circuit of generation 31. After all the pairs and triplets of series inductors along the top of Figure 27.17 are consolidated, it can be seen that the circuit has the equivalent of six inductors horizontally across the top of the circuit and five vertical shunts. Each vertical shunt consists of an inductor and a capacitor (e.g., **L34** and **C18** appear in the first shunt). The effect of the five resonant vertical shunts is to suppress the circuit's output at the common resonant frequency of 1,857 Hz near the boundary of the stopband. This routine simplification (shown in Figure 27.41) makes it clear that this 100%-compliant circuit has the elliptic topology that was invented and patented by Wilhelm Cauer. Sections 27.4 through 27.6 will discuss this rediscovery of the elliptic topology by genetic programming in detail.

Figure 27.3h (made with 200 sample points per decade) shows the behavior in the frequency domain of the best circuit from generation 31.

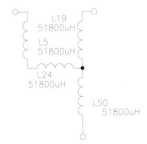

Figure 27.16 **Quintuply called automatically defined function ADF0 from generation 31**

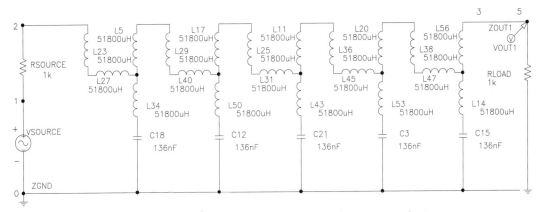

Figure 27.17 **Best circuit of generation 31 illustrating the elliptic (Cauer) filter topology**

27.3.8 Emergence of an Even Better Filter

If a run of genetic programming is continued after the emergence of the first 100%-compliant individual, even better 100%-compliant individuals are usually created. The best-of-run program harvested from generation 35 scores 101 hits (out of 101) and has a fitness of 0.00752. This fitness is about an order of magnitude better than that of the best-of-generation individual from generation 31. The program tree has 34 points in its RPB0 and 4 points in its RPB1 and has 55, 260, 3, and 2 points in ADF0, ADF1, ADF2, and ADF3, respectively.

ADF0 (the only automatically defined function that is actually referenced by the result-producing branches) is invoked four times in the best-of-run program from generation 35. The topology of the substructure created by ADF0 (Figure 27.18) is more complicated than that seen in generation 31 in that the substructure has three ports. The substructure created by ADF0 is used as a building block four times in constructing the overall filter circuit.

Figure 27.19 shows the best-of-run circuit from generation 35 after inserting ADF0 in four places.

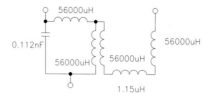

Figure 27.18   ADF0 of the best-of-run circuit from generation 35

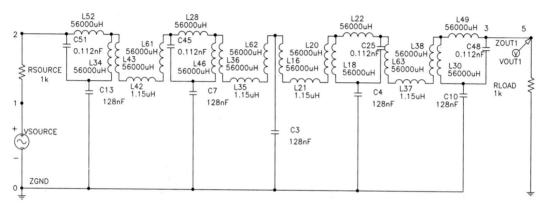

Figure 27.19   Best-of-run circuit from generation 35

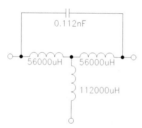

Figure 27.20   Edited version of ADF0 of the best-of-run circuit from generation 35

After simplifying the series composition of three inductors and changing the orientation, it can be seen (Figure 27.20) that ADF0 is a "bridged T" arrangement. Specifically, the 112,000 µH inductor constitutes the vertical part of the "T," the two 56,000 µH inductors constitute the horizontal part of the "T," and the 0.112 nF capacitor is the bridge.

Figure 27.21 shows the best-of-run circuit from generation 35 after inserting the edited version of ADF0 in four places. The four occurrences of the "bridged T" are positioned sideways and thus do not operate in the same fashion in a filter circuit as a canonical "bridged T." Notice that the four capacitors C51, C45, C40, and C48 are unusually small (0.112 nF). When these four capacitors are deleted, the circuit still scores 101 hits.

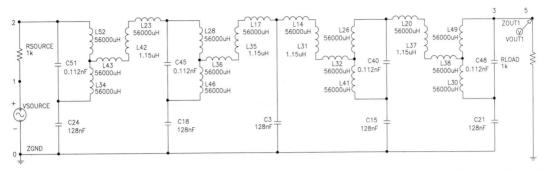

Figure 27.21 Best-of-run circuit from generation 35 with four occurrences of the edited version of ADF0

Notice that if these four capacitors are deleted, the edited circuit has four vertical shunts of the elliptic topology. For example, inductor **L34** and capacitor **C24** together constitute the first of the four vertical inductive-capacitive shunts.

Figure 27.3i shows the behavior in the frequency domain of the best-of-run circuit from generation 35. Notice that the transition between the passband and the stopband is sharper for this best-of-run circuit than for the 100%-compliant best-of-generation circuit from generation 31 (Figure 27.3h). This sharper definition occurs with or without the four small capacitors (**C51, C45, C40,** and **C48**).

27.3.9 Detailed Analysis of a Program Tree with Automatically Defined Functions

The best-of-run circuit from generation 35 is interesting for two reasons. First, its fitness is about an order of magnitude better than that of the elliptic filter from generation 31. Second, it has a quadruply used triangular topology. Third, it presents an opportunity for a step-by-step illustration of the details of transforming a program tree with automatically defined functions into a fully developed circuit (and to thereby illustrate certain subtleties of the developmental process).

When an automatically defined function is encountered during execution of a program tree in a problem of circuit synthesis, the order of execution of the functions in the automatically defined function and the program tree is as if the entire body of the automatically defined function were copied into the program tree at the place where the call to the automatically defined function is encountered.

Figure 27.22 presents the best-of-run individual from generation 35 as a rooted point-labeled tree with ordered branches. The first result-producing branch (RPB0) is rooted at the C function (labeled 6), and the second result-producing branch (RPB1) is rooted at the THREE_VIA3 function (labeled 7). Note that ADF0 is invoked four times—at points 34, 43, 44, and 51. Automatically defined function ADF0 is rooted at the DEFUN (labeled 2). Since ADF0 is the only function-defining branch that is actually referenced by either result-producing branch, the three unreferenced function-defining branches (ADF1, ADF2, and ADF3) are represented by the filled circles (labeled 3, 4, and 5). The arithmetic-performing subtrees are not shown, but instead are abbreviated as V1 (labeled 17), V2 (labeled 45), V3 (labeled 52), V4 (labeled 54), and V5 (labeled 10). We now trace the development of the best-of-run individual from generation 35.

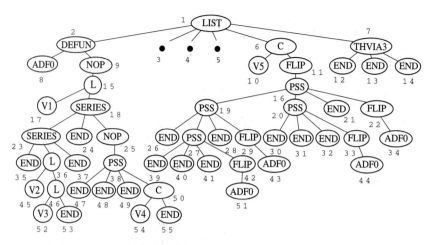

Figure 27.22 **Best-of-run individual from generation 35**

Figure 27.23 shows the one-input, one-output initial circuit used for this problem. The C function (labeled 6 in Figure 27.22 and underlined in the program fragment below) at the root of the first result-producing branch RPB0 converts modifiable wire Z0 into capacitor C3. The 11-point arithmetic-performing subtree rooted at the + function (abbreviated as V5 in Figure 27.22 and underlined in the program fragment below) is immediately executed in its entirety in a depth-first way when the C function (labeled 6) is executed. This subtree returns a value that, when interpreted, causes the value of 128 nF to be assigned to capacitor C3. The writing head now points to capacitor C3.

```
(C (+ (- 0.166 -0.376) (+ (- 0.910 -0.0366) (- -0.297 -0.917)))
(FLIP (PARALLEL0 (PARALLEL0 END (PARALLEL0 END END END (FLIP
(ADF0))) END (FLIP (ADF0))) (PARALLEL0 END END END (FLIP
(ADF0))) END (FLIP (ADF0))))).
```

Figure 27.24 shows the result of executing this C function (labeled 6).

The breadth-first execution of the program tree next causes the execution of the THREE_VIA3 function in RPB1 (labeled 7 in Figure 27.22). This THREE_VIA3 function converts modifiable wire Z1 into one port to layer 3 and three new modifiable wires, Z91, Z93, and Z94 (each with a writing head). Figure 27.25 shows the result of executing this THREE_VIA function (labeled 7).

Since V5 (labeled 10) represents an arithmetic-performing subtree that is immediately executed, in its entirety, in a depth-first way at the time that the C function (labeled 6) is executed, the breadth-first execution of the program tree next causes the execution of the FLIP function (labeled 11 in Figure 27.22 and underlined below) in RPB0. The FLIP function flips the polarity of capacitor C3, and the writing head continues to point to capacitor C3.

```
(C (+ (- 0.166 -0.376) (+ (- 0.910 -0.0366) (- -0.297 -0.917)))
(FLIP (PARALLEL0 (PARALLEL0 END (PARALLEL0 END END END (FLIP
```

```
(ADF0))) END (FLIP (ADF0))) (PARALLEL0 END END END (FLIP
(ADF0))) END (FLIP (ADF0))))).
```

Figure 27.26 shows the change of polarity of capacitor **C3** resulting from the execution of the FLIP function (labeled 11).

The breadth-first execution of the program tree next causes the execution of the three END functions in RPB1 (labeled 12, 13, and 14 in Figure 27.22). These three END functions eliminate all three writing heads spawned by the THREE_VIA3 function (labeled 7).

The first PARALLEL0 function in RPB0 (labeled 16 in Figure 27.22 and underlined below) is then executed. This PARALLEL0 function operates on capacitor **C3** and parallelizes it by creating a duplicate capacitor **C4** and by creating new modifiable wires **Z5** and **Z6**. This PARALLEL0 function spawns four writing heads. Note that the PARALLEL0 function establishes the polarity of the new modifiable wires **Z5** and **Z6**. As it happens, the polarity established here matters when **Z6** is later converted into a component.

```
(C (+ (- 0.166 -0.376) (+ (- 0.910 -0.0366) (- -0.297 -0.917)))
(FLIP (PARALLEL0 (PARALLEL0 END (PARALLEL0 END END END (FLIP
(ADF0))) END (FLIP (ADF0))) (PARALLEL0 END END END (FLIP
(ADF0))) END (FLIP (ADF0))))).
```

Figure 27.27 shows the result of executing the PARALLEL0 function (labeled 16).

The next PARALLEL0 function in RPB0 (labeled 19 in Figure 27.22 and underlined below) then parallelizes capacitor **C3** a second time and creates new capacitor **C7** and modifiable wires **Z8** and **Z9**. This PARALLEL0 function spawns four writing heads.

```
(C (+ (- 0.166 -0.376) (+ (- 0.910 -0.0366) (- -0.297 -0.917)))
(FLIP (PARALLEL0 (PARALLEL0 END (PARALLEL0 END END END (FLIP
(ADF0))) END (FLIP (ADF0))) (PARALLEL0 END END END (FLIP
(ADF0))) END (FLIP (ADF0))))).
```

Figure 27.28 shows the result of executing this PARALLEL0 function (labeled 19).

The breadth-first execution of the program tree next causes the execution of the PARALLEL0 function in RPB0 (labeled 20 in Figure 27.22 and underlined below). This PARALLEL0 function parallelizes capacitor **C4** (i.e., the component to which the second writing head spawned by the PARALLEL0 labeled 16 is pointing). This PARALLEL0 function creates new capacitor **C10** and modifiable wires **Z11** and **Z12**. This PARALLEL0 function spawns four writing heads.

```
(C (+ (- 0.166 -0.376) (+ (- 0.910 -0.0366) (- -0.297 -0.917)))
(FLIP (PARALLEL0 (PARALLEL0 END (PARALLEL0 END END END (FLIP
(ADF0))) END (FLIP (ADF0))) (PARALLEL0 END END END (FLIP
(ADF0))) END (FLIP (ADF0))))).
```

Figure 27.29 shows the result of executing this PARALLEL0 function (labeled 20).

The breadth-first execution of the program tree next causes the execution of the END function (labeled 21 in Figure 27.22). This eliminates the writing head on **Z5** created by the PARALLEL0 function (labeled 16).

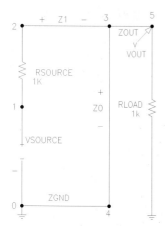

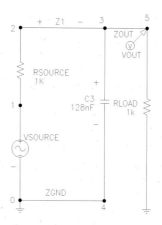

Figure 27.23   One-input, one-output initial circuit with two initial modifiable wires, Z0 and Z1

Figure 27.24   Result of executing the C function (labeled 6)

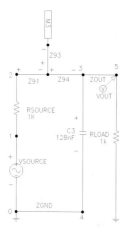

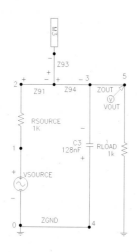

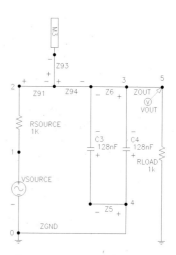

Figure 27.25   Result of executing the THREE_VIA function (labeled 7)

Figure 27.26   Result of executing the FLIP function (labeled 11)

Figure 27.27   Result of executing the PARALLEL0 function (labeled 16)

The breadth-first execution of the program tree next causes the execution of the FLIP function (labeled 22 in Figure 27.22 and underlined below) operating on wire **Z6**. The execution of this FLIP function completes the execution of the functions that are located at the fourth level in the program tree below the topmost LIST function.

On the fifth level of the program tree, the END function (labeled 26 in Figure 27.22 and underlined below) is executed, thereby eliminating a writing head on **C3**. Then the PARALLEL0 function (labeled 27 in Figure 27.22 and underlined below) is executed, causing capacitor **C7** (i.e., the component to which the second writing head spawned by the PARALLEL0 labeled 19 is pointing) to be parallelized. This PARALLEL0 function

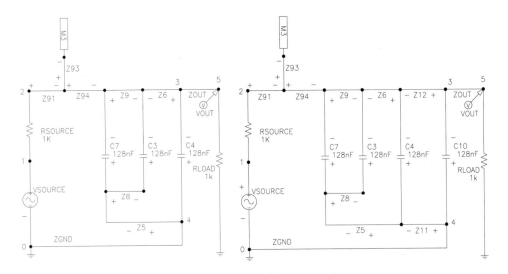

Figure 27.28   Result of executing the PARALLEL0 **function (labeled 19)**

Figure 27.29   Result of executing the PARALLEL0 **function (labeled 20)**

creates new capacitor **C13** and modifiable wires **Z14** and **Z15**. This PARALLEL0 function (labeled 27), in turn, spawns four additional writing heads.

```
(C (+ (- 0.166 -0.376) (+ (- 0.910 -0.0366) (- -0.297 -0.917))))
(FLIP (PARALLEL0 (PARALLEL0 END (PARALLEL0 END END END (FLIP
(ADF0))) END (FLIP (ADF0))) (PARALLEL0 END END END (FLIP
(ADF0))) END (FLIP (ADF0))))).
```

Figure 27.30 shows the result of executing the FLIP function (labeled 22), the END function (labeled 26), and the PARALLEL0 function (labeled 27).

At this point, the remainder of the program tree of Figure 27.22 consists only of END functions (at 28, 30, 31, and 32) and four occurrences of the two-point composition

```
(FLIP (ADF0)).
```

These four occurrences are located in Figure 27.22 at the pairs of points labeled

- 22 and 34 (already discussed),
- 29 and 43,
- 33 and 44, and
- 42 and 51.

It is interesting to note that all four invocations of ADF0 involve the two-point composition

```
(FLIP (ADF0))
```

invoked by a PARALLEL0 function.

The END functions at 28, 30, 31, and 32 eliminate the writing heads at **Z8**, **C4**, **C10**, and **Z11**.

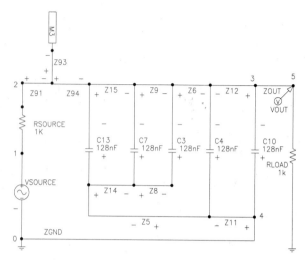

Figure 27.30 Result of executing the FLIP function (labeled 22), the END function (labeled 26), and the PARALLEL0 function (labeled 27)

27.3.10 Detailed Analysis of ADF0

Now consider the (FLIP (ADF0)) subexpression that is located at the points labeled 22 and 34 in Figure 27.22.

```
(C (+ (- 0.166 -0.376) (+ (- 0.910 -0.0366) (- -0.297 -0.917))))
(FLIP (PARALLEL0 (PARALLEL0 END (PARALLEL0 END END END (FLIP
(ADF0))) END (FLIP (ADF0))) (PARALLEL0 END END END (FLIP
(ADF0))) END (FLIP (ADF0)))))).
```

As already mentioned, the FLIP (labeled 22) is executed on the fourth level of the program tree, and ADF0 (labeled 34) remains to be executed on the fifth level. Figure 27.31 shows a cutaway portion of Figure 27.30 with the writing head pointing to modifiable wire **Z6**.

The first function-defining branch of the overall program tree defines automatically defined function ADF0 and is shown in Figure 27.22 starting at the DEFUN (labeled 2). The body of ADF0 begins with the NOP function (labeled 9). ADF0 is as follows:

```
(NOP (L (+ 0.504 (- (+ (+ (+ 0.0830 0.406) (- -0.243 0.658)) (-
(- (+ (+ 0.809 0.407) (- 0.893 -0.113)) -0.212) (- (+ (- -0.506
-0.0313) (- -0.243 0.658)) (- (- 0.556 0.0370) -0.946))))
-0.000741)) (SERIES (SERIES END (L -0.000741 (L 0.0609 END))
END) END (NOP (PARALLEL0 END END END (C -0.949 END)))))))).
```

After the initial NOP function (labeled 9 in Figure 27.22) is executed, the inductor-creating function L (labeled 15 and underlined above) converts modifiable wire **Z6** into

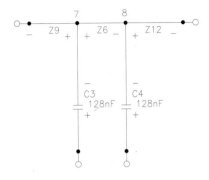

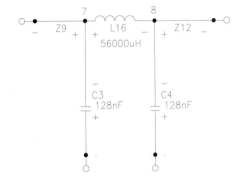

Figure 27.31 Cutaway portion of developing circuit structure where ADF0 (labeled 34) is about to be applied

Figure 27.32 Result of executing the NOP function (labeled 9) and the L function (labeled 15) in ADF0

inductor **L16**. The 34-point arithmetic-performing subtree (underlined above) assigns a value of 56,000 µH to new inductor **L16**. This 34-point subtree is abbreviated in Figure 27.22 as value V1 (labeled 17). Figure 27.32 shows the result of executing the NOP and L functions in ADF0 (labeled 34).

The developmental process then encounters the first SERIES function in ADF0 (labeled 18 in Figure 27.22 and underlined below).

```
(NOP (L (+ 0.504 (- (+ (+ (+ 0.0830 0.406) (- -0.243 0.658)) (-
(- (+ (+ 8.086497E-01 0.407) (-0.893 -0.113)) -0.212) (- (+ (-
-0.506 -0.0313) (- -0.243 0.658)) (- (- 0.556 0.0370)
-0.946)))) -0.000741)) (SERIES (SERIES END (L -0.000741 (L
0.0609 END)) END) END (NOP (PARALLEL0 END END END (C -0.949
END)))))).
```

This SERIES function (labeled 18) creates a series composition consisting of the original inductor **L16**, a new modifiable wire **Z17**, and a duplicate 56,000 µH inductor **L18**. This SERIES function spawns three writing heads. Figure 27.33 shows the result of executing the first SERIES function (labeled 18) in ADF0.

Control then passes to the second SERIES function in ADF0 (labeled 23 in Figure 27.22 and underlined below). This SERIES function is applied to inductor **L16**.

```
(NOP (L (+ 0.504 (- (+ (+ (+ 0.0830 0.406) (- -0.243 0.658)) (-
(- (+ (+ 8.086497E-01 0.407) (-0.893 -0.113)) -0.212) (- (+ (-
-0.506 -0.0313) (- -0.243 0.658)) (- (- 0.556 0.0370)
-0.946)))) -0.000741)) (SERIES (SERIES END (L -0.000741 (L
0.0609 END)) END) END (NOP (PARALLEL0 END END END (C -0.949
END)))))).
```

This second SERIES function (labeled 23) creates a series composition consisting of inductor L16 (i.e., the component to which the first writing head spawned by the first SERIES labeled 18 is pointing), a new modifiable wire Z19, and another duplicate 56,000 µH inductor L20. This SERIES function also spawns three writing heads. Figure 27.34 shows the result of executing the second SERIES function (labeled 23) in ADF0.

The breadth-first execution of the program tree next causes the execution of the END function (labeled 24 in Figure 27.22)—thereby eliminating the writing head on Z17 created by the first SERIES function (labeled 18). Then, the NOP function (labeled 25) is executed. As it happens, the four executions of ADF0 do not interact in this particular program, so the NOP function does not influence the electrical circuit that is ultimately developed.

Control then passes to the END function (labeled 35 in Figure 27.22) that eliminates the writing head on L16.

Development then proceeds to the L function (labeled 36 in Figure 27.22 and underlined below) in ADF0. This component-creating function operates on Z19 and converts it into inductor L21. The small numerical value −0.000741 (underlined below and abbreviated as V2 at point 45 of Figure 27.22) causes the value of inductor L21 to be set to 0.998 µH.

```
(NOP (L (+ 0.504 (- (+ (+ (+ 0.0830 0.406) (- -0.243 0.658)) (-
(- (+ (+ 8.086497E-01 0.407) (-0.893 -0.113)) -0.212) (- (+ (-
-0.506 -0.0313) (- -0.243 0.658)) (- (- 0.556 0.0370)
-0.946)))) -0.000741)) (SERIES (SERIES END (L -0.000741 (L
0.0609 END)) END) END (NOP (PARALLEL0 END END END (C -0.949
END)))))).
```

Figure 27.35 shows the result of executing the L function (labeled 36) in ADF0.

Control then passes to the END function (labeled 37 in Figure 27.22) that eliminates the writing head on L20. Then control passes to the PARALLEL0 parallel division function (labeled 38). We defer discussing this PARALLEL0 function for a moment so we can complete the developmental story concerning inductor L21. The L function in ADF0 (labeled 46 in Figure 27.22 and underlined below) converts it into a differently valued inductor. Specifically, the numerical value 0.0609 (also underlined below and abbreviated in Figure 27.22 as V3 at point 52) revalues L21 to 1.15 µH.

```
NOP (L (+ 0.504 (- (+ (+ (+ 0.0830 0.406) (- -0.243 0.658)) (-
(- (+ (+ 8.086497E-01 0.407) (-0.893 -0.113)) -0.212) (- (+ (-
-0.506 -0.0313) (- -0.243 0.658)) (- (- 0.556 0.0370)
-0.946)))) -0.000741)) (SERIES (SERIES END (L -0.000741
(L 0.0609 END)) END) END (NOP (PARALLEL0 END END END
(C -0.949 END)))))).
```

Figure 27.36 shows the result of executing the L function (labeled 46) in ADF0.

Return now to the PARALLEL0 parallel division function (labeled 38 and underlined below) that operates on L18 and creates a parallel composition consisting of new inductor L22, two new wires (Z23 and Z24), and L18. This PARALLEL0 function spawns four writing heads.

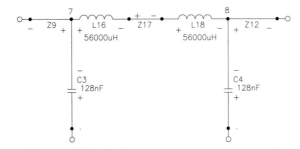

Figure 27.33   Result of executing the first SERIES function (labeled 18) in ADF0

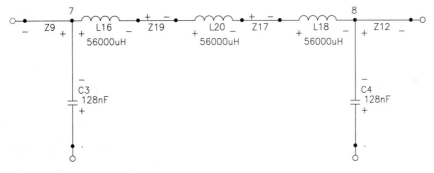

Figure 27.34   Result of executing the second SERIES function (labeled 23) in ADF0

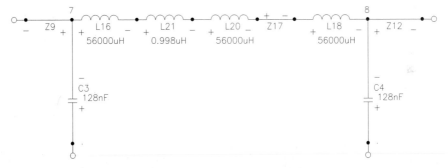

Figure 27.35   Result of executing the L function (labeled 36) in ADF0

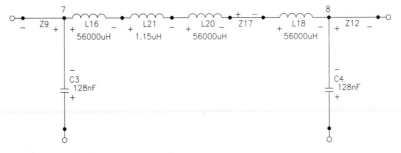

Figure 27.36   Result of executing the L function (labeled 46) in ADF0

```
(NOP (L (+ 0.504 (- (+ (+ (+ 0.0830 0.406) (- -0.243 0.658)) (-
(- (+ (+ 8.086497E-01 0.407) (-0.893 -0.113)) -0.212) (- (+ (-
-0.506 -0.0313) (- -0.243 0.658)) (- (- 0.556 0.0370)
-0.946)))) -0.000741)) (SERIES (SERIES END (L -0.000741 (L
0.0609 END)) END) END (NOP (PARALLEL0 END END END (C -0.949
END))))))).
```

Figure 27.37 shows the result of executing the PARALLEL0 function (labeled 38) in ADF0.

Figure 27.37 illustrates an interesting aspect of the developmental process. Note that at this particular point in the developmental process, nodes 8 and 9 are connected only by modifiable wire Z24. If Z24 is never subsequently converted into a nonwire component, the result will be two inductors in series (L22 and L18). In this event, just before the circuit is submitted to SPICE, L22 and L18 will be consolidated into one inductor, nodes 8 and 9 will be compressed into one node, and Z24 will disappear. However, if Z24 were to be cut (as was the case in generation 24), L18 and C4 would then constitute an inductive-capacitive shunt (to ground). As will be seen momentarily (in Figure 27.39), Z24 will be converted into a capacitor, thereby creating a triangular substructure consisting of L22, L18, and C25.

Three of these writing heads spawned by the PARALLEL0 function (labeled 38) are quickly terminated by END functions (at 47, 48, and 49).

Now consider the C function (labeled 50 and underlined below). This C function operates on modifiable wire Z24 and converts it into capacitor C25. The small numerical value –0.949 (underlined below and abbreviated as V4 at point 54 of Figure 27.22) causes capacitor C25 to acquire the component value of 0.112 nF.

```
(NOP (L (+ 0.504 (- (+ (+ (+ 0.0830 0.406) (- -0.243 0.658)) (-
(- (+ (+ 8.086497E-01 0.407) (-0.893 -0.113)) -0.212) (- (+ (-
-0.506 -0.0313) (- -0.243 0.658)) (- (- 0.556 0.0370)
-0.946)))) -0.000741)) (SERIES (SERIES END (L -0.000741 (L
0.0609 END)) END) END (NOP (PARALLEL0 END END END (C -0.949
END))))))).
```

Figure 27.38 shows the result of executing the three END functions (labeled 47, 48, and 49) and the C function (labeled 50) in ADF0.

Note that L16, L21, L20, Z17, L22, Z23, L18, and C25 are all created from modifiable wire Z6 by ADF0. Note also that even though Z6 was a mere wire with two leads (at nodes 7 and 8 of Figure 27.38), the result of executing ADF0 is a substructure with three ports (at nodes 7, 8, and 9 of this figure). These three ports arise as a consequence of the execution of the PARALLEL0 function (labeled 38) followed by the execution of C function (labeled 50), which causes nodes 8 and 9 of this figure to become separated by an intervening component (i.e., capacitor C25).

The END functions (labeled 53 and 55) eliminate the writing heads on L21 and C25. Figure 27.39 shows the three-port substructure created by ADF0.

Figure 27.40 presents the best-of-run circuit from generation 35 (presented earlier as Figures 27.19 and 27.21) using the triangular three-port substructure created by ADF0.

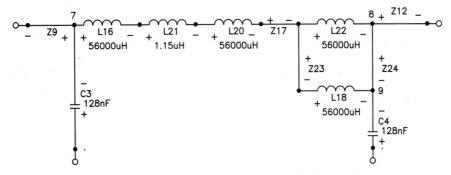

Figure 27.37 Result of executing the PARALLEL0 function (labeled 38) in ADF0

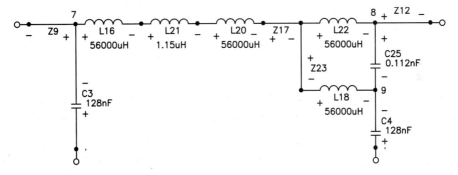

Figure 27.38 Result of executing the C function (labeled 50) in ADF0

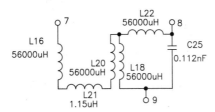

Figure 27.39 The generic three-port substructure created by ADF0

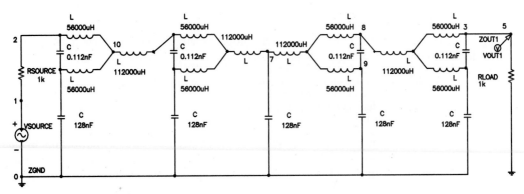

Figure 27.40 Different presentation of the best-of-run circuit from generation 35

27.4 INVENTION AND CREATIVITY IN GENETIC PROGRAMMING

Figure 27.41 consolidates the pairs and triplets of series inductors (and deletes the four tiny 0.112 nF capacitors) from the best circuit (Figure 27.17) of generation 31 of this run of genetic programming. This circuit represents the rediscovery, by genetic programming, of the elliptic filter topology for which Wilhelm Cauer of Gottingen, Germany, received three U.S. patents (Cauer 1934, 1935, 1936).

As Cauer explained in U.S. patent 1,989,545 (Cauer 1935),

> One of the objects of this invention is to provide new and improved electric-wave filters, some of them of new types, never known before . . .

> It is further an object of my invention to improve upon filters of types already known, to the ends that their efficiency may be improved, their cost of manufacture lessened, and the number of elements, of which they are composed, reduced.

The Cauer filter was a significant advance (both theoretically and commercially) over the previously known Campbell, Zobel, Johnson, Butterworth, and Chebychev filters. For example, for one commercially important set of specifications for telephones, a fifth-order elliptic filter matches the behavior of a 17th-order Butterworth filter or an eighth-order Chebychev filter. Most pertinently, the fifth-order elliptic filter has one less inductor than the eighth-order Chebychev filter. As Van Valkenburg (1982, page 379) relates in connection with the history of the elliptic filter,

> Cauer first used his new theory in solving a filter problem for the German telephone industry. His new design achieved specifications with one less inductor than had ever been done before. The world first learned of the Cauer method not through scholarly publication but through a patent disclosure, which eventually reached the Bell Laboratories. Legend has it that the entire Mathematics Department of Bell Laboratories spent the next two weeks at the New York Public Library studying elliptic functions. Cauer had studied mathematics under Hilbert at Goettingen, and so elliptic functions and their applications were familiar to him.

Genetic programming did not, of course, study mathematics under Hilbert or anybody else. Nonetheless, the elliptic topology invented and patented by Cauer emerged in generation 31 of this run of genetic programming using automatically defined functions. The elliptic topology emerged during this run of genetic programming as a natural consequence of the problem's fitness measure and natural selection—not because the run was primed with domain knowledge about elliptic functions. That is, genetic programming opportunistically *reinvented* the elliptic topology in this run because, as they say, necessity is the mother of invention.

Cauer received a patent for his invention of the elliptic filter because it satisfied the legal criteria for obtaining a U.S. patent, namely, that his filter was "new and useful" and

> . . . the differences between the subject matter sought to be patented and the prior art are such that the subject matter as a whole would [not] have been obvious at the time the invention was made to a person having ordinary skill in the art to which said subject matter pertains. (35 *United States Code* 103a.)

The fact that genetic programming rediscovered an electrical circuit that was unobvious "to a person having ordinary skill in the art" establishes that this evolved result satisfies Arthur Samuel's criterion (1983) for artificial intelligence and machine learning:

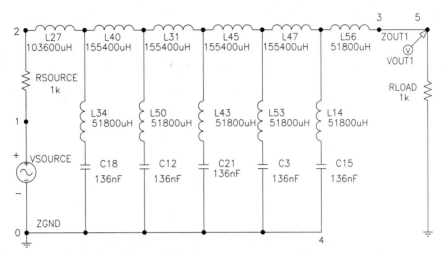

Figure 27.41   Reinvention by genetic programming of the Cauer (elliptic) filter topology

The aim [is] . . . to get machines to exhibit behavior, which if done by humans, would be assumed to involve the use of intelligence.

Referring to the eight criteria in Chapter 1 for establishing that an automatically created result is competitive with a human-produced result, this result satisfies the following two of the eight criteria:

A. The result was patented as an invention in the past, is an improvement over a patented invention, or would qualify today as a patentable new invention.

F. The result is equal to or better than a result that was considered an achievement in its field at the time it was first discovered.

Therefore, we make the following claim:

- **CLAIM NO. 5** We claim that the reinvention by genetic programming of the patented Cauer (elliptic) topology for filters is an instance where genetic programming has produced a result that is competitive with a result created by a creative and inventive human.

Cauer received a patent on the elliptic filter because his idea satisfied the threshold statutory test of being unobvious "to a person having ordinary skill in the art." In contrast, a new idea that can be logically deduced from facts that are known in a field, using transformations that are known in a field, is not patentable. The patent law requires what is called an "illogical step" to distinguish a proposed invention from that which is easily deducible from current knowledge. In the invention process, the human inventor provides the required illogic.

The following gedankenexperiment clarifies the difference between a deterministic logic-driven and knowledge-based technique of automated reasoning and a probabilistic problem-solving technique (such as genetic programming).

Suppose we tried to assemble a set of if-then rules for designing a filter. One of the rules might state that if a lowpass filter is desired, then the topology of the circuit should be a Campbell ladder composed of a capacitor in the vertical shunt of each of the ladder's rungs and a series inductor horizontally in each rung. A set of additional rules might specify the number of rungs in the ladder. For example, one rule might state that if the requirements of the desired filter lie in a certain specified range (perhaps stated in terms of its modular angle and reflection coefficient), then the ladder should have exactly k rungs. Yet another group of rules might state that if the requirements of the desired filter lie in a certain specified range, then the correct sizing for capacitor i ($1 \leq i \leq k$) of the ladder is given by a particular entry in a precomputed table (specific to k-rung ladders). Similarly, the correct sizing for inductor i ($1 \leq i \leq k$) might be given by an entry in another precomputed table (specific to k-rung ladders).

In fact, "cookbooks" with tables such as just described exist for standard ladder filters and other types of standard filters (Williams and Taylor 1995). Such cookbooks are commonly used nowadays for designing standard filters, and these, in turn, often serve as a starting point for human engineers designing nonstandard filters.

It is clear that a vast number of different standard lowpass Campbell ladder filters can be designed using codified knowledge and logical rules. However, this kind of knowledge-based, logic-driven system is closed, deterministic, and brittle. No matter how many times such a system for lowpass ladder filters is exercised, it will never invent the Cauer (elliptic) topology or Zobel's M-derived half section.

If the desired filter is anything other than a standard lowpass filter, the system just described must be significantly modified in order to solve the problem. If, for example, a standard highpass filter (such as the one discussed in Chapter 26) is desired, new rules must be added to the system to reflect the fact that the locations of the capacitor and inductor are reversed in each rung of the ladder in a highpass filter. If a standard bandpass filter is desired, additional, more complicated rules must be added to grapple with the greater complexity of a filter with two stopbands and one passband. Different additional rules are required for a standard bandstop filter. Different tables (and, in some cases, rules) may be required for Chebychev filters (Chapter 37) than Butterworth filters.

More importantly, all of these comments apply only to standard "textbook" filters. No one knows, in general, how to write rules for automatically synthesizing the nonstandard filters that constitute the bulk of contemporary design work in the real world (e.g., the asymmetric bandpass filter of Chapter 31).

As we have already seen, genetic programming differs considerably from logic-driven and knowledge-based techniques in terms of ease of grappling with a new problem. This point was made, for example, in the discussion of the minor differences in the preparatory steps of genetic programming for the problem of synthesizing a highpass filter, a bandstop filter, and a frequency-measuring circuit (Chapter 26) versus the problem of synthesizing a lowpass filter (Chapter 25). This point will be reinforced later (in Chapter 31) by the minor differences in the preparatory steps of genetic programming for the problem of synthesizing a highly nonstandard asymmetric bandpass filter versus the problem of synthesizing a lowpass filter.

However, the differences between genetic programming and conventional logic-driven and knowledge-based techniques go far beyond brittleness and the convenience of handling the perpetual novelty of real-world environments. The more important difference is that genetic programming can be creative and inventive. The ability of genetic programming to be creative and inventive is directly related to five of the seven fundamental differences cited in Chapter 1 between genetic programming and conventional logic-driven and knowledge-based techniques of artificial intelligence and machine learning. In particular, genetic programming

- conducts its search probabilistically,
- employs a population (as opposed to a point-to-point search),
- does not rely exclusively on greedy hill climbing,
- does not use an explicit knowledge base, and
- does not rely on formal logic to guide the search.

The fact that genetic programming conducts its search probabilistically and does not rely exclusively on greedy hill climbing contributes directly to its ability to be inventive and creative. As Hofstadter observed in *Fluid Concepts and Creative Analogies* (Hofstadter and the Fluid Analogies Research Group 1995, page 115), both of these aspects of the search are advantageous in a space about which there are numerous unknown relationships:

> The advantage of choosing at random is that you don't waste precious time worrying over matters that you can't possibly anticipate—you simply make a snap educated guess, plunge forward, and see what happens. . . .

> This [random] strategy should not be confused with blindness. Although the "choices" at branch-points are made at random, there are powerful biases built in. Not everything has an equal chance; indeed, smart ideas will tend to be assigned high urgencies, and dumb ones low urgencies. . . .

> There is another aspect to the hope based on randomness: to a program that exploits randomness, *all pathways are open*, even if most have very low probabilities; conversely, to a program whose choices are always made by consulting a fixed deterministic strategy, many pathways are *a priori* completely closed off. This means that many creative ideas will simply never get discovered by a program that relies totally on [conventional artificial] "intelligence." In many circumstances, the most interesting routes will be more likely to be discovered by accidental exploration than if the "best" route at each junction is invariably chosen. [Emphasis in original.]

The use of a population contributes to the inventiveness and creativity of genetic programming because the availability of a population of points from the search space (i.e., not just a single point) is the precondition for a recombinative operation such as crossover. As an example of the role of crossover in relation to inventiveness, recall that the female parent in the crossover described in Section 25.17.1 had a good topology, but poor component sizing. The male parent in this mating had good sizing, but poor topology. The offspring had both good topology and good sizing. Sections 25.17.2, 25.17.3, and 56.5 similarly show how superior individuals result from the recombination of useful parts of one parent from the population and useful parts of another parent. In other words, the crossover operation in genetic programming can be viewed as a mechanism for combining preexisting ideas in new ways. As the French mathematician Hadamard (1945) noted in *The Psychology of Invention in the Mathematical Field*,

> The possibility of imputing discovery to pure chance is already excluded. . . . Indeed, it is obvious that invention or discovery, be it in mathematics or anywhere else, takes place by combining ideas.

Genetic programming does not employ an explicit knowledge base or formal logic. It therefore avoids the brittle and closed nature of such systems. Of course, when we say that genetic programming does not employ formal logic, we do not mean that it lacks a sound mathematical justification, that its operational steps are not precisely defined, or that it is illogical in a pejorative sense. We simply mean that the mathematical justification for genetic programming is statistical, not logical. The mathematical justification for the probabilistic fitness-weighted allocation of trials in genetic programming is the same as that for genetic algorithms (Holland 1975) and is closely related to the mathematical justification for simulated annealing (Kirkpatrick, Gelatt, and Vecchi 1983; Aarts and Korst 1989).

27.5 GENETIC PROGRAMMING AS AN INVENTION MACHINE

Interestingly, the remainder of 35 *United States Code* 103a (quoted in the preceding section) goes on to state:

> Patentability shall not be negatived by the manner in which the invention was made.

This wording suggests the possibility that genetic programming can potentially be used as an "invention machine" to produce patentable inventions. Unencumbered by preconceptions that may channel human thinking along well-trodden paths, genetic programming starts each run as a new adventure that is free to innovate in any manner that satisfies the requirements of the problem. Genetic programming is a search that is guided by the necessities articulated by the fitness measure of the particular problem at hand. Genetic programming approaches each new problem in terms of "what needs to be done"—not "how to do it."

27.6 THE DARWINIAN INVENTION MACHINE

We have already demonstrated that genetic programming is capable of automatically creating entities that satisfy useful design requirements. However, genetic programming can serve as an invention machine only if, additionally, it can generate entities that are novel. Novelty is a precondition for an invention and for obtaining a patent. Using the terminology of the patent law, a proposed new patent will not be granted if it "reads on" (i.e., possesses the key characteristics of) the "prior art." The prior art consists of all of the previously known solutions to the problem at hand—whether patented or not.

In this section, we show that genetic programming can be used to automatically create designs that are both useful and novel. This is accomplished by employing a two-element fitness measure that incorporates both the degree to which a candidate design satisfies the problem's design requirements and the degree to which the candidate design avoids characteristics that read on the relevant prior art.

The idea of novelty-driven evolution will be illustrated using the problem of synthesizing the design for a lowpass filter circuit (having the same design requirements as used earlier in this chapter and in Chapter 25).

Imagine that the clock has been turned back to the early 1920s when the Campbell ladder filter was known, but Cauer had not yet invented the elliptic filter. At that point in time, the prior art consisted of ladder filters (such as the seven-rung ladder filter shown in Figure 25.57). There was a long-standing need in the telephone industry for filters that would be less expensive to manufacture while satisfying the particular technical requirements of filters for telephones.

Imagine further that Cauer had not studied elliptic functions under Hilbert at Goettingen but, instead, had studied genetic programming.

If Cauer were applying genetic programming in the 1920s to invent a new type of filter to satisfy the industrial need for more efficient filters, he would first need to satisfy the technical requirements for filters in telephones. Cauer could accomplish this objective simply by using the weighted sum of the absolute value of the differences between a candidate circuit's frequency response and the desired frequency response (i.e., the same fitness measure used earlier in this chapter and described in detail in Section 25.14.4).

If Cauer further desired to create a design that differed from the prior art of the 1920s, he would additionally need to give the fitness measure a means for measuring the similarity between a circuit employing the relevant prior art and a candidate circuit in the population being bred by genetic programming. There are numerous alternative ways to implement this element of the fitness measure. Since circuits can be conveniently represented by labeled graphs, one approach is to use a graph isomorphism algorithm to compute the degree of similarity between a graph representing a candidate circuit and one (or more) template graphs representing the key characteristics of the field's relevant prior art. In particular, a measure of similarity based on the size of the maximal common subgraph between a candidate circuit and one template circuit representing the relevant prior art (i.e., the Campbell ladder filter) works for this particular problem.

Of course, graph isomorphism is only one of numerous possible approaches for measuring the degree of similarity between the prior art and a candidate design in a population being bred by genetic programming. In many instances, a rule-based system will be an especially convenient way to ascertain whether a candidate design reads on a field's prior art. Regardless of the chosen approach, the measurement of the degree of similarity between the relevant prior art and a candidate design represents a marriage between genetic programming and a knowledge-based approach.

27.6.1 Preparatory Steps

The initial circuit, program architecture, function set, and terminal set are the same as those used in Sections 25.14.1 through 25.14.3.

Fitness

The fitness measure for a circuit is measured in terms of two factors. The first factor measures the circuit's behavior in the frequency domain (in the same manner as Section 25.14.4) while the second factor measures the circuit's similarity to a Campbell ladder filter.

The second factor is measured in terms of the largest number of nodes and edges (circuit components) of a subgraph of the given circuit that is isomorphic to a subgraph of a template representing the prior art. The template is a ladder that is far larger than would ever be needed to solve the problem at hand. The template (Figure 27.42) consists of 16 shunt capacitors, 17 series inductors, and the circuit's voltage source and source resistor.

The score is determined by a graph isomorphism algorithm (Ullman 1976; Lingas 1981) with the cost function being based on the number of shared nodes and edges (instead of just the number of nodes). Since this graph isomorphism algorithm works with graph adjacency matrices and since circuits often contain parallel compositions of

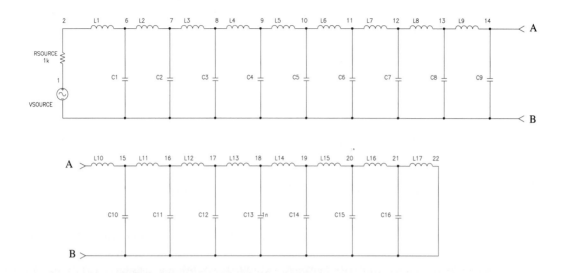

Figure 27.42 **Prior art template for Campbell ladder filter**

two different components, each pair of parallel components that is encountered is treated as if it were a type of component different from either a single capacitor or single inductor.

A lower value of each of the above two fitness factors is better. For circuits not scoring the maximum number of hits (101), the fitness of a circuit is the product of the two factors. For circuits scoring 101 hits (100%-compliant individuals), fitness is the number of shared nodes and edges divided by 10,000. This arrangement almost always assigns a better (lower) fitness to any individual scoring 101 hits than to any individual not scoring 101 hits.

The smaller the overall value of fitness, the better. A value of zero is unattainable because no actual analog filter can perfectly satisfy the problem's requirements in the frequency domain and because every actual circuit has a nonzero number of nodes and edges that also appear in the template (even those associated with just a single inductor or capacitor).

For reference, the factor pertaining to the frequency response of the seven-rung ladder of Figure 25.57 is 0.00784, and its isomorphism factor is 25. (The calculation of the isomorphism score will be explained and illustrated in detail in Tables 27.2 and 27.3 in connection with two other circuits).

As usual, unsimulatable circuits receive a high penalty value of fitness (10^8).

Control Parameters

The population size, M, is 1,950,000 (with $Q = 30,000$; $D = 65$). This run was made on 65 nodes of our 70-node Beowulf-style parallel computer (described in Section 62.1.5). On each generation, four boatloads of emigrants, each consisting of $B = 2\%$ (the migration rate) of the node's subpopulation (selected on the basis of fitness) were dispatched

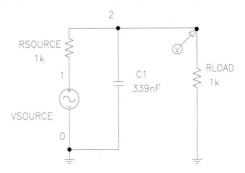

Figure 27.43 Best circuit of generation 0

to each of the four adjacent processing nodes. A maximum size of 300 points was established for each branch of each circuit-constructing program tree.

Termination Criterion and Result Designation

Since the goal was to generate a variety of 100%-compliant circuits for post run examination, the run was not automatically terminated upon evolution of the first 100%-compliant individual. Instead, the maximum number of generations, G, is set to an arbitrary, large number (e.g., 501); numerous 100%-compliant circuits were harvested; and the run was manually monitored and manually terminated.

27.6.2 Results

The best-of-generation circuit from generation 0 (Figure 27.43) scores 52 hits (out of 101). In this circuit, the incoming signal **VSOURCE** passes through the source resistor **RSOURCE**. Node 2 is then connected to a single 339 nF shunt capacitor connected to ground and to the load resistor **RLOAD** connected to ground.

The overall fitness of this best-of-generation circuit from generation 0 is 296.5 because the factor pertaining to this circuit's frequency response is 59.30 and because this circuit's isomorphism factor is 5. The isomorphism factor is 5 because the largest number of nodes and edges of a subgraph of this circuit that is isomorphic to a subgraph of the 17-inductor, 16-capacitor template (Figure 27.42) consists of the five nodes and edges shown in Table 27.2. Note that capacitor **C1** does not contribute to the isomorphism score because it is parallel with the source resistor in this best-of-generation circuit.

Figure 27.44a shows the behavior in the frequency domain of the best circuit of generation 0. As can be seen, the behavior of this circuit bears very little resemblance to the desired lowpass filter. The circuit delivers a full volt only for frequencies up to about 50 Hz. The circuit suppresses the incoming signal only for a handful of frequencies near 100,000 Hz. There is a very large and leisurely transition region in between.

The best-of-generation circuit from generation 16 (Figure 27.45) has three inductors and four capacitors and scores 95 hits. Capacitors **C1**, **C2**, **C3**, and **C4** are shunt capacitors and constitute the rungs of a classical ladder, while inductors **L1**, **L4**, and **L3** (horizontally across the top of the figure) are the ladder's series inductors. This circuit

Table 27.2 Explanation of isomorphism factor of 5

Node or edge of best circuit of generation 0	Node or edge of template
Node 0	Node 0
VSOURCE	VSOURCE
Node 1	Node 1
RSOURCE	RSOURCE
Node2	Node2

constitutes the rediscovery by genetic programming of the Campbell ladder topology. Accordingly, when this is compared with the template, this circuit is assigned a high (undesirable) isomorphism factor. The overall fitness of this circuit from generation 16 is 32.32 because the factor pertaining to this circuit's frequency response is 2.694 and this circuit's isomorphism factor is 12.

Figure 27.44b shows the behavior in the frequency domain of the best circuit of generation 16. As can be seen, the behavior of this circuit bears some resemblance to the desired lowpass filter. Its transition region is more sharply defined than that of the best circuit of generation 0 (Figure 27.44a).

Some circuits that are evolved during the run score well primarily because of the factor pertaining to the circuit's frequency response while others score well because of the isomorphism factor. Two circuits from generation 18 illustrate the competitive tension between the two factors of the fitness measure. Both are pace-setting circuits; the second one is, in fact, the best-of-generation circuit from generation 18.

The overall fitness of one of the pace-setting circuits (called "A") from early in generation 18 (Figure 27.46) is 30.585. The factor of the fitness measure pertaining to this circuit's frequency response is 6.117, and its isomorphism factor is only 5 (reflecting the great dissimilarity between this topologically novel circuit and the 17-inductor, 16-capacitor template of Figure 27.42).

The best-of-generation circuit (called circuit "B") from generation 18 has five inductors and four capacitors (Figure 27.47). The overall fitness of circuit B from generation 18 is 11.556 because the factor pertaining to this circuit's frequency response is 0.7704 and this circuit's isomorphism factor is high (15). The isomorphism factor is 15 because the largest number of nodes and edges of a subgraph of this circuit that is isomorphic to a subgraph of the 17-inductor, 16-capacitor template (Figure 27.42) consists of the 15 nodes and edges shown in Table 27.3.

The fitness of the best-of-generation individuals improves as the run proceeds from generation to generation. Circuits begin to appear that score well because of both the isomorphism factor and the factor pertaining to the circuit's frequency response. Finally, circuits appear that are 100%-compliant (i.e., circuits scoring 101 hits).

Table 27.4 shows the factor pertaining to the circuit's frequency response, the isomorphism factor, and the overall fitness for eight different 100%-compliant circuits that were harvested from this run. As can be seen, the factors pertaining to the frequency response of all of these 100%-compliant circuits are each about 3 orders of magnitude better than that of the best circuit of generation 0.

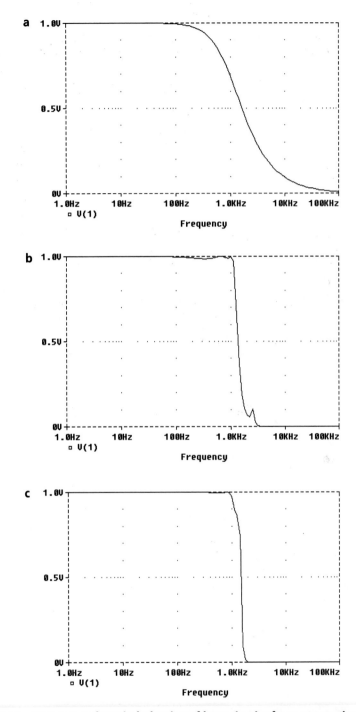

Figure 27.44 Frequency domain behavior of best circuits from generation (*a*) 0, (*b*) 16, and (*c*) solution 8 (100%-compliant circuit with one form of the elliptic topology)

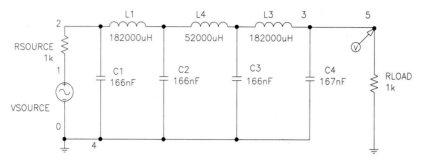

Figure 27.45 Best circuit of generation 16

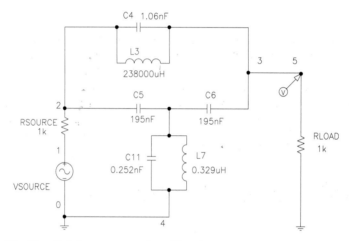

Figure 27.46 Circuit A from generation 18

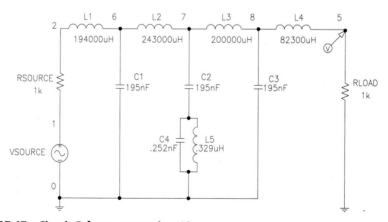

Figure 27.47 Circuit B from generation 18

Table 27.3 Explanation of isomorphism factor of 15 for circuit B from generation 18

Node or edge of best circuit B	Node or edge of template
Node 0	Node0
VSOURCE	VSOURCE
Node 1	Node 1
RSOURCE	RSOURCE
Node 2	Node 2
L1	L1
C1	C1
Node 6	Node 6
L2	L2
Node 7	Node 7
L3	L3
Node 8	Node 8
C3	C3
L4	L4
Node5	Node 9

Table 27.4 Fitness of eight 100%-compliant circuits

Solution	Frequency response factor	Isomorphism factor	Overall fitness	Figure
1	0.051039	7	0.357273	Figure 27.48
2	0.117093	7	0.819651	Figure 27.49
3	0.103064	7	0.721448	Figure 27.50
4	0.161101	7	1.127707	Figure 27.51
5	0.044382	13	0.044382	Figure 27.52
6	0.133877	7	0.937139	Figure 27.53
7	0.059993	5	0.299965	Figure 27.54
8	0.062345	11	0.685795	Figure 27.55

None of the 100%-compliant circuits from this run have the Campbell ladder topology. Figures 27.48 through 27.55 show eight topologically novel 100%-compliant circuits that were created by this run.

In general, almost all of the components of each of these eight 100%-compliant circuits are necessary to achieve the circuit's 100% compliance (101 hits). For example, Table 27.5 shows the number of hits achieved by a circuit created by deleting a particular inductor or capacitor from Figure 27.54 (solution 7). For purposes of this analysis, a deletion is implemented by setting the component's value to zero (so that a capacitor becomes an open circuit and an inductor becomes a wire). As can be seen, all but one of these single-component deletions significantly degrade the circuit's behavior and reduce

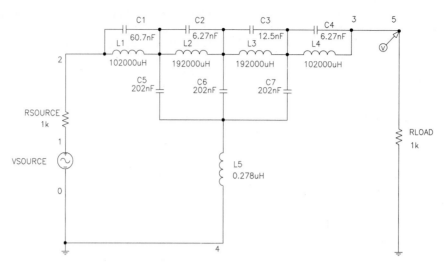

Figure 27.48 Solution 1

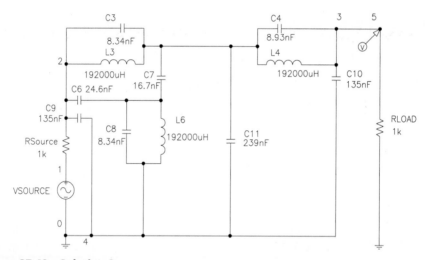

Figure 27.49 Solution 2

the number of hits below 101 (the exception being the deletion of the minuscule 21.6 μH inductor **L3**).

Figure 27.55 (solution 8) is the chronologically first individual scoring 101 hits that appeared in the run. This circuit has an overall fitness of 0.685795. The factor of the fitness measure pertaining to the circuit's frequency response is 0.062345 while the isomorphism factor is 11. The result-producing branches of its circuit-constructing program tree contain 181 and 115 points, respectively. This circuit has four inductors and seven capacitors. The circuit consists of four parallel compositions of an inductor and a capacitor (appearing horizontally across the top of the figure) and three shunt capacitors

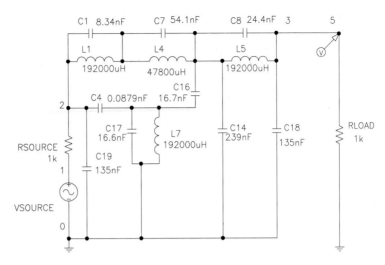

Figure 27.50   Solution 3

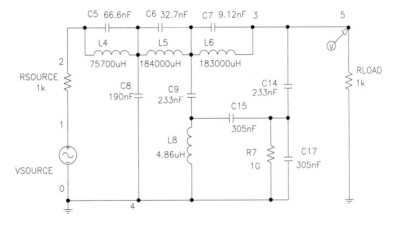

Figure 27.51   Solution 4

(appearing vertically in the figure). Figure 27.44c shows the behavior in the frequency domain of the circuit from Figure 27.55. As can be seen, the circuit delivers nearly a full volt for frequencies up to 1,000 Hz; there is a very sharp drop-off between 1,000 Hz and 2,000 Hz; and the circuit effectively suppresses the output above 2,000 Hz.

Thus, genetic programming evolved multiple novel solutions in this run to the given problem. Each of the evolved solutions avoided the prior art (i.e., the ladder topology).

Once genetic programming has successfully created one or more novel solutions to the given problem, a design engineer may examine them. Some may have unexpected virtues. For example, solution 8 (Figure 27.55) is one form of the elliptic filter that Cauer invented and patented (Cauer 1934, 1935, 1936). Notice that the elliptic topology of Figure 27.55 differs from the elliptic topology of Figure 27.17. The reason is that there

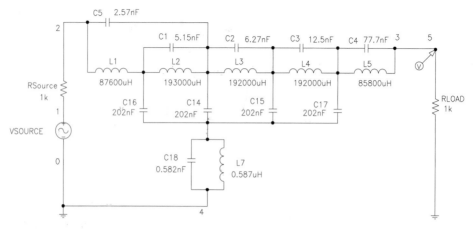

Figure 27.52 Solution 5

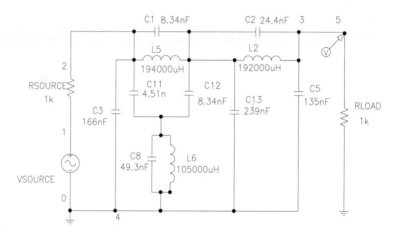

Figure 27.53 Solution 6

are two behaviorally equivalent alternative topologies for elliptic (and other) filters composed of inductors and capacitors.

Cauer invented the elliptic filter topology using the mathematical principles of elliptic functions. In contrast, genetic programming used evolution and natural selection. In Section 27.3, genetic programming rediscovered one form of the elliptic filter topology using a fitness measure based only on frequency response. In this section, genetic programming rediscovered a second form of the elliptic filter topology (and seven other novel solutions) using a fitness measure based on both frequency response and novelty. This section demonstrates the principle that novelty-driven evolution can be used to automate the invention process and that genetic programming can be used as an invention machine.

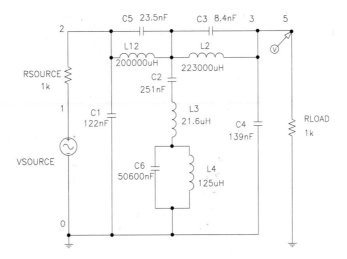

Figure 27.54   Solution 7

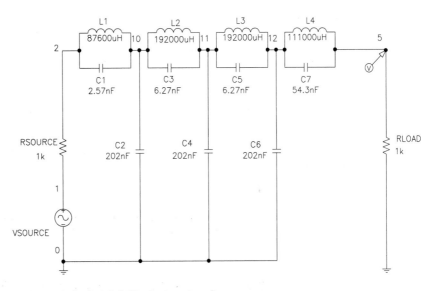

Figure 27.55   Solution 8 (elliptic topology)

27.6.3   Engineering around the Prior Art

The above imaginary scenario for reinventing the elliptic filter assumed Cauer's goal was to obtain a patent for himself. However, sometimes the goal is simply to avoid infringing on a preexisting patent. For example, practicing engineers in industry are often called upon to create a design that does not read on the claims of unexpired patents (notably those held by competing companies). Novelty-driven evolution can be used to "engineer around" a field's prior art in order to avoid patent infringement.

Table 27.5 Effect of deleting particular components from Solution 7

Component	Value	Number of hits
C1	122 nF	73
C2	251 nF	57
C3	8.4 nF	92
C4	139 nF	65
C5	23.5 nF	97
C6	50,600 nF	94
L2	223,000 µH	57
L3	21.6 µH	101
L4	125 µH	100
L12	200,000 µH	53

Emergence of Hierarchy Using Architecture-Altering Operations

Chapter 25 showed that genetic programming is capable of synthesizing the design of a lowpass filter circuit, and Chapter 27 showed that automatically defined functions can be advantageous for synthesizing the design for that circuit.

However, for any particular given problem of circuit synthesis, it may not be obvious a priori whether automatically defined functions should be employed at all. If they are employed, it may not be obvious as to how many automatically defined functions should be employed, how many arguments each automatically defined function should possess, and what hierarchical references, if any, should be permitted among the automatically defined functions. Part 3 of this book demonstrated that it is possible to evolve the architecture of an overall program dynamically during a run of genetic programming using architecture-altering operations.

This chapter illustrates that the architecture-altering operations for automatically defined functions may be useful in evolving the design for a lowpass filter that satisfies the same design requirements as in Section 25.13. In this chapter, the architectural arrangement of the automatically defined functions will not be specified in advance, but instead will be dynamically evolved during the run of genetic programming using the architecture-altering operations.

28.1 DESIGN GOALS

The goal is to evolve, using automatically defined functions and the architecture-altering operations, the design for a lowpass filter that satisfies the same design characteristics as in Section 25.13.

28.2 PREPARATORY STEPS

28.2.1 Embryo and Test Fixture

The initial circuit (Figure 25.6) for this problem is the same as that of Chapters 25, 26, and 27. It is created by embedding the embryo with two modifiable wires and three ports (Figure 25.5) into the one-input, one-output test fixture with three ports (Figure 25.4).

28.2.2   Program Architecture

Since the embryo of the initial circuit has two modifiable wires—one associated with each of the result-producing branches—there are two result-producing branches in each program tree in the population.

Each program in generation 0 has a uniform architecture with two result-producing branches and no automatically defined functions. That is, the architecture of each program tree in generation 0 consists of two result-producing branches joined by a connective LIST function.

Automatically defined functions will be created during the run by the architecture-altering operations. The yet-to-be-created automatically defined functions will each possess zero arguments. Hierarchical references will be permitted between automatically defined functions.

28.2.3   Functions and Terminals

The initial function set for each construction-continuing subtree of a result-producing branch, $F_{\text{ccs-rpb-initial}}$, is

$F_{\text{ccs-rpb-initial}} = \{$C, L, SERIES, PARALLEL0, FLIP, NOP, THREE_GROUND, THREE_VIA0, THREE_VIA1, THREE_VIA2, THREE_VIA3, THREE_VIA4, THREE_VIA5, THREE_VIA6, THREE_VIA7$\}$.

The first seven functions take 2, 2, 3, 4, 1, 1, and 3 arguments, respectively. The eight THREE_VIA functions each take 3 arguments.

The initial terminal set for each construction-continuing subtree of a result-producing branch, $T_{\text{ccs-rpb-initial}}$, is

$T_{\text{ccs-rpb-initial}} = \{END, CUT\}$.

Since there are no automatically defined functions in generation 0 of this problem, $T_{\text{ccs-adf-initial}}$ and $F_{\text{ccs-adf-initial}}$ are empty.

The set of potential functions for each construction-continuing subtree of a result-producing branch, $F_{\text{ccs-rpb-potential}}$, is

$F_{\text{ccs-rpb-potential}} = \{$ADF0, ADF1, ADF2, ADF3$\}$.

The set of potential terminals for each construction-continuing subtree of a result-producing branch, $T_{\text{ccs-rpb-potential}}$, is empty:

$T_{\text{ccs-rpb-potential}} = \phi$.

The newly created automatically defined functions do not hierarchically refer to one another. The set of potential functions for each construction-continuing subtree of an automatically defined function, $F_{\text{ccs-adf-potential}}$, is

$F_{\text{ccs-adf-potential}} = \{$C, L, SERIES, PARALLEL0, FLIP, NOP, THREE_GROUND, THREE_VIA0, THREE_VIA1, THREE_VIA2, THREE_VIA3, THREE_VIA4, THREE_VIA5, THREE_VIA6, THREE_VIA7$\}$.

Since the newly created automatically defined functions possess no arguments, the set of potential terminals for each construction-continuing subtree of an automatically defined function, $T_{\text{ccs-adf-potential}}$, is empty.

$T_{\text{ccs-adf-potential}} = \{\texttt{END, CUT}\}.$

The function set, F_{aps}, for each arithmetic-performing subtree in any branch and the terminal set, T_{aps}, for each arithmetic-performing subtree in any branch are the same as for the lowpass filter problem in Section 25.14.3.

28.2.4   Fitness

The fitness measure is the same as in Section 25.14.4.

28.2.5   Parameters

The control parameters for this chapter are in the tableau (Table 28.1), the tables of percentages of genetic operations in Appendix D, and the default values specified in Appendix D.

28.2.6   Tableau

Table 28.1 summarizes the key features of the problem of designing a lowpass filter using architecture-altering operations.

28.3   RESULTS WITH A REUSED COMMON COMPONENT

One of the most basic (and important) uses for automatically defined functions is that of defining a particular substructure and reusing it multiple times for the purpose of creating *matched* values for components appearing in more than one place in a circuit. (It is also possible to create matched values for components with the crossover operation, as shown in Section 25.17.3).

The best-of-run individual program from generation 77 scores 101 hits (out of 101) and has a fitness of 0.000765. The program tree has 87 points in its RPB0 and 2 points in its RPB1 and has 65, 66, 94, and 9 points in ADF0, ADF1, ADF2, and ADF3, respectively.

This program acquired four automatically defined functions as a result of the architecture-altering operations. ADF0 is invoked six times, and ADF1 is invoked three times. The multiple reuse for these two automatically defined functions creates matched values in six and three different places, respectively.

Figure 28.1 shows the substructure created by ADF0. The substructure in ADF0 consists of a series composition of three inductors (which is, of course, electrically equivalent to one 155,400 μH inductor). The six invocations of ADF0 permit this value to be defined once and then reused on multiple occasions—thereby creating matched values in the six places.

ADF1 consists of one 37,300 μH inductor. The three invocations of ADF1 permit the value of this substructure to be created once and then reused on multiple occasions—thereby creating matched values in three places.

ADF2 consists only of one 28,600 μH inductor and is invoked only once.

ADF3 does not cause the creation of any components because it consists only of topology-modifying functions:

```
(PARALLEL0 END (SERIES END END (FLIP END)) END END).
```

Table 28.1 Tableau for lowpass filter using architecture-altering operations

Objective	Use the architecture-altering operations to design a lowpass filter composed of inductors and capacitors with a passband below 1,000 Hz, a stopband above 2,000 Hz, a maximum allowable passband deviation of 30 millivolts, and a maximum allowable stopband deviation of 1 millivolt.
Test fixture and embryo	One-input, one-output initial circuit with a source resistor, load resistor, and two modifiable wires
Program architecture	Two result-producing branches, RPB0 and RPB1, in generation 0. Zero-argument automatically defined functions will be created during the run by the architecture-altering operations.
Initial function set for the RPBs	For construction-continuing subtrees: $F_{ccs\text{-}rpb\text{-}initial}$ = {C, L, SERIES, PARALLEL0, FLIP, NOP, THREE_GROUND, THREE_VIA0, THREE_VIA1, THREE_VIA2, THREE_VIA3, THREE_VIA4, THREE_VIA5, THREE_VIA6, THREE_VIA7}. For arithmetic-performing subtrees: F_{aps} = {+, -}.
Initial terminal set for the RPBs	For construction-continuing subtrees: $T_{ccs\text{-}rpb\text{-}initial}$ = {END, CUT}. For arithmetic-performing subtrees: T_{aps} = {$\Re_{smaller\text{-}reals}$}.
Initial function set for the ADFs	No automatically defined functions in generation 0. $F_{ccs\text{-}adf\text{-}initial}$ = ϕ.
Initial terminal set for the ADFs	No automatically defined functions in generation 0. $T_{ccs\text{-}adf\text{-}initial}$ = ϕ.
Potential function set for the RPBs	$F_{ccs\text{-}rpb\text{-}potential}$ = {ADF0, ADF1, ADF2, ADF3}
Potential terminal set for the RPBs	$T_{ccs\text{-}rpb\text{-}potential}$ = ϕ
Potential function set for the ADFs	$F_{ccs\text{-}adf\text{-}potential}$ = {C, L, SERIES, PARALLEL0, FLIP, NOP, THREE_GROUND, THREE_VIA0, THREE_VIA1, THREE_VIA2, THREE_VIA3, THREE_VIA4, THREE_VIA5, THREE_VIA6, THREE_VIA7}
Potential terminal set for the ADFs	$T_{ccs\text{-}adf\text{-}potential}$ = {END, CUT}
Fitness cases	101 frequency values in an interval of five decades of frequency values between 1 Hz and 100,000 Hz
Raw fitness	The sum, over these 101 fitness cases, of the absolute weighted deviation between the actual value of the voltage that is produced by the circuit at the probe point and the target value for voltage
Standardized fitness	Same as raw fitness
Hits	The number of hits is defined as the number of fitness cases (out of 101) for which the voltage is acceptable or ideal or that lie in the "don't care" band.

Wrapper	None
Parameters	$M = 640{,}000$. $G = 501$. $Q = 10{,}000$. $D = 64$. $B = 2\%$. $S_{rpb} = 300$. $S_{adf} = 300$. $N_{rpb} = 2$. $N_{max\text{-}adf} = 4$. $N_{max\text{-}argument\text{-}adf} = 0$.
Result designation	Best-so-far pace-setting individual
Success predicate	A program scores the maximum number (101) of hits.

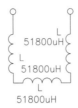

Figure 28.1 Substructure created by automatically defined function ADF0 of the best-of-run circuit from generation 77

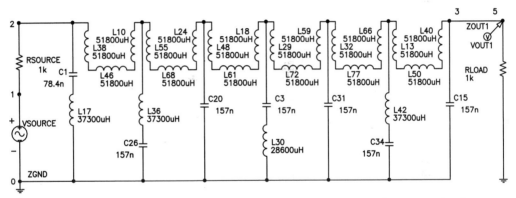

Figure 28.2 Best-of-run circuit from generation 77 produced using architecture-altering operations and with six invocations of ADF0 and three invocations of ADF1

Figure 28.2 shows the 100%-compliant best-of-run circuit from generation 77. The multiple occurrences of 157 nF capacitors in this circuit are the consequence of the PARALLEL function.

Figure 28.3 shows the behavior, in the frequency domain, of this 100%-compliant best-of-run circuit from generation 77 (made with 25 points per decade). The horizontal axis ranges over four decades of frequencies from 10 Hz to 100,000 Hz on a logarithmic scale. The vertical axis ranges from 0 to 1 volt on a linear scale.

For comparison, in another run of this problem (made using the preparatory steps of Section 27.2), a 100%-compliant best-of-run circuit appears in generation 68 with a fitness of 0.08 and 101 hits. ADF0 is used five times in the evolved solution.

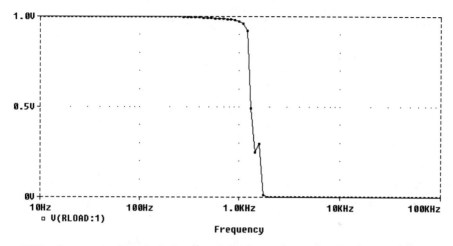

Figure 28.3 **Frequency domain behavior of the best-of-run circuit of generation 77**

Figure 28.4 **Substructure created by quintuply called ADF0 of best circuit of generation 68**

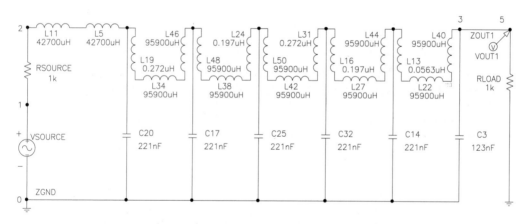

Figure 28.5 **Circuit from generation 68 created by five invocations of a common valued substructure created by ADF0**

Figure 28.4 shows the substructure created by the quintuply called ADF0 of this best-of-run individual. The substructure consists of two inductors, both valued at 95,900 µH, so that the entire substructure is equivalent to one inductor of 191,800 µH.

Figure 28.5 shows the best-of-run circuit from generation 68. Figure 28.6 shows the frequency domain behavior of this circuit from generation 68.

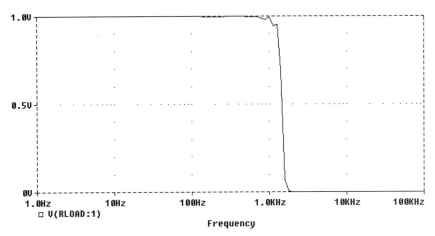

Figure 28.6 **Frequency domain behavior of the best-of-run circuit from generation 68**

28.4 RESULTS SHOWING EVOLUTION OF HIERARCHY

The architecture-altering operations can automatically determine not only the existence of automatically defined functions, the number of automatically defined functions, and the number of arguments that they each possess, but also can automatically create hierarchical references between automatically defined functions. This ability to create hierarchical references between subroutines is demonstrated by

- a hierarchy from the result-producing branch to ADF1 to ADF0 in the solution evolved in run B of the even-3-parity problem using the architecture-altering operations (Section 12.3),
- a hierarchy from one iteration-performing branch to ADF1 to ADF0 and from the second iteration-performing branch to ADF0 to ADF1 in the best-of-run program from the transmembrane segment identification problem with iteration creation (Section 17.2.10), and
- a hierarchy from result-producing branch RPB0 to ADF3 to ADF2, from RPB1 to ADF3 to ADF2, and from RPB2 to ADF4 to ADF2 in the best-of-run circuit two-band crossover (woofer-tweeter) problem using the architecture-altering operations (Section 33.3.2).

In yet another run of the problem of synthesizing a lowpass filter using the architecture-altering operations (using the preparatory steps in this chapter), the best-of-run individual program emerges on generation 46. It has a fitness of 0.0188 and scores 101 hits (out of 101). Between generations 0 and 46, this program acquired four automatically defined functions as a result of the architecture-altering operations. The program tree has 70 points in its RPB0 and 39 points in its RPB1 and has 50, 94, 60, and 115 points in ADF0, ADF1, ADF2, and ADF3, respectively.

Figure 28.7 shows the call tree for the best-of-generation circuit-constructing program tree from generation 46. ADF1 is not used at all. RPB1 uses ADF0 once. RPB0 uses ADF3 once and ADF0 once. ADF3 hierarchically refers five times to another automatically defined function, ADF2. In addition, ADF3 refers to ADF0 once.

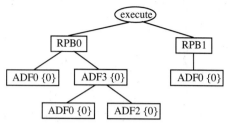

Figure 28.7 Call tree for best-of-generation circuit-constructing program tree from generation 46

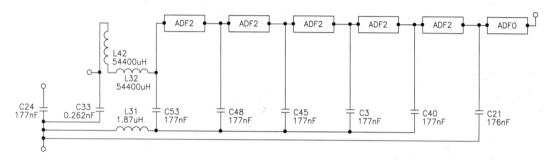

Figure 28.8 Substructure created by automatically defined function ADF3 of the best-of-run circuit from generation 46

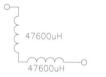

Figure 28.9 Substructure created by automatically defined function ADF0 of the best-of-run circuit from generation 46

Figure 28.10 Substructure created by automatically defined function ADF2 of the best-of-run circuit from generation 46

Figure 28.8 shows the substructure created by ADF3. The multiple occurrences of 177 nF capacitors (**C53, C48, C45, C3, C40,** and **C21**) in this circuit is the consequence of the PARALLEL function. Figure 28.9 shows the substructure created by ADF0. Figure 28.10 shows the substructure created by ADF2.

ADF0 is directly called by RPB0 and RPB1. In addition, ADF0 is separately and indirectly called by RPB0 because RPB0 directly calls ADF3, which, in turn, calls ADF0.

Also, ADF2 is indirectly called by RPB0 because RPB0 directly calls ADF3, which, in turn, calls ADF2 five times.

Figure 28.11 shows the 100%-compliant best-of-run circuit from generation 46. Figure 28.12 shows the frequency domain behavior of this circuit.

Thus, we have demonstrated that a hierarchy can be automatically evolved using the architecture-altering operations on a problem of circuit synthesis.

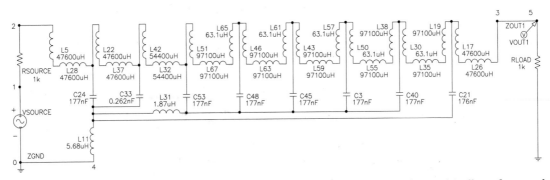

Figure 28.11   Best-of-run circuit from generation 46 produced using hierarchically referenced architecture-altering operations

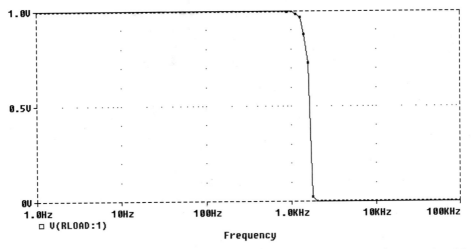

Figure 28.12   Frequency domain behavior of the best-of-run circuit of generation 46

Embryos and Test Fixtures

In each of the previous four Chapters (25 through 28), we used an initial circuit consisting of a one-input, one-output test fixture (Figure 25.4) and an embryo with two modifiable wires (Figure 25.5). Since the next chapter will contain the first use of a different embryo, we take this opportunity to present the eight different test fixtures and eight different embryos that are used throughout this book.

The starting point of the developmental process for transforming an individual program tree in the population into a potentially useful electrical circuit is an initial circuit. The initial circuit consists of two parts: an embryo and a test fixture. Both are very simple. All the test fixtures used in this book contain only resistors and wires (in addition to the circuit's input, output, and connection to ground). All the embryos used in this book contain only modifiable wires (except for the special embryo in Chapter 52). Neither the embryo not the test fixture is a valid electrical circuit. After an embryo is embedded into its test fixture, the combination of the two constitutes a valid electrical circuit. However, this combination (the initial circuit) is still a very simple (and useless) circuit.

29.1 THE EIGHT TEST FIXTURES

The test fixture contains the external input(s) and output point(s) of the overall circuit. Thus, the choice of test fixture for a particular problem of circuit synthesis should be consistent with the number of external inputs and outputs of the overall circuit. In addition, the test fixture has ports that connect with the embryo embedded in the test fixture. Thus, the choice of test fixture for a particular problem must also be consistent (in terms of the number of ports) with the embryo that will be embedded in it.

Figure 29.1 shows the one-input, one-output test fixture (discussed in detail in Section 25.14.1) with three ports to the embryo that has been used in Chapters 25 through 28.

Suppose, for the sake of argument, that a to-be-designed one-input circuit has two outputs (instead of the single output of the lowpass and highpass filters of Chapters 25 through 28). Since the to-be-designed overall circuit has two outputs, it will require two probe points. Each separate voltage probe point requires a separate nonmodifiable isolating wire and a load resistor. Moreover, since the embryo will be expected to develop into a fully developed circuit that has two distinct outputs, both the embryo and test fixture must each have two ports dedicated to communicating the two output signals between the embryo and the test fixture. Thus, the test fixture for a two-output circuit differs from the test fixture for a one-output circuit in that the two-output test fixture has an additional probe point, an additional nonmodifiable isolating wire, an additional load resistor, and an additional port for connecting the embryo and test fixture. Figure 29.2 shows a one-input, two-output test fixture with four ports to the embryo. Nodes 2, 3, 4, and 6 are the four ports of this test fixture that are intended to be attached to an embryo. This test fixture consists of the following nine elements:

- an incoming signal (input to the overall circuit) in the form of a voltage source **VSOURCE** between nodes 0 and 1,
- a source resistor **RSOURCE** between nodes 1 and 2,
- a nonmodifiable wire **ZOUT1** between nodes 3 and 5,
- a first voltage probe point **VOUT1** at node 5,
- a load resistor **RLOAD1** between nodes 5 and 0,
- a nonmodifiable wire **ZOUT2** between nodes 6 and 7,
- a second voltage probe point **VOUT2** at node 7,
- a load resistor **RLOAD2** between nodes 7 and 0, and
- a nonmodifiable wire **ZGND** between nodes 4 and 0.

Now suppose that a to-be-designed one-input circuit has three outputs. In this case, the to-be-designed overall circuit will have three voltage probe points (each with its own separate nonmodifiable isolating wire and a load resistor). Since the embryo will be expected to develop into a fully developed circuit that has three distinct outputs, both the embryo and test fixture must each have three ports dedicated to the task of communicating these two signals between the embryo and the test fixture. Thus, the test fixture for a three-output circuit has three probe points, three nonmodifiable isolating wires, three load resistors, and three ports dedicated to communicating the three output signals between the embryo and the test fixture. Figure 29.3 shows a one-input, three-output test fixture with five ports to the embryo. Nodes 2, 3, 4, 6, and 8 are the five ports of this test fixture that are intended to be attached to an embryo. This test fixture consists of the following 12 elements:

- an incoming signal (input to the overall circuit) in the form of a voltage source **VSOURCE** between nodes 0 and 1,
- a source resistor **RSOURCE** between nodes 1 and 2,
- a nonmodifiable wire **ZOUT1** between nodes 3 and 5,
- a first voltage probe point **VOUT1** at node 5,
- a load resistor **RLOAD1** between nodes 5 and 0,
- a nonmodifiable wire **ZOUT2** between nodes 6 and 7,
- a second voltage probe point **VOUT2** at node 7,
- a load resistor **RLOAD2** between nodes 7 and 0,
- a nonmodifiable wire **ZOUT3** between nodes 8 and 9,
- a second voltage probe point **VOUT3** at node 9,
- a load resistor **RLOAD3** between nodes 9 and 0, and
- a nonmodifiable wire **ZGND** between nodes 4 and 0.

Figure 29.4 is a two-input, one-output test fixture with four ports to the embryo. This test fixture is used for evolving a real-time robot controller (Chapter 48). Nodes 2, 3, 4, and 6 are the four ports of this test fixture that are intended to be attached to an embryo. This test fixture consists of the following eight elements:

- a first incoming signal (input to the overall circuit) in the form of a voltage source **VSOURCE1** between nodes 0 and 1,
- a first source resistor **RSOURCE1** between nodes 1 and 2,
- a second incoming signal in the form of a voltage source **VSOURCE2** between nodes 0 and 7,
- a second source resistor **RSOURCE2** between nodes 7 and 6,
- a nonmodifiable wire **ZOUT** between nodes 3 and 5,
- a voltage probe point **VOUT** at node 5,
- a load resistor **RLOAD** between nodes 5 and 0, and
- a nonmodifiable wire **ZGND** between nodes 4 and 0.

The foregoing test fixtures illustrate how to handle circuits with various numbers of inputs and outputs. However, not all circuits have an explicit input. For example, the temperature-sensing circuit (Chapter 49) senses the ambient temperature and produces a single output voltage indicating the ambient temperature. It has no explicit input signal. Figure 29.5 is a zero-input, one-output test fixture with two ports to the embryo. Nodes 3 and 4 are the two ports of this test fixture that are intended to be attached to an embryo. This test fixture consists of the following four elements:

- a nonmodifiable wire **ZOUT** between nodes 3 and 5,
- a voltage probe point **VOUT** (the output of the overall circuit) at node 5,
- a load resistor **RLOAD** between nodes 5 and 0, and
- a nonmodifiable wire **ZGND** between nodes 4 and 0.

Figure 29.6 shows a test fixture that is identical to Figure 29.1 (a one-input, one-output test fixture with three ports) except that it has no source resistor. This test fixture was tried as part of an experiment for one particular problem in this book (Chapter 43) and never used again.

All of the foregoing test fixtures have output points that probe voltage. Figure 29.7 is a one-input, one-output test fixture for measuring current (Chapter 51) with three ports to the embryo. This test fixture is identical to Figure 29.1, except that it has a current probe point **IOUT** (i.e., the output current of the overall circuit) and a fixed voltage load **VLOAD** (instead of the fixed load resistor typically used when voltage is being probed). The fixed voltage load is shown as a battery in the figure. Nodes 2, 3, and 4 are the three ports of this test fixture that are intended to be attached to an embryo. This test fixture consists of the following six elements:

- an incoming signal (input to the overall circuit) in the form of voltage source **VSOURCE** whose negative end is connected to node 0 (ground) and whose positive end is connected to node 1,
- a source resistor **RSOURCE** between nodes 1 and 2,
- a nonmodifiable wire **ZOUT** between nodes 3 and 5,
- a current probe point **IOUT** (the output of the overall circuit) at node 5,
- a fixed voltage load **VLOAD** between nodes 5 and 0, and
- a nonmodifiable wire **ZGND** between nodes 4 and 0.

Figure 29.8 is a one-input, one-output test fixture with four ports to the embryo that is specifically designed for would-be amplifier circuits. The special test fixture for would-be amplifiers has five resistors:

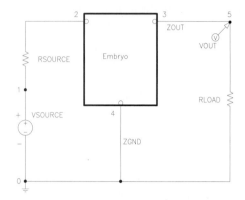

Figure 29.1 One-input, one-output test fixture with three ports to the embryo

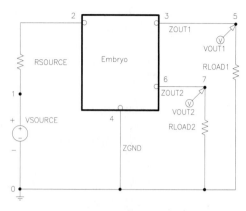

Figure 29.2 One-input, two-output test fixture with four ports to the embryo

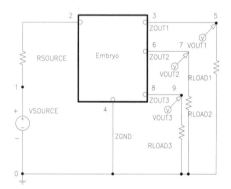

Figure 29.3 One-input, three-output test fixture with five ports to the embryo

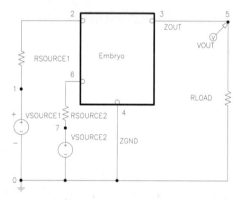

Figure 29.4 Two-input, one-output feedback test fixture with four ports to the embryo

- the usual **RSOURCE** source resistor,
- the usual **RLOAD** load resistor,
- a feedback resistor **RFEEDBACK**,
- a balancing resistor **RBALANCE_SOURCE**, and
- a balancing resistor **RBALANCE_FEEDBACK**.

This new arrangement limits the maximum possible amplification of the circuit as explained in Section 44.2.1. This test fixture is used in Chapters 44, 45, and 46. Nodes 8, 9, 10, and 4 are the four ports of this test fixture that are intended to be attached to an embryo. This test fixture consists of the following 10 elements:

- an incoming signal (input to the overall circuit) in the form of voltage source **VSOURCE** whose negative end is connected to node 0 (ground) and whose positive end is connected to node 1,
- a source resistor **RSOURCE** between nodes 1 and 2,

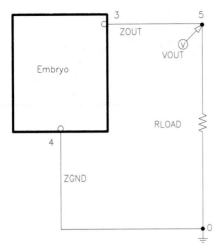

Figure 29.5   Zero-input, one-output test fixture with two ports to the embryo

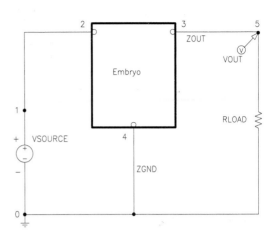

Figure 29.6   One-input, one-output test fixture with three ports to the embryo with no source resistor

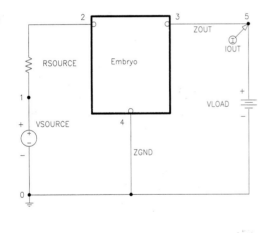

Figure 29.7   One-input, one-output test fixture with three ports to the embryo, a current probe point IOUT, and a fixed voltage load VLOAD

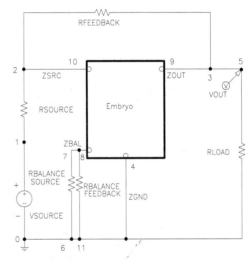

Figure 29.8   One-input, one-output feedback test fixture with five ports to the embryo

- a nonmodifiable wire ZSRC between nodes 2 and 10,
- a nonmodifiable wire ZOUT between nodes 9 and 3,
- a voltage probe point VOUT (the output of the overall circuit) at node 5,
- a load resistor RLOAD between nodes 5 and 0,
- a nonmodifiable wire ZGND between nodes 4 and 0,
- a feedback resistor RFEEDBACK between nodes 3 and 2,

Table 29.1 Problems using the eight test fixtures

Test fixture	Reference
Figure 29.1 (Figure 25.4)	Chapters 25–28, 30, 31, 35–39, 42, 47, 50; Section 52.2; Chapters 53–54, 55
Figure 29.2	Chapters 32, 33
Figure 29.3	Chapter 34
Figure 29.4	Chapter 48
Figure 29.5	Chapter 49
Figure 29.6	Chapter 43
Figure 29.7	Chapter 51
Figure 29.8	Chapters 44–46

- a balancing resistor **RBALANCE_SOURCE** between nodes 6 and 7, and
- a balancing resistor **RBALANCE_FEEDBACK** between nodes 11 and 8.

Table 29.1 shows the sections of this book that employ each of the eight test fixtures. Note that Figure 25.4 represents the same test fixture as Figure 29.1.

Of course, these eight test fixtures (and the eight embryos below) are not the only possible test fixtures(and embryos).

29.2   THE EIGHT EMBRYOS

An embryo contains at least one modifiable wire. Each modifiable wire in the embryo corresponds to a result-producing branch in the overall circuit-constructing program tree. Thus, the choice of embryo for a particular problem of circuit synthesis must be consistent with the number of result-producing branches being used for a particular problem.

The test fixture for a particular problem makes connection with the external input(s) and output(s) of the overall circuit. An embryo that satisfies the design goals of a particular problem must, in some way, service the external input(s) and output(s) of the overall circuit. Thus, the choice of embryo must also be consistent with the number of the external input(s) and output(s) of the overall circuit.

Figure 29.9 shows an embryo with two modifiable wires (Z0 and Z1) and three ports to the test fixture (Embryo_Input, Embryo_Output, and Embryo_Ground). This embryo was discussed in detail in connection with the lowpass filter in Section 25.14.1 and has been used in the previous four chapters (25 through 28).

Figure 29.10 shows an embryo with one modifiable wire (Z0) and three ports to the test fixture (Embryo_Input, Embryo_Output, and Embryo_Ground).

Figure 29.11 shows an embryo with three modifiable wires (Z0, Z1, and Z2) and four ports to the test fixture (Embryo_Input, Embryo_Output1, Embryo_Output2, and Embryo_Ground).

Figure 29.12 shows an embryo with three modifiable wires (Z0, Z1, and Z2) and five ports to the test fixture (Embryo_Input, Embryo_Output1, Embryo_Output2, Embryo_ Output3, and Embryo_Ground).

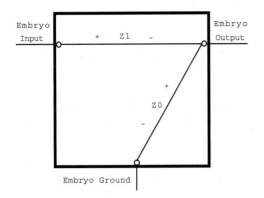

Figure 29.9 Embryo with two modifiable wires (Z0 and Z1) and three ports (Embryo_ Input, Embryo_ Output, and Embryo_Ground)

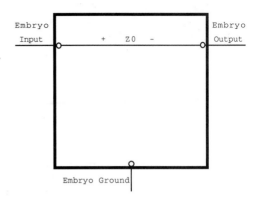

Figure 29.10 Embryo with one modifiable wire (Z0) and three ports (Embryo_Input, Embryo_ Output, and Embryo_Ground)

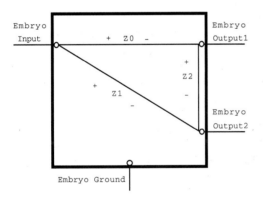

Figure 29.11 Embryo with three modifiable wires (Z0, Z1, and Z2) and four ports (Embryo_Input, Embryo_Output1, Embryo_ Output2, and Embryo_Ground)

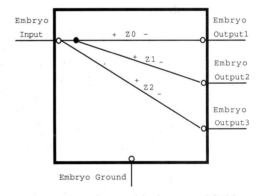

Figure 29.12 Embryo with three modifiable wires (Z0, Z1, and Z2) and five ports (Embryo_ Input, Embryo_Output1, Embryo_Output2, Embryo_ Output3, and Embryo_Ground)

Figure 29.13 shows an embryo with two modifiable wires ($Z0$ and $Z1$) and three ports to the test fixture (Embryo_Input, Embryo_Output, and Embryo_Ground). There is no explicit connection to the circuit's external input, external output, or ground.

Figure 29.14 shows an embryo with three modifiable wires ($Z0$, $Z1$, and $Z2$) and three ports to the test fixture (Embryo_Input, Embryo_Output, and Embryo_Ground).

Figure 29.15 shows an embryo with three modifiable wires ($Z0$, $Z1$, and $Z2$) and four ports to the test fixture (Embryo_Input1, Embryo_Input2, Embryo_Output, and Embryo_Ground).

Figure 29.16 shows an embryo with two modifiable wires ($Z0$ and $Z1$) and two ports to the test fixture (Embryo_Output and Embryo_Ground).

Table 29.2 shows the sections of this book that employ each of the eight embryos. Chapter 52 contains an additional special embryo. Note that Figure 25.5 represents the same embryo as Figure 29.9.

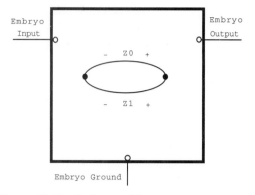

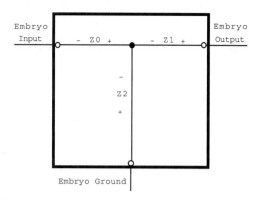

Figure 29.13 Embryo with two modifiable wires (Z0 and Z1) and three ports (Embryo_Input, Embryo_Output, and Embryo_Ground)

Figure 29.14 Embryo with three modifiable wires (Z0, Z1, and Z2) and three ports (Embryo_Input, Embryo_Output, and Embryo_Ground)

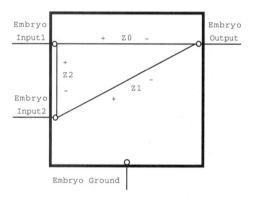

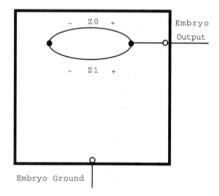

Figure 29.15 Embryo with three modifiable wires (Z0, Z1, and Z2) and four ports (Embryo_Input1, Embryo_Input2, Embryo_Output, and Embryo_Ground)

Figure 29.16 Embryo with two modifiable wires (Z0 and Z1) and two ports (Embryo_Output and Embryo_Ground)

Table 29.2 Problems using the eight embryos

Embryo	Reference
Figure 29.9 (Figure 25.5)	Chapters 25–28, 31, 37, 40, 42, 43, 54
Figure 29.10	Chapters 30, 35, 36, 38, 39, 47, 50, 51, 55
Figure 29.11	Chapters 32, 33
Figure 29.12	Chapter 34
Figure 29.13	Chapter 53
Figure 29.14	Section 52.1
Figure 29.15	Chapters 44–46, 48
Figure 29.16	Chapter 49

Synthesis of a Lowpass Filter Using Automatically Defined Copy

Three previous chapters demonstrated that genetic programming is capable of synthesizing both the topology and sizing for a lowpass filter circuit

- without automatically defined functions (Chapter 25),
- with automatically defined functions, but without architecture-altering operations (Chapter 27), and
- with automatically defined functions and architecture-altering operations (Chapter 28).

Many of the 100%-compliant filters that were evolved using these three approaches employed the repetitive ladder topology of a Campbell filter (where each rung of the ladder is composed of sections consisting of one inductor and one capacitor). Other evolved circuits employed the repetitive topology of the elliptic (Cauer) filter (where each section consists of two inductors and one capacitor). Msany of the other evolved filters contain a ladder as a substructure.

The observed repetitiveness of these evolved circuits suggests that an iterative operation might be useful in synthesizing circuits. Specifically, it might be useful to iteratively copy a useful substructure (such as a rung of a ladder) in order to progressively construct a complex overall structure. Similarly, nonfilter circuits are often replete with the reuse of certain basic arrangements of components.

This chapter describes a new quasi-iterative operator that facilitates the reuse of substructures in circuits created by developmental genetic programming. This quasi-iterative operator is illustrated by applying it to the problem of synthesizing the design of a lowpass filter satisfying the same design requirements as Section 25.13.

30.1 AUTOMATICALLY DEFINED COPY

Chapter 6 described the automatically defined iteration (ADI). In an ADI, a single iteration-performing branch performs an iteration that is restricted to a problem-specific preestablished finite sequence, vector, or array. The number of iterations that are performed with this approach is controlled (and fixed) by the length of the preestablished sequence, vector, or array. The single iteration-performing branch of an automatically defined iteration is subject to evolutionary modification during the run of genetic programming; however, the preestablished sequence, vector, or array is not.

Chapter 7 described the more general concept of an automatically defined loop (ADL) with four branches (the loop initialization branch, loop condition branch, loop body branch, and loop update branch). Each of the four branches is subject to evolutionary modification during the run of genetic programming. The number of iterations that are performed is variable and is controlled by the numerical value calculated and returned by the loop condition branch.

The automatically defined iteration is inappropriate for synthesizing circuits because there is no obvious sequence, vector, or array available to act as a template for controlling the iteration. The topology of a satisfactory circuit is not known a priori. In the case of a lowpass filter, the number of rungs that might be needed in a satisfactory ladder is not known a priori. In fact, the discovery of the topology of an analog circuit is a major part of the problem of synthesizing circuits.

Likewise, the automatically defined loop is inappropriate for synthesizing circuits because there is no obvious numerical calculation that seems appropriate for controlling the number of iterations to be performed.

In addition, automatically defined iterations and automatically defined loops are inappropriate for developmental genetic programming. The iteration-performing branch of an automatically defined iteration and all four branches of an automatically defined loop are trees. A tree has many external points (leaves). Ignoring the obvious and irrelevant exception of arithmetic-performing subtrees, the external points (leaves) of a circuit-constructing program tree typically contain the development-controlling END function. Each END function discards its writing head. An external point (leaf) sometimes contains a CUT or SAFE_CUT function. They too discard their writing head. Suppose one writing head was associated with the topmost point of the iteration-performing branch of an automatically defined iteration and the loop initialization branch of an automatically defined loop. Then that writing head would be lost upon completion of execution of the iteration-performing branch or the loop initialization branch. Thus, there is no natural and convenient way to pass along exactly one writing head between successive invocations of automatically defined iterations or automatically defined loops.

This chapter deals with a quasi-iterative approach that is well suited to developmental genetic programming. This approach has some of the characteristics of an iterative operator and some of the characteristics of an automatically defined function. This approach entails a new structure with two distinct branches, each of which is subject to evolutionary modification during the run of genetic programming. Specifically, an automatically defined copy (ADC) consists of

- a copy control branch, CCB, and
- a copy body branch, CBB.

The execution of an automatically defined copy is controlled in the same manner as the execution of an automatically defined function that hierarchically calls another automatically defined function. Specifically, when the automatically defined copy is invoked (say, by the result-producing branch of the overall program), the copy control branch, CCB, is executed. The copy control branch, CCB, then hierarchically calls the copy body branch, CBB. Typically the copy control branch will repeatedly call the copy body branch.

The automatically defined copy is distinguished by the fact that it is created in accordance with the following constrained syntactic structure:

- The copy control branch, CCB, is composed only of topology-modifying functions, development-controlling functions, and invocations of the copy body branch, CBB. That is, there are no component-creating functions or functions of value-setting (arithmetic-performing) subtrees.
- The copy body branch, CBB, is composed of component-creating functions, topology-modifying functions, development-controlling functions, and the functions of value-setting (arithmetic-performing) subtrees.

A nonnumeric method for controlling variability seems especially appropriate for electrical circuits. The number of times that the iteration is performed by an automatically defined copy is controlled by the number of occurrences of invocations of the copy body branch (CBB) contained in the copy control branch (CCB). The automatically defined copy differs from the automatically defined iteration (where the iteration is performed over a fixed and preestablished sequence, vector, or array) in that the number of iterations can be varied by evolution. The automatically defined copy differs from the automatically defined loop (where the number of iterations is controlled by the numerical result of a calculation in the loop condition branch) in that the variability in the number of iterations of the automatically defined copy is controlled in a nonnumerical way by the topology-modifying functions in its copy control branch.

30.2 PREPARATORY STEPS

30.2.1 Embryo and Test Fixture

We used an embryo with one modifiable wire for this problem.

The initial circuit for this problem is created by embedding the embryo with one modifiable wire and three ports (Figure 29.10) into the one-input, one-output test fixture with three ports (Figure 29.1). That is, we used the same test fixture used in Chapters 25–28, but embedded a different embryo in it (i.e., with just one modifiable wire). Figure 30.1 shows the one-input, one-output initial circuit with one modifiable wire used for this problem.

Our choice here of an embryo with one modifiable wire does not reflect any judgment that one modifiable wire is especially well suited to the automatically defined copy. As previously mentioned, the organization of this book is topical, not chronological. We happened to start our first work on automatic circuit synthesis in 1995 on the lowpass filter problem (Chapter 25) with an initial circuit containing an embryo with two modifiable wires (Figure 29.9). We later employed an embryo with three modifiable wires on several problems and subsequently started using an embryo with one modifiable wire. The automatically defined copy was formulated in this later period.

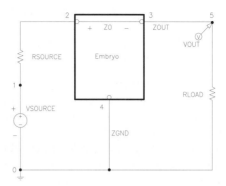

Figure 30.1   One-input, one-output initial circuit with one modifiable wire

30.2.2   Program Architecture

Since the embryo has one modifiable wire, there is one result-producing branch in each program tree in the population.

Each program has one zero-argument automatically defined copy (called ADC0) consisting of a copy control branch, CCB0, and a copy body branch, CBB0. No architecture-altering operations are used. Thus, the architecture of each program tree in the population consists of a total of three branches (i.e., a copy control branch, a copy body branch, and a result-producing branch).

Figure 30.2 shows the call tree for a program with one automatically defined copy, ADC0 (consisting of a one-argument copy control branch, CCB0, and a one-argument copy body branch, CBB0), and one result-producing branch, RPB0. As can be seen, the result-producing branch, RPB0, can call the copy control branch, CCB0, which, in turn, can hierarchically call the copy body branch, CBB0.

30.2.3   Functions and Terminals

The result-producing branch is composed of the same functions and terminals as were used in Chapter 28 except for the addition of the copy control branch, CCB. That is, the function set, $F_{\text{ccs-rpb-initial}}$, for each construction-continuing subtree of the result-producing branches is

$F_{\text{ccs-rpb-initial}} = \{\text{CCB, C, L, SERIES, PARALLEL0, FLIP, NOP,}$
$\text{THREE\_GROUND, THREE\_VIA0, THREE\_VIA1, THREE\_VIA2, THREE\_VIA3,}$
$\text{THREE\_VIA4, THREE\_VIA5, THREE\_VIA6, THREE\_VIA7}\}.$

The terminal set, $T_{\text{ccs-rpb-initial}}$, for each construction-continuing subtree of the result-producing branches is

$T_{\text{ccs-rpb-initial}} = \{\text{END, CUT}\}.$

The copy control branch, CCB, of the automatically defined copy, ADC0, is composed of topology-modifying functions, development-controlling functions, and invocations of the copy body branch, CBB. That is, the initial function set, $F_{\text{ccs-ccb-initial}}$, for each

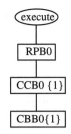

Figure 30.2   Call tree for a program with one automatically defined copy, ADC0 (consisting of a copy control branch, CCB0, and a copy body branch, CBB0), and one result-producing branch, RPB0

construction-continuing subtree of the copy control branch, CCB, of the automatically defined copy is

$F_{\text{ccs-ccb-initial}}$ = {CBB, SERIES, PARALLEL0, FLIP, NOP, THREE_GROUND, THREE_VIA0, THREE_VIA1, THREE_VIA2, THREE_VIA3, THREE_VIA4, THREE_VIA5, THREE_VIA6, THREE_VIA7}.

The initial terminal set, $T_{\text{ccs-ccb-initial}}$, for each construction-continuing subtree of the copy control branch, CCB, of the automatically defined copy is

$T_{\text{ccs-ccb-initial}}$ = {END, CUT}.

The copy body branch, CBB, of the automatically defined copy, ADC0, is composed of the same functions and terminals as the result-producing branch (except for CCB). That is, the initial function set, $F_{\text{ccs-cbb-initial}}$, for each construction-continuing subtree of the copy body branch, CBB, of the automatically defined copy is

$F_{\text{ccs-cbb-initial}}$ = {C, L, SERIES, PARALLEL0, FLIP, NOP, THREE_GROUND, THREE_VIA0, THREE_VIA1, THREE_VIA2, THREE_VIA3, THREE_VIA4, THREE_VIA5, THREE_VIA6, THREE_VIA7}.

The initial terminal set, $T_{\text{ccs-cbb-initial}}$, for each construction-continuing subtree of the function-defining branches is

$T_{\text{ccs-cbb-initial}}$ = {END, CUT}.

Since there are no architecture-altering operations in this problem, $T_{\text{rpb-potential}}$, $F_{\text{rpb-potential}}$, $T_{\text{ccb-potential}}$, $F_{\text{ccb-potential}}$, $T_{\text{cbb-potential}}$, and $F_{\text{cbb-potential}}$ are empty.

The function set, F_{aps}, for each arithmetic-performing subtree and the terminal set, T_{aps}, for each arithmetic-performing subtree in the result-producing branch, RPB, and the copy body branch, CBB, are the same as for the lowpass filter problem in Section 25.14.3.

30.2.4   Fitness

The fitness measure is the same as in Section 25.14.4.

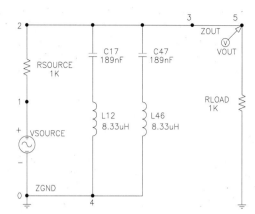

Figure 30.3   Best-of-generation circuit from generation 4

30.2.5   Parameters

This problem has several control parameters that have not appeared previously in this book:

- The maximum size of the copy control branch, S_{ccb}, is 100 points.
- The maximum size of the copy body branch, S_{cbb}, is 250 points.
- The number of arguments in the copy control branch and the copy body branch ($N_{max\text{-}argument\text{-}ccb}$ and $N_{max\text{-}argument\text{-}cbb}$, respectively) is zero.
- The maximum size of the result-producing branch, S_{rpb}, is 250 points.

The control parameters for this chapter are in the tableau (Table 30.1), the tables of percentages of genetic operations in Appendix D, and the default values specified in Appendix D.

30.2.6   Tableau

Table 30.1 summarizes the key features of the problem of designing a lowpass filter using the automatically defined copy.

30.3   RESULTS

In the first run of this problem with the automatically defined copy, the best-of-generation circuit from generation 0 has a fitness of 116.3 and scores 38 hits (out of 101).

30.3.1   Emergence of Copied Inductive-Capacitive Shunt

The first best-of-generation circuit (Figure 30.3) that usefully employs an automatically defined copy appears in generation 4. The fitness of the circuit is 58.3, and it scores 52 hits. This circuit has four capacitors and two inductors (prior to editing), and two capacitors and two inductors (after editing). As can be seen, the circuit has two identical vertical shunts, each consisting of a 189 nF capacitor and an 8.33 µH inductor. The component values produced by the automatically defined copy are identical in both shunts

Table 30.1 Tableau for lowpass filter using the automatically defined copy

Objective	Design, using the automatically defined copy, a lowpass filter composed of inductors and capacitors with a passband below 1,000 Hz, a stopband above 2,000 Hz, a maximum allowable passband deviation of 30 millivolts, and a maximum allowable stopband deviation of 1 millivolt.
Test fixture and embryo	One-input, one-output initial circuit with a source resistor, load resistor, and one modifiable wire
Program architecture	One result-producing branch, RPB0, and one automatically defined copy (called ADC0) consisting of a copy control branch, CCB, and a copy body branch, CBB
Initial function set for the RPB	For construction-continuing subtrees: $F_{ccs\text{-}rpb\text{-}initial}$ = {CCB, C, L, SERIES, PARALLEL0, FLIP, NOP, THREE_GROUND, THREE_VIA0, THREE_VIA1, THREE_VIA2, THREE_VIA3, THREE_VIA4, THREE_VIA5, THREE_VIA6, THREE_VIA7}. For arithmetic-performing subtrees: F_{aps} = {+, -}.
Initial terminal set for the RPB	For construction-continuing subtrees: $T_{ccs\text{-}rpb\text{-}initial}$ = {END, CUT}. For arithmetic-performing subtrees: T_{aps} = {$\Re_{smaller\text{-}reals}$}.
Initial function set for the copy control branch	For construction-continuing subtrees: $F_{ccs\text{-}ccb\text{-}initial}$ = {CBB, SERIES, PARALLEL0, FLIP, NOP, THREE_GROUND, THREE_VIA0, THREE_VIA1, THREE_VIA2, THREE_VIA3, THREE_VIA4, THREE_VIA5, THREE_VIA6, THREE_VIA7}.
Initial terminal set for the copy control branch	For construction-continuing subtrees: $T_{ccs\text{-}ccb\text{-}initial}$ = {END, CUT}.
Initial function set for the copy body branch	For construction-continuing subtrees: $F_{ccs\text{-}cbb\text{-}initial}$ = {C, L, SERIES, PARALLEL0, FLIP, NOP, THREE_GROUND, THREE_VIA0, THREE_VIA1, THREE_VIA2, THREE_VIA3, THREE_VIA4, THREE_VIA5, THREE_VIA6, THREE_VIA7}. For arithmetic-performing subtrees: F_{aps} = {+, -}.
Initial terminal set for the copy body branch	For construction-continuing subtrees: $T_{ccs\text{-}cbb\text{-}initial}$ = {END, CUT}. For arithmetic-performing subtrees: T_{aps} = {$\Re_{smaller\text{-}reals}$}.
Potential function set for the RPB	Architecture-altering operations are not used.
Potential terminal set for the RPB	Architecture-altering operations are not used.
Potential function set for the copy control branch	Architecture-altering operations are not used.

(continued)

Table 30.1 *(continued)*

Potential terminal set for the copy control branch	Architecture-altering operations are not used.
Potential function set for the copy body branch	Architecture-altering operations are not used.
Potential terminal set for the copy body branch	Architecture-altering operations are not used.
Fitness cases	101 frequency values in an interval of five decades of frequency values between 1 Hz and 100,000 Hz
Raw fitness	The sum, over these 101 fitness cases, of the absolute weighted deviation between the actual value of the voltage that is produced by the circuit at the probe point and the target value for voltage
Standardized fitness	Same as raw fitness
Hits	The number of hits is defined as the number of fitness cases (out of 101) for which the voltage is acceptable or ideal or that lie in the "don't care" band.
Wrapper	None
Parameters	$M = 640{,}000$. $G = 501$. $Q = 10{,}000$. $D = 64$. $B = 2\%$. $S_{rpb} = 250$. $S_{ccb} = 100$. $S_{cbb} = 250$. $N_{rpb} = 2$. $N_{max\text{-}argument\text{-}ccb} = 0$. $N_{max\text{-}argument\text{-}cbb} = 0$.
Result designation	Best-so-far pace-setting individual
Success predicate	A program scores the maximum number (101) of hits.

because the automatically defined copy is invoked by the result-producing branch with no numerical arguments in this problem.

Figure 30.4a shows the frequency domain behavior of the best-of-generation circuit from generation 4. The horizontal axis represents the frequency of the incoming signal and ranges over six decades of frequencies from 1 Hz to 1 MHz on a logarithmic scale. The vertical axis represents peak output voltage and ranges from 0 to 1 volt on a linear scale.

The result-producing branch has five points and can be simplified to the four-point program below. Note that it contains one invocation of the copy control branch, CCB, of the automatically defined copy.

```
(SERIES END END CCB).
```

Figure 30.5 shows the result of expressing the result-producing branch of the best circuit from generation 4. As can be seen, there is one invocation of the copy control branch, CCB.

The copy control branch, CCB, of the automatically defined copy of the best circuit from generation 4 has 32 points. As can be seen, it contains two invocations of the copy

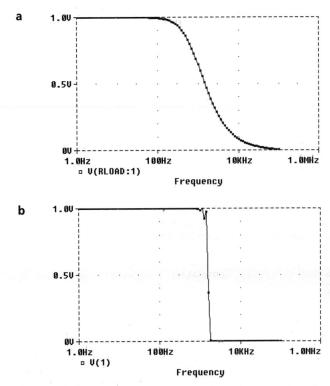

Figure 30.4 Frequency domain behavior of the best-of-generation circuits from generations (*a*) 4 and (*b*) 19

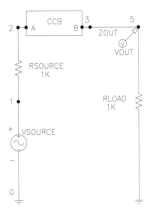

Figure 30.5 Result of expressing result-producing branch of best generation 4

body branch, CBB (underlined). Note that this branch is composed only of topology-modifying functions, development-controlling functions, and invocations of the copy body branch, CBB.

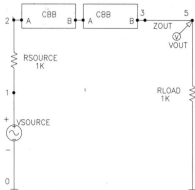

Figure 30.6 Result of expressing the copy control branch, CCB, of the best circuit from generation 4

Figure 30.7 Result of expressing the copy body branch, CBB, of the best circuit from generation 4

```
(SERIES END (SERIES END (SERIES (NOP END) END END) (NOP (NOP
(SERIES (NOP (SERIES END END END)) (SERIES (SERIES END END END)
(SERIES END END (NOP (NOP (CBB)))) (NOP END)) END)))) (CBB)).
```

Figure 30.6 shows the result of expressing the copy control branch, CCB, of the best circuit from generation 4. As can be seen, the resulting circuit now has two invocations of the copy body branch, CBB.

The copy body branch, CBB, has 63 points. This branch is composed of the same functions and terminals as the result-producing branch (except for CCB). After editing, it is equivalent to the following:

```
(PARALLEL0 (TWO_GROUND (L 0.9207610 END) END END) END (C
-2.57675 (SERIES END END END)) (THREE_VIA7 END (SERIES CUT END
END) END)).
```

Figure 30.7 shows the result (in isolation) of expressing the copy body branch, CBB. The resulting two-ported substructure consists of one inductor created by the L function, a connection to ground created by the TWO_GROUND function, and one capacitor created by the C function. As can be seen, this substructure has the classical topology of an inductive-capacitive shunt.

Because there are two occurrences of the copy body branch, CBB, in the one occurrence of the copy control branch, CCB, the result of executing the CCB is to insert two copies of the inductive-capacitive shunt.

30.3.2 Additional Incremental Progress

The fitness of the best-of-generation circuits of generations 7, 11, 14, and 18 are 13.3, 9.7, 3.8, and 0.72, respectively. This is an improvement of almost two orders of magnitude over the fitness of 58.3 in generation 4.

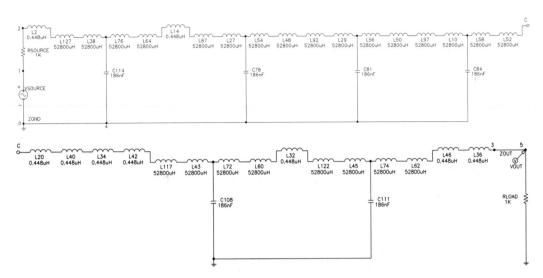

Figure 30.8 Best-of-run circuit from generation 19

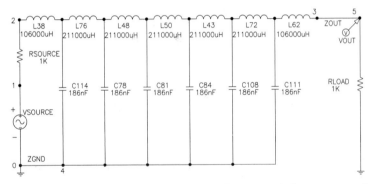

Figure 30.9 Edited version of the best-of-run circuit from generation 19

30.3.3 Emergence of a Six-Rung Ladder

The first 100%-compliant circuit (Figure 30.8) emerged in generation 19. The fitness of the circuit is 0.0374. Prior to editing, the circuit has six capacitors and 33 inductors. Note that the long horizontal row of inductors across the top of the figure is continued, as shown by connector C, with the horizontal row in the middle of the figure.

In Figure 30.9, each group of multiple inductors in series in Figure 30.8 has been consolidated into a single inductor with appropriate value. After editing, there are seven inductors and six capacitors in this best-of-run circuit from generation 19. The figure shows the ladder filter that was evolved using the iterative capabilities of the automatically defined copy.

Notice that the leftmost inductor L38 of Figure 30.9 is 106,000 μH and the right-most inductor L62 is also 106,000 μH. Each of the five 211,000 μH inductors (L76, L48, L50, L43, and L72) located horizontally across the top of this figure can be viewed (approximately) as a series composition of two 106,000 μH inductors. When so viewed, the evolved circuit can be seen as consisting of a cascade of six identical symmetric T-sections (Section 25.12.2). Each T-section consists of the incoming 106,000 µH inductor, a junction point from which a 186 nF capacitor is shunted off to ground, and an outgoing 106,000 µH inductor. Filters constructed of cascades of such symmetric T-sections are referred to as "constant K" filters (Johnson 1950, p. 331). Such filters are characterized by two key parameters. The first parameter is the filter's characteristic resistance (impedance). This characteristic resistance should match the circuit's fixed load resistance **RLOAD** (1,000 Ω in the figure). The second parameter is the nominal cutoff frequency that separates the filter's passband from its stopband.

The characteristic resistance, R, is given by the formula

$$R = \sqrt{L/C}$$

When the inductance, L, is 211,000 µH and the capacitance, C, is 186 nF, then the characteristic resistance, R, is 1,065 Ω according to this formula. This value is very close to the value of the evolved circuit's 1,000 Ω load resistance.

The nominal cutoff frequency, f_c, is given by the formula

$$f_c = \frac{1}{\pi\sqrt{LC}}$$

When the inductance, L, is 211,000 µH and the capacitance, C, is 186 nF, then the nominal cutoff frequency, f_c, is 1,607 Hz. This value is roughly in the middle of the transition band for the desired lowpass filter.

In other words, both of the key parameters of the evolved circuit of Figure 30.9 are very close to those of a "constant K" filter designed with the aim of satisfying the problem's design requirements.

Figure 30.4b shows the frequency domain behavior of this 100%-compliant best-of-run circuit from generation 19.

The result-producing branch of the best-of-run circuit from generation 19 has 61 points. It contains one invocation of the copy control branch, CCB. After editing, it is equivalent to

```
(L -0.349 (CCB)).
```

At the beginning of the developmental process, the embryo consists of a single modifiable wire, and the single writing head points to it. Execution of the result-producing branch starts with the L function, which converts the modifiable wire into an inductor. After execution of the L function, the writing head points to the newly created inductor. The copy control branch, CCB, is in the construction-continuing subtree of the L function. Figure 30.10 shows the result of expressing the result-producing branch of the best-of-run circuit from generation 19.

The copy control branch, CCB, of the automatically defined copy has 78 points and contains six invocations of the copy body branch, CBB:

```
(SERIES (NOP (SERIES (NOP END) (SERIES (NOP (SERIES (NOP (NOP
END)) (NOP (NOP END)) (NOP (CBB)))) END END) (NOP END)))
(SERIES (SERIES (SERIES END END END) (NOP END) (SERIES END END
END)) (NOP (SERIES END (CBB) END)) (SERIES (SERIES END (CBB)
END) (NOP END) (NOP END))) (NOP (SERIES (NOP (CBB)) (NOP END))
(SERIES (SERIES (SERIES END END END) (NOP END) (SERIES END END
```

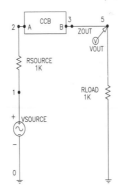

Figure 30.10   Result of expressing the result-producing branch of the best-of-run circuit from generation 19

```
END)) (NOP (SERIES END (CBB) END)) (SERIES (SERIES END (CBB)
END) (NOP END) (NOP END))))))).
```

Figure 30.11 shows the result of expressing the copy control branch, CCB, of the automatically defined copy. As can be seen, the resulting circuit has a succession of nine inductors and six invocations of the copy body branch, CBB. Note that nine inductors are all very small (0.448 µH) in relation to the four 52,800 µH inductors created by each of the six invocations of the CBB.

The copy body branch, CBB, has 102 points. After editing, it is equivalent to

```
(L 5.54794
  (SERIES
    (SERIES
      (SERIES
        (SERIES END END END)
      END
      (TWO_GROUND
        END
        END
        (C 2.26985 END))
    )
  END
  END
  )
  END
  END)
).
```

Figure 30.12 shows the result of expressing (in isolation) the copy body branch, CBB. The resulting two-ported substructure consists of four inductors created by the four calls to the SERIES function following the initial L function, a connection to ground created by the TWO_GROUND function, and one capacitor created by the C function.

Because there are six occurrences of the copy body branch, CBB, in the one occurrence of the copy control branch, CCB, the result of executing the CCB is to insert six copies of the capacitive shunt.

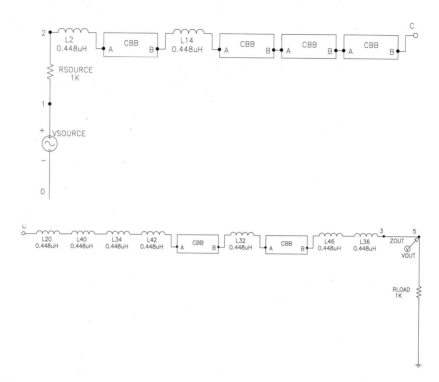

Figure 30.11   Result of expressing the copy control branch, CCB, of the best-of-run circuit from generation 19

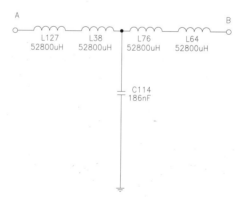

Figure 30.12   Result of expressing the copy body branch, CBB, of the best-of-run circuit from generation 19

The lowpass filter circuit of Figure 30.9 evolved using the automatically defined copy has all the elements of claim 2 of U.S. patent 1,227,113 (Campbell 1917a) as discussed in detail in Section 25.15.1. In particular, this evolved circuit matches Figure 7 of Campbell's 1917 patent. But for the fact that this patent has long since expired, this evolved circuit would infringe on Campbell's patent.

Synthesis of an Asymmetric Bandpass Filter

This chapter describes how genetic programming created both the topology and sizing for an asymmetric bandpass filter that satisfactorily solves a problem of circuit synthesis that was characterized in a leading journal as being difficult to design.

In a paper in *Analog Integrated Circuits and Signal Processing*, Ivan Riis Nielsen (1995) described a new continuous-time filter design tool and applied this new method to a difficult-to-design bandpass filter. The filter involved is considered difficult to design because its specifications are both stringent and highly asymmetric.

Filter design begins with a specification of the desired boundaries for the passband(s) and the stopband(s), the desired attenuation, the maximum passband attenuation, and the minimum stopband attenuation.

The topology and sizing for certain standard lowpass filters have been tabulated in various books (cookbooks) on filter design (Zverev 1967; Van Valkenburg 1982; Williams and Taylor 1995). Many standard highpass, bandpass, or bandstop filters can be designed by transforming the design requirements into the design requirements for a normalized lowpass filter. Once the problem of designing a standard highpass, bandpass, or bandstop filter is recast in this way, the user can choose a standard Butterworth, Chebychev, or Cauer (elliptic) filter that satisfies the normalized lowpass filter specification. The normalized lowpass ladder filter is then designed (often by referring to a cookbook) and transformed into the required highpass, bandpass, or bandstop filter using now-standard transformations (Nielsen 1995). Various computer programs, such as XFILT from the University of Glasgow (Ping, Henderson, and Sewell 1991) are also available to implement the design process for standard filters.

The design of filters becomes increasingly difficult as the user increases the stringency of individual design goals or increases the number of conflicting design goals. Depending on the application, the user may impose requirements relating to factors such as

- the monotonicity of the voltage in the passband and stopband as a function of frequency,
- the phase shift of the output signal relative to the input signal,
- the degree of monotonicity of the voltage in the transitional region between the passband and the stopband as a function of frequency,
- the uniformity of the time delay through the filter as a function of frequency,

- the amount of voltage in the passband and stopband near the boundaries, and
- the amount of *overshoot* (i.e., the voltage in the time domain in excess of the target in response to a step input).

Filter design becomes even more difficult if the user specifies asymmetric or nonuniform requirements for certain critical frequencies. For example, in designing a modem, it may be important to shape the spectrum so that there is a large amount of attenuation in the region that separates two frequencies that represent different digital values. Similarly, it is difficult to design a filter where constant delay is required. There are no general mathematical techniques for designing filters when the user's requirements go substantially beyond those of standard filters (Nielsen 1995).

In contrast, the problem-specific information required for applying genetic programming to different types of circuits is minimal. The requisite new information consists primarily of the number of inputs and outputs of the desired circuit, the types of components to be used, and a fitness measure that expresses the high-level statement of the circuit's desired behavior as a measurable mathematical quantity. There are only a relatively small number of differences between the preparatory steps required for synthesizing the asymmetric bandpass filter in this chapter compared to the more pedestrian lowpass filter of Chapters 25, 27, 28, and 30 and the highpass, bandstop, and bandpass filters of Chapter 26.

31.1   DESIGN GOALS

The goal is to create both the topology and sizing for an asymmetric bandpass filter composed of inductors and capacitors that satisfies Nielsen's specifications (1995).

Nielsen's bandpass filter is targeted for a modem application where one band of frequencies (31.2 KHz to 45.6 KHz) must be isolated from another (69.6 KHz to 84.0 KHz). The desired passband lies between 31.2 KHz and 45.6 KHz. Nielsen specifies that it would be ideal if

- the relative voltage within the passband were in the narrow region between –0.6 dB and 0.6 dB, and
- all the relative voltages outside the passband were below –120 dB (i.e., the attenuation is at least 120 dB or 1,000,000-to-1).

In addition to the ideal characteristics, Nielsen defined the following set of acceptable characteristics:

- Because of the importance of isolating the band of frequencies between 69.6 and 84.0 KHz, the attenuation there should be at least 73 dB (i.e., the relative voltage is below –73 dB). Less stringency is demanded elsewhere.
- The attenuation for frequencies below 20 KHz should be at least 38 dB (i.e., the relative voltage is below –38 dB).
- The relative voltages in the frequency band between 20 KHz and 31.2 KHz and in the band between 45.6 KHz and 69.6 KHz should be below 0 dB.
- The relative voltages in the band above 84.0 KHz should be below –55 dB.

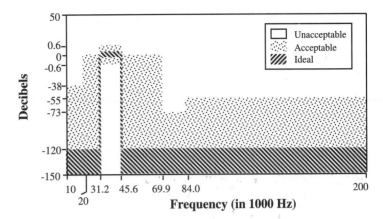

Figure 31.1 **Design goals for Nielsen's asymmetric bandpass filter**

The asymmetry and stringency of these design goals make it difficult to design a filter satisfying these requirements.

Figure 31.1 shows the design goals for Nielsen's asymmetric bandpass filter. Throughout this chapter, the scale of the horizontal axis is linear and ranges from 10 KHz to 200 KHz. The vertical axis represents relative voltage and is scaled in decibels. The vertical axis of this figure (and throughout this chapter) is artistically distorted to highlight certain very narrow ranges of relative voltage of interest. Ideal behavior in the frequency domain is shown with dark shading, acceptable behavior is shown with light shading, and unacceptable behavior is shown in white. Thus, if a circuit were ideal, the plot of the signal (not shown in this figure) would lie entirely in the dark areas.

Nielsen's process starts with the design by hand of a prototype filter (thereby establishing the topology of the solution). This hand-designed prototype (Figure 31.2) is the starting point for Nielsen's system for continuous-time filter compiling (the "C-T compiler"). This hand-designed prototype is already a very good circuit. In this figure, the voltage source **VSOURCE** is 22 volts, the source resistor **RSOURCE** is 1 Ω, and the load resistor **RLOAD** is 0.007641 Ω. In Nielsen's system, the prototype is analyzed by a signal flow graph generator that finds better values for various variables.

31.2 PREPARATORY STEPS

31.2.1 Embryo and Test Fixture

The one-input, one-output initial circuit (Figure 25.6) for this problem is created by embedding the embryo with two modifiable wires and three ports to the test fixture (Figure 29.9) into the one-input, one-output test fixture with three ports to the embryo (Figure 29.1). The source resistance in the test fixture is 1 Ω, the load resistance is 0.1 Ω, and the incoming signal is 22 volts.

Note that the initial circuits used throughout this book (and, in particular, the initial circuit used in this problem) are entirely different in character from Nielsen's human-

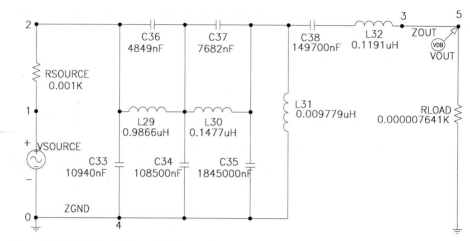

Figure 31.2 Nielsen's hand-designed prototype

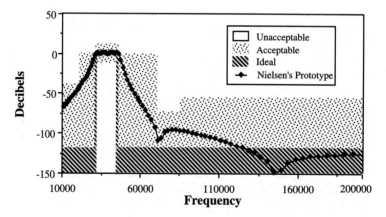

Figure 31.3 Frequency domain behavior of Nielsen's human-designed prototype circuit

designed "prototype circuit" in Figure 31.2. Nielsen's technique makes small adjustments to the component values (sizing) of the prototype circuit. In contrast, genetic programming starts from a virtually degenerate initial circuit consisting only of wires, an incoming signal, an output probe point, and source and load resistors and creates both the topology and sizing of a working, compliant circuit.

Figure 31.3 shows the behavior of Nielsen's human-designed prototype circuit of Figure 31.2 in the frequency domain. As can be seen, 100% of the points on the curve lie in the ideal regions (dark shading) or acceptable regions (light shading). That is, Nielsen's human-designed prototype circuit is an already working 100%-compliant circuit. Figure 31.4 shows the behavior of our one-input, one-output initial circuit (Figure 25.6) for this problem. The output of our initial circuit is always zero, independent of input.

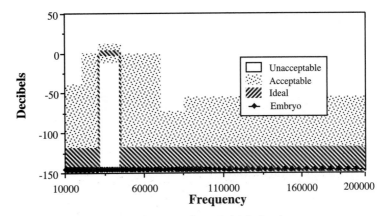

Figure 31.4 Frequency domain behavior of our initial circuit

When the output is zero, the relative voltage is $-\infty$. The value of $-\infty$ is shown in this figure as -150 dB.

31.2.2 Program Architecture

The architecture of each program tree in the population is the same as that used in the lowpass filter problem (Section 25.14.2).

31.2.3 Functions and Terminals

The terminal and function sets are identical to those used in the lowpass filter problem (Section 25.14.3).

31.2.4 Fitness

Note that the initial circuit, the program architecture, and the function and terminal sets are identical to those for the problem of designing the lowpass filter (Sections 25.14.1–25.14.3). That is, these preparatory steps can be applied to *any* one-input, one-output circuit composed of inductors and capacitors.

Given that the preparatory steps above are the same, what is the difference between the problem of synthesizing a standard lowpass filter and the problem of synthesizing a difficult-to-design asymmetric bandpass filter?

The difference is the user-provided fitness measure. It is the fitness measure that directs the evolutionary process to find a circuit that satisfies Nielsen's specifications (as opposed to the specifications for the lowpass filter). In other words, the desired circuit structure arises from fitness.

For this problem, the SPICE simulator is instructed to perform an AC small-signal analysis and to report the circuit's behavior for each of 101 frequency values chosen from the range between 10 KHz and 200 KHz (in equal increments on a logarithmic scale). As it happens, the decade between 10 KHz and 100 KHz has 77 frequency values, and the frequency range between 100 KHz and 200 KHz has 24 points. Note that our choice of a different range of frequencies (as compared to previous chapters) reflects the range used by Nielsen in stating the requirements for his problem. Specifically, this choice does not reflect any judgment on our part that this range of frequencies is somehow preferable to any other.

Fitness is measured in terms of the sum, over these 101 fitness cases, of the absolute weighted deviation between the actual value of the relative voltage (in decibels) that is produced by the circuit at the probe point **VOUT** at node 5 and the target value for relative voltage.

Specifically, the standardized fitness, F, is

$$F = \sum_{i=0}^{100} [W(d(f_i), f_i)d(f_i)]$$

where f_i is the frequency (in hertz) of fitness case i, $d(x)$ is the absolute value of the difference between the target and observed values at frequency x, and $W(y, x)$ is the weighting for difference y at frequency x.

The fitness measure does not penalize ideal values, it slightly penalizes every acceptable deviation, and it heavily penalizes every unacceptable deviation.

The procedure for each of the 14 frequencies inside the desired passband is as follows:

- If the relative voltage is exactly 0 dB (i.e., the ratio of the output voltage to the reference voltage is 1), then the deviation is deemed to be zero for that fitness case.
- If the relative voltage is between –0.6 dB and 0.6 dB, the absolute value of the deviation from 0 dB is weighted by a factor of 10.
- If the relative voltage lies outside that narrow region, the absolute value of the deviation from 0 dB is weighted by a factor of 100.

The procedure for each of the 87 frequencies outside the desired passband is as follows:

- If the relative voltage is below –120 dB for a particular fitness case outside the desired passband, then the deviation is deemed to be zero for that fitness case.
- If the relative voltage is in the acceptable region for a particular fitness case outside the desired passband, the absolute value of the deviation from the target value of relative voltage (–38 dB, 0 dB, –73 dB, –55 dB) is weighted by 1 for that fitness case.
- If the relative voltage is in the unacceptable region for a particular fitness case outside the desired passband, the absolute value of the deviation from –120 dB is weighted by 10 for that fitness case.

The factors of 10 and 100 (rather than the factors of 1 and 10 used on the lowpass filter problem of Section 25.14.4) were selected to approximately equalize the weight given to the relatively few sample points (14) within the desired passband as compared to the relatively large number of sample points (87) outside the desired passband.

The number of hits is defined as the number of fitness cases for which the relative voltage is acceptable or ideal. Note that there are no "don't care" fitness cases for this problem. Thus, the number of hits ranges from 0 to 101.

Using the terminology of Section 25.18.1, the fitness cases in the passband for this problem are points of the type for which we are "CONCERNED_ABOUT_DEVIATIONS_IN_

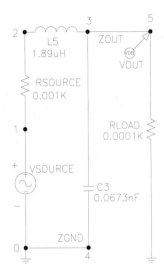

Figure 31.5 Median circuit of generation 0

BOTH _DIRECTIONS", and the fitness cases outside of the passband are points of the type where we are "CONCERNED_ONLY_ABOUT_UPPER_BOUND." There are no fitness cases for this particular problem for which we are "CONCERNED_ONLY_ABOUT_LOWER_BOUND" or "DONT_CARE."

31.2.5 Parameters

The control parameters are the same as in Section 25.14.5.

31.2.6 Tableau

Table 31.1 summarizes the key features of the problem of designing an asymmetric band-pass filter.

31.3 RESULTS

This problem was run three times. All three runs produced nearly 100%-compliant individuals. The run that produced a 100%-compliant individual scoring 101 hits is discussed below.

The median circuit of the simulatable circuits from generation 0 (Figure 31.5) has a fitness of 115,280.0 and scores 0 hits.

Figure 31.6 shows the frequency domain behavior of this median circuit. The horizontal axis represents the frequency of the incoming signal and ranges linearly from 10 KHz to 200 KHz. The vertical axis represents relative voltage in decibels. As can be seen, the curve is almost flat. The circuit does not differentially pass frequencies in any significant way.

Table 31.1 Tableau for asymmetric bandpass filter

Objective	Design an asymmetric bandpass filter satisfying Nielsen's specifications.
Test fixture and embryo	One-input, one-output initial circuit with source resistor, load resistor, and two modifiable wires
Program architecture	Two result-producing branches, RPB0 and RPB1
Initial function set for the RPBs	For construction-continuing subtrees: $F_{ccs\text{-}initial}$ = {C, L, SERIES, PARALLEL0, FLIP, NOP, TWO_GROUND, TWO_VIA0, TWO_VIA1, TWO_VIA2, TWO_VIA3, TWO_VIA4, TWO_VIA5, TWO_VIA6, TWO_VIA7}. For arithmetic-performing subtrees: F_{aps} = {+, -}.
Initial terminal set for the RPBs	For construction-continuing subtrees: $T_{ccs\text{-}initial}$ = {END}. For arithmetic-performing subtrees: $T_{aps} = \{\Re_{smaller\text{-}reals}\}$.
Initial function set for the ADFs	Automatically defined functions are not used.
Initial terminal set for the ADFs	Automatically defined functions are not used.
Potential function set for the RPBs	Architecture-altering operations are not used.
Potential terminal set for the RPBs	Architecture-altering operations are not used.
Potential function set for the ADFs	Architecture-altering operations are not used.
Potential terminal set for the ADFs	Architecture-altering operations are not used.
Fitness cases	101 frequency values in an interval between 10 KHz and 200 KHz
Raw fitness	The sum, over the 101 fitness cases, of the absolute weighted deviation between the actual value of the voltage that is produced by the circuit at the probe point and the target value for voltage
Standardized fitness	Same as raw fitness
Hits	The number of hits is defined as the number of fitness cases (out of 101) for which the voltage is acceptable or ideal.
Wrapper	None
Parameters	M = 640,000. G = 501. S_{rpb} = 200. N_{rpb} = 2.
Result designation	Best-so-far pace-setting individual
Success predicate	A program scores the maximum number (101) of hits.

The best circuit from generation 0 (Figure 31.7) has a fitness of 59,191.7 and scores 72 hits. The first result-producing branch of this program tree has 10 points; the second result-producing branch has 67 points.

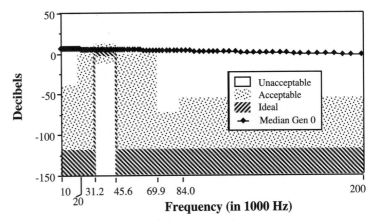

Figure 31.6   Frequency domain behavior of median circuit of generation 0

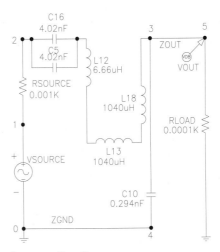

Figure 31.7   Best circuit of generation 0

Figure 31.8a shows the behavior of the best circuit from generation 0. As can be seen, the curve in this figure peaks at −14.7 dB when the frequency is 38.40 KHz. This behavior does not even remotely satisfy the specifications for Nielsen's asymmetric bandpass filter; however, this highly inadequate circuit differentially passes frequencies. The narrow peak at 38.40 KHz falls far short of the desired height; however, it at least occurs within the desired passband (31.2 KHz to 45.6 KHz).

As the run proceeds from generation to generation, the fitness of the best-of-generation individual tends to improve. Figure 31.9 shows, by generation, the standardized fitness and number of hits for the best-of-generation program of each generation of this run. As can be seen, standardized fitness generally improves (i.e., drops) from generation to generation, while the number of hits (i.e., compliant sample points) also generally improves (i.e., rises).

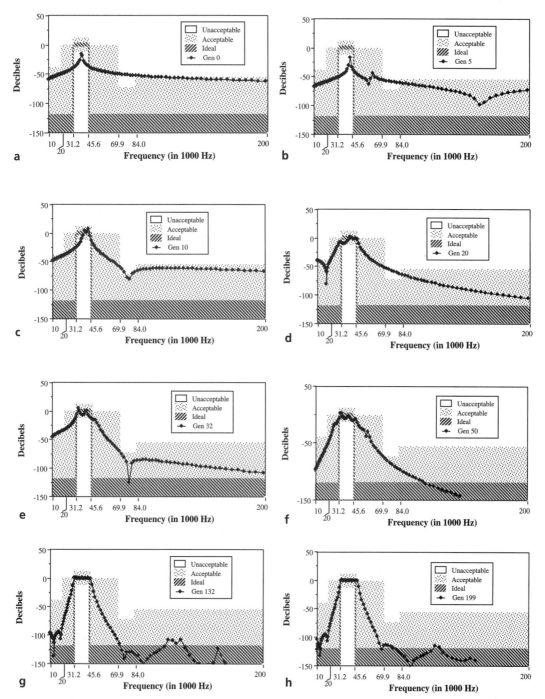

Figure 31.8 Frequency domain behavior of best-of-generation circuits of generations (*a*) 0, (*b*) 5, (*c*) 10, (*d*) 20, (*e*) 32, (*f*) 50, (*g*) 132, and (*h*) 199

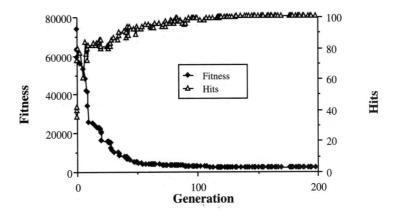

Figure 31.9   Fitness and hits

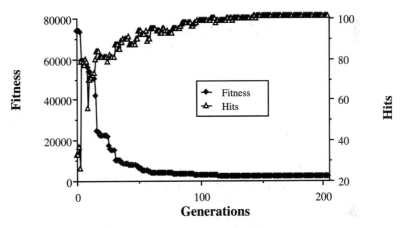

Figure 31.10   Fitness and hits for processing node 59

One processing node of the parallel computer system (the node producing the best-of-run individual) was used for making the computation of the adjusted average population fitness. Figure 31.10 shows the standardized fitness and number of hits for the best-of-generation program of each generation of this run for the 10,000 individuals residing on processing node 59. Note that it is very similar to the figure for the entire population of 640,000 (Figure 31.9).

On processing node 59, 7,768 of the 10,000 programs of generation 0 for this problem produce circuits that cannot be simulated by SPICE. However, the percentage of unsimulatable circuits drops rapidly. The percentage of unsimulatable circuits drops to 37% by generation 1 and 14% by generation 2. Between generations 3 and 202, the maximum percentage of unsimulatable circuits is 18.2%; the minimum is 9.7%; and the average is 13.7%. That is, starting as early as the third generation, six-sevenths of the offspring are simulatable. Figure 31.11 shows, by generation, the percentage of unsimulatable circuits in this run of this problem for processing node 59.

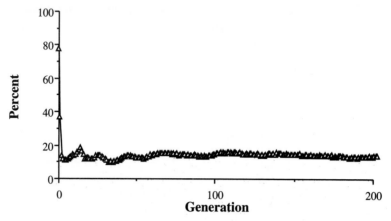

Figure 31.11 Percentage of unsimulatable circuits

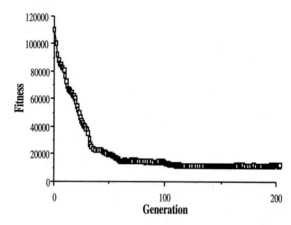

Figure 31.12 Average fitness of the simulatable circuits in the population for processing node 59

Figure 31.12 shows, by generation, the average fitness of the portion of the population that can be analyzed by SPICE (that is, after excluding individuals receiving the penalty value of fitness) for processing node 59. As can be seen, the average fitness of the population as a whole is 109,901.1 for generation 0, 85,871.7 for generation 5, 76,960.6 for generation 10, 19,773.0 for generation 50, 13,681.7 for generation 100, and 12,137.6 for generation 200.

The best individual program in generation 5 has a fitness of 53,238.8 (i.e., slightly better than the 59,191.7 of generation 0) and scores 61 hits. Figure 31.13 shows the best-of-generation circuit for generation 5. The program has 11 points in its first result-producing branch and 30 points in its second result-producing branch. Figure 31.8b shows the behavior of this circuit in the frequency domain for the best-of-generation circuit from generation 5. Notice that the curve peaks at 3.7 dB when the frequency is 42.01 KHz. This peak, in fact, lies within the desired passband from 31.2 KHz to 45.6

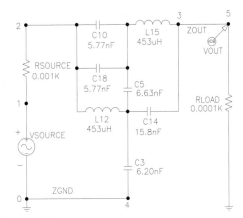

Figure 31.13   Best circuit of generation 5

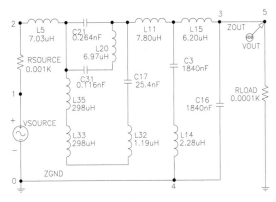

Figure 31.14   Best circuit of generation 10

KHz. Moreover, this peak is closer to the desired value than the peak at generation 0. Thus, although this behavior is still very distant from Nielsen's specifications, this circuit from generation 5 represents an improvement over its predecessors.

The best individual program in generation 10 (Figure 31.14) has a fitness of 25,508.0 and scores 82 hits. The program has 29 points in its first result-producing branch and 95 points in its second result-producing branch. This circuit has two shunts.

Figure 31.8c shows the frequency domain behavior of this circuit from generation 10. Notice the beginning of the formation of a plateau. The peak is at 7.80 dB at 42.01 KHz. The second highest peak to the left is at 5.39 dB at 38.41 KHz. This shows the emergence of the passband that, when fully formed, is intended to run between 31.2 KHz and 45.6 KHz (with relative voltages of between –0.6 dB and 0.6 dB). Note also that the peak here is higher than the peak in the previously shown best circuit. The curve also shows a dip at –81.0 dB to 78.72 KHz (which occurs at frequencies in the band between 69.6 KHz and 84.0 KHz, where asymmetrically greater attenuation is required by the design specifications so that the modem can perform well).

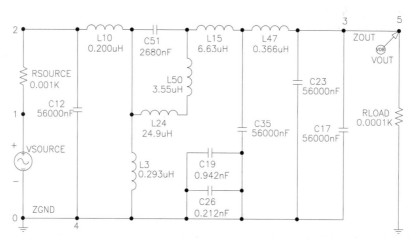

Figure 31.15 Best circuit of generation 20

The best individual circuit in generation 20 (Figure 31.15) has a fitness of 15,999.4 and scores 81 hits. The program has 156 points in its first result-producing branch and 7 points in its second result-producing branch. Capacitors **C19** and **C26** are completely useless.

Figure 31.8d shows the behavior of this circuit in the frequency domain for the best-of-generation circuit from generation 20. Notice the broadening of the emergent pass-band. Also, notice that this individual is doing well in meeting the attenuation requirements to the left of the passband.

The best individual program in generation 32 (Figure 31.16) has a fitness of 10,343.0 and scores 87 hits. The program has 162 points in its first result-producing branch and 52 points in its second result-producing branch. Figure 31.8e shows the behavior of this circuit in the frequency domain for the best-of-generation circuit from generation 32. If we compare this curve with the curve from generation 20 (Figure 31.8d), we see that this curve is doing well in developing the required dip between 69.6 KHz and 84.0 KHz, but does not do as well as the individual from generation 20 in dealing with the low frequencies to the left of the passband.

The best individual program in generation 50 (Figure 31.17) has a fitness of 4,894.2 and scores 94 hits. Figure 31.8f shows the behavior of this circuit in the frequency domain for the best-of-generation circuit from generation 50. The peak of this curve occurs at 2.45 dB at 32.1 KHz. The desired passband starts at 31.2 KHz, so this circuit delivers a strong signal inside the desired passband. A local peak occurs at −9.0 dB at 45.96 KHz, close to the desired end of the passband at 45.6 KHz.

Between generations 132 and 199, there were 42 pace-setting best-of-generation individuals that scored 101 hits in this run. There were also an unknown (but probably large) number of 100%-compliant best-of-generation individuals that were not pace-setting individuals at the time that they arrived at the host processor of the parallel computer system (and hence not stored in the output file for the run). In addition, there were also an unknown (and undoubtedly even larger) number of 100%-compliant individuals

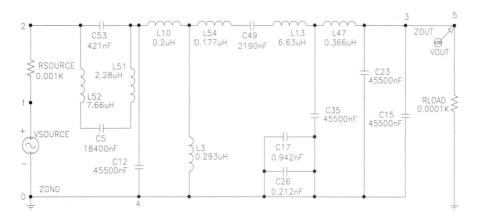

Figure 31.16   Best circuit of generation 32

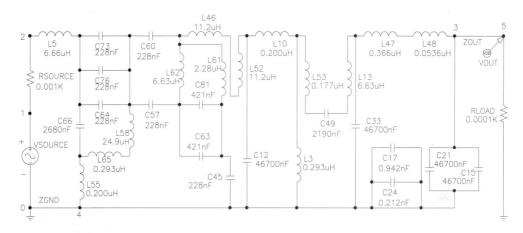

Figure 31.17   Best circuit of generation 50

that were not the very best individual of their generation at their particular processing nodes (and hence not even reported to the host processor by the processing node). In other words, the run produced a multiplicity of solutions to the problem.

The diversity of solutions created in just one run of genetic programming is illustrated by the following six topologically different 100%-compliant circuits:

- The first 100%-compliant circuit created in the run (created at generation 132 with a fitness of 2,252.5).
- The best circuit created in the run (created at generation 199 with a fitness of 2,024.0).
- Three other 100%-compliant circuits (from generations 142, 165, and 185 with fitness values of 2,186.6, 2,130.7, and 2,082.5, respectively). These three individuals were chosen because their fitness values occur at approximately equal increments

along the way between 2,252.5 and 2,024.0 and because they illustrate distinctly different topologies in solving the problem.

- The second 100%-compliant circuit created in the run (created at generation 135) with fitness 2,233.8. This individual was chosen because its topology resembles the topology of the first 100%-compliant circuit created in the run (created at generation 132).

The first pace-setting program achieving 101 hits appears in generation 132. This program has a fitness of 2,252.5. It has 192 points in its first result-producing branch and 200 points in its second result-producing branch. The fact that this individual and many of the other 100%-compliant individuals on this run have 200 (or slightly fewer) points suggests that the individuals in the population repeatedly bumped up against the limit on the maximum number of points established for the run. Figure 31.18 shows the best-of-generation circuit from generation 132.

Figure 31.8g shows the behavior of this circuit in the frequency domain for the best-of-generation circuit from generation 132. As can be seen, 100% of the points are in compliance with the design specifications. In particular, the points in the passband are well within ±0.6 dB of 0 dB required by the specifications.

When a run of genetic programming is continued after the emergence of the first 100%-compliant individual, additional 100%-compliant individuals usually emerge. These additional solutions usually differ, to some degree, in topology, component sizing, or both.

The best-of-run individual program emerged in generation 199 on processor 59 of the parallel computer system. This individual (shown in Figure 31.19) has a fitness of 2,024.0 and scores 101 hits. The program has 199 points in its first result-producing branch and 200 points in its second result-producing branch.

Figure 31.8h shows the behavior of this circuit in the frequency domain for the best-of-run individual from generation 199. As can be seen, 100% of the points are in compliance with the design specifications. Moreover, all the points in the passband are within ±0.39 dB of 0 dB; the specifications merely require a variation of less than ±0.6 dB.

After a circuit is evolved by genetic programming, it may be edited using well-known transformations in several ways. The simplest of these transformations is to combine all series and parallel compositions of like passive components. For example, the evolved best-of-run individual from generation 199 (Figure 31.20) has two 11.2 μH inductors (L37 and L44) in series in the top middle part of the circuit. These two inductors can be replaced by one 22.4 μH inductor. Similarly, the two 53,700 nF capacitors (C15 and C20) can be replaced by one 107,400 nF capacitor.

In addition, evolved circuits can be further improved using numerous other existing techniques by using a 100%-compliant (or nearly 100%-compliant) evolved circuit as a starting point. For example, simulated annealing (Kirkpatrick, Gelatt, and Vecchi 1983; Aarts and Korst 1989) or the genetic algorithm operating on fixed-length character strings (Holland 1975; Goldberg 1989a) can potentially improve the component values of a good evolved circuit (leaving the evolved topology fixed). As another example, the optimization procedure described in Nielsen's 1995 paper can potentially improve a good evolved circuit.

Figure 31.21 shows the circuit for the best-of-generation individual from generation 142. It has a fitness of 2,186.6 and scores 101 hits. Figure 31.22 shows the behavior of this circuit in the frequency domain.

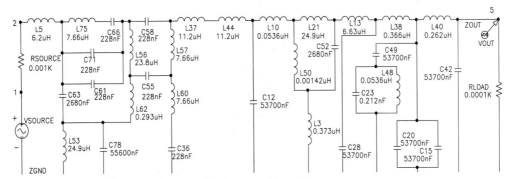

Figure 31.18 Best-of-generation circuit of generation 132

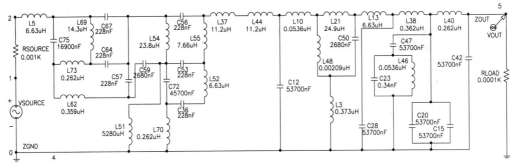

Figure 31.19 Best-of-run circuit from generation 199

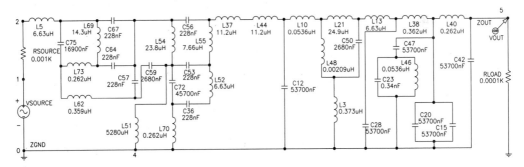

Figure 31.20 Simplification of best-of-run circuit from generation 199

Figure 31.23 shows the circuit for the best-of-generation individual from generation 165. It has a fitness of 2,130.7 and scores 101 hits. The program has 189 points in its first result-producing branch and 198 points in its second result-producing branch. Figure 31.24 shows the behavior of this circuit in the frequency domain.

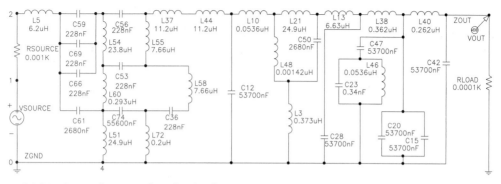

Figure 31.21 Best-of-generation circuit of generation 142

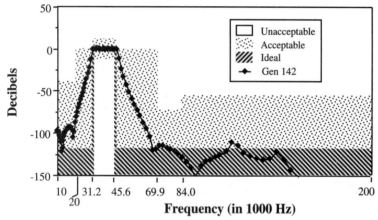

Figure 31.22 Frequency domain behavior of best-of-generation circuit of generation 142

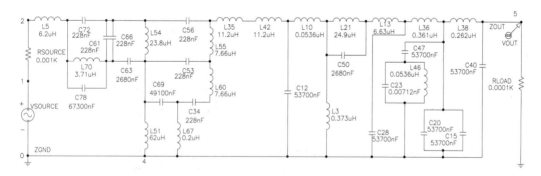

Figure 31.23 Best-of-generation circuit of generation 165

Figure 31.25 shows the circuit for the best-of-generation individual from generation 185. It has a fitness of 2,082.5 and scores 101 hits. Figure 31.26 shows the behavior of this circuit.

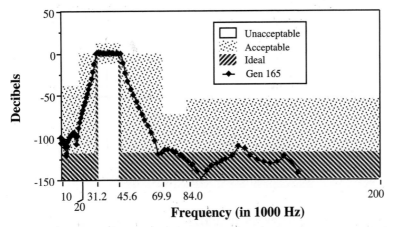

Figure 31.24   Frequency domain behavior of best-of-generation circuit of generation 165

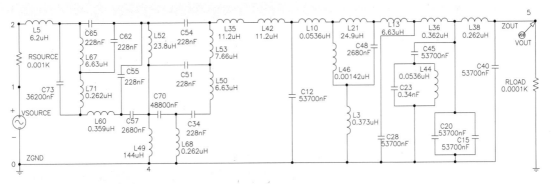

Figure 31.25   Best-of-generation circuit of generation 185

The first 100%-compliant circuit evolved in this run emerged on generation 132 with fitness 2,252.5 (Figure 31.18). The second one emerged on generation 135 with a fitness of 2,233.8 (Figure 31.27). These two circuits are very similar. Other than differences in the numbering of the component values, the only changes occur in two parts of the circuit. First, capacitor **C78** in the bottom-left part of both circuits is 55,600 nF in the circuit from generation 132, but 76,000 nF in the circuit from generation 135. Second, the two-part series composition consisting of 7.66 µH inductor **L75** and 228 nF capacitor **C66** in the upper-left part of the best circuit from generation 132 is replaced by the three-part series composition consisting of 228 nF capacitor **C80**, 6.2 µH inductor **L79**, and 0.2 µH inductor **L70** for the best circuit from generation 135. The topologies of these two circuits are identical, except for this insertion of one inductor. Figure 31.28 shows the behavior of the best-of-generation circuit from generation 135 in the frequency domain.

This chapter demonstrated the evolution of a nonstandard filter of a type that cannot be found in any filter "cookbook."

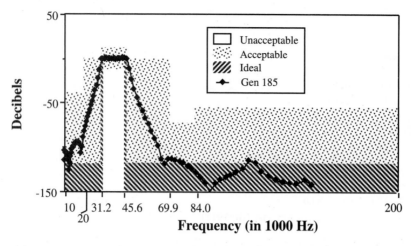

Figure 31.26 **Frequency domain behavior of best-of-generation circuit of generation 185**

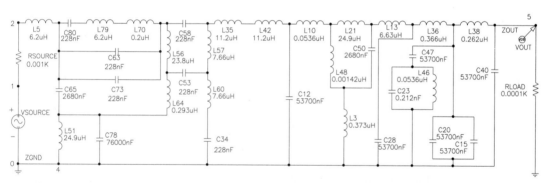

Figure 31.27 **Best-of-generation circuit of generation 135**

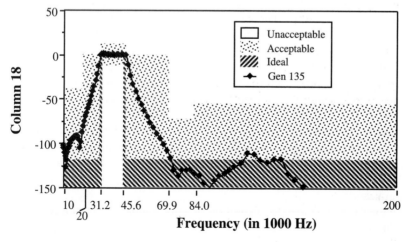

Figure 31.28 **Frequency domain behavior of best-of-generation circuit of generation 135**

Synthesis of a Two-Band Crossover (Woofer-Tweeter) Filter

A *two-band crossover* (woofer-tweeter) filter is a one-input, two-output circuit that passes all frequencies below a certain specified frequency (the *crossover frequency*) to its first output port and that passes all higher frequencies to its second output port while, at the same time, suppressing all frequencies above the crossover frequency to its first port and suppressing the lower frequencies at its second port. High-fidelity sound systems typically contain a crossover filter to channel the low frequencies to the woofer speaker and the high frequencies to the tweeter speaker.

32.1 DESIGN GOALS

The goal is to evolve a design for a two-band crossover filter with a crossover frequency of 2,512 Hz.

32.2 PREPARATORY STEPS

Note the relatively small number of differences between the preparatory steps required for the problem of synthesizing the crossover filter as compared to the problem of synthesizing a lowpass filter (Chapters 25, 27, 28, and 30) and the asymmetric bandpass filter (Chapter 31). The differences arise because the crossover filter has two outputs and the fitness calculation must consider the two different outputs.

32.2.1 Embryo and Test Fixture

A crossover (woofer and tweeter) filter differs from the lowpass filter (Chapters 25, 27, 28, and 30), the highpass filter (Chapter 26), and the asymmetric bandpass filter (Chapter 31) in that the crossover filter has two outputs, not just one. Therefore, the test fixture for the crossover filter must be different from previously used test fixtures because it must have two probe points, **VOUT1** and **VOUT2**, and because each probe point must have its own separate load resistor. In addition, the test fixture must have one external input. A circuit with one external input and two outputs requires an embryo that is different from previously used embryos.

Figure 32.1 shows a one-input, two-output initial circuit for the two-band crossover filter. This initial circuit is the result of embedding a new embryo into a new test fixture. Specifically, the embryo of Figure 29.11, with three modifiable wires (Z0, Z1, and Z2) and four ports (Embryo_Input, Embryo_Output1, Embryo_Output2, and Embryo_ Ground), is embedded into the test fixture of Figure 29.2, with one input, two outputs, and four ports to the embryo.

The input (left) portion of the new test fixture in Figure 32.1 is essentially the same as that used for the previous one-input, one-output circuits. Specifically, the incoming signal VSOURCE is connected to node 0 (ground) and node 1, and there is a source resistor RSOURCE between nodes 1 and 2. However, the output (right) portion of the new test fixture is distinguished from previously used test fixtures by virtue of having two probe points, VOUT1 and VOUT2. As a consequence of having two probe points, there is a nonmodifiable (isolating) wire ZOUT1 between nodes 3 and 5, a voltage probe labeled VOUT1 at node 5, and a fixed load resistor RLOAD1 between nodes 5 and ground. Also, there is a similar nonmodifiable (isolating) wire ZOUT2 between nodes 6 and 7, a voltage probe labeled VOUT2 at node 7, and a load resistor RLOAD2 between nodes 7 and ground.

The new embryo of Figure 32.1 is different from those used previously. In particular, it has four ports (Embryo_Input, Embryo_Output1, Embryo_Output2, and Embryo_Ground). The embryo achieves full connectivity between the Embryo_Input, Embryo_Output1, and Embryo_Output2 by means of the three modifiable wires (Z0, Z1, and Z2). Specifically, there is one modifiable wire Z0 between nodes 2 and 3, a second modifiable wire Z1 between nodes 2 and 6, and a third modifiable wire Z2 between nodes 3 and 6.

As in previous chapters, the initial circuit of Figure 32.1 is designed so that the number of lines impinging at any one node in the circuit is either two or three. This condition is maintained by all of the circuit-constructing functions on the program tree. The isolating (nonmodifiable) wires ZOUT1 and ZOUT2 protect the probe points VOUT1 and VOUT2 during the developmental process.

In the test fixture, the energy source is a 2-volt peak alternating current voltage, the source resistor is 7.94 Ω, and the two load resistors are 7.94 Ω. Except for these minor details involving the incoming voltage level and the values of the load and source resistors, this initial circuit is potentially applicable to any one-input, two-output circuit.

Note that this initial circuit (and all earlier and later ones in this book) contains only resistors, wires, and sources. It is well known that a crossover (woofer and tweeter) filter cannot be created merely from these components. The initial circuit is merely the starting point of a multistep developmental process that transforms an initial circuit into a potentially useful fully developed circuit.

Before proceeding, note the minimal amount of domain knowledge that goes into the initial circuit of Figure 32.1 for this problem. This knowledge consists of the facts that

- the initial circuit has one input (and a source resistor reflecting the reality that all real sources have resistance),
- the initial circuit has two outputs (and two load resistors reflecting the requirement that each output of a circuit must drive a specified load),

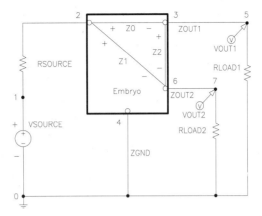

Figure 32.1   One-input, two-output initial circuit for the two-band crossover (woofer-tweeter) filter

- the elements of the to-be-evolved circuit are to be located between the Embryo_Input, Embryo_Output1, Embryo_Output2, and Embryo_Ground in lieu of the three modifiable wires of the embryo, and
- the initial circuit is a valid circuit.

It is important to spotlight one important piece of domain knowledge that we did not use in choosing this embryo. An electrical engineer knows that one well-known effective way to solve the problem of synthesizing a crossover filter is to decompose the problem into two subproblems, namely, synthesizing a lowpass filter and synthesizing a highpass filter. The lowpass filter is inserted between the incoming signal at VSOURCE and the first output port VOUT1 (the intended woofer), while the highpass filter is inserted between the input VSOURCE and the second output port VOUT2 (the intended tweeter). The lowpass and highpass filters operate separately, and their only point of contact is the incoming signal. The embryo here does not incorporate foreknowledge concerning this well-known way of decomposing this problem. Instead, the three modifiable wires (Z0, Z1, and Z2) provide the opportunity for complete connectivity between the two outputs and the one input. There is no bias in favor of the well-known decomposition. In particular, modifiable wire Z2 of the embryo provides an inviting opportunity to connect Embryo_Output1 and Embryo_Output2. As will be seen shortly in the particular run described in detail below, genetic programming happens to decompose this problem by creating a recognizable lowpass filter and a recognizable highpass filter. However, genetic programming does not decompose this problem in this particular way on all runs.

A practicing engineer whose goal is to synthesize a crossover filter has a different orientation from that of, say, a researcher into automated learning techniques. The engineer would have no reason to intentionally avoid using known domain knowledge in solving a particular problem. Instead, the practicing engineer would probably intentionally bias the evolutionary process in the direction of evolving two disconnected substructures by deleting modifiable wire Z2 from the embryo. Because of the TWO_VIA function, the deletion of Z2 does not preclude connectivity between Embryo_Output1 and

Embryo_Output2; however, this deletion would certainly bias the run against such connectivity.

On the other hand, a researcher into automated learning techniques using genetic programming as an "invention machine" might leave all three modifiable wires in place and make 100 runs of the problem in an attempt to discover a new design for a crossover filter (perhaps involving sharing some components in a novel and holistic way).

32.2.2 Program Architecture

Since the embryo has three modifiable wires, there are three result-producing branches.

Neither automatically defined functions nor architecture-altering operations are used on this problem. Thus, the architecture of the overall program tree consists of three result-producing branches.

32.2.3 Functions and Terminals

The function and terminal sets are identical to those used in the problem of synthesizing the lowpass filter (Section 25.14.3).

32.2.4 Fitness

Since a two-band crossover (woofer and tweeter) filter has two outputs, not just one, the fitness measure must be based on both outputs.

The SPICE simulator is instructed to perform an AC small-signal analysis and to report the circuit's behavior at the two probe points, **VOUT1** and **VOUT2**, for each of 101 frequency values chosen from the range between 10 Hz and 100,000 Hz. Each of these four decades of frequency is divided into 25 parts (using a logarithmic scale). Since there are 101 sampled frequencies for each probe point and there are two probe points, there are a total of 202 fitness cases for this problem.

As in previous problems, the fitness measure for this problem is based on a weighted sum of the discrepancies between the actual behavior of the circuit and the desired behavior.

Standardized fitness is measured in terms of the sum, over the 101 frequency values, of the absolute weighted deviation between the actual value of voltage that is produced by the circuit at the first probe point **VOUT1** and the target value for voltage for that first probe point *plus* the sum, over the 101 frequency values, of the absolute weighted deviation between the actual value of voltage that is produced by the circuit at the second probe point **VOUT2** and the target value for voltage for that second probe point. The smaller the value of this two-part fitness measure, the better.

Specifically, the standardized fitness is

$$F = \sum_{i=0}^{100} [W_1(d_1(f_i), f_i)d_1(f_i) + W_2(d_2(f_i), f_i)d_2(f_i)]$$

where f_i is the frequency (in hertz) of fitness case i, $d_1(x)$ is the difference between the target and observed values at frequency x for probe point **VOUT1**, $d_2(x)$ is the difference between the target and observed values at frequency x for probe point **VOUT2**, $W_1(y, x)$ is the weighting for difference y at frequency x for probe point **VOUT1**, and $W_2(y, x)$ is the weighting for difference y at frequency x for probe point **VOUT2**.

Consider the woofer portion and **VOUT1** first. The desired behavior at the woofer output at **VOUT1** of a two-band crossover filter is that of a lowpass filter.

The procedure for each of the 58 points in the interval from 10 Hz to 1,905 Hz is as follows:

- If the voltage equals the ideal value of 1.0 volt in this interval, the deviation is 0.0.
- If the voltage is between 970 millivolts and 1,000 millivolts, the absolute value of the deviation from 1,000 millivolts is weighted by a factor of 1.0.
- If the voltage is less than 970 millivolts, the absolute value of the deviation from 1,000 millivolts is weighted by a factor of 10.0.

This arrangement reflects the fact that the ideal voltage in the passband is 1.0 volt, the fact that a 30 millivolt shortfall satisfies the design goals of the problem, and the fact that a voltage below 970 millivolts in the passband is not acceptable.

The procedure for the 38 fitness cases representing frequencies in the interval from 3,311 Hz to 100,000 Hz is as follows:

- If the voltage equals the ideal value of 0 volts in this interval, the deviation is 0.0.
- If the voltage is between 0 millivolts and 1 millivolt, the absolute value of the deviation from 0 millivolts is weighted by a factor of 1.0.
- If the voltage is more than 1 millivolt, the absolute value of the deviation from 0 millivolts is weighted by a factor of 10.0.

The five frequencies nearest 2,512 Hz belong to the transitional region. The first two points represent the falloff from the 1-volt level and therefore should be reasonably close to 1 volt, the middle point should be around ½ volts, and the last two points represent the falloff toward the 0-volt level and therefore should be reasonably close to 0 volts. The procedure for each of the five frequencies nearest 2,512 Hz is as follows:

- For the two fitness cases at 2,089 Hz and 2,291 Hz, the absolute value of the deviation from 1,000 millivolts is weighted by a factor of 1.0.
- For the fitness case at 2,512 Hz, the absolute value of the deviation from 500 millivolts is weighted by a factor of 1.0.
- For the two fitness cases at 2,754 Hz and 3,020 Hz, the absolute value of the deviation from 0 millivolts is weighted by a factor of 1.0.

We considered the number of fitness cases (61 and 35) in the two main bands to be sufficiently close that we did not bother to equalize the weight given to the differing numbers of fitness cases in these two main bands.

Now consider the tweeter portion at **VOUT2**. The desired behavior at **VOUT2** of a two-band crossover filter is that of a highpass filter. The components of the fitness measure for the tweeter portion is a mirror image of the above arrangement for the woofer portion.

The number of hits is defined as the number of fitness cases for which the voltage is acceptable. For this purpose, the five points that lie in the transitional region between 2,089 Hz and 3,020 Hz for both **VOUT1** and **VOUT2** are unconditionally deemed to be acceptable. Thus, the number of hits ranges from 10 to 202.

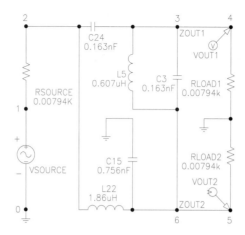

Figure 32.2   Median circuit of generation 0

32.2.5   Parameters

The control parameters are the same as in Section 25.14.5.

32.2.6   Tableau

Table 32.1 summarizes the key features of the problem of designing a two-band cross-over (woofer-tweeter) filter.

32.3   RESULTS

The median simulatable circuit (Figure 32.2) from generation 0 has a fitness of 964.3 and scores 10 hits. Figure 32.3 shows the behavior of this median circuit from generation 0 in the frequency domain. The horizontal scale represents frequency and ranges logarithmically over four decades of frequencies from 10 Hz to 100,000 Hz. The vertical axis represents peak output voltage and ranges linearly from 0 volts to 1 volt. The frequency domain behavior of both outputs is shown in the figure; however, they almost overlap and are indistinguishable on the scale of this figure. It can be seen that neither of the two outputs of this circuit are near the desired levels of 1 volt and 0 volts for the two passbands and stopbands. Based on the scale of this figure, this circuit does not appear to differentially pass frequencies in any significant way.

Figure 32.4 shows an enlarged view of the vertical axis between 662 millivolts and 668 millivolts. This figure shows that the two outputs are, in fact, slightly different and that slightly less power is passed to the woofer at the higher frequencies.

The best individual circuit of generation 0 (Figure 32.5) has a fitness of 159.0 and scores 85 hits (out of 202). The first result-producing branch of its program tree has 181 points, its second result-producing branch has 181 points, and its third result-producing branch has 18 points. The two substructures feeding **VOUT1** and **VOUT2** are connected by capacitor **C5**. This circuit acquires its status as the best circuit of generation 0 because the single inductor **L3** (feeding into the **VOUT1** probe point) has the desirable effect of

Table 32.1 Tableau for two-band crossover (woofer-tweeter) filter

Objective	Design a two-band crossover (woofer-tweeter) filter.
Test fixture and embryo	One-input, two-output initial circuit with a source resistor, two load resistors, and three modifiable wires
Program architecture	Three result-producing branches, RPB0, RPB1, and RPB2
Initial function set for the RPBs	For construction-continuing subtrees: $F_{ccs\text{-}initial}$ = {C, L, SERIES, PARALLEL0, FLIP, NOP, TWO_GROUND, TWO_VIA0, TWO_VIA1, TWO_VIA2, TWO_VIA3, TWO_VIA4, TWO_VIA5, TWO_VIA6, TWO_VIA7}. For arithmetic-performing subtrees: F_{aps} = {+, -}.
Initial terminal set for the RPBs	For construction-continuing subtrees: $T_{ccs\text{-}initial}$ = {END}. For arithmetic-performing subtrees: T_{aps} = {$\Re_{smaller\text{-}reals}$}.
Initial function set for the ADFs	Automatically defined functions are not used.
Initial terminal set for the ADFs	Automatically defined functions are not used.
Potential function set for the RPBs	Architecture-altering operations are not used.
Potential terminal set for the RPBs	Architecture-altering operations are not used.
Potential function set for the ADFs	Architecture-altering operations are not used.
Potential terminal set for the ADFs	Architecture-altering operations are not used.
Fitness cases	There are a total of 202 fitness cases. There are 101 frequency values in an interval of four decades between 10 Hz and 100,000 Hz that are applicable to the probe point for the woofer and another 101 frequency values that are applicable to the probe point for the tweeter.
Raw fitness	The sum, over the 202 fitness cases, of the absolute weighted deviation between the actual value of the voltage that is produced by the circuit at the probe points and the target value for voltage
Standardized fitness	Same as raw fitness
Hits	The number of hits is defined as the number of fitness cases (out of 202) for which the voltage is acceptable or ideal.
Wrapper	None
Parameters	M = 640,000. G = 501. S_{rpb} = 200. N_{rpb} = 3.
Result designation	Best-so-far pace-setting individual
Success predicate	A program scores the maximum number (202) of hits.

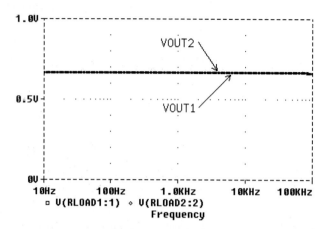

Figure 32.3   Frequency domain behavior of the median circuit of generation 0

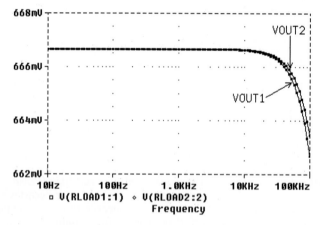

Figure 32.4   Frequency domain behavior of the median circuit of generation 0 using an exploded vertical axis

tending to block the higher frequencies, while the single capacitor **C4** (feeding into the **VOUT2** probe point) has the desirable effect of tending to block the lower frequencies.

Figure 32.6a shows the frequency domain behavior of the two outputs of the best-of-generation circuit from generation 0. The first output resembles that of a poor lowpass filter in that it is near 1.0 volt from 10 Hz to about 500 Hz and then starts dropping off toward 0 volts in a leisurely way as the frequency increases. The only resemblance between the second output and the desired highpass behavior is that it is near 0 volts for the lowest frequencies and climbs slightly between 1,000 Hz and 10,000 Hz.

Figure 32.7 shows the circuit for the best-of-generation individual from generation 12. It has a fitness of 80.3 and scores 116 hits (out of 202). The three result-producing

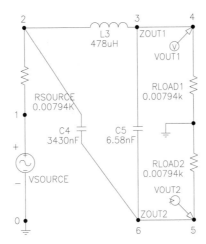

Figure 32.5   Best circuit of generation 0

branches of its program tree have 102, 29, and 148 points, respectively. Notice that two distinct clusters of components have emerged near output ports **VOUT1** and **VOUT2**. Nodes 2, 3, and 6 are fully connected via three modifiable wires (**Z0**, **Z1**, and **Z2**) in a triangular arrangement in the embryo; however, the evolutionary process created the bifurcation that separates the cluster of components feeding **VOUT1** from the cluster feeding **VOUT2**. **L3** and **C24** constitute one rung of a classical ladder topology for a lowpass filter feeding **VOUT1**. **C4** and the series composition **L46** and **L58** constitute one rung of a classical ladder topology for a highpass filter feeding **VOUT2**. **C14** and **C16** are useless appendices.

Figure 32.6b shows the behavior in the frequency domain of the best-of-generation circuit from generation 12. Notice the emergence of a crossover area in the general neighborhood of 2,512 Hz (and 0.5 volts). This crossover area was not present in the corresponding figure for the best circuit of generation 0. Notice that the second output now resembles that of a poor highpass filter.

Figure 32.8 shows the circuit for the best-of-generation individual from generation 20. It has a fitness of 38.8 and scores 125 hits. The three result-producing branches of the program tree have 186, 78, and 41 points, respectively. **L3** and **C5** constitute one rung of a classical ladder topology for a lowpass filter feeding **VOUT1**. **L4** is minuscule and can be ignored. Then **C21** and **L14** constitute one rung of a classical ladder topology for a highpass filter feeding **VOUT2**.

Figure 32.6c shows the behavior in the frequency domain for the best-of-generation circuit from generation 20. Notice that the crossover area around 2,512 Hz is considerably tighter than that of generation 12 (but that the crossover occurs at about 0.7 volts).

The best circuit of generation 79 (Figure 32.9) has a fitness of 1.06 and scores 196 hits. The three result-producing branches of the program tree have 142, 200, and 173 points, respectively.

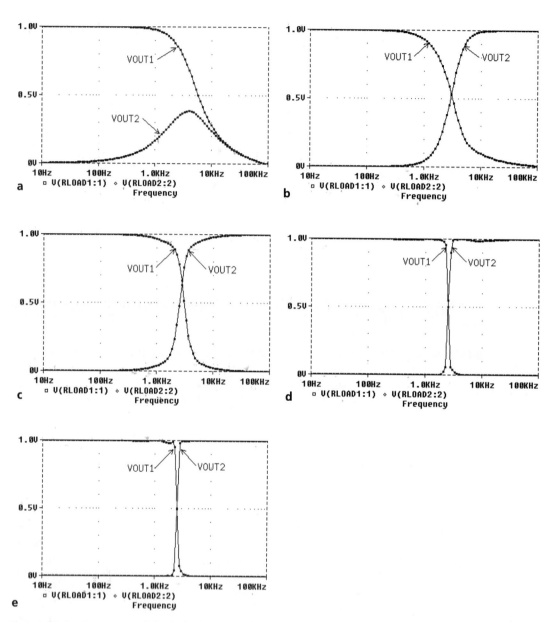

Figure 32.6 Frequency domain behavior of best circuits of generations (*a*) 0, (*b*) 12, (*c*) 20, (*d*) 79, and (*e*) 137

Figure 32.6d shows the behavior in the frequency domain for the best-of-generation circuit from generation 79. Compare the tightness of the crossover region in this figure to that of generations 12 and 20. In particular, notice that the crossover region here around 2,512 Hz is considerably tighter than that of earlier generations and that the two curves now cross around 0.5 volts.

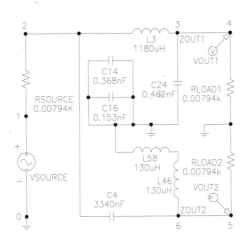

Figure 32.7 Best circuit of generation 12

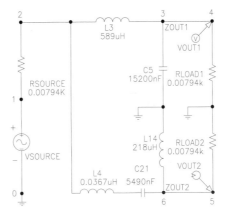

Figure 32.8 Best circuit of generation 20

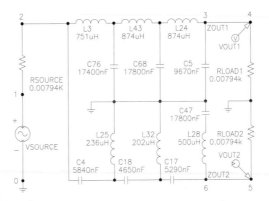

Figure 32.9 Best circuit of generation 79

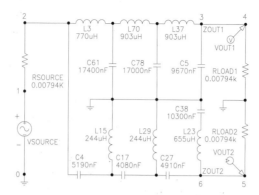

Figure 32.10 Best-of-run circuit from generation 137

The best-of-run circuit of generation 137 (Figure 32.10) has a fitness of 0.7807 and scores 192 hits (out of 202). The three result-producing branches of the program tree have 187, 198, and 191 points, respectively.

The best-of-run circuit from generation 137 has the same topology as the best-of-run circuit from generation 79. All but two of the 13 components have different values; however, the component values are all within 73% of one another. That is, the practical effect of the second half of this particular run is to refine the component values (rather than create new circuit topology). Table 32.2 compares the component values from the two circuits. The names of the corresponding components from the two circuits are shown in the first column of the table. The names of corresponding components are identical in 3 of the 13 cases. In the remaining 10 cases, the name of the component from the best-of-generation circuit from generation 79 is shown first. The values of C5 and C76 / C61 are identical in both generations.

Figure 32.6e shows the frequency domain behavior for the best-of-run individual from generation 137. Notice that the best-of-run circuit from generation 137 does not score a full 202 hits because of the shortcoming in the lowpass part of this figure around 2,000 Hz. (A circuit scoring 200 hits is evolved in Chapter 33 using the architecture-altering operations.) The highpass filter portion of the evolved crossover filter in Figure 32.10 (i.e., the lower half of the figure) possesses the topology and approximately possesses the numerical values of a canonical "M-derived half section" appended to two "constant K" prototype sections. The "M-derived half section" was invented and patented by Zobel (Zobel 1925). It is discussed in detail in Section 25.15.3 and in connection with Figure 26.5.

To see that the two filter sections in the left two-thirds of the highpass filter portion (lower half) of Figure 32.10 constitute two "constant K" prototype sections, note that the two inductors L15 and L29 in the two vertical inductive shunts have the same value (244 µH). Since the capacitance of two equal capacitors in series is half the capacitance of either of them, Figure 32.10 can be recast by replacing the 4,080 nF capacitor C17 with a series composition of two 8,160 nF capacitors and replacing the 4,910 nF capacitor C27 with a series composition of two 9,820 nF capacitors. Suppose, for sake of argument, that we are willing to replace each of the resulting five capacitors (5,190 nF; 8,160 nF; 8,160 nF; 9,820 nF; and 9,820 nF) by their average value (8,230 nF). The result can

Table 32.2 Comparison of component values

Component	Generation 79	Generation 137
L3	751 µH	770 µH
L43 / L70	874 µH	903 µH
L24 / L37	874 µH	903 µH
C76 / C61	17,400 nF	17,400 nF
C68 / C78	17,800 nF	17,000 nF
C5	9,670 nF	9,670 nF
C4	5,840 nF	5,190 nF
C18 / C17	4,650 nF	4,080 nF
C17 / C27	5,290 nF	4,910 nF
L25 / L15	236 µH	244 µH
L32 / L29	202 µH	244 µH
L28 / L23	500 µH	655 µH
C47 / C38	17,800 nF	10,300 nF

then be viewed as five identical 8,230 nF capacitors in series (one to the left of the first vertical shunt, two lying between the first and second vertical shunts, and two lying between the second and third vertical shunts). After the above admittedly approximate substitution, the left two-thirds of the evolved highpass filter portion (lower half) of Figure 32.10 can be viewed as consisting of a cascade of two identical symmetric T sections. Each T section consists of an incoming 8,230 nF capacitor of capacitance $2C$ (where C is 4,115 nF), a junction point from which an inductor of inductance L (where L is 244 µH) is shunted off to ground, and an outgoing capacitor of capacitance $2C$. The two symmetric T sections are referred to as "constant K" filter sections (Johnson 1950, p. 331).

Such sections are characterized by two key parameters. The first parameter is the section's characteristic resistance (impedance). The second parameter is the nominal cutoff frequency. The characteristic resistance, R, of each of the two symmetric T sections is given by the formula

$$R = \sqrt{L/C}$$

When the inductance, L, is 244 µH and the capacitance, C, is 4,115 nF, then the characteristic resistance, R, is 7.70 Ω according to this formula. In principle, the characteristic resistance should match the circuit's fixed load resistance RLOAD. This value is within 3% of the value of the fixed load resistance of 7.94 Ω in the test fixture for this problem. The nominal cutoff frequency, f_c, of each of the T-sections of a highpass filter is given by the formula

$$f_c = 1/(4\pi\sqrt{(LC)}).$$

In principle, this parameter should be in the neighborhood of 2,512 Hz for the crossover filter here. When the inductance, L, is 244 µH and the capacitance, C, is 4,115 nF, then the nominal cutoff frequency, f_c, is 2,511 Hz. In other words, both of the key parameters of the two evolved T sections of Figure 32.10 are very close to the canonical values for two "constant K" sections designed with the aim of satisfying this problem's design requirements.

Now consider the final section of the highpass filter portion (lower half) of Figure 32.10.

To see that this final section approximates an "M-derived half section," note that the value of inductor L23 is 655 µH. Let m be the ratio of the common inductive value (244 µH) in the first two sections to the inductive value in the final section (655 µH), so that $m = 0.37$ here.

Given this choice of m, the final section of the filter has one incoming capacitor of capacitance $2C$, a junction point, and a shunt consisting of a series composition of 10,300 nF capacitor C38 and inductor L23 of inductance L/m (where L is 244 µH). In an "M-derived half section" that is derived from the above two "constant K" prototype sections, the inductance in the vertical shunt of the half section is L/m (Johnson 1950). Of course, the actual value of inductor L23 (655 µH) in the inductive-capacitive shunt here is exactly L/m (where L is 244 µH) because m was so chosen.

The actual value of the series capacitor C27 in the horizontal part of the half section is 4,910 nF. This may be viewed as an 8,230 nF capacitor and a final 12,171 nF capacitor (for the "M-derived half section"). The value of the series capacitor in an "M-derived half section" is given by the formula C/m (where C is 4,115 nF). This expression evaluates to 11,122 nF (which is within 8% of 12,171 nF).

The value of the capacitor C38 in the inductive-capacitive shunt of an "M-derived half section" is given by the formula

$$4\,m\,C\,/\,(1 - m^2).$$

This expression evaluates to 7,056 nF (which is within 31% of the actual value of 10,300 nF for capacitor C38 in the inductive-capacitive shunt).

Thus, the numerical component values of the highpass filter portion of the evolved crossover filter in Figure 32.10 are reasonably close to the expected numerical values of the components of the two "constant K" prototype sections and an "M-derived half section" as described in U.S. patent 1,538,964 (Zobel 1925).

The woofer part of the best-of-generation circuit from generation 79 (Figure 32.9) has a three-rung lowpass ladder topology (with inductors L3, L43, and L24 in series horizontally across the top of the figure and capacitors C76, C68, and C5 as shunts vertically to ground). As we proceed from node 2 toward the two outputs, there is a bifurcation at L3 and C4, after which there is no further contact between the upper (woofer) portion of the circuit (leading to VOUT1) and the lower (tweeter) portion of the circuit (leading to VOUT2). That is, the evolutionary process created two distinct and separate substructures—one for the woofer output and one for the tweeter output. This evolved circuit is a parallel decomposition into a woofer substructure and a tweeter substructure.

The fact that the problem of the design of a crossover filter can be decomposed in this manner is now well known to electrical engineers. In fact, Otto Zobel of American Telephone and Telegraph invented this approach and received U.S. patent 1,538,964 for this invention (Zobel 1925). Genetic programming was not supplied with any knowledge to suggest that it would be advisable to approach this particular problem of circuit synthesis by creating two separate and distinct substructures. Certainly nothing in the fitness measure favored a decomposition (as opposed to a holistic) approach. Moreover, the choice of the embryo did not bias the run of genetic programming in favor of creating separate and distinct substructures. In fact, it was deliberately chosen to be neutral. Instead, this beneficial decomposition emerged automatically during the run of genetic programming. That is, the evolutionary process opportunistically reinvented the well-known decomposition because it was needed. The user-supplied fitness measure specified "what needs to be done," and genetic programming automatically determined "how to do it." This decomposition is precisely the kind of problem decomposition that a system for automatically creating computer programs should be able to perform automatically. And it is precisely the kind of problem decomposition that usually must be performed, by hand, prior to the start-up of a run of most existing techniques for machine learning and artificial intelligence.

In U.S. patent 1,538,964, Otto Zobel (1925) pointed out that the crossover filter addresses the problem of making

> a long telephone circuit available not only for the ordinary telephoning frequencies but also for "carrier currents" of higher frequency, which may be modulated for additional telegraph or telephone uses. At the receiving station it becomes necessary to separate the frequencies so that those of the ordinary telephone range may go to an ordinary telephone receiving instrument and those of higher frequency may go to proper modulating apparatus. In Fig. 5 [of the patent] the incoming line from the left branches to two wave-filters in parallel, which lead respectively to the apparatus J and K, J for ordinary telephone frequencies, K for higher frequencies. Leading to J is a low-pass wave-filter and to K is a high-pass wave-filter. . . . To insure that frequencies of one range shall not go to the other apparatus from that for which they are intended, there must necessarily be an intermediate band of "lost frequencies," which it is desirable to make as narrow as possible.

Referring to the eight criteria in Chapter 1 for establishing that an automatically created result is competitive with a human-produced result, this result satisfies the following two criteria:

A.   The result was patented as an invention in the past, is an improvement over a patented invention, or would qualify today as a patentable new invention.

F.   The result is equal to or better than a result that was considered an achievement in its field at the time it was first discovered.

Therefore, we make the following claim:

- **CLAIM NO. 6**   We claim the rediscovery of the decomposition of the problem of synthesizing a crossover filter is an instance where genetic programming has produced a result that is competitive with a result produced by creative and inventive humans.

The automatic discovery of the usefulness of this parallel decomposition satisfies Arthur Samuel's criterion (1983) for artificial intelligence and machine learning:

> The aim [is] . . . to get machines to exhibit behavior, which if done by humans, would be assumed to involve the use of intelligence.

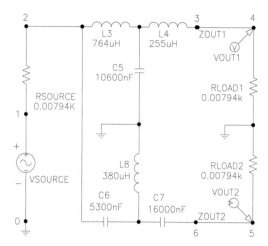

Figure 32.11   Circuit for a combination of lowpass and highpass third-order Butter-worth filters

32.4   COMPARISON WITH BUTTERWORTH FILTERS

The Butterworth filters (Section 37.1.1) are a graded series of benchmark "ladder" filters parameterized by n, where n is the number of inductors and capacitors in the circuit (Van Valkenburg 1982).

Figure 32.11 shows a lowpass third-order Butterworth filter connected to **VOUT1** and a highpass third-order Butterworth filter connected to **VOUT2**. The two together create a crossover filter.

Figure 32.12a shows the frequency domain response of a combination of a third-order lowpass Butterworth filter and a third-order highpass Butterworth filter. When we apply the same fitness and hit measures as just used in evolving the crossover filter (Section 32.2.4) to a combined circuit composed of a lowpass (with its passband ending at 2,512 Hz) and a highpass third-order Butterworth filter (with its passband beginning at 2,512 Hz), the combined circuit scores 162 hits (out of 202).

Figure 32.13 shows a lowpass fifth-order Butterworth filter connected to **VOUT1** and a highpass fifth-order Butterworth filter connected to **VOUT2**.

Figure 32.12b shows the frequency domain response of a combination of a fifth-order lowpass Butterworth filter and a fifth-order highpass Butterworth filter. When we apply our fitness measure and our definition of hits to a combination of lowpass and highpass fifth-order Butterworth filters, the combined circuit scores 184 hits (out of 202).

Figure 32.14 shows a lowpass seventh-order Butterworth filter connected to **VOUT1** and a highpass seventh-order Butterworth filter connected to **VOUT2**.

Figure 32.12c shows the frequency domain response of a combination of a seventh-order lowpass Butterworth filter and a seventh-order highpass Butterworth filter. When we apply our fitness measure and our definition of hits to a combination of lowpass and highpass third-order Butterworth filters, the combined circuit scores 190 hits (out of 202).

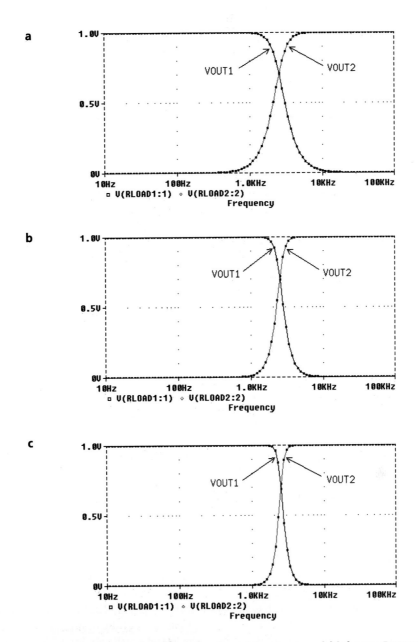

Figure 32.12   Frequency domain behavior of lowpass and highpass Butterworth filters: (a) third-order, (b) fifth-order, and (c) seventh-order

The best-of-run circuit from generation 137 (Figure 32.10) scores 192 hits and thus can be said to deliver a response that is slightly better than a parallel composition of lowpass and highpass seventh-order Butterworth filters. The combination of lowpass and

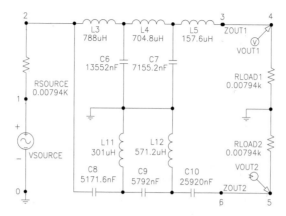

Figure 32.13   Circuit for a combination of lowpass and highpass fifth-order Butterworth filters

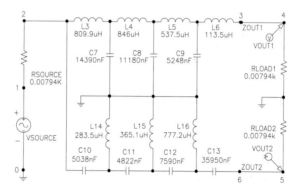

Figure 32.14   Circuit for a combination of lowpass and highpass seventh-order Butterworth filters

highpass seventh-order Butterworth filters requires seven inductors and seven capacitors, while the evolved best-of-run circuit requires only six inductors and seven capacitors. Thus, the evolved filter circuit has a response that is slightly better than a seventh-order Butterworth filter and is slightly more parsimonious. Notice that the lowpass part of the best-of-run circuit has the Butterworth topology (but not the Butterworth values for the components). In contrast, the highpass part of the best-of-run circuit has an extra capacitor and therefore does not have the Butterworth topology. There is a sharper and cleaner boundary around 2,512 Hz for the highpass part (i.e., the part with the extra capacitor) of the frequency response in Figure 32.6e than for the lowpass part. This observed sharper and cleaner boundary is precisely the advantage claimed by Otto Zobel (1925) for his "M-derived half section" consisting of a final inductive-capacitive shunt.

Synthesis of a Two-Band Crossover (Woofer-Tweeter) Filter Using Architecture-Altering Operations

This chapter shows how the problem of designing a two-band crossover filter from the preceding chapter can be solved using the architecture-altering operations (from Part 3). This chapter specifically demonstrates the ability of the architecture-altering operations to automatically organize automatically defined functions into a hierarchy in which one automatically defined function invokes another. In addition, this chapter again demonstrates the ability of the architecture-altering operations to automatically determine the number of automatically defined functions and the number of arguments that they each possess.

33.1 DESIGN GOALS

The goal is to evolve the design of a two-band crossover filter with a crossover frequency of 2,512 Hz using the architecture-altering operations.

33.2 PREPARATORY STEPS

33.2.1 Embryo and Test Fixture

The one-input, two-output initial circuit (Figure 32.1) for this problem is created by embedding the embryo with three modifiable wires and four ports (Figure 29.11) into the one-input, two-output test fixture with four ports (Figure 29.2).

33.2.2 Program Architecture

Since the embryo has three modifiable wires, there are three result-producing branches.

Each program in generation 0 has a uniform architecture with no automatically defined functions (i.e., only three result-producing branches). The architecture-altering operations can create one-argument automatically defined functions as well as dummy variables. Hierarchical references are permitted between the yet-to-be-created automatically defined functions.

33.2.3 Functions and Terminals

The initial function set for each construction-continuing subtree of a result-producing branch, $F_{ccs-rpb-initial}$, is

$F_{ccs-rpb-initial}$ = {C, L, SERIES, PARALLEL0, PARALLEL1, FLIP, NOP, THREE_GROUND, PAIR_CONNECT_0, PAIR_CONNECT_1}.

The initial terminal set for each construction-continuing subtree of a result-producing branch, $T_{ccs-rpb-initial}$, is

$T_{ccs-rpb-initial}$ = {END, SAFE_CUT}.

Since there are no automatically defined functions in generation 0 of this problem, $T_{ccs-adf-initial}$ and $F_{ccs-adf-initial}$ are empty.

The set of potential functions for each construction-continuing subtree of a result-producing branch, $F_{ccs-rpb-potential}$, is

$F_{ccs-rpb-potential}$ = {ADF0, ADF1, ADF2, ADF3, ADF4}.

The set of potential terminals for each construction-continuing subtree of a result-producing branch, $T_{ccs-rpb-potential}$, is empty:

$T_{ccs-rpb-potential}$ = ϕ.

The newly created automatically defined functions do not hierarchically refer to one another. The set of potential functions for each construction-continuing subtree of an automatically defined function, $F_{ccs-adf-potential}$, is

$F_{ccs-adf-potential}$ = {C, L, SERIES, PARALLEL0, PARALLEL1, FLIP, NOP, THREE_GROUND, PAIR_CONNECT_0, PAIR_CONNECT_1}.

The set of potential terminals for each construction-continuing subtree of an automatically defined function, $T_{ccs-adf-potential}$, is

$T_{ccs-adf-potential}$ = {ARG0, END, SAFE_CUT}.

The function set, F_{aps}, for each arithmetic-performing subtree in any branch and the terminal set, T_{aps}, for each arithmetic-performing subtree in any branch are the same as for the lowpass filter problem in Section 25.14.3.

33.2.4 Fitness

The fitness measure is the same as in Section 25.14.4.

33.2.5 Parameters

The control parameters are the same as for the problem of synthesizing a lowpass filter with architecture-altering operations (Section 28.2.5).

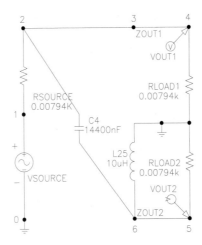

Figure 33.1   Best circuit of generation 0

Tableau

Table 33.1 summarizes the key features of the problem of designing a two-band crossover (woofer-tweeter) filter using architecture-altering operations.

33.3   RESULTS

The best individual circuit of generation 0 has a fitness of 410.3 and scores 98 hits (out of 202). The first result-producing branch of its program tree has 15 points, its second result-producing branch has 103 points, and its third result-producing branch has 12 points.

Figure 33.1 shows the best-of-generation circuit from generation 0. Notice that inductor **L25** is the shunt element and capacitor **C4** is the "series" element of a one-rung ladder for the intended highpass (tweeter) output **VOUT2**. This construction is a well-known topological arrangement for a highpass filter.

Figure 33.2a shows the behavior of the best-of-generation circuit from generation 0 in the frequency domain. The horizontal axis represents the frequency of the incoming signal and ranges over four decades of frequencies from 10 Hz to 100,000 Hz on a logarithmic scale. The vertical axis represents peak voltage and ranges linearly from 0 volts to 1 volt. The convention in this book is that whenever the vertical axis lacks tick marks, a linear scale is being used. As can be seen, the intended highpass (tweeter) output **VOUT2** has the desired value of 0 volts for low frequencies but then rises slowly (and only to about ½ volt) for higher frequencies. The intended lowpass (woofer) output **VOUT1** has the desired value of 1 volt for low frequencies, but then drops off in a very leisurely way until 13.4 KHz and then reverses and rises to around ½ volt for higher frequencies. There appears to be a zero in the woofer transfer function at the resonant frequency of **C4** and **L25** (i.e., 13.4 KHz).

Table 33.1 Tableau for two-band crossover (woofer-tweeter) filter using architecture-altering operations

Objective	Use the architecture-altering operations to design a two-band crossover (woofer-tweeter) filter.
Test fixture and embryo	One-input, two-output initial circuit with a source resistor, two load resistors, and three modifiable wires
Program architecture	Three result-producing branches, RPB0, RPB1, and RPB2, in generation 0. Additional automatically defined functions will be created during the run by the architecture-altering operations.
Initial function set for the RPBs	For construction-continuing subtrees: $F_{\text{ccs-rpb-initial}}$ = {C, L, SERIES, PARALLEL0, PARALLEL1, FLIP, NOP, THREE_GROUND, PAIR_CONNECT_0, PAIR_CONNECT_1}. For arithmetic-performing subtrees: F_{aps} = {+, -}.
Initial terminal set for the RPBs	For construction-continuing subtrees: $T_{\text{ccs-rpb-initial}}$ = {END, SAFE_CUT}. For arithmetic-performing subtrees: T_{aps} = {$\Re_{\text{smaller-reals}}$}.
Initial function set for the ADFs	No automatically defined functions in generation 0. $F_{\text{ccs-adf-initial}}$ = ϕ.
Initial terminal set for the ADFs	No automatically defined functions in generation 0. $T_{\text{ccs-adf-initial}}$ = ϕ.
Potential function set for the RPBs	$F_{\text{ccs-rpb-potential}}$ = {ADF0, ADF1, ADF2, ADF3, ADF4}
Potential terminal set for the RPBs	$T_{\text{ccs-rpb-potential}}$ = ϕ
Potential function set for the ADFs	$F_{\text{ccs-adf-potential}}$ = {C, L, SERIES, PARALLEL0, PARALLEL1, FLIP, NOP, THREE_GROUND, PAIR_CONNECT_0, PAIR_CONNECT_1}
Potential terminal set for the ADFs	$T_{\text{ccs-adf-potential}}$ = {ARG0, END, SAFE_CUT}
Fitness cases	There are a total of 202 fitness cases. There are 101 frequency values in an interval of four decades between 10 Hz and 100,000 Hz that are applicable to the probe point for the woofer and another 101 frequency values that are applicable to the probe point for the tweeter.
Raw fitness	The sum, over the 202 fitness cases, of the absolute weighted deviation between the actual value of the voltage that is produced by the circuit at the probe point and the target value for voltage
Standardized fitness	Same as raw fitness
Hits	The number of hits is defined as the number of fitness cases (out of 202) for which the voltage is acceptable or ideal.
Wrapper	None

Parameters	$M = 640{,}000$. $G = 501$. $Q = 10{,}000$. $D = 64$. $B = 2\%$. $S_{rpb} = 200$. $S_{adf} = 200$. $N_{rpb} = 2$. $N_{max\text{-}adf} = 5$. $N_{max\text{-}argument\text{-}adf} = 1$.
Result designation	Best-so-far pace-setting individual
Success predicate	A program scores the maximum number (202) of hits.

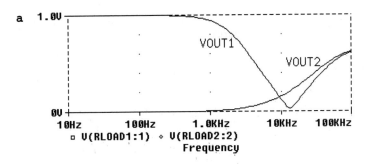

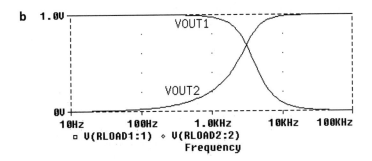

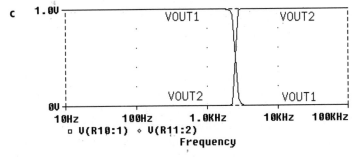

Figure 33.2 Frequency domain behavior of best circuits of generations (*a*) 0, (*b*) 8, and (*c*) 158

33.3.1   Emergence of Automatically Defined Functions

Automatically defined functions are created starting in generation 1; however, the first pace-setting individual with an automatically defined function does not appear until generation 8.

Figure 33.3 shows the circuit for the best-of-generation individual from generation 8. It has a fitness of 108.1 and scores 91 hits (out of 202). The three result-producing branches of the program tree have 187, 7, and 183 points, respectively. Its one automatically defined function, ADF0, has 17 points. The box labeled ADF0 represents the portion of the circuit supplied by automatically defined function ADF0. Notice that inductor **L3** is the "series" element and capacitor **C14** is the shunt element of a one-rung ladder for the intended lowpass (woofer) output **VOUT1**. This is the classical arrangement of a capacitor and an inductor for a single rung of a ladder for a lowpass filter. However, the highpass part of this circuit is not conventional.

Figure 33.4 shows ADF0 of the best-of-generation circuit from generation 8. ADF0 has two ports and supplies one unparameterized 4,210 nF capacitor **C4**. Its dummy variable (formal parameter), ARG0, plays no role in ADF0.

Figure 33.2b shows the behavior of the best-of-generation circuit from generation 8 in the frequency domain. As can be seen, **VOUT1** is 1 volt for low frequencies and drops off to 0 volts for higher frequencies; **VOUT2** is 0 volts for low frequencies and rises to 1 volt for higher frequencies. Although the general shape of the two curves now resembles that of a crossover filter, the rise and fall of the two curves is very leisurely.

33.3.2   Emergence of a Parameterized Argument in a Circuit Substructure

The best-of-run individual from generation 158 has a fitness of 0.107 and scores 200 hits (out of 202). The three result-producing branches of the program tree have 69, 158, and 127 points, respectively. This circuit has five automatically defined functions with 6, 24, 101, 185, and 196 points, respectively. ADF0 and ADF1 are not used. The fitness of this nearly 100%-compliant circuit compares favorably with the fitness of 0.7807 and 192 hits scored by the best-of-run individual from generation 137 of the run of this same problem without the architecture-altering operations (Section 32.3).

Figure 33.5 shows the call tree for the best-of-run circuit-constructing program tree from generation 158. As can be seen, the automatically defined functions are organized in a complicated hierarchy. Three automatically defined functions (ADF2, ADF3, and ADF4) are actually called. Result-producing branch RPB0 calls ADF3 once, RPB1 calls ADF3 once, and RPB2 calls ADF4 once and ADF2 once. ADF2 is hierarchically called once by both ADF3 and ADF4. Note that ADF2 is called a total of five times—once by RPB2 directly, twice by ADF3 (which is called once by RPB0 and RPB1), and once by ADF4.

The 69-point first result-producing branch, RPB0, is shown below. It calls ADF3.

```
(PARALLEL0 (L (+ (- 1.883196E-01 (- -9.095883E-02 5.724576E-
01)) (- 9.737455E-01 -9.452780E-01)) (FLIP END)) (SERIES (C (+
(+ -6.668774E-01 -8.770285E-01) 4.587758E-02) (NOP END))
(SERIES END END (PARALLEL1 END END END END)) (FLIP (SAFE_CUT)))
(PAIR_CONNECT_0 END END END) (PAIR_CONNECT_0 (L (+ -7.220122E-
01 4.896697E-01) END) (L (- -7.195599E-01 3.651142E-02)
```

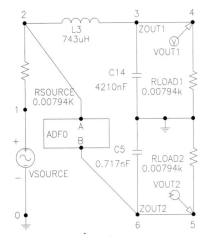

Figure 33.3 Best circuit of generation 8 with ADF0

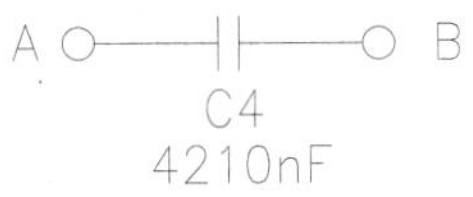

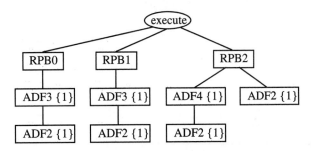

Figure 33.4 Two-ported automatically defined function ADF0 of the best circuit of generation 8

Figure 33.5 Call tree for the best-of-run circuit-constructing program tree from generation 158

```
(SERIES (C (+ -5.111248E-01 (- (- -6.137950E-01 -5.111248E-01)
(- 1.883196E-01 (- -9.095883E-02 5.724576E-01)))) END) (SERIES
END END (ADF3 6.196514E-01)) (NOP END))) (NOP END)))
```

The 158-point second result-producing branch, RPB1, is shown below. It also calls ADF3.

```
(C (+ (- (+ (+ (+ 5.630820E-01 (- 9.737455E-01 -9.452780E-01))
(+ (- (- -7.195599E-01 3.651142E-02) -9.761651E-01) 6.953752E-
02)) (+ (+ 1.883196E-01 (+ 9.346950E-02 (+ -7.220122E-01 (+
2.710414E-02 1.397491E-02)))) 3.660116E-01)) (+ (+ 1.883196E-
01 (+ 9.346950E-02 (+ -7.220122E-01 (+ 2.710414E-02 1.397491E-
02)))) 3.660116E-01)) 9.496355E-01) (NOP (NOP (PAIR_CONNECT_1
(THREE_GROUND_0 (PARALLEL1 (THREE_GROUND_0 END END END)
(PARALLEL1 END END END END) (PARALLEL1 END END END END) END)
```

```
(PARALLEL0 (C -1.877563E-01 END) (L 9.249641E-01 (SAFE_CUT))
(NOP (SAFE_CUT)) (PAIR_CONNECT_1 END END END)) (PARALLEL1
(PARALLEL1 END END END (PARALLEL1 END END (PARALLEL1 END END
END END) END)) (THREE_GROUND_1 END END END) (L (+ (+ 2.398261E-
01 -7.220122E-01) (- 4.587758E-02 -2.340137E-01)) (NOP END))
(SERIES (SAFE_CUT) END END))) (L (+ (- -9.452780E-01
9.628006E-01) (- (- (- (+ 4.587758E-02 -9.404392E-01) (-
-7.788187E-01 -6.885135E-01)) 4.276574E-02) 4.896697E-01))
(PARALLEL0 (PARALLEL1 END END END END) (PARALLEL1 END END END
END) (PAIR_CONNECT_1 (SAFE_CUT) (ADF3 -9.335563E-01) END) (NOP
END))) (C (- (+ (- 2.710414E-02 -2.807583E-01) (+ -6.137950E-
01 -8.554120E-01)) (+ -5.720272E-01 -4.866569E-01)) (C (+
-4.762180E-01 3.651142E-02) (FLIP (NOP END)))))))))
```

The 127-point third result-producing branch, RPB2, is shown below. It calls ADF4 twice and ADF2 once.

```
(THREE_GROUND_0 (ADF4 (- (- -7.195599E-01 (+ (+ 8.741845E-01
1.566386E-01) (- (- -7.195599E-01 3.651142E-02) -2.340137E-01)))
-9.761651E-01)) (FLIP (SERIES END (NOP END) (C (-
(- 9.998040E-01 -8.770285E-01) (+ -6.668774E-01 -8.770285E-
01)) (NOP (NOP (PAIR_CONNECT_1 (THREE_GROUND_0 (PARALLEL1
(FLIP (NOP END)) (PARALLEL1 END END END END) (PARALLEL1 END END
END END) (L -8.554120E-01 END)) (PARALLEL0 (C -1.877563E-01
END) (L 9.249641E-01 (SAFE_CUT)) (NOP (SAFE_CUT))
(PAIR_CONNECT_1 END END END)) (PARALLEL1 (L -3.465674E-01 END)
(THREE_GROUND_1 END END END) (L -3.465674E-01 END) (SERIES
(FLIP (L (- 4.587758E-02 -7.195599E-01) END)) END END))) (L (+
(- -9.452780E-01 9.628006E-01) (- -9.131658E-01 4.896697E-01))
(PARALLEL0 (PARALLEL1 END END END END) (PARALLEL1 END END END
END) (PAIR_CONNECT_1 (SAFE_CUT) (ADF4 -9.335563E-01) END) (NOP
END))) (C (+ 9.786230E-01 (+ 7.194393E-01 3.226026E-01)) (C (-
(+ -4.762180E-01 3.651142E-02) 7.759459E-01) (SERIES
(SAFE_CUT) END END)))))))))) (FLIP (ADF2 9.737455E-01)))
```

Automatically defined function ADF2 has 101 points and is shown below. As explained in detail shortly, it inserts an inductor into the developing circuit whose sizing is a function of the dummy variable (formal parameter), ARG0.

```
(L (+ (+ (+ (+ 8.741845E-01 1.566386E-01) (- (- -7.195599E-01
3.651142E-02) -2.340137E-01)) (+ (- (- 4.037348E-01 4.343444E-
01) (+ -7.788187E-01 (+ (+ (- -8.786904E-01 1.397491E-02) (-
-6.137950E-01 -5.111248E-01)) (+ (+ (- (+ (+ (+ 2.398261E-01
-7.220122E-01) (- 4.587758E-02 -2.340137E-01)) (+ (+ (- (+
(- 2.710414E-02 -2.807583E-01) (+ -6.137950E-01 -8.554120E-
01)) (+ -5.720272E-01 -4.866569E-01)) (+ -8.198292E-01
-6.885135E-01)) (- ARG0 -7.195599E-01))) -2.192044E-02)
1.883196E-01) (+ 7.733750E-01 4.343444E-01))))) (- (-
```

```
-9.389297E-01 5.630820E-01) (+ -5.840433E-02 3.568947E-01))))
(+ (- (+ 9.737455E-01 7.057463E-01) (+ 2.398261E-01 -
7.220122E-01)) (+ + 6.384465E-01 -1.671993E-01) (- (- (+ -
4.762180E-01 3.651142E-02) 7.759459E-01) (- -9.095883E-02
5.724576E-01))))) (NOP (FLIP (FLIP (L (+ (- ARG0 -7.195599E-01)
7.194393E-01) (NOP END))))))
```

Automatically defined function ADF3 has 185 points and is shown below. As explained in detail shortly, ADF3 performs three distinct functions.

```
(C (+ (- (+ (+ (+ 5.630820E-01 (- 9.737455E-01 -9.452780E-01))
(+ ARG0 6.953752E-02)) (- (- 5.627716E-02 (+ 2.273517E-01 (+
1.883196E-01 (+ 9.346950E-02 (+ -7.220122E-01 (+ 2.710414E-02
1.397491E-02)))))) (- (+ (- 2.710414E-02 -2.807583E-01) (+
-6.137950E-01 -8.554120E-01)) (- -8.770285E-01 (- -4.049602E-
01 -2.192044E-02))))) (+ (+ 1.883196E-01 (+ (+ (+ (+ 9.346950E-
02 (+ -7.220122E-01 (+ 2.710414E-02 1.397491E-02))) (-
4.587758E-02 -2.340137E-01)) 3.226026E-01) (+ -7.220122E-01 (-
-9.131658E-01 6.595502E-01)))) 3.660116E-01)) 9.496355E-01)
(THREE_GROUND_0 (C (+ (- (+ (+ (+ 5.630820E-01 (- 9.737455E-01
-9.452780E-01)) (+ (- (- -7.195599E-01 3.651142E-02)
-9.761651E-01) (- (+ (- (- -7.195599E-01 3.651142E-02)
-9.761651E-01) 6.953752E-02) 3.651142E-02))) (- (- 5.627716E-
02 (- 1.883196E-01 (- -9.095883E-02 5.724576E-01)))) (- (+
(- 2.710414E-02 -2.807583E-01) (+ -6.137950E-01 (+ ARG0
6.953752E-02))) (- -8.770285E-01 (- -4.049602E-01 -2.192044E-
02))))) (+ (+ 1.883196E-01 -7.195599E-01) 3.660116E-01))
9.496355E-01) (NOP (FLIP (PAIR_CONNECT_0 END END END)))) (FLIP
(SERIES (FLIP (FLIP (FLIP END))) (C (- (+ 6.238477E-01
6.196514E-01) (+ (+ (- (- 4.037348E-01 4.343444E-01) (+
-7.788187E-01 (+ (+ (- -8.786904E-01 1.397491E-02) (-
-6.137950E-01 (- (+ (- 2.710414E-02 -2.807583E-01) (+
-6.137950E-01 -8.554120E-01)) (- -8.770285E-01 (- -4.049602E-
01 -2.192044E-02))))) (+ (+ 7.215142E-03 1.883196E-01) (+
7.733750E-01 4.343444E-01))))) (- (- -9.389297E-01 5.630820E-
01) (+ -5.840433E-02 3.568947E-01))) -8.554120E-01)) (NOP
END)) END)) (FLIP (ADF2 9.737455E-01)))))
```

Automatically defined function ADF4 has 196 points:

```
(C (+ (- (+ (+ (+ 5.630820E-01 (- 9.737455E-01 -9.452780E-01))
(+ ARG0 6.953752E-02)) (- (- 5.627716E-02 (- 1.883196E-01 (-
-9.095883E-02 5.724576E-01))) (- (+ (- 2.710414E-02
-2.807583E-01) (+ -6.137950E-01 -8.554120E-01)) (- -8.770285E-
01 (- -4.049602E-01 -2.192044E-02))))) (+ (+ 1.883196E-01 (+
9.346950E-02 (+ -7.220122E-01 (- -9.131658E-01 6.595502E-
01)))) 3.660116E-01)) 9.496355E-01) (C (+ (- (+ (+ (+
5.630820E-01 (- 9.737455E-01 -9.452780E-01)) (+ ARG0
```

```
6.953752E-02)) (- (- 5.627716E-02 (- 1.883196E-01 (-
-9.095883E-02 5.724576E-01))) (- (+ (- 2.710414E-02 -
2.807583E-01) (+ -6.137950E-01 -8.554120E-01)) (- -8.770285E-
01 (- -4.049602E-01 (+ 2.710414E-02 1.397491E-02)))))) (+ (+
1.883196E-01 (+ 9.346950E-02 (+ -7.220122E-01 (+ 2.710414E-02
1.397491E-02)))) 3.660116E-01)) 9.496355E-01) (THREE_GROUND_0
(C (+ (- (+ (+ (+ 5.630820E-01 (- 9.737455E-01 -9.452780E-01))
(+ (- (- -6.137950E-01 3.651142E-02) -9.761651E-01) 6.953752E-
02)) (- (- 5.627716E-02 (- 1.883196E-01 (- -9.095883E-02
5.724576E-01))) (- (+ (- (- 4.037348E-01 4.343444E-01) (+
-7.788187E-01 (+ (+ (- -8.786904E-01 1.397491E-02) (-
-6.137950E-01 -5.111248E-01)) (+ (+ 7.215142E-03 1.883196E-01)
(+ 7.733750E-01 4.343444E-01))))) (+ -6.137950E-01 -8.554120E-
01)) (- -8.770285E-01 (- -4.049602E-01 -2.192044E-02))))) (+
(+ 1.883196E-01 (+ 9.346950E-02 (+ -7.220122E-01 (+ 2.710414E-
02 1.397491E-02)))) 3.660116E-01)) 9.496355E-01) (NOP END))
(FLIP (SERIES (NOP END) (C (- (+ 6.238477E-01 6.196514E-01) (+
(+ (- 2.710414E-02 -2.807583E-01) (- (- -9.389297E-01
5.630820E-01) (+ -5.840433E-02 3.568947E-01))) -8.554120E-01))
(NOP (FLIP (FLIP END)))) (FLIP END))) (FLIP (**ADF2 9.737455E-
01**)))))
```

Figure 33.6 shows the best-of-run circuit from generation 158. This circuit has 15 capacitors and 13 inductors (not counting the three resistors in the test fixture). Boxes are used in this figure to indicate the automatically defined functions ADF2, ADF3, and ADF4. The gigaohm resistor **R16** in this figure was introduced (at the automatic editing stage) to avoid a "floating node" of the type that SPICE cannot simulate.

ADF2 is parameterized by a dummy variable (formal parameter) that establishes the sizing of an inductor. Figure 33.7 shows ADF2 of the best-of-run circuit from generation 158. ADF2 has two ports and develops in an inductor whose sizing is determined by the dummy variable (formal parameter) ARG0. As it happens, both invocations of ADF2 (one from ADF3 and one from ADF4) invoke ADF2 with the very same constant argument. In particular, ADF2 is, coincidentally, invoked in both cases with

(ADF2 9.737455E-01).

Thus, even though ADF2 produces an inductor whose sizing is a function of ARG0, ARG0 happens to be the same constant for both invocations. Thus, on all five occasions when ADF2 is called (once by RPB2 directly, twice by ADF3, and twice by ADF4), the result is a 259 μH inductor **L147**.

ADF3 is also parameterized by a dummy variable (formal parameter) that is used to establish the sizing of a component. Figure 33.8 shows the T section that develops from ADF3 of the best-of-run circuit from generation 158. ADF3 has two ports (and one connection to ground).

ADF3 does three things:

1. The structure that develops out of ADF3 includes a capacitor **C112** whose value (5,130 nF) is not a function of its dummy variable, ARG0.

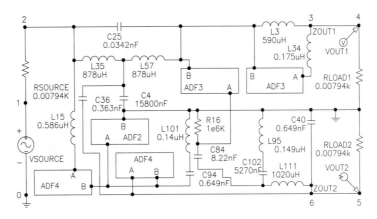

Figure 33.6   Best circuit of generation 158

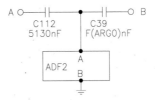

Figure 33.7   Two-ported parameterized automatically defined function ADF2 of the best-of-run circuit from generation 158

A ○─┤├────●────┤├─○ B
C112   C39
5130nF   F(ARG0)nF

ADF2

Figure 33.8   Three-ported automatically defined function ADF3 of the best-of-run circuit from generation 158. ADF3 contains capacitor C39 parameterized by dummy variable ARG0. ADF3 also invokes ADF2 (which produces a 259 μH inductor).

2.   The structure that develops out of ADF3 has one hierarchical reference to ADF2. As previously mentioned, the invocation of ADF2 is done with a constant (9.737455E-01) so this invocation of ADF2 produces a 259 μH inductor.

3.   Most importantly, the structure that develops out of ADF3 creates a capacitor (**C39**) whose sizing, F(ARG0), is a function of the dummy variable, ARG0, of automatically defined function ADF3. In other words, genetic programming creates a reusable structure containing a parameterized component. Capacitor **C39** has different sizings on different invocations of automatically defined function ADF3.

Thus, the combined effect of ADF3 is to insert the following three components:

•   an unparameterized 5,130 nF capacitor,

- a parameterized capacitor **C39** whose component value is dependent on ARG0 of ADF3, and
- a parameterized inductor (created by ADF2) whose sizing is parameterized, but which, in practice, is called with a constant value.

In addition to this instance of a parameterized subroutine used to construct an electrical circuit, this book contains numerous other evolved solutions that contain parameterized subroutines, including

- parameterized subroutines in runs A, B, C, and D of parity problems (Chapter 12),
- thrice-used parameterized subroutine for the time-optimal robot controller (Section 13.4.4),
- the parameterized recursive call in the Fibonacci sequence problem (Chapter 18),
- parameterized subroutines in the quadratic polynomial problem with GPPS 2.0 (Section 23.1.2),
- parameterized subroutines in the cart-centering problem with GPPS 2.0 (Section 23.3.2), and
- parameterized subroutines in the even-6-parity problem with GPPS 2.0 (Section 23.4.2).

Previous work on genetic programming, including *Genetic Programming* (Koza 1992e), *Genetic Programming II* (Koza 1994g), and hundreds of published papers, has demonstrated the use of parameterized subroutines.

Thus, genetic programming possesses the following attribute of a system for automatically creating computer programs (Chapter 1):

- **ATTRIBUTE NO. 6** (Parameterized reuse): It has the ability to reuse groups of steps with different instantiations of values (formal parameters or dummy variables).

As far as we know, genetic programming is unique among techniques of artificial intelligence, machine learning, neural networks, adaptive systems, reinforcement learning, or automated logic in that it provides a general and automatic mechanism for parameterized reuse.

Figure 33.9 shows the T section that develops from ADF4 of the best-of-run circuit from generation 158. ADF4 has two ports (and one connection to ground). It supplies one unparameterized 3,900 nF capacitor **C137** and one unparameterized 5,010 nF capacitor **C149**. ADF4 has one hierarchical reference to ADF2 (which, in turn, supplies one unparameterized 259 μH inductor). Thus, the combined effect of ADF4 is to supply two capacitors and one inductor.

Figure 33.10 shows the best-of-run circuit from generation 158 after all components have been substituted in lieu of the automatically defined functions. An electrical engineer knows that one conventional way to realize a crossover filter is to insert a lowpass filter between the input and the first output port (the intended woofer) and to insert a highpass filter between the input and the second output port (the intended tweeter). In the conventional decomposition, the only point of contact between the woofer part of the circuit feeding **VOUT1** and the tweeter part feeding **VOUT2** is the node that provides the incoming signal from **VSOURCE** and **RSOURCE**. However, we did not introduce any bias into the preparatory steps (in the form of the embryo, a fitness incentive, or anything else) that favored the conventional decomposition. This evolved circuit clearly has

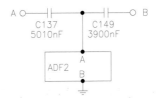

Figure 33.9   Three-ported automatically defined function ADF4 of the best-of-run circuit from generation 158 with capacitor parameterized by dummy variable and with hierarchical reference to ADF2

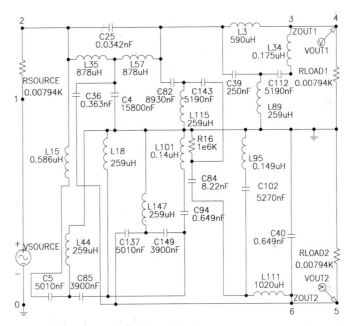

Figure 33.10   Best-of-run circuit from generation 158 after all components have been substituted in lieu of the automatically defined functions

two main parts; however, these two main parts are nominally connected by capacitor **C36** and a pair of capacitors (**C84** and **C143**). In spite of this nominal connection, when **C36** is removed from the circuit, there is no effect (as indicated by a simulation of the modified circuit using MicroSim's PC SPICE). Furthermore, when **C84** and **C143** are removed from the circuit, there is only a very small effect. However, **L15**, **C5**, and **L44** are shared and affect both **VOUT1** and **VOUT2**.

Figure 33.2c shows the behavior of the best-of-run circuit from generation 158 in the frequency domain. As can be seen, this circuit (scoring 200 hits out of 202) provides a sharp transition between the passbands and stopbands for the two outputs.

This best-of-run individual contains an instance where a parameterized subroutine establishes different numerical component values for a capacitor on the two occasions when it is called.

Synthesis of a Three-Band Crossover (Woofer-Midrange-Tweeter) Filter

A *three-band crossover* (woofer-midrange-tweeter) filter is a one-input, three-output circuit that passes all frequencies below a certain specified frequency to its first output port (the woofer), passes the intermediate frequencies to its second output port (the midrange), and passes all frequencies above a certain higher specified frequency to its third output port (the tweeter).

34.1 DESIGN GOALS

The goal is to design a three-band crossover filter with a first crossover frequency of 251.2 Hz between the woofer and midrange and a second crossover frequency of 2,512 Hz between the midrange and tweeter.

34.2 PREPARATORY STEPS

34.2.1 Embryo and Test Fixture

The embryo for this problem must reflect the fact that a three-band crossover (woofer-midrange-tweeter) filter has three outputs and one input (i.e., a total of four ports).

The test fixture for this problem will be different from previously used test fixtures because it must have three probe points, **VOUT1**, **VOUT2**, and **VOUT3**, and also because each probe point must have its own separate load resistor.

When a circuit has a total of one input and three outputs, six modifiable wires are required to provide full connectivity in the embryo between these four ports. The program tree then necessarily has the somewhat unwieldy total of six result-producing branches. One alternative is to provide partial connectivity between the four ports and rely on the THREE_VIA functions to create any needed additional connectivity. This alternative slightly biases the eventual evolved solution in favor of a three-way decomposition consisting of a lowpass, bandpass, and highpass filter.

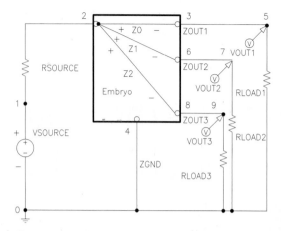

Figure 34.1   One-input, three-output initial circuit for the three-band crossover (woofer-midrange-tweeter) filter

Figure 34.1 shows the one-input, three-output initial circuit with three modifiable wires that is used for this problem. This initial circuit is the result of embedding the embryo of Figure 29.12, with three modifiable wires, Z0, Z1, and Z2, and five ports, into the test fixture of Figure 29.3, with one input, three outputs, and five ports to the embryo.

The input (left) portion of the test fixture is essentially the same as that used for the previous one-input, one-output circuits. Specifically, the incoming signal VSOURCE is connected to node 0 (ground) and node 1, and there is a source resistor RSOURCE between nodes 1 and 2. The output (right) portion of the test fixture has three probe points, VOUT1, VOUT2, and VOUT3. There is a nonmodifiable (isolating) wire ZOUT1 between nodes 3 and 5, a voltage probe labeled VOUT1 at node 5, and a fixed load resistor RLOAD1 between nodes 5 and ground. Second, there is a nonmodifiable (isolating) wire ZOUT2 between nodes 6 and 7, a voltage probe labeled VOUT2 at node 7, and a load resistor RLOAD2 between nodes 7 and ground. Third, there is a nonmodifiable (isolating) wire ZOUT3 between nodes 8 and 9, a voltage probe labeled VOUT3 at node 9, and a load resistor RLOAD3 between nodes 9 and ground.

The embryo achieves partial connectivity between the three outputs and the one input by means of the three modifiable wires, Z0, Z1, and Z2. There is one modifiable wire Z0 between nodes 2 and 3, a second modifiable wire Z1 between nodes 2 and 6, and a third modifiable wire Z2 between nodes 2 and 8.

In the test fixture, the energy source is a 2-volt alternating current sinusoidal voltage, and the source resistor as well as the three load resistors are 7.94 Ω.

34.2.2   Program Architecture

Since the embryo has three modifiable wires, there are three result-producing branches in each program tree.

Neither automatically defined functions nor architecture-altering operations are used on this problem. Thus, the architecture of the overall program tree consists of three result-producing branches.

34.2.3   Functions and Terminals

The terminal sets are identical for all three result-producing branches for this problem. The function sets are identical for all three result-producing branches.

The initial function set, $F_{ccs-rpb-initial}$, for the construction-continuing subtrees of the result-producing branches is

$F_{ccs-rpb-initial}$ = {C, L, SERIES, PARALLEL0, FLIP, NOP, THREE_GROUND, THREE_VIA0, THREE_VIA1, THREE_VIA2, THREE_VIA3, THREE_VIA4, THREE_VIA5, THREE_VIA6, THREE_VIA7}.

The initial terminal set, $T_{ccs-rpb-initial}$, for the construction-continuing subtrees of the result-producing branches is

$T_{ccs-rpb-initial}$ = {END}.

Since there are no automatically defined functions in this problem, $T_{adf-initial}$ and $F_{adf-initial}$ are empty.

Since there are no architecture-altering operations in this problem, $T_{rpb-potential}$, $F_{rpb-potential}$, $T_{adf-potential}$, and $F_{adf-potential}$ are empty.

The function set, F_{aps}, for each arithmetic-performing subtree in any branch and the terminal set, T_{aps}, for each arithmetic-performing subtree in any branch are the same as for the lowpass filter problem in Section 25.14.3.

34.2.4   Fitness

The fitness measure for this problem is constructed in a manner similar to that of the lowpass filter (Section 25.14.4) and the two-band crossover filter (Chapters 32 and 33). Since there are three probe points, the SPICE simulator is instructed to perform an AC small-signal analysis and to report the circuit's behavior at the three probe points, **VOUT1** (for the woofer), **VOUT2** (for the midrange), and **VOUT3** (for the tweeter), for each of 101 frequency values chosen from the range between 10 Hz and 100,000 Hz. Each of these four decades of frequency is divided into 25 parts (using a logarithmic scale). Since there are 101 sampled frequencies and there are three probe points, there are a total of 303 fitness cases for this problem.

Fitness is measured in terms of the sum, over these 303 fitness cases, of the absolute weighted deviation between the actual value of the voltage that is produced by the circuit at the three probe points and the target value for voltage.

The number of hits (0 to 303) is defined as the number of fitness cases for which the voltage is acceptable.

34.2.5   Parameters

The control parameters for this problem are found in the tableau (Table 34.1), the tables of percentages of genetic operations in Appendix D, and the default values specified in Appendix D.

Table 34.1 Tableau for three-band crossover (woofer-midrange-tweeter) filter

Objective	Design a three-band crossover (woofer-midrange-tweeter) filter.
Test fixture and embryo	One-input, three-output initial circuit with a source resistor, three load resistors, and three modifiable wires
Program architecture	Three result-producing branches (RPB0, RPB1, and RPB0)
Initial function set for the RPBs	For construction-continuing subtrees: $F_{\text{ccs-rpb-initial}}$ = {C, L, SERIES, PARALLEL0, FLIP, NOP, THREE_GROUND, THREE_VIA0, THREE_VIA1, THREE_VIA2, THREE_VIA3, THREE_VIA4, THREE_VIA5, THREE_VIA6, THREE_VIA7}. For arithmetic-performing subtrees: F_{aps} = {+, -}.
Initial terminal set for the RPBs	For construction-continuing subtrees: $T_{\text{ccs-rpb-initial}}$ = {END}. For arithmetic-performing subtrees: T_{aps} = {$\Re_{\text{smaller-reals}}$}.
Initial function set for the ADFs	Architecture-altering operations are not used.
Initial terminal set for the ADFs	Architecture-altering operations are not used.
Potential function set for the RPBs	Architecture-altering operations are not used.
Potential terminal set for the RPBs	Architecture-altering operations are not used.
Potential function set for the ADFs	Architecture-altering operations are not used.
Potential terminal set for the ADFs	Architecture-altering operations are not used.
Fitness cases	There are a total of 303 fitness cases. There are 101 frequency values in an interval of four decades between 10 Hz and 100,000 Hz that are applicable to the probe point for the woofer, another 101 frequency values that are applicable to the probe point for the tweeter, and another 101 frequency values that are applicable to the probe point for the midrange.
Raw fitness	The sum, over the 303 fitness cases, of the absolute weighted deviation between the actual value of the voltage that is produced by the circuit at the probe points and the target value for voltage
Standardized fitness	Same as raw fitness
Hits	The number of hits is defined as the number of fitness cases (out of 303) for which the voltage is acceptable or ideal.
Wrapper	None
Parameters	M = 640,000. G = 501. Q = 10,000. D = 64. B = 2%. S_{rpb} = 200. N_{rpb} = 3.

Result designation	Best-so-far pace-setting individual
Success predicate	A program scores the maximum number (303) of hits.

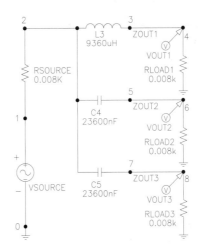

Figure 34.2   Best circuit of generation 0

34.2.6   Tableau

Table 34.1 summarizes the key features of the problem of designing a three-band cross-over (woofer-midrange-tweeter) filter.

34.3   RESULTS

The best individual program tree of generation 0 has a fitness of 1070.1 and scores 37 hits (out of 303). Its first result-producing branch has 181 points, its second result-producing branch has 181 points, and its third result-producing branch has 182 points.

Figure 34.2 shows this best-of-generation circuit from generation 0. As can be seen, there is only one component (**L3**, **C4**, and **C5**) between the incoming signal and each of the three probe points, **VOUT1**, **VOUT2**, and **VOUT3**, respectively.

Figure 34.3a shows the behavior in the frequency domain of this circuit. The horizontal axis represents the frequency of the incoming signal and ranges over four decades of frequencies from 10 Hz to 100,000 Hz on a logarithmic scale. The vertical axis represents peak voltage and ranges linearly from 0 volts to 1 volt. Note that the curves for **VOUT1** and **VOUT2** overlap for this particular circuit (because **C4** and **C5** happen to have identical values).

Figure 34.4 shows the circuit for the best-of-generation individual from generation 54. It has a fitness of 341.2 and scores 99 hits (out of 303). The three result-producing

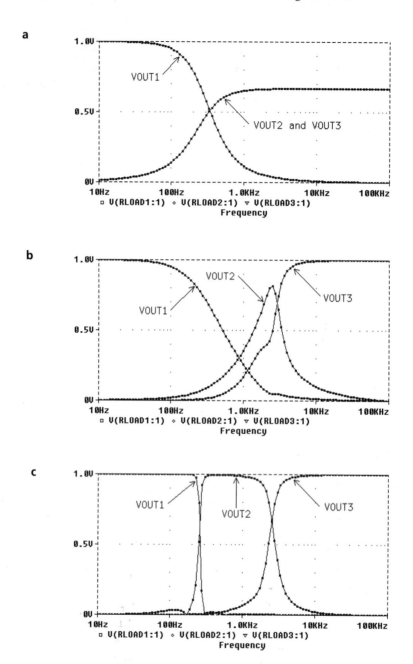

Figure 34.3 Frequency domain behavior of the best circuits of generations (a) 0, (b) 54, and (c) 184

branches of the program tree have 16, 149, and 9 points, respectively. Note that **C25** and **L61** (which are connected directly to **VOUT3**) have the topology of a single rung of a highpass ladder filter.

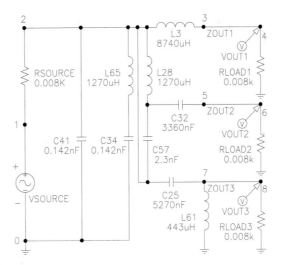

Figure 34.4   Best circuit of generation 54

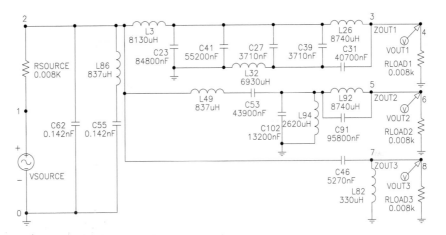

Figure 34.5   Best circuit of generation 184

Figure 34.3b shows the behavior of this circuit in the frequency domain for the best of generation 54. Notice the substantial progress toward formation of the lowpass and highpass behavior, but the relatively small amount of progress toward formation of the bandpass (midrange) behavior.

The best-of-generation individual from generation 184 (Figure 34.5) has a fitness of 138.2 and scores 174 hits (out of 303). The three result-producing branches of the program tree have 198, 198, and 141 points, respectively. Note that **L3** and the two parallel capacitors **C23** and **C41** have the topology of a single rung of a lowpass ladder filter. Also, **C46** and **L82** (which are connected directly to **VOUT3**) have the topology of a single rung of a highpass filter.

Figure 34.3c shows the behavior of this circuit in the frequency domain for the best of generation 184. Notice that the lowpass behavior is well defined and the highpass behavior is reasonably well-defined. The bandpass behavior indicates considerable progress toward the goal, but is not yet sharply defined.

This run (which was stopped at generation 184) indicates considerable progress toward evolving a 100%-compliant three-band crossover (woofer-midrange-tweeter) filter. We believe that a larger population size is probably required to evolve a 100%-compliant circuit for this particular three-output problem. Nonetheless, this filter from generation 184 would be considered usable for many audio applications.

Synthesis of a Double Bandpass Filter Using Subcircuits

The components from which circuits are composed need not be as primitive as resistors, capacitors, inductors, diodes, and transistors.

SPICE supports subcircuit definition using the SUBCKT command. The SUBCKT command enables a particular topological combination of components (each with associated component values) to be defined once and thereafter be included in the netlist of a circuit as if they were a single primitive component. Subcircuits may have one or more leads.

Each SUBCKT definition in SPICE consists of the name of the subcircuit, one or more formal parameters that identify its leads, a netlist that defines the subcircuit, and the ENDS command (which must include the name of the subcircuit if nested subcircuit definitions are being used). Each SUBCKT definition has its own local numbering of components and nodes.

For example, the following is a subcircuit definition in SPICE for a two-leaded fifth-order elliptic lowpass filter named ELIP5_LP_1. The boundary for the passband for this lowpass filter is at 34,258 Hz.

```
.SUBCKT ELIP5_LP_1 1 2
L1 1 3 5.76E+03UH
L2 3 4 3.46E+02UH
C3 4 0 5.90NF
L4 3 5 8.99E+03UH
L5 5 6 9.40E+02UH
C6 6 0 5.26NF
L7 5 2 5.24E+03UH
.ENDS ELIP5_LP_1
```

The first line of this subcircuit definition establishes that the name of the subcircuit is ELIP5_LP_1 and that the subcircuit has two leads (at nodes 1 and 2 in the local numbering scheme of the subcircuit). The next seven lines specify the seven components of the subcircuit (i.e., five inductors and two capacitors). These seven lines specify the values and connectivity for the seven components of the subcircuit. The last line is the ENDS command, which terminates the subcircuit definition.

Figure 35.1 shows this fifth-order elliptic lowpass filter subcircuit.

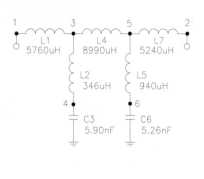

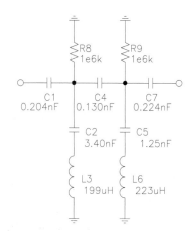

Figure 35.1 A fifth-order elliptic lowpass filter subcircuit ELIP5_LP_1

Figure 35.2 A fifth-order elliptic highpass filter subcircuit ELIP5_HP_1

A subcircuit is invoked by a line of a netlist that begins with an X, a unique number, one or more node numbers, and the name of a subcircuit. For example, the above two-leaded subcircuit for the fifth-order elliptic lowpass filter can be invoked by the following line in a netlist:

```
X99 17 23 ELIP5_LP_1.
```

This invocation of the subcircuit is equivalent to including the entire seven-component ELIP5_LP_1 subcircuit in the main circuit. The subcircuit is connected such that node 17 of the main circuit is connected to lead 1 of the subcircuit and node 23 of the main circuit is connected to lead 2 of the subcircuit.

A subcircuit in SPICE bears some resemblance to a subroutine in a computer program or an automatically defined function in genetic programming. However, there is an important difference between a subcircuit definition in SPICE and an automatically defined function in genetic programming. Subcircuits in SPICE are defined *prior to the run* of SPICE. In contrast, an automatically defined function is a function-defining branch whose body is dynamically evolved *during the run* of genetic programming.

Automatically defined functions typically contain compositions of topology-modifying functions and component-creating functions.

Figure 35.2 shows a fifth-order elliptic highpass filter subcircuit called ELIP5_HP_1. The boundary for the passband for this highpass filter begins at 34,258 Hz. The two resistors, R8 and R9, with high resistance are added to prevent floating nodes (which cannot be simulated by SPICE). These resistors do not have to be included in a physical circuit.

35.1 DESIGN GOALS

The subcircuit facility of SPICE will be illustrated by evolving the design for a double bandpass filter using lowpass and highpass filters as primitive components. Specifically, the goal is to evolve the design of a double bandpass filter whose first passband is to start at 100 Hz and end at 200 Hz and whose second passband is to start at 10,000 Hz and end at 20,000 Hz. The passband cutoff frequency, stopband cutoff frequency, maximum passband attenuation, and minimum stopband attenuation can be satisfied by fifth-order elliptic filters.

35.2 PREPARATORY STEPS

35.2.1 Embryo and Test Fixture

The initial circuit (Figure 30.1) for this problem is created by embedding the embryo with one modifiable wire and three ports (Figure 29.10) into the one-input, one-output test fixture with three ports (Figure 29.1).

35.2.2 Program Architecture

Since the embryo has one modifiable wire, there is one result-producing branch in each program tree.

Neither automatically defined functions nor architecture-altering operations are used on this problem.

35.2.3 Functions and Terminals

The initial function set, $F_{ccs-rpb-initial}$, for the construction-continuing subtrees of the result-producing branches is

$F_{ccs-rpb-initial}$ = {ELIP5_LP, ELIP5_HP, SERIES, PARALLEL0, FLIP, NOP, THREE_GROUND, CUT, THREE_VIA0, THREE_VIA1, THREE_VIA2, THREE_VIA3, THREE_VIA4, THREE_VIA5, THREE_VIA6, THREE_VIA7}.

The one-argument ELIP5_LP function acts as a component-creating function and inserts a subcircuit that acts as a fifth-order lowpass filter. Similarly, the one-argument ELIP5_HP function inserts a subcircuit that acts as a fifth-order highpass filter. The one argument of the ELIP5_LP function and the one argument of the ELIP5_HP function specify the cutoff frequency of the filter. These arguments are contained in the arithmetic-performing subtrees.

The initial terminal set, $T_{ccs-rpb-initial}$, for the construction-continuing subtrees of the result-producing branches is

$T_{ccs-rpb-initial}$ = {END, CUT}.

Since there are no automatically defined functions in this problem, $T_{adf-initial}$ and $F_{adf-initial}$ are empty.

Since there are no architecture-altering operations in this problem, $T_{rpb-potential}$, $F_{rpb-potential}$, $T_{adf-potential}$, and $F_{adf-potential}$ are empty.

The function set, F_{aps}, for each arithmetic-performing subtree in any branch and the terminal set, T_{aps}, for each arithmetic-performing subtree in any branch are the same as for the lowpass filter problem in Section 25.14.3.

35.2.4 Fitness

For this problem, the voltage **VOUT** is probed, and the circuit is measured in the frequency domain. The SPICE simulator is instructed to perform an AC small-signal analysis and to report the circuit's behavior for each of 101 frequency values chosen over four decades of frequency (from 10 Hz to 100,000 Hz). Each decade is divided into 25 parts (using a logarithmic scale).

Fitness is measured in terms of the sum, over these 101 fitness cases, of the absolute weighted deviation between the actual value of the voltage that is produced by the circuit at the probe point **VOUT** and the target value for voltage.

The frequency range is divided into two passbands, three stopbands, and four "don't care" transitional regions.

The procedure for each of the 8 points in each of the two passbands (a total of 16 points) is as follows:

- If the voltage equals the ideal value of 1.0 volt in this interval, the deviation is 0.0.
- If the voltage is between 950 millivolts and 1,000 millivolts, the absolute value of the deviation from 1,000 millivolts is weighted by a factor of 1.0.
- If the voltage is less than 950 millivolts, the absolute value of the deviation from 1,000 millivolts is weighted by a factor of 10.0.

This arrangement reflects the fact that the ideal voltage in the passband is 1.0 volt, the fact that a 50-millivolt shortfall is acceptable, and the fact that a voltage below 950 millivolts in the passband is not acceptable.

The procedure for each of the 53 points in the three stopbands is as follows:

- If the voltage is between 0 millivolts and 2 millivolts, the absolute value of the deviation from 0 millivolts is weighted by a factor of 1.0.
- If the voltage is more than 2 millivolts, the absolute value of the deviation from 0 millivolts is weighted by a factor of 10.0.

There are eight "don't care" points just before each passband and eight "don't care" points just after each passband. The deviation is deemed to be zero for each of these 32 points.

The number of hits is defined as the number of fitness cases for which the voltage is acceptable or ideal or that lie in the "don't care" region. Thus, the number of hits ranges from 32 to 101 for this problem.

35.2.5 Parameters

The control parameters for this problem are found in the tableau (Table 35.1), the tables of percentages of genetic operations in Appendix D, and the default values specified in Appendix D.

35.2.6 Tableau

Table 35.1 summarizes the key features of the problem of designing a double bandpass filter using subcircuits.

Table 35.1 Tableau for double bandpass filter using subcircuits

Objective	Design, using subcircuits, a double bandpass filter whose first passband begins at 100 Hz and ends at 200 Hz and whose second passband begins at 10 KHz and ends at 20 KHz.
Test fixture and embryo	One-input, one-output initial circuit with a source resistor, load resistor, and one modifiable wire
Program architecture	One result-producing branch, RPB.
Initial function set for the RPBs	For construction-continuing subtrees: $F_{ccs\text{-}rpb\text{-}initial}$ = {ELIP5_LP, ELIP5_HP, SERIES, PARALLEL0, FLIP, NOP, THREE_GROUND, CUT, THREE_VIA0, THREE_VIA1, THREE_VIA2, THREE_VIA3, THREE_VIA4, THREE_VIA5, THREE_VIA6, THREE_VIA7}. For arithmetic-performing subtrees: F_{aps} = {+, -}.
Initial terminal set for the RPBs	For construction-continuing subtrees: $T_{ccs\text{-}rpb\text{-}initial}$ = {END, CUT}. For arithmetic-performing subtrees: T_{aps} = {$\Re_{smaller\text{-}reals}$}.
Initial function set for the ADFs	Automatically defined functions are not used.
Initial terminal set for the ADFs	Automatically defined functions are not used.
Potential function set for the RPBs	Architecture-altering operations are not used.
Potential terminal set for the RPBs	Architecture-altering operations are not used.
Potential function set for the ADFs	Architecture-altering operations are not used.
Potential terminal set for the ADFs	Architecture-altering operations are not used.
Fitness cases	101 frequency values in an interval of four decades of frequency values between 10 Hz and 100,000 Hz
Raw fitness	The sum, over these 101 fitness cases, of the absolute weighted deviation between the actual value of the voltage that is produced by the circuit at the probe point and the target value for voltage
Standardized fitness	Same as raw fitness
Hits	The number of hits is defined as the number of fitness cases (32 to 101) for which the voltage is acceptable or ideal or that lie in the "don't care" band.
Wrapper	None

(continued)

Table 35.1 *(continued)*

Parameters	M = 640,000. G = 501. Q =10,000. D = 64. B = 2%. S_{rpb} = 300. N_{rpb} = 1.
Result designation	Best-so-far pace-setting individual
Success predicate	A program scores the maximum number (101) of hits.

35.3 RESULTS

A 100%-compliant circuit (Figure 35.3) emerged in generation 25. This best-of-run circuit has a fitness of 0.197 and scores 101 hits (out of 101). As can be seen, the two passbands are defined by a series and parallel composition of the available lowpass and highpass elliptic filter subcircuits. The numerical parameter associated with each subcircuit is the cutoff frequency for that filter. Each of these numerical parameters comes from an arithmetic-performing subtree.

Figure 35.4 shows the frequency domain behavior of the 100%-compliant best-of-run double bandpass filter from generation 25. The horizontal axis represents the frequency of the incoming signal and ranges over the four decades of frequency between 10 Hz and 100,000 Hz on a logarithmic scale. The vertical axis represents peak voltage and ranges linearly from 0 volts to 1 volt.

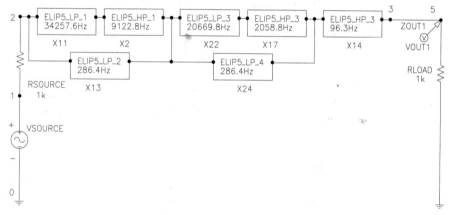

Figure 35.3   Best-of-run double bandpass filter from generation 25

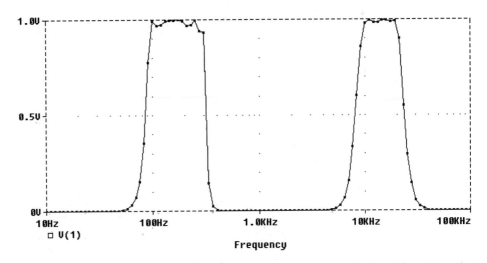

Figure 35.4 Frequency domain behavior of best-of-run double bandpass filter from generation 25

Synthesis of a Double Bandpass Filter Using Architecture-Altering Operations

In Chapter 35, a double bandpass filter was evolved in which complete, already-designed lowpass and highpass filters were available as primitive components. In this chapter, only capacitors and inductors are the primitive components.

36.1 DESIGN GOALS

The goal here is to use the architecture-altering operations to evolve the design of a double bandpass filter using inductors and capacitors as components. Specifically, the goal is to evolve the design of a double bandpass filter whose first passband starts at 1,000 Hz (1 KHz) and ends at 2,000 Hz (2 KHz) and whose second passband starts at 1,000,000 Hz (1 MHz) and ends at 2,000,000 Hz (2 MHz). The passband cutoff frequency, stopband cutoff frequency, maximum passband attenuation, and minimum stopband attenuation can be satisfied by a fifth-order elliptic filter.

The modularity, symmetry, and regularity of the two passbands suggests that automatically defined functions may potentially be useful for this problem.

36.2 PREPARATORY STEPS

36.2.1 Embryo and Test Fixture

The initial circuit (Figure 30.1) for this problem is created by embedding the embryo with one modifiable wire and three ports (Figure 29.10) into the one-input, one-output test fixture with three ports (Figure 29.1).

36.2.2 Program Architecture

Since the embryo has one modifiable wire, each program in generation 0 has one result-producing branch.

Each program tree in the initial random population at generation 0 also has a single one-argument automatically defined function. Thus, each program tree at generation 0 has a uniform architecture consisting of two branches.

One-argument automatically defined functions will be created during the run by the architecture-altering operations. No hierarchical references will be permitted between automatically defined functions.

36.2.3 Functions and Terminals

The initial function set for each construction-continuing subtree of a result-producing branch, $F_{\text{ccs-rpb-initial}}$, is

$F_{\text{ccs-rpb-initial}} = \{$ADF0, C, L, RTINY, SERIES, PARALLEL0, FLIP, NOP, THREE_GROUND, THREE_VIA0, THREE_VIA1, THREE_VIA2, THREE_VIA3, THREE_VIA4, THREE_VIA5, THREE_VIA6, THREE_VIA7$\}$.

The first nine functions take 1, 2, 2, 1, 3, 4, 1, 1, and 3 arguments, respectively. The eight THREE_VIA functions each take 3 arguments.

The one-argument RTINY function (used only on this problem) is identical to the two-argument R function, except that the value of the inserted resistor is always 10^{-9} Ω (and therefore the function possesses only one, instead of two, arguments).

The initial terminal set for each construction-continuing subtree of a result-producing branch, $T_{\text{ccs-rpb-initial}}$, is

$T_{\text{ccs-rpb-initial}} = \{END, CUT\}$.

The initial function set for each construction-continuing subtree of the automatically defined function, $F_{\text{ccs-adf-initial}}$, is

$F_{\text{ccs-adf-initial}} = \{$ADF0, C, L, SERIES, PARALLEL0, FLIP, NOP, THREE_GROUND, THREE_VIA0, THREE_VIA1, THREE_VIA2, THREE_VIA3, THREE_VIA4, THREE_VIA5, THREE_VIA6, THREE_VIA7$\}$.

The initial terminal set for each construction-continuing subtree of the automatically defined function, $T_{\text{ccs-adf-initial}}$, is

$T_{\text{ccs-adf-initial}} = \{$END, CUT, ARG0$\}$.

The set of potential functions for each construction-continuing subtree of a result-producing branch, $F_{\text{ccs-rpb-potential}}$, is

$F_{\text{ccs-rpb-potential}} = \{$ADF1, ADF2, ADF3, ADF4$\}$.

The set of potential terminals for each construction-continuing subtree of a result-producing branch, $T_{\text{ccs-rpb-potential}}$, is empty:

$T_{\text{ccs-rpb-potential}} = \phi$.

The set of potential functions for each construction-continuing subtree of an automatically defined function, $F_{\text{ccs-adf-potential}}$, is empty:

$F_{\text{ccs-adf-potential}} = \phi$.

The set of potential terminals for each construction-continuing subtree of an automatically defined function, $T_{ccs\text{-}adf\text{-}potential}$, is empty:

$$T_{ccs\text{-}adf\text{-}potential} = \phi.$$

The function set, F_{aps}, for each arithmetic-performing subtree in any branch and the terminal set, T_{aps}, for each arithmetic-performing subtree in any branch are the same as for the lowpass filter problem in Section 25.14.3.

36.2.4   Fitness

For this problem, the voltage VOUT is probed and the circuit is measured in the frequency domain. The SPICE simulator is instructed to perform an AC small-signal analysis and to report the circuit's behavior for each of 176 frequency values chosen over seven decades of frequency from 10 Hz to 100 MHz. Each decade is divided into 25 parts (using a logarithmic scale).

Fitness is measured in terms of the sum, over these 176 fitness cases, of the absolute weighted deviation between the actual value of the voltage that is produced by the circuit at the probe point VOUT and the target value for voltage.

The frequency range is divided into two passbands, three stopbands, and four "don't care" transition regions.

The procedure for each of the 8 points in each of the two passbands (a total of 16 points) is as follows:

- If the voltage equals the ideal value of 1.0 volt in this interval, the deviation is 0.0.
- If the voltage is between 960 millivolts and 1,000 millivolts, the absolute value of the deviation from 1,000 millivolts is weighted by a factor of 1.0.
- If the voltage is less than 960 millivolts, the absolute value of the deviation from 1,000 millivolts is weighted by a factor of 10.0.

This arrangement reflects the fact that the ideal voltage in the passband is 1.0 volt, the fact that a 40-millivolt shortfall is acceptable, and the fact that a voltage below 960 millivolts in the passband is not acceptable.

The procedure for each of the 120 points in the three stopbands is as follows:

- If the voltage is between 0 millivolts and 40 millivolts, the absolute value of the deviation from 0 millivolts is weighted by a factor of 1.0.
- If the voltage is more than 40 millivolts, the absolute value of the deviation from 0 millivolts is weighted by a factor of 10.0.

There are 10 "don't care" points just before each passband and 10 "don't care" points just after each passband. The deviation is deemed to be zero for each of the 40 points in these four "don't care" bands.

The number of hits is defined as the number (between 40 and 176) of fitness cases for which the voltage is acceptable or ideal or that lie in one of the "don't care" transition regions.

Table 36.1 Tableau for double bandpass filter using architecture-altering operations

Objective	Design a double bandpass filter using architecture-altering operations whose first passband starts at 1 KHz and ends at 2 KHz and whose second passband starts at 1 MHz and ends at 2 MHz.
Test fixture and embryo	One-input, one-output initial circuit with a source resistor, load resistor, and one modifiable wire
Program architecture	One result-producing branch, RPB, and a single one-argument automatically defined function, ADF0, in generation 0. Additional one-argument automatically defined functions will be created during the run by the architecture-altering operations.
Initial function set for the RPBs	For construction-continuing subtrees: $F_{ccs-rpb-initial}$ = {ADF0, C, L, RTINY, SERIES, PARALLEL0, FLIP, NOP, THREE_GROUND, THREE_VIA0, THREE_VIA1, THREE_VIA2, THREE_VIA3, THREE_VIA4, THREE_VIA5, THREE_VIA6, THREE_VIA7}. For arithmetic-performing subtrees: F_{aps} = {+, -}.
Initial terminal set for the RPBs	For construction-continuing subtrees: $T_{ccs-rpb-initial}$ = {END, CUT, ARG0}. For arithmetic-performing subtrees: T_{aps} = {$\Re_{smaller-reals}$}.
Initial function set for the ADFs	For construction-continuing subtrees: $F_{ccs-adf-initial}$ = {ADF0, C, L, SERIES, PARALLEL0, FLIP, NOP, THREE_GROUND, THREE_VIA0, THREE_VIA1, THREE_VIA2, THREE_VIA3, THREE_VIA4, THREE_VIA5, THREE_VIA6, THREE_VIA7}. For arithmetic-performing subtrees: F_{aps} = {+, -}.
Initial terminal set for the ADFs	For construction-continuing subtrees: $T_{ccs-adf-initial}$ = {END, CUT, ARG0}. For arithmetic-performing subtrees: T_{aps} = {$\Re_{smaller-reals}$}.
Potential function set for the RPBs	$F_{ccs-rpb-potential}$ = {ADF1, ADF2, ADF3, ADF4}
Potential terminal set for the RPBs	$T_{ccs-rpb-potential}$ = ϕ
Potential function set for the ADFs	$F_{ccs-adf-potential}$ = ϕ
Potential terminal set for the ADFs	$T_{ccs-adf-potential}$ = ϕ
Fitness cases	176 frequency values in an interval of seven decades of frequency values between 10 Hz and 100 MHz

Raw fitness	The sum, over these 176 fitness cases, of the absolute weighted deviation between the actual value of the voltage that is produced by the circuit at the probe point and the target value for voltage
Standardized fitness	Same as raw fitness
Hits	The number of hits is defined as the number of fitness cases (40 to 176) for which the voltage is acceptable or ideal or that lie in the "don't care" band.
Wrapper	None
Parameters	$M = 640,000$. $G = 501$. $Q = 10,000$. $D = 64$. $B = 2\%$. $S_{rpb} = 300$. $S_{adf} = 300$. $N_{rpb} = 2$. $N_{max\text{-}adf} = 5$. $N_{max\text{-}argument\text{-}adf} = 1$.
Result designation	Best-so-far pace-setting individual
Success predicate	A program scores the maximum number (176) of hits.

36.2.5   Parameters

The control parameters for this problem are found in the tableau (Table 36.1), the tables of percentages of genetic operations in Appendix D, and the default values specified in Appendix D.

36.2.6   Tableau

Table 36.1 summarizes the key features of the problem of designing a double bandpass filter using architecture-altering operations.

36.3   RESULTS

This run illustrates the progressive addition of function-defining branches and references to them.

The best circuit from generation 0 has a fitness of 720.3 and scores 54 hits; however, the result-producing branch of the program tree does not reference its 45-point automatically defined function.

In generation 2, the first best-of-generation individual with a referenced automatically defined function appears (with a fitness of 697.3 and 58 hits).

The first best-of-generation individual with two automatically defined functions appears in generation 22 (with a fitness of 184.7 and 110 hits); however, there are no references to either automatically defined function. In generation 29, the first best-of-generation individual with two *referenced* automatically defined functions appears (with a fitness of 105.4 and 128 hits).

The first circuit scoring a full 176 hits is produced in generation 82 (with a fitness of 0.731).

The best-of-run individual emerged at generation 89 with four automatically defined functions. This 100%-compliant individual has a fitness of 0.549 and scores 176 hits. ADF0 is called four times, ADF1 is called once, ADF2 is ignored, and ADF3 is called

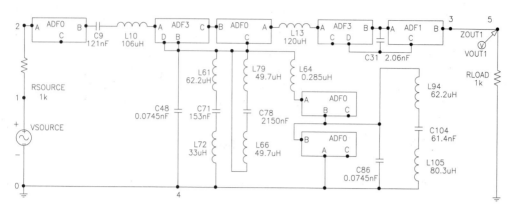

Figure 36.1 Best-of-run circuit from generation 89

twice. The result-producing branch has 296 points, and the function-defining branches have 82, 71, 64, and 82 points, respectively.

Figure 36.1 shows the best-of-run individual from generation 89. Note that **L79**, **C78**, and **L66** are superfluous. Boxes are used to indicate the parts of the overall circuit that are developed by the automatically defined functions. The letters, A, B, and C (and D in the case of ADF3) indicate how the substructure specified by each automatically defined function connects to the overall circuit.

Figure 36.2 shows the substructure developed from ADF0 at each of the four places in the result-producing branch where ADF0 is invoked. The figure shows ADF0's three ports (A, B, and C).

Figure 36.3 shows the substructure developed from ADF1 at the one place in the result-producing branch where ADF1 is invoked.

Figure 36.4 shows the substructure developed from ADF3 at each of the two places in the result-producing branch where ADF3 is invoked. The figure shows ADF3's four ports (A, B, C, and D) indicating how the substructure specified by ADF3 connects to the overall circuit.

Figure 36.5 shows the behavior in the frequency domain of the 100%-compliant best-of-run circuit from generation 89. The horizontal axis represents the frequency of the incoming signal and ranges over the seven decades of frequency between 10 Hz and 100 MHz on a logarithmic scale. The vertical axis represents peak voltage and ranges linearly from 0 volts to 1 volt. All 136 fitness cases that are not part of the "don't care" bands satisfy the design goals of this problem. The two small spikes lie in the "don't care" bands.

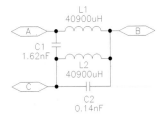

Figure 36.2   Substructure developed from ADF0

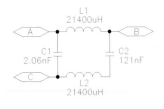

Figure 36.3   Substructure developed from ADF1

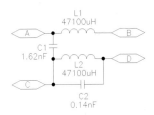

Figure 36.4   Substructure developed from ADF3

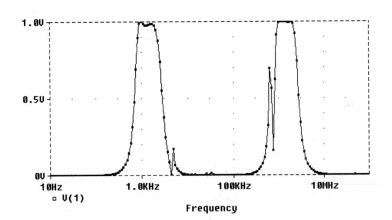

Figure 36.5   Frequency domain behavior of the 100%-compliant best-of-run circuit from generation 89

Synthesis of Butterworth, Chebychev, and Elliptic Filters

Previous chapters have demonstrated that the design of a particular lowpass filter circuit can be successfully evolved using

- genetic programming without automatically defined functions (Chapter 25),
- genetic programming with prespecified automatically defined functions (Chapter 27),
- genetic programming with the architecture-altering operations for automatically defined functions (Chapter 28), and
- genetic programming with the automatically defined copy (Chapter 30).

But suppose the user desires a lowpass filter whose power decreases (or increases) monotonically with the frequency (as is the case for Butterworth filters). Or suppose the user desires that the frequencies just inside the passband are passed with maximum power and that the frequencies just inside the stopband are maximally attenuated (as is the case for elliptic and Chebychev filters).

The Butterworth, Chebychev, and elliptic families of filters each satisfy particular design objectives. Elliptic, Chebychev, and Butterworth filters constitute well-studied benchmarks that are graded in terms of their order (which either equals, or is directly related to, the number of key components in the filter).

This chapter starts by briefly summarizing the main characteristics of the Butterworth, Chebychev, and elliptic (Cauer) families of filters (Section 37.1) and then shows the preparatory steps (Section 37.2) for evolving the design for a filter whose behavior is equivalent to

- a lowpass third-order Butterworth filter,
- a lowpass fifth-order Butterworth filter,
- a lowpass seventh-order Butterworth filter,
- a highpass seventh-order Butterworth filter,
- a highpass seventh-order Chebychev filter, and
- a highpass seventh-order elliptic filter.

Finally, Sections 37.3 through 37.8 show the six evolved filters.

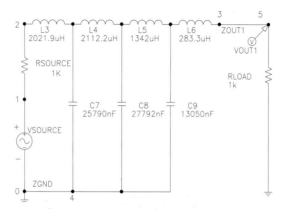

Figure 37.1   Seventh-order Butterworth lowpass filter

The important point of this chapter is that six of the seven preparatory steps are the same as for the problem of designing the lowpass filter (Section 25.14). The only change required to design each of the six filters is the fitness measure.

37.1   CHARACTERISTICS OF VARIOUS FAMILIES OF FILTERS

This section briefly describes the characteristics of the Butterworth, Chebychev, and elliptic families of filters and shows canonical examples of lowpass seventh-order Butterworth, Chebychev, and elliptic filters. The values of the inductors and capacitors for these canonical filters are taken from Van Valkenburg 1982.

37.1.1   Butterworth Filters

Butterworth filters were first described by S. Butterworth in 1930 in *Experimental Wireless and the Wireless Engineer* (Butterworth 1930).

> An ideal electrical filter should not only completely reject the unwanted frequencies but should also have uniform sensitivity for the wanted frequencies. In the usual type of filter circuit, the first condition is generally approximately fulfilled, but the second condition is usually either not obtained or is approximately arrived at by an empirical adjustment of the resistances of the elements.

Figure 37.1 shows a canonical seventh-order Butterworth lowpass filter. The topology of the Butterworth lowpass filter is a ladder in which inductors appear in series along the horizontal line at the top of this figure and the capacitors appear along the vertical lines (called *shunts* to ground). The family of Butterworth filters is parameterized by n, where n is the number of shunt and series lines in the circuit. For Butterworth filters, the number of shunt and series lines equals the number of inductors and capacitors in the circuit. Thus, there are four inductors and three capacitors in the seventh-order lowpass Butterworth filter.

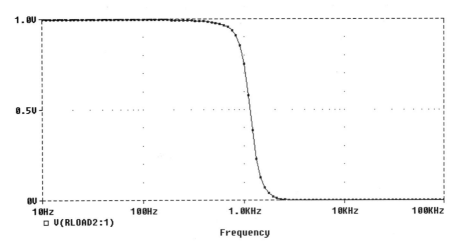

Figure 37.2   Frequency domain behavior of a seventh-order Butterworth filter

Figure 37.2 shows the frequency domain behavior of a lowpass seventh-order Butterworth filter. The horizontal axis here ranges over the four decades of frequency between 10 Hz and 100 KHz on a logarithmic scale. The vertical axis ranges linearly between 0 volts and 1 volt. Butterworth filters are characterized by monotonicity change in voltage as a function of frequency. Also, a lowpass Butterworth filter achieves a uniform, near-maximum power (i.e., a full 1 volt) for most frequencies of its passband (Williams and Taylor 1995). As the frequency increases, the voltage starts to drop off. One consequence of this monotonicity is that the voltage at the boundary of the passband necessarily is not maximal (i.e., near 1 volt).

As will be discussed shortly, a canonical highpass Butterworth filter has the same ladder topology; however, capacitors appear horizontally in series, and inductors appear vertically as shunts. For a highpass filter, the voltage increases monotonically with frequency.

37.1.2   Chebychev Filters

Figure 37.3 shows a canonical seventh-order Chebychev lowpass filter. The topology of a lowpass Chebychev filter is, like a Butterworth filter, a ladder in which a series of inductors appear horizontally across the top of the figure and capacitors appear vertically as shunts. For Chebychev filters (like Butterworth filters), the order of the filter equals the number of inductors and capacitors in the circuit.

Figure 37.4 shows the behavior of the seventh-order Chebychev filter in the frequency domain. Chebychev filters are characterized by a sharper, more rectangular response near the passband boundary (Williams and Taylor 1995). The passband is nonmonotonic in exchange for achieving the objective of getting near-maximal voltage at the edge of the stopband. However, the Chebychev filter is monotonic in the stopband. Thus, the Butterworth filter delivers monotonicity for both the passband and stopband while the Chebychev filter delivers a sharp transition (with some nonmonotonicity in the passband).

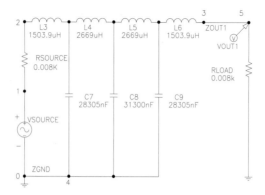

Figure 37.3 Seventh-order Chebychev lowpass filter

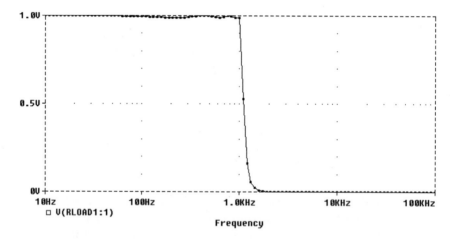

Figure 37.4 Frequency domain behavior of a seventh-order Chebychev filter

Figure 37.5 is a cutaway portion of Figure 37.4 showing the behavior of this lowpass seventh-order Chebychev filter for frequencies in the limited range between 1 Hz and 1,000 Hz and voltages in the highly limited range between 988 millivolts and 1,000 millivolts. As can be seen, the voltage bounces back up to almost a full volt near 1,000 Hz. This return to full voltage near the boundary is achieved at the expense of monotonicity in the passband.

37.1.3   Elliptic Filters

Figure 37.6 shows a canonical seventh-order elliptic lowpass filter. Elliptic filters can be realized with two different topologies. In one topology (Figure 37.6), the lowpass elliptic filter consists of a ladder in which a series of inductors appear horizontally across the top of the figure (like the Butterworth and Chebychev filters), but inductor-capacitor pairs appear vertically as shunts. Elliptic filters are parameterized by n, where n is the number

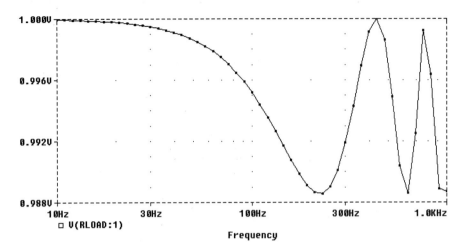

Figure 37.5 Cutaway portion of frequency domain behavior in the passband of a seventh-order Chebychev filter

of shunt and series lines in the circuit. That is, the order of an elliptic filter is not a count of the number of inductors and capacitors. (Figures 25.3, 27.55, and 31.2 are examples of the second topology for realizing elliptic filters.)

Figure 37.7 shows the behavior of the seventh-order elliptic filter in the frequency domain. Monotonicity is not required in the passband or the stopband for elliptic filters. Instead, elliptic filters maximize the steepness of the brick wall of the transition region and are monotonic in the transition region.

Figure 37.8 is a cutaway portion of Figure 37.7 showing the behavior of a seventh-order elliptic filter for frequencies in the limited range between 1 Hz and 1,000 Hz and voltages in the highly limited range between 850 millivolts and 1,000 millivolts.

Figure 37.9 is a cutaway portion of Figure 37.7 showing the behavior of a seventh-order elliptic filter for frequencies in the limited range between 2 KHz and 100 KHz and voltages in the highly limited range between 0 volts and 4 millivolts.

37.2   PREPARATORY STEPS FOR THE SIX FILTERS

The purpose of this section is to synthesize the design for the following six different filters:

- a lowpass third-order Butterworth filter,
- a lowpass fifth-order Butterworth filter,
- a lowpass seventh-order Butterworth filter,
- a highpass seventh-order Butterworth filter,
- a highpass seventh-order Chebychev filter, and
- a highpass seventh-order elliptic (Cauer) filter.

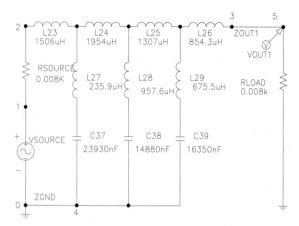

Figure 37.6   Seventh-order elliptic lowpass filter

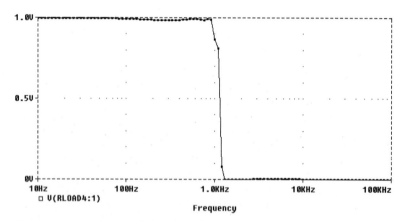

Figure 37.7   Frequency domain behavior of a seventh-order elliptic filter

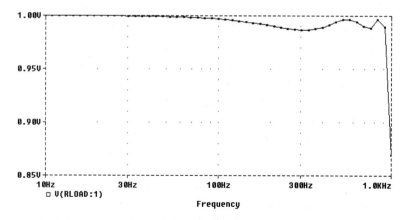

Figure 37.8   Cutaway portion of frequency domain behavior in the passband of a seventh-order elliptic filter

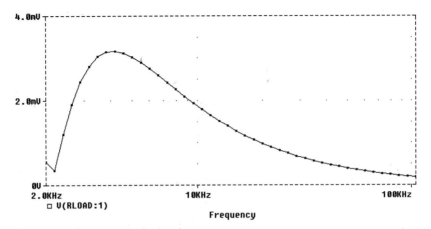

Figure 37.9 Cutaway portion of frequency domain behavior in the stopband of a seventh-order elliptic filter

For each filter, six of the seven preparatory steps are the same as they were for the problem of designing the lowpass filter. In particular, all six runs of genetic programming use

- the same one-input, one-output test fixture and the same embryo with two modifiable wires (Figure 25.6 in Section 25.14.1),
- the same two-branch program architecture (Section 25.14.2),
- the same terminal set (Section 25.14.3),
- the same function set (Section 25.14.3),
- the same population size and other parameters (Section 25.14.5), and
- the same termination criterion and method of result designation (Section 25.14.6).

The difference for the six problems is the fitness measure. As will be seen, various circuit structures will arise from the differences in the fitness measures. Generally, filters from a particular family that are of higher order achieve the family's objectives better than lower-order filters from the same family. Generally, design objectives for filters conflict with one another, so the achievement of one objective is at the expense of achieving other objectives.

Table 37.1 shows the characteristics of the fitness measures for the six filter design problems. The specifications for each of the six filters were chosen to be representative of filters of the type and order that appear in the tables of Williams and Taylor (1995). The first column gives the type and order of the to-be-designed filter. The second and third columns show the start and end, respectively, of the transition region between the passband and the stopband. Generally, these numbers are closer together for high-order filters. The fourth column shows the number of points in the transition region. Generally, this number is smaller for a high-order filter. The fifth and sixth columns show the start and end, respectively, of the region where monotonicity is required. The seventh column shows the passband tolerance in millivolts. The eighth column shows the stopband tolerance in millivolts.

Table 37.1 Characteristics of the fitness measures for the six filter design problems

Type and order of filter	Start of transition region (Hz)	End of transition region (Hz)	Number of points in transition region	Start of monotonic region (Hz)	End of monotonic region (Hz)	Passband tolerance (mv)	Stopband tolerance (mv)
Lowpass third-order Butterworth filter	479	12,020	36	10	100,000	5	0.5
Lowpass fifth-order Butterworth filter	692	4,365	21	10	100,000	5	0.5
Lowpass seventh-order Butterworth filter	759	2,754	15	10	100,000	5	0.5
Highpass seventh-order Butterworth filter	363	1,318	15	10	100,000	0.5	5
Highpass seventh-order Chebychev filter	525	1,000	8	10	912	0.5	30
Highpass seventh-order elliptic filter	1,096	1,445	4	1,096	1,445	3	30

For each point in the monotonic region for the lowpass filters in the first three rows of the table, a point is counted as being monotonic if the output value of the voltage for its frequency is less than or equal to the output value of the voltage of the previous point (or greater than or equal for the highpass filters in the last three rows of the table). If the point is monotonic, fitness and the number of hits are computed in the usual way. If the point is not monotonic, then its contribution to fitness is weighted by 10 in the usual way for noncompliant points (and the point is not counted as a hit).

37.3   LOWPASS THIRD-ORDER BUTTERWORTH FILTER

Figure 37.10 shows a 100%-compliant lowpass filter that is equivalent to a third-order Butterworth filter. It was created in generation 33 of one run. Its fitness is very nearly zero (0.00060). The two result-producing branches of the circuit-constructing program have 63 and 110 points, respectively. The circuit has two capacitors and two inductors. This circuit has one more component than a textbook third-order Butterworth filter, but the same behavior.

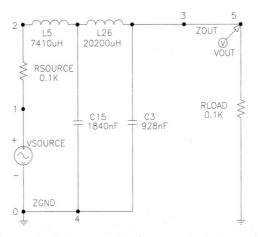

Figure 37.10   Evolved lowpass filter equivalent to a third-order Butterworth filter

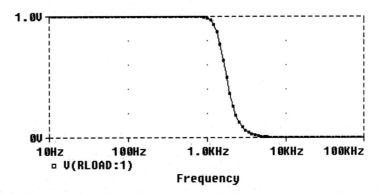

Figure 37.11   Frequency domain behavior of lowpass filter equivalent to a third-order Butterworth filter

Figure 37.11 shows the frequency domain behavior of the evolved lowpass filter that is equivalent to a third-order Butterworth filter. The horizontal axis represents the frequency of the incoming signal and ranges logarithmically over four decades of frequency between 10 Hz and 100 KHz. The vertical axis represents peak voltage and ranges linearly from 0 volts to 1 volt.

37.4   LOWPASS FIFTH-ORDER BUTTERWORTH FILTER

Figure 37.12 shows a 100%-compliant lowpass filter that is equivalent to a fifth-order Butterworth filter. It was created in generation 20 of one run. Its fitness is very nearly zero (0.00578). The two result-producing branches of the circuit-constructing program have 41 and 261 points, respectively. The circuit has three capacitors and three inductors. Notice that this circuit has more components and one more vertical shunt than the

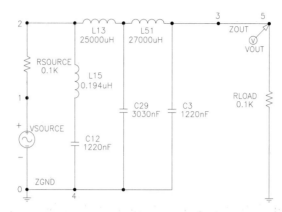

Figure 37.12 Evolved lowpass filter equivalent to a fifth-order Butterworth filter

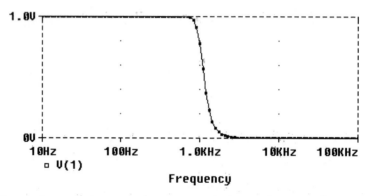

Figure 37.13 Frequency domain behavior of lowpass filter equivalent to a fifth-order Butterworth filter

evolved third-order Butterworth filter. The inductor and capacitor of its first shunt are reminiscent of the topology of an elliptic (i.e., nonmonotonic) filter.

This circuit satisfies the design goals of this problem because the value of **L15** (0.194 μH) is too small to create a noticeable nonmonotonicity for the frequencies of interest. This same comment applies to Figure 37.14. However, it should be remembered that the goal throughout this chapter is to evolve a circuit that satisfies the requirements associated with a particular type of filter of a particular order (e.g., "fifth-order Butterworth compliance"). However, in accomplishing this, the evolutionary process is not constrained to evolve a circuit whose topology and sizing is that of a textbook fifth-order Butterworth filter.

Figure 37.13 shows the frequency domain behavior of the evolved lowpass filter that is equivalent to a fifth-order Butterworth filter. The horizontal axis here ranges over the four decades of frequency between 10 Hz and 100 KHz on a logarithmic scale. The vertical axis ranges linearly between 0 volts and 1 volt.

37.5 LOWPASS SEVENTH-ORDER BUTTERWORTH FILTER

Figure 37.14 shows a 100%-compliant lowpass filter that is equivalent to a seventh-order Butterworth filter. It was created in generation 32 of one run. Its fitness is very nearly zero (0.0243). The two result-producing branches of the circuit-constructing program have 152 and 190 points, respectively. The evolved circuit has four capacitors and five inductors. Notice the two inductors, L17 and L36, on two of the four vertical shunts. These shunts are similar in topology to the shunts found in elliptic filters, not Butterworth filters. Moreover, this evolved circuit has nine components—that is, two more than are found in a canonical seventh-order Butterworth filter. However, both of these two shunt inductors are tiny. In fact, if these two inductors are deleted, the circuit's behavior is not appreciably altered, and in particular, the modified circuit still scores 101 hits. Note that C11 and C27 can be combined once L17 is deleted.

Figure 37.15 shows the frequency domain behavior of the evolved lowpass filter that is equivalent to a seventh-order Butterworth filter. The horizontal axis here ranges over the four decades of frequency between 10 Hz and 100 KHz on a logarithmic scale. The vertical axis ranges linearly between 0 volts and 1 volt.

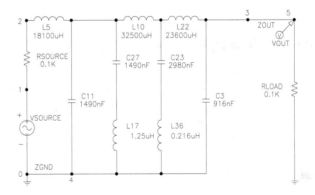

Figure 37.14   Evolved lowpass filter equivalent to a seventh-order Butterworth filter

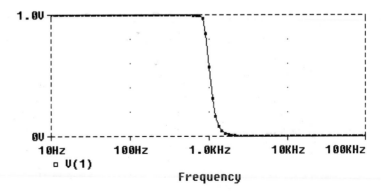

Figure 37.15   Frequency domain behavior of lowpass filter equivalent to a seventh-order Butterworth filter

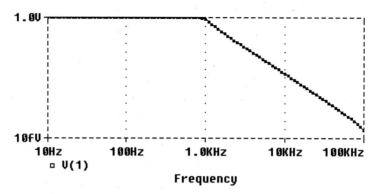

Figure 37.16 Frequency domain behavior using a logarithmic scale for lowpass filter equivalent to a seventh-order Butterworth filter

Figure 37.16 has a logarithmic scale on the vertical axis to better show the monotonicity of the frequency domain behavior of the evolved lowpass filter that is equivalent to a seventh-order Butterworth filter. The horizontal axis here ranges over the four decades of frequency between 10 Hz and 100 KHz on a logarithmic scale. The vertical axis ranges from 10 femtovolts to 1.0 volt.

37.6 HIGHPASS SEVENTH-ORDER ELLIPTIC FILTER

Figure 37.17 shows a 100%-compliant highpass filter that is equivalent to a seventh-order elliptic filter. It was created in generation 39 of one run. Its fitness is very nearly zero (0.0568). The two result-producing branches of the circuit-constructing program have 278 and 263 points, respectively. The circuit has four capacitors and five inductors. Note that the circuit that was evolved to satisfy the design requirements of this problem is not, in fact, an elliptic filter. It is an all-pole filter with a ladder topology. Genetic programming is not cognizant of the topology of elliptic, Butterworth, and Chebychev filters. It was instructed to evolve a circuit that satisfied a particular set of high-level design requirements, and it did so.

Figure 37.18 shows the frequency domain behavior of the evolved highpass filter that is equivalent to a seventh-order elliptic filter.

37.7 HIGHPASS SEVENTH-ORDER CHEBYCHEV FILTER

Figure 37.19 shows a 100%-compliant highpass filter that is equivalent to a seventh-order Chebychev filter. It was created in generation 28 of one run. Its fitness is very nearly zero (0.049). The two result-producing branches of the circuit-constructing program have 247 and 235 points, respectively. The circuit has four capacitors and five inductors. Figure 37.20 shows the frequency domain behavior of the evolved highpass filter that is equivalent to a seventh-order Chebychev filter.

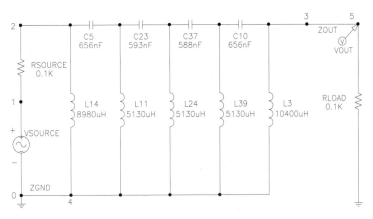

Figure 37.17 Evolved highpass filter equivalent to a seventh-order elliptic filter

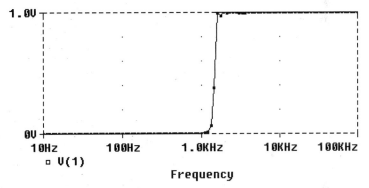

Figure 37.18 Frequency domain behavior of evolved highpass filter equivalent to a seventh-order elliptic filter

37.8 HIGHPASS SEVENTH-ORDER BUTTERWORTH FILTER

We made two runs in an attempt to evolve a 100%-compliant highpass filter that is equivalent to a seventh-order Butterworth filter. The best-of-run circuit from one run scores 98 hits (out of 101) and has a near-zero fitness of 0.568. The best-of-run circuit from the better run (Figure 37.21) produced a highpass filter in generation 50 that scores 99 hits and has a near-zero fitness of 0.0322. The two result-producing branches of the better circuit-constructing program have 216 and 131 points, respectively. This almost-compliant circuit has five capacitors and three inductors.

Figure 37.22 shows the frequency domain behavior of the evolved highpass filter that is nearly equivalent to a seventh-order Butterworth filter. One of the two noncompliant points is at the right end of the stopband. The second noncompliant point is the fourth point in the passband (whose nonmonotonicity manifests itself in the fourth decimal place).

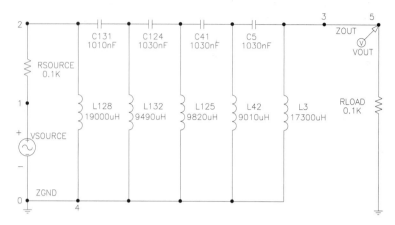

Figure 37.19 Evolved highpass filter equivalent to a seventh-order Chebychev filter

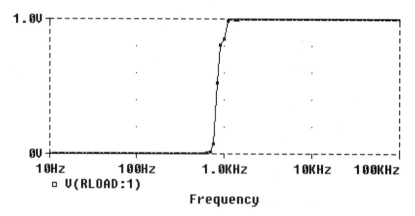

Figure 37.20 Frequency domain behavior of evolved highpass filter equivalent to a seventh-order Chebychev filter

Figure 37.23 has a logarithmic scale on the vertical axis to better show the monotonicity of the frequency domain behavior of the evolved highpass filter that is nearly equivalent to a seventh-order Butterworth filter. The vertical axis of this figure and the two following figures ranges from 10^{-8} volts (10 nanovolts) to 10^{-4} volts (100 microvolts) to 1 volt in steps of 10^{-4} volts. The horizontal axis here ranges over the four decades of frequency between 10 Hz and 100 KHz on a logarithmic scale.

The five capacitors and three inductors of this near-perfect circuit are one more than the number found in a canonical seventh-order Butterworth filter. However, the removal of **C17** from the evolved circuit has no effect on the appearance of the plot of frequency behavior, the fitness of the circuit, or its number of hits. If the circuit is considered without **C17**, then it has the same component count as a textbook seventh-order highpass Butterworth filter (i.e., four capacitors and three inductors).

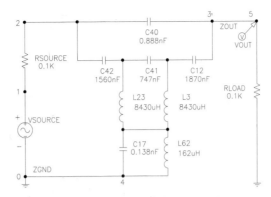

Figure 37.21   Evolved highpass filter equivalent to a seventh-order Butterworth filter

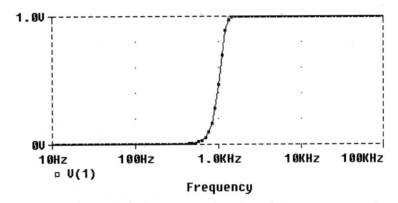

Figure 37.22   Frequency domain behavior of evolved highpass filter equivalent to a seventh-order Butterworth filter

Notice the unusual topological position of capacitor C40 in the evolved circuit of Figure 37.21. Figure 37.24 shows the frequency domain behavior (using the same logarithmic scale as Figure 37.23) when C40 is deleted. C40 is important in this evolved circuit because C40 serves to smooth out the zero that otherwise occurs in the stopband at 275 Hz. However, this smoothing comes at the price of reducing the stopband attenuation. With C40 in the circuit, there is a bend in the stopband at 275 Hz, but the curve remains monotonic. With C40 removed from the circuit, the stopband attenuation is greater, but the zero at 275 Hz becomes nonmonotonic. With C40 removed from the circuit, three new nonmonotonic points appear in the stopband (at the third-to-last, fourth-to-last, and fifth-to-last positions); however, the increase in stopband attenuation causes the previously noncompliant point at the edge of the transition band to become compliant. With C40 removed, the fitness actually drops to 0.0247 (because of the increased stopband attenuation), while the number of hits degrades to 97 (because of the three nonmonotonic points and the one compliant point that are created).

Figure 37.25 superimposes the curves from the two previous figures (using the same logarithmic scale as Figure 27.23).

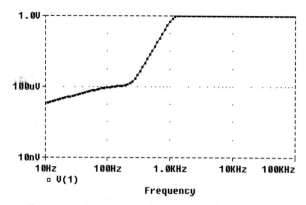

Figure 37.23 **Frequency domain behavior of evolved highpass filter that is nearly equivalent to a seventh-order Butterworth filter (logarithmic scale)**

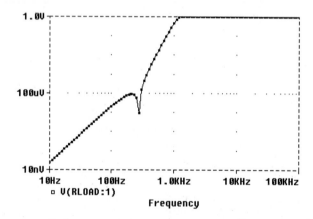

Figure 37.24 **Frequency domain behavior using a logarithmic scale of evolved high-pass filter with C40 deleted**

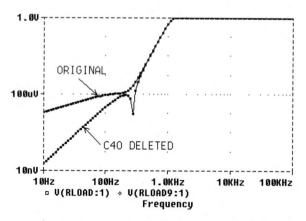

Figure 37.25 **Comparison of original frequency domain behavior and modified behavior**

Synthesis of a Three-Way Source Identification Circuit

The problem of source identification involves correctly classifying an incoming signal into a category that identifies the signal's source. The problem is difficult because information is not provided in advance concerning each source's distinguishing characteristics and because successive signals from the same source generally differ.

A *frequency discriminator* is a circuit that produces a distinctive output according to which of two or more ranges of frequencies an incoming signal belongs. Although successive incoming signals from the same source are usually different, these differences are small in comparison to signals coming from another source.

The work in this chapter was done by the authors in collaboration with Frank Dunlap of Enabling Systems, Palo Alto, California, and Jason D. Lohn, NASA Ames Research Laboratory, Mountain View, California (Koza, Bennett, Lohn, Dunlap et al. 1997b, 1997c).

38.1   DESIGN GOALS

The goal is to evolve the design for a circuit that is composed of resistors, capacitors, and inductors, that acts as a three-way frequency discriminator, and that emits a 1-volt AC signal if the incoming signal is close to 2,560 Hz, a $\frac{1}{2}$-volt AC signal if the incoming signal is close to 256 Hz, and 0 volts otherwise. Specifically, the desired circuit is to produce

- an output of 1 volt (plus or minus 240 millivolts) at the incoming frequency if the frequency of the incoming signal is within 10% of 2,560 Hz,
- an output of $\frac{1}{2}$ volt (plus or minus 240 millivolts) at the incoming frequency if the frequency of the incoming signal is within 10% of 256 Hz, and
- an output of 0 volts (plus 240 millivolts) at the incoming frequency for all other frequencies.

The tolerance of 240 (rather than 250) millivolts is chosen to make the output distinctive for each category.

A three-way frequency discriminator bears some resemblance to a filter with two passbands and three stopbands, but it differs from the previously discussed filters in that it is required to perform a classification by producing three distinct output voltage levels (1 volt, $\frac{1}{2}$ volt, or 0 volts).

38.2 PREPARATORY STEPS

38.2.1 Embryo and Test Fixture

A one-input, one-output test fixture with three ports (Figure 29.1) and an embryo with one modifiable wire and three ports (Figure 29.10) are used for this problem.

38.2.2 Program Architecture

Since the embryo has one modifiable wire, there is one result-producing branch in each program tree.

No automatically defined functions or architecture-altering operations were used for this problem. Thus, the architecture of each program tree in the population consists of one result-producing branch.

38.2.3 Functions and Terminals

The initial function set, $F_{ccs-rpb-initial}$, for the construction-continuing subtrees of the result-producing branches is

$F_{ccs-rpb-initial}$ = {R, L, C, SERIES, PARALLEL0, PARALLEL1, FLIP, NOP, PAIR_CONNECT_0, PAIR_CONNECT_1}.

The initial terminal set, $T_{ccs-rpb-initial}$, for the construction-continuing subtrees of the result-producing branches is

$T_{ccs-rpb-initial}$ = {END, SAFE_CUT}.

Since there are no automatically defined functions in this problem, $T_{adf-initial}$ and $F_{adf-initial}$ are empty.

Since there are no architecture-altering operations in this problem, $T_{rpb-potential}$, $F_{rpb-potential}$, $T_{adf-potential}$, and $F_{adf-potential}$ are empty.

The function set, F_{aps}, for each arithmetic-performing subtree in any branch and the terminal set, T_{aps}, for each arithmetic-performing subtree in any branch are the same as for the lowpass filter problem in Section 25.14.3.

38.2.4 Fitness

For this problem, the voltage **VOUT** is probed at node 5 and the circuit is measured in the frequency domain. The SPICE simulator is instructed to perform an AC small-signal analysis and to report the circuit's behavior for each of 101 frequency values chosen over four decades of frequency (between 1 Hz and 10,000 Hz). Each decade is divided into 25 parts (using a logarithmic scale).

Fitness is measured in terms of the sum, over these 101 fitness cases, of the absolute weighted deviation between the actual value of the voltage that is produced by the circuit at the probe point **VOUT** at node 5 and the target value for voltage.

The three points that are closest to the band located within 10% of 256 Hz are 229.1 Hz, 251.2 Hz, and 275.4 Hz. The procedure for each of these three points is as follows:

- If the voltage equals the ideal value of ½ volt in this interval, the deviation is 0.0.

- If the voltage is less than 240 millivolts away from $\frac{1}{2}$ volt, the absolute value of the deviation from $\frac{1}{2}$ volt is weighted by a factor of 20.
- If the voltage is more than 240 millivolts away from $\frac{1}{2}$ volt, the absolute value of the deviation from $\frac{1}{2}$ volt is weighted by a factor of 200.

This arrangement reflects the fact that the ideal output voltage for this range of frequencies is $\frac{1}{2}$ volt, the fact that a 240-millivolt discrepancy is acceptable, and the fact that a larger discrepancy is not acceptable.

The three points that are closest to the band located within 10% of 2,560 Hz are 2,291 Hz, 2,512 Hz, and 2,754 Hz. The procedure for each of these three points is as follows:

- If the voltage equals the ideal value of 1 volt in this interval, the deviation is 0.0.
- If the voltage is within 240 millivolts of 1 volt, the absolute value of the deviation from 1 volt is weighted by a factor of 20.
- If the voltage is more than 240 millivolts from 1 volt, the absolute value of the deviation from 1 volt is weighted by a factor of 200.

The procedure for each of the remaining 95 points is as follows:

- If the voltage equals the ideal value of 0 volts, the deviation is 0.0.
- If the voltage is within 240 millivolts of 0 volts, the absolute value of the deviation from 0 volts is weighted by a factor of 1.0.
- If the voltage is more than 240 millivolts from 0 volts, the absolute value of the deviation from 0 volts is weighted by a factor of 10.

Note that the weights (20 and 200) in the two passbands are greater than those used previously because only 6 of the 101 points lie in the two passbands.

The number of hits is defined as the number of fitness cases for which the voltage is acceptable or ideal. Thus, the number of hits ranges from a low of 0 to a high of 101 for this problem.

38.2.5 Parameters

The control parameters for this problem are found in the tableau (Table 38.1), the tables of percentages of genetic operations in Appendix D, and the default values specified in Appendix D.

38.2.6 Tableau

Table 38.1 summarizes the key features of the problem of designing a three-way frequency discriminator.

38.3 RESULTS

The best circuit (Figure 38.1) from generation 0 has a fitness of 286.2 and scores 64 hits. It has no inductors, two capacitors, and two resistors (in addition to the source and load resistors in the test fixture). Its circuit-constructing program tree has 67 points.

Figure 38.2a shows the behavior of this circuit in the frequency domain. The horizontal axis is logarithmic and ranges between 1 Hz and 10,000 Hz. The vertical axis ranges

Table 38.1 Tableau for three-way frequency discriminator

Objective	Design a three-way frequency discriminator that emits 1 volt if the incoming signal is close to 2,560 Hz, $1/2$ volt if the incoming signal is close to 256 Hz, and 0 volts otherwise.
Test fixture and embryo	One-input, one-output initial circuit with source resistor, load resistor, and two modifiable wires
Program architecture	Two result-producing branches
Initial function set for the RPBs	For construction-continuing subtrees: $F_{ccs\text{-}rpb\text{-}initial}$ = {R, L, C, SERIES, PARALLEL0, PARALLEL1, FLIP, NOP, PAIR_CONNECT_0, PAIR_CONNECT_1}. For arithmetic-performing subtrees: F_{aps} = {+, -}.
Initial terminal set for the RPBs	For construction-continuing subtrees: $T_{ccs\text{-}rpb\text{-}initial}$ = {END, SAFE_CUT}. For arithmetic-performing subtrees: T_{aps} = {$\Re_{smaller\text{-}reals}$}
Initial function set for the ADFs	Automatically defined functions are not used.
Initial terminal set for the ADFs	Automatically defined functions are not used.
Potential function set for the RPBs	Architecture-altering operations are not used.
Potential terminal set for the RPBs	Architecture-altering operations are not used.
Potential function set for the ADFs	Architecture-altering operations are not used.
Potential terminal set for the ADFs	Architecture-altering operations are not used.
Fitness cases	101 frequency values in an interval of four decades of frequency values between 1 Hz and 10,000 Hz
Raw fitness	The sum, over the 101 sampled frequencies (fitness cases), of the absolute weighted deviation between the actual value of the output voltage that is produced by the circuit at the probe point and the target value for voltage
Standardized fitness	Same as raw fitness
Hits	The number of hits is defined as the number of fitness cases (out of 101) for which the voltage is acceptable or ideal.
Wrapper	None
Parameters	M = 640,000. G = 501. Q =10,000. D = 64. B = 2%. S_{rpb} = 600. N_{rpb} = 1.
Result designation	Best-so-far pace-setting individual
Success predicate	A program scores the maximum number (101) of hits.

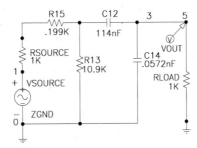

Figure 38.1   Best circuit from generation 0

linearly between 0 volts and 1 volt. The two boxes indicate the range of allowable output voltages (vertical) for the specified range of input frequencies (horizontal). Notice that the frequencies just beyond 256 Hz and 2,560 Hz are not treated in any distinctive way by this best circuit from generation 0.

The best circuit (Figure 38.3) from generation 20 achieves a fitness of 129.1 and scores 76 hits. It has three inductors, four capacitors, and one resistor (in addition to the source and load resistors in the test fixture). Its circuit-constructing program tree has 365 points.

Figure 38.2b shows the behavior of this circuit in the frequency domain. Notice the emergence of a distinctive area around 2,560 Hz and the beginnings of a distinctive area around 256 Hz.

A 100%-compliant circuit (Figure 38.4) emerges in generation 106. This best-of-run circuit achieves a fitness of 21.4 and scores 101 hits (out of 101). It has seven inductors, 15 capacitors, and two resistors (in addition to the source and load resistors in the test fixture and the two **RLARGE** resistors added for simulation purposes). Its circuit-constructing program tree has 551 points.

Figure 38.2c shows the frequency domain behavior of this circuit. As can be seen, the circuit produces output that is close to the desired 1-volt and ½-volt outputs (each within the 240-millivolt tolerance and hence inside the boxes) for the two specified narrow bands of frequencies and also produces the desired near-zero output (i.e., between 0 volts and 240 millivolts) for all other frequencies. This circuit therefore performs the desired three-way frequency discrimination task.

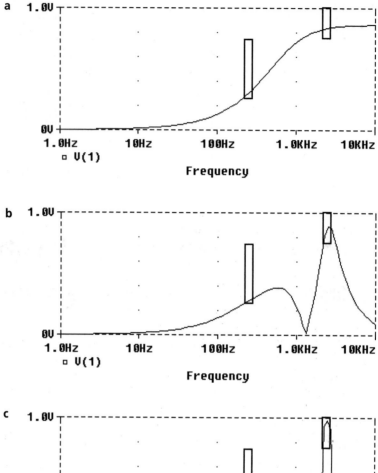

Figure 38.2 Frequency domain behavior of the best circuits of generations (a) 0, (b) 20, and (c) 106

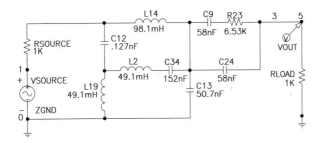

Figure 38.3   Best circuit from generation 20

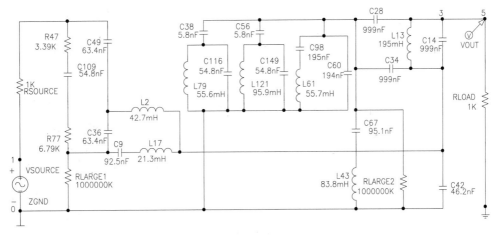

Figure 38.4   Best-of-run circuit from generation 106

Synthesis of a Source Identification Circuit with a Changing Number of Sources

In many practical source identification problems, the exact number of different sources is not known in advance. Moreover, the number of sources may vary over a period of time. Thus, the ability to react to changing environments is especially important in source identification problems.

Genetic methods, in general, have the ability to incrementally and robustly modify an already evolved solution to handle a slightly different environment. The ability of genetic programming to adapt to changing environments was illustrated by a problem of symbolic regression in which the environment varies among seven different Boolean functions (Koza, 1992e, Section 23.4) and the biathlon problem in which the environment alternated between a numerical problem of symbolic regression of a quartic polynomial and the control problem of the artificial ant on the Santa Fe trail (Koza, 1992e, Section 23.5).

This chapter shows how genetic programming can be used to evolve a circuit to perform the task of source identification when the number of sources changes while the evolutionary process is underway.

39.1 DESIGN GOALS

The goal in this section is to evolve the design for a circuit that changes its structure, during the run of genetic programming, as the number of different sources increases. Initially the circuit must classify the incoming signals into three categories. Then the circuit is modified, during the run of genetic programming, so that it can successfully classify incoming signals into four categories.

During the first phase, the requirements for the desired circuit are similar to those for the three-way frequency discriminator discussed previously (Chapter 38). However, the three outputs in the first phase are 1 volt, $\frac{1}{3}$ volt (instead of $\frac{1}{2}$ volt), and 0 volts so that a fourth category ($\frac{2}{3}$ volt) can be conveniently squeezed in during the second phase. Specifically, the desired circuit in the first phase is to produce

- an output of $\frac{1}{3}$ volt (plus or minus 166 millivolts) if the frequency of the incoming signal is within 10% of 256 Hz,
- an output of 1 volt (plus or minus 166 millivolts) if the frequency of the incoming signal is within 10% of 2,560 Hz, and
- an output of 0 volts (plus or minus 166 millivolts) for all other frequencies.

After a circuit is evolved that performs the three-way source identification task on a given processing node of the parallel computer system, the requirements of the problem are changed for that processing node, while the run of genetic programming is underway, to include an additional frequency band. The run is continued with the existing population until a new circuit is evolved that performs a four-way source identification task. The four outputs in the second phase are to be 1 volt, $\frac{2}{3}$ volt, $\frac{1}{3}$ volt, and 0 volts. Specifically, during the second phase, the desired circuit is to produce

- an output of $\frac{2}{3}$ volt (plus or minus 166 millivolts) if the frequency of the incoming signal is within 10% of 750 Hz and
- an output of $\frac{1}{3}$ volt, 1 volt, and 0 volts as above.

39.2   PREPARATORY STEPS

39.2.1   Embryo and Test Fixture

The initial circuit (Figure 30.1) for this problem is created by embedding the embryo with one modifiable wire and three ports (Figure 29.10) into the one-input, one-output test fixture with three ports (Figure 29.1).

39.2.2   Program Architecture

Since the embryo circuit has one modifiable wire, there is one result-producing branch in each circuit-constructing program tree. Thus, each program in generation 0 has a uniform architecture with no automatically defined functions (i.e., one result-producing branch).

One-argument automatically defined functions will be created during the run by the architecture-altering operations. No hierarchical references will be permitted between automatically defined functions.

39.2.3   Functions and Terminals

The initial function set, $F_{ccs-rpb-initial}$, for the construction-continuing subtrees of the result-producing branches is

$F_{ccs-rpb-initial}$ = {R, L, C, SERIES, PARALLEL0, PARALLEL1, FLIP, NOP, PAIR_CONNECT_0, PAIR_CONNECT_1}.

The initial terminal set, $T_{ccs-rpb-initial}$, for the construction-continuing subtrees of the result-producing branches is

$T_{ccs-rpb-initial}$ = {END, SAFE_CUT}.

Since there are no automatically defined functions in generation 0 of this problem, $T_{adf-initial}$ and $F_{adf-initial}$ are empty.

The set of potential functions for each construction-continuing subtree of a result-producing branch, $F_{ccs-rpb-potential}$, is

$$F_{ccs-rpb-potential} = \{ADF0, \ ADF1\}.$$

The set of potential terminals for each construction-continuing subtree of a result-producing branch, $T_{ccs-rpb-potential}$, is empty:

$$T_{ccs-rpb-potential} = \phi.$$

The newly created automatically defined functions do not hierarchically refer to one another. The set of potential functions for each construction-continuing subtree of an automatically defined function, $F_{ccs-adf-potential}$, is

$$F_{ccs-adf-potential} = \{R, \ L, \ C, \ SERIES, \ PARALLEL0, \ PARALLEL1, \ FLIP, \ NOP, \\ PAIR\_CONNECT\_0, \ PAIR\_CONNECT\_1\}.$$

The set of potential terminals for each construction-continuing subtree of an automatically defined function, $T_{ccs-adf-potential}$, is

$$T_{ccs-adf-potential} = \{ARG0, \ END, \ SAFE\_CUT\}.$$

The function set, F_{aps}, for each arithmetic-performing subtree in any branch and the terminal set, T_{aps}, for each arithmetic-performing subtree in any branch are the same as for the lowpass filter problem in Section 25.14.3.

39.2.4   Fitness Measure

For this problem, the voltage **VOUT** is probed at node 5, and the circuit is measured in the frequency domain. The SPICE simulator is instructed to perform an AC small-signal analysis and to report the circuit's behavior for each of 101 frequency values chosen over four decades of frequency (between 1 Hz and 10,000 Hz). Each decade is divided into 25 parts (using a logarithmic scale).

Fitness is measured in terms of the sum, over these 101 fitness cases, of the absolute weighted deviation between the actual value of the voltage that is produced by the circuit at the probe point **VOUT** at node 5 and the target value for voltage.

During the first phase, there are only two frequencies of interest (256 Hz and 2,560 Hz); however, in the second phase, there are three frequencies of interest (750 Hz in addition to the two just mentioned).

In the first phase, fitness is computed as follows. The three points that are closest to the band located within 10% of 256 Hz are 229.1 Hz, 251.2 Hz, and 275.4 Hz. The procedure for each of these three points is as follows:

- If the voltage equals the ideal value of $\frac{1}{3}$ volt in this interval, the deviation is 0.0.
- If the voltage is less than 166 millivolts from $\frac{1}{3}$ volt, the absolute value of the deviation from $\frac{1}{3}$ volt is weighted by a factor of 20.
- If the voltage is more than 166 millivolts from $\frac{1}{3}$ volt, the absolute value of the deviation from $\frac{1}{3}$ volt is weighted by a factor of 200.

This arrangement reflects the fact that the ideal output voltage for this range of frequencies is ⅓ volt, the fact that a 166-millivolt discrepancy is acceptable, and the fact that a larger discrepancy is not acceptable.

The three points that are closest to the band located within 10% of 2,560 Hz are 2,291 Hz, 2,512 Hz, and 2,754 Hz. The procedure for each of these three points is as follows:

- If the voltage equals the ideal value of 1 volt in this interval, the deviation is 0.0.
- If the voltage is within 166 millivolts of 1 volt, the absolute value of the deviation from 1 volt is weighted by a factor of 20.
- If the voltage is more than 166 millivolts from 1 volt, the absolute value of the deviation from 1 volt is weighted by a factor of 200.

The procedure for each of the 95 points outside the passbands is as follows:

- If the voltage equals the ideal value of 0 volts, the deviation is 0.0.
- If the voltage is within 166 millivolts of 0 volts, the absolute value of the deviation from 0 volts is weighted by a factor of 1.0.
- If the voltage is more than 166 millivolts from 0 volts, the absolute value of the deviation from 0 volts is weighted by a factor of 10.

Note that greater weights (20 and 200) are used in the two passbands to compensate for the fact that only 6 of the 101 points lie in the passbands.

In the second phase, there is a source with a frequency of around 750 Hz. The three points that are closest to the band located within 10% of 750 Hz are 758.6 Hz, 791.8 Hz, and 831.8 Hz. The procedure for each of these three points is as follows:

- If the voltage equals the ideal value of ⅔ volt in this interval, the deviation is 0.0.
- If the voltage is less than 166 millivolts from ⅔ volt, the absolute value of the deviation from ⅔ volt is weighted by a factor of 15.
- If the voltage is more than 166 millivolts from ⅔ volt, the absolute value of the deviation from ⅔ volt is weighted by a factor of 150.

In the second phase, the procedure for the six points nearest 256 Hz and 2,560 Hz are the same as above, except that the weight is 15 and 150 (instead of 20 and 200) for the acceptable and unacceptable points, respectively. Lesser weights (15 and 150) are used in the three passbands because 9 of the 101 points lie in the passbands.

In the second phase, the procedure for each of the remaining 92 points is as follows:

- If the voltage equals the ideal value of 0 volts, the deviation is 0.0.
- If the voltage is within 166 millivolts of 0 volts, the absolute value of the deviation from 0 volts is weighted by a factor of 1.0.
- If the voltage is more than 166 millivolts from 0 volts, the absolute value of the deviation from 0 volts is weighted by a factor of 10.

For each phase, the number of hits is defined as the number of fitness cases for which the voltage is acceptable or ideal.

39.2.5   Parameters

The control parameters are the same as for the problem of synthesizing a lowpass filter with architecture-altering operations (Section 28.2.5).

39.2.6 Tableau

Table 39.1 summarizes the key features of the problem of designing a circuit to perform the task of source identification with a changing number of sources.

Table 39.1 Tableau for frequency discriminator with changing number of sources

Objective	Evolve a circuit to perform the task of source identification when the number of sources to be distinguished increases from three to four while the run of genetic programming is underway.
Test fixture and embryo	One-input, one-output initial circuit with a source resistor, load resistor, and one modifiable wire
Program architecture	One result-producing branch, RPB
Initial function set for the RPBs	$F_{ccs\text{-}rpb\text{-}initial}$ = {R, L, C, SERIES, PARALLEL0, PARALLEL1, FLIP, NOP, PAIR_CONNECT_0, PAIR_CONNECT_1}
Initial terminal set for the RPBs	$T_{ccs\text{-}rpb\text{-}initial}$ = {END, SAFE_CUT}
Initial function set for the ADFs	$F_{adf\text{-}initial}$ = ϕ
Initial terminal set for the ADFs	$T_{adf\text{-}initial}$ = ϕ
Potential function set for the RPBs	$F_{ccs\text{-}rpb\text{-}potential}$ = {ADF0, ADF1}
Potential terminal set for the RPBs	$T_{ccs\text{-}rpb\text{-}potential}$ = ϕ
Potential function set for the ADFs	$F_{ccs\text{-}adf\text{-}potential}$ = {R, L, C, SERIES, PARALLEL0, PARALLEL1, FLIP, NOP, PAIR_CONNECT_0, PAIR_CONNECT_1}
Potential terminal set for the ADFs	$T_{ccs\text{-}adf\text{-}potential}$ = {ARG0, END, SAFE_CUT}
Fitness cases	101 frequency values in an interval of four decades of frequency values between 10Hz and 10,000 Hz
Raw fitness	The fitness measure changes during the problem (see text).
Standardized fitness	Same as raw fitness
Hits	The number of hits is defined as the number of fitness cases for which the voltage is acceptable or ideal.
Wrapper	None
Parameters	M = 640,000. G = 501. Q = 10,000. D = 64. B = 2%. S_{rpb} = 600. S_{adf} = 300. N_{rpb} = 1. $N_{max\text{-}adf}$ = 2. $N_{max\text{-}argument\text{-}adf}$ = 1.
Result designation	Best-so-far pace-setting individual
Success predicate	A program scores the maximum number (101) of hits in the second phase.

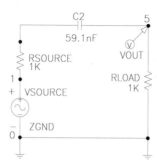

Figure 39.1   Best circuit from generation 0

39.3   RESULTS

The best circuit from generation 0 (Figure 39.1) has a fitness of 200,246.8 and scores 68 hits. It has no inductors, one capacitor, and no resistors (not counting the source and load resistors in the test fixture).

Figure 39.2a shows the behavior of the best circuit of generation 0 in the frequency domain. The horizontal axis represents the frequency of the incoming signal and ranges over four decades of frequencies from 10 Hz to 10,000 Hz on a logarithmic scale. The vertical axis represents peak voltage and ranges linearly from 0 volts to 1 volt.

The best circuit from generation 41 (Figure 39.3) achieves a fitness of 200,015.5 and 100 hits. It has 12 inductors, 13 capacitors, and two resistors (in addition to the source and load resistors in the test fixture). Because of the action of the architecture-altering operations, there is one automatically defined function in the program tree for this circuit. ADF0 is invoked three times by the result-producing branch of the circuit-constructing program tree.

Interestingly, ADF0 develops differently in different contexts in generation 41. In two instances (labeled ADF0-1 and ADF0-2 in Figure 39.3), ADF0 develops into one 296 nF capacitor, as shown in Figure 39.4.

However, for its third instance (labeled ADF0-3 in Figure 39.3), ADF0 develops into a four-ported substructure with two inductors and three capacitors, as shown in Figure 39.5.

Figure 39.6 shows the best circuit from generation 41 after expanding the three occurrences of ADF0.

Figure 39.2b shows the behavior of the best circuit of generation 41 in the frequency domain. Notice the emergence of two distinct peaks around 256 Hz and 2,560 Hz. As can be seen, the circuit produces output that is close to the desired 1-volt and ⅓-volt outputs for the two specified narrow bands of frequencies and also produces the desired near-zero output for all other frequencies.

The first occurrence of the second phase occurs at generation 45. The best circuit from generation 45 achieves a fitness of 100,299.9 and scores 198 hits. It has 12 inductors, 13 capacitors, and two resistors (in addition to the source and load resistors in the test fixture). Because of the action of the architecture-altering operations, there is one automatically defined function in the program tree for this circuit. ADF0 is invoked three times. Figure 39.7 shows the best circuit from generation 45.

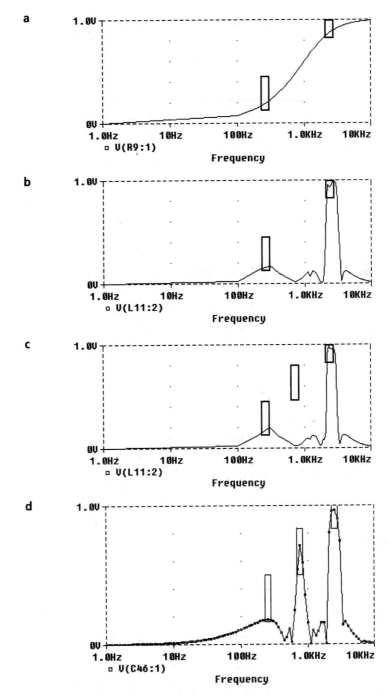

Figure 39.2 Frequency domain behavior of the best circuits of generations (*a*) 0, (*b*) 41, (*c*) 45, and (*d*) 85

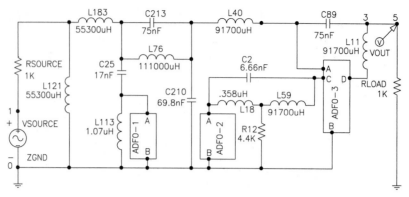

Figure 39.3 Best circuit from generation 41 before the three occurrences of ADF0 (ADF0-1, ADF0-2, and ADF0-3) are expanded

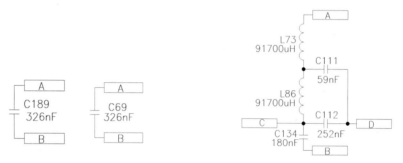

Figure 39.4 ADF0 develops identically in two instances (ADF0-1 and ADF0-2) for generation 41

Figure 39.5 ADF0 develops differently for ADF0-3 than for ADF0-1 and ADF0-2 in generation 41

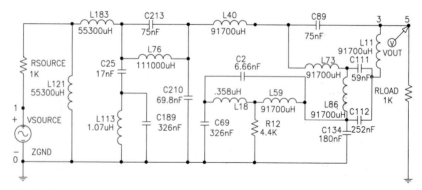

Figure 39.6 Best circuit from generation 41 after expanding the three occurrences of ADF0

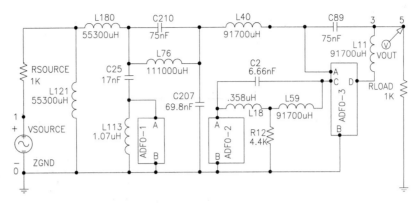

Figure 39.7   Best circuit from generation 45

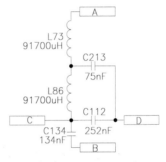

Figure 39.8   ADF0 develops differently for ADF0-3 than for ADF0-1 and ADF0-2 in generation 45

Again, ADF0 develops differently in different contexts for this best circuit of generation 45. In two instances (labeled ADF0-1 and ADF0-2 in Figure 39.7), ADF0 develops into a two-ported substructure that is equivalent to those of Figure 39.4, except that both ADF0-1 and ADF0-2 develop into a 296 nF capacitor. However, for its third instance (labeled ADF0-3 in Figure 39.7), ADF0 develops into a four-ported substructure with two inductors and three capacitors, as shown in Figure 39.8.

Figure 39.9 shows the best circuit from generation 45 after expanding the three occurrences of ADF0.

Figure 39.2c shows the behavior of the best circuit of generation 45 in the frequency domain. This figure contains a new box for the narrow band of frequencies that is supposed to produce an output that is close to ⅔ volt. As can be seen, the circuit's actual response does not lie inside the new box.

The best-of-run circuit from generation 85 (Figure 39.10) achieves a fitness of 404.3. It scores a total of 199 hits, including all 101 hits possible from the first phase. It has 14 inductors, 11 capacitors, and no resistors (except for the source and load resistors in the test fixture). ADF0 is invoked twice and develops into two structures (ADF0-1 and ADF0-2); however, no current flows through ADF0-2.

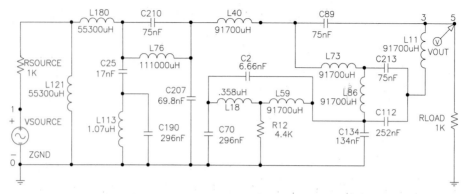

Figure 39.9   Best circuit from generation 45 after expanding the three occurrences of ADF0

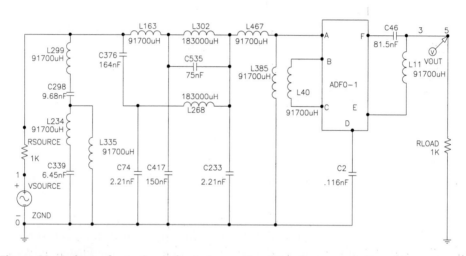

Figure 39.10 Best-of-run circuit from generation 85 before expansion of its automatically defined functions

As shown in Figure 39.11, ADF0 develops into a six-ported substructure with four inductors and two capacitors.

Figure 39.12 shows the best-of-run circuit from generation 85 after expanding its two automatically defined functions, ADF0 and ADF1. Although we made resistors available in this run, they were not actually incorporated into the best-of-run individual. We thought that resistors were necessary (or would at least be helpful) in creating this circuit; however, the evolved result proved us wrong.

Figure 39.2d shows the behavior of the best-of-run circuit of generation 85 in the frequency domain. The three boxes in the figure show the circuit produces the desired 1 volt, 2/3 volt, and 1/3 volt (each within the 1/6-volt tolerance) for the three specified narrow bands of frequencies. The circuit produces the desired near-zero output for all other frequencies.

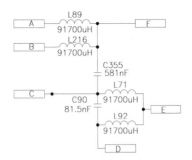

Figure 39.11 Result of developing ADF0 for best-of-run circuit from generation 85

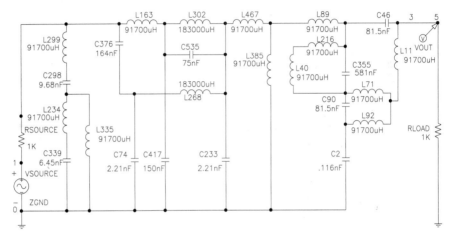

Figure 39.12 Best-of-run circuit from generation 85 after expansion of its automatically defined functions

Lowpass Filter with Parsimony

Multiobjective fitness measures are especially pertinent to design problems because practical design problems typically entail trade-offs among various competing considerations.

The evolutionary process is driven by the fitness measure. In the foregoing chapters on circuit synthesis, fitness was most frequently measured in terms of a single factor—the weighted sum of the absolute values of the deviations between the actual behavior of the circuit and the desired behavior of the circuit in the frequency domain. However, since the fitness measure is a user-written computer program, a fitness measure may incorporate any calculable or measurable behavior or characteristic of the circuit (or combination of such behaviors or characteristics).

The parts count is often an important consideration in designing a practical electrical circuit because of considerations of cost and physical size. Parsimony may be explicitly incorporated into runs of genetic programming in several ways, including minimum description length (Iba, Kurita, de Garis, and Sato 1993; Iba, de Garis, and Sato 1994), the individual objective switching method for evolving compact individuals (Blickle 1997), and other methods for balancing accuracy and parsimony (Zhang and Mühlenbein 1993, 1994, 1995).

40.1 DESIGN GOALS

The goal is to evolve the design for a lowpass filter that satisfies the same design characteristics as in Section 25.13 while minimizing the parts count of the evolved circuit.

40.2 PREPARATORY STEPS

The preparatory steps are identical to those of Section 25.14, except that the fitness measure is modified to reflect the number of inductors and capacitors in the evolved circuit.

Construction of a multiobjective fitness measure requires that appropriate weight be given to competing objectives having entirely different metrics (e.g., apples and oranges). This run employs a straightforward weighted (blended) sum of two different factors. The fitness measure is a blended measure consisting of the fitness measure of Section 25.14.4 plus an additional term of 0.001 times the total number of inductors and capacitors in the circuit. We made three observations in connection with constructing a fitness measure that suitably combines the two factors.

First, a 100%-compliant lowpass filter produces acceptable voltages for all 101 fitness cases over five decades of frequency between 1 Hz and 100,000 Hz. A frequency in the intended passband becomes unacceptable if it is more than 0.030 volt away from the target of 1.000 volt; a frequency in the intended stopband becomes unacceptable if it is more than 0.001 volt away from the target of 0.000 volts. Using the fitness measure of Section 25.14.4, the deviation from the target for an unacceptable voltage in either the passband or the stopband is multiplied by 10. Thus, an individual scoring 100 out of 101 possible hits would have one noncompliant fitness case. If the noncompliant fitness case were in the passband, it would contribute at least 0.300 volt to the original fitness measure of Section 25.14.4. If the noncompliant fitness case were in the stopband, one unacceptable fitness case in the stopband would contribute at least 0.010 volt.

Second, the fitness of the 100%-compliant evolved circuits (scoring 101 hits out of a possible 101) in Chapter 25 ranged over values such as 0.00114 and 0.0650.

Third, the total of 14 inductors and capacitors in the evolved circuit of run A was fewer components than the evolved circuits of runs B, C, D, and E.

Taking these three observations into consideration, an additive term of 0.001 times the total number of inductors and capacitors in the circuit will be considerably below 1.000 (given the maximum number of points allowed in the program trees). This additive term will therefore be in the same general range as the values of fitness for 100%-compliant circuits in Chapter 25. However, early in the run (before achievement of 101 hits), this additive term would be comparatively insignificant. Moreover, since tournament selection is used throughout this book, small additive terms will usually have no effect at all until late in the run.

40.3 RESULTS

In one run, the best circuit of generation 0 has a fitness of 99.1 and scores 62 hits (out of 101).

The first 100%-compliant circuit (Figure 40.1) appears in generation 27. The two result-producing branches of the program tree have 246 and 249 points, respectively. The circuit has a total of 18 components (10 inductors and 8 capacitors).

Between generations 28 and 48, numerous 100%-compliant circuits were evolved (each with between 9 and 17 inductors and capacitors).

A 100%-compliant circuit (Figure 40.2) with a total of eight components (four inductors and four capacitors) appears in generation 49. The two result-producing branches of the program tree have 299 and 134 points. The fitness of this circuit is 0.02523 (of which about 0.017 is due to the frequency response and of which 0.008 is due to the parts count).

Figure 40.3 shows the frequency domain behavior of the 100%-compliant circuit from generation 49. The horizontal axis represents the frequency of the incoming signal and ranges over five decades of frequencies from 1 Hz to 100,000 Hz on a logarithmic scale. The vertical axis represents peak voltage and ranges linearly from 0 volts to 1 volt.

In generation 50, a different 100%-compliant circuit appears on processing node 56 (which is toroidally two steps away from node 15 in the 8×8 mesh of processing nodes on our 64-node parallel computer). This circuit has slightly better fitness (0.02446) than

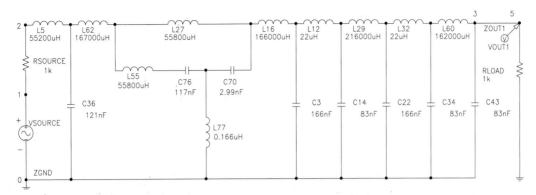

Figure 40.1 **100%-compliant circuit from generation 27 with a total of 10 inductors and 8 capacitors**

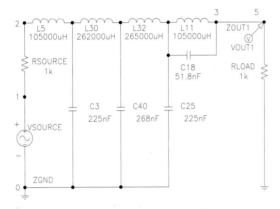

Figure 40.2 **100%-compliant circuit from generation 49 with four inductors and four capacitors**

that of the circuit above from generation 49. The circuit from generation 50 has a total of eight inductors and capacitors and has the very same topology as the circuit above from generation 49. It is likely that both circuits have a common ancestor.

Table 40.1 shows that five of the eight components of these 100%-compliant circuits from generations 49 and 50 are exactly the same, while the last three components in the table are slightly different. Note that the table contains component numbers for the circuit from generation 49 and the value of the corresponding component for the circuit from generation 50.

This run demonstrates that it is possible (1) to evolve electronic circuits using genetic programming using a multiobjective fitness measure that incorporates a primary factor based on the circuit's performance as a satisfactory lowpass filter and a secondary factor based on parts count and (2) to produce improvements in the fitness (as measured by both factors) during the run.

During this run, the parts count for 100%-compliant circuits dropped from 18 to 8 (only one higher than the minimum number of inductors and capacitors that are capable of satisfying the design requirements of this particular problem).

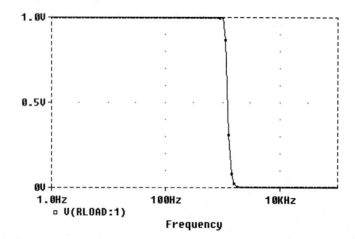

Figure 40.3   Frequency domain behavior of 100%-compliant circuit from generation 49 with four inductors and four capacitors

Table 40.1   Comparison of two 100%-compliant circuits with four inductors and four capacitors

Component	Generation 49	Generation 50
C3	225 nF	225 nF
L5	105,000 μH	105,000 μH
L11	105,000 μH	105,000 μH
C18	51.8 nF	51.8 nF
C25	225 nF	225 nF
L30	262,000 μH	261,000 μH
L32	265,000 μH	269,000 μH
C40	268 nF	270 nF

Complete Repertoire of Circuit-Constructing Functions

This chapter presents the complete repertoire of circuit-constructing functions, including

- component-creating functions (Section 41.1),
- topology-modifying functions (Section 41.2), and
- development-controlling functions (Section 41.3).

41.1 COMPLETE REPERTOIRE OF COMPONENT-CREATING FUNCTIONS

Component-creating functions insert a particular component into a location within the topology of the developing circuit structure in lieu of a modifiable wire or modifiable component and specify the sizing for each such inserted component by means of value-setting subtree(s). This section presents a complete repertoire of component-creating functions used in this book (as well as some additional functions that are illustrative of the flexibility of our system for automatic circuit synthesis).

Each component-creating function in a circuit-constructing program tree is linked to a particular modifiable wire or modifiable component and inserts a particular electrical component into the developing circuit structure in some way. Each component-creating function establishes the value(s) of each component that it inserts into a developing circuit structure by means of value-setting (arithmetic-performing) subtree(s). Component-creating functions usually have zero or one construction-continuing subtrees. Each component-creating function in this book leaves the number of lines impinging at any one node in the circuit at either two or three.

Some of the component-creating functions are context-free and some are context-sensitive. When a component-creating function is context-free, the outcome depends only on the single modifiable wire or modifiable component to which the component-creating function is linked. When a component-creating function is context-sensitive, the outcome also depends on other nearby elements of the circuit structure.

Table 41.1 presents a complete repertoire of component-creating functions and shows the name of the function, a description of the function, the arity of the function, and a reference to the section where it is defined.

Table 41.1 Component-creating functions

Name	Short description	Arity	Section
`AC`	AC power supply	2	41.1.8
`C`	Capacitor	2	25.6.2
`D`	Diode	1	41.1.5
`DC`	DC power supply	2	41.1.7
`DIGITAL_AND0` through `DIGITAL_AND11`	Digital AND gate	3	41.1.24
`DIGITAL_INVERTER`	Digital INVERTER	2	41.1.23
`DIGITAL_OR0` through `DIGITAL_OR11`	Digital OR gate	3	41.1.25
`FIVE_LEAD_OP_AMP0` through `FIVE_LEAD_OP_AMP3`	Five-leaded op amp	5	41.1.29
`L`	Inductor	2	25.6.3
`M_DIODE_NMOS`	MOSFET diode created from *NMOS* transistor	2	51.1.2
`M_DIODE_PMOS`	MOSFET diode created from *PMOS* transistor	2	51.1.3
`M_POS5V_DRAIN_NMOS`	MOSFET *NMOS* transistor with its drain connected to the positive power supply	2	51.1.4
`M_POS5V_GATE_NMOS`	MOSFET *NMOS* transistor with its gate connected to the positive power supply	2	51.1.5
`M_NEG5V_SOURCE_NMOS`	MOSFET *NMOS* transistor with its source connected to the negative power supply	2	51.1.6
`M_NEG5V_DRAIN_PMOS`	MOSFET *PMOS* transistor with its drain connected to the negative power supply	2	51.1.7
`M_NEG5V_GATE_PMOS`	MOSFET *PMOS* transistor with its gate connected to the negative power supply	2	51.1.8
`M_POS5V_SOURCE_PMOS`	MOSFET *PMOS* transistor with its source connected to the positive power supply	2	51.1.9
`M_THREE_NMOS0` through `M_THREE_NMOS11`	*NMOS* transistor	4	51.1.10
`M_THREE_PMOS0` through `M_THREE_PMOS11`	*PMOS* transistor	4	51.1.11
`NEON`	Neon bulb	2	41.1.6

`Q_DIODE_NPN`	A diode created from an *npn* transistor whose collector and base are connected	1	41.1.19
`Q_DIODE_PNP`	A diode created from a *pnp* transistor whose collector and base are connected	1	41.1.20
`Q_GND_EMIT_NPN`	An *npn* transistor whose emitter lead is connected to ground	1	41.1.9
`Q_GND_EMIT_PNP`	A *pnp* transistor whose emitter lead is connected to ground	1	41.1.10
`Q_NEG15V_EMIT_NPN`	An *npn* transistor whose emitter lead is connected to a −15-volt power supply	1	41.1.13
`Q_NEG15V_COLL_PNP`	A *pnp* transistor whose emitter lead is connected to a −15-volt power supply	1	41.1.14
`Q_POS15V_COLL_NPN`	An *npn* transistor whose collector lead is connected to a +15-volt power supply	1	41.1.11
`Q_POS15V_COLL_PNP`	A *pnp* transistor whose collector lead is connected to a +15-volt power supply	1	41.1.12
`Q_POS15V_EMIT_NPN`	An *npn* transistor whose emitter lead is connected to a +15-volt power supply	1	41.1.15
`Q_POS15V_EMIT_PNP`	A *pnp* transistor whose emitter lead is connected to a +15-volt power supply	1	41.1.15
`QVIAB`	Transistor with via from its base	0	41.1.17
`QVIAC`	Transistor with via from its collector	0	41.1.16
`QVIAE`	Transistor with via from its emitter	0	41.1.18
`Q_THREE_NPN0` through `Q_THREE_NPN11`	An *npn* transistor	3	41.1.21
`Q_THREE_PNP0` through `Q_THREE_PNP11`	A *pnp* transistor	3	41.1.22
`R`	Resistor	2	25.6.1
`RTINY`	Tiny resistor	1	41.1.2
`THREE_LEAD_OP_AMP0` through `THREE_LEAD_OP_AMP11`	Three-leaded op amp	3	41.1.28
`TRANSFORMER0` through `TRANSFORMER5`	Transformer	5	41.1.26
`TWO_LEAD_OP_AMP0` and `TWO_LEAD_OP_AMP1`	Two-leaded op amp	2	41.1.27

41.1.1 R Function

The two-argument resistor-creating R function causes the modifiable wire or modifiable component in the developing circuit structure that is linked to this function in the circuit-constructing program tree to be changed into a resistor, as previously described in Section 25.6.1.

41.1.2 RTINY Function

The one-argument RTINY function is identical to the two-argument R function, except that the value of the inserted resistor is always $10^{-9}\Omega$.

Since the value of the inserted resistor is inherent in the definition of this function, the RTINY function possesses only one argument (its construction-continuing subtree).

41.1.3 C Function

The two-argument capacitor-creating C function causes the modifiable wire or modifiable component to which it is linked to be changed into a capacitor, as previously described in Section 25.6.2.

41.1.4 L Function

The two-argument inductor-creating L function causes the modifiable wire or modifiable component to which it is linked to be changed into an inductor, as previously described in Section 25.6.3.

41.1.5 D Function

The one-argument diode-creating D function causes the modifiable wire or modifiable component to which it is linked to be changed into a diode. Diodes have no explicit numerical component value. Hence the D function has no arithmetic-performing subtree. The D function has only a construction-continuing subtree and is therefore a one-argument function.

Figure 41.1 shows the result of applying the D function to the modifiable wire Z0 of Figure 25.9, thereby creating a diode D1 connecting nodes 1 and 2. Note that the polarity of the newly created diode D1 matches that of the modifiable wire Z0 from Figure 25.9 that it replaces. The newly created diode D1 remains modifiable. D1 is linked to the topmost function in the construction-continuing subtree (the argument of the D function). In other words, D1 retains the writing head that originally linked the D function of the program tree to the modifiable wire Z0 of the developing partial circuit of Figure 25.9.

An example of the one line in the netlist created by the D function is

```
D1  2  1  D1N4148
```

The interpretation is that the anode (+ end) of diode D1 is connected to node 2, the cathode (− end) is connected to node 1, and the diode is the D1N4148 model.

Note that although a diode has no explicit numerical component value, the specification of the model implicitly specifies the values of a large number of parameters to the SPICE simulator. In the extreme case, every one of the model parameters for the diode might be viewed as a potential separate component value (and assigned a separate arithmetic-performing subtree).

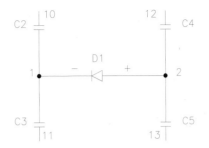

Figure 41.1   Result of applying the D function

For each type of electrical device, the SPICE simulator contains mathematical routines that enable it to simulate the behavior of the device. For example, for capacitors and inductors, SPICE contains routines that implement the derivatives and integrals relating voltage and current for that type of device. In addition, SPICE contains a set (called a *model*) of additional values (called *model parameter values*) that specify the detailed electrical characteristics for each specific component of a particular device type. Note that, for some problems, it may be desirable to make the name of the model a component value for the component. The name of the model is an example of a nonnumerical component value. The possible alternative values of the name of the model would then range over the different available models for the component.

41.1.6   NEON Function

The one-argument NEON ("neon bulb") function causes the modifiable wire or modifiable component to which it is linked to be changed into a neon bulb.

A neon bulb fires when a certain voltage is applied to its leads (e.g., 67 volts). Because the firing voltage is a fixed property of the neon gas, there need not be any explicit component value associated with the NEON function. Hence, there is no need for an arithmetic-performing subtree. The NEON function has only a construction-continuing subtree, and the NEON function is a one-argument function.

Figure 41.2 shows the result of applying the NEON function to the modifiable wire Z0 of Figure 25.9, thereby creating a neon bulb NE1 connecting nodes 1 and 2.

41.1.7   DC Function

The two-argument DC ("DC power supply") function causes the modifiable wire or modifiable component to which it is linked to be changed into a DC power supply.

The component value for the DC function is the value of its DC voltage. The arithmetic-performing subtree specifies the numerical value of the component by returning a floating-point value that is, in turn, interpreted as the value of the component. The method of interpretation is different for the DC function than for other component-creating functions; it is designed to produce voltage levels within a narrower range than is appropriate for other components used in this book. Specifically, the arithmetic-performing subtree of the DC function returns a floating-point value that is, in turn,

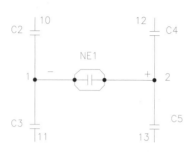

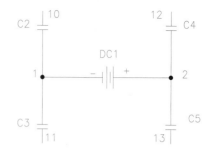

Figure 41.2 Result of applying the NEON function

Figure 41.3 Result of applying the DC function

interpreted as the value of the component in the following way: If the return value is between −100 and +100, U is equated to the value returned by the subtree. If the return value is less than −100, U is set to −100 volts DC; however, if the return value is greater than +100, U is set to +100 volts DC.

Figure 41.3 shows the result of applying the DC function to the modifiable wire Z0 of Figure 25.9, thereby creating a DC voltage source DC1 connecting nodes 1 and 2.

41.1.8   AC Function

The six-argument AC ("AC power supply") function causes the modifiable wire or modifiable component to which it is linked to be changed into an AC sinusoidal power supply. Although this particular function is not used in this book, it is included here to illustrate the myriad possibilities associated with component-creating functions.

The five component values associated with an AC power supply are its offset voltage, its amplitude voltage, its frequency, its time delay (in seconds), and its damping factor.

The five arithmetic-performing subtrees specify these five numerical values by returning five floating-point values that are interpreted in the following way (which is different for the AC function than for other component-creating functions). For amplitude and frequency, the floating-point value returned by each arithmetic-performing subtree of the AC function is interpreted in the following way: If the return value is between −100 and +100, U is equated to the absolute value returned by the subtree. If the return value is less than −100 or greater than +100, U is set to +100 volts AC. For the offset voltage, time delay, and damping factor, the floating-point value returned by each arithmetic-performing subtree of the AC function is interpreted in the following way: If the return value is between −100 and +100, U is equated to the value returned by the subtree. If the return value is less than −100, U is set to −100 volts AC. If the return value is greater than +100, U is set to +100 volts AC.

Figure 41.4 shows the result of applying the AC function to the modifiable wire Z0 of Figure 25.9, thereby creating an AC voltage source AC1 connecting nodes 1 and 2.

41.1.9   Q_GND_EMIT_NPN Function

A *bipolar junction transistor* (BJT) is a three-leaded component with a nonlinear transfer function. The two-argument Q_GND_EMIT_NPN ("npn transistor with grounded emit-

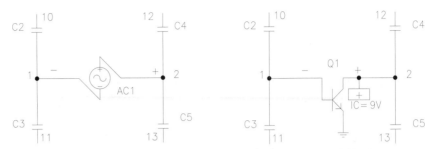

Figure 41.4   Result of applying the AC function

Figure 41.5   Result of applying the Q_GND_EMIT_NPN function

ter") function causes the modifiable wire or modifiable component to which it is linked to be changed into an *npn* transistor whose emitter is connected to ground.

Note that although a transistor ordinarily has no explicit numerical component value, the specification of the model implicitly specifies the values of a large number of parameters to the SPICE simulator.

The insertion of a transistor into a developing circuit structure is, in general, complicated by the fact that transistors have three leads. This function (and several functions that follow in this chapter) avoids this complication because one of the transistor's leads is connected directly to a designated special place (e.g., ground or a power supply).

Figure 41.5 shows the result of applying the Q_GND_EMIT_NPN function to the modifiable wire **Z0** between nodes 1 and 2 of Figure 25.9, thereby creating a transistor **Q1**. The collector of the newly created transistor is connected to the positive end of **Z0** (node 2 of Figure 25.9), and the base is connected to the negative end of **Z0** (node 1 of Figure 25.9). The emitter is connected to ground.

The following line for the netlist is created for the Q_GND_EMIT_NPN function:

```
Q1 2 1 0 Q2N3904
```

The interpretation is that the collector of transistor Q1 is connected to node 2 of Figure 41.5, the base is connected to node 1 of Figure 41.5, the emitter is connected to node 0 (ground), and the model of the bipolar junction transistor is the Q2N3904 model.

For some problems in this book, models other than Q2N3904 are sometimes used for *npn* bipolar junction transistors (e.g., Q2N3055, Q2N2222, and DH3725C).

A component may occasionally require additional numerical component values in situations where it is necessary to specify the initial condition of the component (e.g., the initial voltage on a capacitor, the initial current on an inductor). Initial conditions are not ordinarily used with transistors; however, they are required by the SPICE simulator in certain situations (e.g., certain oscillators). In these unusual situations, the one-argument Q_GND_EMIT_NPN function must be changed into a two-argument function so that it possesses an arithmetic-performing subtree for the initial condition. The arithmetic-performing subtree is in addition to the usual construction-continuing subtree of the Q_GND_EMIT_NPN function. The netlist for the two-argument version of the Q_GND_EMIT_NPN function might be as follows:

```
Q1 2 1 0 Q2N3904
.IC V(2) = 9VOLTS
```

The interpretation of the second line above is that the initial condition for the collector node (node 2) is 9 volts. Figure 41.5 shows this initial condition for the collector of transistor **Q1**.

41.1.10 Q_GND_EMIT_PNP Function

The two-argument Q_GND_EMIT_PNP ("*pnp* transistor with grounded emitter") function causes the modifiable wire or modifiable component to which it is linked to be changed into a *pnp* transistor whose emitter is connected to ground in a manner similar to the Q_GND_EMIT_NPN function described above.

Figure 41.6 shows the result of applying the Q_GND_EMIT_PNP function to the modifiable wire **Z0** connecting nodes 1 and 2 of Figure 25.9, thereby creating a transistor **Q6**. The collector of the transistor is connected to the positive end of **Z0** (node 2 of Figure 25.9), and the base is connected to the negative end of **Z0** (node 1 of Figure 25.9). The emitter is connected to ground. Notice the direction of the arrow on the emitter in this figure compared to Figure 41.5.

41.1.11 Q_POS15V_COLL_NPN Function

The two-argument Q_POS15V_COLL_NPN ("*npn* transistor whose collector is connected to the positive power supply") function causes the modifiable wire or modifiable component to which it is linked to be changed into an *npn* transistor whose collector is connected to a positive power supply for the circuit (e.g., 15 volts DC at node 50).

Figure 41.7 shows the result of applying the Q_POS15V_COLL_NPN function to the modifiable wire **Z0** of Figure 25.9, thereby creating a transistor **Q1** connecting nodes 1 and 2. The base of the transistor is connected to what was the positive end of **Z0** (node 2 of Figure 25.9), and the emitter is connected to what was the negative end of **Z0** (node 1 of Figure 25.9). The collector is connected to a +15-volt DC positive power supply **POS** at node 50.

If an initial condition is required, the netlist for the Q_POS15V_COLL_NPN function would be as follows:

```
Q1 50 2 1 NE Q2N3904
.IC V(2) = 9VOLTS
```

The interpretation of the first line above is that the collector of transistor Q1 is connected to node 50, which is a +15-volt DC power source; the base of the transistor is connected to node 2 of Figure 41.7; the emitter of the transistor is connected to node 1 of Figure 41.7; and the model of the *npn* bipolar junction transistor is Q2N3904. The interpretation of the optional second line is that the optional initial condition for the base node 2 is 9 volts. Figure 41.7 shows the initial condition for the base of the newly created transistor **Q1**.

41.1.12 Q_POS15V_COLL_PNP Function

The two-argument Q_POS15V_COLL_PNP ("*pnp* transistor whose collector is connected to the positive power supply") function causes the modifiable wire or modifiable compo-

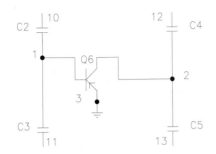

Figure 41.6   Result of applying the Q_GND_EMIT_PNP function

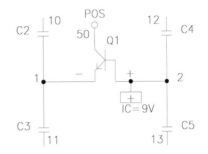

Figure 41.7   Result of applying the Q_POS15V_COLL_NPN function

nent to which it is linked to be changed into a *pnp* transistor whose collector is connected to a positive power supply for the circuit (e.g., 15 volts DC at node 50) in the same manner as the Q_POS15V_COLL_NPN function.

41.1.13   Q_NEG15V_EMIT_NPN Function

The two-argument Q_NEG15V_EMIT_NPN ("*npn* transistor with negative connected emitter") function causes the modifiable wire or modifiable component to which it is linked to be changed into an *npn* transistor whose emitter is connected to the –15-volt DC voltage source.

Figure 41.8 shows the result of applying the Q_NEG15V_EMIT_NPN function to the modifiable wire **Z0** of Figure 25.9, thereby creating a transistor **Q6** connecting nodes 1 and 2. The collector of the transistor is connected to what was the positive end of **Z0** (node 2 of Figure 25.9), and the base is connected to what was the negative end of **Z0** (node 1 of Figure 25.9).

41.1.14   Q_NEG15V_COLL_PNP Function

The two-argument Q_NEG15V_COLL_PNP ("*pnp* transistor with negative connected collector") function causes the modifiable wire or modifiable component to which it is linked to be changed into a *pnp* transistor whose collector is connected to the negative DC voltage source.

Figure 41.9 shows the result of applying the Q_NEG15V_COLL_PNP function to the modifiable wire **Z0** of Figure 25.9, thereby creating a transistor **Q6** connecting nodes 1 and 2. The base of the transistor is connected to what was the positive end of **Z0** (node 2 of Figure 25.9), and the emitter is connected to what was the negative end of **Z0** (node 1 of Figure 25.9).

41.1.15   Q_POS15V_EMIT_PNP and Q_POS15V_EMIT_NPN Functions

The two-argument Q_POS15V_EMIT_PNP ("*pnp* transistor with positive connected emitter") function causes the modifiable wire or modifiable component to which it is linked to be changed into a *pnp* transistor whose emitter is connected to the positive DC voltage source.

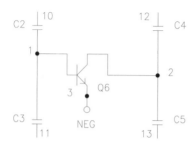

Figure 41.8   Result of applying the Q_NEG15V_EMIT_NPN function

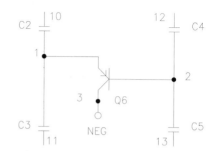

Figure 41.9   Result of applying the Q_NEG15V_COLL_PNP function

Figure 41.10 shows the result of applying the Q_POS15V_EMIT_PNP function to the modifiable wire Z0 of Figure 25.9, thereby creating a transistor **Q6** connecting nodes 1 and 2. The collector of the transistor is connected to what was the positive end of Z0 (node 2 of Figure 25.9), and the base is connected to what was the negative end of Z0 (node 1 of Figure 25.9).

The two-argument Q_POS15V_EMIT_NPN ("*npn* transistor with positive connected emitter") function operates in a similar manner for *npn* transistors.

41.1.16   QVIAC Functions

The eight functions in the QVIAC ("transistor with via from collector") family of zero-argument functions (called QVIAC0, . . . , QVIAC7) cause the modifiable wire or modifiable component in the developing circuit structure that is linked to this function in the circuit-constructing program tree to be changed into a transistor whose collector is connected to a numbered port (called a *via*). A QVIAC function does not possess a construction-continuing subtree. That is, the writing head is lost by the execution of a QVIAC function. Since there is no writing head on the newly created transistor, the transistor remains in the developing circuit structure once it is inserted by a QVIAC function. (These comments also apply to the closely related QVIAB or QVIAE functions described in the next sections.)

The QVIAC function replaces the modifiable wire or modifiable component with a transistor whose base is connected to the negative end of the modifiable wire or modifiable component, whose emitter is connected to the positive end of the modifiable wire or modifiable component, and whose collector is connected to a particular numbered port. The port is connected to a designated one of eight imaginary layers (numbered from 0 to 7) of an imaginary wafer.

If no other part of the fully developed circuit connects to a particular numbered layer designated by a QVIAC (or QVIAB or QVIAE or other via) function, then the port connecting to that layer is useless. In that event, the port is deleted and the now-unattached lead of the transistor is reattached to the node to which the positive end of the modifiable wire or modifiable component is connected. This deletion and reattachment is done just prior to the creation of the netlist for the circuit.

Figure 41.11 shows the result of applying the QVIAC7 function to the modifiable wire Z0 of Figure 25.9, thereby creating a transistor **Q6** positioned between node 1, node 2,

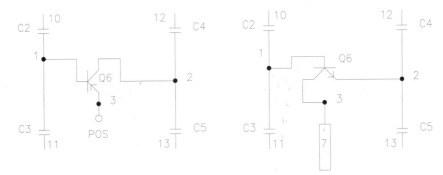

Figure 41.10   Result of applying the
Q_POS15V_EMIT_PNP function

Figure 41.11   Result of applying the
QVIAC7 function

and the port numbered 7. The base of the transistor is connected to the negative end of the modifiable wire or modifiable component (node 1) and the emitter is connected to its positive end (node 2). The collector is connected to the port numbered 7.

41.1.17   QVIAB Functions

Each of the eight functions in the QVIAB ("transistor with via from base") family of zero-argument functions (called QVIAB0, . . . , QVIAB7) causes the modifiable wire or modifiable component in the developing circuit structure that is linked to this function in the circuit-constructing program tree to be changed into a transistor whose base is connected to a numbered port (via). The writing head is lost by the execution of a QVIAB function. This function resembles the QVIAC function.

The QVIAB function replaces the modifiable wire or modifiable component with a transistor whose emitter is connected to the negative end of the modifiable wire or modifiable component, whose collector is connected to the positive end of the modifiable wire or modifiable component, and whose base is connected to a particular numbered port.

Figure 41.12 shows the result of applying the QVIAB7 function to the modifiable wire Z0 of Figure 25.9, thereby creating a transistor Q6 positioned between node 1, node 2, and the port numbered 7.

41.1.18   QVIAE Functions

Each of the eight functions in the QVIAE ("transistor with via from emitter") family of zero-argument functions (called QVIAE0, . . . , QVIAE7) causes the modifiable wire or modifiable component in the developing circuit structure that is linked to this function in the circuit-constructing program tree to be changed into a transistor whose emitter is connected to a numbered port (via). The writing hed is lost by the execution of a QVIAE function. This function resembles the QVIAC function.

The QVIAE function replaces the modifiable wire or modifiable component with a transistor whose collector is connected to the negative end of the modifiable wire or modifiable component, whose base is connected to the positive end of the modifiable

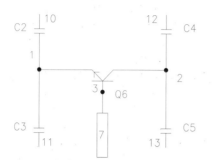

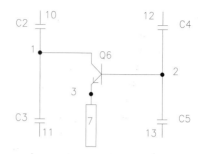

Figure 41.12 Result of applying the QVIAB7 function

Figure 41.13 Result of applying the QVIAE7 function

wire or modifiable component, and whose emitter is connected to a particular numbered port.

Figure 41.13 shows the result of applying the QVIAE7 function to the modifiable wire **Z0** of Figure 25.9, thereby creating a transistor **Q6** between node 1, node 2, and the port numbered 7.

41.1.19 Q_DIODE_NPN Function

The one-argument Q_DIODE_NPN function causes the modifiable wire or modifiable component to which it is linked to be changed into the equivalent of a diode. Specifically, an *npn* transistor is inserted in lieu of the modifiable wire or modifiable component in such a way that its collector and base are connected to each other and are, in turn, connected to the node at the positive end of the modifiable wire or modifiable component. The emitter of the new transistor is connected to the node at the negative end of the modifiable wire or modifiable component.

Figure 41.14 shows the result of applying the Q_DIODE_NPN function to the modifiable wire **Z0** of Figure 25.9.

41.1.20 Q_DIODE_PNP Function

The one-argument Q_DIODE_PNP function causes the modifiable wire or modifiable component to which it is linked to be changed into the equivalent of a diode. Specifically, a *pnp* transistor is inserted in lieu of the modifiable wire or modifiable component in such a way that its collector and base are connected to each other and are, in turn, connected to the node at the negative end of the modifiable wire or modifiable component. The emitter of the new transistor is connected to the node at the positive end of the modifiable wire or modifiable component.

Figure 41.15 shows the result of applying the Q_DIODE_PNP function to the modifiable wire **Z0** of Figure 25.9.

41.1.21 Q_THREE_NPN Functions

All of the foregoing transistor-inserting functions were simplified by restraining the connectivity of one of the three leads of the transistor (e.g., to ground, to a specified power

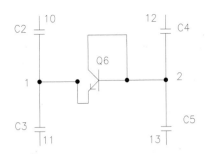

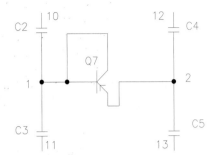

Figure 41.14   Result of Q_DIODE_NPN
function

Figure 41.15   Result of Q_DIODE_PNP
function

supply, or to a via). The Q_THREE_NPN transistor-inserting functions described in this section are more complicated than the foregoing functions because none of the three leads of the transistor are similarly restrained. This flexibility means that there are 12 possible ways of executing this function. The modifiable wire that is altered by the Q_THREE_NPN function has only two leads (preexisting nodes 1 and 2 in Figure 25.9), whereas the to-be-inserted transistor has three leads. The third lead is accommodated by bifurcating one of the two preexisting nodes. There are 12 members of the Q_THREE_NPN family of functions because there are two choices of the node to be bifurcated (either preexisting node 1 or 2) and there are six ways of attaching the transistor's base, collector, and emitter to the three nodes that exist after the bifurcation. Since we require that all circuit-constructing functions be deterministic, there are 12 members (called Q_THREE_NPN0, . . . , Q_THREE_NPN11) in the family of Q_THREE_NPN transistor-inserting functions.

Each of the 12 functions in the Q_THREE_NPN family of three-argument transistor-creating functions causes an *npn* transistor to be inserted in place of the modifiable wire or modifiable component and one of the nodes to which the modifiable wire or modifiable component is connected. Each Q_THREE_NPN function also creates five new nodes and three new modifiable wires. After execution of a Q_THREE_NPN function, there are three writing heads that point to three new modifiable wires. Since there is no writing head on the new transistor itself, a transistor remains in the developing circuit structure once it is inserted by a Q_THREE_NPN function. That is, a transistor created by the Q_THREE_NPN function cannot be overwritten during the developmental process.

The 12 Q_THREE_NPN functions operate in slightly different ways depending on the polarity of the original modifiable wire or modifiable component, the numbering of existing components in the circuit, and the degree of the nodes to which the modifiable wire or modifiable component is connected.

First Case

First consider the case where both nodes of the modifiable wire or modifiable component (i.e., nodes 1 and 2 of the modifiable wire of Figure 25.9) are of degree 3. As will be seen, the 12 Q_THREE_NPN functions produce 12 distinct results in this situation.

The first six functions ($Q\_THREE\_NPN0, \ldots, Q\_THREE\_NPN5$) insert the transistor at the node to which the positive end of the modifiable wire or modifiable component is connected; the second six functions ($Q\_THREE\_NPN6, \ldots, Q\_THREE\_NPN11$) insert the transistor at the negative end. That is, $Q\_THREE\_NPN0, \ldots, Q\_THREE\_NPN5$ cause the node to which the positive end of the modifiable wire or modifiable component is connected to become the "active" node; $Q\_THREE\_NPN6, \ldots, Q\_THREE\_NPN11$ cause the node to which the negative end of the modifiable wire or modifiable component is connected to become the "active" node.

The operation of the six functions in these two subsets depends on the numbering of three existing components in the circuit that are connected to the "active" node (i.e., the node that is to be converted into a transistor). Since there are six possible permutations of three objects, there are six possible ways of connecting the collector, base, and emitter of the new transistor.

Table 41.2 identifies the lead of the new transistor (collector, base, and emitter) that is to become connected to the lowest-numbered, middle-numbered, and highest-numbered existing component at an active node of degree 3.

For example, suppose that the Q_THREE_NPN0 function is applied to the modifiable wire **Z0** of Figure 25.9. Since Q_THREE_NPN0 is in the first subset (i.e., $Q\_THREE\_NPN0, \ldots, Q\_THREE\_NPN5$), Q_THREE_NPN0 operates on the positive end of the modifiable wire or modifiable component, **Z0**. That is, node 2 is the "active" node that will be converted into a transistor (and node 1 is the "passive" node). The three existing components at active node 2 of Figure 25.9 are **Z0**, **C4**, and **C5**. Table 41.2 specifies that the collector of the new transistor is to be connected to the lowest-numbered component, that the base is to be connected to the middle-numbered component (i.e., **C4** of Figure 25.9), and that the emitter is to be connected to the highest-numbered component (i.e., **C5** of Figure 25.9).

Figure 41.16 shows the result of applying the Q_THREE_NPN0 function to the modifiable wire **Z0** of Figure 25.9, thereby creating a transistor **Q6** in lieu of **R1** and node 2:

1. The Q_THREE_NPN0 function creates three new modifiable wires (**Z7**, **Z8**, and **Z9**) and five new nodes (14, 15, 16, 17, and 18).

2. The first new wire (**Z7**) connects the passive node (i.e., node 1) and one lead of the new transistor at new node 18. The polarity of this new wire is established by the polarity of the end of the original component that is connected to the passive node (i.e., by the fact that the negative end of the original modifiable wire **Z0** is connected to node 1). Thus, node 1 is connected to the negative end of **Z7** and node 18 is connected to the positive end of **Z7**.

3. The active node (i.e., node 2) is replaced by the two new nodes 14 and 16.

4. The second new wire (**Z8**) connects new node 14 to new node 15. This new wire acquires its polarity based on whether the positive or negative end of the original modifiable wire or modifiable component is positive or negative at the active node (i.e., node 2).

5. The third new wire (**Z9**) connects new node 16 to new node 17. This new wire acquires its polarity in the same manner as new wire **Z8**.

Table 41.2 Operation of the Q_THREE_NPN functions when the active node is of degree 3

Functions	Lowest-numbered component	Middle-numbered component	Highest-numbered component
Q_THREE_NPN0, Q_THREE_NPN6	Collector	Base	Emitter
Q_THREE_NPN1, Q_THREE_NPN7	Collector	Emitter	Base
Q_THREE_NPN2, Q_THREE_NPN8	Base	Collector	Emitter
Q_THREE_NPN3, Q_THREE_NPN9	Base	Emitter	Collector
Q_THREE_NPN4, Q_THREE_NPN10	Emitter	Collector	Base
Q_THREE_NPN5, Q_THREE_NPN11	Emitter	Base	Collector

6. The collector, base, and emitter leads of the new transistor are connected to new nodes 18, 15, and 17, respectively, in the manner specified by the entries in Table 41.2 for the particular Q_THREE_NPN function being executed.

The following one line is the netlist created by this Q_THREE_NPN0 function:

```
Q6 18 15 17 Q2N3904
```

The interpretation of this one line is that the collector of transistor Q6 is connected to node 18, the base of the transistor is connected to node 15, the emitter of the transistor is connected to node 17, and the model of the *npn* bipolar junction transistor is Q2N3904.

As a second example, suppose that the Q_THREE_NPN8 function is applied to the modifiable wire **Z0** of Figure 25.9. Since Q_THREE_NPN8 is in the second subset (i.e., Q_THREE_NPN6, . . . , Q_THREE_NPN11), Q_THREE_NPN8 operates on the negative end of the modifiable wire, **Z0**. That is, node 1 is the "active" node that will be converted into a transistor, and node 2 is the "passive" node. The three existing components at node 2 are **Z0**, **C2**, and **C3**.

Table 41.2 shows that the base of the new transistor is to be connected to the lowest-numbered component (i.e., **Z0**), that the collector is to be connected to the middle-numbered component (i.e., **C2**), and that the emitter is to be connected to the highest-numbered component (i.e., **C3**).

Figure 41.17 shows the result of applying the Q_THREE_NPN8 function to the modifiable wire **Z0** of Figure 25.9, thereby creating a transistor **Q6**.

Second Case

Now consider the case where one node of the modifiable wire or modifiable component is of degree 3 and the other node is of degree 2. In this case, the one node of degree 3 is the active node, and the other node is the inactive node. Table 41.2 applies in the same manner as before.

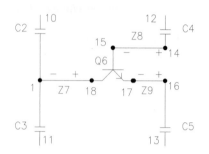

Figure 41.16 Result of applying the Q_THREE_NPN0 function

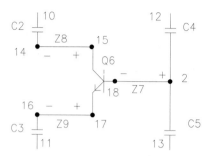

Figure 41.17 Result of applying the Q_THREE_NPN8 function

Third Case

Finally, consider the case where both nodes of the modifiable wire or modifiable component are of degree 2. Figure 41.18 shows a modifiable wire or modifiable component that is connected to two nodes of degree 2.

As before, the first six functions (Q_THREE_NPN0, . . . , Q_THREE_NPN5) insert the transistor at the node to which the positive end of the modifiable wire or modifiable component is connected, while the second six functions (Q_THREE_NPN6, . . . , Q_THREE_NPN11) insert the transistor at the negative end.

Table 41.3 identifies the lead (collector, base, or emitter) of the new transistor that is to become connected to the modifiable wire or modifiable component at the passive node and the two leads that are to become connected to the new modifiable wires that connect to the other component at the active node.

For example, suppose that the Q_THREE_NPN7 (or Q_THREE_NPN10) function is applied to the modifiable component **R1** of Figure 41.18. Since Q_THREE_NPN7 is in the second subset (i.e., Q_THREE_NPN6, . . . , Q_THREE_NPN11), Q_THREE_NPN7 operates on the negative end of the modifiable component, **R1**. That is, node 1 is the "active" node that will be converted into a transistor, and node 2 is the "passive" node. The two existing components at active node 1 are **R1** and **C2**. New wire **Z7** is connected to the passive node. Table 41.3 shows that the base of the new transistor is to be connected to the new wire at the passive node and that the collector and emitter are both to be connected to the other component that is connected to the new modifiable wires that are connected to the active node (i.e., **C2**).

Figure 41.19 shows the result of applying the Q_THREE_NPN7 function to the resistor **R1** of Figure 41.18, thereby creating a transistor **Q6**.

For purposes of creating the initial random population at generation 0, all the functions that belong to a family of functions are weighted so that the cumulative probability of choosing one of the functions of the family equals the probability of selecting any other function from the function set. Thus, for example, each of the 12 Q_THREE_NPN functions has a probability of being chosen equal to $\frac{1}{12}$ of the probability of choosing, say, the inductor-creating L function or the capacitor-creating C function. This weighted approach is used for all other similar families of functions in this book.

Table 41.3 Operation of the `Q_THREE_NPN` **functions when both the active and inactive nodes are of degree 2**

Functions	New wire at passive node	The other component at the active node
`Q_THREE_NPN0`, `Q_THREE_NPN2`, `Q_THREE_NPN6`, `Q_THREE_NPN8`	Emitter	Collector and Base
`Q_THREE_NPN1`, `Q_THREE_NPN4`, `Q_THREE_NPN7`, `Q_THREE_NPN10`	Base	Collector and Emitter
`Q_THREE_NPN3`, `Q_THREE_NPN5`, `Q_THREE_NPN9`, `Q_THREE_NPN11`	Collector	Base and Emitter

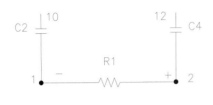

Figure 41.18   Resistor R1 connected to two nodes of degree 2

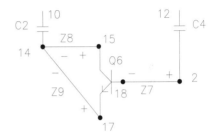

Figure 41.19   Result of applying the `Q_THREE_NPN7` **function when both the active and inactive nodes are of degree 2**

41.1.22   `Q_THREE_PNP` Functions

Each of the 12 functions in the `Q_THREE_PNP` family of three-argument transistor-creating functions (called `Q_THREE_PNP0`, ..., `Q_THREE_PNP11`) operates in a manner similar to the `Q_THREE_NPN` functions and causes a *pnp* transistor to be inserted in place of the modifiable wire or modifiable component and one of the nodes to which the modifiable wire or modifiable component is connected.

41.1.23   `DIGITAL_INVERTER` Function

The two-argument `DIGITAL_INVERTER` (negation) function causes the modifiable wire or modifiable component to which it is linked to be changed into a digital inverter component.

Figure 41.20 shows the result of applying the `DIGITAL_INVERTER` function to the modifiable wire Z0 of Figure 25.9, thereby creating a digital inverter NOT7 connecting nodes 1 and 2 in lieu of modifiable wire Z0 of Figure 25.9.

41.1.24   `DIGITAL_AND` Gate Functions

The 12 functions in the family of three-argument `DIGITAL_AND` functions (`DIGITAL_AND0`, ..., `DIGITAL_AND11`) convert the modifiable wire or modifiable component into a `DIGITAL_AND` gate in the same manner as the `Q_THREE_NPN` functions convert a modifiable wire or modifiable component into a three-leaded transistor. The

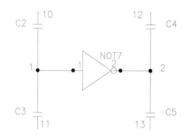

Figure 41.20   Result of applying the DIGITAL_INVERTER function to modifiable wire Z0

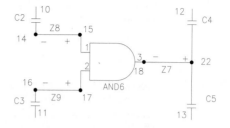

Figure 41.21   Result of applying the DIGITAL_AND6 function to modifiable wire Z0

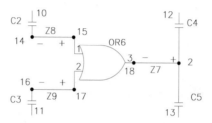

Figure 41.22   Result of applying the DIGITAL_OR6 function to modifiable wire Z0

DIGITAL_AND function creates three new modifiable wires and has three construction-continuing subtrees.

Figure 41.21 shows the result of applying the DIGITAL_AND6 function to the modifiable wire Z0 of Figure 25.9, thereby creating an AND gate AND6.

41.1.25   DIGITAL_OR Gate Functions

The 12 functions in the family of three-argument DIGITAL_OR functions (OR0, ..., OR11) convert the modifiable wire or modifiable component into a DIGITAL_OR gate in the same manner as the Q_THREE_NPN functions convert a modifiable wire or modifiable component into a three-leaded transistor. The DIGITAL_OR function creates three new modifiable wires and has three construction-continuing subtrees.

Figure 41.22 shows the result of applying the DIGITAL_OR6 function to the modifiable wire Z0 of Figure 25.9, thereby creating a digital OR gate OR6.

41.1.26   TRANSFORMER Functions

Although we do not use transformers in any circuit in this book, we include a discussion of the TRANSFORMER functions in order to illustrate how our system for automatically synthesizing circuits might be used to handle a four-leaded component.

A transformer changes the voltage of an alternating current signal on its two coils in accordance with its turns ratio. For example, a transformer might step up the voltage of the signal on its primary coil by a factor of 10 and make the new higher voltage signal available on its secondary coil. The turns ratio is fixed at the time of manufacture of the transformer.

The six functions in the TRANSFORMER family of five-argument functions (called TRANSFORMER0, . . . , TRANSFORMER5) create eight new nodes and four new modifiable wires and cause the modifiable wire or modifiable component to be changed into a transformer. After execution of a TRANSFORMER function, there are four writing heads. That is, the TRANSFORMER function creates four new modifiable wires and has four construction-continuing subtrees. They point to four new modifiable wires that are connected to the four leads of the new transformer. Since there is no writing head on the new transformer itself, a transformer remains in the developing circuit structure once it is inserted by a TRANSFORMER function.

The arity of a TRANSFORMER function is five because one of its arguments is the arithmetic-performing subtree to establish the turns ratio and the remaining arguments are the four construction-continuing subtrees. If there were only one transformer available for insertion into a developing circuit structure, the arithmetic-performing subtree for the turns ratio could be eliminated, and the TRANSFORMER function would then have four arguments.

Two of the four leads of a transformer relate to one coil of the transformer, and the other two leads relate to the second coil. The two leads relating to any one coil are interchangeable. However, the two coils are not interchangeable; one is the primary coil, and the other is the secondary coil. Thus, the six potentially different results produced by the TRANSFORMER function arise from the three different ways of partitioning four objects into two subsets of two objects and the two different ways of assigning the two coils.

When both nodes of the modifiable wire or modifiable component (i.e., nodes 1 and 2 of Figure 25.9) are of degree 3, the six TRANSFORMER functions produce six distinct results. The results of applying any of the TRANSFORMER functions to nodes 1 and 2 of Figure 25.9 are as follows:

1. The TRANSFORMER function creates four new modifiable wires (Z6, Z7, Z8, and Z9) and eight new nodes (3, 4, 5, 6, 14, 15, 16, and 17).
2. The two leads of the primary coil (marked "Hi" in Figures 41.23–41.28) of the transformer are connected to new nodes 3 and 4.
3. The two leads of the secondary coil (marked "Lo" in Figures 41.23–41.28) of the transformer are connected to new nodes 5 and 6.
4. Node 1 is replaced by two new nodes, 14 and 15. Node 2 is replaced by two new nodes, 16 and 17.

Table 41.4 applies when both nodes of the modifiable wire or modifiable component are of degree 3. The table identifies the four new nodes (3, 4, 5, and 6) that are to become connected to the lower-numbered component at the positive end of the modifiable wire or modifiable component, the higher-numbered component at the positive end of the modifiable wire or modifiable component, the lower-numbered component at the negative end of the modifiable wire or modifiable component, and the higher-numbered component at the negative end of the modifiable wire or modifiable component.

Figures 41.23 through 41.28 illustrate the result of applying the TRANSFORMER functions to modifiable wire Z0 of Figure 25.9.

If node 1 is of degree 2, then wires Z6 and Z8 terminate at the same point. Similarly, if node 2 is of degree 2, then wires Z7 and Z9 terminate at the same node.

Table 41.4 Operation of the TRANSFORMER functions when both nodes of the modifiable wire or modifiable component are of degree 3

Functions	Lower-numbered component at positive end	Higher-numbered component at positive end	Lower-numbered component at negative end	Higher-numbered component at negative end
TRANSFORMER0	3	4	5	6
TRANSFORMER1	3	5	4	6
TRANSFORMER2	3	6	5	4
TRANSFORMER3	6	5	4	3
TRANSFORMER4	6	4	5	3
TRANSFORMER5	6	3	4	5

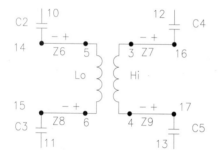

Figure 41.23   Result of applying the TRANSFORMER0 function

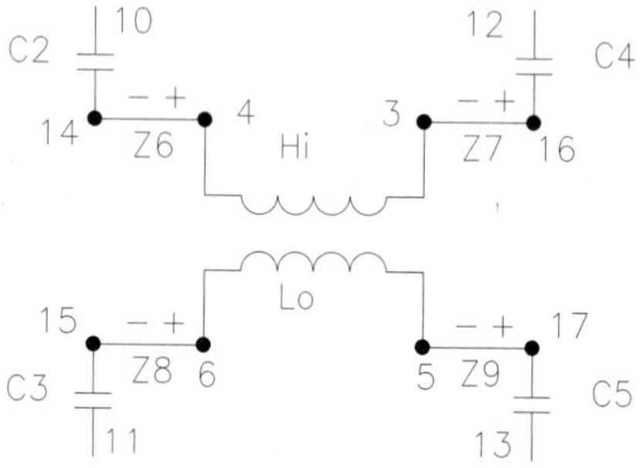

Figure 41.24   Result of applying the TRANSFORMER1 function

Transformers are unusual in that the two leads going to each of their coils are interchangeable provided that the phase is not an issue. If the phase is an issue, all four leads of the transformer are behaviorally distinct. In that event, there would be 24 members of the transformer-inserting family of functions. The general principles used in defining the TRANSFORMER family of functions can be applied to any four-leaded component with four behaviorally distinct leads.

41.1.27   TWO_LEAD_OP_AMP Functions

The functions that are inserted into developing circuit structures by component-creating functions need not be as elementary as resistors, capacitors, inductors, diodes, and transistors. Instead, a complex predefined structure can be inserted into a developing circuit structure.

For example, although an operational amplifier (op amp) may itself be composed of dozens of primitive components (e.g., transistors and capacitors), a component-creating function may be defined that inserts an op amp into a developing circuit structure as if the op amp were merely a single component. Filters may be similarly treated as primi-

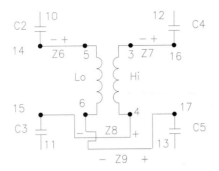

Figure 41.25 Result of applying the TRANSFORMER2 function

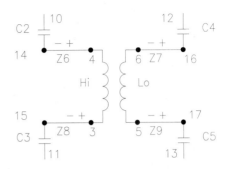

Figure 41.26 Result of applying the TRANSFORMER3 function

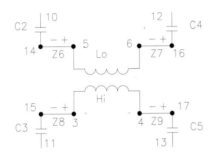

Figure 41.27 Result of applying the TRANSFORMER4 function

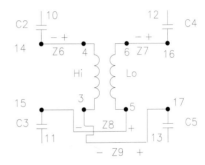

Figure 41.28 Result of applying the TRANSFORMER5 function

tives (as we did in Chapter 35), so that large and complex circuits can be synthesized from compositions of filters, amplifiers, and other devices.

In its most common form, an op amp is a component with five distinct leads. Its first two leads are the inputs to the op amp. A third lead is typically connected to a fixed positive power supply, and a fourth lead is typically connected to a fixed negative power supply. An op amp takes the difference between its two input voltages and produces the product of that difference and a constant A (the voltage amplification factor) as its output at the fifth lead.

It is sometimes useful to consider op amps with fewer than five distinct leads. For example, it is common to connect the third and fourth leads of an op amp to two fixed voltage sources. Thus, in the three-leaded version of an op amp, these two leads are not free, but instead are hard-wired to these two fixed voltage sources. Moreover, in the simplest form of op amp, one of the two input leads is connected to ground. In this special case, the op amp merely amplifies the one input signal by the voltage amplification factor, A.

First consider the TWO_LEAD_OP_AMP functions. The two functions in the TWO_LEAD_OP_AMP family of two-argument functions (TWO_LEAD_OP_AMP0 and TWO_LEAD_OP_AMP1) convert the modifiable wire or modifiable component into an op

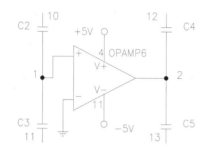

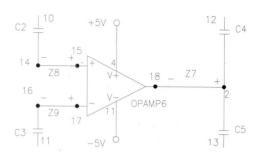

Figure 41.29 Result of applying the TWO_LEAD_OP_AMP1 function to modifiable wire Z0

Figure 41.30 Result of applying the THREE_LEAD_OP_AMP1 function to modifiable wire Z̄0

amp. After execution of a TWO_LEAD_OP_AMP function, there is one writing head. It points to the original component and the two copies.

The TWO_LEAD_OP_AMP0 function converts the modifiable wire or modifiable component into an op amp whose positive input lead is connected to the positive end of the modifiable wire or modifiable component (node 2 in Figure 25.9) and whose output lead is connected to the negative end of the modifiable wire or modifiable component (node 1 in Figure 25.9). The TWO_LEAD_OP_AMP1 function inserts the op amp in the opposite orientation. Figure 41.29 shows the result of applying the TWO_LEAD_OP_AMP1 function.

41.1.28 THREE_LEAD_OP_AMP Functions

When an op amp is being used to take the difference between two input voltages and then amplify the difference by the voltage amplification factor, it is useful to have the THREE_LEAD_OP_AMP functions.

The 12 functions in the THREE_LEAD_OP_AMP family of three-argument functions (THREE_LEAD_OP_AMP0, . . . , THREE_LEAD_OP_AMP11) convert the modifiable wire or modifiable component into an op amp in the same manner that the Q_THREE_NPN functions convert a modifiable wire or modifiable component into a three-lead transistor. After execution of a THREE_LEAD_OP_AMP function, there are three writing heads that point to three new modifiable wires. The THREE_LEAD_OP_AMP functions are sufficient for a wide range of practical circuits.

Figure 41.30 shows the result of applying the THREE_LEAD_OP_AMP1 function. Its positive input lead is connected to the new modifiable wire connected to the lower-numbered component connected to the negative end of the modifiable wire or modifiable component. Its negative lead is connected to the new modifiable wire connected to the higher-numbered component connected to the negative end of the modifiable wire or modifiable component. Its output lead is connected to the positive end of the modifiable wire or modifiable component (node 2 in Figure 25.9).

41.1.29 FIVE_LEAD_OP_AMP Functions

The five-argument FIVE_LEAD_OP_AMP functions provide more flexibility in assigning the leads of an op amp.

There are 120 possible ways of permuting the five distinct leads of an op amp. In addition, there are four distinct ways of inserting an op amp into a developing circuit structure when each node of the modifiable wire or modifiable component is of degree 3 (using the method described below). Thus, there are potentially 480 different FIVE_LEAD_OP_AMP functions in this family of functions. Only one of the 120 permutations will be described here (namely, the four of the 480 distinct FIVE_LEAD_OP_AMP functions that apply to the case where the five leads of the op amp are not permuted at all).

The principles used in defining the FIVE_LEAD_OP_AMP family of component-creating functions can be applied to any component with five behaviorally distinct leads.

The four functions in the FIVE_LEAD_OP_AMP family of five-argument functions (called FIVE_LEAD_OP_AMP0, . . . , FIVE_LEAD_OP_AMP3) create seven new nodes and five new modifiable wires and cause the modifiable wire or modifiable component along with another existing component to be changed into an op amp. After execution of a FIVE_LEAD_OP_AMP function, there are five writing heads. They point to five new modifiable wires that are connected to the five leads of the new op amp. Since there is no writing head on the new op amp itself, an op amp remains in the developing circuit structure once it is inserted by a FIVE_LEAD_OP_AMP function.

Figure 41.31 shows a portion of a circuit in which a resistor R1 has a writing head and both of its leads are connected to nodes of degree 3. Note that resistor R7 is the higher-numbered component that is connected to the same node as the positive end of the modifiable component (R1).

When both nodes of the modifiable wire or modifiable component (i.e., nodes 1 and 2 for resistor R1 in Figure 41.31) are of degree 3 and the end of the second to-be-deleted component (R7) that is not shared with the first to-be-deleted component at node 3 is of degree 3, then the four FIVE_LEAD_OP_AMP functions (associated with one of the 120 permutations) produce four distinct results.

The FIVE_LEAD_OP_AMP functions will delete the modifiable component R1 as well as one additional component that is connected to one of the nodes of R1. The distinction among FIVE_LEAD_OP_AMP0, . . . , FIVE_LEAD_OP_AMP3 lies in the identity of the second to-be-deleted component. For example, FIVE_LEAD_OP_AMP1 deletes the higher-numbered component at the node to which the positive end of R1 is connected, namely, R7.

The results of applying the FIVE_LEAD_OP_AMP3 function to nodes 1 and 2 of the figure are as follows:

1. The FIVE_LEAD_OP_AMP3 function creates five new modifiable wires (Z8, Z9, Z10, Z11, and Z12) and seven new nodes (15, 16, 17, 18, 19, 20, and 21).
2. The positive input of the op amp is connected to new node 18, and the negative input of the op amp is connected to new node 17.
3. The lead that is typically connected to a positive power supply (conventionally designated V+ in the literature for op amps) is connected to new node 19, and the lead that is typically connected to a negative power supply (conventionally designated V−) is connected to new node 16.
4. The output of the op amp is connected to new node 15.
5. The node to which the negative end of R1 was originally connected is replaced with new node 20. The lower-numbered component (excluding R1) to which the

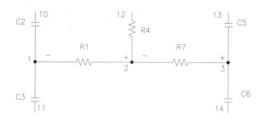

Figure 41.31   Circuit with resistor R1

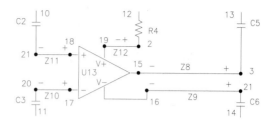

**Figure 41.32   Result of applying the
FIVE_LEAD_OP_AMP3 function to resistor R1**

negative end of R1 was originally connected (i.e., capacitor C2) is connected to node 21, while the higher-numbered component (i.e., capacitor C3) is connected to new node 20.

6. The node connected to the second-to-be-deleted component (and that is not connected to R1) (i.e., node 3) is replaced with new node 21. The lower-numbered component (excluding the second to-be-deleted component) to which node 3 was originally connected remains connected to node 3, while the higher-numbered component becomes connected to new node 21.

7. Node 2 is disconnected from both R1 and the second to-be-deleted component.

8. New modifiable wire Z8 is connected between nodes 15 and 3. Z9 is connected between nodes 16 and 21. Z10 is connected between nodes 17 and 20. Z11 is connected between nodes 21 and 18. Z12 is connected between nodes 19 and 2.

Figure 41.32 illustrates the result of applying the FIVE_LEAD_OP_AMP3 function to resistor R1 of Figure 41.31.

The FIVE_LEAD_OP_AMP function illustrates how any other component with five (or more) leads may be inserted so as to replace a node (point), an edge (line), and additional adjacent component(s).

41.1.30   Subcircuit Definitions in SPICE

SPICE supports subcircuit definition using the SUBCKT command. Subcircuits permit combinations of components to be defined once and then included in the netlist of a circuit. The subcircuit definitions may or may not have formal parameters (dummy variables). See Chapter 35 for an example of a run of genetic programming using subcircuits.

41.1.31   Other Component-Creating Functions

The above component-creating functions are illustrative of the generality and flexibility of the automated design system. Many other component-creating functions can be utilized to accommodate the requirements of particular classes of circuits or particular topological arrangements of circuit elements.

41.2   COMPLETE REPERTOIRE OF TOPOLOGY-MODIFYING FUNCTIONS

The topology of a circuit is determined by the topology-modifying functions. This section presents a complete repertoire of topology-modifying functions that are used in this book (as well as some additional functions that are illustrative of the flexibility of our system for automatic circuit synthesis).

Each topology-modifying function in a circuit-constructing program tree is linked to a particular modifiable wire or modifiable component and modifies the topology of the developing circuit structure in some way. Each topology-modifying function has a specified number (zero, one, or more) of construction-continuing subtrees. Each topology-modifying function (except CUT) leaves the number of lines impinging at any one node in the circuit at either two or three.

Some topology-modifying functions are context-free, and some are context-sensitive. When a topology-modifying function is context-free, the outcome depends only on the single modifiable wire or modifiable component to which the topology-modifying function is linked. When a topology-modifying function is context-sensitive, the outcome also depends on other nearby elements of the circuit structure.

Table 41.5 is a complete repertoire of the topology-modifying functions. The table shows the name of the function, a description of the function, its arity, and a reference to a section in this book.

The set of functions in this table is illustrative of the many possible different topology-modifying functions that may be employed in an automated circuit synthesis methodology using genetic programming. Many other topology-modifying functions can be created.

41.2.1   SERIES Division Function

The three-argument SERIES division function was previously described in Section 25.8.1.

41.2.2   PARALLEL0 and PARALLEL1 Parallel Division Functions

The two four-argument functions in the PARALLEL family of parallel division functions (PARALLEL0 and PARALLEL1) were previously described in Section 25.8.2.

41.2.3   FLIP Function

The one-argument polarity-reversing FLIP function was previously described in Section 25.8.3.

41.2.4   The Y Division Functions

The two functions in the Y family of three-argument division functions (called Y0 and Y1) operate on one modifiable wire or modifiable component and create a Y-shaped composition consisting of the modifiable wire or modifiable component, two copies of the modifiable wire or modifiable component, and two new nodes. After execution of a Y function, there are three writing heads. They point to the original component and the two copies.

The Y functions insert the two copies at the "active" node of the modifiable wire or modifiable component. For the Y0 function, the active node is the node to which the

Table 41.5 Topology-modifying functions

Name	Short description	Arity	Section
CUT	Cuts a component out of a circuit	0	25.8.8
DELTA0, DELTA1	Triangle-shaped division	6	41.2.5
FLIP	Polarity-reversing function	1	25.8.3
INPUT	Zero-argument via to circuit's input	0	53.1
OUTPUT	Zero-argument via to circuit's output	0	53.1
PAIR_CONNECT0, PAIR_CONNECT1	Connects a pair of nodes	3	25.8.10
PARALLEL0, PARALLEL1	Parallel division	4	25.8.2
RETAINING_THREE_GROUND_0, RETAINING_THREE_GROUND_1	Retaining version of three-argument ground	3	41.2.14
RETAINING_THREE_POS5V0, RETAINING_THREE_POS5V_1	Retaining version of three-argument via to a +5.0-volt power supply	3	41.2.15
RETAINING_THREE_NEG5V0, RETAINING_THREE_NEG5V_1	Retaining version of three-argument via to a −5.0-volt power supply	3	41.2.15
RETAINING_THREE_POS15V_0, RETAINING_THREE_POS15V_1	Retaining version of three-argument via to a +15.0-volt power supply	3	41.2.16
RETAINING_THREE_NEG15V_0, RETAINING_THREE_NEG15V_1	Retaining version of three-argument via to a −15.0-volt power supply	3	41.2.16
SAFE_CUT	Protected version of CUT	0	25.8.9
SERIES	Series division	3	25.8.1
THREE_GROUND	Three-argument via to ground	3	25.8.7
THREE_NEG15V	Three-argument via to a −15.0-volt power supply	3	41.2.13
THREE_POS15V	Three-argument via to a +15.0-volt power supply	3	41.2.13
THREE_VIA0 through THREE_VIA7	Three-argument via functions	3	25.8.6
TWO_GROUND	Two-argument ground	2	25.8.5
TWO_NEG15V	Two-argument −15-volt power supply	2	41.2.10
TWO_POS15V	Two-argument +15-volt power supply	2	41.2.10
TWO_VIA0 through TWO_VIA7	Two-argument via functions	2	25.8.4
Y0, Y1	Y-shaped division	3	41.2.4
ZERO_GROUND	Zero-argument via to ground	0	53.1

positive end of the modifiable wire or modifiable component is connected. For the Y1 function, it is the negative end.

To illustrate the Y function, consider the results of applying the function to nodes 1 and 2 of resistor R1 of Figure 25.10:

1. The Y function renames the active node as node 3.
2. If the degree of the active node is 3, then the Y function creates two new nodes, 4 and 5; however, if the degree of the active node is only 2, then the Y function creates only one new node, 4.
3. The Y function inserts one duplicate (named R6) of the original component (including all its component values) between new node 3 and new node 4 (with the positive end of the duplicate being connected to node 3).
4. If the degree of the active node is 3, the Y function inserts a second duplicate (named R7) of the original component (including all its component values) between new node 3 and new node 5 (with the positive end of the duplicate being connected to node 3). However, if the degree of the active node is 2, then the Y function inserts the second duplicate (R7) of the original component between new node 3 and new node 4 (so that R6 and R7 are in parallel with each other between nodes 3 and 4). Nodes 4 and 5 connect to the negative end of R1.

Figure 41.33 illustrates the result of applying the Y1 division function to resistor R1 of Figure 25.10. Note that node 1 of Figure 25.10 is the active node for Y1 and is of degree 3.

The portion of the netlist for Figure 25.10 describing the single 5 Ω resistor R1 consists of the following five lines:

```
R1 2 1 5OHMS
C2 1 10
C3 1 11
C4 2 12
C5 2 13
```

The Y1 function changes the above into the following:

```
R1 2 3 5OHMS
R6 3 4 5OHMS
R7 3 5 5OHMS
C2 4 10
C3 5 11
C4 2 12
C5 2 13
```

If node 1 of Figure 25.10 were of degree 2, then the result would be the following (with the two differences from the above in bold):

```
R1 2 3 5OHMS
R6 3 4 5OHMS
R7 3 4 5OHMS
C2 4 10
C3 4 11
C4 2 12
C5 2 13
```

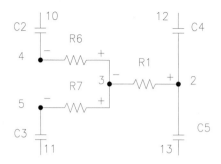

Figure 41.33 Result of applying the Y1 division function to resistor R1

Note that the Y0 and Y1 functions are examples (of several in this chapter) of context-sensitive component-creating functions.

41.2.5 DELTA Division Functions

The two functions in the DELTA family of six-argument functions (called DELTA0 and DELTA1) operate on one modifiable wire or modifiable component by eliminating it (and one adjacent node) and creating a triangular Δ–shaped composition consisting of three copies of the original modifiable wire or modifiable component (and all of its component values), three new modifiable wires, and five new nodes. After execution of a DELTA function, there are six writing heads. They point to the three copies and the three new wires.

The DELTA functions create the triangular composition at the "active" node of the modifiable wire or modifiable component. If the two nodes of the modifiable wire or modifiable component have different degrees, the active node is the node of degree 3. Otherwise, for the DELTA0 function, the active node is the node to which the positive end of the modifiable wire or modifiable component is connected, but, for the DELTA1 function, the active node is the node to which the negative end of the modifiable wire or modifiable component is connected.

When the active node is of degree 3, the DELTA1 function produces the following results when it is applied to nodes 1 and 2 of resistor R1 of Figure 25.10:

1. The DELTA1 function eliminates the modifiable wire or modifiable component, renames the active node as node 3, and creates a new modifiable wire Z5 between node 3 and the passive node.
2. The DELTA1 function creates four new nodes (4, 5, 6, and 7).
3. The DELTA1 function inserts one duplicate (named R6) of the original component (including all its component values) between new node 3 and new node 4 (with the positive end of the duplicate being connected to node 3) and a new modifiable wire (Z9) between new node 4 and new node 6.
4. The DELTA1 function inserts a second duplicate (named R7) of the original component between new nodes 3 and 5 (with the positive end of the duplicate being connected to node 3) and a new modifiable wire (Z10) between new node 5 and new node 7.

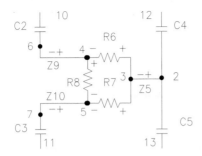 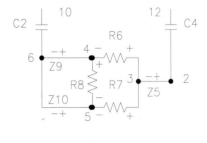

Figure 41.34   Result of applying the DELTA1 **division function to resistor R1 when the active node (node 1) is of degree 3**

Figure 41.35   Result of applying the DELTA1 **division function to resistor R1 when the active node (node 1) is of degree 2**

5.   The DELTA function inserts a third duplicate (named R8) of the original component between new nodes 4 and 5 (with the positive end of the duplicate being connected to node 4).

Figure 41.34 illustrates the result of applying the DELTA1 division function to resistor R1 of Figure 25.10 when the active node (node 1) is of degree 3.

When the active node is of degree 2, the DELTA1 function produces the following results when it is applied to nodes 1 and 2 of resistor R1 of Figure 25.10:

1.   The DELTA1 function renames the active node as node 3 and creates a new modifiable wire Z5 between node 3 and the passive node.
2.   The DELTA1 function creates three new nodes (4, 5, and 6).
3.   The DELTA1 function inserts one duplicate (named R6) of the original component (including all its component values) between new node 3 and new node 4 (with the positive end of the duplicate being connected to node 3) and a new modifiable wire (Z9) between new node 4 and new node 6.
4.   The DELTA1 function inserts a second duplicate (named R7) of the original component between new nodes 3 and 5 (with the positive end of the duplicate being connected to node 3) and a new modifiable wire (Z10) between new node 5 and new node 6.
5.   The DELTA1 function inserts a third duplicate (named R8) of the original component between new nodes 4 and 5 (with the positive end of the duplicate being connected to node 4).

Figure 41.35 illustrates the result of applying the DELTA1 division function to resistor R1 of Figure 25.10 when the active node (node 1) is of degree 2.

41.2.6   CUT **Function**

The zero-argument CUT function causes the modifiable wire or modifiable component in the developing circuit structure that is linked to this function in the circuit-constructing program tree to be removed from the circuit, as previously described in Section 25.8.8.

41.2.7   SAFE_CUT Function

The zero-argument SAFE_CUT function is similar to the CUT function, except that it only removes the modifiable wire or modifiable component if the degree of the nodes at both leads of the modifiable wire or modifiable component is more than two, as previously described in Section 25.8.9.

41.2.8   Two-Argument TWO_VIA Functions

The eight two-argument functions in the TWO_VIA family of functions (called TWO_VIA0, . . . , TWO_VIA7) enable distant parts of a circuit to be connected together, as previously described in Section 25.8.4.

41.2.9   Two-Argument TWO_GROUND Function

The two-argument TWO_GROUND ("ground") function enables any part of a circuit to be connected to ground, as previously described in Section 25.8.5.

41.2.10   Two-Argument TWO_POS15V and TWO_NEG15V Functions

The two-argument TWO_POS15V ("positive reference voltage source") function enables any part of a circuit to be connected to the constant positive (e.g., +15.0 volts) DC power source (e.g., a battery).

The TWO_NEG15V ("negative reference voltage source") function operates in a similar way.

41.2.11   Three-Argument THREE_VIA Functions

The eight three-argument functions in the THREE_VIA family of functions (called THREE_VIA0, . . . , THREE_VIA7) each enable distant parts of a circuit to be connected together, as described previously in Section 25.8.6.

41.2.12   Three-Argument THREE_GROUND Function

The three-argument THREE_GROUND function enables a part of a circuit to be connected directly to ground, as described previously in Section 25.8.7.

41.2.13   Three-Argument THREE_POS15V and THREE_NEG15V Functions

The three-argument THREE_POS15V function enables any part of a circuit to be connected to the +15.0-volt reference voltage source. The THREE_POS15V function creates a via to the +15.0-volt reference voltage source in a manner similar to the way that the three-argument THREE_GROUND function creates a via to ground. After execution of a THREE_POS15V function, there are three writing heads. They point to the three new modifiable wires.

Similarly, the three-argument THREE_NEG15V function enables any part of a circuit to be connected to the –15.0-volt DC power source.

41.2.14   Three-Argument RETAINING_THREE_GROUND Functions

The two functions in the RETAINING_THREE_GROUND family of three-argument functions (called RETAINING_THREE_GROUND0 and RETAINING_THREE_GROUND1) enable

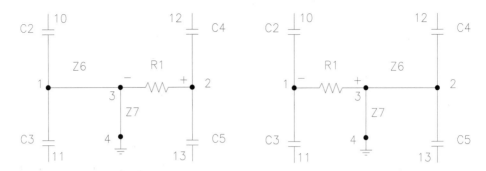

Figure 41.36   **The RETAINING_
THREE_GROUND_0 operator**

Figure 41.37   **The RETAINING_
THREE_GROUND_1 operator**

any part of a circuit to be connected to ground in a manner similar to the THREE_VIA functions. However, instead of replacing the modifiable wire or modifiable component with a wire, these functions retain the modifiable wire or modifiable component connected at its positive or negative end (for RETAINING_THREE_GROUND0 and RETAINING_THREE_GROUND1, respectively). Two new modifiable wires are created, and there are three writing heads after execution of a RETAINING_THREE_GROUND function. The three writing heads point to the two new wires and the preexisting modifiable wire or modifiable component.

We adopted this new pair of functions because we thought it might be desirable to have a version of the function that did not overwrite and obliterate the component on which it acts.

Figure 41.36 shows the results of applying the RETAINING_THREE_GROUND0 function to modifiable wire **R1** of Figure 25.10. The RETAINING_THREE_GROUND0 function changes the circuit by first severing the connection between the node at the negative end of **R1**, then connecting the negative end of **R1** to new node 3, adding a new modifiable wire **Z6** between node 1 and new node 3, and finally adding a new modifiable wire **Z7** between new node 3 and ground.

RETAINING_THREE_GROUND1 works similarly, but leaves the negative end of **R1** connected. Figure 41.37 shows the results of applying RETAINING_THREE_GROUND1 to Figure 25.10.

41.2.15   Three-Argument RETAINING_THREE_POS5V and RETAINING_THREE_NEG5V Functions

In a manner similar to the family of RETAINING_THREE_GROUND functions, the two RETAINING_THREE_POS5V_0 and RETAINING_THREE_POS5V_1 functions allow connections to the +5.0-volt DC voltage source. Similarly, the family of RETAINING_THREE_NEG5V_0 and RETAINING_THREE_NEG5V_1 functions allows connections to the −5.0-volt DC voltage source.

Table 41.6 Development-controlling functions

Name	Short description	Arity	Section
NOP	No operation	1	25.9.1
END	End	0	25.9.2

41.2.16 Three-Argument RETAINING_THREE_POS15V and RETAINING_THREE_NEG15V Functions

In a manner similar to the family of RETAINING_THREE_POS5V functions, the two RETAINING_THREE_POS15V_0 and RETAINING_THREE_POS15V_1 functions allow connections to the +15.0-volt DC voltage source. Similarly, the family of RETAINING_ THREE_NEG15V_0 and RETAINING_THREE_NEG15V_1 functions allows connections to the −15.0-volt DC voltage source.

41.2.17 PAIR_CONNECT Function

The three-argument PAIR_CONNECT function (previously described in Section 25.8.10) enables distant parts of a circuit to be connected together in a seemingly better manner than the THREE_VIA functions.

41.3 COMPLETE REPERTOIRE OF DEVELOPMENT-CONTROLLING FUNCTIONS

Development-controlling functions control the process of developing an initial circuit into a fully developed circuit.

Table 41.6 is a complete repertoire of the development-controlling functions. The table shows the name of the function, a short description of the function, its arity, and a reference to the section where the function is fully described.

The CUT function (Section 25.8.8) and SAFE_CUT function (Section 25.8.9) have characteristics of both development-controlling and topology-modifying functions. They appear above among the topology-modifying functions.

41.3.1 NOP Function

The one-argument NOP (no operation) function was previously described in Section 25.9.1.

41.3.2 END Function

The zero-argument development-terminating END function was previously described in Section 25.9.2.

41.4 COMPLETENESS OF CIRCUIT TOPOLOGIES

The topology-modifying functions (Section 41.2) and the development-controlling functions (Section 41.3) are capable of creating every possible circuit topology (Andre, Bennett, Koza, and Keane 1998).

Synthesis of a 10 dB Amplifier Using Transistors

In its simplest form, an amplifier is a one-input, one-output circuit that multiplies the voltage of its input signal by a voltage amplification factor, A, over a specified range of frequencies.

Amplifiers are active circuits in the sense that the signal power of the output can be greater than the signal power of the input. Active circuits cannot be realized merely with passive components such as resistors, capacitors, and inductors, but instead require active components, such as transistors and power sources.

The introduction of transistors into the parts bin significantly increases the complexity of problems of circuit synthesis. Transistors are more complex than resistors, capacitors, and inductors because they have three leads and their behavior is nonlinear.

This chapter describes our first evolved circuit employing transistors. This book continues the practice of *Genetic Programming* and *Genetic Programming II* of not merely presenting a single final result from a long series of experiments, but, instead, of also trying to convey a feeling for the progressive decision-making process by which we developed our system for automatic circuit synthesis. Thus, the discussion of our efforts to solve the problem of synthesizing active circuits starts with the initial low-gain amplifier described in this chapter. Even though the run in this chapter employed a highly simplified fitness measure and even though the evolved circuit delivers only a modest amount of amplification, the successful synthesis of this first amplifier established the principle that genetic programming can be successfully used to automatically synthesize (create) the design for both the topology and sizing of an analog electrical circuit employing transistors. Subsequent chapters (43 through 46) show the progression of our efforts to apply genetic programming to amplifiers that satisfy more stringent requirements. Each successive chapter reports on an experiment that, a priori, might or might not have succeeded. Each experiment that worked immediately led to an attempt to synthesize a more difficult circuit. Each experiment that revealed limitations in our methodology led to one or more modifications in the succeeding chapters.

The evolved 10 dB amplifier described in this chapter is interesting because, like the filters and other passive circuits appearing earlier in this book, it contains some topological substructures that are recognizable to electrical engineers.

We believe that the results concerning amplifiers in Chapters 42 through 46 (augmented by the results for the numerous other active circuits in Chapters 47 through 51) establish the principle that both active and passive electrical circuits can be designed by means of genetic programming.

Once this principle is established, we think that an appropriate future challenge is to extend the techniques described in this book so as to synthesize the design of circuits that satisfy the requirements of commercial circuits. Looking further into the future, the next extension would be to use genetic programming as an invention machine to create innovative designs for novel circuits.

42.1 DESIGN GOALS

The starting point for the design of an amplifier is the specification by the user of the voltage amplification factor, A, and the range of frequencies over which the amplifier is expected to deliver the desired amplification. In this section, the goal is to synthesize the design of an amplifier with a voltage amplification factor of 3.5 (10 dB) over the frequency range from 20 Hz to 20,000 Hz.

42.2 PREPARATORY STEPS

42.2.1 Embryo and Test Fixture

The one-input, one-output initial circuit (Figure 25.6) for this problem is created by embedding the embryo with two modifiable wires and three ports (Figure 29.9) into the one-input, one-output test fixture with three ports to the embryo (Figure 29.1).

The source resistor **RSOURCE** of the test fixture is 1,000 Ω, and the load resistor **RLOAD** is 8 Ω. The incoming alternating current signal source **VSOURCE** is 500 millivolts in peak amplitude. Since the desired voltage amplification factor is 3.5, the output amplitude should be 1.75 volts. This is equivalent to 10.88 dB of amplification (because 20 times the common logarithm of 3.5 is 10.88).

The initial circuit used on this problem contains only resistors and wires (in addition to the circuit's input, output, and connection to ground). It is well known that an amplifier cannot be created merely from these elements. The initial circuit composed of wires and resistors is merely the starting point of a multistep developmental process that transforms an initial circuit into a potentially useful fully developed circuit.

42.2.2 Program Architecture

Since the embryo has two modifiable wires, there are two result-producing branches in each program tree.

Neither automatically defined functions nor architecture-altering operations are used on this problem. Thus, the architecture of each program tree in the population consists uniformly of two result-producing branches.

42.2.3 Functions and Terminals

The terminal sets are identical for both result-producing branches of the program trees for this problem. The function sets are identical for both result-producing branches. The desired amplifier is to be composed of transistors, resistors, and capacitors.

The initial function set, $F_{\text{ccs-rpb-initial}}$, for the construction-continuing subtrees of the result-producing branches is

$F_{\text{ccs-rpb-initial}}$ = {R, C, Q_THREE_NPN0, . . . , Q_THREE_NPN11, SERIES, PARALLEL0, FLIP, NOP, THREE_GROUND, THREE_POS15V, THREE_VIA0, . . . , THREE_VIA7}.

The THREE_POS15V function and the 12 Q_THREE_NPN0, ..., Q_THREE_NPN11 functions are defined in Chapter 41. The Q_THREE_NPN0, ..., Q_THREE_NPN11 transistor-creating functions use the Q2N2222 model of an *npn* transistor for this problem. Note that *pnp* transistors are not used for this problem.

Circuits in this problem have access to the positive power supply (through the THREE_POS15V functions), but not the negative power supply.

The initial terminal set, $T_{\text{ccs-rpb-initial}}$, for the construction-continuing subtrees of the result-producing branches is

$T_{\text{ccs-rpb-initial}}$ = {END, CUT}.

Since there are no automatically defined functions in this problem, $T_{\text{adf-initial}}$ and $F_{\text{adf-initial}}$ are empty.

Since there are no architecture-altering operations in this problem, $T_{\text{rpb-potential}}$, $F_{\text{rpb-potential}}$, $T_{\text{adf-potential}}$, and $F_{\text{adf-potential}}$ are empty.

The function set, F_{aps}, for each arithmetic-performing subtree in any branch and the terminal set, T_{aps}, for each arithmetic-performing subtree in any branch are the same as for the lowpass filter problem in Section 25.14.3.

42.2.4   Fitness

For this problem, the voltage **VOUT** is viewed in the frequency domain.

The SPICE simulator is instructed to perform an AC small-signal analysis and to report the circuit's behavior for each of 151 frequency values chosen over three decades of frequency (from 20 Hz to 20,000 Hz). Each decade is divided into 50 parts (using a logarithmic scale).

Fitness is the sum, over the 151 fitness cases, of the absolute weighted deviation between the actual value of the relative voltage (i.e., relative to 1 volt) in the frequency domain that is produced by the circuit at the probe point **VOUT** at node 5 of Figure 25.6 and the target value of 10 dB of relative voltage.

The procedure for each of the 151 points in the interval from 20 Hz to 20,000 Hz is as follows:

- If the relative voltage is between 8 dB and 12 dB, the absolute value of the deviation from 10 dB is weighted by a factor of 1.0.
- If the relative voltage is outside this range, the absolute value of the deviation from 10 dB is weighted by a factor of 10.0.

This arrangement reflects the fact that the ideal relative voltage is 10 dB, the fact that a 2 dB variation is acceptable, and the fact that a deviation in relative voltage of more than 2 dB is not acceptable.

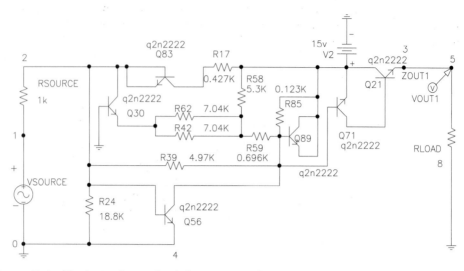

Figure 42.1   The best-of-run circuit from generation 45

The number of hits is defined as the number of fitness cases for which the voltage is acceptable or ideal. There are no "don't care" fitness cases for this problem. Thus, the number of hits ranges from 0 to 151 for this problem.

42.2.5   Parameters

The control parameters for this problem are found in the tableau (Table 42.1), the tables of percentages of genetic operations in Appendix D, and the default values specified in Appendix D.

42.2.6   Tableau

Table 42.1 summarizes the key features of the problem of designing a 10 dB amplifier.

42.3   RESULTS

The best-of-run circuit from generation 45 (Figure 42.1) has a fitness of 0.00329 and scores 151 hits (out of 151). The program tree has 109 and 115 points in its first and second result-producing branches, respectively. Since the sum of the weighted deviations from the target relative voltage is nearly zero, the desired voltage amplification factor of 3.5 (10 dB) is achieved over the desired frequency range.

Figure 42.2 shows the voltage delivered by the best-of-run circuit from generation 45. The horizontal axis represents the frequency of the incoming signal and ranges between 20 Hz and 20,000 Hz on a logarithmic scale. The vertical axis ranges linearly in the very narrow range between 1.778295 volts and 1.778310 volts.

Figure 42.3 shows the relative voltage in decibels delivered by the best circuit from generation 45. The horizontal axis is a logarithmic scale ranging between 20 Hz and

Table 42.1 Tableau for 10 dB amplifier

Objective	Design a 10 dB amplifier.
Test fixture and embryo	One-input, one-output initial circuit with a source resistor, load resistor, and two modifiable wires
Program architecture	Two result-producing branches
Initial function set for the RPBs	For construction-continuing subtrees: $F_{ccs\text{-}rpb\text{-}initial}$ = {R, C, Q_THREE_NPN0, . . . , Q_THREE_NPN11, SERIES, PARALLEL0, FLIP , NOP, THREE_GROUND, THREE_POS15V, THREE_VIA0, . . . , THREE_VIA7}. For arithmetic-performing subtrees: F_{aps} = {+, -}.
Initial terminal set for the RPBs	For construction-continuing subtrees: $T_{ccs\text{-}rpb\text{-}initial}$ = {END, CUT}. For arithmetic-performing subtrees: T_{aps} = {$\Re_{smaller\text{-}reals}$}.
Initial function set for the ADFs	Automatically defined functions are not used.
Initial terminal set for the ADFs	Automatically defined functions are not used.
Potential function set for the RPBs	Architecture-altering operations are not used.
Potential terminal set for the RPBs	Architecture-altering operations are not used.
Potential function set for the ADFs	Architecture-altering operations are not used.
Potential terminal set for the ADFs	Architecture-altering operations are not used.
Fitness cases	151 frequency values in an interval of three decades of frequency values between 20 Hz and 20,000 Hz
Raw fitness	The sum, over the 151 fitness cases, of the absolute weighted deviation between the actual value of relative voltage that is produced by the circuit at the probe point and the target value for relative voltage
Standardized fitness	Same as raw fitness
Hits	The number of hits is defined as the number of fitness cases (out of 151) for which the voltage is acceptable or ideal.
Wrapper	None
Parameters	M = 640,000. G = 501. Q = 10,000. D = 64. B = 2%. S_{rpb} = 300. N_{rpb} = 2.
Result designation	Best-so-far pace-setting individual
Success predicate	A program scores the maximum number (151) of hits.

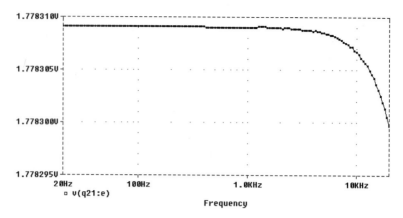

Figure 42.2 **Voltage output of the best-of-run circuit from generation 45**

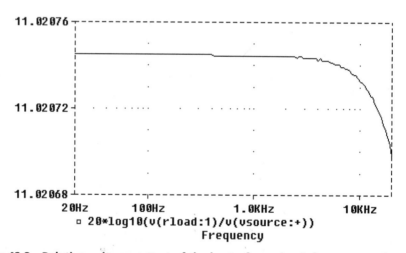

Figure 42.3 **Relative voltage output of the best-of-run circuit from generation 45**

200,000 Hz. The vertical axis ranges linearly over a very narrow range between 11.02068 dB and 11.02076 dB.

The best-of-run circuit from generation 45 can be viewed as being composed of two stages. This can be seen by redrawing Figure 42.1 as shown in Figure 42.4. V_{cc} in Figure 42.4 represents the +15-volt power supply.

One portion of the best-of-run circuit from generation 45 (shown in Figure 42.5) can be interpreted as a voltage gain stage.

A second portion of the best-of-run circuit from generation 45 (shown in Figure 42.6) resembles a Darlington emitter-follower. In this quasi-Darlington emitter-follower, transistor **Q71** is inverted from its conventional positioning. This substructure would be a canonical Darlington emitter-follower if the collector and emitter of **Q71** were

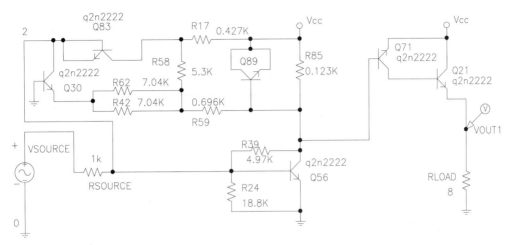

Figure 42.4 **Redrawn best-of-run circuit from generation 45**

exchanged. The noncanonical substructure here works because of the nearly symmetric geometry of the collector and emitter in a solid-state transistor. The quasi-Darlington emitter-follower provides current gain, thus isolating the voltage gain state of the amplifier from the low impedance (8 Ω) load. Of course, genetic programming was not provided with any knowledge relating to voltage gain stages or emitter-followers. These structures arose during the run of genetic programming as a consequence of the competitive pressure exerted by the problem's fitness measure.

Figure 42.7 shows the best-of-run circuit from generation 45 with its voltage gain stage and quasi-Darlington emitter-follower section highlighted by boxes.

It is a common occurrence for genetic programming to evolve an entity that satisfies all the requirements that the user incorporated into the fitness measure in a form that includes extraneous material (often referred to as an "intron" or an "appendix"). The best-of-run circuit from generation 45 of this run contains such extraneous material.

Figure 42.8 shows the best-of-run circuit from generation 45 after the excision of everything except for the voltage gain stage and the quasi-Darlington emitter-follower section. When retested, the excised circuit proves to be an amplifier with a gain almost identical to that of the entire circuit (Figure 42.7). Specifically, the excised circuit achieves an output voltage of 1.78800; the entire best-of-run circuit achieves an output voltage of 1.7783. The excised circuit achieves a gain of 11.067 dB over the frequency range from 20 Hz to 20,000 Hz; the entire best-of-run circuit achieves a gain of 11.021 dB.

Figure 42.9 shows the time domain behavior of the best-of-run circuit from generation 45. The horizontal axis represents time and ranges linearly from 0 to 2 milliseconds; the vertical axis represents voltage from −4 volts to +8 volts. The input is the 1,000 Hz sinusoidal signal shown in the bottom part of the figure. The input signal oscillates around the 0-volt axis and has a peak amplitude of ½ volt. The output is the signal shown in the top part of the figure. The specified amplification is achieved at the specified frequency. Note that the output signal is shifted in phase relative to the input signal by 180° (i.e., the output is inverted relative to the input).

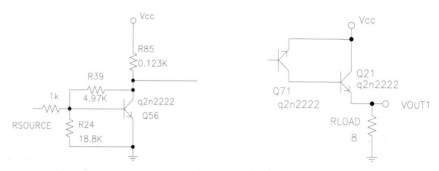

Figure 42.5   Voltage gain stage of best-of-run circuit from generation 45

Figure 42.6   Quasi-Darlington emitter-follower section of the best-of-run circuit from generation 45

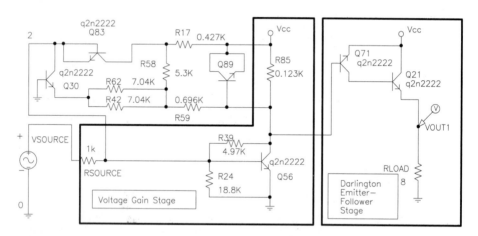

Figure 42.7   Another view of the best-of-run circuit from generation 45

Notice that the output signal in Figure 42.9 is an undistorted sine wave. That is, this particular run fortuitously delivered a circuit with near-zero distortion even though distortion was not explicitly incorporated into the problem's fitness measure. There was generalization in the sense that genetic programming evolved a circuit with an unrequested desirable characteristic (low distortion). We did not ask for low distortion, we were not entitled to low distortion, but we got it.

On the other hand, Figure 42.9 also shows that the output signal has a +5-volt bias relative to the input signal (i.e., the sinusoidal output is centered around +5 volts as opposed to being centered around 0 volts). Although circuit designers can easily correct for bias with additional circuitry, bias is often considered undesirable. The bias arose because the simplified fitness measure used for this problem ignored the issue of bias (and because the function set for this problem included the THREE_POS15V function, but not the THREE_NEG15V function). We did not ask for unbiased output, we were not entitled to unbiased output, and we did not get it.

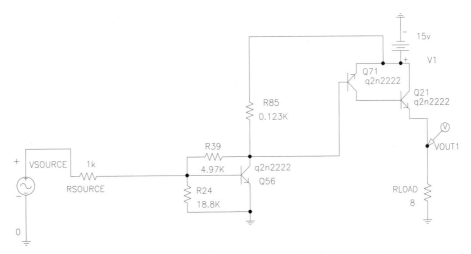

Figure 42.8 **Excised circuit consisting of only the evolved voltage gain stage and the evolved quasi-Darlington emitter-follower section from the best-of-run circuit of generation 45**

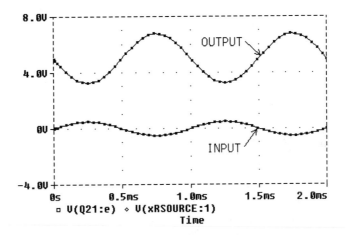

Figure 42.9 **Time domain behavior of best-of-run circuit from generation 45**

We called the emitter-follower section of Figure 42.6 a "quasi-Darlington" emitter-follower section because it differed slightly from the canonical form of this well-known circuit substructure. However, canonical Darlington emitter-follower sections were evolved on numerous occasions in the process of solving problems of analog circuit synthesis in this book.

Sidney Darlington of the Bell Telephone Laboratories was a towering pioneer in the field of analog circuit design. He obtained some 40 patents on numerous fundamental circuits. In particular, he obtained U.S. patent 2,663,806 for what is now called the Darlington emitter-follower section. Claim 1 of this patent (Darlington 1952) covers

A signal translating device comprising a pair of transistors of like conductivity type and each including a base, an emitter and a collector, means directly connecting the collectors together, means directly connecting the emitter of one transistor to the base of the other, and individual electrical connections to the other emitter and base.

In a similar vein, claim 3 of U.S. patent 2,663,806 covers

A signal translating device comprising a pair of transistors of like conductivity type and each including a base, an emitter and a collector, means directly connecting the emitters together, means directly connecting the collector of one transistor to the base of the other, and individual electrical connections to the other collector and base.

Claim 5 is somewhat more general and covers the case where any two like electrodes of the transistor are connected:

A signal translating device comprising a pair of transistors of like conductivity type and each including a base, an emitter and a collector, means directly connecting two like electrodes of said transistors together, means directly connecting another electrode of one transistor to an unlike electrode, other than one of said like electrodes of the other transistor, and individual electrical connections to the other emitter and base.

Claim 10 covers the case where there are three transistors in which collectors are connected:

A signal translating device comprising three transistors of like conductivity type and each including an emitter, a collector and a base, means directly connecting the collectors together electrically, means connecting the base of one transistor directly to the emitter of a second transistor, means connecting the base of said second transistor to the emitter of the third transistor, and individual electrical connections to the emitter of said one transistor and the base of said third transistor.

The Darlington patent also refers to an optional external connection to the connection between the leads of the two transistors. For example, claim 2 is a dependent claim based on claim 1 (where the collectors are connected together) and covers

A signal translating device in accordance with claim 1 comprising an additional electrical connection to the connected emitter and base.

Similarly, claim 4 is based on claim 3 (where the emitters are connected together) and covers

A signal translating device in accordance with claim 3 comprising an additional electrical connection to the connected collector and base.

Figure 42.10 is a cutaway of Figure 45.16, showing *npn* transistors **Q25** and **Q5** from the best circuit of generation 86 of a run of genetic programming of the 96 dB amplifier problem (Chapter 45). This figure shows a recognizable Darlington emitter-follower section in the canonical form, as described in claim 1 of patent 2,663,806. The figure shows "means [namely, a wire] directly connecting the collectors together." It also shows "means directly connecting the emitter of one transistor [namely, **Q5**] to the base of the other [namely, **Q25**]."

Table 42.2 shows 12 instances in which genetic programming evolved a circuit containing a canonical Darlington section. The table identifies the particular transistors involved and the particular claims (1, 2, 3, or 4) of U.S. patent 2,663,806 that genetic programming appears to have infringed (subject to discussion later in this chapter).

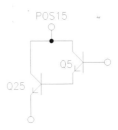

Figure 42.10   A canonical emitter-follower in best circuit from generation 86 of a run of the 96 dB amplifier problem

Darlington received a patent for his invention of the emitter-follower section because it satisfied the legal criteria for obtaining a U.S. patent, namely, that it was "new and useful" and

> . . . the differences between the subject matter sought to be patented and the prior art are such that the subject matter as a whole would [not] have been obvious at the time the invention was made to a person having ordinary skill in the art to which said subject matter pertains. [35 *United States Code* 103a]

Genetic programming reinvented the emitter-follower section. This automated discovery satisfies Arthur Samuel's criterion (1983) for artificial intelligence and machine learning:

> The aim [is] . . . to get machines to exhibit behavior, which if done by humans, would be assumed to involve the use of intelligence.

The successful evolution of this 10 dB amplifier established the principle that an active circuit containing transistors can be evolved using genetic programming with the same general approach that works successfully for the filters and other passive RLC circuits. The gratuitous achievement of the unrequested additional characteristic of low distortion was encouraging. The appearance of extraneous material (introns) in the evolved circuit structure was normal for a run of genetic programming.

Referring to the eight criteria in Chapter 1 for establishing that an automatically created result is competitive with a human-produced result, this result satisfies the following two of the eight criteria:

A.   The result was patented as an invention in the past, is an improvement over a patented invention, or would qualify today as a patentable new invention.

F.   The result is equal to or better than a result that was considered an achievement in its field at the time it was first discovered.

Therefore, we make the following claim:

- **CLAIM NO. 7**   We claim that the reinvention by genetic programming of a recognizable voltage gain stage and a Darlington emitter-follower section is an instance where genetic programming has produced a result that is competitive with a result produced by creative and inventive humans.

Table 42.2 Twelve instances where genetic programming appears to have infringed U.S. patent 2,663,806

Figure	Problem	Generation	Transistors	Type	Patent claim
45.16 (and 42.10)	96 dB amplifier	86	Q5 and Q25	npn	1
45.16	96 dB amplifier	86	Q53 and Q32	npn	3
47.6	Squaring circuit	37	Q101 and Q119	npn	1
47.6	Squaring circuit	37	Q29 and Q88	pnp	4
47.10	Cubing circuit	29	Q27 and Q46	pnp	3
47.10	Cubing circuit	29	Q46 and Q35	pnp	3
47.11	Cubing circuit	74	Q35 and Q49	pnp	3
47.12	Square root circuit	57	Q120 and Q155	pnp	2
47.15	Cube root circuit	17	QNC19 and QNC24	pnp	2
47.16	Cube root circuit	60	QNC73 and QNC74	pnp	1
47.16	Cube root circuit	60	QNC74 and QNC48	pnp	2
47.17	Logarithmic circuit	55	Q22 and Q66	pnp	4

Two things should be noted lest genetic programming be accused of infringing on Darlington's patent. For one thing, this 1952 patent has long since expired. More interestingly, although an electrical engineer would say that all 12 instances in Table 42.2 are examples of Darlington emitter-follower sections, none of these instances actually infringe on Darlington's patent. As explained in Darlington's biography at the Web site (*http://ece.unh.edu/faculty/sidney/SDOther.html*) of the Electrical Engineering Department at the University of New Hampshire (where Darlington was an adjunct professor from 1971 until his death)

> Just after the transistor was invented at Bell Labs, Sidney checked out for the weekend two of the few existing transistors from the head of Bell Labs. Transistors were not generally available, and the head of the Labs kept the few that had been made in his desk. Sidney played with them at home on the weekend and discovered/invented the Darlington pair. He realized that they could be put in one package ("on one chip"), and that, in fact, any number of transistors could be put in one package. The next week he was encouraged to have the lawyers draw up the patent application. He said it should be written for any number in one package, but the lawyers only wanted to do it for two—which is what was applied for. As it turned out, if it had not been restricted to two transistors, Bell Labs and Dr. Darlington would [have] receive[d] a royalty on every IC chip made.

Synthesis of a 40 dB Amplifier

When electrical engineers design amplifiers, they usually seek an unbiased and undistorted output signal. The fitness measure that was used to evolve the 10 dB amplifier in Chapter 42 was highly simplified in that it did not consider either bias or distortion. The evolved amplifier in the previous chapter has a substantial bias (i.e., the output signal was not centered around 0 volts, but was instead centered around +5 volts). As it happened, the circuit was fortuitously free of distortion even though the fitness measure did not explicitly consider this factor.

In this chapter the goal is to evolve the design of a low-bias, low-distortion amplifier with an amount of amplification (40 dB) that is typical of a single-stage amplifier. Five major changes are introduced in this chapter:

1. We use the Fourier components of the output signal as the basis for the fitness measure.
2. We adopted a multiobjective fitness measure that explicitly incorporated amplification, bias, and distortion.
3. We introduced automatically defined functions because of our general belief that they are helpful for solving more difficult problems.
4. No source resistor was used on this particular problem.
5. At the recommendation of Andrei Vladimirescu of Cadence, Inc., of San Jose, author of *The SPICE Book*, we included the *npn* and *pnp* transistor models described in his book (1994, pages 234–235) in the repertoire of components for this problem. The SPICE commands required for inserting the models for these *npn* and *pnp* transistors are found in Appendix E.

The methods used in this chapter proved to be sufficient to evolve a design of a circuit that satisfied the immediate design goals of this chapter; however, they were immediately superseded by different approaches in subsequent chapters.

43.1   DESIGN GOALS

The goal is to evolve the design of a low-bias, low-distortion amplifier that delivers amplification in the neighborhood of 40 dB (100-to-1) at a frequency of 1,000 Hz.

43.2   PREPARATORY STEPS

43.2.1   Embryo and Test Fixture

This problem was run without a source resistor. The initial circuit for this problem is created by embedding the embryo with two modifiable wires and three ports (Figure 29.9) that has appeared repeatedly in this book into the one-input, one-output test fixture without a source resistor (Figure 29.6).

The load resistor **RLOAD** of the test fixture is 1,000 Ω. The incoming alternating current signal source **VSOURCE** is 1 volt in amplitude for this problem.

43.2.2   Program Architecture

Since the embryo has two modifiable wires, there are two result-producing branches in each program tree.

Two one-argument automatically defined functions are used in each program tree. The argument to each automatically defined function is an arithmetic-performing subtree. No hierarchical references among the automatically defined functions are allowed. Consequently, the architecture of each program tree in the population consists of a total of four branches (i.e., two function-defining branches and two result-producing branches).

The architecture-altering operations are not used in this problem.

43.2.3   Functions and Terminals

The terminal sets are identical for both result-producing branches of the program trees for this problem. The function sets are identical for both result-producing branches. The desired amplifier is to be composed of transistors, resistors, and capacitors.

The function set, $F_{ccs\text{-}rpb\text{-}initial}$, for each construction-continuing subtree of the result-producing branches is

$F_{ccs\text{-}rpb\text{-}initial}$ = {ADF0, ADF1, R, C, SERIES, PARALLEL0, FLIP, NOP, THREE_GROUND, THREE_POS15V, THREE_NEG15V, THREE_VIA0, . . . , THREE_VIA7, Q_THREE_NPN0, . . . , Q_THREE_NPN11, Q_THREE_PNP0, . . . , Q_THREE_PNP11, Q_DIODE_NPN, Q_DIODE_PNP}.

Note that this problem has access to both positive and negative power supplies (created by the THREE_POS15V and THREE_NEG15V functions, respectively).

The terminal set, $T_{ccs\text{-}rpb\text{-}initial}$, for each construction-continuing subtree of the result-producing branches is

$T_{ccs\text{-}rpb\text{-}initial}$ = {END, SAFE_CUT}.

The function set, $F_{ccs\text{-}adf\text{-}initial}$, for each construction-continuing subtree of the automatically defined functions is

$F_{ccs\text{-}adf\text{-}initial}$ = {R, C, SERIES, PARALLEL0, FLIP, NOP, THREE_GROUND, THREE_POS15V, THREE_NEG15V, THREE_VIA0, . . . , THREE_VIA7, Q_THREE_NPN0, . . . , Q_THREE_PNP0, . . . , Q_THREE_PNP11, Q_DIODE_NPN, Q_DIODE_PNP}.

The terminal set, $T_{ccs-adf-initial}$, for each construction-continuing subtree of the function-defining branches is

$T_{ccs-adf-initial}$ = {ARG0, END, SAFE_CUT}.

Since there are no architecture-altering operations in this problem, $T_{rpb-potential}$, $F_{rpb-potential}$, $T_{adf-potential}$, and $F_{adf-potential}$ are empty.

The function set, F_{aps}, for each arithmetic-performing subtree in any branch and the terminal set, T_{aps}, for each arithmetic-performing subtree in any branch are the same as for the lowpass filter problem in Section 25.14.3.

43.2.4   Fitness

An ideal amplifier circuit receives a sinusoidal input of a certain amplitude (centered around 0 volts) as its input and produces an undistorted (possibly phase-shifted) sinusoidal output of a considerably increased amplitude (also centered around 0 volts) as its output.

A circuit is flawed to the extent that it does not achieve the desired amplification, to the extent that the output signal is not centered around 0 volts (i.e., it has a bias), or to the extent that the shape of the output signal is not sinusoidal for a sinusoidal input (i.e., is distorted). The Fourier components of the transient response of the circuit to a 1,000 Hz sinusoidal input signal, as computed by SPICE, are used to test for the presence of any of these flaws.

A total of 11 fitness cases (Fourier components) are used:

- The first fitness case represents the DC component (i.e., 0 Hz) and tests for bias. If this Fourier component is zero, the output is centered around 0 volts and there is no bias.
- The second fitness case represents the fundamental frequency of 1,000 Hz (the input source frequency to the circuit). This Fourier component indicates if the circuit is amplifying its 1,000 Hz input signal. If the voltage of this Fourier component is the desired multiple of the amplitude of the incoming AC signal, the desired amplification has been achieved.
- The remaining nine fitness cases represent the harmonics of 1,000 Hz lying between 2,000 Hz and 10,000 Hz. If any of the nine (or other higher) Fourier components are nonzero, the waveform is not a perfect 1,000 Hz sine wave.

Thus, the first Fourier component (i.e., the DC component) of an ideal output signal would be zero; the second Fourier component (i.e., the fundamental frequency) of an ideal output signal would equal the voltage amplification factor times the amplitude of the incoming signal; and the remaining Fourier components of an ideal output signal would be zero.

Figure 43.1 is a histogram (spectrum) of the Fourier components of a biased, but undistorted hypothetical signal. The horizontal axis represents frequency. It starts at 0 Hz (the DC component) and runs from 1,000 Hz to 10,000 Hz in increments of 1,000 Hz. The vertical axis represents voltage. The hypothetical signal shown in the figure has a DC component (bias) of +6 volts and a Fourier component at 1,000 Hz of +3 volts. The Fourier components from 2,000 Hz through 10,000Hz have coefficients of 0 (i.e., are

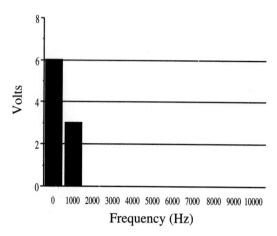

Figure 43.1 Fourier components of a biased, but undistorted signal

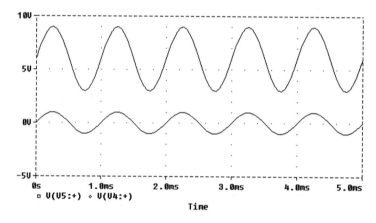

Figure 43.2 Time domain behavior of a biased, but undistorted signal

absent from this illustrative signal). The absence of all Fourier components above 1,000 Hz indicates that the signal has no harmonics and is undistorted.

Figure 43.2 illustrates bias and amplification in the time domain. The horizontal axis represents time and ranges linearly from 0 milliseconds to 5 milliseconds. The vertical axis ranges linearly from –5 volts to +10 volts. The 1,000 Hz input signal (the lower sine wave in the figure) has no bias (i.e., is centered around 0 volts) and has a peak amplitude of 1 volt. The output signal (the upper sine wave in the figure) has a bias of +6 volts (i.e., is centered around +6 volts) and has a peak amplitude of 3 volts (i.e., is amplified by a factor of 3). Both signals are 1,000 Hz (i.e., there are five full cycles in 5 milliseconds). The output is biased and amplified; however, it is not distorted (i.e., the output signal is a perfect sine wave). The Fourier components of the output signal in this figure are those of Figure 43.1.

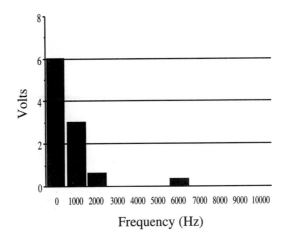

Figure 43.3 **Fourier components of a biased and distorted signal**

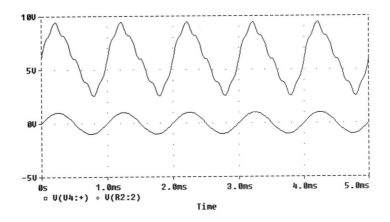

Figure 43.4 **Time domain behavior of a biased and distorted signal**

Figure 43.3 is a histogram of Fourier components of a hypothetical biased and distorted signal. This hypothetical signal has a DC component (bias) of +6 volts (as shown for the 0 Hz frequency at the far left of the figure). It also has a Fourier component at 1,000 Hz of 3 volts. In addition, it has nonzero Fourier components at 2,000 Hz and 6,000 Hz (i.e., the signal is distorted).

Figure 43.4 illustrates bias, amplification, and distortion in the time domain. The 1,000 Hz input signal (the lower sine wave in the figure) has a peak amplitude of 1 volt with no bias (i.e., it is centered around 0 volts). The output signal (the upper signal in the figure) has an amplitude of 3 volts (i.e., is amplified by a factor of 3) and a bias of 6 volts (i.e., is centered around 6 volts). As can be seen, the output signal is not a perfect sine wave, but is instead distorted because of the nonzero harmonics at 2,000 Hz and 6,000 Hz. The Fourier components of the output signal in this figure are those of Figure 43.3.

Fitness is measured in terms of the sum, over these 11 fitness cases, of the absolute weighted deviation between the actual value (in volts) of the Fourier component that is produced by the circuit at the probe point **VOUT** at node 6 of the test fixture (Figure 29.6) and the target value of the Fourier component. The 11 fitness cases are considered in three groups:

- the DC component (i.e., the bias),
- the fundamental frequency component (i.e., 1,000 Hz), and
- the nine harmonics (e.g., 2,000 Hz, 3,000 Hz, and so forth).

First, the procedure for the DC component is as follows:

- If the output voltage is exactly zero (i.e., there is no bias at all), the deviation is deemed to be zero.
- If the output voltage is between 0.0 volts and 0.1 volt, the absolute value of the deviation from 0 is weighted by a factor of 1.0.
- If the voltage is outside this range, the absolute value of the deviation from 0 is weighted by a factor of 10.0.

Second, the goal in this problem is to attain amplification of 40 dB (a voltage amplification factor of 100-to-1). We constructed the fitness measure based on a somewhat larger range of gains, namely, up to 50 dB (i.e., 316-to-1). Therefore, the procedure for the Fourier component of the fundamental frequency of 1,000 Hz is as follows:

- If the output voltage is 316 volts (i.e., a 50 dB amplification), the deviation is deemed to be zero.
- If the output voltage is between 315 volts and 316 volts, the absolute value of the deviation from 316 volts is weighted by a factor of 1.0.
- If the voltage is outside this range, the absolute value of the deviation from 316 volts is weighted by a factor of 10.0.

Third, the procedure for the Fourier component for the nine harmonics is as follows:

- If the output voltage is exactly zero, the deviation is deemed to be zero (i.e., there is no distortion at all).
- If the output voltage is between 0 volts and 7 volts, the absolute value of the deviation from 0 is weighted by a factor of 1.0.
- If the voltage is outside this range, the absolute value of the deviation from 0 is weighted by a factor of 10.0. We obtained the boundary of 7 volts by taking 20% of 316 volts and dividing this over the nine harmonics.

An amplification of 40 dB is not possible with the 1-volt input and the 15-volt DC power supplies (the rails); however, when the evolved circuit is subsequently tested on input signals with lower amplitude, we do obtain amplification approaching 40 dB.

The number of hits is defined as the number of fitness cases for which the voltage is acceptable or ideal. Thus, the number of hits ranges from 0 to 11 for this problem.

43.2.5 Parameters

The control parameters for this problem are found in the tableau (Table 43.1), the tables of percentages of genetic operations in Appendix D, and the default values specified in Appendix D.

43.2.6 Tableau

Table 43.1 summarizes the key features of the problem of designing a 40 dB amplifier.

Table 43.1 Tableau for 40 dB amplifier

Objective	Design a 40 dB amplifier.
Test fixture and embryo	One-input, one-output initial circuit with a load resistor (but no source resistor) and two modifiable wires
Program architecture	Two result-producing branches and two one-argument automatically defined functions
Initial function set for the RPBs	For construction-continuing subtrees: $F_{\text{ccs-rpb-initial}}$ = {ADF0, ADF1, R, C, SERIES, PARALLEL0, FLIP, NOP, THREE_GROUND, THREE_POS15V, THREE_NEG15V, THREE_VIA0, . . . , THREE_VIA7, Q_THREE_NPN0, . . . , Q_THREE_NPN11, Q_THREE_PNP0, . . . , Q_THREE_PNP11, Q_DIODE_NPN, Q_DIODE_PNP}. For arithmetic-performing subtrees: F_{aps} = {+, -}.
Initial terminal set for the RPBs	For construction-continuing subtrees: $T_{\text{ccs-rpb-initial}}$ = {END, SAFE_CUT}. For arithmetic-performing subtrees: T_{aps} = {$\Re_{\text{smaller-reals}}$}.
Initial function set for the ADFs	For construction-continuing subtrees: $F_{\text{ccs-adf-initial}}$ = {R, C, SERIES, PARALLEL0, FLIP, NOP, THREE_GROUND, THREE_POS15V, THREE_NEG15V, THREE_VIA0, . . . , THREE_VIA7, Q_THREE_NPN0, . . . , Q_THREE_PNP0, . . . , Q_THREE_PNP11, Q_DIODE_NPN, Q_DIODE_PNP}. For arithmetic-performing subtrees: F_{aps} = {+, -}.
Initial terminal set for the ADFs	For construction-continuing subtrees: $T_{\text{ccs-adf-initial}}$ = {ARG0, END, SAFE_CUT}. For arithmetic-performing subtrees: T_{aps} = {$\Re_{\text{smaller-reals}}$}.
Potential function set for the RPBs	Architecture-altering operations are not used.
Potential terminal set for the RPBs	Architecture-altering operations are not used.
Potential function set for the ADFs	Architecture-altering operations are not used.
Potential terminal set for the ADFs	Architecture-altering operations are not used.

(continued)

Table 43.2 (continued)

Fitness cases	11 fitness cases representing the frequencies 0, 1,000, 2,000, . . . , 10,000 Hz.
Raw fitness	The sum, over the 11 fitness cases, of the absolute weighted deviation between the actual value of voltage that is produced by the circuit at the probe point and the target value
Standardized fitness	Same as raw fitness
Hits	The number of hits is the number of fitness cases (out of 11) for which the voltage is acceptable or ideal.
Wrapper	None
Parameters	$M = 640,000$. $G = 501$. $Q = 10,000$. $D = 64$. $B = 2\%$. $S_{rpb} = 300$. $S_{adf} = 300$. $N_{rpb} = 2$. $N_{max\text{-}adf} = 2$. $N_{max\text{-}argument\text{-}adf} = 1$.
Result designation	Best-so-far pace-setting individual
Success predicate	A program scores the maximum number (11) of hits.

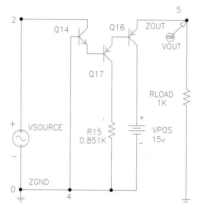

Figure 43.5 Best circuit from generation 0

43.3 RESULTS

The best circuit from generation 0 (Figure 43.5) has three transistors and one resistor (in addition to the load resistor of the test fixture). It achieves a fitness of 3,144.7. The result-producing branches in its circuit-constructing program tree have 2 and 34 points, respectively. The two automatically defined functions in its circuit-constructing program tree have 19 and 45 points, respectively. Notice that there are no capacitors in this circuit (or any other best-of-generation circuit in this section) even though the capacitor-creating C function is in the function set of this problem.

Figure 43.6 shows the time domain behavior of the best circuit from generation 0. The horizontal axis represents time and ranges linearly from 0 milliseconds to 5 milliseconds; the vertical axis represents peak output voltage and ranges linearly from −1 volt to

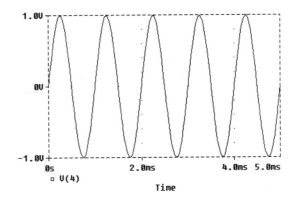

Figure 43.6   Time domain behavior of the best circuit of generation 0

Table 43.2 Fourier components for best circuit of generation 0

Harmonic	Frequency (Hz)	Fourier component
0	DC component	–0.00179
1	1,000	0.995
2	2,000	0.00126
3	3,000	0.000610
4	4,000	0.000694
5	5,000	0.000332
6	6,000	0.000492
7	7,000	0.000134
8	8,000	0.000192
9	9,000	0.0000443
10	10,000	0.0000945

+1 volt. This circuit's output is a 0.995-volt almost-sinusoidal signal oscillating around a midpoint of –0.00179 volt. It is visually indistinguishable from the input (a 1.000-volt, 1,000 Hz perfect sine wave oscillating around 0 volts).

Table 43.2 shows 11 Fourier components of the transient response for the best circuit from generation 0. As can be seen, the only significant Fourier component (0.995) is at 1,000 Hz. The output signal contains no significant DC component and no substantial components for any of the harmonics.

Figure 43.7a is a histogram of the 11 Fourier components. The horizontal axis represents frequency and runs from 0 Hz (the DC component) to 10,000 Hz. The vertical axis represents voltage and runs from 0 volts to 15 volts.

The amplification of an amplifier can be measured from the DC sweep. Figure 43.8 shows the result of performing SPICE's DC sweep on the best-of-generation circuit from generation 0. The horizontal axis represents input DC values ranging linearly from –100

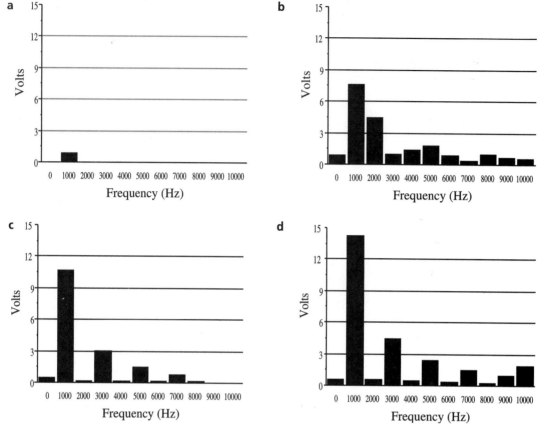

Figure 43.7   Fourier components for best circuits of generations (a) 0, (b) 7, (c) 13, and (d) 30

millivolts to +100 millivolts. The vertical axis represents the output voltage on a linear scale. The diagonal line shows that the input equals the output. The amplification in decibels is 20 times the common logarithm of the ratio of the change in the output divided by the total change of the input (i.e., 200 millivolts). This ratio is 0 dB here since the circuit provides no amplification and merely passes the incoming signal.

The amplification of an amplifier can also be measured from an AC sweep. Figure 43.9 shows the AC sweep for the best circuit of generation 0. The horizontal axis of this figure represents frequency from 1 Hz to 1 MHz. The vertical axis ranges from –1 microdecibels (μdB) to +1 μdB and represents amplification. As can be seen, the amplification is 0 μdB for all frequencies.

About 43% of the programs in generation 0 for this problem produce circuits that cannot be simulated by SPICE. However, the percentage of unsimulatable circuits drops to 8% by generation 1, 6% by generation 2, ranges between 3% and 9% until generation 25, and then drops below 1% after generation 25.

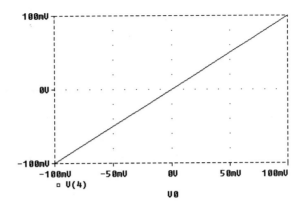

Figure 43.8 DC sweep for the best circuit from generation 0

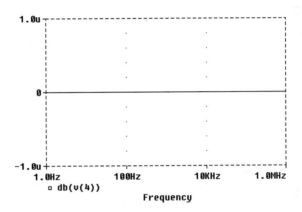

Figure 43.9 AC sweep for the best circuit from generation 0

The best circuit from generation 7 (Figure 43.10) has eight transistors and no resistors (beyond the load resistor of the test fixture). It achieves the somewhat better value of fitness of 3,104.1.

Figure 43.7b shows the magnitude of the 11 Fourier components as a histogram. The DC component of this circuit is –0.84 volt. The Fourier component for 1,000 Hz is the largest. However, there are substantial Fourier components at 2,000, 4,000, and 5,000 Hz.

Figure 43.11 shows the time domain behavior of the best circuit from generation 7. The output signal is still a highly nonsinusoidal waveform. However, in contrast to the time domain behavior of the best circuit of generation 0, the output signal spends a considerable amount of time below the 0-volt horizontal axis.

The best circuit of generation 7, as measured by a DC sweep, produces a constant zero output, regardless of input.

Figure 43.12 shows the AC sweep for the best circuit of generation 7. The vertical scale runs from –200 dB to –100 dB. As can be seen, the amplification is –141 dB at 1,000

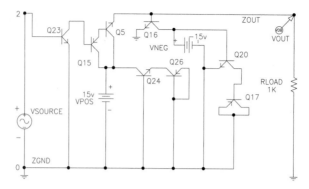

Figure 43.10 Best circuit from generation 7

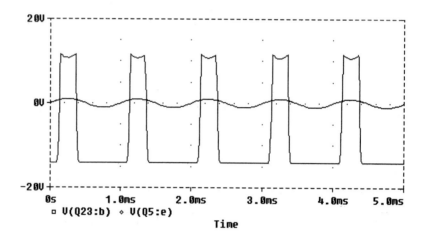

Figure 43.11 Time domain behavior of the best circuit from generation 7

Hz and negative throughout the domain, so this circuit is a deamplifier when evaluated by the AC sweep.

The best circuit from generation 13 (Figure 43.13) has five transistors and one resistor. It scores a fitness of 3,064.0.

Figure 43.7c shows the magnitude of the 11 Fourier components as a histogram for the best circuit of generation 13. The DC component of this circuit is –0.445 volt (as compared with –0.84 volt for the best circuit of generation 7. The Fourier component for 1,000 Hz continues to be the largest. There are substantial Fourier components only at three odd harmonics, namely, 3,000, 5,000, and 7,000 Hz.

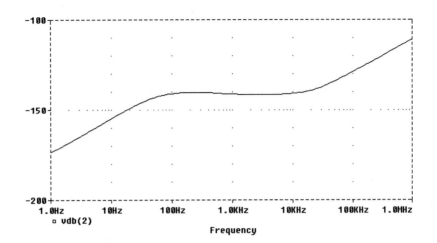

Figure 43.12   AC sweep for the best circuit from generation 7

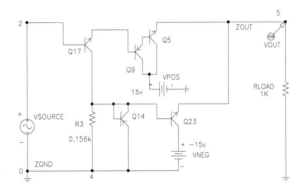

Figure 43.13   Best circuit from generation 13

Figure 43.14 shows the time domain behavior of the best circuit from generation 13. Unlike the time domain behavior of the previous circuits, the output signal now spends about the same amount of time above and below the horizontal axis. The output signal resembles a 1,000 Hz square wave. This near-square output in the time domain is consistent with the existence of substantial nonzero odd harmonics (i.e., 1, 3, 5, and 7 KHz).

Figure 43.15 shows the AC sweep for the best circuit of generation 13. The horizontal axis ranges over six decades of frequencies from 1 Hz to 1 MHz on a logarithmic scale. The vertical axis ranges from −20 dB to +40 dB. As can be seen, a gain of +32.32 dB is achieved between 1 Hz and almost 10,000 Hz. The gain of the circuit decreases with

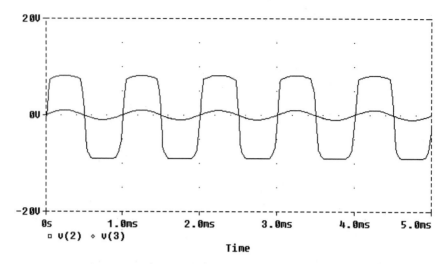

Figure 43.14 Time domain behavior of the best circuit from generation 13

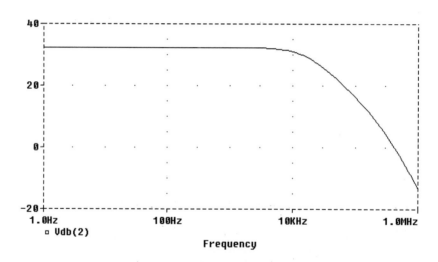

Figure 43.15 AC sweep for the best circuit from generation 13

increasing frequency because the transistors yield decreasing gain (and actually attenuate the signal at high frequencies). Note that the fitness measure is based on the DC sweep and does not include any consideration of the AC sweep. Nonetheless, the value of amplification observed using the AC sweep is almost identical to that observed using the Fourier analysis.

Figure 43.16 shows the result of performing SPICE's DC sweep on the best-of-generation circuit from generation 13. Because of the larger scale (in volts) needed on the vertical axis of this graph, the input (ranging from −100 millivolts to 100 millivolts) appears as the hori-

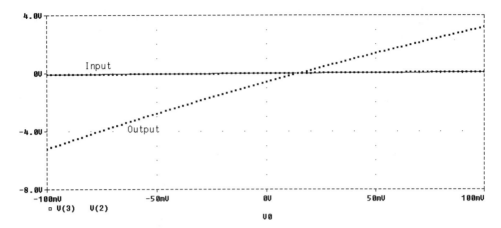

Figure 43.16 DC sweep for the best circuit from generation 13

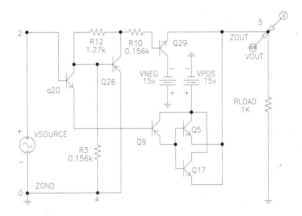

Figure 43.17 Best-of-run circuit from generation 30

zontal line that you see in this figure. The diagonal then represents the output and shows the amplification of the input signal. The amplification, as measured by a DC sweep, is 32.44 dB for the best of generation 13.

The best circuit from generation 30 (Figure 43.17) has six transistors and three resistors (in addition to the load resistor of the test fixture). It achieves a fitness of 3,033.8. Its circuit-constructing program tree has 33 and 39 points in its first and second result-producing branches, respectively, and 19 and 45 points in its first and second automatically defined functions, respectively.

Table 43.3 shows the Fourier components of the transient response for the best circuit from generation 30.

Figure 43.7d shows the 11 Fourier components as a histogram for the best circuit of generation 30. The bias for this circuit is 0.53 volt, and the total harmonic distortion is 36.5%.

Table 43.3 Fourier components for best circuit of generation 30

Harmonic	Frequency (Hz)	Fourier component
0	DC component	0.53
1	1,000	14.14
2	2,000	0.50
3	3,000	4.389
4	4,000	0.3854
5	5,000	2.362
6	6,000	0.3154
7	7,000	1.444
8	8,000	0.2541
9	9,000	0.9080
10	10,000	0.1856

Table 43.4 Bias and total harmonic distortion

Generation	Bias	Total harmonic distortion
0	−0.00179	0.17%
7	−0.84	68.35%
13	−0.44	31.56%
30	0.53	37.65%

The formula for the total harmonic distortion (THD) is

$$THD = \frac{\sqrt{\sum_{i=2}^{9} A_i^2}}{A_1}$$

where A_1 is the fundamental frequency and the A_i are the harmonics (Vladimirescu 1994).

Table 43.4 shows the changes in bias and total harmonic distortion for the best circuits of generations 0, 7, 13, and 30.

Figure 43.18 shows the time domain behavior of the best-of-run circuit from generation 30. Note that the peak is at 12.04 volts (as compared to 8.24 volts for the corresponding peaks of generation 13). The actual output signal shown in this figure is not a perfect sine wave because of the 37.65% total harmonic distortion.

Figure 43.19 shows the result of performing SPICE's DC sweep on the best-of-generation circuit from generation 30. The horizontal axis ranges linearly from −100 millivolts to 100 millivolts. The vertical axis ranges linearly from −10 volts to +10 volts. The amplification, as measured by a DC sweep, is 37.67 dB.

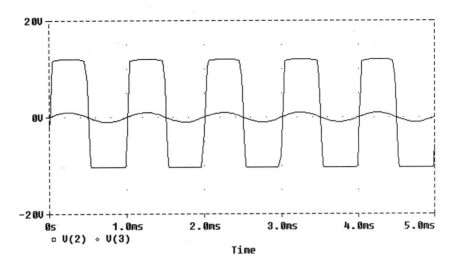

Figure 43.18 Time domain behavior of the best-of-run circuit from generation 30

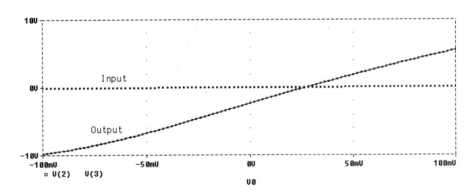

Figure 43.19 DC sweep for the best-of-run circuit from generation 30

Figure 43.20 shows the AC sweep for the best-of-run circuit from generation 30. The horizontal axis ranges over six decades of frequencies from 1 Hz to 1 MHz on a logarithmic scale. The vertical axis ranges from –20 dB to +40 dB. As can be seen, the amplification delivered by this circuit is nearly constant from 1 Hz to 1,900 Hz and the circuit's flatband gain is 39 dB. The 3 dB bandwidth of an amplifier is the frequency at which the amplification is 3 dB below the flatband gain. The 3 dB bandwidth is 16,600 Hz. Thus, even though the evolutionary process was based on a transient analysis whose fundamental frequency was 1,000 Hz, the evolved circuit delivered significant amplification for frequencies considerably above 1,000 Hz. That is, there was generalization of a desirable characteristic outside the range explicitly considered by the fitness measure.

Table 43.5 summarizes the performance of the best-of-generation circuits from generations 0, 7, 13, and 30 of this run. The best-of-run circuit produces an amplification of

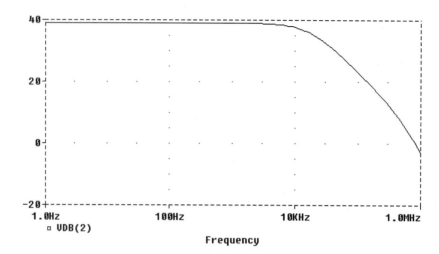

Figure 43.20   AC sweep for the best circuit from generation 30

Table 43.5 Summary of amplification

Generation	Amplification in voltage measured by Fourier	Amplification in dB measured by Fourier	Amplification in dB measured in DC sweep	Amplification in dB measured in AC sweep
0	1.00	0.0	0.0	0.0
7	7.507	17.5	−∞	−141
13	10.66	20.6	32.44	32.32
30	14.12	23.0	37.67	38.99

39 dB when measured by the AC sweep and 38 dB when measured by the DC sweep. Note that the voltage amplification factor reported for generation 30 in the third column is considerably lower than the target of 40 dB because the output is limited by the rails (i.e., the +15-volt and −15-volt DC power supplies). Although the fitness measure only uses the Fourier domain, there was generalization that yielded this additional desirable performance measured by the AC and DC sweeps.

Synthesis of a 60 dB Amplifier

After evolving the 39 dB amplifier (Chapter 43), we successfully applied the same techniques to evolve several different amplifiers with amplification in the range of 30 dB to 50 dB. However, after trying several runs, these techniques did not appear capable of evolving a 60 dB amplifier.

Thus, our effort to synthesize a 60 dB amplifier became the occasion for significantly reexamining and modifying our entire approach to the problem of designing amplifiers:

1. We abandoned the THREE_VIA functions (Section 25.8.6) in favor of the PAIR_CONNECT functions (Section 25.8.10).
2. We introduced diodes as an explicit separate type of component. In previous runs, diodes were created by joining the base and collector nodes of a single transistor.
3. We introduced a new test fixture that was specifically designed for would-be amplifier circuits.
4. We adopted a new fitness measure. In the previous chapter, fitness was measured in the Fourier domain. Our new fitness measure was based on the amplification, bias, and linearity of the amplification as measured by a DC sweep (weighting them equally as we did in the previous chapter).

These four changes did not produce the desired results.

We then discovered that the problem was the equal weighting of the three components of the fitness measure. In particular, in generation 0, numerous circuits have perfect (i.e., zero) bias (thereby incurring no bias penalty), but deliver no amplification. A small number of biased circuits in generation 0 delivered some amplification, but incurred such a heavy bias penalty that their tiny amplification credit was overwhelmed. Consequently, the perfectly unbiased circuits prematurely drove out all the weak amplifier circuits from the population. The solution was to rearrange the factors in the fitness measure so as to make the voltage amplification factor dominant (as described in detail below).

44.1 DESIGN GOALS

The goal is to evolve the design of an amplifier that delivers amplification of 60 dB (1,000-to-1) with low distortion and little, if any, bias.

44.2 PREPARATORY STEPS

44.2.1 Embryo and Test Fixture

The combination of the embryo and test fixture used in this chapter (and Chapters 45 and 46) is specifically designed for would-be amplifier circuits. The initial circuit for this problem is created by embedding the embryo with three modifiable wires and four ports (Figure 29.15) into a one-input, one-output test fixture with four ports (Figure 29.8).

Figure 44.1 shows a one-input, one-output initial circuit that serves as a test fixture for would-be amplifier circuits. **VSOURCE** is the input signal. **VOUT** is the output signal. The special test fixture for would-be amplifiers has five resistors:

- the usual **RSOURCE** source resistor,
- the usual **RLOAD** load resistor,
- a feedback resistor **RFEEDBACK**,
- a source-balancing resistor **RBALANCE_SOURCE**, and
- a feedback-balancing resistor **RBALANCE_FEEDBACK**.

The source resistor **RSOURCE** and the load resistor **RLOAD** are each 1,000 Ω. This test fixture limits the maximum possible amplification of the circuit to the ratio of the feedback resistor to the source resistor (Graeme, Tobey, and Huelsman 1971). The feedback resistor **RFEEDBACK** is 1,000,000 Ω, and the source resistor **RSOURCE** is 1,000 Ω, thereby establishing a 1,000-to-1 ratio (equal to 60 dB of amplification). The feedback-balancing resistor **RBALANCE_FEEDBACK** is 1,000,000 Ω, and the source-balancing resistor **RBALANCE_SOURCE** is 1,000 Ω. The embryo (Figure 29.15) has three modifiable wires (**Z0**, **Z1**, and **Z2**) arranged in a triangle so as to provide full connectivity between nodes 8, 9, and 10. These three nodes, in turn, connect to the balance, load, and source resistors, respectively. As usual, all development occurs in the embryo and originates from the modifiable wires.

Note that this initial circuit (and all earlier and later ones in this book) contains only resistors and wires. It is well known that an amplifier cannot be created merely from wires and resistors.

44.2.2 Program Architecture

Since the embryo has three modifiable wires, there are three result-producing branches in each program tree.

Two one-argument automatically defined functions are used in each program tree. The argument to each automatically defined function is an arithmetic-performing subtree. No hierarchical references among the automatically defined functions are allowed. Consequently, the architecture of each program tree in the population consists of a total of five branches (i.e., two function-defining branches and three result-producing branches).

The architecture-altering operations are not used on this problem.

44.2.3 Functions and Terminals

The desired amplifier is to be composed of transistors, diodes, resistors, and capacitors.

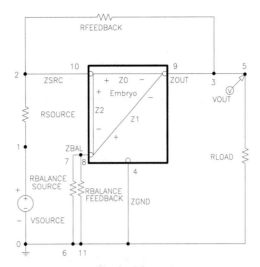

Figure 44.1   Initial circuit for the 60 dB amplifier

The function set, $F_{ccs-rpb-initial}$, for each construction-continuing subtree of each result-producing branch is

$F_{ccs-rpb-initial}$ = {ADF0, ADF1, R, C, SERIES, PARALLEL0, PARALLEL1, FLIP, NOP, RETAINING_THREE_GROUND_0, RETAINING_THREE_GROUND_1, RETAINING_THREE_POS15V_0, RETAINING_THREE_POS15V_1, RETAINING_THREE_NEG15V_0, RETAINING_THREE_NEG15V_1, PAIR_CONNECT_0, PAIR_CONNECT_1, Q_DIODE_NPN, Q_DIODE_PNP, Q_THREE_NPN0, . . . , Q_THREE_NPN11, Q_THREE_PNP0, . . . , Q_THREE_PNP11, Q_POS15V_COLL_NPN, Q_GND_EMIT_NPN, Q_NEG15V_EMIT_NPN, Q_GND_EMIT_PNP, Q_POS15V_EMIT_PNP, Q_NEG15V_COLL_PNP}

For the *npn* transistors, the Q2N3904 model is used. For *pnp* transistors, the Q2N3906 model is used.

The terminal set, $T_{ccs-rpb-initial}$, for each construction-continuing subtree of the result-producing branches is

$T_{ccs-rpb-initial}$ = {END, SAFE_CUT}.

The function set, $F_{ccs-adf-initial}$, for each construction-continuing subtree of the automatically defined functions is

$F_{ccs-adf-initial}$ = $F_{ccs-rpb-initial}$ − {ADF0, ADF1}.

The terminal set, $T_{ccs-adf-initial}$, for each construction-continuing subtree of the function-defining branches is

$T_{ccs-adf-initial}$ = {ARG0, END, SAFE_CUT}.

Since there are no architecture-altering operations in this problem, $T_{rpb\text{-potential}}$, $F_{rpb\text{-potential}}$, $T_{adf\text{-potential}}$, and $F_{adf\text{-potential}}$ are empty.

The function set, F_{aps}, for each arithmetic-performing subtree in any branch and the terminal set, T_{aps}, for each arithmetic-performing subtree in any branch are the same as for the lowpass filter problem in Section 25.14.3.

44.2.4   Fitness

In the previous chapter, fitness is defined in terms of the 11 Fourier components of the transient response of the circuit to a 1,000 Hz sinusoidal input signal. The performance of a would-be amplifier can also be viewed in terms of its response to a DC input. An ideal inverting amplifier circuit receives a DC input, inverts it, and multiplies it by the voltage amplification factor.

In this scheme, a circuit is flawed to the extent that it does not achieve the desired amplification, to the extent that the DC response of the circuit is not linear, or to the extent that the output signal is not centered around 0 volts (i.e., it has a bias).

Thus, for this problem, we used a fitness measure based on SPICE's DC sweep. The DC sweep analysis measures the DC response of the circuit at several different DC input voltages. The circuits are analyzed with a five-point DC sweep at –10, –5, 0, +5, and +10 millivolts. SPICE then produces the circuit's output voltage for each of these five DC input values. Since there are five DC output values, there are five fitness cases for this problem.

Fitness is then calculated from four penalties derived from these five DC input values. Fitness is the sum of the amplification penalty, the bias penalty, and the two nonlinearity penalties.

First, the overall voltage amplification factor of the circuit is measured by the slope of the straight line between the output for –10 millivolts and the output for +10 millivolts (i.e., between the outputs for the endpoints of the DC sweep).

$$gain = \frac{out(-10 \text{ millivolts}) - out(10 \text{ millivolts})}{20 \text{ millivolts}}$$

If the voltage amplification factor is less than the maximum possible amplification (1,000-to-1 for this problem), the amplification penalty is equal to the numerical difference between the maximum possible gain and the actual gain. For example, if the gain were 100-to-1, there would be a penalty of 900 to the fitness measure.

Second, the linearity is measured by the deviation between the slope of each of two line segments and the circuit's overall voltage amplification factor. The first line segment connects the output values associated with inputs of –10 millivolts through –5 millivolts.

$$sub\_gain_0 = \frac{out(-10 \text{ millivolts}) - out(-5 \text{ millivolts})}{5 \text{ millivolts}}$$

The second line segment connects the output values associated with inputs of +5 millivolts and +10 millivolts.

$$sub\_gain_1 = \frac{out(+5 \text{ millivolts}) - out(+10 \text{ millivolts})}{5 \text{ millivolts}}$$

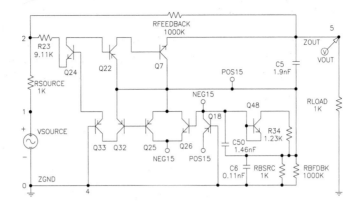

Figure 44.2   Best circuit from generation 0

The nonlinearity penalty for each of these line segments is equal to the absolute value of the difference in slope between the respective line segment and the circuit's voltage amplification factor.

Third, the bias is computed using the DC output associated with a DC input of 0 volts:

$$bias = out(0 \text{ millivolts})$$

The bias penalty is equal to the bias times a weight (which, for this problem, is 0.1).

Hits were not defined for this problem.

44.2.5   Parameters

The control parameters for this problem are found in the tableau (Table 44.1), the tables of percentages of genetic operations in Appendix D, and the default values specified in Appendix D.

44.2.6   Tableau

Table 44.1 summarizes the key features of the problem of designing a 60 dB amplifier.

44.3   RESULTS

The best circuit from generation 0 (Figure 44.2) achieves a fitness of 986.1 and has nine transistors, no diodes, three capacitors, and two resistors (in addition to the five resistors of the test fixture). Its circuit-constructing program tree has 16, 51, and 3 points in its three result-producing branches and 13 and 10 points in its two function-defining branches. When we say that this circuit (and other circuits in this book) has no diodes, we mean that it has no diodes that are created by diode-creating functions. This circuit does, in fact, contain diodes that are created by transistor-creating functions by joining the transistor's leads.

Figure 44.3 shows the time domain behavior of the best circuit from generation 0. The horizontal axis represents time (on a linear scale from 0 milliseconds to 5 milliseconds); the vertical axis represents peak output voltage ranging linearly from −1.0 volt to

Table 44.1 Tableau for 60 dB amplifier

Objective	Design a 60 dB amplifier.
Test fixture and embryo	One-input, one-output initial circuit with three modifiable wires providing feedback and permitting a maximum amplification of 60 dB
Program architecture	Two result-producing branches and two one-argument automatically defined functions (ADF0 and ADF1)
Initial function set for the RPBs	For construction-continuing subtrees: $F_{ccs-rpb-initial}$ = {ADF0, ADF1, R, C, SERIES, PARALLEL0, PARALLEL1, FLIP, NOP, RETAINING_GND_0, RETAINING_GND_1, RETAINING_POS15V_0, RETAINING_POS15V_1, RETAINING_NEG15V_0, RETAINING_NEG15V_1, PAIR_CONNECT_0, PAIR_CONNECT_1, Q_DIODE_NPN, Q_DIODE_PNP, Q_THREE_NPN0, . . . , Q_THREE_NPN11, Q_THREE_PNP0, . . . , Q_THREE_PNP11, QPC_NPN, QGE_NPN, QNE_NPN, QGE_PNP, QPE_PNP, QNC_PNP}. For arithmetic-performing subtrees: F_{aps} = {+, -}.
Initial terminal set for the RPBs	For construction-continuing subtrees: $T_{ccs-rpb-initial}$ = {END, SAFE_CUT}. For arithmetic-performing subtrees: T_{aps} = {$\Re_{smaller-reals}$}.
Initial function set for the ADFs	For construction-continuing subtrees: $F_{ccs-adf-initial}$ = $F_{ccs-rpb-initial}$ − {ADF0, ADF1}. For arithmetic-performing subtrees: F_{aps} = {+, -}.
Initial terminal set for the ADFs	For construction-continuing subtrees: $T_{ccs-adf-initial}$ = {ARG0, END, SAFE_CUT}. For arithmetic-performing subtrees: T_{aps} = {$\Re_{smaller-reals}$}.
Potential function set for the RPBs	Architecture-altering operations are not used.
Potential terminal set for the RPBs	Architecture-altering operations are not used.
Potential function set for the ADFs	Architecture-altering operations are not used.
Potential terminal set for the ADFs	Architecture-altering operations are not used.
Fitness cases	Five DC voltage values
Raw fitness	The sum of an amplification penalty, a bias penalty, and two nonlinearity penalties.
Standardized fitness	Same as raw fitness
Hits	Not used for this problem
Wrapper	None

Parameters	M = 640,000. G = 501. Q = 10,000. D = 64. B = 2%. S_{rpb} = 300. S_{adf} = 300. N_{rpb} = 2. $N_{max\text{-}adf}$ = 2. $N_{max\text{-}argument\text{-}adf}$ = 1.
Result designation	Best-so-far pace-setting individual
Success predicate	Fitness appears to have reached a plateau.

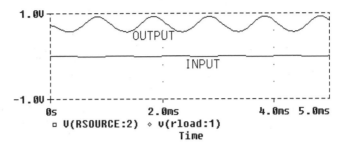

Figure 44.3   Time domain behavior of the best circuit from generation 0

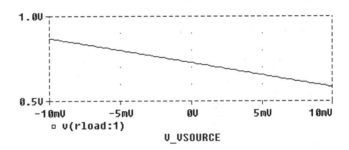

Figure 44.4   DC sweep for the best circuit from generation 0

+1.0 volt. The input is a 10-millivolt 1,000 Hz sinusoidal signal (whose oscillatory behavior is not visible in the figure). At 1,000 Hz, the amplification measured by a transient analysis is 24.8 dB, the bias is 740 millivolts, and the total harmonic distortion is 5.07%.

Figure 44.4 shows the result of performing SPICE's DC sweep on the best-of-generation circuit from generation 0. The horizontal axis ranges linearly from −10 millivolts to +10 millivolts. The vertical axis ranges from +0.5 volt to +1.0 volt. The amplification of an amplifier can be measured from the DC sweep. The amplification in decibels is 20 times the logarithm of the ratio of the change in the output divided by the change (20 millivolts) of the input. The amplification is 23.0 dB here. The DC sweep measures the bias to be 726 millivolts.

Figure 44.5 shows the AC sweep for the best circuit of generation 0. The amplification of an amplifier can also be measured from an AC sweep. The AC sweep, the transient analysis, and the circuit's time domain behavior played no role in the fitness measure for this problem. The horizontal axis of this figure represents frequency from 1 Hz to 1 MHz.

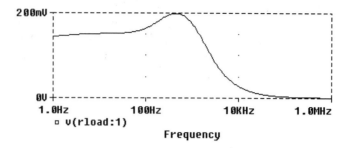

Figure 44.5   AC sweep for the best circuit from generation 0

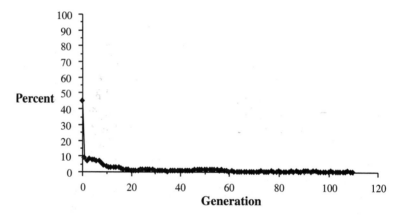

Figure 44.6   Percentage of unsimulatable circuits

The vertical axis ranges from 0 millivolts to 200 millivolts. The amplification at 1,000 Hz is 24.9 dB. The 3 dB bandwidth is 2,476 Hz. This circuit has a low frequency gain of 23.3 dB.

Figure 44.6 shows, by generation, the percentage of unsimulatable circuits in this run of this problem. About 45% of the programs of generation 0 produce circuits that cannot be simulated by SPICE. However, the percentage of unsimulatable circuits drops to 8% by generation 1. This percentage does not exceed 2% after generation 16 and does not exceed 1% after generation 58.

The best circuit (Figure 44.7) from generation 19 has 11 transistors, no diodes, one capacitor, and three resistors (in addition to the five resistors of the test fixture). It achieves a fitness of 691.1.

Figure 44.8 shows the time domain behavior of this circuit. The horizontal axis represents time ranging linearly from 0 milliseconds to 5 milliseconds. The vertical axis represents voltage ranging linearly from −10 volts to +10 volts. The input is a 10-millivolt 1,000 Hz sinusoidal signal (which appears as a straight line because of the scale of the figure). At 1,000 Hz, the amplification measured by a transient analysis is 49.8 dB, the bias is 5.1 volts, and the total harmonic distortion is 1.93%.

Figure 44.9 shows the result of performing SPICE's DC sweep on the best-of-generation circuit from generation 19. The horizontal axis represents voltage ranging linearly from −10

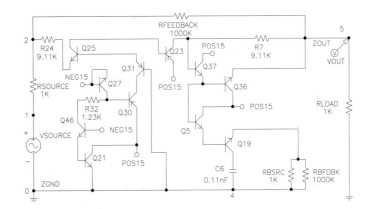

Figure 44.7   Best circuit from generation 19

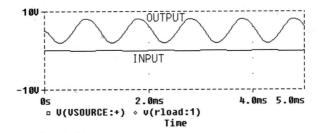

Figure 44.8   Time domain behavior of the best circuit from generation 19

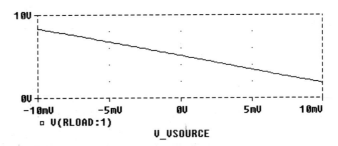

Figure 44.9   DC sweep of the best circuit from generation 19

millivolts to +10 millivolts. The vertical axis represents voltage and ranges linearly from 0 volts to 10 volts. The amplification is 50.2 dB here. There is a bias of 5.1 volts. The DC sweep shows a negative gain because the fitness measure requires a negative gain in order to achieve the goal of evolving an inverting amplifier.

Figure 44.10 shows the AC sweep for this circuit. The horizontal axis ranges over six decades of frequencies from 1 Hz to 1 MHz on a logarithmic scale. The vertical axis

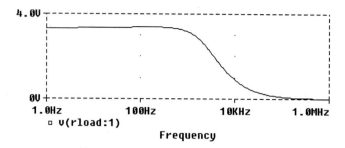

Figure 44.10   AC sweep for the best circuit from generation 19

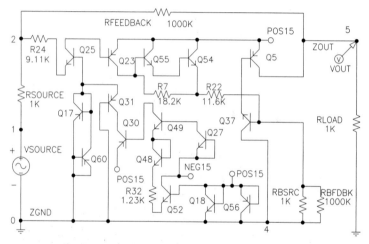

Figure 44.11   Best circuit from generation 49

ranges linearly from 0 volts to +4 volts. The 3 dB bandwidth is 2,699 Hz. The circuit has a flatband gain of 50.4 dB.

The best circuit (Figure 44.11) from generation 49 has 15 transistors, one diode (**Q48**) that was created with the diode-creating function (rather than by joining two leads of a transistor), no capacitors, and four resistors (in addition to the five resistors of the test fixture). This circuit achieves a fitness of 404.0.

Figure 44.12 shows the time domain behavior this circuit. The vertical axis represents voltage and ranges linearly from −20 volts to +20 volts. The input is a 10-millivolt 1,000 Hz sinusoidal signal (which appears as a straight line because of the scale of the figure). At 1,000 Hz, the amplification measured by a transient analysis is 56.9 dB, the bias is 7.3 volts, and the total harmonic distortion is 5.7%.

Figure 44.13 shows the result of performing SPICE's DC sweep on the best-of-generation circuit from generation 49. The amplification is 57.3 dB here. There is a bias of 7.2 volts.

Figure 44.14 shows the AC sweep for this circuit. The vertical axis ranges linearly from 0 volts to 10 volts. The 3 dB bandwidth is 3,981 Hz. The circuit has a flatband gain of 58.2 dB.

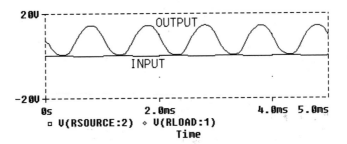

Figure 44.12   Time domain behavior of the best circuit from generation 49

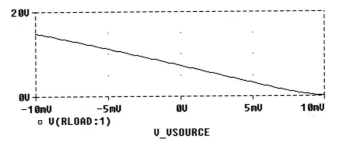

Figure 44.13   DC sweep of the best circuit from generation 49

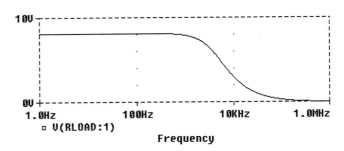

Figure 44.14   AC sweep for the best circuit from generation 49

The best circuit from generation 109 (Figure 44.15) has 22 transistors, no diodes, no capacitors, and 11 resistors (in addition to the 5 resistors of the test fixture). It achieves a fitness of 0.178. Its circuit-constructing program tree has 40, 98, and 27 points in its first, second, and third result-producing branches, respectively, and 33 and 144 points in its first and second automatically defined functions, respectively.

Figure 44.16 shows the time domain behavior of this circuit. The vertical axis represents voltage and ranges linearly from −10 volts to +10 volts. The input is a 10-millivolt 1,000 Hz sinusoidal signal; however, it appears here as a nearly straight line because of

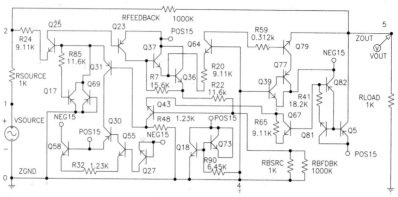

Figure 44.15 Best circuit from generation 109

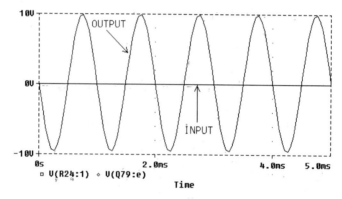

Figure 44.16 Time domain behavior of the best circuit from generation 109

the scale of this figure. At 1,000 Hz, the amplification measured by a transient analysis is 59.7 dB, the bias has dropped to 0.18 volt, and the total harmonic distortion is 0.17%.

Figure 44.17 shows the result of performing SPICE's DC sweep on the best-of-generation circuit from generation 109. The amplification is 60 dB here (i.e., 1,000-to-1 ratio). There is a bias of 0.2 volt. The *input-referred bias* is the ratio of 0.2 volt to the gain (1,000) and is therefore 0.0002 volt here. That is, a change of 0.0002 volt at the input would compensate and eliminate the 0.2-volt bias.

Figure 44.18 shows the AC sweep for this circuit. The vertical axis ranges linearly from 0 volts to 20 volts. The flatband gain is 60 dB, and the 3 dB bandwidth is 79,333 Hz.

Since the fitness measure and test fixture consider only the DC characteristics of the circuit, capacitors could have been left out of the function set for this problem. Nonetheless, we included capacitors with an eye toward examining the AC characteristics of the circuit and later adding factors to the fitness measure relating to AC characteristics. Even though capacitors were available for this problem, genetic programming tended not to use them. Table 44.2 shows the number of capacitors in the best circuits from generations 0, 19, 49, and 109. There are capacitors in the best-of-generation circuits early in the run, but there are none in the best-of-generation circuits in the table later in the run.

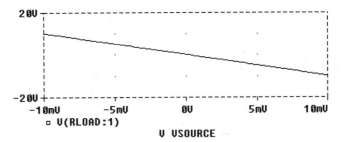

Figure 44.17   DC sweep of the best circuit from generation 109

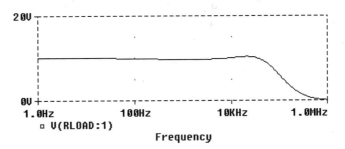

Figure 44.18   AC sweep for the best circuit from generation 109

Table 44.2 Number of capacitors in best-of-generation circuits

Generation	Number of capacitors
0	3
19	1
49	0
109	0

Similarly, there were no capacitors in any of the best-of-generation circuits shown for the 40 dB amplifier problem (Chapter 43) and the power supply rejection ratio problem (Chapter 46).

In summary, the best-of-run circuit of generation 109 achieves 60 dB amplification (based on the DC sweep), has almost no bias, has almost no total harmonic distortion, and generalizes well over the frequency domain.

We then embedded the evolved 22-transistor best circuit from generation 109 in a new test fixture that is appropriate for testing whether amplification of up to 80 dB is achieved. Specifically, the resistance of both **RFEEDBACK** and **RBALANCE_FEED-BACK** in this new 80 dB test fixture are multiplied by a factor of 10 and become 10,000,000 Ω. At the same time, there is a decrease by a factor of 10 in the input voltages in the 80 dB test fixture for the DC sweep, the AC sweep, and the transient analysis.

Figure 44.19 shows the result of performing SPICE's DC sweep on the best circuit from generation 109 when it is embedded in the new 80 dB test fixture. The input to the DC sweep ranges from –1 millivolt to +1 millivolt. The amplification is 80.15 dB here. There is a bias of 2.14 volts.

Figure 44.20 shows the time domain behavior of the best circuit from generation 109 when it is embedded in the new 80 dB test fixture. The vertical axis ranges from –20 volts to +20 volts. The input is the 1-millivolt 1,000 Hz sinusoidal signal; however, it appears here as a nearly straight line because of the scale of this figure. The amplification is 77.79 dB at 1,000 Hz. The bias is 2.08 volts. The total harmonic distortion is 1.56%.

Figure 44.21 shows the AC sweep for this circuit when it is embedded in the new 80 dB test fixture. The vertical axis ranges from 0 volts to 20 volts. The circuit delivers over 80 dB of amplification from 1 Hz to 36 Hz and over 77.86 dB from 36 Hz to 55,000 Hz. Amplification falls off above 55,000 Hz.

In summary, the evolved 22-transistor best-of-run circuit from generation 109 generalizes so as to deliver 80 dB of amplification (as measured by the DC sweep) when it is embedded in a test fixture that allows 80 dB of amplification. That is, there was generalization that yielded a desirable unrequested characteristic that was not incorporated into the fitness measure used in the run of genetic programming.

We then targeted a goal of amplification of 80 dB (using a fitness measure based on a maximum gain of 100 dB) and successfully evolved three additional amplifiers whose gain was in the mid-80s in terms of decibels.

The fitness measures for this problem (and all the other circuit synthesis problems involving transistors in this book) are limited in that they incorporate only some of the characteristics that are ordinarily demanded of commercial-quality circuits. For example, the fitness measure for the amplifier in this chapter explicitly incorporated three important characteristics: gain, bias, and distortion. As it happened, the evolved circuit generalized beyond these explicitly requested characteristics and also possessed certain unrequested additional desirable characteristics (e.g., reasonable bandwidth, reasonable parts count). A later chapter (46) will describe the addition of the power supply rejection ratio to the list of characteristics that are explicitly incorporated into the fitness measure of an amplifier. Nonetheless, the data sheet for a commercial-quality op amp includes numerous additional requirements (e.g., slew rate, power consumption) beyond those described in this book. Moreover, the design of commercial-quality circuits entails the use of more complex component models than those used here (Appendix E). Thus, we specifically do not claim that genetic programming has, at the present time, evolved a commercial-grade analog circuit involving transistors.

We do claim that we have established the principle that genetic programming can evolve both the topology and sizing for both passive circuits (e.g., filters) and active circuits (involving transistors). We also assert that the design of a circuit satisfying the characteristics that were explicitly incorporated into the fitness measure here (i.e., gain, bias, and distortion) is nontrivial and that there is no previously known general technique for automatically creating an entire analog circuit (i.e., both the topological arrangement of the components and the values of all of its components) from a high-level statement of the design goals of the circuit (e.g., the circuit's measurable behaviors and characteristics).

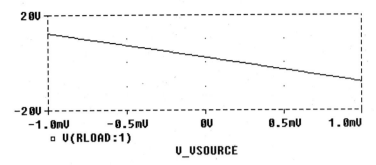

Figure 44.19   DC sweep of the best circuit from generation 109 with 80 dB test fixture

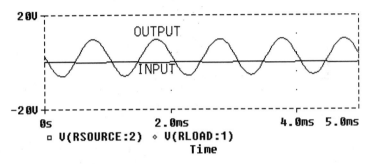

Figure 44.20   Time domain behavior of the best circuit from generation 109 with 80 dB test fixture

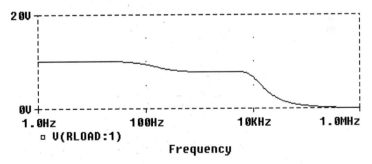

Figure 44.21   AC sweep for the best circuit from generation 109 with 80 dB test fixture

Synthesis of a 96 dB Amplifier with Architecture-Altering Operations

After evolving the 60 dB amplifier and three amplifiers with slightly more than 80 dB of amplification (Chapter 44), we tried to apply the same techniques to evolve an amplifier with amplification in the range of 100 dB (100,000-to-1). However, after trying several runs, these techniques did not appear capable of evolving a 100 dB amplifier. We therefore reexamined our techniques.

We noticed that one or both of the two power supplies (positive and negative) in some evolved circuits were shorted to ground or to each other. We speculated it might be useful to eliminate such circuits entirely from the population. Accordingly, we made a run in which the penalty value of fitness (10^8) was assigned to such circuits. However, this change was apparently ill advised (possibly because this penalization was so heavy-handed that it excessively reduced the diversity of the genetic material remaining in the circuit-constructing program trees). Thus, we abandoned this approach.

We then introduced three other changes that enabled genetic programming to evolve a high-gain 96 dB amplifier. First, we introduced the architecture-altering operations based on the conviction that, for more complex problems, we should rely on the evolutionary process to dynamically determine the number of automatically defined functions that are to be used in the solution to the problem.

Second, we noted the paper at the Genetic Programming 1996 Conference (Luke and Spector 1996b) describing the successful use of branch typing (Section 5.7.2) applied to result-producing branches in a problem of evolving teamwork in a multiagent system. Branch typing is commonly used for automatically defined functions (Koza 1994g). However, none of the problems in Koza 1994g had multiple result-producing branches. It had not previously occurred to us that branch typing might be relevant for the multiple result-producing branches of circuit problems—particularly the types of circuit problems (such as amplifiers) that human engineers frequently design in distinct stages. When only about 30 to 50 dB of amplification is required, a typical design for an amplifier might have just one stage. When additional amplification is required (say, about 50 to 70 dB), an amplifier might have two stages. Amplification in the neighborhood of about 100 dB might employ three stages. Because amplifiers are commonly designed by humans in stages, restriction of crossover to corresponding branches of a three-branch program seemed especially appropriate to the synthesis of a high-gain amplifier.

Third, we noticed that the Berkeley SPICE simulator that is embedded in our genetic programming system was reporting that some circuits were producing output voltages that exceeded the power supply voltages (i.e., the voltages on the rails). Beyond-the-rail voltages sometimes occur by bootstrapping when capacitors are present or because of parasitic capacitance. However, it should not be possible for the output voltage to go beyond the rails in a DC analysis. The beyond-the-rail results could not be replicated when the circuits were simulated offline with MicroSim's PSPICE simulator on a PC Pentium–type computer. We concluded that the evolutionary process had discovered and exploited a subtle anomaly of the Berkeley SPICE simulator. Therefore, we adopted the policy of assigning the penalty value of fitness (10^8) to circuits whose output voltage is beyond-the-rail. After this change, we no longer encountered this kind of discrepancy between the offline MicroSim PSPICE simulator and our modified version of the Berkeley SPICE simulator that is embedded in our genetic programming system.

45.1   DESIGN GOALS

The goal is to evolve the design of an amplifier that delivers around 100 dB (100,000-to-1) of amplification with low distortion and little, if any, bias.

45.2   PREPARATORY STEPS

45.2.1   Embryo and Test Fixture

The combination of the embryo and test fixture on this problem is designed to facilitate observation and measurement of would-be amplifier circuits. The initial circuit for this problem is created by embedding the embryo with three modifiable wires and four ports (Figure 29.15) into a one-input, one-output test fixture with four ports (Figure 29.8).

Figure 45.1 shows the one-input, one-output initial circuit that serves as a test fixture for would-be amplifier circuits. As explained in Section 44.2.1, the ratio of the feedback resistor to the source resistor establishes a ceiling on the possible amplification. The maximum possible amplification is limited to 120 dB (a 1,000,000-to-1 gain). This is a value that is greater than we are actually seeking. A choice of 100,000,000 Ω for feedback resistor **RFEEDBACK** and a choice of 100 Ω for the source resistor **RSOURCE** establishes this 1,000,000-to-1 ratio. The balance feedback resistor **RBALANCE_FEEDBACK** is 100,000,000 Ω, and the balance source resistor **RBALANCE_SOURCE** is 100 Ω.

45.2.2   Program Architecture

Since the embryo has three modifiable wires, there are three result-producing branches in each program tree.

Each program in generation 0 has a uniform architecture with three result-producing branches and no automatically defined functions. One-argument automatically defined functions will be created during the run by the architecture-altering operations. The argument to each automatically defined function is a value-setting (arithmetic-performing) subtree.

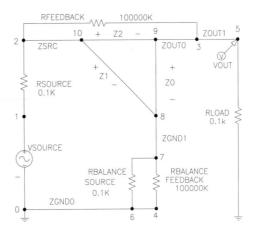

Figure 45.1   Initial circuit for the 96 dB amplifier

45.2.3   Functions and Terminals

The terminal sets are identical for all three result-producing branches of the program trees for this problem. The function sets are identical for all three result-producing branches. The desired amplifier is to be composed of transistors, diodes, resistors, and capacitors.

The initial function set, $F_{ccs-rpb-initial}$, for the construction-continuing subtrees of the result-producing branches is

$F_{ccs-rpb-initial}$ = {R, C, SERIES, PARALLEL0, PARALLEL1, FLIP, NOP, RETAINING_THREE_GROUND_0, RETAINING_THREE_GROUND_1, RETAINING_THREE_POS15V_0, RETAINING_THREE_POS15V_1, RETAINING_THREE_NEG15V_0, RETAINING_THREE_NEG15V_1, PAIR_CONNECT_0, PAIR_CONNECT_1, Q_DIODE_NPN, Q_DIODE_PNP, Q_THREE_NPN0, . . . , Q_THREE_NPN11, Q_THREE_PNP0, . . . , Q_THREE_PNP11, Q_POS15V_COLL_NPN, Q_GND_EMIT_NPN, Q_NEG15V_EMIT_NPN, Q_GND_EMIT_PNP, Q_POS15V_EMIT_PNP, Q_NEG15V_COLL_PNP}.

For the *npn* transistors, the Q2N3904 model is used. For *pnp* transistors, the Q2N3906 model is used.

The initial terminal set, $T_{ccs-rpb-initial}$, for the construction-continuing subtrees of the result-producing branches is

$T_{ccs-rpb-initial}$ = {END, SAFE_CUT}.

Since there are no automatically defined functions in generation 0 of this problem, $T_{ccs-adf-initial}$ and $F_{ccs-adf-initial}$ are empty.

The set of potential functions for each construction-continuing subtree of a result-producing branch, $F_{ccs-rpb-potential}$, is

$F_{ccs-rpb-potential}$ = {ADF0, ADF1, ADF2, ADF3}.

The set of potential terminals for each construction-continuing subtree of a result-producing branch, $T_{ccs-rpb-potential}$, is empty:

$$T_{ccs-rpb-potential} = \phi.$$

The newly created automatically defined functions do not hierarchically refer to one another. The set of potential functions for each construction-continuing subtree of an automatically defined function, $F_{ccs-adf-potential}$, is

```
Fccs-adf-potential = {R, C, SERIES, PARALLEL0, PARALLEL1, FLIP, NOP,
RETAINING_THREE_GROUND_0, RETAINING_THREE_GROUND_1,
RETAINING_THREE_POS15V_0, RETAINING_THREE_POS15V_1,
RETAINING_THREE_NEG15V_0, RETAINING_THREE_NEG15V_1,
PAIR_CONNECT_0, PAIR_CONNECT_1, Q_DIODE_NPN, Q_DIODE_PNP,
Q_THREE_NPN0, . . . , Q_THREE_NPN11, Q_THREE_PNP0, . . . ,
Q_THREE_PNP11, Q_POS15V_COLL_NPN, Q_GND_EMIT_NPN,
Q_NEG15V_EMIT_NPN, Q_GND_EMIT_PNP, Q_POS15V_EMIT_PNP,
Q_NEG15V_COLL_PNP}.
```

The set of potential terminals for each construction-continuing subtree of an automatically defined function, $T_{ccs-adf-potential}$, is

$$T_{ccs-adf-potential} = \{ARG0, END, SAFE\_CUT\}.$$

The function set, F_{aps}, for each arithmetic-performing subtree in any branch and the terminal set, T_{aps}, for each arithmetic-performing subtree in any branch are the same as for the lowpass filter problem in Section 25.14.3.

45.2.4   Fitness

An amplifier can be viewed in terms of its response to a DC input. An ideal inverting amplifier circuit receives a DC input, inverts it, and multiplies it by the voltage amplification factor.

A circuit is flawed to the extent that it does not achieve the desired amplification, to the extent that the DC response of the circuit at several different DC input voltages is not linear, or to the extent that the output signal is not centered around 0 volts (i.e., it has a bias).

Thus, for this problem, the fitness measure is based on SPICE's DC sweep. The DC sweep analysis measures the DC response of the circuit at several different DC input voltages. The circuits are analyzed with a five-point DC sweep ranging from –10 microvolts to +10 microvolts, with input points at –10, –5, 0, +5, and +10 microvolts. SPICE then produces the circuit's output voltages for each of these five DC input values.

Since there are five DC output values, there are five fitness cases for this problem. Fitness is then calculated from four penalties derived from these five DC output values. Fitness is the sum of the amplification penalty, the bias penalty, and the two nonlinearity penalties.

First, the overall voltage amplification factor of the circuit is measured using the overall value for the gain of the circuit as measured by the slope of the straight line between the output for –10 microvolts and the output for +10 microvolts (i.e., between the outputs for the endpoints of the DC sweep).

$$gain = \frac{out(-10 \text{ microvolts}) - out(10 \text{ microvolts})}{20 \text{ microvolts}}$$

If the voltage amplification factor is less than the maximum possible amplification (1,000,000-to-1 for this problem), the amplification penalty is equal to the numerical difference between the maximum possible gain and the actual gain. For example, if the gain were 100,000-to-1, there would be a penalty of 900,000 to the fitness measure.

Second, the linearity is measured by the deviation between the slope of each of two line segments and the circuit's overall voltage amplification factor. The first line segment connects the output values associated with inputs of –10 microvolts through –5 microvolts.

$$sub\_gain_0 = \frac{out(-10 \text{ microvolts}) - out(-5 \text{ microvolts})}{5 \text{ microvolts}}$$

The second line segment connects the output values associated with inputs of +5 microvolts and +10 microvolts.

$$sub\_gain_1 = \frac{out(+5 \text{ microvolts}) - out(+10 \text{ microvolts})}{5 \text{ microvolts}}$$

The nonlinearity penalty for each of these line segments is equal to the absolute value of the difference in slope between the respective line segment and the circuit's voltage amplification factor.

Third, the bias is computed using the DC output associated with a DC input of 0 volts:

$$bias = out \, (0 \text{ microvolts})$$

The bias penalty is equal to the bias times a weight (which, for this problem, is 0.1).

Thus, fitness ranges from a worst value of 1,000,000 to a potential best value of 0.

To facilitate monitoring of the run, the number of hits is defined as the integral number of decibels of amplification.

45.2.5 Parameters

The control parameters are the same as for the problem of synthesizing a lowpass filter with architecture-altering operations (Section 28.2.5).

45.2.6 Tableau

Table 45.1 summarizes the key features of the problem of designing a 96 dB amplifier.

45.3 RESULTS

The best circuit from generation 0 (Figure 45.2) has a fitness of 999,992.1. It has five transistors, no diodes, no capacitors, and one resistor (in addition to the five resistors of the test fixture). The three result-producing branches of its circuit-constructing program tree have 15, 6, and 13 points. In generation 0 of this run, there are no automatically

Table 45.1 Tableau for a 96 dB amplifier with architecture-altering operations

Objective	Design an amplifier with amplification approaching 100 dB.
Test fixture and embryo	One-input, one-output initial circuit composed of an embryo with three modifiable wires and a test fixture providing feedback and a maximum possible amplification of 120 dB
Program architecture	Three result-producing branches in generation 0. Additional one-argument automatically defined functions will be created during the run by the architecture-altering operations.
Initial function set for the RPBs	For construction-continuing subtrees: $F_{ccs-rpb-initial}$ = {R, C, SERIES, PARALLEL0, PARALLEL1, FLIP, NOP, RETAINING_GND_0, RETAINING_GND_1, RETAINING_POS15V_0, RETAINING_POS15V_1, RETAINING_NEG15V_0, RETAINING_NEG15V_1, PAIR_CONNECT_0, PAIR_CONNECT_1, Q_DIODE_NPN, Q_DIODE_PNP, Q_THREE_NPN0, . . . , Q_THREE_NPN11, Q_THREE_PNP0, . . . , Q_THREE_PNP11, QPC_NPN, QGE_NPN, QNE_NPN, QGE_PNP, QPE_PNP, QNC_PNP}. For arithmetic-performing subtrees: F_{aps} = {+, -}.
Initial terminal set for the RPBs	For construction-continuing subtrees: $T_{ccs-rpb-initial}$ = {END, SAFE_CUT}. For arithmetic-performing subtrees: T_{aps} = {$\Re_{smaller-reals}$}.
Initial function set for the ADFs	$F_{ccs-adf-initial}$ = ϕ
Initial terminal set for the ADFs	$T_{ccs-adf-initial}$ = ϕ
Potential function set for the RPBs	$F_{ccs-rpb-potential}$ = {ADF0, ADF1, ADF2, ADF3}
Potential terminal set for the RPBs	$T_{ccs-rpb-potential}$ = ϕ
Potential function set for the ADFs	$F_{ccs-adf-potential}$ = {R, C, SERIES, PARALLEL0, PARALLEL1, FLIP, NOP, RETAINING_THREE_GROUND_0, RETAINING_THREE_GROUND_1, RETAINING_THREE_POS15V_0, RETAINING_THREE_POS15V_1, RETAINING_THREE_NEG15V_0, RETAINING_THREE_NEG15V_1, PAIR_CONNECT_0, PAIR_CONNECT_1, Q_DIODE_NPN, Q_DIODE_PNP, Q_THREE_NPN0, . . . , Q_THREE_NPN11, Q_THREE_PNP0, . . . , Q_THREE_PNP11, Q_POS15V_COLL_NPN, Q_GND_EMIT_NPN, Q_NEG15V_EMIT_NPN, Q_GND_EMIT_PNP, Q_POS15V_EMIT_PNP, Q_NEG15V_COLL_PNP}.
Potential terminal set for the ADFs	$T_{ccs-adf-potential}$ = {ARG0, END, SAFE_CUT}
Fitness cases	Five DC values as fitness cases
Raw fitness	The sum of an amplification penalty, a bias penalty, and two nonlinearity penalties

Standardized fitness	Same as raw fitness
Hits	The number of hits is defined as the number of decibels of amplification.
Wrapper	None
Parameters	$M = 640{,}000$. $G = 501$. $Q = 10{,}000$. $D = 64$. $B = 2\%$. $S_{rpb} = 300$. $S_{adf} = 200$. $N_{rpb} = 3$. $N_{max\text{-}adf} = 4$. $N_{max\text{-}argument\text{-}adf} = 1$.
Result designation	Best-so-far pace-setting individual
Success predicate	Fitness appears to have reached a plateau.

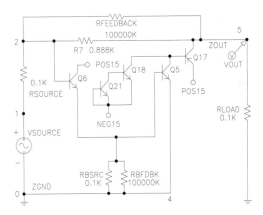

Figure 45.2 Best circuit from generation 0

defined functions in any individual in the population; however, they are introduced in later generations by the architecture-altering operations.

Figure 45.3 shows the time domain behavior produced by a SPICE transient analysis at 1,000 Hz of the best circuit from generation 0. The common horizontal axis represents time (from 0 milliseconds to 5 milliseconds). The two vertical axes represent voltage on a linear scale. Note that the scales on the two vertical axes differ by six orders of magnitude (microvolts to volts). The top half of this figure shows the 10-microvolt 1,000 Hz sinusoidal input signal (for which the vertical axis ranges linearly over peak voltages from −10 microvolts to +10 microvolts). The bottom half shows the resulting output (for which the vertical axis ranges linearly over peak voltages ranging linearly between +13.050 volts and +13.051 volts). Note that the output is inverted, almost undistorted, and has a DC bias. Based on this transient analysis, the amplification is 19.6 dB, the bias is 13.8505 volts, and the total harmonic distortion is 0.3%.

Figure 45.4 shows the result of performing SPICE's DC sweep on the best-of-generation circuit from generation 0. The horizontal axis represents input DC values ranging linearly from −10 microvolts to +10 microvolts. The vertical axis represents the output voltage ranging linearly from +13.850 volts to +13.851 volts. The amplification of an amplifier can be measured from the DC sweep. Based on the DC sweep, the amplification is 19.6 dB, and the bias is 13.85 volts.

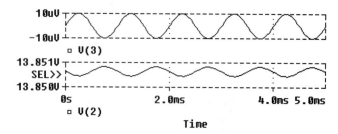

Figure 45.3 Time domain behavior of the best circuit from generation 0

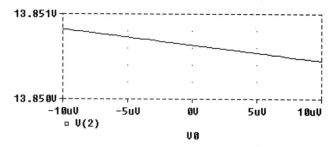

Figure 45.4 DC sweep for the best circuit from generation 0

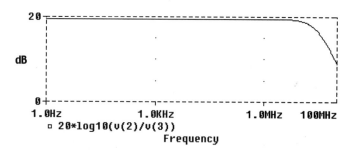

Figure 45.5 AC sweep for the best circuit from generation 0

Figure 45.5 shows the frequency response of this circuit as shown by an AC sweep. The horizontal axis ranges over eight decades of frequencies from 1 Hz to 100 MHz. The vertical axis ranges from 0 dB to 20 dB. The amplification of an amplifier can also be measured from an AC sweep. Of course, the results of the AC sweep played no role in the fitness measure for this problem. The 3 dB bandwidth is 30.1 MHz. The circuit has a flat-band gain of 19.5 dB.

Figure 45.6 shows, by generation, the percentage of unsimulatable circuits in this run of this problem. About 41% of the circuits of generation 0 cannot be simulated by SPICE; however, the percentage of unsimulatable circuits drops to between 2% and 4% between generations 1 and 10 and never exceeds 8% thereafter.

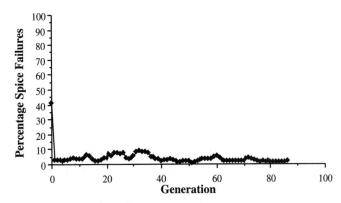

Figure 45.6   Percentage of unsimulatable circuits

Starting with generation 1, the architecture-altering operations begin to introduce automatically defined functions into some of the individuals in the population. The first pace-setting individual with an automatically defined function appears in generation 12.

The best circuit (Figure 45.7) from generation 42 has 28 transistors, no diodes, four capacitors, and two resistors (in addition to the five resistors of the test fixture). It achieves a fitness of 989,101.4. Because of the operation of the architecture-altering operations, there is one automatically defined function ADF0 in the program tree. Two-ported ADF0 is called only once. As shown in Figure 45.8, two-ported ADF0 has seven transistors, no diodes, one capacitor, and one resistor.

Figure 45.9 shows the time domain behavior produced by a SPICE transient analysis at 1,000 Hz for the best circuit from generation 42. The common horizontal axis represents time (from 0 milliseconds to 5 milliseconds) on a linear scale. Both vertical axes represent voltage on a linear scale. Note that the scales on the two vertical axes differ by six orders of magnitude (microvolts and volts). The top half of this figure shows the 10-microvolt 1,000 Hz sinusoidal input signal (for which the vertical axis ranges linearly over peak voltages from −10 microvolts to +10 microvolts). The bottom half shows the resulting output (for which the vertical axis ranges linearly over peak voltages from +5 volts to +7 volts). Based on this transient analysis, the amplification is 82.8 dB (13,800-to-1), the bias is 6.05 volts, and the total harmonic distortion is 7.62%.

Figure 45.10 shows the result of performing SPICE's DC sweep on the best-of-generation circuit from generation 42. Based on the DC sweep, the amplification is 81.8 dB (12,315-to-1), and the bias is 6.00 volts.

Figure 45.11 shows the AC sweep for this circuit of generation 42. The horizontal axis ranges over seven decades of frequencies from 1 Hz to 10 MHz on a logarithmic scale. The vertical axis ranges from 0 dB to 100 dB. The 3 dB bandwidth is 4,770 Hz. The circuit has a flatband gain of 81.7 dB.

The best circuit (Figure 45.12) from generation 50 has 33 transistors, no diodes, eight capacitors, and five resistors (in addition to the five resistors of the test fixture). It achieves a fitness of 971,076.4. No automatically defined functions are present.

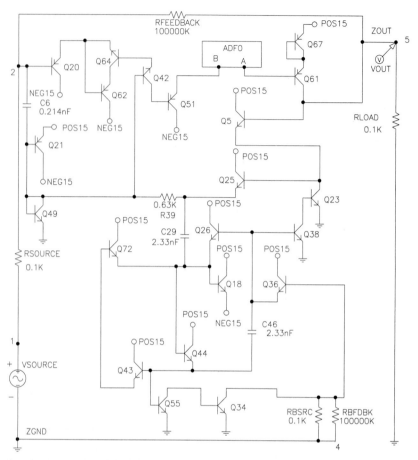

Figure 45.7   Best circuit from generation 42

Figure 45.13 shows the time domain behavior produced by a SPICE transient analysis at 1,000 Hz of this circuit from generation 50. The common horizontal axis represents time (from 0 milliseconds to 5 milliseconds) on a linear scale. The two vertical axes represent voltage on a linear scale. Note that the scales on the two vertical axes differ by six orders of magnitude (microvolts to volts). The top half of this figure shows the 10-microvolt 1,000 Hz sinusoidal input signal (for which the vertical axis ranges over voltages from –10 microvolts to +10 microvolts). The bottom half shows the resulting output (for which the vertical axis ranges over voltages from +8 volts to +12 volts). Based on this transient analysis, the amplification is 89.7 dB (30,500-to-1), the bias is 9.76 volts, and the total harmonic distortion is 6.29%.

Figure 45.14 shows the result of performing SPICE's DC sweep on the best-of-generation circuit from generation 50. Based on the DC sweep, the amplification is 89.7 dB (30,545-to-1), and the bias is 9.77 volts.

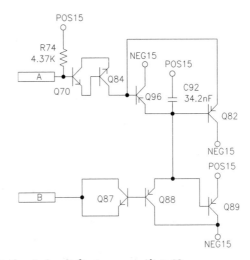

Figure 45.8 ADF0 for best circuit from generation 42

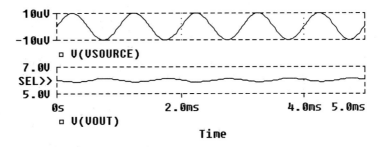

Figure 45.9 Time domain behavior of the best circuit from generation 42

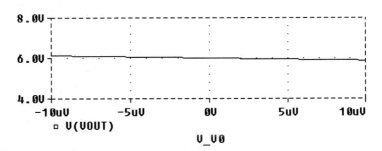

Figure 45.10 DC sweep of the best circuit from generation 42

Figure 45.15 shows the AC sweep for this circuit of generation 50. The vertical axis ranges from 0 dB to +100 dB. The 3 dB bandwidth is 2,300 Hz. This circuit has a flatband gain of 89.7 dB.

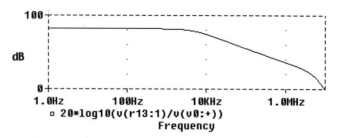

Figure 45.11   AC sweep for the best circuit from generation 42

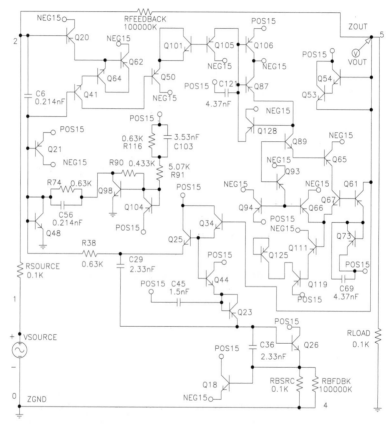

Figure 45.12   Best circuit from generation 50

The best circuit (Figure 45.16) from generation 86 achieves a fitness of 938,427.3. The program has two automatically defined functions. ADF0 is called once; ADF1 is not called. The circuit (without ADF0) has 25 transistors, no diodes, two capacitors, and two resistors (in addition to the five resistors of the test fixture). There are 75, 141, and 34 points in the three result-producing branches, and there are 86 and 153 points in the two function-defining branches.

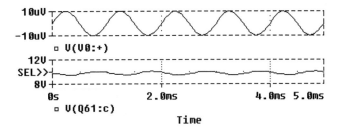

Figure 45.13 **Time domain behavior of the best circuit from generation 50**

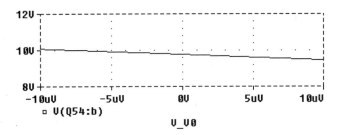

Figure 45.14 **DC sweep of the best circuit from generation 50**

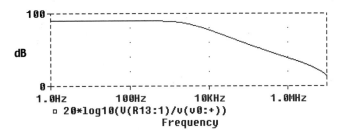

Figure 45.15 **AC sweep for the best circuit from generation 50**

As shown in Figure 45.17, ADF0 of the best circuit from generation 86 has 12 transistors, no diodes, one capacitor, and two resistors.

Figure 45.18 shows the time domain behavior produced by a SPICE transient analysis at 1,000 Hz of the best circuit from generation 86. The common horizontal axis represents time (from 0 milliseconds to 5 milliseconds) on a linear scale. The two vertical axes represent voltage on a linear scale. Note that the scales on the two vertical axes differ by six orders of magnitude (microvolts to volts). The top half of this figure shows the 10-microvolt 1,000 Hz sinusoidal input signal (for which the vertical axis ranges over voltages from −10 microvolts to +10 microvolts). The bottom half shows the resulting output (for which the vertical axis ranges over voltages from +6 volts to +8 volts). Based on this transient analysis, the amplification is 94.1 dB, the bias is 7.46 volts, and the total harmonic distortion is 7.07%. Note that the output is inverted.

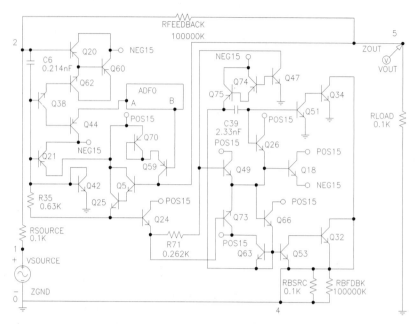

Figure 45.16 Best circuit from generation 86

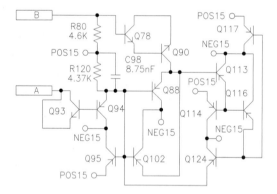

Figure 45.17 ADF0 for best circuit from generation 86

Figure 45.19 shows the result of performing SPICE's DC sweep on the best-of-generation circuit from generation 86. The horizontal axis represents input DC values ranging linearly from –10 microvolts to +10 microvolts. The vertical axis represents the output voltage on a linear scale. Based on the DC sweep, the amplification is 96.2 dB (64,860-to-1), and the bias is 7.44 volts. The input-referred bias here is the ratio of 7.44 volts to the gain (64,860) and is therefore 0.0002 volts. That is, a change of 0.000115 volt at the input would compensate and eliminate the 7.44-volt bias.

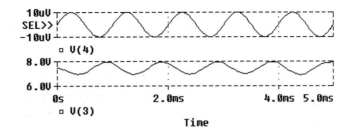

Figure 45.18   Time domain behavior of the best circuit from generation 86

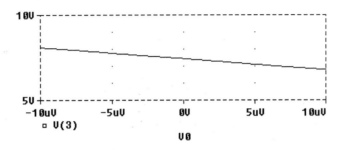

Figure 45.19   DC sweep of the best circuit from generation 86

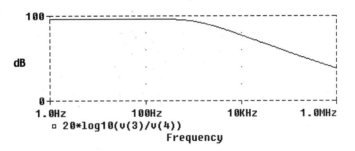

Figure 45.20   AC sweep for the best circuit from generation 86

Figure 45.20 shows the frequency response of this circuit as shown by an AC sweep. The horizontal axis ranges over six decades of frequencies from 1 Hz to 1 MHz on a logarithmic scale. The vertical axis ranges from 0 dB to +100 dB. The 3 dB bandwidth is 1,078.4 Hz. The circuit has a flatband gain of 96.3 dB.

The task of designing an amplifier is known to be nontrivial. Hundreds of patents for amplifiers have been issued over the years. Harold S. Black (mentioned in Chapter 1 in connection with his invention of the negative feedback amplifier while crossing the Hudson River on the Lackawanna Ferry in 1927) himself received numerous patents for amplifiers. In particular, Black received two early and fundamental patents on amplifiers in 1935 and 1937 (Black 1935, 1937).

This chapter and Chapter 44 showed that both the topology and component sizing for 60 dB and 96 dB amplifiers can be created by genetic programming. In addition, the next chapter demonstrates the evolution of a 40 dB amplifier with a high power supply rejection ratio, and Chapters 42 and 43 demonstrated the evolution of a 10 dB and a 39 dB amplifier, respectively.

Referring to the eight criteria in Chapter 1 for establishing that an automatically created result is competitive with a human-produced result, these results satisfy the following criteria:

A. The result was patented as an invention in the past, is an improvement over a patented invention, or would qualify today as a patentable new invention.

F. The result is equal to or better than a result that was considered an achievement in its field at the time it was first discovered.

Therefore, we make the following claim:

- **CLAIM NO. 8** We claim that the automatic synthesis by genetic programming of 60 and 96 decibel amplifiers is an instance where genetic programming has produced a result that is competitive with a result produced by creative and inventive humans.

These instances of automated design satisfy Arthur Samuel's criterion (1983) for artificial intelligence and machine learning:

The aim [is] . . . to get machines to exhibit behavior, which if done by humans, would be assumed to involve the use of intelligence.

Synthesis of an Amplifier with a High Power Supply Rejection Ratio

Chapters 42 through 45 demonstrate that it is possible to evolve amplifier circuits with high gain, low bias, and low distortion (high linearity).

The data sheet for a commercial-quality op amp, such as the μ741 op amp, includes numerous additional requirements, such as power supply rejection ratio, slew rate, power consumption, and so forth. Thus, it is important to demonstrate that it is possible to expand a multiobjective fitness measure so as to include more and more factors.

The power supply rejection ratio is important in designing amplifiers (and other circuits) because it is desirable that the output of a circuit not be unduly affected by fluctuations in the voltage provided by the circuit's external power supply.

The *power supply rejection ratio* is defined as 20 times the common logarithm of the quotient of the change in power supply voltage and the change in output voltage. A higher value of the power supply rejection ratio is more desirable.

46.1 DESIGN GOALS

The goal is to evolve the design of a low-bias, low-distortion 40 dB (100-to-1) amplifier with a high power supply rejection ratio.

46.2 PREPARATORY STEPS

46.2.1 Embryo and Test Fixture

The combination of the embryo and test fixture on this problem is designed to facilitate observation and measurement of would-be amplifier circuits. The initial circuit for this problem is created by embedding the embryo with three modifiable wires and four ports (Figure 29.15) into a one-input, one-output test fixture with four ports (Figure 29.8).

Figure 46.1 shows a one-input, one-output initial circuit that serves as a test fixture for would-be amplifier circuits that limits the possible amplification of the circuit to a

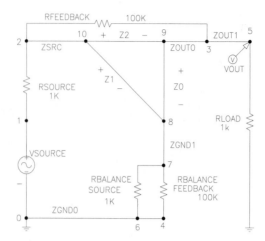

Figure 46.1 Initial circuit for a 40 dB amplifier

100-to-1 ratio (40 dB). The test fixture contains a fixed 1,000 Ω load resistor **RLOAD**, a fixed 1,000 Ω source resistor **RSOURCE**, a fixed 100,000 Ω feedback resistor **RFEED-BACK**, a fixed 1,000 Ω balancing source resistor **RBALANCE_SOURCE**, and a fixed 100,000 Ω balancing feedback resistor **RBALANCE_FEEDBACK**.

46.2.2   Architecture

Since the embryo has three modifiable wires, there are three result-producing branches in each program tree.

Each program tree contains two one-argument automatically defined functions. The argument to each automatically defined function is an arithmetic-performing subtree. No hierarchical references are allowed among the automatically defined functions.

No architecture-altering operations are used in this problem.

Consequently, the architecture of each program tree in the population consists of a total of five branches (i.e., two automatically defined functions and three result-producing branches).

46.2.3   Functions and Terminals

The terminal sets are identical for all three result-producing branches of the program trees. The function sets are identical for all three result-producing branches.

The initial function set, $F_{ccs-rpb-initial}$, for each construction-continuing subtree of each result-producing branch is

```
Fccs-rpb-initial = {ADF0, ADF1, R, C, SERIES, PARALLEL0, PARALLEL1,
FLIP, NOP, RETAINING_THREE_GROUND_0, RETAINING_THREE_GROUND_1,
RETAINING_THREE_POS15V_0, RETAINING_THREE_POS15V_1,
RETAINING_THREE_NEG15V_0, RETAINING_THREE_NEG15V_1,
PAIR_CONNECT_0, PAIR_CONNECT_1, Q_DIODE_NPN, Q_DIODE_PNP,
Q_THREE_NPN0, . . . , Q_THREE_NPN11, Q_THREE_PNP0, . . . ,
Q_THREE_PNP11, Q_POS15V_COLL_NPN, Q_GND_EMIT_NPN,
```

```
Q_NEG15V_EMIT_NPN, Q_GND_EMIT_PNP, Q_POS15V_EMIT_PNP,
Q_NEG15V_COLL_PNP}.
```

The initial terminal set, $T_{ccs-rpb-initial}$, for each construction-continuing subtree of each result-producing branch is

$T_{ccs-rpb-initial}$ = {END, SAFE_CUT}.

The terminal sets are identical for both function-defining branches (automatically defined functions). The function sets are identical for both.

The function set, $F_{ccs-adf-initial}$, for each construction-continuing subtree of each automatically defined function is

```
Fccs-adf-initial = Fccs-rpb-initial − {ADF0, ADF1} = {R, C, SERIES,
PARALLEL0, PARALLEL1, FLIP, NOP, RETAINING_THREE_GROUND_0,
RETAINING_THREE_GROUND_1, RETAINING_THREE_POS15V_0,
RETAINING_THREE_POS15V_1, RETAINING_THREE_NEG15V_0,
RETAINING_THREE_NEG15V_1, PAIR_CONNECT_0, PAIR_CONNECT_1,
Q_DIODE_NPN, Q_DIODE_PNP, Q_THREE_NPN0, . . . , Q_THREE_NPN11,
Q_THREE_PNP0, . . . , Q_THREE_PNP11, Q_POS15V_COLL_NPN,
Q_GND_EMIT_NPN, Q_NEG15V_EMIT_NPN, Q_GND_EMIT_PNP,
Q_POS15V_EMIT_PNP, Q_NEG15V_COLL_PNP}.
```

The terminal set, $T_{ccs-adf-initial}$, for each construction-continuing subtree of each automatically defined function is

$T_{ccs-adf-initial}$ = {ARG0, END, SAFE_CUT}.

Since there are no architecture-altering operations in this problem, $T_{rpb-potential}$, $F_{rpb-potential}$, $T_{adf-potential}$, and $F_{adf-potential}$ are empty.

The function set, F_{aps}, for each arithmetic-performing subtree in any branch and the terminal set, T_{aps}, for each arithmetic-performing subtree in any branch are the same as for the lowpass filter problem in Section 25.14.3.

46.2.4   Fitness

The starting point for evaluating the fitness of a circuit in this chapter is its response to a DC input. An ideal inverting amplifier circuit would receive a DC input, invert it, and multiply it by the voltage amplification factor.

A circuit is flawed to the extent that it does not achieve the desired amplification, to the extent that the output signal is not centered around 0 volts (i.e., it has a bias), to the extent that the DC response is not linear, and to the extent that the power supply rejection ratio is small.

Thus, for this problem, the fitness measure is based on three DC sweeps in SPICE. The DC sweep analysis measures the DC response of the circuit at several different DC input voltages.

1.   The circuit is analyzed with a five-point DC sweep of **VSOURCE** at –100, –50, 0, +50, and +100 millivolts. SPICE then produces the circuit's output for each of these five DC voltages.

2. The circuit is analyzed with a two-point DC sweep over the nominal +15-volt power supply, **POS15**, ranging from +14 volts to +16 volts. SPICE then produces the circuit's output for each of these two DC voltages.

3. The circuit is analyzed with a two-point DC sweep over the nominal −15-volt power supply, **NEG15**, ranging from −16 volts to −14 volts. SPICE then produces the circuit's output for each of these two DC voltages.

Thus, there are nine fitness cases for this problem.

Fitness is the sum of six penalties based on these nine fitness cases. The first four penalties (amplification penalty, bias penalty, two nonlinearity penalties) arise from the five-point DC sweep over **VSOURCE**. The fifth penalty arises from the two-point DC sweep over **POS15**. The sixth penalty arises from the two-point DC sweep over **NEG15**.

The first penalty is computed as follows: The circuit's voltage amplification factor is measured by the slope of the straight line between the output for −100 millivolts and the output for +100 millivolts (i.e., between the outputs for the endpoints of the DC sweep). If the voltage amplification factor is less than the maximum allowed by the feedback resistor (40 dB), there is a penalty equal to the shortfall in amplification.

The second penalty is computed as follows: The bias is computed using the DC output associated with a DC input of 0 volts. The bias penalty is equal to the bias times a weight. The weight is 0.1 for the bias penalty for this problem (with all other penalties receiving a weight of 1.0).

The third and fourth penalties are computed as follows: The linearity is measured by the deviation between the slope of each of two line segments and the circuit's overall voltage amplification factor. The first line segment spans the output values associated with inputs of −100 millivolts and −50 millivolts. The second line segment spans the output values associated with inputs of +50 millivolts and +100 millivolts. The penalty for each of these line segments is equal to the absolute value of the difference in slope between the respective line segment and the circuit's voltage amplification factor.

The fifth penalty is computed as follows: The power supply rejection ratio of the circuit is measured by the negative of the slope of the straight line between the output for +14 volts and the output for +16 volts (i.e., between the outputs for the endpoints of the two-point DC sweep for **POS15**). The penalty is the reciprocal of this number.

The sixth penalty is computed as follows: The power supply rejection ratio of the circuit is measured by the negative of the slope of the straight line between the output for −16 volts and the output for −14 volts (i.e., between the outputs for the endpoints of the two-point DC sweep for **NEG15**). The penalty is the reciprocal of this number.

If a particular circuit fails to use a particular power supply (**POS15** or **NEG15**), that penalty is set to zero.

46.2.5 Parameters

The population size, M, is 600,000. There is no significance to the use of a slightly different population size for this problem (and other problems in this book run with this population size). Four of the processing nodes of our 64-node parallel computer system were being repaired at the time that this problem was run, so we reconfigured the parallel system computer as a 6×10 toroidal mesh.

The control parameters for this problem are found in the tableau (Table 46.1), the tables of percentages of genetic operations in Appendix D, and the default values specified in Appendix D.

46.2.6 Tableau

Table 46.1 summarizes the key features of the problem of synthesizing an amplifier with a high power supply rejection ratio.

46.3 RESULTS

The best circuit (Figure 46.2) from generation 0 has five transistors, one diode, no capacitors, and one resistor (in addition to the resistors of the test fixture) and achieves a fitness of 99.85. ADF0 and ADF1 are not used. The three result-producing branches have 10, 3, and 10 points and the two automatically defined functions have 25 and 3 points. The DC sweep of **VSOURCE** shows that the circuit has an amplification of 1.38 dB (1.17-to-1) and a bias of 7.26 volts. Based on the AC sweep, the 3 dB bandwidth is 6.12 MHz. Based on a DC sweep of the power supply **POS15**, the power supply rejection ratio is 13.4 dB. The total power dissipation is 268 milliwatts.

Figure 46.3 shows the time domain behavior produced by a SPICE transient analysis at 1,000 Hz of the best circuit from generation 0. The common horizontal axis represents time (from 0 milliseconds to 5 milliseconds) on a linear scale. Both vertical axes represent voltage on a linear scale. Note that the scales on the two vertical axes differ by three orders of magnitude (millivolts and volts). The top half of this figure shows a 100-millivolt 1,000 Hz sinusoidal input signal (for which the vertical axis ranges linearly over peak voltages from −100 millivolts to +100 millivolts). The bottom half shows the resulting output (for which the vertical axis ranges linearly over peak voltages from +7.0 volts to +7.50 volts). Note that the output is inverted, almost undistorted, and has a DC bias. Based on this transient analysis, the amplification is 1.34 dB, the bias is 7.3 volts, and the total harmonic distortion is 0.94%.

Figure 46.4 shows the result of performing SPICE's DC sweep on the best-of-generation circuit from generation 0. The horizontal axis represents input DC values ranging linearly from −100 millivolts to +100 millivolts. The vertical axis represents the output voltage on a linear scale between +7.00 volts and +7.50 volts. The amplification of an amplifier can be measured from the DC sweep. Based on the DC sweep, the amplification is 1.38 dB, and the bias is 7.26 volts.

Figure 46.5 shows the frequency response of this circuit as shown by an AC sweep for the best circuit from generation 0. The amplification of an amplifier can also be measured from an AC sweep. The results of the AC sweep played no role in the fitness measure for this problem. The horizontal axis ranges over seven decades of frequencies from 1 Hz to 10 MHz on a logarithmic scale. The vertical axis ranges from −5 dB to +5 dB. The 3 dB bandwidth is 6.12 MHz. The circuit has a flatband gain of 1.37 dB.

The fitness measure for this problem did not incorporate power consumption. According to an offline simulation made in MicroSim's PSPICE, the total power dissipation is 268 milliwatts for the best-of-generation circuit from generation 0. The penalty in

Table 46.1 Tableau for amplifier with a high power supply rejection ratio

Objective	Design of a low-bias, low-distortion 40 dB (100-to-1) amplifier with a high power supply rejection ratio.
Test fixture and embryo	One-input, one-output initial circuit with three modifiable wires providing feedback and permitting a maximum amplification of 40 dB
Program architecture	Three result-producing branches and two one-argument automatically defined functions
Initial function set for the RPBs	For construction-continuing subtrees: $F_{ccs\text{-}rpb\text{-}initial}$ = {ADF0, ADF1, R, C, SERIES, PARALLEL0, PARALLEL1, FLIP, NOP, RETAINING_THREE_GROUND_0, RETAINING_THREE_GROUND_1, RETAINING_THREE_POS15V_0, RETAINING_THREE_POS15V_1, RETAINING_THREE_NEG15V_0, RETAINING_THREE_NEG15V_1, PAIR_CONNECT_0, PAIR_CONNECT_1, Q_DIODE_NPN, Q_DIODE_PNP, Q_THREE_NPN0, . . . , Q_THREE_NPN11, Q_THREE_PNP0, . . . , Q_THREE_PNP11, Q_POS15V_COLL_NPN, Q_GND_EMIT_NPN, Q_NEG15V_EMIT_NPN, Q_GND_EMIT_PNP, Q_POS15V_EMIT_PNP, Q_NEG15V_COLL_PNP}. For arithmetic-performing subtrees: F_{aps} = {+, -}.
Initial terminal set for the RPBs	For construction-continuing subtrees: $T_{ccs\text{-}rpb\text{-}initial}$ = {END, SAFE_CUT}. For arithmetic-performing subtrees: T_{aps} = {$\Re_{smaller\text{-}reals}$}.
Initial function set for the ADFs	For construction-continuing subtrees: $F_{ccs\text{-}adf\text{-}initial}$ = $F_{ccs\text{-}rpb\text{-}initial}$ - {ADF0, ADF1} = {R, C, SERIES, PARALLEL0, PARALLEL1, FLIP, NOP, RETAINING_THREE_GROUND_0, RETAINING_THREE_GROUND_1, RETAINING_THREE_POS15V_0, RETAINING_THREE_POS15V_1, RETAINING_THREE_NEG15V_0, RETAINING_THREE_NEG15V_1, PAIR_CONNECT_0, PAIR_CONNECT_1, Q_DIODE_NPN, Q_DIODE_PNP, Q_THREE_NPN0, . . . , Q_THREE_NPN11, Q_THREE_PNP0, . . . , Q_THREE_PNP11, Q_POS15V_COLL_NPN, Q_GND_EMIT_NPN, Q_NEG15V_EMIT_NPN, Q_GND_EMIT_PNP, Q_POS15V_EMIT_PNP, Q_NEG15V_COLL_PNP}. For arithmetic-performing subtrees: F_{aps} = {+, -}.
Initial terminal set for the ADFs	For construction-continuing subtrees: $T_{ccs\text{-}adf\text{-}initial}$ = {ARG0, END, SAFE_CUT}. For arithmetic-performing subtrees: T_{aps} = {$\Re_{smaller\text{-}reals}$}.
Potential function set for the RPBs	Architecture-altering operations are not used.

Potential terminal set for the RPBs	Architecture-altering operations are not used.
Potential function set for the ADFs	Architecture-altering operations are not used.
Potential terminal set for the ADFs	Architecture-altering operations are not used.
Fitness cases	Nine fitness cases from three DC sweeps (see text)
Raw fitness	The sum of six penalties (see text)
Standardized fitness	Same as raw fitness
Hits	Not used for this problem
Wrapper	None
Parameters	$M = 600,000$. $G = 501$. $Q = 10,000$. $D = 60$. $B = 2\%$. $S_{rpb} = 300$. $S_{adf} = 300$. $N_{rpb} = 3$. $N_{max\text{-}adf} = 2$. $N_{max\text{-}argument\text{-}adf} = 1$.
Result designation	Best-so-far pace-setting individual
Success predicate	Fitness appears to have reached a plateau.

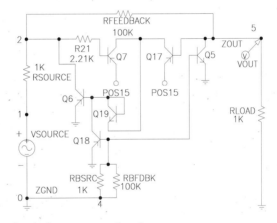

Figure 46.2   Best circuit from generation 0

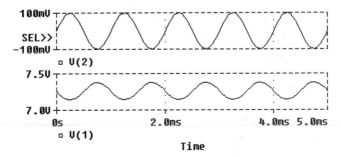

Figure 46.3   Time domain behavior of the best circuit from generation 0

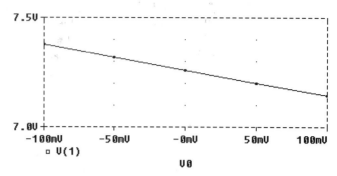

Figure 46.4 DC sweep for the best circuit from generation 0

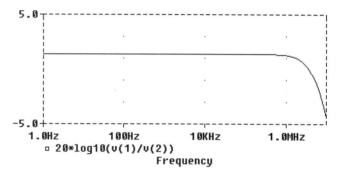

Figure 46.5 AC sweep for the best circuit from generation 0

fitness associated with the positive power supply is +0.213. The penalty in fitness associated with the negative power supply is 0 (meaning the power supply is not being used in this circuit). The positive power supply rejection ratio is +13.44 dB.

About 40% of the circuits of generation 0 cannot be simulated; however, the percentage of unsimulatable circuits drops to about 1% after a few generations.

The best circuit (Figure 46.6) from generation 12 has five transistors, four diodes, no capacitors, and one resistor (in addition to the five resistors of the test fixture) and achieves a fitness of 79.80. ADF0 is not used, and ADF1 is used once.

Figure 46.7 shows automatically defined function ADF1 of the best circuit from generation 12. The component that ADF1 inserts into the circuit acts as a diode.

Figure 46.8 shows the time domain behavior produced by a SPICE transient analysis at 1,000 Hz of the best circuit from generation 12. The common horizontal axis represents time (from 0 milliseconds to 5 milliseconds) on a linear scale. The two vertical axes represent voltage on a linear scale. Note that the scales on the two vertical axes differ by three orders of magnitude (millivolts to volts). The top half of this figure shows a 100-millivolt 1,000 Hz sinusoidal input signal (for which the vertical axis ranges over voltages from −100 millivolts to +100 millivolts). The bottom half shows the resulting output (for which the vertical axis ranges over voltages from 0 volts to +20 volts). Note that the output is inverted, almost undistorted, and has a DC bias. Based on this transient

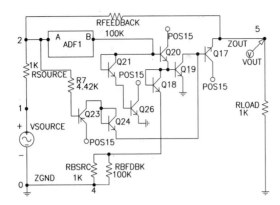

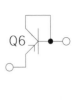

Figure 46.6 Best circuit from generation 12

Figure 46.7 ADF1 **for best circuit from generation 12**

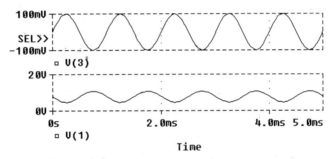

Figure 46.8 Time domain behavior of the best circuit from generation 12

analysis, the amplification is 29.2 dB, the bias is 7.72 volts, and the total harmonic distortion is 2.24%.

Figure 46.9 shows the result of performing SPICE's DC sweep on the best-of-generation circuit from generation 12. The horizontal axis represents input DC values ranging linearly from −100 millivolts to +100 millivolts. The vertical axis represents the output voltage on a linear scale between 0 volts and +20 volts. Based on the DC sweep, the amplification is 29.3 dB, and the bias is 7.68 volts.

Figure 46.10 shows the frequency response with an AC sweep for the best circuit from generation 12. The horizontal axis ranges over seven decades of frequencies from 1 Hz to 10 MHz on a logarithmic scale. The vertical axis ranges from 0 dB to +40 dB. The 3 dB bandwidth is 5.67 MHz. The circuit has a flatband gain of 29.6 dB.

According to an offline simulation made in MicroSim's PSPICE, the maximum current through the circuit is −26.7 milliamperes, and the total power dissipation is 377 milliwatts for the best circuit from generation 12. The penalty in fitness associated with the positive power supply is +3.46. The penalty in fitness associated with the negative power supply is 0 (meaning the power supply is not being used in this circuit). The positive power supply rejection ratio is −10.78 dB (i.e., the circuit is amplifying, instead of rejecting, the power supply voltage, as indicated by the negative sign).

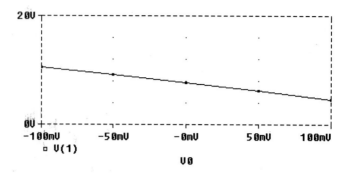

Figure 46.9 DC sweep for the best circuit from generation 12

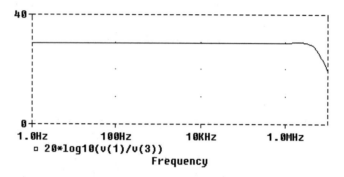

Figure 46.10 AC sweep for the best circuit from generation 12

The best-of-run circuit (Figure 46.11) appeared in generation 46. This circuit has 24 transistors, four diodes, no capacitors, and no resistors (not counting the five resistors of the test fixture) and achieves a fitness of 35.47. ADF0 is not used, and ADF1 is used twice. However, one of the invocations of ADF1 is in a disconnected circuit fragment and is not shown in the figure. The three result-producing branches have 60, 129, and 20 points, and the two automatically defined functions have 47 and 9 points.

Figure 46.12 shows automatically defined function ADF1 of the best circuit from generation 46.

Figure 46.13 shows the time domain behavior produced by a SPICE transient analysis at 1,000 Hz of the best circuit from generation 46. The common horizontal axis represents time (from 0 milliseconds to 5 milliseconds) on a linear scale. The two vertical axes represent voltage on a linear scale. Note that the scales on the two vertical axes differ by three orders of magnitude (millivolts to volts). The top half of this figure shows a 100-millivolt 1,000 Hz sinusoidal input signal (for which the vertical axis ranges over voltages from −100 millivolts to +100 millivolts). The bottom half shows the resulting output (for which the vertical axis ranges over voltages from 0 volts to +20 volts). Note that the output is inverted, almost undistorted, and has a DC bias. Based on this transient analysis, the amplification is 36.6 dB, the bias is 6.93 volts, and the total harmonic distortion is 0.719%.

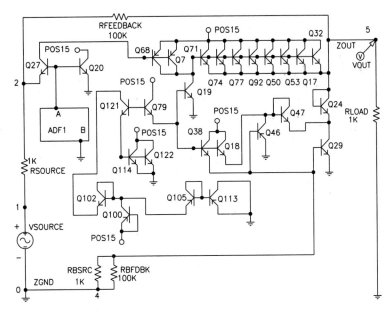

Figure 46.11 Best circuit from generation 46

Figure 46.12 ADF1 for best circuit from generation 46

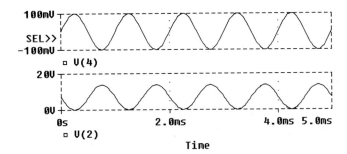

Figure 46.13 Time domain behavior of the best circuit from generation 46

Figure 46.14 shows the result of performing SPICE's DC sweep on the best-of-generation circuit from generation 46. The horizontal axis represents input DC values ranging linearly from −100 millivolts to +100 millivolts. The vertical axis represents the output voltage on a linear scale from 0 volts to +20 volts. Based on the DC sweep, the

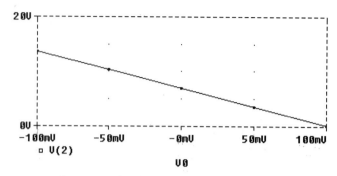

Figure 46.14 DC sweep for the best circuit from generation 46

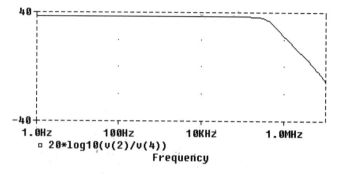

Figure 46.15 AC sweep for the best circuit from generation 46

amplification is 36.6 dB (67.6-to-1), and the bias is 6.96 volts. The input-referred bias here is the ratio of 6.96 volts to the gain (67.6) and is therefore 0.103 volt. That is, a change of 0.103 volt at the input would compensate and eliminate the 6.96-volt bias.

Figure 46.15 shows the frequency response of this circuit as shown by an AC sweep for the best circuit from generation 46. The horizontal axis ranges over seven decades of frequencies from 1 Hz to 10 MHz on a logarithmic scale. The vertical axis ranges from –40 dB to +40 dB. The 3 dB bandwidth is 417 KHz. The circuit has a flatband gain of 36.8 dB.

The total power dissipation is 128 milliwatts for the best-of-generation circuit from generation 46, according to an offline simulation made in MicroSim's PSPICE. Although total power dissipation was not part of the fitness measure for this problem (or any preceding problem in this book), the evolutionary process produced a circuit with this relatively modest power dissipation.

The penalty in fitness associated with the positive power supply is +0.062. The penalty in fitness associated with the negative power supply is 0 (meaning the power supply is not being used in this circuit). The positive power supply rejection ratio is +24.2 dB (i.e., the variations in the power supply are being rejected, as desired). Thus, genetic programming successfully evolved an amplifier that satisfied the design goals of high gain, low distortion, and high power supply rejection ratio. In addition, the evolved amplifier also has reasonable bandwidth, total power dissipation, and parts count. This circuit was evolved with only incremental changes in the fitness measures used in previous chapters.

Synthesis of Computational Circuits

An analog electrical circuit whose output is a mathematical function (e.g., logarithm, square, square root, cube, cube root, and Gaussian) is called a *computational circuit*.

An analog computational circuit may be desirable when the need for just one or two particular mathematical functions does not warrant the considerable overhead associated with converting an analog signal into a digital signal, performing the mathematical calculation in the digital domain with a digital microprocessor, and then converting the result back to the analog domain. An analog computational circuit may be necessary if the mathematical function must be calculated faster than is possible using a digital microprocessor (and after performing the associated analog-to-digital and digital-to-analog conversions).

The design of computational circuits is exceedingly difficult even for seemingly mundane mathematical functions. Success often relies on the clever exploitation of some aspect of the underlying device physics of a particular electrical component. The implementation of each mathematical function typically requires an entirely different clever insight and an entirely different circuit (Gilbert 1968; Sheingold 1976; Babanezhad and Temes 1986).

This chapter demonstrates that genetic programming can automatically create, without relying on function-specific insights, analog computational circuits for the following mathematical functions:

- squaring (Section 47.1),
- cubing (Section 47.2),
- square root (Section 47.3),
- cube root (Section 47.4), and
- logarithm (Section 47.5).

In Chapter 51, a Gaussian computational circuit is synthesized in MOSFET technology.

Most of the work in this chapter was done by the authors in collaboration with Frank Dunlap of Enabling Systems, Palo Alto, California, and Jason D. Lohn, NASA Ames Research Laboratory, Mountain View, California (Koza, Bennett, Lohn, Dunlap, Andre, and Keane 1997a).

47.1 SQUARING CIRCUIT

47.1.1 Design Goals

The goal is to evolve the design of a circuit whose output voltage is the square of its input voltage.

47.1.2 Preparatory Steps

Embryo and Test Fixture

The initial circuit (Figure 30.1) for this problem is created by embedding the embryo with one modifiable wire and three ports (Figure 29.10) into the one-input, one-output test fixture with three ports (Figure 29.1).

Program Architecture

Since the embryo has one modifiable wire, there is one result-producing branch in each circuit-constructing program tree.

Neither automatically defined functions nor architecture-altering operations are used in this problem. Thus, the architecture of each program tree in the population consists of one result-producing branch.

Functions and Terminals

The initial function set, $F_{ccs-rpb-initial}$, for the construction-continuing subtrees of the result-producing branches is

$F_{ccs-rpb-initial}$ = {R, SERIES, PARALLEL0, PARALLEL1, FLIP, NOP,
RETAINING_THREE_GROUND_0, RETAINING_THREE_GROUND_1,
RETAINING_THREE_POS15V_0, RETAINING_THREE_POS15V_1,
RETAINING_THREE_NEG15V_0, RETAINING_THREE_NEG15V_1,
PAIR_CONNECT_0, PAIR_CONNECT_1, Q_DIODE_NPN, Q_DIODE_PNP,
Q_THREE_NPN0, . . . , Q_THREE_NPN11, Q_THREE_PNP0, . . . ,
Q_THREE_PNP11, Q_POS15V_COLL_NPN, Q_GND_EMIT_NPN,
Q_NEG15V_EMIT_NPN, Q_GND_EMIT_PNP, Q_POS15V_EMIT_PNP,
Q_NEG15V_COLL_PNP}.

SPICE's default *npn* and *pnp* transistor model parameters are used.

The initial terminal set, $T_{ccs-rpb-initial}$, for the construction-continuing subtrees of the result-producing branches is

$T_{ccs-rpb-initial}$ = {END, SAFE_CUT}.

Since there are no automatically defined functions in this problem, $T_{adf-initial}$ and $F_{adf-initial}$ are empty.

Since there are no architecture-altering operations in this problem, $T_{rpb-potential}$, $F_{rpb-potential}$, $T_{adf-potential}$, and $F_{adf-potential}$ are empty.

The function set, F_{aps}, for each arithmetic-performing subtree in any branch and the terminal set, T_{aps}, for each arithmetic-performing subtree in any branch are the same as for the lowpass filter problem in Section 25.14.3.

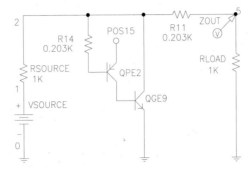

Figure 47.1   Best squaring circuit from generation 0

Fitness

The SPICE simulator is instructed to perform a DC sweep analysis at 21 equidistant voltages between –250 millivolts and +250 millivolts.

Fitness is the sum, over these 21 fitness cases, of the absolute weighted deviation between the actual value of the voltage that is produced by the circuit at the probe point VOUT at node 5 and the target value for voltage (i.e., the square of the input). The smaller the value of fitness, the better. A fitness of zero represents an ideal squaring circuit.

The procedure for the 21 fitness cases is as follows:

- If the output voltage is within 1% of the target voltage value for a particular fitness case, the absolute value of the deviation is weighted by 1.0 for that fitness case.
- If the output voltage is not within 1% of the target voltage value, the deviation is weighted by 10.0 for that fitness case.

This arrangement reflects the fact that a deviation of 1% from the ideal voltage is acceptable, but that greater deviations are unacceptable.

The number of hits is defined as the number of fitness cases for which the voltage is acceptable or ideal.

Parameters

The control parameters for this problem are found in the tableau (Table 47.1), the tables of percentages of genetic operations in Appendix D, and the default values specified in Appendix D.

Tableau

Table 47.1 summarizes the key features of the problem of designing a computational circuit for the squaring function.

47.1.3   Results

The best circuit from generation 0 (Figure 47.1) achieves a fitness of 3.61 and has two transistors, no diodes, no capacitors, and two resistors (in addition to the source and load resistors in the test fixture). Its circuit-constructing program tree has 52 points.

Table 47.1 Tableau for squaring circuit

Objective	Design a computational circuit whose output voltage is the square of its input voltage.
Test fixture and embryo	One-input, one-output initial circuit with source resistor, load resistor, and one modifiable wire
Program architecture	One result-producing branch
Initial function set for the RPBs	For construction-continuing subtrees: $F_{ccs-rpb-initial}$ = {R, SERIES, PARALLEL0, PARALLEL1, FLIP, NOP, RETAINING_THREE_GROUND_0, RETAINING_THREE_GROUND_1, RETAINING_THREE_POS15V_0, RETAINING_THREE_POS15V_1, RETAINING_THREE_NEG15V_0, RETAINING_THREE_NEG15V_1, PAIR_CONNECT_0, PAIR_CONNECT_1, Q_DIODE_NPN, Q_DIODE_PNP, Q_THREE_NPN0, . . . , Q_THREE_NPN11, Q_THREE_PNP0, . . . , Q_THREE_PNP11, Q_POS15V_COLL_NPN, Q_GND_EMIT_NPN, Q_NEG15V_EMIT_NPN, Q_GND_EMIT_PNP, Q_POS15V_EMIT_PNP, Q_NEG15V_COLL_PNP}. For arithmetic-performing subtrees: F_{aps} = {+, −}.
Initial terminal set for the RPBs	For construction-continuing subtrees: $T_{ccs-rpb-initial}$ = {END, SAFE_CUT}. For arithmetic-performing subtrees: T_{aps} = {$\mathfrak{R}_{smaller-reals}$}.
Initial function set for the ADFs	Automatically defined functions are not used.
Initial terminal set for the ADFs	Automatically defined functions are not used.
Potential function set for the RPBs	Architecture-altering operations are not used.
Potential terminal set for the RPBs	Architecture-altering operations are not used.
Potential function set for the ADFs	Architecture-altering operations are not used.
Potential terminal set for the ADFs	Architecture-altering operations are not used.
Fitness cases	21 values of voltage between −250 millivolts and +250 millivolts
Raw fitness	The sum, over the 21 fitness cases, of the absolute weighted deviation between the actual value of the voltage that is produced by the circuit at the probe point and the target value for voltage (i.e., the square of the input)
Standardized fitness	Same as raw fitness
Hits	The number of hits is defined as the number of fitness cases for which the voltage is acceptable or ideal.
Wrapper	None

Parameters	M = 640,000. G = 501. Q = 10,000. D = 64. B = 2%. S_{rpb} = 600. N_{rpb} = 1.
Result designation	Best-so-far pace-setting individual
Success predicate	A program scores the maximum number (21) of hits.

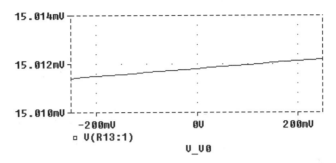

Figure 47.2   **DC sweep of best squaring circuit of generation 0**

Figure 47.2 shows the output of a DC sweep for the best circuit from generation 0. The horizontal axis represents the DC input between −250 millivolts and +250 millivolts; the vertical axis represents the DC output on a scale between 15.010 millivolts and 15.014 millivolts. The DC output is almost flat because almost all of the current is being drained away by the stacked transistors **QPE2** and **QGE9**.

Figure 47.3a compares the nearly flat output produced by the best circuit from generation 0 with the target (i.e., the square of the input voltage). The horizontal axis represents the DC input between −300 millivolts and +300 millivolts; the vertical axis represents the DC output on a linear scale between 0 millivolts and +100 millivolts. The plot of the output voltage has a very slight upward slope; however, it is not discernible because of the scale of this figure.

Figure 47.4 shows the absolute value of the discrepancy (error) between the output produced by the best circuit from generation 0 and the target. The horizontal axis represents the DC input between −300 millivolts and +300 millivolts; the vertical axis represents the error on a scale between 0 millivolts and +50 millivolts.

The best circuit from generation 16 (Figure 47.5) achieves a fitness of 1.10 and has 25 transistors, four diodes, no capacitors, and one resistor (in addition to the source and load resistors in the test fixture).

Figure 47.3b compares the output produced by the best circuit from generation 16 with the target. As can be seen, the output matches the target reasonably well when **VSOURCE** is greater than −150 millivolts, but does poorly when **VSOURCE** is less than −150 millivolts.

The best-of-run circuit from generation 37 (Figure 47.6) achieves a fitness of 0.2090 and has 33 transistors, five diodes, no capacitors, and one resistor (in addition to the source and load resistors in the test fixture). Its circuit-constructing program tree has 191 points.

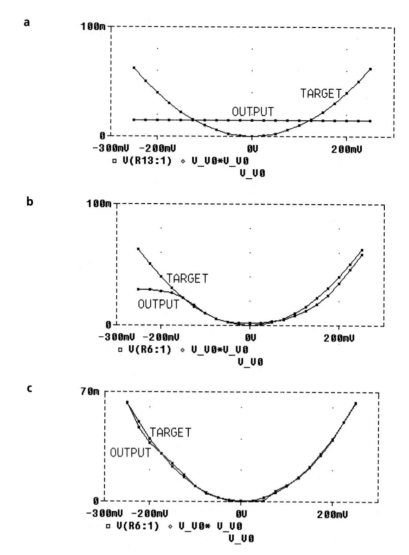

Figure 47.3 Comparison of actual output and target for best circuits of generations (a) 0, (b) 16, and (c) 37

This best-of-run circuit builds a squaring function by combining the output of two subcircuits, one producing the output for negative input voltages and the other producing the output for positive inputs. For negative input voltages, the power supply on the emitter of transistor **QPE19** biases **QPE19** and **QPC10** so as to create a current waveform resembling **VSOURCE**. This current is then routed through the collector of **Q11** and the emitter of **Q26** to node 5. For positive input voltages, most of the output current is supplied by the power supply connected to the collector of **QPC45**, which flows through the emitter and base of transistor **Q23** into node 5. The two currents flowing

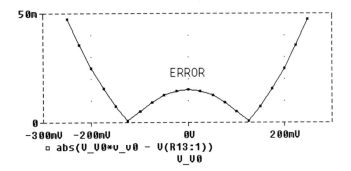

Figure 47.4 Error for generation 0

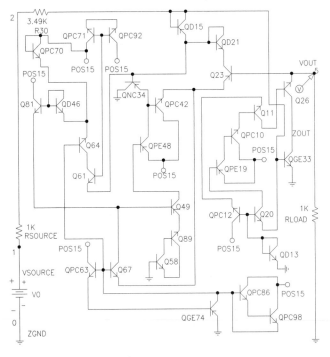

Figure 47.5 Best circuit from generation 16

into node 5 sum to produce a current (only a few microamps) that is converted into the desired voltage levels when it flows through the 1,000 Ω load resistor RLOAD.

Figure 47.3c compares the output produced by the best-of-run circuit from generation 37 with the target (i.e., the square of the input voltage). The horizontal axis represents the DC input between –300 millivolts and +300 millivolts; the vertical axis represents the error on a scale between 0 millivolts and +70 millivolts. As can be seen, the output closely matches the target. In fact, the output is so close to the target that the two cannot be readily distinguished on the scale of this figure.

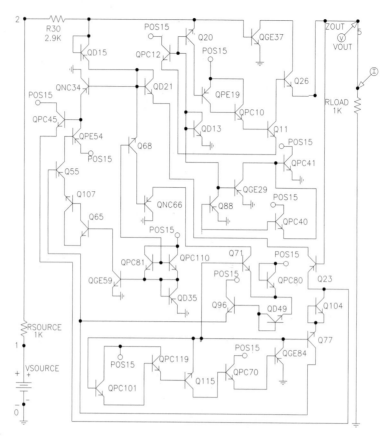

Figure 47.6 Best-of-run squaring circuit from generation 37

47.2 CUBING CIRCUIT

47.2.1 Design Goals

The goal is to evolve the design of a circuit whose output voltage is the cube of its input voltage.

47.2.2 Preparatory Steps

The preparatory steps for the cubing circuit are identical to those for the squaring circuit (Section 47.1), except that the target function is the cube of the input.

47.2.3 Results

The best circuit from generation 0 (Figure 47.7) achieves a fitness of 0.471 and has no transistors, no diodes, no capacitors, and one resistor (in addition to the source and load resistors in the test fixture). Its circuit-constructing program tree has 10 points.

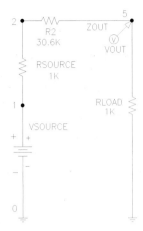

Figure 47.7   Best circuit from generation 0

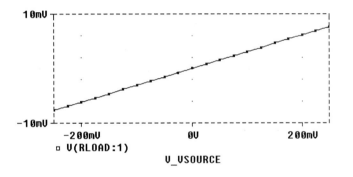

Figure 47.8   DC sweep of circuit of generation 0

Figure 47.8 shows the output of a DC transfer characteristic produced by SPICE's DC sweep for the best circuit from generation 0. The horizontal axis represents the DC input between −250 millivolts and +250 millivolts; the vertical axis represents the DC output on a scale between −10 millivolts and +10 millivolts. Since the circuit merely divides the voltage across R2, RSOURCE, and RLOAD, the output voltage rises linearly with the input voltage.

Figure 47.9a compares the output produced by the best circuit from generation 0 with the target (i.e., the cube of the input voltage). The horizontal axis represents the DC input between −300 millivolts and +300 millivolts; the vertical axis represents the DC output on a linear scale between −20 millivolts and +20 millivolts.

The best circuit from generation 29 (Figure 47.10) achieves a fitness of 0.22225 and has 20 transistors, nine diodes, no capacitors, and 14 resistors (in addition to the source and load resistors in the test fixture).

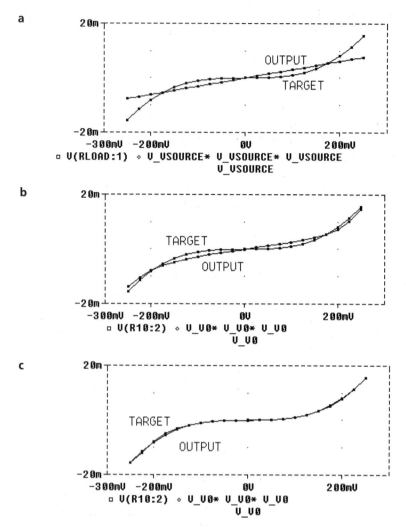

Figure 47.9 Comparison of actual output and target for best circuits of generations (a) 0, (b) 29, and (c) 74

Figure 47.9b compares the output produced by the best circuit from generation 29 with the target (i.e., the cube of the input voltage).

The best-of-run circuit from generation 74 (Figure 47.11) achieves a fitness of 0.01710 and has 30 transistors, five diodes, no capacitors, and 21 resistors (in addition to the source and load resistors in the test fixture). Its circuit-constructing program tree has 450 points.

Figure 47.9c compares the output produced by the best circuit from generation 74 with the target (i.e., the cube of the input voltage). The horizontal axis represents the DC input between −300 millivolts and +300 millivolts; the vertical axis represents the DC output on a scale between −20 millivolts and +20 millivolts. As can be seen, the output is so close to the target that the two curves cannot be distinguished on the scale of this figure.

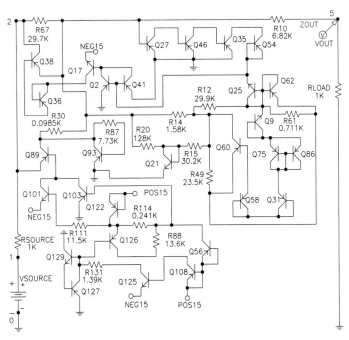

Figure 47.10 Best circuit from generation 29

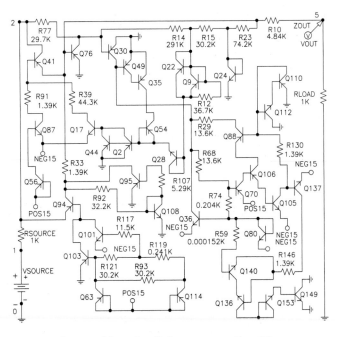

Figure 47.11 Best-of-run cubing circuit from generation 74

47.3   SQUARE ROOT CIRCUIT

47.3.1   Design Goals

The goal is to evolve the design of a circuit whose output voltage is the square root of its (positive) input voltage.

47.3.2   Preparatory Steps

The preparatory steps for the square root circuit are identical to those for the squaring circuit (Section 47.1) with the following two exceptions. First, the target function is the square root of the input. Second, the SPICE simulator is instructed to perform a DC sweep analysis at 21 equidistant voltages between 0 millivolts and +500 millivolts in increments of 25 millivolts. Note that only positive voltages are scanned in order to avoid asking for the square root of a negative number.

47.3.3   Results

The best-of-run circuit from generation 57 (Figure 47.12) achieves a fitness of 1.19 and has 38 transistors, seven diodes, and 18 resistors (in addition to the source and load resistors in the test fixture). Its circuit-constructing program tree has 539 points.

Figure 47.13 compares the output produced by the best-of-run circuit from generation 57 with the target (i.e., the square root of the input voltages from 0 millivolts to 500 millivolts). The horizontal axis represents the DC input between 0 millivolts and +500 millivolts; the vertical axis represents the output voltage on a scale ranging linearly between 0 volts and +1 volt. As can be seen, the output is so close to the target that the two cannot be readily distinguished on the scale of this figure (except near zero).

47.4   CUBE ROOT CIRCUIT

47.4.1   Design Goals

The goal is to evolve the design of a circuit whose output voltage is the cube root of its input voltage.

47.4.2   Preparatory Steps

The preparatory steps for the cube root circuit are identical to those for the squaring circuit (Section 47.1), except that the target function is the cube root of the input.

47.4.3   Results

The best circuit from generation 0 achieves a fitness of 77.7 and has two transistors, no diodes, no capacitors, and two resistors (in addition to the source and load resistors in the test fixture). Its circuit-constructing program tree has eight points. Figure 47.14a compares the output produced by the best circuit from generation 0 with the target (i.e., the cube root of the input voltage). As can be seen, the output resembles the target only in that it has a positive slope.

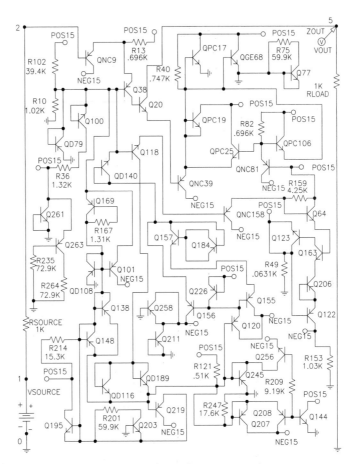

Figure 47.12   Best-of-run square root circuit from generation 57

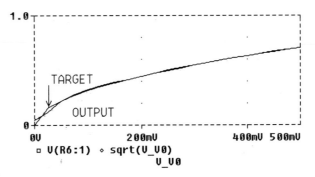

Figure 47.13   Comparison for best-of-run square root circuit from generation 57

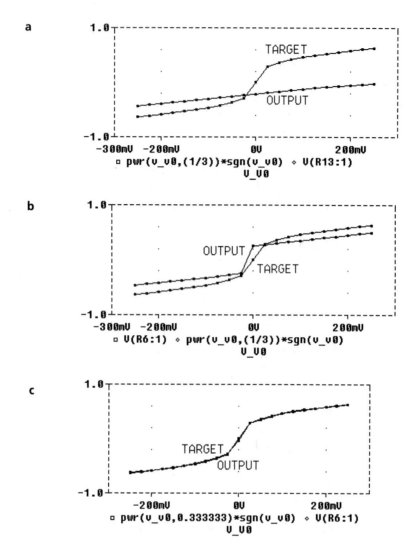

Figure 47.14 Comparison of actual output and target for best circuits of generations (*a*) 0, (*b*) 17, and (*c*) 60

The best circuit from generation 17 (Figure 47.15) achieves a fitness of 26.7 and has 13 transistors, three diodes, no capacitors, and two resistors (in addition to the source and load resistors in the test fixture).

Figure 47.14b compares the output produced by the best circuit from generation 17 with the target (i.e., the cube root of the input voltage).

The best-of-run circuit from generation 60 (Figure 47.16) achieves a fitness of 1.68. It has 36 transistors, two diodes, no capacitors, and 12 resistors (in addition to the source and load resistors in the test fixture).

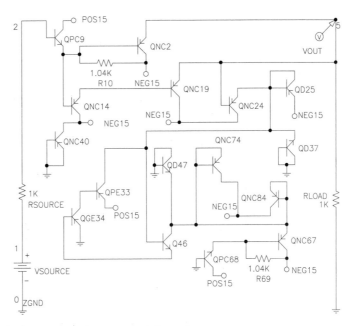

Figure 47.15   Best circuit from generation 17

Figure 47.14c compares the output produced by this circuit from generation 60 with the target (i.e., the cube root of the input voltage). The output is so close to the target that the two cannot be distinguished on the scale of this figure.

47.5   LOGARITHMIC CIRCUIT

47.5.1   Design Goals

The goal is to evolve the design of a circuit whose output voltage is the natural logarithm of its (positive) input voltage.

47.5.2   Preparatory Steps

The preparatory steps for the logarithmic circuit are identical to those for the squaring circuit (Section 47.1) with the following two exceptions. First, the target function is the logarithm of the input. Second, the SPICE simulator is instructed to perform a DC sweep analysis at 51 equidistant voltages between 0 volts and +10.0 volts in increments of 0.1 volt. Only positive voltages are scanned for the logarithmic circuit.

47.5.3   Results

The best-of-run circuit (Figure 47.17) appears in generation 55 and achieves a fitness of 40.77. The one result-producing branch of this program has 413 points. The circuit has 26 transistors, 12 diodes, and 17 resistors.

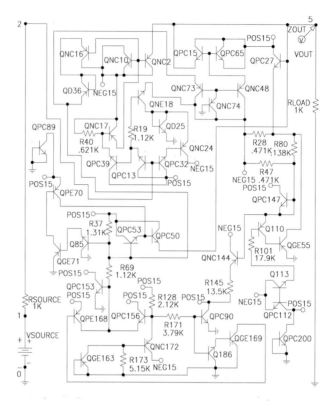

Figure 47.16 Best-of-run cube root circuit from generation 60

Figure 47.18 shows the output voltage produced by the best circuit from generation 55. The horizontal axis ranges linearly from 0 volts to 10 volts. The vertical axis ranges linearly from −10 volts to +5 volts.

In addition to the above five computational circuits, a circuit for the Gaussian function is created in Chapter 51 using MOSFET semiconductor technology.

The problem of designing analog computational circuits for specified mathematical functions is recognized as being exceedingly difficult. Dozens of computational circuits have been patented, including square root circuits (Newbold 1962; Schlatter 1973), logarithmic circuits (Green 1958; Platzer 1965; Gilbert 1991), and multiplier circuits (Gilbert 1979).

Referring to the eight criteria in Chapter 1 for establishing that an automatically created result is competitive with a human-produced result, these six results satisfy the following three of the eight criteria:

A. The result was patented as an invention in the past, is an improvement over a patented invention, or would qualify today as a patentable new invention.
D. The result is publishable in its own right as a new scientific result (independent of the fact that the result was mechanically created).
G. The result solves a problem of indisputable difficulty in its field.

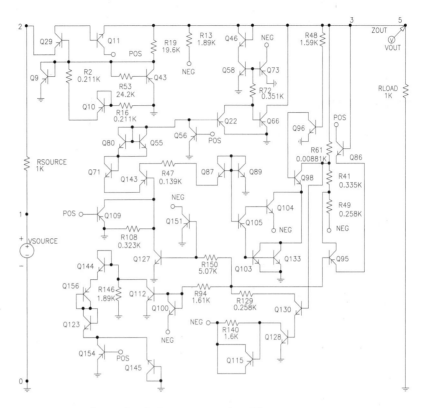

Figure 47.17 Best-of-run circuit from generation 55

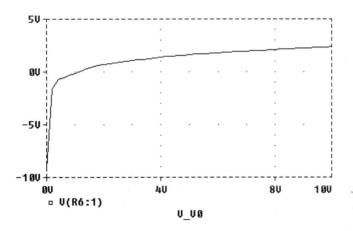

Figure 47.18 Behavior of best-of-run circuit from generation 55

Therefore, we make the following claim:

- **CLAIM NO. 9** We claim that the automatic synthesis by genetic programming of analog computational circuits for the squaring, square root, cubing, cube root, logarithm, and Gaussian functions are instances where genetic programming has produced results that are competitive with results produced by creative and inventive humans.

These instances of automated design satisfy Arthur Samuel's criterion (1983) for artificial intelligence and machine learning:

> The aim [is] . . . to get machines to exhibit behavior, which if done by humans, would be assumed to involve the use of intelligence.

Synthesis of a Real-Time Robot Controller Circuit with Architecture-Altering Operations

In Chapter 13, genetic programming was used to solve a time-optimal navigation problem in which the goal was to find a strategy for continuously moving a constant-speed robot with a nonzero turning radius to an arbitrary destination point. In Chapter 21, this same problem was solved using the Genetic Programming Problem Solver (GPPS 1.0), and it was solved yet again in Chapter 23 using GPPS 2.0.

An evolved computer program can be installed in an actual robot by writing a computer program for an embedded digital controller residing in the robot. The function set employed by genetic programming in both of these previous chapters included addition, subtraction, multiplication, division, and a conditional branching operator. The robot's embedded digital controller will therefore contain numerous instances of these arithmetic functions and conditional operations. When the robot with this embedded digital computer is operating, the robot's current location is sensed in analog form. This analog input is then converted into digital form using an analog-to-digital converter. Then the embedded digital processor performs a digital calculation consisting of a sequence of arithmetic and conditional operations on the digital data. Finally, the digital output is passed to a digital-to-analog converter (DAC) that would convert the program's digital output into an analog signal. The resulting analog signal, in turn, causes the robot to move in the specified direction.

Notice that the above approach entails five steps: analog sensing, analog-to-digital conversion, the actual computation in the digital domain to determine the robot's movement, digital-to-analog conversion, and physical implementation of the final analog signal by the robot. The amount of time required to perform the digital computation is potentially significant for certain applications. In addition, the analog-to-digital and digital-to-analog conversions are not instantaneous. This chapter contemplates a more holistic approach to this robot control problem in which the three middle steps are consolidated into one (entirely analog) step. In particular, the goal in this chapter is to evolve the design for a real-time analog circuit for directly controlling a robot in a time-optimal way. In this approach, there is no computer program performing addition, subtraction, multiplication, division, or conditional branching operations. There will be no conversions to and from the analog domain. In addition, there will be no digital processor resident in the robot.

48.1   DESIGN GOALS

The goal is to evolve the design for a real-time circuit for controlling the trajectory of a robot with nonzero turning radius (moving at constant speed) such that the robot moves to an arbitrary destination point in minimal time (as described in Chapter 13).

48.2   PREPARATORY STEPS

48.2.1   Embryo and Test Fixture

This is the first circuit in this book with two inputs. The inputs are the robot's current two-dimensional location (expressed as a pair of voltages) with respect to the destination point in the robot's frame of reference. The single output consists of a voltage that is interpreted by the problem-specific wrapper (output interface) as the robot's turn angle Θ.

The initial circuit for this problem (Figure 48.1) is created by embedding the embryo with three modifiable wires (Figure 29.15) into the two-input, one-output test fixture (Figure 29.4). Notice that the test fixture has two separate source resistors (**RSOURCE1** and **RSOURCE2**) to accommodate the two inputs.

48.2.2   Program Architecture

Since the embryo has three modifiable wires, there are three writing heads and three result-producing branches in each circuit-constructing program tree.

Each program in generation 0 has a uniform architecture, consisting of three result-producing branches and no automatically defined functions.

One-argument automatically defined functions can be created during the run by the architecture-altering operations.

48.2.3   Functions and Terminals

The initial function set, $F_{ccs\text{-}rpb\text{-}initial}$, for the construction-continuing subtrees of the result-producing branches is

$F_{ccs\text{-}rpb\text{-}initial}$ = {R, SERIES, PARALLEL0, PARALLEL1, FLIP, NOP,
RETAINING_THREE_GROUND_0, RETAINING_THREE_GROUND_1,
RETAINING_THREE_POS15V_0, RETAINING_THREE_POS15V_1,
RETAINING_THREE_NEG15V_0, RETAINING_THREE_NEG15V_1,
PAIR_CONNECT_0, PAIR_CONNECT_1, Q_DIODE_NPN, Q_DIODE_PNP,
Q_THREE_NPN0, . . . , Q_THREE_NPN11, Q_THREE_PNP0, . . . ,
Q_THREE_PNP11, Q_POS15V_COLL_NPN, Q_GND_EMIT_NPN,
Q_NEG15V_EMIT_NPN, Q_GND_EMIT_PNP, Q_POS15V_EMIT_PNP,
Q_NEG15V_COLL_PNP}.

SPICE's default *npn* and *pnp* transistor model parameters are used.

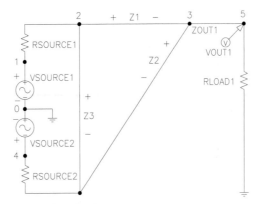

Figure 48.1 Two-input, one-output initial circuit for the real-time robot controller

The initial terminal set, $T_{\text{ccs-rpb-initial}}$, for the construction-continuing subtrees of the result-producing branches is

$$T_{\text{ccs-rpb-initial}} = \{\text{END, SAFE\_CUT}\}.$$

Since there are no automatically defined functions in generation 0, $T_{\text{adf-initial}}$ and $F_{\text{adf-initial}}$ are empty.

The set of potential functions for each construction-continuing subtree of a result-producing branch, $F_{\text{ccs-rpb-potential}}$, is

$$F_{\text{ccs-rpb-potential}} = \{\text{ADF0, ADF1}\}.$$

The set of potential terminals for each construction-continuing subtree of a result-producing branch, $T_{\text{ccs-rpb-potential}}$, is empty:

$$T_{\text{ccs-rpb-potential}} = \phi.$$

Since the newly created automatically defined functions do not hierarchically refer to one another, the set of potential functions for each construction-continuing subtree of an automatically defined function, $F_{\text{ccs-adf-potential}}$, is

$$
\begin{aligned}
F_{\text{ccs-adf-potential}} = &\{\text{R, SERIES, PARALLEL0, PARALLEL1, FLIP, NOP,} \\
&\text{RETAINING\_THREE\_GROUND\_0, RETAINING\_THREE\_GROUND\_1,} \\
&\text{RETAINING\_THREE\_POS15V\_0, RETAINING\_THREE\_POS15V\_1,} \\
&\text{RETAINING\_THREE\_NEG15V\_0, RETAINING\_THREE\_NEG15V\_1,} \\
&\text{PAIR\_CONNECT\_0, PAIR\_CONNECT\_1, Q\_DIODE\_NPN, Q\_DIODE\_PNP,} \\
&\text{Q\_THREE\_NPN0, . . . , Q\_THREE\_NPN11, Q\_THREE\_PNP0, . . . ,} \\
&\text{Q\_THREE\_PNP11, Q\_POS15V\_COLL\_NPN, Q\_GND\_EMIT\_NPN,} \\
&\text{Q\_NEG15V\_EMIT\_NPN, Q\_GND\_EMIT\_PNP, Q\_POS15V\_EMIT\_PNP,} \\
&\text{Q\_NEG15V\_COLL\_PNP}\}.
\end{aligned}
$$

The set of potential terminals for each construction-continuing subtree of an automatically defined function, $T_{\text{ccs-adf-potential}}$, is empty:

$$T_{\text{ccs-adf-potential}} = \{\text{ARG0, END, SAFE\_CUT}\}.$$

The function set, F_{aps}, for each arithmetic-performing subtree in any branch and the terminal set, T_{aps}, for each arithmetic-performing subtree in any branch are the same as for the lowpass filter problem in Section 25.14.3.

48.2.4 Fitness

For this problem, the voltage **VOUT** is probed at node 5.

The SPICE simulator is instructed to perform a nested DC sweep. The nested DC sweep provides a way to simulate the DC behavior of a circuit with two inputs. A nested DC sweep resembles a nested pair of FOR loops in a computer program in that both of the loops have a starting value for the voltage, an increment, and an ending value for the voltage. For each voltage value in the outer loop, the inner loop simulates the behavior of the circuit by stepping through its range of voltages. Specifically for both loops, the starting value for the voltage is –4 volts, the step size is 0.2 volt, and the ending value is +4 volts. These voltage values correspond to the locations in the robot's world of 64 square meters, extending 4 meters in each of the four directions from the origin of a coordinate system, with 1 volt equaling 1 meter. The output voltage produced by the circuit is then passed to the same wrapper as previously used (Section 13.3.3) in order to yield a turn angle, Θ, for the robot. The wrapper modularizes and clamps the output voltage produced by the circuit so that the final turn angle Θ lies between $-\Theta_{max}$ and $+\Theta_{max}$, as shown in Figure 13.5.

48.2.5 Parameters

The control parameters are the same as for the problem of synthesizing a lowpass filter with architecture-altering operations (Section 28.2.5).

48.2.6 Tableau

Table 48.1 summarizes the key features of the problem of designing a real-time robot controller circuit with the architecture-altering operations.

48.3 RESULTS

The best circuit from generation 0 (Figure 48.2) scores 61 hits (out of 72) and achieves a fitness of 3.005 hours. It has seven transistors, one diode, and one resistor (not counting the three resistors of the test fixture and those contained in the power supplies). Its circuit-constructing program tree has 4, 48, and 11 points in its three result-producing branches.

Note that the fitness (3.005 hours) of the best-of-generation circuit from generation 0 for the electrical circuits version of the robot controller problem happens to be very close to the fitness (3.010 hours) of the best-of-generation controller from generation 0 for the original nonelectrical circuit version of this problem (Chapter 13). They both, coincidentally, score 61 hits. This circuit has two transistors that simply drain power. **QNE5** is connected to the negative power supply, the positive power supply, and ground. **QGE12** acts as a diode between the positive power supply and ground. If this circuit had otherwise desirable behavior, components such as these could be easily edited out of the circuit (manually or mechanically).

Table 48.1 Tableau for real-time robot controller circuit with architecture-altering operations

Objective	Design a circuit for controlling the trajectory of a real-time robot with nonzero turning radius (moving at constant speed) such that the robot moves to an arbitrary destination point in minimal time.
Test fixture and embryo	Two-input, one-output initial circuit with two source resistors, one load resistor, and three modifiable wires
Program architecture	Three result-producing branches in generation 0. Automatically defined functions and arguments will be created during the run by the architecture-altering operations.
Initial function set for the RPBs	For construction-continuing subtrees: $F_{ccs\text{-}rpb\text{-}initial}$ = {R, SERIES, PARALLEL0, PARALLEL1, FLIP, NOP, RETAINING_THREE_GROUND_0, RETAINING_THREE_GROUND_1, RETAINING_THREE_POS15V_0, RETAINING_THREE_POS15V_1, RETAINING_THREE_NEG15V_0, RETAINING_THREE_NEG15V_1, PAIR_CONNECT_0, PAIR_CONNECT_1, Q_DIODE_NPN, Q_DIODE_PNP, Q_THREE_NPN0, . . . , Q_THREE_NPN11, Q_THREE_PNP0, . . . , Q_THREE_PNP11, Q_POS15V_COLL_NPN, Q_GND_EMIT_NPN, Q_NEG15V_EMIT_NPN, Q_GND_EMIT_PNP, Q_POS15V_EMIT_PNP, Q_NEG15V_COLL_PNP} For arithmetic-performing subtrees: F_{aps} = {+, -}.
Initial terminal set for the RPBs	For construction-continuing subtrees: $T_{ccs\text{-}rpb\text{-}initial}$ = {END, SAFE_CUT}. For arithmetic-performing subtrees: T_{aps} = {$\Re_{smaller\text{-}reals}$}.
Initial function set for the ADFs	No automatically defined functions in generation 0. $F_{adf\text{-}initial}$ = ϕ.
Initial terminal set for the ADFs	No automatically defined functions in generation 0. $T_{adf\text{-}initial}$ = ϕ.
Potential function set for the RPBs	$F_{ccs\text{-}rpb\text{-}potential}$ = {ADF0, ADF1}
Potential terminal set for the RPBs	$T_{ccs\text{-}rpb\text{-}potential}$ = ϕ
Potential function set for the ADFs	$F_{ccs\text{-}adf\text{-}potential}$ = {R, SERIES, PARALLEL0, PARALLEL1, FLIP, NOP, RETAINING_THREE_GROUND_0, RETAINING_THREE_GROUND_1, RETAINING_THREE_POS15V_0, RETAINING_THREE_POS15V_1, RETAINING_THREE_NEG15V_0, RETAINING_THREE_NEG15V_1, PAIR_CONNECT_0, PAIR_CONNECT_1, Q_DIODE_NPN, Q_DIODE_PNP, Q_THREE_NPN0, . . . , Q_THREE_NPN11, Q_THREE_PNP0, . . . , Q_THREE_PNP11, Q_POS15V_COLL_NPN, Q_GND_EMIT_NPN, Q_NEG15V_EMIT_NPN, Q_GND_EMIT_PNP, Q_POS15V_EMIT_PNP, Q_NEG15V_COLL_PNP}.
Potential terminal set for the ADFs	$T_{ccs\text{-}adf\text{-}potential}$ = {ARG0, END SAFE_CUT}

(continued)

Table 48.1 *(continued)*

Fitness cases	72 random destinations (x_i, y_i) for the robot
Raw fitness	The sum, over the 72 destinations, of the time for the robot to reach the destination
Standardized fitness	Same as raw fitness
Hits	Number of fitness cases that do not time out
Wrapper	The wrapper modularizes and clamps the output voltage produced by the circuit so that the final turn angle Θ lies between $-\Theta_{max}$ and $+\Theta_{max}$.
Parameters	$M = 640{,}000.$ $G = 501.$ $Q = 10{,}000.$ $D = 64.$ $B = 2\%.$ $S_{rpb} = 300.$ $S_{adf} = 300.$ $N_{rpb} = 3.$ $N_{max\text{-}adf} = 2.$ $N_{max\text{-}argument\text{-}adf} = 1.$
Result designation	Best-so-far pace-setting individual
Success predicate	A program scores the maximum number (72) of hits.

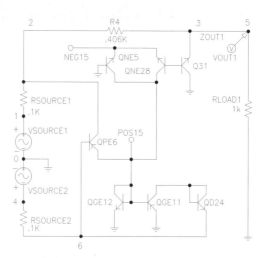

Figure 48.2   Best circuit of generation 0

The best circuit (Figure 48.3) from generation 8 scores 67 hits and achieves a fitness of 2.57 hours. It has seven transistors, one diode, and one resistor (not counting the three resistors of the test fixture and those contained in the power supplies).

The best circuit (Figure 48.4) from generation 17 scores 69 hits and achieves a fitness of 2.06 hours. It has 12 transistors, no diodes, and one resistor (not counting the three resistors of the test fixture and those contained in the power supplies).

The best circuit of generation 20 scores 72 hits (out of 72) and achieves a fitness of 1.602 hours. It is the first robot controller circuit that reaches all 72 destinations within the allotted time (80 time steps, each representing 0.001 hour).

The best-of-run circuit (Figure 48.5), appearing in generation 31, scores 72 hits and achieves a near-optimal fitness of 1.541 hours. This circuit has 10 transistors and four

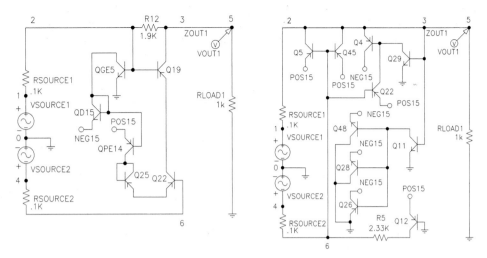

Figure 48.3 Best circuit of generation 8   **Figure 48.4 Best circuit of generation 17**

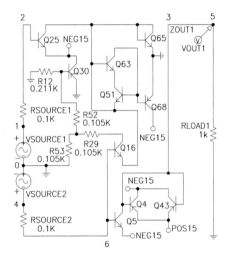

Figure 48.5 Best-of-run circuit from generation 31

resistors. The result-producing branches have 24, 11, and 54 points. ADF0 has 12 points and is called twice.

The creation (in Chapters 13, 21, and 23) of a mathematical formula consisting of addition, subtraction, multiplication, division, and conditional operations to solve this nonlinear optimal control problem is a nontrivial and interesting result. As mentioned in Chapter 47, the synthesis of a design for an analog circuit to implement a given mathematical formula is, in general, a problem of recognized difficulty. This chapter combines these two tasks and presents a procedure for creating, in one integrated and holistic process, an analog real-time circuit directly from the high-level requirements for a time-optimal controller.

Referring to the eight criteria in Chapter 1 for establishing that an automatically created result is competitive with a human-produced result, this result satisfies the following criterion:

G. The result solves a problem of indisputable difficulty in its field.

Therefore, we make the following claim:

- **CLAIM NO. 10** We claim that the synthesis by genetic programming of a real-time analog computational circuit for time-optimal control of a robot is an instance where genetic programming has produced a result that is competitive with an algorithm produced by creative and inventive humans.

This instance of holistic design satisfies Arthur Samuel's criterion (1983) for artificial intelligence and machine learning:

> The aim [is] . . . to get machines to exhibit behavior, which if done by humans, would be assumed to involve the use of intelligence.

48.4 TWO-INPUT AMPLIFIER

In this section, the goal is to evolve a 40 dB three-leaded two-input op amp. A three-leaded operational amplifier (op amp) is a two-input circuit whose output has an amplitude that is a multiple of the difference between its two inputs (Sections 41.1.27 and 41.1.28).

There are two reasons why evolving a two-input op amp is more difficult than evolving a one-input amplifier. First, the op amp must include circuitry for computing the difference between its two input signals. Second, as just seen in the robot controller, the number of fitness cases required to evolve a two-input circuit is considerably larger than the number of fitness cases for a similar one-input circuit. Fitness for the two-input op amp is measured using a nested DC sweep over five voltage values (–50, –25, 0, +25, and +50 millivolts) for each of the two inputs. Thus, 25 fitness cases are used (whereas only five fitness cases were used in Section 44.2.4 for evolving a one-input amplifier). As in Section 44.2.4, fitness is calculated on the basis of four penalties (an amplification penalty, a bias penalty, and two nonlinearity penalties) derived from these 25 fitness cases. The function and terminal set is the same as used in Section 44.2.3 with two exceptions. First, the capacitor-creating function is removed (since capacitors do not pass the DC values used by the fitness measure). Second, the two-argument resistor-creating function (with its arithmetic-performing subtree for setting the numerical value for resistance) is replaced by three one-argument functions for creating resistors with fixed values. That is, a parts bin containing only 1 KΩ, 10 KΩ, and 100 KΩ resistors is used. This problem was run on our 70-node Beowulf-style parallel computer (with 533 MHz processors at each node [described in Section 62.1.5]) using a population size of 2,100,000 (i.e., $Q = 30,000$ and $D = 70$). In our only run of this problem on our 70-node Beowulf-style parallel computer, a highly linear 39.4 dB two-input op amp with a 0.228 volt bias appears on generation 83 with 29 transistors and 25 resistors.

Prior to running this problem on our 70-node Beowulf-style parallel computer, we ran this problem several times on our considerably slower 64-node parallel computer (with 80 MHz processors at each node) with a population size of 640,000. None of these runs were successful. This problem is another example of a problem that was not solved with a slower computer, but was subsequently solved when additional computational resources were provided (i.e., a faster computer working with a larger population).

48.5   ACTIVE FILTER EMPLOYING TWO-INPUT AMPLIFIERS

Chapter 25, among others, demonstrated that genetic programming is capable of evolving a lowpass filter circuit composed of passive components (such as capacitors and inductors). However, filters are commonly constructed from active components, such as three-leaded transistors or operational amplifiers. Genetic programming can be used to evolve an active filter (instead of a passive filter) merely by changing the preparatory step pertaining to the problem's function set. Specifically, the inductor-creating L function in the function set is replaced with the component-creating function for three-leaded (two-input) op amps (Section 41.1.28). In addition, the resistor-creating R function (Section 25.6.1) is added to the problem's function set. All the other specifications are the same as in Section 25.14. In our only run of this problem, a 100%-compliant circuit appears in generation 51 with a fitness of 0.157. This evolved active filter consists of 13 op amps, 15 capacitors, and five resistors.

Synthesis of a Temperature-Sensing Circuit

Since electrical components operate differently at different temperatures, it is possible to design a zero-input circuit that senses the temperature of the environment in which the circuit is operating. Bruce Moore (1998) observed:

> IC temperature sensors have come of age. Driven by PC and automotive applications, designers have embedded these ubiquitous heat sniffers in almost every electronic system larger than a pager. Cellular phones usually include one or more sensors in the battery pack, and notebook computers might have four or more sensors for checking temperatures in the CPU, battery, AC adapter, and PCMCIA card cage. Consequently, the design and manufacture of IC temperature sensors has become a $300 million/year industry.

> These applications do not cover the enormous number of thermal-shutdown and -protection circuits that designers build into all sorts of ICs. . . . They cannot always replace the traditional temperature sensors—resistance temperature detectors, thermistors, and thermocouples—but IC temperature sensors offer many advantages. They require no linearization or cold-junction compensation, for instance. . . . They generally provide better noise immunity through higher level output signals, and some provide logic outputs that can interface directly to digital systems.

49.1   DESIGN GOALS

The goal is to evolve the design of a circuit whose output voltage is proportional to the circuit's ambient temperature over a wide range (water's freezing and boiling points). Unlike all the other circuits in this book, this one-output circuit has no explicit input. Instead, its task is to infer the ambient temperature from the fact that its own electrical components behave differently at different temperatures.

The circuit will operate in an environment whose temperature ranges between 0°C and 100°C and will be expected to report the ambient temperature using a linear scale in which 0 volts equals 0°C and 10 volts equals 100°C.

49.2   PREPARATORY STEPS

49.2.1   Embryo and Test Fixture

The desired temperature-sensing circuit has no explicit input and one output.

The initial circuit for this problem (Figure 49.1) is created by embedding the embryo with two modifiable wires and two ports (Figure 29.16) into a zero-input, one-output test fixture with two ports (Figure 29.5). The test fixture has no source resistor since it has no external input. Since the circuit has no explicit input, the two modifiable wires (Z0 and Z1) are arranged as a loop between nodes 2 and 3.

49.2.2   Program Architecture

Since the embryo has two modifiable wires, there are two result-producing branches in each program tree. Thus, the architecture of each program tree in the population consists of two result-producing branches.

No automatically defined functions or architecture-altering operations are used for this problem.

49.2.3   Functions and Terminals

The initial function set, $F_{ccs\text{-}rpb\text{-}initial}$, for the construction-continuing subtrees of the result-producing branches is

$F_{ccs\text{-}rpb\text{-}initial}$ = {R, C, SERIES, PARALLEL0, PARALLEL1, FLIP, NOP, RETAINING_THREE_GROUND_0, RETAINING_THREE_GROUND_1, RETAINING_THREE_POS15V_0, RETAINING_THREE_POS15V_1, RETAINING_THREE_NEG15V_0, RETAINING_THREE_NEG15V_1, PAIR_CONNECT_0, PAIR_CONNECT_1, Q_DIODE_NPN, Q_DIODE_PNP, Q_THREE_NPN0, . . . , Q_THREE_NPN11, Q_THREE_PNP0, . . . , Q_THREE_PNP11, Q_POS15V_COLL_NPN, Q_GND_EMIT_NPN, Q_NEG15V_EMIT_NPN, Q_GND_EMIT_PNP, Q_POS15V_EMIT_PNP, Q_NEG15V_COLL_PNP}.

For the *npn* transistors, the Q2N3904 model is used. For *pnp* transistors, the Q2N3906 model is used.

The initial terminal set, $T_{ccs\text{-}rpb\text{-}initial}$, for the construction-continuing subtrees of the result-producing branches is

$T_{ccs\text{-}rpb\text{-}initial}$ = {END, SAFE_CUT}.

Since there are no automatically defined functions in this problem, $T_{adf\text{-}initial}$ and $F_{adf\text{-}initial}$ are empty.

Since there are no architecture-altering operations in this problem, $T_{rpb\text{-}potential}$, $F_{rpb\text{-}potential}$, $T_{adf\text{-}potential}$, and $F_{adf\text{-}potential}$ are empty.

The function set, F_{aps}, for each arithmetic-performing subtree in any branch and the terminal set, T_{aps}, for each arithmetic-performing subtree in any branch are the same as for the lowpass filter problem in Section 25.14.3.

49.2.4   Fitness

For this problem, the voltage **VOUT** is probed at node 5.

The SPICE simulator is instructed to perform 21 consecutive DC operating point analyses for temperatures between 0°C and 100°C in increments of 5°. Fitness is the sum, over the 21 fitness cases, of the absolute value of the weighted difference between the output voltage and the target voltage. If the output voltage is within the acceptable range

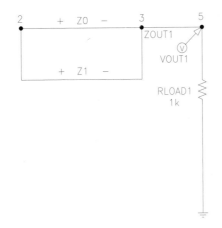

Figure 49.1   Zero-input, one-output initial circuit for temperature-sensing circuit

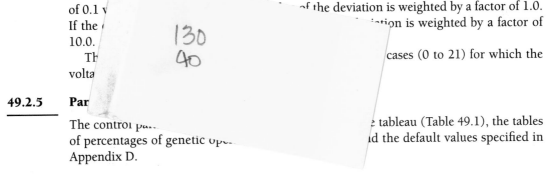

of 0.1 v   of the deviation is weighted by a factor of 1.0.
If the   tion is weighted by a factor of
10.0.

Th   cases (0 to 21) for which the
volta

49.2.5   Par

The control pa   e tableau (Table 49.1), the tables
of percentages of genetic ope   d the default values specified in
Appendix D.

49.2.6   Tableau

Table 49.1 summarizes the key features of the problem of designing a temperature-sensing circuit.

49.3   RESULTS

The best circuit from generation 0 (Figure 49.2) achieves a fitness of 211.7 and scores 1 hit (out of 21). It is composed of seven transistors, no diodes, and no resistors (not counting the one fixed resistor of the test fixture).

Figure 49.3a shows the behavior of this circuit from generation 0. The horizontal axis represents temperature and ranges linearly from 0°C to 100°C. The vertical axis represents voltage and ranges linearly from 0 volts to 10 volts. As can be seen, the output is not a linear function of the temperature.

The best circuit from generation 9 (Figure 49.4) achieves a fitness of 67.3 and scores 8 hits (out of 21). It is composed of eight transistors, no diodes, and no resistors (not counting the one fixed resistor of the test fixture).

Table 49.1 Tableau for temperature-sensing circuit

Objective	Design an inputless circuit whose output voltage is proportional to the circuit's ambient temperature (between 0°C and 100°C).
Test fixture and embryo	Zero-input, one-output initial circuit with a load resistor and two modifiable wires (arranged as a loop).
Program architecture	Two result-producing branches
Initial function set for the RPBs	For construction-continuing subtrees: $F_{ccs\text{-}rpb\text{-}initial}$ = {R, C, SERIES, PARALLEL0, PARALLEL1, FLIP, NOP, RETAINING_THREE_GROUND_0, RETAINING_THREE_GROUND_1, RETAINING_THREE_POS15V_0, RETAINING_THREE_POS15V_1, RETAINING_THREE_NEG15V_0, RETAINING_THREE_NEG15V_1, PAIR_CONNECT_0, PAIR_CONNECT_1, Q_DIODE_NPN, Q_DIODE_PNP, Q_THREE_NPN0, . . . , Q_THREE_NPN11, Q_THREE_PNP0, . . . , Q_THREE_PNP11, Q_POS15V_COLL_NPN, Q_GND_EMIT_NPN, Q_NEG15V_EMIT_NPN, Q_GND_EMIT_PNP, Q_POS15V_EMIT_PNP, Q_NEG15V_COLL_PNP}. For arithmetic-performing subtrees: F_{aps} = {+, -}.
Initial terminal set for the RPBs	For construction-continuing subtrees: $T_{ccs\text{-}rpb\text{-}initial}$ = {END, SAFE_CUT}. For arithmetic-performing subtrees: T_{aps} = {$\Re_{smaller\text{-}reals}$}.
Initial function set for the ADFs	Automatically defined functions are not used.
Initial terminal set for the ADFs	Automatically defined functions are not used.
Potential function set for the RPBs	Architecture-altering operations are not used.
Potential terminal set for the RPBs	Architecture-altering operations are not used.
Potential function set for the ADFs	Architecture-altering operations are not used.
Potential terminal set for the ADFs	Architecture-altering operations are not used.
Fitness cases	21 temperatures between 0°C and 100°C in increments of 5°.
Raw fitness	The sum, over the 21 fitness cases, of the absolute value of the weighted difference between the output voltage and the target voltage
Standardized fitness	Same as raw fitness
Hits	The number of hits is defined as the number of fitness cases (0 to 21) for which the voltage is acceptable.
Wrapper	None

Parameters	M = 640,000. G = 501. Q = 10,000. D = 64. B = 2%. S_{rpb} = 400. N_{rpb} = 2.
Result designation	Best-so-far pace-setting individual
Success predicate	A program scores the maximum number (21) of hits.

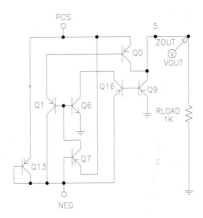

Figure 49.2   Best of generation 0 temperature-sensing circuit

Figure 49.3b shows the behavior of this circuit from generation 9. As can be seen, the output is closer to a linear function of temperature than was the case for generation 0.

The best circuit from generation 25 (Figure 49.5) achieves a fitness of 26.4 and scores 16 hits (out of 21). It is composed of 42 transistors, six diodes, and six resistors (not counting the one fixed resistor of the test fixture). The program tree has 205 and 120 points in its two result-producing branches. As it happens, everything to the left of the vertical line starting at **POS** at the top middle of the figure is disconnected from the circuit's output and therefore could be edited out of the circuit.

Figure 49.3c shows the output of the best-of-run temperature-sensing circuit from generation 25 as a function of temperature. As can be seen, the evolved circuit produces output that is an almost linear function of the input. The output is imperfect for temperatures near the freezing temperature of water.

The design of a zero-input electronic thermometer is a problem of recognized difficulty. At least two dozen temperature-sensing circuits have been patented, including ones by Massey (1970) and Haeusler (1976). Sidney Darlington received a patent for a temperature-compensated transistor amplifier in 1959 (Darlington 1959).

Referring to the eight criteria in Chapter 1 for establishing that an automatically created result is competitive with a human-produced result, this result satisfies the following two criteria:

A. The result was patented as an invention in the past, is an improvement over a patented invention, or would qualify today as a patentable new invention.

G. The result solves a problem of indisputable difficulty in its field.

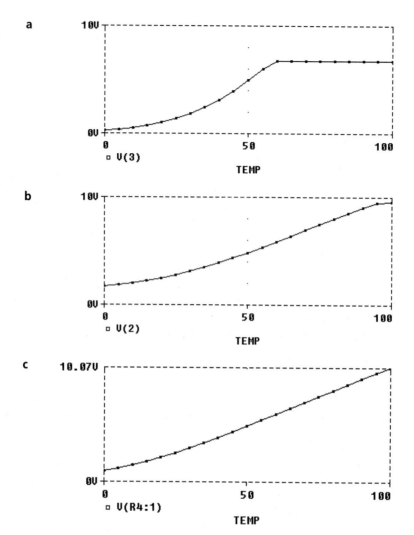

Figure 49.3 Comparison of actual output and target for best circuits of generations (a) 0, (b) 9, and (c) 25

Therefore, we make the following claim:

- **CLAIM NO. 11** We claim that the synthesis by genetic programming of a temperature-sensing circuit is an instance where genetic programming has produced a result that is competitive with a result produced by creative and inventive humans.

This automatically created circuit satisfies Arthur Samuel's criterion (1983) for artificial intelligence and machine learning:

The aim [is] ... to get machines to exhibit behavior, which if done by humans, would be assumed to involve the use of intelligence.

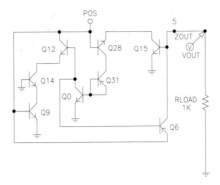

Figure 49.4   Best of generation 9 temperature-sensing circuit

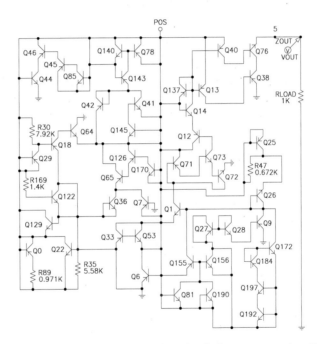

Figure 49.5   Best-of-run temperature-sensing circuit from generation 25

Synthesis of a Voltage Reference Circuit

The voltage supplied by all practical sources of electrical power is subject to variation. However, many circuits operate properly only when they are supplied with one or more reference voltages that can be relied upon to vary only slightly from their specified values. Moreover, the behavior of all circuits is subject to variation because of temperature. A voltage reference circuit supplies a prespecified constant voltage (with a small prespecified tolerance) in spite of variation in the incoming power supply and in spite of variation in the ambient temperature.

50.1 DESIGN GOALS

The goal is to design a voltage reference circuit that delivers a constant 2 volts in spite of ± 20% variations in the voltage of the incoming 5-volt power supply (i.e., from 4 volts to 6 volts) and in spite of variations in the circuit's ambient temperature between 0°C and 100°C. The output is a function of two variables (incoming voltage and temperature); however, the incoming power supply voltage is the only explicit input. Temperature is implicit (in the same sense as for the temperature-sensing circuit of Chapter 49).

50.2 PREPARATORY STEPS

50.2.1 Embryo and Test Fixture

The initial circuit (Figure 30.1) for this problem is created by embedding the embryo with one modifiable wire and three ports (Figure 29.10) into the one-input, one-output test fixture with three ports (Figure 29.1).

50.2.2 Program Architecture

Since the embryo has one modifiable wire, there is one result-producing branch in each circuit-constructing program tree.

No automatically defined functions or architecture-altering operations are used for this problem.

50.2.3 Functions and Terminals

The initial function set, $F_{ccs-rpb-initial}$, for the construction-continuing subtrees of the result-producing branches is

$F_{ccs-rpb-initial}$ = {R, SERIES, PARALLEL0, PARALLEL1, FLIP, NOP,
RETAINING_THREE_GROUND_0, RETAINING_THREE_GROUND_1,
PAIR_CONNECT_0, PAIR_CONNECT_1, Q_DIODE_NPN, Q_DIODE_PNP,
Q_THREE_NPN0, . . . , Q_THREE_NPN11, Q_THREE_PNP0, . . . ,
Q_THREE_PNP11, Q_GND_EMIT_NPN, Q_GND_EMIT_PNP}.

Note that there are no component-creating functions relating to power supplies in the above function set, since the goal of this problem is to create a reliable power source.

The initial terminal set, $T_{ccs-rpb-initial}$, for the construction-continuing subtrees of the result-producing branches is

$T_{ccs-rpb-initial}$ = {END, SAFE_CUT}.

Since there are no automatically defined functions in this problem, $T_{adf-initial}$ and $F_{adf-initial}$ are empty.

Since there are no architecture-altering operations in this problem, $T_{rpb-potential}$, $F_{rpb-potential}$, $T_{adf-potential}$, and $F_{adf-potential}$ are empty.

The function set, F_{aps}, for each arithmetic-performing subtree in any branch and the terminal set, T_{aps}, for each arithmetic-performing subtree in any branch are the same as for the lowpass filter problem in Section 25.14.3.

50.2.4 Fitness

The SPICE simulator is instructed to perform five consecutive DC sweeps. Each DC sweep is performed for a particular temperature—0°, 25°, 50°, 75°, and 100°C. Each DC sweep runs between 4 volts and 6 volts in 21 increments of 0.1 volt. A total of 105 fitness cases are created by pairing each of the five temperatures with each of the 21 voltages.

Fitness is the sum, over the 105 fitness cases, of the absolute value of the weighted difference between the output voltage and the target voltage. If the output voltage is within the acceptable range of 0.02 volt of the target, the absolute value of the deviation is weighted by a factor of 1.0. If the deviation is greater, the absolute value of the deviation is weighted by a factor of 10.0.

The number of hits is defined as the number of fitness cases (0 to 105) for which the voltage is acceptable.

50.2.5 Parameters

The control parameters for this problem are found in the tableau (Table 50.1), the tables of percentages of genetic operations in Appendix D, and the default values specified in Appendix D.

50.2.6 Tableau

Table 50.1 summarizes the key features of the problem of designing a voltage reference circuit.

Table 50.1 Tableau for voltage reference circuit

Objective	Design a voltage reference circuit that delivers a constant 2 volts in spite of ± 20% variations in the voltage of the incoming 5-volt power supply and in spite of variations in the circuit's ambient temperature between 0°C and 100°C.
Test fixture and embryo	One-input, one-output initial circuit with source resistor, load resistor, and two modifiable wires
Program architecture	Two result-producing branches
Initial function set for the RPBs	For construction-continuing subtrees: $F_{ccs-rpb-initial}$ = {R, SERIES, PARALLEL0, PARALLEL1, FLIP, NOP, RETAINING_THREE_GROUND_0, RETAINING_THREE_GROUND_1, PAIR_CONNECT_0, PAIR_CONNECT_1, Q_DIODE_NPN, Q_DIODE_PNP, Q_THREE_NPN0, . . . , Q_THREE_NPN11, Q_THREE_PNP0, . . . , Q_THREE_PNP11, Q_GND_EMIT_NPN, Q_GND_EMIT_PNP}. For arithmetic-performing subtrees: F_{aps} = {+, -}.
Initial terminal set for the RPBs	For construction-continuing subtrees: $T_{ccs-rpb-initial}$ = {END, SAFE_CUT}. For arithmetic-performing subtrees: T_{aps} = {$\Re_{smaller-reals}$}.
Initial function set for the ADFs	Automatically defined functions are not used.
Initial terminal set for the ADFs	Automatically defined functions are not used.
Potential function set for the RPBs	Architecture-altering operations are not used.
Potential terminal set for the RPBs	Architecture-altering operations are not used.
Potential function set for the ADFs	Architecture-altering operations are not used.
Potential terminal set for the ADFs	Architecture-altering operations are not used.
Fitness cases	105 fitness cases obtained by pairing each of five temperatures (0°, 25°, 50°, 75°, and 100°C) with 21 values of DC voltage ranging between 4 volts and 6 volts in 21 increments of 0.1 volt
Raw fitness	The sum, over the 105 fitness cases, of the absolute value of the weighted difference between the output voltage and the target voltage
Standardized fitness	Same as raw fitness
Hits	The number of hits is defined as the number of fitness cases (0 to 105) for which the voltage is acceptable.
Wrapper	None

(continued)

Table 50.1 *(continued)*

Parameters	M = 640,000. G = 501. Q = 10,000. D = 64. B = 2%. S_{rpb} = 600. N_{rpb} = 1.
Result designation	Best-so-far pace-setting individual
Success predicate	A program scores the maximum number (105) of hits.

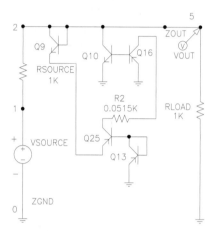

Figure 50.1   Best circuit from generation 0

50.3   RESULTS

The best circuit from generation 0 (Figure 50.1) achieves a fitness of 131.1 and scores 10 hits. It is composed of three transistors, two diodes, and one resistor (not counting the two fixed resistors in the test fixture). The circuit-constructing program tree has 32 points.

Figure 50.2 shows the voltages produced by the best circuit of generation 0. The horizontal axis represents the actual incoming voltage provided by the power supply and ranges linearly from 4 volts to 6 volts. The vertical axis represents output voltage on a linear scale. The top graph indicates the voltages produced at 0°C. The four remaining graphs in this figure represent 25°, 50°, 75°, and 100°C.

Figure 50.3 shows the voltage produced by the best circuit of generations 0, 6, 49, and 80. As can be seen, as we proceed from earlier to later generations of the run, there is a progressive flattening of the five graphs and a progressive coalescence of the five graphs around the desired target output of 2 volts. The best circuit from generation 80 delivers a voltage that is almost independent of the temperature and almost independent of the actual incoming voltage provided by the power supply.

The best circuit from generation 6 (Figure 50.4) achieves a fitness of 65.7 and scores 16 hits. The circuit has six transistors, two diodes, and two resistors.

Figure 50.5 shows a close-up of the output voltage in the narrow range between 1.8 volts and 2.13 volts for this circuit from generation 6.

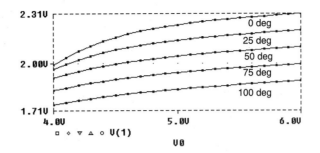

Figure 50.2   Close-up of the output voltage of the best circuit from generation 0

The best circuit from generation 49 (Figure 50.6) achieves a fitness of 35.2 and scores 49 hits. The circuit has 11 transistors, four diodes, and four resistors.

Figure 50.7 shows a close-up of the output voltage in the range between 1.9 and 2.1 volts for this circuit.

The best-of-run circuit from generation 80 (Figure 50.8) achieves a fitness of 6.6 and scores 90 hits (out of 105). The circuit has 40 transistors, 14 diodes, and 13 resistors. The program tree has 522 points.

Figure 50.9 shows a close-up of the output voltage in the narrow range starting at 1.93 volts for this circuit from generation 80. As can be seen, the output voltages are within about 1% of 2 volts for most incoming voltages (and within about 3% at the low end of the range of incoming voltages).

The design of a voltage reference circuit is a problem of recognized difficulty. As Schweber (1998) states:

> Since the beginning days of instrumentation in the 19th century, electrical systems have needed a compact source of well-defined potential difference—a voltage—that remains accurate, stable, repeatable, and inexpensive. Although laboratories have used carefully constructed, wet electrochemical cells, called Weston cells, for primary references, these are hopelessly impractical for most systems. . . .

> The legendary, late Bob Widlar [1970] described a reference that simply and cleverly employed the two opposing temperature coefficients together in a mutually canceling way. The resulting device was a bandgap voltage reference, which [David] Fullagar notes was "one of the most elegant pieces of design work in our industry."

Also,

> A voltage reference has a higher ratio of design-in subtlety to the number of active devices than any other linear component. For an IC with just two or three terminals, the voltage reference packs a lot of mystery into its design, packaging, and application.

Robert C. Dobkin and Robert J. Widlar of National Semiconductor Corporation received U.S. patent 3,617,859 for the voltage reference circuit (Dobkin and Widlar 1971). While the genetically evolved circuit does not employ the cleverness and elegance of the design in the Dobkin-Widlar patent, it achieves the same overall objective. Subsequent to the Dobkin-Widlar patent, other patents have been issued for voltage reference circuits, including U.S. patent 3,743,923 to Goetz Wolfgang Steudel of RCA Corporation (Steudel 1973).

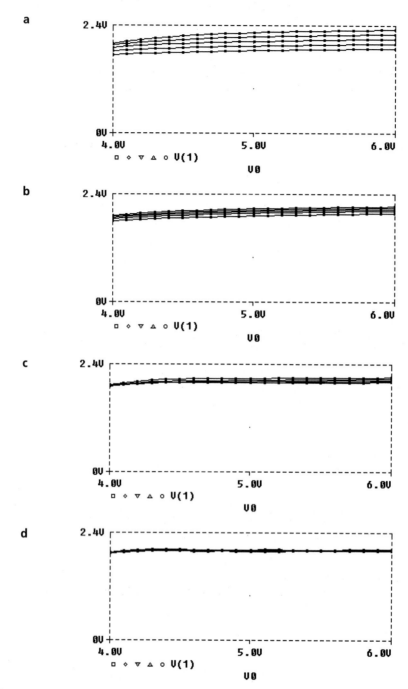

Figure 50.3 Output voltage of the best circuits of generations (a) 0, (b) 6, (c) 49, and (d) 80 for temperatures of 0°, 25°, 50°, 75°, and 100°C

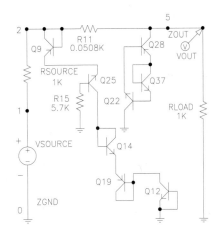

Figure 50.4 Best circuit from generation 6

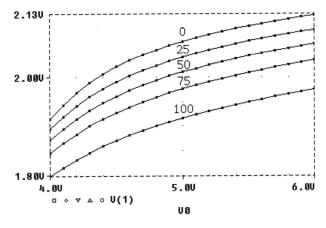

Figure 50.5 Close-up of the output voltage of the best circuit from generation 6

Referring to the eight criteria in Chapter 1 for establishing that an automatically created result is competitive with a human-produced result, this result satisfies the following two criteria:

A. The result was patented as an invention in the past, is an improvement over a patented invention, or would qualify today as a patentable new invention.
G. The result solves a problem of indisputable difficulty in its field.

Therefore, we make the following claim:

- **CLAIM NO. 12** We claim that the synthesis by genetic programming of a voltage reference circuit is an instance where genetic programming has produced a result that is competitive with a result produced by creative and inventive humans.

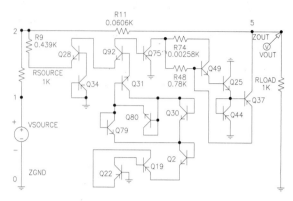

Figure 50.6   Best circuit from generation 49

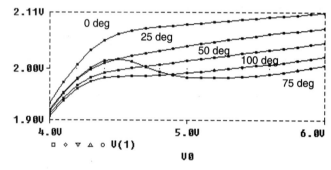

Figure 50.7   Close-up of the output voltage of the best circuit from generation 49

This automatically created circuit satisfies Arthur Samuel's criterion (1983) for artificial intelligence and machine learning:

> The aim [is] . . . to get machines to exhibit behavior, which if done by humans, would be assumed to involve the use of intelligence.

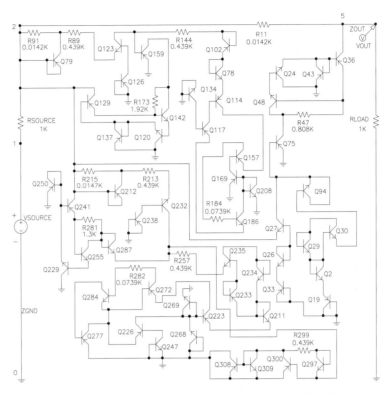

Figure 50.8 Best-of-run voltage reference circuit from generation 80

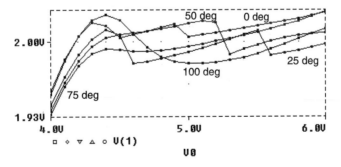

Figure 50.9 Close-up of the output voltage for the best-of-run circuit from generation 80

Synthesis of a MOSFET Circuit

All the transistors appearing in previous chapters were bipolar junction transistors (BJTs). One of the shortcomings of BJT technology is that the number of transistors that can be fabricated in a single integrated circuit is severely constrained by the power consumed and dissipated by the circuit (Wakerly 1990).

A metal-oxide semiconductor (MOS) transistor is a four-leaded device that acts like a voltage-controlled resistance (Wakerly 1990). The four terminals of an MOS transistor are called the *drain*, *gate*, *source*, and *bulk*. The gate of an MOS transistor has a very high impedance. MOS transistors are often called field-effect (or MOSFET) transistors because the gate voltage creates an electric field that enhances or retards the flow of current between source and drain.

There are both n-channel MOS transistors and p-channel MOS transistors. In an n-channel MOS (*NMOS*) transistor, the voltage from gate to source is usually made to be zero or positive. If this voltage from gate to source is zero, then the resistance from drain to source is very high (perhaps measured in megaohms); however, as this voltage is increasingly made more positive, the resistance from drain to source decreases dramatically. In a p-channel MOS (*PMOS*) transistor, the voltage from gate to source is normally zero or negative. If this voltage from gate to source is zero, then the resistance from source to drain is very high; however, as this voltage is increasingly made more negative, the resistance from source to drain decreases dramatically (Wakerly 1990).

MOSFET transistors are usually manufactured with a different semiconductor process technology than bipolar junction transistors. Once a digital circuit is designed using one technology, the same design can usually be substantially reused when it comes time to migrate the circuit to a new technology. The behavior of interest in digital circuits is expressed in terms of two-valued logic—not in terms of a continuous range of analog values. The behavior of digital circuits is governed by well-understood basic principles of Boolean logic that are independent of whether a digital circuit is implemented with mechanical devices (as in Boole's 19th-century design), electromagnetic relays (as in early computers), vacuum tubes, BJT transistors, or MOSFET transistors. In contrast, the design of analog circuits is highly dependent on the particular technology being used. In general, if an analog circuit is designed using one technology, the circuit must be substantially (often entirely) redesigned in order to implement it using a different technology. The task of migrating existing analog designs between each new semiconductor process technology entails an enormous amount of work (and creativity).

This chapter will demonstrate the design of a computational circuit (specifically, a Gaussian computational circuit) using MOSFET (instead of BJT) technology. The changes necessary to apply genetic programming to a problem of analog circuit synthesis using MOSFET technology are minimal. The changes consist of defining a new set of component-creating functions for MOSFET components. MOSFET transistors are implemented in SPICE using models that are applicable to MOSFET transistors that are available in SPICE's library of models. Once the new component-creating functions are defined, genetic programming can be applied to MOSFET technology in precisely the same way that it is applied to BJT technology. As will be seen, the task of defining the required new MOSFET component-creating functions in the next section does not require any detailed knowledge about the behavior of MOSFET circuits.

51.1   MOSFET COMPONENT-CREATING FUNCTIONS

In general, the component values for MOSFET components are a channel length, L_{mosfet}, and a channel width, W_{mosfet}. For simplicity, in this book, the channel length of all MOSFET components is fixed at 10 micrometers (μm). The channel width is expressed in micrometers and is typically different for each component that is inserted into a circuit. Consequently, the MOSFET component-creating functions in this book each take two (or four) arguments—one for the value-setting subtree to establish the channel width and the other for the one (or three) construction-continuing subtree(s).

51.1.1   Value-Setting Subtrees for MOSFET Component-Creating Functions

The value-setting subtree for the MOSFET component-creating functions is an arithmetic-performing subtree composed of addition and subtraction and random constants. A range of 10 μm to 200 μm is permitted for widths in this book. The purpose of the arithmetic-performing subtree is to establish a value between 10 μm and 200 μm as the width of the component.

A three-step process is used to interpret the arithmetic-performing subtree:

1. The arithmetic-performing subtree is evaluated. We call the floating-point number that it returns, X.
2. X is used to produce an intermediate value U_{mosfet} in the range of 1.0 (the common logarithm of 10) and 2.3 (the common logarithm of 200) in the following way:
    - If the return value X is between -5.0 and $+5.0$, the intermediate value U_{mosfet} is found from the straight line connecting the points $(-5, +1)$ and $(+5, +2.3)$.
    - If the return value X is less than -100 or greater than $+100$, U_{mosfet} is set to a saturating value of 1.65.
    - If the return value X is between -100 and -5.0, the intermediate value U_{mosfet} is found from the straight line connecting the points $(-100, 1.65)$ and $(-5, +1.0)$.
    - If the return value X is between $+5.0$ and $+100$, the intermediate value U_{mosfet} is found from the straight line connecting $(5, 2.3)$ and $(100, 1.65)$.

Figure 51.1 shows the mapping between the value X returned by the subtree and U_{mosfet}.

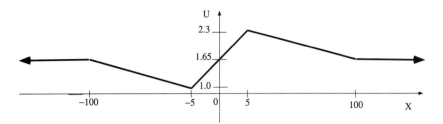

Figure 51.1 Mapping between *X* and *U*mosfet

3. The actual width, W_{mosfet}, in micrometers of a MOSFET component is the anti-logarithm (base 10) of the intermediate value U_{mosfet}. That is, W_{mosfet} is $10^{U_{mosfet}}$.

51.1.2   The M_DIODE_NMOS Function

The two-argument M_DIODE_NMOS function causes a modifiable wire or modifiable component in the developing circuit structure that is linked to this function in the circuit-constructing program tree to be changed into the equivalent of a MOSFET diode. Specifically, this function inserts a MOSFET *NMOS* transistor in lieu of a modifiable wire or modifiable component in such a way that its drain and gate are connected to each other, and these two leads are, in turn, connected to the node at the positive end of the modifiable wire or modifiable component. The source of the new MOSFET transistor is connected to the node at the negative end of the modifiable wire or modifiable component. The bulk terminal of all MOSFET *NMOS* transistors in this book is connected to the most negative voltage in the circuit involved (usually the negative power supply). One of the two arguments to the M_DIODE_NMOS function is a value-setting (arithmetic-performing) subtree, and the other is a construction-continuing subtree. The width of the MOSFET component is established by the arithmetic-performing subtree of the function (as described in Section 51.1.1). Figure 51.2 shows the result of applying the M_DIODE_NMOS function to the modifiable wire **Z0** of Figure 25.9.

51.1.3   The M_DIODE_PMOS Function

The two-argument M_DIODE_PMOS function causes a modifiable wire or modifiable component to be changed into the equivalent of a MOSFET diode. Specifically, this function inserts a MOSFET *PMOS* transistor in lieu of a modifiable wire or modifiable component in such a way that its drain and gate are connected to each other, and these two leads are, in turn, connected to the node at the positive end of the modifiable wire or modifiable component. The source of the new MOSFET transistor is connected to the node at the negative end of the modifiable wire or modifiable component. The bulk terminal of all MOSFET *PMOS* transistors in this book is connected to the most positive voltage in the circuit involved (usually the positive power supply). The width of the MOSFET component is established by the arithmetic-performing subtree. Figure 51.3 shows the result of applying the M_DIODE_PMOS function to the modifiable wire **Z0** of Figure 25.9.

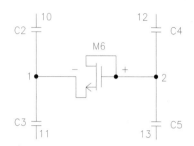

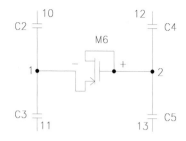

Figure 51.2   Result of M_DIODE_NMOS function

Figure 51.3   Result of M_DIODE_PMOS function

51.1.4   The M_POS5V_DRAIN_NMOS Function

The two-argument MOSFET-transistor-creating M_POS5V_DRAIN_NMOS function causes a modifiable wire or modifiable component to be changed into a MOSFET transistor. Specifically, this function inserts a MOSFET *NMOS* transistor in lieu of a modifiable wire or modifiable component in such a way that its drain is connected to the + 5-volt power supply POS, its gate is connected to the node at the positive end of the modifiable wire or modifiable component, and its source is connected to the negative end of the modifiable wire or modifiable component. The width of the newly created MOSFET component is established by the arithmetic-performing subtree. Figure 51.4 shows the result of applying the M_POS5V_DRAIN_NMOS function to the modifiable wire Z0 of Figure 25.9.

51.1.5   The M_POS5V_GATE_NMOS Function

The two-argument MOSFET-transistor-creating M_POS5V_GATE_NMOS function inserts a MOSFET *NMOS* transistor in lieu of a modifiable wire or modifiable component in such a way that its gate is connected to the +5-volt power supply POS, its drain is connected to the node at the positive end of the modifiable wire or modifiable component, and its source is connected to the negative end of the modifiable wire or modifiable component, as shown in Figure 51.5.

51.1.6   The M_NEG5V_SOURCE_NMOS Function

The two-argument MOSFET-transistor-creating M_NEG5V_SOURCE_NMOS function inserts a MOSFET *NMOS* transistor in lieu of a modifiable wire or modifiable component in such a way that its source is connected to the –5-volt power supply NEG, its drain is connected to the node at the negative end of the modifiable wire or modifiable component, and its gate is connected to the positive end of the modifiable wire or modifiable component, as shown in Figure 51.6.

51.1.7   The M_NEG5V_DRAIN_PMOS Function

The two-argument MOSFET-transistor-creating M_NEG5V_DRAIN_PMOS function inserts a MOSFET *PMOS* transistor in lieu of a modifiable wire or modifiable component in such a way that its drain is connected to the –5-volt power supply NEG, its gate is

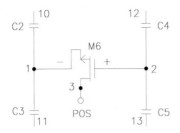

Figure 51.4 Result of
M_POS5V_DRAIN_NMOS function

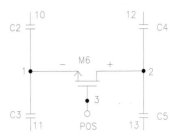

Figure 51.5 Result of
M_POS5V_GATE_NMOS function

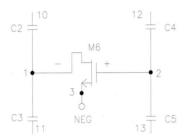

Figure 51.6 Result of
M_NEG5V_SOURCE_NMOS function

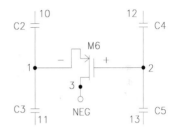

Figure 51.7 Result of
M_NEG5V_DRAIN_PMOS function

connected to the node at the positive end of the modifiable wire or modifiable component, and its source is connected to the negative end of the modifiable wire or modifiable component, as shown in Figure 51.7.

51.1.8 The M_NEG5V_GATE_PMOS Function

The two-argument MOSFET-transistor-creating M_NEG5V_GATE_PMOS function inserts a MOSFET *PMOS* transistor in lieu of a modifiable wire or modifiable component in such a way that its gate is connected to the − 5-volt power supply **NEG**, its drain is connected to the node at the positive end of the modifiable wire or modifiable component, and its source is connected to the negative end of the modifiable wire or modifiable component, as shown in Figure 51.8.

51.1.9 The M_POS5V_SOURCE_PMOS Function

The two-argument M_POS5V_SOURCE_PMOS function inserts a MOSFET *PMOS* transistor in lieu of a modifiable wire or modifiable component in such a way that its source is connected to the +5-volt power supply **POS**, its drain is connected to the node at the negative end of the modifiable wire or modifiable component, and its gate is connected to the positive end of the modifiable wire or modifiable component, as shown in Figure 51.9.

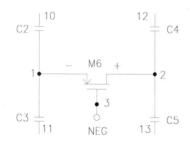

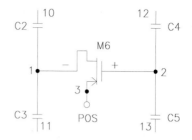

Figure 51.8   Result of M_NEG5V_GATE_PMOS function

Figure 51.9   Result of M_POS5V_SOURCE_PMOS function

51.1.10   The M_THREE_NMOS Functions

Each of the 12 functions in the family of four-argument MOSFET-transistor-creating M_THREE_NMOS functions (called M_THREE_NMOS0, . . . , M_THREE_NMOS11) causes an NMOS transistor to be inserted in place of a modifiable wire or modifiable component and one of the nodes to which a modifiable wire or modifiable component is connected. Each M_THREE_NMOS function also creates five new nodes and three new modifiable wires. After execution of an M_THREE_NMOS function, there are three writing heads that point to the three new modifiable wires. Since there is no writing head on the new transistor itself, a transistor remains in the developing circuit structure once it is inserted by an M_THREE_NMOS function. The MOSFET-transistor-creating M_THREE_NMOS functions are similar to the Q_THREE_NPN functions (Section 41.1.21), but differ in that there are four arguments because the width of the newly created MOSFET component is established by the arithmetic-performing subtree.

The 12 M_THREE_NMOS functions (like the Q_THREE_NPN functions) operate in slightly different ways depending on the polarity of the original modifiable wire or modifiable component, the numbering of existing components in the circuit, and the degree of the nodes to which the modifiable wire or modifiable component is connected. Thus, Table 41.2 for the case where both the active and inactive nodes are of degree 3 applies to the M_THREE_NMOS functions, except that "collector" becomes "drain," "base" becomes "gate," and "emitter" becomes "source." Similarly, Table 41.3 for degree 2 applies to the M_THREE_NMOS functions with the same substitutions.

Figure 51.10 shows the result of applying the M_THREE_NMOS0 function to the modifiable wire Z0 of Figure 25.9.

51.1.11   The M_THREE_PMOS Functions

Each of the 12 functions in the family of four-argument MOSFET-transistor-creating M_THREE_PMOS functions (called M_THREE_PMOS0, . . . , M_THREE_PMOS11) operates in the same manner as the M_THREE_NMOS functions, except that a *PMOS* transistor is inserted. Figure 51.11 shows the result of applying the M_THREE_PMOS0 function to the modifiable wire Z0 of Figure 25.9.

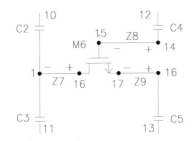

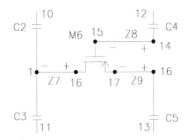

Figure 51.10   Result of M_THREE_NMOS0 function

Figure 51.11   Result of M_THREE_PMOS0 function

51.2   DESIGN GOALS

The goal is to evolve the design of a circuit with sized MOSFET transistors whose output current is a Gaussian function of its input voltage. The target Gaussian function peaks at 80 nanoamperes in current. It has a mean of 2.5 volts and a variance of 0.1 (multiplied by the scaling quotient of $20/10^{-9}$). This problem was suggested to us by Adrian Stroica of JPL in Pasadena, California.

51.3   PREPARATORY STEPS

51.3.1   Embryo and Test Fixture

This is the first circuit in this book where the probe point of the circuit measures current (instead of voltage).

The one-input, one-output initial circuit (Figure 51.12) for this problem involving MOSFET technology is created by combining an embryo that has been repeatedly used previously in this book with a new test fixture. Specifically, the initial circuit uses the embryo (Figure 29.10) with one modifiable wire and three ports to the test fixture. The new test fixture (Figure 29.7) has one input, one output, and three ports to the embryo. The input (left) portion of this new test fixture is familiar and has a 1 Ω source resistor **RSOURCE** associated with the incoming signal **VSOURCE**. However, the output (right) portion of the new test fixture differs from other test fixtures because it has a probe point for output current, **IOUT**, and a fixed voltage load **VLOAD** (shown by the icon for a battery in this figure). The output current **IOUT** is measured in nanoamperes. The +2.5-volt fixed voltage load **VLOAD** permits the output current **IOUT** flowing in **VLOAD** to be probed.

51.3.2   Program Architecture

Since the embryo has one modifiable wire, there is one result-producing branch in each program tree.

Each program in the initial population of programs has a uniform architecture with a single result-producing branch.

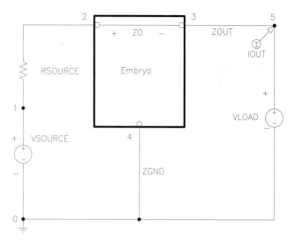

Figure 51.12   Initial circuit for the Gaussian computation circuit using MOSFET technology

Automatically defined functions and architecture-altering operations are not used on this problem.

51.3.3   Functions and Terminals

The initial function set, $F_{ccs\text{-}rpb\text{-}initial}$, for the construction-continuing subtrees of the result-producing branches is

$F_{ccs\text{-}rpb\text{-}initial}$ = {R, SERIES, PARALLEL0, PARALLEL1, FLIP, NOP, RETAINING_THREE_GROUND_0, RETAINING_THREE_GROUND_1, RETAINING_THREE_POS5V_0, RETAINING_THREE_POS5V_1, PAIR_CONNECT_0, PAIR_CONNECT_1, M_D_NMOS, M_D_PMOS, M_THREE_NMOS0, . . . , M_THREE_NMOS11, M_THREE_PMOS0, . . . , M_THREE_PMOS11, M_POS5V_DRAIN_NMOS, M_POS5V_SOURCE_PMOS, M_POS5V_GAIN_NMOS}.

SPICE's default *NMOS* and *PMOS* MOSFET transistor model parameters are used.

The initial terminal set, $T_{ccs\text{-}rpb\text{-}initial}$, for the construction-continuing subtrees of the result-producing branches is

$T_{ccs\text{-}rpb\text{-}initial}$ = {END, SAFE_CUT}.

Since there are no automatically defined functions in this problem, $T_{adf\text{-}initial}$ and $F_{adf\text{-}initial}$ are empty.

Since there are no architecture-altering operations in this problem, $T_{rpb\text{-}potential}$, $F_{rpb\text{-}potential}$, $T_{adf\text{-}potential}$, and $F_{adf\text{-}potential}$ are empty.

The function set, F_{aps}, for each arithmetic-performing subtree in any branch and the terminal set, T_{aps}, for each arithmetic-performing subtree in any branch are the same as for the lowpass filter problem in Section 25.14.3.

51.3.4 Fitness

The input to the desired circuit is measured as a voltage, while the output is measured as a current.

The SPICE simulator is instructed to perform a DC sweep analysis at 101 equidistant voltages between +2.00 volts and +3.00 volts. We chose this range because the mean of the desired Gaussian is 2.5 volts and its variance is 0.1.

Fitness is measured in terms of the sum, over these 101 fitness cases, of the absolute weighted deviation between the actual value of the current that is produced by the circuit through a +2.5-volt voltage source and the target value for current (i.e., the Gaussian function of the input voltage).

The fitness measure does not penalize output currents that perfectly match the target current. It penalizes every acceptable deviation from the target current, and it heavily penalizes every unacceptable deviation. There is a 10-to-1 ratio between the penalties for the acceptable and unacceptable deviations.

The procedure for the 101 fitness cases is as follows:

- If the output current is within 5 nanoamperes of the target current value for a particular fitness case, the absolute value of the deviation is weighted by 10^6 for that fitness case.
- If the output current is not within 5 nanoamperes of the target current value, the deviation is weighted by 10^7 for that fitness case.

The number of hits is defined as the number of fitness cases for which the current is acceptable or ideal.

51.3.5 Parameters

The control parameters for this problem are found in the tableau (Table 51.1), the tables of percentages of genetic operations in Appendix D, and the default values specified in Appendix D.

51.3.6 Tableau

Table 51.1 summarizes the key features of the problem of designing a Gaussian computational circuit using MOSFET technology.

51.4 RESULTS

The best-of-generation program from generation 0 (Figure 51.13) has a fitness of 17.45 and scores 60 hits (out of 101). The circuit has four transistors (one used as a diode) and one resistor (outside of the test fixture). The result-producing branch of this program has 87 points.

Figure 51.14 shows the output current produced by this circuit. The horizontal axis represents input voltage and ranges linearly from 2 volts to 3 volts. The vertical axis represents peak current output and ranges linearly from −1 microampere to +1 microampere. The output current is flat and zero because the input is effectively disconnected

Table 51.1   Tableau for Gaussian computational circuit using MOSFET technology

Objective	Design a MOSFET circuit with sized transistors whose output current is a Gaussian function of its input voltage.
Test fixture and embryo	One-input, one-output initial circuit with a voltage source, a 1 Ω source resistor, and a fixed +2.5-volt voltage load that is used to probe current
Program architecture	One result-producing branch
Initial function set for the RPBs	For construction-continuing subtrees: $F_{ccs\text{-}rpb\text{-}initial}$ = {R, SERIES, PARALLEL0, PARALLEL1, FLIP, NOP, RETAINING_THREE_GROUND_0, RETAINING_THREE_GROUND_1, RETAINING_THREE_POS5V_0, RETAINING_THREE_POS5V_1, PAIR_CONNECT_0, PAIR_CONNECT_1, M_D_NMOS, M_D_PMOS, M_THREE_NMOS0, . . . , M_THREE_NMOS11, M_THREE_PMOS0, ... , M_THREE_PMOS11, M_POS5V_DRAIN_NMOS, M_POS5V_SOURCE_PMOS, M_POS5V_GAIN_NMOS}. For arithmetic-performing subtrees: F_{aps} = {+, -}.
Initial terminal set for the RPBs	For construction-continuing subtrees: $T_{ccs\text{-}rpb\text{-}initial}$ = {END, SAFE_CUT}. For arithmetic-performing subtrees: $T_{aps} = \{\Re_{smaller\text{-}reals}\}$.
Initial function set for the ADFs	Automatically defined functions are not used.
Initial terminal set for the ADFs	Automatically defined functions are not used.
Potential function set for the RPBs	Architecture-altering operations are not used.
Potential terminal set for the RPBs	Architecture-altering operations are not used.
Potential function set for the ADFs	Architecture-altering operations are not used.
Potential terminal set for the ADFs	Architecture-altering operations are not used.
Fitness cases	101 equidistant voltages between +2.00 volts and +3.00 volts
Raw fitness	The sum, over the 101 fitness cases, of the absolute weighted deviation between the actual value of the current that is produced by the circuit through a +2.5-volt voltage load and the target value for current (i.e., the Gaussian function of the input voltage)
Standardized fitness	Same as raw fitness
Hits	The number of hits is defined as the number of fitness cases for which the current is acceptable or ideal
Wrapper	None

Parameters	$M = 640{,}000$. $G = 501$. $Q = 10{,}000$. $D = 64$. $B = 2\%$. $S_{rpb} = 600$. $N_{rpb} = 1$.
Result designation	Best-so-far pace-setting individual
Success predicate	A program scores the maximum number (101) of hits.

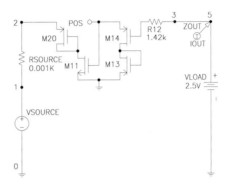

Figure 51.13 Best-of-generation circuit from generation 0

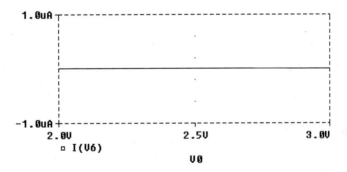

Figure 51.14 Output current for best circuit of generation 0

from the output. This individual scores as many as 60 hits only because the tails of the Gaussian curve are near zero.

The best circuit from generation 19 (Figure 51.15) has a fitness of 4.58 and scores 81 hits. The circuit has 11 transistors (two used as diodes) and two resistors (outside the test fixture).

Figure 51.16 shows the output current produced by this circuit. The horizontal axis represents input voltage and ranges linearly from 2 volts to 3 volts. The vertical axis represents output current and ranges linearly from 0 nanoamperes to +120 nanoamperes. As can be seen, the output bears some resemblance to the target Gaussian function with a mean of 2.5 volts. However, the peak current of this particular circuit is almost 50% higher than the desired level of 80 nanoamperes for a 2.5-volt input.

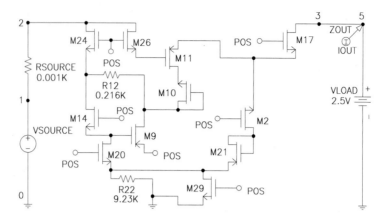

Figure 51.15 Best-of-generation circuit from generation 19

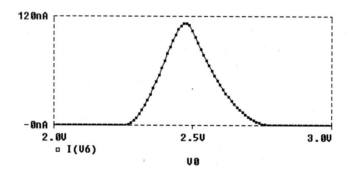

Figure 51.16 Output current for best circuit of generation 19

The first program that scores 101 hits appears at generation 29 with a fitness of 0.64.

The best-of-run circuit (Figure 51.17) appears in generation 36 and achieves a fitness of 0.094. The result-producing branch of this program has 215 points. The circuit has 13 transistors (five used as diodes) and one resistor (outside of the test fixture). Components M9, M14, M20, M24, and M29 of this circuit operate in the milliampere range.

Figure 51.18 shows the 100%-compliant output current produced by the best-of-run circuit from generation 36. The horizontal axis represents input voltage and ranges linearly from 2 volts to 3 volts. The vertical axis represents output current and ranges linearly from 0 nanoamperes to +80 nanoamperes. As can be seen, the target Gaussian function peaks at the desired level of 80 nanoamperes for a 2.5-volt input.

Table 51.2 shows the width, W_{mosfet}, in micrometers of each of the 13 transistors in the best-of-run circuit from generation 36.

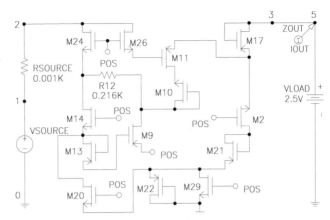

Figure 51.17 Best-of-run circuit from generation 36

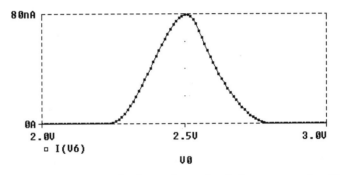

Figure 51.18 Output current for best-of-run circuit from generation 36

Table 51.2 Component values for 13 transistors in the best-of-run circuit from generation 36

Component	Created by function	Width (µm)
MPG2	M_POS5V_GATE_NMOS	40.19
MPS9	M_POS5V_SOURCE_PMOS	34.71
MD10	M_DIODE_NMOS	35.48
M11	M_THREE_PMOS	10.82
MD13	M_DIODE_PMOS	51.99
MPG14	M_POS5V_GATE_NMOS	61.31
MD17	M_DIODE_PMOS	32.69
MPG20	M_POS5V_GATE_NMOS	43.22
MD21	M_DIODE_PMOS	36.87
MD22	M_DIODE_PMOS	36.87
MPG24	M_POS5V_GATE_NMOS	58.69
MPG2	M_POS5V_GATE_NMOS	61.31
MPG29	M_POS5V_GATE_NMOS	58.64

51.5   FUTURE WORK

We are aware that this evolved circuit (and many of the other evolved active circuits in this book) possess only some of the characteristics that would be required of a commercial version of the type of circuit under discussion. For example, the data sheet for a commercial-quality op amp (e.g., the μ741) includes requirements that are more stringent than those used in this book (e.g., distortion, bandwidth) and also includes requirements in addition to those incorporated into the fitness measures of the problems in this book (e.g., slew rate, total power dissipation).

The models that are supplied with the SPICE simulator (although very good in general) have been crafted to be most accurate when the devices are operating in everyday regimes. These models do not necessarily accurately represent every conceivable operating regime—particularly those that practicing engineers would be unlikely to devise (but which an evolutionary process might be very likely to devise). It is therefore likely that some of the devices in some of the evolved circuits in this book are operating in regimes in which their underlying models in SPICE are not representative of real devices.

Thus, we make no claim that the evolved active circuits in this book are, in their present state, equal to commercial circuits designed by human engineers.

Nonetheless, we believe that we have established the principle that both the topology and sizing of analog electrical circuits (and other complex structures) can be evolved using genetic programming.

Future work in this area will focus on determining whether circuits approaching commercial usefulness can be designed with currently available computational resources. In particular, we intend to incorporate more and more of the characteristics from the commercial data sheets into the fitness measures for our runs. As we add requirements from the data sheets of practical circuits, it will be interesting to see whether genetic programming will create more substructures that are recognizable to electrical engineers and will invent new and useful circuits.

Constraints Involving Subcircuits or Topologies

There are numerous situations in which a designer may want to incorporate certain domain knowledge to bias the search for a satisfactory design. This chapter describes how certain constraints involving topologies and subcircuits can be implemented with special test fixtures and embryos.

52.1 TOPOLOGICAL CONSTRAINTS

It is sometimes desirable to require that a particular circuit be divided into distinct stages. For example, amplifiers are often designed in stages.

If a two-stage circuit is desired, this requirement can be easily implemented in genetic programming by embedding two embryos in one test fixture, as shown in Figure 52.1. The test fixture receives the circuit's input at **VSOURCE** and feeds it through source resistor **RSOURCE** to node 2 of the first embryo (Embryo1). The first embryo (Figure 29.14) consists of three modifiable wires **Z0**, **Z1**, and **Z2** and three ports. The output port of the first embryo at node 6 is then connected to a nonmodifiable wire **ZNONMOD** of the test fixture. This nonmodifiable intermediate wire runs to the input port of the second embryo (Embryo2) at node 7. The second embryo also consists of three modifiable wires **Z3**, **Z4**, and **Z5** and three ports. The output port of the second embryo at node 3 is then connected to the circuit's voltage probe point at node 5 and a load resistor **RLOAD**. Thus, connectivity is established in the test fixture between the circuit's input port and the circuit's output port.

The test fixture here is based on the one-input, one-output test fixture of Figure 29.1. The differences are that the test fixture here has two grounding wires **ZGND1** and **ZGND2** (the extra grounding wire being for the extra embryo) and a nonmodifiable wire **ZNONMOD**. No part of the first embryo has direct access to the circuit's output port. No part of the second embryo has direct access to the circuit's input. Since the intermediate wire **ZNONMOD** connecting the two embryos cannot be modified, every circuit that is produced throughout the entire developmental and evolutionary process is guaranteed to consist of two distinct stages. If the TWO_VIA or PAIR_CONNECT topology-modifying functions are being used, they must be modified so that they permit connectivity only within the now-distinct two stages of the overall circuit. In addition, it is also possible,

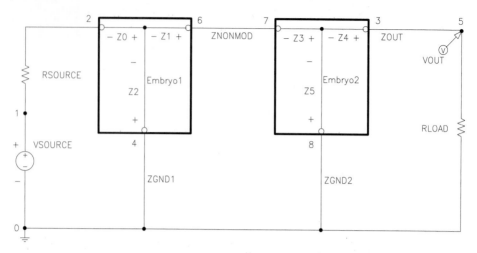

Figure 52.1 Special test fixture and embryos for a two-stage circuit

by using different function sets in the result-producing branches of each stage, to make different components available to the now-distinct two stages of the to-be-evolved circuit.

52.2 SUBCIRCUIT CONSTRAINTS

For reasons of cost, physical size, availability of parts, packaging constraints, or power consumption, many practical design problems contain a requirement that a certain substructure be embedded in a particular way into the final circuit.

Lamey (1995, page 118) poses a problem in which it is necessary to design a class B push-pull amplifier in which the final circuit must incorporate two specified transistors in a specified arrangement. Constraints such as this can be easily implemented in genetic programming by incorporating the required arrangement of the required transistors into a special embryo, as shown in Figure 52.2. The test fixture in this figure is the one-input, one-output test fixture of Figure 29.1. The test fixture receives the circuit's input at **VSOURCE** and feeds it through source resistor **RSOURCE** to node 2 at the input port of the embryo. The output port of the embryo at node 3 is connected to the circuit's voltage probe point at node 5 and drives load resistor **RLOAD**. The special embryo contains three modifiable wires **Z0**, **Z1**, and **Z2**. It also contains certain hard-wired components and connections specified by Lamey. These hard-wired elements include a hard-wired *npn* transistor **Q3**, a hard-wired *pnp* transistor **Q4**, a hard-wired connection between the emitter of **Q3** and the collector of **Q4**, and a hard-wired connection from the collector of **Q3** to the 12-volt DC power supply **POS12**. These hard-wired components and connections are not modifiable. Only the three modifiable wires (**Z0**, **Z1**, and **Z2**) are modifiable. Thus, every circuit that is produced in the developmental process and every circuit that is created in every generation of a run of genetic programming will be guaranteed to satisfy Lamey's requirements.

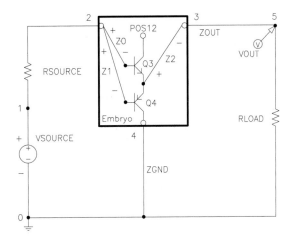

Figure 52.2   Special embryo with two hard-wired transistors

Minimal Embryo

Section 53.1 describes a minimal embryo and a minimal function set that can be used for evolving circuits. Section 53.2 describes how the embryo itself may be created by the evolutionary process.

53.1 DESCRIPTION

Throughout this book, the embryo has been embedded in the test fixture so as to give the embryo access to the circuit's external input(s) and external output(s). It is not necessary to provide the embryo with such direct access in this manner. In fact, it is possible to solve the problem of synthesizing a lowpass filter (Chapter 25) with a minimalist embryo.

Figure 29.13 shows an embryo with two modifiable wires (Z0 and Z1) and three ports (Embryo_Input, Embryo_Output, and Embryo_Ground). There is no explicit connection in the embryo to the circuit's external input, external output, or ground.

Figure 29.1 shows the one-input, one-output test fixture (discussed in detail in Section 29.1) with three ports.

Figure 53.1 shows the result of embedding the embryo of Figure 29.13 into the test fixture of Figure 29.1. The result is not a typical initial circuit because it is not a valid circuit.

In spite of this embryo's lack of connection to the input, output, and ground, a lowpass filter satisfying the requirements of Section 25.13 can nonetheless be successfully evolved using this embryo as a starting point. In fact, a lowpass filter can be successfully evolved with the parallel division function PARALLEL and the zero-argument CUT function as the only topology-modifying functions. That is, functions such as the topology-modifying SERIES and TWO_VIA functions are not required.

Specifically, the initial terminal set, $T_{\text{ccs-rpb-initial}}$, for the construction-continuing subtrees of the result-producing branches is

$$T_{\text{ccs-rpb-initial}} = \{\text{CUT, END, NOP}\}.$$

The initial function set, $F_{\text{ccs-rpb-initial}}$, for the construction-continuing subtrees of the result-producing branches is

$$F_{\text{ccs-rpb-initial}} = \{\text{C, L, PARALLEL0, PARALLEL1, ZERO\_GROUND, INPUT, OUTPUT}\}.$$

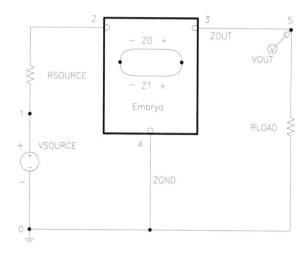

Figure 53.1   Result of embedding an embryo with two modifiable wires (Z0 and Z1) and three ports in a one-input, one-output test fixture with three ports to the embryo

The zero-argument INPUT function enables a part of the developing circuit structure to become connected to the input for the circuit. Figure 53.2 shows the results of applying the INPUT function to modifiable wire Z0 of Figure 25.9. The INPUT function creates one new node. The modifiable wire Z0 is replaced by a nonmodifiable wire between preexisting node 1 and newly created node 3 and a nonmodifiable wire between preexisting node 2 and new node 3. The INPUT function connects new node 3 to the input port. Note that the two new nonmodifiable wires replace any preexisting modifiable wire or component.

Similarly, the zero-argument OUTPUT function enables any part of a circuit to be connected to the circuit's output, and the zero-argument ZERO_GROUND function enables any part of a circuit to be connected to ground.

Since no power supplies are included in the parts bin, the only potential source of energy for this circuit is the incoming signal. If the circuit's external output never becomes connected to the circuit's external input, the circuit will produce only a constant-zero output. Since the evolutionary process is aimed at evolving a lowpass filter, a circuit producing a constant-zero output will necessarily receive a very poor value of fitness and will rarely be selected to participate in the fitness-based genetic operations of reproduction, crossover, and mutation.

In one run of this problem (with a population of 640,000), most of the circuits in generation 0 fail to establish a connection to the circuit's external input or output or both. Because such circuits have poor fitness, there is immediate selection pressure in favor of circuits that make a connection to both the input and the output.

Figure 53.3 shows the 100%-compliant best-of-run circuit from generation 90, consisting of seven capacitors and three inductors.

Figure 53.4 shows the frequency domain behavior of this circuit. The horizontal axis represents frequency and the vertical axis represents voltage logarithmically in terms of

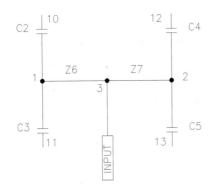

Figure 53.2 **Result of applying the INPUT function to modifiable wire Z0**

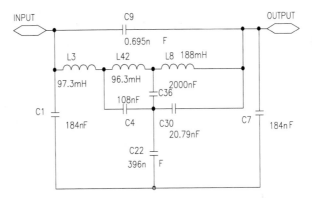

Figure 53.3 **Best-of-run circuit from generation 90**

decibels of attenuation. As can be seen, the circuit delivers a full volt (0 dB of attenuation) up to 1,000 Hz (the boundary of the desired passband). It also delivers 60 dB of attenuation (a 1,000-to-1 reduction from 1 volt to 1 millivolt) at 2,000 Hz (the boundary of the desired stopband). This evolved circuit also delivers 60dB or better attenuation for frequencies above 2,000 Hz. The evolved circuit of Figure 53.3 is noteworthy because of its novel topology and because its behavior in the frequency domain approximates that of an elliptic filter. For example, the peaks in the ripple of the stopband of an elliptic filter are equal. The figure shows that the first two peaks in the ripple in the stopband are indeed equal (at 60 dB). Note that the achievement of the 60 dB of attenuation is achieved because of the zero at about 2,100 Hz. All the components in the circuit contribute to its behavior, including, in particular, the small 0.695 nF capacitor **C9**. This capacitor is responsible for the zero at about 3,800 Hz.

The absence of a guaranteed connection to both the input and output and the minimalist function set has the effect of slowing the evolutionary process considerably (roughly doubling the number of generations needed to solve this particular problem).

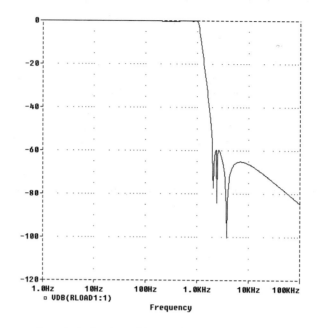

Figure 53.4   Frequency domain behavior of best-of-run circuit from generation 90

In summary, it is possible to solve the problem of synthesizing a lowpass filter with a minimalist embryo and a minimalist function set containing only PARALLEL and CUT as topology-modifying functions.

53.2   COEVOLUTION WITH AN EMBRYO

Throughout this book, the user specified the embryo to be used on a particular problem of circuit synthesis. Once this choice is made, the same embryo, the same test fixture, and the same initial circuit are used as a starting point for development for all individuals in the population of a given run.

However, for some problems, it may be advantageous to coevolve an embryo along with the circuit-constructing program tree. In this approach, each individual in the population consists of a pair of entities—a program tree along with an associated embryo. Starting at generation 0 of the run, the population is architecturally diverse in terms of the embryos. When a circuit-constructing program tree is evaluated, the evaluation applies its functions to the particular embryo associated with that particular program tree. The evolutionary process will tend to favor an entity in the population whose circuit-constructing program tree, acting in concert with its embryo, more rapidly accrues fitness.

Comparative Experiments Involving the Lowpass Filter

This chapter compares various alternative ways of implementing genetic programming on problems of circuit synthesis. Before proceeding, three limitations should be recognized concerning all the results in this chapter (and the next two chapters).

First, the persuasiveness of the results of any comparative experiment inevitably depends on both the difficulty and representativeness of the benchmark problem(s) in the experiment. Since no one problem or set of problems can encompass all the complexities and subtleties of the entire universe of problems, we must be wary of drawing overly strong conclusions from comparative experiments. As Whitley, Rana, Dzubera, and Mathias (1996) observed,

> Test functions are commonly used to evaluate the effectiveness of different search algorithms. However, the results of evaluation are as dependent on the test problems as they are on the algorithms that are the subject of comparison.

The comparisons in this chapter are based on the easiest problem of circuit synthesis in this book—the problem of synthesizing a lowpass filter (Chapter 25). This problem is the most difficult problem in this book for which we could currently afford to make numerous runs (56, 60, or 64 runs for each competing approach) within a reasonable amount of computer time. We did not do any comparative experiments on problems involving transistors because such circuits require considerably more computer resources than the problems involving only capacitors, inductors, and resistors. Although this problem is the easiest problem of circuit synthesis in this book, it is far from being a "toy" problem. This problem is certainly more difficult than the vast majority of the benchmark problems used in experimental comparative studies in the field of evolutionary computation and related fields. In fact, it may well be the most difficult problem ever used in any such comparative study. Nonetheless, as discussed in detail shortly, an important shortcoming of all comparative experiments of probabilistic search algorithms is that, for any given allocation of computational resources, the benchmark problem is inevitably considerably easier (typically by at least two orders of magnitude) than whatever problem can currently be solved with the available computational resources. For example, if two groups of 50 to 100 independent runs are required to achieve an acceptable level of statistical significance in studying two competing approaches to solving a problem, then the benchmark problem must be downscaled so that it is about 100 to 200 times easier than whatever problem can currently be solved with the same available allocation of computational resources.

Second, only one particular attribute of the problem is varied in each comparative experiment. This is both advantageous and disadvantageous. The illusory advantage of varying only a single attribute of a problem is that it isolates the effect of the varied attribute. However, the inevitable disadvantage is that any conclusion regarding the effect of the varied attribute is qualified by the fact that the observed effect applies *only* for the particular settings of all the numerous other attributes of the run. These other attributes include, but are not limited to, the major and minor parameters that control runs of genetic programming (Appendix D). Experience indicates that the control parameters of runs of evolutionary algorithms are often interrelated in highly nonlinear and counterintuitive ways. Thus, even though all attributes but one are held constant for the comparative experiments in this chapter, there is no guarantee that the observed effect of varying the single attribute applies when two or more attributes are simultaneously varied. That is, "isolating" one variable is appropriate only when the effect of the variable is independent of the effect of the problem's other variables—*something we know not to be the case.* Unfortunately, it is all too common for "rules of thumb" derived from a comparative experiment to insinuate themselves in the folklore of a field while all the qualifications concerning the limited set of applicable conditions are jettisoned.

Third, the comparisons in this chapter are based on only one particular problem of analog circuit synthesis. The representativeness of any conclusion arising from an experiment based on only one (or only a few) problems is always subject to doubt. However, if numerous benchmark problems are included in a test suite for a comparative experiment, the amount of downscaling in problem difficulty necessarily increases to three or more orders of magnitude. We do not believe that the benefit of including additional problems of synthesis of analog electrical circuits involving only capacitors, inductors, and resistors is worth the cost of a further downscaling in problem difficulty.

Section 54.1 describes implementation details that apply to the entire chapter. Section 54.2 presents a base case for the comparative experiments in this chapter using the problem of synthesizing a lowpass filter (Chapter 25). Subsequent sections consider the effect of the following variations in the base case:

- small population (1,000 versus 30,000) (Section 54.3),
- addition of an extraneous new component (diodes) (Section 54.4),
- addition of resistors (Section 54.5),
- addition of automatically defined copy (Section 54.6),
- deletion of the CUT function (Section 54.7),
- use of branch typing on the two result-producing branches (Section 54.8),
- immediate release of writing heads (Section 54.9), and
- depth-first (instead of breadth-first) order of evaluation (Section 54.10).

Chapter 56 considers the effect of not using crossover.

54.1 COMMON IMPLEMENTATION DETAILS

Except as specifically noted, all preparatory steps for runs in this chapter are the same as those found in Section 25.14.

The computational effort is computed from 64 independent runs, each with a population size of 30,000. The 64 runs are implemented by squelching migration (i.e., the migration rate $B = 0\%$) and making one run on a 64-node parallel computer with $D = 64$ subpopulations of size $Q = 30,000$. With migration squelched, the effect is to make 64 independent runs simultaneously (each with a population size of 30,000 with panmictic selection within the population at each processing node). Pace-setting individuals are recorded separately for each of the 64 processing nodes. Some performance curves in this chapter are based on 60 independent runs because the runs were made during times when our parallel computer was reconfigured from 64 to 60 nodes for maintenance reasons. The maximum size, S_{rpb}, of each of the two result-producing branches is 300 points, so each individual program in the population has a maximum of 600 points. We made these choices of population size and the maximum branch size based on practical considerations concerning the amount of memory on a single processing node of our parallel computer (32 megabytes). Given these choices, the population (along with certain supporting information in the data structure for each individual) occupies about 19 megabytes of RAM. The SPICE simulator, the genetic programming system, and various buffers fill up the remainder of the available 32 megabytes of memory.

All performance curves in this chapter are constructed in the manner described in Section 12.6 (except that the ceiling function for rounding up to the next highest integer is not used).

54.2 BASE CASE

Figure 54.1 presents the performance curve based on 64 independent runs of the base case for the comparative experiments in this chapter on the problem of synthesizing a lowpass filter (Chapter 25). The first generation for which the experimentally observed cumulative probability of success, $P(M, x)$, is nonzero is generation 22. Since one of the 64 runs was successful at generation 22, $P(M, x)$ is 1.56% for that generation. The cumulative probability of success, $P(M, x)$, reaches 85.9% at generation 81. The $I(M, x, z)$ curve reaches a minimum value at the best generation $i^* = 42$ (as shown by the shaded vertical line in the figure). The cumulative probability of success, $P(M, x)$, is 71.9% at generation 42. When the probability of success is 71.9%, 3.63 runs are necessary to yield a solution to the problem with a probability of $z = 99\%$. That is, $R(z)$ is 3.63. The two numbers in the oval indicate that running this problem 3.63 times through to generation 42 and thereby processing a total computational effort of $E = 4,683,183$ individuals (i.e., $30,000 \times 43$ generations $\times 3.63$ runs) is sufficient to yield a solution to this problem with 99% probability.

The runs used to create every performance curve in this book inherently contain information concerning the results of trying to solve the given problem with blind random search. For example, the values of fitness and hits obtained in generation 0 of the 64 runs are the results of a blind random search of 1,920,000 individuals from the search space of this problem. The best value of fitness attained among these 1,920,000 individuals from generation 0 is 90.5. A fitness of 90.5 over the 101 fitness cases of this problem represents an average weighted error of about 0.9 volt per fitness case. To further put this value in perspective, recall that a value of fitness of 90.5 is four or five orders of magnitude worse (larger) than the value of fitness associated with most 100%-compliant

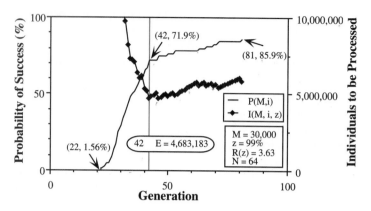

Figure 54.1   **Performance curves showing that *E* = 4,683,183 for the base case**

solutions to this problem reported in this book (e.g., Section 25.15.1). The best value of hits attained in generation 0 from the 1,920,000 individuals is 72 (out of 101). These poor results of blind random search are consistent with the well-established fact that blind random search is unlikely to solve any nontrivial problem of interest in any reasonable amount of time.

54.3   POPULATION OF 1,000

The question arises as to whether the problem of synthesizing a lowpass filter can be efficiently solved with a population of 1,000, instead of the larger population (30,000) used in the base case (Section 54.2).

Figure 54.2 presents the performance curve based on 60 independent runs with a population of 1,000 (instead of 30,000). The first generation for which the experimentally observed cumulative probability of success, $P(M, x)$, is nonzero is generation 54; $P(M, x)$ is 1.67% for that generation. The cumulative probability of success, $P(M, x)$, reaches 36.7% at generation 2,439. The $I(M, x, z)$ curve reaches a minimum value at the best generation $i^* = 136$. The cumulative probability of success, $P(M, x)$, is 11.7% at generation 136, so $R(z)$ is 37.1. The two numbers in the oval indicate that running this problem 37.1 times through to generation 136 and thereby processing a total computational effort of $E = 5,085,812$ individuals (i.e., 1,000 × 137 generations × 37.1 runs) is sufficient to yield a solution to this problem with 99% probability. This figure (encompassing almost 2,500 generations) shows the minimum value (at generation 136) of the $I(M, x, z)$ curve with unusual clarity.

This computational effort of 5,085,812 is only about 9% more than the computational effort of 4,683,183 for the base case for this problem. That is, a small population (1,000) can be used to solve this problem with only slightly more computational effort over the base case (with a population of 30,000).

Figure 54.2 highlights two important points about solving problems with probabilistic algorithms in general and genetic programming in particular. First, the ability to solve a problem with a probabilistic algorithm does not depend on every run being successful.

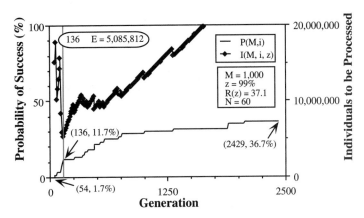

Figure 54.2 Performance curves showing that E = 5,085,812 for runs of genetic programming with a population of 1,000

Second, it is often more productive to make a counterintuitively large number of short runs, rather than one long run.

The population size of the runs here (1,000) is $\frac{1}{30}$ of the population size used elsewhere in this chapter (30,000). You might expect that it would be best to run this problem for several thousand generations in order to compensate for the smaller population. However, as can be seen from Figure 54.2 (which covers 2,500 generations), the optimal choice, i^*, for the number of generations is a counterintuitively small number (136). This optimal choice (136) is only about three times greater than the optimal choice (42) for the base case (Section 54.2). Only about one in nine runs (11.7%) is successful as a consequence of stopping each run at this counterintuitively early generation (136). When only 11.7% of the runs are successful, it takes 37.1 independent runs to yield a solution with 99% probability. Nonetheless, this problem can be solved (with 99% probability) with the least computational effort (with a population of 1,000) by making multiple independent runs and stopping each run at generation 136. Note that it is, of course, incorrect and misleading to report that this problem can be solved with only 137,000 fitness evaluations (i.e., 1,000 × 137 generations) with a population size of 1,000.

For the base case (where the population size is 30,000), 55 of 64 runs (i.e., 86% of the runs) solved by generation 81. At generation 2,429 (the equivalent, in terms of fitness evaluations, to generation 81 when a population of 1,000 is used instead of 30,000), the runs of genetic programming with a population of 1,000 solved on only 22 out of 60 runs (i.e., 37% of the runs). The differences in these results are statistically significant at generation 81 (and 2,429), according to a X^2 test (Freedman, Pisani, Purves, and Adhikari 1991). The likelihood that the difference between the base case and the runs with a population size of 1,000 is attributable to chance is very small ($p \sim 10^{-8}$).

The above test for statistical significance was made at a reasonable common point (e.g., generation 2,429). We will highlight a similarly chosen common generation number in this and succeeding chapters. However, the X^2 test could have been applied at other common points during the two runs. Figure 54.3 shows the result, p, of the X^2 test

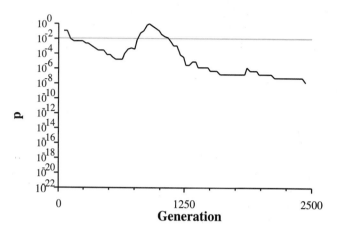

Figure 54.3   Values of *p* for runs of genetic programming with a population of 1,000

performed at various other common generations for the comparison between the base case and the runs of genetic programming with a population size of 1,000. The horizontal axis of this figure represents generations (in terms of the run with a population size of 1,000). The corresponding generation number for a population size of 30,000 is obtained by dividing by 30. The vertical axis shows the result, p, of the X^2 test on a logarithmic scale. A shaded horizontal line is shown for $p = 0.01$. Thus, if the value of p is below the shaded line (as it is for a majority of this figure), the likelihood is less than 1% that the experimentally observed difference between the base case and the runs with a population size of 1,000 is attributable to chance.

54.4   ADDITION OF DIODES

It is known that a lowpass filter can be constructed from capacitors and inductors. Diodes are not generally used in constructing a lowpass filter (if, indeed, there is any way to use them). What happens if the user did not possess (or did not want to use) the knowledge that the parts bin (for a passive filter) should include capacitors and inductors, but not diodes?

There is, of course, some evidence that genetic programming generally overcomes the potentially deleterious effects of extraneous functions at the expense of increased computational effort (Koza 1992e, Section 24.3). The question arises as to whether developmental genetic programming can overcome the potentially deleterious effect of a component-creating function that adds an extraneous component to a problem of synthesizing an analog circuit. Thus, we performed an experiment to test whether developmental genetic programming can overcome the potentially deleterious effects of adding the component-creating function for diodes (Section 41.1.5) to the function set used in the base case (Section 54.2) for this problem.

Figure 54.4 presents the performance curve based on 60 independent runs with diodes added to the parts bin of the problem. The first generation for which the experi-

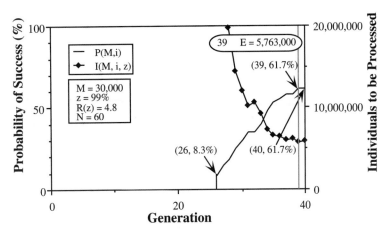

Figure 54.4 Performance curves showing that E = 5,763,000 for runs with diodes added to the parts bin

mentally observed cumulative probability of success, $P(M, x)$, is nonzero is generation 26; $P(M, x)$ is 8.3% for that generation. The cumulative probability of success, $P(M, x)$, reaches 61.7% at generation 40. The $I(M, x, z)$ curve reaches a minimum value at the best generation $i^* = 39$. The cumulative probability of success, $P(M, x)$, is 61.7% at generation 39, so $R(z)$ is 4.8. The two numbers in the oval indicate that running this problem 4.8 times through to generation 39 and thereby processing a total computational effort of $E = 5,763,000$ individuals (i.e., $30,000 \times 39$ generations $\times 4.8$ runs) is sufficient to yield a solution to this problem with 99% probability. A computational effort of 5,763,000 is 23% more than the computational effort of 4,683,183 for the base case for this problem (Section 54.2).

Generation 40 is the largest generation number for which the probability of success is shown by both this performance curve and the performance curve for the base case (Figure 54.1). For the base case, 42 of the 64 runs (i.e., 65.6% of the runs) solved by generation 40. At generation 40, the runs using diodes solved on 37 out of 60 runs (i.e., 61.6% of the runs). These are more or less the same. According to a X^2 test, the two different sets of runs are not significantly different at generation 40. The likelihood that the difference is attributable to chance is high ($p = 0.65$). It is far higher than that required for statistical significance (typically small values of p such as 0.01).

Figure 54.5 shows the result, p, of the X^2 test performed at various other common generations for the comparison between the base case and the runs with diodes added to the parts bin. The horizontal axis of this figure represents generations. The vertical axis shows the result, p, of the X^2 test on a logarithmic scale (with a shaded horizontal line at $p = 0.01$). As can be seen, the value of p is substantial for all common generations of these two runs. Therefore, the likelihood is substantial that the experimentally observed difference between the base case and the runs with diodes added to the parts bin is attributable to chance.

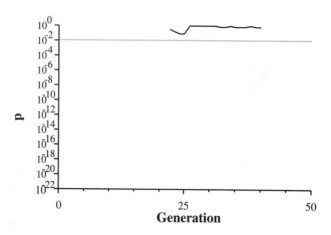

Figure 54.5   Values of _p_ for runs with diodes added to the parts bin

54.5   ADDITION OF RESISTORS

Although it is known that a lowpass filter can be constructed from capacitors and inductors, it is not clear a priori whether the inclusion of resistors in the parts bin would be helpful in synthesizing a lowpass filter.

There are two possible reasons for thinking that resistors might be deleterious to a run of genetic programming on this problem. First, the essential purpose of a filter is differential treatment of frequencies, and resistors usually do not themselves differentially treat frequencies. Second, resistors drain power. Thus, it is possible that resistors would make it difficult to deliver an acceptably high voltage (i.e., 970 millivolts) in the passband.

On the other hand, there are two reasons for thinking that resistors might accelerate a run of genetic programming on this problem. First, the addition of resistors in a filter circuit may broaden a filter's bandwidth (i.e., reduce its frequency selectivity). This might enable a run of genetic programming to create a filter that satisfactorily handles the required range of frequencies in both the stopband and passband more quickly than would otherwise be the case. Second, the addition of small resistors to a circuit enables some otherwise pathological circuits to become simulatable by SPICE. The reduction of unsimulatable circuits is generally beneficial because it increases the effective size of the population available during the run.

Figure 54.6 presents the performance curve based on 64 independent runs with resistors added to the parts bin of the problem. The first generation for which the experimentally observed cumulative probability of success, $P(M, x)$, is nonzero is generation 24. Two satisfactory solutions appeared in generation 24, so $P(M, x)$ is 3.1% for that generation. The cumulative probability of success, $P(M, x)$, reaches 82.8% at generation 92. The $I(M, x, z)$ curve reaches a minimum value at the best generation $i^* = 46$. The cumulative probability of success, $P(M, x)$, is 78.1% at generation 46, so $R(z)$ is 3.03. The two numbers in the oval indicate that running this problem 3.03 times through to generation 46 and thereby processing a total computational effort of $E = 4,272,392$ individuals (i.e., $30,000 \times 47$ generations $\times 3.03$ runs) is sufficient to yield a solution to this problem with

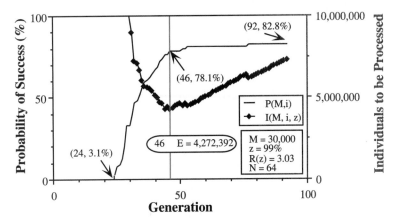

Figure 54.6   Performance curves showing that _E_ = 4,272,392 with resistors added to the parts bin

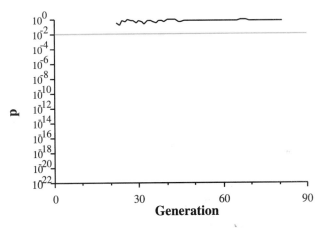

Figure 54.7   Values of _p_ for runs with resistors added to the parts bin

99% probability. A computational effort of 4,272,392 is 9% less than the computational effort of 4,683,183 for the base case for this problem (Section 54.2).

For the base case, 55 of 64 runs solved by generation 81. At generation 81, the runs using resistors solved on 53 out of 64 runs. The two different sets of runs are not significantly different at generation 81, according to a X^2 test. The likelihood that the difference is attributable to chance ($p = 0.626$) is far too high.

Figure 54.7 shows the result, p, of the X^2 test performed at various other common generations for the comparison between the base case and the runs with resistors added to the parts bin. As can be seen, the value of p is substantial for all common generations of these two runs. Therefore, the likelihood is substantial that the experimentally observed difference between the base case and the runs with resistors added to the parts bin is attributable to chance.

54.6 AUTOMATICALLY DEFINED COPY

The observed repetitive structure of human-designed electrical circuits suggests that a mechanism for reuse might be beneficial when genetic programming is evolving the design of electrical circuits. This section compares runs of genetic programming with the automatically defined copy (Chapter 30) to runs without them (the base case of Section 54.2).

Figure 54.8 presents the performance curve based on 60 independent runs with the automatically defined copy. The first generation for which the experimentally observed cumulative probability of success, $P(M, x)$, is nonzero is generation 16. Two satisfactory solutions appeared in generation 16, so $P(M, x)$ is 3.3% for that generation. The cumulative probability of success, $P(M, x)$, reaches 88.3% at generation 91. The $I(M, x, z)$ curve reaches a minimum value at the best generation $i^* = 36$. The cumulative probability of success, $P(M, x)$, is 75% at generation 36, so $R(z)$ is 3.3. The two numbers in the oval indicate that running this problem 3.3 times through to generation 36 and thereby processing a total computational effort of $E = 3,687,341$ individuals (i.e., $30,000 \times 37$ generations $\times 3.3$ runs) is sufficient to yield a solution to this problem with 99% probability. A computational effort of 3,687,341 is 21% less than the computational effort of 4,683,183 for the base case for this problem (Section 54.2).

For the base case, 50 of 64 runs solved by generation 58. At generation 58, the runs with the automatically defined copy solved on 52 out of 60 runs. The two different sets of runs are not significantly different at generation 58, according to a X^2 test. The likelihood that the difference is attributable to chance ($p = 0.9$) is far too high for generation 58.

Figure 54.9 shows the result, p, of the X^2 test performed at various other common generations for the comparison between the base case and the runs with the automatically defined copy. The vertical axis shows the result, p, of the X^2 test on a logarithmic scale (with a shaded horizontal line at $p = 0.01$). As can be seen, the value of p is below (or near) the shaded line between generations 18 and 36, so the likelihood is less than 1% *for those generations* that the experimentally observed difference between the base case and the runs with the automatically defined copy is attributable to chance. After generation 36, the value of p in Figure 54.9 is consistently above the shaded line, so the likelihood is substantial *for those generations* that the experimentally observed difference between the base case and the runs with the automatically defined copy is attributable to chance.

Figure 54.9 suggests some of the pitfalls inherent in ascertaining statistical significance using the X^2 test. For all the comparative experiments in this chapter and Chapters 55 and 56, the problem is solvable, to some degree, using both the methodology of the base case and the methodology of the alternative approach under consideration. The only issue is whether one method yields solutions faster than the other. Moreover, the entire comparative experiment is influenced by the artifact that each method is run for only a fixed and finite number of times.

If one method produces solutions significantly faster than the other, p will be well below the shaded line for a certain block of early generations. That is, the likelihood will be less than 1% (or whatever threshold is chosen for the shaded line) that the observed differences in the probability of success between the base case and the alternative

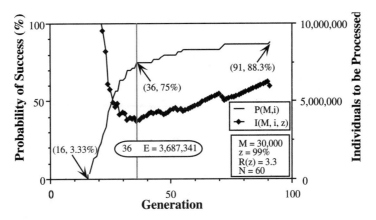

Figure 54.8   Performance curves showing that E = 3,687,341 with the automatically defined copy

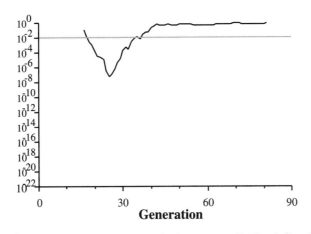

Figure 54.9   Values of p for runs with the automatically defined copy

method is attributable to chance. Figure 54.9 illustrates this situation between generations 18 and 36.

However, assuming that the slower method is capable of eventually producing solutions to the given problem, the probability of success will approach 100% for both methods (for some high generation number) when the number of runs is fixed and finite (as it is here). (Of course, neither method may reach a 100% probability of success when the number of runs is open-ended.) As the probability of success approaches 100% for both methods, p also trends toward 100% because there is no longer any statistically significant difference in the two probabilities of success at the high generation number where both methods appear to solve the problem with 100% probability of success (given the fixed and finite number of runs). Figure 54.9 illustrates this situation for later generations. Figures 54.1 and 54.8 show that the probability of success is trending toward

100% for both the base case and the runs with automatically defined copy in the first 100 generations. In turn, Figure 54.9 shows that p is also trending toward 100%.

54.7   DELETION OF CUT FUNCTION

The question arises as to the importance of the CUT function in solving problems of circuit synthesis.

Figure 54.10 presents the performance curve based on 60 independent runs without the CUT function. The first generation for which the experimentally observed cumulative probability of success, $P(M, x)$, is nonzero is generation 24. Three satisfactory solutions appeared in generation 24, so $P(M, x)$ is 5% for that generation. The cumulative probability of success, $P(M, x)$, reaches 76.7% at generation 58. The $I(M, x, z)$ curve reaches a minimum value at the best generation $i^* = 55$. The cumulative probability of success, $P(M, x)$, is 76.7% at generation 55, so $R(z)$ is 3.16. The two numbers in the oval indicate that running this problem 3.16 times through to generation 55 and thereby processing a total computational effort of $E = 5,316,262$ individuals (i.e., $30,000 \times 56$ generations $\times$ 3.16 runs) is sufficient to yield a solution to this problem with 99% probability. A computational effort of 5,316,262 is 14% more than the computational effort of 4,683,183 for the base case.

For the base case (Section 54.2), 50 of 64 runs solved by generation 58. At generation 58, the runs without the CUT function solved on 46 out of 60 runs. The two different sets of runs are not significantly different, according to a X^2 test for generation 58. The likelihood that the difference is attributable to chance ($p = 0.85$) is far too high.

Figure 54.11 shows the result, p, of the X^2 test performed at various other common generations for the comparison between the base case and the runs without the CUT function. The value of p is consistently above the shaded line, so the likelihood is substantial that the experimentally observed difference between the base case and the runs without the CUT function is attributable to chance.

54.8   BRANCH TYPING VERSUS LIKE-BRANCH TYPING

The number of modifiable wires in the embryo of the initial circuit determines the number of result-producing branches in circuit-constructing program trees. For example, two result-producing branches are used on the problem of synthesizing a lowpass filter in this chapter. When there is more than one result-producing branch in a program, the question arises as to whether to use branch typing, like-branch typing, or point typing in performing structure-preserving crossover (Section 5.7.2). When we started evolving circuits, we adopted the use of like-branch typing for the result-producing branches.

Figure 54.12 presents the performance curve based on 60 independent runs with branch typing. The first generation for which the experimentally observed cumulative probability of success, $P(M, x)$, is nonzero is generation 30. Two satisfactory solutions appeared in generation 30, so $P(M, x)$ is 3.3% for that generation. The cumulative probability of success, $P(M, x)$, reaches 30% at generation 111. The $I(M, x, z)$ curve reaches a minimum value at the best generation $i^* = 71$. The cumulative probability of success, $P(M, x)$, is 30% at generation 71, so $R(z)$ is 12.9. The two numbers in the oval indicate that running this problem 12.9 times through to generation 71 and thereby processing a

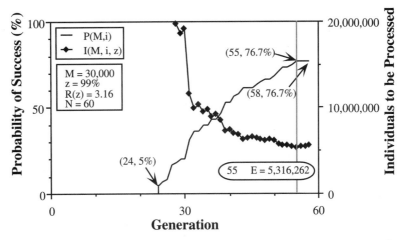

Figure 54.10 Performance curves showing that $E = 5,316,262$ without the CUT function

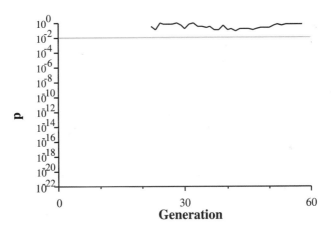

Figure 54.11 Values of p for runs without the CUT function

total computational effort of $E = 27,888,612$ individuals (i.e., $30,000 \times 72$ generations $\times 12.9$ runs) is sufficient to yield a solution to this problem with 99% probability. A computational effort of 27,888,612 is 596% more than the computational effort of 4,683,183 for the base case (Section 54.2) for this problem.

For the base case, 55 of 64 runs solved by generation 81. At generation 81, the runs with branch typing solved on only 18 out of 60 runs. The differences in these results are statistically significant, according to a X^2 test for generation 81. The likelihood that the difference is attributable to chance is very small ($p \sim 10^{-10}$) at generation 81. Note that there were no additional solutions even at generation 111.

Figure 54.13 shows the result, p, of the X^2 test performed at various other common generations for the comparison between the base case and the runs with branch typing.

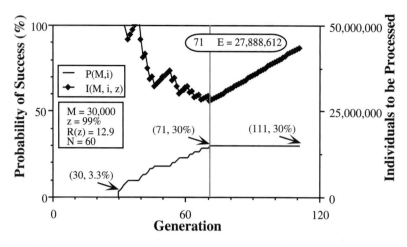

Figure 54.12 Performance curves showing that $E = 27,888,612$ with branch typing

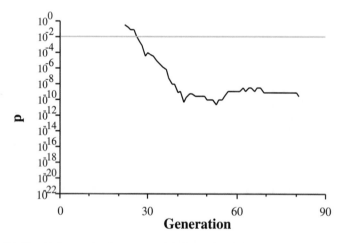

Figure 54.13 Values of p for runs with branch typing

The value of p is below the shaded line for most generations in this figure so the likelihood is less than 1% that the experimentally observed difference between the base case and the runs with branch typing is attributable to chance for those generations.

Even though branch typing is clearly not helpful for the lowpass filter problem, branch typing appears to us to be helpful for other problems such as high-gain amplifiers (Chapter 45). We believe that it may be easier for genetic programming to construct a high-gain amplifier circuit in distinct stages (just as human engineers typically design such amplifiers in stages). Since amplifiers are large, active circuits using transistors, it generally takes considerably more computer time to simulate and evolve an amplifier than to simulate and evolve a passive circuit involving only linear components (such as a lowpass LC filter). Thus, we cannot support our belief that branch typing is helpful for designing amplifiers with a series of numerous runs.

54.9 IMMEDIATE RELEASE OF WRITING HEADS

This series of 64 runs is identical to the base case (Section 54.2), except that the two component-creating functions for this problem are modified so that the writing head is released as part of the execution of the function. In other words, once a component-creating function inserts a capacitor or inductor in this series of runs, no writing head is left pointing to the newly inserted component. Therefore, once a component is inserted into a developing circuit structure in this series or runs, it is never overwritten by another component. For this experiment, both the capacitor-creating and inductor-creating functions become one-argument functions (i.e., they possess an arithmetic-performing subtree, but no construction-continuing subtree).

Our original design choice (involving retention of the writing head) was more or less arbitrary. When we first started using three-leaded transistors as components, it was simpler and more straightforward to define the transistor-creating functions so that the writing head was released immediately upon insertion of the transistor. This difference in treatment between transistors and two-leaded components raised the question of whether the component-creating functions for two-leaded components might work better if the writing head was released immediately upon insertion of the component.

Figure 54.14 presents the performance curve based on 64 independent runs with an immediate release of the writing heads on the capacitor-creating and inductor-creating functions. The first generation for which the experimentally observed cumulative probability of success, $P(M, x)$, is nonzero is generation 34; $P(M, x)$ is 1.56% for that generation. The cumulative probability of success, $P(M, x)$, reaches 29.7% at generation 97. The $I(M, x, z)$ curve reaches a minimum value at the best generation $i* = 89$. The cumulative probability of success, $P(M, x)$, is 28.1% at generation 89, so $R(z)$ is 13.1. The two numbers in the oval indicate that running this problem 13.1 times through to generation 89 and thereby processing a total computational effort of $E = 35,301,632$ individuals (i.e., $30,000 \times 89$ generations $\times 13.1$ runs) is sufficient to yield a solution to this problem with 99% probability. A computational effort of 35,301,632 is 754% more than the computational effort of 4,683,183 for the base case for this problem (Section 54.2).

For the base case, 55 of 64 runs solved by generation 81. At generation 81, the runs with the immediate release of the writing heads solved on only 16 out of 64 runs. The differences in these results are statistically significant at generation 81, according to a X^2 test. The likelihood that the difference is attributable to chance is very small ($p \sim 10^{-18}$). Even if the test is applied on generation 97 (where 19 of 64 runs solved), the likelihood that the difference is attributable to chance is still very small ($p \sim 10^{-10}$).

Figure 54.15 shows the result, p, of the X^2 test performed at various other common generations for the comparison between the base case and the runs with immediate release of the writing heads. The value of p is below the shaded line for most generations in this figure, so the likelihood is less than 1% that the experimentally observed difference between the base case and the runs with immediate release of the writing heads is attributable to chance for those generations.

We were surprised by the fact that performance degraded with the immediate release of the writing heads, and we were surprised by the magnitude of the degradation (about seven times more computational effort than the base case). This result may be an artifact of the fact that the immediate release of the writing heads results in smaller program

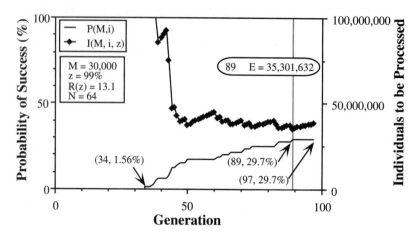

Figure 54.14 Performance curves showing that $E = 35{,}301{,}632$ with the immediate release of the writing heads

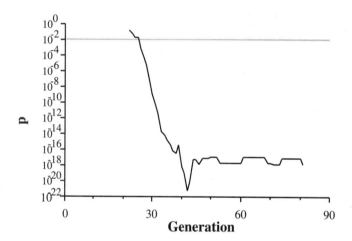

Figure 54.15 Values of p for runs with immediate release of the writing heads

trees (when everything else is kept constant) and that it is harder to solve this problem by crossing small circuit-constructing program trees.

54.10 BREADTH-FIRST VERSUS DEPTH-FIRST EXECUTION

This series of 64 runs is identical to the base case (Section 54.2) except that the order of evaluation of functions (outside arithmetic-performing subtrees) is changed from a breadth-first order to a depth-first order.

When we first implemented genetic programming on problems of circuit synthesis, we followed the convention used in Gruau's work on cellular encoding of neural networks (Gruau 1992a, 1992b, 1993, 1994a, 1994b; Gruau and Whitley 1993) of executing the functions in breadth-first order (starting at the left). This breadth-first order of evaluation contrasts with the convention used in Common LISP (Steele 1990) of evaluating symbolic expressions in a depth-first way (starting at the left).

As time passed, we began to question our early decision to adopt Gruau's breadth-first approach. The question arises as to whether one approach is better than the other.

The component-creating and topology-modifying functions predominantly affect only a local area of the developing circuit. This locality arises from the fact that the writing heads of the circuit-constructing functions are passed only to nearby wires or components of the developing circuit.

With a depth-first order of evaluation, all the circuit-constructing functions of a subtree (outside of an arithmetic-performing subtree) are executed before the execution of any functions from outside the subtree. In contrast, the breadth-first order of evaluation consecutively executes one function in one subtree and then another function from a distant subtree.

In the crossover operation (Figures 2.5 through 2.8), a subtree from one individual (selected probabilistically on the basis of fitness) is inserted at a randomly chosen point into another individual (selected on the basis of fitness). With depth-first execution, all the functions in a subtree inserted by crossover are executed before any functions from outside the subtree inserted by crossover.

Genetic algorithms and genetic programming work on the principle that there is something about the structure of a high-fitness individual in the population that contributes to the individual's high fitness. The crossover operation attempts to create new individuals by recombining parts of the structure of high-fitness individuals.

Consequently, it seems reasonable that this recombination will work better if the parts of a program that are kept together and moved by the crossover operation more closely correspond to a sequence of component-creating and topology-modifying functions that predominantly affect a local area of a circuit.

Figure 54.16 presents the performance curve based on 64 independent runs with depth-first evaluation of the entire circuit-constructing program tree. The first generation for which the experimentally observed cumulative probability of success, $P(M, x)$, is nonzero is generation 20; $P(M, x)$ is 1.56% for that generation. The cumulative probability of success, $P(M, x)$, reaches 85.9% at generation 54. The $I(M, x, z)$ curve reaches a minimum value at the best generation $i^* = 39$. The cumulative probability of success, $P(M, x)$, is 79.7% at generation 39, so $R(z)$ is 3.03. The two numbers in the oval indicate that running this problem 3.03 times through to generation 39 and thereby processing a total computational effort of $E = 3,636,078$ individuals (i.e., $30,000 \times 40$ generations $\times$ 3.03 runs) is sufficient to yield a solution to this problem with 99% probability. A computational effort of 3,636,078 is 22% less than the computational effort of 4,683,183 for the base case for this problem (Section 54.2).

For the base case, 50 of 64 runs solved by generation 54. At generation 54, the runs with depth-first evaluation solved on 55 of 64 runs. The two different sets of runs are not significantly different at generation 54, according to a X^2 test. The likelihood that the difference is attributable to chance ($p = 0.25$) is far too high.

Figure 54.17 shows the result, p, of the X^2 test performed at various other common generations for the comparison between the base case and the runs with depth-first

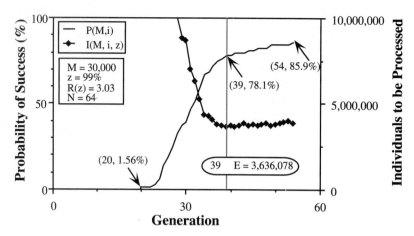

Figure 54.16 Performance curves showing that E = 3,636,078 with depth-first evaluation

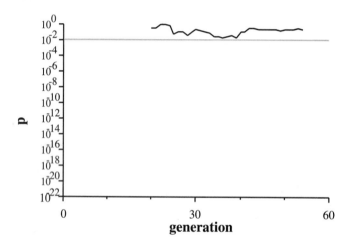

Figure 54.17 Values of p for runs with depth-first evaluation

evaluation. The value of p is consistently above the shaded line, so the likelihood is substantial that the experimentally observed difference between the base case and the runs with depth-first evaluation is attributable to chance.

Although the observed difference between the two approaches is small, although Figure 54.17 shows the difference to be statistically insignificant, and although we have performed this experiment only on one particular problem (with only one particular set of choices for all the other major and minor parameters), we nonetheless continue to suspect (based on the analytical reasons given above) that depth-first evaluation is preferable to breadth-first for problems of analog circuit synthesis using developmental genetic programming.

54.11 SUMMARY OF EIGHT COMPARATIVE EXPERIMENTS

In the above comparisons between the base case and six of the eight competing approaches for implementing our system for synthesizing circuits, the difference between the competing approaches was not statistically significant (for most generations considered).

When we were planning our approach to the problem of automated synthesis of analog circuits using genetic programming, we were faced with several hundred different choices concerning alternative ways in which genetic programming might have been applied to the problem. You might mistakenly credit the authors with great astuteness in making correct choices concerning the precisely right way of creating test fixtures and embryos, the precisely right way of defining the details of the numerous topology-modifying and component-creating functions, and the precisely right way of choosing all the major and minor parameters governing each run. While we would like to take credit for the astute discovery of such a unique "needle in the haystack" combination of choices, we think that the better conclusion is that there are numerous satisfactory alternative implementations for a great many aspects of our system for synthesizing circuits using developmental genetic programming. We claim to have found one set of satisfactory choices and to have demonstrated the principle that the design of nontrivial analog electrical circuits (and, by inference, other similar complex structures) can be automatically synthesized using genetic programming.

Comparative Experiments Involving the Lowpass Elliptic Filter and the Automatically Defined Copy

This chapter shows the computational effort, E, for a scaled series of three problems (elliptic lowpass filters of order 3, 5, and 7) using the automatically defined copy (Chapter 30).

All details of runs in this chapter are the same as those found in Section 54.2 except that we used an embryo with one modifiable wire (Figure 29.10). The performance curves in this chapter are based on 60 independent runs, each with a population of 30,000. The runs are implemented by making one run on 60 nodes of a parallel computer with migration squelched. The performance curves in this chapter are constructed in the manner described in Section 12.6 (except that the ceiling function for rounding up to the next highest integer is not used).

55.1   THIRD-ORDER ELLIPTIC FILTER

For the third-order elliptic filter, the boundary of the passband is 1,000 Hz, and the boundary of the stopband is 3,020 Hz, thereby making the modular angle $\Theta = 19.34°$.

Figure 55.1 presents the performance curve based on 60 independent runs of the problem of synthesizing this third-order elliptic filter with the automatically defined copy. The first generation for which the experimentally observed cumulative probability of success, $P(M, x)$, is nonzero is generation 12; $P(M, x)$ is 1.67% for that generation. The cumulative probability of success, $P(M, x)$, reaches 46.7% at generation 60. The $I(M, x, z)$ curve reaches a minimum value at the best generation $i^* = 35$. The cumulative probability of success, $P(M, x)$, is 36.7% at generation 35, so $R(z)$ is 10.1. The two numbers in the oval indicate that running this problem 10.1 times through to generation 35 and thereby processing a total computational effort of $E = 10,888,874$ individuals (i.e., $30,000 \times 36$ generations $\times 10.1$ runs) is sufficient to yield a solution to this problem with 99% probability.

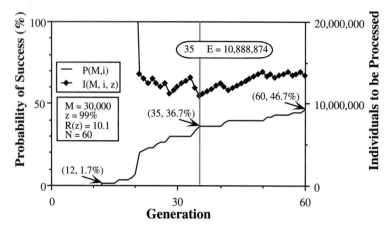

Figure 55.1   Performance curves for the problem of synthesizing a third-order elliptic lowpass filter with the automatically defined copy

55.2   FIFTH-ORDER ELLIPTIC FILTER

For the fifth-order elliptic filter, the boundary of the passband is 1,000 Hz, and the boundary of the stopband is 1,738 Hz, thereby making the modular angle $\Theta = 35.13°$.

Figure 55.2 presents the performance curve based on 60 independent runs of the problem of synthesizing this fifth-order elliptic filter with the automatically defined copy. The first generation for which the experimentally observed cumulative probability of success, $P(M, x)$, is nonzero is generation 20; $P(M, x)$ is 1.67% for that generation. The cumulative probability of success, $P(M, x)$, reaches 41.7% at generation 174. The $I(M, x, z)$ curve reaches a minimum value at the best generation $i^* = 159$. The cumulative probability of success, $P(M, x)$, is 41.7% at generation 159, so $R(z)$ is 8.54. The two numbers in the oval indicate that running this problem 8.54 times through to generation 159 and thereby processing a total computational effort of $E = 41,011,072$ individuals (i.e., $30,000 \times 160$ generations $\times$ 8.54 runs) is sufficient to yield a solution to this problem with 99% probability.

55.3   SEVENTH-ORDER ELLIPTIC FILTER

For the seventh-order elliptic filter, the boundary of the passband is 1,000 Hz, and the boundary of the stopband is 1,259 Hz, thereby making the modular angle $\Theta = 52.6°$.

Figure 55.3 presents the performance curve based on 60 independent runs of the problem of synthesizing this seventh-order elliptic filter with the automatically defined copy. The first generation for which the experimentally observed cumulative probability of success, $P(M, x)$, is nonzero is generation 24; $P(M, x)$ is 1.67% for that generation. The cumulative probability of success, $P(M, x)$, reaches 28.3% at generation 186. The $I(M, x, z)$ curve reaches a minimum value at the best generation $i^* = 68$. The cumulative probability of success, $P(M, x)$, is 16.7% at generation 68, so $R(z)$ is 25.3. The two numbers in the oval indicate that running this problem 25.3 times through to generation 68 and thereby processing

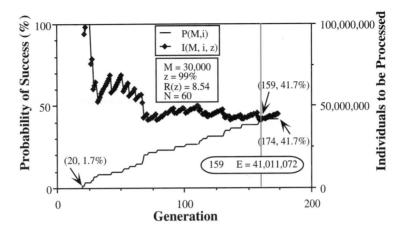

Figure 55.2 Performance curves for the problem of synthesizing a fifth-order elliptic lowpass filter with the automatically defined copy

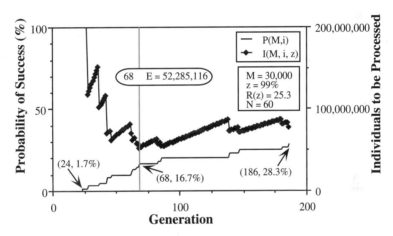

Figure 55.3 Performance curves for the problem of synthesizing a seventh-order elliptic lowpass filter with the automatically defined copy

a total computational effort of $E = 52,285,116$ individuals (i.e., $30,000 \times 69$ generations $\times 25.3$ runs) is sufficient to yield a solution to this problem with 99% probability.

55.4 SUMMARY

Table 55.1 summarizes the computational effort required for evolving the design of a third-, fifth-, and seventh-order elliptic filter with the automatically defined copy. Although the data in this table is manifestly sparse, the three values of computational effort for these progressively more stringent filters do not suggest unfavorable scaling.

Table 55.1 **Computational effort for elliptic filters with the automatically defined copy**

Order	Computational effort, E
3	10,888,874
5	41,011,072
7	52,285,116

The Role of Crossover in Genetic Programming

The canonical forms of evolutionary programming (L. Fogel 1962; L. Fogel, Owens, and Walsh 1966; D. Fogel 1991) and evolution strategies (Rechenberg 1965, 1973) employ Darwinian selection and asexual mutation, but not the crossover operation.

In contrast, the canonical form of the genetic algorithm (Holland 1975) and genetic programming employs the crossover (sexual recombination) operation in addition to Darwinian selection and asexual mutation. Crossover is not only used in runs of the genetic algorithm and genetic programming; it is the preeminent operation.

The practitioners of evolutionary programming, evolution strategies, genetic algorithms, and genetic programming all agree on the utility of Darwinian selection and the asexual mutation operation. However, the practitioners of evolutionary programming and evolution strategies frequently (and rather strenuously) argue that the crossover operation is not useful in general and may be deleted from the repertoire of operations used in evolutionary computation.

This chapter contains

- a comparative experiment on the effect of deleting crossover in runs of genetic programming on the problem of synthesizing a lowpass filter,
- a discussion of a common framework for viewing crossover, mutation, and blind random search,
- a discussion of certain published studies purporting to show that it is advantageous to delete the crossover operation in genetic programming, and
- an analysis of how the crossover operation serves as a reservoir of information and thereby contributes to the solution of problems.

56.1 COMPARATIVE EXPERIMENT ON THE EFFECT OF DELETING CROSSOVER

In this section, a series of 64 runs of genetic programming is made on the problem of synthesizing a lowpass filter. The runs are identical to the base case (Section 54.2), except that the crossover operation is deleted.

The percentages of the genetic operations (Section 2.3.2) on each generation for the base case are values that we commonly use with genetic programming (Appendix D):

- 1% mutation,
- 10% reproduction, and
- 89% crossover.

The percentages of genetic operations on each generation for the series of 64 runs without crossover in this section are

- 90% mutation and
- 10% reproduction.

As always, the genetic operations are applied to individuals that are selected probabilistically from the population on the basis of fitness.

Figure 56.1 presents the performance curve based on 64 independent runs of genetic programming without crossover.

Without crossover, the first generation for which the experimentally observed cumulative probability of success, $P(M, x)$, is nonzero is generation 64; $P(M, x)$ is 1.56% for that generation. This compares to generation 22 for the base case (which used crossover).

Recall that 42 is the best generation number, i^*, for the base case and that 71.9% of the 64 runs yielded solutions by generation 42 of the base case (Section 54.2). In other words, not one of 64 runs without crossover solved the problem by the generation at which our experiments indicate is optimal for terminating runs with crossover.

Without crossover, the second solution (out of 64 runs) does not occur until generation 91.

The $I(M, x, z)$ curve reaches a minimum value at the best generation $i^* = 134$. The cumulative probability of success, $P(M, x)$, is 14.1% at generation 134. When the probability of success is 14.1%, 30.4 runs are necessary to yield a solution to the problem with a probability of $z = 99\%$. The two numbers in the oval indicate that running this problem 30.4 times through to generation 134 and thereby processing a total computational effort of $E = 123,068,000$ individuals (i.e., $30,000 \times 134$ generations $\times$ 30.4 runs) is sufficient to yield a solution to this problem with 99% probability.

The computational effort, $E = 123,068,000$, required to solve this problem using genetic programming with a population of 30,000 without crossover is 26.2 times the computational effort required to solve it with crossover (i.e., in the base case of Section 54.2 where the computational effort, E, is 4,683,183).

For the base case, 55 of 64 runs solved by generation 81. At generation 81, the runs of genetic programming without crossover solved on only 1 run out of 64. The differences in these results are statistically significant at generation 81, according to a X^2 test. The likelihood that the difference is attributable to chance is infinitesimal ($p \sim 10^{-22}$). If the X^2 test is applied on generation 134 (where 9 of 64 runs solved), the likelihood that the difference is attributable to chance is still infinitesimal ($p \sim 10^{-16}$).

Figure 56.2 shows the result, p, of the X^2 test performed at various other common generations for the comparison between the base case and the runs of genetic programming without crossover (with a population of 30,000). The horizontal axis of this figure represents generations. The vertical axis shows the result, p, of the X^2 test on a logarithmic scale. A shaded horizontal line is shown for $p = 0.01$. Since the value of p is below the shaded line for almost all of this figure, the likelihood is less than 1% (in fact, consid-

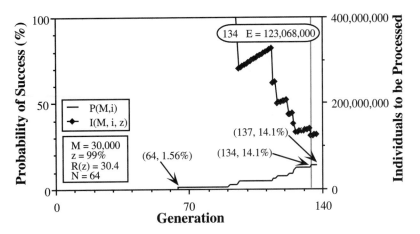

Figure 56.1 Performance curves showing that E = 123,068,000 in runs of genetic programming with a population of 30,000, without crossover

erably less than 1%) that the experimentally observed difference between the base case and the runs without crossover (with a population of 30,000) is attributable to chance.

The conclusion of this experiment (with a population of 30,000) is that this problem can indeed be solved with genetic programming without crossover (i.e., using only Darwinian selection and mutation). However, although genetic programming without crossover works, it works far more slowly. This conclusion is consistent with similar comparisons for numerous other problems where crossover was deleted from the repertoire of genetic operations in the genetic algorithm (Goldberg 1989a).

56.1.1 Population of 1,000 without Crossover

Since both the asexual mutation and reproduction operations act on single individuals in the population, a smaller population may be preferable when crossover is deleted from genetic programming (Luke and Spector 1997). Therefore, we redid the above experiment of genetic programming without crossover and used a population size of 1,000 (and redid it yet again in the next section with a population size of 100). When the population size is smaller, correspondingly more generations are run (in order to keep the number of fitness evaluations constant).

Figure 56.3 presents the performance curve based on 60 independent runs of genetic programming without crossover and with a population of 1,000. The first generation for which the experimentally observed cumulative probability of success, $P(M, x)$, is nonzero is generation 256; $P(M, x)$ is 1.67% for that generation. The cumulative probability of success, $P(M, x)$, reaches 8.3% at generation 2,559. The $I(M, x, z)$ curve reaches a minimum value at the best generation $i^* = 256$. The cumulative probability of success, $P(M, x)$, is 1.67% at generation 256, so $R(z)$ is 274. The two numbers in the oval indicate that running this problem 274 times through to generation 256 and thereby processing a total computational effort of E = 70,418,312 individuals (i.e., 1,000 × 257 generations × 274 runs) is sufficient to yield a solution to this problem with 99% probability.

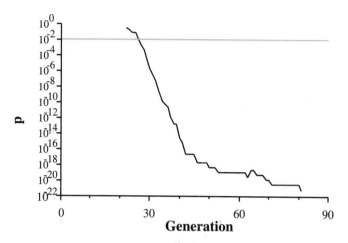

Figure 56.2   Values of *p* for runs of genetic programming with a population of 30,000, without crossover

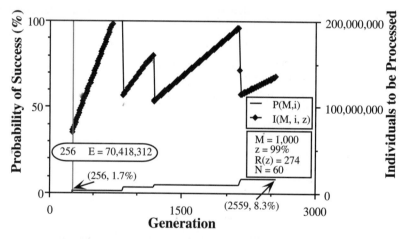

Figure 56.3   Performance curves showing that *E* = 70,418,312 in runs of genetic programming with a population of 1,000, without crossover

The computational effort, E = 70,418,312, required to solve this problem using genetic programming with a population of 1,000 without crossover is 15.04 times the computational effort required to solve it with crossover (i.e., in the base case of Section 54.2 where the computational effort, E, is 4,683,183).

For the base case (with a population of 30,000), 55 of 64 runs solved by generation 81. At generation 2,430 (the equivalent to generation 81 when a population of 1,000 is used instead of a population of 30,000), the runs of genetic programming without crossover solved on only 5 out of 60 runs. The differences in these results are statistically significant at generation 81 (and 2,430), according to a X^2 test. The likelihood that the difference is attributable to chance is very small ($p \sim 10^{-18}$).

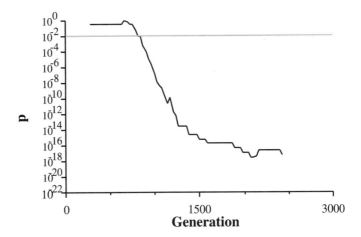

Figure 56.4   Values of p for runs of genetic programming with a population of 1,000, without crossover

Figure 56.4 shows the result, p, of the X^2 test performed at various other common generations for the comparison between the base case and the runs of genetic programming without crossover (and with a population of 1,000). Since the value of p is below the shaded line (representing $p = 0.01$) for almost all of this figure, the likelihood is less than 1% that the experimentally observed difference between the base case and the runs of genetic programming without crossover (and with a population of 1,000) is attributable to chance.

56.1.2   Population of 100 without Crossover

Figure 56.5 presents the performance curve based on 56 independent runs of genetic programming without crossover and with a population of 100 (instead of the populations of 30,000 and 1,000 used in the previous two sections). The first generation for which the experimentally observed cumulative probability of success, $P(M, x)$, is nonzero is generation 2,100; $P(M, x)$ is 1.8% for that generation. The cumulative probability of success, $P(M, x)$, reaches 14.3% at generation 75,400. The $I(M, x, z)$ curve reaches a minimum value at the best generation $i^* = 4,700$. The cumulative probability of success, $P(M, x)$, is 7.14% at generation 4,700, so $R(z)$ is 62. The two numbers in the oval indicate that running this problem 62 times through to generation 4,700 and thereby processing a total computational effort of $E = 29,210,000$ individuals (i.e., $100 \times 4,701$ generations $\times$ 62 runs) is sufficient to yield a solution to this problem with 99% probability. For the record, this particular series of 56 runs was made on 56 nodes of our Beowulf-style parallel computer (described in Section 62.1.5); however, the choice of computing platform has no effect on the results.

Recall that 42 is the best generation number, i^*, for the base case (Section 54.2). When the population is 100, generation 12,900 corresponds to generation 42 (i.e., $43 \times 30,000 = 1,290,000$ individuals processed). However, only 4 of the 56 runs (7.14%) with a population of 100 yielded a solution by generation 12,900 whereas 46 of the 64

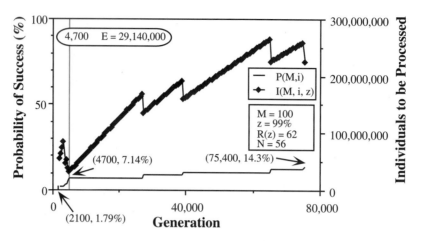

Figure 56.5 Performance curves showing that $E = 29,210,000$ in runs of genetic programming with a population of 100, without crossover

runs (71.9%) yielded solutions by generation 42 of the base case (with a population of 30,000).

The computational effort, $E = 29,210,000$, required to solve this problem using genetic programming without crossover (and with a population of 100) is 6.24 times the computational effort required to solve it with crossover (i.e., in the base case of Section 54.2 where the computational effort, E, is 4,683,183).

For the base case (with a population of 30,000), 55 of 64 runs solved by generation 81. At generation 24,330 (the equivalent to generation 81 when a population of 100 is used instead of a population of 30,000), the runs of genetic programming without crossover solved on only 4 out of 56 runs. The differences in these results are statistically significant at generation 81, according to a X^2 test. The likelihood that the difference is attributable to chance is very small ($p \sim 10^{-18}$).

Figure 56.6 shows the result, p, of the X^2 test performed at various other common (equivalent) generations for the comparison between the base case and the runs of genetic programming without crossover (and with a population of 100). Since the value of p is below the shaded line (representing $p = 0.01$) for almost all of this figure, the likelihood is less than 1% that the experimentally observed difference between the base case and the runs of genetic programming without crossover (and with a population of 100) is attributable to chance.

56.2   COMMON FRAMEWORK FOR CROSSOVER, MUTATION, AND BLIND RANDOM SEARCH

The mutation operation in genetic programming operates on one parental computer program selected with a probability based on fitness and creates one new offspring program for the new population at the next generation. In the mutation operation, a point is randomly chosen in the parental program. The subtree rooted at the chosen mutation point is deleted from the program, and a new subtree is randomly grown using the available

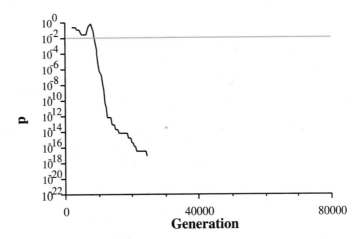

Figure 56.6 **Values of *p* for runs of genetic programming with a population of 100, without crossover**

functions and terminals in the same manner as trees are grown in creating the initial random population of generation 0. The random subtree is then implanted at the chosen mutation point.

In understanding the mutation operation in genetic programming, it is important to notice that it can be viewed as a special case of the crossover operation. The subtree that is grown and implanted by the mutation operation (in lieu of the deleted subtree) can be viewed as having come from a randomly chosen subtree from a randomly created individual, created by the same probabilistic process as was used to create individuals for generation 0. That is, a mutation operation in generation i can be viewed as a crossover in which the remainder comes from a *fitness-selected parent* from *the current generation i,* and the crossover fragment consists of a randomly chosen subtree from a *randomly selected parent* from *generation 0.* In saying this, we mean that the subtree that is grown and implanted by the mutation operation is produced by the same random process that is used to produce individuals in the initial random generation. We do not mean that the particular subtree that is grown and implanted by the mutation operation is itself necessarily present in generation 0 of the particular run involved. In a crossover operation in generation i, the remainder comes from a *fitness-selected parent* from *the current generation i* (i.e., the same source as used by the mutation operation), but the crossover fragment consists of a randomly chosen subtree from a *fitness-selected parent* from *the current generation i.*

The crossover and mutation operations are not identical, even in generation 0. The subtree that is implanted by the mutation operation in generation 0 consists of the equivalent of a randomly chosen subtree from a *randomly selected parent*; the subtree that is implanted by the crossover operation consists of a randomly chosen subtree from a *fitness-selected parent.*

In the same vein, a blind random search in the space of computer programs can be viewed as a special case of the crossover operation. The individual program created by blind random search can be viewed as the offspring of a crossover in which the remainder comes from a *randomly selected parent* from *generation 0,* and the crossover fragment consists of a randomly chosen subtree from a *randomly selected parent* from *generation 0.*

Viewing the crossover operation, the mutation operation, and blind random search as special cases of the crossover operation puts all three operations into a common framework. By doing this, we can see that the crucial differences between these three operations are the statistical properties of the *source* of the fragment and the *source* of the remainder used to construct the offspring. The differences among the three operations concern only whether the fragment or remainder is randomly chosen versus fitness-selected, and whether the fragment or remainder comes from the current generation i or is created in the same way as generation 0.

Table 56.1 compares the crossover operation, the mutation operation, and blind random search in terms of the source of the crossover fragment and remainder used to construct the offspring.

Everyone agrees that nontrivial problems of interest cannot be solved in any reasonable amount of time by blind random search. That is, everyone agrees that it is not advantageous to choose both the fragment and remainder from a randomly chosen subtree of a randomly chosen individual created in the same way as generation 0.

Practitioners of evolutionary programming, evolution strategies, the genetic algorithm, and genetic programming all share the view that choosing the remainder based on fitness from the current generation i is essential to the operation of any successful evolutionary algorithm. It is well established that all the techniques of evolutionary computation usually produce results that are far superior to blind random search on nontrival problems of interest to engineers, mathematicians, and designers.

Practitioners of evolutionary programming and evolution strategies differ from practitioners of the genetic algorithm and genetic programming over the issue of the more advantageous source for the fragment that is to be implanted in the remainder in constructing the offspring. Practitioners of evolutionary programming and evolution strategies advocate choosing a randomly chosen subtree from the equivalent of a randomly chosen individual from generation 0; practitioners of the canonical genetic algorithm and genetic programming advocate choosing a randomly chosen subtree from a fitness-selected individual from the current generation i.

Thus, the difference in opinion concerns only whether it is more advantageous that the fragment that is to be implanted in the remainder comes from a randomly chosen subtree of

- a randomly chosen parent from generation 0 or
- a fitness-selected parent from current generation i.

Thus, it seems reasonable to pose the following question concerning not using crossover:

Since everyone agrees that it is advantageous for the remainder to come from a fitness-selected individual from the current generation i, why is it not likewise advantageous for the fragment to come from a fitness-selected individual from the current generation i? What is the argument for treating the two parts differently?

Table 56.1 Comparison of crossover, mutation, and blind random search

	Remainder comes from a randomly chosen subtree of	Fragment comes from a randomly chosen subtree of
Blind random search	Random parent from current generation 0	Random parent from current generation 0
Mutation	Fitness-selected parent from current generation i	Random parent from generation 0
Crossover	Fitness-selected parent from current generation i	Fitness-selected parent from current generation i

Similarly, it seems reasonable to pose the following question concerning the use of crossover:

Since crossover can only be advantageous if the fitness-selected fragments from the current generation i are different from a set of random fragments in a way that significantly contributes to discovering a solution to the problem, can the existence of this alleged difference be demonstrated?

56.3   THE ASSERTED USELESSNESS OF CROSSOVER

We are not aware of anything in the literature where practitioners of evolutionary programming and evolution strategies directly address the first question posed above (in Section 56.2). However, there are numerous published papers that purport to experimentally show that it is not advantageous to use crossover for solving particular sets of problems.

It must be acknowledged that it is exceedingly difficult to avoid methodological flaws in structuring a comparative experiment of a probabilistic algorithm that is capable of solving a variety of problems. Having acknowledged the inherent difficulty faced by all authors of all comparative studies, it is nonetheless entirely appropriate to critically examine the methodology of each comparative experiment before accepting its conclusions.

The most common methodological flaws in comparative experiments stem from the choice (usually unconscious) of control parameters that hamper the problem-solving ability of one of the algorithms in the comparative study and from the choice of an unpersuasive suite of test problems. In the case of the published papers purporting to show experimentally that crossover is not advantageous, we focus here on methodological problems concerning the choices of

- population size,
- limits on program size,
- distributions of crossover points, and
- the suite of test problems.

The most extensive (and recent) comparative study in the genre of papers purporting to show experimentally that crossover is not advantageous is found in Chellapilla 1997b. This paper performs comparative experiments on 14 problems taken directly from (or derived from) problems in the 1992 book *Genetic Programming* (Koza 1992e). In Chellapilla's study, one series of runs is made with crossover, and a second series of runs is made without crossover. The computational effort, E, is then computed for the two series of runs for 10 of the 14 problems. We also review two other comparative studies based on suites of between three to five problems (Angeline 1997a, 1997b; O'Reilly and Oppacher 1994, 1996). (See also Chellapilla 1997a, 1998.)

56.3.1   Population Size

Let us begin with the choice of population size. Chellapilla (1997b) used a population size of 500 for all 14 problems in his comparative study. To appreciate the decisive impact of this choice of a population size on the particular suite of test problems involved in this comparative study, consider the following points.

First, the ability of genetic programming to solve the odd-3-parity problem (Boolean rule 150) is known to be very sensitive to population size. There is almost a 50-to-1 difference in the computational effort necessary to solve this problem depending on the choice of population size between 50 and 1,000. Specifically, Figure 9.3 in *Genetic Programming* (Koza 1992e) showed that the following number of individuals must be processed per solution to the odd-3-parity problem:

- 999,750 for a population of 50,
- 665,923 for a population of 100,
- 379,876 for a population of 200,
- 122,754 for a population of 500, and
- 20,285 for a population size of 1,000.

Notice, in particular, that there is a 6.05-to-1 difference (i.e., 122,754 versus 20,285) in the number of individuals that must be processed per solution for a population size of 500 versus a population size of 1,000. That is, Chellapilla's decision to use a population size of 500 versus 1,000 in a comparative study of evolutionary programming versus genetic programming on the odd-3-parity problem decreased the ability of genetic programming to solve the problem by a factor of 6.05-to-1. Tellingly, the largest advantage reported for evolutionary programming for any problem in his entire comparative study of 14 problems (Chellapilla 1997b, Table III) is only 3.36-to-1. Moreover, this largest reported advantage was achieved on this very problem.

Second, a population size of 1,000 was used in the truck backer upper problem in *Genetic Programming* (Koza 1992e, Section 11.2). As Table 26.7 in *Genetic Programming* shows, about half of the problems in the 1992 book were efficiently solved using a population size of 500. In fact, our practice was to first try to tackle each problem (including the truck backer upper problem) in the 1992 book with a population size of 500. Whenever we realized that a larger population size was required to make progress on a particular problem in *Genetic Programming*, our practice was to then try the same problem with a larger population size. After several attempts, genetic programming was unable to solve the truck backer upper problem with a population size of 500. When we increased the population size to 1,000 on the truck backer upper problem, the problem solved on the very first run. This experience suggests that the computational effort necessary to solve this problem is—like that of the 3-parity problem above—highly sensitive to the choice of a population size (in the range of population sizes between 500 and 1,000 here).

Again, Chellapilla's decision to use a population size of 500 for the truck backer upper problem substantially decreased the probability of success for the runs with crossover.

Third, the Boolean 6-multiplexer problem is also known to be highly sensitive to the choice of population size in the range between 300 and 1,000. When we previously tried population sizes of 300 and 500, the probability of success was exceedingly low. We quickly realized that a larger population size would be far more efficient for this problem; that is, the increased probability of success with the larger population size would more than compensate for the increased effort required to process the larger population on each generation. Accordingly, a population size of 1,000 was used for all the experiments involving the 6-multiplexer problem throughout Chapter 25 of *Genetic Programming*. Chellapilla's decision to use a population size of 500 for studying the differences between mutation and crossover on this problem substantially decreased the probability of success for the runs with crossover.

Fourth, a population size of 4,000 was used on the even-3-parity, even-4-parity, and even-5-parity problems in *Genetic Programming* (Chapters 20 and 21, Section 25.11). Again, a population of 4,000 was used precisely because our experience was that the performance of genetic programming on these particular problems was adversely affected by smaller population sizes. The decision (Chellapilla 1997b) to use a population size of 500 for the comparative study of mutation versus crossover dramatically decreased the ability of genetic programming to solve this problem.

Fifth, a population size of 10,000 was used on the reported successful run of the intertwined spiral problem in *Genetic Programming* (Chapter 17). This was the largest population size used in the 1992 book, and it, too, was not chosen by accident. We first tried various smaller population sizes. We were unable, after several attempts, to solve the problem with a population of 2,000, 4,000, or 8,000. When we tried a population size of 10,000, the problem solved on the first (and only) run that we made with that population size. The decision (Chellapilla 1997b) to use a population size of 500 for the comparative study of mutation versus crossover dramatically decreased the ability of genetic programming to solve this problem.

In the same vein, Angeline (1997a, 1997b) studied the crossover operation using a population size of 300 for the intertwined spiral problem (in comparison to the population size of 10,000 that was used in *Genetic Programming*). That is, Angeline used a population size on this problem that was 33.3 times smaller than that used by the result reported in the genetic programming literature.

Angeline's work also used a population size of 500 on the even-6-parity problem. As mentioned above, we used a population size of 4,000 for parity problems of orders 3, 4, and 5. The even-6-parity problem is considerably more formidable than its lower-order counterparts. *Genetic Programming II* (Koza 1994g) specifically mentioned that we had been unable to solve the even-6-parity problem after trying 19 separate runs with a population of 16,000 using our LISP machine. When we first started using our 64-node parallel transputer system in 1994, we ran the even-6-parity problem and obtained a solution on our first (and only) run using a population size of 96,000. The number of fitness evaluations required to evolve a solution to the even-6-parity problem were within 3% of the estimate of 70,176,000 published in *Genetic Programming II* (Koza 1994g, Section 6.6). Here Angeline used a population size on this problem that was 192 times smaller than that used by the result reported in the genetic programming literature.

Angeline (1997a, 1997b) also did a comparison (apparently with a population size of 500) with the work of Oakley (1994) on the Mackey-Glass equations (where Oakley used populations of up to 5,000 in his runs of genetic programming). On this problem, Angeline used a population size that was 10 times smaller than that used by the result reported in the genetic programming literature.

Angeline's decision to use a population size that was appreciably smaller than that used by the practitioners of genetic programming dramatically decreased the ability of genetic programming to solve all three problems.

O'Reilly and Oppacher (1994, 1996) used a population of only 500 on the Boolean 6-multiplexer problem in a comparison of genetic programming, simulated annealing (Kirkpatrick, Gelatt, and Vecchi 1983; Aarts and Korst 1989), and stochastic iterative hill climbing. The search space was the usual space of computer programs used in genetic programming. Crossover and mutation were used in the usual way for the runs with genetic programming. The usual mutation operation for program trees was used for the runs with simulated annealing and stochastic iterative hill climbing. As previously mentioned, the 6-multiplexer problem is known to be exquisitely sensitive to the choice of population size in the range between 300 and 1,000. Smaller population sizes are known to be inefficient for the 6-multiplexer problem, and a population of 1,000 was used in *Genetic Programming* (Koza 1992e, Chapter 25). In addition, O'Reilly and Oppacher (1994) used the same small population size of 500 on the considerably more difficult Boolean 11-multiplexer problem. In contrast, *Genetic Programming* (Section 7.4) used a population of 4,000 on the 11-multiplexer problem. The decision to use population sizes of 500 on these problems clearly hampered the ability of genetic programming to solve each of these problems.

If the population is indeed a reservoir of useful information for runs of the genetic algorithm and genetic programming (as will be discussed in greater detail below), the choice of population size is critical and decisive in determining the success of a run of the genetic algorithm and genetic programming. In contrast, the mutation operation operates on single individuals in the population (and does not draw on cohorts in the same generation of the population).

56.3.2   Program Size

Consider now the question of program size. For 13 of the 14 problems for which Chellapilla (1997b) did comparisons on problems (or variants of problems) that appeared in *Genetic Programming* (Koza 1992e), 50 was established as the maximum number of functions and terminals for a program.

It is well known that the ability of genetic programming to solve a problem drops dramatically when the size of programs is overly constrained. The size of an evolving program in the population of a run of genetic programming expands and contracts as the various genetic operations are applied. The programs that exist during a run of genetic programming need considerable working area so that they can freely expand and contract during the run. The size of the single program that is designated as the final result of a run is often considerably less than the size of its largest ancestor over the many generations of the run.

A constraint on the maximum number of points in a program is a fortiori an even more severe constraint on the size of the subtrees that may be exchanged in a crossover. Moreover, if the population is indeed a reservoir of useful information (as will be discussed in greater detail below), the quality of crossover fragments is essential to successful crossovers. An abnormally low limit on program size throttles genetic programming because crossover depends on fitness-selected fragments from the current generation being significantly different from a set of random fragments in a way that significantly contributes to discovering a solution to the problem.

Chellapilla's choice of 50 is extraordinarily small and is far below (by about an order of magnitude) the effective maximum used throughout *Genetic Programming* (Section 6.9). To appreciate the severity of this constraint on program size, consider the following.

First, *Genetic Programming* (Section 20.2) presented illustrative solutions to the even-3-parity, even-4-parity, and even-5-parity problems having 45, 149, and 347 points, respectively. In addition, *Genetic Programming II* (Koza 1994g, Tables 6.4, 6.5, and 6.6) reported that the average size of the evolved solutions for the even-3-parity, even-4-parity, and even-5-parity problems are 44.2, 112.6, and 299.9 points, respectively. Since these latter numbers are averages, a maximum size of 50 is restrictive even for the 3-parity problem. Such a limit has a suffocating effect on runs of the 4-parity and 5-parity problems. It excludes virtually every solution that is likely to have evolved using crossover. In addition, Figure 20.8 of *Genetic Programming* graphically shows that the size of the average program in the population for the even-4-parity problem significantly exceeds 50 as early as generation 2. This figure is accompanied by the statement, "As can be seen, the average size . . . is well over one hundred for the majority of this run." Figure 21.6 of *Genetic Programming* makes a similar point. Finally, as another indication of the insufficiency of programs that are limited to 50 functions and terminals, consider the fact that a solution to the 4-parity problem written in disjunctive normal form (DNF) occupies 81 points (using one commonly used arrangement).

Second, the evolved solution to the intertwined spiral problem is reported in *Genetic Programming* (Chapter 17) to contain 179 points. Moreover, Figure 17.15 therein shows that the size of the average program in the population exceeds 50 for virtually every generation of the run.

Third, Figure 25.23 in *Genetic Programming* also shows that a choice of 50 for program size is restrictive for the 6-multiplexer problem. The figure shows that the size of the average program in the population exceeds 50 for virtually every generation of the run.

Fourth, as a further point of reference, when we ran the cart-centering problem in this book (Chapter 19), we established the maximum number of points, S_{rpb}, in the result-producing branch at 500. Moreover, we established a limit of 500 in the context of a run where the programs had the ability to expand their total size by means of the architecture-altering operations.

Angeline (1997a, 1997b) did not specify the maximum program size for the even-6-parity and intertwined spiral problems. Angeline has informed the authors by means of a personal communication that his maximum size was 250. O'Reilly and Oppacher (1994) did not specify their maximum program size.

56.3.3   Distribution of Crossover Points

The probability distribution used to choose crossover points in genetic programming has a significant effect on the outcome of a run of genetic programming. Since a significant fraction (usually about half) of the points in a typical program tree are terminals, it is common for practitioners of genetic programming to bias the two independent random choices of crossover points so as to favor the choosing of internal points of the program tree (Section 2.3.2, "Crossover Operation").

Without this bias, a significant fraction (about a quarter) of the crossovers will involve simply swapping two terminals. That is, the crossover operation degenerates into a point mutation operation in about 25% of the instances of crossover. In addition, about 50% of the instances of crossover consist merely of a stunted form of crossover in which a terminal is exchanged with a subtree. The substitution of a single terminal for a subtree is a form of pruning. It manifestly does not give the receiving parent the benefit of a non-degenerate subtree from elsewhere in the current generation of the population. Only about 25% of the instances of crossover entail exchanging two nondegenerate subtrees. Thus, without the bias commonly used by practitioners of genetic programming, the result is only an enfeebled form of the crossover operation.

The commonly used biasing was not used, for example, by O'Reilly and Oppacher (1994). Chellapilla (1997a, 1997b) and Angeline (1997a, 1997b) are silent on this aspect concerning the runs of genetic programming. However, both Chellapilla and Angeline have informed the authors by means of personal communications that they did, in fact, use this biasing.

56.3.4   Problem Downscaling

Any one of the above three methodological flaws is alone sufficient to invalidate the conclusions derived from the above comparative experiments. However, there is a far more significant methodological shortcoming common to virtually all such comparative experiments of this genre, namely, the triviality of the problems in the test suite.

For any given allocation of computational resources, the problem(s) that are included in the test suite for a comparative experiment must inevitably be considerably easier than whatever problem can currently be solved with the available resources. For example, if 50 independent runs are required to achieve an acceptable level of statistical significance in studying two competing approaches, then the difficulty of the test problem in the comparative experiment must be two orders of magnitude easier than whatever problem can currently be solved with the available allocation of computational resources.

This shortcoming is exacerbated when contemplating the construction of a comparative experiment with a multiplicity of problems in the test suite. For example, Chellapilla (1997b, Table III) studied 14 problems and reported the computational effort for 10 of them (understandably omitting the computational effort for the four less trivial problems that used large amounts of computer time). When a comparative study includes 10 test problems (and if 50 independent runs are required to achieve an acceptable level of statistical significance in studying two competing approaches), then each test problem must be *three* orders of magnitude easier than whatever problem can currently be solved with the available allocation of computational resources.

This 1,000-to-1 downscaling in problem difficulty is not an option for the researcher conducting the experiments; it is an inherent limitation in achieving a reasonable level of statistical validity for a comparative experiment with a multiplicity of problems in its test suite. This limitation applies to all such comparative experiments and is not a criticism of any particular experiment or any particular individual who may have conducted such an experiment. (Note that the authors also report on several comparative experiments of their own throughout this book, and these experiments suffer from this same limitation.)

This inherently required 1,000-to-1 downscaling in problem difficulty (which we call the "dumbing down" dilemma) is especially vexatious at the present time for two reasons.

First, given the present-day speed of computers, it is currently barely possible to make one run of genetic programming on a problem whose evolved solution can reasonably be said to be competitive with human-produced results (as shown, for example, in Table 61.1). Except for the lowpass filter problem, this book reports on only one run (or only a few runs) of each of the 14 problems in this book for which we claim that genetic programming produced results that are competitive with human-produced results. In doing the research that led to this book, we made a conscious management decision to allocate our computational resources to the question of whether genetic programming could produce results that could be plausibly described as competitive with human-produced results. The present-day speed of computers precludes doing meaningful comparative experiments on problems of this level of difficulty within the amount of computer time available to us.

Second, more importantly, this 1,000-to-1 downscaling in problem difficulty has the effect (at the present time) of eliminating (from comparative studies) nontrivial problems that possess any interesting substructure in the form of modularities, symmetries, and regularities. For example, to obtain suitably easy problems for his 1997 comparative study, Chellapilla (1997b) delved into the 1992 book *Genetic Programming*. Most of the problems in the 1992 book originated from the literature of the fields of machine learning and artificial intelligence in the late 1980s. The 1992 book claimed that genetic programming could solve a variety of problems from a variety of fields. The persuasiveness of that claim was enhanced, at the time, by the fact that most of the problems in the book were previously studied benchmark problems that had been independently formulated by contemporary researchers from the fields of machine learning and artificial intelligence. However, whatever merits those problems possessed in 1992, no one can view them as meaningful benchmark problems today. Moreover, although the persuasiveness of the 1992 book may have been somewhat enhanced by using independently formulated problems, the origin of these problems was a double-edged sword. Because these problems originated from work in the fields of machine learning and artificial intelligence in the late 1980s, these problems reflected the fact that the fields of machine learning and artificial intelligence had not given much attention to problems with interesting substructure in the form of modularities, symmetries, and regularities.

The artificial ant (Santa Fe trail) problem from Koza (1992e) used by Chellapilla (1997b) illustrates the issue of downscaling in problem difficulty. There is almost no substructure to this problem. A solution to the artificial ant problem requires that a certain sequence of primitive operations be performed in one of two allowable orders.

Although certain superfluous motions are permitted, the required sequence of primitive operations must always be performed in order to solve the problem. When we contemplated using the Santa Fe trail version of the artificial ant problem to study automatically defined functions for *Genetic Programming II* (Koza 1994g, Chapter 12.1), we quickly realized that the artificial ant problem could not be used to study reuse because there is next to nothing to reuse. Consequently, we constructed a more difficult version of the problem (the San Mateo trail) for the 1994 book. The more difficult version of the problem required considerably more computer time to run (because of the more complex geometry of the food trail, the more complex sequence of motions required, the greater number of time steps necessitated by the more complex geometry, and the need for multiple fitness cases). Moreover, this substantial increase in computational resources merely yielded a problem with the possibility of reusing a sequence of steps *one time* (i.e., for a grand total of two uses). After making the required larger investment of computer time, automatically defined functions proved to be beneficial on the more difficult version of the problem by a factor of 2.0 (as shown in Table 12.3 of Koza 1994g and in the videotape Koza 1994h). The original Santa Fe trail version of the artificial ant problem from the 1992 book is unsuitable for studying the crossover operation for the same reason that it was unsuitable for studying automatically defined functions—there is next to nothing to reuse. It is unsuitable for studying the question of mutation and crossover for the same reason.

In contrast to most of the "toy" problems appearing in the literature of the 1980s and early 1990s, most problems in the real world are replete with modularities, symmetries, and regularities and interesting substructure. Solving such problems usually depends on using the leverage gained from the exploitation of a problem's inherent modularities, symmetries, and regularities.

For example, designers of microprocessor chips reuse certain standard circuits, each performing a certain elementary function, throughout the chip. The design of a microprocessor chip containing hundreds of occurrences of a standard cell would be impractical if the chip designer had to start from first principles and separately reinvent the design of each such cell on each occasion when it is needed. Instead, there is massive reuse of certain basic constructions.

Similarly, computer programmers invoke a similar process of reuse when they make multiple calls to a subroutine from a calling program. The writing of computer programs would be utterly impractical if programmers had to rewrite, from scratch, the code for the square root, cosine, array access, file handling, and printing on each separate occasion when they needed those functions. Again, there is massive reuse of certain basic constructions.

The human body contains approximately five trillion cells. The structure of all of these cells is specified by only six billion bits of information (contained in the three billion nucleotide bases of the human genome). The human body is produced through the massive reuse of certain basic constructions.

An adult human possesses about 10^{21} molecules of hemoglobin (just one of about 100,000 different proteins specified by the human genome). Again, there is massive reuse of a basic structure.

56.4   GEDANKENEXPERIMENT ON THE DIFFERENCES BETWEEN CROSSOVER AND MUTATION

Before proceeding, consider the following gedanken experiment concerning a run of genetic programming on a modified version of a simple problem of symbolic regression (system identification).

The goal is to evolve a one-output computer program whose output matches that of an unidentified system (the output of which is produced by the sextic polynomial $x^6 + x^4 + x^2$). The function set for this problem contains the four ordinary arithmetic functions. Fitness is the sum of absolute errors, over 20 randomly chosen values (fitness cases) of the independent variable x between -1.0 and $+1.0$. The actual values produced by the sextic polynomial range between only 0.0 and $+3.0$ in the interval $[-1.0, +1.0]$.

The terminal set for this problem contains the independent variable X and an extraneous variable Y. The variable Y returns an independently created random number (Gaussian distributed with a mean of 1,000 and a standard deviation of 100) on each separate occasion on which it is encountered in a program. In 299 out of 300 instances, any program tree containing a single occurrence of Y will return a value that is somewhere between 700 and 1,300 greater than would otherwise be the case. A program with even a single Y in it will, almost always, be highly unfit.

Suppose, for the sake of argument, that the average number of terminals in the randomly created program in generation 0 is 20. Since about half of the randomly chosen terminals are Ys, only about 1 program in 1,024 will be Y-free (i.e., there is a 99.9% probability that a program in generation 0 has at least one Y). If the population size is 5,000, then we can expect about five Y-free programs in generation 0. Selection will heavily favor the Y-free programs. Selection will also favor programs with fewer Ys because each Y in a program increases (worsens) the program's fitness by an average of 20,000 (1,000 times the 20 fitness cases). As a run of genetic programming progresses from generation to generation, descendents of the Y-free programs from generation 0 will tend to dominate the population, and the population will rapidly become largely Y-free (say, by generation i).

When a crossover is performed in generation i, the remainder comes from a fitness-selected parent from generation i, and the inserted fragment consists of a randomly chosen subtree from a fitness-selected parent from generation i. A crossover between two Y-free parents will always beget a Y-free offspring. The relatively unchallenging problem of symbolic regression of the sextic polynomial $x^6 + x^4 + x^2$ will be solved quickly as soon as the evolutionary process starts mating with Y-free programs.

When a mutation is performed in generation i, the remainder comes from a fitness-selected parent from generation i and the inserted fragment consists of a subtree produced in the same manner as an individual in generation 0. The offspring produced by a mutation of a Y-free parent will, with 99.9% probability, contain the poison pill (Y) and therefore will be very unfit.

This gedankenexperiment for the "poison pill" problem highlights the fact that the characteristics of the set of fitness-selected fragments from the current generation i can be significantly different from characteristics of the set of randomly created fragments. Moreover, the characteristics of the set of fitness-selected fragments from the current generation *i* are different in a way that significantly contributes to discovering a solution to this problem.

We do not, of course, assert that a poison pill as dramatic as the one described above appears in practical problems (although less dramatic forms of poison pills do appear in practical problems, including the unsimulatable circuits depicted in Figure 25.51 of this book and the exponential, logarithm, sine, and cosine functions of the symbolic regression in Section 7.3 of *Genetic Programming*). We do assert that this gedankenexperiment serves to highlight a fundamental difference between the operations of crossover and mutation. In particular, the experiment shows how the population, at an advanced generation, can serve as a reservoir of information that can aid the crossover operation in finding a solution to a problem. In the next section, we demonstrate how the population *does* serve as such a reservoir.

56.5 THE POPULATION AS A RESERVOIR OF INFORMATION IN A NONTRIVIAL PROBLEM

The problem of synthesizing the design of a lowpass filter differs in two ways from almost all of the problems used in previously published comparative studies on the role of crossover.

First, the problem is a nontoy problem. We are not talking about problems involving the artificial ant, the exclusive-or function, the Boolean multiplexer, or a simple polynomial regression. This problem is far more difficult than the vast majority of the problems used in experimental comparative studies on a computer in the field of evolutionary computation (and related areas of machine learning and artificial intelligence as well).

Second, more importantly, the problem possesses interesting substructure in the form of modularity, symmetry, and regularity.

We believe that the problem of synthesizing the design of a lowpass filter directly addresses the second question (posed in Section 56.2) of whether the set of fitness-selected fragments from the current generation can be significantly different from a set of random fragments in a way that aids in discovering a solution.

The discussion below continues the discussion concerning run G of the lowpass filter problem from Section 25.17 (see Section 25.17 for background information).

Crossover created the best-of-generation individual of generation 18 from two reasonably good parents from generation 17. The contributing (male) parent in the crossover of interest was a two-rung ladder circuit (Figure 25.73) consisting of a series of two inductors (L105 and L111) and two vertical shunts (C112 and C103). The receiving (female) parent (Figure 25.72) consisted of a series of two inductors (L225 and L212), two capacitive shunts (C226 and C213), and one inductive-capacitive shunt (inductor L210 and capacitor C211). The offspring circuit (Figure 25.74) produced in generation 18 by the crossover of the two parents was a significant improvement over both of its parents:

- The fitness of two parents was 12.20 and 12.22, respectively. The fitness of the offspring is 3.143.
- The number of hits for the two parents was 85 and 77 hits, respectively. The number of hits for the offspring is 95.

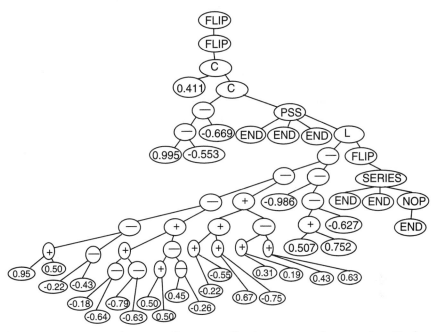

Figure 56.7   Crossover fragment from contributing parent of generation 17 of run G

Figure 56.7 shows the 69-point crossover fragment (from the first result-producing branch of the contributing parent from generation 17) that actually produced this improved offspring. This crossover fragment was a randomly chosen subtree from a fitness-selected individual from the population of 30,000 individuals in generation 17.

At the moment when the best-of-generation individual of generation 18 was created in run G, a mutation might have been performed in lieu of the crossover that was actually performed in run G. Moreover, a different crossover might have been performed in lieu of the crossover that was actually performed in run G. Thus, we now perform two experiments that demonstrate the likely outcome of these two alternative scenarios.

We performed 1,000,000 alternative crossover operations. The contributing parent was fixed. First, 1,000,000 independent fitness-based selections were made of individuals from the population of 30,000 at generation 17 (with reselection allowed). Second, a point was randomly and independently chosen from each of these 1,000,000 selected individuals. Third, the subtree from the fixed contributing parent was implanted in each of the 1,000,000 selected individuals.

We also performed 1,000,000 alternative mutation operations. The parent was fixed. Then a new subtree was randomly grown in the same manner as trees are grown in creating the initial random population of generation 0.

What are the characteristics of these 1,000,000 crossovers as compared to these 1,000,000 mutations? In particular, which operation produced more offspring that were superior to both of their parents?

- 202,538 of the 1,000,000 circuits produced by crossovers were better than both parents (i.e., have a fitness of better than 12.20).

- 18,328 of the 1,000,000 circuits produced by mutation were better than its single parent.

In other words, 20.2% of the crossovers produced an improvement, but only 1.8% of the mutations did so. The reason is that the crossover operation draws its fragments from a reservoir that has undergone 17 generations of improvement; the mutation operation draws its fragments from the equivalent of generation 0. A glance back at Figure 56.7 reminds us that it took a fairly large subtree to improve a receiving parent in generation 17 in the crossover that was actually performed in run G. It is difficult to create a subtree at random that will yield an improvement when inserted into a receiving parent at an advanced generation of a run of a nontrivial problem such as this.

Which operation produced the best single outcome?

- The best fitness produced by 1,000,000 crossovers is 3.140 (i.e., slightly better than the actual crossover that was performed in run G).
- The best fitness produced by 1,000,000 mutations is 8.652.

Here again, the best single offspring (out of 202,538 improved offspring) produced by the crossover operation is far better than the best single offspring (out of 18,328 improved offspring) produced by the mutation operation.

Which operation produced more offspring with fitness better than 4.0 (i.e., near the best single outcome of 3.140)?

- 97 of the 1,000,000 offspring have a fitness of less than 4.0.
- 0 of the 1,000,000 circuits produced by mutation have a fitness of less than 4.0.

Again, when we focus on what happens at the tail of the distribution (which is, in the final analysis, the source of solutions to problems), crossover produces many more distinctly improved offspring than does the mutation operation. Notice that the number of distinctly improved offspring is not enormous when the above probability (97 in 1,000,000) is applied to an actual population of size 30,000. Crossover can be expected to yield only about three distinctly improved offspring in going from generation 17 to 18 in an actual population of size 30,000. Nonetheless, the creation of a modest number of distinctly improved individuals in one generation of an evolutionary search is more than sufficient to advance a run toward its ultimate goal of solving the problem.

Which operation produced the best average outcome?

- The mean fitness over all 1,000,000 circuits produced by crossover is 4,391,460.
- The mean fitness over all 1,000,000 circuits produced by mutation is 9,207,167.

Again, the mean of the offspring produced by the crossover operation is far better than the mean of the offspring produced by the mutation operation. Both means are large because they both include numerous unsimulatable circuits (whose fitness is the 10^8 penalty). Thus, we also ask the following question:

Which operation produced fewer unsimulatable circuits?

- 43,940 of the 1,000,000 circuits produced by crossover were unsimulatable by SPICE.
- 92,052 of the 1,000,000 circuits produced by mutation were unsimulatable by SPICE.

The crossover operation produces less than half as many unsimulatable circuits as the mutation operation. In other words, when a subtree is inserted into a circuit-constructing program tree, the chances of producing a nonpathological (i.e., simulatable) circuit are more than doubled if the inserted subtree came from a nonpathological circuit.

Which operation produced the best average outcome if only the simulatable circuits are considered?

- If only the 956,060 simulatable circuits produced by crossover are considered, the mean is 66.15.
- If only the 907,948 simulatable circuits produced by mutation are considered, the mean is 91.04.

Again, the mean of the circuits produced by the crossover operation is better than the mean of the circuits produced by the mutation operation.

In summary, the above demonstration based on 1,000,000 alternative crossovers and mutations addresses the second question posed in Section 56.2. The population acts as a reservoir of useful information during a run of genetic programming, and the crossover operation exploits the richness of this reservoir of information in order to advance the discovery of solutions to problems.

56.5.1 Relation to Evolutionary Programming

The above experiment concerned runs of genetic programming without crossover—that is, a run with Darwinian reproduction and the mutation operation (Section 2.3.2) *of genetic programming.*

Canonical evolutionary programming (L. Fogel 1962; L. Fogel, Owens, and Walsh 1966; D. Fogel 1991) also uses Darwinian reproduction and mutation, but does not use crossover. The above experiment is thus relevant to runs of evolutionary programming on the lowpass filter; however, the above experiment is not equivalent to a run of evolutionary programming.

Evolution of computer programs is only one of many areas to which the technique of evolutionary programming has been applied. There are several possible ways that evolutionary programming may be applied to the evolution of computer programs. Chellapilla (1997b) describes an approach in which six different mutation operations are employed when applying evolutionary programming to the evolution of computer programs. The six operations are applied to individual computer programs that are selected probabilistically from the population on the basis of fitness.

One of the six mutation operations (called "Grow") corresponds to the mutation operation of genetic programming (Section 2.3.2).

The "Truncation" operation randomly chooses an internal point of the program tree (a node with a function), deletes the subtree rooted at the chosen point, and inserts a randomly chosen terminal at the chosen point.

The "One Node" operation randomly chooses a point of the program tree and replaces the function at that point with another function of the same arity. The chosen point may be a terminal (i.e., a function of arity zero).

The "All Node" operation applies the "One Node" operation to every point of the program tree. This operation preserves the topology of the tree, but randomly replaces every function and terminal in it.

The "Swap" operation randomly chooses a function (internal point of the program tree) with arity of at least two, randomly picks two of the arguments to the chosen function, and swaps the two picked argument subtrees.

The sixth mutation operation (called "Gaussian") is specialized. It is used only to perturb numerical constants in a program tree (using a Gaussian distribution with a specified standard deviation). This operation is similar to the Gaussian mutation operators that are commonly used in evolution strategies (Rechenberg 1965, 1973) and in some genetic algorithm work (e.g., the Gaussian creep operator described in Montana and Davis 1989; Davis 1991).

The six mutation operations share the characteristic of operating without reference to any cohort individual in the current generation of the population. That is, no use is made of any information that may be residing elsewhere in the population at the time the operation is performed. Crossover is advantageous because it exploits the reservoir of information present in cohorts of the individual residing in the current generation of the population. In particular, the fitness-selected crossover fragments from the current generation i are different from randomly created fragments in a way that significantly contributes to discovering a solution to the problem. None of the six mutation operations of evolutionary programming are designed to exploit the reservoir of information stored in the current population. Therefore, we believe that no combination of the above mutation operations can be as effective as crossover in rapidly advancing the search in nontrivial problems with modularities, symmetries, and regularity.

Having said that, we should add that we believe that the method of adjusting the numerical values returned by the arithmetic-performing subtrees in our current implementation of development genetic programming is not very effective. In fact, we believe that the Gaussian mutation operation of evolutionary programming is probably superior to the approach used in this book for numerical constants (as perhaps would be the other alternatives mentioned in Section 25.7). We do not know whether the advantage conferred by correcting this known weakness of our current treatment of numerical constants in genetic programming is greater or less than the disadvantage incurred by deleting crossover in solving the lowpass filter problem. This point concerning the fact that evolutionary programming may handle numerical constants better than genetic programming underscores a point that was previously made concerning the various comparative studies purporting to show that crossover is disadvantageous, namely, that the results of these studies are obscured and overshadowed by numerous uncontrolled, significant variables (e.g., the choice of overly small population sizes, overly constrained program sizes, and nonstandard methods of selecting crossover points).

56.5.2   Relation to Simulated Annealing

Simulated annealing (Kirkpatrick, Gelatt, and Vecchi 1983; Aarts and Korst 1989) can potentially be used to conduct the search for a satisfactory computer program in the space of computer programs.

Simulated annealing is a point-to-point search technique that uses a problem-specific probabilistic modification operator (often called a "mutation") for modifying the current point in the search space in order to obtain its successor. At each step of the search, the current point in the search space is modified using the modification operator, and the new point's fitness (usually called the "energy level") is determined. The Metropolis algorithm is applied to determine whether to accept the newly created point. If the fitness of the new point is an improvement (in terms of its fitness), the new point is always accepted, and the search continues from the new point. However, if the fitness of the new point is not an improvement, the modification may still be accepted with a certain probability determined by the Boltzmann equation. The entire run of simulated annealing is governed by an annealing schedule in which a temperature T changes as the run proceeds (typically in an exponentially decreasing way). The probability of acceptance of a nonimproving modification is greater if the fitness difference is small or if the temperature T is high. Thus, fairly large nonimproving modifications are likely to be accepted early in the run (when the temperature is usually high), while only small nonimproving modifications are likely to be accepted later in the run. If a modification is not accepted at any step of the run of simulated annealing, the probabilistic modification operator is reinvoked to produce another new point. The beginning of a run of simulated annealing conducts a broad-based search for promising regions of the search space; the end of the run predominantly does hill climbing in a localized area.

Simulated annealing differs from genetic programming in that there is no population (and hence no crossover operation). Simulated annealing also differs from genetic programming in that simulated annealing always accepts an improving modification. Simulated annealing is similar to genetic programming in that it sometimes accepts a newly created point that is known to be inferior in the hope that it will lead to better points.

When simulated annealing is applied to the space of computer programs (O'Reilly and Oppacher 1994, 1996), the mutation operation of genetic programming (Section 2.3.2) may be used as the modification operator.

Since there is no population in simulated annealing, it cannot exploit the reservoir of information that resides in the current generation of the population. As in evolutionary programming, each execution of the probabilistic mutation operation is an independent event. As demonstrated above, the fitness-selected crossover fragments from the current generation i are different from the randomly created fragments created by the mutation operation in a way that significantly contributes to discovering a solution to the problem. Therefore, we do not believe that simulated annealing would be as effective as genetic programming with crossover in rapidly advancing the search for a computer program to solve nontrivial problems with modularities, symmetries, and regularity.

Part 6: EVOLVABLE HARDWARE

The idea of evolvable hardware (Higuchi et al. 1993a, 1993b; Sanchez and Tomassini 1996; Higuchi, Iwata, and Liu 1997) and the commercial availability of rapidly reconfigurable field-programmable gate arrays (FPGAs) open the possibility of embodying each individual of an evolving population of a run of an evolutionary algorithm into hardware. This approach offers the possibility of exploiting the massive parallelism of such hardware to greatly accelerate the computationally burdensome fitness evaluation task of evolutionary algorithms.

Evolvable Hardware and Rapidly Reconfigurable Field-Programmable Gate Arrays

This chapter brings evolvable hardware to bear on the problem of synthesizing a minimal sorting network (previously solved in Section 21.4 with the Genetic Programming Problem Solver).

Section 57.1 introduces field-programmable gate arrays. Section 57.2 highlights the rapid reconfigurability of certain FPGAs. Section 57.3 describes the Xilinx XC6200 series of field-programmable gate arrays. Section 57.4 discusses the types of problems in evolutionary computation for which rapidly reconfigurable FPGAs may be suitable.

In Section 21.4.1, we described the problem of synthesizing the design of minimal sorting networks. Section 57.5 is a statement of the problem here. Section 57.6 presents the preparatory steps for applying genetic programming to this problem. Section 57.7 shows how this problem is mapped into the Xilinx XC6216 chip.

Section 57.8 shows an evolved 16-step seven-sorter that has two fewer steps than the sorting network described in the O'Connor and Nelson patent (1962) on sorting networks and that has the same number of steps as the minimal seven-sorter devised by Floyd and Knuth (Knuth 1973) subsequent to the patent.

Section 57.9 compares the style of human-written sorting networks with the incremental style of the evolved networks.

The work in this chapter was done in collaboration with Jeffrey L. Hutchings and Stephen L. Bade of Convergent Design, L.L.C. (Koza, Bennett, Hutchings, Bade, Keane, and Andre 1997a, 1997b, 1997c, 1998).

57.1 FIELD-PROGRAMMABLE GATE ARRAYS

The dominant component of the computational burden of solving nontrivial problems with the genetic algorithm or genetic programming is the task of measuring the fitness of each individual in each generation of the evolving population. (Relatively little computer time is expended on other tasks of the algorithm, such as the creation of the initial random population at the beginning of the run and the execution of the genetic operations during the run). In a run of the genetic algorithm or genetic programming, the population may contain thousands or even millions of individuals, and the algorithm may be run for dozens, hundreds, or thousands of generations. Moreover, the measurement of fitness for just one individual in just one generation typically involves exposing the individual program to hundreds or thousands of different combinations of inputs (called *fitness cases*). Executing one individual program for just one fitness case may, in turn, entail hundreds or thousands of steps.

A *field-programmable gate array* is a type of digital chip that contains a regular two-dimensional array of thousands of logical cells and a regular network of interconnection lines in which both the functionality of each cell and the connectivity between the cells can be programmed by the user in the field (rather than at the chip fabrication factory).

FPGAs were commercially introduced in the mid-1980s by Xilinx and are typically used to facilitate rapid prototyping of new electronic products—particularly those for which low initial product volume and time-to-market considerations preclude the design and fabrication of a custom application-specific integrated circuit (ASIC). Thus, many new electronic products contain an FPGA when they are first marketed. After the market is established for the product and its design has stabilized, an ASIC may be used in later versions of the product.

Some FPGAs are of the anti-fuse type that are irreversibly programmed by the user in the field by the one-time application of a high voltage. Other types can be reprogrammed, but only with significant limitations. For example, some FPGAs must be physically removed from their operating environment and erased with ultraviolet light before they can be electrically reprogrammed. Moreover, these types of FPGAs can be reprogrammed only a few hundred times. The focus here is on the infinitely reprogrammable type of FPGA where the functionality of each function unit and the connectivity between the function units is stored in static random access memory (SRAM). This type of FPGA can be electrically programmed and reprogrammed.

Engineers working with FPGAs typically employ a multistep process involving a computer-aided design (CAD) tool to design and optimize their FPGA circuits:

1. The engineer conceives the design (which often incorporates subcircuits from a library).
2. The engineer's design of the desired circuit is captured by the CAD tool in the form of a schematic diagram, a set of Boolean expressions, or a general-purpose high-level description language such as VHDL (an acronym for "VHSIC Hardware Description Language," in which VHSIC is, in turn, an acronym for "Very High Speed Integrated Circuits").
3. A technology mapping converts the description of the circuit into logical function units of the particular type that are present on the particular FPGA chip that is to be used.
4. A time-consuming placement step places the logical function units into particular locations on the FPGA.
5. A routing between the logical function units on the chip is created using the FPGA's interconnection resources. This routing process may be difficult because interconnection resources are extremely scarce for almost all commercially available FPGAs.

6. Hundreds of thousands of configuration bits are created. The encoding scheme for the configuration bits of almost all commercially available FPGAs are kept confidential by the FPGA manufacturers for a variety of reasons (including deterrence of reverse engineering of the prototype products that account for much of the FPGA market).
7. The configuration bits are downloaded into the FPGA's memory.

An engineer might spend several days or weeks designing a circuit and perhaps an hour entering the design into the CAD tool via its schematic editor (the first two steps in the multistep process above). The CAD tool may then require hours (or, at best, many minutes) to perform the technology mapping, placement, routing, and bit creation tasks (the next four steps above). Then the downloading of the configuration bits for a single design into memory may take about a half second. For almost all FPGAs (other than Xilinx's XC6000 series), 100% of the configuration bits must be reloaded if even one bit changes. Moreover, the downloading of the configuration bits is typically accomplished bit by bit through a serial port for almost all FPGAs (other than Xilinx's XC6000 series).

The above elapsed times measured in hours, minutes, and seconds for an FPGA compare very favorably with the weeks or months that may be required for performing the same steps using an ASIC—thereby giving the FPGA an advantage over an ASIC in the time required to launch a new product.

Additional information on FPGAs can be found in Trimberger 1994; Brown, Francis, Rose, and Vranesic 1992; Chan and Mourad 1994; Jenkins 1994; Murgai, Brayton, and Sangiovanni-Vincentelli 1995; Oldfield and Dorf 1995. Sources of additional information on recent research on FPGAs are described in the proceedings of the IEEE Symposium on FPGAs for Custom Computing Machines (IEEE 1996), the ACM International Symposium on Field-Programmable Gate Arrays (ACM 1997), the Oxford International Workshop on Field-Programmable Logic and Applications (Moore and Luk 1995), and the International Workshop on Field-Programmable Gate Arrays and Applications (Grunbacher and Hartenstein 1993).

57.2 RECONFIGURABILITY VERSUS RAPID RECONFIGURABILITY

The previous section described the kind of reconfigurability that has been commercially available for about a decade with field-programmable gate arrays.

Field-programmable gate arrays are massively parallel computational devices. The advent of rapidly reconfigurable field-programmable gate arrays and the idea of evolvable hardware (Higuchi et al. 1993a, 1993b; Higuchi, Iwata, and Liu 1997; de Garis 1993, 1996; Korkin, de Garis, Gers, and Hemmi 1997; Sanchez and Tomassini 1996; Thompson 1995, 1996a, 1996c, 1997; Harvey and Thompson 1996; Thompson, Harvey, and Husbands 1996) opens the possibility of embodying each individual of the evolving population into hardware. Once an FPGA is configured, its thousands of logical function units operate in parallel at the chip's clock rate.

Since the fitness measurement task residing in the inner loop of a run of the genetic algorithm or genetic programming constitutes the main component of the computational burden of a run, the question arises as to whether the massive parallelism of FPGAs can be exploited to accelerate this time-consuming task. This alluring possibility cannot, in practice, be realized with previously available FPGAs for four reasons.

First, the encoding schemes for the configuration bits of almost all commercially available FPGAs are complex and kept confidential by the FPGA manufacturers.

Second, the tasks of technology mapping, placement, routing, and creation of the configuration bits consume so much time as to preclude practical use of an FPGA in the inner loop of the genetic algorithm or genetic programming. Even if these four tasks could be reduced from the usual hours or minutes to as little as 10 seconds for each individual in the population, these four tasks would consume 10^6 seconds (278 hours) in a run involving a population as minuscule as 1,000 for as short as 100 generations. A run involving a population of 1,000,000 individuals would multiply the above unacceptably long time (278 hours) by 1,000.

Third, the 500 milliseconds typically required for the task of downloading the configuration bits to an FPGA is insignificantly small for an engineer who has spent hours, days, or months on a single prototype design. However, this downloading time would consume 14 hours for even a minuscule population of 1,000 that was run for as few as 100 generations. Again, a run involving a population of 1,000,000 individuals would multiply this already unacceptably long time (14 hours) by 1,000. What's worse—both of these unacceptably long times (278 hours and 14 hours) are merely *preliminary* to the time required by the FPGA for the actual problem-specific fitness measurement. That is, there is a discrepancy of numerous orders of magnitude between the time required for the technology mapping, placement, routing, bit creation, and downloading tasks and the time available for these preliminaries in the inner loop of a practical run of the genetic algorithm or genetic programming.

Thus, reconfigurability is not enough for practical work on FPGAs with genetic algorithms and genetic programming. *Rapid reconfigurability* is what is needed—where "rapid" means a total time of microseconds or milliseconds for all five preliminary tasks (technology mapping, placement, routing, bit creation, and downloading).

Fourth, the genetic algorithm starts with an initial population of randomly created individuals and uses probabilistic operations to breed new candidate individuals. These randomly created individuals do not conform to the design principles that are employed by humans. Most commercially available FPGAs are vulnerable to damage caused by combinations of configuration bits that connect contending digital signals to the same line. The process of verifying the acceptability of genetically created combinations of configuration bits is complex and would be prohibitively slow in the inner loop of the genetic algorithm or genetic programming. Invulnerability (or near invulnerability) to damage is needed in order to make FPGAs practical for the inner loop of the genetic algorithm or genetic programming.

As will be seen in the next section, the Xilinx XC6200 series of rapidly reconfigurable field-programmable gate arrays addresses the above four issues of

- openness,
- rapid technology mapping, placement, routing, and creation of the configuration bits,
- rapid downloading of configuration bits, and
- invulnerability to damage,

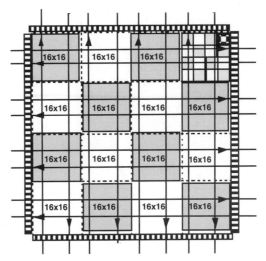

Figure 57.1   Hierarchical view of Xilinx XC6216 field-programmable gate array

thereby opening the possibility of exploiting the massive parallelism of FPGAs in the inner loop of the genetic algorithm and genetic programming.

57.3   XILINX XC6216 FIELD-PROGRAMMABLE GATE ARRAY

The Xilinx XC6216 chip contains a 64×64 two-dimensional array of identical cells (Xilinx 1997). Figure 57.1 shows the hierarchical arrangement of the 4,096 cells on the chip. At the highest level, there is a 4×4 arrangement of regions, with each region containing a total of $16 \times 16 = 256$ individual cells. At the next lower level of the hierarchy, there is a 4×4 arrangement of subregions, with each subregion containing $4 \times 4 = 16$ individual cells.

Figure 57.2 shows additional detail of the lower-left corner of the Xilinx XC6216 chip. This figure shows a 5×5 area containing 25 of the chip's 4,096 cells. An arrow points to one of the 25 cells. It also shows 10 of 256 input-output blocks (IOBs) near the periphery of the chip (at the left and bottom of the figure); some of the long, intermediate, and short interconnection lines that provide connectivity between pairs of cells on the chip; and some of the interconnection lines that provide connectivity between one of the 4,096 cells and one of the input-output blocks. The switch boxes (located in switch blocks) between the chip's fourth and fifth rows and between the chip's fourth and fifth columns are the sites where signals are attached to the various long, intermediate, and short interconnection lines.

The functionality and local routing of each of the chip's 4,096 cells are controlled by 24 configuration bits per cell. Additional configuration bits are used to establish nonlocal interconnections between cells and the functionality of the 256 input-output blocks located on the periphery of the chip. The meaning of all configuration bits is simple, straightforward, and publicly available.

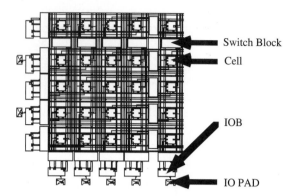

Figure 57.2 Small 5 × 5 corner of Xilinx XC6216 FPGA

Figure 57.3 shows the contents of one of the chip's 4,096 cells. Each cell can directly receive inputs from its four neighbors (as well as certain more distant cells).

Eight configuration bits (two associated with each of the four directions) determine whether the cell's outputs in each of the four directions (N_{out}, E_{out}, W_{out}, S_{out}) is the output F of the cell's function unit or is a "flyover" output consisting of the output of one of the cell's three adjacent neighbors. For example, N_{out} of a cell can be F or the north-going, east-going, or west-going outputs of the cell to the south, west, or east, respectively.

Three configuration bits associated with each of the three inputs (X1, X2, and X3) to the function unit in the center of the figure (i.e., a total of nine configuration bits) determine to which of eight possible sources each of these three inputs is connected. The possible sources include the outputs of the four adjacent cells (N, E, W, and S) and the outputs of four more distant cells (N4, E4, W4, and S4).

Another configuration bit determines which of two inputs (from among X2 and X3) becomes a special ("magic") output of the cell, useful for efficient routing and turning of data lines.

Six configuration bits control the operation of the function unit of each cell. The function unit contains a flip-flop for storing one bit of information and combinatorial logic that is capable of implementing all possible two-argument Boolean functions (as well as many useful three-argument Boolean functions).

Figure 57.4 shows the function unit of one cell of the Xilinx XC6216 FPGA. The function unit has one output (F), three inputs (X1, X2, and X3), as well as clock (Clk) and clear (Clr) inputs. The function unit contains five multiplexers. Boolean logic is performed on the inputs X1, X2, and X3 and flip-flop output $\overline{Q}$, using the three multiplexers on the left half of the figure. Two configuration bits determine whether input X3, the negation of X3, flip-flop output $\overline{Q}$, or the negation of $\overline{Q}$ becomes multiplexer output Y3. Similarly, two additional configuration bits determine whether input X2, the negation of X2, flip-flop output $\overline{Q}$, or the negation of $\overline{Q}$ becomes multiplexer output Y2. In any event, input X1 controls whether Y2 or Y3 becomes the combinatorial logic output **C** of the inverting multiplexer. The configuration bit for the input of multiplexer **CS** determines whether the output F of the function unit is the combinatorial logic output **C** or

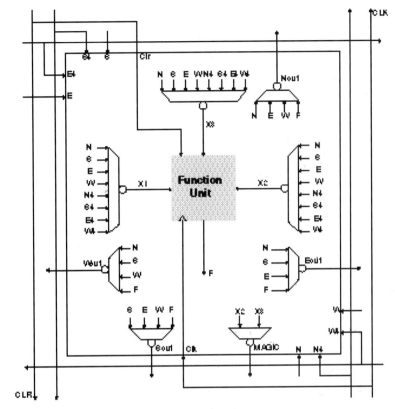

Figure 57.3   One cell of the Xilinx XC6216

the previously stored bit S in the flip-flop. The configuration bit for the input of multi-plexer **RP** determines whether flip-flop input **D** is the negation of combinatorial logic output **C** or flip-flop output $\overline{Q}$.

Unlike other FPGAs available at the time of this writing, the configuration bits of the XC6216 can be randomly accessed, and the memory containing the configuration bits is directly memory-mapped onto the address space of the host processor.

Most importantly, the Xilinx XC6216 FPGA is designed so that no combination of configuration bits for cells can cause internal contention (i.e., conflicting 1 and 0 signals simultaneously driving a destination) and thereby potentially damage the chip. Specifi-cally, it is not possible for two or more signal sources to ever simultaneously drive a rout-ing line or input node of a cell. This is accomplished by obtaining the driving signal for each routing line and each input node from a single multiplexer. Thus, only a single driving signal can be selected regardless of the choice of configuration bits. In contrast, in most other FPGAs, the driving signal is selected by multiple independently program-mable interface points (pips). Nonetheless, care must still be taken with the configura-tion bits that control the XC6216's input-output blocks because an outside signal (with unknown voltage) connected to one of the chip's input pins can potentially get chan-neled onto the chip.

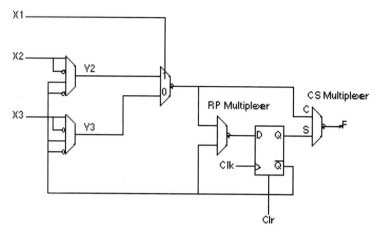

Figure 57.4 Function unit for one cell of the Xilinx XC6216

The work in this chapter was done on a low-cost H.O.T. (Hardware Object Technology) Works expansion board for PC-type computers that is available from Virtual Computer Corporation (*www.vcc.com*). The board contains the Xilinx XC6216 reconfigurable programming unit (RPU), SRAM memory, a programmable oscillator that establishes a suitable clock rate for operating the XC6216, and a PCI interface for the board housed on a Xilinx XC4013E field-programmable gate array. It is interesting to note that Virtual Computer Corporation implemented the board's PCI interface on an FPGA (rather than an ASIC) in order to help bring this product to market rapidly.

57.4 PROBLEMS SUITABLE FOR RAPIDLY RECONFIGURABLE FIELD-PROGRAMMABLE GATE ARRAYS

The Xilinx XC6216 rapidly reconfigurable field-programmable gate array addresses several of the obstacles to using FPGAs for the fitness evaluation task of genetic algorithms.

First, the XC6216 streamlines the task of downloading the configuration bits. The fact that the configuration bits reside in the address space of the host processor accelerates the downloading and also makes it possible to change single configuration bits without downloading any others. Moreover, the downloading of the configuration bits is faster for the Xilinx XC6000 series than almost all other FPGAs because the downloading is done via a memory bus that handles 32 bits simultaneously and that operates at speeds far in excess of those of current serial interfaces. Also, the Xilinx XC6000 series has a wild-card feature that facilitates loading of regular bit patterns.

Second, the encoding scheme for the configuration bits is public. This openness enables us to rapidly generate the configuration bits in our own software.

Third, the encoding scheme for the configuration bits is simple in comparison to most other FPGAs, thereby potentially significantly accelerating the technology mapping, placement, routing, and bit creation tasks. This simplicity is critical because these tasks are so time-consuming as to preclude practical use of conventional FPGAs in the inner loop of a genetic algorithm.

The above positive features of the XC6216 must be considered in light of two important negative factors affecting all FPGAs. First, the clock rate (established by a programmable oscillator) at which an FPGA actually operates is often much slower (typically around 10-fold) than that of contemporary microprocessor chips. Second, the operations that can be performed by the logical function units of an FPGA are extremely primitive in comparison to the 32-bit arithmetic operations that can be performed by contemporary microprocessor chips.

However, the above negative factors may, in turn, be counterbalanced by the fact that the FPGA's logical function units operate in parallel. The existing XC6216 chip has 4,096 cells. Chips of this same 6200 series are forthcoming, at the time of this writing, with four times as many logical function units. A 10-fold slowing of the clock rate can be more than compensated by a 1,000-fold acceleration due to parallelization.

Thus, rapidly reconfigurable field-programmable gate arrays can be highly beneficial for certain types of problems (while useless or counterproductive for others). Effective use of these devices depends on correctly identifying suitable problems.

One indicator of the possible suitability of a problem for FPGAs is the prominence of bit-level operations (or operations that can be conveniently and efficiently recast as bit-level operations). For example, for problems of image processing, pattern recognition, and manipulation of sequential data, a single multiplexer or flip-flop can often perform the same computation that a conventional microprocessor will perform with a 32-bit operation. There are many well-developed techniques for mapping problems that initially appear to be ill suited for FPGAs into the FPGA architecture (Trimberger 1994; Brown, Francis, Rose, and Vranesic 1992; Chan and Mourad 1994; Jenkins 1994; Murgai, Brayton, and Sangiovanni-Vincentelli 1995; Oldfield and Dorf 1995; Moore and Luk 1995; Grunbacher and Hartenstein 1993).

A second indicator of the possible suitability of a problem for FPGAs is the prominence of parallelizable computations. Problems containing a large number of identical parallelizable computations (e.g., cellular automata problems or problems that can be conveniently recast as cellular automata problems) are especially suitable for FPGAs because they can potentially maximize the benefits of the device's fine-grained parallelism.

Problems containing numerous disparate parallelizable computations that must be performed serially in a conventional microprocessor are also suitable for FPGAs. For these problems, the disparate parallelizable computations are housed in different areas of the FPGA.

A third indicator of the possible suitability of a problem for FPGAs is the prominence of computations that can be pipelined. The stages of the pipeline may correspond to different fitness cases or different steps of a simulation or computation. The benefit of pipelining rises proportionately with the number of stages in the pipeline that the FPGA can process simultaneously.

The next sections describe a problem that exploits, in several different ways, the advantages for evolutionary computation of the Xilinx XC6216 rapidly reconfigurable field-programmable gate array.

57.5   STATEMENT OF THE PROBLEM

The goal is to synthesize the design of a minimal sorting network (Section 21.4.1) for sorting seven items.

57.6   PREPARATORY STEPS

57.6.1   Program Architecture

Each program in the population has a uniform architecture consisting of one result-producing branch. Automatically defined functions and architecture-altering operations are not used.

57.6.2   Function and Terminal Sets

The initial terminal set for the result-producing branch, $T_{rpb\text{-}initial}$, for the problem of synthesizing the design of a sorting network for seven items is

$$T_{rpb\text{-}initial} = \{D1, \ . \ . \ . \ , \ D7\}.$$

The initial function set for the result-producing branch, $F_{rpb\text{-}initial}$, is

$$F_{rpb\text{-}initial} = \{COMPARE\text{-}EXCHANGE, \ NOP, \ PROG2, \ PROG3, \ PROG4\}.$$

None of these functions have return values. They operate solely by their side effects on the vector of bits being sorted.

The two-argument COMPARE-EXCHANGE function changes the order of the to-be-sorted bits. The result of executing a (COMPARE-EXCHANGE i j) is that the bit currently in position i of the vector is compared with the bit currently in position j of the vector. If the first bit is greater than the second bit, the two bits are exchanged. That is, the effect of executing a (COMPARE-EXCHANGE i j) is that the two bits are sorted into nondecreasing order.

Table 57.1 shows the two results R_i and R_j produced by executing a (COMPARE-EXCHANGE i j). Note that column R_i is simply the Boolean **AND** function and column R_j is the Boolean **OR** function. Here NOP is the zero-argument "no operation" function.

The PROG2, PROG3, and PROG4 connective functions are versions of the PROGN function that sequentially evaluate their two, three, or four arguments, respectively.

Each individual in the population consists of a constrained syntactic structure composed of primitive functions from the function set, $F_{rpb\text{-}initial}$, and terminals from the terminal set, $T_{rpb\text{-}initial}$, such that the root of each program tree is a PROG2, PROG3, or PROG4; each argument to PROG2, PROG3, and PROG4 must be a NOP or a function from $F_{rpb\text{-}initial}$; and both arguments to every COMPARE-EXCHANGE function must be from $F_{rpb\text{-}initial}$ (but not NOP).

Figure 57.5 shows a program tree produced in accordance with this constrained syntactic structure. This program tree is a minimal five-step sorting network for four items. As can be seen, the sorting network performs the five operations of (COMPARE-EXCHANGE 0 1), (COMPARE-EXCHANGE 2 3), (COMPARE-EXCHANGE 0 2), (COMPARE-EXCHANGE 1 3), and (COMPARE-EXCHANGE 1 2).

Table 57.1 The COMPARE–EXCHANGE function

Two Arguments		Two Results	
A_i	A_j	R_i	R_j
0	0	0	0
0	1	0	1
1	0	0	1
1	1	1	1

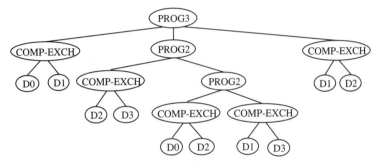

Figure 57.5   Program tree for a minimal sorting network for four items

Since there are no automatically defined functions in this problem, $F_{\text{adf-initial}}$ and $T_{\text{adf-initial}}$ are empty.

Since there are no architecture-altering operations in this problem, $F_{\text{rpb-potential}}$, $T_{\text{rpb-potential}}$, $F_{\text{adf-potential}}$, and $T_{\text{adf-potential}}$ are all empty.

57.6.3   Fitness

The fitness of each individual program in the population is based on the correctness of its sorting of the 2^k fitness cases consisting of all possible vectors of k bits. If, after an individual program is executed on a particular fitness case, all the 1s appear below all the 0s, the program is deemed to have correctly sorted that particular fitness case.

Since the goal is to evolve small (and preferably minimal) sorting networks, exchanges where $i = j$ and exchanges that are identical to the previous exchange are ignored. Moreover, during the depth-first execution of a program tree, only the first C_{max} COMPARE–EXCHANGE functions in a program are actually executed (thereby relegating the remainder of the program to be unused code). C_{max} is set to five more than the currently best known sorting network. Thus, $C_{max} = 65$ for the 16-sorter since Green's 60-step 16-sorter is the currently best known 16-sorter, and $C_{max} = 21$ for the seven-sorter since 16 steps are known to be minimal (Knuth 1973).

The number of hits is defined as the number of fitness cases (0 to 2^k) for which the sort is performed correctly.

The fitness measure for this problem is multiobjective in that it involves both the correctness of the sorting network and its size (i.e., number of steps). Standardized fitness is defined to be 1 plus the number of bits (0 to 7×128) that are incorrectly positioned upon completion of the sort plus 0.01 times the number (1 to C_{max}) of COMPARE-EXCHANGE operations that are actually executed (i.e., excluding those COMPARE-EXCHANGE operations for which $i = j$ or that are identical to the previous exchange). Since we use tournament selection throughout this book, this blended fitness measure operates in a lexical fashion. In particular, an individual that makes fewer mistakes in sorting always has a better (lower) fitness (regardless of its number of COMPARE-EXCHANGE operations) than an individual that makes more mistakes.

57.6.4 Parameters

The control parameters for this problem are shown in the tableau (Table 57.2) and the default values specified in Koza 1994g, Appendix D.

57.6.5 Tableau

Table 57.2 summarizes the key features of the problem of synthesizing the design of a sorting network for seven items using a field-programmable gate array for the fitness evaluation task.

57.7 MAPPING THE FITNESS EVALUATION TASK ONTO THE XILINX XC6216 CHIP

The problem of synthesizing the design of sorting networks was run on a host PC Pentium–type computer with a Virtual Computer Corporation H.O.T. Works PCI board containing a Xilinx XC6216 field-programmable gate array. This combination permits the field-programmable gate array to be advantageously used for the computationally burdensome fitness evaluation task while permitting the general-purpose host computer to perform all the other tasks.

In this arrangement, the host PC begins the run by creating the initial random population (with the XC6216 waiting). Then, for generation 0 (and each succeeding generation), the PC creates the necessary configuration bits to enable the XC6216 to measure the fitness of the first individual program in the population (with the XC6216 waiting). Thereafter, the XC6216 measures the fitness of one individual. Note that the PC can simultaneously prepare the configuration bits for the next individual in the population while the XC6216 is testing the fitness cases. After the fitness of each individual in the current generation of the population is measured, the genetic operations (reproduction, crossover, and mutation) are performed (with the XC6216 waiting). Since the tasks of creating the initial random population and of executing the genetic operations can be performed very rapidly in comparison with the fitness evaluation task, it is acceptable to leave the XC6216 waiting while these tasks are being performed.

The clock rate at which a field-programmable gate array can be run on a problem is considerably slower than that of a contemporary serial microprocessor (e.g., Pentium or PowerPC) that might run a software version of the same problem. Thus, in order to advantageously use the Xilinx XC6216 field-programmable gate array, it is necessary to find a mapping of the fitness evaluation task onto the XC6216 that exploits at least some of the massive parallelism of the 4,096 cells of the XC6216.

Table 57.2 Tableau for sorting network for seven items using field-programmable gate array

Objective	Synthesize the design of a minimal sorting network for sorting seven items using a field-programmable gate array for the fitness evaluation task.
Program architecture	One result-producing branch
Initial function set for the RPBs	$F_{\text{rpb-initial}}$ = {COMPARE-EXCHANGE, NOP, PROG2, PROG3, PROG4}
Initial terminal set for the RPBs	$T_{\text{rpb-initial}}$ = {D1, . . . , D7} for sorting seven items
Initial function set for the ADFs	Automatically defined functions are not used.
Initial terminal set for the ADFs	Automatically defined functions are not used.
Potential function set for the RPBs	Architecture-altering operations are not used.
Potential terminal set for the RPBs	Architecture-altering operations are not used.
Potential function set for the ADFs	Architecture-altering operations are not used.
Potential terminal set for the ADFs	Architecture-altering operations are not used.
Fitness cases	All 128 possible vectors of seven bits
Raw fitness	1 plus the number of bits (0 to 7×2^7) for which the bits are incorrectly positioned after execution of the network plus 0.01 times the number of COMPARE-EXCHANGE functions that are actually executed
Standardized fitness	Same as raw fitness
Hits	The number of COMPARE-EXCHANGE functions that are actually executed
Wrapper	Exchanges where $i = j$ and exchanges that are identical to the previous exchange are ignored. Only the first C_{max} COMPARE-EXCHANGE functions in a program are executed.
Parameters	M = 1,000 (for sorting seven items). G = 501. S_{rpb} = 300. N_{rpb} = 1.
Result designation	Best-so-far pace-setting individual
Success predicate	Fitness reaches 1.16.

Figure 57.6 shows our placement of eight major computational elements (labeled A through H) on 32 horizontal rows and 64 vertical columns of the XC6216 chip. Broadly, fitness cases are created in area B, are sorted in areas C, D, and E, and are evaluated in F and G. The figure does not show the ring of input-output blocks on the periphery of the

chip that surround the 64×64 area of cells or the physical input-output pins that connect the chip to the outside. The figure also does not reflect the fact that two such 32×64 areas operate in parallel on the same chip.

For a k-sorter ($k \leq 16$), a 16-bit counter **B** (near the upper-left corner of the chip in Figure 57.6) counts down from $2^k - 2$ to 0 under control of control logic **A** (upper-left corner). The vector of k bits resident in counter **B** on a given time step represents one fitness case of the sorting network problem. The vector of bits from counter **B** is fed into the first (leftmost) 16×1 vertical column of cells of the large 16×40 area **C**.

Each 16×1 vertical column of cells in **C** (and each cell in the similar area **E** in Figure 57.6) corresponds to one COMPARE–EXCHANGE operation of an individual candidate sorting network. The vector of 16 bits produced by the 40th (rightmost) sorting step of area **C** then proceeds to area **D**.

Area **D** is a U-turn area that channels the vector of 16 bits from the rightmost column of area **C** into the first (rightmost) column of the large 16×40 area **E**.

The final output from area **E** in Figure 57.6 is checked by answer logic **F** for whether the individual candidate sorting network has correctly rearranged the original incoming vector of bits so that all the 0s are above all the 1s. The 16-bit accumulator **G** is incremented by one if the bits are correctly sorted. Note that the 16 bits of accumulator **G** are sufficient for tallying the number of correctly sorted fitness cases because the host computer starts counter **B** at $2^k - 2$, thereby skipping the uninteresting fitness case consisting of all 1s (which cannot be incorrectly sorted by any network). The final value of raw fitness is reported in 16-bit register **H** after all the $2^k - 2$ fitness cases have been processed.

The logical function units and interconnection resources of areas **A**, **B**, **D**, **F**, **G**, and **H** of Figure 57.6 are permanently configured to handle the sorting network problem for all $k \leq 16$.

The two large areas, **C** and **E**, together represent the individual candidate sorting network. The configuration of the logical function units and interconnection resources of the 1,280 cells in areas **C** and **E** become personalized to the current individual candidate sorting network.

For area **C** in Figure 57.6, each cell in a 16×1 vertical column is configured in one of three main ways. First, the logical function unit of exactly one of the 16 cells is configured as a two-argument Boolean **AND** function (corresponding to result R_i of Table 57.1). Second, the logical function unit of exactly one other cell is configured as a two-argument Boolean **OR** function (corresponding to result R_j of Table 57.1). Bits i and j become sorted into the correct order by virtue of the fact that the single **AND** cell in each 16×1 vertical column always appears above the single **OR** cell. Third, the logical function units of 14 of the 16 cells are configured as "passthrough" cells that horizontally pass their input from one vertical column to the next.

For area **E** in Figure 57.6, each cell in a 16×1 vertical column is configured in one of three similar main ways.

There are four subtypes each of **AND** and **OR** cells and four types of passthrough cells. Half of these subtypes are required because all the cells in area **E** differ in chirality (handedness) from those in area **C** in that they receive their input from their right and deliver output to their left.

If the sorting network has fewer than 80 COMPARE–EXCHANGE operations, the last vertical columns of area **E** each contain 16 passthrough cells. Note that the genetic oper-

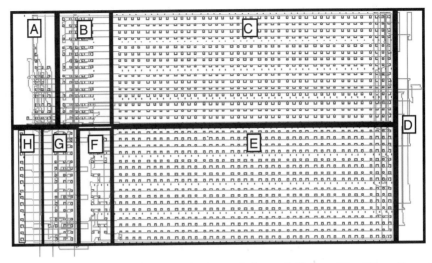

Figure 57.6 **Arrangement of major elements A through H on a 32 × 64 portion of the Xilinx XC6216 chip**

ations are constrained so as to not produce networks with more than 80 steps and, as previously mentioned, only the first $C_{max} < 80$ steps are actually executed.

Within each cell of areas **C** and **E** of Figure 57.6, the one-bit output of the cell's logical function unit is stored in a flip-flop. The contents of the 16 flip-flops in one vertical column become the inputs to the next vertical column on the next time step.

The overall arrangement of Figure 57.6 operates as an 87-stage pipeline (the 80 stages of areas **C** and **E**, the 3 stages of answer logic **F**, and 4 stages of padding at both ends of **C** and **E**).

Figure 57.7 shows six cells of an illustrative vertical column from area **C** whose purpose is to implement a (COMPARE-EXCHANGE 2 5) operation. The cells in this figure are numbered from 1 to 6 from the top to the bottom of the figure. As can be seen, cell 2 is configured as a two-argument Boolean **AND** function (indicated by an × in the figure), and cell 5 is configured as a two-argument **OR** function (indicated by a + in the figure). All the remaining cells of the vertical column (of which only four are shown in this abbreviated figure) are passthrough cells (indicated by a triangle in the figure). These passthrough cells horizontally convey the bit in the previous vertical column to the next vertical column. Every cell in the Xilinx XC6216 has the additional capacity of being able to convey one signal in each direction as a flyover signal that plays no role in the cell's own computation. Thus, each of the two "intervening" passthrough cells (3 and 4) that lie between the **AND** and **OR** cells (1 and 5) is configured so that it conveys one signal vertically upwards and one signal vertically downwards as flyover signals. These flyovers of the two intervening cells (3 and 4) enable cell 2's input to be shared with cell 5 and cell 5's input to be shared with cell 2. Specifically, the input coming into cell 2 horizontally from the previous vertical column (i.e., from the left in the figure) is bifurcated so that it feeds both the two-argument **AND** in cell 2 and the two-argument **OR** in cell 5 (and similarly for the input coming into cell 5).

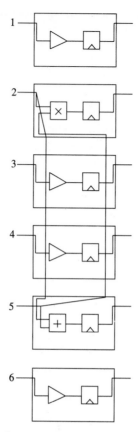

Figure 57.7 Implementation of (COMPARE–EXCHANGE 2 5)

Notice that when a 1 is received from the previous vertical column on horizontal row 2 of Figure 57.7 and a 0 is received on horizontal row 5 (i.e., the two bits are out of order), the **AND** of cell 2 and the **OR** of cell 5 cause a 0 to be emitted as output on horizontal row 2 and a 1 to be emitted as output on horizontal row 5 (i.e., the two bits have become sorted into the correct order).

The remaining passthrough cells (i.e., cells 1 and 6 in Figure 57.7 and cells 7 through 16 in the full 1×16 vertical column of Figure 57.6) are of a subtype that is not configured with the vertical flyovers of the intervening cells (3 and 4). The design of this subtype prevents possible reading of signals (of unknown voltage) from the input-output blocks that surround the main 64×64 area of the chip. All **AND** and **OR** cells are similarly designed since they necessarily sometimes occur at the top or bottom of a vertical column.

The intervening passthrough cells (cells 3 and 4 of Figure 57.7) invert their flyover signals. Thus, if there is an odd number of passthrough cells intervening vertically between the **AND** cells and **OR** cells, the signals being conveyed upwards and downwards in a vertical column will arrive at their destinations in inverted form. Accordingly, special subtypes of the **AND** cells and **OR** cells reinvert (and thereby correct) such arriving signals.

Answer logic F determines whether the 16 bits coming from the 80th column of the pipeline (from the left end of area E of Figure 57.6) are properly sorted—that is, the bits are of the form 0^j1^{16-j}.

When the XC6216 begins operation for a particular individual sorting network, all the 16×80 flip-flops in C and E of Figure 57.6 (as well as the flip-flops in three-stage answer logic F, the four insulative stages, and the "done bit" flip-flop) are initialized to 0. Thus, the first 87 output vectors received by answer logic F each consist of 16 0s. Since answer logic F treats a vector of 16 0s as incorrect, accumulator G is not incremented for these first 87 vectors.

A "past zero" flip-flop is set when counter B counts down to 0 in Figure 57.6. As B continues counting, it rolls over to $2^{16} - 1 = 65,535$ and continues counting down. When counter B reaches $2^{16} - 87$ (with the "past zero" flip-flop being set), control logic A stops further incrementation of accumulator G. The raw fitness from G appears in reporting register H, and the "done bit" flip-flop is set to 1. The host computer polls this "done bit" to determine that the XC6216 has completed its fitness evaluation task for the current individual.

The flip-flop toggle rate of the XC6216 chip is 220 MHz (i.e., about the same as a contemporary Pentium or PowerPC microprocessor device). The flip-flop toggle rate of the chip is an upper bound on the speed at which a field-programmable gate array can be run. In practice, the speed at which an FPGA can be run is governed by the longest routing delay. It is common to see a 10-to-1 reduction in clock rate in FPGAs because of routing delays. Indeed, the current (unoptimized) version of the FPGA design for the sorting network problem is run at 20 MHz.

The above approach exploits the massive parallelism of the XC6216 chip in six different ways:

1. The tasks performed by areas A, B, C, D, E, F, G, and H of Figure 57.6 are examples of performing disparate tasks in parallel in physically different areas of the FPGA.

2. The two separate 32×64 areas operating in parallel on the chip are an example (at a higher level) of performing identical tasks in parallel in physically different areas of the FPGA.

3. The XC6216 evaluates the 2^k fitness cases independently of the activity of the host PC Pentium–type computer (which simultaneously can prepare the next individual(s) for the XC6216). This is an example (at the highest level) of performing disparate tasks in parallel.

4. The Boolean AND functions and OR functions of each COMPARE–EXCHANGE operation are performed in parallel (in each of the vertical columns of areas C and E of Figure 57.6). This is an example of recasting a key operation (i.e., the COMPARE–EXCHANGE operation) as a bit-level operation so that the FPGA can be advantageously used. It is also an example of performing two disparate operations (AND and OR) in parallel in physically different areas of the FPGA (i.e., different locations in the vertical columns of areas C and E).

5. Numerous operations are performed in parallel inside control logic A, counter B, answer logic F, accumulator G, and reporting register H. The parallelization inside answer logic F is especially advantageous because numerous sequential

steps are required on a conventional serial microprocessor to determine whether k bits are properly sorted. Answer logic F is an example of a multistep task that is both successfully parallelized and pipelined on the FPGA.

6. Most importantly, the 87-step pipeline (80 steps for areas C and E and 7 steps for answer logic F and accumulator G of Figure 57.6) enables 87 fitness cases to be processed in parallel in the pipeline.

A comparison of the speed of executing this problem in reconfigurable hardware versus software depends on several factors. First, the outcome of the comparison depends on the nature of the task being performed in each different area of the chip. Software can be very efficient when a machine code instruction operating on multibit binary numbers exists to perform the required task. Second, the outcome depends on the amount of time and effort that a programmer is willing to expend in implementing the problem in software. A clever programmer (perhaps exploiting certain assembly code instructions for manipulating bits) might be able to write code that performs certain tasks faster than the code that a typical programmer might write. Third, the outcome also depends on the clock rate of the reconfigurable chip versus the clock rate of the particular computer on which the software would be run (say, 10 times faster).

Counter B of Figure 57.6 is a 16-bit binary counter for which all 16 bits are separately addressable and available. In one clock cycle, counter B can be decremented with all 16 new bits being immediately available as separate bits. One way to implement this same functionality in software is to decrement a designated 16-bit variable by one and to then execute a series of 16 divisions to convert the resulting 16-bit variable into 16 separate variables (each 0 or 1). With a little more thought and effort, the divisions could be avoided by extracting the 16 separate bits using 16 masks. This approach requires a constant amount of time. A second implementation (variable-time) involves maintaining a vector of 16 separate variables and simulating the subtraction of one (with borrowing and cascades of borrowing, as necessary). In any event, the number of clock cycles required for the software implementation would be so large as to give the advantage to the reconfigurable chip. This conclusion appears correct for the way a typical programmer would probably approach this task; however, a clever programmer might reverse this conclusion.

In areas C and E of Figure 57.6, the execution of the **AND** and **OR** functions (shown in Figure 57.7) in any one vertical column of the chip occurs in parallel in one clock cycle. In software, the two variables would be fetched and the two Boolean operations would then be performed. The software implementation requires more than one clock cycle, but it is faster for any one vertical column because the clock rate for the computer on which the software will be run is considerably faster than that of the reconfigurable chip. However, when the pipelining of all 80 vertical columns is considered, the advantage ends up with the reconfigurable architecture.

Answer logic F of Figure 57.6 is implemented in a three-stage pipeline. One way (constant-time) to implement this same functionality in software is to loop through the 16 variables and verify that the sequence of 16 variables never switched from 1 to 0 and switched from 0 to 1 at most one time. A second way is to convert the 16 separate variables to a 16-bit binary number and compare it to the 17 correct configurations (i.e., those of the form $0^j 1^{16-j}$). In any event, the number of clock cycles required for the software implementation by a typical programmer would be so large as to give the advantage to the reconfigurable chip.

Accumulator **G** of Figure 57.6 is incremented by one for each fitness case that is correctly sorted.

The Xilinx XC6216 field-programmable gate array can evaluate all 2^{16} fitness cases for a 16-sorter in 3.28 milliseconds. In contrast, a 90 MHz Pentium executing an assembly code implementation of a sorting network takes 153 milliseconds to evaluate the 2^{16} fitness cases. This is a speedup of better than 46-to-1. This speedup occurs in spite of the fact that the Pentium computer operates at 15 times the clock rate at which the FPGA operates for this problem.

57.8   RESULTS

57.8.1   Evolved Seven-Sorter

The design of a 16-step seven-sorter (Figure 57.8) was evolved in 69 minutes on the FPGA. The evolved sorting network has two fewer steps than the sorting network described in the 1962 O'Connor and Nelson patent on sorting networks. The evolved seven-sorter has the same number of steps as the seven-sorter devised by Floyd and Knuth subsequent to the patent and that has been proven to be minimal (Knuth 1973). The evolved sorter was produced on generation 31.

The rediscovery by genetic programming of a sorting network for seven items with only 16 steps has already been claimed (in Chapter 21 involving GPPS 1.0) as an instance where genetic programming has produced a result that is competitive with that produced by creative and inventive humans. This problem was also solved in Chapter 23 using GPPS 2.0.

57.8.2   Evolved Eight-Sorter

Using a population size of $M = 60,000$, a 19-step eight-sorter (Figure 57.9) was evolved on generation 58. This sorter is known to be minimal (Knuth 1973).

57.8.3   Evolved Nine-Sorter

Using a population size of $M = 100,000$, a 25-step nine-sorter (Figure 57.10) was evolved on generation 105. This sorter is known to be minimal (Knuth 1973).

57.9   EVOLUTIONARY INCREMENTALISM VERSUS DEFAULT HIERARCHIES

A *default hierarchy* is a set of problem-solving rules in which one or possibly more *default rules* satisfactorily handle the vast majority of instances of a problem, while a set of *exception-handling rules* makes the corrections necessary to satisfactorily handle the remaining instances. A familiar example of a default hierarchy is the spelling rule "*i* before *e*, except after *c*." An example of a more complex default hierarchy is the rule that states that a year divisible by four is a leap year, except a year divisible by 100 is not a leap year; however, a year that is divisible by 400 is a leap year. It has been observed that

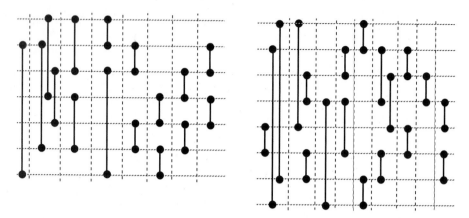

Figure 57.8 Evolved seven-sorter with two fewer steps than the 1962 O'Connor and Nelson seven-sorter

Figure 57.9 Evolved 19-step eight-sorter

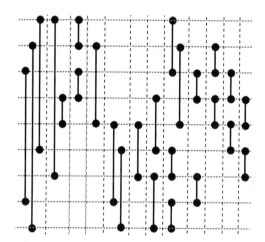

Figure 57.10 Evolved 25-step nine-sorter

human problem solving often employs the style of default hierarchies (Holland 1986, 1987; Holland, Holyoak, Nisbett, and Thagard 1986).

57.9.1 Evolved Seven-Sorter

Figure 57.11 shows the percentage of the $2^k = 128$ fitness cases that become correctly sorted on each of the 16 steps of the evolved minimal sorting network for seven items (Figure 57.8). Once the k bits of any one of the 2^k fitness cases are arranged into the correct order, no COMPARE–EXCHANGE operation occurring later in the sorting network can change the ordering of the k bits for that fitness case. Thus, the percentage of fitness cases that are correctly sorted is a nondecreasing function of the number of executed steps of the network. As can be seen, the graph is approximately linear. That is, the number of fitness cases that become correctly sorted after each time step is approximately equal for each of the 16 steps. The largest single increase is 15 (about twice the average of 8 fitness cases per step).

The graphs for all three of the other evolved 16-step seven-sorters are similar, approximately linear progressions. That is, each step of all four evolved seven-sorters makes steady incremental progress toward the goal of correctly sorting the given items.

Figure 57.12 shows the change in percentage of the fitness cases that become correctly sorted on each of its 16 steps of the evolved minimal sorting network for seven items (Figure 57.8).

Figure 57.13 shows the percentage of the fitness cases that are correctly sorted after deletion of single step *i* from the evolved minimal 16-step seven-sorter (Figure 57.8). Admittedly, the steps of a sorting network are intended to be executed in consecutive order. Nonetheless, the deletion of single steps gives a rough indication of the importance of each step. As can be seen, the degradation caused by most single deletions is relatively small. The graphs of the effect of single deletions for all three of the other evolved minimal 16-step seven-sorters are similar to Figure 57.13.

57.9.2 Evolved Eight-Sorter

Figure 57.14 shows the percentage of the $2^k = 256$ fitness cases that become correctly sorted on each of the 19 steps of the evolved minimal eight-sorter (Figure 57.9). Each step of the evolved eight-sorter makes steady incremental progress toward the goal of correctly sorting the given items.

Figure 57.15 shows the change in percentage of the fitness cases that become correctly sorted on each of the 19 steps of the evolved minimal sorting network for eight items (Figure 57.9).

Figure 57.16 shows the percentage of the fitness cases that are correctly sorted after deletion of single step *i* from the evolved minimal 19-step eight-sorter (Figure 57.9).

57.9.3 Evolved Nine-Sorter

Figure 57.17 shows the percentage of the $2^k = 512$ fitness cases that become correctly sorted on each of the 25 steps of the evolved minimal nine-sorter (Figure 57.10). Each step of the evolved nine-sorter makes steady incremental progress toward the goal of correctly sorting the given items. The largest single increase is 50 at step 21 (about two and a half times the average of 20.5 fitness cases per step).

Figure 57.18 shows the change in percentage of the fitness cases that become correctly sorted on each of the 25 steps of the evolved minimal sorting network for nine items (Figure 57.10).

Figure 57.19 shows the percentage of the fitness cases that are correctly sorted after deletion of single step *i* from the evolved minimal 25-step nine-sorter (Figure 57.10).

57.9.4 Human-Written Nine-Sorter

Figure 57.20 shows the percentage of the $2^k = 512$ fitness cases that become correctly sorted on each of the 25 steps of a human-designed nine-sorter presented in Knuth 1973 (which does not show a minimal seven-sorter). As can be seen, most steps of the sorting network satisfactorily dispose of relatively few of the fitness cases; however, one step disposes of 42% of the fitness cases (216 out of 512).

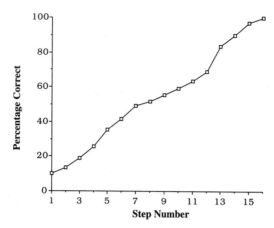

Figure 57.11 **Percentage of correctly sorted fitness cases after each step for evolved minimal seven-sorter**

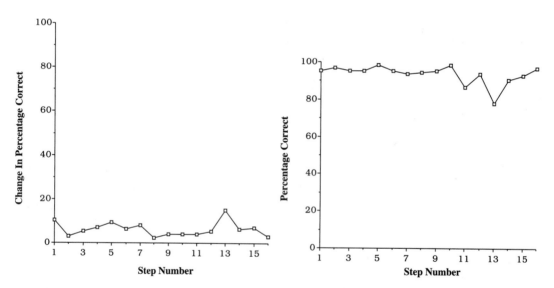

Figure 57.12 **Percentage change in correctly sorted fitness cases after each step for evolved minimal seven-sorter**

Figure 57.13 **Percentage of fitness cases that remain correctly sorted upon deletion of particular single steps from the evolved minimal seven-sorter**

Figure 57.21 shows the change in percentage of the fitness cases that become correctly sorted on each of the 25 steps of the human-designed 25-step nine-sorter.

The graphs for several other human-designed minimal sorting networks display a similar highly nonlinear progression. For example, Juille (1995) observed that Green's 60-step 16-sorter correctly arranges most of the 65,536 fitness cases in its first 32 steps. The second half of the network is spent on fixing up a relatively few exceptions. The first

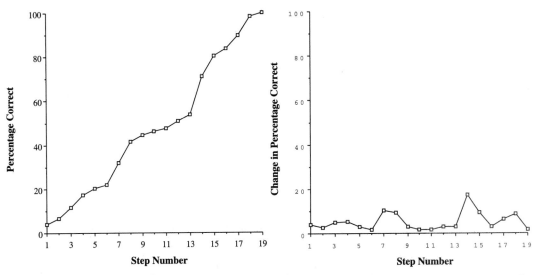

Figure 57.14   **Percentage of correctly sorted fitness cases after each step for the evolved minimal eight-sorter**

Figure 57.15   **Percentage change in correctly sorted fitness cases after each step for the evolved minimal eight-sorter**

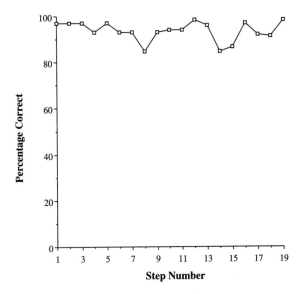

Figure 57.16   **Percentage of fitness cases that remain correctly sorted upon deletion of particular single steps from the evolved minimal eight-sorter**

32 steps of Green's front-loaded 60-step 16-sorter can be viewed as a default rule, while the last half can be viewed as exception handling.

Figure 57.22 shows the percentage of the 2^k fitness cases that are correctly sorted after deletion of single step i from the human-designed nine-sorter in Knuth 1973. As can be

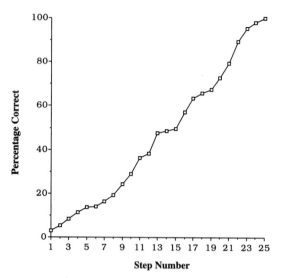

Figure 57.17 Percentage of correctly sorted fitness cases after each step for the evolved minimal nine-sorter

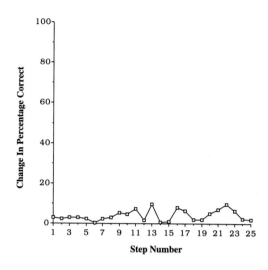

Figure 57.18 Percentage change in correctly sorted fitness cases after each step for evolved inimal nine-sorter

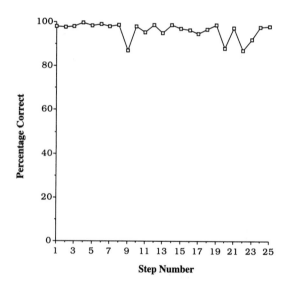

Figure 57.19 Percentage of fitness cases that remain correctly sorted upon deletion of particular single steps from the evolved minimal nine-sorter

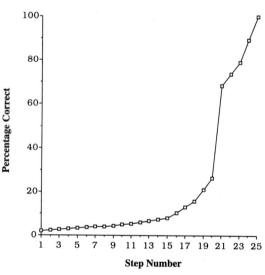

Figure 57.20 Percentage of correctly sorted fitness cases after each step for human-designed nine-sorter

seen, many of the single deletions cause comparatively greater degradation than those of Figure 57.19 (which shows the percentage of the fitness cases that are correctly sorted after deletion of single step *i* from the evolved minimal 25-step nine-sorter of Figure

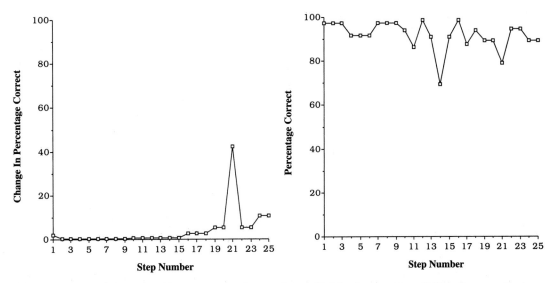

Figure 57.21   Percentage change in correctly sorted fitness cases after each step for the human-designed 25-step nine-sorter

Figure 57.22   Percentage of fitness cases that remain correctly sorted upon deletion of single steps for human-designed nine-sorter

57.10). The graphs for several other human-designed minimal sorting networks similarly displayed relatively large degradation caused by single deletions.

Although the above observations are admittedly limited to specific instances of one particular problem, they raise the interesting question of whether there is a general tendency of evolved solutions to problems to exhibit steady incrementalism, while human-written solutions for the same problem tend to employ the style of default hierarchies.

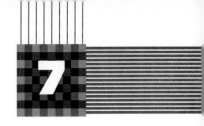

Part 7:
DISCOVERY OF CELLULAR AUTOMATA RULES

This part describes how genetic programming evolved a cellular automata rule that performs better than a succession of human-written algorithms developed over the past two decades for the vexatious majority classification problem for one-dimensional, two-state, radius-three cellular automata.

Discovery of a Cellular Automata Rule for the Majority Classification Problem

Massively parallel computing devices are seemingly very attractive for solving problems. However, it is generally difficult to write programs for such machines. Cellular automata are one type of parallel computing device that is especially difficult to program. Since each individual automaton in the cellular space can communicate with only a limited local group of neighbors, the difficulty of writing programs for cellular automata is compounded when the desired computation inherently requires global integration of information that is distributed over the cellular space.

In the past two decades, various human-written algorithms have appeared for the majority classification problem for one-dimensional two-state cellular automata. This chapter describes how genetic programming evolved a rule in 1995 for this task with an accuracy of 82.326%. This level of accuracy exceeds that of the original 1978 Gacs-Kurdyumov-Levin (GKL) rule, all known subsequent human-written rules, and all known rules produced by automated methods. As will be seen, the rule evolved by genetic programming is qualitatively different from all previous rules in that it employs a larger and more intricate repertoire of space-time structures to communicate information in the cellular space.

Section 58.1 provides background on cellular automata. Section 58.2 describes the majority classification task and previous work. Section 58.3 details the preparatory steps required to apply genetic programming to the problem. Section 58.4 examines the results of our most successful run using genetic programming. Section 58.4.1 examines the intricate communication patterns employed by the best rule evolved by genetic programming.

58.1 CELLULAR AUTOMATA

Local rules govern the interactions of many animate and inanimate entities. It has been frequently observed that the simultaneous execution of a single relatively simple rule at multiple local sites leads to the emergence of interesting and complex global behavior

(Langton 1989). This global behavior is especially interesting when entities have access only to information about their immediate local environment, but need to engage in both long-distance communication of information and long-distance integration of information in order to perform the required task.

Cellular automata (CA) are an abstract way of studying and analyzing the simultaneous execution of local rules (Burks 1970; Farmer, Toffoli, and Wolfram 1983; Wolfram 1986; Gutowitz 1991; Wuensche and Lesser 1992; Sipper 1997a, 1997b).

A cellular space is a uniform array of cells arranged in a certain topological arrangement in a certain number of dimensions. Each cell in a cellular space is occupied by an identical automaton (each with its own current state). The next state of each individual automaton in the cellular space depends on its own current state and on the current states of the other automata in a specified local neighborhood around the individual automaton. The state of each automaton at time 0 is called its *initial condition*.

The best-known cellular automata system is John Conway's game of Life (Berlekamp, Conway, and Guy 1985). It involves a two-dimensional arrangement of identical two-state automata. In the game of Life, the next state of each automaton depends on its current state and on the states of its eight immediately adjacent neighbors in the two-dimensional cellular space. Certain patterns (such as gliders and blinkers) reproduce themselves in different locations in the space over time.

In a one-dimensional cellular automata system, the cellular space is a linear arrangement of identical automata. The next state of each individual automaton in the cellular space depends on the current state of that automaton and the current states of its neighbors at a particular specified distance. For example, if the distance is three, the states of seven automata determine the next state of the given automaton. The seven automata involved are conventionally called X (for the automaton at the center of the group of seven), W (the adjacent automaton to the left), E (the adjacent automaton to the right), WW (the automaton at distance 2 to the west), EE (the automaton at distance 2 to the east), WWW, and EEE. A cellular space is said to have *periodic boundary conditions* when the cellular space is toroidal. If the automaton located in each cell has only two states, the state transition function of the automaton is a Boolean function of its own current state and the states of the specified neighbors. The behavior of a two-state cellular automata system operating at distance three is specified by a state transition table that maps the $2^7 = 128$ combinations of seven binary inputs into a single bit representing the next state of the cell at the center of the group of seven cells.

Figure 58.1 shows a one-dimensional cellular automata system composed of 12 two-state automata. The next state of automaton X is determined by the previous states of X, W, WW, WWW, E, EE, and EEE. Specifically, the current states of the seven automata that participate in the creation of the new state for automaton X are 1, 0, 1, 0, 1, 0, and 1 in the figure. The two 0s at the far left and the three 0s at the far right do not participate. If the transition rule happened to be the Boolean seven-argument majority function, then the next state of automaton X would be 1.

Cellular automata are dynamical systems that are discrete in time, in space (the cells), and in site value (the states). Cellular automata are the discrete counterparts of continuous dynamical systems defined by partial differential equations and the physicist's concept of field (Toffoli and Margolus 1987). Simulations of fluid flow and other complex processes that depend only on local states are well suited to cellular automata.

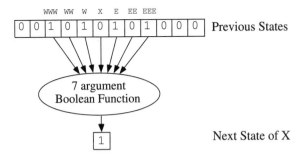

Figure 58.1   One-dimensional cellular automata system composed of two-state automata that receive their input from a distance of three

It is extremely difficult, in general, to design a single state transition rule that, when it operates in each cell of the cellular space, produces a desired global behavior.

Genetic algorithms operating on fixed-length character strings have been previously used to evolve the initial conditions and state transition rules for cellular automata (Packard 1990; Meyer, Richards, and Packard 1991).

Evolvable hardware employing genetic algorithms has been used to solve various cellular automata problems (Sipper 1997a, 1997b; Sipper et al. 1997).

Genetic programming has been previously used for the discovery of cellular automata rules (Koza 1992e, Chapter 14; Koza and Rice 1992e).

58.2   THE MAJORITY CLASSIFICATION PROBLEM

The majority classification problem presents the issue of how complex calculations can be performed over large expanses of time and space using rules of interaction that operate over a comparatively small distance.

In one frequently studied version of this vexatious problem, there is a one-dimensional linear arrangement of 149 two-state automata whose update rule uses only information within a distance of three from a given location. The same state transition rule appears in all 149 locations. The 149 locations differ only in their current states (0 or 1). The initial states of all 149 automata (called the *initial configuration*) are viewed as the inputs to a calculation. If all 149 automata relax to a common state (0 or 1) after the system operates for a certain number of time steps, the automata is said to have *converged*. The common state (0 or 1) to which all 149 locations have converged is considered to be the answer produced by the calculation. For the majority classification task, convergence to 149 0s is considered correct if a majority of the 149 bits of the initial configuration are 0; convergence to 149 1s is considered correct if a majority of the bits of the initial configuration are 1. Thus, the goal in this problem is to find a seven-argument Boolean transition rule such that, when it is situated at all 149 cells of a one-dimensional cellular automata system, the automata converge to the correct configuration of 149 0s or 149 1s after some maximum allowed amount of time (say, 600 time steps). The fitness of a rule for this task is measured by its ability to correctly classify any of the 2^{149} possible initial configurations.

It is difficult to construct a two-state seven-neighborhood cellular automata rule that performs this majority classification task on a 149-bit input configuration. Seven bits cannot store an integer as large as 149 (if, for example, we contemplated storing and transmitting a signal reporting a locally observed surplus or deficit of 0s). A large percentage of the 2^{149} possible initial configurations have approximately equal numbers of 0s and 1s. It is known that a perfect solution to this problem does not exist (Land and Belew 1995a). It is interesting to note that a two-state cellular automata system can perfectly solve an altered version of the problem (Capcarrere, Sipper, and Tomassini 1996).

The difficulty of this problem is illustrated by the long history of attempts by human programmers to write good rules for it. In 1978, Gacs, Kurdyumov, and Levin (1978) developed a two-state seven-neighbor rule in connection with their study of reliable computation under random perturbations (Gacs 1983, 1986). This Gacs-Kurdyumov-Levin (GKL) rule performs the majority classification task reasonably well. The GKL rule is successful on 81.6% of the possible initial configurations. Gonzaga de Sa and Maes (1992) proved that this rule does indeed relax to a common state.

The majority classification task has been the subject of extensive study (Mitchell, Hraber, and Crutchfield 1993; Das, Mitchell, and Crutchfield 1994; Mitchell, Crutchfield, and Hraber 1994; Crutchfield and Mitchell 1995; Das, Crutchfield, Mitchell, and Hanson 1995; Mitchell 1996). Sipper (1997a, 1997b) has studied this problem using evolvable hardware. In addition, many variations of this problem have been studied (e.g., using nonuniform cellular automata in Sipper 1996 and Sipper and Rippin 1997).

In 1993, Lawrence Davis (1995) cleverly modified the GKL rule and created a rule that achieved an accuracy of about 81.8%.

Rajarshi Das (1995) created another clever rule that achieved 82.178% accuracy—slightly better than the GKL rule and the Davis rule.

Table 58.1 shows the GKL rule, the Davis rule, the Das rule, and the rule evolved by genetic programming described in this chapter. The 128 bits are presented in the natural order that they would appear in a state transition table starting with state 0000000 and ending at state 1111111 (i.e., 0 to 127).

Das, Mitchell, and Crutchfield (1994) evolved rules using a version of the genetic algorithm operating on fixed-length strings. These rules sometimes exhibited some of the same qualitative behaviors as the GKL rule. However, quantitatively, none of the rules evolved using the genetic algorithm operating on fixed-length strings even approached the accuracy of the original GKL rule. Most of the runs using the genetic algorithm found only relatively uninteresting block-expanding rules with 65% to 70% accuracy. The best result from a very substantial number of runs using the genetic algorithm had an accuracy of only 76.9%.

Land and Belew (1995b) suggested that evolution may actually be hindered by the standard representation of the cellular automata rule as a chromosome string of length 128 used in previous work using the genetic algorithm. They suggest that higher-level representations (such as condition-action pairs) may aid the evolutionary process because of the higher degree of locality in the condition-action pairs. Given Land and Belew's view, the tree representation employed by genetic programming seems well suited for this task. The size and shape of the ultimate solution is free to undergo evolution in genetic programming. Genetic programming supports automatically defined functions, whereas the conventional genetic algorithm operating on fixed-length strings does not have a similar facility for exploiting modularities, symmetries, and regularity of the problem environment.

Table 58.1 Various cellular automata rules for the majority classification task

Rule	State transitions
GKL rule—human-written (Gacs, Kurdyumov, and Levin 1978)	00000000 01011111 00000000 01011111 00000000 01011111 00000000 01011111 00000000 01011111 11111111 01011111 00000000 01011111 11111111 01011111
Davis rule—human-written (Davis 1995)	00000000 00101111 00000011 01011111 00000000 00011111 11001111 00011111 00000000 00101111 11111100 01011111 00000000 00011111 11111111 00011111
Das rule—human-written (Das 1995)	00000111 00000000 00000111 11111111 00001111 00000000 00001111 11111111 00001111 00000000 00000111 11111111 00001111 00110001 00001111 11111111
Best rule evolved by genetic programming (described in this chapter)	00000101 00000000 01010101 00000101 00000101 00000000 01010101 00000101 01010101 11111111 01010101 11111111 01010101 11111111 01010101 11111111

Although this problem involves discovering a single seven-argument Boolean function, this problem is not a mere problem of symbolic regression of a Boolean function in which the 2^7 fitness cases (i.e., the 2^7 lines in the truth table) are independent. Such problems can be solved by many search techniques, including simple hill climbing (Juels and Wattenberg 1994). Such problems can also be trivially and mechanically solved by merely stepping through the 2^7 fitness cases, toggling the Boolean answer for each fitness case, and choosing the Boolean answer for the just-toggled fitness case that improves the fitness measure. However, this approach cannot be used when a Boolean function is embedded in multiple cells of a cellular automata system so that the same Boolean function is simultaneously executed in a multiplicity of intercommunicating locations.

58.3 PREPARATORY STEPS

58.3.1 Program Architecture

Each program in the population has a uniform architecture consisting of one result-producing branch, one two-argument automatically defined function (ADF0), and one three-argument automatically defined function (ADF1). ADF1 can refer hierarchically to ADF0. Automatically defined functions and architecture-altering operations are not used.

58.3.2 Function and Terminal Sets

The initial terminal set for the result-producing branch, $T_{rpb\text{-}initial}$, is

$$T_{rpb\text{-}initial} = \{X, E, EE, EEE, W, WW, WWW\}.$$

The initial function set for the result-producing branch, $F_{rpb\text{-}initial}$, is

$$F_{rpb\text{-}initial} = \{AND, OR, NAND, NOR, NOT, IF, XOR, ADF0, ADF1\}.$$

Note that the IF function here need not be implemented as a macro (as described in Section 13.3.2) since none of the other functions in this problem have side effects.

The initial terminal set for the first automatically defined function (ADF0), $T_{\text{adf0-initial}}$, is

$$T_{\text{adf0-initial}} = \{\text{ARG0, ARG1, X, E, EE, EEE, W, WW, WWW}\}.$$

Because the second automatically defined function (ADF1) has three arguments, the initial terminal set for the second automatically defined function, $T_{\text{adf1-initial}}$, is

$$T_{\text{adf1-initial}} = T_{\text{adf0-initial}} \cup \{\text{ARG2}\}.$$

The initial function set for the first automatically defined function (ADF0), $F_{\text{adf0-initial}}$, is

$$F_{\text{adf0-initial}} = \{\text{AND, OR, NAND, NOR, NOT, IF, XOR}\}.$$

Because the second automatically defined function (ADF1) can refer hierarchically to the first automatically defined function (ADF0), the initial function set for the second automatically defined function, $F_{\text{adf1-initial}}$, is

$$F_{\text{adf1-initial}} = F_{\text{adf0-initial}} \cup \{\text{ADF0}\}.$$

Since there are no architecture-altering operations in this problem, $F_{\text{rpb-potential}}$, $T_{\text{rpb-potential}}$, $F_{\text{adf-potential}}$, and $T_{\text{adf-potential}}$ are all empty.

58.3.3 Fitness

The in-sample fitness cases consist of 1,000 randomly created initial 149-bit configurations (created with no bias in the sense that 0 and 1 each have an independent 50% probability of being chosen for each bit). This is, of course, an extremely small sampling of the 2^{149} possible initial configurations. Note that the fitness evaluation of each individual in the population at each generation of the run entails executing the 149 automata for 600 time steps on each of the 1,000 fitness cases (i.e., 89,400,000 executions of a seven-input program).

The out-of-sample fitness cases consist of 1,000,000 (and later 10,000,000 and 15,000,000) similarly created random initial configurations of 149 bits.

Raw fitness is the number of fitness cases for which the system stabilizes to a correct configuration of 149 0s or 149 1s after 600 time steps. Standardized fitness is 1,000 minus raw fitness.

A considerable amount of computer time was saved by converting the result-producing branch (representing a seven-argument Boolean function) and automatically defined functions to a truth table (thereby eliminating repeated evaluation of the program tree). In addition, if the state of all 149 automata were equal for two consecutive time steps (i.e., the system reached a fixed point), the simulation was stopped. Additional computer time might possibly have been saved if we had programmed a test to see if the system had become recognizably periodic (i.e., the state of all 149 automata were equal for two time steps within some specified number of time steps). However, we were not convinced that the savings would outweigh the cost of this testing.

58.3.4 Parameters

The control parameters for runs in this chapter are either in the tableau (Table 58.2) or are the default values specified in Koza 1994g, Appendix D.

58.3.5 Tableau

Table 58.2 summarizes the key features of the majority classification problem for one-dimensional cellular automata.

58.4 RESULTS

We made five runs of this problem. Each run produced numerous individuals that are reminiscent of the GKL rule in various ways. Each of the runs yielded numerous individuals that scored well above the best accuracy of 76.9% achieved by the best previous run of the genetic algorithm operating on fixed-length character strings.

On the best run, many interesting individuals appeared prior to the creation of the best-of-run individual in generation 17.

The best-of-generation program of generation 0 of the best run indiscriminately classifies all fitness cases as having a majority of 1s and scores 525 hits (out of 1,000) on the in-sample fitness cases. This best-of-generation individual is an artifact of the fact that 525 of the 1,000 randomly created fitness cases used on this particular run happened to have a majority of 1s. It is interesting to note that if we used a fitness measure based on, say, correlation (instead of accuracy), this individual would not have been the best individual of generation 0.

The best-of-generation individual from generation 1 scores 650 hits on the in-sample fitness cases. The behavior of a one-dimensional cellular automata system can be presented as a two-dimensional grid (called a *space-time diagram*) in which the top horizontal row contains the states (0 or 1) of the 149 cells at time 0 (i.e., the initial configuration of the system) and in which each successive row represents the states of the 149 cells at successive time steps. A complete space-time diagram for this problem would contain 149 columns and 600 rows.

Figure 58.2 shows a small part of the space-time diagram for this best-of-generation individual from generation 1. This space-time diagram does not start at time step 0, but instead shows the behavior for some intermediate time steps. In this space-time diagram, there are large areas dominated by solid blocks of repeated simple patterns (repeated single bits in the case of this particular space-time diagram). Such blocks are called *domains*. Domains can be specified by a regular expression. The two domains shown in the figure are the domain denoted by the regular expression 1* and the domain denoted by the expression 0*. In space-time diagrams, 1s are considered to be black, and 0s are considered to be white. The 1* domain is designated by B and the 0* domain is designated by W.

The B and W domains in Figure 58.2 for this best-of-generation individual from generation 1 interact in time and space. When a domain consisting of a solid block of 1s is to the left of a domain consisting of a solid block of 0s, the interface between the domains consists of . . .1111000. . . . The interface between any two domains is called a *particle*. Following Das, Mitchell, and Crutchfield (1994), a particle is denoted P(XY), where X is the domain on the left and Y the domain on the right. The interface that comprises a

Table 58.2 Tableau for the majority classification problem for one-dimensional cellular automata

Objective	Find a seven-argument Boolean function that performs the majority classification task for a 149-wide one-dimensional cellular automata system.
Program architecture	One result-producing branch, one two-argument automatically defined function, ADF0, and one three-argument automatically defined function, ADF1. ADF1 can refer hierarchically to ADF0.
Initial function set for the RPBs	F_{rpb} = {AND, OR, NAND, NOR, NOT, IF, XOR, ADF0, ADF1}
Initial terminal set for the RPBs	T_{rpb} = {X, E, EE, EEE, W, WW, WWW}

Initial function set for the ADFs	For automatically defined function ADF0:
	    F_{adf0} = {AND, OR, NAND, NOR, NOT, IF, XOR}.
	For automatically defined function ADF1:
	    F_{adf1} = F_{adf0} ∪ {ADF0}.

Initial terminal set for the ADFs	For automatically defined function ADF0:
	    T_{adf0} = {ARG0, ARG1, X, E, EE, EEE, W, WW, WWW}.
	For automatically defined function ADF1:
	    T_{adf1} = T_{adf0} ∪ {ARG2}.

Potential function set for the RPBs	Architecture-altering operations are not used.
Potential terminal set for the RPBs	Architecture-altering operations are not used.
Potential function set for the ADFs	Architecture-altering operations are not used.
Potential terminal set for the ADFs	Architecture-altering operations are not used.
Fitness cases	The in-sample fitness cases consist of 1,000 randomly created 149-bit configurations (created with no bias). The out-of-sample fitness cases consist of 1,000,000 (and later 10,000,000 and 15,000,000) similarly created initial configurations.
Raw fitness	The number of fitness cases for which the system stabilizes to a correct configuration of 149 0s or 149 1s after 600 time steps
Standardized fitness	1,000 minus raw fitness
Hits	Same as raw fitness
Wrapper	None
Parameters	M = 51,200. G = 51. Q = 800. D = 64. B = 3%. S_{rpb} = 500. S_{adf} = 250. N_{rpb} = 1. $N_{max\text{-}adf}$ = 2.
Result designation	Best-so-far pace-setting individual
Success predicate	A program scores the maximum number of hits (1,000).

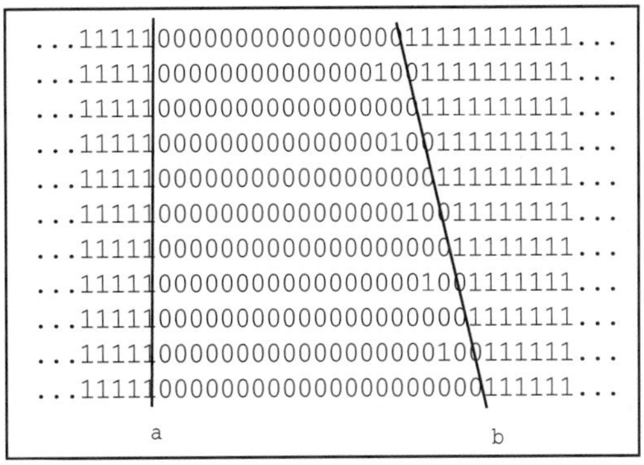

```
...11111|000000000000000011111111111...
...11111|000000000000000100|1111111111...
...11111|000000000000000001111111111...
...11111|000000000000000100|111111111...
...11111|000000000000000001111111111...
...11111|000000000000000010|011111111...
...11111|000000000000000000|11111111...
...11111|000000000000000010|01111111...
...11111|000000000000000001111111...
...11111|000000000000000010|0111111...
...11111|000000000000000000|111111...
```

a   b

Figure 58.2   Eleven time steps of a part of the space-time behavior for one fitness case of the best individual of generation 1

particle need not be a simple one. It can consist of a set of interactions that extends temporally over several time steps and extends spatially across several cells. Domains and particles provide a way to describe how a cellular automata system operates and, in particular, how information is communicated across large distances in time and space in a cellular space. Thus, the particle consisting of the interface between the solid block of 1s (the **B** domain) and the solid block of 0s (the **W** domain) in this figure is denoted by P(**BW**). At the next time step (i.e., the next lower row of the space-time diagram), the corresponding positions consist of the identical interface (i.e., . . .1111000. . .) in the very same locations of the cellular space. That is, these particular two domains do not move left or right over time. Consequently, the particle P(**BW**) is said to have a *velocity* of zero. In Figure 58.2, line **a** shows the perfect vertical path of the stationary P(**BW**) particle.

Table 58.3 shows the eight combinations of the seven inputs that define the stationary particle P(**BW**) for the best-of-generation individual from generation 1. As can be seen, when the seven inputs to central cell X are 1110000 (row 112), 1100000 (96), 1000000 (64), or 0000000 (0), cell X stays in state 0. However, when the seven inputs to central cell X are 1111000 (row 120), 1111100 (124), 1111110 (126), or 1111111 (127), cell X stays in state 1.

Line **b** in Figure 58.2 shows the particle P(**WB**) consisting of the interface between the solid block of 0s (the **W** domain) on the left and the solid block of 1s (the **B** domain) on the right. Note that particle P(**WB**) consists of a two-step region where the **W** domain meets the **B** domain as well as the extra 1 that appears two cells to the west on every second time step. Line **b** is not stationary, but instead trends diagonally to the east at the rate of one location to the east for every two time steps (down). Consequently, particle P(**WB**) is said to have a velocity of ½.

The best-of-generation individual from generation 1 is an example of what Mitchell, Hraber, and Crutchfield (1993) call a *block-expanding rule* (i.e., a rule that relentlessly expands a block of contiguous identical bits in the input). A block-expanding rule will eventually invade all 149 locations of the cellular space unless there is a sufficiently large

Table 58.3 Stationary particle P(BW) for best of generation 1

#	WWW	WW	W	X	E	EE	EEE	Best-of-generation 1 rule
0	0	0	0	0	0	0	0	0
64	1	0	0	0	0	0	0	0
96	1	1	0	0	0	0	0	0
112	1	1	1	0	0	0	0	0
120	1	1	1	1	0	0	0	1
124	1	1	1	1	1	0	0	1
126	1	1	1	1	1	1	0	1
127	1	1	1	1	1	1	1	1

block of adjacent (or nearly adjacent) opposite bits. This rule overpredicts a majority of 1s and underpredicts a majority of 0s.

The best program of generation 6 scores 706 hits on the 1,000 in-sample fitness cases. A portion of its space-time behavior for an illustrative fitness case is shown in Figure 58.3. The granularity of this figure (and other similar figures in this chapter) is such that the black domains (represented by the regular expression 1*) appear as black areas and the white domains (0*) appear as white areas. The behavior of this individual is similar to the best-of-generation individual of generation 1. However, it scores slightly better because it has modified the conditions under which it expands a block. The interaction between the domain of 0s on the left and 1s on the right for the particle P(WB) is quite complex, and the interface between the two domains is quite large. The particle P(WB) travels at a velocity of $\frac{2}{7}$.

The best individual of generation 10 scores 739 hits. Its space-time behavior for one fitness case is shown in Figure 58.4. It has some interesting behavior in that it is the first example in this run of a rule that uses the black, white, and gray domains in a manner reminiscent of the GKL rule (although considerably less effectively). The gray domains separate domains of white (0s) on the left and black (1s) on the right. The gray domain closes in on the white domain (slowly) while remaining constant with the black domain. The white domain slowly grows into the black domain, but at a slower rate than the rate at which gray encroaches into white. This might seem to indicate that white will always disappear from the diagrams. However, when a white domain is next to a gray domain on its left, the white quickly encroaches into the gray domain's space.

The best individual of generation 15 scores 815 hits on the in-sample fitness cases. Although it scores less than 80% on the out-of-sample fitness cases, its behavior is reminiscent of the GKL rule. Figure 58.5 is a space-time diagram for this individual for an illustrative fitness case. Like the GKL rule, this rule has a gray domain (half white and half black). As can be seen in the center portion of this figure, the gray domain acts as a separator and pushes the white domain to the left and the black domain to the right. When black is to the left of white (as it is to the right in the upper middle of the figure), the interaction consists of a zero-velocity P(BW) particle. Note that there is no P(WB)

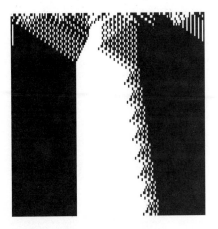

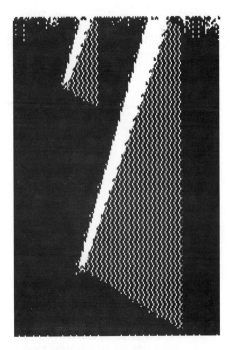

Figure 58.3 Partial space-time behavior for one fitness case of the best individual of generation 6

Figure 58.4 Space-time behavior for one fitness case of the best rule from generation 10

particle because the gray domain always separates a black area that is to the right of a white area. The space-time diagram for this particular fitness case converges to 149 0s (all white) at the bottom of the figure. As shown in Figure 58.5 for an illustrative fitness case, the best individual of generation 15 uses the same basic mechanism as employed by the GKL rule to compute a global measure of density. If the white domain 0* is larger, it will eventually dominate the black domain 1*, and vice versa.

The best individual of generation 15 has several additional shades of gray that are not found in the GKL rule. Figure 58.6 shows the interaction of these new grayish domains for another illustrative fitness case. The space-time diagram for this particular fitness case converges to 149 1s (all black) at the bottom of the figure. In this figure, all of the primary computation is performed by the new gray domains. Significantly, the black domain does not enter into the computation until the very end. However, the new gray domains do not interact particularly well in this best individual of generation 15. This individual often makes mistakes when it relies on the new gray domains.

The best-of-run individual emerged on generation 17. Its 36-point result-producing branch is

```
(NAND (XOR (OR (ADF0 X (NOT WWW)) (NOT WWW)) (ADF0 (ADF0 E X)
(OR E W))) (OR (NAND (IF EEE E X) (IF EEE W (AND EE WWW)))
(ADF1 (NAND W E) (XOR WWW W) E))).
```

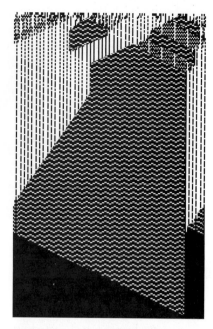

Figure 58.5   A complete space-time behavior for one fitness case of the best individual of generation 15

Figure 58.6   A complete space-time behavior of the best individual of generation 15 where there are no all-black or all-white domains until the end

Note that the result-producing branch makes repeated references to both ADF0 and ADF1.

The 10-point automatically defined function ADF0 of this best-of-run individual from generation 17 is

```
(IF (NOR (OR X X) (NOR ARG1 ARG0)) EEE WWW).
```

Its 44-point automatically defined function ADF1 is

```
(XOR W (XOR (ADF0 (ADF0 (IF (OR (NOT W) (ADF0 WWW ARG2)) (XOR
(ADF0 WWW X) (NOR WW WWW)) (NAND (XOR X X) (OR X WW))) (NOR (OR
(IF ARG2 EEE ARG2) (NOR ARG2 ARG1)) (NOT (XOR W E)))) (XOR W
(NOT ARG2))) EEE)).
```

Note that ADFi makes repeated hierarchical references to ADF0.

This best-of-run individual from generation 17 scores 824 hits on the 1,000 in-sample fitness cases. When cross-validated on out-of-sample fitness cases, it achieves 82.4% accuracy on 100,000 out-of-sample cases and 82.326% accuracy over 10,000,000 additional out-of-sample cases. There are, of course, 2^{149} fitness cases in total.

Table 58.4 shows the result of testing this best-of-run individual from generation 17 against the GKL rule, the Das rule (1995), and the Davis rule (1995) (all shown in Table 58.1) using the same 10^6 or 10^7 fitness cases. Table 58.4 also includes the scores of the

Table 58.4 Out-of-sample performance of various rules for the majority classification task

Rule	Accuracy	Number of out-of-sample fitness cases
Best rule evolved by bit-string genetic algorithm (Das, Mitchell, and Crutchfield 1994)	76.9%	10^6
GKL rule—human-written (Gacs, Kurdyumov, and Levin 1978)	81.6%	10^6
Davis rule—human-written (Davis 1995)	81.8%	10^6
Das rule—human-written (Das 1995)	82.178%	10^7
Best rule evolved by genetic programming (described in this chapter)	82.326%	10^7

best rule produced by the genetic algorithm operating on fixed-length character strings as reported by Das, Mitchell, and Crutchfield (1994). The GKL rule (Gacs, Kurdyumov, and Levin 1978; Gacs 1983, 1986) achieves an accuracy of 81.6% based on the fitness cases used in this comparison.

As can be seen, the best cellular automata rule for the majority classification task evolved by genetic programming achieves an accuracy that exceeds that of the GKL rule, all other known human-written rules, and all other known rules produced by automated approaches. Nonparametric X^2 tests with one degree of freedom were performed. The probability, p, that the pairwise differences between the best rule evolved by genetic programming and each of the other three rules are attributable to chance is less than 0.001 (i.e., the differences are statistically significant because $p < 0.001$).

Referring to the eight criteria in Chapter 1 for establishing that an automatically created result is competitive with a human-produced result, these four results satisfy the following two of the eight criteria:

D. The result is publishable in its own right as a new scientific result (independent of the fact that the result was mechanically created).

E. The result is equal to or better than the most recent human-created solution to a long-standing problem for which there has been a succession of increasingly better human-created solutions.

Therefore, we make the following claim:

- **CLAIM NO. 13** We claim that the automatic creation by genetic programming of a cellular automata rule for the majority classification problem that is better than the Gacs-Kurdyumov-Levin rule and better than all other known rules written by humans over the past 20 years is an instance where genetic programming has produced a result that is competitive with a result produced by creative and inventive humans.

This automatically created cellular automata rule satisfies Arthur Samuel's criterion (1983) for artificial intelligence and machine learning:

> The aim [is] . . . to get machines to exhibit behavior, which if done by humans, would be assumed to involve the use of intelligence.

58.4.1 Analysis of the Best-of-Run Rule

Tables 58.5 through 58.12 show the combinations of inputs with 0, 1, 2, 3, 4, 5, 6, and 7 active inputs (1s), respectively, for the best-of-run rule created by genetic programming and the GKL rule. The GKL rule can be explained as follows:

- If cell X is 0, then the new value of X is the Boolean majority function applied to X, W, and WWW.
- If cell X is 1, then the new value of X is the Boolean majority function applied to X, E, and EEE.

As can be seen, except for the fitness cases with 0 or 1 active or inactive inputs, there is a considerable difference between the best-of-run rule created by genetic programming and the GKL rule. We know of no simple restatement of the best rule created by genetic programming.

Table 58.5 The 1 fitness case with 0 active inputs

#	WWW	WW	W	X	E	EE	EEE	GP rule	GKL rule
0	0	0	0	0	0	0	0	0	0

Table 58.6 The 7 fitness cases with 1 active input

#	WWW	WW	W	X	E	EE	EEE	GP rule	GKL rule
1	0	0	0	0	0	0	1	0	0
2	0	0	0	0	0	1	0	0	0
4	0	0	0	0	1	0	0	0	0
8	0	0	0	1	0	0	0	0	0
16	0	0	1	0	0	0	0	0	0
32	0	1	0	0	0	0	0	0	0
64	1	0	0	0	0	0	0	0	0

Table 58.7 The 21 fitness cases with 2 active inputs

#	WWW	WW	W	X	E	EE	EEE	GP rule	GKL rule
3	0	0	0	0	0	1	1	0	0
5	0	0	0	0	1	0	1	1	0
6	0	0	0	0	1	1	0	0	0
9	0	0	0	1	0	0	1	0	1

#									
10	0	0	0	1	0	1	0	0	0
12	0	0	0	1	1	0	0	0	1
17	0	0	1	0	0	0	1	1	0
18	0	0	1	0	0	1	0	0	0
20	0	0	1	0	1	0	0	0	0
24	0	0	1	1	0	0	0	0	0
33	0	1	0	0	0	0	1	0	0
34	0	1	0	0	0	1	0	0	0
36	0	1	0	0	1	0	0	0	0
40	0	1	0	1	0	0	0	0	0
48	0	1	1	0	0	0	0	0	0
65	1	0	0	0	0	0	1	1	0
66	1	0	0	0	0	1	0	0	0
68	1	0	0	0	1	0	0	0	0
72	1	0	0	1	0	0	0	1	0
80	1	0	1	0	0	0	0	0	1
96	1	1	0	0	0	0	0	0	0

Table 58.8 The 35 fitness cases with 3 active inputs

#	WWW	WW	W	X	E	EE	EEE	GP rule	GKL rule
7	0	0	0	0	1	1	1	1	0
11	0	0	0	1	0	1	1	0	1
13	0	0	0	1	1	0	1	0	1
14	0	0	0	1	1	1	0	0	1
19	0	0	1	0	0	1	1	1	0
21	0	0	1	0	1	0	1	1	0
22	0	0	1	0	1	1	0	0	0
25	0	0	1	1	0	0	1	0	1
26	0	0	1	1	0	1	0	0	0
28	0	0	1	1	1	0	0	0	1
35	0	1	0	0	0	1	1	0	0
37	0	1	0	0	1	0	1	1	0
38	0	1	0	0	1	1	0	0	0
41	0	1	0	1	0	0	1	0	1
42	0	1	0	1	0	1	0	0	0
44	0	1	0	1	1	0	0	0	1
49	0	1	1	0	0	0	1	1	0
50	0	1	1	0	0	1	0	0	0
52	0	1	1	0	1	0	0	0	0
56	0	1	1	1	0	0	0	0	0

(continued)

Table 58.8 *(continued)*

#	WWW	WW	W	X	E	EE	EEE	GP rule	GKL rule
67	1	0	0	0	0	1	1	1	0
69	1	0	0	0	1	0	1	1	0
70	1	0	0	0	1	1	0	0	0
73	1	0	0	1	0	0	1	1	1
74	1	0	0	1	0	1	0	1	0
76	1	0	0	1	1	0	0	1	1
81	1	0	1	0	0	0	1	1	1
82	1	0	1	0	0	1	0	0	1
84	1	0	1	0	1	0	0	0	1
88	1	0	1	1	0	0	0	1	0
97	1	1	0	0	0	0	1	1	0
98	1	1	0	0	0	1	0	0	0
104	1	1	0	1	0	0	0	1	0
112	1	1	1	0	0	0	0	0	1
100	1	1	0	0	1	0	0	0	0

Table 58.9 The 35 fitness cases with 4 active inputs

#	WWW	WW	W	X	E	EE	EEE	GP rule	GKL rule
15	0	0	0	1	1	1	1	0	1
23	0	0	1	0	1	1	1	1	0
27	0	0	1	1	0	1	1	0	1
29	0	0	1	1	1	0	1	1	1
30	0	0	1	1	1	1	0	0	1
39	0	1	0	0	1	1	1	1	0
43	0	1	0	1	0	1	1	0	1
45	0	1	0	1	1	0	1	0	1
46	0	1	0	1	1	1	0	0	1
51	0	1	1	0	0	1	1	1	0
53	0	1	1	0	1	0	1	1	0
54	0	1	1	0	1	1	0	0	0
57	0	1	1	1	0	0	1	0	1
58	0	1	1	1	0	1	0	0	0
60	0	1	1	1	1	0	0	0	1
71	1	0	0	0	1	1	1	1	0
75	1	0	0	1	0	1	1	1	1
77	1	0	0	1	1	0	1	1	1
78	1	0	0	1	1	1	0	1	1
83	1	0	1	0	0	1	1	1	1

85	1	0	1	0	1	0	1	1	1
86	1	0	1	0	1	1	0	0	1
89	1	0	1	1	0	0	1	1	1
90	1	0	1	1	0	1	0	1	0
92	1	0	1	1	1	0	0	1	1
99	1	1	0	0	0	1	1	1	0
101	1	1	0	0	1	0	1	1	0
102	1	1	0	0	1	1	0	0	0
105	1	1	0	1	0	0	1	1	1
106	1	1	0	1	0	1	0	1	0
108	1	1	0	1	1	0	0	1	1
113	1	1	1	0	0	0	1	1	1
114	1	1	1	0	0	1	0	0	1
116	1	1	1	0	1	0	0	0	1
120	1	1	1	1	0	0	0	1	0

Table 58.10 The 21 fitness cases with 5 active inputs

#	WWW	WW	W	X	E	EE	EEE	GP rule	GKL rule
31	0	0	1	1	1	1	1	1	1
47	0	1	0	1	1	1	1	0	1
55	0	1	1	0	1	1	1	1	0
59	0	1	1	1	0	1	1	0	1
61	0	1	1	1	1	0	1	1	1
62	0	1	1	1	1	1	0	0	1
79	1	0	0	1	1	1	1	1	1
87	1	0	1	0	1	1	1	1	1
91	1	0	1	1	0	1	1	1	1
93	1	0	1	1	1	0	1	1	1
94	1	0	1	1	1	1	0	1	1
103	1	1	0	0	1	1	1	1	0
107	1	1	0	1	0	1	1	1	1
109	1	1	0	1	1	0	1	1	1
110	1	1	0	1	1	1	0	1	1
115	1	1	1	0	0	1	1	1	1
117	1	1	1	0	1	0	1	1	1
118	1	1	1	0	1	1	0	0	1
121	1	1	1	1	0	0	1	1	1
122	1	1	1	1	0	1	0	1	0
124	1	1	1	1	1	0	0	1	1

Table 58.11 The 7 fitness cases with 6 active inputs

#	WWW	WW	W	X	E	EE	EEE	GP rule	GKL rule
63	0	1	1	1	1	1	1	1	1
95	1	0	1	1	1	1	1	1	1
111	1	1	0	1	1	1	1	1	1
119	1	1	1	0	1	1	1	1	1
123	1	1	1	1	0	1	1	1	1
125	1	1	1	1	1	0	1	1	1
126	1	1	1	1	1	1	0	1	1

Table 58.12 The 1 fitness case with 7 active inputs

#	WWW	WW	W	X	E	EE	EEE	GP rule	GKL rule
127	1	1	1	1	1	1	1	1	1

Table 58.13 The 11 domains of the best rule evolved by genetic programming

Domain name	Color	Regular expression for the domain	Kernel size
W	White	0*	1
B	Black	1*	1
1	Very light gray	(000001)* ∪ (100000)* ∪ (010000)* ∪ (001000)* ∪ (000100)* ∪ (000010)*	6
2	Light gray	(000101)* ∪ (100010)* ∪ (010001)* ∪ (101000)* ∪ (010100)* ∪ (001010)*	6
3	Light gray	(001)* ∪ (100)* ∪ (010)*	3
4	Gray	(001101)* ∪ (100110)* ∪ (010011)* ∪ (101001)* ∪ (110100)* ∪ (011010)*	6
5	Gray	(001011)* ∪ (100101)* ∪ (110010)* ∪ (011001)* ∪ (101100)* ∪ (010110)*	6
6	Gray	(01)* ∪ (10)*	2
7	Dark gray	(011101)* ∪ (101110)* ∪ (010111)* ∪ (101011)* ∪ (110101)* ∪ (111010)*	6
8	Dark gray	(011)* ∪ (101)* ∪ (110)*	3
9	Very dark gray	(011111)* ∪ (101111)* ∪ (110111)* ∪ (111011)* ∪ (111101)* ∪ (111110)*	6

Why does the best-of-run rule evolved by genetic programming on generation 17 score better than the previously known (human-written) rules?

First, it has more domains than the GKL rule. The 11 domains of the rule evolved by genetic programming (Table 58.13) classify the density of 1s into finer levels of gray than do the black, white, and checkerboard gray domains of the GKL rule (analyzed in detail in Das, Mitchell, and Crutchfield 1994).

The checkerboard gray domain of the GKL rule corresponds to the regular expression (10)* ∪ (01)* (Das, Mitchell, and Crutchfield 1994). The rule evolved by genetic programming employs a larger number of particles. The rule evolved by genetic programming employs 10 particles that are identical to the particles (Das, Mitchell, and Crutchfield 1994) in the GKL rule; however, it also discovered at least 40 additional particles that involve the new gray domains. All the new particles have velocity 0, +3, or −3.

The question arises as to whether the additional domains in the rule evolved by genetic programming affect the outcome of the computation performed by the overall system. If these additional domains affect the outcome, a second question also arises, namely, whether the effect of the additional domains accounts for the improved performance of the rule evolved by genetic programming.

Concerning the first question, the new gray domains do affect the outcome of the computation. In the behavior shown in Figure 58.7, for example, the new gray areas are critical to the success of the rule. If all the grays acted identically, then the automata would not converge in this example. Specifically, the interactions of the several gray domains in the area indicated by the arrow represent a computation that is trying to integrate density information from the initial states and is trying to decide whether the balance favors white or black. In this example, the computation decides in favor of white. Consequently, the white domain to the right of the arrowhead starts to expand to the left and becomes dominant at the bottom of the figure.

In addition, there are periods (as shown in Figure 58.8) during the behavior of the best rule evolved by genetic programming where none of the GKL domains exist. Thus, the new gray domains certainly do affect the outcome of the computation.

Concerning the second question, the new gray domains account for at least some of the difference in score between the best rule evolved by genetic programming and the GKL rule. The behavior of both rules (Figure 58.9) indicates that the finer levels of gray do confer an advantage on the best rule evolved by genetic programming. On the left of the initial state vector, there are two fairly large regions of white (0s) separated by a region of black (1s) marked in the diagrams by the arrows. Under the GKL rule (top part of the figure), the black area is eliminated by the two adjacent white domains. In the best rule evolved by genetic programming (bottom part of the figure), these two white areas are classified as light gray domains, and the black area becomes a dark gray domain (all shifted to the right slightly). Because it can make use of extra domains, the best rule evolved by genetic programming retains the information that there is a significant density of black (1s) in the vicinity of the arrow until additional global information can resolve the local dispute. In essence, the ability of the evolved rule to classify domains of the input as intermediate gray values allows it to avoid the "rounding off" error that the GKL rule makes.

The basic mechanism of the best rule evolved by genetic programming is similar to that of the GKL rule in that there is a race among the black, white, and gray domains. Figure 58.10 is a stylized space-time diagram showing the behavior of the best rule evolved by genetic programming for an illustrative fitness case. The darkness of each domain corresponds to the density of 1s.

In the best rule evolved by genetic programming, a white domain **W** is separated on the right from a black domain **B** by a growing domain of checkerboard gray **6**. The white

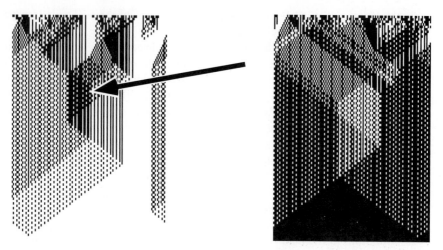

Figure 58.7 Space-time diagram for one fitness case showing the behavior of the best rule evolved by genetic programming

Figure 58.8 The behavior of the best rule evolved by genetic programming on one set of initial states

Figure 58.9 The space-time behavior of the GKL rule (*left*) and the best rule evolved by genetic programming (*right*) on the same initial state vector

domain W is separated on the left from the black domain B by one or both of the separator domains, 3 and 8, which are domains whose interactions with either white or black have zero velocity. In the case shown in Figure 58.10, the B domain is larger, and the

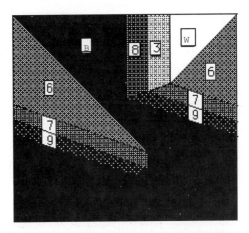

Figure 58.10 **Stylized space-time domain diagram for the best rule evolved by genetic programming showing its behavior for an illustrative fitness case**

gray 6 domain cuts off the white domain W, allowing the black domain B to break through. In this case, the extra gray domains of 7 and 9 are not important; however, these domains play a role in other fitness cases.

The GKL rule is able to correctly solve the majority classification problem for many initial conditions; however, it sometimes fails to compute the correct answer when the black B and white W domains are of approximately equal width (Figure 58.11). When the black B domain and the white W domain are nearly the same width, the gray 6 domain completes its encroachment into both of them at nearly the same time. The complete encroachment of the gray 6 domain into the black B domain creates a new white W domain. Similarly, the complete encroachment of the gray 6 domain into the white W domain creates a new black B domain. This near-tie situation creates a new gray 6 domain located between the new black B domain and the new white W domain. The new black B domain and the new white W domain are then in a race to not be the first domain that is completely encroached upon by the gray 6 domain. This strategy is not able to distinguish near-ties in all cases.

The best rule evolved by genetic programming differs from the GKL rule in two ways. First, the best rule evolved by genetic programming handles near-ties in a more complex fashion. It recodes the computation into a multiplicity of gray domains (whereas the GKL rule only employs the gray 6 domain). Second, the best rule evolved by genetic programming uses two separator domains, 8 and 3, that form vertical bands between the black B domain and white W domain. The two separator domains (8 and 3) represent an intermediate classification of the density between the extremes of the black B domain and the white W domain. Thus, the two separator domains perform a more fine-grained calculation than is possible with the GKL rule.

If there is a near-tie, new domains emerge after the collision instead of the black and white domains, and there is no immediate gray separator domain. The new gray domains of 7 and 9 represent the complete encroachment of the gray 6 domain into the white W domain. Domains 1 and 2 represent the complete encroachment of the gray 6 domain

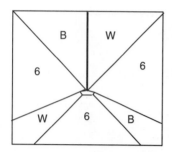

Figure 58.11   Collisions for the GKL rule

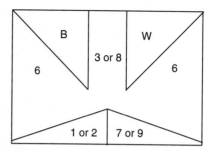

Figure 58.12   Collisions for the best rule evolved by genetic programming

into the black **B** domain. Thus, when there is a near-tie in the best rule evolved by genetic programming, the original black and white domains disappear completely, and the computation is carried out entirely by the gray domains. An abstract schematic for this interaction is shown in Figure 58.12.

In the circumstance shown in Figure 58.13, the black **B** and white **W** domains are separated by the **3** domain. When the gray **6** domain completely cuts off and eliminates the black **B** domain, a new **1** domain is created (to represent the complete encroachment of the gray **6** domain into the black **B** domain). When the gray **6** domain completely cuts off and eliminates the white **W** domain, a new **7** domain is created (to represent the complete encroachment of the gray **6** domain into the white **W** domain). Thus after the gray **6** domain has fully encroached on both the black **B** domain and the white **W** domain, then the representation has been changed from a contest of **B** versus **W** into a contest of **1** versus **7** (where **1** encodes that white **W** is winning and **7** encodes that black **B** is winning).

In the new contest between the **1** domain and the **7** domain, the **1** domain completely eliminates the separator domain **3** before the **7** domain is able to encroach at all on the **3** domain. The collision of the **1** domain into the **7** domain from the left to the right creates a zero-velocity particle that appears as a vertical line between these two domains in Figure 58.13. But the collision of the **1** domain into the **7** domain from the right to the left creates a new **5** domain. This new **5** domain creates a zero-velocity particle between **5** and **1**, but the **5** domain also encroaches on the **7** domain to the left. Once the **5** domain has eliminated the **7** domain, then the **1** domain encroaches on the **5** domain. The **1** domain ends up dominating the entire space. After the **1** domain has completely encroached on the entire space, then the final collision of particle P(**15**) with particle P(**51**) creates a new white domain. The entire space converges to the white **W** domain, which is the correct result for the calculation.

Figure 58.14 shows a slightly more complex fitness case. In this case, there are two separator domains, domain **8** and domain **3**. As before, the complete encroachment of the gray **6** domain into the white **W** domain creates the new **7** domain. But in this case, the complete encroachment of the gray **6** domain into the black **B** domain creates the new **2** domain (instead of the new **1** domain as in the previous example). The difference is caused by the fact that this case has an **8** separator domain next to the black **B** domain (instead of a **3** separator domain as before). So this time the complete encroachment of

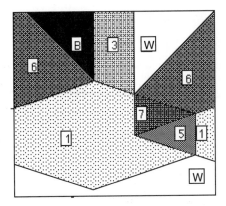

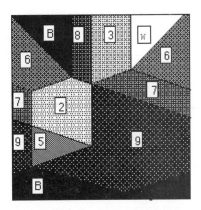

Figure 58.13   The abstracted space-time domain behavior of the best evolved rule on a near-tie where the correct answer is white W. The automata correctly converged to W.

Figure 58.14   The behavior of the best evolved rule on a near-tie where the correct answer is black. The automata correctly converged to all-black B.

gray **6** into black **B** leads to a collision between particle P(**6B**) and particle P(**B8**), which creates the new **2** domain.

The **2** domain acts similarly to the **1** domain in the previous example in that it completely encroaches into both the gray **6** domain and the separator **8** domain. As in the previous example, the **7** domain completely encroaches into both the separator **3** domain and the gray **6** domain.

Unlike the previous example, the collision in the middle of Figure 58.14 between particle P(**28**) and particle P(**37**) creates new domain **9**, which completely takes over the space. After the **9** domain has completely encroached into the entire space, then the final collision between particle P(**95**) and particle P(**59**) creates a new black **B** domain. The entire space converges to the black **B** domain, which is the correct result for the calculation.

The asymmetry of the best rule evolved by genetic programming suggests that there may be other rules that are better yet at performing the majority classification task.

One problem that a rule utilizing zero-velocity particles can have is that the initial state vector could either be in a state or relax to a state where convergence does not take place. If the automata either start in or reach a state where the automata are filled with domains that have zero-velocity interactions with the adjacent patterns, the automata cannot converge. Thus, one potential downside to the best rule evolved by genetic programming is that because it utilizes more domains in its computation that have zero-velocity particles, it may be more likely to be nonconvergent. After testing 15,000,000 fitness cases, only one fitness case was found for which the best rule evolved by genetic programming failed to converge in the allotted time. Figure 58.15 shows the behavior of the best rule evolved by genetic programming on the initial state vector where the rule does not converge. Note the numerous particles of zero velocity (vertical) in this space-time diagram. Given that the best rule evolved by genetic programming scores better than any other known rule, however, it is possible that the occasional nonconvergence represents a strategic trade-off rather than a defect.

Figure 58.15 Example of a nonconvergent fitness case for the best rule evolved by genetic programming

The best rule evolved by genetic programming differs qualitatively from the other published rules. It utilizes a very fine internal representation of density information, it employs a large number of different domains and particles, and it uses an intricate set of signals for communicating information over large distances in time and space.

58.5 SUBSEQUENT RESULT

The above run was made on September 27, 1995. In July 1998, Juille and Pollack (1998) reported that they had successfully used coevolution in conjunction with the genetic algorithm to achieve an even better cellular automata rule for the majority classification problem.

Part 8:
DISCOVERY OF MOTIFS AND PROGRAMMATIC MOTIFS FOR MOLECULAR BIOLOGY

This part describes two problems from the field of computational molecular biology. These problems rely on the background on molecular biology contained in Chapters 16 and 17 concerning the transmembrane segment identification problem. Both problems in this part deal with classifying an entire protein sequence, rather than just a segment of the protein. The first problem here makes a decision concerning the entire protein based on a small local area of the protein; the second problem makes a decision concerning the entire protein based on a computation involving the entire sequence.

Chapter 59 describes how genetic programming can be used to evolve one motif for detecting the D–E–A–D box family of proteins and a second motif for detecting the manganese superoxide dismutase family.

Chapter 60 describes how genetic programming can be used to evolve programmatic motifs for classifying proteins as to their cellular location.

59

Automatic Discovery of Protein Motifs

This chapter describes how genetic programming successfully evolved motifs for detecting the D–E–A–D box family of proteins and for detecting the manganese superoxide dismutase family. Both motifs were evolved without prespecifying their length. Both evolved motifs employed automatically defined functions to capture the repeated use of common subexpressions. When tested against the SWISS-PROT database of proteins, the two evolved consensus motifs detect the two families either as well as, or slightly better than, the comparable human-written motifs found in the PROSITE database.

59.1   INTRODUCTION

Most proteins appear in many different species; however, the sequence of amino acid residues in functionally equivalent proteins in two different species are usually not exactly identical. For one thing, the primary sequences of the "same" protein in two different species often differ slightly in length. Moreover, even after using an alignment algorithm (e.g., Smith and Waterman 1981) to align related sequences of different lengths, the residues found at a particular aligned position often will still differ slightly. The reason is that only a relative handful of the amino acids in the overall sequence are responsible for the biological function, activity, and structure of the protein. Over millions of years, evolution has substituted dissimilar amino acid residues at noncritical positions. Moreover, evolution often substitutes a chemically similar amino acid residue for a particular residue even for the relatively small part of the overall protein that is responsible for the protein's biological activity. Thus, only a small subset of the residues of two functionally equivalent proteins are actually absolutely identical (that is, *conserved*).

Sometimes, amidst all the differences, it is possible to identify certain high-specificity, high-sensitivity patterns (called *motifs*, *sites*, *signatures*, or *fingerprints*) in the sequences of biologically similar proteins. If a motif is defined well, it will correspond to a biologically important common property. The residues in such motifs are often directly responsible for the essential function and activity of the protein.

SWISS-PROT is a massive, systematically collected, periodically reviewed, annotated database of protein sequences that is maintained by the University of Geneva and the European Molecular Biology Laboratory (Bairoch and Boeckmann 1991). Release 30

(October 1994) of SWISS-PROT contains 14,147,368 amino acid residues from 40,292 sequences from hundreds of different species. The Human Genome Project and other research efforts in molecular biology are rapidly increasing the number of entries in SWISS-PROT and other databases of protein sequences and genomic DNA sequences. Automated techniques (such as those of machine learning) may prove useful or necessary for analyzing this accumulating data.

PROSITE is a database of biologically meaningful patterns found in protein sequences (Bairoch and Bucher 1994). Release 12 (June 1994) of PROSITE contains 1,029 different motifs. Motifs are entered in the PROSITE database after careful consideration by Amos Bairoch at the University of Geneva and his colleagues. Since the intended primary purpose of the PROSITE database is to detect families of proteins in computerized databases, a motif is included in PROSITE if it detects most (preferably all) sequences that have a particular biological property (i.e., has few false negatives), while detecting few (preferably zero) unrelated sequences (i.e., has few false positives).

Automated methods of machine learning may be useful in discovering biologically meaningful patterns that are hidden in the rapidly growing databases of genomic and protein sequences. Unfortunately, almost all existing methods of automated discovery require that the user specify, in advance, the size and shape of the to-be-discovered pattern. However, in practice, the discovery of the size and shape of the pattern may, in fact, be the problem (or, at the very least, a major part of the problem). None of the existing methods of automated discovery have a workable analog of the idea of a reusable, parameterized subroutine to capture and exploit repeated occurrences of regularities or subpatterns of the problem environment.

The problem of discovering biologically meaningful patterns in databases can be rephrased as a search for an unknown-size computer program. When the motif discovery problem is so rephrased, genetic programming becomes a candidate for approaching the problem. Genetic programming may be appropriate for this problem because it is capable of evolving complicated problem-solving expressions of unspecified size and shape. Moreover, when automatically defined functions are added to genetic programming, genetic programming becomes capable of efficiently capturing and exploiting recurring subpatterns.

Section 59.2 of this chapter provides background on the D–E–A-D box family of proteins and the manganese superoxide dismutase family. Section 59.3 describes how motifs can be represented by automatically defined functions. Section 59.4 identifies the preparatory steps required to apply genetic programming to the D–E–A-D box family of proteins. Section 59.5 discusses the jury method for creating a consensus motif. Section 59.6 presents an evolved consensus motif that is slightly better than the human-written motif found in the PROSITE database for detecting the D–E–A-D box family of proteins. Section 59.7 identifies the preparatory steps required to apply genetic programming to the manganese superoxide dismutase family of proteins. Section 59.8 presents an evolved consensus motif for detecting the manganese superoxide dismutase family that is as good as the human-written motif found in the PROSITE database.

59.2 BACKGROUND ON MOTIFS AND PROTEINS

The D–E–A-D box family of proteins and the manganese superoxide dismutase family of proteins will be used to illustrate how genetic programming may be applied to the problem of discovering motifs in protein sequences.

59.2.1 The D–E–A-D Box Family of Proteins

In an article entitled "Birth of the D–E–A-D box," Linder et al. (1989) described a family of proteins (called *helicases*) involved in the unwinding of the double helix of the DNA molecule during DNA replication (Chang, Arenas, and Abelson 1990; Dorer, Christensen, and Johnson 1990; Hodgman 1988). This family of proteins gets its name from the fact that the amino acid residues D (aspartic acid), E (glutamic acid), A (alanine), and D appear, in that order, at the core of one of its biologically critical subsequences. There are 34 proteins from this family among the 40,292 proteins appearing in release 30 of SWISS-PROT. Proteins of this family can be detected effectively (but not perfectly) by the following motif of length 9 (called ATP_HELICASE_1) that is included by Amos Bairoch and his colleagues at the University of Geneva in the PROSITE database:

[LIVM]-[LIVM]-D-E-A-D-x-[LIVM]-[LIVM].

In interpreting this expression, the first pair of square brackets indicates that the first residue of the nine is to be chosen from the set consisting of the amino acid residues L, I, V, and M. The second pair of square brackets indicates that the second residue is chosen (independently from the first) from the same set of four possibilities. Then the third, fourth, fifth, and sixth residues must be D, E, A, and D, respectively. The X in the motif indicates that the seventh residue can be any of the 20 possible amino acid residues. The eighth and ninth residues are chosen from the same set of four, namely, L, I, V, and M.

D and E are negatively charged and hence hydrophilic (water-loving) at normal pH values. A (alanine) is small, uncharged, and hydrophobic (water-hating). L (leucine), I (isoleucine), V (valine), or M (methionine) are moderately sized, uncharged, and hydrophobic. Thus, ignoring the X, this motif calls for three hydrophilic residues accompanied, on each side, by two moderately sized hydrophobic residues.

The above PROSITE expression detects any of $4^4 \times 20 = 5,120$ different possible sequences of length 9 (out of approximately 5×10^{11} possible sequences of length 9). When SWISS-PROT is searched using the above PROSITE motif, there are 34 true positives, 14,147,333 true negatives (among the 40,292 proteins), 1 false positive, and no false negatives. This corresponds to a correlation coefficient, C, of 0.99 (Matthews 1975) (described in Section 16.4.3).

Table 59.1 shows subsequences from 6 of the 34 proteins containing the D-E–A-D box motif in release 30 of the SWISS-PROT database. The table shows the position of the start of the D–E–A-D box motif in its second column. The third column shows the three amino acid residues in the primary sequence before the onset of the motif, the nine residues (in boldface) of the D–E–A-D box itself, and the five residues following the D–E–A-D box.

The number of possible PROSITE expressions (composed of disjunctions such as shown above) covering exactly nine positions is $(2^{20})^9 \sim 10^{54}$. Since the length of an expression that is capable of detecting a particular family of proteins is, in actual

Table 59.1 Six examples of D–E–A-D box motif

Protein	Start	Subsequence
Human putative ATP-dependent RNA helicase P54	244	QMI**VLDEADKLL**SQDFV
Rabbit eukaryotic initiation factor 4A	168	KMF**VLDEADEML**SRGFK
Fruit fly vasa protein	397	RFV**VLDEADRML**DMGFS
C. elegans putative ATP-dependent RNA helicase	192	KFL**IMDEADRIL**NMDFE
E. coli ATP-dependent RNA helicase	155	ETL**ILDEADRML**DMGFA
Fruit fly putative ATP-dependent RNA helicase	303	KFL**VIDEADRIM**DAVFQ

practice, not known in advance, the search space of the motif discovery problem is considerably larger than 10^{54}.

The question arises as to whether it is possible to use an automated machine learning technique to examine a large set of protein sequences and extract biologically meaningful motifs. Such a technique should, of course, not require advance specification of the length of the motif. Moreover, such a technique should capture modularities, symmetries, and regularities in the problem environment (e.g., the repetition of a pattern such as [LIVM]).

59.2.2   The Manganese Superoxide Dismutase Family of Proteins

The oxygen radicals that are normally produced in living cells have been implicated in many degenerative processes, including cancer and aging. Proteins belonging to the manganese superoxide dismutase family prevent oxidative damage to DNA and other molecules by catalyzing the conversion of these toxic superoxide radicals to oxygen and hydrogen peroxide (Ludwig, Metzger, Pattridge, and Stallings 1991; Stoddard, Ringe, and Petsko 1990; Bannister, Bannister, and Rotilio 1987). The four ligands of the manganese atom are conserved in all the known sequences of the manganese superoxide dismutase family. Amos Bairoch selected a short conserved region that includes two of the four ligands, namely, one **D** (aspartic acid) and one nearby **H** (histidine), to create the following motif of length 8 (called SOD_MN) for detecting proteins belonging to this family:

D-X-W-E-H-[STA]-[FY][FY].

For example, for human manganese superoxide dismutase (whose length is 198), the above motif correctly identifies the protein as belonging to this family because residues 159 to 166 of this protein are

DVWEHAYY.

When it is tested against all of SWISS-PROT, the above motif scored 40 true positives, 14,147,328 true negatives, no false positives, and no false negatives (for a correlation of 1.00).

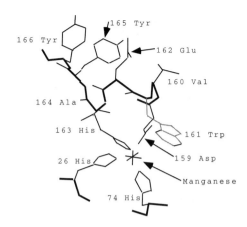

Figure 59.1   Active site of human manganese superoxide dismutase

The Protein Data Bank (PDB), maintained by the Brookhaven National Laboratory in Upton, New York (Bernstein et al. 1977), is the worldwide computerized repository of the three-dimensional coordinates of the atomic structure of proteins. Proteins from the PDB can be interactively displayed by making a three-dimensional *kinemage* of the protein using the PREKIN software and viewing the kinemage with the MAGE software (Richardson and Richardson 1992). Figure 59.1 shows residues 159 to 166 of human manganese superoxide dismutase (1ABM in the Protein Data Bank) as well as the histidines at positions 26 and 74 of the protein sequence. The manganese is ligated by Asp 159, His 163, His 26, and His 74.

59.3 MOTIFS AND AUTOMATICALLY DEFINED FUNCTIONS

When humans write programs, they use subroutines to exploit, by reuse, the modularities, symmetries, and regularities of nontrivial problems (Koza 1994g). Automatically defined functions enable genetic programming to evolve multipart programs consisting of a main program and one or more reusable hierarchically callable subprograms.

The PROSITE language has no facility for defining and using subroutines; however, the D–E–A–D box motif found in the PROSITE database contains a repeatedly used subexpression consisting of four moderately sized, uncharged, hydrophobic residues (L, I, V, and M). Similarly, the manganese superoxide dismutase motif contains a repeatedly used subexpression consisting of Y and F. Because of this manifest modularity, genetic programming with automatically defined functions may be appropriate for evolving a motif-detecting program for the D–E–A–D box family of proteins.

Genetic programming with automatically defined functions has been applied to the transmembrane segment identification problem (Chapters 16 and 17). Genetic programming has also been used to identify omega loops in proteins (Koza 1994g, Chapter 19), to predict whether a residue in a protein sequence is in an α-helix (Handley 1993a, 1994a), to predict the degree to which a protein sequence is exposed to solvent (Handley 1994d), to predict whether or not a nucleic acid sequence is an *E. coli* promoter region

(Handley 1995b), to predict whether or not a 60-base DNA sequence contains a centrally located splice site (Handley 1995c), and to classify a nucleic acid subsequence as being an intron or exon (Handley 1995a).

59.4   PREPARATORY STEPS FOR THE D–E–A–D BOX FAMILY

59.4.1   Program Architecture

The nature of this problem of evolving a motif-detecting program suggests using automatically defined functions to organize the amino acid residues into various subsets of interchangeable residues (corresponding to the square brackets of PROSITE expressions) and using the result-producing branch to decide whether or not a given protein subsequence is an instance of the motif by conjunctively joining the outcomes of the matching at each position of the protein sequence.

The overall architecture for each program in the population consists of two zero-argument automatically defined functions and one result-producing branch. The architecture-altering operations are not used in this problem.

59.4.2   Functions and Terminals

After analyzing the problem, it seems reasonable that the ingredients of the to-be-evolved computer programs should include 20 zero-argument logical functions capable of interrogating the current position of a protein sequence (described in Section 16.4.2).

Square brackets are used in a PROSITE expression to form disjunctive sets of residues. The two-argument MOR function (reminiscent of a Boolean OR function) can be used to define disjunctions of the values returned by the 20 residue-detecting functions.

The dash is used in a PROSITE expression to lengthen the PROSITE expression. The two-argument MAND function (reminiscent of a Boolean AND function) corresponds to the dash of the PROSITE language.

The terminal set, $T_{\text{adf-initial}}$, for the two function-defining branches (ADF0 and ADF1) contains the 20 zero-argument residue-detecting functions:

$$T_{\text{adf-initial}} = \{ (A?), (C?), (D?), \ldots, (Y?) \}.$$

The initial function set, $F_{\text{adf-initial}}$, for the two function-defining branches is

$$F_{\text{adf-initial}} = \{MOR\}.$$

The initial terminal set for the result-producing branch, $T_{\text{rpb-initial}}$, consists of the now-defined automatically defined functions (ADF0 and ADF1) and the 20 zero-argument residue-detecting functions:

$$T_{\text{rpb-initial}} = \{ADF0, ADF1, (A?), (C?), (D?), \ldots, (Y?)\}.$$

The initial function set for the result-producing branch, $F_{\text{rpb-initial}}$, is

$$F_{\text{rpb-initial}} = \{MAND\}.$$

Both function-defining branches of each program in the population for this problem are compositions of the functions from $F_{\text{adf-initial}}$ and terminals from $T_{\text{adf-initial}}$. The result-producing branch is composed of functions from $F_{\text{rpb-initial}}$ and terminals from $T_{\text{rpb-initial}}$.

Note that we do not prespecify the length of the motif that is to be evolved. Both the size and content of each branch of the multipart program are to be evolved by genetic programming.

If the result-producing branch of a program returns a logically true value at a particular position in a protein sequence, that position will be identified as the beginning of an occurrence of the motif; otherwise that position will be classified negatively. If a program examines a residue that is beyond the C-terminal (end) of the protein, the position will be classified negatively.

Since there are no architecture-altering operations in this problem, $F_{\text{rpb-potential}}$, $T_{\text{rpb-potential}}$, $F_{\text{adf-potential}}$, and $T_{\text{adf-potential}}$ are all empty.

59.4.3   Fitness

The fitness measure must assign a value as to how well a particular evolved motif-detecting program predicts whether a particular amino acid residue is the beginning of a D–E–A–D box.

A set of in-sample fitness cases (i.e., the training set) is used to measure the fitness of programs during the evolutionary process. The fitness cases for this problem are individual amino acid residues of proteins. The single residue indicating the start of the occurrence of the motif is a positive fitness case, and all other residues are negative fitness cases.

When an individual motif-detecting program in the population is tested against a particular fitness case, the outcome can be a true positive, a true negative, a false positive (an overprediction), or a false negative (an underprediction).

The set of positive in-sample fitness cases contains all the residues of 26 of the 34 proteins in SWISS-PROT belonging to the D–E–A–D box family.

Because of the rarity of the motif among the 14,147,368 residues in SWISS-PROT and in order to save computer time, we constructed the set of negative in-sample fitness cases by extracting 210 30-residue fragments that did not belong to the D–E–A–D box family, did not contain the D–E–A–D box motif, but did contain a sizable partial match with the D–E–A–D box motif (such as all X-X-D-E-A-D-X-X-X or V-X-X-E-A-D-X-X-X that are not in the D–E–A–D box family). In the end, the in-sample fitness cases consisted of 19,200 amino acid residues from 236 proteins (26 residues being positive instances and 19,174 being negative instances of the D–E–A–D box motif).

Correlation is appropriate as a measure of raw fitness for an individual motif-detecting program in a two-way classification problem (as described in Section 16.4.3). Standardized fitness can then be defined as $1 - C/2$. Thus, fitness ranges between 0.0 and +1.0, so that lower values of fitness are better than higher values and a value of 0 corresponds to the best.

After a motif-detecting program is evolved using the in-sample fitness cases, the question arises as to how well it generalizes to unseen different fitness cases from the same problem environment. A set of out-of-sample fitness cases consisting of 5,605 amino acid residues from 53 proteins (8 residues being positive instances and 5,597 being negative instances of the D–E–A–D box motif) is used to validate the performance of an evolved motif-detecting program. For reference, when the D–E–A–D box motif found in the

PROSITE database is tested against the out-of-sample fitness cases, there are 8 true positives, 5,596 true negatives, 1 false positive, and no false negatives (for a correlation of 0.94). When it is tested against all of SWISS-PROT, it scored 34 true positives, 14,147,333 true negatives, 1 false positive, and no false negatives (for a correlation of 0.99).

59.4.4   Parameters

The control parameters for runs in this chapter are either in the tableau (Table 59.2) or are the default values specified in Koza 1994g, Appendix D.

59.4.5   Termination

The success predicate for any one run of this problem is emergence of an evolved program with an in-sample correlation of 1.00 on the in-sample fitness cases. That program is designated as the result of the run.

59.4.6   Tableau

Table 59.2 summarizes the key features of the protein motif discovery problem for the D–E–A-D box family.

59.5   JURY METHOD FOR CREATING A CONSENSUS MOTIF

Because the 1,029 PROSITE motifs partition the existing protein database into relatively small subsets and because the PROSITE database is intentionally oriented toward highly overfitted descriptions, there is a poverty of instances of any given motif in the protein database. The difficulties of evolving a motif from such an impoverished database can be compensated for by using a jury (Rost and Sander 1993) of at least two evolved results having an in-sample correlation of 1.00. A jury consisting of the best-of-run solutions from various independent runs was used to make the final decision. A unanimous jury decision was required in order to classify a position of a protein sequence as the beginning of the motif. Otherwise, the position was classified negatively.

59.6   RESULTS FOR THE D–E–A-D BOX FAMILY

In one run, the best motif-detecting program from generation 0 scored 20 true positives, 19,152 true negatives, 22 false positives, and 6 false negatives (for an in-sample correlation of 0.60). Like all programs in all generations of this problem, this program consists of two automatically defined functions (ADF0 and ADF1) followed by one result-producing branch:

```
(PROGN (DEFUN ADF0 ()
    (VALUES (MOR (L?) (N?))))
(DEFUN ADF1 ()
    (VALUES (MOR (R?) (V?))))
    (VALUES (MAND (V?) (MAND (L?) (D?))))).
```

Table 59.2 Tableau for protein motif discovery problem for the D–E–A-D box family of proteins

Objective	Discover a program that classifies a protein as to whether it belongs to the D–E–A–D box family of proteins.
Program architecture	One result-producing branch and two zero-argument automatically defined functions
Initial function set for the RPBs	$F_{rpb-initial}$ = {MAND}
Initial terminal set for the RPBs	$T_{rpb-initial}$ = {ADF0, ADF1, (A?), (C?), (D?), . . . , (Y?)}
Initial function set for the ADFs	$T_{adf-initial}$ = {(A?), (C?), (D?), . . . , (Y?)}
Initial terminal set for the ADFs	$F_{adf-initial}$ = {MOR}
Potential function set for the RPBs	Architecture-altering operations are not used.
Potential terminal set for the RPBs	Architecture-altering operations are not used.
Potential function set for the ADFs	Architecture-altering operations are not used.
Potential terminal set for the ADFs	Architecture-altering operations are not used.
Fitness cases	The in-sample fitness cases consist of 19,200 amino acid residues from 236 proteins (26 residues being positive instances and 19,174 being negative instances of the D–E–A-D box motif).
	The out-of-sample fitness cases consist of 5,605 amino acid residues from 53 proteins (8 residues being positive instances and 5,597 being negative instances).
Raw fitness	Correlation C (ranging from –1.0 to +1.0)
Standardized fitness	$1 - C/2$ (ranging from 0.0 to 1.0)
Hits	Not used
Wrapper	None
Parameters	M = 256,000. G = 201. Q = 4,000. D = 64. B = 8%. S_{rpb} = 50. S_{adf} = 50. N_{rpb} = 1. $N_{max-adf}$ = 2. $N_{max-argument-adf}$ = 0.
Result designation	Best-so-far pace-setting individual
Success predicate	A program achieves an in-sample correlation of 1.00 on the in-sample fitness cases.

The result-producing branch of this best-of-generation program from generation 0 defines the motif **V-L-D** of length 3. The motif in this result-producing branch admits no alternatives in any of its three positions. This result-producing branch entirely ignores the subsets defined by its two automatically defined functions, ADF0 and ADF1.

In subsequent generations, the programs in the population became more complex and their fitness improved apace. There is a wide-ranging search among possible lengths for the motifs and possible ways of using and reusing the automatically defined functions. The length of the motifs started to increase (sometimes beyond 9). The result-producing branches started to refer to one or both of their automatically defined functions. The automatically defined functions started to be used two or more times by the result-producing branches.

On generation 42 of one run, the best-of-generation program (shown below) scored 26 true positives, 19,174 true negatives, no false positives, and no false negatives (for an in-sample correlation of 1.00):

```
(PROGN (DEFUN ADF0 ()
   (VALUES (MOR (MOR (MOR (MOR (W?) (M?)) (MOR (C?) (A?))) (M?))
(MOR (MOR (MOR (MOR (W?) (M?)) (MOR (M?) (I?))) (L?)) (I?)))))
(DEFUN ADF1 ()
   (VALUES (MOR (MOR (MOR (A?) (E?)) (MOR (MOR (MOR (MOR (A?)
(K?)) (MOR (V?) (N?))) (MOR (MOR (E?) (R?)) (MOR (MOR (A?)
(W?)) (MOR (K?) (Q?))))) (MOR (V?) (K?)))) (MOR (MOR (I?) (C?))
(A?)))))
   (VALUES (MAND (MAND (MAND (MAND (MAND (MAND (MAND (ADF1)
(ADF0)) (MAND (D?) (E?))) (ADF0)) (D?)) (ADF1)) (ADF0))
(ADF0))).
```

This best-of-generation program defines the following motif of length 9:

[VIAEKNRWQC]-[LIMCAW]-D-E-[LIMCAW]-D-
[RNEKVIAWQC]-[LIMCAW]-[LIMCAW].

Note that the common subexpression [LIMCAW] defined in ADF0 is used a total of four times in the above overall expression. When tested on the 5,605 out-of-sample fitness cases, this expression scored 8 true positives, 5,597 true negatives, no false positives, and no false negatives (for a correlation of 1.00). When tested against SWISS-PROT, this program scored 34 true positives, 14,147,328 true negatives, 6 false positives, and no false negatives (for a correlation of 0.92).

In another run, the best-of-generation program from generation 64 has an in-sample correlation of 1.00 and defined the following motif of length 10:

[FVIAC]-[LIM EQDNRSK]-D-E-[AFVIC]-D-[LIMEQDNRSK]-[LIMEQDNRSK] -
[LIMEQDNRSK]-[LIMEQDNRSK].

Note that the common subexpression [LIMEQDNRSK] defined in ADF1 is used a total of five times in the above overall expression. When tested on the out-of-sample fitness cases, this program has a correlation of 0.94. When tested against SWISS-PROT, this program scored 34 true positives, 14,147,272 true negatives, 62 false positives, and no false negatives (for a correlation of 0.60).

In other runs, 10 additional evolved programs each have an in-sample correlation of 1.00. These 12 results participated in a jury that created an evolved consensus motif of length 10 (shown below) that scored 26 true positives, 19,174 true negatives, no false positives, and no false negatives (for an in-sample correlation of 1.00):

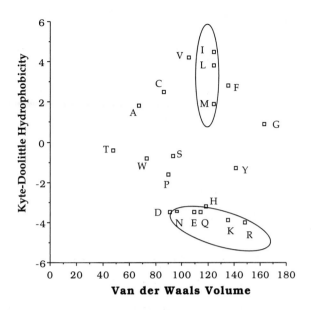

Figure 59.2   Scatter diagram of hydrophobicity and van der Waals volume of the 20 amino acid residues

[IV]-[LIM]-D-E-[AI]-D-[RNEK]-[LIM]-[LIM]-[LIMEQDNRSK].

Note that [LIM] is used three times in this expression. When tested on the 5,605 out-of-sample fitness cases, this expression scored 8 true positives, 5,597 true negatives, no false positives, and no false negatives (for a correlation of 1.00). When tested against SWISS-PROT, this program scored 34 true positives, 14,147,334 true negatives, no false positives, and no false negatives (for a correlation of 1.00). Thus, the evolved consensus motif created by the jury scored slightly better than the human-written motif found in the PROSITE database on the problem of detecting the D–E–A–D box family of proteins.

Recalling that the motif found in the PROSITE database for the D–E–A–D box family is

[LIVM]-[LIVM]-D-E-A-D-x-[LIVM]-[LIVM],

we can see that the evolved consensus motif differs in the following four ways from the motif found in the PROSITE database.

First, position 7 of the motif has a definite character. The X in position 7 of the PRO-SITE motif is replaced by [RNEK] in the consensus motif. Figure 59.2 is a scatter diagram relating the van der Waals volume (Creighton 1993) and the hydrophobicity values (Kyte and Doolittle 1982) of the 20 amino acids. In this figure, E, K, N, and R are located in the same general area (circled in the lower right) indicating that they are all highly hydrophilic and bulky.

Second, the [LIVM] in positions 2, 8, and 9 of the PROSITE motif is replaced by the somewhat more precise [LIM] in the consensus motif. As can be seen in the circled area at the top right of Figure 59.2, residues I, L, and M have virtually identical volumes, but V has a different volume.

Third, the [LIVM] in position 1 of the PROSITE motif is replaced by the somewhat more precise [IV] in the consensus motif.

Fourth, the evolved consensus motif specifies that position 10 (beyond the last position specified by the PROSITE motif) contains [LIMEQDNRSK].

59.7 PREPARATORY STEPS FOR THE MANGANESE SUPEROXIDE DISMUTASE FAMILY

The motif found in the PROSITE database for the manganese superoxide dismutase family of proteins is

D-X-W-E-H-[STA]-[FY][FY].

The preparatory steps for this problem are the same as those for the D–E–A–D box family with two exceptions.

First, the fitness cases are different. Specifically, the in-sample fitness cases for the problem of detecting the manganese superoxide dismutase family of proteins consisted of 13,518 amino acid residues from 270 proteins (30 residues being positive instances and 13,488 being negative instances). The out-of-sample fitness cases are constructed using the same approach as described above and consisted of 3,280 residues from 53 proteins (10 residues being positive instances and 3,270 being negative instances). When the manganese superoxide dismutase motif found in the PROSITE database is tested against the out-of-sample fitness cases, there are 10 true positives, 3,270 true negatives, no false positives, and no false negatives (for a correlation of 1.00). When it is tested against all of SWISS-PROT, it scores a correlation of 1.00.

Second, three zero-argument automatically defined functions are used on this problem because this motif for this family is known to be more complex than that of the D–E–A–D box family.

59.8 RESULTS FOR THE MANGANESE SUPEROXIDE DISMUTASE FAMILY

As before, the evolved motifs participated in a jury that created the following consensus motif of length 9 that has an in-sample correlation of 1.00:

D–[VAML]–W–E–H–[SA]–[YFH]–[YFAHS]–[YFADHLIS].

When tested on the 3,280 out-of-sample fitness cases, this expression has an out-of-sample correlation of 1.00. When tested against SWISS-PROT, this program scored 40 true positives, 14,147,328 true negatives, no false positives, and no false negatives (for a correlation of 1.00). That is, the evolved consensus motif created by the jury scored as well as the human-written motif found in the PROSITE database on the problem of detecting the manganese superoxide dismutase family of proteins.

The evolved consensus motif differs in the following ways from the motif found in the PROSITE database.

First, the X in position 2 of the PROSITE motif is replaced by the set of hydrophobic residues [VAML]. As can be seen from Figure 59.3, position 2 of the motif (i.e., position 160 of the protein) is buried (in contrast to, for example, electrically charged Glu 162,

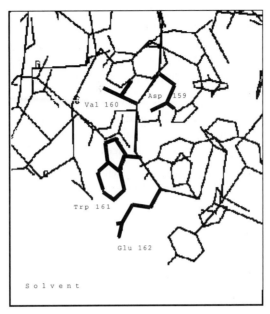

Figure 59.3   Section of manganese superoxide dismutase showing that position 160 is buried

which is exposed to the solvent). Thus, it is reasonable that whatever appears at position 2 should be hydrophobic.

Second, the [STA] in position 6 of the PROSITE motif is replaced by the somewhat more precise [SA] in the consensus motif.

Third, the evolved consensus motif specifies that position 9 (beyond the last position specified by the PROSITE motif) contains [YFADHLIS].

In summary, genetic programming was successfully used to create motifs for the D–E–A–D box family of proteins and the manganese superoxide dismutase family. Both motifs are evolved without prespecifying their length. Both evolved motifs employed automatically defined functions to capture the repeated use of a common subexpression. When tested against the SWISS-PROT database of proteins, the two evolved consensus motifs detect the two families as well as, or slightly better than, the human-written motifs placed in the PROSITE database by an international committee of human experts on molecular biology.

Referring to the eight criteria in Chapter 1 for establishing that an automatically created result is competitive with a human-produced result, this result satisfies the following criterion:

C.   The result is equal to or better than a result that was placed into a database or archive of results maintained by an internationally recognized panel of scientific experts.

Therefore, we make the following claim:

- **CLAIM NO. 14** We claim that the automatic creation by genetic programming of motifs that detect the D–E–A-D box family of proteins and the manganese superoxide dismutase family as well as, or slightly better than, the human-written motifs found in the PROSITE database are instances where genetic programming has produced results that are competitive with a result produced by creative and inventive humans.

The programs created by genetic programming for these two problems constitute additional instances of automatically created algorithms that satisfy Arthur Samuel's criterion (1983) for artificial intelligence and machine learning:

> The aim [is] . . . to get machines to exhibit behavior, which if done by humans, would be assumed to involve the use of intelligence.

Programmatic Motifs and the Cellular Location Problem

As soon as a newly sequenced protein is deposited into the world's ever-growing archive of protein sequences, the question immediately arises as to the biological structure and function of the protein. One question about a new protein involves its cellular location—that is, where the protein resides in a living organism. After a protein is produced inside the cell, it may perform its work from an intracellular location, it may be secreted from the cell and operate from an extracellular location, it may become embedded in the membrane of the cell (or other membrane), or it may reside in the cell's nucleus (if the cell has one).

Figure 60.1 shows a living cell with a cellular membrane dividing the cell's inside (intracellular region) from its outside (extracellular region). The cell shown has a nucleus containing DNA.

Proteins are often classified into five classes based on their cellular location—extracellular (E), intracellular (I), nuclear (N), membrane integral (M), and membrane anchored (A).

For example, hemagglutinin/amebocyte aggregation factor precursor (called HAAF_LIMPO in the SWISS-PROT database of proteins) consists of the following 172 amino acid residues:

MNSPAIVIIFSTLTFSEAWVNDWDGALNFQCQLKDSIKTISSIHSNHHEDRR
WNFGCERTLRDPSCYFTNYVNDWDKLLHFTCKSGEAIAGFNSYHDNRRE
DRRWKIYCCKDKNKCTDYRTCAWTGYVNSWDGDLHYTVPKDYVLTGVISE
HDNHREDRRWKFQHCRLKNC

and is an example of an extracellular (E) protein.

Peptidyl-prolyl cis-trans isomerase (CYPH_STRCH) consists of the following 165 residues:

MTTKVYFDITIDDAPAGRITFNLFDDVVPKTAENFRALATGEKGFGYAGSSF
HRVITDFMLQGGDFTRGDGTGGKSIYGEKFADENFQLKHDRVGLLSMAN
AGKNTNGSQFFITTVLTPWLDGKHVVFGEVADDDSMALVRKIEALGSSSG
RTSAKVTIAESGAL

and is an example of an intracellular (I) protein.

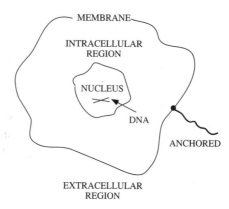

Figure 60.1   Living cell

Prostaglandin-H2-D-isomerase precursor (PGHD_RAT) consists of the following 188 residues:

MAALPMLWTGLVLLGLLGFPQTPAQGHDTVQPNFQQDKFLGRWYSAGLA
SNSSWFREKKELLFMCQTVVAPSTEGGLNLTSTFLRKNQCETKVMVLQPA
GVPGQYTYNSPHWQLPLPLSVETDYDEYAFLFSKRTKGPGQDFRMATLYS
RAQLLKEELKEKF ITFSKDQGLTEEDIVFLPQPDKCIQE

and is an example of a nuclear (N) protein.

Halocyanin precursor (HCY_NATPH) consists of the following 163 residues:

MKDISRRRFVLGTGATVAAATLAGCNGNGNGNGNGNGNGEPDTPEGRA
DQFLTDNDALMYDGDITDETGQDEVVVVTGAGNNGFAFDPAAIRVDVGTT
VTWEWTGDGGAHNVVSEPESDFEFESDRVDEEGFTFEQTFDDEGVALY
VCTPHRAQGMYGAVIVE

and is an example of a membrane (M) protein.

T-cell surface glycoprotein CD3 delta chain precursor (CD3D_HUMAN) consists of the following 171 residues:

MEHSTFLSGLVLATLLSQVSPFKIPIEELEDRVFVNCNTSITWVEGTVGTLLS
DITRLDLGKRILDPRGIYRCNGTDIYKDKESTVQVHYRMCQSCVELDPATVAGI
IVT DVIATLLLALGVFCFAGHETGRLSGAADTQALLRNDQVYQPLRDRDDA
QYSHLG GNWARNK

and is an example of an anchored (A) membrane protein.

Numerous methods, including statistics, motifs, neural networks, decision trees, and inductive logic programming, have been used to uncover patterns in protein and DNA sequences that are related to the biological function of the sequence.

For example, statistical methods are typically used to uncover relationships between the biological activity of a sequence and occurrences (single or multiple) of some elementary event (such as the appearance of an amino acid residue in a protein sequence). One statistical approach is based on computing the protein's amino acid composition (i.e., the percentage of occurrence of each of the 20 amino acids in the protein).

As another example, motifs are regular expressions that are matched to short subsequences of proteins to predict whether a particular protein belongs to a particular family (as described in Chapter 59). Neural networks typically examine a sequence using a fixed-sized window and compute an arithmetic weighted sum of signals (Rost and Sander 1993) to make various predictions about the sequence.

However, for each of these types of computation, the allowable computation is predetermined and highly constrained. Highly constrained types of computations have many limitations in attempting to capture the exceedingly complex relationship that links a protein's primary sequence to its biological structure and function.

In contrast, ordinary computer programs bring a large and varied arsenal of computational capabilities to bear in solving problems. These capabilities include arithmetic functions, conditional operations, logical operations, internal storage, parameterizable subroutines, data structures (named memory, indexed memory, matrices, stacks, queues, lists, relational memory), iteration, recursion, macro definitions, hierarchical compositions of subprograms, multiple inputs, multiple outputs, and so forth.

This chapter introduces the idea of a programmatic motif and applies it to the problem of cellular location.

60.1 TYPES OF COMPUTATION

Statistics, motifs, neural networks, decision trees, inductive logic programming, and computer programs are among the many techniques that have been used to uncover biologically interesting patterns in protein and DNA sequences.

60.1.1 Single-Residue Statistics

Cedano, Aloy, Perez-Pons, and Querol (1997) recently reported, in the *Journal of Molecular Biology*, a single-residue statistical algorithm with 76% accuracy that used the protein's amino acid composition for classifying a protein sequence according to its cellular location using the five classes we discussed previously: extracellular, intracellular, nuclear, membrane integral, and membrane anchored.

Their single-residue statistical algorithm works reasonably well because there are several relatively simple relationships between a protein's cellular location and the frequency of occurrence of particular amino acids. For example, extracellular proteins have comparatively low percentages of hydrophobic (water-hating) or polar residues and comparatively high percentages of cysteine residues (which often form extremely stable extracellular disulfide bonds). Integral membrane and anchored membrane proteins are comparatively rich in hydrophobic residues because portion(s) of the protein sequence are embedded in the lipid membrane and hydrophobic residues are congenial to nonpolar environments (Chapters 16 and 17). Nuclear proteins have comparatively very high percentages of positively charged residues (to partially compensate for the negative charge of the phosphate backbone of the DNA residing in the nucleus), but comparatively low percentages of aromatic residues. Intracellular (cytoplasmic) proteins have comparatively high percentages of negatively charged residues and aliphatic residues, but relatively low percentages of cysteine.

Another reason for variation in the frequency of occurrence of particular amino acids by cellular location is that the amino acids on the protein's surface interact directly with the physiochemical environments of different cellular locations. For example, about 40% of the amino acid residues on the surfaces of intracellular and nuclear proteins are electrically charged (reflecting the ionic strength of these two environments), while only about 16% of the amino acid residues on the surfaces of extracellular proteins are electrically charged. Another study of cellular location (Andrade, O'Donoghue, and Rost 1998) used the amino acid composition on the protein's surface for classifying a protein sequence according to its cellular location into three classes (extracellular, intracellular, and nuclear) with 77% accuracy. This approach assumes the existence of substantial additional information in the form of the protein's tertiary structure (which establishes which amino acid residues actually lie on the protein's surface after the protein folds itself into its three-dimensional conformation).

Other subcellular compartments (such as the mitochondria, ribosomes, lysosomes, and endoplasmic reticulum) are not specifically considered in the work of Cedano, Aloy, Perez-Pons, and Querol (1997), the work of Andrade, O'Donoghue, and Rost (1998), or the work described in this chapter.

60.1.2 Adjacent-Pair Statistics

Cedano, Aloy, Perez-Pons, and Querol (1997) themselves acknowledged that their single-residue statistical algorithm "is an apparently simple relationship between amino acid composition and protein class (location)" and that it alone cannot pinpoint the cellular location of a protein. For example, it is known that augmenting single-residue percentages with two-residue percentages can improve the accuracy of classification (Nakashima and Nishikawa 1994).

60.1.3 Motifs

Another type of computation for examining the primary structure of a protein is to scan a protein sequence for an occurrence of a biologically important short subsequence of consecutive amino acid residues (motifs). A protein is said to satisfy this motif if there is a consecutive subsequence *anywhere* along the entire protein sequence that matches the defining expression. As explained in Chapter 59, motifs are defined by regular expressions, such as

[LIVM]-[LIVM]-D-E-A-D-X-[LIVM]-[LIVM],

and consequently represent a highly constrained method of computation.

60.1.4 Shortcomings of Highly Constrained Types of Computations

Highly constrained types of computations have many limitations in attempting to capture the exceedingly complex relationship that links a protein's primary sequence to its biological structure and function.

Single-residue statistics reduce the entire protein sequence to 20 percentages. Because single-residue statistics look at the protein through a window of a fixed size (one), they cannot take into account relationships between a combination of two or more residues. Adjacent-pair statistics similarly employ a fixed window size of two and similarly ignore relationships involving three or more adjacent residues. They also ignore relationships between two or more nonadjacent residues. Similarly, motifs have a fixed window size and are constrained to set-manipulating operations (e.g., matching, disjunction, conjunction) and cannot do any arithmetic or conditional calculations. They are also narrowly focused on a short localized subsequence of consecutive residues. Neural network approaches are limited to using a fixed window size and to performing a particular single type of arithmetic calculation (layers of weighted sums of inputs).

In addition, motifs, single-residue statistics, adjacent-pair statistics, neural networks, decision trees, inductive logic programming, and other machine learning techniques are not open-ended: they all require that the human investigator decide in advance the detailed nature of the computation that is to be performed. However, for most complex problems, deciding on the nature of the requisite computation is often, in fact, the problem (or at least a major part of it).

The problem of discovering biologically meaningful patterns in protein sequences can be recast as a search for a classification-performing computer program of unknown size and shape. When the problem is recast in this way, genetic programming becomes a candidate for solving the problem.

60.2   PROGRAMMATIC MOTIFS

A computer program resembles a conventional motif (and the other highly constrained types of computation mentioned above) in that it is a deterministic computation that is performed on a protein sequence in order to decide whether or not the protein has a certain property. However, a computer program differs from a motif in that it employs a large and varied arsenal of computational capabilities, including arithmetic functions, conditional operations, subroutines, iterations, memory, data structures, set-creating operations, macro definitions, recursion, and so forth.

We view a computer program as an extension of the conventional concept of "motif." We call the program that genetic programming produces for analyzing a protein a *programmatic motif.*

60.3   PREPARATORY STEPS

60.3.1   Architecture

Each program has a uniform seven-branch architecture, including

- three set-creating automatically defined functions (ADF0, ADF1, and ADF2),
- two arithmetic-performing automatically defined functions (ADF3 and ADF4),
- one iteration-performing branch (IPB), and
- one result-producing branch (RPB).

The architecture-altering operations are not used.

60.3.2   Functions and Terminals

The three set-creating automatically defined functions (ADF0, ADF1, and ADF2) provide a mechanism for defining subsets of the 20 amino acids (that is, for reducing the 20-letter alphabet to a smaller alphabet).

The initial terminal set for the three set-creating automatically defined functions, $T_{\text{adf-sc-initial}}$, contains the 20 zero-argument numerically valued residue-detecting functions (as described in Section 16.4.2):

$$T_{\text{adf-sc-initial}} = \{ (A?), (C?), \ldots, (Y?) \}.$$

The initial function set for the three set-creating automatically defined functions, $F_{\text{adf-sc-initial}}$, contains only the two-argument numerically valued disjunctive function (as described in Section 16.4.2):

$$F_{\text{adf-sc-initial}} = \{ORN\}.$$

The two arithmetic-performing automatically defined functions (ADF3 and ADF4) provide a mechanism for performing arithmetic.

The initial terminal set for the arithmetic-performing automatically defined functions, $T_{\text{adf-ap-initial}}$, contains the 20 zero-argument numerically valued residue-detecting functions:

$$T_{\text{adf-ap-initial}} = \{ (A?), (C?), \ldots, (Y?), \Re_{\text{bigger-reals}} \}.$$

The initial function set for the two arithmetic-performing automatically defined functions, $F_{\text{adf-ap-initial}}$, is

$$F_{\text{adf-ap-initial}} = \{+, -, *, \%, \text{IFGTZ}, \text{ORN}\}.$$

The iteration-performing branch provides a mechanism for integrating information over the entire protein sequence by performing an iterative calculation. The proteins are of different length. The sequence of steps in the iteration-performing branch are performed iteratively for each of the amino acid residues of the given protein sequence. The iteration over the protein sequence is indexed by the iterative variable, INDEX. At the beginning of each step of the iteration, the ACTIVE residue of the protein is the same as the iterative variable, INDEX. The distinction between the ACTIVE residue and the iterative variable, INDEX, is important because the ACTIVE residue can be incremented inside a given step (INDEX) of the iteration using the FORWARD function (described below).

Memory cells can be used to store the intermediate and final results during the iterative calculation. There are two types of memory:

- 5 cells of named memory and
- 20 cells of indexed memory.

The contents of all cells of named and indexed memory are initialized to zero before execution of the iteration-performing branch for a particular fitness case.

The calculation in the iteration-performing branch can involve arithmetic functions, conditional operations, the residue-detecting functions, the numerically valued disjunctive function, the contents of named memory, the contents of indexed memory, the memory-setting functions for named memory, the memory-setting functions for indexed memory, and the results produced by the set-creating and arithmetic-performing automatically defined functions.

The initial terminal set for the iteration-performing branch, $T_{\text{adi-initial}}$, contains the five automatically defined functions (ADF0, ADF1, ADF2, ADF3, ADF4), 20 zero-argument numerically valued residue-detecting functions, five settable named variables (M0, M1, M2, M3, and M4), the READ-RESIDUE function, and floating-point random constants ($\mathfrak{R}_{\text{bigger-reals}}$):

$$T_{\text{adi-initial}} = \{\text{ADF0, ADF1, ADF2, ADF3, ADF4, (A?), (C?), \ldots ,}$$
$$\text{(Y?), M0, M1, M2, M3, M4, READ-RESIDUE, } \mathfrak{R}_{\text{bigger-reals}}\}.$$

The terminal M0 returns the value contained in memory cell M0 (and similarly for the four other terminals M1, M2, M3, and M4). The terminal READ-RESIDUE returns the value contained in the cell of indexed memory implicitly indexed by the active residue.

The function set for the iteration-performing branch, $F_{\text{adi-initial}}$, contains the numerically valued Boolean disjunction ORN, the conditional operator IFGTZ, the WRITE-RESIDUE function, the FORWARD function, the five named setting functions (SETM0, SETM1, ..., SETM4), and the four arithmetic functions:

$$F_{\text{adi-initial}} = \{\text{ORN, SETM0, SETM1, SETM2, SETM3, SETM4, IFGTZ, WRITE-}$$
$$\text{RESIDUE, FORWARD, +, -, *, \%}\}.$$

The one-argument setting functions SETM0, SETM1, SETM2, SETM3, SETM4 are described in Section 6.1.2. The three-argument conditional operator IFGTZ ("if greater than zero") is described in Section 15.2.2. The two-argument protected division function, %, is described in Section 13.3.2.

The one-argument WRITE-RESIDUE function sets the cell of indexed memory implicitly indexed by the active residue to the value of its argument.

The one-argument FORWARD function increments the ACTIVE residue by one and returns the value of its one argument using the current value of ACTIVE. Upon completion of the evaluation of the argument of the FORWARD function, the ACTIVE residue is restored to its previous value. If the FORWARD function attempts to increment the ACTIVE residue beyond the length of the protein, the ACTIVE residue remains unchanged. Note that the values returned by the five automatically defined functions depend on the ACTIVE residue.

The result-producing branch provides a mechanism for performing a final calculation that classifies the protein into one of two classes.

The initial terminal set, $T_{\text{rpb-initial}}$, for the result-producing branch is

$$T_{\text{rpb-initial}} = \{\text{M0, M1, M2, M3, M4, } \mathfrak{R}_{\text{bigger-reals}}\}.$$

The initial function set for the result-producing branch, $F_{\text{rpb-initial}}$, is

$$F_{\text{rpb-initial}} = \{\text{ORN, IFGTZ, +, -, *, \%, READ}\}.$$

The one-argument READ function returns the value stored in the indexed memory cell J, where J is the value of its one argument (adjusted by flooring it and then taking it modulo the size, 20, of the indexed memory).

Since there are no architecture-altering operations in this problem, $F_{\text{rpb-potential}}$, $T_{\text{rpb-potential}}$, $F_{\text{adi-potential}}$, $T_{\text{adi-potential}}$, $F_{\text{adf-potential}}$, and $T_{\text{adf-potential}}$ are all empty.

The wrapper (output interface) for the result-producing branch consists of the IFGTZ function, so a positive return value is interpreted as YES, and a zero or negative return value is interpreted as NO.

60.3.3   Fitness

The fitness measure indicates how well a particular evolved program classifies protein sequences. Fitness is measured over a number of protein sequences (fitness cases). When a classifying program is tested against a particular protein sequence, the outcome can be a true positive, true negative, false positive, or false negative. The total number of true positives, true negatives, false positives, and false negatives for a set of protein sequences, in turn, can be used to compute the correlation coefficient, C (Section 16.4.3). The fitness of a classifying program can then be defined as $1 - C/2$. Thus, fitness ranges between 0.0 and +1.0, so that lower values of fitness are better than higher values and a value of 0 corresponds to the best.

Cedano, Aloy, Perez-Pons, and Querol (1997) used 1,000 proteins (200 from each of five classes) as their in-sample fitness cases. We saved a substantial amount of computer time (about three fourths) by randomly choosing 50% of the proteins of length less than 600 as the in-sample fitness cases. Since the average protein contains about 300 residues, a cutoff of 600 permits the inclusion of many proteins that are up to twice the average length. This approach yielded 471 in-sample fitness cases (88 membrane, 91 nuclear, 108 intracellular, 124 extracellular, and 70 anchored proteins) having a total of 122,489 residues.

The true measure of performance for a classifying program is how well it generalizes to unseen additional (out-of-sample) fitness cases. The results were first cross-validated using the remaining proteins of length less than 600. Then the results were further cross-validated using the same 200 out-of-sample fitness cases as Cedano et al. (1997) (specifically, 41 membrane, 46 nuclear, 55 intracellular, 33 extracellular, and 25 anchored proteins), having a total of 100,029 residues.

Considerable computer time was saved by caching the result of executing each set-creating and arithmetic-performing automatically defined function for each of the 20 residues.

60.3.4   Parameters

The control parameters for this problem are found in the tableau (Table 60.1), the tables of percentages of genetic operations in Appendix D, and the default values specified in Appendix D.

60.3.5   Tableau

Table 60.1 summarizes the key features of the problem of designing a classification program for cellular location.

60.4   RESULTS FOR NUCLEAR PROTEINS

The results below were obtained on our first run of the cellular location problem for nuclear proteins. This run used a population size, M, of 320,000.

The best-of-run two-way classification program for nuclear proteins appears on generation 7 with 86% in-sample accuracy, 91% out-of-sample accuracy (online), and 84% accuracy on the 200 out-of-sample proteins of Cedano et al. (1997).

Table 60.1 Tableau for cellular location problem

Objective	Discover a program to classify a protein sequence as to whether or not it resides in a particular cellular location.
Program architecture	One result-producing branch (RPB), three set-creating automatically defined functions (ADF0, ADF1, and ADF2), two arithmetic-performing automatically defined functions (ADF3 and ADF4), and one iteration-performing branch (IPB).
Initial function set for the RPBs	$F_{rpb\text{-}initial}$ = {ORN, IFGTZ, +, -, *, %, READ}
Initial terminal set for the RPBs	$T_{rpb\text{-}initial}$ = {M0, M1, M2, M3, M4, $\Re_{bigger\text{-}reals}$}
Initial function set for the set-creating ADFs	$F_{adf\text{-}sc\text{-}initial}$ = {ORN}
Initial terminal set for the set-creating ADFs	$T_{adf\text{-}sc\text{-}initial}$ = {(A?), (C?), . . . , (Y?)}
Initial function set for the arithmetic-performing ADFs	$F_{adf\text{-}ap\text{-}initial}$ = {+, -, *, %, IFGTZ, ORN}
Initial terminal set for the arithmetic-performing ADFs	$T_{adf\text{-}ap\text{-}initial}$ = {(A?), (C?), . . . , (Y?), $\Re_{bigger\text{-}reals}$}
Initial function set for the IPB	$F_{adi\text{-}initial}$ = {ORN, SETM0, SETM1, SETM2, SETM3, SETM4, IFGTZ, WRITE-RESIDUE, FORWARD, +, -, *, %}
Initial terminal set for the IPB	$T_{adi\text{-}initial}$ = {ADF0, ADF1, ADF2, ADF3, ADF4, (A?), (C?), . . . , (Y?), M0, M1, M2, M3, M4, READ-RESIDUE, $\Re_{bigger\text{-}reals}$}.
Potential function set for the RPBs	Architecture-altering operations are not used.
Potential terminal set for the RPBs	Architecture-altering operations are not used.
Potential function set for the set-creating ADFs	Architecture-altering operations are not used.
Potential terminal set for the set-creating ADFs	Architecture-altering operations are not used.
Potential function set for the arithmetic-performing ADFs	Architecture-altering operations are not used.

(continued)

Table 60.1 (continued)

Potential terminal set for the arithmetic-performing ADFs	Architecture-altering operations are not used.
Potential function set for the IPB	Architecture-altering operations are not used.
Potential terminal set for the IPB	Architecture-altering operations are not used.
Fitness cases	471 proteins (Section 60.3.3)
Raw fitness	Correlation C (ranging from −1.0 to +1.0)
Standardized fitness	$1 - C/2$ (ranging from 0.0 to 1.0).
Hits	Not used for this problem
Wrapper	The wrapper (output interface) for the result-producing branch consists of the IFGTZ function, so a positive return value is interpreted as YES and a zero or negative return value is interpreted as NO.
Parameters	$M = 320,000$. $G = 201$. $Q = 5,000$. $D = 64$. $B = 2\%$. $S_{rpb} = 400$. $S_{adf} = 40$. $N_{rpb} = 1$. $N_{max\text{-}adf} = 5$. $N_{adi\text{-}max} = 1$.
Result designation	Best-so-far pace-setting individual
Success predicate	Fitness appears to have reached a plateau.

Table 60.2 shows the performance of the best-of-run classifying program for nuclear proteins from generation 7 from the run with a population size of 320,000 based on the 200 out-of-sample proteins of Cedano et al. (1997). The rows of the table represent the classification made by the evolved program. The columns represent the correct classification. The table shows that the best-of-run program from generation 7 scores 26 true positives, 143 true negatives, 11 false positives, and 20 false negatives. Most of the false positives are incorrect intracellular classifications. Intracellular proteins, like nuclear proteins, tend to be negatively charged. No errors were made for either the membrane or anchored membrane proteins.

The evolved program actually invokes its result-producing branch and iteration-performing branch, but no automatically defined functions. It uses three cells of named memory (M1, M2, and M4) for communication between its iteration-performing branch and the result-producing branch.

The 36-point iteration-performing branch is

```
(SETM2 (SETM0 (SETM3 (+ (- (P?) (L?)) (SETM2 (SETM0 (SETM3 (+
(SETM1 (FORWARD (- (R?) (V?)))) (SETM3 (SETM1 (SETM3 (+ (- (Q?)
(V?)) (SETM1 (SETM0 (SETM3 (+ (SETM1 (FORWARD (- (R?) (V?))))
(SETM3 (SETM1 (SETM1 M0)))))))))))))))))))).
```

The six-point result-producing branch is

```
(+ (IFGTZ M4 M1 -3.337654) M2).
```

Table 60.2 Performance of the best-of-run classifying program for nuclear proteins (population size of 320,000)

	I	E	A	M	N
N	7	4	0	0	26
Other	48	29	25	32	20

Notice that no multiplications or divisions appear in these branches. Note also that

```
(SETM1 (FORWARD (- (R?) (V?))))
```

appears twice in the iteration-performing branch. This duplication was almost certainly produced by a crossover.

When the current residue is arginine R, the subexpression `(- (R?) (V?))` evaluates to +2. When the current residue is valine V, this subexpression evaluates to –2. When the current expression is neither R nor V, this subexpression evaluates to 0. Although the FORWARD function can be used to test for patterns that involve multiple positions in the protein sequence, the effect of this FORWARD here is merely to (almost) double the effect of the subexpression `(- (R?) (V?))`. The effect is not exactly a doubling since the contribution of the very first residue of the protein sequence is not doubled.

When analyzed, the evolved solution for classifying a protein as nuclear is, subject to the above minor qualification, equivalent to the following:

- Increment the running sum, M0, by adding the number in Table 60.3 to M0 for each residue of the protein.
- If $-3.34 + M0 > 0$, then classify the protein as a nuclear protein; otherwise, classify the protein as nonnuclear.

DNA carries a net negative charge. The arginine R residue is positively charged while the glutamine residue Q is polar. Proline P, leucine L, and valine V are not electrically charged.

We subsequently made a second run of this problem for nuclear proteins on 56 nodes of our 70-node Beowulf-style parallel computer (described in Section 62.1.5). Because of the higher speed of the Beowulf-style computer (a 533 MHz microprocessor instead of an 80 MHz microprocessor) and the greater amount of RAM memory per microprocessor (64 megabytes instead of 32 megabytes), we were able to run this problem with a population size of 1,120,000 (i.e., $Q = 20,000$ and $D = 56$) instead of the 320,000 used above. In addition, because of the higher speed of the Beowulf-style computer, we were able to use 800 in-sample fitness cases (instead of the 471 proteins used above). Moreover, we were able to use proteins of all lengths and did not filter out the longer proteins (as we did above).

The best-of-run two-way classification program for nuclear proteins appears on generation 14 with 90% in-sample accuracy, 90% out-of-sample accuracy (online), and 87% accuracy on the 200 out-of-sample proteins of Cedano et al. (1997).

Table 60.4 shows the performance of the best-of-run classifying program for nuclear proteins from generation 14 of the run with a population size of 1,120,000 based on the

Table 60.3 Increments used for nuclear proteins

Residue	Increment
R	+4
Q	+2
P	+2
L	−2
V	−6
Other	0

Table 60.4 Performance of the best-of-run classifying program for nuclear proteins (population size of 1,120,000)

	I	E	A	M	N
N	5	3	0	0	29
Other	50	30	25	41	17

200 out-of-sample proteins of Cedano et al. (1997). The table shows that the best-of-run program from generation 14 scores 29 true positives, 146 true negatives, 8 false positives, and 17 false negatives. None of the false positives are membrane or anchored proteins. Membrane or anchored proteins tend to have a considerable percentage of hydrophobic amino acid residues. On the other hand, all of the false positives are intracellular and extracellular proteins, which tend to be electrically charged (negatively or positively, respectively).

The evolved program invokes its result-producing branch and iteration-performing branch. The iteration-performing branch invokes an arithmetic-performing automatically defined function (ADF4). The remaining four automatically defined functions are ignored. Only cell M0 of named memory is used for communication between the result-producing branch and the iteration-performing branch.

The 30-point iteration-performing branch is

```
(SETM1 (SETM3 (+ (+ (SETM2 (IFGTZ (V?) (E?) (P?))) (* (ADF4)
(ORN (ORN (V?) (L?)) (ORN (L?) (W?))))) (- (SETM0 M1) (% (ORN
(+ (M?) (I?)) (- (S?) (Y?))) (A?)))))))).
```

The 12-point result-producing branch is

```
(+ (IFGTZ 3.254503 (+ (READ M0) (READ (* M0 4.084754))) M4)
M0).
```

The 31-point automatically defined function ADF4 is

```
(- -2.002551 (ORN (ORN (ORN (ORN (ORN (ORN (ORN (E?) (K?)) (ORN
(N?) (K?))) (ORN (ORN (W?) (V?)) (ORN (M?) (K?)))) (ORN (ORN
(R?) (Q?)) (K?))) (P?)) (ORN (S?) (V?))) (E?))).
```

60.5   RESULTS FOR MEMBRANE PROTEINS

The results below were obtained on the first and only run of the cellular location problem for membrane proteins. This run used a population size, M, of 320,000.

The best-of-run two-way classification program for membrane proteins appears on generation 10 with 85% in-sample accuracy, 87% out-of-sample accuracy (online), and 89% accuracy on the 200 out-of-sample proteins (offline) of Cedano et al. (1997).

Table 60.5 shows the performance of this best-of-run classifying program for membrane proteins based on the 200 out-of-sample proteins of Cedano et al. (1997). The table shows that the best-of-run program scores 24 true positives, 154 true negatives, 5 false positives, and 17 false negatives. Since a portion of each membrane protein is extracellular and intracellular, membrane proteins are most easily mistaken for extracellular and intracellular proteins. Similarly, membrane proteins may be easily mistaken for anchored membrane proteins. However, membrane proteins are most dissimilar to nuclear proteins and are, accordingly, not misclassified as nuclear at all by this program.

One set-creating automatically defined function (ADF0) is actually referenced. The iteration-performing branch writes to indexed memory extensively (in seven different places) and also employs named memory to store intermediate results. One cell of named memory (M1) is used for communication between the iteration-performing branch and the result-producing branch.

The three-point automatically defined function ADF0 is

```
(ORN (P?) (K?)).
```

The 37-point iteration-performing branch is

```
(WRITE-RESIDUE (SETM4 (+ (SETM0 (- (WRITE-RESIDUE (SETM4 (+
(SETM0 (- (SETM2 M4) (+ (N?) M1))) (WRITE-RESIDUE (IFGTZ
(WRITE-RESIDUE (V?)) (SETM4 (F?)) (WRITE-RESIDUE (I?))))))) (+
(SETM0 (ADF0)) M1))) (WRITE-RESIDUE (IFGTZ (WRITE-RESIDUE (-
(N?) (S?))) (SETM4 (F?)) (SETM4 (F?))))))).
```

The two-point result-producing branch is

```
(READ-RESIDUE M1).
```

Since M1 is never set, it is 0, and the result-producing branch is equivalent to

```
(READ-RESIDUE 0).
```

That is, the final result is the number stored in the zeroth cell of indexed memory. Since alanine **A** is alphabetically the first amino acid residue, the final result comes from the position of indexed memory associated with alanine.

The overall program operates by incrementing a running sum, M4, by adding the number in Table 60.6 to M4 for each residue of the protein. For each residue, the program writes the current value of M4 into the cell of indexed memory whose index equals the current residue. In particular, the program writes the current value of M4 into the zeroth cell of indexed memory for the last alanine of the protein sequence. If the zeroth cell of indexed memory is positive, then the program classifies the protein as a membrane protein; otherwise, it classifies the protein as nonmembrane.

Table 60.5 Performance of best-of-run classifying program for membrane proteins (population size of 320,000)

	I	E	A	M	N
M	2	2	1	24	0
Other	53	31	24	17	46

Table 60.6 Increments used for membrane proteins

Residue	Increment
F	+2
I	+2
P	−2
N	−2
K	−2
Other	0

Notice that no multiplications or divisions appear in any of these three branches. When analyzed, the evolved solution for classifying a protein as a membrane can be restated as follows:

- Increment a running sum, SUM, by adding the number in Table 60.6 to SUM for each residue of the protein until reaching the last alanine of the protein sequence.
- If SUM is positive, then classify the protein as a membrane protein; otherwise, classify the protein as nonmembrane.

60.6   RESULTS FOR EXTRACELLULAR PROTEINS

The results below were obtained on the first and only run of the cellular location problem for extracellular proteins. This run used a population size, M, of 320,000.

On generation 26, genetic programming evolved a two-way classification program for extracellular proteins with 82% in-sample accuracy, 87% out-of-sample accuracy (online), and 83% accuracy on the 200 out-of-sample proteins (offline) of Cedano et al. (1997).

Table 60.7 shows the performance of this best-of-run classifying program for extracellular proteins based on the 200 out-of-sample proteins of Cedano et al. (1997). The table shows that the best-of-run program scores 7 true positives, 160 true negatives, 7 false positives, and 26 false negatives.

The evolved program refers once to one of its arithmetic-performing automatically defined functions (ADF4) and repeatedly refers to one of its set-creating automatically defined functions (ADF1). It twice uses the FORWARD function to examine downstream residues. It uses one cell of named memory (M0) for communication between its iteration-performing branch and the result-producing branch.

Table 60.7 Performance of best-of-run classifying program for extracellular proteins (population size of 320,000)

	I	E	A	M	N
E	4	7	0	2	1
Other	51	26	25	39	45

The 69-point iteration-performing branch is

```
(SET0 (IFGTZ (ORN (SET4 (+ (E?) (Y?))) (% M0 (SET0 (IFGTZ (ORN
(SET4 (+ (E?) (Y?))) (% M0 (* (* (% (A?) (- (Y?) (* (- (Y?)
(ORN (H?) (E?))) (T?)))) (N?)) (- (N?) (I?))))) (SET1 (+ (SET2
M0) (- (ADF1) (ORN (C?) (Y?))))) (SET2 (SET4 (SET2
(ADF4)))))))) (SET1 (+ (SET2 M0) (- (ADF1) (ORN (C?) (SET3
(SET3 (- (Y?) (P?))))))) (% (* (FORWARD (I?)) (R?)) (SET4
(FORWARD (R?)))))).
```

The 119-point result-producing branch is

```
(+ (- (- (IFGTZ (ORN M0 M3) (READ-RESIDUE -1.176145) (IFGTZ M1
M0 M2)) (* (+ 4.536757 M3) (+ M0 M2))) (+ (READ-RESIDUE (IFGTZ
M3 M2 M0)) (ORN (ORN -1.090041 M0) (ORN M0 M0)))) (% (- (%
(IFGTZ M2 M4 2.438198) (IFGTZ M2 -2.261266 M1)) (% (- M2 M4) (-
2.807559 M1))) (- (READ-RESIDUE (* (- (% (IFGTZ M2 M4 2.438198)
(+ 2.519011 M3)) (% (- (* (% (ORN M3 M2) (- M1 M2)) (- (* M2 -
2.070116) (% (- (% (IFGTZ M2 M4 2.438198) (IFGTZ M2 -2.261266
M1)) (% (- M2 M4) (- 2.807559 M1))) (- (READ-RESIDUE (-
2.807559 M1)) (- (ORN M3 M2) (* M3 M4)))))) M4) (- 2.807559
M1))) 1.836927)) (- (ORN M3 M2) (* M3 M4))))).
```

The three-point set-creating automatically defined function ADF1 is

```
(ORN (F?) (R?)).
```

The nine-point arithmetic-performing automatically defined function ADF4 is

```
(% (A?) (- (Y?) (* (- (Y?) (S?)) (T?)))).
```

60.7   RESULTS FOR INTRACELLULAR PROTEINS

The results below were obtained on our first and only run of the cellular location problem for intracellular proteins. This run used a population size, M, of 320,000.

On generation 12, genetic programming evolved a two-way classification program for intracellular proteins with 78% in-sample accuracy, 79% out-of-sample accuracy (online), and 78% accuracy on the 200 out-of-sample proteins of Cedano et al. (1997).

Table 60.8 shows the performance of this best-of-run classifying program for anchored proteins based on the 200 out-of-sample proteins of Cedano et al. (1997). The

Table 60.8 Performance of best-of-run classifying program for intracellular proteins (population size of 320,000)

	I	E	A	M	N
I	37	5	5	4	12
Other	18	28	20	37	34

table shows that the best-of-run program scores 37 true positives, 119 true negatives, 26 false positives, and 18 false negatives.

The evolved program repeatedly referred to set-creating automatically defined functions ADF0 and ADF2 and referred once to one arithmetic-performing automatically defined function (ADF4).

60.8 RESULTS FOR ANCHORED PROTEINS

The results below were obtained on our first run of the cellular location problem for anchored proteins. This run used a population size, M, of 320,000.

The best-of-run two-way classification program for anchored proteins appears on generation 11 with 80% in-sample accuracy, 85% out-of-sample accuracy (online), and 83% accuracy on the 200 out-of-sample proteins of Cedano et al. (1997).

Table 60.9 shows the performance of this best-of-run classifying program for anchored proteins based on the 200 out-of-sample proteins of Cedano et al. (1997). The table shows that the best-of-run program scores 6 true positives, 160 true negatives, 15 false positives, and 19 false negatives.

The iteration-performing branch uses both indexed memory and named memory. The program actually invokes one set-creating automatically defined function (ADF2) and one arithmetic-performing automatically defined function (ADF3).

We subsequently made a second run of this problem for anchored proteins on 56 nodes of our 70-node Beowulf-style parallel computer (described in Section 62.1.5). The larger machine enabled us to run this problem with a population size of 1,120,000 (i.e., $Q = 20,000$ and $D = 56$) and the full 800 in-sample fitness cases.

The best-of-run two-way classification program for anchored proteins appears on generation 12 with 72% in-sample accuracy, 69% out-of-sample accuracy (online), and 75% accuracy on the 200 out-of-sample proteins of Cedano et al. (1997).

Table 60.10 shows the performance of the best-of-run classifying program for anchored proteins from generation 12 of the run with a population size of 1,120,000 based on the 200 out-of-sample proteins of Cedano et al. (1997). The table shows that the best-of-run program from generation 12 scores 14 true positives, 137 true negatives, 38 false positives, and 11 false negatives.

60.9 SUMMARY

This chapter describes two-way classification algorithms evolved using genetic programming for the cellular location problem. On the 200 out-of-sample proteins of Cedano et

Table 60.9 Performance of best-of-run classifying program for anchored proteins (with a population size of 320,000)

	I	E	A	M	N
A	8	2	6	5	0
Other	47	31	19	36	46

Table 60.10 Performance of the best-of-run classifying program for anchored proteins from run (with a population size of 1,120,000)

	I	E	A	M	N
N	7	14	14	13	4
Other	48	19	11	28	42

al. (1997), these two-way classifiers have an 83% accuracy for extracellular proteins, 87% for nuclear proteins (the better of the two runs), 89% accuracy for membrane proteins, 78% for intracellular proteins, and 83% for anchored membrane proteins (the better of the two runs). All five two-way accuracies of these are better than the 76% accuracy reported for the human-created five-way algorithm (Cedano et al. 1997). These two-way levels of accuracy are also better than the human-created three-way algorithm using protein tertiary structure (Andrade, O'Donoghue, and Rost 1998). The evolved classifying programs employed a large variety of types of computation (such as iteration, memory, subroutines, arithmetic and conditional operations, set-creating operations, and lookahead) that are available in genetic programming, but not available in conventional automated techniques. These results are suggestive of the potential usefulness of programmatic motifs for other problems of classification involving proteins (and other biological sequence data).

Part 9: PARALLELIZATION AND IMPLEMENTATION ISSUES

Genetic programming starts with a high-level specification of the problem to be solved and creates a computer program to solve the problem. Since genetic programming creates the computer program using a minimum of user-supplied information, runs of genetic programming on nontrivial problems typically require considerable computer resources. Thus, a discussion of genetic programming inevitably leads to a discussion of practical issues of computer implementation.

Chapter 61 tallies the computer time that was consumed by the runs that yielded the 14 instances (from Table 1.1) where we claim that genetic programming has produced results that are competitive with human-produced results. Chapter 62 describes the implementation of parallel genetic programming. Chapter 63 discusses other implementation issues concerning genetic programming.

Computer Time

Table 61.1 tallies the computer time that was consumed by the 23 runs that yielded the 14 instances (from table 1.1) where we claim that genetic programming has produced results that are competitive with human-produced results.

For each run, Table 61.1 shows the population size, M, and the generation number, i, that yielded the best-of-run individual presented in this book. The column labeled "$M \times (i + 1)$" is the product of the population size, M, and the number of generations run. This number is equivalent to the number of fitness evaluations necessary to produce the best-of-run individual. No adjustment is made for the fact that, in practice, no fitness evaluation is actually performed for some individuals (typically the 9% or 10% of the population that is simply reproduced and the offspring of semantics-preserving architecture-altering operations such as subroutine duplication and argument duplication).

Table 61.1 also shows the number of minutes needed to create the best-of-run individual for the particular run and the number of petacycles (10^{15} cycles) consumed by the run. All problems in this table were run on the 64-node Parsytec parallel computer with an 80 MHz PowerPC 601 microprocessor at each processing node (described in Chapter 62), except for the D–E–A-D box problem (last row of the table). The 64-node Parsytec parallel computer operates at 5.12 GHz, or 307.2 gigacycles per minute. For reference, the SPECfp95 rating of a PowerPC 601 80 MHz processor is 2.97, so the 64-node Parsytec system delivers about 190 SPECfp95 in the aggregate. The D–E–A-D box problem was run on the 64-node Transtech parallel computer with an INMOS T-805 30 MHz transputer at each processing node (Chapter 62). The INMOS T-805 30 MHz transputer is roughly equivalent to an Intel 486/33 microprocessor on the genetic programming application. The 64-node Transtech parallel computer operates at 1.92 GHz, or 115.2 gigacycles per minute. Our limited internal experimentation indicates that the SPECfp95 measurements are a reasonably accurate gauge of performance of our genetic programming system in C over a number of platforms. SPECfp95 measurements are not available for the transputer. Our 64-node Parsytec computer system is approximately 22 times faster than our 64-node Transtech transputer system on our application. Therefore, we estimate that the 64-node Transtech transputer system delivers about 8.64 SPECfp95 in the aggregate. The remaining discussion in this chapter is based on the admittedly imperfect metric of clock speed.

The 23 runs in Table 61.1 executed an average of 32,797,983 fitness evaluations. These runs averaged 5,034 minutes (about 3.5 days) and 1.5 petacycles. This average was heavily influenced by the temperature-sensing circuit (Chapter 49), the voltage reference circuit (Chapter 50), and the real-time robot controller (Chapter 48).

Table 61.1 Computer time consumed by runs of genetic programming that produced the 14 results that are competitive with human-produced results

	Claimed instance	Population M	Generation i	$M \times (i + 1)$	Minutes	Petacycles	Reference
1	Transmembrane segment identification problem with architecture-altering operations for subroutines	128,000	28	3,712,000	312	0.096	Chapter 16
1	Transmembrane segment identification problem with iteration creation	64,000	42	2,752,000	163	0.050	Chapter 17
2	Minimal sorting network (GPPS 1.0)	640,000	31	20,480,000	145	0.045	Figure 21.6
2	Minimal sorting network (GPPS 2.0)	300,000	33	10,200,000	30	0.009	Figure 23.2
3	Recognizable ladder topology for filters	320,000	49	16,000,000	138	0.042	Figure 25.57
4	Recognizable M-derived half sections for filters	320,000	53	17,280,000	481	0.148	Figure 25.59
5	Recognizable elliptic topology for filters	640,000	31	20,480,000	899	0.276	Figure 27.41
6	Crossover filter	640,000	137	88,320,000	2,673	0.821	Figure 32.10
6	Crossover filter	640,000	158	101,760,000	5,436	1.670	Figure 33.10
7	Recognizable voltage gain stage and a Darlington emitter-follower section	640,000	45	29,440,000	1,056	0.324	Figure 42.7
8	60 dB amplifier	640,000	109	70,400,000	3,139	0.964	Figure 44.15
8	96 dB amplifier	640,000	86	55,680,000	4,786	1.470	Figure 45.16
9	Squaring computational circuit	640,000	37	24,320,000	2,504	0.769	Figure 47.6
9	Cubing computational circuit	640,000	74	48,000,000	2,545	0.782	Figure 47.11
9	Square root computational circuit	640,000	57	37,120,000	2,817	0.865	Figure 47.12
9	Cube root computational circuit	640,000	60	39,040,000	2,179	0.669	Figure 47.16
9	Logarithmic computational circuit	640,000	55	35,840,000	4,309	1.324	Figure 47.17
9	Gaussian computational circuit (MOSFET)	640,000	36	23,680,000	1,190	0.366	Figure 51.18
10	Real-time robot controller	640,000	31	20,480,000	22,103	6.790	Figure 48.5
11	Temperature-sensing circuit	640,000	25	16,640,000	14,204	4.363	Figure 49.5
12	Voltage reference circuit	640,000	80	51,840,000	37,147	11.412	Figure 50.8
13	Cellular automata rule for the majority classification problem	51,200	17	921,600	4,231	1.300	Chapter 58
14	Motifs for the D–E–A–D box family of proteins	256,000	42	11,008,000	3,297	1.013	Chapter 59

The 80 MHz microprocessors used to produce most of the results in Table 61.1 were almost obsolete by the time that this book was completed. A single DEC Alpha 21164 microprocessor of 1998 vintage operates at 533 MHz (6.7 times faster). Thus, if the 23 runs in Table 61.1 were run on a system composed of an identical number of 533 MHz microprocessors (64), each run might average approximately only 751 minutes (about 12.5 hours).

If available computer capacity continues to double approximately every 18 months in accordance with Moore's law (Moore 1996), a computation requiring 751 minutes in 1998 would only require about 47 minutes in 2004 and 2.93 minutes in 2010.

Petaflop computers (Sterling, Messina, and Smith 1995) capable of executing 10^{15} operations per second are expected to be available to high-end institutional users by 2010. Thus, it will be possible to run the foregoing examples of automated circuit synthesis in one second in little more than a decade.

The times required to run the circuit synthesis problems in Table 61.1 can all be improved considerably by software optimizations. Each fitness evaluation in such problems requires a separate SPICE simulation consisting of an average of 2.3×10^7 computer operations (i.e., a single fitness evaluation consumed an average of about 0.25 second of computer time on an 80 MHz processor). None of the computer times for circuit synthesis problems in Table 61.1 reflect known optimizations that could be implemented today. For example, SPICE can be accelerated by a factor of at least three by using versions of SPICE that are currently commercially available (as opposed to the public domain SPICE simulator that we modified and used). In addition, SPICE simulations can be accelerated by several fold (Kielkowski 1994) by using known techniques to tune its control parameters to the specific type of circuit being designed. Our technique for circuit synthesis could also be modified (e.g., implementing the depth-first evaluation of the circuit-constructing program tree described in Section 54.10). The combined effect of all of these known optimizations is approximately one order of magnitude for problems of circuit synthesis.

Parallelization of Genetic Programming

Although many moderately sized problems can be solved by the genetic algorithm using currently available single-processor workstations, more substantial problems usually require a large population, a large number of generations, or both. Increases in computing power can be realized either by increasing the speed of computation or by parallelizing the application.

The electronics industry has delivered components with increased speed of computation (i.e., an approximate doubling every 18 months) for several decades in accordance with Moore's law (Moore 1996). Continued increases at approximately the same rate (or greater) are predicted for at least an additional decade and a half (Case 1998). For example, petaflop computers capable of executing 10^{15} operations per second are expected to be available to high-end institutional users by 2010 (Sterling, Messina, and Smith 1995). Moreover, this increase in computational speed has been accompanied by declining cost. For applications that can be parallelized efficiently (such as genetic algorithms and genetic programming), parallelization provides an efficient means for increasing computing power.

With respect to computer time, the dominant component of the computational burden of solving nontrivial problems with the genetic algorithm or genetic programming is the task of measuring the fitness of each individual in each generation of the evolving population. Relatively little computer time is expended on other tasks of the algorithm, such as the creation of the initial random population at the beginning of the run and the execution of the genetic operations during the run.

With respect to memory, the dominant component of the computational burden is the storage of the population of individuals (since the population typically involves large numbers of individuals for nontrivial problems). In fact, the population is the only data that must be stored in a run of the genetic algorithm or genetic programming (although it is common practice to carry a small data structure containing various statistics along with the population and the cached best-so-far individual). For the genetic algorithm operating on fixed-length character strings, storage of the population almost never constitutes a major concern. For genetic programming (where the individuals in the population are potentially corpulent program trees), memory usage is sometimes an important consideration. However, in practice, the choice of population size is usually constrained by considerations of time rather than space. Thus, this chapter focuses on issues of computer time.

Because the task of measuring the fitness of one particular individual in the population is decoupled from the task of measuring the fitness of all other individuals, nearly 100% efficiency can be realized from a parallel computer system running genetic algorithms and genetic programming. In fact, the decoupled nature of genetic algorithms and genetic programming usually also extends to the level of fitness cases. In any event, amenability to parallelization is a recognized feature of genetic algorithms and genetic programming (Holland 1975; Robertson 1987; Tanese 1989; Goldberg 1989a; Stender 1993; Oussaidene 1996).

In fact, runs of genetic algorithms and genetic programming can frequently be beneficially mapped onto a parallel computing device in several different ways, including

- mapping a semi-isolated subpopulation (deme) to each processor,
- mapping a single individual to each processor,
- mapping a single fitness case to each processor,
- mapping a single time step to particular processors (as in the pipeline of the field-programmable gate array of Chapter 57), and
- mapping a particular independent run to a processor.

These mappings may be dynamic (as in schemes where work is farmed out to various processors) or static (where a particular subpopulation, individual, fitness case, time step, or run is assigned to a particular processor on a one-time basis).

The remainder of this chapter focuses on the first approach, namely, the *distributed genetic algorithm* or *island model* of parallelization. In this approach, the population for a given run is divided into semi-isolated subpopulations (Tanese 1989). The subpopulations are called *demes* (as per Sewall Wright 1943). Each subpopulation is assigned to a processor of the parallel computing device. In the typical case where the initial population is randomly created, each subpopulation is created locally on each processor. Then the time-consuming task of measuring the fitness of each individual in the subpopulation is performed separately at each processor. Because this task is performed independently for each individual and independently at each processing node, this approach delivers an overall increase in the total amount of work performed that is nearly linear with the number of independent processing nodes. The genetic operations such as reproduction, crossover, and mutation are also performed separately at each processor. In particular, mating is localized within the subpopulation. Upon completion of a generation, a certain relatively small percentage of the individuals in each subpopulation are probabilistically selected (based on fitness) for emigration from each processor. The selected individuals then emigrate to other processing nodes (typically neighboring ones). The subpopulations usually operate independently in the sense that generations start and end asynchronously from node to node. The immigrants to each node typically wait in a buffer at their destination until the destination is ready to assimilate its immigrants. The immigrants are inserted in lieu of the just-departed emigrants. On the relatively rare occasions when the full complement of immigrants have not yet been received, the deficiency is made up from randomly chosen copies of the just-departed emigrants. The overall iterative process then proceeds to the next generation, beginning with the measurement of fitness of the new subpopulation (which contains many new individuals because of both the genetic operations and the immigration).

The amount of migration may be small (thereby potentially creating distinct subspecies within the overall population) or large (thereby approaching, for all practical purposes, panmictic selection throughout the overall population). In either event, the dominant component of the computational burden of solving nontrivial problems is the task of measuring the fitness of each individual in each generation of the evolving population. Thus, the interprocessor communication requirements of migration are low because the migration is spread over a considerable amount of time.

The distributed genetic algorithm is well suited to loosely coupled, low-bandwidth, parallel computation. It is possible to readily implement the distributed genetic algorithm on a medium-grained parallel computer or on a network of workstations.

There have been numerous parallel implementations of genetic algorithms (Stender 1993; Robertson 1987; Tanese 1989; Abramson, Mills, and Perkins 1994; Bianchini and Brown 1993; Cui and Fogarty 1992; Kroger, Schwenderling, and Vornberger 1992; Schwehm 1992; Tout, Ribeiro-Filho, Mignot, and Idlebi 1994; Juric, Potter, and Plaksin 1995).

Section 62.1 describes the hardware of our parallel genetic programming system, and Section 62.2 describes the software.

Section 62.3 contains a comparative experiment concerning the computational effort required to solve a problem using the parallel computer system with semi-isolated subpopulations with various migration rates and a serial computer using panmictic selection (i.e., where the individual selected to participate in a genetic operation can come from anywhere in the population). As will be seen, a modest migration rate is most favorable for the particular problem. The use of semi-isolated subpopulations (apart from the parallel or serial nature of the computer) often delivers a *superlinear* speedup in terms of the computational effort required to yield a solution to the problem.

62.1 HARDWARE

Almost every run of genetic programming reported in this book was executed on a parallel computer device of some type.

The sorting network problem (Chapter 57) was done using a 4,096-processor field-programmable gate array. It will not be discussed further in this chapter.

All other problems in this book were executed on one of the following four parallel computing systems:

- a 64-node parallel computer system consisting of 64 Transtech TRAM boards (each containing an INMOS T-805 30 MHz processor with 4 megabytes of RAM memory) arranged in a two-dimensional 8×8 toroidal mesh with a host PC 486–type computer,
- a 64-node Parsytec parallel computer system consisting of 64 PowerPC 601 80 MHz processors (each with 32 megabytes of RAM) arranged in a two-dimensional 8×8 toroidal mesh with a host PC Pentium–type computer,
- a four-node Parsytec parallel computer system consisting of four PowerPC 601 80 MHz processors (each with 32 megabytes of RAM) arranged in a two-dimensional 2×2 toroidal mesh with a host PC Pentium–type computer, and

- a 70-node home-built Beowulf-style parallel computer system consisting of 70 processing nodes (each containing a 533 MHz DEC Alpha microprocessor and 64 megabytes of RAM) arranged in a two-dimensional 7×10 toroidal mesh with a host DEC Alpha–type computer.

The vast majority of the runs in this book were done using a 64-node Parsytec parallel computer system.

The machine from Transtech (of Ithaca, New York) was acquired in the spring of 1994. The machine from Parsytec (of Aachen, West Germany) was acquired in the spring of 1995. The 70-node machine was built in May 1998. The DEC Alpha computers were acquired from DCG Computers of New Hampshire.

62.1.1   Transputers

The first three of these systems are based on transputers—either for communications alone or for both communications and computation. A transputer is a single VLSI device containing an on-chip processor, on-chip memory, and several independent serial bidirectional physical on-chip communication links. Manufactured by INMOS (a division of SGS-Thomson Microelectronics), the transputer was one of the first 32-bit microprocessors and was the first microprocessor that was designed with the specific primary goal of supporting multiprocessing. The on-chip communication links and multiprocessing capabilities of transputers were specifically designed to facilitate parallel supercomputing. The communication between transputers is through one-way point-to-point unbuffered channels. Transputers are typically mounted on small boards with up to 16 megabytes of additional RAM memory above and beyond the on-chip memory. These small boards are called TRAMS. One popular model of TRAM has 4 megabytes of RAM memory and an INMOS T-805 transputer featuring a 30 MHz 32-bit floating-point processor, 4 kilobytes of on-chip memory, and four communication links.

One important reason for choosing transputer-based systems for parallel genetic programming at the time of our purchase in 1994 and 1995 was that the transputer (and its supporting tools) were designed, from the beginning, to support parallel computation involving multiple intercommunicating processes on each processor and interprocessor communication. The transputer was designed so that

- the executable code could be easily distributed to all the processing nodes of a network at the beginning of each run,
- the processes on each node could be easily started up,
- messages could be easily sent and received between two processes on the same or different processing nodes,
- messages could be easily sent and received between one processing node and a central supervisory program,
- messages could be easily sent and received by the host computer from the central supervisory program, and
- the processes on each node could be easily stopped.

62.1.2   Transtech 64-Node System

The 64-node Transtech machine (called the "farm") has a PC 486–type computer (running Windows 3.11) acting as the host and as the file server for the overall system. Two

TRAMs are physically housed on a B008 expansion board within the host computer. One TRAM runs the central supervisory process for running genetic programming (the boss process described below). The other TRAM runs the INMOS debugger process for transputer systems.

The remaining 64 TRAMs (the processing nodes) are physically housed on eight Transtech boards in a VME box. Each processing node has an INMOS T-805 30 MHz processor with 4 megabytes of RAM memory. The 64 processing nodes are arranged in a toroidal network in which 62 of the 64 processing nodes are physically connected to four neighbors (in the N, E, W, and S directions). Two of the 64 nodes of the network are exceptional in that they are physically connected to the boss node and are thus connected to only three other (of the 64) processing nodes. The boss node is physically linked only to these two exceptional nodes of the network.

The communication between processes on different transputers is through one-way point-to-point channels. The channels are laid out along the physical links of the transputers using a virtual router provided in the INMOS toolkit for transputers. The virtual router creates a two-dimensional toroidal mesh among the 64 processing nodes. All communications and process scheduling for the 64 nodes are handled by the hardware of the transputer.

Our tests indicate that a single INMOS T-805 30 MHz microprocessor is approximately equivalent to an Intel 486/33 microprocessor for a run of genetic programming written in the C programming language. Thus, the 64-node Transtech machine is equivalent to about 64 Intel 486/33 microprocessors. The 64-node Transtech system operates at about 1.92 GHz in the aggregate.

62.1.3   Parsytec 64-Node System

The 64-node Parsytec machine (called the "ranch") also has a PC Pentium–type computer (running Windows 3.11) acting as the host and as the file server for the overall system. The boss process runs on a TRAM that is separate from the host PC and separate from the 64 processing nodes.

The processing nodes are packaged as 16 Parsytec XPlorer units, each containing four processing nodes. Each processing node has an 80 MHz PowerPC 601 microprocessor, 32 megabytes of RAM memory, and an INMOS T-805 transputer. The PowerPC microprocessor is used for computational purposes, and the INMOS transputer is used solely for communication purposes. The 64 processing nodes are arranged in a toroidal network that is essentially the same as that of the Transtech machine. The communication between processing nodes is by means of the one-way point-to-point channels of the transputer on each processing node. The channels are laid out along the physical links of the transputers using a virtual router provided by Parsytec. The virtual router creates a toroidal mesh among the 64 processing nodes. The 64 nodes run a specialized transputer microkernel operating system developed by Parsytec.

The 64-node Parsytec system operates at about 5.12 GHz in the aggregate. Apart from the difference in clock rates, the PowerPC microprocessor used for computation in the Parsytec system is considerably more powerful than the INMOS T-805 transputer. The former uses a RISC architecture that is particularly well suited for genetic programming work; the latter is based on one-byte machine instructions. The SPECfp95 rating of a PowerPC 601 80 MHz processor is 2.97, so the 64-node Parsytec system delivers about

190 SPECfp95 in the aggregate. The 64-node Parsytec system delivers a speedup of about 22 times over the 64-node Transtech system.

62.1.4 Parsytec Four-Node System

The four-node Parsytec machine (called the "garden") consists of one Parsytec XPlorer unit with four processing nodes. It is used primarily for development and testing of programs. Its configuration is similar to that of the 64-node Parsytec system, except for the size of the system.

62.1.5 Alpha 70-Node Beowulf-Style System

Each processing node of the 70-node Alpha system contains a 533 MHz DEC Alpha microprocessor and 64 megabytes of RAM. The system has one DEC Alpha processor as host. The system is configured in a Beowulf style (Sterling 1996, 1998; Sterling, Salmon, Becker, and Savarese 1999). The processing nodes are connected with a 100 megabit-per-second Ethernet. The processing nodes and the host use the Linux operating system.

The 70-node Alpha system operates at about 37.31 GHz in the aggregate (i.e., about 7.3 times faster than the 64-node Parsytec system). The SPECfp95 rating of a 533 MHz DEC 21164 Alpha microprocessor is 23.985 (about 8.08 times that of the PowerPC 601 80 MHz microprocessor), so the 70-node Alpha system delivers about 1,679 SPECfp95 in the aggregate (about 8.8 times the 64-node Parsytec system).

An expanded version of this Beowulf system is being planned.

62.2 SOFTWARE

A single, unified genetic programming software system runs on all four of our parallel computing platforms as well as the PC Pentium–type computers that we use for program development. Ordinarily, we first test a new program on a PC Pentium–type computer and then retest it on the four-node Parsytec parallel computer. The program is then run on the 64-node Parsytec parallel computer (or the 64-node Transtech system). We have used both the 64-node Parsytec system and the 64-node Transtech system on problems with a population in excess of three million. However, the most common population size used for problems in this book is 640,000—that is, a subpopulation (deme) size of $Q = 10,000$ on each of the $D = 64$ nodes of the Parsytec system.

Because of our single unified genetic programming software system, the transition from the earlier 64-node Transtech system to the 64-node Parsytec system was accomplished in four days. Similarly, the transition from the 64-node Parsytec system to the 70-node Alpha system took less than a week.

Except for minor differences, the description below of our implementation of parallel genetic programming applies to all four systems.

The host computer for the Transtech and Parsytec systems is a PC-type computer and consists of a keyboard, a video display monitor, and a large disk for memory. The host computer for the 70-node Alpha system is an Alpha workstation.

Figure 62.1 shows the various physical elements of the parallel genetic programming system in terms of a small illustrative system with a 3×3 arrangement of processing nodes. The boxes denote the various computers, including the host computer, the debugger node (applicable only to the Transtech system), the boss node, and the net-

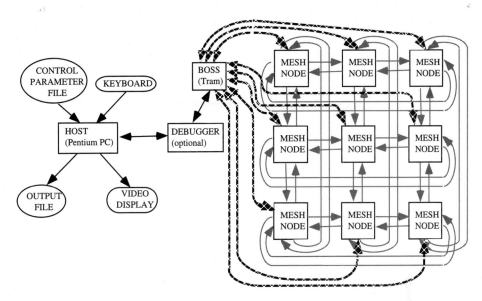

Figure 62.1 Illustrative parallel genetic programming system with a host computer and a 3 × 3 arrangement of processing nodes arranged in a toroidal mesh

work of processing nodes. The ovals denote the various major files on the host computer, including the control parameter file for each run and the output file. The rounded boxes denote the input-output devices of the host computer (i.e., the keyboard and video display). Heavy unbroken lines are used to show the physical linkages between the various elements of the system. Heavy broken lines show the lines of virtual communication between the boss node and all of the processing nodes. The light unbroken lines show the actual physical channels connecting each processing node with its four toroidally adjacent neighbors.

The host process runs on the host computer (PC or Alpha). The boss process runs on a TRAM for the Transtech and Parsytec systems and on an Alpha for the Alpha system.

Each of the 64 processing nodes concurrently run the following four intercommunicating processes:

- a monitor process,
- a breeder process,
- an exporter process, and
- an importer process.

The 64 processing nodes do not access files or input-output devices.

Figure 62.2 shows the four intercommunicating processes on each of the 64 processing nodes. The primary process on each of the processing nodes is the breeder process, which executes the bulk of the steps of genetic programming. The other three processes permit asynchronous communication between the processing nodes of the system. The monitor process of a given processing node of the network communicates with the boss process and the breeder process of the node. The breeder also communicates with the importer and exporter processes of the processing node. The importer and exporter each

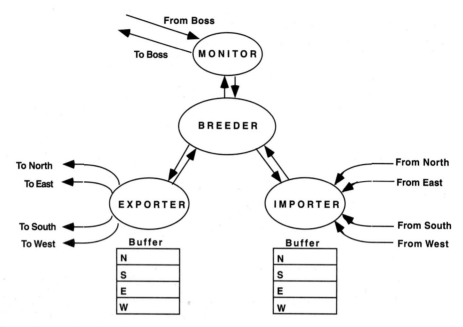

Figure 62.2 The four intercommunicating processes on each of the 64 processing nodes

have four buffers for storing emigrants and arriving immigrants, respectively, from the four toroidally adjacent processing nodes.

62.2.1 The Host Process

The host computer runs the host process, which receives input from the keyboard, reads an input file containing the parameters for controlling the run, and writes the output files and communicates with the boss process.

62.2.2 The Boss Process

The boss process is responsible for communicating with the host process of the host computer and the 64 processing nodes of the network.

The boss process sends the initial start-up messages to each of the 64 processors in the network, receives and tabulates information sent to it from each processor, sends information to the host process of the host computer, and handles various error conditions.

At the beginning of a run of genetic programming, the boss process initializes various data structures, creates the set of fitness cases (either by computing them or by obtaining information from a file on the host), creates a different random seed for each processor, pings each processor to be sure it is ready, and reads in a set of control parameters from a file on the host computer.

Then the boss process sends a start-up message to the monitor process of each processing node of the network (which will, in turn, be sent by the monitor process to the breeder process of that particular processing node). The start-up message includes the following:

- the size of the subpopulation that is to be created at the processing node,
- the control parameters for creating the initial random subpopulation at that processing node, including the method of generation and the maximum size for the initial random individuals (and each function-defining branch, each iteration-performing branch, and each result-producing branch, as the case may be),
- the common networkwide table of 200+ random constants for the problem (if any),
- the control parameters specifying the percentage of each genetic operation (e.g., reproduction, crossover, mutation) to be performed for each generation,
- the perpetual run number for the run,
- a node-specific seed for the randomizer (which is used in conjunction with the perpetual run number to seed the randomizer for creating the initial random population at the node),
- one of the following:
  - the actual fitness cases for the problem if the fitness cases are being supplied from an outside database (e.g., protein sequences or economic data),
  - the common networkwide randomizer seed for creating fitness cases for the run if the fitness cases for the problem are being randomly created at the processing node, or
  - nothing if the fitness cases for the problem are being created programmatically at the processing node (e.g., all 2^k fitness cases for a problem of symbolic regression of a k-argument Boolean function),
- the targeted maximum number of generations to be run and the absolute maximum number of generations to be run at the processing node (usually 120% of the former), and
- the number of primed individuals (and, if there are any, the primed individuals themselves).

After sending the start-up message, the boss process enters a loop where it handles the various messages that each monitor sends until an error condition occurs, a solution is found, or all processors have completed a specified number of generations.

62.2.3 The Monitor Process

The monitor process of each processing node is continually awaiting messages from both the boss process of the boss node and the breeder process of its processing node. Upon receipt of a start-up message from the boss process, the monitor process passes this message along to the breeder process on its node.

The monitor process also passes the following messages from the breeder process of its node along to the boss process of the boss node:

- *End-of-generation*: The end-of-generation message contains the best-of-generation individual for the current subpopulation on the processing node and statistics about that individual such as its fitness and number of hits. This message also contains the fitness (and hits) for the worst-of-generation individual of the processing node, the average fitness (and hits) for the subpopulation as a whole, and the variance of the fitness (and hits) of the subpopulation as a whole.

- *Eureka*: The eureka message announces that the processing node has just created an individual in its subpopulation that satisfies the success predicate of the problem and contains the just-created individual and various statistics about it. If the termination criterion for the problem specifies that the run ends with achievement of the success predicate, this message will cause the run to end, and the just-created individual from the processing node will ordinarily become the best-of-run individual.
- *Trace*: The trace message announces that the breeder process has reached certain milestones in its code (e.g., received its start-up message, completed creation of the initial random subpopulation for the node, encountered a problem-specific event that is worthy of reporting to the boss process).
- *Error*: The error message announces that the breeder process has encountered certain anticipatable error conditions.

62.2.4   The Breeder Process

After the breeder process of a processing node receives the start-up message, it performs the following steps in connection with generation 0:

- It creates the initial random subpopulation of individuals for the node.
- It creates the fitness cases for the problem at the processing node (unless the fitness cases are transmitted from the boss process).

In the main generational loop, the breeder process of a processing node iteratively performs the following steps:

- *Fitness evaluation task:* Evaluates the fitness of every individual in the subpopulation.
- *Emigration:* Selects, probabilistically based on fitness, a small number of individuals to be emigrants at the end of generation (except generation 0) and sends these emigrants to a buffer of the exporter process of the processing node.
- *Immigration:* Assimilates the immigrants currently waiting in the buffers of the importer process.
- *Reporting:* Creates an end-of-generation report for the subpopulation.
- *Genetic operations:* Performs the genetic operations on the subpopulation.

The entire network runs until one individual is created that satisfies the success predicate of the problem or until every processing node has completed an originally targeted maximum number of generations to be run. A processing node that reaches the originally targeted maximum number of generations before all the other nodes have reached that originally targeted generation is permitted to continue running up to an absolute maximum number of generations (usually 120% of the originally targeted maximum number).

For most problems the amount of computer time required to measure the fitness of individuals varies considerably among subpopulations. The presence of just one or a few time-consuming programs in a particular subpopulation can dramatically affect the amount of computer time consumed by one processing node in running a generation. Any attempt to synchronize the activities of the algorithm at the various processing nodes would require slowing every processing node to the speed of the slowest. Therefore, each processing node operates asynchronously with respect to all other processing nodes. After a few generations, the various processing nodes of the system will typically be working on different generations.

This variation arises from numerous factors, including the different sizes of the individual programs that are prevalent in a population in genetic programming; the mix of faster and slower primitive functions within the programs; and the number, nature, and content of the function-defining branches or iteration-performing branches of the overall program. In particular, each invocation of an automatically defined function requires execution of its body, so that the effective size of the overall program at the time of execution is considerably larger than the visible number of points actually appearing in the overall program. Moreover, when one automatically defined function can hierarchically refer to another, the effective size (and the execution time) of the program may be an exponential function of the visible number of points actually appearing in the overall program. In addition, if the programs in the population are architecturally diverse, additional variation is introduced. This variation is further magnified if the architecture of a program changes during the run as a result of architecture-altering operations. For problems involving a simulation of behavior over many time steps, many separate experiments, or many probabilistic scenarios, some programs may finish the simulation considerably earlier or later than others. Indeed, for some problems (e.g., time-optimal control problems), variation in program duration is the very objective of the problem.

The asynchrony of the generations on nearby processors requires that the exporting and importing of migrating programs take place in a manner that does not require that the breeder ever wait for a neighboring process to finish a generation. To allow the breeder nearly uninterrupted computing time, the exporter process and the importer process were created to handle the communication. The monitor process acts in a similar fashion for communication with the boss process. The use of multiple processes is also important in preventing deadlocks.

62.2.5 The Exporter Process

In our current implementation, emigrants are sent to the four toroidally adjacent nodes (north, east, south, and west) of the given processing node. The exporter process interacts with the breeder process of its processing node toward the end of the breeder's main generational loop for each generation (except generation 0). At that time, the breeder sends four boatloads of emigrants to a buffer of the exporter process. The number of individuals in each boatload is specified by the migration percentage, B. The exporter process then immediately sends one boatload of emigrants to the importer process of each of the four neighboring processing nodes of the network. Because the exporter process is a separate process, it enables the breeder process to immediately resume its work without waiting for the successful completion of shipment of the emigrants to their destinations.

62.2.6 The Importer Process

The purpose of the importer is to store incoming boatloads of emigrants in its four buffers until the breeder is ready to incorporate them into the subpopulation at the processing node. When a boatload of immigrants arrives via any one of the four channels connecting the importer process to the exporter processes of its four neighboring processing nodes, the importer consumes the immigrants from that channel and places them into the buffer associated with that channel.

The importer process interacts with the breeder process when the breeder process is ready to assimilate immigrants. This occurs immediately after the breeder process deals with the exporter process for a given generation. At that time, the breeder process calls for the contents of the importer's four buffers. If all four buffers are full, the four boatloads of immigrants replace the emigrants that were just dispatched by the breeder process to the exporter process of the node. If fewer than four buffers of the importer process are full, the new immigrants replace as many of the just-dispatched emigrants as possible. Since the emigrants that are dispatched to the exporter process are copies, a few emigrants become duplicated in the case when fewer than four buffers of the importer process are full.

Since the generations run asynchronously at each processing node, one of the neighbors of a particular processing node may complete processing of two generations while the given processing node completes only one generation. In that event, the second boatload of immigrants will arrive from the faster neighbor at the importer process at the destination node before the buffers of the importer process at the destination node have been emptied by the breeder process of that node. In that event, the newly arriving immigrants overwrite the previously arrived, but not yet assimilated, immigrants in that particular buffer. This overwriting seems appropriate since individuals coming from a later generation of a given processing node are likely to be more fit than immigrants from an earlier generation of the same node.

62.2.7 Visual Monitoring Process

A monitoring process (written in Visual Basic) on the host computer can display information about the run on its video display monitor.

One window of this display consists of a multicolor grid presenting information about the last reporting generation for each of the 64 processing nodes. The number of hits for the best-of-generation individual is shown for each node; the nodes with the best and worst number of hits are highlighted. Each processing node is colored green, yellow, red, or gray depending on the amount of time since the last end-of-generation report from that node (based on problem-specific timing parameters). Green indicates that a report was received reasonably recently in accordance with our expectations, yellow indicates that the processing node is slower than our expectations, red indicates that the processing node is very tardy, and gray indicates that the node is dead. The fastest and slowest nodes are highlighted.

A second window shows, by generation, the best fitness and best number of hits for the system as a whole. A third window shows a histogram of the number of hits.

62.2.8 Reliability

The 64-node Parsytec machine has been in continuous use (24 hours per day, seven days per week) for more than three years, from April 1995 to December 1998. During this time, the machine as a whole was never inoperative due to reliability problems attributable to the machine. There have been seven occasions (i.e., about one every six months) when a problem developed in one of the 16 physical units (each containing four processing nodes). At such times, the machine was reconfigured and operated as a 60-node system (6 × 10 toroidal mesh) while the physical unit involved was being repaired by the manufacturer. Excluding test runs, approximately 500 different runs of genetic programming (averaging about two days each) were made during this three-year period.

The most significant operational problems for both our 64-node Transtech system and 64-node Parsytec system related to air conditioning. The summer of 1996 was unusually hot and we experienced memory errors in the part of the Parsytec machine near what we subsequently identified as a "hot spot" in our air-conditioned computer room. We resolved this problem in two ways.

First, we had additional ducting and fans installed to route cool air directly from the air conditioner to the known hot spot in the computer room.

Second, while we were waiting for the additional ducting and fans to be installed, we introduced a software solution to keep the machine running. Since less than about 10% of the RAM memory on each processing node is used to store program code, about 90% of the heat-induced memory errors corrupt the syntactic structure of individuals in the population (rather than the program code for the genetic programming system). Therefore, when a branch of an individual program in the population becomes corrupted, we replace the entire corrupted branch with a newly created branch (as if we had chosen the topmost point of the corrupted branch as the mutation point for applying the ordinary mutation operator). Each invocation of this "summertime mutation" operator is recorded in the output file. Since we commonly apply the mutation operator to about 1% of the individuals in the population on each generation of a run of genetic programming (Appendix D), this incremental number of mutations is an irrelevant increase in the total number of mutations. The historical record indicates that this operator is invoked about a dozen times per year.

62.3   COMPARISON OF COMPUTATIONAL EFFORT FOR DIFFERENT MIGRATION RATES

This section compares the computational effort associated with different migration rates between the processing nodes using the problem of symbolic regression of the Boolean even-5-parity function.

Numerous runs of this problem with a total population size of $M = 32,000$ were made using 10 different approaches. This particular population size (which is much smaller than the population size that can be supported on the parallel system) was chosen because it was possible for us to run this size of population on a single serial computer (PC Pentium–type) with panmictic selection (i.e., where the individual to be selected to participate in a genetic operation can be from anywhere in the population) and thereby compare serial versus parallel processing using a common population size of 32,000.

The first approach tested runs on a single processor with a panmictic population of 32,000.

The second approach tested runs on the parallel system with $D = 64$ demes, a population size of $Q = 500$ per deme, and a migration rate of $B = 12\%$ (in each of four directions on each generation of each deme).

The third through tenth approaches tested runs on the parallel system with the same $D = 64$ demes, the same population size of $Q = 500$ per deme, but migration rates of $B = 8\%$, 6%, 5%, 4%, 3%, 2%, 1%, and 0%, respectively.

For all 10 approaches, the maximum number of generations, G, to be run is 76; the maximum size, S_{rpb}, for the result-producing branch is 500 points. Other minor parameters for the runs were selected as in Koza 1994g, Appendix D.

Figure 62.3 presents the performance curves for approach 5. This figure is based on the 34 runs of the problem of symbolic regression of the Boolean even-5-parity function with $D = 64$ subpopulations of size $Q = 500$ and a migration rate of $B = 5\%$ (in each of four directions on each generation of each subpopulation).

The first value of x for which the experimentally observed cumulative probability of success, $P(M, x)$, is nonzero occurs at $x = 1,202,000$ individuals ($i = 37.6$ equivalent synchronous generations); $P(M, x)$ is 3% for that x. The experimentally observed value of $P(M, x)$ over the 34 runs is 94% after making 1,671,000 fitness evaluations ($i = 52.2$ equivalent synchronous generations) and 97% after making 2,417,500 fitness evaluations ($i = 75.5$ equivalent synchronous generations).

The second curve in Figure 62.3 shows the number of individuals that must be processed, $I(M, x, z)$, to yield, with probability z, a solution to the problem after making x fitness evaluations. The right vertical axis applies to $I(M, x, z)$. $I(M, x, z)$ is derived from the experimentally observed values of $P(M, x)$ as the product of the number of fitness evaluations, x, and the number of independent runs, $R(z)$, necessary to yield a solution to the problem with a required probability, z, after making x fitness evaluations. In turn, $R(z)$ is given by

$$R(z) = \frac{\log(1 - z)}{\log(1 - P(M, x))}$$

The required probability, z, is 99% throughout this book. This equation for $R(z)$ differs slightly from the equation used in Section 12.6 in that the value of $R(z)$ is not rounded to the nearest larger integer.

The $I(M, x, z)$ curve reaches a minimum value of 2,716,081 at the best value $x^* = 1,671,000$ (equivalent to $i^* = 52.2$ synchronous generations) as shown by the shaded vertical line in Figure 62.3. For the observed value of $P(M, x^*) = 94\%$ associated with the best x^*, the number of independent runs necessary to yield a solution to the problem with a 99% probability is $R(z) = 1.63$. The three summary numbers ($x^* = 1,671,000$, $i^* = 52.2$, and $E = 2,716,081$) in the oval indicate making multiple runs of $x^* = 1,671,000$ fitness evaluations (equivalent to $i^* = 52.2$ synchronous generations) is sufficient to yield a solution to this problem with 99% probability after making a total of $E = 2,716,081$ fitness evaluations (i.e., 32,000 population size $\times$ 52.2 equivalent synchronous generations $\times$ 1.63 runs). E is a measure of the computational effort necessary to yield a solution to this problem with 99% probability.

Table 62.1 compares the computational effort $I(M, x, z)$ for the 10 approaches to migration. As can be seen, the computational effort, E, is smallest for a migration rate of $B = 5\%$ (approach 5). The computational effort for all of the parallel runs except for those runs with an extreme (0% or 12%) migration rate is less than the computational effort required with the panmictic population. In other words, creating semi-isolated

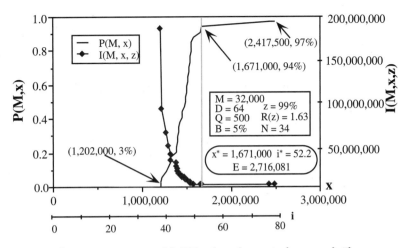

Figure 62.3   Performance curves with 5% migration rate (approach 5)

Table 62.1 Comparison of ten approaches to migration

	Approach	Migration rate B	Computational effort $I(M, x, z)$
1	Panmictic	No demes	5,929,442
2	Parallel	12%	7,072,500
3	Parallel	8%	3,822,500
4	Parallel	6%	3,078,551
5	Parallel	5%	2,716,081
6	Parallel	4%	3,667,221
7	Parallel	3%	3,101,285
8	Parallel	2%	3,822,500
9	Parallel	1%	3,426,878
10	Parallel	0%	16,898,000

demes produced the bonus of also improving the performance of genetic programming for all moderate migration rates for this problem.

The parallel system delivers two speedups:

- the nearly linear speedup in executing a fixed amount of code in parallel inherent in the island model of genetic programming and
- the superlinear speedup in terms of the speed of the genetic programming algorithm in solving the problem.

In other words, not only does the problem solve more quickly because of the distribution of the computation over many processors, but less computational effort is needed because of the multiple semi-isolated populations. This result is consistent with the analysis of Sewall Wright (1943) regarding demes of biological populations. This superlinear speedup has been repeatedly observed by many researchers in runs of the parallel genetic algorithm and parallel genetic programming (Andre and Koza 1996a). Of course, a parallel computer is not required to implement semi-isolated subpopulations; they can readily be implemented on a serial machine.

Implementation Issues

This chapter discusses
- our choice of the C programming language (instead of LISP) for work in this book,
- the vector method of representing program trees,
- the four categories of functions in genetic programming,
- the data structures for branches and functions,
- the one-byte-per-point method for storing a program in a vector and implementation of the EVAL function, and
- memory-efficient crossover

63.1   CHOICE OF PROGRAMMING LANGUAGE

As discussed in Section 2.2, LISP is a natural language for genetic programming. Both programs and data are represented in a uniform way (by S-expressions). The EVAL function provided by LISP permits an S-expression to be evaluated on the fly within a genetic programming system. Moreover, the COMPILE function in LISP can improve the performance of repeatedly executed LISP code by enabling an S-expression to be compiled on the fly within a genetic programming system.

In spite of these advantages, LISP can be exceedingly time-consuming (in part because of its interpretative operation). Execution of programs in LISP typically also requires a large amount of memory. Moreover, LISP (or at least efficient versions of LISP) are not available for certain computer architectures (e.g., transputers).

For these and other reasons, all the work reported in this book was done in the C programming language.

63.2   VECTOR REPRESENTATION FOR PROGRAMS

When implementing genetic programming in a language other than LISP, the question arises of how to represent the program trees.

One possible approach was implemented by Walter Tackett (1994) and is called SGPC (Simple Genetic Programming Code in C). This code uses a pointer-based system in which each internal point in a program tree is represented by a structure that points to the arguments of each function. Although SGPC ran considerably faster than contemporary LISP systems, this approach requires a large amount of memory and either dynamic allocation of memory or a memory management system.

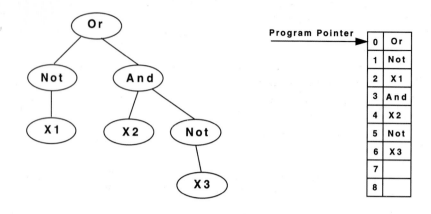

(Or (Not x1) (And x2 (Not x3)))

Figure 63.1 Representation of a program tree as a vector

Our genetic programming system represents program trees in Polish notation. This approach is implemented in our genetic programming system using DGPC (Dave's Genetic Programming Code in C). Polish notation was previously used, for the sake of efficiency, within our earlier LISP machine for representing LISP S-expressions for certain problems (Koza 1994g, Appendix D).

Figure 63.1 shows the program tree representing the S-expression

```
(OR (NOT X1) (AND X2 (NOT X3)))
```

and the corresponding vector in Polish notation. Each element of this particular vector contains the name of a function that is to be executed (AND, OR, or NOT) or the name of a terminal (X1, X2, or X3). When using Polish notation, each function must have a unique arity so that the vector can be unambiguously interpreted. For example, the Boolean AND and OR functions each have an arity of two in the above example, while the NOT function has an arity of one. If it is necessary that a particular function be available with multiple arities, the function is simply given multiple names for each separate arity. For example, if both a two-argument and three-argument version of the Boolean AND function were required, the function set would include an AND2 and an AND3 function.

In this approach, a subtree of a program tree corresponds to a particular contiguous subsequence of the vector. When a single point is picked from a program tree for a genetic operation based on a subtree (e.g., crossover, mutation, or an architecture-altering operation requiring a subtree), the appropriate contiguous subsequence of the vector is located. Keith and Martin's study (1994) on how to efficiently store program trees in genetic programming indicates that Polish notation uses memory efficiently and is easy to implement.

63.3 FOUR CATEGORIES OF FUNCTIONS

Table 63.1 describes the four categories of functions typically used in genetic programming:

- constants (zero-arity functions),
- terminals (zero-arity functions),
- ordinary functions, and
- macros.

63.3.1   Data Structure for Branches and Functions

Each branch of a multipart program has its own function set and terminal set. In an architecturally diverse population, each individual program in the population has its own function and terminal set for each of its branches. In addition, when the architecture-altering operations are being used, the number of branches and the function and terminal sets of the branches vary during the run of genetic programming.

A data structure is maintained for recording information about the function set of each branch of each individual program in the population. If the population is not architecturally diverse, one common data structure suffices for the entire population. In this data structure, constants, terminals, ordinary functions, and macros are all considered to be functions (belonging to one of the four categories above). This data structure contains the following information about each function of each branch of each individual program:

- its name,
- its arity, and
- its category (constant, terminal, ordinary function, or macro).

When architecture-altering operations are being used, the elements of this data structure are progressively modified during the run.

A second data structure is maintained for recording information about each function, including

- its arity,
- its category (constant, terminal, ordinary function, or macro),
- a function pointer to a function that will execute the given function, and
- a string description of how the function should be printed.

63.3.2   One-Byte Representation and the EVAL Function

The implementation of genetic programming should be efficient in terms of both time and space. An individual program in the population of a run of genetic programming may contain 500, 1,000, 2,000 or more points (i.e., functions and terminals). Thus, the storage of a population of 10,000 individuals entails storing information on 5 million, 10 million, 20 million, or more points. Thus, it is important to store individuals in an efficient way.

We store individuals so that each point in the program tree occupies one byte of storage. Since a byte can represent 256 possibilities, this encoding sets a limit of 256 different functions—that is, constants, terminals, ordinary functions, and macros. The problems in this book have no more than a few dozen terminals, ordinary functions, and macros.

The remaining (approximately 200) possibilities are used for random constants. Thus, in a typical problem in this book, there is a limited repertoire of about 200 possible

Table 63.1 Four categories of functions

Category	Arity	Description
Constants	0	Constants are zero-arity functions that obtain a value once and only once during their existence. In particular, their value does not vary over the fitness cases.
Terminals	0	Terminals are zero-arity functions whose return value is variable. The return value of a terminal is determined outside the program tree (typically varying from fitness case to fitness case). Dummy variables (formal parameters) are considered to be terminals. The values returned by an iteration-performing branch of an automatically defined iteration and the values returned by each of the four branches of an automatically defined loop are also considered to be terminals.
Ordinary functions	N	Ordinary functions (often just called "functions") possess N arguments. The arguments of an ordinary function are evaluated prior to execution of the function. Ordinary functions may possess zero arguments. Zero-arity ordinary functions are typically side-effecting functions that alter the state of the world.
Macros	N	Macros possess N arguments. Macros differ from ordinary functions in that their arguments are not evaluated prior to execution of the function. Instead the macro is responsible for the evaluation of its own arguments. Macros may possess zero arguments. Examples of macros are the IFLTE ("if less than or equal") operator and other similar conditional branching operators (Section 13.3.2).

different random constants. Since problems that use random constants usually also use arithmetic operations, many thousands of different numerical values are created during a typical run.

When implementing genetic programming in a language other than LISP, it is necessary to write code to implement an equivalent of the LISP EVAL function. An excellent discussion of how to efficiently implement an EVAL function for genetic programming is found in Keith and Martin (1994).

63.4 MEMORY-EFFICIENT CROSSOVER

Many implementations of genetic programming require an allocation of memory sufficient to store $2M$ individuals for a population of size M. In this conventional approach, one copy of the population serves as the active population. The parents for all the genetic operations are selected from this copy. The offspring produced by the genetic operations are inserted into the second copy.

However, it is possible to perform all the genetic operations with memory sufficient only to store $M + 2$ individuals (assuming single offspring crossover). This can be accomplished by dividing each operation into two phases. The first phase involves deciding which parents will actually be selected to participate in the operation. The second phase involves actually executing the operation. This division into two phases allows us to identify the individuals that will not participate in subsequent operations and to organize the sequence of operations so that a single copy of the population is sufficient for storing both the parents and the offspring. The memory occupied by individuals that are no longer needed can be marked and used to store the offspring of subsequent operations. Because all of the individuals in the population may sometimes be involved in subsequent operations, it is necessary to allocate a small amount of additional storage. Although it is not obvious, a simple pigeonhole argument can be used to show that memory space for only two additional individuals is sufficient for two-parent crossover. Thus, for a population of size M, an allocation of memory for $M + 2$ individuals is sufficient. A small data structure for bookkeeping (whose size is about an order of magnitude less than that required for storing the entire population) must be created to store information concerning the operations in which each individual will participate. The net effect of this approach is that it almost doubles the size of a population that can be accommodated by a given available amount of memory.

To implement this technique, the bookkeeping data structure is introduced to store the details of each operation to be performed. In the first phase, the operations to be performed are identified. The additional bookkeeping data structure is used to store the type of each operation and its parents. This data structure also stores the number of operations in which each parent will participate. Each parent is initially placed onto one of four lists. The first list identifies the parents that are involved in no remaining operations. This list is thus available to hold the offspring of subsequent operations. The second, third, and fourth lists identify the parents that are involved in one, two, or more remaining operations, respectively. The two additional slots for the offspring are initially placed on the first list. The genetic operations are performed as follows: First, an operation is chosen such that the involved parents are on the list indicating the smallest (but nonzero) number of remaining operations. For example, if there are parents on the 1-list, operations involving those parents are chosen first. Second, the operation is performed, and the offspring are placed into memory locations held by individuals on the empty list (0-list). These are now removed from the lists, as they are now full of offspring. Third, the parents of the operation are then moved to the appropriate new list, given that the operation is now complete. For example, if an operation involving a parent with only one remaining operation is performed, then that parent is moved to the empty list (0-list), as it is no longer needed. The previously mentioned pigeonhole argument guarantees that there will always be enough memory locations on the empty list, given that there are at least two placed there initially.

Part 10: CONCLUSION

Conclusion

At the beginning of Chapter 1, we presented a nondefinitional list of 16 attributes for a system for automatically creating computer programs. As stated in Chapter 1, the main point of this book is that genetic programming currently unconditionally possesses the first 13 of these 16 attributes of a system for automatically creating computer programs and that genetic programming at least partially possesses the remaining three attributes. To see this, we now review the 16 attributes from Chapter 1.

64.1 ATTRIBUTE NO. 1—STARTS WITH "WHAT NEEDS TO BE DONE"

Attribute no. 1 requires that a putative system for automatically creating computer programs starts from a high-level statement of the requirements for a solution to a problem. This attribute is a restatement of Arthur Samuel's characterization (1959) of one of the central challenges of computer science:

> How can computers be made to do what needs to be done, without being told exactly how to do it?

It is also a familiar statement of the main goal of artificial intelligence and machine learning.

Of course, there must be some method of communicating "what it is to do" to the system before it can start. As Friedberg, another pioneer in machine learning, observed (1958),

> If a machine is not told *how* to do something, at least some indication must be given of *what* it is to do; otherwise we could not direct its effort toward a particular problem. [Emphasis in original.]

The preparatory steps of genetic programming are the user's way of communicating the high-level statement of the problem to the genetic programming system. The preparatory steps identify what the user must provide to the genetic programming system before launching a run of genetic programming.

The first two preparatory steps of genetic programming concern the ingredients that are to be used to create the computer programs (often just the four arithmetic operations of addition, subtraction, multiplication, and division; a conditional branching operator; the inputs; and constants).

The fitness measure provided by the user is the primary mechanism for communicating a high-level statement of the requirements for the solution to a problem to the genetic programming system. The first two preparatory steps define the search space; the fitness measure determines the outcome of the search.

For example, if the problem entails navigating a robot with a nonzero turning radius to a destination in minimum time (Chapter 13), the fitness measure for the problem is based on elapsed time. This fitness measure indicates "what needs to be done"—get the robot to the destination in a time-optimal way. This fitness measure provides a method of comparing any two candidate control strategies as to which is quicker (i.e., it establishes a partial order between any two candidate points in the search space of the problem). However, the fitness measure does not specify "how to do it." In particular, the fitness measure conveys no hint about the critical (and counterintuitive) tactic needed to minimize elapsed time in this time-optimal control problem—that it is sometimes necessary to veer away from the destination in order to reach it in minimal time.

The fitness measure for the problem of learning the Boolean parity functions (Chapter 12; Sections 21.1, 21.2, and 23.4) scores a candidate program according to the number of errors that it makes. This fitness measure indicates "what needs to be done" (i.e., make no errors)—not "how to do it." In particular, the fitness measure does not instruct genetic programming to use, say, an iteration (counting the number of ones among the inputs), a subroutine (assembling intermediate-order parity functions into the desired higher-order parity function), a decision tree containing a chain of conditional tests, a recursion (taking successive two-parities until some base case is reached), disjunctive normal form, or some combination of the above approaches. Instead, the fitness measure merely indicates "what needs to be done" without conveying any information about the way of doing it.

The fitness measure for each problem of analog circuit synthesis (Part 5) is couched in terms of the high-level behavior (and other measurable characteristics) of the desired circuit. For example, if a lowpass filter is desired, the fitness measure calls for delivery of a near-maximum output voltage for low frequencies and a near-zero output voltage for high frequencies. The fitness measure is concerned with "what needs to be done"—produce the desired output voltage at the specified frequencies. The fitness measure does not disclose "how to do it." The fitness measure provides no information about the number of components that may be needed in order to achieve the desired behavior, the topological arrangement of the components, or the numerical values of the components. Similarly, the fitness measure contains no information about integro-differential equations, Kirchhoff's node law, poles, zeros, or Laplace transforms. It certainly does not represent or codify the considerable knowledge, mathematical abstractions, or expertise that human engineers bring to bear in designing filters.

Likewise, the fitness measure for the problem of devising a rule for a cellular automaton (Chapter 58) is couched in terms of the accuracy of the automaton at performing the majority classification task. The fitness measure indicates "what needs to be done" (i.e., get the right answer)—not "how to do it." This fitness measure conveys no hint that it is advisable to construct, transmit, receive, and decode space-time signals in order to solve this problem. Achieving high accuracy in classification is the problem's high-level requirement. Creating space-time signals is an advisable tactic. It is the job of genetic programming to discover this tactic.

Similarly, correlation is the fitness measure for the various classification problems of molecular biology in this book (Chapters 16, 17, 59, and 60). In particular, fitness is the correlation between the classification produced by a candidate program and the correct answer. The fitness measure is concerned with "what needs to be done"—get the correct answer (by maximizing correlation). The fitness measure does not reveal "how to do it." This fitness measure provides no information about the biochemistry of living cells that may aid in making the correct classification.

These same comments about fitness measures apply equally to all the other fitness measures appearing in this book as well as the fitness measures in *Genetic Programming* (Koza 1992e), *Genetic Programming II* (Koza 1994g), and nearly all of the fitness measures used in about 1,400 published papers by over 300 other authors in the field of genetic programming.

Thus, genetic programming possesses attribute no. 1 (from Chapter 1):

- **ATTRIBUTE NO. 1** (Starts with "what needs to be done"): It starts from a high-level statement specifying the requirements of the problem.

64.2 ATTRIBUTE NO. 2—TELLS US "HOW TO DO IT"

A run of genetic programming starts with a population of programs, each with a different random sequence of programmatic steps. The genetic operations of crossover, mutation, and the architecture-altering operations (Part 3) produce offspring that usually contain a different sequence of steps than their parent(s).

A run of genetic programming is a competition (beam search) among a diverse population of computer programs that is governed by the goal of discovering a satisfactory program for solving the given problem. The universe of possible compositions of the available functions and terminals defines the search space of possible computer programs. The competitive pressures of the environment (as expressed by the problem's fitness measure) determine the outcome of the competition. A run of genetic programming ends when the termination criterion is satisfied, and the result of the run is determined by the method of result designation (as provided by the user in the fifth major preparatory step for genetic programming). The exact sequence of functions and terminals in the designated final result of a run is not predetermined by the user, but instead emerges from the evolutionary process during the run.

In the genetic programming system, the fitness measure specifies "what needs to be done" in terms of a high-level statement of the requirements for a solution to a problem. The particular sequence of steps that emerges in the designated final result of a run of genetic programming tells the user "how to do it."

Thus, genetic programming possesses attribute no. 2:

- **ATTRIBUTE NO. 2** (Tells us "how to do it"): It produces a result in the form of a sequence of steps that satisfactorily solves the problem.

64.3 ATTRIBUTE NO. 3—PRODUCES A COMPUTER PROGRAM

Manifestly, genetic programming possesses the following attribute of a system for automatically creating computer programs:

- **ATTRIBUTE NO. 3** (Produces a computer program): It produces an entity that can run on a computer.

64.4 ATTRIBUTE NO. 4—AUTOMATIC DETERMINATION OF PROGRAM SIZE

Some techniques of machine learning, reinforcement learning, adaptive systems, neural networks, artificial intelligence, and automated logic require the user to analyze the problem and to specify the exact size of the solution in advance.

The exact number of points (i.e., functions and terminals) that actually appear in a computer program that is eventually evolved by genetic programming is not prespecified by the user. And, of course, the exact sequence of functions and terminals that actually appear in an evolved program is not prespecified by the user.

Genetic programming is an open-ended process in the sense that the size of the solution is part of the *answer* produced by the process, not part of the *question* posed by the user.

Therefore, we can say that genetic programming possesses attribute no. 4:

- **ATTRIBUTE NO. 4** (Automatic determination of program size): It has the ability to automatically determine the number of steps that must be performed and thus does not require the user to prespecify the exact size of the solution.

64.5 ATTRIBUTE NO. 5—CODE REUSE

We believe that reuse is required if a system for automatically creating computer programs is ever to be scaled up from small problems to large problems.

Code reuse goes hand in hand with generality. Thus, we also believe that reuse is desirable in a system for automatically creating computer programs because reused code tends to be general.

Genetic programming provides several mechanisms for code reuse. Subroutines are implemented in genetic programming as automatically defined functions (Koza 1992e, Chapters 20 and 21; Koza and Rice 1992b; Koza 1994g). Automatically defined iterations (Chapter 6), automatically defined loops (Chapter 7), and automatically defined recursions (Chapter 8) are additional mechanisms by which genetic programming can organize useful groups of steps so that they can be reused.

Therefore, genetic programming possesses attribute no. 5:

- **ATTRIBUTE NO. 5** (Code reuse): It has the ability to automatically organize useful groups of steps so that they can be reused.

64.6 ATTRIBUTE NO. 6—PARAMETERIZED REUSE

The most powerful form of code reuse is parameterized reuse. Parameterization enables useful sequences of steps to perform a particular task in a variety of similar, but different, ways.

This book contains numerous instances of parameterized subroutines in evolved solutions, including

- a parameterized subroutine establishing a different numerical component value for an electrical component on the two occasions when the subroutine is called (in Section 33.3.2 for the problem of synthesizing a two-band woofer-tweeter filter),
- parameterized subroutines in four runs of parity problems (Chapter 12),
- a thrice-used parameterized subroutine for the time-optimal robot controller (Section 13.4.4),
- parameterized recursive calls in the Fibonacci sequence problem (Chapter 18),
- parameterized subroutines in the quadratic polynomial problem with GPPS 2.0 (Section 23.1.2),
- parameterized subroutines in the cart-centering problem with GPPS 2.0 (Section 23.3.2), and
- parameterized subroutines in the even-6-parity problem with GPPS 2.0 (Section 23.4.2).

Previous work on genetic programming, including *Genetic Programming* (Koza 1992e), *Genetic Programming II* (Koza 1994g), and numerous published papers by various authors have demonstrated additional instances of parameterized reuse.

Thus, genetic programming possesses attribute no. 6:

- **ATTRIBUTE NO. 6** (Parameterized reuse): It has the ability to reuse groups of steps with different instantiations of values (formal parameters or dummy variables).

As far as we know, genetic programming is unique among techniques of artificial intelligence, machine learning, neural networks, adaptive systems, reinforcement learning, or automated logic in that it provides a general and automatic mechanism for parameterized reuse.

64.7 ATTRIBUTE NO. 7—INTERNAL STORAGE

Genetic programming can implement internal storage in numerous forms, including named memory (Koza 1992e, 1994g), indexed (vector) memory (Teller 1994a, 1994b), matrix memory (Andre 1994b), state (Raik and Browne 1997), and relational memory (Brave 1995a, 1996c).

Langdon (1995, 1996a, 1996b, 1996c, 1998) describes the implementation of a wide variety of data structures in genetic programming, including stacks, queues, and lists.

The automatically defined store (Chapter 9) is a general mechanism for creating, using, and deleting internal storage in evolving computer programs.

Therefore, genetic programming possesses attribute no. 7:

- **ATTRIBUTE NO. 7** (Internal storage): It has the ability to use internal storage in the form of single variables, vectors, matrices, arrays, stacks, queues, lists, relational memory, and other data structures.

64.8 ATTRIBUTE NO. 8—ITERATIONS, LOOPS, AND RECURSIONS

Iteration has been successfully implemented previously in genetic programming in various ways (Koza 1992e, Chapter 18; Andre 1994c; Handley 1996a, 1998; Teller 1998).

Recursion has also been successfully implemented in the context of genetic programming in various ways (Brave 1995b, 1996b; Wong and Leung 1996, 1998; Yu and Clack 1997b; Teller 1998).

In addition, this book describes a general approach to creating, using, and deleting automatically defined iterations (Chapter 6), automatically defined loops (Chapter 7), and automatically defined recursions (Chapter 8) in evolving computer programs.

Iterations, loops, and recursions are mechanisms for code reuse. Reused code provides leverage that can accelerate an automated learning system. Because the code appearing in iterations, loops, and recursions is reused, it tends to be general.

We believe that mechanisms for reuse are important for a system for automatically creating computer programs because reuse is required if such a system is ever to be scaled up from small problems to large problems.

Based on this work, genetic programming possesses the following attribute of a system for automatically creating computer programs:

- **ATTRIBUTE NO. 8** (Iterations, loops, and recursions): It has the ability to implement iterations, loops, and recursions.

64.9 ATTRIBUTE NO. 9—SELF-ORGANIZATION OF HIERARCHIES

Hierarchies are central to efficient and effective computer programming. As D. C. Ince (1992) said, in reviewing Alan Turing's 1945 "Proposals for Development in the Mathematics Division of an Automatic Computer Engine (ACE)":

> The third feature of [Turing's 1945] proposal—and almost certainly the most important—was the idea of a hierarchy of programs. This was the first instance of a developer drawing attention to the fact that *certain operations for a computer would be required time and time again, and that some facilities would be required for storing the programs . . . that implement these operations, and for controlling the hierarchical execution of these programs.* Turing's solution . . . is still the preferred method for controlling the execution of software.

> It has been claimed that Turing's ideas represent the invention of the art of programming (Hodges 1983). This claim can be seen as something of a slight exaggeration as Conrad Zuse had, during World War II, worked out some similar ideas; indeed, a good case could be made that Babbage was the real father of programming. Nevertheless, *the description of a software system as a hierarchic series of programs which communicate with each other* is a unique insight which represents a major leap forward from the rather primitive programming ideas that were current in 1945 and 1946. [Emphasis added.]

Chapter 5 presented architecture-altering operations for creating, duplicating, and deleting subroutines (automatically defined functions) and for creating, duplicating, and deleting the arguments possessed by them during the run of genetic programming.

In addition, architecture-altering operations were described for dynamically creating, duplicating, and deleting automatically defined iterations (Chapter 6), automatically defined loops (Chapter 7), and automatically defined recursions (Chapter 8).

The hierarchy of references among the branches of the program can be broadened by the operations of

- subroutine duplication (Section 5.1.2),
- iteration duplication (Section 6.2.2),
- loop duplication (Section 7.2.2), and
- recursion duplication (Section 8.1.3).

The hierarchy of references among the branches of the program can be deepened by the operations of

- subroutine creation (Section 5.3.1),
- iteration creation (Section 6.2.1),
- loop creation (Section 7.2.1), and
- recursion creation (Section 8.1.1).

Broadening may set the stage for subsequent deepening of the hierarchy by crossover.

The hierarchy of references among the branches of the program can be pruned by the operations of

- subroutine deletion (Section 5.5.4),
- iteration deletion (Section 6.2.3),
- loop deletion (Section 7.2.3), and
- recursion deletion (Section 8.1.2).

The ability to create hierarchical references between subroutines is demonstrated by

- a hierarchy from result-producing branch RPB0 to automatically defined function ADF3 to ADF0, and from RPB0 to ADF3 to ADF2 in the lowpass filter problem using the architecture-altering operations (Section 28.4),
- a hierarchy from result-producing branch RPB0 to ADF3 to ADF2, and from RPB1 to ADF3 to ADF2, and from RPB2 to ADF4 to ADF2 in the two-band crossover (woofer-tweeter) problem using the architecture-altering operations (Section 33.3.2),
- a hierarchy from one iteration-performing branch to ADF1 to ADF0 and from the second iteration-performing branch to ADF0 to ADF1 in the transmembrane segment identification problem with iteration creation (Section 17.2.10), and
- a hierarchy from the result-producing branch to ADF1 to ADF0 in run B of the even-3-parity problem using the architecture-altering operations (Section 12.3).

The amount of information that is communicated within the hierarchy of a program can be dynamically changed by the operations of argument duplication (Section 5.2), argument creation (Section 5.4), and argument deletion (Section 5.5) and their counterparts for automatically defined iterations (Chapter 6), automatically defined loops (Chapter 7), and automatically defined recursions (Chapter 8).

In summary, architecture-altering operations for ADFs, ADF arguments, ADIs, ADLs, and ADRs enable genetic programming to automatically create a hierarchical organization of groups of useful steps and to create a hierarchical arrangement of subprograms that pass information between them. That is, genetic programming possesses attribute no. 9:

- **ATTRIBUTE NO. 9** (Self-organization of hierarchies): It has the ability to automatically organize groups of steps into a hierarchy.

64.10 ATTRIBUTE NO. 10—AUTOMATIC DETERMINATION OF PROGRAM ARCHITECTURE

In addition to the architecture-altering operations for ADFs, ADF arguments, ADIs, ADLs, and ADRs mentioned in the previous section, Chapter 9 described the automatically defined store and architecture-altering operations for dynamically creating, duplicating, and deleting internal storage. The operations of storage argument duplication and storage argument deletion permit the dynamic changing of internal storage.

Each offspring produced by the architecture-altering operations for ADFs, ADF arguments, ADIs, ADLs, ADRs, and ADSs constitutes an experimental trial, undertaken during the run of genetic programming, as to whether a particular subroutine, argument, iteration, loop, recursion, or internal storage structure is, in fact, beneficial to the overall effort of solving the problem at hand. The competitive pressures of the environment (as expressed by the problem's fitness measure) ultimately determine the outcome of the trial. These trials are conducted automatically by the ongoing competition for survival among the evolving individuals in the population. Thus, genetic programming is an open-ended process in the sense that the architecture of the solution is part of the *answer* produced by the process, not part of the *question* posed by the user.

Therefore, genetic programming possesses the following attribute of a system for automatically creating computer programs:

- **ATTRIBUTE NO. 10** (Automatic determination of program architecture): It has the ability to automatically determine whether to employ subroutines, iterations, loops, recursions, and internal storage, and to automatically determine the number of arguments possessed by each subroutine, iteration, loop, and recursion.

64.11 ATTRIBUTE NO. 11—WIDE RANGE OF PROGRAMMING CONSTRUCTS

Various researchers have implemented a broad range of useful and familiar programming constructs in the context of genetic programming.

Macros (Spector 1996) have been implemented in genetic programming in the form of automatically defined macros (ADMs).

Libraries and caches of subroutines and modules have been implemented (Koza 1990b; Koza and Rice 1991b; Koza 1992e, Section 6.5.4; Angeline and Pollack 1993, 1994; Angeline 1993, 1994; Kinnear 1994a).

Typing (Montana 1995; Montana and Czerwinski 1996; Janikow 1996; Yu and Clack 1997a) and constrained syntactic structures (Koza 1992e) have also been implemented.

Explicit pointers have been implemented in genetic programming (Andre 1994c).

Basic genetic programming (Koza 1992e) implemented conditional operations, logical functions, integer functions, floating-point functions, complex-valued functions, multiple inputs, and multiple outputs.

Linear machine code instructions (Nordin 1994, 1997; Banzhaf, Nordin, Keller, and Francone 1998) and graphical program structures (Teller and Veloso 1996, 1997; Teller 1998) have also been implemented.

Thus, we can say that genetic programming possesses attribute no. 11:

- **ATTRIBUTE NO. 11** (**Wide range of programming constructs**): It has the ability to implement analogs of the programming constructs that human computer programmers find useful, including macros, libraries, typing, pointers, conditional operations, logical functions, integer functions, floating-point functions, complex-valued functions, multiple inputs, multiple outputs, and machine code instructions.

64.12 ATTRIBUTE NO. 12—WELL-DEFINED

The preparatory steps of genetic programming (Section 2.3.1) unmistakably identify what the user must provide prior to starting a run of genetic programming. There are no hidden preparatory steps in genetic programming.

After the user has performed the preparatory steps for a problem, the run of genetic programming is launched on a computer. Once the run is launched, a sequence of well-defined steps are executed. These executional steps consist of creating the initial population and then executing a main generational loop in which the fitness of each individual in the population is determined and in which the genetic operations are performed.

There are no hidden executional steps required in genetic programming. In particular, there is no discretionary human intervention during a run of genetic programming (although the user may optionally decide when to terminate the run).

Therefore, genetic programming possesses attribute no. 12:

- **ATTRIBUTE NO. 12** (Well-defined): It operates in a well-defined way. It unmistakably distinguishes between what the user must provide and what the system delivers.

64.13 ATTRIBUTE NO. 13—PROBLEM-INDEPENDENT

Genetic programming is problem-independent in the sense that the user does not have to modify the basic sequence of executional steps for each new problem.

Therefore, genetic programming possesses attribute no. 13:

- **ATTRIBUTE NO. 13** (Problem-independent): It is problem-independent in the sense that the user does not have to modify the system's executable steps for each new problem.

64.14 ATTRIBUTE NO. 14—WIDE APPLICABILITY

Genetic programming has automatically produced satisfactory computer programs for a wide variety of problems from many different fields:

- problems described in *Genetic Programming* (Koza 1992e), involving symbolic regression (system identification, empirical discovery, modeling, forecasting, data mining), classification, control, optimization, equation solving, game playing, induction, emergent behavior, coevolution, cellular automata programming, randomizer construction, image compression, symbolic integration and differentiation, inverse problems, and decision tree induction,

- problems described in *Genetic Programming II* (Koza 1994g), involving symbolic regression, control, pattern recognition, classification, and computational molecular biology,
- problems in this book, involving system identification, time-optimal control, classification, design of cellular automata rules, design of minimal sorting networks, multiagent programming, and synthesizing both the topology and sizing for analog electrical circuits, and
- several hundred other problems in about 1,400 published papers by over 300 other authors in the field of genetic programming.

Admittedly, genetic programming has not been demonstrated to be capable of solving all problems of all types from all fields. It has not solved the protein folding problem nor has it evolved a competitor to the Microsoft Windows operating system. Nonetheless, it is fair to say that there is "considerable evidence in favor" of the assertion that genetic programming possesses attribute no. 14:

- **ATTRIBUTE NO. 14** (Wide applicability): It produces a satisfactory solution to a wide variety of problems from many different fields.

Since many researchers are active in applying genetic programming to numerous problems in various fields, it is reasonable to anticipate that additional evidence will accumulate in the future concerning this point.

64.15 ATTRIBUTE NO. 15—SCALABILITY

The assertion that genetic programming scales well with problem size is supported by both experimental evidence and argument. However, since there are many practical difficulties associated with studying scaling, experimental evidence concerning scaling is admittedly limited.

Main point 6 of *Genetic Programming II: Automatic Discovery of Reusable Programs* (Koza 1994g) was

> For the three problems herein for which a progression of several scaled-up versions is studied, the number of fitness evaluations required by genetic programming to yield a solution (with a specified high probability) increases as a function of problem size at a lower rate with automatically defined functions than without them.

Main points 5 and 7 of *Genetic Programming II* (listed in Section 2.3.6 herein) provide some additional evidence that automatically defined functions provide a basis for a scalable system for automatically creating computer programs.

In addition, this book provides some additional evidence on this point in the form of comparisons (Chapter 55) of the computational effort associated with evolving the design of a succession of increasingly stringent filters and the computational effort associated with the automatically defined copy (a variation of the automatically defined function).

Sequences of steps are evolved in automatically defined functions, automatically defined iterations, and automatically defined loops during the run of genetic programming. Once such a sequence of steps is defined, it can be reused repeatedly within the overall program. This reuse means that it is not necessary to evolve a useful sequence of steps anew on each separate occasion on which the sequence of steps is used. We believe that reuse is a precondition for a scalable system for automatically creating computer programs.

Clearly, more experimental evidence as well as theoretical work is needed on this important question of scalability. Nonetheless, it is fair to say that there is "some evidence in favor" of the assertion that genetic programming possesses attribute no. 15:

- **ATTRIBUTE NO. 15** (Scalability): It scales well to larger versions of the same problem.

Additional favorable evidence will accumulate in the future concerning scalability. We believe that genetic programming will prove to scale well because it contains mechanisms for reuse and parameterized reuse such as subroutines, iterations, loops, and recursions.

64.16 ATTRIBUTE NO. 16—COMPETITIVE WITH HUMAN-PRODUCED RESULTS

This book contains 14 instances where genetic programming has produced results that are competitive with results produced by humans. Ten of the 14 genetically evolved results in Table 1.1 involve previously patented inventions. Table 1.1 cites the specific basis (from the list of eight criteria in Chapter 1) for claiming that the 14 genetically evolved results are competitive with human-produced results.

In addition, there are numerous instances outside of this book where genetic programming has succeeded in automatically producing computer programs that are competitive with human-produced results.

Admittedly, the present number of instances where genetic programming has been shown to be competitive with human-produced results is limited. Nonetheless, it is fair to say that there is a "moderate amount of evidence" in favor of the assertion that genetic programming possesses attribute no. 16:

- **ATTRIBUTE NO. 16** (Competitive with human-produced results): It produces results that are competitive with those produced by human programmers, engineers, mathematicians, and designers.

Each new instance of a genetically evolved result that is competitive with a human-produced result adds evidence in support of the above assertion. We believe that additional favorable evidence will accumulate in the future.

64.17 SUMMARY

Table 64.1 recapitulates the degree to which genetic programming currently possesses 16 attributes of a system for automatically creating computer programs.

Table 64.1 Degree to which genetic programming currently possesses 16 attributes of a system for automatically creating computer programs

Attribute	Reference	Current state of compliance
1 Starts with "what needs to be done"	Section 2.3.1	Yes
2 Tells us "how to do it"	Section 2.3.4	Yes
3 Produces a computer program	Section 2.3.3	Yes
4 Automatic determination of program size	Section 2.3.5	Yes
5 Code reuse	Section 2.3.6	Yes
6 Parameterized reuse	Section 33.3.2	Yes
7 Internal storage	Section 9.3	Yes
8 Iterations, loops, and recursions	Section 8.2	Yes
9 Self-organization of hierarchies	Chapter 10	Yes
10 Automatic determination of program architecture	Chapter 10	Yes
11 Wide range of programming constructs	Section 2.3.10	Yes
12 Well-defined	Section 2.3.2	Yes
13 Problem-independent	Section 2.3.2	Yes
14 Wide applicability	Section 2.3	Considerable evidence
15 Scalability	Section 2.3.6	Some evidence
16 Competitive with human-produced results	Table 1.1	Moderate evidence

In conclusion, genetic programming currently unconditionally possesses 13 of the above 16 attributes of a system for automatically creating computer programs and at least partially possesses the remaining 3 attributes. As John Holland said in 1997,

> Genetic programming *is* automatic programming. For the first time since the idea of automatic programming was first discussed in the late 40's and early 50's, we have a set of non-trivial, non-tailored, computer-generated programs that satisfy Samuel's exhortation: "Tell the computer what to do, not how to do it."

APPENDICES

Acronyms and Abbreviations

Acronym	Interpretation	Reference
ADC	automatically defined copy	Chapter 30
ADF	automatically defined function	Section 2.3.6
ADI	automatically defined iteration	Chapter 6
ADL	automatically defined loop	Chapter 7
ADM	automatically defined macro	Spector 1996
ADR	automatically defined recursion	Chapter 8
ADS	automatically defined store	Chapter 9
CBB	copy body branch	Chapter 30
CCB	copy control branch	Chapter 30
F	farad (unit of capacitance)	
GHz	gigahertz (10^9 cycles per second)	
GP	genetic programming	
GPPS	Genetic Programming Problem Solver	Part 4
H	henry (unit of inductance)	
Hz	hertz (cycles per second)	
IPB	iteration-performing branch of an ADI	Chapter 6
KHz	kilohertz (1,000 cycles per second)	
KΩ	kilo-ohm (unit of resistance)	
LBB	loop body branch of an ADL	Chapter 7
LCB	loop condition branch of an ADL	Chapter 7
LIB	loop initialization branch of an ADL	Chapter 7
LUB	loop update branch of an ADL	Chapter 7
MHz	megahertz (10^6 cycles per second)	
μH	microhenry (unit of inductance)	
nF	nanofarad (unit of capacitance)	
RBB	recursion body branch of an ADR	Chapter 8
RCB	recursion condition branch of an ADR	Chapter 8

Acronym	Interpretation	Reference
RGB	recursion ground branch of an ADR	Chapter 8
RPB	result-producing branch (main program)	Section 2.3.2
RUB	recursion update branch of an ADR	Chapter 8
SRB	storage reading branch of an ADS	Chapter 9
SWB	storage writing branch of an ADS	Chapter 9
Ω	Ohm (unit of resistance)	

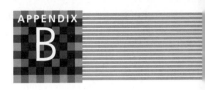

Special Symbols

Symbol	Definition	Reference
B	migration rate (boatload size) in a parallel computer implementing genetic programming	Chapter 62
C	correlation	Section 16.4.3
D	number of demes (semi-isolated subpopulations) on processing nodes of a parallel computer	Chapter 62
E	computational effort as measured by the minimum value of $I(M, i, z)$ over all generations between 0 and G	Section 12.6.1
F	function set	Section 2.3.1
G	maximum number of generations to be run	Sections 2.1, 2.3
i	current generation number	Section 12.6.1
$i*$	best generation number (i.e., the first generation on which the minimum value of $I(M, i, z)$ is achieved)	Section 12.6.1
$I(M, i, z)$	total number of individuals that must be processed to yield a desired result by generation i with probability z using a population of size M	Section 12.6.1
K	number of characters in the alphabet for the genetic algorithm operating on a fixed-length character string	Section 2.1
L	length of string for the genetic algorithm operating on a fixed-length character string	Section 2.1
M	population size	Sections 2.1, 2.3
$N_{max-adf}$	maximum number of ADFs	
$N_{max-adi}$	maximum number of ADIs	
$N_{max-adl}$	maximum number of ADLs	
$N_{max-adl-executions}$	maximum number of executions of ADLs	
$N_{max-adr}$	maximum number of ADRs	

Symbol	Definition	Reference
$N_{\text{max-adr-executions}}$	maximum number of executions of ADRs	
$N_{\text{max-ads}}$	maximum number of ADSs	
$N_{\text{max-ads-dimension}}$	maximum dimensionality of ADSs	
$N_{\text{max-ads-size-index-1}}$	maximum size of array (first dimension) or maximum size of indexed memory	
$N_{\text{max-ads-size-index-2}}$	maximum size of array (second dimension)	
$N_{\text{max-argument-adf}}$	maximum number of arguments for an ADF	
$N_{\text{max-argument-adi}}$	maximum number of arguments for an ADI	
$N_{\text{max-argument-adl}}$	maximum number of arguments for an ADL	
$N_{\text{max-argument-adr}}$	maximum number of arguments for an ADR	
$N_{\text{max-argument-cbb}}$	maximum number of arguments for copy body branch of an ADC	
$N_{\text{max-argument-ccb}}$	maximum number of arguments for copy control branch of an ADC	
$N_{\text{min-adf}}$	minimum number of ADFs	
$N_{\text{min-adi}}$	minimum number of ADIs	
$N_{\text{min-adl}}$	minimum number of ADLs	
$N_{\text{min-adr}}$	minimum number of ADRs	
$N_{\text{min-argument-adf}}$	minimum number of arguments for an ADF	
$N_{\text{min-argument-adi}}$	minimum number of arguments for an ADI	
$N_{\text{min-argument-adl}}$	minimum number of arguments for an ADL	
$N_{\text{min-argument-adr}}$	minimum number of arguments for an ADR	
N_{rpb}	number of result-producing branches in a program	
NIL	Boolean constant denoting false	Section 2.2
p	probability in X^2 test	Section 54.3
$P_{\text{argument-creation}}$	probability of argument creation	
$P_{\text{argument-deletion}}$	probability of argument deletion	
$P_{\text{argument-duplication}}$	probability of argument duplication	
p_c	probability of crossover	
$P_{\text{iteration-creation}}$	probability of iteration creation	
$P_{\text{loop-creation}}$	probability of loop creation	
p_m	probability of mutation	
$P(M, i)$	cumulative probability of success by generation i with population size M	Section 12.6.1
p_r	probability of reproduction	
$P_{\text{subroutine-creation}}$	probability of subroutine creation	

$p_{\text{subroutine-deletion}}$	probability of subroutine deletion	
$p_{\text{subroutine-duplication}}$	probability of subroutine duplication	
Q	subpopulation size (i.e., population per deme or processing node of a parallel computer implementing genetic programming)	Chapter 62
$\Re_{\text{bigger-reals}}$	floating-point random constants ranging between −10.0 and +10.0.	Section 16.4.2
$\Re_{\text{integers}}$	integer random constants ranging between −10 and +10.	Section 18.2.2
$\Re_{\text{smaller-reals}}$	floating-point random constants ranging between −1.0 and +1.0.	Section 13.3.2
$R(z)$	number of independent runs required to yield a desired result with probability z	Section 12.6.1
S_{adf}	maximum size (i.e., number of points) of function-defining branch of ADF	
S_{adi}	maximum size (i.e., number of points) of each branch of an ADI	
S_{adl}	maximum size (i.e., number of points) of each branch of an ADL	
S_{adr}	maximum size (i.e., number of points) of each branch of an ADR	
S_{cbb}	maximum size (i.e., number of points) of copy body branch of ADC	
S_{ccb}	maximum size (i.e., number of points) of copy control branch of ADC	
S_{rpb}	maximum size (i.e., number of points) of result-producing branch	
$\bar{s}$	average structural complexity (number of functions and terminals) in a set of programs (usually the set of successful runs)	Section 12.6
$\mathbb{T}$	Boolean constant denoting true	Section 2.2
T	terminal set	Section 2.3.1
U	intermediate value used in converting value of arithmetic-performing subtree into a specified range of component values	Section 25.7
U_{mosfet}	intermediate value used for MOSFET components	Section 51.1.1
W_{mosfet}	channel width for MOSFET components	Section 51.1
z	probability threshold desired for finding at least one successful run in a series of runs (99% throughout this book)	Section 12.6.1

Special Functions

Function	Name	Number of arguments	Reference
%	protected division	2	Section 13.3.2
FLOOR	floor	1	Chapter 20
IF	if	3	Section 2.2
IFEQZ	if equal to zero	3	Chapter 20
IFGTZ	if greater than zero	3	Section 15.2.2
IFLTE	if less than or equal	4	Section 13.3.2
ORN	numerically valued disjunction	2	Section 16.4.2
RIM	read indexed memory	1	Chapter 20
RLO	read linear output	1	Chapter 20
TAND	numerically valued conjunction	2	Chapter 20
TNOT	numerically valued negation	1	Chapter 20
TOR	numerically valued disjunction	2	Chapter 20
WIM	write indexed memory	2	Chapter 20
WLO	write linear output	2	Chapter 20

Control Parameters

The control parameters for runs of genetic programming are organized into the following three groups:

- default parameters,
- parameters presented in the tableau for each problem, and
- the percentages for the genetic operations.

D.1 DEFAULT PARAMETERS

The first group of control parameters are the default parameters. This book continues the policy of *Genetic Programming* (Koza 1992e) and *Genetic Programming II* (Koza 1994g) of using a fixed set of default values for the minor control parameters for the vast majority of the problems in the book. Thus, unless otherwise indicated for a specific problem, the values of all control parameters for all problems in this book are fixed at the default values specified in this section. Many problems described in this book could undoubtedly be solved more efficiently by making different choices for these control parameters. However, our policy of substantial consistency in the choice of control parameters helps to eliminate superficial concerns that the demonstrated success of genetic programming depends on shrewd or fortuitous choices of the control parameters for each particular problem.

The default values appearing in this section are, in most cases, identical to those used in *Genetic Programming* (Koza 1992e, Section 6.9) and *Genetic Programming II* (Koza 1994g, Appendix D). The differences arise primarily from five causes:

1. the extensive use in this book of multibranch programs,
2. the frequent use in this book of architecturally diverse populations and architecture-altering operations,
3. the almost exclusive use in this book of parallel computers (Chapter 62),
4. the use throughout most of this book of mutation at a low level such as 1% (instead of the previously used 0%), and
5. the use of the C programming language in this book (instead of the LISP programming language that was used previously).

First, the use of multibranch programs creates the need to specify the maximum size of each branch.

Second, the use of architecture-altering operations creates the need to specify the frequency of their invocation. In addition, the architecturally diverse population that results from the architecture-altering operations implies the use of structure-preserving crossover with point typing and the use of single-offspring crossover (instead of two-offspring crossover).

Third, the use of a parallel computer system with semi-isolated subpopulations creates the need to specify parameters for specifying the subpopulation (deme) size, the number of subpopulations (which, in this book, corresponds to the number of processing nodes), and the migration rate between the nodes.

Fourth, the use of mutation at a nonzero level calls for a specification of the mutation percentage, p_m.

Fifth, the use of the C programming language means that it is more convenient to specify the size of individuals in terms of the total number of points (i.e., total number of functions and terminals) rather than the depth of the program tree (as in LISP).

Unless otherwise specified, the following choices are the default choices for parameters in this book:

- Structure-preserving crossover with point typing is used.
- One-offspring crossover is used.
- The generative method for the initial random population is ramped half-and-half (Koza 1992e, Section 6.2).
- The method of selection for reproduction and for the first parent in crossover is tournament selection with a group size of seven (Goldberg and Deb 1991).
- The method of selecting the second parent for a crossover is the same as the method for selecting the first parent (i.e., tournament selection with a group size of seven).
- The adjusted fitness measure and the technique of greedy overselection (used frequently in Koza 1992e) is irrelevant in the context of tournament selection and is not used at all in this book.
- The elitist strategy is not used.
- If there is any randomization involved in the creation of the fitness cases for the problem, the randomization occurs once in a run and remains fixed for all runs of the problem.
- In choosing crossover points, we use a probability distribution that allocates $p_{ip} = 90\%$ of the crossover points equally among the internal points of each program tree and $p_{ep} = 1 - p_{ip} = 10\%$ of the crossover points equally among the external points of each tree (i.e., the terminals). The choice of crossover points is further restricted so that if the root of any branch is chosen as the point of insertion, then the crossover point of the other parent may not be merely a terminal.
- A maximum size (measured by depth), $D_{initial}$, is 6 for the random individuals generated for the initial population.
- The operations of encapsulation, editing, permutation, and decimation (described in Koza 1992e) are not used.

All functions and terminals are weighted equally during the probabilistic process of constructing individuals for generation 0 with two qualifications. First, the terminal representing floating-point random constants (e.g., $\Re_{\text{smaller-reals}}$) is treated as if it were a single terminal for purposes of this weighting (even though $\Re_{\text{smaller-reals}}$ may represent about 200 different floating-point random constants). Second, in problems involving the synthesis of electrical circuits, all functions belonging to a family (e.g., the PARALLEL0 and PARALLEL1 functions in the PARALLEL family of functions and TWO_VIA0, . . . , TWO_VIA7 in the TWO_VIA family of functions) are treated as if they were a single function for purposes of this weighting. For example, suppose a function set includes the capacitor-creating C function, the topology-modifying SERIES function, the development-controlling NOP function, the PARALLEL function, and the TWO_VIA function. In this example, the SERIES function, the C function, and the NOP functions are each equally likely to be chosen during the process of constructing individuals for generation 0. All of the functions of a family (such as PARALLEL and TWO_VIA) together receive the same weight as any one of the functions that do not come in families. Specifically, a relative weight of 1 is assigned to each of the functions of the most populous family for a given problem (the eight TWO_VIA functions in this example), a relative weight of 4 is assigned to each of the two PARALLEL functions (in this example), and a relative weight of 8 is assigned to each of the other functions (C, SERIES, and NOP in this example).

D.2   TABLEAU PARAMETERS

The second group of control parameters are those presented in the tableau for each problem.

The parameters presented in the tableau include the population size, M, and the maximum number of generations to be run, G.

If a parallel computer is being used, the tableau also presents the subpopulation size, Q, for each of the D demes (processing nodes) and the migration rate, B.

The tableau for each problem also presents the maximum size of each branch in the to-be-evolved program. The tableau presents the maximum size of the result-producing branch(es), S_{rpb}, and the number of result-producing branches in each program, N_{rpb}. Problems of circuit synthesis typically employ multiple result-producing branches.

If automatically defined functions are being used, the tableau also presents the size of each function-defining branch of each automatically defined function, S_{adf}; the maximum number of ADFs, $N_{\text{max-adf}}$; the maximum number of arguments for each ADF, $N_{\text{max-argument-adf}}$; and the minimum number of arguments for each ADF, $N_{\text{min-argument-adf}}$.

Similarly, if automatically defined iterations are being used, the tableau also presents the size of the iteration-performing branch, S_{adi}; the maximum number of ADIs, $N_{\text{max-adi}}$; the maximum number of arguments for each ADI, $N_{\text{max-argument-adi}}$; and the minimum number of arguments for each ADI, $N_{\text{min-argument-adi}}$.

If automatically defined loops are being used, the tableau also presents the maximum number of ADLs, $N_{\text{max-adl}}$; the maximum size of each of the four branches of an ADL, S_{adl}; the maximum number of arguments possessed by each ADL, $N_{\text{max-argument-adl}}$; and the minimum number of arguments possessed by each ADL, $N_{\text{min-argument-adl}}$.

If automatically defined recursions are being used, the tableau also presents the maximum number of ADRs, $N_{\text{max-adr}}$; the maximum size of each of the four branches of an

ADR, S_{adr}; the maximum number of arguments possessed by each ADR, $N_{max-argument-adr}$; and the minimum number of arguments possessed by each ADR, $N_{min-argument-adr}$.

If automatically defined stores are being used, the tableau also presents the maximum number of ADSs, N_{ads}; the maximum dimensionality for the automatically defined stores, $N_{max-ads-dimension}$; the maximum size for the array's first dimension, $N_{max-ads-size-index-1}$ (assuming its dimensionality is at least one); and the maximum size for the array's second dimension, $N_{max-ads-size-index-2}$ (assuming its dimensionality is at least two).

For problems involving version 1.0 of the Genetic Programming Problem Solver (GPPS 1.0), the tableau includes the size of the input vector, NINPUTS; the size of the output vector, NOUTPUTS; the size of indexed memory, NINDEXED; and the maximum number of executions of automatically defined loops, $N_{max-adl-executions}$.

For problems involving GPPS 2.0, the tableau includes the size of the input vector, NINPUTS; the size of the output vector, NOUTPUTS; the maximum number of executions of automatically defined loops, $N_{max-adl-executions}$; and the maximum number of recursive calls of automatically defined recursions, $N_{max-adr-executions}$.

D.3 PERCENTAGES OF GENETIC OPERATIONS

The third group of control parameters pertain to the percentages for each genetic operation. Tables D.1, D.3, and D.5 present the percentages of genetic operations that are used on or before generation 5 of runs of the designated problems and Tables D.2, D.4, and D.6 present this information for the genetic operations after generation 5.

Table D.1 Percentages of operations before generation 5

	Parity—runs A, B, C, and D (Chapter 12)	Approaches A, B, D, and E (Section 12.6.1)	Approach C (Section 12.6.1)	Multiagent strategies (Chapter 14)	Fibonacci sequence (Chapter 18)
One-offspring crossover	45%	90%	74%	85%	64%
Reproduction	8%	10%	10%	10%	10%
Mutation	0%	0%	0%	1%	1%
Subroutine duplication	15%	0%	5%	3%	0%
Argument duplication	15%	0%	5%	0%	0%
Subroutine deletion	1%	0%	0.5%	1%	0%
Argument deletion	1%	0%	0.5%	0%	0%
Subroutine creation	15%	0%	5%	0%	0%

Argument creation	0%	0%	0%	0%	0%
Iteration creation	0%	0%	0%	0%	0%
Loop creation	0%	0%	0%	0%	0%
Recursion creation	0%	0%	0%	0%	25%
Storage creation	0%	0%	0%	0%	0%

Table D.2 Percentages of operations after generation 5

	Parity—runs A, B, C, and D (Chapter 12)	Approaches A, B, D, and E (Section 12.6.1)	Approach C (Section 12.6.1)	Multiagent strategies (Chapter 14)	Fibonacci sequence (Chapter 18)
One-offspring crossover	45%	90%	74%	85%	89%
Reproduction	8%	10%	10%	10%	9%
Mutation	0%	0%	0%	1%	1%
Subroutine duplication	15%	0%	5%	3%	0%
Argument duplication	15%	0%	5%	0%	0%
Subroutine deletion	1%	0%	0.5%	1%	0%
Argument deletion	1%	0%	0.5%	0%	0%
Subroutine creation	15%	0%	5%	0%	0%
Argument creation	0%	0%	0%	0%	0%
Iteration creation	0%	0%	0%	0%	0%
Loop creation	0%	0%	0%	0%	0%
Recursion creation	0%	0%	0%	0%	1%
Storage creation	0%	0%	0%	0%	0%

Table D.3 Percentages of operations before generation 5

	Robot controller (Chapter 13)	Digit recognition (Chapter 15)	Transmembrane segment identification with architecture-altering operations for ADFs (Chapter 16)	Transmembrane segment identification problem with iteration creation (Chapter 17)	Cart centering (Chapter 19)
One-offspring crossover	78%	60%	60%	70%	78%
Reproduction	10%	10%	10%	10%	10%
Mutation	1%	0%	0%	0%	2%
Subroutine duplication	5%	0%	0%	2%	0%
Argument duplication	0%	0%	0%	2%	0%
Subroutine deletion	1%	0%	0%	2%	0%
Argument deletion	0%	0%	0%	2%	0%
Subroutine creation	5%	30%	30%	6%	0%
Argument creation	0%	0%	0%	0%	0%
Iteration creation	0%	0%	0%	6%	0%
Loop creation	0%	0%	0%	0%	0%
Recursion creation	0%	0%	0%	0%	0%
Storage creation	0%	0%	0%	0%	10%

Table D.4 Percentages of operations after generation 5

	Robot controller (Chapter 13)	Digit recognition (Chapter 15)	Transmembrane segment identification with architecture-altering operations for ADFs (Chapter 16)	Transmembrane segment identification problem with iteration creation (Chapter 17)	Cart centering (Chapter 19)
One-offspring crossover	86.5%	87%	86%	85%	88%
Reproduction	10%	10%	10%	10%	10%
Mutation	1%	0%	0%	0%	1%
Subroutine duplication	1%	1%	1%	1%	0%
Argument duplication	0%	0%	1%	1%	0%
Subroutine deletion	0.5%	1%	0.5%	0.5%	0%
Argument deletion	0%	0%	0.5%	0.5%	0%
Subroutine creation	1%	1%	1%	1%	0%
Argument creation	0%	0%	0%	0%	0%
Iteration creation	0%	0%	0%	1%	0%
Loop creation	0%	0%	0%	0%	0%
Recursion creation	0%	0%	0%	0%	0%
Storage creation	0%	0%	0%	0%	1%

Table D.5 Percentages of operations before generation 5

	Three problems with GPPS 1.0 (Chapter 21)	Six problems with GPPS 2.0 (Chapter 23)	Four circuit synthesis problems (Chapters 25, 27, 31, 32)	Five circuit synthesis problems with architecture-altering operations (Chapters 28, 33, 39, 45, 48)	Double bandpass filter using architecture-altering operations (Chapter 36)
One-offspring crossover	64%	62%	90%	78%	82%
Reproduction	10%	10%	9%	10%	11%
Mutation	2%	1%	1%	1%	1%
Subroutine duplication	2%	5%	0%	5%	5%
Argument duplication	2%	2%	0%	0%	0%
Subroutine deletion	0%	0%	0%	1%	1%
Argument deletion	0%	0%	0%	0%	0%
Subroutine creation	10%	5%	0%	5%	0%
Argument creation	0%	0%	0%	0%	0%
Iteration creation	0%	0%	0%	0%	0%
Loop creation	10%	5%	0%	0%	0%
Recursion creation	0%	5%	0%	0%	0%
Storage creation	0%	5%	0%	0%	0%

Table D.6 Percentages of operations after generation 5

	Three problems with GPPS 1.0 (Chapter 21)	Six problems with GPPS 2.0 (Chapter 23)	Four circuit synthesis problems (Chapters 25, 27, 31, 32)	Five circuit synthesis problems with architecture-altering operations (Chapters 28, 33, 39, 45, 48)	Double bandpass filter using architecture-altering operations (Chapter 36)
One-offspring crossover	85%	83%	90%	86.5%	87.5%
Reproduction	10%	10%	9%	10%	10%
Mutation	1%	1%	1%	1%	1%
Subroutine duplication	1%	1%	0%	1%	1%
Argument duplication	1%	1%	0%	0%	0%
Subroutine deletion	0%	0%	0%	0.5%	0.5%
Argument deletion	0%	0%	0%	0%	0%
Subroutine creation	1%	1%	0%	1%	0%
Argument creation	0%	0%	0%	0%	0%
Iteration creation	0%	0%	0%	0%	0%
Loop creation	1%	1%	0%	0%	0%
Recursion creation	0%	1%	0%	0%	0%
Storage creation	0%	1%	0%	0%	0%

SPICE Transistor Models

Many of the problems of circuit synthesis in this book use the Q2N3904 *npn* and Q2N3906 *pnp* models for bipolar junction transistors (BJT).

```
.MODEL Q2N3904 NPN IS 6.734F XTI 3 EG 1.11
+ VAF 74.03 BF 416.4 NE 1.259 ISE 6.734F
+ IKF 66.78M XTB 1.5 BR 0.7371 NC 2 ISC 0
+ IKR 0 RC 1 CJC 3.638P VJC 0.75 MJC 0.3085
+ FC 0.5 CJE 4.493P VJE 0.75 MJE 0.2593
+ TR 239.5N TF 301.2P ITF 0.4 XTF 2 RB 10

.MODEL Q2N3906 PNP IS=1.41F XTI=3 EG=1.11
+ VAF=18.7 BF=180.7 NE=1.5 ISE=0 IKF=80M
+ XTB=1.5 BR=4.977 NC=2 ISC=0 IKR=0 RC=2.5
+ CJC=9.728P MJC=.5776 VJC=.75 FC=.5
+ CJE=8.063P MJE=.3677 VJE=.75 TR=33.42N
+ TF=179.3P ITF=.4 VTF=4 XTF=6 RB=10
```

We often use the following default models for transistors:

```
.MODEL Q2N0000 NPN

.MODEL Q2P0000 PNP
```

For power transistors, we use the following models:

```
.MODEL Q2N2222 NPN IS 14.34F XTI 3 EG 1.11
+ VAF 74.03 BF 255.9 NE 1.307 ISE 14.34F
+ IKF 0.2847 XTB 1.5 BR 6.092 NC 2 ISC 0
+ IKR 0 RC 1 CJC 7.306P VJC 0.75 MJC 0.3416
+ FC 0.5 CJE 22.01P VJE 0.75 MJE 0.377
+ TR 46.91N TF 411.1P ITF 0.6 VTF 1.7
+ XTF 3 RB 10

.MODE Q2N3055 NPN IS=974.4F XTI=3 EG=1.11
+ VAF=50 BF=99.49 NE=1.941 ISE=902.5P IKF=4.029
+ XTB=1.5 BR=2.949 NC=2 ISC=0 IKR=0 RC=.1
+ CJC=276P VJC=.75 MJC=.3333 FC=.5 CJE=569.1P
```

```
+ VJE=.75 MJE=.3333 TR=971.7N TF=39.11N ITF=20
+ VTF=10 XTF=2 RB=.1
```

The following commands are used to insert the models for the desired *npn* and *pnp* transistors from Vladimirescu (1994, pages 234–235) into our runs of SPICE:

```
.MODEL Q2NVLAD NPN BF=209 BR=2.5 RB=670 RC=300
+ CCS=1.417P TF=1.15N TR=405N CJE=0.65P
+ CJC=0.36P IS=1.26E-15 VA=178.6 ISE=2.083E-12
+ IK=1.611M NE=2 PE=0.6 ME=0.33 PC=0.45
+ MC=0.33
```

```
.MODEL Q2PVLAD PNP BF=75 BR=3.8 RB=500 RC=150
+ CCS=2.259P TF=27.4N TR=2540N CJE=0.10P
+ CJC=1.05P IS=3.15E-15 VA=55.11 ISE=5.557E-12
+ IK=270U NE=2 PE=0.45 ME=0.33 PC=0.45
+ MC=0.33
```

We also sometimes used a modified version of the above Vladimirescu models with BR set very low (e.g., 10μ).

```
.MODEL Q2NVBR0 NPN BF=209 BR=10.0U RB=670 RC=300
+ CCS=1.417P TF=1.15N TR=405N CJE=0.65P
+ CJC=0.36P IS=1.26E-15 VA=178.6 ISE=2.083E-12
+ IK=1.611M NE=2 PE=0.6 ME=0.33 PC=0.45
+ MC=0.33
```

```
.MODEL Q2PVBR0 PNP BF=75 BR=10.0U RB=500 RC=150
+ CCS=2.259P TF=27.4N TR=2540N CJE=0.10P
+ CJC=1.05P IS=3.15E-15 VA=55.11 ISE=5.557E-12
+ IK=270U NE=2 PE=0.45 ME=0.33 PC=0.45
+ MC=0.33
```

We often use the following default model for diodes:

```
.MODEL DMOD D
```

We often use the following default model for MOSFET transistors:

```
.MODEL MN0000 NMOS
```

```
.MODEL MP0000 PMOS
```

Fonts Used in This Book

Examples	Definition	Font
`IFLTE, i, ADF0, RPB0, M0`	• Computer variables (e.g., if-less-than-or-equal operator `IFLTE`, index `i`) • Parts of a multipart computer program (e.g., automatically defined function `ADF0`, result-producing branch `RPB0`). • Cell of named memory (e.g., `M0`) • Vias in electrical circuit (e.g., a connection to layer `M0`)	Courier
`c`	One of the nucleotide bases found in DNA or RNA (e.g., cytosine `c`)	Courier
C	Electrical components (e.g., capacitor C).	Helvetica
A	One of the 20 amino acid residues found in proteins (e.g., alanine A)	Helvetica
F$_{rpb}$	Names of function and terminal sets (e.g., **F**$_{rpb}$ for a result-producing branch)	Helvetica
B	Names of domains for cellular automata problem (e.g., black B)	Helvetica

Bibliography

Aarts, Emile; and Korst, Jan. 1989. *Simulated Annealing and Boltzmann Machines.* Chichester, England: John Wiley & Sons.

Aaserud, O.; and Nielsen, I. Ring. 1995. Trends in current analog design: A panel debate. *Analog Integrated Circuits and Signal Processing* 7(1):5–9.

Abramson, David; Mills, Graham; and Perkins, Sonya. 1994. Parallelisation of a genetic algorithm for the computation of efficient train schedules. In Arnold, David; Christie, Ruth; Day, John; and Roe, Paul (eds.). *Parallel Computing and Transputers.* Amsterdam: IOS Press. pp.139–149.

ACM. 1997. *Proceedings of the ACM Fifth International Symposium on Field Programmable Gate Arrays.* New York: ACM Press.

Ahlswede, Rudolf; and Wegener, Ingo. 1979. *Search Problems.* Chicester: John Wiley & Sons.

Alander, Jarmo T. (ed.). 1997. *Proceedings of the Third Nordic Workshop on Genetic Algorithms and Their Applications (NWGA).* Espoo, Finland: Finnish Artificial Intelligence Society.

Aler, Ricardo; Barrajo, Daniel; and Isasi, Pedro. 1998. Genetic programming and deductive-inductive learning: A multi-strategy approach. In Shavlik, Jude (ed.). *Machine Learning: Proceedings of the Fifteenth International Conference.* San Francisco: Morgan Kaufmann. pp.10–18.

Alliot, J. M.; Lutton, E.; Ronald, E.; Schoenauer, M.; and Snyers, D. (eds.). 1995. *Artificial Evolution: European Conference, AE 95, Brest, France, September 1995, Selected Papers.* Lecture Notes in Computer Science. Vol.1063. Berlin: Springer-Verlag.

Altman, Russ B.; and Koza, John R. 1995. A programming course in bioinformatics for computer and information science students. In Hunter, Lawrence; and Klein, Teri E. (eds.). *Pacific Symposium on Biocomputing '96.* Singapore: World Scientific. pp.73–84.

Andrade, Miguel A.; O'Donoghue, Sean I.; and Rost, Burkhard. 1998. Adaptation of protein surfaces to subcellular location. *Journal of Molecular Biology* 276(2):517–525.

Andre, David. 1994a. Automatically defined features: The simultaneous evolution of 2-dimensional feature detectors and an algorithm for using them. In Kinnear, Kenneth E., Jr. (ed.). *Advances in Genetic Programming.* Cambridge, MA: MIT Press.

————. 1994b. Evolution of map making: Learning, planning, and memory using genetic programming. *Proceedings of the First IEEE Conference on Evolutionary Computation.* Piscataway, NJ: IEEE Press. Vol.I. pp.250–255.

————. 1994c. Learning and upgrading rules for an OCR system using genetic programming. *Proceedings of the First IEEE Conference on Evolutionary Computation.* Piscataway, NJ: IEEE Press. Vol.I. pp.462–467.

————. 1995a. The automatic programming of agents that learn mental models and create simple plans of action. *Proceedings of the 14th International Joint Conference on Artificial Intelligence.* San Francisco: Morgan Kaufmann. pp.741–747.

————. 1995b. The evolution of agents that build mental models and create simple plans using genetic programming. In Eshelman, Larry J. (ed.). *Proceedings of the Sixth International Conference on Genetic Algorithms.* San Francisco: Morgan Kaufmann. pp.248–255.

————. 1997. Learning and upgrading rules for an OCR system using genetic programming. In Bäck, Thomas; Fogel, David B.; and Michalewicz, Zbigniew (eds.). *Handbook of Evolutionary Computation*. Bristol, UK: Institute of Physics Publishing; New York: Oxford University Press. pp.G8.1:1–G8.1:8.

Andre, David; Bennett, Forrest H, III; and Koza, John R. 1996a. Discovery by genetic programming of a cellular automata rule that is better than any known rule for the majority classification problem. In Koza, John R.; Goldberg, David E.; Fogel, David B.; and Riolo, Rick L. (eds.). *Genetic Programming 1996: Proceedings of the First Annual Conference, July 28–31, 1996, Stanford University*. Cambridge, MA: MIT Press. pp.3–11.

————. 1996b. Evolution of intricate long-distance communication signals in cellular automata using genetic programming. In Langton, Christopher G.; and Shimohara, Katsunori (eds.). 1997. *Artificial Life V: Proceedings of the Fifth International Workshop on the Synthesis and Simulation of Living Systems*. Cambridge, MA: MIT Press. pp.513–520.

Andre, David; Bennett, Forrest H, III; Koza, John R.; and Keane, Martin A. 1998. On the theory of designing circuits using genetic programming and a minimum of domain knowledge. *Proceedings of the 1998 IEEE Conference on Evolutionary Computation*. Piscataway, NJ: IEEE Press. pp.130–135.

Andre, David; and Koza, John R. 1995. Parallel genetic programming on a network of transputers. In Rosca, Justinian (ed.). *Proceedings of the Workshop on Genetic Programming: From Theory to Real-World Applications*. University of Rochester. National Resource Laboratory for the Study of Brain and Behavior. Technical Report 95–2. June. pp.111–120.

————. 1996a. A parallel implementation of genetic programming that achieves super-linear performance. In Arabnia, Hamid R. (ed.). *Proceedings of the International Conference on Parallel and Distributed Processing Techniques and Applications*. Athens, GA: CSREA. Vol.III. pp.1163–1174.

————. 1996b. Parallel genetic programming: A scalable implementation using the transputer network architecture. In Angeline, Peter J.; and Kinnear, Kenneth E., Jr. (eds.). *Advances in Genetic Programming 2*. Cambridge, MA: MIT Press. pp.317–337.

Andre, David; and Teller, Astro. 1998. Evolving team Darwin United. In Asada, Minoru (ed.). *RoboCup-98: Robot Soccer World Cup II*. Lecture Notes in Computer Science. Berlin: Springer-Verlag. Forthcoming.

Anfinsen, C. B. 1973. Principles that govern the folding of protein chains. *Science* 81:223–230.

Angeline, Peter J. 1993. *Evolutionary Algorithms and Emergent Intelligence*. Ph.D. dissertation. Computer and Information Science Department. Ohio State University.

————. 1994. Genetic programming and emergent intelligence. In Kinnear, K. E., Jr. (ed.). *Advances in Genetic Programming*. Cambridge, MA: MIT Press. pp.75–97.

————. 1997a. Comparing subtree crossover with macro mutation. In Angeline, Peter J.; Reynolds, Robert G.; McDonnell, John R.; and Eberhart, Russ (eds.). *Evolutionary Programming VI. 6th International Conference, EP97, Indianapolis, Indiana, April 1997 Proceedings*. Lecture Notes in Computer Science. Berlin: Springer-Verlag. Vol.1213. pp.101–111.

————. 1997b. Subtree crossover: Building block engine or macromutation? In Koza, John R.; Deb, Kalyanmoy; Dorigo, Marco; Fogel, David B.; Garzon, Max H.; Iba, Hitoshi; and Riolo, Rick L. (eds.). *Genetic Programming 1997: Proceedings of the Second Annual Conference, July 13–16, 1997, Stanford University*. San Francisco: Morgan Kaufmann. pp.9–17.

————. 1998. Personal communication. August 5, 1998.

Angeline, Peter J.; and Kinnear, Kenneth E., Jr. (eds.). 1996. *Advances in Genetic Programming 2*. Cambridge, MA: MIT Press.

Angeline, Peter J.; and Pollack, Jordan B. 1992. The evolutionary induction of subroutines. *Proceedings of the Fourteenth Annual Conference of the Cognitive Science Society*. Hillsdale, NJ: Lawrence Erlbaum Associates. pp.236–241.

————. 1993. Competitive environments evolve better solutions for complex tasks. In Forrest, Stephanie (ed.). *Proceedings of the Fifth International Conference on Genetic Algorithms*. San Francisco: Morgan Kaufmann. pp.264–270.

————. 1994. Coevolving high-level representations. In Langton, Christopher G. (ed.). *Artificial Life III, SFI Studies in the Sciences of Complexity*. Redwood City, CA: Addison-Wesley. Vol.XVII. pp.55–71.

Angeline, Peter J.; Reynolds, Robert G.; McDonnell, John R.; and Eberhart, Russ (eds.). 1997. *Evolutionary Programming VI. 6th International Conference, EP97, Indianapolis, Indiana, April 1997 Proceedings*. Lecture Notes in Computer Science. Vol.1213. Berlin: Springer-Verlag.

Axelrod, Robert. 1984. *The Evolution of Cooperation*. New York: Basic Books.

————. 1987. The evolution of strategies in the iterated prisoner's dilemma. In Davis, Lawrence (ed.). *Genetic Algorithms and Simulated Annealing*. London: Pittman.

Baars, B. 1988. *A Cognitive Theory of Consciousness*. Cambridge: Cambridge University Press.

Babanezhad, J. N.; and Temes, G. C. 1986. Analog CMOS computational circuits. *IEEE International Symposium on Circuits and Systems*. Piscataway, NJ: IEEE Press. Vol.3. pp.1156–1160.

Babovic, Vladan. 1996a. *Emergence, Evolution, Intelligence: Hydroinformatics*. Ph.D. thesis. International Institute for Infrastructural, Hydraulic and Environmental Engineering and Technical University. Delft, The Netherlands.

————. 1996b. *Emergence, Evolution, Intelligence: Hydroinformatics*. Rotterdam, The Netherlands: Balkema Publishers.

Bäck, Thomas. 1996. *Evolutionary Algorithms in Theory and Practice*. New York: Oxford University Press.

———— (ed.). 1997. *Genetic Algorithms: Proceedings of the Seventh International Conference*. San Francisco: Morgan Kaufmann.

Bäck, Thomas; Fogel, David B.; and Michalewicz, Zbigniew (eds.). 1997. *Handbook of Evolutionary Computation*. Bristol, UK: Institute of Physics Publishing; New York: Oxford University Press.

Bairoch, Amos; and Boeckmann, B. 1991. The SWISS-PROT protein sequence data bank: Current status. *Nucleic Acids Research* 22(17):3578–3580.

Bairoch, Amos; and Bucher, Philipp. 1994. PROSITE: Recent developments. *Nucleic Acids Research* 22(17):3583–3589.

Bannister, Joe V.; Bannister, William H.; and Rotilio, Giuseppe. 1987. Aspects of the structure, functions, and applications of superoxide dismutase. *CRC Critical Review of Biochemistry* 22:111–154.

Banzhaf, Wolfgang; Nordin, Peter; Keller, Robert E.; and Francone, Frank D. 1998. *Genetic Programming—An Introduction*. San Francisco: Morgan Kaufmann; Heidelberg, Germany: dpunkt.verlag.

Banzhaf, Wolfgang; Poli, Riccardo; Schoenauer, Marc; and Fogarty, Terence C. 1998. *Genetic Programming: First European Workshop. EuroGP'98. Paris, France, April 1998 Proceedings*. Lecture Notes in Computer Science. Vol.1391. Berlin: Springer-Verlag.

Barnsley, Michael. 1988. *Fractals Everywhere*. Boston: Academic Press.

Barricelli, Nils Aall. 1992. Numerical testing of evolution theories: Part 1. *Acta Biotheoretica* 16:69–98.

Bauer, R. J., Jr. 1994. *Genetic Algorithms and Investment Strategies*. New York: John Wiley & Sons.

Beckers, R.; Holland, O. E.; and Deneubourg, J. L. 1994. From local actions to global tasks: Stigmergy and collective robotics. In Brooks, Rodney A.; and Maes, Pattie (eds.). *Artificial Life IV*. Cambridge, MA: MIT Press. pp.181–189.

Belew, Richard; and Vose, Michael D. (eds.). 1997. *Foundations of Genetic Algorithms 4*. San Francisco: Morgan Kaufmann.

Bennett, Forrest H, III. 1996a. Automatic creation of an efficient multi-agent architecture using genetic programming with architecture-altering operations. In Koza, John R.; Goldberg, David E.; Fogel, David B.; and Riolo, Rick L. (eds.). 1996. *Genetic Programming 1996: Proceedings of the First Annual Conference, July 28–31, 1996, Stanford University*. Cambridge, MA: MIT Press. pp.30–38.

————. 1996b. Emergence of a multi-agent architecture and new tactics for the ant colony food foraging problem using genetic programming. In Maes, Pattie; Mataric, Maja J.; Meyer, Jean-Arcady; Pollack, Jordan; and Wilson, Stewart W. (eds.). *From Animals to Animats 4: Proceedings of the Fourth International Conference on Simulation of Adaptive Behavior*. Cambridge, MA: MIT Press. pp.430–439.

————. 1997. Programming computers by means of natural selection: Application to analog circuit synthesis. In Hara, F.; and Yoshida, K. (eds.). *Proceedings of International Symposium on System Life, July 21–22, 1997, Tokyo International Forum.* Tokyo: Japan Society of Mechanical Engineers. pp.41–50.

Bennett, Forrest H, III; Koza, John R.; Andre, David; and Keane, Martin A. 1997. Evolution of a 60 Decibel op amp using genetic programming. In Higuchi, Tetsuya; Iwata, Masaya; and Liu, Weixin (eds.). 1997. *Proceedings of International Conference on Evolvable Systems: From Biology to Hardware (ICES-96).* Lecture Notes in Computer Science. Berlin: Springer-Verlag. Vol.1259. pp.455–469.

Bentley, Peter J. (ed.). 1999. *Evolutionary Design by Computers.* Chapter 16. London: John Wiley & Sons.

Berlekamp, Elwyn R.; Conway, John H.; and Guy, Richard K. 1985. *Winning Ways.* London: Academic Press. Vol.2. pp.817–850.

Bernstein, F. C.; Koetzle, T. F.; Williams, G. J. B.; Meyer, E. J., Jr.; Brice, M. D.; Rodgets, J. R.; Kennard, O.; Shimamouchi, T.; and Tasumi, M. 1977. The protein data bank: A computer based archival file for macromolecular structures. *Journal of Molecular Biology* 112:535–542.

Beyer, Hans-Georg. 1998. *Die Theorie der Evolutionsstrategien.* Stuttgart, Germany: Frommann-Holzboog Verlag.

Bhanu, Bir; and Lee, Sungkee. 1994. *Genetic Learning for Adaptive Image Segmentation.* Boston: Kluwer.

Bianchini, Ricardo; and Brown, Christopher. 1993. Parallel genetic algorithms on distributed-memory architectures. In Atkins, S.; and Wagner, A. S. (eds.). *Transputer Research and Applications 6.* Amsterdam: IOS Press. pp.67–82.

Biethahn, Jorg; and Nissen, Volker (eds.). 1995. *Evolutionary Algorithms in Management Applications.* Berlin: Springer-Verlag.

Black, Harold S. 1935. *Wave Translation System.* U.S. Patent 2,003,282. Filed August 8, 1928. Issued June 4, 1935.

————. 1937. *Wave Translation System.* U.S. Patent 2,102,670. Filed August 8, 1928. Issued December 21, 1937.

————. 1977. Inventing the negative feedback amplifier. *IEEE Spectrum.* December 1977. pp.55–60.

Blickle, Tobias. 1997. *Theory of Evolutionary Algorithms and Application to System Synthesis.* TIK-Schriftenreihe Nr. 17. Zurich, Switzerland: vdf Hochschul Verlag AG and der ETH Zurich.

Bode, Hendrik W. 1931. *Transmission Network.* U.S. Patent 1,828,454. Filed July 3, 1930. Issued October 20, 1931.

————. 1935. *Wave Filter.* U.S. Patent 2,002,216. Filed June 7, 1932. Issued May 21, 1935.

Booker, Lashon; Goldberg, David E.; and Holland, John H. 1989. Classifier systems and genetic algorithms. *Artificial Intelligence* 40:235–282.

Brave, Scott. 1995a. Using genetic programming to evolve mental models. *Proceedings of the Fourth Golden West Conference on Intelligent Systems.* Raleigh, NC: International Society for Computers and Their Applications. pp.91–96.

————. 1995b. Using genetic programming to evolve recursive programs for tree search. *Proceedings of the Fourth Golden West Conference on Intelligent Systems.* Raleigh, NC: International Society for Computers and Their Applications. pp.60–65.

————. 1996a. Evolving deterministic finite automata using cellular encoding. In Koza, John R.; Goldberg, David E.; Fogel, David B.; and Riolo, Rick L. (eds.). 1996. *Genetic Programming 1996: Proceedings of the First Annual Conference, July 28–31, 1996, Stanford University.* Cambridge, MA: MIT Press. pp.39–44.

————. 1996b. Evolving recursive programs for tree search. In Angeline, Peter J.; and Kinnear, Kenneth E., Jr. (eds.). *Advances in Genetic Programming 2.* Cambridge, MA: MIT Press. pp.203–218.

————. 1996c. The evolution of memory and mental models using genetic programming. In Koza, John R.; Goldberg, David E.; Fogel, David B.; and Riolo, Rick L. (eds.). 1996. *Genetic Programming 1996: Proceedings of the First Annual Conference, July 28–31, 1996, Stanford University.* Cambridge, MA: MIT Press. pp.261–266.

Brooks Low, K. 1988. Genetic recombination: A brief overview. In Brooks Low, K. (ed.). *The Recombination of Genetic Material.* San Diego: Academic Press. pp.1–21.

Brown, Stephen D.; Francis, Robert J.; Rose, Jonathan; and Vranesic, Zvonko G. 1992. *Field Programmable Gate Arrays.* Boston: Kluwer.

Bruce, Wilker Shane. 1995. *The Application of Genetic Programming to the Automatic Generation of Object-Oriented Programs*. Ph.D. dissertation. School of Computer and Information Sciences. Nova Southeastern University.

Bryson, Arthur E.; and Ho, Yu-Chi. 1975. *Applied Optimal Control*. New York: Hemisphere Publishing.

Buckles, Bill P.; and Petry, Frederick E. 1992. *Genetic Algorithms*. Los Alamitos, CA: IEEE Computer Society Press.

Burks, Arthur W. 1970. *Essays on Cellular Automata*. Urbana, IL: University of Illinois Press.

Butterworth, S. 1930. On the theory of filter amplifiers. *Experimental Wireless and the Wireless Engineer*. October. pp.536–541.

Campbell, George A. 1917a. *Electric Wave Filter*. U.S. Patent 1,227,113. Filed July 15, 1915. Issued May 22, 1917.

———. 1917b. *Wave Filter*. U.S. Patent 1,227,114. Filed July 15, 1915. Issued May 22, 1917.

Capcarrere, M. S.; Sipper, Moshe; and Tomassini, Marco. 1996. Two-state, r = 1 cellular automaton that classifies density. *Physical Review Letters* 77(24):4969–4971.

Case, James. 1998. Designing and producing the microcircuits of the future: Part I. *SIAM News* 31(4):16.

Cauer, Wilhelm. 1934. *Artificial Network*. U.S. Patent 1,958,742. Filed June 8, 1928, in Germany. Filed December 1, 1930, in United States. Issued May 15, 1934.

———. 1935. *Electric Wave Filter*. U.S. Patent 1,989,545. Filed June 8, 1928, in Germany. Filed December 6, 1930, in United States. Issued January 29, 1935.

———. 1936. *Unsymmetrical Electric Wave Filter*. U.S. Patent 2,048,426. Filed November 10, 1932, in Germany. Filed November 23, 1933 in United States. Issued July 21, 1936.

Cavicchio, Daniel J. 1970. *Adaptive Search Using Simulated Evolution*. Ph.D. dissertation. Department of Computer and Communications Science. University of Michigan.

Cedano, Juan; Aloy, Patrick; Perez-Pons, Josep A.; and Querol, Enrique. 1997. Relation between amino acid composition and cellular location of proteins. *Journal of Molecular Biology* 266(3):594–600.

Chambers, Lance (ed.). 1995. *Practical Handbook of Genetic Algorithms: Applications: Volume I*. Boca Raton, FL: CRC Press.

Chan, Pak K.; and Mourad, Samiha. 1994. *Digital Design Using Field Programmable Gate Arrays*. Englewood Cliffs, NJ: PTR Prentice Hall.

Chang, Tien-Hsien; Arenas, Jaime; and Abelson, John. 1990. Identification of five putative yeast RNA helicase genes. *Proceedings of the National Academy of Sciences U.S.A* 87:1571–1575.

Char, K. Govinda. 1998. *Constructivist AI with Genetic Programming*. Ph.D. thesis. Department of Electronics and Electrical Engineering. University of Glasgow.

Chellapilla, Kumar. 1997a. Evolutionary programming with tree mutations: Evolving computer programs without crossover. In Koza, John R.; Deb, Kalyanmoy; Dorigo, Marco; Fogel, David B.; Garzon, Max H.; Iba, Hitoshi; and Riolo, Rick L. (eds.). *Genetic Programming 1997: Proceedings of the Second Annual Conference, July 13–16, 1997, Stanford University*. San Francisco: Morgan Kaufmann. pp.432–438.

———. 1997b. Evolving computer programs without subtree crossover. *IEEE Transactions on Evolutionary Computation* 1(3):209–216.

———. 1998. A preliminary investigation into evolving modular programs without subtree crossover. In Koza, John R.; Banzhaf, Wolfgang; Chellapilla, Kumar; Deb, Kalyanmoy; Dorigo, Marco; Fogel, David B.; Garzon, Max H.; Goldberg, David E.; Iba, Hitoshi; and Riolo, Rick L. (eds.). *Genetic Programming 1998: Proceedings of the Third Annual Conference, July 22–25, 1998, University of Wisconsin, Madison, Wisconsin*. San Francisco: Morgan Kaufmann. pp.23–31.

Clements, John C. 1990. Minimum-time turn trajectories to fly-to points. *Optimal Control Applications and Methods* 11:39–50.

Conrad, Michael. 1983. *Adaptability*. New York: Plenum.

Conrad, Michael; and Pattee, H. H. 1970. Evolution experiments with an artificial ecosystem. *Journal of Theoretical Biology* 28:393–409.

Corne, David; and Shaprio, Jonathan L. 1997. *Evolutionary Computing: AISB Workshop.* Lecture Notes in Computer Science. Vol.1305. Berlin: Springer-Verlag.

Creighton, T. E. 1993. *Proteins: Structures and Molecular Properties.* Second edition. New York: W. H. Freeman.

Crosbie, Mark; and Spafford, Eugene H. 1995. Defending a computer system using autonomous agents. *Proceedings of the 18th National Information Systems Security Conference.* National Institute of Standards and Technology/ National Computer Security Center. Vol.2. pp.549–558.

Crutchfield, J. P.; and Mitchell, Melanie. 1995. The evolution of emergent computation. *Proceedings of the National Academy of Sciences, USA* 92(23):10,742–10,746.

Cui, J.; and Fogarty, T. C. 1992. Optimization by using a parallel genetic algorithm on a transputer computing surface. In Valero, M; Onate, E.; Jane, M.; Larriba, J. L.; and Suarez, B. (eds.). *Parallel Computing and Transputer Applications.* Amsterdam: IOS Press. pp.246–254.

Darlington, Sidney. 1952. *Semiconductor Signal Translating Device.* U.S. Patent 2,663,806. Filed May 9, 1952. Issued December 22, 1953.

———. 1959. *Temperature Compensated Transistor Amplifier.* U.S. Patent 2,885,494. Filed September 26, 1952. Issued May 5, 1959.

Darwin, Charles. 1859. *On the Origin of Species by Means of Natural Selection.* London: John Murray.

Das, Rajarshi. 1995. Personal communication.

Das, Rajarshi; Crutchfield, J. P.; Mitchell, Melanie; and Hanson, J. E. 1995. Evolving globally synchronized cellular automata. In Eshelman, Larry J. (ed.). *Proceedings of the Sixth International Conference on Genetic Algorithms.* San Francisco: Morgan Kaufmann.

Das, Rajarshi; Mitchell, Melanie; and Crutchfield, J. P. 1994. A genetic algorithm discovers particle-based computation in cellular automata. In Davidor, Yuval; Schwefel, Hans-Paul; and Maenner, Reinhard (eds.). *Parallel Problem Solving from Nature—PPSN III.* Lecture Notes in Computer Science. Berlin: Springer-Verlag. Vol.866. pp.344–353.

Dasgupta, D.; and Michalewicz, Z. (eds.). 1997. *Evolutionary Algorithms in Engineering Applications.* Berlin: Springer-Verlag.

Davidor, Yuval. 1990. *Genetic Algorithms and Robotics.* Singapore: World Scientific.

Davis, Lawrence. 1991. *Handbook of Genetic Algorithms.* New York: Van Nostrand Reinhold.

———. 1995. Personal communication.

——— (ed.). 1987. *Genetic Algorithms and Simulated Annealing.* London: Pittman.

Dawid, Herbert. 1996. *Adaptive Learning by Genetic Algorithms: Analytical Results and Applications to Economic Models.* Lecture Notes in Economics and Mathematical Systems 441. Heidelberg: Springer-Verlag.

de Garis, Hugo. 1993. Evolvable hardware: Genetic programming of a Darwin machine. In Albrecht, R. F.; Reeves, C. R.; and Steele, N. C. (eds.). *Artificial Neural Nets and Genetic Algorithms.* Vienna: Springer-Verlag. pp.441–449.

———. 1996. CAM-BRAIN: The evolutionary engineering of a billion neuron artificial brain by 2001 which grows/ evolves at electronic speeds inside a cellular automata machine (CAM). In Sanchez, Eduardo; and Tomassini, Marco (eds.). *Toward Evolvable Hardware.* Lecture Notes in Computer Science. Berlin: Springer-Verlag. Vol.1062. pp.76–98.

Degrauwe, M. 1987. IDAC: An interactive design tool for analog integrated circuits. *IEEE Journal of Solid State Circuits* 22:1106–1116.

Deneubourg, J. L.; Aron, S.; Goss, S.; Pasteels, J. M.; and Duerinck, G. 1986. Random behavior, amplification processes and number of participants: How they contribute to the foraging properties of ants. In Farmer, Doyne; Lapedes, Alan; Packard, Norman; and Wendroff, Burton (eds.). *Evolution, Games, and Learning.* Amsterdam: North-Holland.

Deneubourg, J. L.; Goss, S.; Franks, N.; Sendova-Franks, A.; Detrain, C.; and Chrétien, L. 1991. The dynamics of collective sorting robot-like ants and ant-like robots. In Meyer, Jean-Arcady; and Wilson, Stewart W. (eds.). *From Animals to Animats: Proceedings of the First International Conference on Simulation of Adaptive Behavior.* Cambridge, MA: MIT Press. pp.356–363.

Dennett, Daniel C. 1991. *Consciousness Explained.* Boston: Little, Brown.

Devaney, Robert L. 1989. *An Introduction to Chaotic Dynamical Systems.* Redwood City, CA: Addison-Wesley.

Dickerson, Richard E.; and Geis, Irving. 1983. *Hemoglobin: Structure, Function, Evolution, and Pathology.* Menlo Park, CA: Benjamin Cummings.

Dietz, H. G. 1992. Common subexpression induction. Parallel Processing Laboratory Technical Report TR-EE-92-5. School of Electrical Engineering. Purdue University.

Dietz, H. G.; and Cohen, W. E. 1992. A massively parallel MIND implemented by SIMD hardware. Parallel Processing Laboratory Technical Report TR-EE-92-4. School of Electrical Engineering. Purdue University.

Diplock, Gary. 1996. *The Application of Evolutionary Computing Techniques to Spatial Interaction Modelling.* Ph.D. thesis. Leeds University.

Dobkin, Robert C.; and Widlar, Robert J. 1971. *Electrical Regulator Apparatus Including a Zero-Temperature Coefficient Voltage Reference Circuit.* U.S. Patent 3,617,859. Filed May 23, 1970. Issued November 2, 1971.

Dorer, Douglas R.; Christensen, Alan C.; and Johnson, Daniel H. 1990. A novel RNA helicase gene tightly linked to the *Triplo-lethal* locus of *Drosophila. Nucleic Acids Research* 18(18):5489–5495.

Dorf, Richard C.; and Bishop, Robert H. 1998. *Modern Control Systems.* Eighth edition. Menlo Park, CA: Addison-Wesley.

Dorigo, Marco; and Colombetti, M. 1997. *Robot Shaping: An Experiment in Behavior Engineering.* Cambridge, MA: MIT Press.

Dracopoulos, Dimitris C. 1997. *Evolutionary Learning Algorithms for Neural Adaptive Control.* London: Springer-Verlag.

Drechsler, Rolf. 1998. *Evolutionary Algorithms for VLSI CAD.* Boston: Kluwer.

Dyson, George B. 1997. Darwin among the machines: The evolution of global intelligence. Reading, MA: Addison-Wesley.

Dyson, Paul; and Sherratt, David. 1985. Molecular mechanisms of duplication, deletion, and transposition of DNA. In Cavalier-Smith, T. (ed.). *The Evolution of Genome Size.* Chichester, England: John Wiley & Sons.

Engelman, D.; Steitz, T.; and Goldman, A. 1986. Identifying nonpolar transbilayer helices in amino acid sequences of membrane proteins. *Annual Review of Biophysics and Biophysiological Chemistry* 15:321–353.

Esparcia-Alcázar, Anna I. 1998. *Genetic Programming for Adaptive Signal Processing.* Ph.D. thesis. Department of Electronics and Electrical Engineering. University of Glasgow.

Esparcia-Alcázar, Anna I.; and Sharman, Ken. 1997. Evolving recurrent neural network architectures by genetic programming. In Koza, John R.; Deb, Kalyanmoy; Dorigo, Marco; Fogel, David B.; Garzon, Max H.; Iba, Hitoshi; and Riolo, Rick L. (eds.). *Genetic Programming 1997: Proceedings of the Second Annual Conference, July 13–16, 1997, Stanford University.* San Francisco: Morgan Kaufmann. pp.89–94.

Falkenauer, Emanuel. 1997. *Genetic Algorithms and Grouping Problems.* Chichester, England: John Wiley & Sons.

Farmer, Doyne; Toffoli, Tommaso; and Wolfram, Stephen (eds.). 1983. *Cellular Automata: Proceedings of an Interdisciplinary Workshop, Los Alamos, New Mexico, March 7–11, 1983.* Amsterdam: North-Holland Physics Publishing. Also in *Physica D* 10.

Fenical, L. H. 1992. *PSpice: A Tutorial.* Englewood Cliffs, NJ: Prentice Hall.

Fittkau, E. J.; and Klinge, H. 1973. On biomass and trophic structure of the central Amazonian rain forest ecosystem. *Biotropica* 5(1):2–14.

Fogarty, Terence C. (ed.). 1995. *Evolutionary Computing: AISB Workshop, Sheffield, U.K., April 1995, Selected Papers.* Lecture Notes in Computer Science. Vol.993. Berlin: Springer-Verlag.

Fogarty, Terence C.; Miller, J. F.; and Thomson, P. 1998. Evolving digital logic circuits on Xilinx 6000 family FPGAs. In Chawdhry, P. K.; Roy, R.; and Pant, R. K. (eds.). *Soft Computing in Engineering Design and Manufacturing.* London: Springer-Verlag. pp.299–305.

Fogel, David B. 1991. *System Identification through Simulated Evolution.* Needham Heights, MA: Ginn Press.

———. 1995. *Evolutionary Computation: Toward a New Philosophy of Machine Intelligence.* Piscataway, NJ: IEEE Press.

———. 1998. *Evolutionary Computation: The Fossil Record* (ed.). Piscataway, NJ: IEEE Press.

Fogel, Lawrence J. 1962. Autonomous automata. *Industrial Research* 4:14–19.

Fogel, Lawrence J.; Owens, Alvin J.; and Walsh, Michael. J. 1966. *Artificial Intelligence through Simulated Evolution.* New York: John Wiley & Sons.

Forrest, Stephanie. 1991. *Parallelism and Programming in Classifier Systems.* London: Pittman.

——— (ed.). 1990. *Emergent Computation: Self-Organizing, Collective, and Cooperative Computing Networks.* Cambridge, MA: MIT Press. Also in *Physica D.* 1990.

——— (ed.). 1993. *Proceedings of the Fifth International Conference on Genetic Algorithms.* San Francisco: Morgan Kaufmann.

Freedman, David; Pisani, Robert; Purves, Roger; and Adhikari, Ani. 1991. *Statistics.* Second edition. New York: W. W. Norton.

Friedberg, R. M. 1958. A learning machine: Part I. *IBM Journal of Research and Development* 2(1):2–13.

Friedberg, R. M.; Dunham, B.; and North, J. H. 1959. A learning machine: Part II. *IBM Journal of Research and Development* 3(3):282–287.

Fukushima, Kunihiko. 1989. Analysis of the process of visual pattern recognition by Neocognitron. *Neural Networks* 2:413–420.

Fukushima, Kunihiko; and Miyake, Sei. 1982. Neocognitron: A new algorithm for pattern recognition tolerant of deformations and shifts in position. *Pattern Recognition* 15(6):455–469.

Fukushima, Kunihiko; Miyake, Sei; and Takatuki, Ito. 1983. *IEEE Transactions on Systems, Man, and Cybernetics* 13(5):826–834.

Gacs, Peter. 1983. Reliable computation with cellular automata. *Proceedings of the 15th ACM Symposium on Theory of Computing.* New York: ACM Press. pp.32–41.

———. 1986. Reliable computation with cellular automata. *Journal of Computer and Systems Science* 32(1):15–78.

Gacs, Peter; Kurdyumov, G. L.; and Levin, L. A. 1978. One dimensional uniform arrays that wash out finite islands. *Problemy Peredachi Informatsii* 12:92–98.

Galli, Joakim; and Wislander, Lars. 1993. Two secretory protein genes in *Chironomus tentans* have arisen by gene duplication and exhibit different developmental expression patterns. *Journal of Molecular Biology* 231:324–334.

———. 1994. Structure of the smallest salivary-gland secretory protein in *Chironomus tentans. Journal of Molecular Evolution* 38:482–488.

Garces-Perez, Jaime; Schoenefeld, Dale A.; and Wainwright, Roger L. 1996. Solving facility layout problems using genetic programming. In Koza, John R.; Goldberg, David E.; Fogel, David B.; and Riolo, Rick L. (eds.). *Genetic Programming 1996: Proceedings of the First Annual Conference, July 28–31, 1996, Stanford University.* Cambridge, MA: MIT Press. pp.182–190.

Gardner, Martin. 1970. The fantastic combinations of John Conway's new solitaire game "Life." *Scientific American* 223(April):120–123.

Gasser, Les; and Huhns, Michael N. 1989. *Distributed Artificial Intelligence, Volume II.* London: Pittman.

Gathercole, Chris. 1998. *An Investigation of Supervised Learning in Genetic Programming.* Ph.D. thesis. University of Edinburgh.

Gen, Mitsuo; and Cheng, Runwei. 1997. *Genetic Algorithms and Engineering Design.* New York: John Wiley & Sons.

Gentilli, P.; Piazza, F.; and Uncini, A. 1994. Evolutionary design of FIR digital filters with power-of-two coefficients. *Proceedings of the First IEEE Conference on Evolutionary Computation.* Piscataway, NJ: IEEE Press. Vol.I. pp.110–114.

Gerstein, Mark. 1997. A structural census of genomes: Comparing bacterical, eukaryotic, and archaeal genomes in terms of protein structure. *Journal of Molecular Biology* 274:562–576.

Geyer-Schulz, Andreas. 1995. *Fuzzy Rule-Based Expert Systems and Genetic Machine Learning.* Heidelberg, Germany: Physica-Verlag.

Gilbert, Barrie. 1968. A precise four-quadrant multiplier with subnanosecond response. *IEEE Journal of Solid-State Circuits* SC-3(4):365–373.

———. 1979. *Multiplier Circuit.* U.S. Patent 4,156,283. Filed October 3, 1977. Issued May 22, 1979.

———. 1991. *Logarithmic Amplifier.* U.S. Patent 4,990,803. Filed March 27, 1989. Issued February 5, 1991.

Gilbert, Scott F. 1991. *Developmental Biology.* Third edition. Sunderland, MA: Sinauer Associates.

Go, Mittko. 1991. Module organization in proteins and exon shuffling. In Osawa, S.; and Honjo, T. (eds.). *Evolution of Life.* Tokyo: Springer-Verlag.

Goldberg, David E. 1983. *Computer-Aided Gas Pipeline Operation Using Genetic Algorithms and Rule Learning.* Ph.D. dissertation. Ann Arbor: University of Michigan.

———. 1989a. *Genetic Algorithms in Search, Optimization, and Machine Learning.* Reading, MA: Addison-Wesley.

———. 1989b. Sizing populations for serial and parallel genetic algorithms. In Schaffer, J. D. (ed.). *Proceedings of the Third International Conference on Genetic Algorithms.* San Francisco: Morgan Kaufmann. pp.70–79.

Goldberg, David E.; and Deb, Kalyanmoy. 1991. A comparative analysis of selection schemes used in genetic algorithms. In Rawlins, Gregory (ed.). *Foundations of Genetic Algorithms.* San Francisco: Morgan Kaufmann. pp.69–93.

Goldberg, David E.; Korb, Bradley; and Deb, Kalyanmoy. 1989. Messy genetic algorithms: Motivation, analysis, and first results. *Complex Systems* 3(5):493–530.

Gomi, Takeshi (ed.). 1998. *Evolutionary Robotics: From Intelligent Robots to Artificial Life (ER'98).* Kanata, Canada: AAI Press.

Gonzaga de Sa, P.; and Maes, C. 1992. The Gacs-Kurdyumov-Levin automaton revisited. *Journal of Statistical Physics* 67(3/4):507–522.

Goodman, Erik D. (ed.). 1996. *Proceedings of the First International Conference on Evolutionary Computation and Its Applications.* Moscow: Presidium of the Russian Academy of Sciences.

Gorne, Thomas; and Schneider, Martin. 1993. Design of digital filters with evolutionary algorithms. In Albrecht, R. F.; Reeves, C. R.; and Steele, N. C. (eds.). *Artificial Neural Nets and Genetic Algorithms.* Vienna: Springer-Verlag. pp.368–374.

Graeme, Jerald G.; Tobey, Gene E; and Huelsman, Lawrence P. 1971. *Operational Amplifers: Design and Application.* New York: McGraw-Hill.

Green, Milton. 1958. *Logarithmic Converter Circuit.* U.S. Patent 2,861,182. Filed June 16, 1953. Issued November 18, 1958.

Greene, Francis. 1997a. *Genetic Synthesis of Signal Processing Networks Utilizing Diploid/Dominance.* Ph.D. thesis. Department of Electrical Engineering. University of Washington, Seattle.

———.1997b. Performance of diploid dominance with genetically synthesized signal processing networks. In Bäck, Thomas (ed.). *Genetic Algorithms: Proceedings of the Seventh International Conference.* San Francisco: Morgan Kaufmann. pp.615–622.

Grimbleby, J. B. 1995. Automatic analogue network synthesis using genetic algorithms. *Proceedings of the First International Conference on Genetic Algorithms in Engineering Systems: Innovations and Applications (GALESIA).* London: Institution of Electrical Engineers. pp.53–58.

Gruau, Frederic. 1992a. *Cellular Encoding of Genetic Neural Networks.* Technical Report 92–21. Laboratoire de l'Informatique du Parallélisme. Ecole Normale Supérieure de Lyon. May.

———. 1992b. Genetic synthesis of Boolean neural networks with a cell rewriting developmental process. In Schaffer, J. D.; and Whitley, Darrell (eds.). *Proceedings of the Workshop on Combinations of Genetic Algorithms and Neural Networks 1992.* Los Alamitos, CA: IEEE Computer Society Press.

———. 1993. Genetic synthesis of modular neural networks. In Forrest, Stephanie (ed.). *Proceedings of the Fifth International Conference on Genetic Algorithms.* San Francisco: Morgan Kaufmann. pp.318–325.

———. 1994a. *Neural Network Synthesis Using Cellular Encoding and the Genetic Algorithm.* Ph.D. thesis. Ecole Normale Supérieure de Lyon.

———. 1994b. Genetic micro programming of neural networks. In Kinnear, Kenneth E., Jr. (ed.). 1994. *Advances in Genetic Programming.* Cambridge, MA: MIT Press. pp.495–518.

Gruau, Frederic; and Whitley, Darrell. 1993. Adding learning to the cellular development process: A comparative study. *Evolutionary Computation* 1(3):213–233.

Grunbacher, Herbert; and Hartenstein, Reiner W. (eds.). 1993. *Field Programmable Gate Arrays: Architectures and Tools for Rapid Prototyping. Second International Workshop on Field Programmable Gate Arrays and Applications, Vienna, Austria, August/September 1992. Selected Papers.* Lecture Notes in Computer Science. Vol.705. Berlin: Springer-Verlag.

Gutowitz, Howard (ed.). 1991. *Cellular Automata: Theory and Experiment.* Cambridge, MA: MIT Press.

Hadamard, J. 1945. *The Psychology of Invention in the Mathematical Field.* Princeton, NJ: Princeton University Press.

Haeusler, Jochen, 1976. *Arrangement for Measuring Temperatures.* U.S. Patent 3,943,434. Filed February 6, 1974. Issued March 9, 1976.

Handley, Simon. 1993a. Automated learning of a detector for α-helices in protein sequences via genetic programming. In Forrest, Stephanie (ed.). *Proceedings of the Fifth International Conference on Genetic Algorithms.* San Francisco: Morgan Kaufmann. pp.271–278.

———. 1993b. The automatic generation of plans for a mobile robot via genetic programming with automatically defined functions. *Proceedings of the Fifth Workshop on Neural Networks: An International Conference on Computational Intelligence: Neural Networks, Fuzzy Systems, Evolutionary Programming, and Virtual Reality.* San Diego, CA: Society for Computer Simulation. pp.73–78.

———. 1993c. The genetic planner: The automatic generation of plans for a mobile robot via genetic programming. *Proceedings of the Eighth IEEE International Symposium on Intelligent Control.* New York: IEEE Control System Society. pp.190–195.

———. 1994a. Automated learning of a detector for the cores of α-helices in protein sequences via genetic programming. *Proceedings of the First IEEE Conference on Evolutionary Computation.* Piscataway, NJ: IEEE Press. Vol.I. pp.474–479.

———. 1994b. On the use of a directed acyclic graph to represent a population of computer programs. *Proceedings of the First IEEE Conference on Evolutionary Computation.* Piscataway, NJ: IEEE Press. Vol.I. pp.154–159.

———. 1994c. The automatic generation of plans for a mobile robot via genetic programming with automatically defined functions. In Kinnear, Kenneth E., Jr. (ed.). *Advances in Genetic Programming.* Cambridge, MA: MIT Press.

———. 1994d. The prediction of the degree of exposure to solvent of amino acid residues via genetic programming. In Altman, Russ; Brutlag, Douglas; Karp, Peter; Lathrop, Richard; and Searls, David (eds.). *Proceedings of the Second International Conference on Intelligent Systems for Molecular Biology.* Menlo Park, CA: AAAI Press. pp.156–159.

———. 1995a. Classifying nucleic acid subsequences as introns or exons using genetic programming. In Rawlings, Christopher; Clark, Dominic; Altman, Russ; Hunter, Lawrence; Lengauer, Thomas; and Wodak, Shoshana (eds.). *Proceedings of the Third International Conference on Intelligent Systems for Molecular Biology.* Menlo Park, CA: AAAI Press. pp.162–169.

———. 1995b. Predicting whether or not a nucleic acid sequence is an *E. coli* promoter region using genetic programming. *Proceedings of First International Symposium on Intelligence in Neural and Biological Systems.* Los Alamitos, CA: IEEE Computer Society Press. pp.122–127.

———. 1995c. Predicting whether or not a 60-base DNA sequence contains a centrally located splice site using genetic programming. In Rosca, Justinian (ed.). *Proceedings of the Workshop on Genetic Programming: From Theory to Real-World Applications.* University of Rochester. National Resource Laboratory for the Study of Brain and Behavior. Technical Report 95-2. June. pp.98–103.

———. 1996a. A new class of function sets for solving sequence problems. In Koza, John R.; Goldberg, David E.; Fogel, David B.; and Riolo, Rick L. (eds.). 1996. *Genetic Programming 1996: Proceedings of the First Annual Conference, July 28–31, 1996, Stanford University.* Cambridge, MA: MIT Press. pp.301–308.

————. 1996b. The prediction of the degree of exposure to solvent of amino acid residues via genetic programming. In Koza, John R.; Goldberg, David E.; Fogel, David B.; and Riolo, Rick L. (eds.). 1996. *Genetic Programming 1996: Proceedings of the First Annual Conference, July 28–31, 1996, Stanford University.* Cambridge, MA: MIT Press. pp.297–300.

————. 1998. *Automatically Discovering Solutions That Flexibly Combine Iterative and Non-Iterative Computations.* Ph.D. thesis. Department of Computer Science. Stanford University.

Handley, S. G.; and Klingler, T. 1993. Automated learning of a detector for α-helices in protein sequences via genetic programming. In Koza, John R. (ed.). *Artificial Life at Stanford 1993.* Stanford, CA: Stanford University Bookstore.

Hao, J. K; Lutton, E.; Ronald, E.; Schoenauer, M.; and Snyers, D. (eds.). 1997. *Artificial Evolution, European Conference, AE '97, Nimes, France, October 1997: Selected Papers.* Lecture Notes in Computer Science. Vol.1063. Berlin: Springer-Verlag.

Harjani, Ramesh. 1989. *OASYS: A Framework for Analog Circuit Synthesis.* Ph.D. thesis. Department of Electrical and Computer Engineering. Carnegie Mellon University.

Harjani, Ramesh; Rutenbar, Rob A.; and Carley, L. Richard. 1987. A prototype framework for knowledge-based analog circuit synthesis. *Proceedings of the 24th Design Automation Conference.* New York: Association for Computing Machinery.

————. 1989. OASYS: A framework for analog circuit synthesis. *IEEE Transactions on Computer Aided Design* 8:1247–1266.

Harris, Christopher. 1997. *An Investigation into the Application of Genetic Programming Techniques to Signal Analysis and Feature Detection.* Ph.D. thesis. Department of Computer Science, University College London, University of London.

Harvey, Inman; and Thompson, Adrian. 1996. Through the labyrinth evolution finds a way: A silicon ridge. In Higuchi, Tetsuya; Iwata, Masaya; and Liu, Weixin (eds.). *Proceedings of International Conference on Evolvable Systems: From Biology to Hardware (ICES-96).* Lecture Notes in Computer Science. Berlin: Springer-Verlag. Vol.1259. pp.406–422.

Haupt, Randy L.; and Haupt, Sue Ellen. 1998. *Practical Genetic Algorithms.* New York: John Wiley & Sons.

Haynes, Thomas. 1998. *Collective Adaptation: The Sharing of Building Blocks.* Ph.D. thesis. Department of Mathematical and Computer Science. University of Tulsa.

Haynes, Thomas; and Sen, Sandip. 1997. Crossover operators for evolving a team. In Koza, John R.; Deb, Kalyanmoy; Dorigo, Marco; Fogel, David B.; Garzon, Max H.; Iba, Hitoshi; and Riolo, Rick L. (eds.). *Genetic Programming: Proceedings of the Second Annual Conference, July 13–16, 1997, Stanford University.* San Francisco: Morgan Kaufmann. pp.162–167.

Hemmi, Hitoshi; Hikage, Tomofumi; and Shimohara, Katsunori. 1994. AdAM: A hardware evolutionary system. *Proceedings of the First IEEE Conference on Evolutionary Computation.* Piscataway, NJ: IEEE Press. Vol.I. pp.193–196.

Hemmi, Hitoshi; Mizoguchi, Jun'ichi; and Shimohara, Katsunori. 1994. Development and evolution of hardware behaviors. In Brooks, Rodney; and Maes, Pattie (eds.). *Artificial Life IV: Proceedings of the Fourth International Workshop on the Synthesis and Simulation of Living Systems.* Cambridge, MA: MIT Press. pp.371–376.

Higuchi, Tetsuya; Hitoshi, I.; and Manderick, Bernard. 1994. Applying evolvable hardware to autonomous agents. In Davidor, Yuval; Schwefel, Hans-Paul; and Maenner, Reinhard (eds.). *Parallel Problem Solving from Nature, PPSN III.* Lecture Notes in Computer Science. Vol.866. Berlin: Springer-Verlag.

Higuchi, Tetsuya; Iwata, Masaya; Kajitani, Isamu; Iba, Hitoshi; Hirao, Yuji; Furuya, Tatsumi; and Manderick, Bernard. 1996. Evolvable hardware and its applications to pattern recognition and fault-tolerant systems. In Sanchez, Eduardo; and Tomassini, Marco (eds.). *Toward Evolvable Hardware.* Lecture Notes in Computer Science. Berlin: Springer-Verlag. Vol.1062. pp.119–135.

Higuchi, Tetsuya; Iwata, Masaya; and Liu, Weixin (eds.). 1997. *Proceedings of International Conference on Evolvable Systems: From Biology to Hardware (ICES-96).* Lecture Notes in Computer Science. Berlin: Springer-Verlag. Vol.1259.

Higuchi, Tetsuya; Niwa, Tatsuya; Tanaka, Toshio; Iba, Hitoshi; de Garis, Hugo; and Furuya, Tatsumi. 1993a. *Evolvable Hardware—Genetic-Based Generation of Electric Circuitry at Gate and Hardware Description Language (HDL) Levels.* Electrotechnical Laboratory Technical Report 93–4. Tsukuba, Japan: Electrotechnical Laboratory.

———. 1993b. Evolving hardware with genetic learning: A first step towards building a Darwin machine. In Meyer, Jean-Arcady; Roitblat, Herbert L.; and Wilson, Stewart W. (eds.). *From Animals to Animats 2: Proceedings of the Second International Conference on Simulation of Adaptive Behavior.* Cambridge, MA: MIT Press. pp.417–424.

Hillis, W. Daniel. 1990. Co-evolving parasites improve simulated evolution as an optimization procedure. In Forrest, Stephanie (ed.). *Emergent Computation: Self-Organizing, Collective, and Cooperative Computing Networks.* Cambridge, MA: MIT Press.

———. 1992. Co-evolving parasites improve simulated evolution as an optimization procedure. In Langton, Christopher; Taylor, Charles; Farmer, J. Doyne; and Rasmussen, Steen (eds.). *Artificial Life II, SFI Studies in the Sciences of Complexity.* Redwood City, CA: Addison-Wesley. Vol.X. pp.313–324.

Hodges, A. 1983. *Alan Turin—The Enigma of Intelligence.* London: Hutchinson.

Hodgman, T. C. 1988. A new superfamily of replicative proteins. *Nature* 333:22–23 and 578 (Errata).

Hofstadter, Douglas; and the Fluid Analogies Research Group. 1995. *Fluid Concepts and Creative Analogies: Computer Models of the Fundamental Mechanisms of Thought.* New York: Basic Books.

Holland, John H. 1975. *Adaptation in Natural and Artificial Systems: An Introductory Analysis with Applications to Biology, Control, and Artificial Intelligence.* First edition. Ann Arbor, MI: University of Michigan Press.

———. 1986. Escaping brittleness: The possibilities of general-purpose learning algorithms applied to parallel rule-based systems. In Michalski, Ryszard S.; Carbonell, Jaime G.; and Mitchell, Tom M. (eds.). *Machine Learning: An Artificial Intelligence Approach, Vol.II.* San Francisco: Morgan Kaufmann. pp.593–623.

———. 1987. Classifier systems, Q-morphisms, and induction. In Davis, Lawrence (ed.). *Genetic Algorithms and Simulated Annealing.* London: Pittman. pp.116–128.

———. 1992. *Adaptation in Natural and Artificial Systems: An Introductory Analysis with Applications to Biology, Control, and Artificial Intelligence.* Second edition. Cambridge, MA: MIT Press.

Holland, John H.; and Burks, Arthur W. 1987. *Adaptive Computing System Capable of Learning and Discovery.* U.S. Patent 4,697,242. Issued September 29, 1987.

———. 1989. *Method of Controlling a Classifier System.* U.S. Patent 4,881,178. Issued November 14, 1989.

Holland, John H.; Holyoak, K. J.; Nisbett, R. E.; and Thagard, P. A. 1986. *Induction: Processes of Inference, Learning, and Discovery.* Cambridge, MA: MIT Press.

Holland, John H.; and Reitman, J. S. 1978. Cognitive systems based on adaptive algorithms. In Waterman, D. A.; and Hayes-Roth, Frederick (eds.). *Pattern-Directed Inference Systems.* New York: Academic Press.

Hölldobler, Bert; and Wilson, Edward O. 1990. *The Ants.* Cambridge, MA: Belknap Press of Harvard University Press.

Hood, Leroy; and Hunkapiller, Tim. 1991. Modular evolution and the immunoglobin gene superfamily. In Osawa, S.; and Honjo, T. (eds.). *Evolution of Life.* Tokyo: Springer-Verlag.

Howley, Brian. 1996. Genetic programming of near-minimum-time spacecraft attitude maneuvers. In Koza, John R.; Goldberg, David E.; Fogel, David B.; and Riolo, Rick L. (eds.). *Genetic Programming 1996: Proceedings of the First Annual Conference, July 28–31, 1996, Stanford University.* Cambridge, MA: MIT Press.

Huhns, Michael N. 1987. *Distributed Artificial Intelligence.* London: Pittman.

Husbands, Philip; and Harvey, Inman (eds.). 1997. *Fourth European Conference on Artificial Life.* Cambridge, MA: MIT Press.

Husbands, Philip; and Meyer, Jean-Arcady (eds.). 1998. *Evolutionary Robotics: First European Workshop, EvoRobot98, Paris, France, April 1998, Proceedings.* Lecture Notes in Computer Science. Vol.1468. Berlin: Springer-Verlag.

Iba, Hitoshi. 1996a. Emergent cooperation for multiple agents using genetic programming. In Voigt, Hans-Michael; Ebeling, Werner; Rechenberg, Ingo; and Schwefel, Hans-Paul (eds.). *Parallel Problem Solving from Nature— PPSN IV.* Berlin: Springer-Verlag. pp.32–41.

———. 1996b. *Genetic Programming.* Tokyo: Tokyo Denki University Press. In Japanese.

————. 1997. Multiple-agent learning for a robot navigation task by genetic programming. In Koza, John R.; Deb, Kalyanmoy; Dorigo, Marco; Fogel, David B.; Garzon, Max H.; Iba, Hitoshi; and Riolo, Rick L. (eds.). *Genetic Programming 1997: Proceedings of the Second Annual Conference, July 13–16, 1997, Stanford University*. San Francisco: Morgan Kaufmann. pp.195–200.

Iba, Hitoshi; de Garis, Hugo; and Sato, Taisuke. 1994. Genetic programming using a minimum description length principle. In Kinnear, Kenneth E., Jr. (ed.). *Advances in Genetic Programming*. Cambridge, MA: MIT Press.

Iba, Hitoshi; Kurita, Takio; de Garis, Hugo; and Sato, Taisuke. 1993. System identification using structured genetic algorithms. In Forrest, Stephanie (ed.). *Proceedings of the Fifth International Conference on Genetic Algorithms*. San Francisco: Morgan Kaufmann. pp.279–286.

Iba, Hitoshi; Nozoe, Toshihide; and Ueda, Kanji. 1997. Evolving communication agents based on genetic programming. *Proceedings of the Fourth IEEE Conference on Evolutionary Computation*. Piscataway, NJ: IEEE Press. pp.297–302.

IEE. 1995. *Proceedings of the First International Conference on Genetic Algorithms in Engineering Systems: Innovations and Applications (GALESIA)*. London: Institution of Electrical Engineers.

IEEE. 1996. *Proceedings of IEEE Symposium on FPGAs for Custom Computing Machines, April 17–19, 1996, Napa Valley, CA*. Los Alamitos, CA: IEEE Computer Society Press.

————. 1997. *Proceedings of the 1997 IEEE Conference on Evolutionary Computation*. Piscataway, NJ: IEEE Press.

Ince, D. C. (ed.). 1992. *Mechanical Intelligence: Collected Works of A. M. Turing*. Amsterdam: North-Holland.

Jacob, Christian. 1995. *MathEvolvica—Simulierte Evolution von Entwicklungsprogrammen der Natur*. Ph.D. dissertation. Arbeitsberichte des Instituts fur Mathematische Maschinen und Datenverarbeitung (IMMD), Informatik. University of Erlangen. Erlangen, Germany. In German.

————. 1996. Evolving evolution programs: Genetic programming and L-systems. In Koza, John R.; Goldberg, David E.; Fogel, David B.; and Riolo, Rick L. (eds.). *Genetic Programming 1996: Proceedings of the First Annual Conference, July 28–31, 1996, Stanford University*. Cambridge, MA: MIT Press. pp.107–115.

————. 1997. *Principia Evolvica: Simulierte Evolution mit Mathematica*. Heidelberg, Germany: dpunkt.verlag. In German. English translation forthcoming from Morgan Kaufmann in 2000.

Janikow, Cezary Z. 1996. A methodology for processing problem constraints in genetic programming. *Computers and Mathematics with Applications* 32(8):97–113.

Jenkins, Jesse H. 1994. *Designing with FPGAs and CPLDs*. Englewood Cliffs, NJ: PTR Prentice Hall.

Jiang, M. 1992. *A Hierarchical Genetic System for Symbolic Function Identification*. Ph.D. dissertation. University of Montana.

Johnson, Kenneth S. 1926. *Electric-Wave Transmission*. U.S. Patent 1,611,916. Filed March 9, 1923. Issued December 28, 1926.

Johnson, Walter C. 1950. *Transmission Lines and Networks*. New York: McGraw-Hill.

Jones, William Evan, III. 1996. *Simultaneous Topology Selection and Sizing/Biasing for Analog Synthesis in ASTRX/OBLX*. Master's thesis. Department of Electrical and Computer Engineering. Carnegie Mellon University.

Juels, Ari; and Wattenberg, Martin. 1994. *Stochastic Hillclimbing as a Baseline Method for Evaluating Genetic Algorithms*. University of California Computer Science Department Technical Report CSD-94-834. September 28, 1994.

Juille, Hugues. 1995. Evolution of non-deterministic incremental algorithms as a new approach for search in state spaces. In Eshelman, L. J. (ed.). *Proceedings of the Sixth International Conference on Genetic Algorithms*. San Francisco: Morgan Kaufmann. pp.351–358.

————. 1997. Personal communication.

Juille, Hugues; and Pollack, Jordan B. 1998. Coevolving the "ideal" trainer: Application to the discovery of cellular automata rules. In Koza, John R.; Banzhaf, Wolfgang; Chellapilla, Kumar; Deb, Kalyanmoy; Dorigo, Marco; Fogel, David B.; Garzon, Max H.; Goldberg, David E.; Iba, Hitoshi; and Riolo, Rick L. (eds.). *Genetic Programming 1998: Proceedings of the Third Annual Conference, July 22–25, 1998, University of Wisconsin, Madison*. San Francisco: Morgan Kaufmann. pp.519–527.

Juric, M.; Potter, W. D.; and Plaksin, M. 1995. Using the parallel virtual machine for hunting snake-in-the-box codes. In Arabnia, Hamid R. (ed.). *Transputer Research and Applications 7*. Amsterdam: IOS Press.

Keane, Martin A.; Koza, John R.; and Rice, James P. 1993. Finding an impulse response function using genetic programming. *Proceedings of the 1993 American Control Conference*. Evanston, IL: American Automatic Control Council. Vol.III. pp.2345–2350.

Keith, Mike J.; and Martin, Martin C. 1994. Genetic programming in C++: Implementation issues. In Kinnear, Kenneth E., Jr. (ed.). *Advances in Genetic Programming*. Cambridge, MA: MIT Press. Chapter 13. pp.285–310.

Kennelly, Robert A., Jr. 1997. Genetic evolution of shape-altering programs for supersonic aerodynamics. In Koza, John R. (ed.). *Genetic Algorithms and Genetic Programming at Stanford 1997*. Stanford, CA: Stanford University Bookstore. pp.100–109.

Kielkowski, Ron M. 1994. *Inside SPICE: Overcoming the Obstacles of Circuit Simulation*. New York: McGraw-Hill.

Kinnear, Kenneth E., Jr. 1993a. Evolving a sort: Lessons in genetic programming. *1993 IEEE International Conference on Neural Networks, San Francisco*. Piscataway, NJ: IEEE Press. Vol.2. pp.881–888.

———. 1993b. Generality and difficulty in genetic programming: Evolving a sort. In Forrest, Stephanie (ed.). *Proceedings of the Fifth International Conference on Genetic Algorithms*. San Francisco: Morgan Kaufmann. pp.287–294.

———. 1994a. Alternatives in automatic function definition: A comparison of performance. In Kinnear, Kenneth E., Jr. (ed.). *Advances in Genetic Programming*. Cambridge, MA: MIT Press.

——— (ed.). 1994b. *Advances in Genetic Programming*. Cambridge, MA: MIT Press.

Kirkpatrick, S.; Gelatt, C. D.; and Vecchi, M. P. 1983. Optimization by simulated annealing. *Science* 220:671–680.

Kitano, Hiroaki. 1990. Designing neural networks using genetic algorithms with graph generation system. *Complex Systems* 4:461–476.

———. 1993. *Genetic Algorithms*. Tokyo: Sangyoutosyo Publishers. In Japanese.

———. 1994. Neurogenetic learning: An integrated method of designing and training neural networks using genetic algorithms. *Physica D* 75:225–238.

———. 1995. *Genetic Algorithms 2*. Tokyo: Sangyoutosyo Publishers. In Japanese.

———. 1996. Morphogenesis for evolvable systems. In Sanchez, Eduardo; and Tomassini, Marco (eds.). *Toward Evolvable Hardware*. Lecture Notes in Computer Science. Berlin: Springer-Verlag. Vol.1062. pp.99–117.

———. 1997. *Genetic Algorithms 3*. Tokyo: Sangyoutosyo Publishers. In Japanese.

Klockgether, Jürgen; and Schwefel, Hans-Paul. 1970. Two-phase nozzle and hollow core jet experiments. In Elliott, D. G. (ed.). *Proceedings of the Eleventh Symposium on the Engineering Aspects of Magnetohydrodynamics*. Pasadena, CA: California Institute of Technology. pp.141–148.

Knuth, Donald E. 1973. *The Art of Computer Programming*. Vol.3. Reading, MA: Addison-Wesley.

Koh, H. Y.; Sequin, C. H.; and Gray, P. R. 1987. Automatic synthesis of operational amplifiers based on analytic circuit models. *Proceedings of IEEE International Conference on Computer-Aided Design*. Piscataway, NJ: IEEE Press.

Korkin, Michael; de Garis, Hugo; Gers, Felix; and Hemmi, Hitoshi. 1997. CBM (CAM-Brain Machine):A hardware tool which evolves a neural net module in a fraction of a second and runs a million neuron artificial brain in real time. In Koza, John R.; Deb, Kalyanmoy; Dorigo, Marco; Fogel, David B.; Garzon, Max H.; Iba, Hitoshi; and Riolo, Rick L. (eds.). *Genetic Programming 1997: Proceedings of the Second Annual Conference, July 13–16, 1997, Stanford University*. San Francisco: Morgan Kaufmann. pp.498–503.

Koza, John R. 1972. *On Inducing a Nontrivial, Parsimonious, Hierarchical Grammar for a Given Sample of Sentences*. Ph.D. dissertation. Department of Computer Science. University of Michigan.

———. 1988. *Non-Linear Genetic Algorithms for Solving Problems*. U.S. Patent Application filed May 20, 1988.

———. 1989. Hierarchical genetic algorithms operating on populations of computer programs. *Proceedings of the 11th International Joint Conference on Artificial Intelligence*. San Francisco: Morgan Kaufmann. Vol.I. pp.768–774.

———. 1990a. A genetic approach to econometric modeling. Paper presented at Sixth World Congress of the Econometric Society, Barcelona, Spain. August 27, 1990.

———. 1990b. *Genetic Programming: A Paradigm for Genetically Breeding Populations of Computer Programs to Solve Problems.* Stanford University Computer Science Department Technical Report STAN-CS-90-1314. June.

———. 1990c. Genetically breeding populations of computer programs to solve problems in artificial intelligence. *Proceedings of the Second International Conference on Tools for AI.* Herndon, Virginia. November 6–9, 1990. Los Alamitos, CA: IEEE Computer Society Press. pp.819–827.

———. 1990d. Integrating symbolic processing into genetic algorithms. Presented at the Workshop on Integrating Symbolic and Neural Processes at AAAI-90 in Boston. July 29, 1990.

———. 1990e. *Non-Linear Genetic Algorithms for Solving Problems.* U.S. Patent 4,935,877. Filed May 20, 1988. Issued June 19, 1990.

———. 1990f. *Non-Linear Genetic Algorithms for Solving Problems by Finding a Fit Composition of Functions.* U.S. Patent Application filed March 28, 1990.

———. 1991a. A genetic approach to econometric modeling. In Bourgine, Paul; and Walliser, Bernard. *Economics and Cognitive Science.* Oxford: Pergamon Press. pp.57–75.

———. 1991b. A hierarchical approach to learning the Boolean multiplexer function. In Rawlins, Gregory (ed.). *Foundations of Genetic Algorithms.* San Francisco: Morgan Kaufmann. pp.171–192.

———. 1991c. Concept formation and decision tree induction using the genetic programming paradigm. In Schwefel, Hans-Paul; and Maenner, Reinhard (eds.). *Parallel Problem Solving from Nature.* Berlin: Springer-Verlag. pp.124–128.

———. 1991d. Evolution and co-evolution of computer programs to control independent-acting agents. In Meyer, Jean-Arcady; and Wilson, Stewart W. *From Animals to Animats: Proceedings of the First International Conference on Simulation of Adaptive Behavior.* Paris. September 24–28, 1990. Cambridge, MA: MIT Press. pp.366–375.

———. 1991e. Evolving a computer program to generate random numbers using the genetic programming paradigm. In Belew, Rik; and Booker, Lashon (eds.). *Proceedings of the Fourth International Conference on Genetic Algorithms.* San Francisco: Morgan Kaufmann. pp.37–44.

———. 1991f. Genetic evolution and co-evolution of computer programs. In Langton, Christopher; Taylor, Charles; Farmer, J. Doyne; and Rasmussen, Steen (eds.). *Artificial Life II, SFI Studies in the Sciences of Complexity.* Redwood City, CA: Addison-Wesley. Vol.X. pp.603–629.

———. 1991g. *Non-Linear Genetic Algorithms for Solving Problems.* Australian Patent 611,350. Issued September 21, 1991.

———. 1992a. A genetic approach to finding a controller to back up a tractor-trailer truck. *Proceedings of the 1992 American Control Conference.* Evanston, IL: American Automatic Control Council. Vol.III. pp.2307–2311.

———. 1992b. A genetic approach to the truck backer upper problem and the intertwined spirals problem. *Proceedings of IJCNN International Joint Conference on Neural Networks.* Piscataway, NJ: IEEE Press. Vol.IV. pp.310–318.

———. 1992c. Evolution of subsumption using genetic programming. In Varela, Francisco J.; and Bourgine, Paul (eds.). *Toward a Practice of Autonomous Systems: Proceedings of the First European Conference on Artificial Life.* Cambridge, MA: MIT Press. pp.110–119.

———. 1992d. Genetic evolution and co-evolution of game strategies. Paper presented at the International Conference on Game Theory and Its Applications, Stony Brook, New York. July 15, 1992.

———. 1992e. *Genetic Programming: On the Programming of Computers by Means of Natural Selection.* Cambridge, MA: MIT Press.

———. 1992f. Hierarchical automatic function definition in genetic programming. In Whitley, Darrell (ed.). 1993. *Foundations of Genetic Algorithms 2.* San Francisco: Morgan Kaufmann. pp.297–318.

———. 1992g. *Non-Linear Genetic Algorithms for Solving Problems.* Canadian Patent 1,311,561. Issued December 15, 1992.

———. 1992h. *Non-Linear Genetic Algorithms for Solving Problems by Finding a Fit Composition of Functions.* U.S. Patent 5,136,686. Filed March 28, 1990. Issued August 4, 1992.

——. 1992i. The genetic programming paradigm: Genetically breeding populations of computer programs to solve problems. In Soucek, Branko; and the IRIS Group (eds.). *Dynamic, Genetic, and Chaotic Programming*. New York: John Wiley & Sons. pp.203–321.

——. 1993a. Discovery of a main program and reusable subroutines using genetic programming. *Proceedings of the Fifth Workshop on Neural Networks: An International Conference on Computational Intelligence: Neural Networks, Fuzzy Systems, Evolutionary Programming, and Virtual Reality*. San Diego, CA: Society for Computer Simulation. pp.109–118.

——. 1993b. Discovery of rewrite rules in Lindenmayer systems and state transition rules in cellular automata via genetic programming. Symposium on Pattern Formation (SPF-93), Claremont, CA. February 13, 1993.

——. 1993c. Simultaneous discovery of detectors and a way of using the detectors via genetic programming. *1993 IEEE International Conference on Neural Networks, San Francisco*. Piscataway, NJ: IEEE Press. Vol.III. pp.1794–1801.

——. 1993d. Simultaneous discovery of reusable detectors and subroutines using genetic programming. In Forrest, Stephanie (ed.). *Proceedings of the Fifth International Conference on Genetic Algorithms*. San Francisco: Morgan Kaufmann. pp.295–302.

——. 1994a. *Architecture-Altering Operations for Evolving the Architecture of a Multi-Part Program in Genetic Programming*. Stanford University Computer Science Department Technical Report stan-cs-tr-94-1528. October 21, 1994.

——. 1994b. Automated discovery of detectors and iteration-performing calculations to recognize patterns in protein sequences using genetic programming. *Proceedings of the Conference on Computer Vision and Pattern Recognition*. Los Alamitos, CA: IEEE Computer Society Press. pp.684–689.

——. 1994c. Evolution of a computer program for classifying protein segments as transmembrane domains using genetic programming. In Altman, Russ; Brutlag, Douglas; Karp, Peter; Lathrop, Richard; and Searls, David (eds.). *Proceedings of the Second International Conference on Intelligent Systems for Molecular Biology*. Menlo Park, CA: AAAI Press. pp.244–252.

——. 1994d. Evolution of a subsumption architecture that performs a wall following task for an autonomous mobile robot via genetic programming. In Hanson, Stephen Jose; Petsche, Thomas; Kearns, Michael; and Rivest, Ronald L. (eds.). *Computational Learning Theory and Natural Learning Systems*. Cambridge, MA: MIT Press. Vol.2. pp.321–346.

——. 1994e. Evolution of emergent cooperative behavior using genetic programming. In Paton, Ray (ed.). *Computing with Biological Metaphors*. London: Chapman & Hall. pp.280–297.

——. 1994f. Genetic programming as a means for programming computers by natural selection. *Statistics and Computing* 4:87–112.

——. 1994g. *Genetic Programming II: Automatic Discovery of Reusable Programs*. Cambridge, MA: MIT Press.

——. 1994h. *Genetic Programming II Videotape: The Next Generation*. Cambridge, MA: MIT Press.

——. 1994i. Introduction to genetic programming. In Kinnear, Kenneth E., Jr. (ed.). *Advances in Genetic Programming*. Cambridge, MA: MIT Press. Chapter 2. pp.21–45.

——. 1994j. Recognizing patterns in protein sequences using iteration-performing calculations in genetic programming. *Proceedings of the First IEEE Conference on Evolutionary Computation*. Piscataway, NJ: IEEE Press. Vol.I. pp.244–249.

——. 1994k. Scalable learning in genetic programming using automatic function definition. In Kinnear, Kenneth E., Jr. (ed.). *Advances in Genetic Programming*. Cambridge, MA: MIT Press. Chapter 5. pp.99–117.

——. 1994l. Spontaneous emergence of self-replicating and evolutionarily self-improving computer programs. In Langton, Christopher G. (ed.). *Artificial Life III, SFI Studies in the Sciences of Complexity*. Redwood City, CA: Addison-Wesley. Vol.XVII. pp.225–262.

——. 1995a. Evolving the architecture of a multi-part program in genetic programming using architecture-altering operations. In McDonnell, John R.; Reynolds, Robert G.; and Fogel, David B. (eds.). *Evolutionary Programming IV: Proceedings of the Fourth Annual Conference on Evolutionary Programming*. Cambridge, MA: MIT Press. pp.695–717.

———. 1995b. Gene duplication to enable genetic programming to concurrently evolve both the architecture and work-performing steps of a computer program. *Proceedings of the 14th International Joint Conference on Artificial Intelligence*. San Francisco: Morgan Kaufmann. pp.734–740.

———. 1995c. Genetic Programming for econometric modeling. In Goonatilaje, Susan; and Treleaven, P. (eds.). *Intelligent Systems for Finance and Business*. London: John Wiley & Sons. pp.251–269.

———. 1995d. Survey of genetic algorithms and genetic programming. *Proceedings of 1995 WESCON Conference*. Piscataway, NJ: IEEE. pp.589–594.

———. 1995e. Two ways of discovering the size and shape of a computer program to solve a problem. In Eshelman, Larry J. (ed.). *Proceedings of the Sixth International Conference on Genetic Algorithms*. San Francisco: Morgan Kaufmann. pp.287–294.

———. 1997a. Classifying protein segments as transmembrane domains using genetic programming and architecture-altering operations. In Bäck, Thomas; Fogel, David B.; and Michalewicz, Zbigniew (eds.). *Handbook of Evolutionary Computation*. Bristol, UK: Institute of Physics Publishing; New York: Oxford University Press. pp.G6.1:1–5.

———. 1997b. Future work and practical applications of genetic programming. In Bäck, Thomas; Fogel, David B.; and Michalewicz, Zbigniew (eds.). *Handbook of Evolutionary Computation*. Bristol, UK: Institute of Physics Publishing; New York: Oxford University Press. pp.H1.1:1–6.

———. 1997c. Introduction to evolutionary computation. In Jain, Lakhmi C. (ed.). *Soft Computing Techniques in Knowledge-Based Intelligent Engineering Systems*. Heidelberg, Germany: Springer-Verlag. Chapter 5. pp.71–111.

———. 1997d. *Non-Linear Genetic Algorithms for Solving Problems*. German Patent No. 3916328.8–53. Issued June 18, 1997.

———. 1998a. Genetic programming. In Williams, James G.; and Kent, Allen (eds.). *Encyclopedia of Computer Science and Technology*. New York: Marcel-Dekker. Vol.39. Supplement 24. pp.29–43.

———. 1998b. *Non-Linear Genetic Algorithms for Solving Problems*. Japanese Patent Application No. 126512/89 in 1989. Japanese Patent 2,818,802. Issued August 28, 1998.

———. 1998c. Using biology to solve a problem in automated machine learning. In Wynne, Clive; and Staddon, John (eds.). *Models of Action: Mechanisms for Adaptive Behavior*. Mahwah, NJ: Lawrence Erlbaum Associates. Chapter 5. pp.157–199.

——— (ed.). 1993a. *Artificial Life at Stanford 1993*. Stanford, CA: Stanford University Bookstore.

——— (ed.). 1993b. *Course Reader for CS 425 (Artificial Life) for Winter Quarter 1993*. Stanford, CA: Stanford University Bookstore.

——— (ed.). 1993c. *Genetic Algorithms at Stanford 1993*. Stanford, CA: Stanford University Bookstore.

——— (ed.). 1994a. *Artificial Life at Stanford 1994*. Stanford, CA: Stanford University Bookstore.

——— (ed.). 1994b. *Course Reader for Computer Science 425 (Artificial Life) for Spring Quarter 1994*. Stanford, CA: Stanford University Bookstore.

——— (ed.). 1994c. *Course Reader for Computer Science 426 (Genetic Algorithms and Genetic Programming) for Fall Quarter 1994*. Stanford, CA: Stanford University Bookstore.

——— (ed.). 1994d. *Genetic Algorithms at Stanford 1994*. Stanford, CA: Stanford University Bookstore.

——— (ed.). 1995a. *Course Reader for Computer Science 426 (Genetic Algorithms and Genetic Programming) for Fall Quarter 1995*. Stanford, CA: Stanford University Bookstore.

——— (ed.). 1995b. *Genetic Algorithms and Genetic Programming at Stanford 1995*. Stanford, CA: Stanford University Bookstore.

——— (ed.). 1995c. *University Courses on Genetic Algorithms 1995. Edition No. 1*. December. Stanford, CA: Stanford University Bookstore.

——— (ed.). 1996. *Genetic Algorithms at Stanford 1996*. Stanford, CA: Stanford University Bookstore.

———— (ed.). 1997a. *Genetic Algorithms and Genetic Programming at Stanford 1997.* Stanford, CA: Stanford University Bookstore.

———— (ed.). 1997b. *Late Breaking Papers at the Genetic Programming 1997 Conference, Stanford University, July 13–16, 1997.* Stanford, CA: Stanford University Bookstore.

———— (ed.). 1998. *Genetic Algorithms and Genetic Programming at Stanford 1998.* Stanford, CA: Stanford University Bookstore.

Koza, John R.; and Andre, David. 1995a. A case study where biology inspired a solution to a computer science problem. In Hunter, Lawrence; and Klein, Teri E. (eds.). 1995. *Pacific Symposium on Biocomputing '96.* Singapore: World Scientific. pp.500–511.

————. 1995b. Automated discovery of protein motifs with genetic programming. In Siegel, Eric (ed.). *Proceedings of AAAI-95 Fall Symposium Series—Genetic Programming.* Menlo Park, CA: AAAI Press.

————. 1995c. Automatic discovery using genetic programming of an unknown-sized detector of protein motifs containing repeatedly used subexpressions. In Rosca, Justinian (ed.). *Proceedings of the Workshop on Genetic Programming: From Theory to Real-World Applications.* University of Rochester. National Resource Laboratory for the Study of Brain and Behavior. Technical Report 95–2. June. pp.89–97.

————. 1995d. Evolution of both the architecture and the sequence of work-performing steps of a computer program using genetic programming with architecture-altering operations. In Siegel, Eric (ed.). *Proceedings of AAAI-95 Fall Symposium Series—Genetic Programming.* Menlo Park, CA: AAAI Press.

————. 1995e. *Parallel Genetic Programming on a Network of Transputers.* Stanford University Computer Science Department Technical Report stan-cs-tr-95-1542. January 30, 1995.

————. 1996a. Classifying protein segments as transmembrane domains using architecture-altering operations in genetic programming. In Angeline, Peter J.; and Kinnear, Kenneth E., Jr. (eds.). *Advances in Genetic Programming 2.* Cambridge, MA: MIT Press. pp.155–176.

————. 1996b. Evolution of iteration in genetic programming. In Fogel, Lawrence J.; Angeline, Peter J.; and Baeck, T. *Evolutionary Programming V: Proceedings of the Fifth Annual Conference on Evolutionary Programming.* Cambridge, MA: MIT Press. pp.469–478.

Koza, John R.; Andre, David; Bennett, Forrest H, III; and Keane, Martin A. 1996a. Design of a 96 decibel operational amplifier and other problems for which a computer program evolved by genetic programming is competitive with human performance. In Gen, Mitsuo; and Zu, Weixuan (eds.). *Proceedings of 1996 Japan-China Joint International Workshop on Information Systems.* Ashikaga, Japan: Ashikaga Institute of Technology. pp.30–49.

————. 1996b. Evolution of a low-distortion, low-bias 60 decibel op amp with good frequency generalization using genetic programming. In Koza, John R. (ed.). *Late Breaking Papers at the Genetic Programming 1996 Conference, Stanford University, July 28–31, 1996.* Stanford, CA: Stanford University Bookstore. pp.94–100.

————. 1996c. Use of automatically defined functions and architecture-altering operations in automated circuit synthesis with genetic programming. In Koza, John R.; Goldberg, David E.; Fogel, David B.; and Riolo, Rick L. (eds.). *Genetic Programming 1996: Proceedings of the First Annual Conference, July 28–31, 1996, Stanford University.* Cambridge, MA: MIT Press. pp.132–140.

————. 1997. Design of a high-gain operational amplifier and other circuits by means of genetic programming. In Angeline, Peter J.; Reynolds, Robert G.; McDonnell, John R.; and Eberhart, Russ (eds.). *Evolutionary Programming VI. 6th International Conference, EP97, Indianapolis, Indiana, April 1997 Proceedings.* Lecture Notes in Computer Science. Berlin: Springer-Verlag. Vol.1213. pp.125–136.

Koza, John R.; Andre, David; and Tackett, Walter Alden. 1994. *Simultaneous Evolution of the Architecture of a Multi-Part Program to Solve a Problem Using Architecture Altering Operations.* U.S. Patent Application filed August 4, 1994.

————. 1998. *Simultaneous Evolution of the Architecture of a Multi-Part Program to Solve a Problem Using Architecture Altering Operations.* U.S. Patent 5,742,738. Filed August 4, 1994. Issued April 21, 1998.

Koza, John R.; Banzhaf, Wolfgang; Chellapilla, Kumar; Deb, Kalyanmoy; Dorigo, Marco; Fogel, David B.; Garzon, Max H.; Goldberg, David E.; Iba, Hitoshi; and Riolo, Rick L. (eds.). 1998. *Genetic Programming 1998: Proceedings of the Third Annual Conference, July 22–25, 1998, University of Wisconsin, Madison*. San Francisco: Morgan Kaufmann.

Koza, John R.; Bennett, Forrest H, III; and Andre, David. 1998a. Classifying proteins as extracellular using programmatic motifs and genetic programming. *Proceedings of the 1998 IEEE Conference on Evolutionary Computation*. Piscataway, NJ: IEEE Press. pp.212–217.

———. 1998b. Using programmatic motifs and genetic programming to classify protein sequences as to extracellular and membrane cellular location. *Evolutionary Programming VII. 7h International Conference, EP98, San Diego, March 1998. Proceedings*. Lecture Notes in Computer Science. Berlin: Springer-Verlag. Vol.1447 pp.437–447

Koza, John R.; Bennett, Forrest H, III; Andre, David; and Keane, Martin A. 1996a. Automated design of both the topology and sizing of analog electrical circuits using genetic programming. In Gero, John S.; and Sudweeks, Fay (eds.). *Artificial Intelligence in Design '96*. Dordrecht, The Netherlands: Kluwer. pp.151–170.

———. 1996b. Automated WYWIWYG design of both the topology and component values of analog electrical circuits using genetic programming. In Koza, John R.; Goldberg, David E.; Fogel, David B.; and Riolo, Rick L. (eds.). *Genetic Programming 1996: Proceedings of the First Annual Conference, July 28–31, 1996, Stanford University*. Cambridge, MA: MIT Press. pp.123–131.

———. 1996c. Four problems for which a computer program evolved by genetic programming is competitive with human performance. *Proceedings of the 1996 IEEE International Conference on Evolutionary Computation*. Piscataway, NJ: IEEE Press. pp.1–10.

———. 1996d. *Method and Apparatus for Automated Design of Electrical Circuits Using Genetic Programming*. U.S. Patent Application filed February 20, 1996.

———. 1996e. Reuse, parameterized reuse, and hierarchical reuse of substructures in evolving electrical circuits using genetic programming. In Higuchi, Tetsuya; Iwata, Masaya; and Liu, Weixin (eds.). *Proceedings of International Conference on Evolvable Systems: From Biology to Hardware (ICES-96)*. Lecture Notes in Computer Science. Berlin: Springer-Verlag. Vol.1259. pp.312–326.

———. 1997a. Evolution using genetic programming of a low-distortion 96 decibel operational amplifier. *Proceedings of the 1997 ACM Symposium on Applied Computing, San Jose, CA, February 28–March 2, 1997*. New York: Association for Computing Machinery. pp.207–216.

———. 1997b. Toward evolution of electronic animals using genetic programming. In Langton, Christopher G.; and Shimohara, Katsunori (eds.). *Artificial Life V: Proceedings of the Fifth International Workshop on the Synthesis and Simulation of Living Systems*. Cambridge, MA: MIT Press. pp.327–334.

———. 1998a. Evolutionary design of analog electrical circuits using genetic programming. In Parmee, I. C. (ed.). *Adaptive Computing in Design and Manufacture*. London: Springer. pp.177–192.

———. 1998b. Fourteen instances where genetic programming has produced results that are competitive with results produced by humans. In Gomi, Takeshi (ed.). *Evolutionary Robotics: From Intelligent Robots to Artificial Life (ER'98)*. Kanata, Canada: AAI Press. pp.37–76.

———. 1999a Automatic design of analog electrical circuits using genetic programming. In Cartwright, Hugh M. (ed.). *Intelligent Data Analysis in Science: A Handbook*. Oxford, England: Oxford University Press.

———. 1999b. *Method and Apparatus for Automated Designs of Complex Structures Using Genetic Programming*. U.S. Patent 5,867,397. Filed February 20, 1996. Issued February 2, 1999.

———. 1999c. The design of analog circuits by means of genetic programming. In Bentley, Peter J. (ed.). *Evolutionary Design by Computers*. Chapter 16. John Wiley & Sons. pp.365–385.

Koza, John R.; Bennett, Forrest H, III; Andre, David; Keane, Martin A.; and Dunlap, Frank. 1997. Automated synthesis of analog electrical circuits by means of genetic programming. *IEEE Transactions on Evolutionary Computation* 1(2):109–128.

Koza, John R.; Bennett, Forrest H, III; Hutchings, Jeffrey L.; Bade, Stephen L.; Keane, Martin A.; and Andre, David. 1997a. Evolving sorting networks using genetic programming and rapidly reconfigurable field-programmable gate arrays. In Higuchi, Tetsuya (ed.). *Workshop on Evolvable Systems. International Joint Conference on Artificial Intelligence. Nagoya*. pp.27–32.

———. 1997b. Evolving sorting networks using genetic programming and the rapidly reconfigurable Xilinx 6216 field-programmable gate array. *Proceedings of the 31st Asilomar Conference on Signals, Systems, and Computers*. Piscataway, NJ: IEEE Press. pp.404–410.

———. 1997c. Rapidly reconfigurable field-programmable gate arrays for accelerating fitness evaluation in genetic programming. In Koza, John R. (ed.). *Late Breaking Papers at the Genetic Programming 1997 Conference, Stanford University, July 13–16, 1997*. Stanford, CA: Stanford University Bookstore. pp.121–131.

———. 1998. Evolving computer programs using rapidly reconfigurable field-programmable gate arrays and genetic programming. *Proceedings of the ACM Sixth International Symposium on Field Programmable Gate Arrays*. New York: ACM Press. pp.209–219.

Koza, John R.; Bennett, Forrest H, III; Keane, Martin A.; and Andre, David. 1997a. Automatic programming of a time-optimal robot controller and an analog electrical circuit to implement the robot controller by means of genetic programming. *Proceedings of 1997 IEEE International Symposium on Computational Intelligence in Robotics and Automation*. Los Alamitos, CA: Computer Society Press. pp.340–346.

———. 1997b. Evolution of a time-optimal fly-to controller circuit using genetic programming. In Koza, John R.; Deb, Kalyanmoy; Dorigo, Marco; Fogel, David B.; Garzon, Max H.; Iba, Hitoshi; and Riolo, Rick L. (eds.). 1997. *Genetic Programming 1997: Proceedings of the Second Annual Conference, July 13–16, 1997, Stanford University*. San Francisco: Morgan Kaufmann. pp.207–212.

Koza, John R.; Bennett, Forrest H, III; Lohn, Jason; Dunlap, Frank; Andre, David; and Keane, Martin A. 1997a. Automated synthesis of computational circuits using genetic programming. *Proceedings of the 1997 IEEE Conference on Evolutionary Computation*. Piscataway, NJ: IEEE Press. pp.447–452.

———. 1997b. Evolution of a tri-state frequency discriminator for the source identification problem using genetic programming. In Wang, Paul P. (ed.). *Proceedings of Joint Conference of Information Sciences*. Vol.I. pp.95–99.

———. 1997c. Use of architecture-altering operations to dynamically adapt a three-way analog source identification circuit to accommodate a new source. In Koza, John R.; Deb, Kalyanmoy; Dorigo, Marco; Fogel, David B.; Garzon, Max H.; Iba, Hitoshi; and Riolo, Rick L. (eds.). *Genetic Programming 1997: Proceedings of the Second Annual Conference, July 13–16, 1997, Stanford University*. San Francisco: Morgan Kaufmann. pp.213–221.

Koza, John R.; Deb, Kalyanmoy; Dorigo, Marco; Fogel, David B.; Garzon, Max H.; Iba, Hitoshi; and Riolo, Rick L. (eds.). 1997. *Genetic Programming 1997: Proceedings of the Second Annual Conference, July 13–16, 1997, Stanford University*. San Francisco: Morgan Kaufmann.

Koza, John R.; Goldberg, David E.; Fogel, David B.; and Riolo, Rick L. (eds.). 1996. *Genetic Programming 1996: Proceedings of the First Annual Conference, July 28–31, 1996, Stanford University*. Cambridge, MA: MIT Press.

Koza, John R.; and Keane, Martin A. 1990a. Cart centering and broom balancing by genetically breeding populations of control strategy programs. *Proceedings of International Joint Conference on Neural Networks, Washington, DC, January 15–19, 1990*. Hillsdale, NJ: Lawrence Erlbaum. Vol.I. pp.198–201.

———. 1990b. Genetic breeding of non-linear optimal control strategies for broom balancing. *Proceedings of the Ninth International Conference on Analysis and Optimization of Systems. Antibes, France, June, 1990*. Berlin: Springer-Verlag. pp.47–56.

Koza, John R.; Keane, Martin A.; and Rice, James P. 1993. Performance improvement of machine learning via automatic discovery of facilitating functions as applied to a problem of symbolic system identification. *1993 IEEE International Conference on Neural Networks, San Francisco*. Piscataway, NJ: IEEE Press. Vol.I. pp.191–198.

Koza, John R.; and Rice, James P. 1990. *A Non-Linear Genetic Process for Use with Plural Co-Evolving Populations*. U.S. Patent Application filed September 18, 1990.

———. 1991a. A genetic approach to artificial intelligence. In Langton, C. G. (ed.). *Artificial Life II Video Proceedings*. Redwood City, CA: Addison-Wesley.

————. 1991b. Genetic generation of both the weights and architecture for a neural network. *Proceedings of International Joint Conference on Neural Networks, Seattle, July 1991*. Los Alamitos, CA: IEEE Press. Vol.II. pp.397–404.

————. 1992a. *A Non-Linear Genetic Process for Data Encoding and for Solving Problems Using Automatically Defined Functions*. U.S. Patent Application filed May 11, 1992.

————. 1992b. *A Non-Linear Genetic Process for Problem Solving Using Spontaneously Emergent Self-Replicating and Self-Improving Entities*. U.S. Patent Application filed June 16, 1992.

————. 1992c. *A Non-Linear Genetic Process for Use with Plural Co-Evolving Populations*. U.S. Patent 5,148,513. Filed September 18, 1990. Issued September 15, 1992.

————. 1992d. Automatic programming of robots using genetic programming. *Proceedings of Tenth National Conference on Artificial Intelligence*. Menlo Park, CA: AAAI Press/MIT Press. pp.194–201.

————. 1992e. *Genetic Programming: The Movie*. Cambridge, MA: MIT Press.

————. 1994. *A Non-Linear Genetic Process for Data Encoding and for Solving Problems Using Automatically Defined Functions*. U.S. Patent 5,343,554. Filed May 11, 1992. Issued August 30, 1994.

————. 1995. *Process for Problem Solving Using Spontaneously Emergent Self-Replicating and Self-Improving Entities*. U.S. Patent 5,390,282. Filed June 16, 1992. Issued February 14, 1995.

Koza, John R.; Rice, James P.; and Roughgarden, Jonathan. 1992a. Evolution of food foraging strategies for the Caribbean *Anolis* lizard using genetic programming. *Adaptive Behavior* 1(2):47–74.

————. 1992b. *Evolution of Food Foraging Strategies for the Caribbean Anolis Lizard Using Genetic Programming*. Santa Fe Institute Working Paper 92-06-028. June.

Kroger, Berthold; Schwenderling, Peter; and Vornberger, Oliver. 1992. Massive parallel genetic packing. In Reijns, G. L.; and Luo, J. (eds.). *Transputing in Numerical and Neural Network Applications*. Amsterdam: IOS Press. pp.214–230.

Kruiskamp, Marinum Wilhelmus. 1996. *Analog Design Automation Using Genetic Algorithms and Polytopes*. Eindhoven, The Netherlands: Data Library Technische Universiteit Eindhoven.

Kruiskamp, Marinum Wilhelmus; and Leenaerts, Domine. 1995. DARWIN: CMOS opamp synthesis by means of a genetic algorithm. *Proceedings of the 32nd Design Automation Conference*. New York: Association for Computing Machinery. pp.433–438.

Kyte, J.; and Doolittle, R. 1982. A simple method for displaying the hydropathic character of proteins. *Journal of Molecular Biology* 157:105–132.

Lai, Loi Lei. 1998. *Intelligent System Applications in Power Engineering: Evolutionary Programming and Neural Networks*. Chichester, England: John Wiley & Sons.

Laird, John E.; Rosenbloom, Paul S.; and Newell, Allen. 1986a. Chunking in Soar: The anatomy of a general learning mechanism. *Machine Learning* 1(1):11–46.

————. 1986b. *Universal Subgoaling and Chunking*. Boston: Kluwer.

Lamey, Robert. 1995. *The Illustrated Guide to PSpice*. Albany, NY: Delmar.

Land, Mark; and Belew, Richard K. 1995a. No perfect two-state cellular automata for density classification exists. *Physical Review Letters* 74(25):5148–5150.

————. 1995b. Toward a self-replicating language for computation. In McDonnell, John R.; Reynolds, Robert G.; and Fogel, David B. (eds.). *Evolutionary Programming IV: Proceedings of the Fourth Annual Conference on Evolutionary Programming*. Cambridge, MA: MIT Press. pp.403–434.

Lang, Kevin. 1995. Hill climbing beats genetic search on a Boolean circuit synthesis problem of Koza's. *Proceedings of the Twelfth International Conference on Machine Learning*. San Francisco: Morgan Kaufmann.

Lang, Kevin J.; and Witbrock, Michael J. 1989. Learning to tell two spirals apart. In Touretzky, David S.; Hinton, Geoffrey E.; and Sejnowski, Terrence J. (eds.). *Proceedings of the 1988 Connectionist Models Summer School*. San Francisco: Morgan Kaufmann. pp.52–59.

Langdon, William B. 1995. Evolving data structures using genetic programming. In Eshelman, Larry J. (ed.). *Proceedings of the Sixth International Conference on Genetic Algorithms*. San Francisco: Morgan Kaufmann. pp.295–302.

———. 1996a. Data structures and genetic programming. In Angeline, Peter J.; and Kinnear, Kenneth E., Jr. (eds.). *Advances in Genetic Programming 2*. Cambridge, MA: MIT Press. pp.395–414.

———. 1996b. *Data Structures and Genetic Programming*. Ph.D. thesis. University College, London.

———. 1996c. Using data structures within genetic programming. In Koza, John R.; Goldberg, David E.; Fogel, David B.; and Riolo, Rick L. (eds.). *Genetic Programming 1996: Proceedings of the First Annual Conference, July 28–31, 1996, Stanford University*. Cambridge, MA: MIT Press. pp.141–149.

———. 1998. *Genetic Programming and Data Structures: Genetic Programming + Data Structures = Automatic Programming!* Amsterdam: Kluwer.

Langton, Christopher G. (ed.). 1989. *Artificial Life, Santa Fe Institute Studies in the Sciences of Complexity*. Vol.VI. Redwood City, CA: Addison-Wesley.

——— (ed.). 1991. *Artificial Life II Video Proceedings*. Reading, MA: Addison-Wesley.

——— (ed.). 1994. *Artificial Life III, SFI Studies in the Sciences of Complexity*. Vol.XVII. Redwood City, CA: Addison-Wesley.

Langton, Christopher G.; and Shimohara, Katsunori (eds.). 1997. *Artificial Life V: Proceedings of the Fifth International Workshop on the Synthesis and Simulation of Living Systems*. Cambridge, MA: MIT Press.

Langton, Christopher G.; Taylor, Charles; Farmer, J. Doyne; and Rasmussen, Steen (eds.). 1991. *Artificial Life II, SFI Studies in the Sciences of Complexity*. Vol.X. Redwood City, CA: Addison-Wesley.

Lazcano, A.; and Miller, S. L. 1994. How long did it take for life to begin and evolve to cyanobacteria? *Journal of Molecular Evolution* 39:546–554.

Le Cun, Y.; Boser, B.; Denker, J. S.; Henderson, D.; Howard, R. E.; Hubbard, W.; and Jackel, L. D. 1990. Handwritten digit recognition with a back-propagation network. In Touretzky, David S. (ed.) *Advances in Neural Information Processing Systems 2*. San Francisco: Morgan Kaufmann.

Lee, Tsu-Chang. 1991. *Structure Level Adaptation for Artificial Neural Networks*. Boston: Kluwer.

Lee, Wei-Po. 1997. *Evolving Robots: From Simple Behaviours to Complete Systems*. Ph.D. thesis. Department of Artificial Intelligence. University of Edinburgh.

Lenat, Douglas B. 1983. The role of heuristics in learning by discovery: Three case studies. In Michalski, Ryszard S.; Carbonell, Jaime G.; and Mitchell, Tom M. (eds.). *Machine Learning: An Artificial Intelligence Approach, Vol.I*. San Francisco: Morgan Kaufmann. pp.243–306.

Lewin, Benjamin. 1994. *Genes V*. Oxford: Oxford University Press.

Lindenmayer, Aristid. 1968. Mathematical models for cellular interactions in development, I & II. *Journal of Theoretical Biology* 18:280–315.

Lindenmayer, Aristid; and Rozenberg, G. (eds.). 1976. *Automata, Languages, Development*. Amsterdam: North-Holland.

Linder, P.; Lasko, P.; Ashburner, M.; Leroy, P.; Nielsen, P. J.; Nishi, J.; Schneir, J.; and Slonimski, P. P. 1989. Birth of the D–E–A–D box. *Nature* 337:121–122.

Lindgren, Kristian. 1991. Evolutionary phenomena in simple dynamics. In Langton, Christopher; Taylor, Charles; Farmer, J. Doyne; and Rasmussen, Steen (eds.). *Artificial Life II, SFI Studies in the Sciences of Complexity*. Redwood City, CA: Addison-Wesley. Vol.X. pp.295–312.

Lingas, Andrzej. 1981. Certain algorithms for subgraph isomorphism problems. In Astesiano, E.; and Bohm, C. (eds.). *Proceedings of the Sixth Colloquium on Trees in Algebra and Programming*. Lecture Notes on Computer Science. Berlin: Springer-Verlag. Vol.112. pp.290–307.

Lohn, Jason D.; and Colombano, Silvano P. 1998. Automated analog circuit synthesis using a linear representation. In Sipper, Moshe; Mange, Daniel; and Perez-Uribe, Andres (eds.). *Evolvable Systems: From Biology to Hardware. Second International Conference, ICES 98, Lausanne, Switzerland, September 1998, Proceedings*. Lecture Notes in Computer Science. Berlin: Spring-Verlag. Vol.1478. pp.125–143.

Ludwig, M. I.; Metzger, A. I.; Pattridge, R. A.; and Stallings, W. C. 1991. Manganese superoxide dismutase from *Thermus thermophilus*: A structural model refined at 1.8 Å resolution. *Journal of Molecular Biology* 219:335–358.

Luke, Sean; and Spector, Lee. 1996a. Evolving graphs and networks with edge encoding: Preliminary report. In Koza, John R. (ed.). *Late-Breaking Papers at the Genetic Programming 1996 Conference*. Stanford, CA: Stanford University Bookstore. pp.117–124.

————. 1996b. Evolving teamwork and coordination with genetic programming. In Koza, John R.; Goldberg, David E.; Fogel, David B.; and Riolo, Rick L. (eds.). *Genetic Programming 1996: Proceedings of the First Annual Conference, July 28–31, 1996, Stanford University*. Cambridge, MA: MIT Press. pp.150–156.

————. 1997. A comparison of crossover and mutation in genetic programming. In Koza, John R.; Deb, Kalyanmoy; Dorigo, Marco; Fogel, David B.; Garzon, Max H.; Iba, Hitoshi; and Riolo, Rick L. (eds.). *Genetic Programming 1997: Proceedings of the Second Annual Conference, July 13–16, 1997, Stanford University*. San Francisco: Morgan Kaufmann. pp.240–248.

————. 1998. Genetic programming produced competitive soccer softbot teams for RoboCup97. In Koza, John R.; Banzhaf, Wolfgang; Chellapilla, Kumar; Deb, Kalyanmoy; Dorigo, Marco; Fogel, David B.; Garzon, Max H.; Goldberg, David E.; Iba, Hitoshi; and Riolo, Rick L. (eds.). *Genetic Programming 1998: Proceedings of the Third Annual Conference, July 22–25, 1998, University of Wisconsin, Madison*. San Francisco: Morgan Kaufmann. pp.214–222.

Lundh, Dan; Olsson, Bjorn; and Narayanan, Ajit (eds.). 1997. *Biocomputing and Emergent Computation—Proceedings of Bio-Computing and Emergent Computation 97*. Singapore: World Scientific.

Macki, Jack; and Strauss, Aaron. 1982. *Introduction to Optimal Control*. New York: Springer-Verlag.

Maeda, Nobuyo; and Smithies, Oliver. 1986. The evolution of multigene families: Human haptoglobin genes. *Annual Review of Genetics* 20:81–108.

Maes, Pattie; Mataric, Maja J.; Meyer, Jean-Arcady; Pollack, Jordan; and Wilson, Stewart W. (eds.). 1996. *From Animals to Animats 4: Proceedings of the Fourth International Conference on Simulation of Adaptive Behavior*. Cambridge, MA: MIT Press.

Man, K. F.; Tang, K. S.; Kwong, S.; and Halang, W. A. 1997. *Genetic Algorithms for Control and Signal Processing*. London: Springer-Verlag.

Mange, Daniel; and Tomassini, Marco (eds.). 1998. *Bio-Inspired Computing Machines*. Lausanne, Switzerland: Presses Polytechniques et Universitaries Romandes.

Massey, John. 1970. *Compensated Resistance Bridge-Type Electrical Thermometer*. U.S. Patent 3,541,857. Filed November 27, 1968. Issued November 24, 1970.

Mattfield, Dirk C. 1996. *Evolutionary Search and the Job Shop*. Heidelberg: Physica-Verlag.

Matthews, B. W. 1975. Comparison of the predicted and observed secondary structure of T4 phage lysozyme. *Biochemica et Biophysica Acta* 405:442–451.

Maulik, P. C.; Carley, L. Richard; and Rutenbar, R. A. 1992. A mixed-integer nonlinear programming approach to analog circuit synthesis. *Proceedings of the 29th Design Automation Conference*. Los Alamitos, CA: IEEE Press. pp.698–703.

Maxwell, Sidney R., III. 1994. Experiments with a coroutine execution model for genetic programming. *Proceedings of the First IEEE Conference on Evolutionary Computation*. Piscataway, NJ: IEEE Press. Vol.I. pp.413–417a.

Meyer, Thomas P.; Richards, Fred C.; and Packard, Norman H. 1991. Extracting cellular automaton rules directly from experimental data. In Gutowitz, Howard (ed.). *Cellular Automata: Theory and Experiment*. Cambridge, MA: MIT Press.

Michalewicz, Z. 1996. *Genetic Algorithms + Data Structures = Evolution Programs*. Third edition. New York: Springer-Verlag.

Miller, Geoffrey F.; Todd, Peter M.; and Hegde, S. U. 1989. Designing neural networks using genetic algorithms. In Schaffer, J. D. (ed.). *Proceedings of the Third International Conference on Genetic Algorithms*. San Francisco: Morgan Kaufmann. pp.65–80.

Miller, J. F.; Thomson, P.; and Fogarty, T. C. 1998. Designing electronic circuits using evolutionary algorithms: Arithmetic circuits: A case study. In Quagliarella, D.; Periaux, J.; Poloni, C.; and Winter G. (eds.). *Genetic Algorithms in Engineering and Computer Science: Recent Advancements and Applications.* Chapter 6. New York: John Wiley & Sons.

Min, Shermann L. 1994. Feasibility of evolving self-learned pattern recognition applied toward the solution of a constrained system using genetic programming. In Koza, John R. (ed.). *Genetic Algorithms at Stanford 1994.* Stanford, CA: Stanford University Bookstore.

Minsky, Marvin. 1985. *The Society of Mind.* New York: Simon and Schuster.

Mitchell, Melanie. 1996. *An Introduction to Genetic Algorithms.* Cambridge, MA: MIT Press.

Mitchell, Melanie; Crutchfield, J. P.; and Hraber, P. T. 1994. Dynamics, computation, and the "edge of chaos": A reexamination. In Cowan, G.; Pines, D.; and Melzner, D. (eds.). *Complexity: Metaphors, Models, and Reality.* Santa Fe Institute Studies in the Sciences of Complexity, Proceedings. Vol.19. Reading, MA: Addison-Wesley.

Mitchell, Melanie; Hraber, P. T.; and Crutchfield, J. P. 1993. Revisiting the edge of chaos: Evolving cellular automata to perform computations. *Complex Systems* 7:89–130.

Mizoguchi, Junichi; Hemmi, Hitoshi; and Shimohara, Katsunori. 1994. Production genetic algorithms for automated hardware design through an evolutionary process. *Proceedings of the First IEEE Conference on Evolutionary Computation.* Piscataway, NJ: IEEE Press. Vol.I. pp.661–664.

Monsseen, Franz. 1993. *PSpice with Circuit Analysis.* New York: Macmillan.

Montana, David J. 1995. Strongly typed genetic programming. *Evolutionary Computation* 3(2):199–230.

Montana, David J.; and Czerwinski, Steven. 1996. Evolving control laws for a network of traffic signals. In Koza, John R.; Goldberg, David E.; Fogel, David B.; and Riolo, Rick L. (eds.). *Genetic Programming 1996: Proceedings of the First Annual Conference, July 28–31, 1996, Stanford University.* Cambridge, MA: MIT Press. pp.333–338.

Montana, David J.; and Davis, Lawrence. 1989. Training feedforward neural networks using genetic algorithms. *Proceedings of the 11th International Joint Conference on Artificial Intelligence.* San Francisco: Morgan Kaufmann. Vol.I. pp.762–767.

Moore, Bruce D. 1998. IC temperature sensors find the hot spots. *EDN.* July 2, 1998. pp.99–110.

Moore, Frank William. 1997. *A Methodology for Strategy Optimization under Uncertainty.* Ph.D. thesis. Department of Computer Science and Engineering. Wright State University.

Moore, Gordon E. 1996. Can Moore's law continue indefinitely? *Computerworld Leadership Series* 2(6):2–7. July 15, 1996.

Moore, Will R.; and Luk, Wayne (eds.). 1995. *Field Programmable Logic and Applications: 5th International Workshop, FLP '96, Oxford, United Kingdom, August/September 1995 Proceedings.* Lecture Notes in Computer Science. Vol.975. Berlin: Springer-Verlag.

Mukherjee, Tamal. 1995. *Efficient Handling of Operating Range and Manufacturing Line Variations in Analog Cell Synthesis.* Ph.D. thesis. Department of Electrical and Computer Engineering. Carnegie Mellon University. December.

Murgai, Rajeev; Brayton, Robert K.; and Sangiovanni-Vincentelli, Alberto. 1995. *Logic Synthesis for Field Programmable Gate Arrays.* Boston: Kluwer.

Nachbar, Robert B. 1995. Genetic programming. *Mathematica Journal* 5:36–47.

———. 1998. Molecular evolution: A hierarchical representation for chemical topology and its automated manipulation. In Koza, John R.; Banzhaf, Wolfgang; Chellapilla, Kumar; Deb, Kalyanmoy; Dorigo, Marco; Fogel, David B.; Garzon, Max H.; Goldberg, David E.; Iba, Hitoshi; and Riolo, Rick L. (eds.). *Genetic Programming 1998:Proceedings of the Third Annual Conference, July 22–25, 1998, University of Wisconsin, Madison.* San Francisco: Morgan Kaufmann. pp.246–253.

Nakashima, J.; and Nishikawa, K. 1994. Discrimination of intercellular and extracellular proteins using amino acid composition and residue-pair frequencies. *Journal of Molecular Biology* 238:54–61.

Nei, Masatoshi. 1987. *Molecular Evolutionary Genetics.* New York: Columbia University Press.

Neubauer, Andre. 1994. Genetic design of analog IIR filters with variable time delays for optically controlled microwave signal processors. *Proceedings of the First IEEE Conference on Evolutionary Computation.* Piscataway, NJ: IEEE Press. Vol.I. pp.437–442.

Newbold, William F. 1962. *Square Root Extracting Integrator.* U.S. Patent 3,016,197. Filed September 15, 1958. Issued January 9, 1962.

Nielsen, Ivan Riis. 1995. A C-T filter compiler—From specification to layout. *Analog Integrated Circuits and Signal Processing* 7(1):21–33.

Ning, Z.; Kole, M.; Mouthaan, T.; and Wallings, H. 1992. Analog circuit design automation for performance. *Proceedings of the 14th IEEE CICC.* New York: IEEE Press. pp.8.2.1–8.2.4.

Nissen, Volker. 1994. *Evolutionaere Algorithmen. Darstellung, Beispiele.* Wiesbaden, Germany: betriebswirtschaftliche Anwendungsmoeglichkeiten. Deutscher Universitaets Verlag. In German.

————. 1997. *Einfuehrung in Evolutionaere Algorithmen. Optimierung nach dem Vorbild der Evolution.* Wiesbaden, Germany: Vieweg Verlag. In German.

Nordin, Peter. 1994. A compiling genetic programming system that directly manipulates the machine code. In Kinnear, Kenneth E., Jr. (ed.). *Advances in Genetic Programming.* Cambridge, MA: MIT Press.

————. 1997. *Evolutionary Program Induction of Binary Machine Code and Its Application.* Munster, Germany: Krehl Verlag.

Nordin, Peter; and Banzhaf, Wolfgang. 1995. Evolving Turing-complete programs for a register machine with self-modifying code. In Eshelman, Larry J. (ed.). *Proceedings of the Sixth International Conference on Genetic Algorithms.* San Francisco: Morgan Kaufmann. pp.318–325.

Oakley, E. H. N. 1994. Two scientific applications of genetic programming: Stack filters and nonlinear equation fitting to chaotic data. In Kinnear, Kenneth E., Jr. (ed.). *Advances in Genetic Programming.* Cambridge, MA: MIT Press.

Ochotta, Emil Stephen. 1994. *Synthesis of High-Performance Analog Cells in ASTRX/OBLX.* Ph.D. thesis. Department of Electrical and Computer Engineering. Carnegie Mellon University.

Ochotta, Emil S.; Rutenbar, Rob A.; and Carley, L. Richard. 1996. Synthesis of high-performance analog circuits in ASTRX/OBLX. *IEEE Transactions on Computer-Aided Design of Integrated Circuits and Systems* 15(3):273–294.

O'Connor, Daniel G.; and Nelson, Raymond J. 1962. *Sorting System with N-Line Sorting Switch.* U.S. Patent 3,029,413. Issued April 10, 1962.

Ohno, Susumu. 1970. *Evolution by Gene Duplication.* New York: Springer-Verlag.

Oldfield, John V.; and Dorf, Richard C. 1995. *Field Programmable Gate Arrays: Reconfigurable Logic for Rapid Prototyping and Implementation of Digital Systems.* New York: John Wiley & Sons.

Olsson, Jan Roland. 1994a. Inductive functional programming using incremental program transformation. *Artificial Intelligence* 74:55–81.

————. 1994b. *Inductive Functional Programming Using Incremental Program Transformation.* Dr. Scient. thesis. University of Oslo.

O'Reilly, Una-May. 1995. *An Analysis of Genetic Programming.* Ph.D. dissertation. Ottawa-Carleton Institute for Computer Science. Carleton University. Ottawa, Ontario, Canada.

O'Reilly, Una-May; and Oppacher, Franz. 1994. Program search with a hierarchical variable length representation: Genetic programming, simulated annealing, and hill climbing. In Davidor, Yuval; Schwefel, Hans-Paul; and Maenner, Reinhard (eds.). *Parallel Problem Solving from Nature—PPSN III.* Lecture Notes in Computer Science. Berlin: Springer-Verlag. Vol.866. pp.397–406.

————. 1996. A comparative analysis of genetic programming. In Angeline, Peter J.; and Kinnear, Kenneth E., Jr. (eds.). *Advances in Genetic Programming 2.* Cambridge, MA: MIT Press. Chapter 2. pp.23–44.

Oster, G. H.; and Wilson, E. O. 1978. *Caste and Ecology in the Social Insects.* Monographs in Population Biology, no. 12. Princeton, NJ: Princeton University Press.

Oussaidene, Mouloud. 1996. *Genetic Programming: Methodology, Parallelization and Applications.* Ph.D. thesis. Computer Science Department. University of Geneva.

Packard, Norman H. 1990. A genetic learning algorithm for the analysis of complex data. *Complex Systems* 4(5):543–572.

Pal, Sankar K.; and Wang, Paul P. 1996. *Genetic Algorithms and Pattern Recognition.* Boca Raton, FL: CRC Press.

Parmee, I. C. (ed.). 1998. *Adaptive Computing in Design and Manufacture.* London: Springer.

Patthy, Laszlo. 1991. Modular exchange principles in proteins. *Current Opinion in Structural Biology* 1:351–361.

Pearson, D. W.; Steele, N. C.; and Albrecht, R. F. 1995. *Artificial Neural Nets and Genetic Algorithms.* Vienna: Springer-Verlag.

Pedrycz, Witold. 1997. *Fuzzy Evolutionary Computation.* Boston: Kluwer.

Perkis, Tim. 1994. Stack-based genetic programming. *Proceedings of the First IEEE Conference on Evolutionary Computation.* Piscataway, NJ: IEEE Press. Vol.I. pp.148–153.

Perry, Tekla S. 1998. Donald O. Pederson—The Father of SPICE. *IEEE Spectrum* 35(6):22–27.

Perutz, Max. 1990. *Mechanisms of Cooperativity and Allosteric Regulation in Proteins.* Cambridge: Cambridge University Press.

———. 1997. *Science Is Not a Quiet Life: Unraveling the Atomic Mechanism of Haemoglobin.* Singapore: World Scientific.

Ping, Li; Henderson, R. K.; and Sewell, J. I. 1991. A methodology for integrated ladder filter design. *IEEE Transactions on Circuits and Systems* 38(8):853–868.

Platzer, George E. 1965. *Logarithmic Multiplier-Divider.* U.S. Patent 3,197,626. Filed January 8, 1962. Issued July 27, 1965.

Poli, Riccardo. 1997a. Evolution of graph-like programs with parallel distributed genetic programming. In Bäck, Thomas. (ed.). *Genetic Algorithms: Proceedings of the Seventh International Conference.* San Francisco: Morgan Kaufmann. pp.19–23.

———. 1997b. Evolution of recursive transition networks for natural language recognition with parallel distributed genetic programming. In Corne, David; and Shaprio, Jonathan L. *Evolutionary Computing: AISB Workshop.* Lecture Notes in Computer Science. Berlin: Springer-Verlag. Vol.1305. pp.163–177.

Poli, Riccardo; and Cagnoni, Stefano. 1997. Genetic programming with user-driven selection: Experiments on the evolution of algorithms for image enhancement. In Koza, John R.; Deb, Kalyanmoy; Dorigo, Marco; Fogel, David B.; Garzon, Max H.; Iba, Hitoshi; and Riolo, Rick L. (eds.). *Genetic Programming 1997: Proceedings of the Second Annual Conference, July 13–16, 1997, Stanford University.* San Francisco: Morgan Kaufmann. pp.269–277.

Poli, Riccardo; and Langdon, W. B. 1997. A new schema theory for genetic programming with one-point crossover and point mutation. In Koza, John R.; Deb, Kalyanmoy; Dorigo, Marco; Fogel, David B.; Garzon, Max H.; Iba, Hitoshi; and Riolo, Rick L. (eds.). *Genetic Programming 1997: Proceedings of the Second Annual Conference, July 13–16, 1997, Stanford University.* San Francisco: Morgan Kaufmann. pp.278–285.

Prusinkiewicz, Przemyslaw; and Hanan, James. 1980. *Lindenmayer Systems, Fractals, and Plants.* New York: Springer-Verlag.

Prusinkiewicz, Przemyslaw; and Lindenmayer, Aristid. 1990. *The Algorithmic Beauty of Plants.* New York: Springer-Verlag.

Quagliarella, D.; Periaux, J.; Poloni, C.; and Winter, G. 1998. *Genetic Algorithms and Evolution Strategy in Engineering and Computer Science.* Chichester, England: John Wiley & Sons.

Quarles, Thomas; Newton, A. R.; Pederson, D. O.; and Sangiovanni-Vincentelli, A. 1994. *SPICE 3 Version 3F5 User's Manual.* Department of Electrical Engineering and Computer Science, University of California, Berkeley. March.

Quinlan, J. R. 1986. Induction of decision trees. *Machine Learning* 1(1):81–106.

Qureshi, Adil. 1996. Evolving agents. In Koza, John R.; Goldberg, David E.; Fogel, David B.; and Riolo, Rick L. (eds.). *Genetic Programming 1996: Proceedings of the First Annual Conference, July 28–31, 1996, Stanford University.* Cambridge, MA: MIT Press. pp.369–374.

Raik, Simon E.; and Browne, David G. 1997. Evolving state and memory in genetic programming. In Yao, Xin; Kim, J.-H.; and Furuhashi, T. (eds.). *Simulated Evolution and Learning. First Asia-Pacific Conference, SEAL '96. Taejon, Korea, November 1996, Selected Papers.* Lecture Notes in Artificial Intelligence. Heidelberg, Germany: Springer-Verlag. Vol.1285. pp.73–80.

Rechenberg, Ingo. 1965. *Cybernetic Solution Path of an Experimental Problem.* Royal Aircraft Establishments, Library Translation 1112. Farnborough, U.K.

———. 1973. *Evolutionsstrategie: Optimierung technischer Systeme nach Prinzipien der biologischen Evolution.* Stuttgart, Germany: Frommann-Holzboog.

———. 1994. *Evolutionsstrategie.* Stuttgart, Germany: Frommann-Holzboog.

Resnick, Mitchel. 1991. Animal simulations with *Logo: Massive parallelism for the masses. In Meyer, Jean-Arcady; and Wilson, Stewart W. *From Animals to Animats: Proceedings of the First International Conference on Simulation of Adaptive Behavior.* Paris. September 24–28, 1990. Cambridge, MA: MIT Press. pp.534–539.

Reynolds, Craig W. 1993. An evolved vision-based behavioral model of coordinated group motion. In Meyer, Jean-Arcady; Roitblat, Herbert L.; and Wilson, Stewart W. (eds.). *From Animals to Animats 2: Proceedings of the Second International Conference on Simulation of Adaptive Behavior.* Cambridge, MA: MIT Press. pp.384–392.

———. 1994a. An evolved vision-based model of obstacle avoidance behavior. In Langton, Christopher G. (ed.). *Artificial Life III, SFI Studies in the Sciences of Complexity.* Redwood City, CA: Addison-Wesley. Vol.XVII. pp.327–346.

———. 1994b. Competition, coevolution and the game of tag. In Brooks, Rodney; and Maes, Pattie (eds.). 1994. *Artificial Life IV: Proceedings of the Fourth International Workshop on the Synthesis and Simulation of Living Systems.* Cambridge, MA: MIT Press. pp.59–69.

———. 1994c. Evolution of corridor following behavior in a noisy world. In Cliff, Dave; Husbands, Philip; Meyer, Jean-Arcady; and Wilson, Stewart W. (eds.). *From Animals to Animats 3: Proceedings of the Third International Conference on Simulation of Adaptive Behavior.* Cambridge, MA: MIT Press. pp.402–410.

———. 1994d. Evolution of obstacle avoidance behavior: Using noise to promote robust solutions. In Kinnear, Kenneth E., Jr. (ed.). *Advances in Genetic Programming.* Cambridge, MA: MIT Press.

Richardson, D. C.; and Richardson, J. S. 1992. The kinemage: A tool for scientific communication. *Protein Science* 1(1):3–9.

Riley, M. 1993. Functions of the gene products of *Escherichia coli. Reviews of Microbiology* 32:519–560.

Robertson, George. 1987. Parallel implementation of genetic algorithms in a classifier system. In Davis, Lawrence (ed.). *Genetic Algorithms and Simulated Annealing.* London: Pittman.

Rosca, Justinian P. 1995. Genetic programming exploratory power and the discovery of functions. In McDonnell, John R.; Reynolds, Robert G.; and Fogel, David B. (eds.). *Evolutionary Programming IV: Proceedings of the Fourth Annual Conference on Evolutionary Programming.* Cambridge, MA: MIT Press.

———. 1997. *Hierarchical Learning with Procedural Abstraction Mechanisms.* Ph.D. thesis. Computer Science Department. University of Rochester.

——— (ed.). 1995. *Proceedings of the Workshop on Genetic Programming: From Theory to Real-World Applications.* University of Rochester. National Resource Laboratory for the Study of Brain and Behavior. Technical Report 95–2. June.

Rosca, Justinian P.; and Ballard, Dana H. 1994a. Hierarchical self-organization in genetic programming. *Proceedings of the Eleventh International Conference on Machine Learning.* San Francisco: Morgan Kaufmann.

———. 1994b. Learning by adapting representations in genetic programming. *Proceedings of the First IEEE Conference on Evolutionary Computation.* Piscataway, NJ: IEEE Press. Vol.I. pp.407–412.

Rose, Carolyn P. 1997. *Robust Interactive Dialogue Interpretation.* Ph.D. dissertation. Language Technologies Insititute. Carnegie Mellon University. Technical Report CMU-LTI-97-151.

Rosenbloom, Paul S.; Laird, John E.; and Newell, Allen (eds.). 1993. *The Soar Papers.* Volumes I and II. Cambridge, MA: MIT Press.

Rost, Burkhard. 1998. Marrying structure and genomics. *Structure* 6(3):259–263.

Rost, Burkhard; and Sander, C. 1993. Prediction of protein secondary structure at better than 70% accuracy. *Journal of Molecular Biology* 232:584–599.

Roston, Gerald P. 1994. *A Genetic Methodology for Configuration Design.* Technical Report CMU-RI-TR-94-42. Ph.D. thesis. Mechanical Engineering. Carnegie Mellon University. December.

Rudolph, Guenter. 1997. *Convergence Properties of Evolutionary Algorithms.* Hamburg: Verlag Kovač.

Rumelhart, D. E.; McClelland, J. L.; and the PDP Research Group (eds.). 1986. *Parallel Distributed Processing.* Cambridge, MA: MIT Press.

Rutenbar, R. A. 1993. Analog design automation: Where are we? Where are we going? *Proceedings of the 15th IEEE CICC.* New York: IEEE Press. pp.13.1.1–13.1.8.

Ryan, Conor. 1995. GP robots and GP teams—competition, co-evolution and co-operation in genetic programming. *Proceedings of the AAAI-95 Fall Symposium Series on Genetic Programming.* pp.86–93.

———. 1996a. Paragen: A novel technique for the autoparallelisation of sequential programs using GP. In Koza, John R.; Goldberg, David E.; Fogel, David B.; and Riolo, Rick L. (eds.). *Genetic Programming 1996: Proceedings of the First Annual Conference, July 28–31, 1996, Stanford University.* Cambridge, MA: MIT Press. pp.406–409.

———. 1996b. *Reducing Premature Convergence in Evolutionary Algorithms.* Ph.D. dissertation. University College, Cork, Ireland.

———. 1997. The evolution of provable parallel programs. In Koza, John R.; Deb, Kalyanmoy; Dorigo, Marco; Fogel, David B.; Garzon, Max H.; Iba, Hitoshi; and Riolo, Rick L. (eds.). *Genetic Programming 1997: Proceedings of the Second Annual Conference, July 13–16, 1997, Stanford University.* San Francisco: Morgan Kaufmann. pp.295–302.

Salustowicz, Rafal; and Schmidhuber, Jürgen. 1997. Probabilistic incremental program evolution. *Evolutionary Computation* 5(2):123–141.

Samuel, Arthur L. 1959. Some studies in machine learning using the game of checkers. *IBM Journal of Research and Development* 3(3):210–229.

———. 1983. AI: Where it has been and where it is going. *Proceedings of the Eighth International Joint Conference on Artificial Intelligence.* San Francisco: Morgan Kaufmann. pp.1152–1157.

Sanchez, Eduardo; and Tomassini, Marco (eds.). 1996. *Toward Evolvable Hardware.* Lecture Notes in Computer Science. Vol.1062. Berlin: Springer-Verlag.

Schaffer, J. D.; and Whitley, Darrell (eds.). 1992. *Proceedings of the Workshop on Combinations of Genetic Algorithms and Neural Networks 1992.* Los Alamitos, CA: IEEE Computer Society Press.

Schirmer, Tilman; and Cowan, Sandra W. 1993. Prediction of membrane-spanning β-strands and its application to maltoporin. *Protein Science* 2(August):1361–1363.

Schlatter, Gerald Lance. 1973. *Analog Multiplier and Square Root Extractor Having a Plurality of Strain Gages Connected in a Bridge Circuit.* U.S. Patent 3,732,406. Filed July 8, 1971. Issued May 8, 1973.

Schweber, Bill. 1998. Investment in voltage references pays big system dividends. *EDN.* April 23, 1998.

Schwefel, Hans-Paul. 1968. Experimentelle Optimierung einer Zweiphasend. Technical Report no. 35 of the Project MHD—Staustrahlrohr. 11.034/68. Berlin: AEG Research Institute. October.

———. 1995. *Evolution and Optimum Seeking.* New York: John Wiley & Sons.

———. 1998. Personal communication. February 19.

Schwehm, M. 1992. Implementation of genetic algorithms on various interconnection networks. In Valero, M.; Onate, E.; Jane, M.; Larriba, J. L.; and Suarez, B. (eds.). *Parallel Computing and Transputer Applications.* Amsterdam: IOS Press. pp.195–203.

Sheingold, Daniel H. (ed.). 1976. *Nonlinear Circuits Handbook.* Norwood, MA: Analog Devices.

Siegel, Eric. 1998. *Linguistic Indicators for Language Understanding: Using Machine Learning Methods to Combine Corpus-Based Indicators for Aspectual Classification of Clauses.* Ph.D. thesis. Computer Science Department. Columbia University.

Sims, Karl. 1991a. Artificial evolution for computer graphics. *Computer Graphics* 25(4):319–328.

————. 1991b. Panspermia. In Langton, Christopher G. (ed.). *Artificial Life II Video Proceedings*. Reading, MA: Addison-Wesley.

————. 1992. Interactive evolution of dynamical systems. In Varela, Francisco J.; and Bourgine, Paul (eds.). *Toward a Practice of Autonomous Systems: Proceedings of the First European Conference on Artificial Life*. Cambridge, MA: MIT Press. pp.171–178.

————. 1993. Interactive evolution of equations for procedural models. *The Visual Computer* 9:466–476.

Singleton, Andrew. 1994. Personal communication.

Sipper, Moshe. 1996. Co-evolving non-uniform cellular automata to perform computations. *Physica D* 92:193–208.

————. 1997a. *Evolution of Parallel Cellular Machines*. Lecture Notes in Computer Science. Vol.1194. Berlin: Springer-Verlag.

————. 1997b. The evolution of parallel cellular machines: Toward evolware. *Biosystems* 42:29–43.

Sipper, Moshe; Mange, Daniel; and Perez-Uribe, Andres (eds.). 1998. *Evolvable Systems: From Biology to Hardware. Second International Conference, ICES 98, Lausanne, Switzerland, September 1998, Proceedings*. Lecture Notes in Computer Science. Vol.1478. Berlin: Spring-Verlag.

Sipper, Moshe; and Rippin, E. 1997. Co-evolving architectures for cellular machines. *Physica D* 99:428–441.

Sipper, Moshe; Sanchez, Eduardo; Mange, Daniel; Tomassini, Marco; Perez-Uribe, Andres; and Stauffer, A. 1997. A phylogenetic, ontogenetic, and epigenetic view of bio-inspired hardware systems. *IEEE Transactions on Evolutionary Computation* 1(1):83–97.

Smith, G. D.; Steele, N. C.; and Albrecht, R. F. (eds.). 1997. *Proceedings of the Third International Conference on Artificial Neural Networks and Genetic Algorithms (ICANNGA97)*. Vienna: Springer-Verlag.

Smith, Robert E.; and Valenzuela-Rendon, Manuel (eds.). 1994. Special issue on classifier systems. *Evolutionary Computation* 2(1):1–91.

Smith, Steven. 1980. *A Learning System Based on Genetic Adaptive Algorithms*. Ph.D. dissertation. University of Pittsburgh.

————. 1983. Flexible learning of problem solving heuristics through adaptive search. *Proceedings of the Eighth International Conference on Artificial Intelligence*. San Francisco: Morgan Kaufmann.

Smith, T. F.; and Waterman, M. S. 1981. Identification of common molecular subsequences. *Journal of Molecular Biology* 147:195–197.

Soule, Terence. 1998. *Code Growth in Genetic Programming*. Ph.D. thesis. University of Idaho. Moscow, Idaho.

Spector, Lee. 1996. Simultaneous evolution of programs and their control structures. In Angeline, P.; and Kinnear, K. (eds.). *Advances in Genetic Programming* 2. Cambridge, MA: MIT Press. pp.137–154.

Spector, Lee; Langdon, William B.; O'Reilly, Una-May; and Angeline, Peter (eds.). 1999. *Advances in Genetic Programming 3*. Cambridge, MA: MIT Press.

Spector, Lee; and Luke, Sean. 1996a. Culture enhances the evolvability of cognition. In Cottrell, Gary (ed.). *Proceedings of the Eighteenth Annual Conference of the Cognitive Society*. Mahwah, NJ: Lawrence Erlbaum Associates. pp.672–677.

————. 1996b. Cultural transmission of information in genetic programming. In Koza, John R.; Goldberg, David E.; Fogel, David B.; and Riolo, Rick L. (eds.). *Genetic Programming 1996: Proceedings of the First Annual Conference, July 28–31, 1996, Stanford University*. Cambridge, MA: MIT Press. pp.209–214.

Spector, Lee; and Stoffel, Kilian. 1996a. Automatic generation of adaptive programs. In Maes, Pattie; Mataric, Maja J.; Meyer, Jean-Arcady; Pollack, Jordan; and Wilson, Stewart W. (eds.). *From Animals to Animats 4: Proceedings of the Fourth International Conference on Simulation of Adaptive Behavior*. Cambridge, MA: MIT Press. pp.476–483.

————. 1996b. Ontogenetic programming. In Koza, John R.; Goldberg, David E.; Fogel, David B.; and Riolo, Rick L. (eds.). *Genetic Programming 1996: Proceedings of the First Annual Conference, July 28–31, 1996, Stanford University*. Cambridge, MA: MIT Press. pp.394–399.

Steele, Guy L., Jr. 1990. *Common LISP: The Language*. Second edition. Digital Press.

Steels, Luc. 1990. Cooperation between distributed agents using self-organization. In Demazeau, Y.; and Muller, J.-P. (eds.). *Decentralized AI*. Amsterdam: North-Holland.

———. 1991. Toward a theory of emergent functionality. In Meyer, Jean-Arcady; and Wilson, Stewart W. (eds.). *From Animals to Animats: Proceedings of the First International Conference on Simulation of Adaptive Behavior.* Cambridge, MA: MIT Press. pp.451–461.

Stender, Joachim (ed.). 1993. *Parallel Genetic Algorithms*. Amsterdam: IOS Publishing.

Stender, Joachim; Hillebrand, E.; and Kingdon, J. (eds.). 1994. *Genetic Algorithms in Optimization, Simulation, and Modeling*. Amsterdam: IOS Publishing.

Sterling, Thomas. 1996. The scientific workstation of the future may be a pile of PCs. *Communications of the ACM* 39(9):11–12.

———. 1998. Beowulf-class clustered computing: Harnessing the power of parallelism in a pile of PCs. In Koza, John R.; Banzhaf, Wolfgang; Chellapilla, Kumar; Deb, Kalyanmoy; Dorigo, Marco; Fogel, David B.; Garzon, Max H.; Goldberg, David E.; Iba, Hitoshi; and Riolo, Rick L. (eds.). *Genetic Programming 1998: Proceedings of the Third Annual Conference, July 22–25, 1998, University of Wisconsin, Madison.* San Francisco: Morgan Kaufmann. pp.883–887.

Sterling, Thomas; Messina, Paul; and Smith, Paul H. 1995. *Enabling Technologies for Petaflops Computing*. Cambridge, MA: MIT Press.

Sterling, Thomas L.; Salmon, John; Becker, Donald J.; and Savarese, Daniel F. 1999. *How to Build a Beowulf: A Guide to Implementation and Application of PC Clusters*. Cambridge, MA: MIT Press.

Steudel, Goetz Wolfgang. 1973. *Reference Voltage Generator and Regulator*. U.S. Patent 3,743,923. Filed December 2, 1971. Issued July 3, 1973.

Stevenson, George H. 1926. *Electrical Network*. U.S. Patent 1,606,817. Filed December 7, 1925. Issued November 16, 1926.

Stoddard, B. I.; Ringe, D.; and Petsko, G. A. 1990. The structure of iron superoxide dismutase from *Pseudomonas ovalis* complexed with the inhibitor azide. *Protein Engineering* 4:113–199.

Stryer, Lubert. 1995. *Biochemistry*. Fourth edition. New York: W. H. Freeman.

Sussman, Gerald J.; and Stallman, Richard Matthew. 1975. Heuristic techniques in computer-aided circuit analysis. *IEEE Transactions on Circuits and Systems* 22(11):857–865.

———. 1977. Forward reasoning and dependency-directed backtracking in a system for computer-aided circuit analysis. *Artificial Intelligence* 9 (2):135–196.

———. 1979. Problem solving about electrical circuits. In Winston, Patrick Henry; and Brown, Richard Henry (eds.). *Artificial Intelligence: An MIT Perspective*. Cambridge, MA: MIT Press. pp.31–91.

Svingen, Borge. 1997. Using genetic programming for document classification. In Koza, John R. (ed.). *Late-Breaking Papers at the Genetic Programming 1996 Conference*. Stanford, CA: Stanford University Bookstore. pp.240–245.

Syswerda, Gilbert. 1989. Uniform crossover in genetic algorithms. In Schaffer, J. D. (ed.). *Proceedings of the Third International Conference on Genetic Algorithms*. San Francisco: Morgan Kaufmann. pp.2–9.

———. 1991. A study of reproduction in generational and steady state genetic algorithms. In Rawlins, Gregory (ed.). *Foundations of Genetic Algorithms*. San Francisco: Morgan Kaufmann. pp.94–101.

Tackett, Walter Alden. 1994. *Recombination, Selection, and the Genetic Construction of Computer Programs*. Ph.D. dissertation. Computer Engineering Division. Electrical Engineering—Systems Department. University of Southern California. Also available as Technical Report CENG 94–13. April.

Tanese, Reiko. 1989. *Distributed Genetic Algorithm for Function Optimization*. Ph.D. dissertation. Department of Electrical Engineering and Computer Science. University of Michigan.

Teller, Astro. 1994a. Genetic programming, indexed memory, the halting problem, and other curiosities. *Proceedings of the Seventh Florida Artificial Intelligence Research Symposium*. pp.270–274.

———. 1994b. The evolution of mental models. In Kinnear, Kenneth E., Jr. (ed.). *Advances in Genetic Programming.* Cambridge, MA: MIT Press. pp.199–219.

———. 1994c. Turing completeness in the language of genetic programming with indexed memory. *Proceedings of the First IEEE Conference on Evolutionary Computation.* Piscataway, NJ: IEEE Press. Vol.I. pp.136–141.

———. 1998. *Algorithm Evolution with Internal Reinforcement for Signal Understanding.* Ph.D. thesis. School of Computer Science. Carnegie Mellon University.

Teller, Astro, and Veloso, Manuela. 1996. PADO: A new learning architecture for object recognition. In Ikeuchi, Katsushi; and Veloso, Manuela (eds.). *Symbolic Visual Learning.* New York: Oxford University Press.

———. 1997. Neural programming and an internal reinforcement policy. In Yao, Xin; Kim, Jong-Hwan; and Furuhashi, T. (eds.). *Simulated Evolution and Learning.* Lecture Notes in Artificial Intelligence. Heidelberg, Germany: Springer-Verlag. Vol.1285. pp.279–286.

Teufel, Michael; Pompejus, Markus; Humbel, Bruno; Friedrich, Karlheinz; and Fritz, Hans-Joachim. 1993. Properties of bacteriorhodopsin derivatives constructed by insertion of an exogenous epitope into extra-membrane loops. *The EMBO Journal* 12(9):3399–3408.

Thompson, Adrian. 1995. Evolving electronic robot controllers that exploit hardware resources. In Moran, Federico; Moreno, Alvaro; Merelo, Juan Julian; and Chacon, Pablo (eds.). 1995. *Advances in Artificial Life: Third European Conference on Artificial Life, Granada, Spain, June 1995, Proceedings.* Lecture Notes in Computer Science Vol.929. Berlin: Springer-Verlag. pp.640–656.

———. 1996a. An evolved circuit, intrinsic in silicon, entwined with physics. In Higuchi, Tetsuya; Iwata, Masaya; and Liu, Weixin (eds.). *Proceedings of International Conference on Evolvable Systems: From Biology to Hardware (ICES-96).* Lecture Notes in Computer Science. Berlin: Springer-Verlag. Vol.1259. pp.390–405.

———. 1996b. *Hardware Evolution: Automatic Design of Electronic Circuits in Reconfigurable Hardware by Artificial Evolution.* Ph.D. thesis. School of Cognitive and Computing Sciences, University of Sussex.

———. 1996c. Silicon evolution. In Koza, John R.; Goldberg, David E.; Fogel, David B.; and Riolo, Rick L. (eds.). 1996. *Genetic Programming 1996: Proceedings of the First Annual Conference, July 28–31, 1996, Stanford University.* Cambridge, MA: MIT Press. pp.444–452.

———. 1997. Temperature in natural and artificial systems. In Husbands, Philip; and Harvey, Inman (eds.). *Fourth European Conference on Artificial Life.* Cambridge, MA: MIT Press. pp.388–397.

———. 1998. *Hardware Evolution: Automatic Design of Electronic Circuits in Reconfigurable Hardware by Artificial Evolution.* Conference of Professors and Heads of Computing/British Computer Society Distinguished Dissertation series. Berlin: Springer-Verlag.

Thompson, Adrian; Harvey, Inman; and Husbands, Philip. 1996. Unconstrained evolution and hard consequences. In Sanchez, Eduardo; and Tomassini, Marco (eds.). *Toward Evolvable Hardware.* Lecture Notes in Computer Science. Berlin: Springer-Verlag. Vol.1062. pp.136–165.

Toffoli, T.; and Margolus, N. 1987. *Cellular Automata Machines.* Cambridge, MA: MIT Press.

Tout, K.; Ribeiro-Filho, B.; Mignot, B.; and Idlebi, N. A. 1994. Cross-platform parallel genetic algorithms programming environment. *Transputer Applications and Systems '94.* Amsterdam: IOS Press. pp.79–90.

Trenaman, Adrian. 1998. Concurrent genetic programming and the use of explicit state to evolve agents in partially known environments. In Koza, John R.; Banzhaf, Wolfgang; Chellapilla, Kumar; Deb, Kalyanmoy; Dorigo, Marco; Fogel, David B.; Garzon, Max H.; Goldberg, David E.; Iba, Hitoshi; and Riolo, Rick L. (eds.). *Genetic Programming 1998: Proceedings of the Third Annual Conference, July 22–25, 1998, University of Wisconsin, Madison.* San Francisco: Morgan Kaufmann. pp.391–398.

Trimberger, Stephen M. (ed.). 1994. *Field Programmable Gate Array Technology.* Boston: Kluwer.

Trinquier, Georges, and Sanejouand, Yves-Henri. 1998. Which effective property of amino acids is best preserved by the genetic code? *Protein Engineering* 11(3):153–169.

Tuinenga, Paul W. 1995. *SPICE: A Guide to Circuit Simulation and Analysis Using PSpice.* Third edition. Englewood Cliffs, NJ: Prentice Hall.

Tunstel, Edward W. 1996. *Adaptive Hierarchy of Distributed Fuzzy Control: Application to Behavior Control of Rovers.* Ph.D. thesis. Electrical and Computer Engineering. University of New Mexico. Albuquerque, New Mexico.

Tunstel, Edward; and Jamshidi, Mo. 1996. On genetic programming of fuzzy rule-based systems for intelligent control. *International Journal of Intelligent Automation and Soft Computing* 2(3):273–284.

Turing, Alan M. 1945. Proposals for development in the mathematics division of an automatic computer engine (ACE). In Ince, D. C. (ed.). 1992. *Mechanical Intelligence: Collected Works of A. M. Turing.* Amsterdam: North-Holland. pp.1–86.

———. 1948. Intelligent machines. pp.21–23. In Ince, D. C. (ed.). 1992. *Mechanical Intelligence: Collected Works of A. M. Turing.* Amsterdam: North-Holland. pp.107–128.

———. 1950. Computing machinery and intelligence. *Mind* 59(236):433–460. Reprinted in Ince, D. C. (ed.). 1992. *Mechanical Intelligence: Collected Works of A. M. Turing.* Amsterdam: North-Holland. pp.133–160.

Uhr, Leonard; and Vossler, Charles. 1966. A pattern recognition program that generates, evaluates, and adjusts its own operators. In Uhr, Leonard (ed.). *Pattern Recognition.* New York: John Wiley & Sons. pp.349–364.

Ulam, Stanislaw M. 1991. *Adventures of a Mathematician.* Berkeley, CA: University of California Press.

Ullman, J. R. 1976. An algorithm for subgraph isomorphism. *Journal of the Association for Computing Machinery* 23(1):31–42.

Van Valkenburg, M. E. 1982. *Analog Filter Design.* Fort Worth, TX: Harcourt Brace Jovanovich.

Vladimirescu, Andrei. 1994. *The SPICE Book.* New York: John Wiley & Sons.

Voigt, Hans-Michael. 1989. *Evolution and Optimization: An Introduction to Solving Complex Problems by Replicator Networks.* Berlin: Akademie-Verlag.

Voigt, Hans-Michael; Ebeling, Werner; Rechenberg, Ingo; and Schwefel, Hans-Paul (eds.). 1996. *Parallel Problem Solving from Nature–PPSN IV.* Berlin: Springer-Verlag.

von Heijne, G. 1992. Membrane protein structure prediction: Hydrophobicity analysis and the positive-inside rule. *Journal of Molecular Biology* 225:487–494.

Vose, Michael. 1999. *The Simple Genetic Algorithm: Foundations and Theory.* Cambridge, MA: MIT Press.

Wakerly, John F. 1990. *Digital Design Principles and Practices.* Englewood Cliffs, NJ: Prentice Hall.

Wang, Paul P. (ed.). 1997. *Proceedings of Joint Conference of Information Sciences.*

Watson, James D.; Hopkins, Nancy H.; Roberts, Jeffrey W.; Steitz, Joan Argetsinger; and Weiner, Alan M. 1987. *Molecular Biology of the Gene.* Fourth edition. Menlo Park, CA: Benjamin-Cummings.

Weiss, S. M.; Cohen, D. M.; and Indurkhya, N. 1993. Transmembrane segment prediction from protein sequence data. In Hunter, L.; Searls, D.; and Shavlik, J. (eds.). *Proceedings of the First International Conference on Intelligent Systems for Molecular Biology.* Menlo Park, CA: AAAI Press.

Wheeler, Michael. 1998. Explaining the evolved: Homunculi, modules, and internal representation. In Husbands, Philip; and Meyer, Jean-Arcady (eds.). *Evolutionary Robotics: First European Workshop, EvoRobot98, Paris, France, April 1998, Proceedings.* Lecture Notes in Computer Science. Berlin: Springer-Verlag. Vol.1468. pp.87–107.

Whigham, Peter A. 1995a. Grammatically based genetic programming. In Rosca, Justinian (ed.). *Proceedings of the Workshop on Genetic Programming: From Theory to Real-World Applications.* University of Rochester. National Resource Laboratory for the Study of Brain and Behavior. Technical Report 95–2. June. pp.33–41.

———. 1995b. Inductive bias and genetic programming. *Proceedings of the First International Conference on Genetic Algorithms in Engineering Systems: Innovations and Applications (GALESIA).* London: Institution of Electrical Engineers. pp.461–466.

———. 1996a. *Grammatical Bias for Evolutionary Learning.* Ph.D. dissertation. School of Computer Science. University College, University of New South Wales, Australian Defence Force Academy.

———. 1996b. Search bias, language bias, and genetic programming. In Koza, John R.; Goldberg, David E.; Fogel, David B.; and Riolo, Rick L. (eds.). *Genetic Programming 1996: Proceedings of the First Annual Conference, July 28–31, 1996, Stanford University.* Cambridge, MA: MIT Press. pp.230–237.

Whitley, Darrell; Rana, Soraya; Dzubera, John; and Mathias, Keith E. 1996. *Artificial Intelligence* 85:245–276.

Widlar, Robert J. 1970. New developments in IC voltage regulators. *IEEE International Solid-State Circuits Conference.* Session FAM 13.3. New York: IEEE Solid State Circuits Council. pp.158–159.

Williams, Arthur B.; and Taylor, Fred J. 1995. *Electronic Filter Design Handbook.* Third edition. New York: McGraw-Hill.

Winter, G.; Periaux, J.; Galan, M.; and Cuesta, P. (eds.). 1996. *Genetic Algorithms in Engineering and Computer Science.* New York: John Wiley & Sons.

Wolfram, S. (ed.). 1986. *Theory and Applications of Cellular Automata.* Singapore: World Scientific.

Wong, Man Leung. 1995. *Evolutionary Program Induction Directed by Logic Grammars.* Ph.D. thesis. Department of Computer Science and Engineering. Chinese University of Hong Kong.

Wong, Man Leung; and Leung, Kwong Sak. 1995a. An adaptive inductive logic programming system using genetic programming. In McDonnell, John R.; Reynolds, Robert G.; and Fogel, David B. (eds.). 1995. *Evolutionary Programming IV: Proceedings of the Fourth Annual Conference on Evolutionary Programming.* Cambridge, MA: MIT Press. pp.737–752.

————. 1995b. An induction system that learns programs in different programming languages using genetic programming and logic grammars. *Proceedings of the 7th IEEE International Conference on Tools with Artificial Intelligence.* Los Alamitos, CA: IEEE Computer Society Press. pp.380–387.

————. 1995c. Applying logic grammars to induce sub-functions in genetic programming. *Proceedings of the 1995 IEEE Conference on Evolutionary Computation.* Los Alamitos, CA: IEEE Computer Society Press. pp.737–740.

————. 1995d. Combining genetic programming and inductive logic programming using logic grammars. *Proceedings of the 1995 IEEE Conference on Evolutionary Computation.* Los Alamitos, CA: IEEE Computer Society Press. pp.733–736.

————. 1995e. Inducing logic programs with genetic algorithms: The Genetic Logic Programming System. *IEEE Expert* 9(5):68–76.

————. 1996. Evolving recursive functions for the even-parity problem using genetic programming. In Angeline, Peter J.; and Kinnear, Kenneth E., Jr. (eds.). *Advances in Genetic Programming 2.* Cambridge, MA: MIT Press. Chapter 11. pp.221–240.

————. 1997. Evolutionary program induction directed by logic grammars. *Evolutionary Computation* 5(2):143–180.

————. 1998. Learning recursive functions from noisy examples using generic genetic programming. In Koza, John R.; Goldberg, David E.; Fogel, David B.; and Riolo, Rick L. (eds.). 1996. *Genetic Programming 1996: Proceedings of the First Annual Conference, July 28–31, 1996, Stanford University.* Cambridge, MA: MIT Press. pp.238–246.

Wright, Sewall. 1943. Isolation by distance. *Genetics* 28:114–138.

Wuensche, Andrew; and Lesser, Mike. 1992. *The Global Dynamics of Cellular Automata.* Santa Fe Institute Studies in the Sciences of Complexity. Reference Vol.I. Reading, MA: Addison-Wesley.

Xilinx. 1997. *XC6000 Field Programmable Gate Arrays: Advance Product Information.* January 9, 1997. Version 1.8.

Yao, Xin (ed.). 1994. *Progress in Evolutionary Computation: AI '93 and AI '94 Workshops on Evolutionary Computation, Melbourne, Victoria, Australia, November 1993, Armidale, NSW, Australia, November 1994. Selected Papers.* Lecture Notes in Computer Science. Vol.956. Berlin: Springer-Verlag.

Yao, Xin; Kim, Jong-Hwan; and Furuhashi, T. (eds.). 1997. *Simulated Evolution and Learning.* Lecture Notes in Artificial Intelligence. Vol.1285. Heidelberg, Germany: Springer-Verlag.

Yeagle, Philip L. 1993. *The Membranes of Cells.* Second edition. San Diego, CA: Academic Press.

Yu, Tina; and Clack, Chris. 1997a. PolyGP: A polymorphic genetic programming system in Haskell. In Koza, John R.; Deb, Kalyanmoy; Dorigo, Marco; Fogel, David B.; Garzon, Max H.; Iba, Hitoshi; and Riolo, Rick L. (eds.). *Genetic Programming 1997: Proceedings of the Second Annual Conference, July 13–16, 1997, Stanford University.* San Francisco: Morgan Kaufmann. pp.416–421.

———. 1997b. Recursion, lambda abstractions and genetic programming. In Koza, John R.; Deb, Kalyanmoy; Dorigo, Marco; Fogel, David B.; Garzon, Max H.; Iba, Hitoshi; and Riolo, Rick L. (eds.). *Genetic Programming 1997: Proceedings of the Second Annual Conference, July 13–16, 1997, Stanford University.* San Francisco: Morgan Kaufmann. pp.422–430.

Zalzala, A. M. S.; and Fleming, P. J. 1997. *Genetic Algorithms in Engineering Systems.* London: Institution of Electrical Engineers.

Zhang, Byoung-Tak; and Mühlenbein, Heinz. 1993. Genetic programming of minimal neural nets using Occam's razor. In Forrest, Stephanie (ed.). *Proceedings of the Fifth International Conference on Genetic Algorithms.* San Francisco: Morgan Kaufmann. pp.342–349.

———. 1994. Synthesis of sigma-pi neural networks by the breeder genetic programming. *Proceedings of the First IEEE Conference on Evolutionary Computation.* Piscataway, NJ: IEEE Press. Vol.I. pp.342–349.

———. 1995. Balancing accuracy and parsimony in genetic programming. *Evolutionary Computation* 3(1):17–38.

Zobel, Otto Julius. 1925. *Wave Filter.* U.S. Patent 1,538,964. Filed January 15, 1921. Issued May 26, 1925.

———. 1934. *Wave Transmission Network.* U.S. Patent 1,977,751. Filed March 18, 1933. Issued October 23, 1934.

Zverev, A. I. 1967. *Handbook of Filter Synthesis.* New York: John Wiley & Sons.

Index